# Human Biology

## *Concepts and Current Issues*

FIFTH EDITION



**Michael D. Johnson**
*Weill Cornell Medical College in Qatar*

Benjamin Cummings
San Francisco Boston New York
Cape Town Hong Kong London Madrid Mexico City
Montreal Munich Paris Singapore Sydney Tokyo Toronto

**Senior Acquisitions Editor:** Deirdre Espinoza
**Senior Project Editor:** Marie Beaugureau
**Development Manager:** Barbara Yien
**Development Editor:** Alice Fugate
**Assistant Editor:** Shannon Cutt
**Media Editor:** Alex Streczyn
**Managing Editor:** Deborah Cogan
**Production Supervisor:** Beth Masse
**Copyeditor:** Kevin Gleason
**Production Editor:** Sharon Montooth
**Composition:** Pre-Press PMG
**Interior and Cover Designer:** tani hasegawa
**Illustrators:** Electronic Publishing Services Inc., Rolin Graphics
**Art Development Editor:** Kelly Murphy
**Senior Art Editor:** Donna Kalal
**Photo Researcher:** Kristin Piljay
**Image Rights and Permissions Manager:** Zina Arabia
**Manufacturing Buyer:** Michael Penne
**Marketing Director:** Christy Lawrence
**Cover Photo Credit:** Gustoimages/Science Photo Library
**Text Printer:** Courier Kendallville
**Cover Printer:** Phoenix Color

Text, photography, and illustration credits appear on page C-1.



ISBN-10: 0-321-59088-0

ISBN-13: 978-0-321-59088-6



**Benjamin Cummings**
is an imprint of

PEARSON

www.pearsonhighered.com

1 2 3 4 5 6 7 8 9 10—**CRK**—11 12 10 09 08

Manufactured in the United States of America

# About the Author

**Dr. Michael D. Johnson** spent most of his youth in the fields and forests of rural Washington, observing nature. He earned his B.S. degree in Zoology from Washington State University and then moved East to earn a Ph.D. in physiology from the University of Michigan. After completing a Postdoctoral Research Fellowship at Harvard Medical School he joined the faculty of West Virginia University, where he remained for most of his career.

In 2008 Dr. Johnson moved to Qatar, on the Arabian Peninsula, to take the position of Associate Dean for Premedical Education at Weill Cornell Medical College in Qatar. In his new position he directs the premedical education of students from more than 30 countries.

Dr. Johnson received several teaching awards during his career, including the West Virginia University Foundation Outstanding Teacher award and the Distinguished Teacher Award of the School of Medicine. He is a member of the American Physiological Society, the Human Anatomy and Physiology Society, the National Association of Biology Teachers, and the American Association for the Advancement of Science.

Whether teaching undergraduates or medical students, Michael Johnson has a keen interest in instilling in students an appreciation of science. He seeks to show students how the advancement of scientific knowledge sometimes raises unforeseen ethical, political, economic, and social issues for all of us to discuss and solve. Through his teaching and this book, he encourages students to become scientifically literate so that they will feel comfortable making responsible choices as consumers of science.

You can contact Michael Johnson at mdj2002@qatar-med.cornell.edu with comments or questions about this book.

# Brief Contents

# Detailed Contents

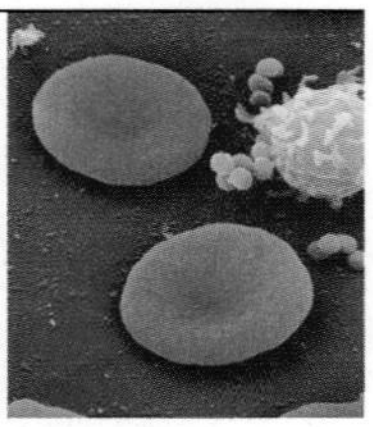



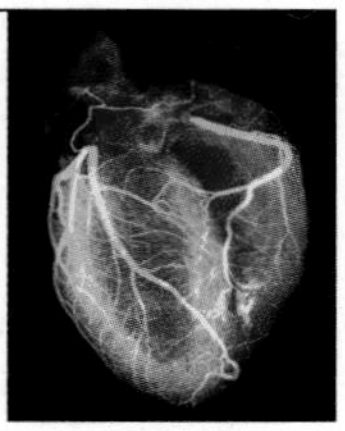

# Preface

**In 1997 scientists cloned an adult animal** for the first time. By 2003 scientists associated with the Human Genome Project published the sequence of all three billion base pairs of the human genome, two years ahead of schedule. Gene therapies for some genetic diseases are on the horizon. And all this is just in the field of genetics!

Those of us who find these discoveries fascinating—and yes, even exciting!—have an obligation to help our students understand the impact of science on their lives. Science is too much fun and far too important to be left to scientists.

## The Focus Is on the Student

This book was written for students who do not yet have a strong background in science, so that they, too, might share in the joy and wonder of science. Every effort was made to make the book accurate and up-to-date while keeping it inviting, accessible, and easy to read. The look and feel of the text is intentionally like that of a news magazine, peppered with short features likely to be of interest to the student and with a strong visual appeal.

Students are naturally curious about how their own bodies work and about human diseases. We capitalize on this curiosity with Health Watch boxes that highlight timely health topics. In addition, organ system chapters generally conclude with a section covering the more common human diseases and disorders.

A specific goal of this book is to help students become sufficiently comfortable with science that they begin to use science in their daily lives. The book shows by example that science is both a body of knowledge and a process for acquiring new knowledge. Directions in Science boxes reveal how scientific knowledge changes over time. Try It Yourself features bring an element of active learning to the course. Current Issues highlight recent discoveries and discuss ethical, social, political, and economic controversies raised by science. Readers are encouraged to continue learning about these hot topics in the *Weighing the Issues* area of the text's Web site, the Human Biology Place.

## Unifying Themes Tie the Subjects Together

Several unifying themes in biology hold the chapters together. *Homeostasis*, the state of dynamic equilibrium in which the internal environment of an organism is maintained fairly constant, is one of those recurrent themes. The concept of homeostasis ties in with another recurrent theme: that *structure and function are related*. Structure/function relationships are the very core of the study of anatomy and physiology, and both of these fields in turn rely on the most unifying concept in all of biology: *evolution*. Only in the context of evolution can anatomy and physiology be fully understood; without the concept of evolution, very little in biology makes sense.

The theme that *science is a process* for gaining new information runs throughout the book. Directions in Science boxes, Try It Yourself activities, and numerous examples within the text show the scientific method in action, highlight examples of scientific progress over time, and demonstrate the process of formulating and testing hypotheses.

A second science theme is that *science has an impact on society*. The Current Issues in particular show how new scientific knowledge can affect society in a variety of ways, both positive and negative. I hope students will formulate their own positions on these interesting and often controversial topics. Indeed, a theme of *personal and societal choices* runs throughout the Current Issues. Students will learn that either by our actions or by inaction, we (both as individuals and as a society) are constantly making choices regarding the use of scientific information. The best choices are likely to be well-informed ones.

## The Organization Fits the Course

This book was designed to accommodate the fairly standard format for college courses in human biology. There are chapters that introduce science and chemistry, chapters that cover basic human biology from cells through the human organ systems, and finally chapters on evolution, ecosystems and populations, and human impacts on the environment.

With such broad coverage, however, there is never enough time to teach all that is interesting, exciting, and relevant about human biology in one semester. Fortunately, because each chapter was written to stand on its own, this book allows for a certain degree of flexibility. Instructors wishing to emphasize the basics of human anatomy and physiology or focus on the medical aspects of human biology could omit or deemphasize the last two chapters. Instructors should feel free to present the organ system chapters in a different order if they feel more comfortable doing so. Within chapters, Diseases and Disorders sections could be omitted or considered optional. Those interested in a more cellular or molecular approach might want to give greater emphasis to Chapters 4 and 17–21 and move quickly through the organ systems chapters. Those more interested in the broader picture of where humans came from and how humans fit into the world order may want to allow sufficient time for the last three chapters, even if it means that they must move quickly or selectively through the organ system chapters. All of these approaches are equally valid.

However much you cover, dig in and enjoy your course!

*Michael D. Johnson*

# Acknowledgments

The Fifth Edition of *Human Biology: Concepts and Current Issues* is the product of the continued hard work and dedication of the people at Benjamin Cummings Publishing, led by Senior Acquisitions Editor **Deirdre Espinoza.** Deirdre directs a team that functions as smoothly and professionally as any in the business. Her association with this book since the very first edition is one reason that each new edition is an improvement over the last. On a day-to-day basis, once again I relied totally on Senior Project Editor **Marie Beaugureau.** Without her organizational skills, broad vision, and gentle persuasiveness over the past three editions, this book would not be what you see today. I am blessed to have had her advice and support.

Three chapters were given special attention in this edition. Development Editor **Alice Fugate** worked closely with content experts and fellow teachers **Andrew Greene,** of Ashland University, on Chapter 19 (Genetics and Inheritance) and **Rosalind Haselbeck,** of the University of San Diego, on Chapters 23 and 24 (Ecosystems and Populations; Human Impacts, Biodiversity, and Environmental Issues). Improvements in these chapters are largely due to their efforts.

The visually appealing new art program in this edition is due to the hard work and vision of Art Development Editor **Kelly Murphy** and Senior Art Editor **Donna Kalal.** Photo researcher **Kristin Piljay** found the new photos you see in this edition.

Accuracy and clarity have been checked and rechecked by the hundreds of insightful faculty members around the country over the past ten years. New to this edition are **Erik Schweitzer,** who contacted me with a suggestion for how best to present the concept of diffusion visually. Our conversations led to the series of photographs (his) that comprise Figure 3.6—certainly the most accurate visual depiction of diffusion I have ever seen. Also new to this edition are **Mike Troyan** of Pennsylvania State University and **Kent Koerner** of Indiana State University, who collaborated with me in producing an expanded set of "Apply What You Know" questions with model answers.

Thanks go to the outstanding administrative support team at Pearson/BenjaminCummings. It includes Assistant Editor **Alex Streczyn,** who produced the Human Biology Place, Course Management Systems, and Instructor Resource DVD; Associate Editor **Emily Portwood,** who managed the revision of the Laboratory Manual and created the new Human Biology Support Manual; and Assistant Editor **Shannon Cutt,** who managed the Instructor Guide and Test Bank, Study Guide, and Teaching Toolbox, provided administrative support, and is helping me with the blog that now supports the book. Production Supervisor **Beth Masse** and Production and Art Coordinator **Sharon Montooth** did a superb job of keeping the entire team organized and on schedule. Copyeditor **Kevin Gleason** fixed typos, questioned my meaning on occasion, and corrected my grammar tactfully and with good humor.

Once again, the textbook is supported by a wonderful set of ancillary materials. Thanks go to **Robert Sullivan** of Marist College, who wrote the Instructor Guide and developed the PowerPoint Lecture Slides, to **David Rivers** of Loyola College in Maryland, who revised the Test Bank, to **Judith Stewart** at the Community College of Southern Nevada, whose Study Guide will certainly help those students who choose to use it, to **Bert Atsma** of Union County College and **Sandra Hsu** of Skyline College, whose Laboratory Manual continues to complement the best human biology courses, and to **Suzanne Long** of Monroe Community College, who provided content for the Human Biology Place and Course Management Systems.

Last but not least, I'd like to thank my wife, Pamela, for her whole-hearted support and understanding over the years.

## Reviewers

Ellen Brisch
*Minnesota State University, Moorhead*

Andrew V. Greene
*Ashland University*

Rosalind Haselbeck
*University of San Diego*

Nickolas Kapp
*Skyline College*

Christopher P. Kemnitz
*University of Wisconsin, Superior*

Kent Koerner
*Indiana State University*

Dominic I. Lannutti
*El Paso Community College*

Marian Leal
*Sacred Heart University*

J. Mitchell Lockheart
*Valdosta State University*

Roberta M. Meehan
*Rio Salado College*

David Rivers
*Loyola College in Maryland*

Kent R. Thomas
*Wichita State University*

Michael Troyan
*Pennsylvania State University*

Sara Van Orden
*Quinebaug Valley Community College*

Wendy Vermillion
*Columbus State Community College*

# Beautiful New Art Reinforces Learning

Providing realistic, beautiful art is a key goal of the Fifth Edition of *Human Biology: Concepts and Current Issues*. Almost every piece of art in the book has been revised to be more realistic and colorful.

## Art That Informs

Newly rendered figurative art is realistic, attractive, and shows students where in the body structures are located.

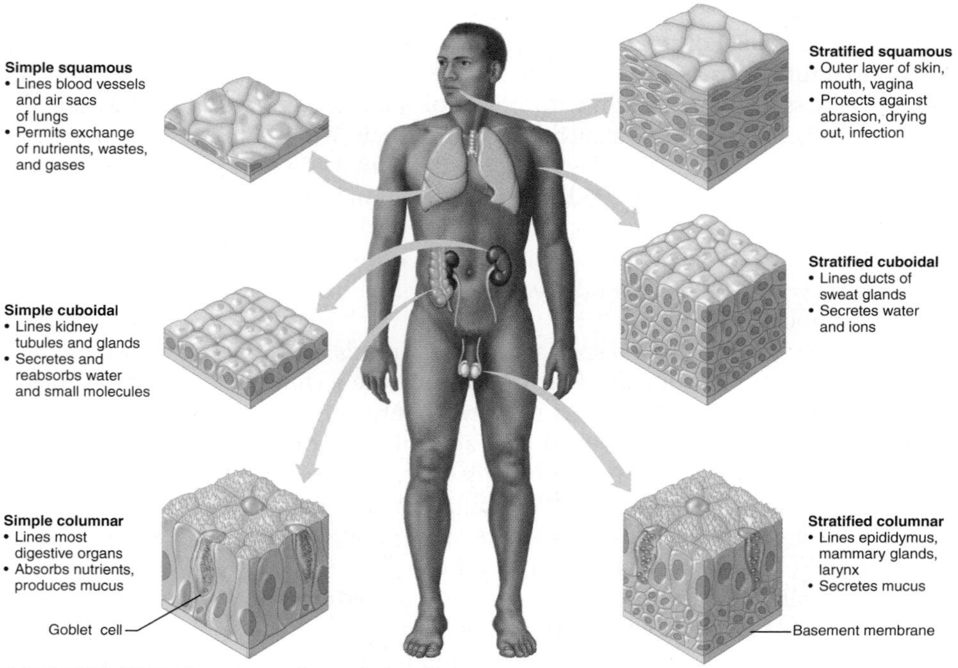


**a) Most epithelial tissues line or cover surfaces or body cavities**

## Art as a Study Tool

Much of the art in *Human Biology: Concepts and Current Issues* can stand alone as a study tool for students or teaching tool for instructors. Step boxes walk students through important processes in an easy-to-interpret manner.

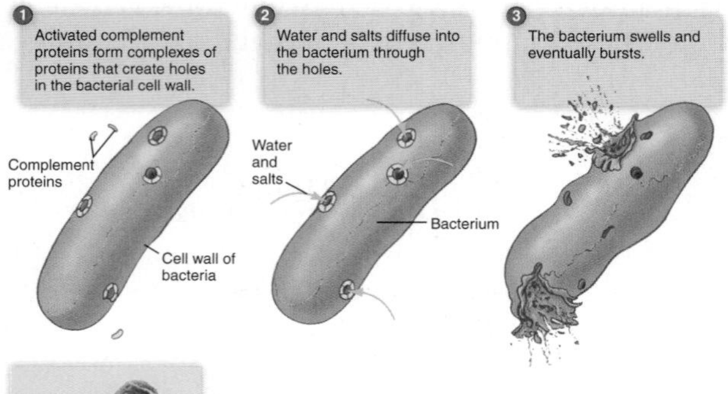


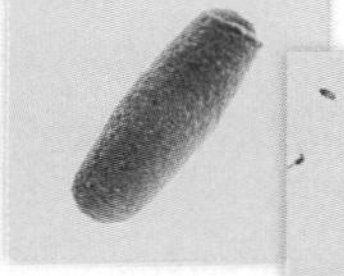

Photomicrograph of an intact bacterium

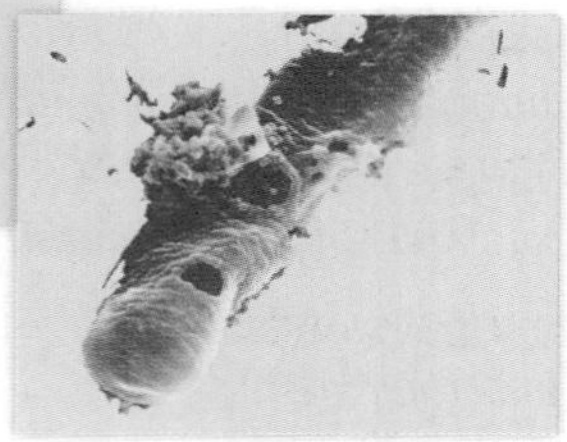

A bacterium after lysis by activated complement proteins

## Art and Life Combined

Using micrographs and illustrations together helps bring concepts to life.

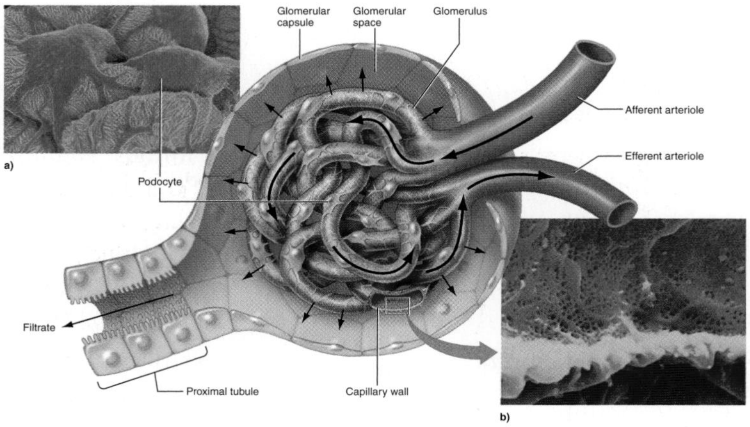

# In-Text Tools Teach and Promote Study Skills

Clearly explaining the concepts and helping students review the material in each chapter are important goals of *Human Biology: Concepts and Current Issues*. A variety of helpful learning tools are built into the book to reinforce students' understanding of human biology topics presented throughout the text.

## Try It Yourself Boxes Promote Active Learning

These short exercises can be performed in minutes, during class or at home, to validate facts found in the text. Students are able to see first-hand how the principles being taught in the text are at work in their own bodies.

**try it** *yourself*

### Stabilizing a Joint

To appreciate the role ligaments, tendons, and muscles play in stabilizing a joint, try this simple experiment. Sit in a low chair, stretch your leg in front of you with your heel resting on the floor, and relax your muscles. Try to move your kneecap (patella) from side to side gently with your hand. Notice how easily you can shift it out of position. Now, without changing position, tense the muscle of your thigh. Can you still move your patella?

The patella is attached to the tibia by a ligament and to the muscles of the thigh by a tendon. When you contract your thigh muscles the patella remains in position because contraction puts tension on the tendon and the ligament. The increased tension holds the patella firmly in place. If you move your hand to just below the kneecap, you can feel the tightening of the patellar ligament as you alternately contract and relax your thigh muscle.

## Conceptual Headings and Recap Paragraphs Explain and Reinforce the Topics

Headings that don't just identify topics but also explain them allow students to understand why a section is important even before reading it, and consistently placed Recap paragraphs rephrase the sections that students just read, helping them to understand the concepts and not just memorize the words before moving on to the next section.

### 1.3 Science is both a body of knowledge and a process

We have already said that science is the study of the natural world. More explicitly, science is two things: *knowledge* (organized, reliable information) about the natural world, and the *process* we use to get that knowledge. *Scientific knowledge* refers to information about the natural world. The process of science, or the way scientific knowledge is acquired, is generally called the **scientific method,** although in practice this term encompasses a variet
book you will be presente
good to remember that thi
over time by the scientific

**RECAP**

The scientific method is a systematic process of observation, hypothesis building, and hypothesis testing. A theory is a broad hypothesis that has withstood numerous tests. ■

## Intro Questions Draw Students into the Chapter

The Intro Questions at the beginning of each chapter pique students' interest and encourage them to read on. Answers and explanations for the Intro Questions appear on the following page.

1 **True or False?** A cell is the smallest unit of life.

2 **True or False?** Each of your cells is surrounded by a rigid, impermeable barrier.

3 **True or False?** The energy your cells need to grow and reproduce comes from the food you eat.

4 When some of your cells become damaged or die, can they be replaced? **a.** Yes **b.** No **c.** It depends on which type of cell.

# An Emphasis on Critical Thinking and Applying Information to Real Life Demonstrates the Relevance of Human Biology

## Current Issue Boxes Connect Human Biology to the World

Current Issue boxes, included in every chapter, provide contrasting views on controversial topics, along with a summary of "The Facts" that help students think critically about commonly reported health and science information.

New essay topics for the Fifth Edition include, lipodissolve, smokers' vs. nonsmokers' rights, the classification of "overweight," and prophylactic breast and ovary removal.

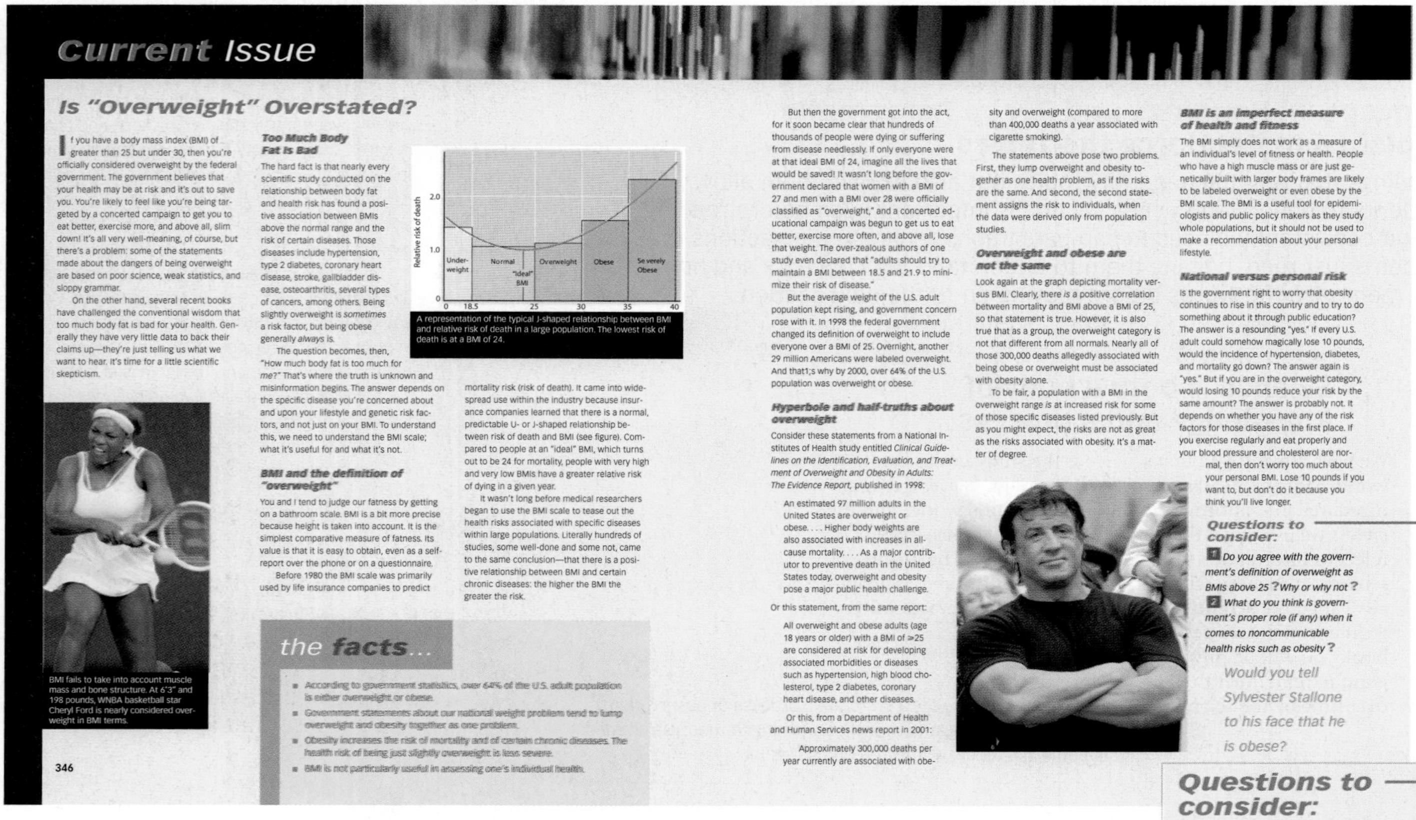

Current Issue

Is "Overweight" Overstated?

If you have a body mass index (BMI) of greater than 25 but under 30, then you're officially considered overweight by the federal government. The government believes that your health may be at risk and it's out to save you. You're likely to feel like you're being targeted by a concerted campaign to get you to eat better, exercise more, and above all, slim down! It's all very well-meaning, of course, but there's a problem: some of the statements made about the dangers of being overweight are based on poor science, weak statistics, and sloppy grammar.

On the other hand, several recent books have challenged the conventional wisdom that too much body fat is bad for your health. Generally they have very little data to back their claims up—they're just telling us what we want to hear. It's time for a little scientific skepticism.

BMI fails to take into account muscle mass and bone structure. At 6'3" and 198 pounds, WNBA basketball star Cheryl Ford is nearly considered overweight in BMI terms.

Too Much Body Fat Is Bad

The hard fact is that nearly every scientific study conducted on the relationship between body fat and health risk has found a positive association between BMIs above the normal range and the risk of certain diseases. Those diseases include hypertension, type 2 diabetes, coronary heart disease, stroke, gallbladder disease, osteoarthritis, several types of cancers, among others. Being slightly overweight is *sometimes* a risk factor, but being obese generally *always* is.

The question becomes, then, "How much body fat is too much for *me*?" That's where the truth is unknown and misinformation begins. The answer depends on the specific disease you're concerned about and upon your lifestyle and genetic risk factors, and not just on your BMI. To understand this, we need to understand the BMI scale; what it's useful for and what it's not.



A representation of the typical J-shaped relationship between BMI and relative risk of death in a large population. The lowest risk of death is at a BMI of 24.

BMI and the definition of "overweight"

You and I tend to judge our fatness by getting on a bathroom scale. BMI is a bit more precise because height is taken into account. It is the simplest comparative measure of fatness. Its value is that it is easy to obtain, even as a self-report over the phone or on a questionnaire.

Before 1980 the BMI scale was primarily used by life insurance companies to predict mortality risk (risk of death). It came into widespread use within the industry because insurance companies learned that there is a normal, predictable U- or J-shaped relationship between risk of death and BMI (see figure). Compared to people at an "ideal" BMI, which turns out to be 24 for mortality, people with very high and very low BMIs have a greater relative risk of dying in a given year.

It wasn't long before medical researchers began to use the BMI scale to tease out the health risks associated with specific diseases within large populations. Literally hundreds of studies, some well-done and some not, came to the same conclusion—that there is a positive relationship between BMI and certain chronic diseases: the higher the BMI the greater the risk.

the facts...

- According to government statistics, over 64% of the U.S. adult population is either overweight or obese.
- Government statements about our national weight problem tend to lump overweight and obesity together as one problem.
- Obesity increases the risk of mortality and of certain chronic diseases. The health risk of being just slightly overweight is less severe.
- BMI is not particularly useful in assessing one's individual health.

346

But then the government got into the act, for it soon became clear that hundreds of thousands of people were dying or suffering from disease needlessly. If only everyone were at that ideal BMI of 24, imagine all the lives that would be saved! It wasn't long before the government declared that women with a BMI of 27 and men with a BMI over 28 were officially classified as "overweight," and a concerted educational campaign was begun to get us to eat better, exercise more often, and above all, lose that weight. The over-zealous authors of one study even declared that "adults should try to maintain a BMI between 18.5 and 21.9 to minimize their risk of disease."

But the average weight of the U.S. adult population kept rising, and government concern rose with it. In 1998 the federal government changed its definition of overweight to include everyone over a BMI of 25. Overnight, another 29 million Americans were labeled overweight. And that1;s why by 2000, over 64% of the U.S. population was overweight or obese.

Hyperbole and half-truths about overweight

Consider these statements from a National Institutes of Health study entitled *Clinical Guidelines on the Identification, Evaluation, and Treatment of Overweight and Obesity in Adults: The Evidence Report*, published in 1998:

> An estimated 97 million adults in the United States are overweight or obese. . . . Higher body weights are also associated with increases in all-cause mortality. . . . As a major contributor to preventive death in the United States today, overweight and obesity pose a major public health challenge.

Or this statement, from the same report:

> All overweight and obese adults (age 18 years or older) with a BMI of ≥25 are considered at risk for developing associated morbidities or diseases such as hypertension, high blood cholesterol, type 2 diabetes, coronary heart disease, and other diseases.

Or this, from a Department of Health and Human Services news report in 2001:

> Approximately 300,000 deaths per year currently are associated with obesity and overweight (compared to more than 400,000 deaths a year associated with cigarette smoking).

The statements above pose two problems. First, they lump overweight and obesity together as one health problem, as if the risks are the same. And second, the second statement assigns the risk to individuals, when the data were derived only from population studies.

Overweight and obese are not the same

Look again at the graph depicting mortality versus BMI. Clearly, there *is* a positive correlation between mortality and BMI above a BMI of 25, so that statement is true. However, it is also true that as a group, the overweight category is not that different from all normals. Nearly all of those 300,000 deaths allegedly associated with being obese or overweight must be associated with obesity alone.

To be fair, a population with a BMI in the overweight range *is* at increased risk for some of those specific diseases listed previously. But as you might expect, the risks are not as great as the risks associated with obesity. It's a matter of degree.

BMI is an imperfect measure of health and fitness

The BMI simply does not work as a measure of an individual's level of fitness or health. People who have a high muscle mass or are just genetically built with larger body frames are likely to be labeled overweight or even obese by the BMI scale. The BMI is a useful tool for epidemiologists and public policy makers as they study whole populations, but it should not be used to make a recommendation about your personal lifestyle.

National versus personal risk

Is the government right to worry that obesity continues to rise in this country and to try to do something about it through public education? The answer is a resounding "yes." If every U.S. adult could somehow magically lose 10 pounds, would the incidence of hypertension, diabetes, and mortality go down? The answer again is "yes." But if you are in the overweight category, would losing 10 pounds reduce your risk by the same amount? The answer is probably not. It depends on whether you have any of the risk factors for those diseases in the first place. If you exercise regularly and eat properly and your blood pressure and cholesterol are normal, then don't worry too much about your personal BMI. Lose 10 pounds if you want to, but don't do it because you think you'll live longer.

Questions to consider:

1 *Do you agree with the government's definition of overweight as BMIs above 25? Why or why not?*

2 *What do you think is government's proper role (if any) when it comes to noncommunicable health risks such as obesity?*

*Would you tell Sylvester Stallone to his face that he is obese?*

**Questions to consider** at the end of each essay prompt critical thinking and ask students to draw their own opinions about these important issues.


**Questions to consider:**

1 *Do you agree with the government's definition of overweight as BMIs above 25? Why or why not?*

2 *What do you think is government's proper role (if any) when it comes to noncommunicable health risks such as obesity?*


**Apply What You Know**

1. Imagine that you are shown two cells under the microscope. One is small, has lots of mitochondria, and contains numerous glycogen granules. The other is somewhat larger and has only a few mitochondria and no glycogen granules. Which cell do you think is more metabolically active? Explain your reasoning.
2. The sodium-potassium pump is a large protein molecule. Where do you think the sodium-potassium pumps are made in the cell, and how do you think they become inserted into the lipid bilayer of the plasma membrane?
3. Mitochondria resemble a bacterial cell in a number of ways. Some scientists hypothesize that mitochondria evolved from aerobic prokaryotes that were engulfed by anaerobic eukaryotes, and now both have evolved together in a mutually advantageous way. Can you think of an explanation for why it might have been advantageous for both cells to enter into such an arrangement?

## Apply What You Know Questions Get Students Thinking Critically

Apply What You Know questions encourage students to apply the information they are learning to novel situations or their own lives. For the Fifth Edition, we have focused on including more questions; now 6 to 8 questions appear at the end of each chapter. Answers to the questions appear on the Human Biology Place Website.

## Health Watch

### The Growing Threat of Antibiotic-Resistant Bacteria

When antibiotics—drugs that kill bacteria—became available in the 1940s, they were hailed as a breakthrough. Indeed, many people owe their lives to them.

But there is a downside: Indiscriminate use of antibiotics increases resistance in some strains of bacteria. If we are not careful, we may soon face deadly microorganisms against which we have no protection except the body's natural immune system. This past year we've been hearing about an antibiotic-resistant strain of the *Staphylococcus aureus* bacterium called MRSA (methicillin-resistant *Staphylococcus aureus*) that is resistant to nearly all antibiotics. It used to show up only in hospitals and long-term care facilities, but it's beginning to appear in locker rooms and even more generally in the community. Approximately 292,000 Americans are hospitalized every year with "staph" infections, about 126,000 of which are now caused by this new strain. This frightening superbug can penetrate bones and lungs, killing approximately 20% of those with severe infections.

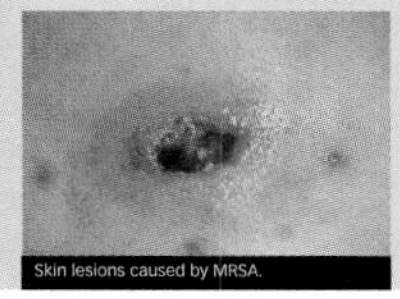

Skin lesions caused by MRSA.

Antibiotic resistance is rapidly becoming a global threat, not just a threat in the United States. The antibiotic Vancomycin was introduced into clinical use in 1972, and according to the World Health Organization, Vancomycin-resistant strains of bacteria were appearing around the world by 1987. In a recent study, almost 25% of intensive-care patients infected with enterococci, bacteria that inhabit the intestinal tract, were resistant to Vancomycin.

The bacteria in (and on) your body compete for your body's resources, just as all organisms do when they occupy the same ecological space. Good bacteria limit the growth of harmful bacteria through this competition. But when you take an antibiotic, you destroy the good bacteria, too. By definition, if a drug kills most but not all of the bacteria, the survivors are those most resistant to the antibiotic's effects. With the total population of bacteria now decreased, these antibiotic-resistant survivors multiply. Any time we take an antibiotic, the percentage of resistant bacteria in the remaining population increases, and the antibiotic is less effective the next time around.

Because antibiotics seem so effective, we tend to use them indiscriminately. In the United States alone we manufacture over 50 million pounds of antibiotics annually, about half of which are fed to livestock or sprayed on fruit trees. Researchers estimate that fully one-third of all antibiotic prescriptions given to non-hospitalized patients in the United States are not needed.

Another problem: To ensure that all bacteria are killed, doctors prescribe a course of antibiotics lasting 7–10 days. Many people feel better within 3 days when most (but by no means all) of the bacteria have been killed, so they stop taking the drug and save the leftover pills for a future illness. They have inadvertently selected the most antibiotic-resistant bacteria for survival!

As a society, we can take several steps to preserve the effectiveness of antibiotics:

- Don't ask your doctor for antibiotics for a viral illness such as a cold or flu. Antibiotics kill bacteria but have no effect on viruses.
- Take the drugs only when needed and as prescribed. Complete the full course of treatment even if you feel like you are back to normal.
- Reduce your use of antibacterial hand creams, soaps, and laundry detergents. Products that leave a residue on skin may favor the growth of resistant germs.
- Encourage farmers and orchard owners to reduce their use of antibiotics in cattle feed and on fruit trees, bearing in mind that these groups have legitimate reasons of their own for antibiotic use.
- Support research efforts to find new antibiotics.

The development of resistance to antibiotics is a global issue that affects us all. Used properly and judiciously, however, antibiotics will remain in our antibacterial arsenal for many years.

## Health Watch

### Suntans, Smoking, and Your Skin

Many of us think suntans are attractive. A suntan indicates we have leisure time to spend basking in the sun, and it gives the skin a healthy-looking "glow." But are suntans really healthy?

The answer is clearly no. Strong light rays, whether from sunlight or tanning beds, can age your skin prematurely and increase your risk for skin cancer. The rays penetrate to the dermis and damage its collagen and elastin fibers. Elastin fibers clump together, leading at first to fine wrinkles and later to a wrinkled, leathery skin texture.

Prolonged exposure to sunlight or tanning lamps can also damage small blood vessels. Sometimes the vessels remain permanently dilated, leading to a condition called *telangiectasis*, or spider veins. Sunlight also damages the keratinocytes and melanocytes in the epidermis. The keratinocytes become rough and thickened and no longer fit together as a smooth interlocking layer. The melanocytes begin to produce melanin unevenly, leading to patches of darker pigmentation known as freckles, age spots, or liver spots.

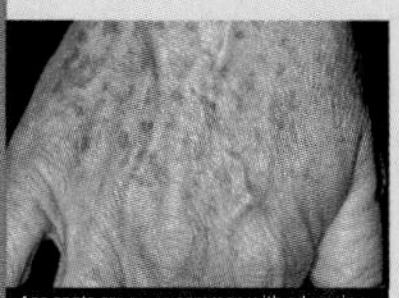

Age spots are more common with advancing age, especially in Caucasians who have had excessive exposure to the sun.

Perhaps you have heard that ultraviolet (UV) rays combine "good" UVA rays that tan your skin and "bad" UVB rays that cause sunburn. Tanning lotions with high SPF (sun protection factor) numbers are designed to block the UVB rays, which at least prevents the acute damage and pain of a sunburn. However, UVA rays are also bad for you. They penetrate more deeply than the UVB rays and in fact cause most of the long-term changes that age skin prematurely.

What about smoking? Heavy smokers are nearly five times more likely to develop premature wrinkles. Smoking damages and thickens the elastin fibers in the dermis. It also dehydrates keratinocytes in the epidermis, causing the epidermis to develop a rough texture. Finally, smoking narrows blood vessels, reducing blood flow to the skin. As a result the skin of smokers heals more slowly from injury than the skin of nonsmokers.

Smoking causes changes in the elastin fibers in the dermis and a loss of water from the cells of the epidermis. The result is dehydrated, wrinkled skin.

## Health Watch Boxes Relate Human Biology to Health

Health Watch boxes provide insights and practical advice on health topics such as antibiotic-resistant bacteria and checking yourself for cancer.

## Directions in Science Boxes Explain the Process of Science

Directions in Science boxes highlight the process of science in an unintimidating manner, and cover hot new topics in human biology. From explaining what scientists learned by studying Lance Armstrong to discussing how a new taste receptor on the tongue was discovered, these boxes show students that science is a process that is always evolving.

## Directions in Science

### Science and Sports: Lessons Learned from Lance Armstrong

Covering over 2,000 miles of variable terrain in about 20 stages, the annual Tour de France bicycle race is one of the most grueling athletic events in the world. How could one man dominate this premier sporting event for *seven consecutive years*?

Scientists are interested in that question, too, and now they may have an answer. Researchers who tested Lance Armstrong over the entire period of his record seven consecutive Tour de France wins report that he increased his muscle efficiency by 8% during those years—in other words, his muscles became more efficient at utilizing the same amount of oxygen. At the same time, his average cycling pace during races rose from 85–95 revolutions per minute to about 105–110 rpm.

A physician who studied Armstrong hypothesizes that the process of ATP turnover within his contracting muscle fibers actually became more efficient. Armstrong may also have increased his percentage of slow-twitch muscle fibers from approximately 60% to 80%, an increase similar to those observed previously in other competitive cyclists. Blood tests showed that he had very low levels of lactate, a component of lactic acid—even lower than those of other competitive cyclists. Enhanced muscle efficiency, plus a planned weight loss of 7% before the race, enabled Armstrong to achieve an overall improvement of 18% in what researchers call his "steady-state power per kilogram" output.

This is remarkable, since researchers have long thought that muscle efficiency is genetically determined. Armstrong may have "good genes," but apparently he also trained smarter. How he did it is still under investigation.

Fifty years ago, an aspiring athlete needed only a set of weights, a place to train, and a lot of determination and hard work. Not today. In an era when winning brings big endorsement contracts, sports have gone high-tech. Downhill ski racers and speed skaters are studied in wind tunnels previously used only to test models of airplanes and buildings. Digital video cameras, remote sensors, and computer programs analyze athletes' motion patterns for speed, power, and direction. Researchers in genetics, biochemistry, and exercise training are unlocking the secrets of athletic success (such as Armstrong's) on a cellular level and applying what they learn to young athletes in training.

In the future, a professional athletics "consultant" firm will be able to approach parents of young children with offers of genetic, biochemical, physical, and psychological testing. They'll promise to determine the child's likelihood of success in every sport, and link parents to just the right training facilities and professional trainers. Future Olympic hopefuls will be selected early and trained according to the latest scientifically proven training methods. Unlikely? Listen to the stories of the Olympics winners over the next 20 years and judge for yourself.

## Directions in Science

### The Discovery of Umami

How many basic taste qualities are there? In ancient Greece, scholars identified seven: sweet, salty, sour, bitter, spicy, astringent, and sandy. In ancient India, yogic principles identified eight. A Chinese medical text written around 1000 B.C.E. described five.

Rigorous application of the scientific method beginning several centuries ago reduced the number of proven taste qualities to just four: sweet, sour, salty, and bitter. To be considered a basic taste quality there had to be evidence of specific receptors on the tongue that responded primarily to specific chemicals, such as sugar (sweet taste), sodium (salty taste), hydrogen ion (sour taste), and certain toxic plant chemicals (bitter taste).

Then in 1908 Kikunae Ikeda, a chemistry professor at the Imperial University of Tokyo, hypothesized that there was a fifth taste and set out to prove it. Ikeda noted that the dominant flavor of dashi, a Japanese soup base, was mild but distinctly different from the four known tastes, and thus might exemplify this mysterious fifth quality. The seaweed *Laminaria japonica* is a major ingredient of dashi, so Ikeda attempted to isolate the chemical source of *Laminaria*'s flavor. In a series of painstaking chemical procedures, he extracted and removed other ingredients until eventually he had crystallized glutamic acid (glutamate), the most common amino acid in proteins. In 1909 Ikeda published an article in a Japanese journal in which he announced that there was indeed a fifth taste that involved the detection of glutamate. Ikeda named his discovery *umami*, a term derived from the Japanese word *umai* (delicious).

Many Asians were receptive to the concept of umami. In fact, commercial production of monosodium glutamate (MSG), a seasoning agent that adds the sensation of umami to food, began the same year that Ikeda published his article.

However, scientists in the U.S. and Europe remained skeptical. One reason may have been that Ikeda's article was published in Japanese, so many of his foreign peers were unable to read his original work. In the 1950s the U.S. FDA classified umami as a flavor enhancer, not a taste. Around 1980 scientists began to investigate whether laboratory animals could detect glutamate. The research was not entirely convincing to the skeptics because different species, and even different strains of lab mice, showed a variety of responses to the chemical. Although an international symposium accepted umami as the fifth basic taste in 1990, many U.S. researchers remained unconvinced.

The development of molecular biology techniques for sequencing and identifying specific proteins provided new tools for studying sensory receptors. Using these techniques, two groups of researchers reported in 2002 the existence of human glutamate taste receptors. Further research showed that a common form of glutamate (L-glutamate) activates these receptors and elicits the sensation of umami. These findings provide powerful independent confirmation of the pioneering work of Dr. Ikeda a century ago.

Research continues into the molecular basis of taste in general and umami in particular. Some scientists are seeking to block molecular activity at glutamate receptors; if this also blocks the perception of umami, the finding would support the link between the two. Other researchers are exploring the paths by which signals travel from glutamate receptors to the brain, to determine whether umami truly is a single taste or a combination of other taste sensations.

Whether or not you accept that umami is an elusive "fifth taste," it is clear that MSG and umami-rich foods can add depth and richness to recipes. Foods said to be high in umami include Parmesan cheese, shiitake mushrooms, scallops, chicken, soy sauce, and Worcestershire sauce.

# Supplements and Media That Make Instructor Preparation Easier Than Ever

## Think Inside the Box! A course planning kit that saves you hours of time

**New!** ***The Teaching Tool Box provides easy access to all your teaching resources in one convenient place.***

By including all the instructor supplements, valuable student supplements, and unique lecture and prep tools in one convenient place, the Teaching Tool Box helps make prepping for class even easier.

### Complete Contents of Teaching Tool Box

- New! Instructor Resource DVD Demo
- New! Human Biology Support Manual
- New! Course-at-a-Glance: Quick Reference Guide
- Instructor Guide and Test Bank
- Computerized Test Bank
- Transparency Acetates
- Interactive Physiology® for Human Biology (IP for HB)

### New! Instructor Resource DVD

Now on DVD and with an easy-to-use file folder structure, the Instructor Resource DVD organizes all instructor media resources into one convenient, chapter-by-chapter resource package. See page xxvi for a full list of the contents of the IRDVD. A demo copy of the Instructor Resource DVD is available inside the Teaching Tool Box. Contact your Pearson sales representative for the full version.

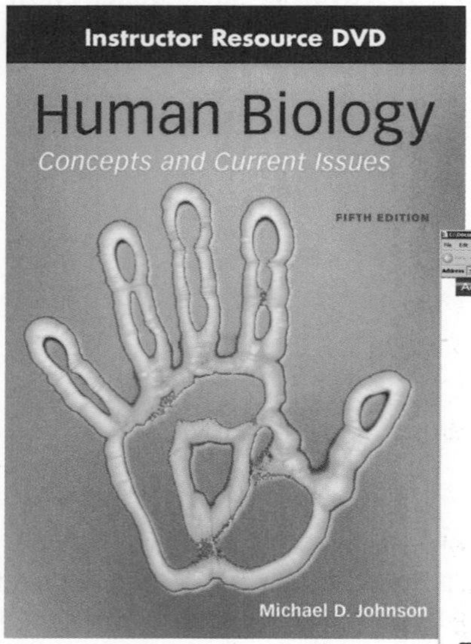


**Animations in the IRDVD**

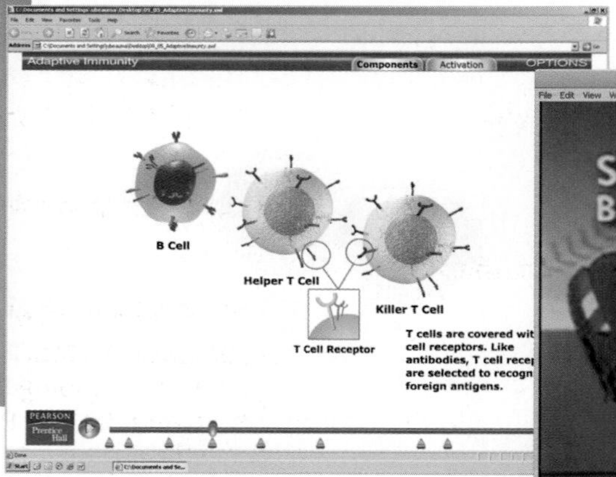


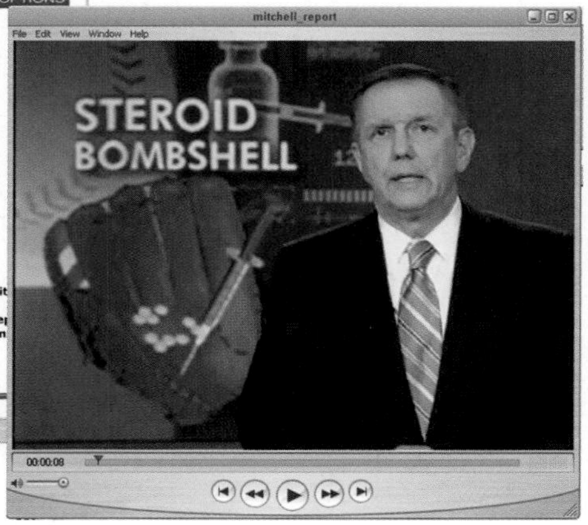


**ABC News video clips in the IRDVD**

### New! Human Biology Support Manual

Created specifically for adjuncts or first-time teachers, the Human Biology Support Manual provides a step-by-step visual lecture outline of all the resources available to instructors, plus helpful teaching tips and sample syllabi.

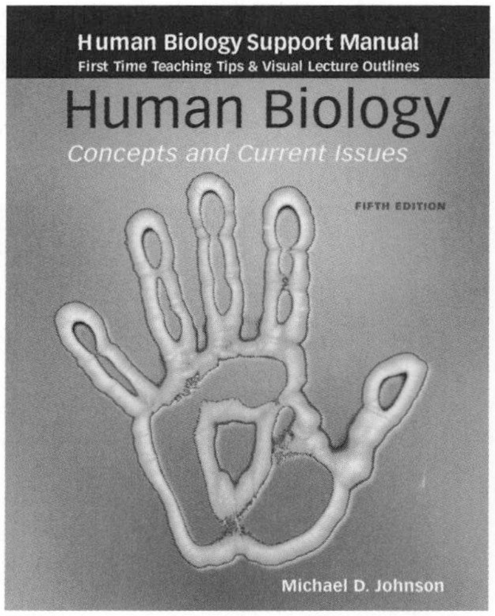

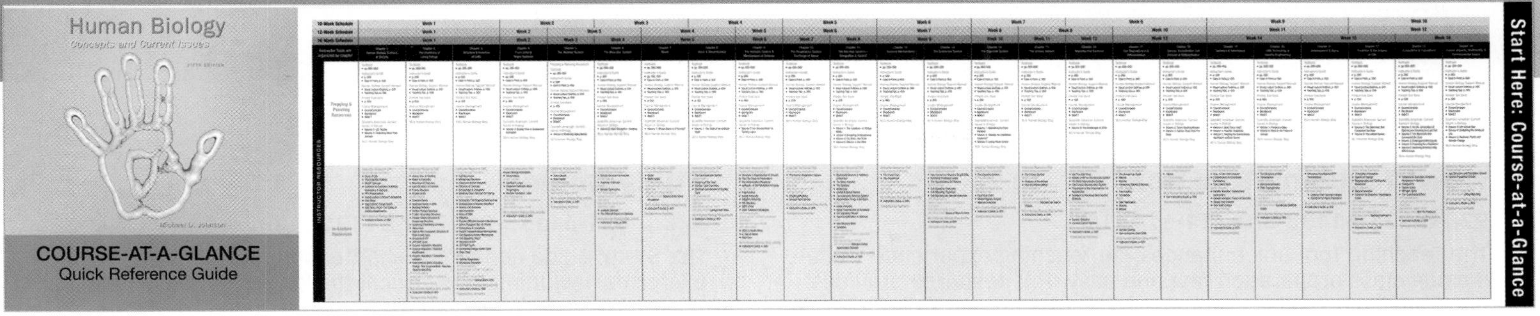


## New! Course-at-a-Glance Quick Reference Guide

This useful guide offers an easy roadmap to all of the contents of the Tool Box, organized for class prep and lecture.

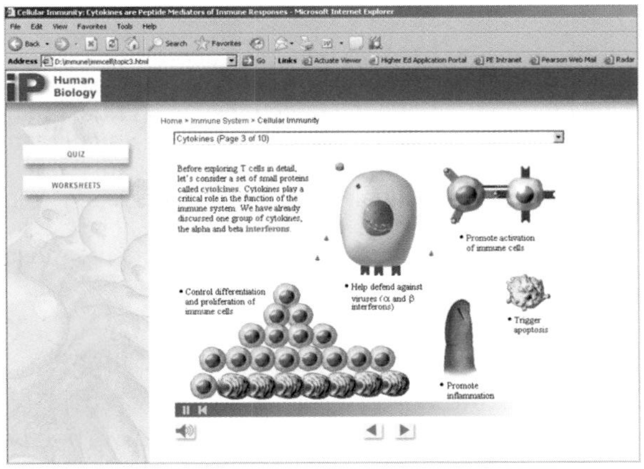


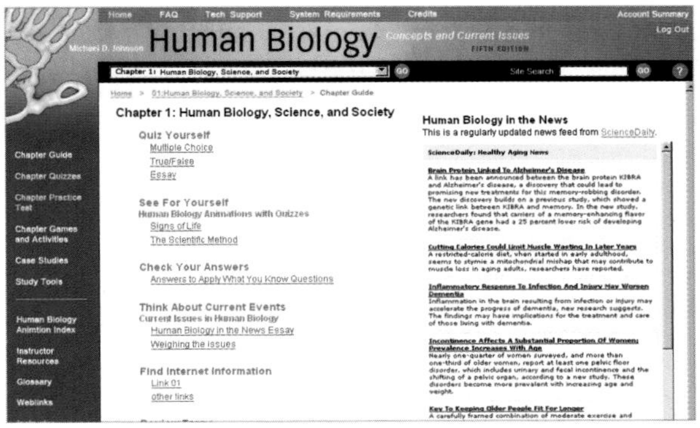


## Interactive Physiology® for Human Biology

Updated with a new Immune System module, Interactive Physiology® for Human Biology is adapted from the award-winning Interactive Physiology series specifically for human biology courses.

## Instructor Guide and Test Bank

This fully updated comprehensive resource contains a printed Test Bank with 75–100 questions per chapter and a chapter-by-chapter Instructor Guide.

## Computerized Test Bank

A Computerized Test Bank is available on a user-friendly cross-platform CD, and contains all the questions from the printed Test Bank to choose from or modify.

## Transparency Acetates

Over 400 transparencies include figures and tables from the text as full-color acetates.

## The Human Biology Place Website

**www.humanbiology.com**

The Human Biology Place offers students many features to independently assess and reinforce their understanding of each chapter. It contains true/false, multiple-choice, and essay self-quizzes for each chapter; animations; answers to Apply What You Know questions; an interactive glossary and flashcards; web links; chapter guides that provide study plans for each chapter; constantly updated RSS feeds of human biology news; and a downloadable free sample chapter of the Student Study Guide. Also included on the Human Biology Place are password-protected instructor teaching tools.

## Course Management

**CourseCompass™**
**www.pearsonhighered.com/coursecompass**

**WebCT** **www.pearsonhighered.com/webct**

**Blackboard** **www.pearsonhighered.com/blackboard**

CourseCompass™, WebCT, and Blackboard courses offer pre-loaded content including testing and assessment plus assets from the Human Biology Place website. These three course management systems are available as pre-built, easy-to-use courses that instructors can use to create sophisticated web-based educational programs.

# Complete Tools for Instructors and Students

## Instructor Supplements

### New! Teaching Tool Box

**978-0-321-61133-8/0-321-61133-0**

The Teaching Tool Box enhances the teaching experience while making class preparation fast and easy. This resource provides unparalleled instructor support. See pages xviii and xix for a full list of contents.

### New! Instructor Resource DVD

**978-0-321-61139-0/0-321-61139-X**

The Instructor Resource DVD organizes all instructor media resources into one convenient, chapter-by-chapter resource package. The Instructor Resource DVD includes: An image library of all the art (with and without labels), tables, and photos from the book; a selection of images with customizable labels and stepped-out art; PowerPoint® lecture presentation slides with embedded links to multimedia; clicker questions; over 150 animations; 28 ABC News video clips; *Scientific American: Current Issues in Biology* PowerPoint® slides; IP for HB slides, worksheets, and answer sheets; interactive Quiz Show games; Lab Manual Answers; and Word files for the Instructor Guide and Test Bank. A demo copy of the Instructor Resource DVD is available inside the Teaching Tool Box. The full version can be ordered by adopters through your Pearson sales representative.

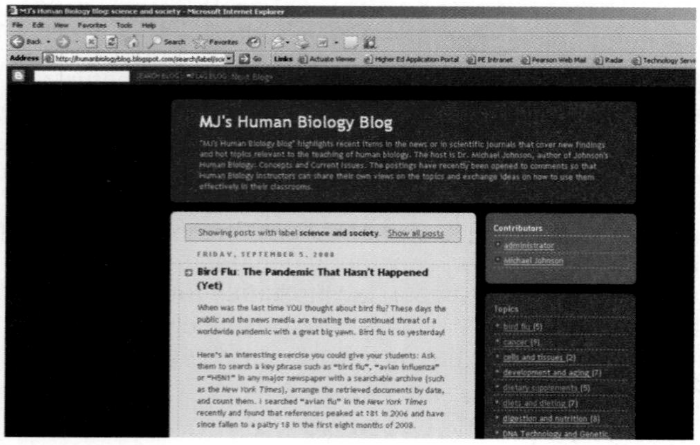


### Mike Johnson's Human Biology Blog

**http://humanbiologyblog.blogspot.com**

Created specifically for instructors, Mike Johnson's Human Biology Blog helps you bring the excitement and relevance of breaking news into your human biology classroom. Mike Johnson continually updates the blog with descriptions of and source information for articles on new, interesting human biology topics and gives tips on how the topic can be used in class. The posts are grouped into categories to make it easy to select topics for each lecture. The Instructor Guide gives tips and examples on how to use the blog as well. Share your thoughts and tips with other instructors with the new commenting feature.

## Student Supplements

### Study Guide

**978-0-321-61135-2/0-321-61135-7**

The Study Guide contains a chapter summary, key concepts, exercises (including new critical thinking questions, matching, short answer, labeling, table completion, fill-in-the-blank, paragraph completion, word choice, true/false, and crossword puzzle), a chapter test, key concept review questions, and an answer key. A sample chapter of the Study Guide appears for free on the Human Biology Place website.

### Laboratory Manual

**978-0-132-44306-7/0-132-44306-6**

Written by Bert Atsma and Sandra Hsu, the Laboratory Manual includes safety guidelines, objectives, materials lists, topic introductions, activities with embedded questions, and critical thinking questions. Figures, tables and photos have been significantly updated and an emphasis on critical thinking is now present throughout the entire lab manual. Exercises 22 and 23, covering evolution and human ecology, have been significantly revised and other topics have been updated to give students the most current information available.

### Interactive Physiology for Human Biology

**978-0-321-59539-3/0-321-59539-4**

Interactive Physiology for Human Biology is a powerful tool to help students understand the key systems of the human body. A copy can be bundled at no additional charge with every new textbook; for more details, contact your Pearson sales representative.

### Human Biology Place Website

**www.humanbiology.com**

The open-access Human Biology Place is an interactive study tool that students can use to understand difficult topics and improve their grades in human biology.

### *Scientific American: Current Issues in Biology,* Volumes 1–5

**Volume 1: 978-0-8053-7507-7 • 0-8053-7507-4**
**Volume 2: 978-0-8053-7108-6 • 0-8053-7108-7**
**Volume 3: 978-0-8053-7527-5 • 0-8053-7527-9**
**Volume 4: 978-0-8053-3566-8 • 0-8053-3566-8**
**Volume 5: 978-0-321-54187-1 • 0-321-54187-1**

Give your students the best of both worlds — accessible, dynamic, relevant articles from *Scientific American* magazine that present key issues in biology, paired with the authority, reliability, and clarity of Benjamin Cummings' biology texts. Each article includes questions to help students check their comprehension and make connections between science and society. *Current Issues* is available at no additional charge when packaged with a new text. Corresponding instructor PowerPoint® lectures that feature images from the articles and are sure to stimulate class discussion can be found in the IRDVD.

# New to This Edition

With each new edition of *Human Biology: Concepts and Current Issues* Mike Johnson and the book team strive to make the text even more engaging, current, and applicable to students' lives. For the Fifth Edition we made a number of changes, globally throughout the text, and also in specific chapters.

## Changes Throughout the Book:

- **New Art Program!** In response to reviewer requests, we've completely revised our art to be more realistic and colorful. Almost every figure in the book has been revised or created anew. The result is beautiful, pedagogically sound art that jumps off the page and engages readers.
- **Emphasis on Critical Thinking** with new Apply What You Know questions. Students need to think critically about the content of the text and not just memorize facts; our book now contains more new and updated Apply What You Know questions.
- **Revised Intro Questions.** We have revised each set of Intro Questions to contain less trivia and to be more applicable to the content of each chapter.
- **Keeping an Eye on Currency and Accuracy.** Every chapter, box, question, and figure has been scrutinized to ensure that they are as current and accurate as possible.

## Chapter-Specific Changes:

Chapter 1, Human Biology, Science, and Society:

- The Current Issue on dietary supplements was substantially rewritten to include "functional foods."
- The recent threat posed by MRSA (methicillin-resistant *S. aureas*) is now mentioned in the Health Watch on antibiotic resistance.
- The relationship between correlation and causation (in Section 1.5) was explained in greater depth.

Chapter 2, The Chemistry of Living Things:

- New Figure 2.7, illustrating hydrogen bonds, shows the structures of water and particularly of ice much better.
- The Current Issue on antioxidants was updated.

Chapter 3, Structure and Function of Cells:

- The discussion of diffusion was improved with a clearer explanation that diffusion only works over very short distances.
- Figure 3.6 (diffusion) was replaced with a new photo that more clearly shows diffusion.
- The Current Issue on human stem cells was updated to include the latest findings that adult cells could be turned back into stem cells.

Chapter 4, From Cells to Organ Systems:

- A new Current Issue on lipodissolve replaces the old one on liposuction.

Chapter 5, The Skeletal System:

- The Black Market in Bones Current Issue was updated to include final resolution of the legal case.
- The topic of osteoporosis was moved from a Health Watch box into the last major subsection of the text on diseases and disorders.

Chapter 6, The Muscular System:

- Figure 6.10, illustrating muscle twitch, summation, and tetanus, was completely rethought.
- The Current Issue entitled Are Anabolic Steroids Dangerous? was entirely recast as a new issue on Drug Abuse by Athletes.

Chapter 7, Blood:

- The Section 7.3 subsection entitled Rh Blood Typing is Based on Rh Factor was substantially rewritten for clarity and accuracy.

Chapter 8, Heart and Blood Vessels:

- The Current Issue entitled Merck Faces Lawsuits over Vioxx was updated to reflect new events in the lawsuits against Merck.

Chapter 9, The Immune System and Mechanisms of Defense:

- Fourth Edition Figures 9.3 and 9.4, illustrating the lymphatic system and its components, were combined into one.
- Fourth Edition Figure 9.13, illustrating the formation and activation of T cells, was rethought and split into two.
- Fourth Edition Table 9.1, on physical and chemical barriers to pathogens, was removed.
- A map of the world was added to the AIDS Current Issue and all AIDS data were updated.

Chapter 10, Respiratory System: Exchange of Gases:

- A new Current Issue on Smokers' Rights replaces the old one on an epidemic of childhood asthma.

Chapter 11, The Nervous System: Integration and Control:

- The Health Watch box on repairing spinal cord injuries now includes the story of Kevin Everett.

Chapter 12, Sensory Mechanisms:

- Discussion of taste buds on the tongue was revised for the new understanding that there are not clear "taste zones" on the tongue.

Chapter 13, The Endocrine System:

- A new Figure 13.10 replaces Fourth Edition Figure 13.9. The new figure better shows the dual control of blood glucose by insulin and glucagons.
- The writing in Section 13.4 on glycogen and insulin was tightened and simplified. So, too, was the cortisol section.

Chapter 14, The Digestive System and Nutrition:

- New Current Issue entitled Is Overweight Overstated?

Chapter 15, The Urinary System:

- The Current Issue was updated with information about patients and donors using the Internet to find organ matches.

Chapter 16, Reproductive Systems:

- Several new figures have been added, illustrating photos of common STIs and contraceptive choices.
- Figure 16.8 shows how a positive feedback cycle causes ovulation every month.

Chapter 17, Cell Reproduction and Differentiation:

- Added detail to the Current Issue on human cloning.

Chapter 18, Cancer: Uncontrolled Cell Division and Differentiation:

- New Current Issue entitled Voluntary Breast and Ovary Removal—Could You Do It?
- New hard-hitting Figure 18.7, showing the human cost of popularizing smoking.

Chapter 19, Genetics and Inheritance:

- This chapter was heavily revised overall.
- More coverage and background of Gregor Mendel's work with pea plants.
- New clarification between dominance and frequency of alleles in a population, using the example of polydactyly in humans and cats, with a new Figure 19.5 to illustrate the concept.
- Expanded coverage of two-trait crosses, with new Figures 19.6 and 19.7 to illustrate the concept.
- New Try It Yourself activity about blood type inheritance.
- Removed the Sex Chromosomes May Have Arisen By Chance Mutation section.

Chapter 20, DNA Technology and Genetic Engineering:

- The Current Issue on genetically modified foods is now entitled Should We Be Harnessing the Potential of GM Plants?, reflecting a neutral, more practical approach to the risks and rewards of GM crops.

Chapter 21, Development and Aging:

- New section on gender determination: Section 21.5,Gender Determination Begins at Six Weeks, with a new Figure 21.12 illustrating the development of the external genitalia.

Chapter 22, Evolution and the Origins of Life:

- The Current Issue, entitled The Flores People Controversy Heats Up, describes the growing controversy over whether *Homo floresiensis* is (or is not) a new hominid species.

Chapter 23, Ecosystems and Populations:

- This chapter was heavily revised overall.
- Updated discussion of carrying capacity of the human population.
- Combined Fourth Edition Figures 23.4 and 23.6 into new Figure 23.0 showing past and projected human population.
- New, more in-depth discussion of climax communities, with a new photo.
- Added new Figure 23.9 illustrating energy flow and chemical recycling in a pond ecosystem.
- Added examples of wetland damage to the water cycle discussion.
- In the Current Issue, all data were updated.

Chapter 24, Human Impacts, Biodiversity, and Environmental Issues:

- This chapter was heavily revised overall.
- Added more examples of pollution and human effects on the environment.
- Added information on the Genuine Progress Indicator (GPI).
- More coverage of sustainable initiatives and renewable energy throughout the chapter, including new and updated Figures 24.11, 24.12, and 24.13.
- Added discussion of water vapor as a greenhouse gas.
- Discussion of biological magnification changed from DDT to mercury, to make it more current and relevant to today.
- Added new Directions in Science box titled Biofuels: The Fuels of the Future?
- In the Current Issue, added discussions of carbon trading and carbon sequestering technologies, as well as a discussion of human adaptations that might become necessary with a warming planet.

# 1 Human Biology, Science, and Society

Crew of the space shuttle Atlantis, November 20, 2007.

**1** **True or False?** The only purpose of science is to improve the **human condition**.

**2** **True or False?** To be useful to a scientist, a **hypothesis** must be testable.

**3** Which of the following is **proof** that you are human? **a.** You can touch the tips of your fingers with your thumbs. **b.** You walk on two legs. **c.** You have a capacity for complex language and can read this book. **d.** Any one of the above.

**4** What is **anecdotal evidence**, and what is wrong with it?

**5** How are you similar to a **bacterium**? **a.** You require some form of energy. **b.** You have the ability to reproduce. **c.** You respond to the environment around you. **d.** All the above.

**You were born into exciting times,** when scientific discoveries are happening more rapidly than at any other time in human history. Like the Industrial Revolution of the nineteenth century and the discovery of DNA in the twentieth, today's scientific innovations will change the human condition forever.

In your lifetime people may be able to select or modify their children's features before they are born. People may even be able to have clones (copies) made of themselves. At the very least, certain diseases that threaten us now will become curable. Perhaps your grandchildren will not even know what AIDS is because the disease will have disappeared.

What you are witnessing is the power of science. **Science** is the study of the *natural world,* which includes all matter and all energy. Because all living organisms are also made of matter and energy, they are part of the natural world (Figure 1.1). Biology is one of many branches of science. More specifically, **biology** (from the Greek words *bios,* life, and *logos,* word or thought) is the study of living organisms and life's processes. It is the study of life. Other branches of science are chemistry, physics, geology, astronomy, and related fields such as medicine.

This text is specifically about *human* biology. We will explore what it means to be alive. We will see how the molecules that make up our bodies are created from molecules in the air and in our food and drink. We will learn how our cells grow and divide, and how we evolved from single-celled organisms that arose from nonliving chemical elements nearly 3.5 billion years ago. We will explore how our bodies function, why we get diseases, and how we manage to survive them. We will look at how we develop into adults, reproduce, and influence the destinies of other organisms on Earth.

With the power of science comes an awesome responsibility. All of us, individually and collectively, must choose how to use the knowledge that science gives us. Will human cloning be acceptable? Can we prevent global warming? Should your insurance company be able to reject you for coverage because genetic testing shows that you may develop cancer 40 years from now?

We all have to make responsible decisions concerning not only our own health and well-being but also the long-term well-being of our species. This book considers many aspects of human interaction with the natural world. We'll contemplate human functioning within the environment and the impact of humans on the environment. Along the way we'll confront a variety of social and personal issues and discuss the choices we might make about them. Because biology is the study of life, we begin by defining life itself.

**RECAP**

Science is the study of the natural world, which consists of all matter and energy. Biology is the study of living organisms. ■

## 1.1 The characteristics of life

What is life? On one hand, this question seems easy and on the other so abstract that it is more like a riddle. We all think we can recognize life even if we can't define it easily. Children learn early to distinguish between living and nonliving things. Remember that childhood game "animal, vegetable, or mineral"? In it, children distinguish what is alive (animals and plants) from what is not (minerals).

Most biologists accept the following criteria as signs of life:

- *Living things have a different molecular composition than nonliving things do.* Everything in the natural world, both living and nonliving, is composed of the same set of approximately 100 different chemical *elements*. However, only a few elements are present in any abundance in living organisms. In addition, living organisms can combine elements in unique ways, creating certain *molecules* (combinations of elements) that nonliving things cannot create. These molecules of life (proteins, carbohydrates, lipids, and nucleic acids) are found in all living organisms and often persist in the remains of dead organisms. Variations in these molecules in different life forms account for the diversity of life.

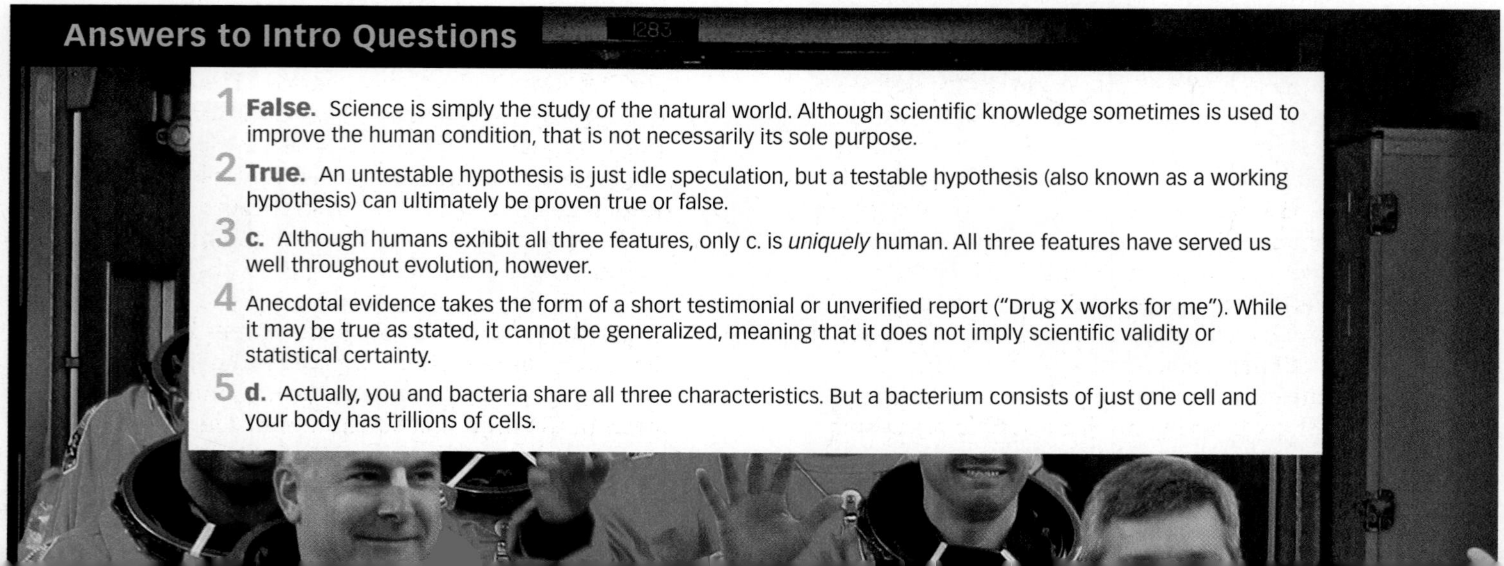

### Answers to Intro Questions

1 **False.** Science is simply the study of the natural world. Although scientific knowledge sometimes is used to improve the human condition, that is not necessarily its sole purpose.

2 **True.** An untestable hypothesis is just idle speculation, but a testable hypothesis (also known as a working hypothesis) can ultimately be proven true or false.

3 **c.** Although humans exhibit all three features, only c. is *uniquely* human. All three features have served us well throughout evolution, however.

4 Anecdotal evidence takes the form of a short testimonial or unverified report ("Drug X works for me"). While it may be true as stated, it cannot be generalized, meaning that it does not imply scientific validity or statistical certainty.

5 **d.** Actually, you and bacteria share all three characteristics. But a bacterium consists of just one cell and your body has trillions of cells.

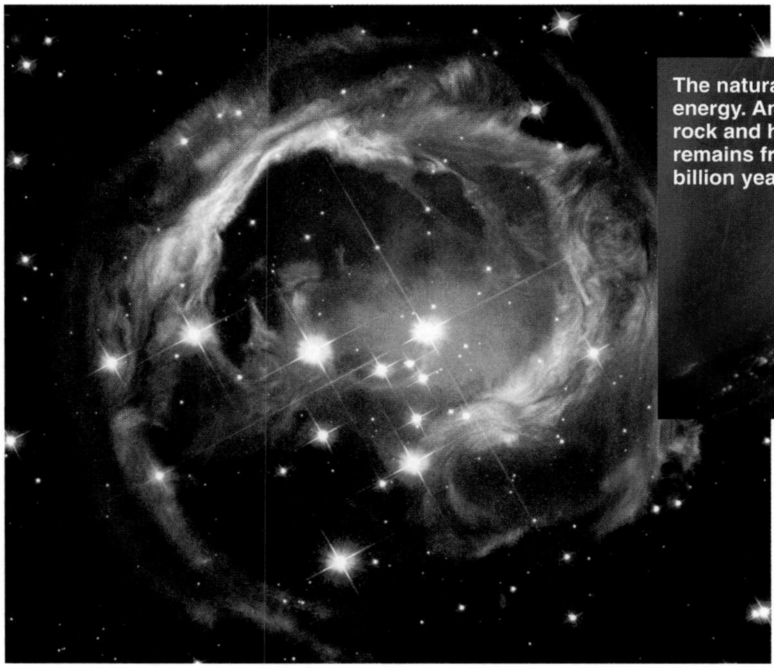

Photo taken from the Hubble Space Telescope showing a tiny portion of the universe. Studies by astronomers have shown that all matter on Earth originated inside stars or with the Big Bang.

**The natural world comprises all matter and energy. An erupting volcano spewing liquid rock and heat is the result of energy that still remains from the creation of Earth nearly 4.6 billion years ago.**

Jane Goodall has dedicated her life to studying the needs and behaviors of chimpanzees. The DNA of humans and chimps is almost the same, yet important physical and behavioral differences are obvious. Evolution examines how these differences arose.

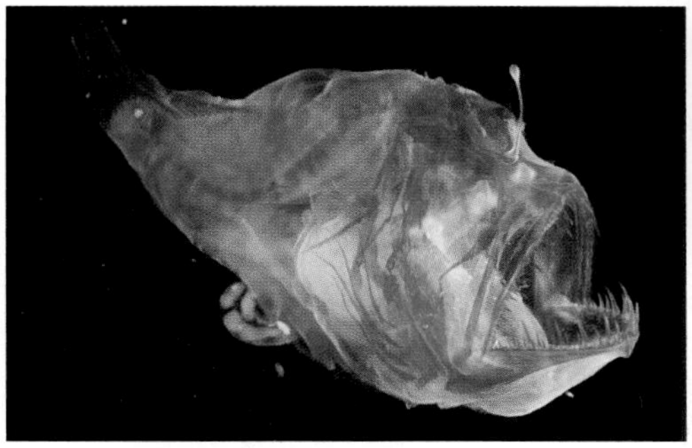

Studying this unusual fish from deep waters off California allows biologists to understand the processes by which a species successfully survives. Many different environments exist in the world, but the same physical and chemical laws govern them all.

**Figure 1.1 Studies of the natural world.**

- *Living things require energy and raw materials.* The creation of the molecules of life doesn't happen by accident, at least under present conditions on Earth. The transformation of molecules from one form to another requires energy. The term **metabolism** refers to the physical and chemical processes involved in transforming energy and molecules so that life can be maintained. All living things take in raw materials and energy from the environment and metabolize them into the molecules and energy that they need to survive. Plants use the energy of sunlight and chemicals obtained from soil, water, and air. Animals and all other forms of life ultimately obtain their energy and raw materials from water, air, plants, or other animals.
- *Living things are composed of cells.* A **cell** is the smallest unit that exhibits all the characteristics of life (Figure 1.2). All cells come only from existing cells. There is always at least one cell in any living thing, and some organisms (called *unicellular* organisms) are *only* one cell. *Multicellular* organisms are composed of many cells or many different types of cells.
- *Living things maintain homeostasis.* All living organisms must maintain an internal environment compatible with life, and the range of chemical and physical conditions compatible with life is very narrow. The maintenance of a relatively constant internal environment is called **homeostasis.** Living things have developed remarkable ways of regulating their internal environment despite sometimes dramatic changes in the external environment. Single cells and unicellular organisms are surrounded by a membrane that allows the cell (or organism) to maintain internal homeostasis by providing a selective barrier to the entry and exit of various substances. In multicellular organisms the tissues, organs, and organ systems work together to maintain homeostasis of the fluid that surrounds all cells. We discuss the importance of homeostasis further in Chapter 4.

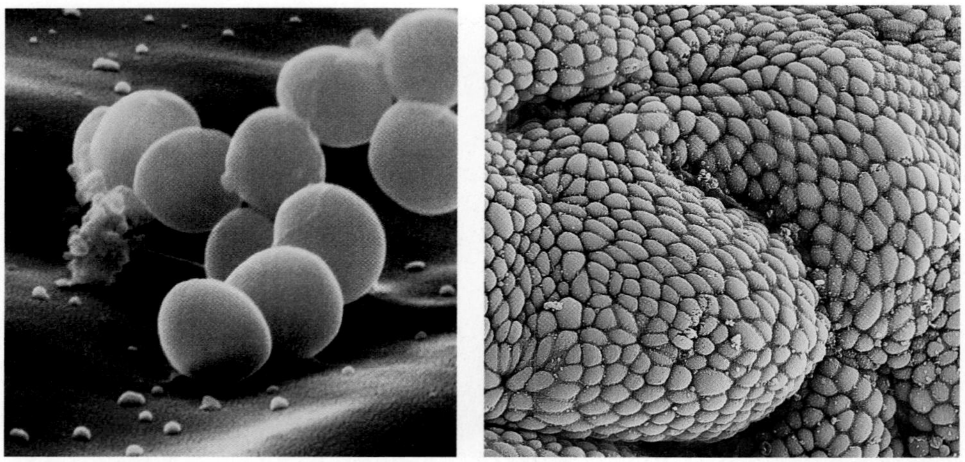

a) b)

**Figure 1.2 Cells are the smallest units of life.** Some organisms consist of just one cell (unicellular), whereas others contain many cells (multicellular). **(a)** *Staphylococcus aureus*, the bacterium that causes food poisoning (SEM × 50,000). **(b)** Some of the many cells that line the inner surface of the human stomach (SEM × 500).

- *Living things respond to their external environment.* Stay out in the cold too long and you are likely to respond by moving to a warm room. Plants respond to their environment by turning their leaves toward light or by growing roots toward sources of nutrients and water. Even bacteria respond to their environment by moving toward nutrients (and away from noxious stimuli) and by increasing their growth rate.
- *Living things grow and reproduce.* Living organisms have the capacity to grow and ultimately produce more living organisms like themselves (Figure 1.3). The ability to grow and reproduce is determined by the genetic material in cells, called DNA. Some nonliving things can get larger, of course; examples are glaciers and volcanic mountains. However, they cannot create copies of themselves.
- *Populations of living things evolve.* The various forms of life may change over many generations in a process known as evolution. Evolution explains why there are so many different forms of life on Earth today.

Although all these characteristics are necessary to describe life fully, not all of them apply to every living thing all the time. Individual organisms do not evolve, nor do they necessarily reproduce or always respond to their surroundings. However, populations of similar organisms have the *capacity* to perform these functions.

**RECAP**

All living things are composed of cells. Living things require energy and raw materials, maintain homeostasis, respond to their external environments, grow and reproduce, and evolve over many generations. ■

## 1.2 How humans fit into the natural world

### Living things are grouped according to their characteristics

To find order in the diversity of life, biologists have long sought ways to categorize living things. In 1969 a classification system of *five kingdoms* was proposed. In this system the fundamental criteria for classifying organisms are the presence or absence of a nucleus, the number of cells, and the type of metabolism. One kingdom comprises organisms lacking a nucleus (the prokaryotes), and the remaining four kingdoms comprise organisms with cell nuclei (the eukaryotes).

The five-kingdom classification system (Figure 1.4a) places all single-celled prokaryotic organisms in the kingdom **Monera,** which comprises the bacteria, some of the oldest, smallest, simplest, and most successful organisms on Earth. Of the four kingdoms of eukaryotes, three of them (**Animalia, Plantae,** and **Fungi**) consist of

**Figure 1.3 Living things grow and reproduce.**

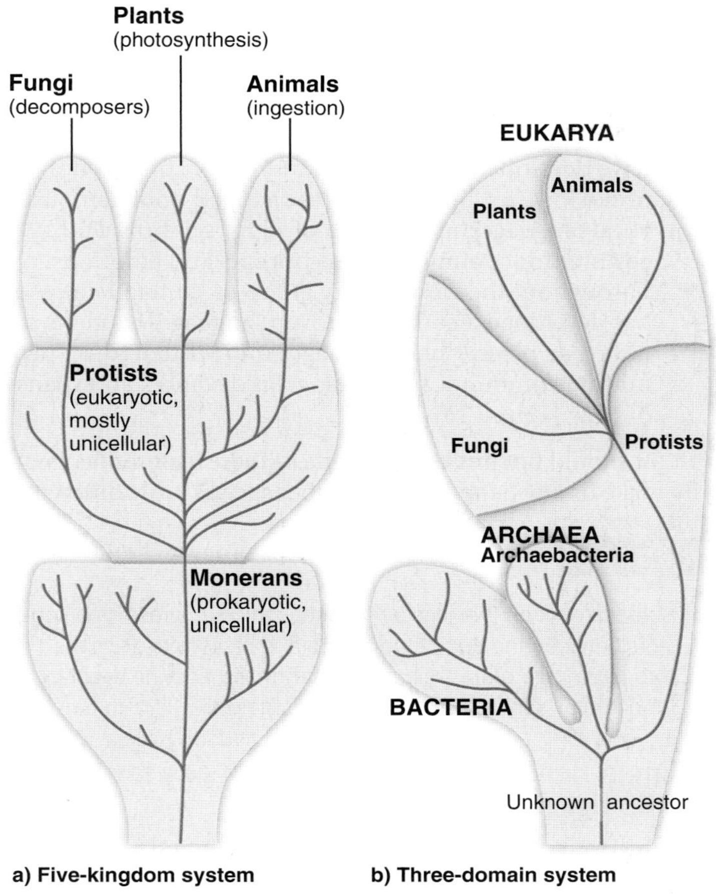


**Figure 1.4 Categorizing organisms. (a)** The five-kingdom system classifies organisms based on the presence or absence of a cell nucleus, cellular structure (multicellular or unicellular), and certain characteristics of structure, life cycle, and mode of nutrition. **(b)** The three-domain system places prokaryotes in one of two domains based on their biochemical and molecular characteristics, and puts all eukaryotes in a single domain.

multicellular organisms. The criteria for classifying animals, plants, and fungi are based largely on the organism's life cycle, structure, and mode of nutrition. Plants, for example, contain a green pigment called chlorophyll that allows them to capture the energy of sunlight, which they convert for their own use in a process called **photosynthesis.** Animals get the energy they need by eating plants or other animals, which requires structures specialized to digest and absorb food. Most animals can move about to obtain food. Fungi (yeasts, molds, and mushrooms) are *decomposers,* meaning that they obtain their energy from decaying material. The fourth group of eukaryotes, the kingdom **Protista,** comprises unicellular and relatively simple multicellular eukaryotes such as protozoa, algae, and slime molds. All animals, plants, and fungi are thought to have evolved from single-celled protistan-type organisms.

In recent years new techniques in molecular biology and biochemistry have distinguished two fundamentally different types of prokaryotes. For this reason, many biologists now advocate a classification system that begins with *domains,* a higher classification level that encompasses kingdoms. In the three-domain system (see Figure 1.4b) the organisms of the kingdom Monera are distributed across two domains (**Bacteria** and **Archaea**), each comprising a kingdom, while all organisms whose cells have nuclei fall into the third domain, the **Eukarya.** The domain Eukarya thus comprises all four eukaryotic kingdoms.

Other classification systems have been proposed, including systems with five, seven, and eight kingdoms. All these systems are subject to change as new information is discovered. There is no debate, however, concerning the classification of humans within the animal kingdom.

Humans belong to a subgroup of the animal kingdom called *vertebrates,* defined as animals with a nerve cord and a backbone. Within the vertebrates, humans are subclassified as *mammals,* defined as vertebrates with mammary glands for nursing their young. Among the mammals, we, along with apes and monkeys, are further classified as *primates.*

The smallest unit of any classification system is the species. A **species** is one or more populations of organisms with similar physical and functional characteristics that interbreed and produce fertile offspring under natural conditions. All living humans belong to the same **genus** (the second smallest unit of classification) and species, called *Homo sapiens.* We share features that make us different from any other species on Earth, and we can interbreed.

No one knows how many species of living organisms exist on Earth. Estimates range from about 3 million to 30 million, but only about 2 million species have been identified so far.

**RECAP**

Classification systems place living things into increasingly inclusive groups. The most inclusive is a domain and the smallest is a species. Humans belong to the kingdom Animalia within the domain Eukarya. Our genus and species is *Homo sapiens*. ■

## The defining features of humans

Humans are not the largest animal, nor the fastest or strongest. Our eyesight and hearing are not the best. We can't fly, we swim poorly, and we don't dig holes in the ground very well with our hands. How have we managed to survive? We possess several features that, taken together, define how we are different from other organisms:

- *Bipedalism.* Humans are the only mammals that prefer to stand upright and walk on two legs. Bipedalism (from the Latin *bi-,* two, and *pes,* foot) frees our hands and forearms for carrying items ranging from weapons to infants. Birds walk upright, too, of course, but they do not have the advantage of being able to carry things with their forelimbs.

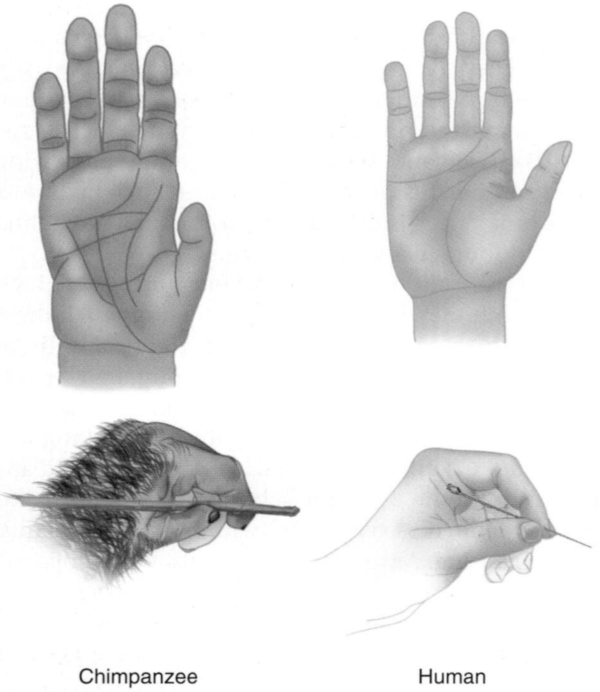


**Figure 1.5 How humans and chimpanzees hold small objects.** Although the hands of humans and chimpanzees seem similar, only humans tend to hold objects between the tip of a thumb and the tips of the fingers.

- *Opposable thumbs.* Humans and several other primates have thumbs that can be moved into position to oppose the tips of the fingers. However, only humans have the well-developed muscles that enable us to exert a certain type of precise control over the thumb and fingers. For instance, we tend to pick up and manipulate small objects between the tip of the thumb and the tip of either the index or second finger (Figure 1.5). In contrast, chimpanzees more naturally grasp objects between the thumb and the side of the index finger. Threading a needle or suturing a wound would be difficult for a chimpanzee.
- *Large brain.* Humans have a large brain mass relative to body size. The evolution of a large brain seems to have coincided with the advent of stone tools, leading some scientists to suggest that a large brain was required for the complex motions associated with tool use. Other scientists believe that a large brain was necessary for language, and that language developed as social interactions among humans became more important.
- *Capacity for complex language.* Many animals vocalize (produce sounds) to warn, threaten, or identify other members of their species, and a few (such as dolphins) have developed fairly complex forms of communication. However, humans have developed both complex vocal language and a system of signs, symbols, and gestures for communicating concepts and emotions. Throughout the world, every group of human beings has developed a complex spoken language. Humans have also placed their languages into written form, permitting communication over great distances and spans of time (Figure 1.6).

**Figure 1.6 Language.** Human societies throughout the world have developed complex written languages.

It should be stressed that none of these features necessarily make us any better than any other species, only different.

**RECAP**

Humans walk on two legs (are bipedal) and can grasp small objects between the tips of the thumb and first finger. Humans also have large brains relative to body mass, and the capacity for complex spoken and written languages. ■

### Human biology can be studied on any level of biological organization

Figure 1.7 shows how humans fit into the grand scheme of things in the natural world. The figure also shows how humans—or any living thing, for that matter—can be studied on any level of biological organization, from the level of the atom to the level of the biosphere. This text examines human biology on progressively larger scales.

Our study of human biology begins with the smallest units of life. Like rocks, water, and air, humans are composed of small units of natural elements called *atoms* and *molecules.* We'll introduce the basic chemistry of living things in Chapter 2. In Chapter 3 we'll see how the atoms and molecules of living things are arranged into the smallest of living units called *cells.* Next, we'll learn how, in multicellular organisms, groups of similar cells become *tissues,* how groups of tissues that carry out a specific function constitute an *organ,* and how organs may work together in an *organ system* to carry out a more general function (Chapter 4). The structures and functions of specific human organs and organ systems are the subjects of Chapters 5–16. For example, we'll learn why—and how—more blood flows through the

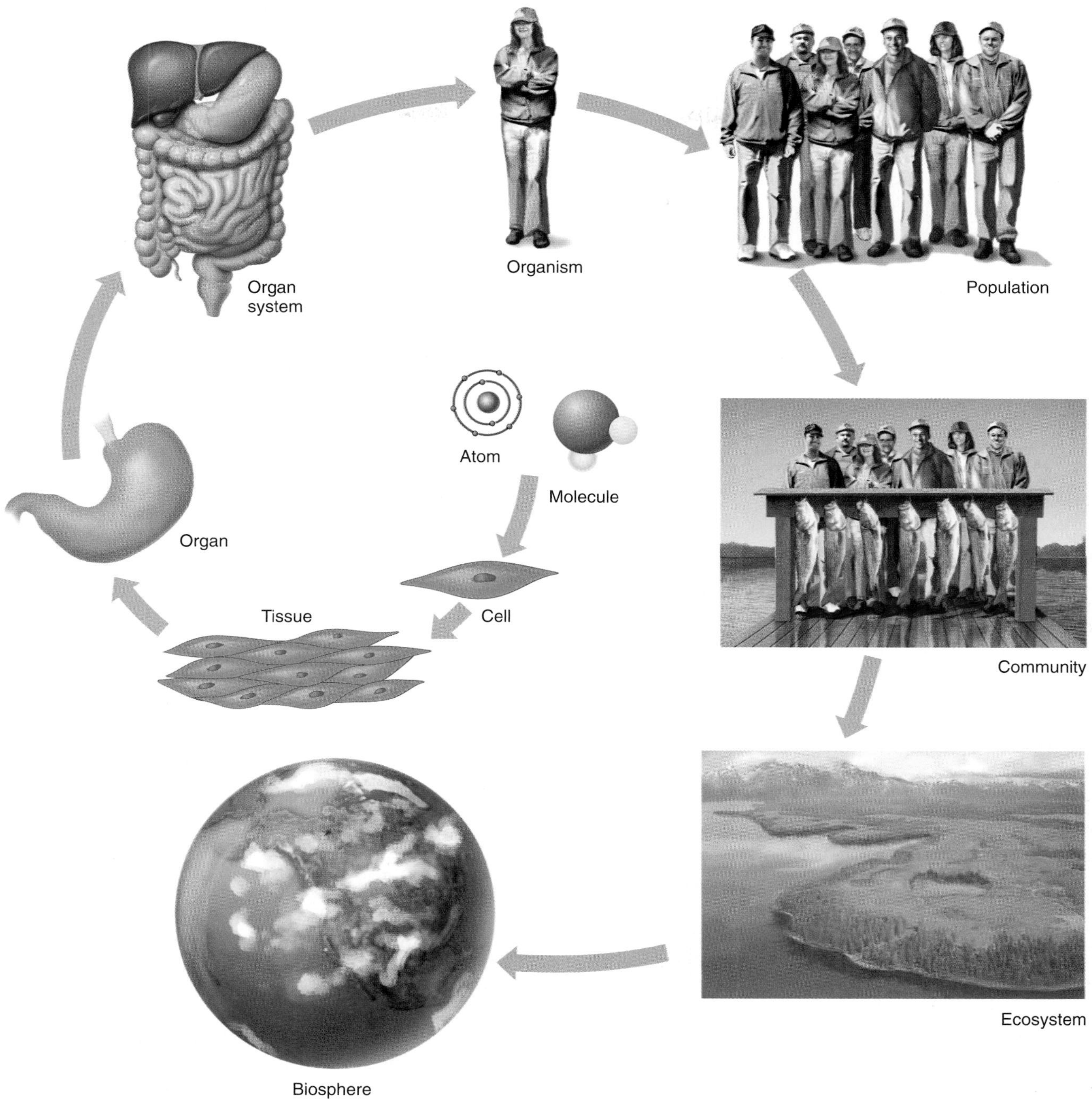


**Figure 1.7 Levels of organization in human biology.** Human biology is at the heart of a number of current issues in our society.

lungs than through any other organ and what happens to your dinner as it makes its way through your digestive system. Chapters 17–21 consider humans as complete *organisms,* including how cells reproduce, how we inherit traits from our parents, and how we develop, age, and die. Finally, we'll discuss how *communities* of living organisms evolved and how life began (Chapter 22), and how humans fit into and alter the *ecosystems* in which we live and the entire *biosphere* of the natural world (Chapters 23 and 24).

Table 1.1 lists some current issues, controversies, and "hot topics" that relate to human biology. Many of these issues and controversies also concern fields outside the sphere of science, such as economics, law, politics, and ethics. What you learn in this course will help you make informed decisions about these and future issues that will come up in your lifetime.

Your ability to make good judgments in the future and to feel comfortable with your decisions will depend on your critical thinking skills. We turn now to a discussion of what science

**Table 1.1 Examples of issues and controversies associated with the levels of human biology**

| Level of organization | Definition | Issues and controversies |
|---|---|---|
| Atom and molecule | **Atom:** smallest unit of an element of matter.<br>**Molecule:** More than one atom in a stable association. | Disposing of radioactive wastes<br>Role of free radicals in cancer and aging |
| Cell | Smallest unit of life. | Cloning adult animals, plants, and humans from a single cell |
| Tissue | An association of cells with the same general structure and function. | Using human fetal tissues in research |
| Organ | An association of several tissue types that carry out a specific function. | Increasing the supply of human organs for transplantation<br>Transplanting animal organs into humans |
| Organ system | Two or more organs that work together to carry out a general function, such as digestion or movement. | Enhancing human performance with drugs or by genetic engineering |
| Organism | An individual living being composed of several organs or organ systems. | Testing for heritable diseases for which there are no cures<br>Abortion<br>Deciding who should pay for human behavior-related illnesses such as those caused by smoking |
| Population | A group of individuals of the same species living in the same area. | Rationing medical care<br>Determining who gets the scarce human organs available for transplantation |
| Community | Several populations of different species who inhabit the same area and interact with each other. | Impact of humans on the well-being and survival of other species<br>Genetic engineering of plants and animals for human purposes<br>Using animals in medical research and cosmetics testing |
| Ecosystem | All of the organisms in a given area plus all of the nonliving matter and energy. | Environmental pollution<br>Destruction of ecosystems due to overuse by humans |
| Biosphere | All ecosystems combined. The portion of Earth occupied by living organisms, plus those organisms. | Global warming<br>Destruction of the ozone layer |

is, how we can use the methodology of science to improve our critical thinking skills, and how science influences our lives.

**RECAP**

Humans, along with all other organisms, live in a world that is highly organized. From atoms to cells, from organ to organism, and from community to biosphere, each level of biological organization is increasingly inclusive. ■

## 1.3 Science is both a body of knowledge and a process

We have already said that science is the study of the natural world. More explicitly, science is two things: *knowledge* (organized, reliable information) about the natural world, and the *process* we use to get that knowledge. *Scientific knowledge* refers to information about the natural world. The process of science, or the way scientific knowledge is acquired, is generally called the **scientific method,** although in practice this term encompasses a variety of methods. Throughout this book you will be presented with scientific knowledge, but it's good to remember that this information was obtained slowly over time by the scientific method.

Scientific knowledge enables us to describe and predict the natural world. Scientific knowledge is also empirical, meaning that it relies on observation and experimentation. Through the scientific method, scientists strive to accumulate information that is as free as possible of bias, embellishment, or interpretation.

### The scientific method is a process for testing ideas

Although there is more than one way to gather information about the natural world, the scientific method is a systematic process for developing and testing predictions (Figure 1.8). You probably already use the scientific method, or at least elements of it, in your own everyday problem solving. Sometimes we go through the steps without thinking about them consciously, but we follow them nevertheless.

**Step 1: Observe and generalize** When we observe the world around us and make generalizations from what we learn, we are employing *inductive reasoning* (extrapolating from the specific to the general case). Usually we don't even think about it and don't bother to put our observations and generalizations into any kind of formal language, but we do it just the same. For example, you are probably convinced that it will *always* be colder in winter than in summer (a generalization) because you have observed that every winter in the past was colder than the preceding summer (specific observation). The difference between common experience and good science is that science uses generalization to make a prediction that can be tested. Taking an example from biological research, let's start with two observations and a generalization:

*Observation 1:* Rats given a particular drug (call it Drug X) have lower blood pressures than rats not fed the drug.

*Observation 2:* Independently, researchers in Canada showed that Drug X lowers blood pressures in dogs and cats.

*Generalization:* Drug X lowers blood pressure in all mammals.

**Step 2: Formulate a hypothesis** Observations and generalizations are used to develop a *hypothesis.* A **hypothesis** is a tentative statement about the natural world. Importantly, it is a statement that can lead to testable deductions.

*Hypothesis:* Drug X would be a safe and effective treatment for high blood pressure in humans.

**Step 3: Make a testable prediction** Hypotheses that cannot be tested are idle speculation, so much hot air. But many hypotheses are so sweeping and comprehensive that ways must be found to test them under a variety of conditions. For example, you probably would not be convinced that Drug X is safe and effective for all people under all conditions until you had at least tested it in quite a few people under many different conditions. To have confidence in your hypothesis, you must make testable predictions (also called *working hypotheses*) based on the hypothesis and then test them one at a time. Predictions employ *deductive reasoning* (applying the

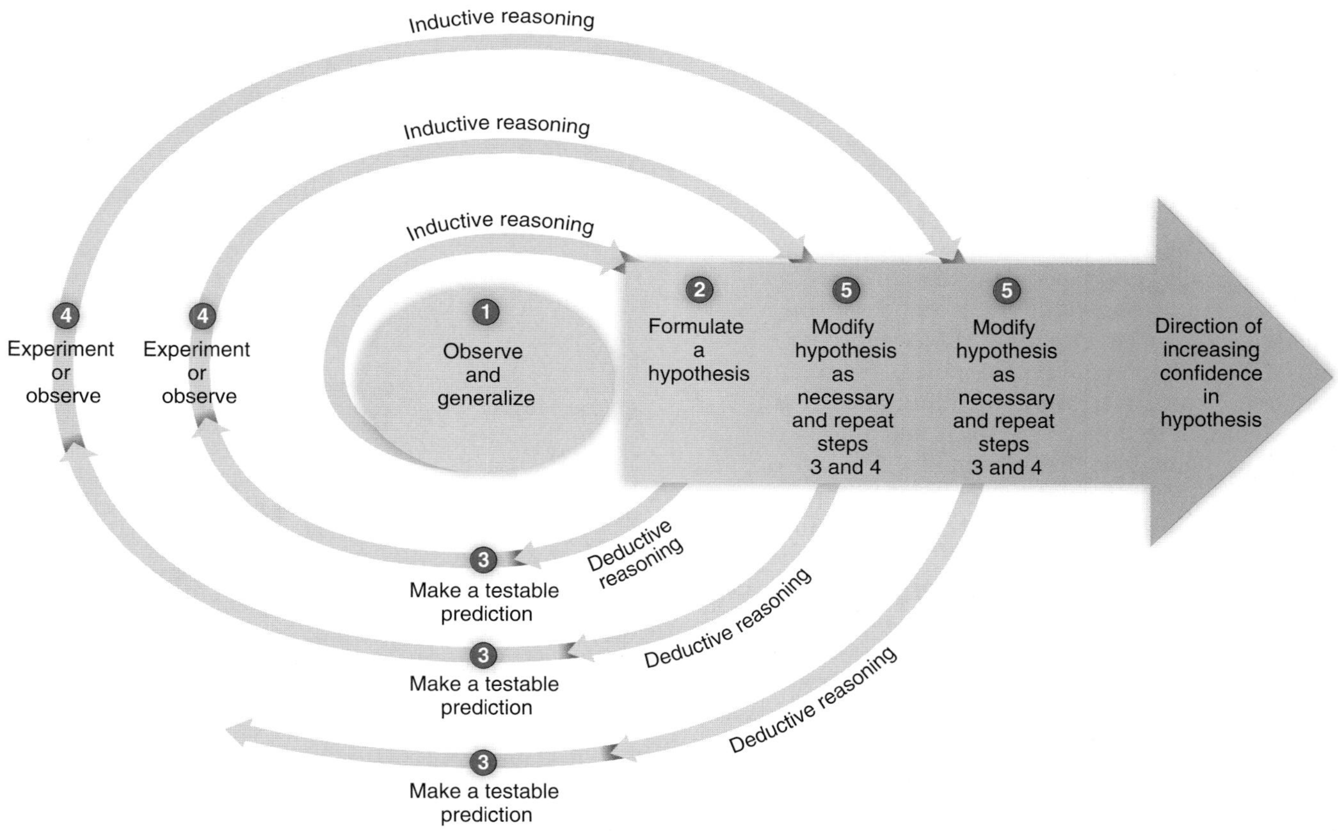


**Figure 1.8 The scientific method.** Observations and generalizations lead to the formulation of a hypothesis. From the hypothesis, specific predictions are made that can be tested by experimentation or observation. The results either support the hypothesis or require that it be modified to fit the new facts. The cycle is repeated. Ultimately the scientific method moves in the direction of increased confidence in the modified hypothesis.

general case to the specific). Often they are put in the form of an "if . . . then" statement, in which the "if" part of the statement is the hypothesis. For example:

*Prediction: If* Drug X is a safe and effective treatment for high blood pressure in humans, *then* 10 mg/day of Drug X will lower blood pressure in people with high blood pressure within one month.

Notice that the prediction is very specific. In this example the prediction specifies the dose of drug, the medical condition of the persons on whom it will be tested, the expected effect of the drug if the prediction is correct, and a specified time period for the test. Its specificity makes it testable—yes or no, true or false.

**Step 4: Experiment or observe** The truth or falsehood of your prediction is determined by observation or by experimentation. An **experiment** is a carefully planned and executed manipulation of the natural world to test your prediction. The experiment that you conduct (or the observations you make) will depend on the specific nature of the prediction.

When testing a prediction, scientists try to design experiments that can be conducted under strictly controlled conditions. Experiments conducted under specific, controlled conditions are called *controlled experiments* because they have the distinct advantage of accounting for all possible **variables** (factors that might vary during the course of the experiment) except for the one variable of interest, called the *controlled variable.* In this case the controlled variable is blood pressure. Therefore, in the example of Drug X, you could follow these steps in your controlled experiment (Figure 1.9):

- Select a large group of human subjects. In this case you would specifically choose people with high blood pressure rather than people with normal blood pressure.
- *Randomly* divide the larger pool of subjects into two groups. Designate one the **experimental group** and the other the **control group.** The importance of random assignment to the two groups is that all other factors that might affect the outcome (such as age or gender differences in responsiveness to the drug, or other previous health problems) are automatically equalized between the two groups. In effect, the control group accounts for all unknown factors. If you treat the experimental and control groups identically at this point, the probability is that the average blood pressures of the groups will be equal, as long as the groups are large enough.
- Treat subjects in the two groups *exactly* the same except that only the experimental group gets the drug. Treat the experimental group with 10 mg/day of Drug X for one month and the control group with a **placebo,** or "false treatment." If you deliver Drug X in a pill, the placebo should be an identical-looking pill with no drug in it. If you administer Drug X as an injection in a saline solution, the placebo should be an injection of the same volume of saline.

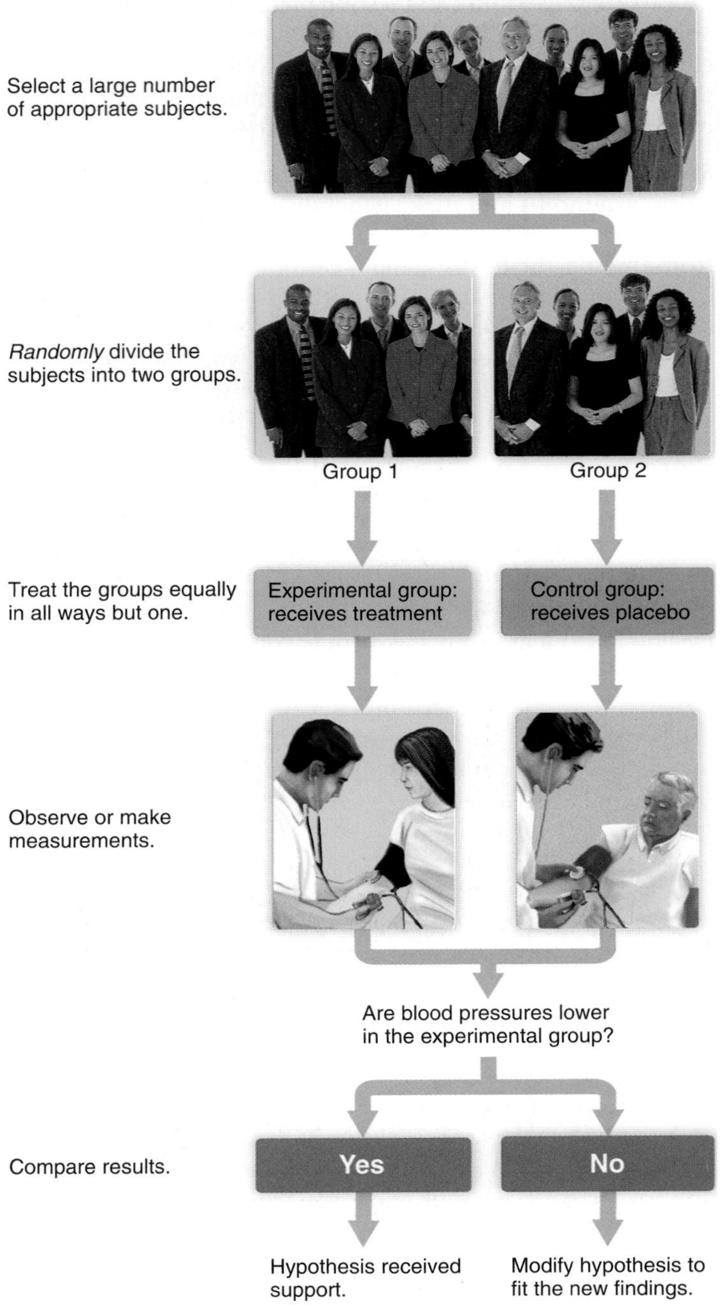


**Figure 1.9 The steps in a controlled experiment.** In this example the experimental variable is blood pressure. Because of the way the experiment is designed, the only difference between the two groups is the presence or absence of the experimental treatment itself.

When working with human subjects, scientists must take the power of suggestion into account. It is important that no subjects in either group know which group has received the drug. If members of the experimental group find out that they are getting a drug to lower their blood pressure, this knowledge may accidentally influence the outcome of the experiment. To eliminate the power of suggestion as a variable, researchers conduct experiments "blind," meaning that the subjects don't know whether they are getting the placebo or the drug. Sometimes experiments are done "double-blind," so that even the person administering the drugs and placebos does not know which is which until the experiment is over.

- Measure blood pressures in both groups at the end of one month and compare them using the appropriate statistical (mathematical) tests. If the experimental group's blood pressures are statistically lower, then your prediction is verified and your hypothesis receives support.

**Step 5: Modify the hypothesis as necessary and repeat steps 3 and 4** If your prediction turns out to be false, you will have to modify your hypothesis to fit the new findings and repeat steps 3 and 4. For example, perhaps the drug would lower blood pressure if you increased the dose or gave it for a longer period of time.

Even if your prediction turns out to be true, you're still not done. This is because you've tested only one small part of the hypothesis (its effectiveness under one specific set of conditions), not all the infinite possibilities. How do we know the drug is safe, and how safe is "safe," anyway? Does it cause a dangerous drop in blood pressure in people with normal blood pressures? Does it cause birth defects if taken by pregnant women? Does long-term use lead to kidney failure? Specific predictions may have to be stated and tested for each of these questions before the drug is allowed on the market.

Only after many scientists have tried repeatedly (and failed) to disprove a hypothesis do they begin to have more confidence in it. A hypothesis cannot be proved true; it can only be supported or disproved. As this example shows, the scientific method is a process of elimination that may be limited by our approach and even by our preconceived notions about what to test. We move toward the best explanation for the moment, with the understanding that it may change in the future.

### Making the findings known

New information is not of much use if hardly anybody knows of it. For that reason, scientists need to let others know of their findings. Often they publish the details in scientific journals to announce their findings to the world. Articles in *peer-reviewed* journals are subjected to the scrutiny of several experts (the scientists' peers) who must approve the article before it can be published. Peer-reviewed journals often contain the most accurate scientific information.

An unspoken assumption in any conclusion is that the results are valid only for the conditions under which the experiment was done. This is why scientific articles go into such detail about exactly how the experiment was performed. Complete documentation allows other scientists to repeat the experiments themselves or to develop and test their own predictions based on the findings of others.

Try to apply the scientific method to a hypothesis dealing with some aspect of evolution or to a global problem such as cancer or AIDS, and you begin to appreciate how scientists can spend a lifetime of discovery in science (and enjoy every minute!). At times the process seems like three steps forward and two steps back. You can bet that at least some of what you learn in this book will not be considered accurate 10 years from now. Nevertheless, even through our mistakes we make important new observations, some of which may lead to rapid advances in science and technology. Just in the last 100 years we've developed antibiotics, sent people to the moon, and put computers on millions of desks.

Many people associate science with certainty, whereas in reality scientists are constantly dealing with uncertainty. That is why we find scientists who don't agree or who change their minds. Building and testing hypotheses is slow, messy work, requiring that scientists constantly question and verify each other.

### A well-tested hypothesis becomes a theory

Many people think that a theory is a form of idle speculation or a guess. Scientists use the word quite differently. To scientists, a **theory** is a broad hypothesis that has been extensively tested and supported over time and that explains a broad range of scientific facts with a high degree of reliability.

A theory is the highest status that any hypothesis can achieve. Even theories, however, may be modified over time as new and better information emerges. Only a few hypotheses have been elevated to the status of theories in biology. Among them are the theory of evolution and the cell theory of life.

**RECAP**

The scientific method is a systematic process of observation, hypothesis building, and hypothesis testing. A theory is a broad hypothesis that has withstood numerous tests. ■

## 1.4 Sources of scientific information vary in style and quality

We are constantly bombarded by scientific information, some of it accurate and some not. What can you believe when the facts seem to change so quickly? All of us need to know how to find good information and evaluate it critically. Different sources of scientific information may have very different goals, so look for those that can best inform you at your own level of understanding and interest.

Some scientific knowledge is highly technical. As a result, scientists have a tendency to speak on a technical level and primarily to each other. As we've already mentioned, scientists often communicate by means of articles in specialized peer-reviewed journals such as *Nature* and *Science*. Articles in peer-reviewed journals are concise, accurate, and documented so thoroughly that another scientist ought to be able to duplicate the work after reading the article. Generally they refer extensively to previous literature on the subject. Articles in peer-reviewed journals make for laborious reading, and they are usually as dry as toast. But bear in mind that their purpose is primarily to inform other experts.

Other helpful print sources are science magazines and nonfiction books meant for the well-educated public. The goal is to inform the interested reader who may have only a limited background in science. The authors are usually science writers or experts who translate the finer scientific points into language that we can all understand. The information is generally accurate and readable, although the reader may not understand some of the details. Generally these articles and books tell readers who want to delve more deeply into the subject where to find more information.

General interest news magazines and daily newspapers also report on selected hot topics in science. Their goal is to get the information out as quickly as possible to a wide audience. Coverage is timely but less in-depth than in science magazines, and may not include the details you need to check the validity of the statements. A decided plus is that magazines and newspapers often discuss social, political, economic, legal, or ethical ramifications of the scientific findings, something generally lacking in the previous sources. Although the scientific information is usually accurate, the reporter may not understand the subject fully and may not provide adequate context. The best articles point readers to the original sources. Television (for instance, the Discovery Channel, *Nova*) also presents science-related topics to the public.

Since the 1980s, scientists and researchers have used the Internet to communicate and share ideas. The recent expansion of the World Wide Web has made the Internet accessible to the general public, opening exciting new sources of scientific information. Nearly all universities now have Web pages; the site addresses end in ".edu" (for "educational") rather than ".com" (for "commercial"). A number of scientific and professional organizations have created Web sites that offer helpful information for both scientists and consumers. Examples of organizations with Web sites include the National Institutes of Health, the American Cancer Society, and the American Heart Association. The Web addresses of government agencies and nonprofit organizations generally end in ".gov" and ".org," respectively.

Be aware that the Internet can also be a source of misinformation. At present the Internet is less closely regulated than print and broadcast media, so it can be difficult to tell the difference between objective reports and advertisements. In addition, participants in online chat rooms and special interest groups may promote their own opinions as proven truths. It pays to be skeptical.

**RECAP**

The best sources of scientific information translate difficult or complex information accurately into understandable terms and have enough references that you can check the information if you wish. ■

## 1.5 Learning to be a critical thinker

Scientists are human. Many are motivated by strong curiosity or a sense of wonder and awe about how the natural world works. Exploring the frontiers of knowledge requires a great deal of creativity and imagination. Like many people, however, scientists may leap to conclusions or resist new ideas. A few may be driven by self-interest. To combat these natural human tendencies, good scientists try to use certain tools of critical thinking. You too can learn to use these tools, regardless of whether you choose a career in science. The Try It Yourself box provides a guide.

**try it yourself**

### Evaluating a Scientific Claim

Throughout your life you will have to evaluate the validity of scientific claims in the popular media. In most cases you'll make your judgment based solely on the information given. As practice, choose an article—from a newspaper, magazine, or the Internet—on a topic related to human biology and do the following:

- State the article's primary claim. It may help to write the claim down.
- List the evidence provided to support the claim.
- Examine each piece of evidence to see whether it meets a basic standard of scientific acceptability.

Three criteria will help you decide whether the evidence is acceptable:

1. Scientific evidence is observation-based and quantifiable (example: "From 1976 to 2006 the number of spotted owls seen per year by hikers in Oregon's national forests declined from 5,000 to 2,000"). In contrast, inferential evidence is merely descriptive (example: "The population of spotted owls declined from 1976 to 2006").
2. The source and quality of the evidence should be apparent. Cited, verifiable references to previous work by others is a big plus. At the very least, the experimental design should be sufficiently described so that you can understand how the data were collected, whether or not there is a control group, what the sample size is, and so on. You should be convinced that the data were collected and presented properly.
3. The evidence should be free of obvious bias. Who presented the data? Is there any reason to suspect a hidden agenda?

If most of the evidence presented does not meet these three simple tests, there is no reason to accept the claim. In such cases you would be wise to reserve judgment until later. Meanwhile, pay attention to what other scientists say about the claim—and be sure to apply the same criteria to their evidence as well.

## Become a skeptic

Good scientists combine creativity and imagination with **skepticism,** a questioning attitude. If you've ever bought something based on claims about how well it works and then been disappointed, you know the value of skepticism. Question everything and dig a little deeper before believing something you read and hear. Here are some questions you might ask yourself:

- Who says that a particular statement is true?
- What evidence is presented?
- Are the persons speaking on a subject qualified by training or skill to speak authoritatively about it?
- Are they being paid, and if so, how might that affect what they have to say?
- Where's the evidence to back up a claim?

Skepticism is particularly important for claims that are new, startling, and not yet verified by other scientists. Listen carefully to the debate between scientists in the public arena. A new scientific claim may take several years to be checked out adequately.

## Appreciate the value of statistics

Statistics is the mathematics of organizing and interpreting numerical information, or **data.** Scientists use statistics to determine how much confidence they should place in information. Most scientists would be willing to accept experimental results with confidence if (according to statistical tests) they would get the same outcome 19 of every 20 times they repeat the experiment, or 95% of the time. When you see numerical averages followed by a smaller "+/−" number, the smaller number represents an expression of confidence in the certainty of the results, called the "standard error." In graphs, the standard errors are represented as small lines that extend above and below the average number.

Statistics are important in many disciplines. During elections, we may hear pollsters report, for example, that "52% of the respondents said that they will vote for the president. The poll has a margin for error of +/−3%." This tells you the pollsters are relatively certain that the actual percentage who will vote for the president is somewhere between 49 and 55%, still too close to call.

## Learn how to read graphs

Just like a picture, a graph is worth a thousand words. Graphs display data obtained from observations and experimental results in a way that is economical and easy to grasp. Graphs can also be used to clarify the meaning of experimental results.

Most graphs are plotted on two lines, or axes (singular: axis). The horizontal axis at the bottom is called the *abscissa* (from math you may know this as the *x*-axis), and the vertical axis is called the *ordinate* (*y*-axis). By convention the *independent variable,* such as time, distance, age, or another category that defines groups, is generally plotted on the abscissa. The *dependent variable,* so called because its variation may depend on the independent variable, is plotted on the ordinate.

Graphs can take a variety of forms, from plots of individual data points to lines or bars of average values (Figure 1.10). When reading a graph, first check the scales and the legends on the abscissa and the ordinate to determine what the graph is about. Be careful to look for a "split axis," in which the scale changes. An example is shown in Figure 1.11. A split axis is sometimes a convenient way of representing data that cover a wide range on one axis, but it can also be used to deliberately mislead people unfamiliar with reading graphs.

## Distinguish anecdotes from scientific evidence

*Anecdotal* evidence takes the form of a testimonial or short unverified report. Although an anecdote may be

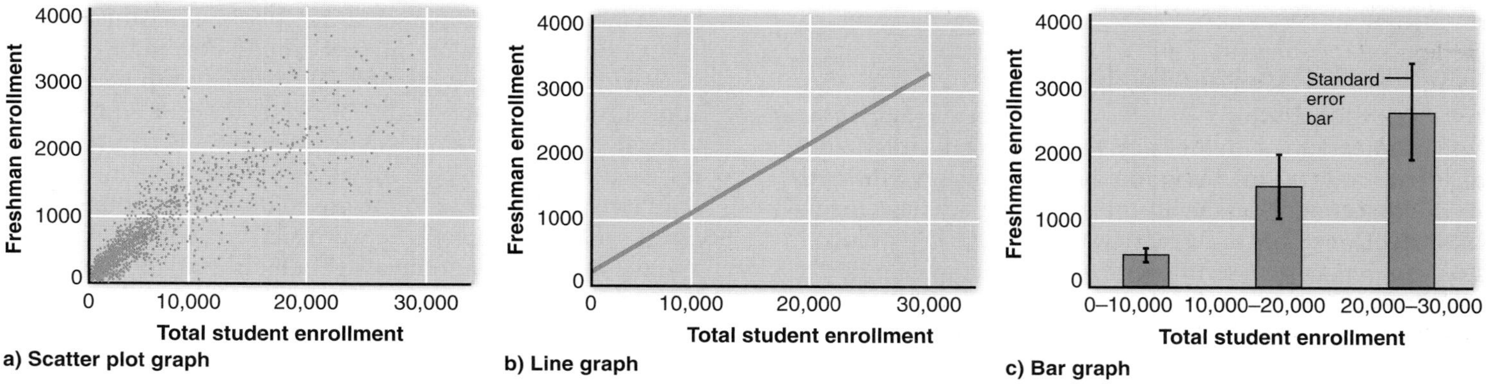


**Figure 1.10 Types of graphs.** Each of these graphs reports the relationship between freshman enrollment and total student enrollment at approximately 1,500 U.S. colleges and universities. **(a)** A scatter plot showing enrollments at each individual college. Each data point is known as an observation. **(b)** A line graph drawn representing the best straight line fit of the data in (a). **(c)** A bar graph in which university enrollments are lumped together in three class sizes and the freshman enrollments are then averaged. This graph also shows typical standard error bars, indicating that the data have been analyzed statistically.

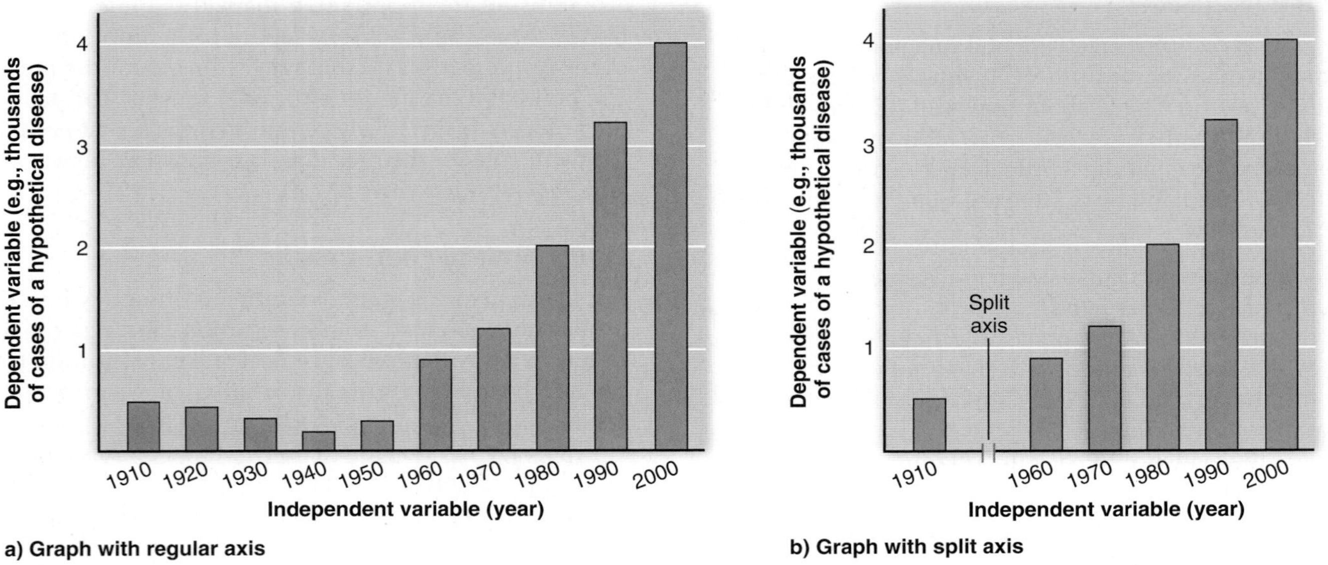


**Figure 1.11 How a split axis affects a graph.** The graph in **(b)** is redrawn from the data in **(a)** by splitting the abscissa and omitting the data for the years 1920–1950. The effect is a consolidated graph that fits in less space, but it might mislead you into thinking that the number of cases of the disease has been rising steadily since 1910, instead of only since 1960.

true as stated, it in no way implies scientific or statistical certainty. It cannot be generalized to the larger population because it is not based on empirical evidence. Advertising agencies sometimes use anecdotes to influence you. The actor on television who looks sincerely into the camera and says "Drug X worked for me" may be telling the truth—the drug may work for him. But this does not prove the drug will work for everyone, or even for 10% of the population.

Nonscientists (and even scientists) often say things like "My grandmother swears by this remedy." Again, the statement may be true, but it is not scientific evidence. Listen carefully to how the evidence for a statement is presented.

### Separate facts from conclusions

A *fact* is a verifiable piece of information, whereas a *conclusion* is a judgment based on the facts. The news media often mix facts with conclusions without indicating which is which. Almost every evening on the business news we hear statements like "The Dow Jones Industrial Average declined 50 points today on renewed concern over the consumer price index." The first half of the sentence (about the decline) is a verifiable fact. The second half is conjecture on the part of the reporter.

Or consider the following: "The average global temperature was 0.1°C higher this year than last year. The rise in temperature proves that global warming is occurring." Again, fact is followed by conclusion. The conclusion may not be warranted if temperature fluctuations up and down of 0.3°C are normal from year to year.

### Understand the difference between correlation and causation

A close pattern or relationship (a correlation) between two variables does not necessarily mean that one causes the other. The catch-phrase is "*correlation does not imply causation.*" A good example of a correlation without causation is the close correlation between ice cream sales and drownings—when ice cream sales are up in the summer months, so are drownings. Does that mean that eating ice cream causes people to drown? Hardly. Ice cream sales and drownings also correlate with (and are most likely caused by) a third factor not mentioned in the original correlation—warmer temperatures during the summer.

If the above example seems too obvious, try this one: in 1999 a study at a major university found that children who slept with a light on were more likely to develop nearsightedness (myopia) later in life. The study received a lot of attention in the popular press, including a CNN report with the headline, "Night-light may lead to nearsightedness." But does it really? In fact, a follow-up study in 2000 found no direct causal relationship between sleeping with a light on and the development of nearsightedness. Instead, the follow-up study showed that children who develop nearsightedness are more likely to have parents who are nearsighted, suggesting (but not proving) a genetic cause. It also showed that parents who are nearsighted are just more likely to leave the light on!

In the above example, the original scientific observation was stated correctly (lights-on *correlates* with nearsightedness). The CNN headline was also technically correct, for it essentially only raised the possibility that sleeping with the lights on *may* be a cause of nearsightedness. But anyone who became convinced that sleeping with a light on *causes* nearsightedness would have been wrong. Be skeptical of causal statements that are based only on a good correlation, for the true cause may not be obvious at first.

Of course, a close correlation is likely whenever a true causal relationship does exist. So although a correlation does not necessarily prove causation, it can be a strong hint that you *may* have found the true cause, or at least that the true cause is nearby and may even be linked to both of the variables you're observing.

**RECAP**

Healthy skepticism, a basic understanding of statistics, and an ability to read graphs are important tools for critical thinking. Know anecdotal evidence when you see it, and appreciate the differences between fact and conclusion and between correlation and causation. ■

## 1.6 The role of science in society

How do we place science in its proper perspective in our society? Why do we bother spending billions of dollars on scientific research when there are people starving in the streets? These are vital questions for all of us, so let's look at why we study the natural world in the first place.

### Science improves technology and the human physical condition

Science gives us information about the natural world upon which we can base our societal decisions. Throughout history some of the greatest benefits of science have been derived from the *application* of science, called **technology,** for the betterment of humankind (Figure 1.12). Time and time again, scientific knowledge has led to technological advances that have increased the productivity and hence prosperity of both industries and nations. Science has given us larger crop yields, more consistent weather predictions, better construction materials, better health care, and more efficient and cleaner sources of power, to name just a few benefits. It has made global transportation and communication possible.

Many people are concerned that overuse of our technological capabilities may lead to problems in the future. Science can help here, too, by helping us identify problems early on. We can see the early warning role of science in the "Health Watch" discussion of bacterial resistance to antibiotics. Only by understanding a problem can we learn how to solve it. Science helps us correct our mistakes.

### Science has limits

Scientific knowledge is limited to physical explanations for observable events in the natural world. It cannot prove or disprove the existence, or importance to us, of things that fall

**a) Modern farmers grow food crops much more efficiently than in the past, thanks to advances in such diverse fields as genetics, chemistry, and even the aerospace industry.** Global positioning satellites and computers allow farmers to administer fertilizers precisely where needed, thereby eliminating waste, reducing environmental degradation, and improving yields.

**b) These scientists are studying the tree-top ecosystem of a rain forest in Panama.** Studies such as this improve our understanding of the interrelationships of organisms in an ecosystem and have yielded rare natural chemical compounds that may prove useful in human and animal medicine.

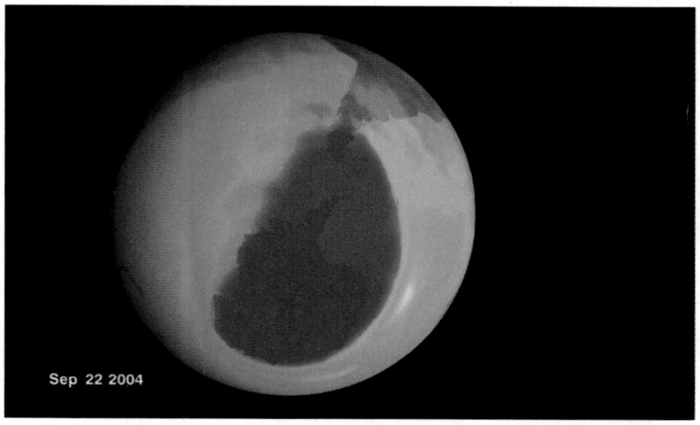


**c) A satellite map documenting depletion of the ozone layer over Antarctica in 2004.** The area of greatest depletion appears dark blue. Studies such as this one allow scientists to document when and where ozone depletion occurs so that they can better understand its causes and cures.

**Figure 1.12 Benefits of science.** These photos show typical scenes of scientists and the application of science (technology) for the betterment of the human condition.

# Functional Foods and Dietary Supplements—Choices, Choices

Red Bull energy drink; sports drinks saturated with oxygen; pills containing glucosamine and chondroitin; whole-grain bread containing wheat bran—we seem to have an increased appetite for functional foods and dietary supplements.

**Functional foods,** also sometimes called "nutraceuticals," are food or drink products that are claimed to have health benefits or physiological effects beyond basic nutrition. Some are natural products; others are fortified foods or completely artificially created products. Red Bull may be considered a functional food because of the manufacturer's claim that it boosts energy levels. Whole-wheat bread can be a functional food, too, if the claim is made that the insoluble fiber in wheat bran contributes to the maintenance of a healthy digestive tract.

Vitamins, minerals, amino acids, plant extracts, and hormonal products that are not normally part of the diet but are added to the diet to improve health or physiological function are called **dietary supplements.** Pills containing purified glucosamine and chondroitin for joint health, extracts of *Echinacea purpurea* to fight infections, or extracts of *Ginkgo biloba* for improved circulation are all dietary supplements.

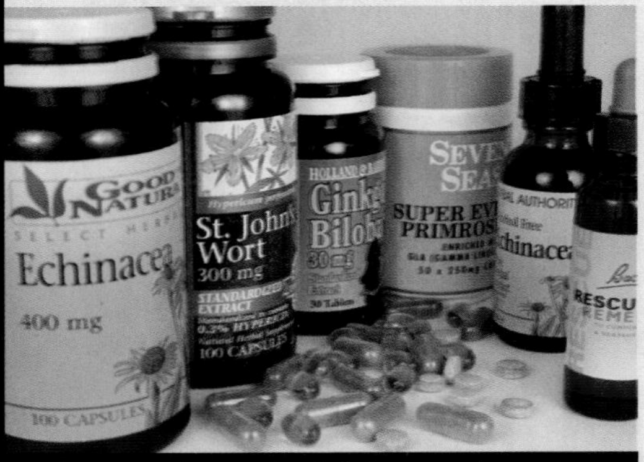


There are thousands of dietary supplements on the market today.

The safety and *efficacy* (i.e., do they work as advertised?) of functional foods and dietary supplements can vary widely from product to product and even between different producers of the same product. One reason is that years ago the dietary supplements industry fought to ensure that dietary supplements would not be regulated in the same way as drugs. How did this state of affairs come about, and is it a good thing? To understand this issue, it will help you to understand how pharmaceutical drugs are regulated (and why they cost so much!).

### The Role of the FDA in Drug Discovery and Regulation

The U.S. Food and Drug Administration (FDA) is responsible for overseeing the safety and efficacy of pharmaceutical drugs (drugs created specifically for the treatment or prevention of disease). Pharmaceutical drugs can have powerful and unpredictable side effects, so safety is a major concern. By law, a pharmaceutical company must prove beyond a reasonable doubt that a new drug is safe and effective in humans before it can be sold to the public. Human testing of a new drug is done in three phases. In Phase I, safety tests are conducted on a small group of healthy volunteers (perhaps 20–80 people). In Phase II, the drug is tested on several hundred people to see if it actually is effective in treating a specific condition or disease. If the drug appears to be both safe and effective, Phase III clinical trials are performed on 1,000–4,000 people to explore the consequences of widespread use.

On average it takes 12–15 years and costs about $800 million to bring one new drug to market. Companies can afford it only because they can patent the drug, giving them exclusive ownership and marketing rights for a certain number of years. Although patients sometimes complain about the high cost of prescription medications, pharmaceutical companies respond that the price reflects their steep development costs.

### Functional Foods and Dietary Supplements Are Not Regulated as Drugs

The ingredients in functional foods and dietary supplements occur naturally. Many of them have been in use for hundreds or even thousands of years. Because anyone can produce them, no one has exclusive rights over them and therefore they cannot be patented. And without the assurance of patent protection, manufacturers and producers simply cannot afford to spend $800 million for product research and testing. Recognizing this, back in 1994 the dietary supplement manufacturers asked for an exemption from the FDA drug approval process. The exemption was granted by the Dietary Supplements Health and Education Act of 1994, which permits dietary supplements (and functional foods) to be produced and sold until they are proven *unsafe*. Note that this shifts the entire burden (and expense) of determining safety completely away from

## the facts...

- Functional foods and dietary supplements are popular with consumers. Americans consume more than $18 billion worth of dietary supplements every year.
- Functional foods and dietary supplements don't pass through the same rigorous approval procedure that is required of all new pharmaceutical drugs.
- Some functional foods and dietary supplements do not live up to their marketing hype, and a few may not be safe.

the manufacturer or producer. Who has the time, money, and interest in trying to prove that a product is unsafe? Essentially no one.

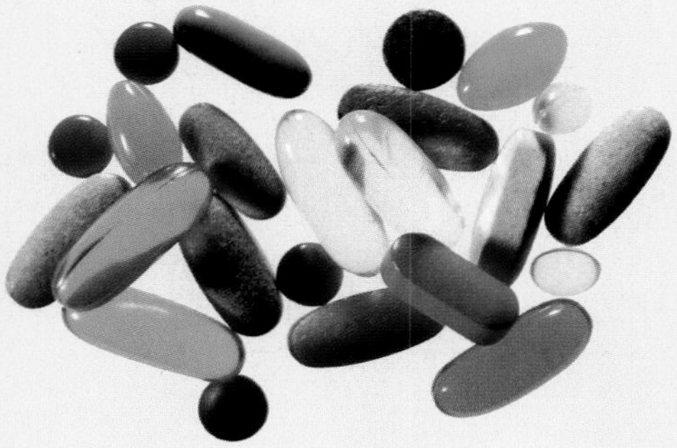

Producers and distributors of functional foods and dietary supplements also have considerable latitude in advertising their products as long as they do not claim that their product prevents or treats specific medical conditions or diseases. For example, producers of cranberry juice products are free to say that cranberry juice "helps maintain urinary tract health" (a rather vague health claim), but they cannot claim that cranberry juice "prevents the recurrence of urinary tract infections" because that would represent a specific medical claim. Nevertheless, many consumers do use cranberry juice to treat urinary tract infections or to prevent their recurrence, simply because they believe that it works. And indeed it may; it's just that it has never been scientifically tested to the standards of a pharmaceutical drug.

With all that latitude in producing and marketing their products, it's not surprising that the functional foods and dietary supplements industries and the advertising industry that supports them have all grown rapidly. U.S. sales of dietary supplements now top $18 billion a year.

### Questions of Safety and Efficacy Remain

Because the ingredients in functional foods and dietary supplements are found in nature and have been eaten by humans in one form or another for perhaps thousands of years, many consumers argue that any adverse effects should have become apparent by now. However, that's not entirely true for some of the newer products. The active ingredients in Red Bull, for example, are all synthetically produced, and so they can be added to the final product in relatively high concentrations. Furthermore, the interactions between dietary supplements and modern drugs are largely unknown and could be potentially dangerous. For instance, recent studies suggest that the popular herbal antidepressant St. John's wort can interfere with a number of commonly prescribed medications, including drugs for birth control, heart conditions, asthma, and HIV infections.

Other safety concerns include inaccurate product labeling and improper manufacturing processes. Manufacturers are not required to report quality control information to the FDA, so consumers have no assurance that a particular dietary supplement contains the stated amount of active ingredient or is free of impurities. Indeed, independent tests found that products labeled as containing the same dosage of ginseng actually varied by a factor of 10 (some contained none at all). And California investigators found that nearly a third of all imported Asian herbal remedies they tested contained lead, arsenic, mercury, or drugs not mentioned on the label at all.

What's in this can? If you don't know, should you be drinking it?

Because there is no requirement that the FDA even be notified of "adverse events" (the FDA must rely on voluntary information supplied by consumers and health professionals), it's hard to tell how safe dietary supplements actually are. During a 5-year period the FDA reported only about 500 adverse events and fewer than 50 deaths per year associated with dietary supplements. In contrast, the American Association of Poison Control Centers received nearly 7,000 reports involving dietary supplements in one year alone.

Consumers want to be assured that the dietary supplements and natural and fortified food products they use are safe. They'd like to know that the health claims about these products are true. How to achieve that goal and still ensure that the products remain available is an ongoing issue. In the meantime, it's up to you to know what is in the products you choose to put in your body.

How will you determine if the supplement you're taking is safe?

### Questions to consider

*1 Who do you think should be responsible for ensuring that dietary supplements and functional foods are safe? Explain your position. 2 What dietary supplements or functional foods do you use? Do you know what's in them and do you understand why you're using them?*

Purple coneflower (*Echinacea purpurea*).

# Health Watch

## The Growing Threat of Antibiotic-Resistant Bacteria

When antibiotics—drugs that kill bacteria—became available in the 1940s, they were hailed as a breakthrough. Indeed, many people owe their lives to them.

But there is a downside: Indiscriminate use of antibiotics increases resistance in some strains of bacteria. If we are not careful, we may soon face deadly microorganisms against which we have no protection except the body's natural immune system. This past year we've been hearing about an antibiotic-resistant strain of the *Staphylococcus aureus* bacterium called MRSA (methicillin-resistant *Staphylococcus aureus*) that is resistant to nearly all antibiotics. It used to show up only in hospitals and long-term care facilities, but it's beginning to appear in locker rooms and even more generally in the community. Approximately 292,000 Americans are hospitalized every year with "staph" infections, about 126,000 of which are now caused by this new strain. This frightening superbug can penetrate bones and lungs, killing approximately 20% of those with severe infections.

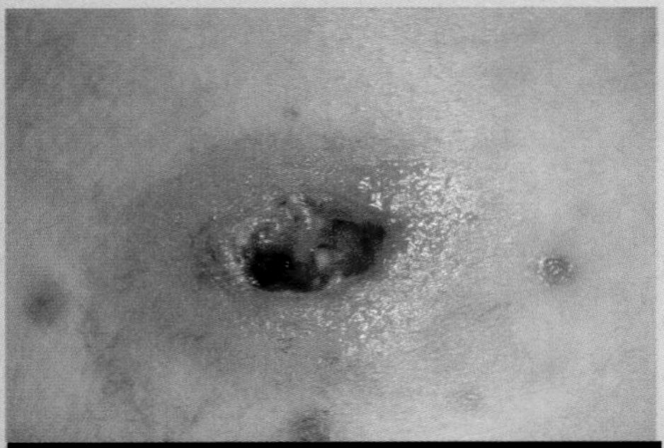

Skin lesions caused by MRSA.

Antibiotic resistance is rapidly becoming a global threat, not just a threat in the United States. The antibiotic Vancomycin was introduced into clinical use in 1972, and according to the World Health Organization, Vancomycin-resistant strains of bacteria were appearing around the world by 1987. In a recent study, almost 25% of intensive-care patients infected with enterococci, bacteria that inhabit the intestinal tract, were resistant to Vancomycin.

The bacteria in (and on) your body compete for your body's resources, just as all organisms do when they occupy the same ecological space. Good bacteria limit the growth of harmful bacteria through this competition. But when you take an antibiotic, you destroy the good bacteria, too. By definition, if a drug kills most but not all of the bacteria, the survivors are those most resistant to the antibiotic's effects. With the total population of bacteria now decreased, these antibiotic-resistant survivors multiply. Any time we take an antibiotic, the percentage of resistant bacteria in the remaining population increases, and the antibiotic is less effective the next time around.

Because antibiotics seem so effective, we tend to use them indiscriminately. In the United States alone we manufacture over 50 million pounds of antibiotics annually, about half of which are fed to livestock or sprayed on fruit trees. Researchers estimate that fully one-third of all antibiotic prescriptions given to non-hospitalized patients in the United States are not needed.

Another problem: To ensure that all bacteria are killed, doctors prescribe a course of antibiotics lasting 7–10 days. Many people feel better within 3 days when most (but by no means all) of the bacteria have been killed, so they stop taking the drug and save the leftover pills for a future illness. They have inadvertently selected the most antibiotic-resistant bacteria for survival.

As a society, we can take several steps to preserve the effectiveness of antibiotics:

- Don't ask your doctor for antibiotics for a viral illness such as a cold or flu. Antibiotics kill bacteria but have no effect on viruses.
- Take the drugs only when needed and as prescribed. Complete the full course of treatment even if you feel like you are back to normal.
- Reduce your use of antibacterial hand creams, soaps, and laundry detergents. Products that leave a residue on skin may favor the growth of resistant germs.
- Encourage farmers and orchard owners to reduce their use of antibiotics in cattle feed and on fruit trees, bearing in mind that these groups have legitimate reasons of their own for antibiotic use.
- Support research efforts to find new antibiotics.

The development of resistance to antibiotics is a global issue that affects us all. Used properly and judiciously, however, antibiotics will remain in our antibacterial arsenal for many years.

outside the realm of the natural world, such as faith or spiritual experiences. Many scientists have a strong faith or belief that cannot be tested by science, because faith does not depend on logical proof or material evidence. They believe that the search for meaning and the search for knowledge are complementary, not contradictory.

In addition, science alone cannot provide us with the "right" answers to political, economic, social, legal, or ethical dilemmas. Humans have minds, a moral sense, and a sense of history and the future. How we use scientific knowledge is up to all of us, not just scientists. For example, given the current state of knowledge about how cells grow and divide, scientists may eventually be able to clone an adult human being. Whether or not we should permit cloning, and under what circumstances, are important topics of public debate. It's not for scientists to decide alone.

This does not mean scientists are without moral obligation. As experts in their fields, they are in a unique position to advise us about the application of scientific knowledge, even if the choices ultimately rest with all of us. Failing to advise the public can sometimes be an abdication of social responsibility.

A practical limitation of science is that some information, including data that may be useful in improving human health, cannot be obtained by observation or experimentation. Our society places a very high value on human life, and therefore we don't experiment on humans unless the experiment is likely to be of direct benefit to the subject (the use of experimental cancer drugs falls into this category). This is why it is hard to investigate the danger of street drugs like cocaine or anabolic steroids. No good scientist would ever deliberately give healthy humans a drug likely to cause injury or death, even if the resulting information could save countless lives in the future. Our society currently permits experimentation on animals as substitutes for human subjects, provided that federal guidelines are strictly followed (Figure 1.13).

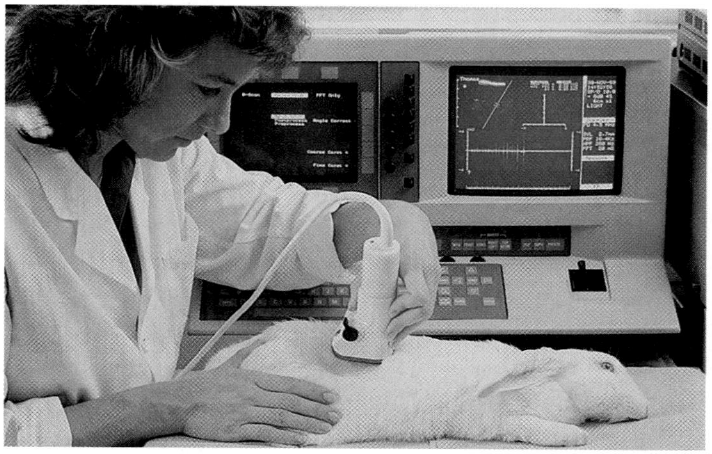

**Figure 1.13 Animals in research.** In this society we allow the use of animals for research in certain circumstances. This researcher is using a noninvasive technique for measuring blood flow in the skin as part of a study of vascular diseases.

## The importance of making informed choices

You live in a science-oriented society. Throughout this book we present a common theme: Every day you make decisions about how you and society choose to use the knowledge that science gives us. Whether or not you are conscious of it, whether or not you deliberately take action, you make these choices daily.

Should Olympic athletes be allowed to use bodybuilding drugs? Do you think the use of pesticides is justified in order to feed more people? How do you feel about the cloning of human beings? Are you willing to eat a proper diet to stay healthy, and by the way, what *is* a proper diet? Who should pay for health care for the poor?

Our knowledge has advanced rapidly. By the end of this book you will know more about genetics and evolution than did the scientists who originally developed the theories about them. With knowledge comes the responsibility for making choices. From global warming to genetic engineering to personal health, each of us must deal with issues that concern our well-being and the future of the biological world in which we live. We owe it to ourselves, as individuals and as a society, to acquire the knowledge and skill we need to make intelligent decisions. Your choices can make a difference.

**RECAP**

Science and technology have improved the human condition. Science cannot, however, resolve moral dilemmas. Scientists can advise us on issues of science, but we as a society must decide how to put this scientific knowledge to use. ■

# Chapter Summary

### The characteristics of life *p. 2*

- All living things acquire both matter and energy from their environment, transforming them for their own purposes.
- The basic unit of life is a single cell.
- Living things maintain homeostasis, respond to their external environments, and reproduce

### How humans fit into the natural world *p. 4*

- The biological world can be organized into kingdoms. A common scheme classifies life into five kingdoms: Monera, Protista, Fungi, Plantae, and Animalia.
- Features that define humans are bipedalism, well-developed opposable thumbs, a large brain, and the capacity for complex language.
- Humans are part of communities of different organisms living together in various ecosystems.

### Science is both a body of knowledge and a process *p. 8*

- Scientific knowledge allows us to describe and predict the natural world.
- The *scientific method* is a way of thinking, a way of testing statements about the natural world *(hypotheses)* by trying to prove them false.
- A *theory* is a hypothesis that has been extensively tested and that explains a broad range of scientific facts with a high degree of reliability.

### Sources of scientific information vary in style and quality *p. 11*

- Articles in peer-reviewed scientific journals are generally written for other scientists. They may be difficult to read but are very accurate.
- Journals, books, and television shows on popular science present scientific knowledge efficiently to the general public.
- Web sites vary widely in the quality and accuracy of the information they present.

### Learning to be a critical thinker *p. 12*

- Skepticism is a questioning attitude ("prove it to me"). Critical thinking requires skepticism.
- Knowing how to read graphs and understand basic statistics can help you evaluate numerical data.
- Being able to recognize an anecdote, tell fact from conclusion, and distinguish between correlation and causation can help you evaluate the truth of a claim.

### The role of science in society *p. 15*

- The application of science is called technology.
- Science is limited to physical explanations of observable events.
- How to use science is up to us.

## Terms You Should Know

biology, *2*
control group, *10*
data, *13*
experiment, *10*
experimental group, *10*
homeostasis, *3*
hypothesis, *9*
science, *2*
scientific method, *8*
theory, *11*
variable, *10*

## Concept Review

1. Living things have a different molecular composition than nonliving things. What makes this possible?
2. Explain the meaning of the term *homeostasis*.
3. Name four features that together contribute to our uniqueness and define us as human.
4. Describe the difference between a hypothesis and a prediction (or working hypothesis).
5. Discuss the role of scientists in helping us solve economic, social, and ethical dilemmas.

## Test Yourself

### Matching Exercise

_____ 1. The domain of life to which humans belong
_____ 2. The kingdom of life to which single-celled organisms lacking a nucleus belong
_____ 3. The process of science
_____ 4. An experiment designed and conducted under strictly controlled conditions
_____ 5. A main hypothesis that has withstood the test of repeated experimentation
_____ 6. The application of science

a. scientific method
b. controlled experiment
c. theory
d. Eukarya
e. technology
f. Monera

### Fill in the Blank

7. The smallest unit of any classification of life system is the _____________.
8. The natural world consists of all _____________ and all _____________.
9. Making observations and then making generalizations based on what we learn is an example of _____________ reasoning.
10. Scientists design and conduct _____________ in order to test their predictions and hypotheses.
11. The _____________ group in a controlled experiment receives the treatment and the _____________ group receives a false treatment called a placebo.
12. In graphs, the independent variable is usually plotted on the _____________ and the dependent variable is usually plotted on the ordinate.

### True or False?

13. Populations of living things evolve.
14. Some of the best scientific evidence is anecdotal.
15. A good correlation between two variables always means that one causes the other.

## References and Additional Reading

Brennan, Richard P. *Dictionary of Scientific Literacy.* New York: Wiley, 1999. 334 pp. (A handy quick reference guide to the vocabulary and core knowledge of science.)

Carey, Stephen S. *A Beginner's Guide to Scientific Method.* Belmont, CA: Wadsworth, 2003. 160 pp. (A description of the methods underlying scientific research. Designed for nonscience students.)

Parker, Sybil P. (ed.). *McGraw-Hill Dictionary of Scientific and Technical Terms.* New York: McGraw-Hill Professional, 2002. (A comprehensive dictionary of over 100,000 terms and definitions, classified into over 100 fields.)

## Apply **What You Know**

1. A magician has a coin that he says (hypothesizes) has heads on both sides, but he's unwilling to show you both sides. To convince you, he flips it three times and gets heads each time. Do you believe that the coin has two heads? What if he gets heads 10 times in a row? 100 times? What would it take (by coin flip) to prove that the coin does *not* have two heads? With this example, explain the difference between having relative confidence in the truth of a hypothesis, proving it to be true, and proving it to be false.
2. Your roommate is writing a paper on the subject of cocaine and birth defects in humans and wonders why there don't seem to be published reports of controlled experiments in humans on the subject; all the studies are on rats! Describe to her how such a controlled experiment would have to be designed and conducted, and convince her that it would never be permitted by any responsible regulatory agency.
3. You have a friend who truly believes in the existence of ghosts and says he has scientific evidence; he and his two roommates have all seen them. Explain to your friend what it means to have scientific evidence. Think about what data are, how they are gathered, and why personal experiences do not meet the criteria to be considered scientific evidence.
4. An episode of an old TV show was about doctors living in a tropical environment where the heat is unusually oppressive. An orderly comes to seek relief from the heat, and one doctor gives a supply of sugar pills to the orderly and tells him they are an experimental drug designed to keep humans cool in hot weather. The gullible orderly takes them, and while others are sweating, he claims to suffer no effects from the heat to the point of not even sweating. He later finds out the drug is fake, and immediately complains of being overheated.

   This is a fictitious demonstration of the "placebo effect." Explain how the placebo effect can be avoided when testing new drugs.
5. You are trying to convince your friend who smokes cigarettes that he should quit. You explain to him that smoking and the incidence of lung cancer are strongly correlated. Your friend says that that does not prove smoking causes lung cancer. Is your friend correct? If so, explain why he is correct. What would you say to him?
6. On the radio, you hear an interview with a climatologist discussing global warming. The interviewer asks the scientist what proof she has that humans are to blame for global warming and the resulting rise in sea levels. The scientist responds that while we cannot prove humans are to blame for global warming, there is much evidence that human activities are responsible for the rising temperatures. The interviewer says, "Aha, so you have no proof that humans are to blame, and this is all nothing more than a theory, and isn't a theory nothing more than an opinion?" What differentiates a scientific theory from an opinion?
7. Explain why religious explanations cannot disprove a scientific theory, and conversely, why science cannot prove or disprove a religious belief.

*Answers can be found on the Human Biology Place.*

Peirce, Andrea. *The American Pharmaceutical Association Practical Guide to Natural Medicines.* New York: Morrow, 1999. (An encyclopedia of dietary supplements and natural medicines.)

Sagan, Carl. *The Demon-Haunted World: Science as a Candle in the Dark.* New York: Ballantine, 1996. 457 pp. (A book that expresses the curiosity, amazement, and skepticism of science by a leading science author.)

### Internet References

Find links to the following Web sites at the Human Biology Place.

**U.S. Food and Drug Administration**
**www.fda.gov**
Federal agency that oversees safety of food, drugs, medical devices, cosmetics, biologics, radiation-admitting products, and animal feed and drugs.

**National Institutes of Health**
**www.nih.gov**
Federal agency that monitors medical and behavioral research at the national level; provides information about health issues and the science behind them.

**ScienceDaily**
**www.sciencedaily.com**
A Web portal to news releases from universities, medical centers, and other research organizations around the world. Not peerreviewed articles, but a good way to view current research in a range of scientific disciplines.

**National Center for Infectious Diseases—Antimicrobial Resistance Homepage**
**www.cdc.gov/drugresistance**
Up-to-date information on drug resistance for the general public and the professional.

# 2 The Chemistry of Living Things

**1 True or False?** Although you hear about the dangers of **high cholesterol**, a certain amount of cholesterol is good for you.

**2** Which of the following are **unsaturated fats?** **a.** Butter **b.** Olive oil **c.** Palm oil **d.** Bacon grease

**3** **About 60%** of your body weight consists of **a.** fat **b.** bone **c.** muscle **d.** water

**4** What is an **enzyme**, and why are enzymes so important in living systems?

Paper chromatograms, used to separate compounds in a mixture.

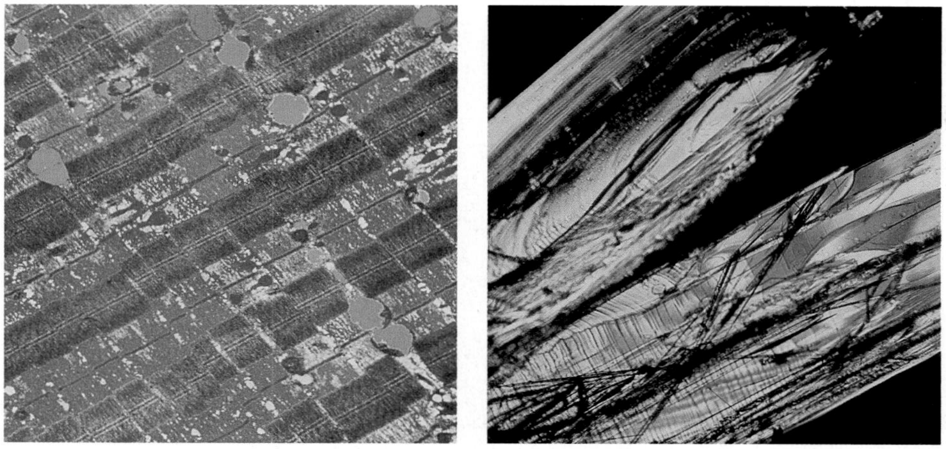

**a) A magnified view (× 15,000) of a portion of a skeletal muscle cell.** **b) A magnified view (× 30) of a crystal of aspirin.**

**Figure 2.1 All matter is made of atoms.** The three most common atoms in both muscle and aspirin are carbon, hydrogen, and oxygen.

**As mentioned in Chapter 1,** the natural world consists of matter and energy. *Chemistry* is the study of matter and the energy that causes matter to combine, break apart, and recombine into all the substances, both living and nonliving, that exist in the natural world. Every substance is made from the same basic units of matter and the same types of energy (Figure 2.1). Everything in the natural world is governed by the laws of chemistry, including you and me.

Yet there is something very special about the chemistry of living things. Living organisms have the ability to grow and reproduce, unlike inanimate objects. Living things have evolved to take advantage of the rules of chemistry that govern the natural world. Living organisms create special combinations of matter not generally found in nonliving things. They also have developed the ability to store energy so that they may later turn it to their own purposes.

In this chapter we consider how the laws of chemistry serve life. We begin with an introduction to basic chemistry.

## 2.1 All matter consists of elements

**Matter** is anything that has mass and occupies space. All matter is composed of elements. An **element** is a fundamental (pure) form of matter that cannot be broken down to a simpler form. Aluminum and iron are elements, and so are oxygen and hydrogen. There are just over 100 known elements, and together they account for all matter on Earth. The *periodic table of elements* arranges all known elements into groups according to their similar properties (Figure 2.2).

### Atoms are the smallest functional units of an element

Elements are made up of particles called atoms. An **atom** is the smallest unit of any element that still retains the physical and chemical properties of that element. Although we now know that atoms can be split apart under unusual circumstances (such as a nuclear reaction), atoms are the smallest units of matter that can take part in chemical reactions. So, for all practical purposes, atoms are the smallest functional units of matter.

Even the largest atoms are so small that we can see them only with specialized microscopes. Chemists can also infer what they look like from studying their physical properties (Figure 2.3).

The central core of an atom is called the *nucleus*. The nucleus is made of positively charged particles called **protons** and a nearly equal number of neutral particles called **neutrons,** all tightly bound together. An exception is the smallest atom, hydrogen, whose nucleus consists of only a single proton. Smaller negatively charged particles called **electrons** orbit the nucleus. Because electrons are constantly moving, their precise position at any one time is unknown. You may think of electrons as occupying one or more spherical clouds of negative charge around the nucleus called *shells*. Each shell can accommodate only a certain number of electrons. The first shell, the one closest to the nucleus, can hold two electrons, the second can accommodate up to eight, and the third shell (if there is one) also accommodates eight. Each type of atom has a unique number of electrons. Under most circumstances the number of electrons equals the number of protons, and, as a result, the entire atom is electrically neutral.

## Answers to Intro Questions

1 **True.** Although high cholesterol levels are a risk factor for cardiovascular disease, our bodies need a certain amount of cholesterol to function properly. In this chapter we will see why.

2 **b. and c.** Unsaturated fats, or oils, are generally liquids at room temperature. Unsaturated fats are considered better for your diet.

3 **d.** Water has unique properties that make life possible. In this chapter we'll see what they are.

4 Enzymes are biological catalysts, meaning that they speed up the rates of biochemical reactions within the body. Without enzymes, most biochemical reactions would occur too slowly to sustain life.

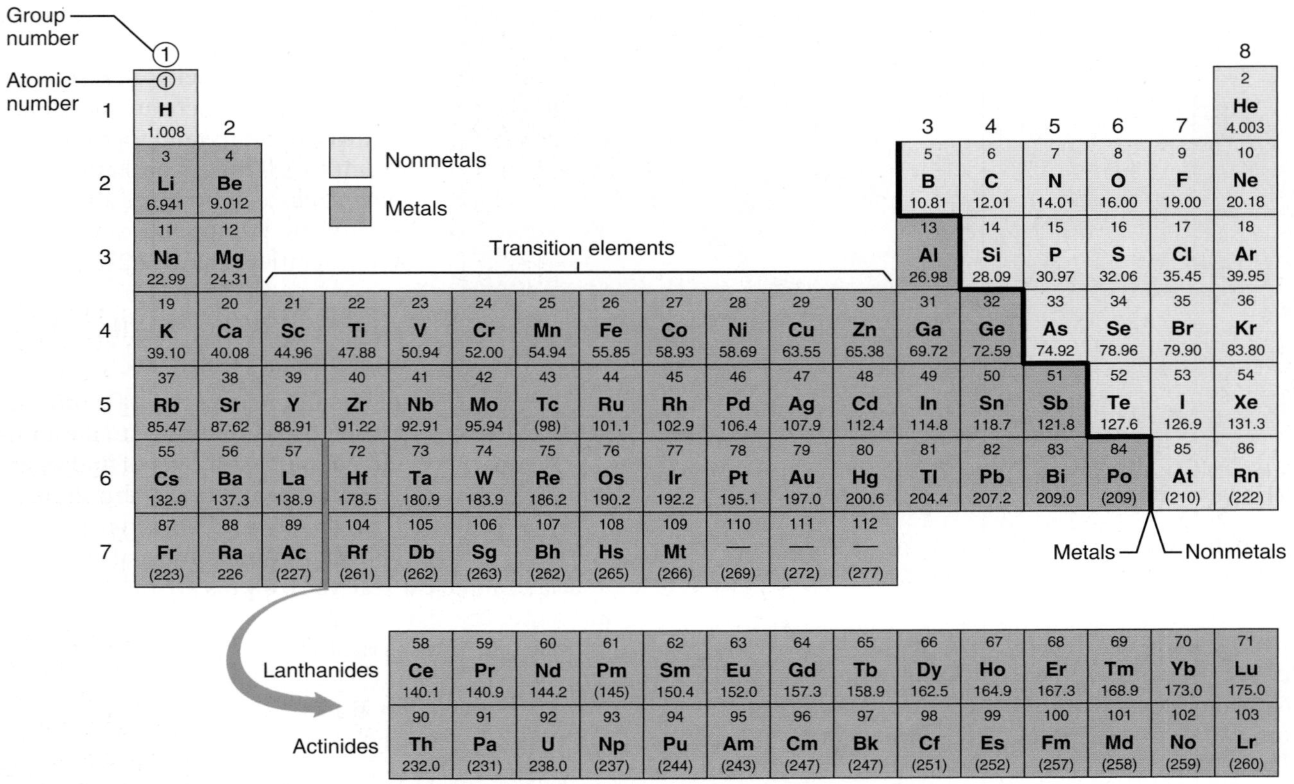


**Figure 2.2 The periodic table shows all known elements in order of increasing atomic number.** For example, nitrogen (N) has 7 protons, so its atomic number is 7. The table also organizes elements into groups based on the number of electrons in their outer shells (elements in group 1 have one electron, those in group 3 have three electrons, and so on). Scientists are interested in the number of electrons in the outer shell because these particles affect how an atom interacts with other elements.

Protons and neutrons have about the same mass and both have much more mass than electrons. (*Mass* is measured chemically and is not dependent on gravity. For the purpose of this text, however, mass and *weight* are about the same. The protons and neutrons in the atom's nucleus account for over 99.9% of the atom's mass.)

In the periodic table and in chemical equations, atoms are designated by one- or two-letter symbols taken from English or Latin. For example, oxygen is designated by the letter O, nitrogen by N, sodium by Na (from the Latin word for sodium, *natrium*), and potassium by K (Latin *kalium*). A subscript numeral following the symbol indicates the numbers of atoms of that element. For example, the chemical formula $O_2$ represents two atoms of oxygen linked together, the most stable form of elemental oxygen.

In addition to a symbol, atoms have an *atomic number* representing the characteristic number of protons in the nucleus and an *atomic mass* (or mass number), which is generally fairly close to the total number of neutrons and protons.

## Isotopes have a different number of neutrons

Although all the atoms of a particular element have the same number of protons, the number of neutrons can vary slightly. Atoms with either more or fewer neutrons than the usual number for that element are called **isotopes.** Isotopes of an element have the same atomic number as the more common atoms but a different atomic mass. For example, elemental carbon typically consists of atoms with six protons and six neutrons, for an atomic mass of 12. The isotope of carbon known as carbon-14 has an atomic mass of 14 because it has two extra neutrons.

Isotopes are always identified by a superscript mass number preceding the symbol. For instance, the carbon-14 isotope is designated $^{14}C$. The superscript mass number of the more common elemental form of carbon is generally omitted because it is understood to be 12.

Many isotopes are unstable. Such isotopes are called *radioisotopes* because they tend to give off energy (in the form of radiation) and particles until they reach a more stable state. The radiation emitted by radioisotopes can be dangerous to living organisms because the energy can damage tissues.

Certain radioisotopes have a number of important scientific and medical uses. Because the rate of decay to more stable energy states is known for each radioisotope, scientists can determine when rocks and fossils were formed by measuring the

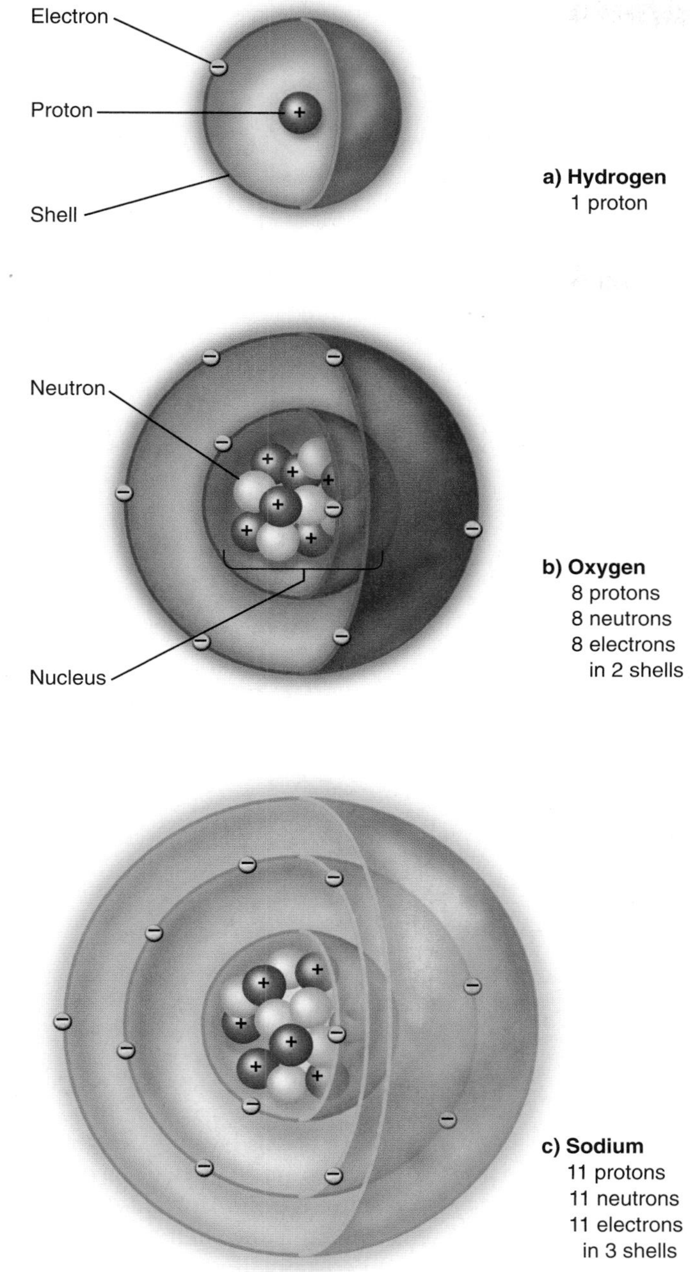


**Figure 2.3 The structure of atoms.** Atoms consist of a nucleus, comprising positively charged protons and neutral neutrons, surrounded by spherical shells of negatively charged electrons.

amount of radioisotope still present. The carbon-14 isotope is commonly used for this purpose. In medicine, radioisotopes are used to "tag" molecules so that radiation sensors can track their location in the body. For example, physicians use radioisotopes to locate areas of damaged tissue in a patient's heart after a heart attack. Radioisotopes are also used to target and kill certain kinds of cancer. Certain radioisotopes that emit energy for long periods of time are used as a power supply in heart pacemakers.

**RECAP**

Atoms are made up of protons, neutrons, and electrons. Radioisotopes are unstable atoms with an unusual number of neutrons that give off energy and particles as they decay to a more stable state. ■

## 2.2 Atoms combine to form molecules

A **molecule** consists of a stable association between two or more atoms. For example, a molecule of water is two atoms of hydrogen plus one atom of oxygen (written $H_2O$). A molecule of ordinary table salt (written NaCl) is one atom of sodium (Na) plus one atom of chlorine (Cl). A molecule of hydrogen gas (written $H_2$) is two atoms of hydrogen. To understand *why* atoms join together to form molecules, we need to know more about energy.

### Energy fuels life's activities

**Energy** is the capacity to do work, the capacity to cause some change in matter. Joining atoms is one type of work, and breaking up molecules is another—and both require energy. Stored energy that is not actually performing any work at the moment is called **potential energy** because it has the *potential* to make things happen. Energy that is actually *doing* work—that is, energy in motion—is called **kinetic energy** (Figure 2.4).

**Figure 2.4 Energy. (a)** Potential energy is locked up in the chemical bonds of the fats, carbohydrates, and other energy-storage molecules in this person's tissues. **(b)** Kinetic energy is energy in motion.

You can visualize the difference between potential energy and kinetic energy in the water held behind a dam: there is tremendous potential energy in the water held in reserve. When the water is released, potential energy is converted into kinetic energy: rushing water that can be put to work turning turbines. Similarly, the spark of a match converts the potential energy in firewood to kinetic energy in the form of heat and light.

Potential energy is stored in the bonds that hold atoms together in all matter, both living and nonliving. Living organisms take advantage of this general principle of chemistry by using certain molecules to store energy for their own use. When the chemical bonds of these energy-storage molecules are broken, potential energy becomes kinetic energy. We rely on this energy to power "work" such as breathing, moving, digesting food, and many other tasks.

Recall that electrons carry a negative charge, whereas protons within the nucleus have a positive charge. Electrons are attracted to the positively charged nucleus and repelled by each other. As a result of these opposing attractive and repulsive forces, each electron occupies a specific shell around the nucleus. Each shell corresponds to a specific level of electron potential energy, and each shell farther out represents a higher potential energy level than the preceding one closer to the nucleus. When an electron moves to a shell closer to the nucleus, it loses energy. To move to a shell that is farther from the nucleus, the electron must absorb energy.

**RECAP**

Stored energy is called potential energy, whereas energy doing work is called kinetic energy. Electrons in the energy level (or shell) closest to the nucleus have the least potential energy; those in the outermost shell have the most potential energy. ■

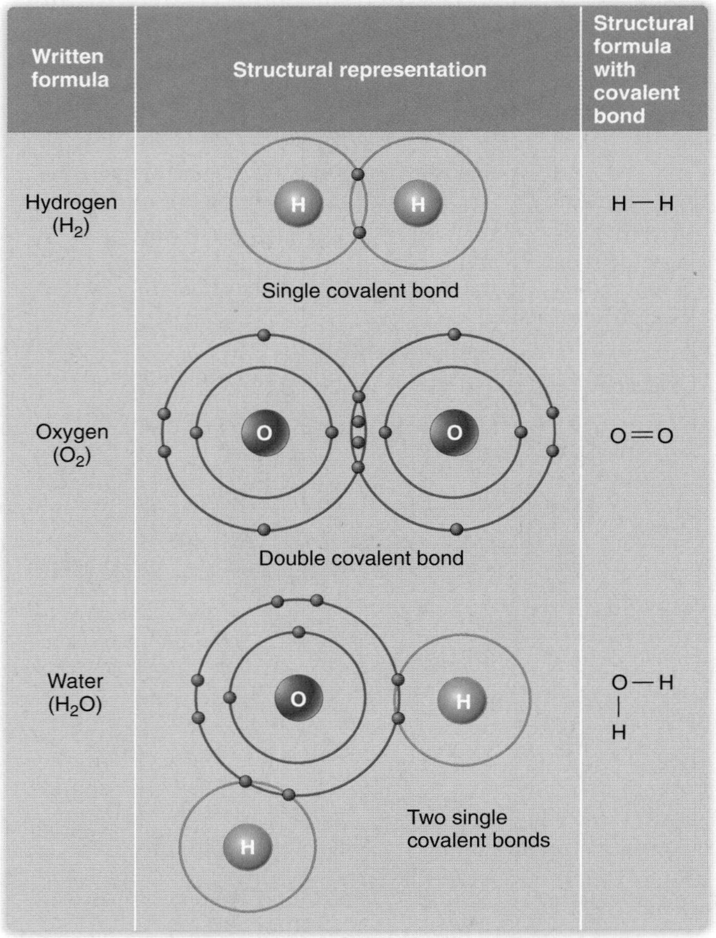


**Figure 2.5 Covalent bonds.** Sharing pairs of electrons is a way for atoms to fill their outermost shell.

## Chemical bonds link atoms to form molecules

A key concept in chemistry is that *atoms are most stable when their outermost occupied electron shell is completely filled.* An atom whose outermost electron shell is not normally filled tends to interact with one or more other atoms in a way that fills its outermost shell. Such interactions generally cause the atoms to be bound to each other by attractive forces called **chemical bonds.** The three principal types of chemical bonds are called covalent, ionic, and hydrogen bonds.

**Covalent bonds involve sharing electrons** One way that an atom can fill its outermost shell is by sharing a pair of electrons with another atom. An electron-sharing bond between atoms is called a **covalent bond** (Figure 2.5). Covalent bonds between atoms are among the strongest chemical bonds in nature, so strong that they rarely break apart. In structural formulas, a covalent bond is depicted as a line drawn between two atoms.

Hydrogen gas offers an example of how a covalent (electron-sharing) bond fills the outermost shells of two atoms. Each of the two hydrogen atoms has just one electron in the first shell, which could accommodate two electrons. When joined together by a covalent bond (forming $H_2$, a gas) each atom has, in effect, a "full" first shell of two electrons. As a result, $H_2$ gas is more stable than the same two hydrogen atoms by themselves. The sharing of one pair of electrons, as in $H_2$, is called a *single* bond.

Oxygen gas is another example of covalent bonding. An oxygen atom has eight electrons: two of these fill the first electron shell, and the remaining six occupy the second electron shell (which can accommodate eight). Two oxygen atoms may join to form a molecule of oxygen gas by sharing two pairs of electrons, thus completing the outer shells of both atoms. When two pairs of electrons are shared, the bond is called a *double bond.* In structural formulas, double bonds are indicated by two parallel lines.

A molecule of water forms from one oxygen and two hydrogen atoms because this combination completely fills the outermost shells of both hydrogen and oxygen. The prevalence of water on Earth follows from the simple rule that matter is most stable when it contains the least potential energy. That is, both hydrogen and oxygen are more stable when bonded together (as $H_2O$) than as independent atoms.

**Ionic bonds occur between oppositely charged ions** A second way that atoms can fill their outer shell of electrons is to give up electrons completely (if they have only one or two electrons in their outermost shell) or to take electrons from other atoms (if they need one or two to fill their outermost shell). Such a loss or gain of electrons gives the atom a net charge, because now there are fewer (or more) electrons than protons in the nucleus. The net charge is positive (+) for each electron lost and negative (–) for each electron gained.

An electrically charged atom or molecule is called an **ion.** Examples of ions are sodium ($Na^+$), chloride ($Cl^-$), calcium ($Ca^{2+}$), and hydrogen phosphate ($HPO_4^-$). Notice that ions can have a shortage or surplus of more than one electron ($Ca^{2+}$ has lost two electrons).

Ever heard the expression "opposites attract"? It should come as no surprise that oppositely charged ions are attracted to each other. When two oppositely charged ions come together, an **ionic bond** is formed (Figure 2.6). In aqueous (watery) solutions, ionic bonds are much weaker than covalent bonds, and so they tend to break rather easily. In the human body, for example, almost all of the sodium is in the form of $Na^+$, and most of the chlorine is in its ionized form, called *chloride* ($Cl^-$). Very little exists as NaCl.

Ions in aqueous solutions are sometimes called *electrolytes* because solutions of water containing ions are good conductors of electricity. As you will see, cells can control the movement of certain ions, creating electrical forces essential to the functioning of nerves, muscles, and other living tissues.

**Weak hydrogen bonds form between polar molecules** A third type of attraction occurs between molecules that do not have a net charge. Glance back at the water molecule in Figure 2.5 and note that the two hydrogen atoms are found not at opposite ends of the water molecule but fairly close together. Although the oxygen and the two hydrogen atoms share electrons, the sharing is unequal. The shared electrons in a water molecule actually spend slightly more of their time near the oxygen atom than near the hydrogen atoms because the oxygen atom attracts electrons more strongly than do the hydrogen atoms. The uneven sharing gives the oxygen region of a water molecule a partial negative charge and the two hydrogen regions a partial positive charge, even though the water molecule as a whole is electrically neutral.

Molecules such as water that are electrically neutral overall but still have partially charged regions, or *poles,* are called *polar* molecules. According to the principle that opposites attract, polar molecules arrange themselves so that the partial negative pole of one molecule is oriented toward (attracted by) the partial positive pole of another molecule. The weak attractive force between oppositely charged regions of polar molecules that contain covalently bonded hydrogen is called a **hydrogen bond** (Figure 2.7). Hydrogen bonds between water molecules are so weak that they continually break and re-form, allowing liquid water to flow. When water gets cold enough to freeze, each water molecule forms four stable, unchanging hydrogen bonds with its neighbors. When water is vaporized (becomes a gas), the hydrogen bonds are broken and stay broken as long as the water is in the gas phase.

Hydrogen bonds are important in biological molecules. They provide the force that gives proteins their three-dimensional shape, and they keep the two strands of the DNA molecule together. The structures of both proteins and DNA are described later in this chapter.

Table 2.1 summarizes covalent, ionic, and hydrogen bonds.

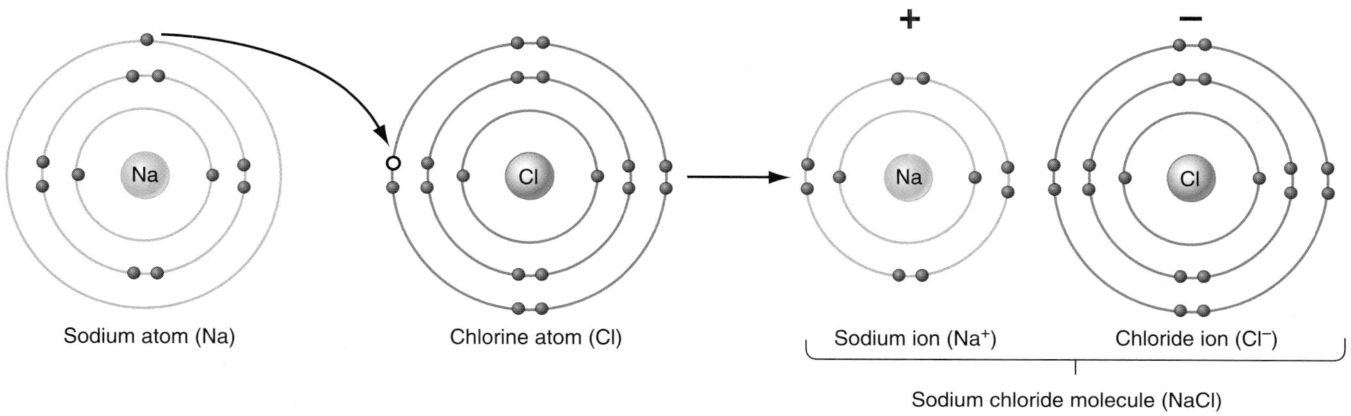


**Figure 2.6 Ionic bonds.** Electrically charged ions form when atoms give up or gain electrons. The oppositely charged ions are attracted to each other, forming an ionic bond.

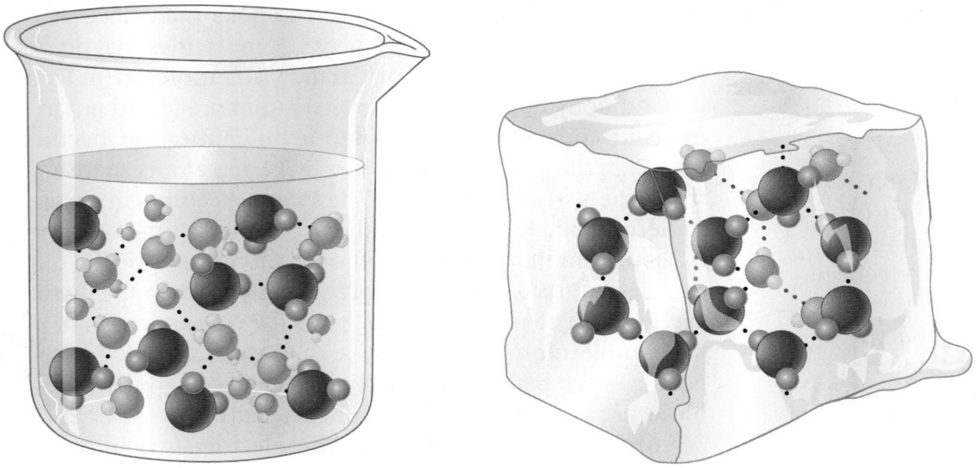


**Figure 2.7 Hydrogen bonds.** In water, weak hydrogen bonds continually form, break, and re-form between hydrogen and oxygen atoms of adjacent water molecules. Ice is a solid because stable hydrogen bonds form between each water molecule and four of its neighbors.

Even the largest atoms are small compared to the structures in living organisms. To appreciate the vast size differences between the atoms, cells, and organs in your body, imagine that a sodium atom is the size of a penny. On this scale, one of your red blood cells would be 1/2 mile in diameter, and your heart would be larger than the entire Earth!

Next, let's look at some of the most important matter of living systems: water, hydrogen ions, and a host of molecules that contain a backbone of carbon atoms.

**RECAP**

Strong covalent bonds form between atoms when they share pairs of electrons, ionic bonds form between oppositely charged ions, and weak hydrogen bonds occur between oppositely charged regions of polar molecules. ■

### Living organisms contain only certain elements

Although there are nearly 100 different elements in nature, living organisms are constructed from a limited number of them. In fact, about 99% of your body weight consists of just six elements: oxygen, carbon, hydrogen, nitrogen, calcium, and phosphorus (Table 2.2). However, the less common elements are still important, and life on Earth as we know it would not be possible without them.

## 2.3 Life depends on water

No molecule is more essential to life than water. Indeed, it accounts for 60% of your body weight. The following properties of water are especially important to living organisms:

- Water molecules are polar.
- Water is a liquid at body temperature.
- Water can absorb and hold heat energy.

These properties make water an ideal solvent and an important factor in temperature regulation.

### Water is the biological solvent

A **solvent** is a liquid in which other substances dissolve, and a **solute** is any dissolved substance. Water is the ideal solvent in living organisms specifically because it is a polar liquid at body temperature. As the solvent of life, water is the substance in which the many chemical reactions of living organisms take place. Let's look at a simple example of a solute dissolving in water to better understand how the polar nature of water facilitates the reaction.

**Table 2.1 Summary of the three types of chemical bonds**

| Type | Strength | Description | Examples |
|---|---|---|---|
| Covalent bond | Strong | A bond in which the sharing of electrons between atoms results in each atom having a maximally filled outermost shell of electrons | The bonds between hydrogen and oxygen in a molecule of water |
| Ionic bond | Moderate | The bond between two oppositely charged ions (atoms or molecules that were formed by the permanent transfer of one or more electrons) | The bond between $Na^+$ and $Cl^-$ in salt |
| Hydrogen bond | Weak | The bond between oppositely charged regions of molecules that contain covalently bonded hydrogen atoms | The bonds between molecules of water |

**Table 2.2 The most common and important elements in living organisms***

| Element | Atomic symbol | Atomic number | Atomic mass | % of Human weight | Functions in life |
|---|---|---|---|---|---|
| Oxygen | O | 8 | 16.0 | 65 | Part of water and most organic molecules; also molecular oxygen |
| Carbon | C | 6 | 12.0 | 18 | The backbone of all organic molecules |
| Hydrogen | H | 1 | 1.0 | 10 | Part of all organic molecules and of water |
| Nitrogen | N | 7 | 14.0 | 3 | Component of proteins and nucleic acids |
| Calcium | Ca | 20 | 40.1 | 2 | Constituent of bone; also essential for the action of nerves and muscles |
| Phosphorus | P | 15 | 31.0 | 1 | Part of cell membranes and of energy storage molecules; also a constituent of bone |
| Potassium | K | 19 | 39.1 | 0.3 | Important in nerve action |
| Sulfur | S | 16 | 32.1 | 0.2 | Structural component of most proteins |
| Sodium | Na | 11 | 23.0 | 0.1 | The primary ion in body fluids; also important for nerve action |
| Chlorine | Cl | 17 | 35.5 | 0.1 | Component of digestive acid; also a major ion in body fluids |
| Magnesium | Mg | 12 | 24.3 | Trace | Important for the action of certain enzymes and for muscle contraction |
| Iron | Fe | 26 | 55.8 | Trace | A constituent of hemoglobin, the oxygen-carrying molecule |

*The elements are listed in descending order of their contribution to total body weight. Atomic number represents the number of protons in the nucleus. Atomic mass is roughly equivalent to the total number of protons and neutrons because electrons have very little mass. Note that 99% of your body weight is accounted for by just six elements.

Consider a common and important solid, crystals of sodium chloride (NaCl), or table salt. Crystals of table salt consist of a regular, repeating pattern of sodium and chloride ions held together by ionic bonds (Figure 2.8). When salt is placed in water, individual ions at the surface of the crystal are pulled away from the crystal and are immediately surrounded by the polar water molecules. The water molecules form such a tight cluster around each ion that the ions are prevented from reassociating back into the crystalline form. In other words, water keeps the ions dissolved. Note that the water molecules are oriented around ions according to the principle that opposite charges attract.

Polar molecules that are attracted to water and interact with it are called **hydrophilic** (from the Greek words *hydor,* water, and *philos,* loving). Nonpolar molecules that are not attracted to water are **hydrophobic** (*hydor* + the Greek *phobos,* fear). You can observe hydrophobic molecules in action by mixing cooking oil and water (see the Try It Yourself box on page 31).

Because water is a liquid at body temperature, it can flow freely. This makes it an excellent medium for transporting solutes from one place to another. Indeed, the blood in our cardiovascular system is over 90% water. As a liquid, water also occupies space. It fills our cells (the intracellular space) and the spaces between cells (the intercellular space).

## Water helps regulate body temperature

An important property of water is that it can absorb and hold a large amount of heat energy with only a modest increase in temperature. In fact, it absorbs heat better than most other liquids. Water thus may prevent large increases

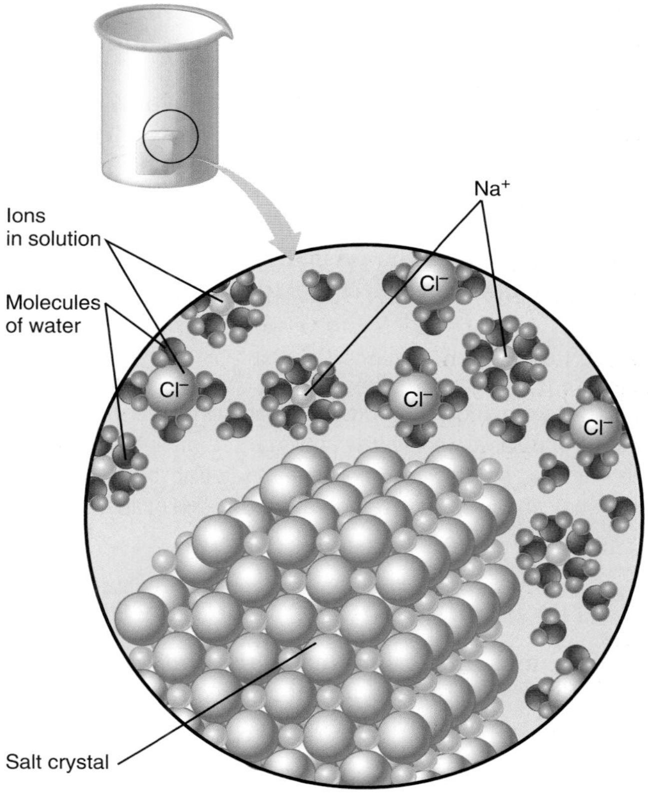


**Figure 2.8 How water keeps ions in solution.** The slightly negative ends of polar water molecules are attracted to positive ions, whereas the slightly positive ends of water molecules are attracted to negative ions. The water molecules pull the ions away from the crystal and prevent them from reassociating with each other.

**Figure 2.9 Water contributes to the regulation of body temperature.**

in body temperature when excess heat is produced. Water also holds heat well when there is a danger of too much heat loss (for instance, when you go outdoors wearing shorts on a cool day). The ability of water to absorb and hold heat helps prevent rapid changes in body temperature when changes occur in metabolism or in the environment.

Our bodies generate heat during metabolism. We usually generate more heat than we need to maintain a constant body temperature of 98.6° Fahrenheit (37° Celsius), so losing heat is generally more of a priority than conserving it. One way we can lose heat quickly is by evaporation of water (Figure 2.9). When water is in contact with air, hydrogen bonds between some of the water molecules at the surface of the water are broken, and water molecules escape into the air as water vapor. It takes energy to break all those hydrogen bonds, and that energy comes from heat generated by the body and transported to the skin by the blood. Evaporation of sweat is just one of the mechanisms for the removal of heat from the body. How the body regulates body temperature is discussed in more detail in Chapter 4.

You can demonstrate the cooling power of evaporation for yourself. The next time you perspire heavily, notice that your exposed skin may actually feel cool to the touch.

**RECAP**

Most biological molecules dissolve readily in water because water is a polar molecule. The liquid nature of water facilitates the transport of biological molecules. Water absorbs and holds heat and can lower body temperature through evaporation. ■

## 2.4 The importance of hydrogen ions

One of the most important ions in the body is the hydrogen ion (a single proton without an electron). In this section we will see how hydrogen ions are created and why it is so important to maintain an appropriate concentration of them.

### Acids donate hydrogen ions, bases accept them

Although the covalent bonds between hydrogen and oxygen in water are strong and thus rarely broken, it can happen. When it does, the electron from one hydrogen atom is transferred to the oxygen atom completely, and the water molecule breaks into two ions—a *hydrogen ion* ($H^+$) and a *hydroxide ion* ($OH^-$).

In pure water, only a very few molecules of water are dissociated (broken apart) into $H^+$ and $OH^-$ at any one time. However, there are other sources of hydrogen ions in aqueous solutions. An **acid** is any molecule that can donate (give up) an $H^+$ ion. When added to pure water, acids produce an *acidic* solution, one with a higher $H^+$ concentration than that of pure water. (By definition, an aqueous solution with the same concentration of $H^+$ as that of pure water is a *neutral* solution). Common acidic solutions are vinegar, carbonated beverages, and orange juice. Conversely, a **base** is any molecule that can accept (combine with) an $H^+$ ion. When added to pure water, bases produce a basic or *alkaline* solution, one with a lower $H^+$ concentration than that of pure water. Common alkaline solutions include baking soda in water, detergents, and drain cleaner.

Because acids and bases have opposite effects on the $H^+$ concentration of solutions, they are said to neutralize each other. You have probably heard that a spoonful of baking soda in water is a time-honored way to counteract an "acid stomach." Now you know that this home remedy is based on sound chemical principles.

### The pH scale expresses hydrogen ion concentration

Scientists use the pH scale to indicate the acidity or alkalinity of a solution. The **pH scale** is a measure of the hydrogen ion concentration of a solution. The scale ranges from 0 to 14, with pure water having a pH of 7.0, the neutral point. A pH of 7 corresponds to a hydrogen ion concentration of $10^{-7}$ moles/liter (a *mole* is a term used by chemists to indicate a certain number of atoms, ions, or molecules). An *acidic* solution has a pH of *less* than 7, whereas a *basic* solution has a pH of *greater* than 7. Each whole number change in pH represents a 10-fold change in the hydrogen ion concentration in the opposite direction. For example, an acidic solution with a pH of 6 has an $H^+$ concentration of $10^{-6}$ moles/liter (10 times greater than pure water), whereas an alkaline solution with a pH of 8 has an $H^+$ concentration of $10^{-8}$ moles/liter (1/10 that of water). Figure 2.10 shows the pH scale and indicates the pH values of some common substances and body fluids.

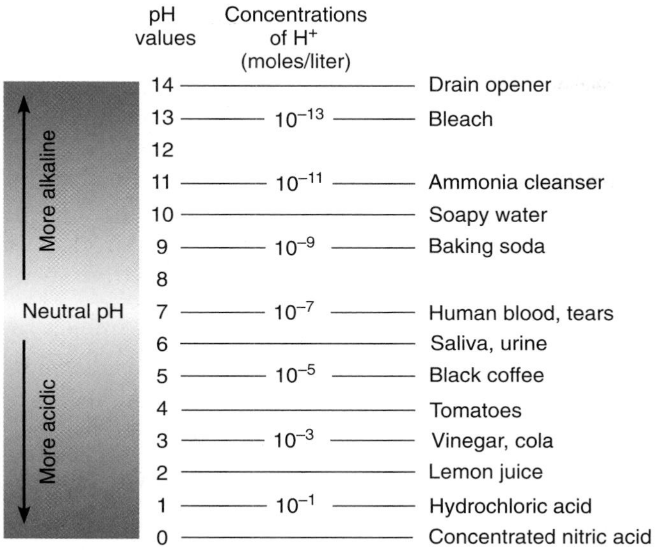


**Figure 2.10 The pH scale.** The pH scale is an indication of the $H^+$ concentration of a solution.

The pH of blood is 7.4, just slightly more alkaline than neutral water. The hydrogen ion concentration of blood plasma is low relative to the concentration of other ions (the hydrogen ion concentration of blood plasma is less than one-*millionth* that of sodium ions, for example). It is important to maintain homeostasis of this low concentration of hydrogen ions in the body because hydrogen ions are small, mobile, positively charged, and highly reactive. Hydrogen ions tend to displace other positive ions in molecules, and when they do they alter molecular structures and change the ability of the molecule to function properly.

Changes in the pH of body fluids can affect how molecules are transported across the cell membrane and how rapidly certain chemical reactions occur. They may even alter the shapes of proteins that are structural elements of the cell. In other words, a change in the hydrogen ion concentration can be dangerous because it threatens homeostasis.

**RECAP**

Acids can donate hydrogen ions to a solution, whereas bases can accept hydrogen ions from a solution. The pH scale indicates the hydrogen ion concentration of a solution. The normal pH of blood is 7.4. ■

## Buffers minimize changes in pH

A **buffer** is any substance that tends to minimize the changes in pH that might otherwise occur when an acid or base is added to a solution. Buffers are essential to our ability to maintain homeostasis of pH in body fluids.

In biological solutions such as blood or urine, buffers are present as *pairs* of related molecules that have opposite effects. One of the pair is the acid form of the molecule (capable of donating an $H^+$ ion), and the other is the base form (capable of accepting an $H^+$ ion). When an acid is added and the number of $H^+$ ions increases, the base form of the buffer pair accepts some of the $H^+$ ions, minimizing the fall in pH that might otherwise occur. Conversely, when a base is added that might take up too many $H^+$ ions, the acid form of the buffer pair releases additional $H^+$ ions and thus minimizes the rise in pH. Buffer pairs are like absorbent sponges that can pick up excess water and then can be wrung out to release water when necessary.

One of the most important buffer pairs in body fluids such as blood is bicarbonate ($HCO_3^-$, the base form) and carbonic acid ($H_2CO_3$, the acid form). When blood becomes too acidic, bicarbonate accepts excess $H^+$ according to the following reaction:

$$HCO_3^- + H^+ \rightarrow H_2CO_3$$

When blood becomes too alkaline, carbonic acid donates $H^+$ by the reverse reaction:

$$HCO_3^- + H^+ \leftarrow H_2CO_3$$

In a biological solution such as blood, bicarbonate and carbonic acid take up and release $H^+$ all the time. Ultimately a chemical *equilibrium* is reached in which the rates of the two chemical reactions are the same, as represented by the following combined equation:

$$HCO_3^- + H^+ \leftrightarrow H_2CO_3$$

**try it yourself**

### Oil and Water Don't Mix

To demonstrate that oil and water don't mix, add two tablespoons of cooking oil to a jar half filled with water. Shake the jar vigorously and then let it stand for a while. Notice that the oil tends to separate from the water, eventually forming a single layer at the top of the jar.

Why does this happen? Recall that water is a polar molecule: although it is electrically neutral overall, it has partially charged positive and negative ends, or "poles." Oils are completely neutral molecules. When water and oil are mixed, the water molecules are attracted to each other. They tend to bond together by weak hydrogen bonds, excluding oil from regions occupied by water. Over time the oil is forced into ever larger droplets until it completely separates from the water. It rises to the top because oil is less dense than water.

Now add an egg yolk to the oil-and-water mixture and try the experiment again. You will see a lot of foam on top of the water because of the denaturation of some of the proteins in the egg yolk. However, the important observation is that the oil no longer separates from the water. This is because egg yolk contains molecules (proteins and phospholipids) that have both polar and nonpolar regions. Their nonpolar regions surround the fat droplets, leaving their polar regions facing outward. The outer polar layer becomes a barrier that prevents the fat droplets from coming in contact with each other, and so the fat droplets remain in solution indefinitely.

When excess acid is produced, the combined equation shifts to the right as the bicarbonate combines with $H^+$. The reverse is true for alkalinity.

There are many other buffers in the body as well. The more buffers that are present in a body fluid, the more stable the pH.

**RECAP**

Buffers tend to minimize changes in pH in a solution. They help us maintain a stable pH in body fluids. ■

## 2.5 The organic molecules of living organisms

**Organic molecules** are molecules that contain carbon and other elements held together by covalent bonds. The name "organic" came about at a time when scientists believed that all organic molecules were created only by living organisms and all "inorganic" molecules came from nonliving matter. Today we know that organic molecules can be synthesized in the laboratory under the right conditions and that they probably existed on Earth before there was life.

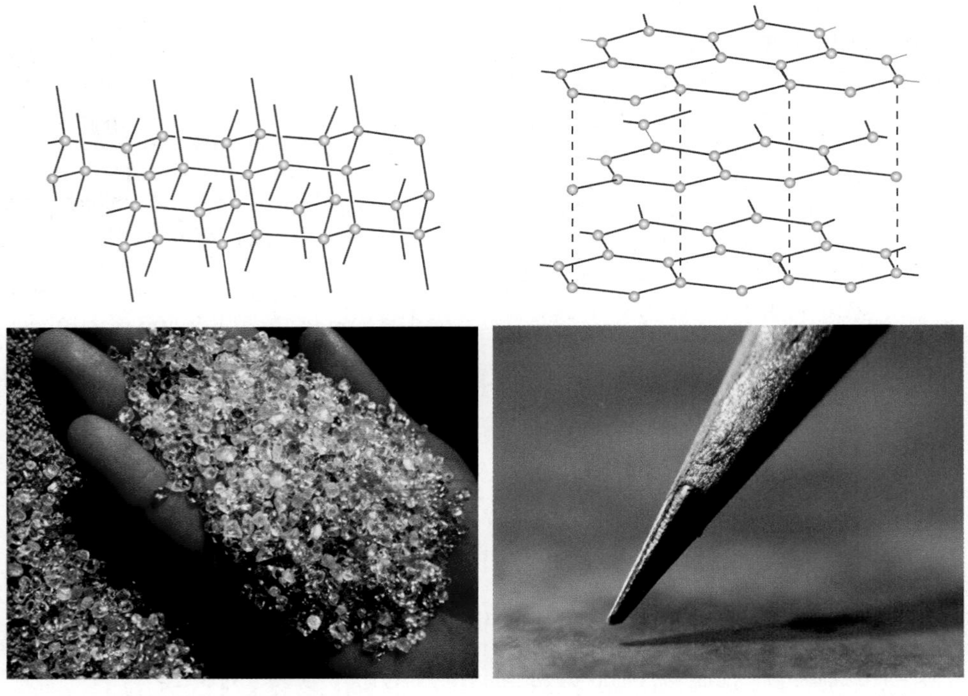

**a) Diamonds are formed only under conditions of extreme temperature and pressure.** The structure of diamond resembles the steel framework of a large building; each atom is covalently bonded to four neighboring carbon atoms. This explains the hardness of diamonds.

**b) Graphite is produced as a result of decay of older carbon-based substances.** Its structure consists of layers of hexagonal rings of carbon atoms. Graphite is fairly soft (hence its use in pencils) because these layers of carbon atoms can slide past one another.

**Figure 2.11 Carbon.** Graphite and diamond are both elemental forms of carbon.

### Carbon is the common building block of organic molecules

Carbon (Figure 2.11) is relatively rare in the natural world, representing less than 0.03% of Earth's crust. However, living organisms actively accumulate it. Carbon accounts for about 18% of body weight in humans.

Carbon is the common building block of all organic molecules because of the many ways it can form strong covalent bonds with other atoms. Carbon has six electrons, two in the first shell and four in the second. Because carbon is most stable when its second shell is filled with eight electrons, *its natural tendency is to form four covalent bonds with other molecules.* This makes carbon an ideal structural component, one that can branch in a multitude of directions.

Using the chemist's convention that a line between the chemical symbols of atoms represents a pair of shared electrons in a covalent bond, Figure 2.12 shows some of the many structural possibilities for carbon. Carbon can form covalent bonds with hydrogen, nitrogen, oxygen, or another carbon. It can form double covalent bonds with oxygen or another carbon. It can even form five- or six-membered carbon rings, with or without double bonds between carbons.

In addition to their complexity, there is almost no limit to the size of organic molecules derived from carbon. Some, called *macromolecules* (from the Greek *makros,* long), consist of thousands or even millions of smaller molecules.

### Macromolecules are synthesized and broken down within the cell

Macromolecules are built (synthesized) within the cell itself. In a process called **dehydration synthesis** (also called the condensation reaction), smaller molecules called subunits are joined by covalent bonds, like pearls on a string. The name of the process accurately describes what is happening: Each time a subunit is added, the equivalent of a water molecule is removed ("dehydration") (Figure 2.13). The subunits needed to synthesize macromolecules come from the foods you eat and from the biochemical reactions in your body that break down other large molecules into smaller ones.

The synthesis of macromolecules from smaller molecules requires energy. That is one reason we need energy to survive and grow. It is no accident that children seem to eat enormous amounts of food. Growing children require energy to make the macromolecules necessary to create new cell membranes, muscle fibers, and other body tissues.

Some macromolecules are synthesized specifically for the purpose of storing energy within our cells. The ability to store energy internally allows organisms to survive even when food is not plentiful. Other macromolecules serve as structural components of cells or of extracellular (outside the cell) structures such as bone. Still others direct the many activities of the cell or serve as signaling molecules between cells.

Organic macromolecules are broken down by a process called **hydrolysis.** During hydrolysis the equivalent of a water molecule is added each time a covalent bond between single subunits in the chain is broken. Notice that hydrolysis is essentially the reverse of dehydration synthesis, and thus it should not surprise you that the breakdown of macromolecules releases energy. The energy was stored as potential energy in the covalent bonds between atoms. The body obtains much of its energy through hydrolysis of energy-storage molecules. Hydrolysis is also used to break down molecules of food during digestion, to recycle materials for reuse, and to get rid of substances that are no longer needed by the body.

Living organisms synthesize four classes of organic molecules, known as *carbohydrates, lipids, proteins,* and *nucleic acids.* The many different molecules within each class are constructed of the same handful of chemical elements. However, there is essentially no limit to the number of different molecules that could be created. No one knows for sure how many different organic molecules there are in humans. On a chemical level, the tremendous diversity among the many species of organisms on Earth is due to differences in their organic molecules, especially their proteins and nucleic acids.

**RECAP**

Carbon is a key element of organic molecules because of the multiple ways it can form strong covalent bonds with other molecules. Organic molecules are synthesized by dehydration synthesis, a process that requires energy, and broken down by hydrolysis, which liberates energy. The four classes of organic molecules are carbohydrates, lipids, proteins, and nucleic acids. ■

## 2.6 Carbohydrates: Used for energy and structural support

A clue to the basic structure of carbohydrates is found in their name. Carbohydrates have a backbone of carbon atoms with hydrogen and oxygen attached in the same proportion as they appear in water (2-to-1); hence the carbon is "hydrated," or combined with water.

Most living organisms use carbohydrates for energy, and plants use at least one carbohydrate (cellulose) as structural support.

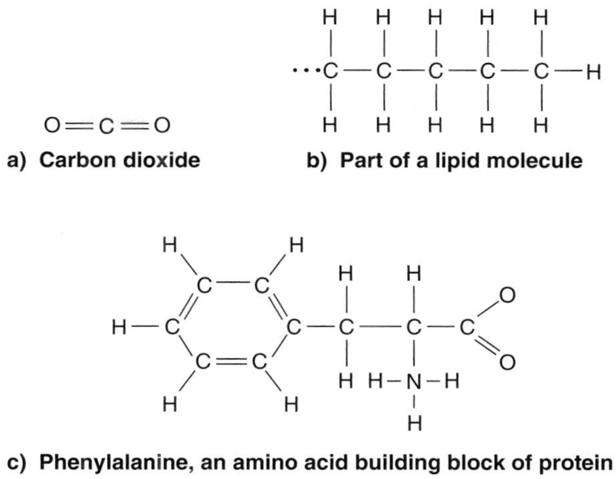


**Figure 2.12 Examples of the structural diversity of carbon.** **(a)** In carbon dioxide, a carbon atom forms two covalent bonds with each oxygen atom. **(b)** Lipid molecules contain long chains of carbon atoms covalently bound to hydrogen. **(c)** Carbon is the backbone of the amino acid phenylalanine.

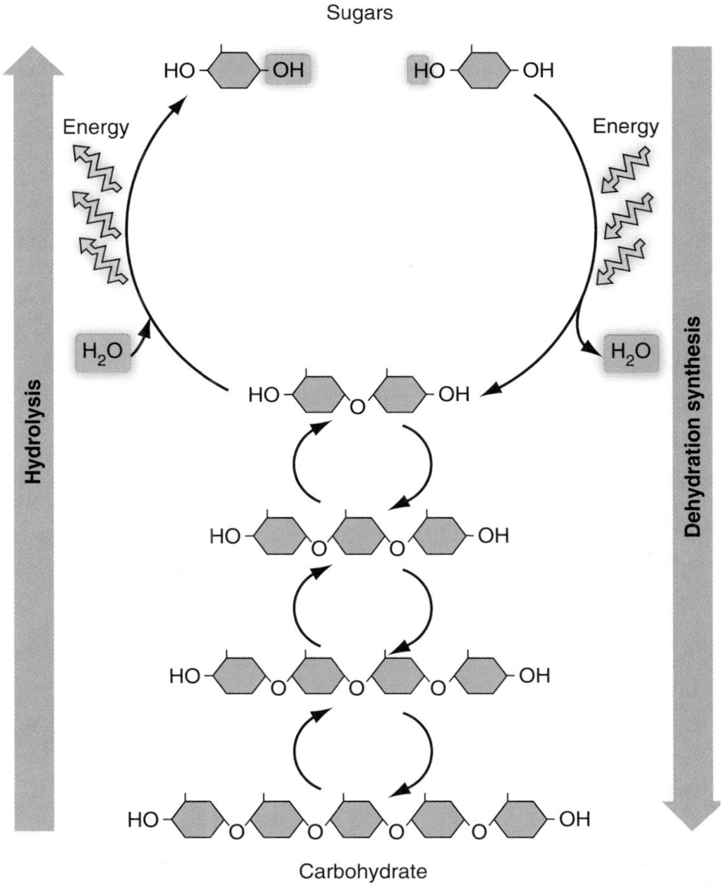


**Figure 2.13 Dehydration synthesis and hydrolysis.** The synthesis of larger molecules by dehydration synthesis requires energy, whereas the breakdown of molecules into smaller units by hydrolysis liberates stored energy. In this example the smallest units are simple sugars and the macromolecule is a carbohydrate.

### Monosaccharides are simple sugars

The simplest kind of carbohydrate is called a **monosaccharide** (meaning "one sugar"). Monosaccharides have relatively simple structures consisting of carbon, hydrogen, and oxygen in a 1-2-1 ratio. The most common monosaccharides contain five or six carbon atoms arranged in either a five-membered or six-membered ring (Figure 2.14).

*Glucose, fructose, ribose,* and *deoxyribose* are four of the most important monosaccharides in humans. Ribose and deoxyribose (Figure 2.14a) are both five-carbon monosaccharides that are components of nucleotide molecules, discussed below. The only difference between the two is that deoxyribose has one less oxygen atom than ribose. Glucose, a six-carbon monosaccharide, is an important source of energy for cells. When more energy is available than can be used right away, glucose molecules can be linked together by dehydration synthesis to form larger carbohydrate molecules (Figure 2.14b).

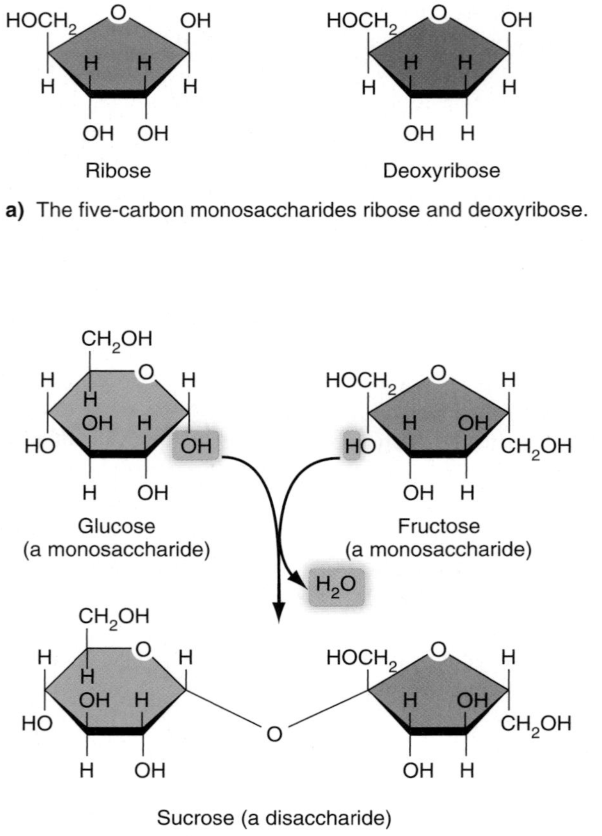


**a)** The five-carbon monosaccharides ribose and deoxyribose.

**b)** Two six-carbon monosaccharides (glucose and fructose) are joined together by dehydration synthesis, forming sucrose.

**Figure 2.14 Monosaccharides.** By convention, in a ringed structure the symbol C for carbon is often omitted because its presence is inferred by the union of two bond lines at an angle.

### Oligosaccharides: More than one monosaccharide linked together

**Oligosaccharides** are short strings of monosaccharides (*oligo* means "a few") linked together by dehydration synthesis. One common oligosaccharide is table sugar, or sucrose. Sucrose is also called a *disaccharide* because it consists of just two monosaccharides (glucose + fructose). Another is maltose (glucose + glucose).

Some oligosaccharides are covalently bonded to certain cell-membrane proteins (called glycoproteins). Glycoproteins participate in linking adjacent cells together and in cell-cell recognition and communication.

### Polysaccharides store energy

Complex carbohydrates called **polysaccharides** (*poly* means "many") form when thousands of monosaccharides are joined together into straight or branched chains by dehydration synthesis. Polysaccharides are a convenient way for cells to stockpile extra energy by locking it in the bonds of the polysaccharide molecule.

The most important polysaccharides in living organisms consist of long chains of glucose monosaccharides. In animals the storage polysaccharide is **glycogen** (Figure 2.15), whereas in plants it is **starch.** The flour we obtain by grinding plant grains is high in starch, which we then utilize for our own energy needs by breaking it down to glucose. Any glucose not consumed for energy in the short term can be used to create glycogen or lipids and stored within our cells for later use.

*Cellulose* is a slightly different form of glucose polysaccharide. Plants use it for structural support rather than for energy storage. The nature of the chemical bonds in cellulose is such that most animals, including humans, cannot break cellulose down to glucose units (which is why we cannot digest wood). But there's plenty of energy locked in the chemical bonds of cellulose, as demonstrated by the heat generated by a wood fire.

Undigested cellulose in the food we eat contributes to the fiber or "roughage" in our diet. A certain amount of fiber is thought to be beneficial because it increases the movement of wastes through the digestive tract. The more rapid excretion of wastes decreases the time of exposure to any carcinogens (cancer-causing agents) that may be in the waste material.

**RECAP**

Carbohydrates contain carbon, hydrogen, and oxygen in a 1-2-1 ratio. Simple sugars such as glucose provide immediate energy for cells. Complex carbohydrates called polysaccharides store energy (in animals and plants) and provide structural support (in plants). ■

## 2.7 Lipids: Insoluble in water

The most important physical characteristic of **lipids** for biology is that they are relatively insoluble in water. The most important subclasses of lipids in your body are *triglycerides, phospholipids,* and *steroids.*

### Triglycerides are energy-storage molecules

**Triglycerides,** also called neutral fats or just fats, are synthesized from a molecule of glycerol and three fatty acids

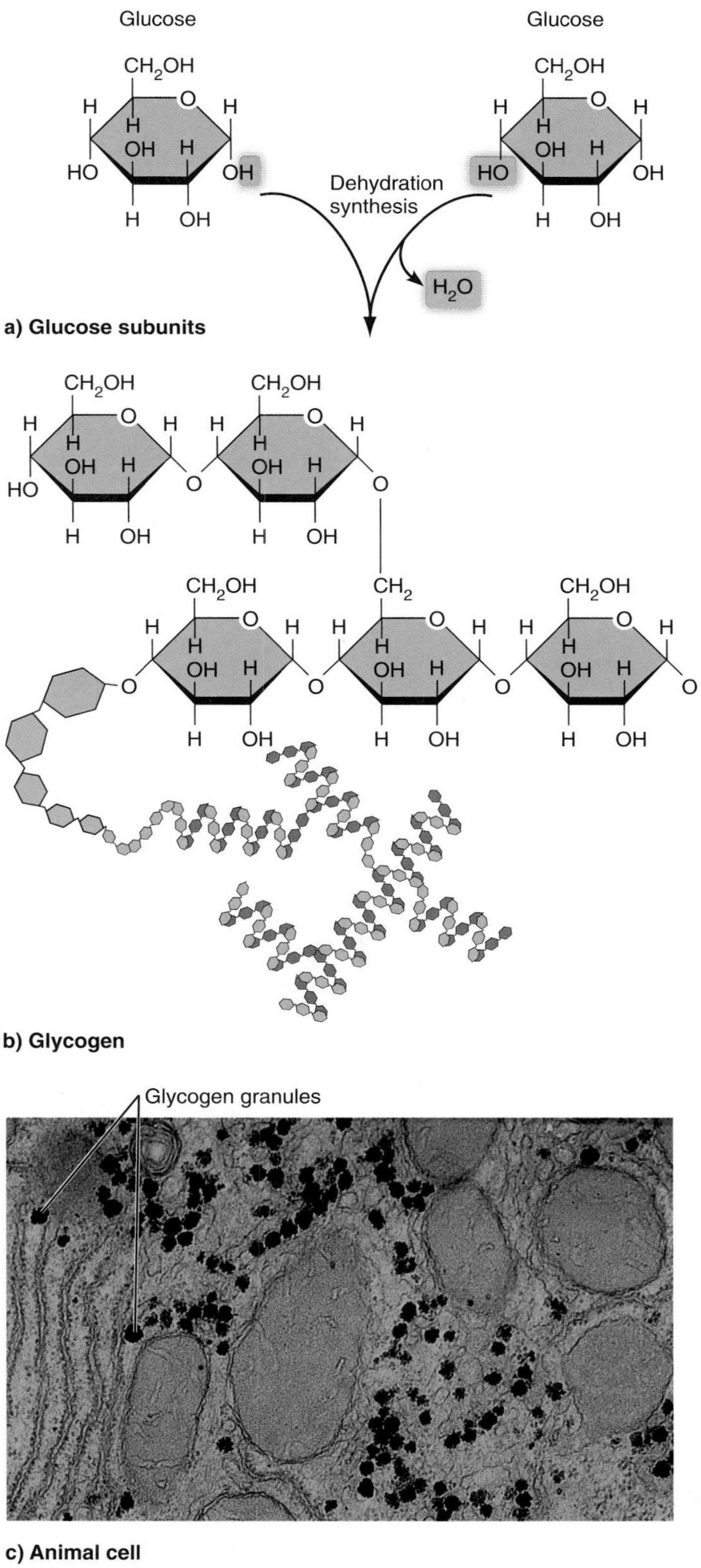


**Figure 2.15 Glycogen is the storage carbohydrate in animals. (a)** Glycogen is formed by dehydration synthesis from glucose subunits. **(b)** A representation of the highly branched nature of glycogen. **(c)** An animal cell with granules of stored glycogen.

(Figure 2.16). **Fatty acids** are chains of hydrocarbons (usually about 16–18 carbons long) that end in a group of atoms known as a carboxyl group (COOH). Fats vary in the length of their fatty acid tails and the ratio of hydrogen atoms to carbon atoms in the tails.

*Saturated fats* have a full complement of two hydrogen atoms for each carbon in their tails. In saturated fats, the tails are fairly straight, allowing them to pack closely together. As a result, saturated fats are generally solid at room temperature. Animal fats, such as butter and bacon grease, are saturated fats. A diet rich in saturated fats is thought to contribute to the development of cardiovascular disease.

*Unsaturated fats,* also called *oils,* have fewer than two hydrogen atoms on one or more of the carbon atoms in the tails. As a result, double bonds form between adjacent carbons, putting kinks in the tails and preventing the fats from associating closely together. As a result, unsaturated fats (oils) are generally liquid at room temperature.

Triglycerides are stored in adipose (fat) tissue and are an important source of stored energy in our bodies. Most of the energy is located in the bonds between carbon and hydrogen in the fatty acid tails.

**RECAP**

Lipids (triglycerides, phospholipids, and steroids) are all relatively insoluble in water. Triglycerides are an important source of stored energy. ■

## Phospholipids are the primary component of cell membranes

**Phospholipids** are a modified form of lipid. They are the primary structural component of cell membranes.

Like fats, phospholipids have a molecule of glycerol as the backbone, but they have only two fatty acid tails. Replacing the third fatty acid is a negatively charged phosphate group ($PO_4^-$) and another group that varies depending on the phospholipid but is generally positively charged (Figure 2.17 on page 37). The presence of charged groups on one end gives the phospholipid a special property: one end of the molecule is polar and thus soluble in water, whereas the other end (represented by the two fatty acid tails) is neutral and therefore relatively insoluble in water.

## Steroids are composed of four rings

**Steroids** do not look at all like the lipids described previously but are classified as lipids because they are relatively insoluble in water. Steroids consist of a backbone of 3 six-membered carbon rings and 1 five-membered carbon ring to which any number of different groups may be attached.

One steroid you may be familiar with is **cholesterol.** High levels of cholesterol in the blood are associated with cardiovascular disease. However, we all need a certain amount of cholesterol. It is a normal and essential structural component of animal cell membranes and is also the source of several important

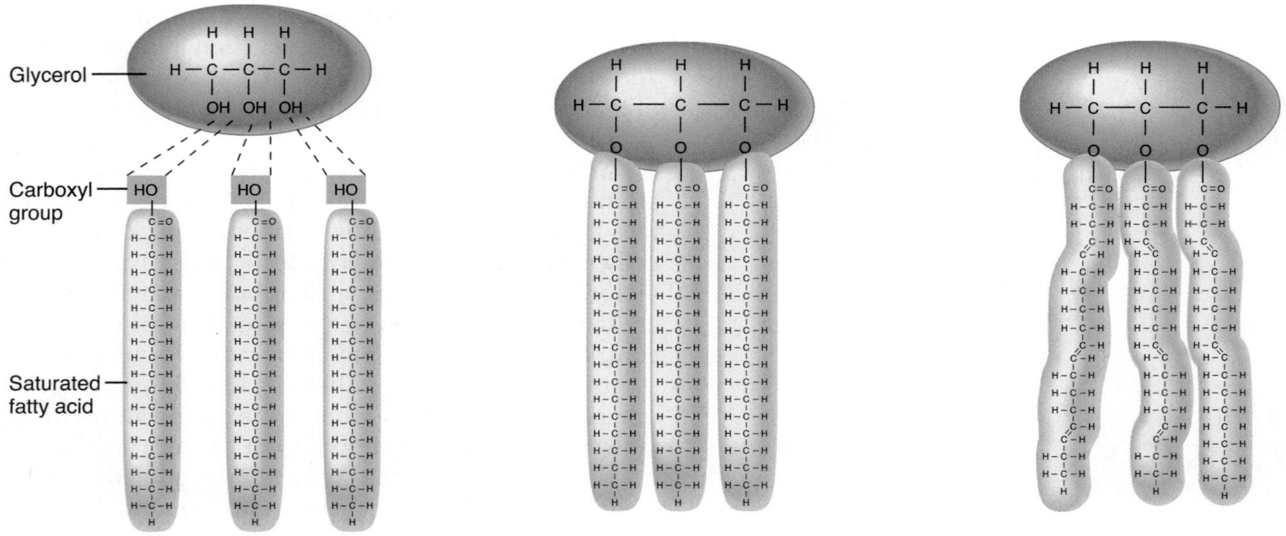


**a) Triglycerides (neutral fats) are synthesized from glycerol and three fatty acids by dehydration synthesis.**

**b) Saturated fats have straight tails, allowing them to pack closely together.**

**c) Unsaturated fats have kinked tails, preventing them from packing closely together.**

**Figure 2.16 Triglycerides.** **(a)** Triglycerides (neutral fats) are synthesized from glycerol and three fatty acids. **(b)** A triglyceride with saturated fatty acid tails. **(c)** A triglyceride with unsaturated fatty acid tails.

hormones, including the sex hormones estrogen and testosterone (Figure 2.18). Our bodies manufacture cholesterol even though we generally get more than we need from our diet.

**RECAP**

Phospholipids, an important component of cell membranes, have a polar (water-soluble) head and two fatty acid (water-insoluble) tails. Steroids, such as cholesterol, have a four-ring structure. ■

## 2.8 Proteins: Complex structures constructed of amino acids

Proteins are macromolecules constructed from long strings of single units called **amino acids.** All human proteins are constructed from only 20 different amino acids (Figure 2.19 on page 38). Each amino acid has an *amino group* ($NH_3$) on one end, a carboxyl acid group on the other, a C-H group in the middle, and an additional group (designated "R") that represents everything else. Some of the R groups are completely neutral, others are neutral but polar, and a few carry a net charge (either positive or negative). Differences in the charge and structure of the amino acids affect the shape and functions of the proteins constructed from them. Our bodies can synthesize (make) 11 of the amino acids if necessary. However, we generally get enough of most of them, including the 9 we cannot synthesize, in the food we eat.

Like complex carbohydrates and fats, proteins are formed by dehydration synthesis (Figure 2.20 on page 39). A single string of 3 to 100 amino acids is called a **polypeptide.** A polypeptide is generally referred to as a **protein** when it is longer than 100 amino acids and has a complex structure and a function. Some proteins consist of several polypeptides linked together.

The function of every protein depends critically on its structure. We can define protein structure on at least three levels and sometimes four levels (Figure 2.21 on page 40):

- *Primary structure.* The primary structure of a protein is represented by its amino acid sequence. In writing, each amino acid is indicated by a three-letter code (review Figure 2.19).
- *Secondary structure.* The secondary structure describes how the chain of amino acids is oriented in space. A common secondary structure of proteins is an *alpha($\alpha$) helix*. An $\alpha$ helix is a right-hand spiral that is stabilized by hydrogen bonds between amino acids at regular intervals. Another common secondary structure also stabilized by hydrogen bonds is a flat ribbon called a *beta* ($\beta$) *sheet*. A $\beta$ sheet is formed when hydrogen bonds join two primary sequences of amino acids side by side. In addition to forming these two structures, proteins can coil into an almost infinite variety of shapes depending on which amino acids make up the sequence.
- *Tertiary structure.* Tertiary structure, the third level, refers to how the protein twists and folds to form a three-dimensional shape. The protein's three-dimensional structure depends in part on its sequence of amino acids, because the locations of the polar and charged groups within the chain detmine the locations of hydrogen bonds that hold the whole sequence together.

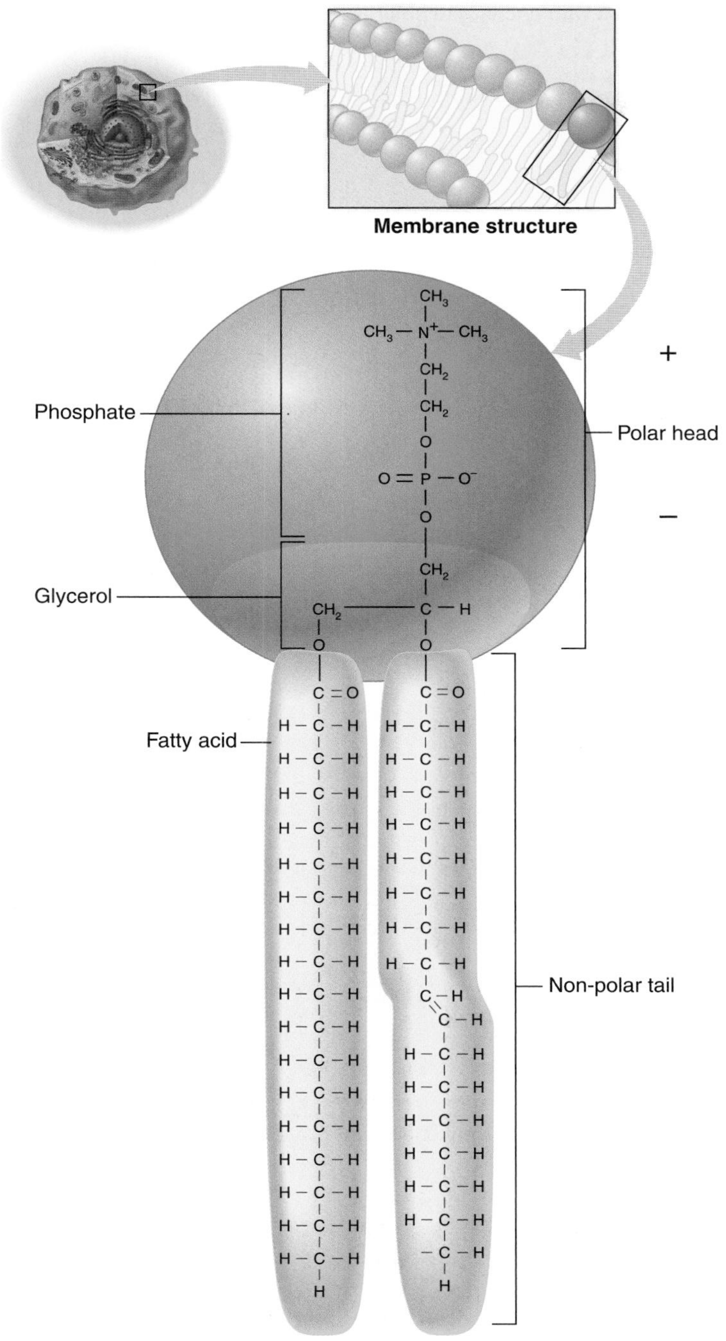


**Figure 2.17 Phospholipids.** Phospholipids are the primary constituent of animal cell membranes.

In addition, occasionally a covalent bond called a disulfide (S-S) bond forms between the sulfur molecules of two cysteine amino acids. Finally, proteins tend to fold in such a way that neutral amino acids are more likely to end up in the interior, whereas charged and polar amino acids are more likely to face the outside (aqueous environment). Proteins acquire their characteristic tertiary structure by a folding process that occurs either during synthesis or shortly thereafter.

- *Quaternary structure.* The quaternary (fourth) structure of some proteins refers to how many polypeptide chains make up the protein (if there is more than one) and how they associate with each other.

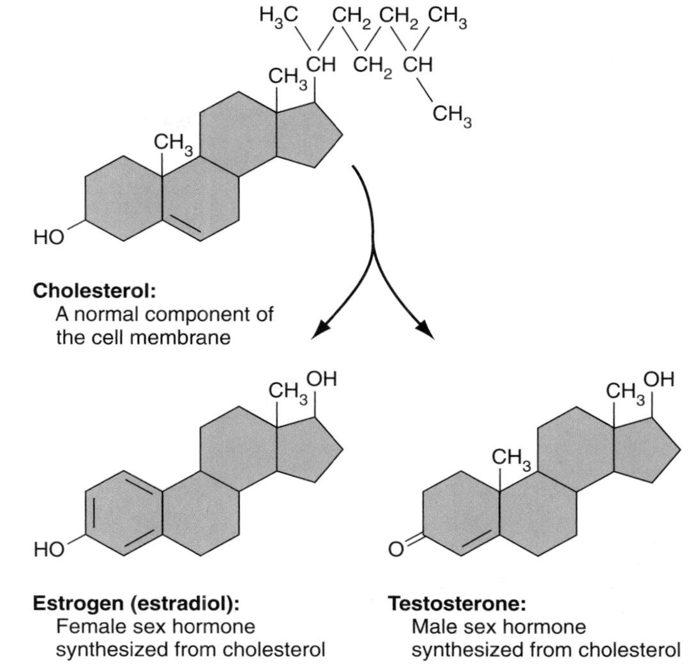


**Figure 2.18 Steroids.**

The human body has thousands of different proteins, each serving a different function. Some proteins are primarily for structural support. Others are involved in muscle contraction. Others form part of the cell membrane, where they help transmit information and materials into and out of cells. Still others, called *enzymes,* regulate the rates of biochemical reactions within cells (see next section).

Because the links that determine the secondary and tertiary structures of protein are relatively weak hydrogen bonds, they may be broken by nearby charged molecules. This means that *the shape of proteins can change* in the presence of charged or polar molecules. The ability to change shape is essential to the functions of certain proteins.

Protein structure can also be damaged, sometimes permanently, by high temperatures or changes in pH. **Denaturation** refers to permanent disruption of protein structure, leading to a loss of biological function. An egg becomes hard when it is exposed to high temperatures because the soluble proteins in the egg become denatured and clump together as a solid mass.

Most proteins are water soluble, meaning that they dissolve in water. There are exceptions, however. Many of the proteins that are part of our cell membranes either are insoluble in water or have water-insoluble regions. You will learn more about why this is important in Chapter 3.

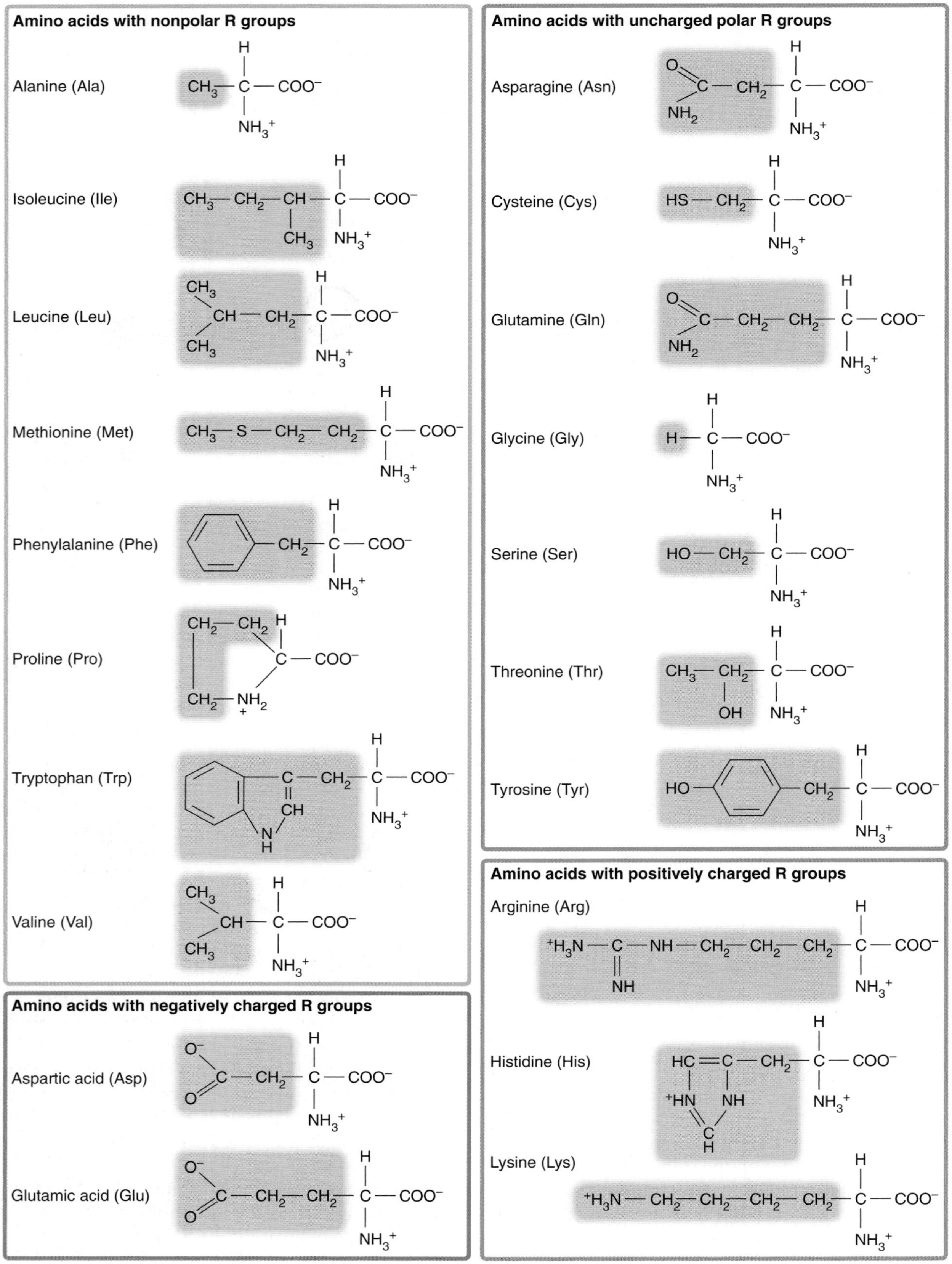


**Figure 2.19 The 20 amino acid building blocks of proteins.** The portions of amino acids that make them different from each other, called R groups, are colored. The three-letter codes in parentheses designate the amino acids in written formulas.

# Directions in Science

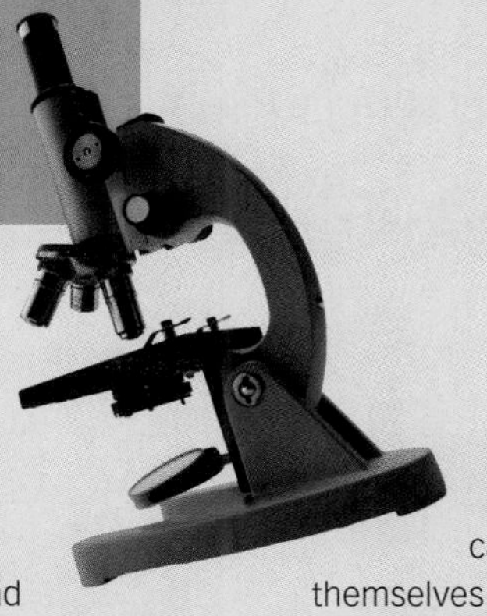

## Why Protein Folding Is Important

A misfolded protein is a useless piece of junk, because protein function depends on protein shape. The shape of a protein, in turn, is determined by how the amino acid chain twists and folds back on itself.

The consequences of misfolding can be catastrophic. Consider cystic fibrosis, the most lethal genetic disease in North America. Patients with cystic fibrosis have a defective version of a critical protein that normally transports chloride ions across the cell membrane. Why is the protein defective? Because the protein folding process goes awry at a critical step.

Misfolded proteins have been linked to several other serious health problems as well. They include the degenerative nerve disorders Parkinson's disease and Alzheimer's disease; atherosclerosis, the "hardening of the arteries" that promotes heart trouble; and Creutzfeldt-Jakob disease, the human form of mad cow disease.

In the 1950s, researchers discovered that the various twists and folds of proteins are caused by weak hydrogen bonds that form between amino acids at different points in the amino acid chain. It soon became apparent that the final shape of a protein is determined by the precise locations of these hydrogen bonds. But what causes the protein to fold into precisely the right shape in the first place so that these bonds can form?

A breakthrough came in 1960 with the discovery that if proteins are made to unfold slightly, most (but not all) will twist back into their proper shape. This implies that at least part of the folding process is automatic, dependent only upon the attractive forces between the protein's amino acids. However, not all proteins can refold themselves or even fold themselves properly in the first place. For some, there is a critical phase during the folding process when they either twist correctly or become hopelessly tangled. Proteins that cannot fold themselves are made to fold properly by special "chaperone proteins," whose sole function is to shepherd the protein into its proper shape at just the right time, like little tugboats pushing a large ship to turn in the right direction.

Current research focuses on identifying molecules that can block errors in the folding process. These substances could form the basis for drugs to treat existing disease or even to prevent a disease from developing in the first place.

**RECAP**

Proteins are complex molecules consisting of strings of amino acids. The function of a protein relates to its shape, which is determined by its amino acid sequence and the twisting and folding of its chain of amino acids. A denatured protein loses its shape and function. ■

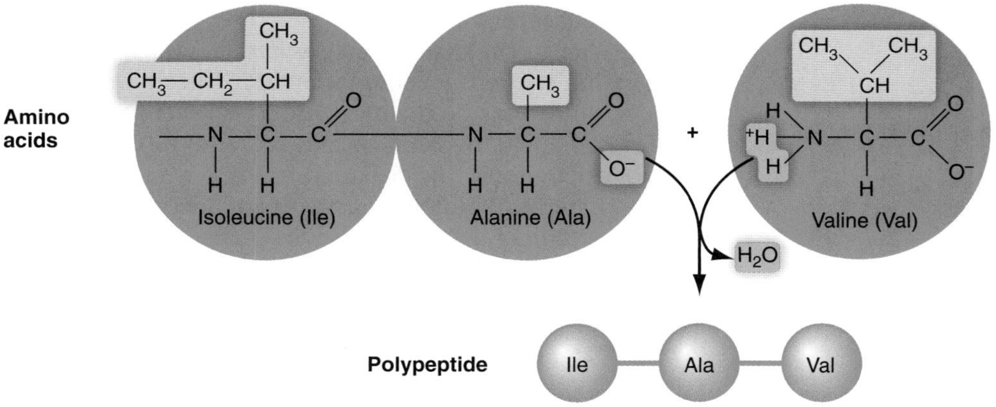


**Figure 2.20 The synthesis of proteins.** Proteins are created from amino acids by dehydration synthesis.

### Enzymes facilitate biochemical reactions

An **enzyme** is a protein that functions as a biological catalyst. A **catalyst** is a substance that speeds up the rate of a chemical reaction without itself being altered or consumed by the reaction. Enzymes help biochemical reactions to occur, but they do not change the final result of the reaction. That is, they can only speed reactions that would have happened anyway, although much more slowly. A chemical reaction that could take hours by itself might reach the same point in minutes or seconds in the presence of an enzyme.

Without help from thousands of enzymes, most biochemical reactions in our cells would occur too slowly to sustain life. Each enzyme facilitates a particular chemical reaction or group of reactions. Some enzymes break molecules apart; others join molecules together. In general, the enzyme takes one or more *reactants* (also called substrates) and turns them into one or more *products*. Enzymes serve as catalysts because, as proteins, they can change shape. The ability to change shape allows them

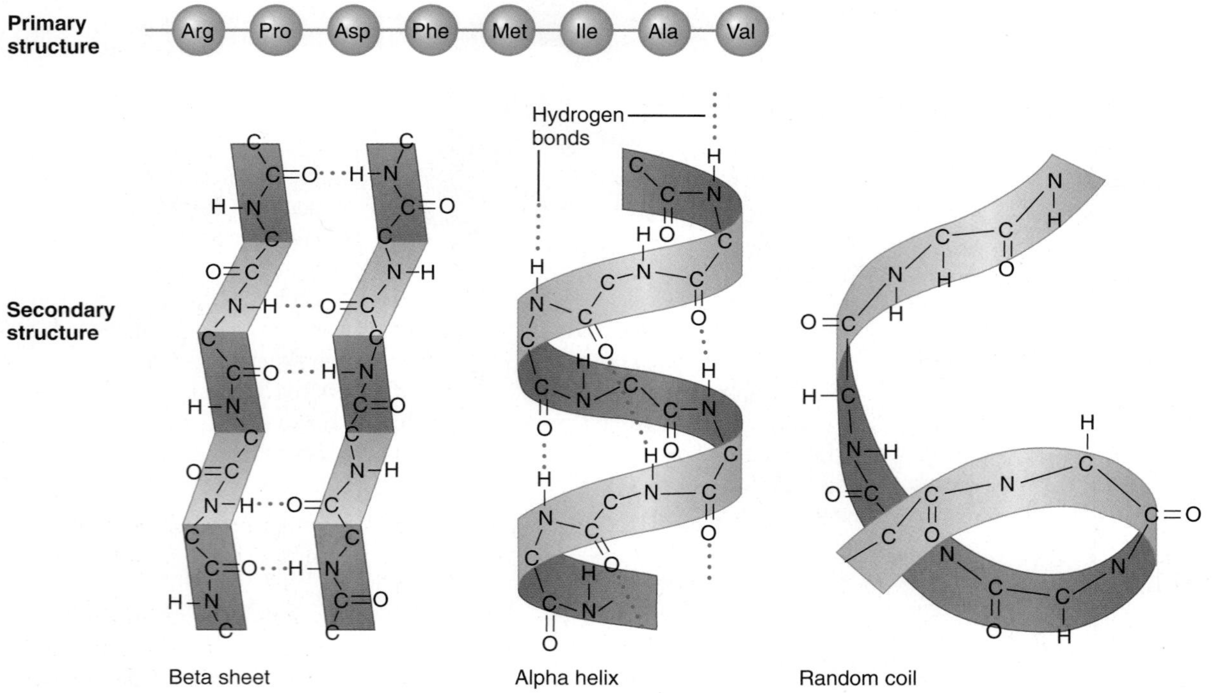


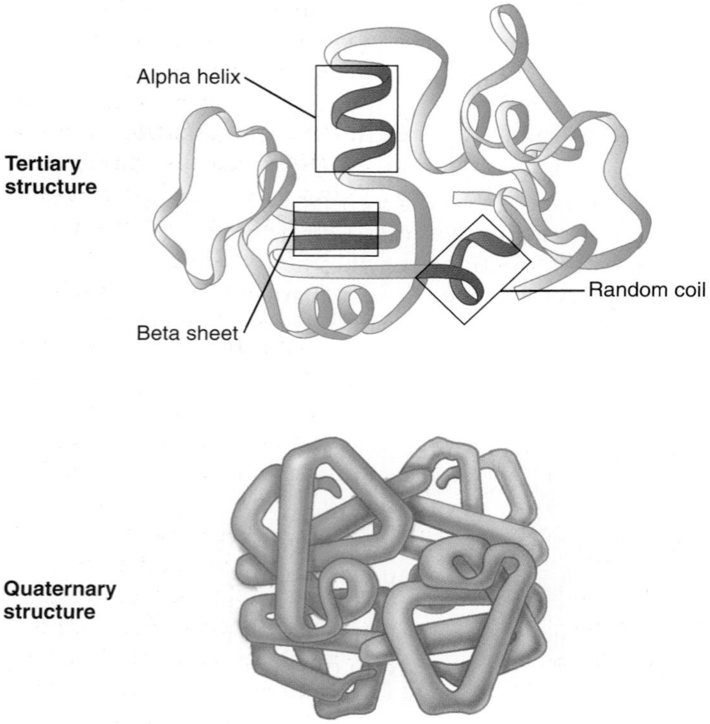


**Figure 2.21 The structure of proteins.** In the diagrams of secondary structure the R groups have been omitted so that the basic backbone can be seen more easily.

to bind to other molecules and orient them so that they may interact. Figure 2.22 illustrates how a typical enzyme works.

Just how important are enzymes? As one example, the reason we can digest glycogen and starch is that we possess specific enzymes that break the chemical bonds between the glucose monosaccharides in these molecules (as you can demonstrate with the Try It Yourself box). In contrast, we cannot digest cellulose because we lack the right enzyme to break it apart. Termites can utilize cellulose only because their digestive systems harbor bacteria that have a cellulose-digesting enzyme.

The changeable shape of an enzyme shows why homeostasis within our cells is so important. Protein shape is in part determined by the chemical and physical environment inside a cell, including temperature, pH, and the concentrations of certain ions. Any deviation from homeostasis can affect the shapes and biological activities of dozens of different enzymes and thus alter the course of biochemical reactions within the cell.

### RECAP

Enzymes are proteins that facilitate biochemical reactions in the body. Without enzymes, many biochemical reactions would occur too slowly to sustain life. ■

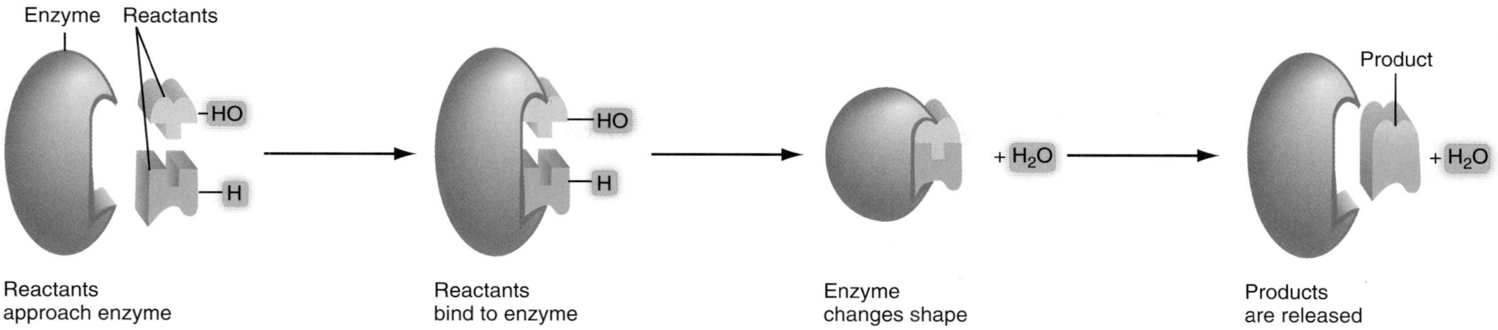


**Figure 2.22 Enzymes facilitate chemical reactions.** This particular enzyme facilitates a dehydration synthesis reaction in which two reactants join to create one larger product plus a molecule of water. Note that the enzyme is not used up during the reaction.

## 2.9 Nucleic acids store genetic information

Another important class of organic molecules is the *nucleic acids*, **DNA (deoxyribonucleic acid)** and **RNA (ribonucleic acid).** You have probably heard of such subjects as cloning, genetic engineering, and DNA "fingerprinting." These subjects relate to the nucleic acids, DNA and RNA.

DNA, the genetic material in living things, directs everything the cell does. It is both the organizational plan and the set of instructions for carrying the plan out. Because it directs and controls all of life's processes including growth, development, and reproduction, DNA is key to life itself. RNA, a closely related macromolecule, is responsible for carrying out the instructions of DNA, and in some cases, of regulating the activity of DNA itself. In some viruses RNA (rather than DNA) serves as the genetic material.

To fully appreciate the importance of DNA and RNA, consider that

- DNA contains the instructions for producing RNA.
- RNA contains the instructions for producing proteins.
- Proteins direct most of life's processes.

Both DNA and RNA are composed of smaller molecular subunits called **nucleotides.** Nucleotides consist of (1) a five-carbon sugar, (2) a single- or double-ringed structure containing nitrogen called *a base,* and (3) one or more phosphate groups. There are only eight different nucleotides, four in DNA and four in RNA.

Figure 2.23 on page 44 shows the structures of the four nucleotides that make up DNA. Each nucleotide is composed of a five-carbon sugar molecule called *deoxyribose* (like the five-carbon sugar ribose but missing one oxygen atom), a phosphate group, and one of four different nitrogen-containing base molecules (*adenine, thymine, cytosine,* or *guanine*). To form a single strand of DNA, these nucleotides hook together by covalent bonds between the phosphate and sugar groups. The complete molecule of DNA is actually composed of two intertwined strands of nucleotides that are held together by weak hydrogen bonds (Figure 2.24 on page 44). The sequence of one strand determines the sequence of the other (they are complementary strands), for adenine can form hydrogen bonds only with thymine (A with T) and cytosine can form bonds only with guanine (C with G).

The "code" for making a specific protein resides in the specific sequence of base pairs in one of the two strands of the DNA molecule. Notice that the entire genetic code is based entirely on the sequence of only four different molecular units (the four nucleotides). You will learn more about DNA, the genetic code, and inheritance in Chapters 17 and 19.

**try it yourself**

### Demonstrating an Enzyme in Your Saliva

You can investigate the presence of an enzyme in one of your own body fluids, saliva, with the following demonstration.

Place a small soda cracker in your mouth and mix it with saliva. Don't swallow it, but move the mixture around in your mouth. After a minute you may experience a sweet taste that was not present initially. This is because your saliva contains an enzyme that can break the bonds in the starch of the cracker, producing the sweet-tasting disaccharide maltose. What you have just demonstrated is that the hydrolysis (digestion) of starch actually begins in your mouth, even before food reaches your stomach.

How can you be sure that the breakdown of starch wasn't caused by the watery component of your saliva instead of an enzyme? You could test that question as an alternative hypothesis. Sprinkle water on another soda cracker, let it stand for the same length of time that you moistened the first one with saliva, and then put it in your mouth. It probably won't taste sweet.

# Antioxidants: Hope or Hype?

As we saw in Chapter 1 (see the Current Issue box), dietary supplements are an $18 billion industry in the United States alone. Many of these vitamins, minerals, food extracts, and herbs are advertised as containing **antioxidants.** What are antioxidants, and is there any scientific basis for claims that they can improve general health, slow down the aging process, and reduce the risk of illnesses such as heart disease and cancer?

## Antioxidants Defend the Body Against Free Radicals

Oxygen free radicals, sometimes just called *free radicals,* are an especially unstable class of molecules. They are produced in small amounts during the normal process of energy transfer within living cells—the higher the rate of metabolism, the greater the rate of free radical production. Free radicals damage body tissues and may accelerate the aging process. Exposure to chemicals, radiation, ultraviolet light, cigarette smoke, alcohol, and air pollution may also produce free radicals.

The body's defenses against free radicals are a group of molecules called antioxidants—certain vitamins, natural nutrients, and enzymes that either prevent the formation of free radicals or inactivate them before they can damage body tissues. Antioxidants include vitamin E, vitamin C, beta-carotene and vitamin A, and the enzyme superoxide dismutase.

*Exposure to cigarette smoke can create free radicals and promote oxidative damage.*

## Scientific Findings on Antioxidant Supplements Are Inconclusive

Some studies conducted in the past supported the hypothesis that naturally occurring antioxidants are beneficial in defending against heart disease. Antioxidants have been found to slow down the progression of the oxidative damage inside blood vessels that can lead to blood clots and heart attacks. Antioxidants may even contribute to the repair process in injured blood vessels.

Based on these and other findings, scientists began to test the hypothesis that maintaining a high level of antioxidants in the body might actually improve general health and slow the aging process. The studies began in animals, of course. In one study, elderly lab rats that were fed antioxidant-rich extracts of strawberries, blueberries, or spinach experienced improvements in short-term memory. The blueberry-eaters also showed improved balance and coordination. In other studies it has been reported that fruit flies bred for long life have higher than normal amounts of superoxide dismutase, and that experimental manipulations that increase their production of superoxide dismutase prolong their average life span.

Studies in humans extended and supported the findings in animals. Several studies have shown that people who eat lots of fresh tomatoes and tomato products (foods high in antioxidants), experience lower rates of cancer. Others have shown that diets high in foods containing beta-carotene, vitamin C, and vitamin E are associated with a reduced risk of cardiovascular disease.

The key phrase here is *associated with*. Research of this type in humans generally involves observational studies that compare the

## the facts...

- Studies in laboratory animals and humans support the hypothesis that diets high in antioxidant-rich foods may improve health and slow the aging process.
- However, studies in humans have failed to confirm any significant health benefits from taking antioxidant supplements in pill form. There may even be some health risks.
- Until more is known about antioxidant supplements, the best course of action may be to eat a balanced diet containing a wide variety of antioxidant-rich foods.

eating patterns and health of large population groups, based largely on self-reporting of dietary intake. The goal is only to determine whether there is an association between a specific dietary intake and health status. Observational studies can provide valuable information, but they cannot prove cause and effect. For instance, people who eat many fruits and vegetables may tend to have more healthy lifestyles in general; they may be less likely to smoke and more likely to exercise. Also, vegetable-based diets tend to exclude less healthy items such as red meat and high-fat foods. It is possible, therefore, that the lower rate of disease in these individuals could be due to their overall lifestyle rather than their consumption of antioxidants.

The observations described above are interesting and could lead to further testable hypotheses. However, they do not prove that taking high doses of antioxidants in pill form will lead to better health or a longer life. Yet that is exactly what the antioxidant supplements industry would like you to believe.

What about carefully controlled experiments in humans of the type that we discussed in Chapter 1, with one group of subjects being given an antioxidant pill and the other receiving only a placebo? As you know, that would be the proper way to do the experiment, especially if the subjects were randomly assigned to the two groups. In fact, such experiments have been done many times in humans. A statistical meta-analysis of 68 different controlled experiments involving over 230,000 human subjects found that, overall, antioxidant supplements did not reduce mortality. But when the authors eliminated the studies that had a high risk of being biased (many dietary supplements studies are supported by funds from the dietary supplements industry), the results seemed to indicate that beta-carotene, vitamin A, and vitamin E dietary supplements may have caused a slight *increase* in mortality. Don't expect to read about this study on the back of a bottle of vitamin E pills, however.

Many packaged products promote their high antioxidant content to appeal to health-conscious consumers.

Can antioxidant supplements improve the health of patients who already have certain diseases that may be related to oxidant stress? Here the results are slightly more encouraging. At least two large studies have shown that high doses of vitamin E can lower the risk of future heart attack and stroke in people who already have heart disease. However, it is unclear whether vitamin E will have any effect on the subjects' overall mortality rate. Other controlled clinical trials have found no effect from antioxidant supplements at all.

Clearly, there is no scientific consensus on the value of antioxidant supplements. This has not stopped dietary supplement companies from marketing their wares aggressively, sometimes with extravagant claims related to health and aging. (Try googling the search term "antioxidants" and see what you get). Encouraged by the media, some consumers have come to view antioxidants as a possible miracle cure. Studies report that 34–65% of prostate cancer patients take dietary supplements and antioxidants to augment their standard medical treatments.

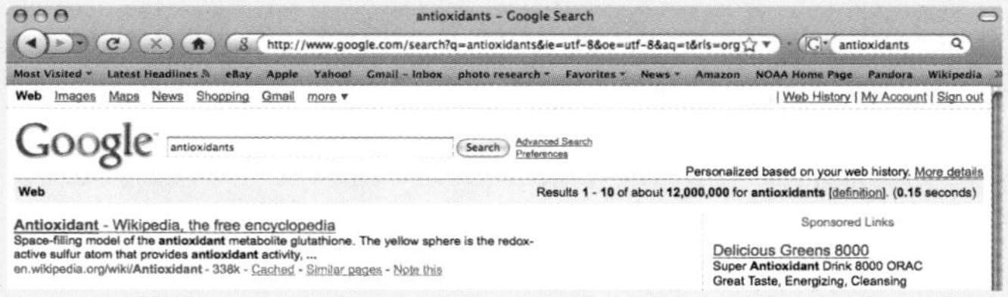


*A Google.com search for "antioxidants" turns up 12 million results.*

### *Eat Wisely and Well*

Research into antioxidants (and the debate over their alleged benefits) will no doubt continue. At the moment, the evidence is not yet convincing that taking antioxidant supplements in pill form will slow the aging process, prevent disease, or prolong life in humans. Nevertheless, it is clear that antioxidant-rich foods are a healthy addition to your diet. Many researchers believe that the observed benefits of antioxidant foods are due not to their content of specific antioxidants but to their interactions with other nutrients in the body. The best course of action may be to eat a wide variety of foods, including antioxidant-rich foods. Good sources of antioxidants include fruit, yellow/orange vegetables, green vegetables, and whole-grain breads and cereals.

## *Questions to consider*

**1** *Do you take dietary supplements? Which ones, and why?* **2** *Of all the foods you ate today, which three would you guess were the highest in antioxidants?* **3** *If you didn't know the answer to the last question and you wanted to learn, where would you go for the information?*

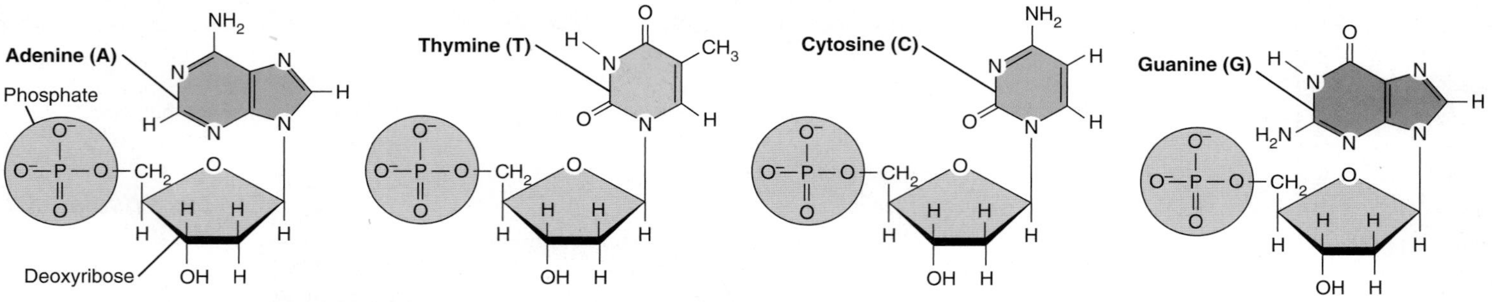


**Figure 2.23 The four nucleotides that compose DNA.** The phosphate and sugar groups are identical in all four nucleotides.

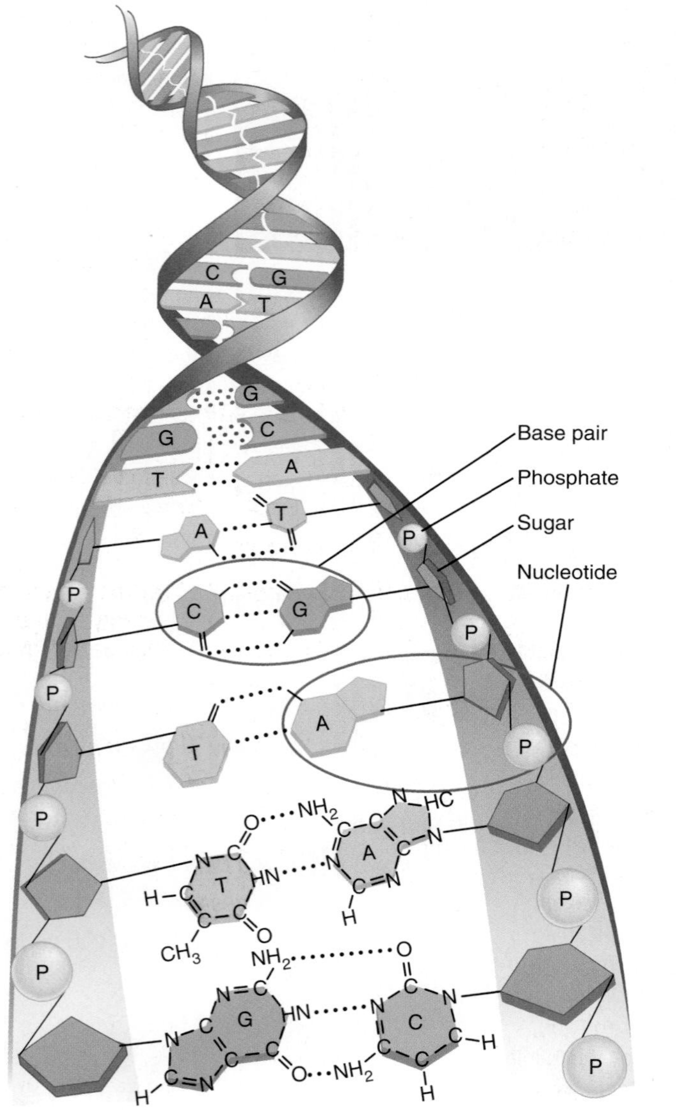


**Figure 2.24 The double helical structure of DNA.** The single strands of DNA are formed by dehydration synthesis. The two strands are held together by two hydrogen bonds between adenine and thymine and three hydrogen bonds between cytosine and guanine.

A single molecule of DNA carries the code for making a lot of different proteins. It is like an entire bookshelf of information, too big to be read all at once. To carry out their function, portions of the DNA molecule are transcribed into smaller fragments of RNA. RNA is structurally like DNA, with a few exceptions (Figure 2.25):

- The sugar unit in all four of the nucleotides in RNA is *ribose* rather than deoxyribose (hence the name ribonucleic acid).
- One of the four nitrogen-containing base molecules is different (uracil is substituted for thymine).
- RNA is a single-stranded molecule, representing a complementary copy of a portion of only *one* strand of DNA.
- RNA is shorter, representing only the segment of DNA that codes for one or more proteins.

In Chapter 17 we discuss how RNA is used to make proteins, as well as RNA's possible role in regulating the activity of DNA.

**RECAP**

DNA and RNA are constructed of long strings of nucleotides. Double-stranded DNA represents the genetic code for life, and RNA is responsible for carrying out those instructions. ■

## 2.10 ATP carries energy

One additional related nucleotide with an important function is **ATP (adenosine triphosphate).** ATP is identical to the adenine-containing nucleotide in RNA except that it has two additional phosphate groups. ATP consists of an adenine base, the five-carbon sugar ribose (together they are called *adenosine*), and three phosphate groups (*triphosphate*) (Figure 2.26). ATP is a universal energy source for cells because the bonds between the phosphate groups contain a great deal of potential energy. Any time a cell needs energy for virtually any function, it can break the bond between the last two phosphate groups of ATP and release energy according to the following equation:

$$ATP \rightarrow ADP + P_i + energy$$

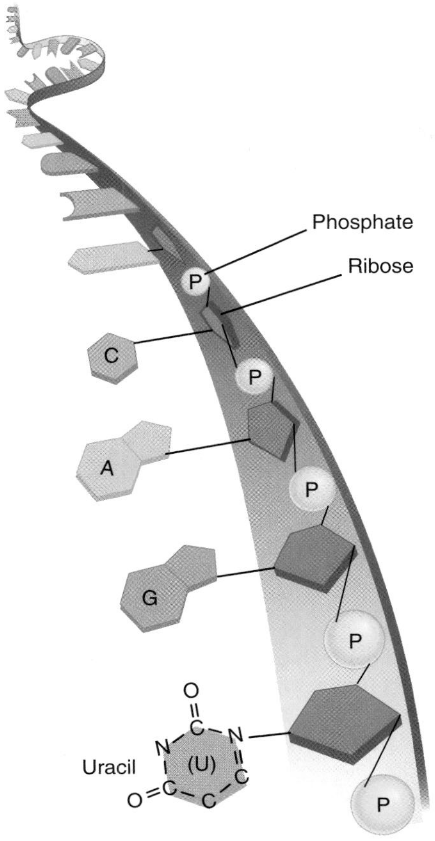


**Figure 2.25 The structure of RNA.** RNA is a single strand of nucleotides in which the base uracil substitutes for thymine. The sugar is ribose.

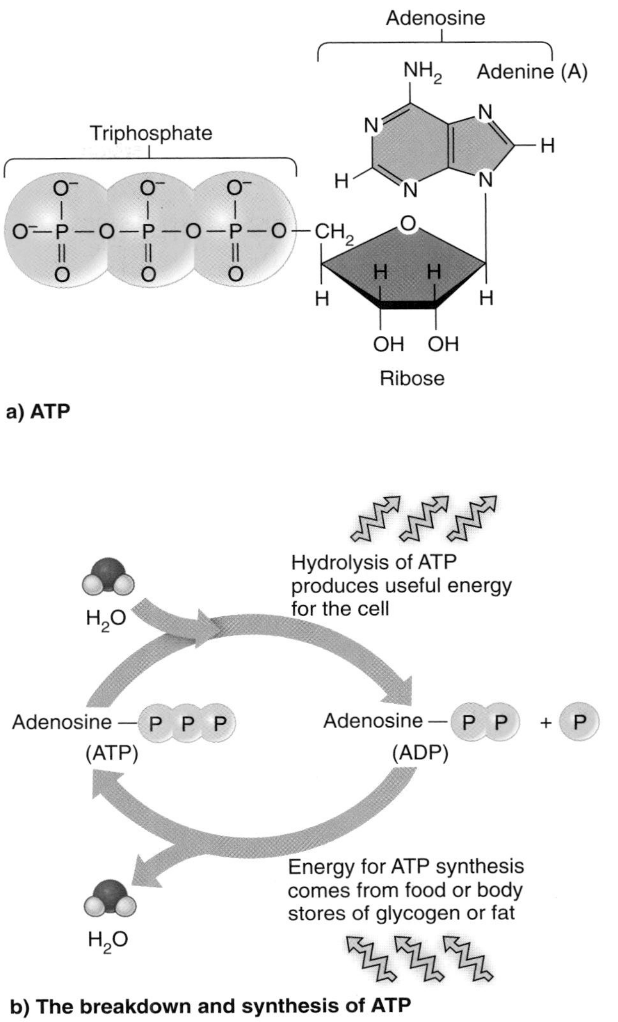


**Figure 2.26 Adenosine triphosphate (ATP) (a)** The structure of ATP. **(b)** The breakdown (hydrolysis) of ATP yields energy for the cell. The reaction is reversible, meaning that ATP may be resynthesized using energy from other sources.

The breakdown of ATP produces **ADP (adenosine diphosphate)** plus an inorganic phosphate group ($P_i$), which is not attached to an organic molecule, plus energy that is now available to do work. The reaction is reversible, meaning that ATP is replenished by using another source of energy to reattach $P_i$ to ADP. The energy to replenish ATP may come from stored energy in the food we eat, or from the breakdown of energy storage molecules such as glycogen or fat. You will learn more about ATP as an energy source when we discuss energy utilization by muscles (Chapter 6).

**RECAP**

ATP is a nearly universal source of quick energy for cells. The energy is stored in the chemical bonds between phosphate groups. ■

# Chapter Summary

### All matter consists of elements *p. 23*

- Atoms, the smallest functional unit of any element, contain a nucleus and a cloud of electrons.
- The protons and neutrons in an atom's nucleus account for most of its mass.
- Radioisotopes are unstable isotopes; an isotope has more or fewer neutrons than the usual number for that atom.

### Atoms combine to form molecules *p. 25*

- Energy exists as either kinetic energy or potential energy.
- Three types of chemical bonds account for the structures of molecules: covalent, ionic, and hydrogen bonds. Covalent bonds are the strongest; hydrogen bonds are the weakest.

- Over 99% of your body weight consists of just six elements: oxygen, carbon, hydrogen, nitrogen, calcium, and phosphorus.

### Life depends on water *p. 28*

- The polar nature of the water molecule accounts for its physical properties and for its unusually good qualities as a solvent for most other molecules and ions.
- Water is important in human temperature regulation.

### The importance of hydrogen ions *p. 30*

- Molecules that can donate a hydrogen ion ($H^+$) are called acids. Molecules that can accept $H^+$ are called bases.
- The hydrogen ion concentration of a solution is expressed as pH.
- Buffers are pairs of molecules that tend to minimize changes in pH when an acid or base is added to a solution.

### The organic molecules of living organisms *p. 32*

- The backbone of all organic molecules is carbon.
- Organic molecules are formed by a process called dehydration synthesis (requiring energy) and broken down by a process called hydrolysis (releasing energy).

### Carbohydrates: Used for energy and structural support *p. 33*

- Monosaccharides, or simple sugars, are a source of quick energy for cells.
- Complex carbohydrates (polysaccharides) are formed by linking simple sugars (monosaccharides) together by dehydration synthesis.
- Carbohydrates are primarily energy-storage molecules. Plants use them for structural support as well.
- In animals the storage molecule is glycogen; in plants it is starch.

### Lipids: Insoluble in water *p. 34*

- Lipids include fats and oils, phospholipids, and steroids. Lipids are insoluble in water.
- Fats store energy. Phospholipids and cholesterol are important structural components of the cell membrane. The sex hormones are steroids synthesized from cholesterol.

### Proteins: Complex structures constructed of amino acids *p. 36*

- Proteins have unique three-dimensional structures that depend on their primary structure (their amino acid sequences). Living organisms construct a tremendous number of different proteins using just 20 different amino acids.
- The human body contains thousands of proteins, each with a different function.
- Enzymes are proteins that facilitate the rates of chemical reactions.

### Nucleic acids store genetic information *p. 41*

- DNA is composed of two long strands of nucleotides intertwined into a double helix. DNA is constructed from just four different DNA nucleotides.
- RNA is a shorter single strand of RNA nucleotides, representing the code for one or more proteins.

### ATP carries energy *p. 44*

- The nucleotide ATP is an energy source for cells. The energy is stored in the bonds between phosphate groups.

## Terms You Should Know

acid, *30*
atom, *23*
ATP, *44*
base, *30*
catalyst, *39*
covalent bond, *26*
DNA, *41*
electron, *23*
enzyme, *39*
hydrogen bond, *27*
ionic bond, *27*
lipid, *34*
molecule, *25*
neutron, *23*
pH scale, *30*
protein, *36*
proton, *23*
RNA, *41*

## Concept Review

1. Describe the electrical charges and relative masses of protons, neutrons, and electrons.
2. Explain why two atoms of hydrogen tend to combine into a molecule of hydrogen gas ($H_2$).
3. Explain why polar and charged molecules tend to be soluble in water.
4. How is a covalent bond different from an ionic bond?
5. Compare and contrast potential energy and kinetic energy.
6. Distinguish between *saturated* and *unsaturated* fats.
7. Describe the role cholesterol plays in cells.
8. Explain why proteins come in an almost unlimited variety of shapes.
9. Discuss the importance of enzymes in living organisms.
10. Describe the role of ATP in energy transfer within a cell.

## Test Yourself

### Matching Exercise

_____ 1. An unstable atom with more or fewer neutrons than its typical number
_____ 2. A simple sugar
_____ 3. The lower-energy form of an important energy-transfer molecule
_____ 4. A steroid in our diet
_____ 5. A common polar molecule in living organisms
_____ 6. Atom that serves as the backbone of organic molecules

a. monosaccharide
b. cholesterol
c. water
d. radioisotope
e. carbon
f. ADP

### Fill in the Blank

7. A(n) _______________ solution has a pH greater than 7.
8. The four classes of organic molecules are *carbohydrates, lipids,* _______________, and *nucleic acids.*
9. The complex carbohydrate that is the storage polysaccharide in animals is _______________.
10. _______________ are proteins that serve as biological catalysts.

11. Triglycerides, the storage form of fat, are composed of one molecule of glycerol and three molecules of ____________.
12. Fats that are liquids at room temperature are called ____________.

**True or False?**

13. Lipids are generally very soluble in water.
14. Electrons have a negative charge.
15. The most common atom (by weight) in the human body is oxygen.

## References and Additional Reading

Chapman, Carolyn. *Basic Chemistry for Biology.* Boston: McGraw-Hill, 1998. (An introduction to biological chemistry for beginners.)

O'Neil, Maryadele J., et al. (Eds.) *The Merck Index: An Encyclopedia of Chemicals, Drugs, & Biologicals,* 13th ed. Whitehouse Station, NJ: Merck, 2001. (A standard reference text to over 10,000 chemicals, drugs, and biological molecules.)

Waites, Gillian, and Percy Harrison. *The Cassell Dictionary of Chemistry.* London: Cassell Academic, 1999. (A reference source designed for students and nonexperts.)

### Internet Reference

Find a link to the following Web site at the Human Biology Place.

**Chemistry.org**
**www.chemistry.org**
Home of the American Chemical Society; features a molecule of the week.

## Apply **What You Know**

1. Athletes are sometimes advised to eat large amounts of complex carbohydrates (such as whole-wheat pasta) for a day or two before a competitive event. Explain the reasoning behind this.
2. Physicians become concerned about the potential for irreversible brain damage when body temperatures approach 105°F. Which of the four classes of macromolecules do you think is most likely affected by high temperatures? Explain.
3. Many people use cholesterol-lowering drugs to reduce their high cholesterol, because they know that a high cholesterol level is a risk factor for heart disease. Would it be advisable to take a little extra dose of these drugs to try to lower your cholesterol to below normal levels, just to be on the safe side?
4. In Miami when it's 90 degrees outside and very humid, the heat feels stifling. Yet most people report feeling fine in Arizona, where the humidity is generally low, even when it is 100 degrees. Why does the humidity have such an effect on our perception of comfort in terms of temperature?
5. Coca Cola is a very acidic drink; its pH is around 3. Blood has a pH of about 7. Yet when you drink a Coke the pH of the blood doesn't change measurably. Why is that?
6. Although normal physiological processes produce small amounts of free radicals, it is possible that your behavior, lifestyle, or environment might contribute to an increased production of free radicals. What behavioral or environmental risks do you think you have that might promote the formation of free radicals?

*Answers can be found on the Human Biology Place.*

# 3 Structure and Function of Cells

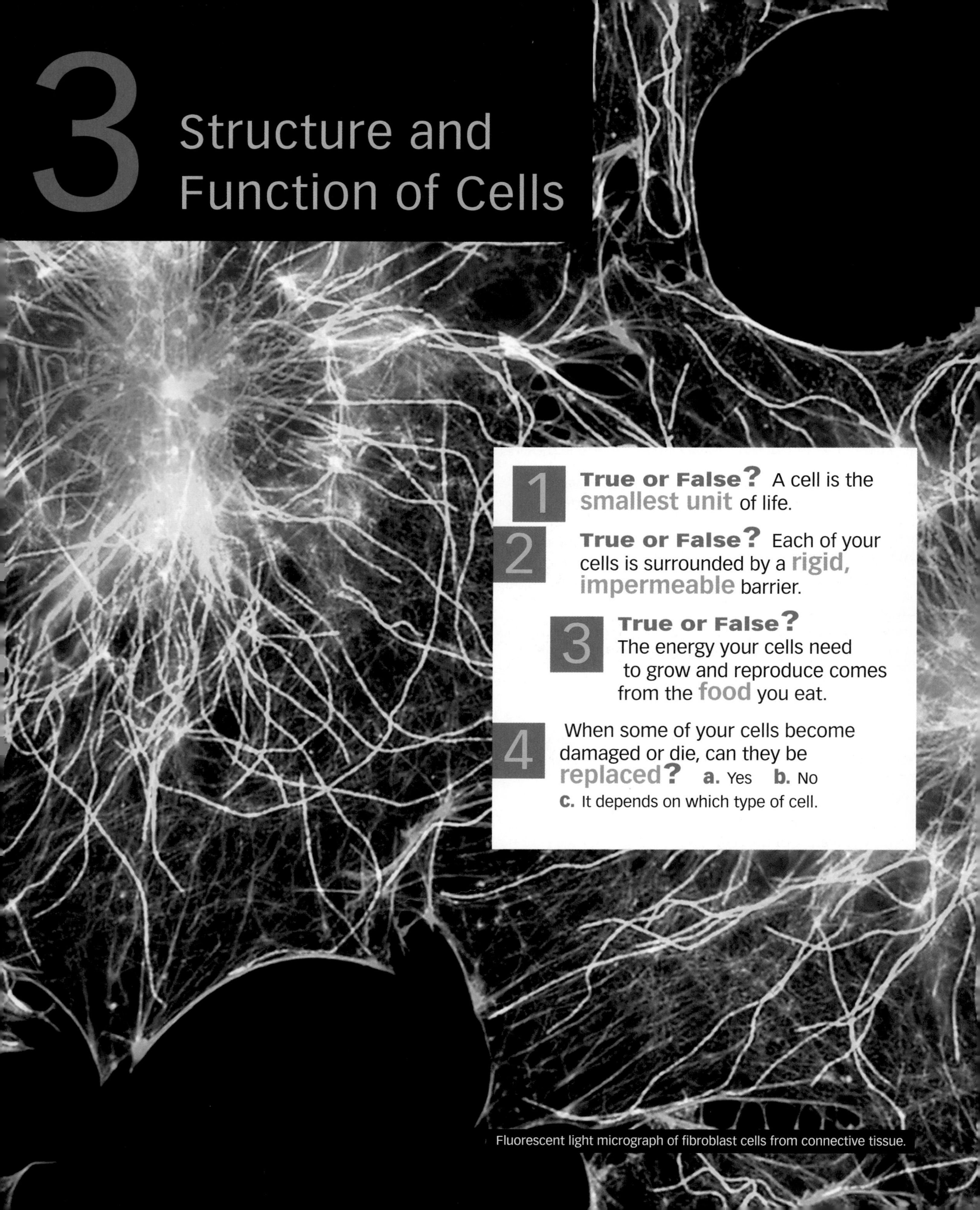

**1** **True or False?** A cell is the **smallest unit** of life.

**2** **True or False?** Each of your cells is surrounded by a **rigid, impermeable** barrier.

**3** **True or False?** The energy your cells need to grow and reproduce comes from the **food** you eat.

**4** When some of your cells become damaged or die, can they be **replaced?** **a.** Yes **b.** No **c.** It depends on which type of cell.

Fluorescent light micrograph of fibroblast cells from connective tissue.

**Scientists first observed living cells** under a microscope in 1674. Since then, countless observations and experiments have confirmed the **cell doctrine,** which consists of three basic principles:

1. All living things are composed of cells and cell products.
2. A single cell is the smallest unit that exhibits all the characteristics of life.
3. All cells come only from preexisting cells.

If we examine any part of the human body under a microscope, we find living cells and/or cell products. "Cell products" include materials composed of dead cells (such as the outer layer of your skin) and substances resulting from cellular activity (such as the hard crystalline elements of bone). There are no living units smaller than cells. All of our cells—all 100 trillion of them—are derived from earlier cells, going all the way back to our first cell, the fertilized egg. Even that original cell came from preexisting cells: the sperm and egg from our parents.

## 3.1 Cells are classified according to their internal organization

All cells are surrounded by an outer membrane called the **plasma membrane.** The plasma membrane encloses the material inside the cell, which is mostly water but also contains ions, enzymes, and other structures the cell requires to maintain life.

All living cells are classified as either eukaryotes or prokaryotes, depending on their internal organization.

### Eukaryotes have a nucleus, cytoplasm, and organelles

Human cells, like those of most species, are **eukaryotes** (*eu-* means "true" and *karyote* means "nucleus"). Nearly every eukaryotic cell has three basic structural components (Figure 3.1):

1. A plasma membrane. The plasma membrane forms the outer covering of the cell.
2. A nucleus. Nucleus is a general term for "core." In the last chapter, we saw that chemists define a nucleus as the core of an atom. In biology, the nucleus is a membrane-bound compartment that houses the cell's genetic material and functions as its "information center." Most eukaryotic cells have one nucleus. There are a few exceptions, to be discussed in later chapters.
3. Cytoplasm ("cell material"). The cytoplasm includes everything inside the cell except the nucleus. It is composed of a soft, gel-like fluid called the *cytosol* ("cell solution"). The cytosol contains a variety of microscopic structures called **organelles** ("little organs") that carry out specialized functions, such as digesting nutrients or packaging cellular products.

### Prokaryotes lack a nucleus and organelles

**Prokaryotes** (*pro-* means "before" and *karyote* means "nucleus") are the bacteria (kingdom Monera). Prokaryotes have a plasma membrane that is surrounded by a rigid cell wall. Their genetic material is concentrated in a particular region, but it is not specifically enclosed within a membrane-bound nucleus. Prokaryotes also lack most of the organelles found in eukaryotes. Nevertheless they are living organisms that fit the definition of a cell according to the cell doctrine.

In the rest of this chapter and throughout the book, we concentrate on the structure and function of eukaryotic cells. However, we discuss bacteria again in terms of how they can make us ill (Chapter 9) and in the context of evolution (Chapter 22).

## 3.2 Cell structure reflects cell function

Eukaryotic cells are remarkably alike in their structural features regardless of which organism they come from. This is because all cells carry out certain activities to maintain life, and there is a strong link between structure and function.

All cells must gather raw materials, excrete wastes, make macromolecules (the molecules of life), and grow and reproduce. These are not easy tasks. The specific activities carried out by a living cell (and the structures required to perform

### Answers to Intro Questions

1 **True.** Some organisms consist of only one cell, whereas others consist of many cells. Cells grow, use energy, and reproduce. In this chapter we will examine the unique features of these tiniest of life-forms.

2 **False.** The plasma membrane around each human cell is a soft, flexible, highly selective barrier—it allows some molecules to cross, but not others. Your cells obtain the nutrients they need and get rid of their waste products across this barrier.

3 **True.** However, this energy is not in usable form when it reaches the cell. Within the cell, tiny "power plants" called *mitochondria* manufacture usable energy for the cell from these raw energy sources.

4 **c.** Some types of cells—heart muscle cells and brain cells, for example—are rarely replaced, if at all. That's part of the reason heart attacks and strokes are so dangerous. You see cell reproduction in action when you cut your skin: the neighboring skin cells reproduce, creating new skin cells that fill the gap.

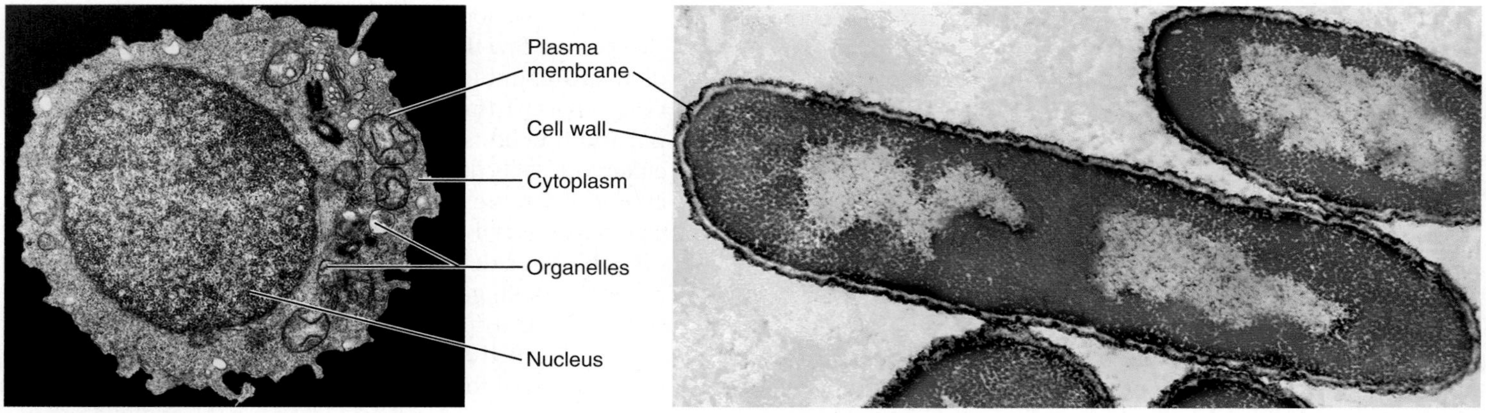


**a) Eukaryotic cell** **b) Prokaryotic cell**

**Figure 3.1 Types of living cells. (a)** A eukaryotic animal cell has a large nucleus (to the left) and numerous small organelles (to the right). The cytoplasm is enclosed by a flexible plasma membrane. **(b)** Prokaryotic cells such as this bacterium have a rigid cell wall surrounding the plasma membrane. The genetic material is not surrounded by a membrane and there are no organelles in the cell. The elongated bacterium in the center of the photo appears to be about ready to divide in two, as its genetic material is concentrated at both ends of the cell.

them) would rival those of any large city or even a country! There is an outer structure that defines its border; an infrastructure for support; an information center; manufacturing facilities; refining, packaging and shipping centers; transportation systems for supplying raw materials and energy; stockpiles of energy; and mechanisms for recycling or removing toxic waste. Cells even possess sophisticated defense mechanisms to combat invaders.

Most of the structural differences between cells reflect differences in function (Figure 3.2). Muscle cells contain numerous organelles to produce the necessary energy for muscle contraction. Many nerve cells are long and thin; the longest nerve cells carry impulses all the way from your toes to your spinal cord. The cells that line the kidney tubules are cube shaped. Essentially every cell has a specialized function of some sort or it would be of little use to the organism.

Cells that serve the same function are often remarkably similar between species. For example, a human nerve cell has more in common (structurally and functionally) with a nerve cell in a cockroach than it does with a human liver cell. Furthermore, cells in a mouse are not that much different in size from those in an elephant; it's just that an elephant has more of them.

**RECAP**

Common features of nearly all eukaryotic cells are a plasma membrane, a nucleus, organelles, and the cytoplasm. Differences in cell shape and internal organization reflect differences in function. ■

## Cells remain small to stay efficient

Despite their structural differences, all cells have at least one feature in common: they are small in one or more dimensions, requiring considerable magnification to be seen (Figure 3.3). Despite the incredible complexity of human cells, not one can be seen with the naked eye. Even nerve cells that are over

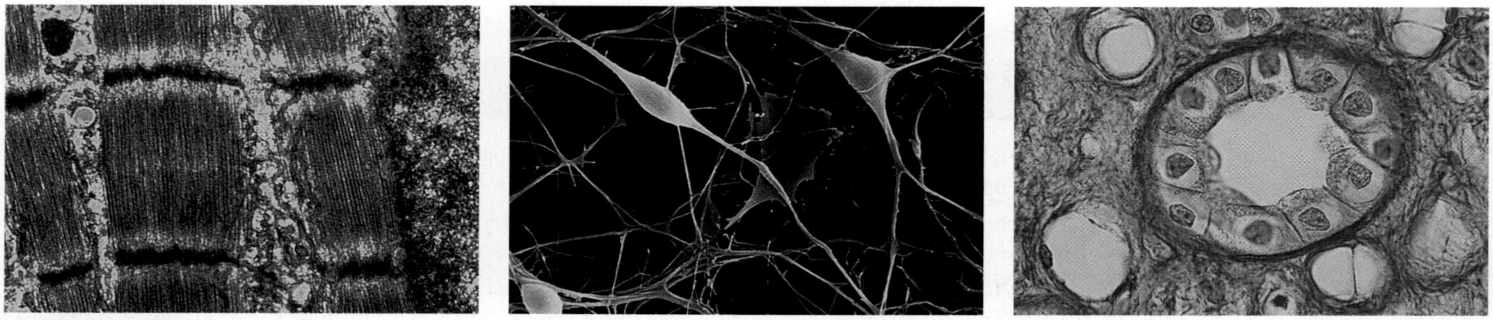

**a) A portion of a muscle cell of the heart (×2,500)** **b) Nerve cells of the central nervous system (×520)** **c) Cells lining a tubule of a kidney (×250)**

**Figure 3.2 Human cells vary in shape.**

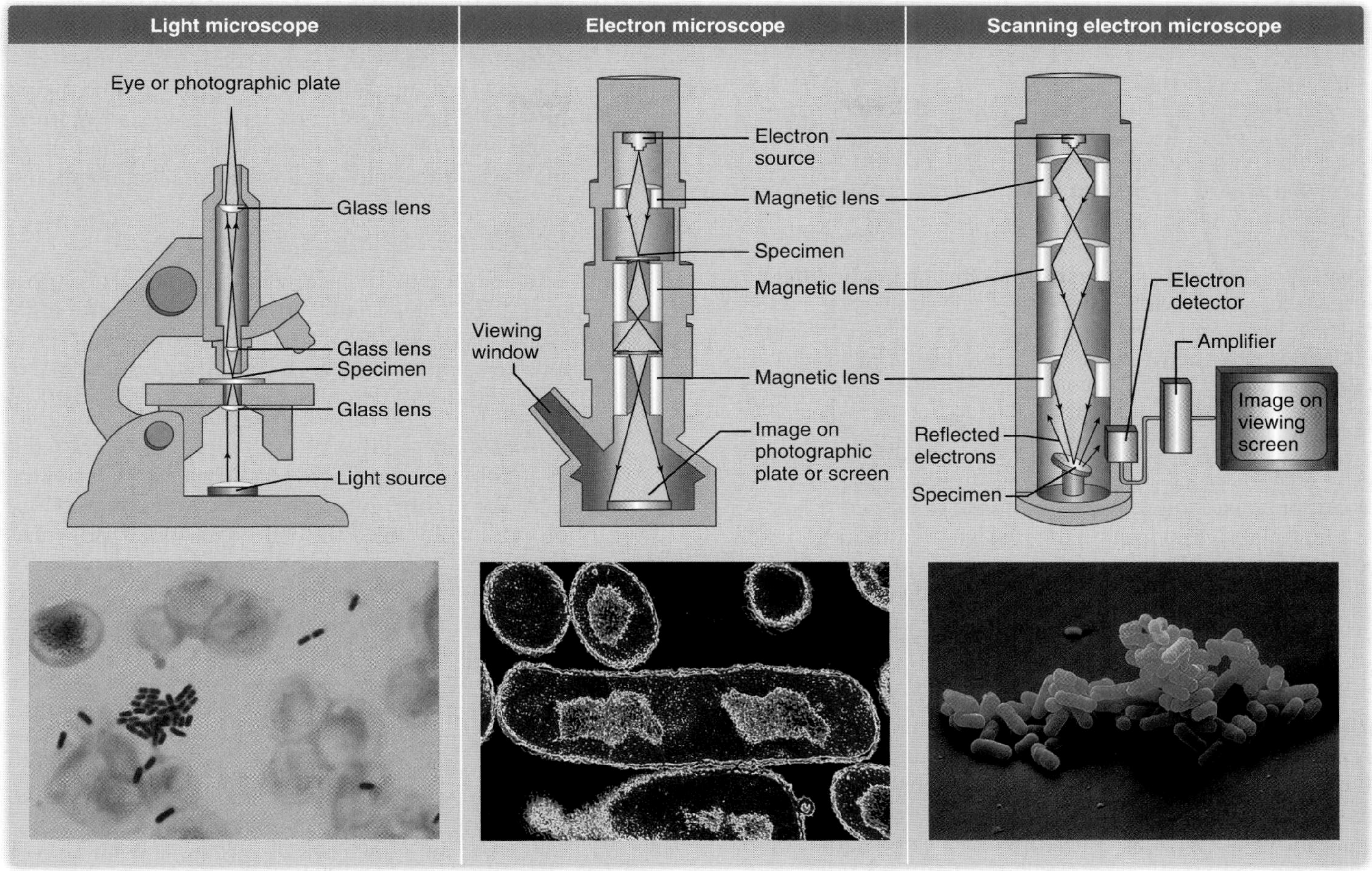


a) **The light microscope (LM).** Most of us have seen or used a light microscope. The light microscope uses visible light and a series of glass lenses to magnify a small sample as much as 1,000-fold. Focus can be difficult to maintain if objects are at different depths in a sample. Light does not transmit well through very dense or thick samples. Light microscopes have been in use for over 300 years.

b) **The transmission electron microscope (TEM).** A transmission electron microscope bombards the sample with a beam of electrons, some of which pass through the sample. Electrons behave like light waves, but since the wavelengths of electrons are shorter than visible light, the image has greater clarity at any magnification. A good electron microscope can magnify up to about 100,000 times, a hundred times greater than the light microscope. The images are two-dimensional (flat) because the sample must be very thin, but the magnification is sufficiently high that one can see the structural details of organelles within single cells.

c) **The scanning electron microscope (SEM).** The scanning electron microscope also focuses beams of electrons on the object. It produces what appears to be a three-dimensional view of the *surface* of an object. A narrow beam of electrons is scanned over the surface of an object that has been coated with a thin coat of metal so that the electron beam cannot penetrate. As the beam passes, the metal gives off secondary electrons, which can be recorded to produce a visual picture of the object's surface. Scanning electron microscopes have revealed stunning images of the relationships between cells and of the outer surfaces of cells. The scanning electron microscope can also magnify up to about 100,000 times.

**Figure 3.3 Visualizing cells with microscopes.** Photographs taken by the various methods of microscopy are called photomicrographs. All three of the photomicrographs shown here are of *Escherichia coli*, a normally harmless bacterium found in the digestive tract.

three feet long are so thin that we can't see them. Given the variety of life forms on Earth, why are there are so few giant cells? (An exception is the egg of some species.)

The answer shows that nature obeys certain simple and understandable principles:

- The total metabolic activities of a cell are proportional to its volume of cytoplasm, which is in effect its size. To support its activities, every cell needs raw materials in proportion to its size. Every cell also needs a way to get rid of its wastes.

**Figure 3.4 Cell size and plasma membrane shape affect surface area and volume.** The volume is the same in these three groups of cells, but the ratio of volume to surface area is different in **(a)**, **(b)**, and **(c)**. Compared to the cell in **(a)**, the eight small cells in **(b)** have twice the surface area. **(c)** The surface area of any cell can be increased by the presence of microvilli.

- All raw materials, energy, and waste can enter or leave the cell only by crossing the plasma membrane.
- As objects get larger, their volume increases more than their surface area. For both spheres and cubes, for example, an eightfold increase in volume is accompanied by only a fourfold increase in surface area.

The larger a cell gets, then, the more likely that its growth and metabolism will be limited by its ability to supply itself across the plasma membrane (Figure 3.4). Put another way, the smaller a cell is, the more effectively it can obtain raw materials and get rid of wastes.

Some cells have numerous microscopic projections of the plasma membrane called *microvilli*. Microvilli are an effective way to increase surface area relative to volume. Plasma membranes with microvilli are especially common in cells that transport substances into and out of the body, such as the cells that line the digestive tract and the tubules of the kidneys.

**RECAP**

Cells exchange materials with their environment across their plasma membrane. Cells divide to remain small, because this makes them more efficient at obtaining nutrients and expelling wastes. ■

## 3.3 A plasma membrane surrounds the cell

Consider a house. Its walls and roof are composed of special materials that prevent rain and wind from entering. They also form a barrier that allows the temperature inside the house to stay warmer or cooler than the temperature outside. At the same time, the house interacts with its environment. Windows allow light in; doors open and close to allow entry and exit. Water and power lines permit the regulated entry of water and energy, and sewer lines remove wastes. The house exchanges information with the outside world through mail slots, telephone lines, and computer cables.

The exterior structure of a living cell is its plasma membrane. Like the roof and walls of a house, the plasma membrane must permit the movement of some substances into and out of the cell yet restrict the movement of others. It must also allow the transfer of information across the membrane.

### The plasma membrane is a lipid bilayer

The plasma membrane is constructed of two layers of phospholipids, called a *lipid bilayer*, plus some cholesterol and various proteins (Figure 3.5). Each of the three components contributes to the membrane's overall structural and functional properties:

- *Phospholipids.* Recall that phospholipids are a particular type of lipid with a polar head and neutral nonpolar tails. In the plasma membrane the two layers of phospholipids are arranged so that the nonpolar tails meet in the center of the membrane. One layer of polar (water-soluble) heads faces the watery solution on the outside of the cell, and the other layer of polar heads faces the watery solution of the cell's cytoplasm.
- *Cholesterol.* By itself, a bilayer of phospholipids would be soft because it would be basically a double layer of oil. Cholesterol molecules make the plasma membrane more rigid.
- *Proteins.* Various proteins are embedded in the phospholipid bilayer of the plasma membrane. Like the doors, windows, and wires of a house, they provide the means for transporting molecules and information across the plasma membrane. A few membrane proteins anchor the cell's internal scaffold-like support network. Some proteins span the entire membrane; others protrude from only one surface. Plasma membrane proteins generally have one region that is electrically neutral and another that is electrically charged (either 1 or 2). The charged regions tend to extend out of the membrane and thus are in contact with water, whereas the neutral portions are often embedded within the phospholipid bilayer.

The phospholipid bilayer of the plasma membrane is only about 3.5 nanometers thick (a nanometer, abbreviated nm, is a billionth of a meter), too small to be seen in detail even with microscopes. To appreciate relative sizes, imagine as we did in Chapter 2 that a single sodium ion is the size of a penny. At this scale the phospholipid bilayer of a typical cell would be about 13 inches thick. It is no wonder that many substances are restricted from passing through the membrane unless there is some sort of channel or transport mechanism available.

Although we have likened the plasma membrane to the exterior of a house, there are two key differences. First, the plasma membrane of animal cells is not rigid. If you could touch a plasma membrane, it would probably feel like a wet sponge, giving way under your touch and springing back when you remove your hand. Most cells do maintain a

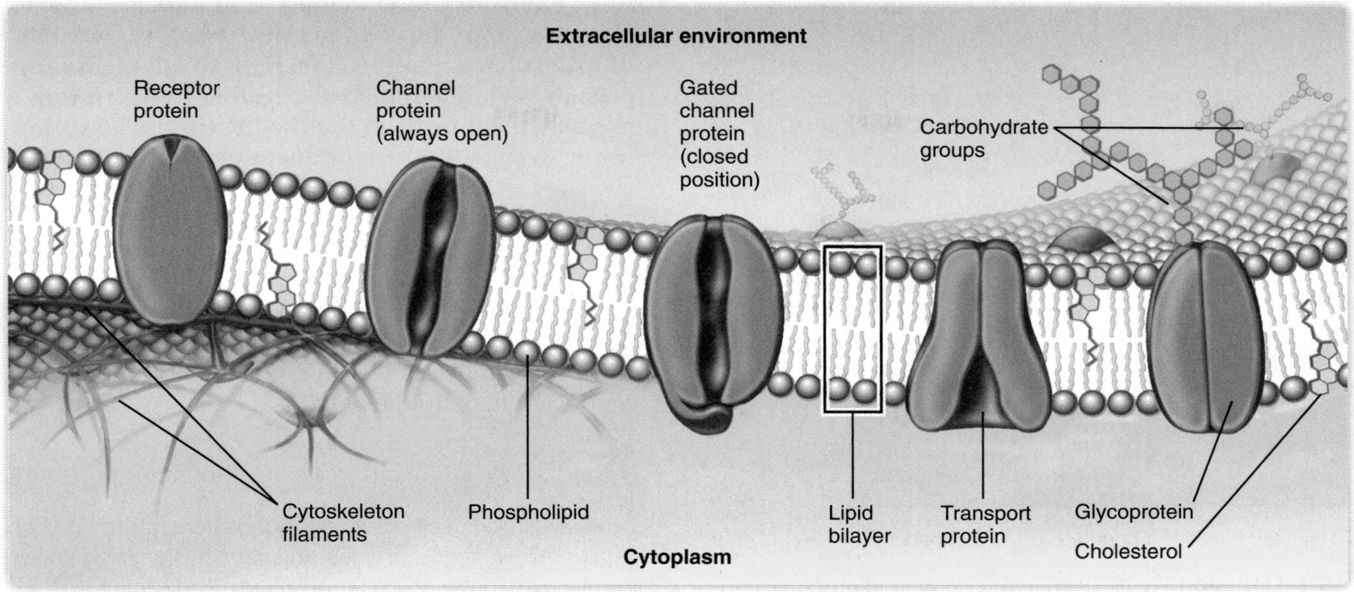


**Figure 3.5 The plasma membrane.**

certain shape, but it is mainly due to a supporting network of fibers inside the cell, the fluid within the cell, and the limitations imposed by contact with surrounding cells, not the stiffness of the plasma membrane itself.

Second, the phospholipids and proteins are not anchored to specific positions in the plasma membrane. Many proteins drift about in the lipid bilayer like icebergs floating on the surface of the sea. Imagine if you were to get up in the morning and find that the front door to your house had moved 3 feet to the left! The plasma membrane of animal cells is often described as a "fluid mosaic" to indicate that it is not a rigid structure and that the pattern of proteins within it constantly changes.

**RECAP**

The plasma membrane allows some substances to move into and out of the cell but restricts others. Its phospholipid bilayer contains cholesterol for rigidity and proteins for information transfer, transport of molecules, and structural support. ■

## 3.4 Molecules cross the plasma membrane in several ways

The plasma membrane creates a barrier between the cell's external environment and the processes of life going on within. Life was impossible until these functions could be enclosed and concentrated in one place, keeping what was needed for growth and reproduction inside and limiting the entry of other materials. Molecules (and ions) cross the plasma membrane in three major ways: (1) passive transport (diffusion and osmosis), (2) active transport, and (3) endocytosis or exocytosis.

### Passive transport: Principles of diffusion and osmosis

**Passive transport** is "passive" because it transports a molecule without requiring the cell to expend any energy. Passive transport relies on the mechanism of diffusion.

**Diffusion** Molecules in a gas or a liquid move about randomly, colliding with other molecules and changing direction. The movement of molecules from one region to another as the result of this random motion is known as **diffusion.**

If there are more molecules in one region than in another, then strictly by chance more molecules will tend to diffuse away from the area of high concentration and toward the region of low concentration. In other words, the *net* diffusion of molecules requires that there be a difference in concentration, called a *concentration gradient,* between two points. Once the concentration of molecules is the same throughout the solution, a state of equilibrium exists in which molecules diffuse randomly but equally in all directions.

Figure 3.6 illustrates diffusion by showing what happens when crystals that dissolve in water are placed at the bottom of a container of water. Over time, the dissolved molecules diffuse away from their region of highest concentration until the entire fluid has the same concentration of dissolved molecules.

Water also diffuses from the region of its highest concentration toward the region of its lowest concentration. However, the concentration of water (the liquid, or solvent) in a

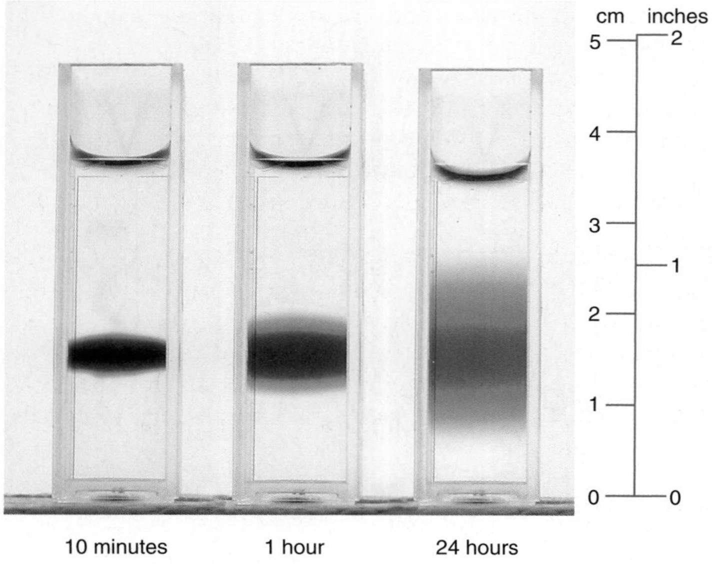


**Figure 3.6 Diffusion.** At time zero a concentrated solution of a blue dye was placed in the middle of a tube of water. To prevent the movement of water by bulk flow, a stabilizing agent had been added previously to the water. Over time the random motion of molecules in solution has caused some molecules of dye to move from the region of highest dye concentration to the region of low dye concentration. Although not visible, water has diffused in the opposite direction, from the region of highest water concentration (pure water) toward the region of lower water concentration (the region occupied by dye). Note that diffusion is effective only over short distances; it has taken 24 hours for the dye to move only 1 cm in any direction.

solution is *opposite* to that of the molecules other than water (the solutes). The higher the concentration of solutes, the lower the concentration of water. Pure water is the solution with the highest possible concentration of water. Net diffusion of water is always toward the solution with the higher concentration of solutes and away from the solution with a higher concentration of water (for a familiar example, see the Try It Yourself box, page 56).

**Osmosis** Not all substances diffuse readily into and out of living cells. The plasma membrane is **selectively permeable,** meaning that it allows some substances to cross by diffusion but not others. It is highly permeable to water but not to all ions or molecules. The net diffusion of water across a selectively permeable membrane is called **osmosis.**

Figure 3.7 demonstrates the process of osmosis. In Figure 3.7a, a selectively permeable membrane—in this case permeable only to water—separates pure water from a solution of glucose in water. Although the glucose cannot diffuse, the water diffuses toward its region of lower concentration, from right to left. As osmosis occurs, the volume in the left chamber rises, creating a fluid pressure that begins to oppose the continued osmosis of water. Eventually the movement of water from left to right (because of differences in fluid pressure) equals the movement from right to left (by osmosis), and there is no further net change in the volume of water on each side of the membrane.

The fluid pressure required to exactly oppose osmosis is called *osmotic pressure.* In Figure 3.7c osmotic pressure is represented by the extra weight of the higher column of water on the left than on the right.

**RECAP**

Molecules diffuse from a region of higher concentration to a region of lower concentration. The net diffusion of water across a selectively permeable membrane is called osmosis. ■

## Passive transport moves with the concentration gradient

Most substances cross cell membranes by passive transport. Passive transport always proceeds "downhill" with respect to the concentration gradient, meaning that it relies on diffusion in some way. Three forms of passive transport across the cell membrane are (1) diffusion through the lipid bilayer, (2) diffusion through channels, and (3) facilitated transport (Figure 3.8).

**Diffusion through the lipid bilayer** The lipid bilayer structure of the plasma membrane allows the free passage of some molecules while restricting others. For instance, small

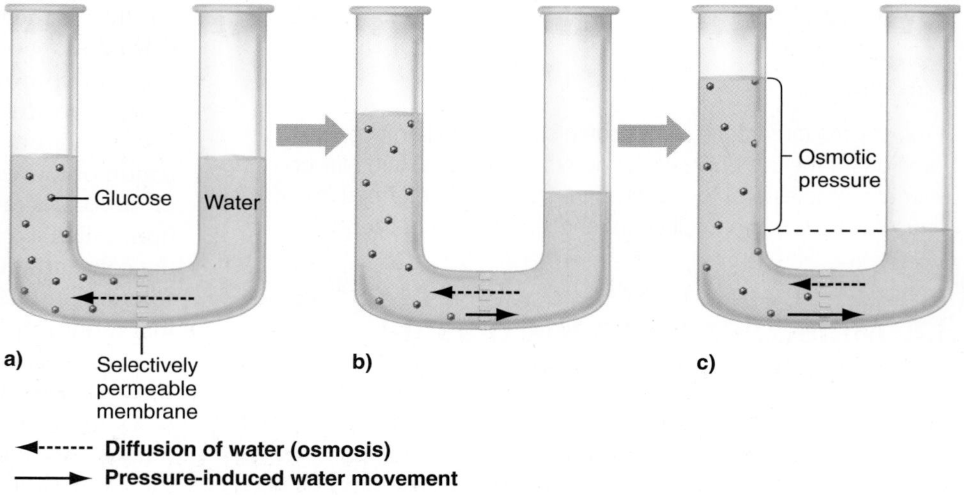


**Figure 3.7 Generation of osmotic pressure by osmosis.** Starting in **(a),** there is a net movement of water from right to left until the diffusion of water (osmosis) is opposed by movement of water due to osmotic pressure **(c).**

uncharged nonpolar molecules can diffuse right through the lipid bilayer as if it did not exist. Such molecules simply dissolve in the lipid bilayer, passing through it like a ghost through a wall. Polar or electrically charged molecules, in contrast, cannot cross the lipid bilayer because they are not soluble in lipids.

Two important lipid-soluble molecules are oxygen ($O_2$), which diffuses into cells and is used up in the process of metabolism, and carbon dioxide ($CO_2$), a waste product of metabolism, which diffuses out of cells and is removed from the body by the lungs. Another substance that crosses the lipid bilayer by diffusion is urea, a neutral waste product removed from the body by the kidneys.

**Diffusion through channels** Water and many ions diffuse through channels in the plasma membrane. The channels are constructed of proteins that span the entire lipid bilayer. The sizes and shapes of these protein channels, as well as the electrical charges on the various amino acid groups that line the channel, determine which molecules can pass through.

Some channels are open all the time (typical of water channels). The diffusion of any molecule through the membrane is largely determined by the number of channels through which the molecule can fit. Other channels are "gated," meaning that they can open and close under certain conditions. Gated channels are particularly important in regulating the transport of ions (sodium, potassium, and calcium) in cells that are electrically excitable, such as nerve cells (Chapter 11). Look at Figure 3.5, which represents a number of the proteins instrumental in transport.

**Facilitated transport** In **facilitated transport,** also called *facilitated diffusion*, the molecule does not pass through a channel at all. Instead it attaches to a membrane protein, triggering a change in the protein's shape or orientation that transfers the molecule to the other side of the membrane and releases it there. Once the molecule is released, the protein returns to its original form. A protein that carries a molecule across the plasma membrane in this manner, rather than opening a channel through it, is called a **transport protein** (carrier protein).

Facilitated transport is highly selective for particular substances. The direction of movement is always from a region of higher concentration to one of lower concentration, and thus it does not require the cell to expend energy. The normal process of diffusion is simply being "facilitated" by the transport protein. Glucose and other simple sugars enter most cells by this method.

**RECAP**

Diffusion and facilitated transport are both forms of passive transport. They do not require the expenditure of energy. ■

## Active transport requires energy

All methods of passive transport allow substances to move only down their concentration gradients, in the direction they would normally diffuse if there were no barrier. However, **active transport** can move substances through the plasma membrane *against* their concentration gradient. Active transport allows a cell to accumulate essential molecules even when their concentration outside the cell is relatively low, and to get rid of molecules that it does not need. Active transport requires the expenditure of energy.

Like facilitated transport, active transport is accomplished by proteins that span the plasma membrane. The difference is that active transport proteins must have some source of energy to transport certain molecules. Some active transport proteins use the high-energy molecule ATP (adenosine triphosphate) for this purpose (Figure 3.9a on page 57). They break ATP down to ADP (adenosine diphosphate) and a phosphate group ($P_i$) and use the released energy to transport one or more molecules across the plasma membrane against their concentration gradient. Imagine that the active transport protein is a conveyor belt moving objects uphill, powered by a gasoline engine. In this analogy, ATP is the gasoline and ADP the exhaust (with one difference: the ADP "exhaust" in the cell can be recycled to ATP).

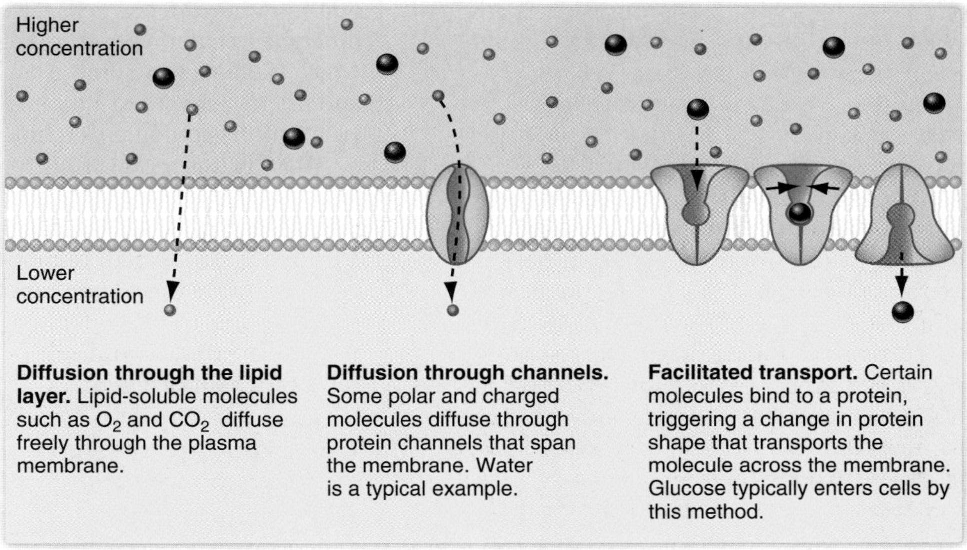


**Figure 3.8 The three forms of passive transport.** All involve transport down a concentration gradient without the expenditure of additional energy.

Proteins that actively transport molecules across the plasma membrane are sometimes called "pumps." Some pumps can transport several different molecules at once and even in both directions at the same time. One of the most important plasma membrane pumps is the **sodium-potassium pump,** which uses energy derived from breaking down ATP to transport sodium out of the cell and potassium into the cell.

Not all active transport pumps use ATP as the energy source. Some derive energy from the "downhill" facilitated transport of one molecule and use it to transport another molecule "uphill," against its concentration gradient (Figure 3.9b). This type of transport is analogous to an old-fashioned mill that grinds grain into flour by using energy derived from the downhill movement of water.

## Endocytosis and exocytosis move materials in bulk

Most ions and small molecules move across the cell membrane by one or more of the passive and active transport mechanisms just described. However, some molecules are too big to be transported by these methods. To move large molecules or transport several kinds of molecules in bulk, some cells resort to endocytosis and/or exocytosis. These two processes are based on the same principle but have different directions of movement. **Endocytosis** moves materials into the cell, and **exocytosis** moves materials out of the cell.

Figure 3.10 shows the processes of endocytosis and exocytosis. In endocytosis, molecules dissolved in the extracellular fluid are surrounded by a pocket formed by an infolding of the plasma membrane. Eventually the pocket pinches off, forming a membrane-bound **vesicle** within the cell. To facilitate the selection of the right molecules for endocytosis, some vesicles have receptors on their surface that bind only to certain specific molecules. Insulin and certain enzymes enter cells by this method. Other vesicles are nonselective, engulfing whatever is in the extracellular fluid, such as nutrients and water. Vesicles of this type are often found in cells lining the digestive tract. Some white blood cells engulf and destroy whole bacteria by endocytosis (Chapter 9).

In exocytosis, a vesicle already present within the cell fuses with the plasma membrane and releases its contents into the fluid surrounding the cell. This is how certain cells release toxic waste products, get rid of indigestible material, or secrete their special products.

## Information can be transferred across the plasma membrane

**Receptor proteins** that span the plasma membrane can receive and transmit information across the membrane. The information received by receptor proteins generally causes something to happen within the cell even though no molecules cross the membrane.

Figure 3.11 on page 58 illustrates how a receptor protein works. A molecule approaches the membrane and binds to a specific *receptor site* in a lock-and-key fashion. This binding triggers a series of biochemical events that ultimately cause changes within the cell. Receptor proteins are highly specific for a particular molecule or a group of similar molecules. For example, the receptor protein for the hormone insulin responds only to insulin and not to any other hormone. Furthermore, different cells have different sets of receptor proteins, which explains why some cells and tissues respond to a particular hormone and others do not.

We discuss receptor proteins and hormones in more detail in Chapter 13. For now, remember that certain molecules can influence what happens inside a cell merely by coming in contact with the cell's outer surface.

## The sodium-potassium pump helps maintain cell volume

Probably the most critical task facing a cell is maintaining its volume. Why? Recall that the plasma membrane is soft and

**try it** *yourself*

### Observing the Effect of Osmosis on Your Skin

The next time you step out of a long, soaking shower or bath or the swimming pool, look at your fingers and toes. They may be wrinkled. Why?

Your body contains water, of course, but it also contains solutes, so the water in your body is less concentrated than the water of your bath or pool (pure freshwater has the highest concentration of water possible). As described in this chapter, water diffuses from a region of high concentration—that is, your bath or the pool—to a region of lower concentration, such as your body. The "shriveled" look of your fingers and toes actually results from being waterlogged. The extra water entering the outer layers of your skin causes them to swell in some places but not others, causing wrinkles.

Why doesn't the rest of your skin become wrinkled too? As we'll see in the next chapter, tiny glands in your skin produce a natural moisturizer that waterproofs it to some extent. These moisturizer-producing glands are associated with hair follicles, so most of the moisturizer is produced by areas of the body that have at least some hair. If your skin remains wet for long enough, what little moisturizer there is on your fingertips quickly washes away or is rubbed off, allowing osmosis to occur. The parts of your body that are covered by hair retain this moisturizer better, which blocks osmosis.

You can observe the same phenomenon after you wash dishes, of course. But that's not a good excuse for not doing the dishes! The wrinkling is not harmful and goes away quickly. If you want to avoid it, wear gloves or try a good moisturizer.

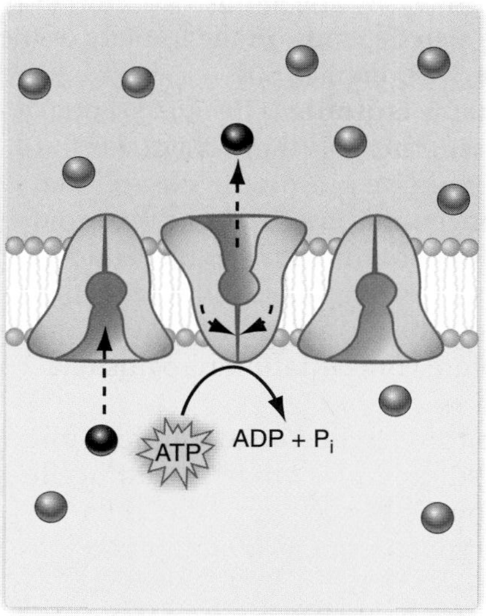


a) Active transport using ATP.

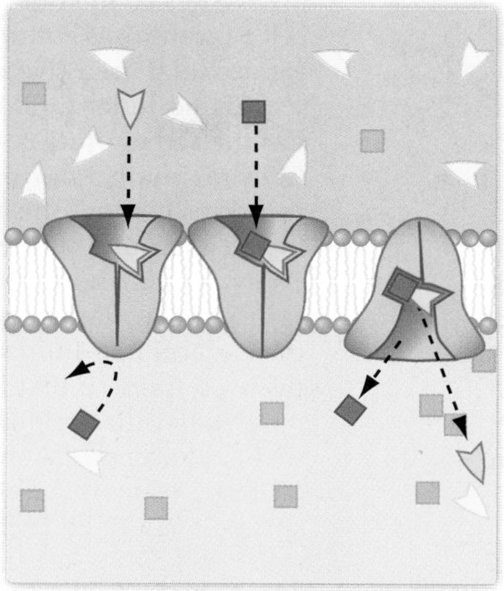

b) Active transport of the square molecules, using the diffusion of the spearhead molecules as the source of energy.

**Figure 3.9 Active transport.** A cell can employ active transport to move a molecule against a concentration gradient. Because this is an "uphill" effort, energy is required. **(a)** ATP offers the energy needed to change the shape of the carrier protein. ATP is converted to ADP + $P_i$ as it liberates energy. **(b)** Some carrier proteins use the energy derived from the downhill transport of one molecule to transport another molecule uphill.

flexible. It cannot withstand much stretching or high fluid pressures. Furthermore, cells tend to accumulate certain materials depending on what is available in their *extracellular* environment (the area outside the cell, beyond the plasma membrane). Cells already contain a nucleus and organelles. In addition, they produce or stockpile molecules, including amino acids, sugars, lipids, ions, and many others. These molecules are necessary for the cell to function normally, but they represent a lot of solute particles within the cell.

Because water can diffuse across the plasma membrane rather easily, you might expect that water would diffuse into the cell, toward the high cytoplasmic solute concentration. This inward diffusion would increase cell volume, eventually causing the cell to swell and even rupture.

The only way to avoid this is for the cell to keep the solute concentration in its cytoplasm identical to the solute concentration of the extracellular fluid. Then there is no net driving force for the diffusion of water. What the cell actually does is get rid of ions it *doesn't* need in large quantities (primarily sodium) in exchange for those it must stockpile. This is the primary function of the sodium-potassium pump.

Figure 3.12a on page 59 shows how the sodium-potassium pump works. The pump has three binding sites for sodium that are accessible from inside the cell. The binding of three cytoplasmic sodium ions triggers the breakdown of an ATP molecule to ADP and an inorganic phosphate. The energy released by ATP causes the pump to change shape, expelling the sodium

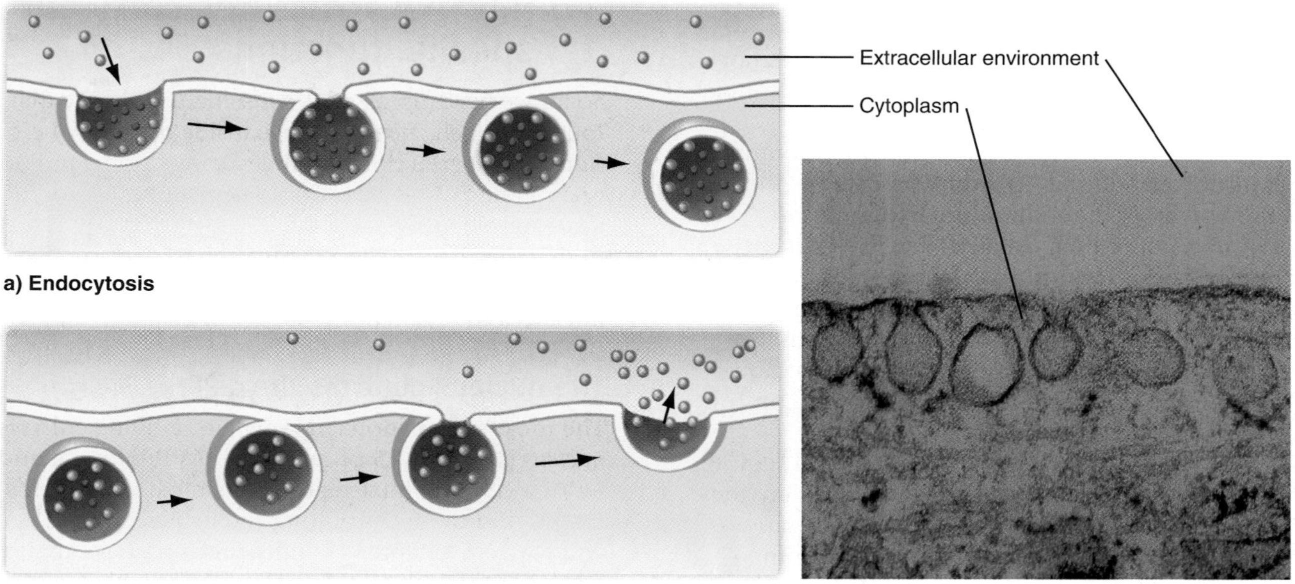


a) Endocytosis

b) Exocytosis

c) Photo of endocytosis

**Figure 3.10 Endocytosis and exocytosis. (a)** In endocytosis, material is surrounded by the cell membrane and brought into the cell. **(b)** In exocytosis, a membranous vesicle fuses with the plasma membrane, expelling its contents outside the cell. **(c)** Photomicrograph showing various stages of endocytosis.

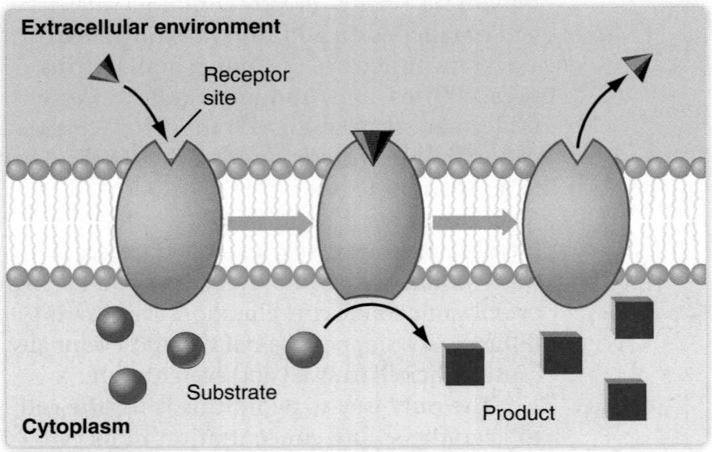


**Figure 3.11 Receptor protein action.** A specific molecule approaches a receptor site on a receptor protein and binds to it. The binding of the molecule to the receptor protein causes a series of chemical reactions within the cell. In this example, a particular cellular product (the squares) is produced from substrate molecules (the circles).

ions and exposing two binding sites for potassium that are accessible only from outside the cell. The binding of potassium triggers another change of shape, and the potassium ions are transported into the cell.

One effect of this three sodium/two potassium exchange is to lower the number of ions within the cell slightly. More importantly, the plasma membrane is much more permeable to potassium than to sodium because it contains many potassium channels but very few sodium channels. Effectively, the cell keeps the number of sodium ions in the cytoplasm low by pumping them out again just as soon as a few leak in. The inward active transport of potassium does not increase the intracellular potassium concentration very much because they can leak back out so easily.

As Figure 3.12b shows, the sodium-potassium pump effectively controls cell volume. To reduce its volume, the cell increases the activity of the sodium-potassium pumps, getting rid of more sodium than usual. Water also exits to maintain osmotic equilibrium. To expand its volume, the cell lowers the activity of the pumps and retains water along with the extra sodium. Because potassium can diffuse so quickly no matter how much is pumped, the rate of potassium transport by the pumps is not relevant to the control of cell volume.

A single red blood cell may have over a hundred sodium-potassium pumps in its plasma membrane. In addition, the pump is essential to the ability of nerve cells to generate an electric current. We discuss the sodium-potassium pump in more detail in Chapter 11.

### Isotonic extracellular fluid also maintains cell volume

*Tonicity* refers to the relative concentrations of solutes in two fluids (*-tonic* means "strength"). Because water can diffuse across the cell membrane so easily, the ability of a human cell to control its volume also depends on the tonicity of the extracellular fluid (Figure 3.13 on page 60).

Extracellular fluid that is **isotonic** (Greek *isos*, equal) has the same solute concentration as the *intracellular* fluid. Cells maintain a normal volume in isotonic extracellular solutions because the concentration of water is the same inside and out. In humans, isotonic extracellular fluid is equivalent to about 9 grams of salt dissolved in a liter of solution. Regulatory mechanisms in the body ensure that the extracellular fluid solute concentration remains relatively constant at that level.

When cells are placed in a **hypertonic** solution, one with a concentration of solutes *higher* than the intracellular fluid, water diffuses out of the cells, and the cells shrink. Eventually this impairs normal function and the cells die.

Conversely, when cells are placed in a **hypotonic** solution with a *lower* concentration of solutes than intracellular fluid, water enters the cells and causes them to swell. Pure water is the most hypotonic solution possible. Most human cells quickly swell, burst, and die when placed in pure water.

**RECAP**

The sodium-potassium pump is an essential mechanism in the regulation of cell volume. In addition, homeostatic regulatory processes keep the tonicity of the extracellular fluid relatively constant. ■

## 3.5 Internal structures carry out specific functions

So far we have discussed the plasma membrane that surrounds the cell. Now we move inside the cell, where we find a number of different membrane-bound and non-membrane-bound structures. The membrane-bound structures are called organelles, because they are like tiny organs in that they have a specific function to perform. Figure 3.14 on page 61 presents a cutaway view of an animal cell with its nucleus and organelles.

### The nucleus controls the cell

The most conspicuous organelle of a living eukaryote is its *nucleus* (Figure 3.15 on page 62). As the information center of a cell, the nucleus contains most of the cell's genetic material in the form of long molecules of DNA. (As you will learn in Chapter 17, mitochondria have their own DNA.) Ultimately, DNA controls nearly all the activities of a cell. Details of how DNA controls cellular function are discussed in Chapters 17 and 19.

The outer surface of the nucleus consists of a double-layered membrane, called the *nuclear membrane,* that keeps the DNA within the nucleus. The nuclear membrane is

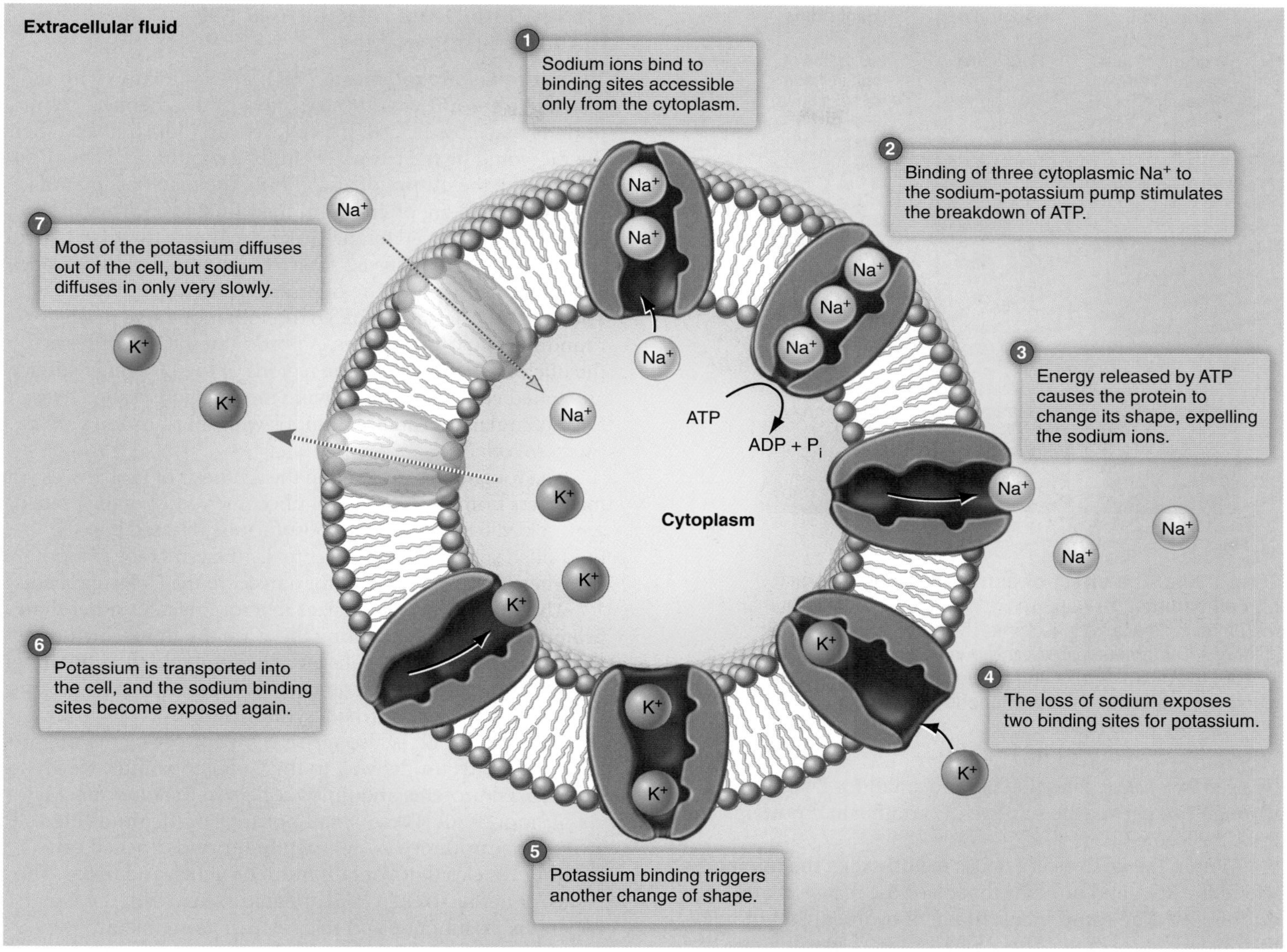


**a) The cell membrane contains $Na^+$ - $K^+$ pumps, and also channels that permit the rapid outward diffusion of $K^+$ but only a slow inward diffusion of $Na^+$.**

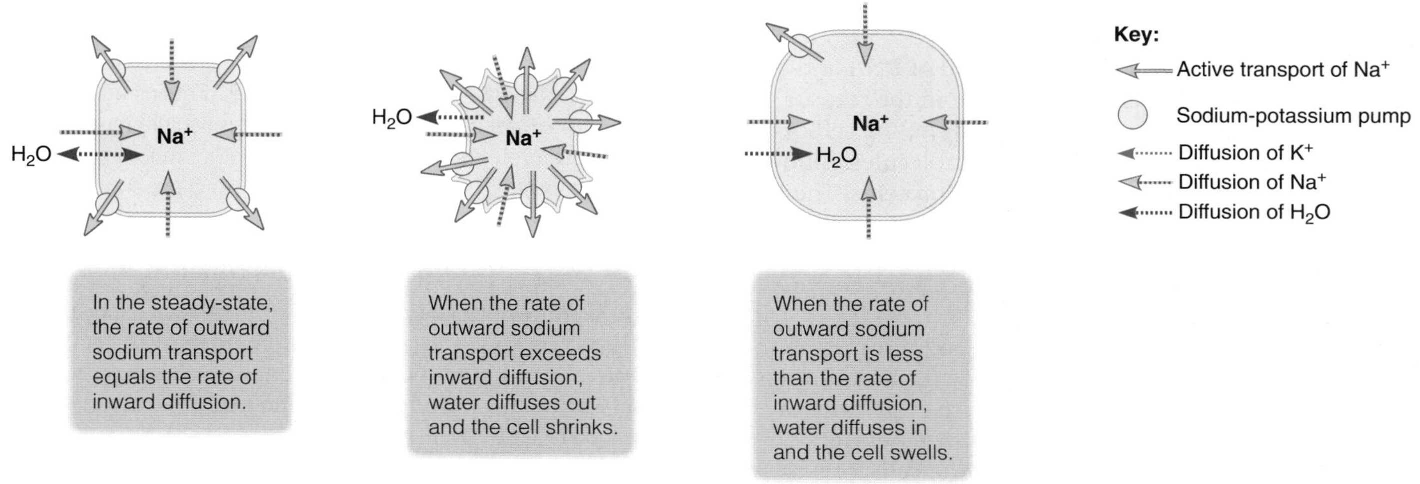


**b) The rate of transport by the $Na^+$ - $K^+$ pumps determines cell volume.**

Figure 3.12 **Control of cell volume by the sodium-potassium pump ($Na^+$-$K^+$ pump).**

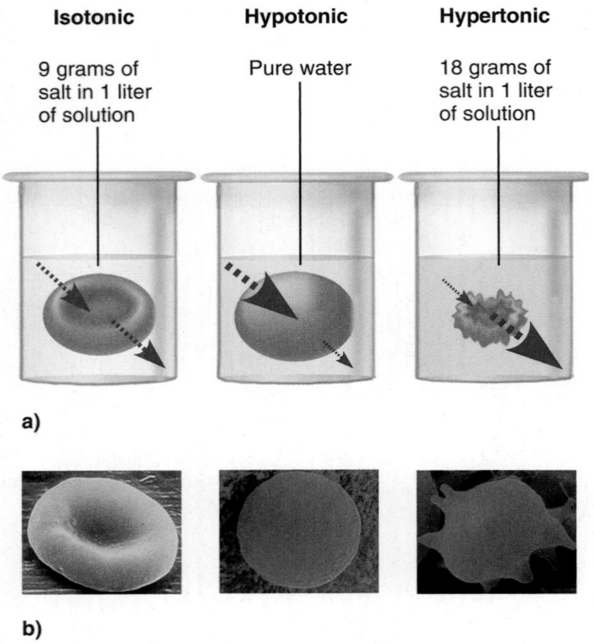


**Figure 3.13 The effect of extracellular fluid tonicity on cell volume. (a)** Water movement into and out of human red blood cells placed in isotonic, hypotonic, or hypertonic solutions. The amount of water movement is indicated by the sizes of the arrows. **(b)** Scanning electron micrographs of red blood cells placed in similar solutions.

bridged by *nuclear pores* that are too small for DNA to pass through but permit the passage of certain small proteins and RNA molecules.

Within the nucleus is a dense region called the **nucleolus,** where the RNA and proteins that compose *ribosomes* are synthesized. The components of the ribosomes pass through the nuclear pores to the cytoplasm for final assembly into ribosomes.

## Ribosomes are responsible for protein synthesis

**Ribosomes** are small structures composed of RNA and certain proteins that are either floating freely in the cytosol or are attached to the endoplasmic reticulum, the cell organelle that synthesizes most biological molecules. Ribosomes are responsible for making specific proteins. They assemble amino acids into proteins by connecting the appropriate amino acids in the correct sequence according to an RNA template. We describe this process in more detail in Chapter 17.

Ribosomes that are attached to the endoplasmic reticulum release their proteins into the folds of the endoplasmic reticulum. Many of these proteins are eventually secreted by the cell. Free-floating ribosomes generally produce proteins for immediate use by the cell, such as enzymes that serve as catalysts for chemical reactions within the cytoplasmic fluid.

## The endoplasmic reticulum is the manufacturing center

The **endoplasmic reticulum (ER),** in conjunction with its attached ribosomes, synthesizes most of the chemical compounds made by the cell. If a cell were an industrial city, then the ER would be the city's steel mills, sawmills, and chemical plants. Like the output of a steel mill, the materials manufactured by the ER are often not in their final form. They are refined and packaged by the Golgi apparatus, discussed later.

Figure 3.16 on page 62 shows the structure of the ER and its role in the manufacture of proteins and other materials. The ER is an extensively folded, membranous system surrounding a fluid-filled space. A portion of the ER connects to the nuclear membrane. Some regions of the ER's outer surface are dotted with ribosomes, giving those regions, called *rough ER,* a granular appearance. Regions without ribosomes are called *smooth ER.*

The rough ER is involved in the synthesis of proteins, as you may guess from the presence of ribosomes. Most of the proteins synthesized by the attached ribosomes are released into the fluid-filled space of the ER. Eventually they enter the smooth ER, where they are packaged for transfer to the Golgi apparatus.

The smooth ER synthesizes macromolecules other than protein. Most notable among these are the lipids, including some hormones. Numerous enzymes embedded in the inner surface of the ER membrane facilitate the chemical reactions necessary for macromolecule synthesis.

The smooth ER is also responsible for packaging the proteins and lipids for delivery to the Golgi apparatus. Newly synthesized proteins and lipids collect in the outermost layers of smooth ER. There, small portions of the fluid-filled space are surrounded by ER membrane and pinched off, forming vesicles that contain fluid, proteins, and lipids. The vesicles migrate to the Golgi apparatus, fuse with the Golgi apparatus membrane, and release their contents into the Golgi apparatus for further processing.

**RECAP**

The nucleus contains most of the cell's genetic material. Ribosomes composed of RNA and ribosomal proteins are responsible for protein assembly. The endoplasmic reticulum modifies some of these proteins, manufactures most other macromolecules in rough form, and transfers them to the Golgi apparatus. ■

## The Golgi apparatus refines, packages, and ships

The **Golgi apparatus** is the cell's refining, packaging, and shipping center. To continue our analogy of the cell as an industrial city, here is where steel bars are shaped into nails and screws, raw lumber assembled into doors and windows, and grain turned into bread.

Figure 3.17 on page 63 diagrams the structure of the Golgi apparatus and the processes that occur there. In cross section the Golgi apparatus appears as a series of interconnected fluid-filled

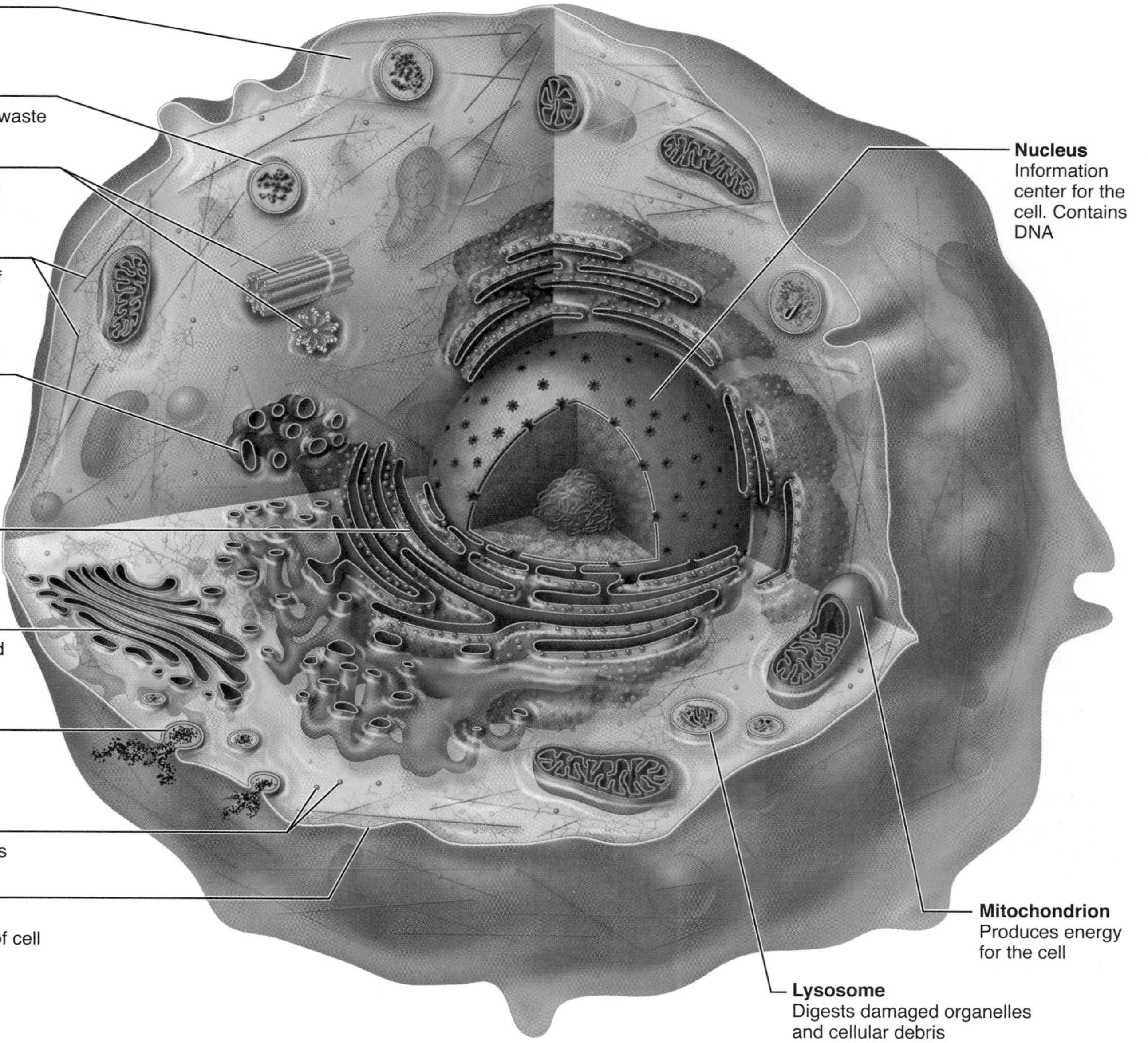


**Figure 3.14 A typical animal cell.** Not shown in this cell are cilia, a flagellum, glycogen granules, or fat deposits, as only certain cells have these features.

spaces surrounded by membrane, much like a stack of plates. Like the ER, it contains enzymes that further refine the products of the ER into final form.

The contents of the Golgi apparatus move outward by a slow but continuous process. At the outermost layer of the Golgi apparatus, the products are finally ready to be packaged into vesicles and shipped to their final destinations.

## Vesicles: Membrane-bound storage and shipping containers

Vesicles are membrane-bound spheres that enclose something within the cell. Sometimes they contain it inside the cell, and sometimes they move it to another location. There are several types of vesicles, each with a different origin and purpose.

**Vesicles that ship and store cellular products** These vesicles enclose and transport the products of the ER and Golgi apparatus. Each vesicle contains only one product out of the thousands of substances made by the Golgi apparatus.

The contents of each vesicle depend on certain proteins in the vesicle membrane that act as "shipping labels." They determine which product is put into the vesicle and where the vesicle is sent. If a vesicle's products are not immediately needed it remains in the cell cytoplasm, like a box stored in a warehouse awaiting shipment.

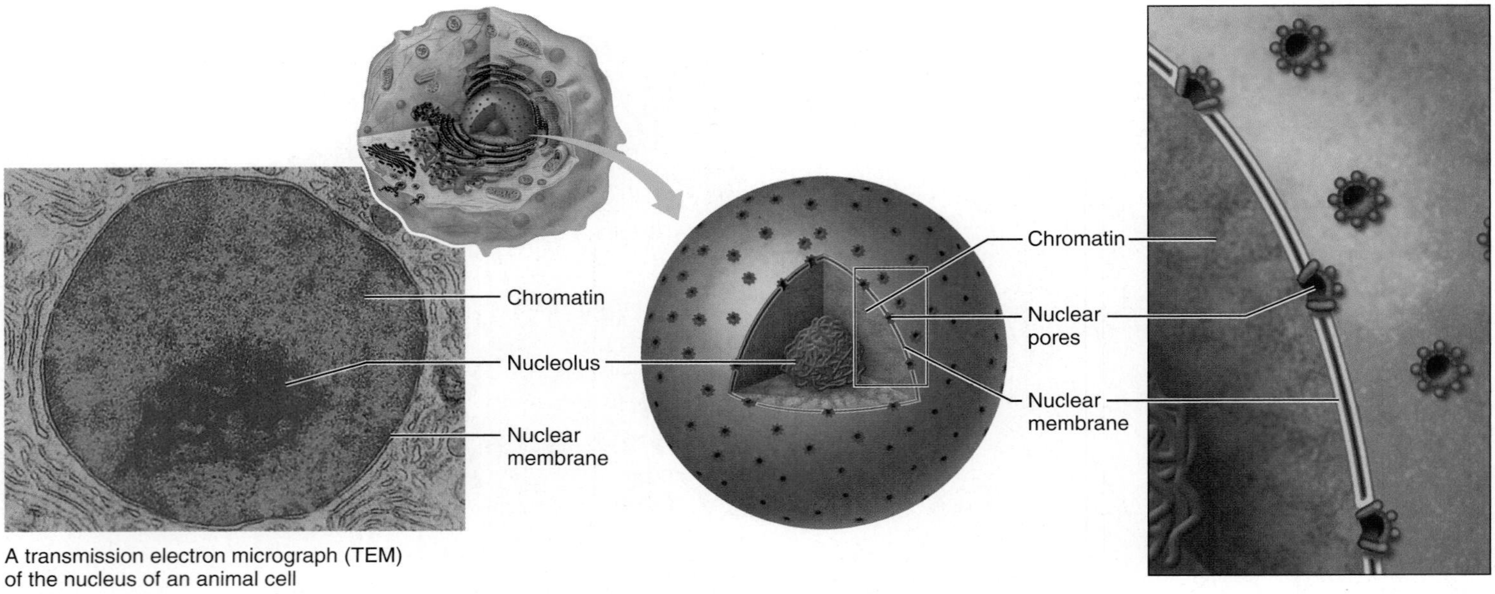


**Figure 3.15 The nucleus.** The nucleus contains the cell's genetic material. The nucleolus produces the protein and RNA components of ribosomes. These components exit the nucleus through nuclear pores.

**Secretory vesicles** Secretory vesicles contain products destined for export from the cell. They migrate to the plasma membrane and release their contents outside the cell by exocytosis. Because most secretory products are made in the Golgi apparatus, secretory vesicles generally derive from Golgi apparatus membrane.

**Endocytotic vesicles** These structures enclose bacteria and raw materials from the extracellular environment. They bring them into the cell by endocytosis.

**Peroxisomes and lysosomes** These vesicles contain enzymes so powerful that they must be kept within the vesicle to avoid damaging the rest of the cell. Both are produced by the Golgi apparatus. Figure 3.18 shows their functions.

The enzymes in **peroxisomes** destroy various toxic wastes produced in the cell, including hydrogen peroxide ($H_2O_2$). They also destroy compounds that have entered the cell from outside, such as alcohol. The detoxification process occurs entirely within the peroxisome.

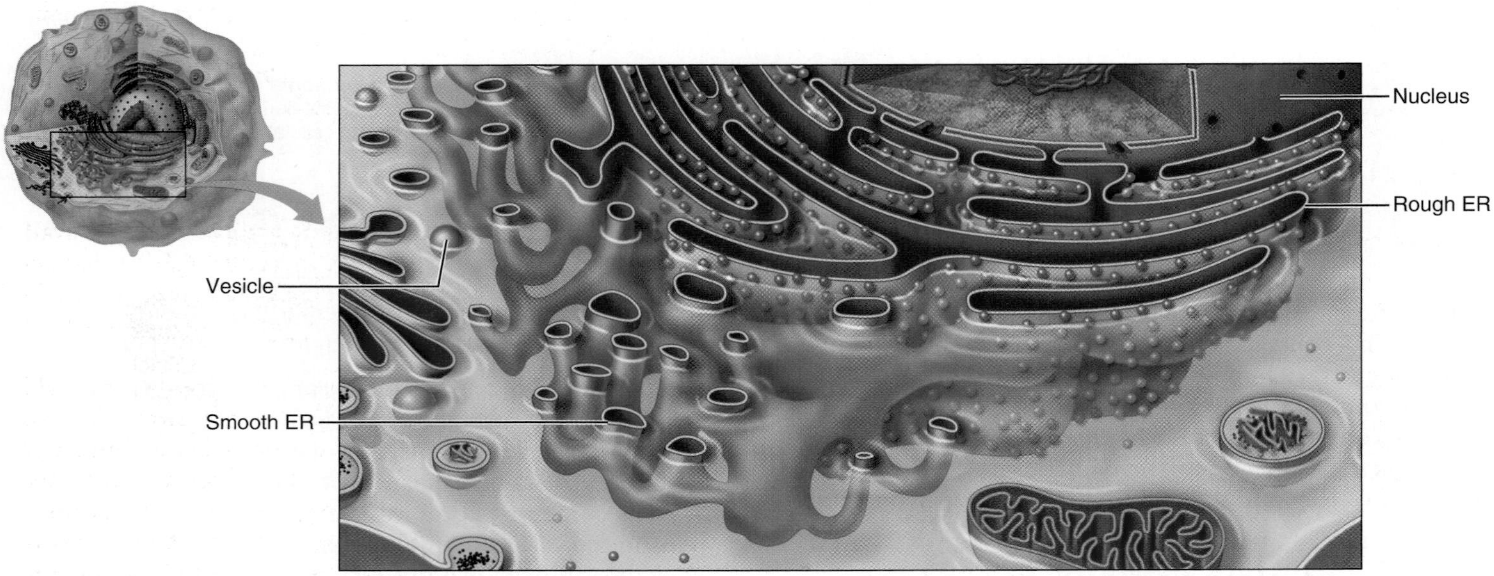


**Figure 3.16 The endoplasmic reticulum (ER).** The rough ER is studded with ribosomes, where proteins are made. The smooth ER packages the proteins and other products of the ER and prepares them for shipment to the Golgi apparatus in vesicles.

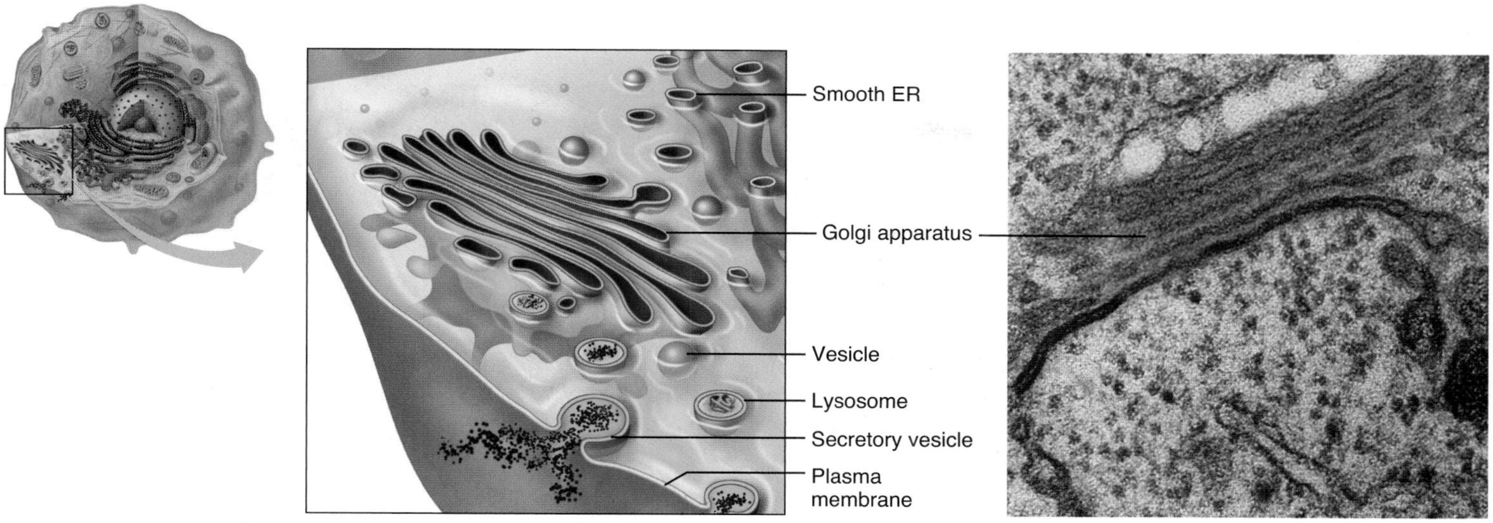


**Figure 3.17 The Golgi apparatus.** The Golgi apparatus receives substances from the ER, refines them into final products, and packages them into vesicles for their final destinations.

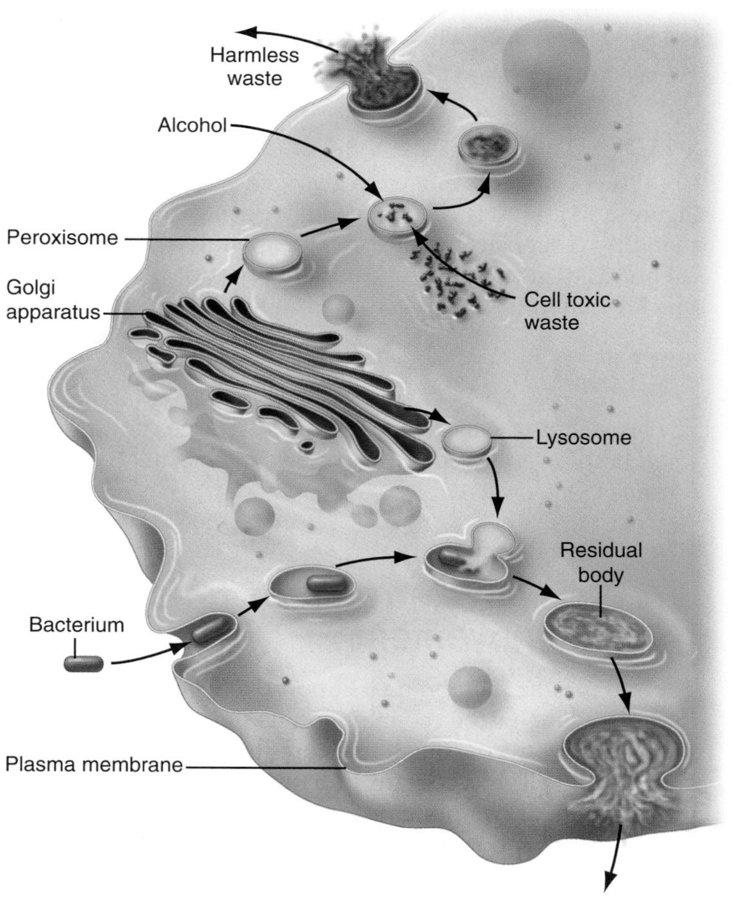


**Figure 3.18 Lysosomes and peroxisomes.** Lysosomes formed by the Golgi apparatus fuse with endocytotic vesicles containing a bacterium. Following digestion of the bacterium the residual waste is excreted by exocytosis. Peroxisomes take up toxic wastes (including alcohol) and degrade them to harmless waste, which is also excreted.

**Lysosomes** (from the Greek *lysis*, dissolution, and *soma*, body) contain powerful digestive enzymes. Lysosomes fuse with endocytotic vesicles within the cell, digesting bacteria and other large objects. Lysosomes also perform certain housekeeping tasks, such as dissolving and removing damaged mitochondria and other cellular debris. When their digestive task is complete they become "residual bodies," analogous to small bags of compacted waste. Residual bodies can be stored in the cell, but usually their contents are eliminated from the cell by exocytosis.

**RECAP**

The Golgi apparatus refines cellular products to their final form and packages them in membrane-bound vesicles. Some vesicles store, ship, and secrete cellular products; others digest and remove toxic waste and cellular debris. ■

## Mitochondria provide energy

Nearly all of a cell's functions require energy. Energy is available in the chemical bonds of the food we eat, but cells cannot use it directly. Most energy in ingested nutrients must be converted to a more usable form before it can power the chemical and physical activities of living cells.

**Mitochondria** are the organelles responsible for providing most of this usable energy; they are often called the cells' "power plants." Not surprisingly, their number within different cells varies widely according to the energy requirements of the cells. A cell with a high rate of energy consumption, such as a muscle cell, may contain over 1,000 mitochondria.

Figure 3.19 shows a photograph of a single mitochondrion and diagrams its structure and function. A smooth outer membrane, similar to the plasma membrane, covers the entire surface. Within the outer membrane is an inner

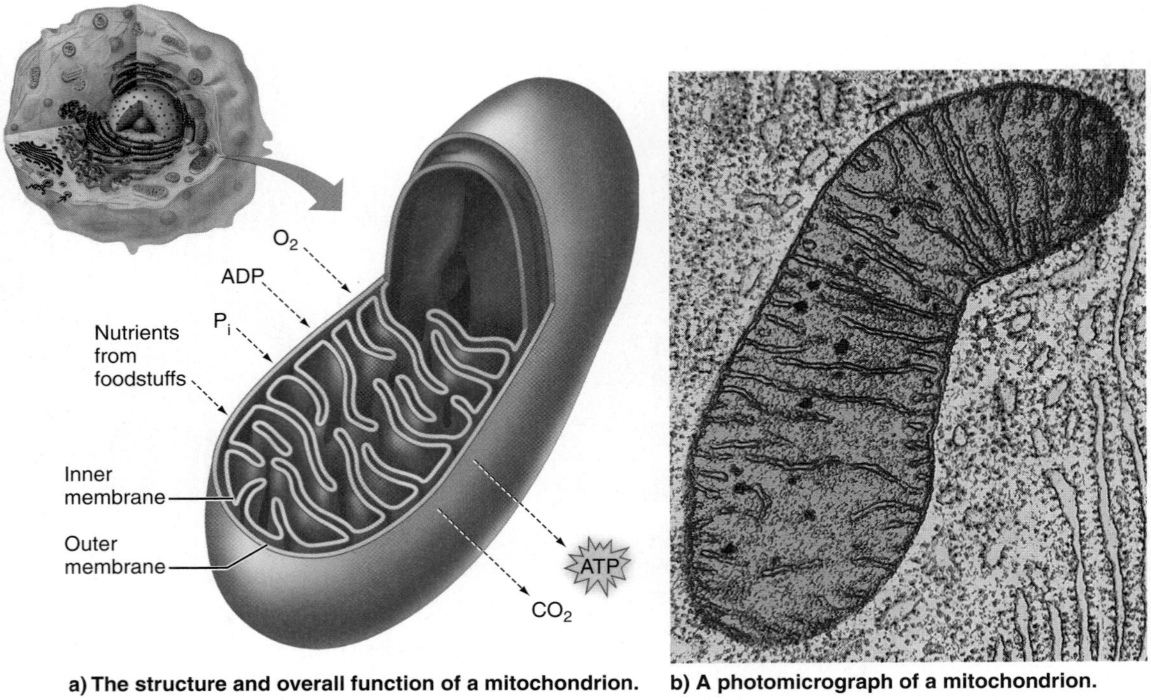


**Figure 3.19 Mitochondria. (a)** The structure and overall function of a mitochondrion. **(b)** A photomicrograph of a mitochondrion.

membrane with numerous folds that increase its surface area. The inner membrane and the fluid in its folds contain hundreds of protein enzymes, which serve as catalysts to break down chemical bonds in our food and release the energy. This process consumes oxygen and produces carbon dioxide.

The energy liberated within the mitochondria is used to create high-energy molecules such as ATP. ATP is then exported from the mitochondria to the cytosol, where it is available as a quick source of energy for the cell. Like electric power, ATP is useful for a variety of purposes. We have already seen one of its uses—providing the energy used to transport sodium and potassium across the plasma membrane.

### Fat and glycogen: Sources of energy

The mitochondria generally manufacture ATP as it is needed. To avoid the possibility of running out of fuel, some cells store energy in raw form. These energy stores are not enclosed in any membrane-bound container. They are more like large piles of coal on the ground, awaiting delivery to the power plants (mitochondria) for conversion to electricity (ATP).

Some cells store raw energy as lipids (fat). Our so-called fat cells are so specialized for this purpose that most of their volume consists of large droplets of stored lipids. Dieting and exercise tend to reduce the amount of stored fat—that is, they make the fat cells leaner. However, dieting and exercise do not reduce their number. The cells are available to store fat again, which is why it is so hard to *keep* lost weight off.

Other cells store energy as glycogen granules (review Figure 2.15). Muscle cells rely on glycogen granules rather than on fat deposits because the energy stored in the chemical bonds of glycogen can be used to produce ATP more quickly than the energy derived from fat.

**RECAP**

Mitochondria manufacture ATP for the cell. Some cells stockpile fats or glycogen, which they can use to make more ATP as needed. ■

## 3.6 Cells have structures for support and movement

The soft plasma membrane is supported by an internal scaffolding that helps the cell maintain its shape. In addition, some cells have specialized structures to help them move around, and all cells contain structures that are involved in moving cellular components during cell division. Structural elements for support and movement include the cytoskeleton, cilia and flagella, and centrioles.

### The cytoskeleton supports the cell

The **cytoskeleton** (Figure 3.20) consists of a loosely structured network of fibers called microtubules and microfilaments. As their names imply, microtubules are tiny hollow

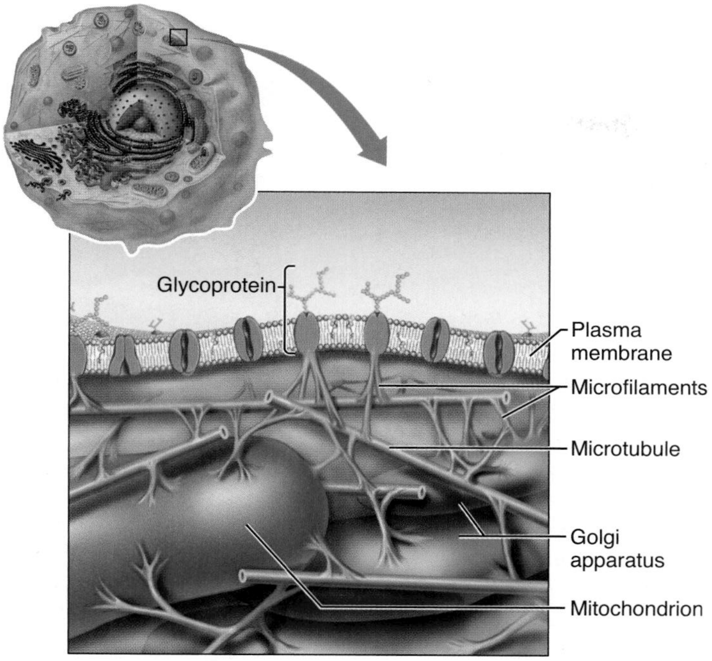


**Figure 3.20 The cytoskeleton.** The cytoskeleton consists of microtubules and microfilaments that attach to and support the cell's organelles and plasma membrane.

tubes, and microfilaments are thin solid fibers. Both are composed of protein. They attach to each other and to proteins in the plasma membrane, called *glycoproteins,* which typically have carbohydrate group components.

The cytoskeleton forms a framework for the soft plasma membrane, much as tent poles support a nylon tent. The cytoskeleton also supports and anchors the other structures within the cell.

### Cilia and flagella are specialized for movement

A few cells have hairlike **cilia** (singular: cilium) or longer **flagella** (singular: flagellum) that extend from the surface. Cilia are generally only 2–10 microns long (1 micron equals one-millionth of a meter). In cells that have them, they are numerous. Cilia move materials along the surface of a cell with a brushing motion. They are common on the surfaces of cells that line the airways and in certain ducts within the body.

In humans, flagella (approximately 200 microns long) are found only on sperm cells (Figure 3.21). The whiplike movement of the flagellum moves the entire sperm cell from one place to another.

Cilia and flagella are similar in structure. They are composed primarily of protein microtubules held together by connecting elements and surrounded by a plasma membrane. Nine pairs of fused microtubules surround two single microtubules in the center. The entire structure bends when temporary linkages form between adjacent pairs of microtubules, causing the pairs to slide past each other. The formation and release of these temporary bonds requires energy in the form of ATP.

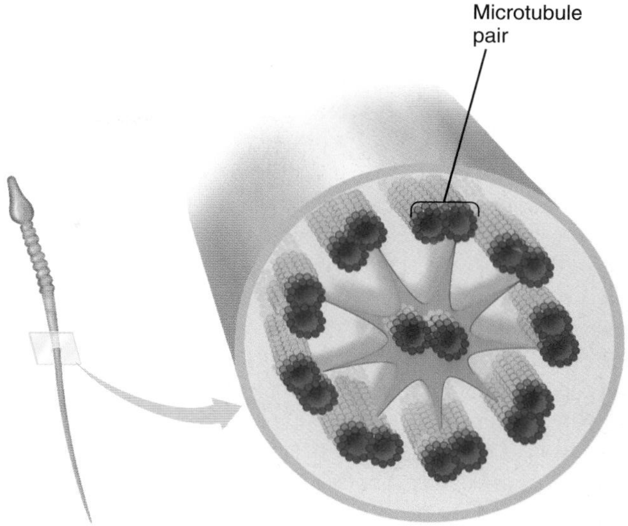


**Figure 3.21 Flagella.** A cross-sectional view of a flagellum showing that it is composed of nine pairs of microtubules surrounding a central pair.

### Centrioles are involved in cell division

**Centrioles** are short, rodlike microtubular structures located near the nucleus. Centrioles are essential to the process of cell division because they participate in aligning and dividing the genetic material of the cell. We discuss them in Chapter 17 when we describe how a cell divides.

**RECAP**

The cytoskeleton forms a supportive framework for the cell. Cilia and flagella are specialized for movement, and centrioles are essential to cell division. ■

## 3.7 Cells use and transform matter and energy

Living cells can release the energy stored in the chemical bonds of molecules and use it to build, store, and break down still other molecules as required to maintain life. **Metabolism** is the sum of all of the chemical reactions in the organism.

In a single cell, thousands of different chemical reactions are possible at any one time. Some of these chemical reactions are organized as *metabolic pathways* in which one reaction follows after another in orderly and predictable patterns (Figure 3.22). Some metabolic pathways are linear, in which the **product** (or end material) from one chemical reaction becomes the **substrate** (starting material) for the next. Other metabolic pathways form a cycle in which substrate molecules enter and product molecules exit, but the basic chemical cycle repeats over and over again.

# Directions in Science

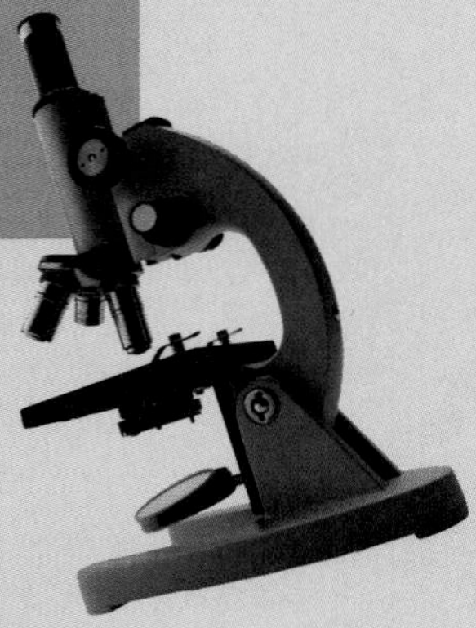

## The First Cultured Human Cells

In the late 1940s researchers were studying a virus that was as huge a public concern as the AIDS virus is today: the microbe that causes polio. One major obstacle was that the polio virus prefers human cells for its growth and reproduction, and there was no way (in the 1940s) to keep human cells alive in the laboratory outside the human body. Most human cells just did not grow properly in laboratory dishes.

That changed on February 8, 1951. Researchers at Johns Hopkins University, led by Dr. G. O. Gey, obtained some living cancer cells from 31-year-old Henrietta Lacks, who had cancer of the cervix. Gey and his associates were able to keep these cells and their offspring alive in the laboratory, thereby establishing the first culture of human cells. Gey named them HeLa cells in honor of the patient who donated them. The pseudonym Helen Lane was initially used to protect her identity, but today it seems appropriate to honor her by using her true name.

Although HeLa cells were first used to grow the polio virus in the laboratory, they proved to have other uses, including the study of cancer itself. Eventually Gey established a stable stock culture of HeLa cells and made it available to other researchers around the world. HeLa cells have proven invaluable not only for our understanding of the mechanisms underlying the development of cancer but also our understanding of cell nutrition, viral growth, protein synthesis, and drug effects on cells.

Henrietta Lacks died a few years after the discovery of her cancer, but her cells live on. Indeed, HeLa cells have become so widely used in human cell research that there are over 1,000 references to HeLa cells in the scientific literature each year.

Henrietta Lacks provided the first human cells to be successfully cultured.

There are two basic types of metabolic pathways:

1. **Anabolism** (from the Greek *anabole,* a throwing up): molecules are assembled into larger molecules that contain more energy, a process that requires energy. The assembly of a protein from many amino acids is an example of an anabolic pathway.
2. **Catabolism** (Greek *katabole,* a throwing down): larger molecules are broken down, a process that releases energy. The breakdown of glucose into water, carbon dioxide, and energy is an example of a catabolic pathway.

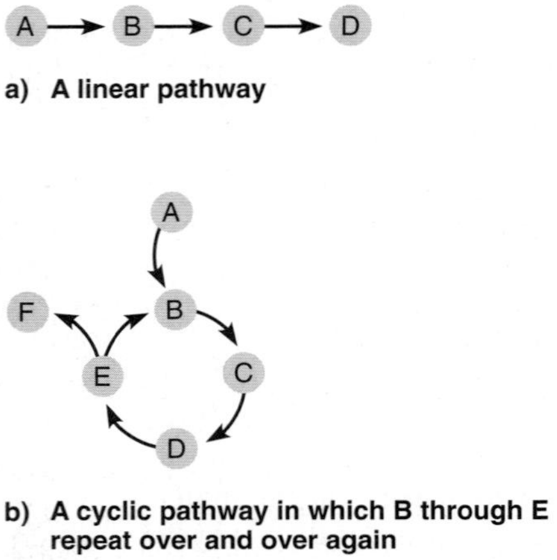


**Figure 3.22 Types of metabolic pathways.**

Two facts are important about metabolic pathways. First, nearly every chemical reaction requires a specific enzyme. The cell regulates and controls the rates of chemical reactions through the specificity and availability of key enzymes. Second, the metabolic activities of a living cell require a lot of energy. Energy is required for building the complex macromolecules found only in living organisms, such as proteins, DNA, cholesterol, and so on. Energy is also used to power cellular activities such as active transport and muscle contraction.

Cells get their energy by catabolism of molecules that serve as chemical stores of energy. The most immediately useful source of energy, a sort of "energy cash" if you will, is ATP. The energy in ATP is locked in the chemical bond between the second and third phosphate group. Every time the third phosphate group is removed from an ATP molecule, energy is released that the cell can use to do work. The reaction is reversible, meaning that the application of energy to ADP in the presence of a phosphate group can *phosphorylate* (add a phosphate group to) ADP again, re-creating ATP. The equation is written as:

$$ATP \leftrightarrow ADP + P_i + \text{energy}$$

In this equation, $P_i$ is used as the abbreviation for the inorganic phosphate ($PO_4^{-2}$) to distinguish it from the chemical symbol for pure phosphorus (P).

**RECAP**

Metabolism refers to all of a cell's chemical processes. Metabolic pathways either create molecules and use energy (anabolism) or break them down and liberate energy (catabolism). ■

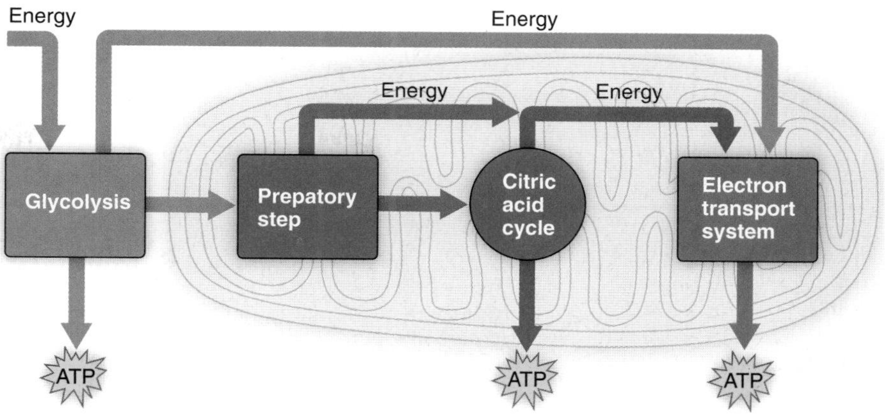


**Figure 3.24 Cellular respiration: An overview.** Glycolysis occurs in the cytoplasm. The products of glycolysis, two molecules of pyruvate, enter mitochondria. The preparatory step and the citric acid cycle result in the complete breakdown of the two pyruvate molecules but only limited ATP production. Most of the ATP is produced in the electron transport system, using energy harvested from the first three steps.

## Glucose provides the cell with energy

Cells can use a variety of fuels to make the ATP energy "cash" they need. The most readily available fuel generally is glucose, derived either from food recently eaten or from stored glycogen. However, if glucose is not available, cells may turn to stored fats and even proteins for fuel. Regardless of the fuel used, most of the ATP is produced by very similar metabolic pathways. Let's look at the use of glucose as a fuel source first, and then we'll describe briefly how other fuels are used.

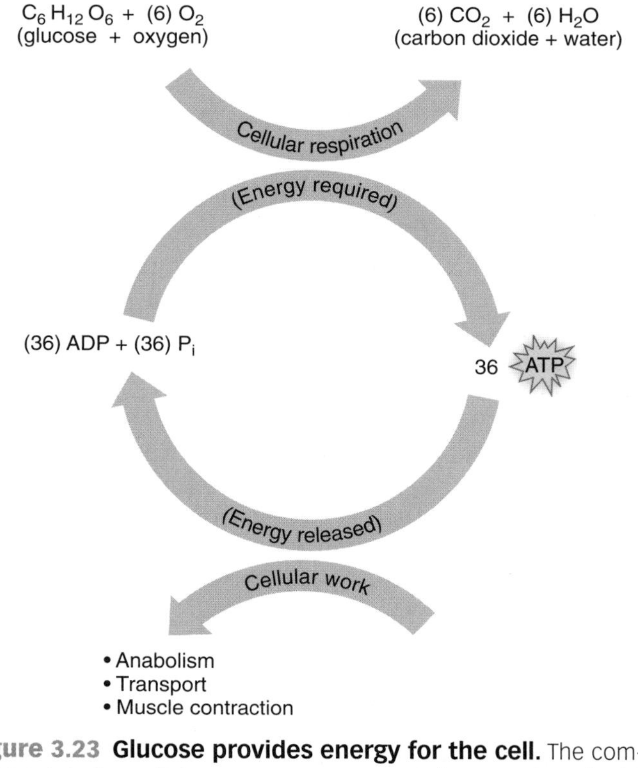


**Figure 3.23 Glucose provides energy for the cell.** The complete catabolism of glucose uses oxygen, produces carbon dioxide and water, and generates 36 molecules of ATP that can be used to do cellular work.

Recall that glucose is a six-carbon sugar molecule with the chemical formula $C_6H_{12}O_6$. This seemingly simple little molecule packs a lot of potential energy in its chemical bonds. Just as a gallon of gas provides enough energy to power your car for 25–30 miles, a single glucose molecule provides the cell enough energy to produce approximately 36 molecules of ATP (Figure 3.23).

The production of ATP from glucose occurs in four stages, summarized in Figure 3.24:

1. *Glycolysis:* The six-carbon glucose molecule is split into two three-carbon pyruvate molecules. Energy is required to get the process started.
2. *The preparatory step:* In preparation for the citric acid cycle, pyruvate enters a mitochondrion. A series of chemical reactions yields a two-carbon molecule called acetyl CoA, plus some energy.
3. *The citric acid cycle:* An acetyl CoA molecule is broken down completely by mitochondrial enzymes, and its energy is released. Most of the energy is captured by certain high-energy electron transport molecules.
4. *The electron transport system:* Most of the energy derived from the original glucose molecule is used to phosphorylate ADP, producing high-energy ATP.

### Glycolysis: Glucose is split into two pyruvate molecules

Figure 3.25 illustrates **glycolysis,** the first stage in the complete breakdown of glucose (*glyco-* means "sweet," referring to sugar, and *-lysis* means "to break"). Glycolyis occurs within the cell's cytoplasm, not within mitochondria. In the first five of the ten chemical reactions that constitute glycolysis, glucose is broken into two 3-carbon molecules called *glyceraldehyde-3-phosphate* (PGAL). Two of these steps require the input of energy (two molecules of ATP)—like putting a match to a bonfire.

Then, each of the two PGAL molecules is converted in a series of steps to *pyruvate*. This process requires several more enzymes. At several of these steps, enzymes carrying high-energy

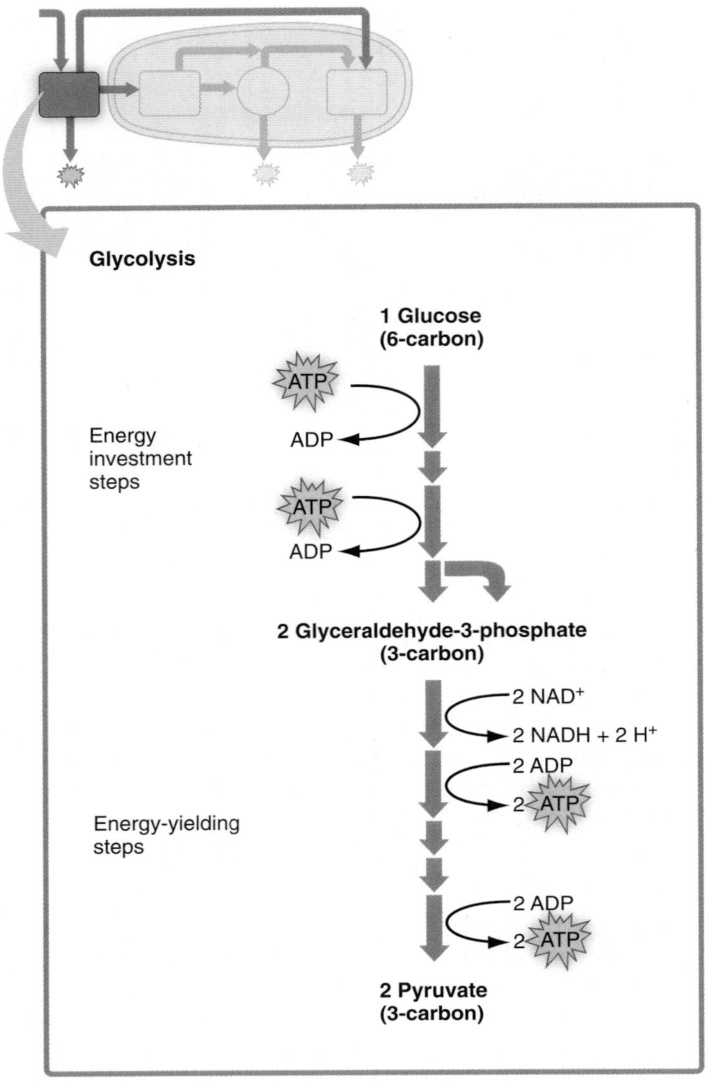


**Figure 3.25 Glycolysis.** This initial breakdown of glucose to two molecules of glyceraldehyde-3-phosphate (PGAL) requires energy. Thereafter, energy is generated as the two PGAL molecules are further degraded to two molecules of pyruvate.

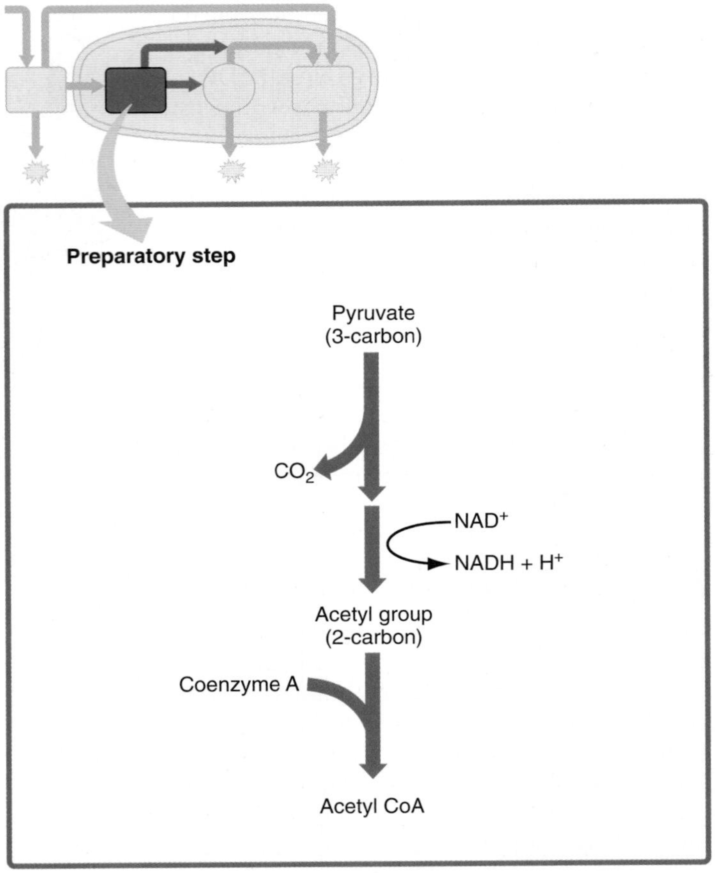


**Figure 3.26 The preparatory step.** Pyruvate is transported into a mitochondrion and catabolized to a two-carbon acetyl group. Energy is released, and the freed carbon is given off as carbon dioxide waste. The acetyl group combines with coenzyme A for delivery to the next step, the citric acid cycle.

phosphate groups pass their phosphate groups directly to ADP, producing ATP. The process, called *substrate-level phosphorylation,* does not require oxygen. During glycolysis, four molecules of ATP are produced by substrate-level phosphorylation.

The rest of the potentially usable energy from glycolysis is released as high-energy hydrogen ions ($H^+$) and electrons ($e^-$). Most of these are picked up by a *coenzyme* called **NAD$^+$** (nicotinamide adenine dinucleotide). A **coenzyme** is a small molecule that assists an enzyme by transporting small molecular groups. In this case NAD$^+$ functions as an energy-carrying molecule. NAD$^+$ picks up one high-energy $H^+$ ion and two high-energy electrons to become the higher-energy molecule **NADH.**

So far, then, the net energy yield from glycolysis is only two molecules of ATP (four were formed, but two were used to get the process started) and two molecules of NADH. The energy carried by NADH is used to make ATP within the mitochondria, as we'll see later.

**The preparatory step: Pyruvate is converted to acetyl CoA** At this point the pyruvate molecules enter the mitochondria, where all the rest of the ATP-generating reactions occur. In a series of steps preparatory to the citric acid cycle, a two-carbon *acetyl group* and a carbon dioxide ($CO_2$) waste molecule are formed from each pyruvate (Figure 3.26). Each acetyl group is then joined with another coenzyme (called *coenzyme A*) to form *acetyl CoA,* which delivers the acetyl group to the *citric acid cycle.* There is a net gain of an additional two NADH molecules from the conversion of two pyruvates to two acetyl CoA molecules in the preparatory step.

**The citric acid cycle harvests energy** The **citric acid cycle,** also called the Krebs cycle for its discoverer, Hans Krebs, is a series of eight sequential steps in which each acetyl group is completely disassembled to $CO_2$ waste and various high-energy products (Figure 3.27). The citric acid cycle begins when acetyl CoA combines with the four-carbon fragment left over from the previous turn of the cycle

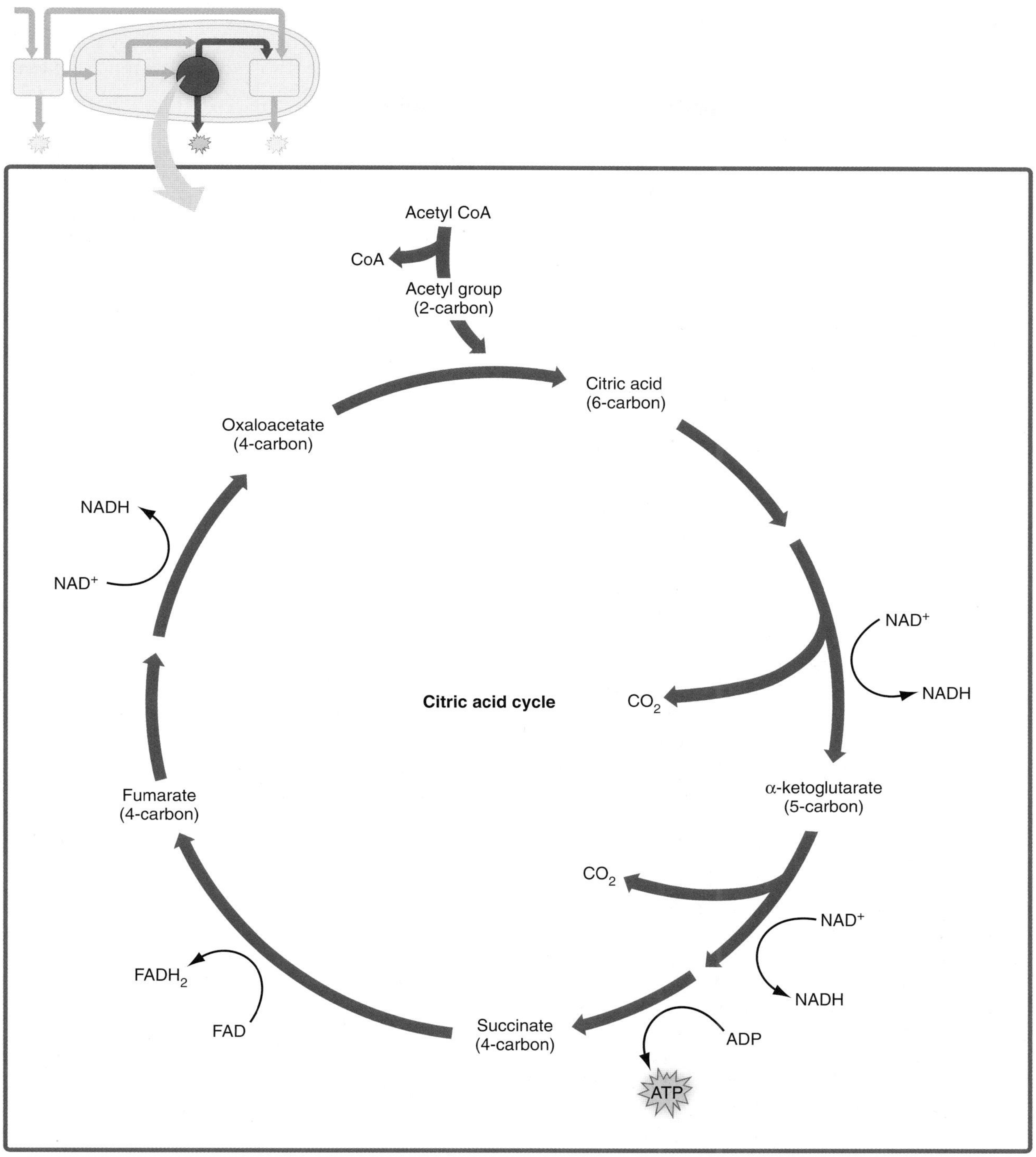


**Figure 3.27 The citric acid cycle.** A complete turn of the citric acid cycle produces two molecules of $CO_2$ waste, an ATP molecule, three molecules of NADH, and a molecule of $FADH_2$ for every 2-carbon acetyl group used as fuel. The cycle occurs twice for each molecule of glucose that undergoes glycolysis to produce two pyruvate molecules. The NADH and $FADH_2$ molecules carry high-energy hydrogen ions and electrons to the electron transport system, where their energy can be used to synthesize ATP.

(oxaloacetic acid) to produce *citric acid,* the six-carbon molecule for which the cycle is named. Citric acid is the starting substrate for seven reactions that end with oxaloacetic acid again. Each reaction is regulated by a different enzyme. The two carbons that are lost during the citric acid cycle are given off as $CO_2$ waste, and one ATP molecule is produced directly by substrate-level phosphorylation. The high-energy hydrogen ions and electrons removed at various points in the cycle are harvested in the form of three molecules of NADH and one molecule of another energy-carrying coenzyme called **FAD** (flavin adenine dinucleotide). FAD picks up two high-energy $H^+$ ions and two electrons to become **$FADH_2$**.

**RECAP**

By the completion of the citric acid cycle, glucose has been broken down completely to $CO_2$ waste and high-energy $H^+$ and electrons carried by NADH and $FADH_2$. Six ATP molecules have been produced by substrate-level phosphorylation, but two others were needed to initiate glycolysis, for a net gain of only four.

**The electron transport system produces ATP** So far, the glucose molecule has been completely dismantled and $CO_2$ has been generated as a waste product, but only four new ATP molecules have been generated. The rest of the energy is still in the electrons and hydrogen ions that are part of NADH and $FADH_2$.

At this point NADH and $FADH_2$ move to the inner membrane of the mitochondria and release their cargo to the **electron transport system** (Figure 3.28). Here, the energy-rich electrons are transferred sequentially from one protein carrier molecule to another. The sequential transfer is important because it allows the energy in the electrons to be released in manageable quantities. The sequence of events is as follows:

1. NADH and $FADH_2$ release the $H^+$ and high-energy electrons they acquired in the citric acid cycle to a carrier protein of the electron transport system.
2. The electrons pass from one protein carrier molecule to the next in the electron transport system.
3. Each time an electron is transferred, the carrier molecule acquires some of its energy and the electron loses energy. The carrier protein uses the energy to transport $H^+$ from the inner compartment of the mitochondria to the outer compartment.

The active transport of $H^+$ into the outer compartment of the mitochondria sets the stage for the actual production of ATP. Since the concentration of $H^+$ is now higher in the outer compartment than in the inner compartment, there is a concentration gradient that favors diffusion of $H^+$ back to the inner compartment. However, $H^+$ can diffuse only through special channels. These channels are actually an enzyme

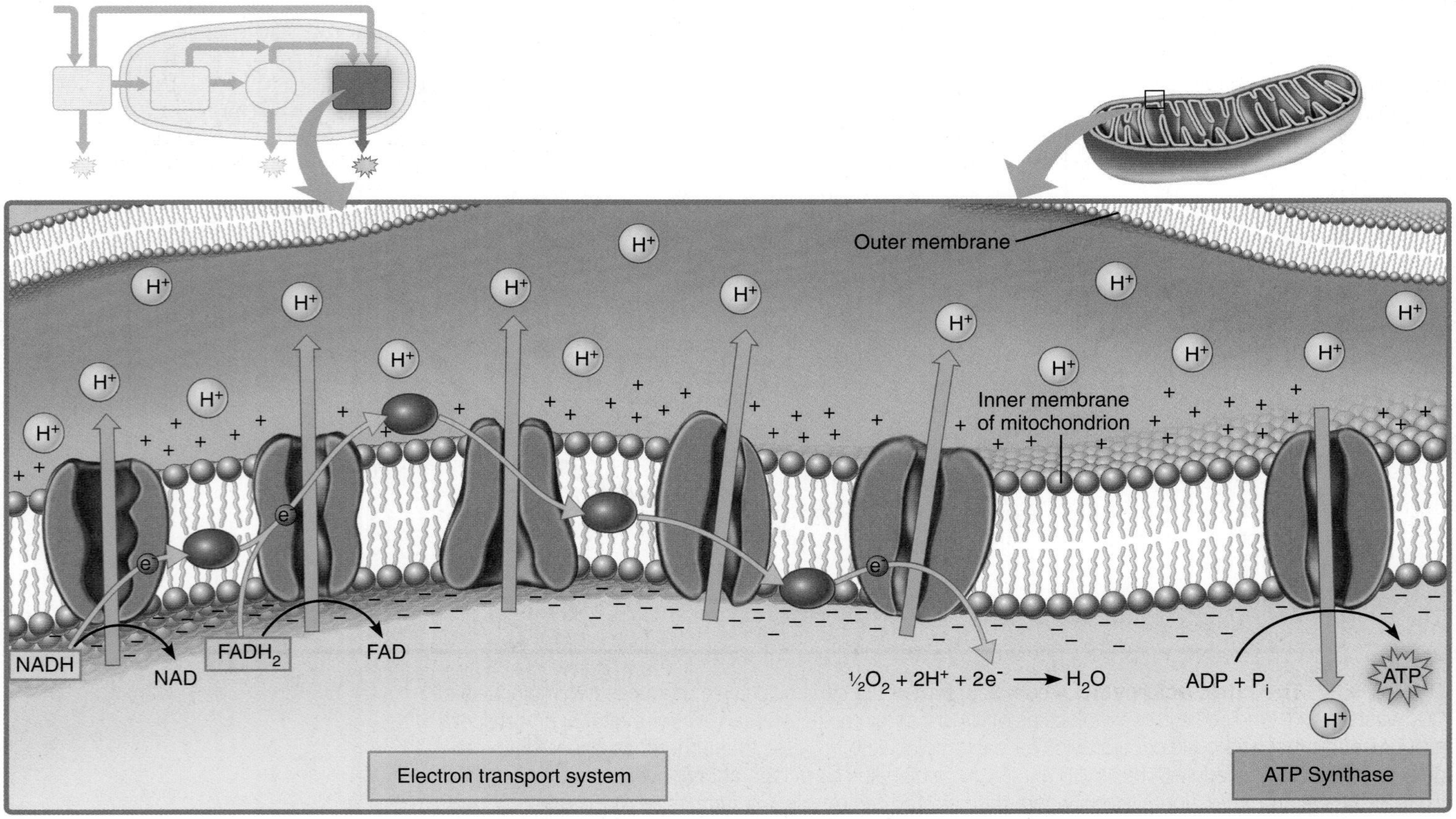


**Figure 3.28 The electron transport system.** During electron transfer, the high-energy molecules of NADH (and $FADH_2$) give up electrons and hydrogen ions. As the electrons are transferred from one molecule in the system to the next, their energy is released and used to transport hydrogen ions into the space between the two mitochondrial membranes. The energy provided by the diffusion of hydrogen ions back into the inner mitochondrial space allows the enzyme ATP synthase to synthesize ATP from ADP and inorganic phosphate ($P_i$).

called *ATP synthase* that uses the energy derived from the diffusion of $H^+$ to catalyze the synthesis of ATP from ADP and $P_i$. Once it is formed, ATP leaves the inner compartment of the mitochondria via a special channel protein, to be used by the cell as an energy source.

As mentioned earlier, *phosphorylation* is the addition of a phosphate group. The process of producing ATP from ADP plus $P_i$, using the energy obtained as electrons are transferred from one molecule to another in the electron transport system, is called **oxidative phosphorylation.** The term *oxidative* indicates that the process uses oxygen and that electrons have been removed.

By the time they have reached the end of the electron transport system, most of the energy of the electrons and $H^+$ has been spent. At this point the spent hydrogen ions and electrons combine with oxygen to form water, a waste product. The low-energy $NAD^+$ and FAD molecules, now lacking hydrogen ions and electrons, are recycled and used again. The ability to recycle $NAD^+$, FAD, and ADP increases cellular efficiency because it means that these do not need to be synthesized anew each time.

Cellular metabolic processes that use oxygen and produce carbon dioxide in the process of making ATP are collectively termed **cellular respiration.** Cellular respiration takes place entirely within mitochondria. Although some ATP is made in the cytoplasm during glycolysis, glycolysis does not require oxygen. Indeed, glycolysis can proceed without oxygen because there are alternative metabolic pathways that pyruvate can take besides entering the preparatory step and citric acid cycle. In contrast, the citric acid cycle *is* considered to be part of cellular respiration, because although it does not use oxygen directly, it would soon come to a complete halt in the absence of oxygen.

**Summary of energy production from glucose** The most effective way to harvest the energy in any fuel, whether gasoline or glucose, is to release the energy *slowly*, under carefully controlled conditions. Holding a match to a gallon of gasoline results in a useless fire or even a potentially dangerous explosion, but burning it drop by drop in the pistons of your car allows the energy to be converted to mechanical work. Similarly, in a living cell, the whole point of glycolysis and cellular respiration is to release the energy in the chemical bonds of glucose *slowly* so that the energy can be harvested effectively.

That is exactly what the cell does (Figure 3.29). The complete breakdown of glucose during glycolysis, the

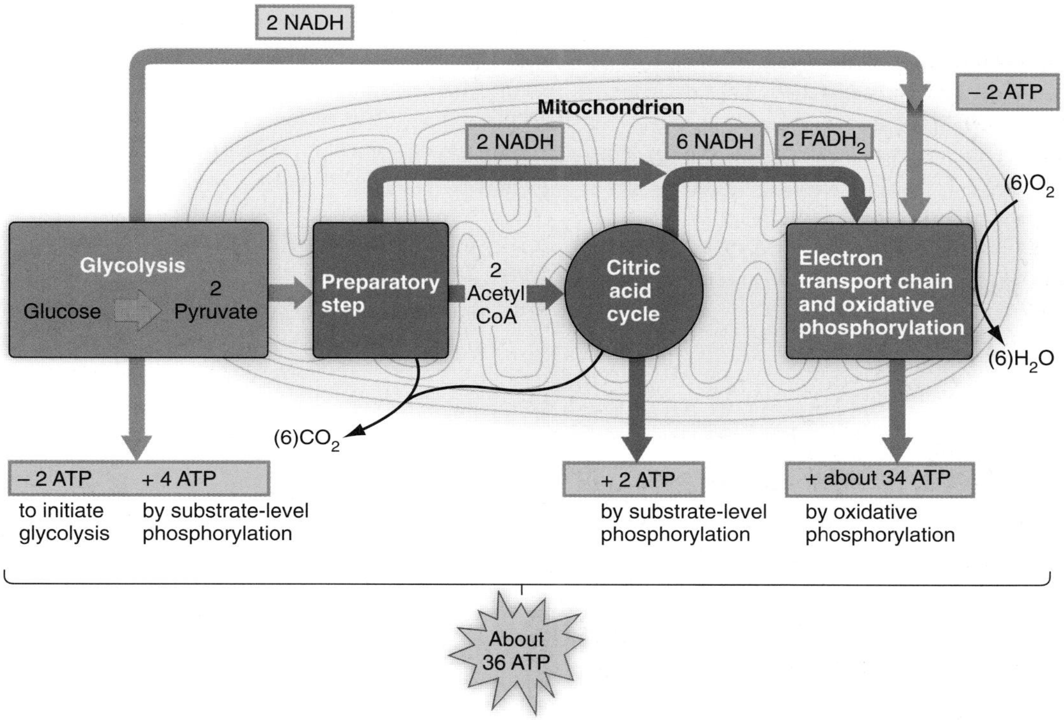


**a) Most of the ATP generated during cellular respiration is synthesized in the electron transport system.**

**b) Cellular respiration powers the activities of humans and many other organisms.**

**Figure 3.29 Cellular respiration: A recap.**

# Should We Use Human Stem Cells for Research and Transplantation?

What do boxing champion Muhammad Ali and actor Michael J. Fox have in common? They both suffer from Parkinson's disease, a debilitating neurological disorder. The key to curing Parkinson's disease and many other diseases and health problems including Alzheimer's disease, leukemia, diabetes, and spinal cord injuries may be a **stem cell,** so called because all of the various types of cells in the body originate (stem) from it.

Muhammad Ali and Michael J. Fox, both sufferers of Parkinson's disease, support stem cell research.

A stem cell is the universal beginning cell, full of potential. Stem cells represent the ancestors of all specialized cells. The ultimate stem cell is the fertilized human egg, from which all the cells in the body develop. All of the cells of the human body originate from that one fertilized egg cell, but as the cells continue to grow and divide again and again they begin to *differentiate,* meaning that they become different from the original. They specialize. Some become muscle; others become skin; still others become nerve cells in the brain.

Stem cells have several properties that may make them (or their early offspring) ideal candidates for the treatment of certain diseases. First, stem cells are easier to work with than adult cells because they don't adhere tightly to each other and they grow in culture better than most adult cells. They are also easy to administer to a patient, because they can be injected and allowed to migrate to their target site rather than having to be surgically transplanted. Finally, a tremendous obstacle to most organ transplants is tissue rejection, which occurs when the recipient's immune system attacks the transplanted (foreign) tissue. Stem cells seem to provoke a weaker immune response than adult cells.

### The Source of Human Stem Cells

Traditionally most human embryonic stem cells have come from very early-stage human embryos, in the first several days after fertilization. At this stage all of the eight or fewer cells are still undifferentiated. Currently, the only available embryos of this age are those created "in excess of clinical need" by *in vitro* fertilization at private fertility clinics. Only a few researchers have access to such embryos.

However, cells used to treat specific diseases don't need to be completely undifferentiated. If nerve cells are needed, a good source of young cells is the very first neural tissue in the human fetus. Already, over 100 people with Parkinson's disease have received fetal nerve cell transplants worldwide, and some have shown measurable improvements in brain function. Nonliving human fetuses are much more common than "extra" embryos as a consequence of the more than one million legal abortions performed in the U.S. each year.

Not surprisingly, the use of human embryonic cells (or fetal tissues) is highly controversial. On one hand, patient advocacy groups recognize their potential benefits and promote efforts to harvest and use them. On the other, some human rights groups object strongly to harvesting or using human embryonic stem cells or fetal cells under any circumstances.

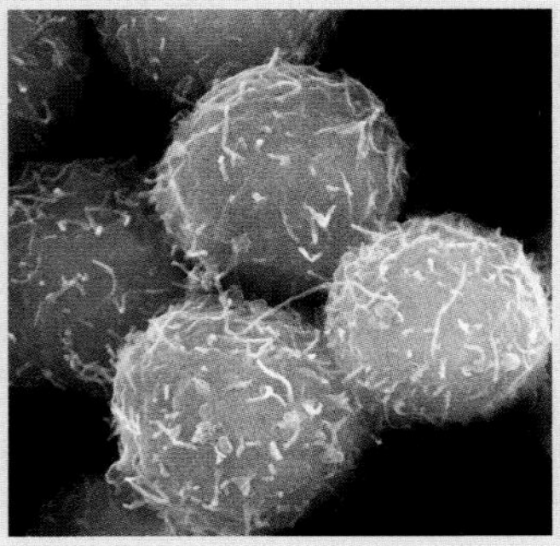

Stem cells.

### Objections to the Use of Human Embryonic Stem Cells

Objections to the use of stem cells generally concern human rights—specifically the status of the embryo or fetus from which they are obtained. Many people argue that an embryo or fetus is a human being, with the same legal rights as any other living person. Since an

## the *facts*...

- Stem cells obtained from human embryos may have the potential to treat or cure numerous diseases.
- The controversy over embryonic stem cell research centers on questions of human and legal rights.
- In the United States, stem cell research is limited by restrictive federal funding guidelines.
- As stem cell research in the United States slows, stem cell researchers are moving to other countries to continue their work.

*Many people object strongly to the harvesting and use of human embryonic stem cells.*

embryo or aborted fetus cannot give informed consent, opponents assert that stem cells derived from them should not be used under any circumstances, not even to help another person.

Others argue that an aborted fetus has the same standing as any other dead person—that is, as a cadaver. Cadaveric tissues and organs are routinely and legally used for research, teaching, and transplantation. According to the Uniform Anatomical Gift Act, the law governing the procurement of tissues or organs from a cadaver, consent may be given by the person before death (not possible for an embryo or fetus) or by family members after death. Although the parents are logically the people to make this decision, one could question whether parents who choose abortion are acting in the best interest of the fetus in the first place. The legal status of a frozen embryo is not clear.

According to current federal guidelines developed under the Bush administration in 2001, federal funds can only be used to study stem cell lines derived from embryos before 2001. (A stem cell "line" is a group of identical cells grown from a single stem cell). In effect, the 2001 federal guidelines prohibited the National Institutes of Health, which funds most biomedical research, from funding any stem cell research that might require the future death of a human embryo. However, the guidelines stopped short of prohibiting human stem cell research altogether; privately funded human embryonic stem cell research is still permitted under certain conditions.

These guidelines are a political compromise at best. They allow selected federally funded research projects to go forward with the few stem cell lines that already existed at the time the law was passed (2001), while respecting concerns about the sanctity of human life. Of course, the guidelines are opposed by stem cell researchers, who contend that only about 10 cell lines are still available today—not enough for medical purposes. They worry that, as the debate rages on, the U.S. will fall farther behind in this important research area. Some stem cell researchers have already moved to Britain, which recently funded a facility for storing thousands of cell lines, or to other places in the world.

Not long after the change in the federal guidelines, several states took steps to allocate state funds for stem cell research, bypassing federal funding mechanisms entirely. In a move that is being closely watched by other states, in 2004 California voters approved a landmark $3 billion in public money over 10 years for stem cell research. The initiative is already under attack by public-interest groups. Some of the top universities are also getting into the act. Harvard University, Stanford University, and the University of Michigan, among others, have all announced plans to develop stem cell research centers without the support of government funds.

Actor Brad Pitt supported California's Proposition 71, which provides public money for stem cell research.

### New Research Offers Hope, But How Much?

In the midst of all this controversy, new research published in 2007 has raised the hope that someday in the far distant future, the use of human embryonic stem cells could simply become a nonissue. Two groups of scientists, one in Kyoto, Japan, and the other in Madison, Wisconsin, have succeeded in reprogramming skin cells so that they became stem cells once again. The feat involved the insertion of a set of four human genes into the cells using viral vectors to deliver the genes. Numerous press reports hailed the research as a breakthrough and speculated that before long, human embryonic stem cells would not be required at all. But some scientists caution that new techniques for creating new stem cell lines may not necessarily translate quickly into cures for specific diseases. It would be a shame if a well-meaning public, convinced that human embryonic stem cells are no longer necessary, came to accept laws that severely restrict human embryonic stem cell research in this country. Although the day may yet come when human embryonic stem cells truly aren't necessary, that day has not yet arrived. Just ask Michael J. Fox.

### Questions to consider

**1** *Do you think the federal government should relax its current restrictive guidelines regarding stem cell research?*

**2** *Suppose that you and your spouse held frozen embryos at a private fertility clinic and that you knew you would never want them. Would you donate them for stem cell research? Why or why not?*

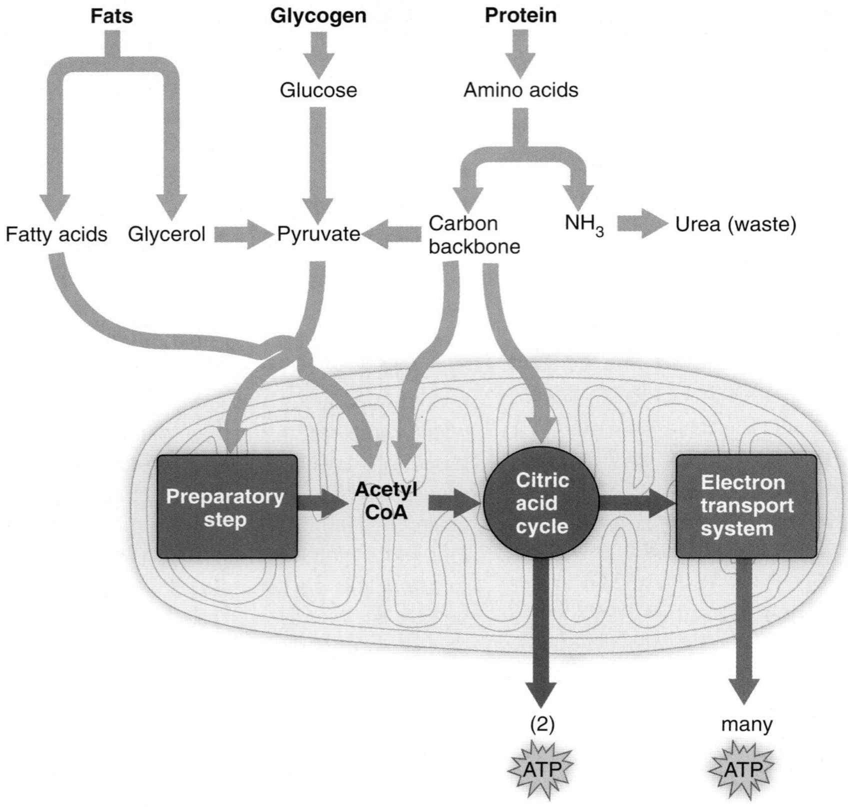


**Figure 3.30 Metabolic pathways for fats, glycogen, and proteins as sources of cellular energy.** All three sources produce pyruvate and acetyl groups. In addition, a few components of protein can enter the citric acid cycle directly.

preparatory step, and the citric acid cycle is accomplished by a sequence of over 20 different chemical reactions, each controlled by an enzyme. The net yield of high-energy molecules (prior to the electron transport chain) is four molecules of ATP, ten molecules of NADH, and two molecules of $FADH_2$. Each NADH carries sufficient energy to produce about three ATP molecules in the electron transport system. $FADH_2$ carries less energy, enters the electron transport chain at a lower energy point, and so produces only about two ATP molecules per $FADH_2$ molecule. Add it all up and you should get about 38 ATP molecules per glucose molecule.

But there's a catch. Two of the NADH (the two produced during glycolysis) were produced in the cytoplasm. Yet the electron transport system utilizes NADH located in the inner compartment of the mitochondria. Since the inner mitochondrial membrane is impermeable to NADH, the cytosolic NADH molecules release their $H^+$ ions and electrons, which are then transported across by transport proteins. Once inside, they may be picked up again by other $NAD^+$ molecules. But every transfer and active transport results in a small energy loss—in this case it's the equivalent of about two ATP molecules. Therefore, the net maximum yield of energy from a single glucose molecule is closer to 36 ATP molecules. In fact it may be even lower than that because some of the energy may be used directly to do other work for the cell, but for the sake of simplicity we'll settle on a number of 36.

**RECAP**

The electron transport system in the inner membrane of mitochondria converts the energy in the $H^+$ ions and electrons carried by $FADH_2$ and NADH to ATP. Stripped of their energy, the low-energy $H^+$ ions and electrons combine with oxygen, yielding water. In total, a single molecule of glucose yields about 36 molecules of ATP for the cell. ■

## Fats and proteins are additional energy sources

So far we have concentrated on the cellular catabolism of glucose. Normally the blood glucose concentration remains fairly constant even between meals because glycogen (the storage form of glucose in humans) is constantly being catabolized to replenish the glucose that is used by cells.

However, most of the body's energy reserves do not take the form of glycogen. In fact, the body stores only about 1% of its total energy reserves as glycogen; about 78% are stored as fats and 21% as protein. After glycogen, our bodies may utilize fats and proteins. Figure 3.30 illustrates the metabolic pathways for fat, glycogen, and protein.

Energy is constantly being transferred into and out of the body. Immediately after a meal, when plenty of glucose, lipids, and amino acids are readily available in the blood, we tend to use primarily glucose as an energy source. When we eat more calories than we can use immediately, some of the excess energy goes to replenish the body's stores of glycogen and the rest is converted to fat and stored in fat tissue. After we have not eaten for hours, the body uses glycogen and eventually fats and even proteins for energy.

Pound for pound, fats carry more than twice the energy of carbohydrates such as glycogen. During fat catabolism, triglycerides (the storage form of fat) are first broken down to glycerol and fatty acids. The glycerol can be converted to glucose in the liver or it can be converted to pyruvic acid, which then enters the citric acid cycle. Enzymes break down the fatty acid tails to two-carbon acetyl groups, which also enter the citric acid cycle. Each molecule of triglyceride yields a great deal of ATP because the fatty acid tails are generally 16–18 carbons long and so generate many acetyl groups.

Proteins carry about the same amount of energy per pound as glycogen. Proteins are first broken down to amino acids, and the amine group ($-NH_2$) of each amino acid is removed. The carbon backbones then enter the citric acid cycle at various points, depending on the specific amino acid. The amine groups are converted to urea by the liver and then excreted in urine as waste.

Proteins serve primarily as enzymes and structural components of the body, not as a stored form of energy. Nevertheless, protein catabolism increases significantly during starvation. Prolonged protein catabolism causes muscle wasting, but at least it keeps the individual alive.

## Anaerobic pathways make energy available without oxygen

As we have seen, cellular respiration requires oxygen to complete the chemical reactions of the citric acid cycle and the electron transport chain. However, a small amount of ATP *can* be made in humans by anaerobic metabolism (without oxygen) for at least brief periods of time. Glycolysis, for example, is an anaerobic metabolic pathway. In the absence of oxygen, glucose is broken down to pyruvate (glycolysis occurs), but then the pyruvate cannot proceed through the citric acid cycle and electron transport chain (Figure 3.31). Instead, the pyruvate is converted to *lactic acid*. The buildup of lactic acid is what causes the burning sensation and cramps associated with muscle fatigue when not enough oxygen is available to muscle tissue. When oxygen becomes available again, the lactic acid is metabolized by aerobic pathways.

Because glycolysis is the only step that can occur without oxygen, glucose (and glucose derived from glycogen) is the only fuel that can be used under anaerobic conditions. The amounts of ATP are very limited, however; only two molecules of ATP are produced per molecule of glucose instead of the usual 36.

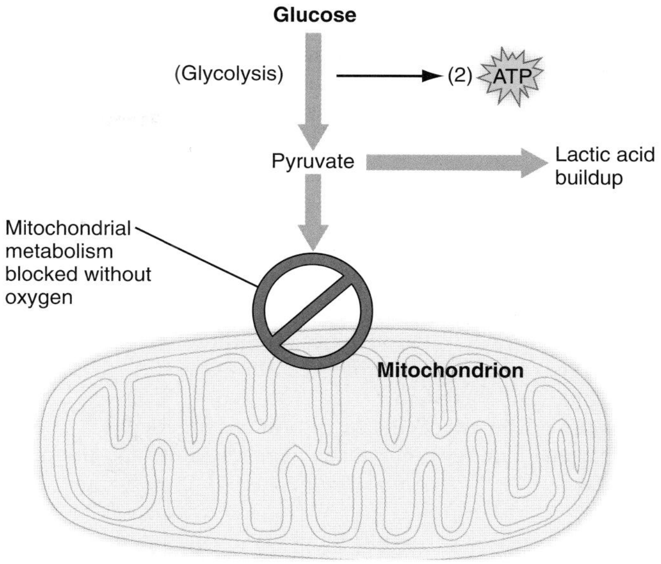


**Figure 3.31 Anaerobic metabolism.** In the absence of oxygen, glycolysis is the only ATP-producing step available. Glycolysis without oxygen results in lactic acid buildup.

**RECAP**

Carbohydrates and fats are the main sources of stored energy for making ATP, although proteins can be used if necessary. In the absence of oxygen, only glucose can be used, and only very limited amounts of ATP are produced. ■

# Chapter Summary

### Cells are classified according to their internal organization *p. 49*

- All cells have a plasma membrane that surrounds and encloses the cytoplasm.
- Eukaryotic cells have a nucleus.

### Cell structure reflects cell function *p. 49*

- Limits to cell size are imposed by the mathematical relationship between cell volume and cell surface area.
- Various types of microscopes with magnifications up to 100,000-fold enable us to visualize cells and their structures.

### A plasma membrane surrounds the cell *p. 52*

- The plasma membrane is a bilayer of phospholipids that also contains cholesterol and various proteins.

### Molecules cross the plasma membrane in several ways *p. 53*

- Some molecules are transported across the plasma membrane passively (by diffusion), whereas others are transported by active processes requiring the expenditure of energy.
- Receptor proteins transfer information across the plasma membrane.
- The sodium-potassium pump is a plasma membrane protein with a critical role in the maintenance of cell volume.

### Internal structures carry out specific functions *p. 58*

- The nucleus directs all of the cell's activities.
- Ribosomes, the endoplasmic reticulum, and the Golgi apparatus participate in the synthesis of life's molecules.
- Vesicles are membrane-bound spheres that transport, store, and ship cellular products and toxic or dangerous materials.
- Mitochondria make energy available for the cell in the form of the high-energy molecule ATP.

### Cells have structures for support and movement *p. 64*

- A cytoskeleton of microtubules and microfilaments serves as structural support and anchors the various organelles.
- Cilia and flagella provide for movement in certain types of cells. Both cilia and flagella are made of pairs of protein microtubules.

### Cells use and transform matter and energy *p. 65*

- The creation and destruction of molecules either requires energy or liberates energy.
- The most readily useful form of energy for cells is ATP.
- The production of ATP from glucose requires four consecutive stages: glycolysis, a preparatory step, the citric acid cycle, and the electron transport system.
- Cells can utilize glycogen, fats, or proteins for energy.
- Only a small amount of ATP can be made in the absence of oxygen.

## Terms You Should Know

active transport, *55*
citric acid cycle, *68*
cytoskeleton, *64*
diffusion, *53*
electron transport system, *70*
endocytosis/exocytosis, *56*
endoplasmic reticulum (ER), *60*
glycolysis, *67*
Golgi apparatus, *60*
metabolism, *65*
mitochondria, *63*
$NAD^+$/NADH, *68*
osmosis, *54*
passive transport, *53*
plasma membrane, *49*
ribosome, *60*
sodium-potassium pump, *56*
vesicles, *56*

## Concept Review

1. Explain why being small is advantageous to a cell.
2. List the basic tenets of the *cell doctrine*.
3. Describe how phospholipids are oriented in the plasma membrane and why they orient naturally that way.
4. Define *passive transport* and name the three passive transport methods that are used to transport different molecules across the plasma membrane.
5. Compare and contrast endocytosis and exocytosis.
6. Describe the activity of the sodium-potassium pump and indicate its importance to the cell.
7. Explain what happens to cells placed in a high-salt or a low-salt environment, and why.
8. Define *vesicles* and name at least two different types of vesicles.
9. What are the four stages of ATP production from glucose, and which one yields the most ATP?
10. Describe what happens to a cell's ability to produce ATP when oxygen is not available.

## Test Yourself

### Matching Exercise

_____ 1. Microscopic structures within the cell other than the nucleus
_____ 2. The net diffusion of water across a selectively permeable membrane
_____ 3. Diffusion of molecules across the cell membrane using transport proteins
_____ 4. The information center of a living cell
_____ 5. The packaging and shipping center of the cell
_____ 6. The process whereby glucose is split into two 3-carbon molecules, yielding two molecules of ATP

a. facilitated transport
b. glycolysis
c. organelles
d. golgi apparatus
e. nucleus
f. osmosis

### Fill in the Blank

7. The plasma membrane consists of phospholipids, _______________, and proteins.
8. Cells that have a nucleus and organelles are called _______________, while those that lack these structures are called _______________.
9. Ribosomes may float freely in the cell or may be attached to the _______________.
10. Vesicles in the cell called _______________ contain digestive enzymes that fuse with other vesicles containing bacteria.
11. The _______________ is a repetitive cycle in which two-carbon acetyl groups are broken down to $CO_2$, $H^+$, and electrons.
12. In the absence of oxygen, the catabolism of glucose produces _______________, which can cause a burning sensation and may contribute to muscle cramps.

### True or False?

13. Large animals have correspondingly larger cells.
14. The most immediately useful form of energy for most cells is ATP.
15. The sodium-potassium pump actively transports both sodium and potassium out of the cell.

## References and Additional Reading

Becker, Wayne M., Jane B. Reece, and Martin F. Phoenie. *The World of the Cell.* Menlo Park, CA: Benjamin Cummings, 2008. (A comprehensive textbook of cell biology for the student particularly interested in this subject.)

Financial Times & Scientific American Special Report 2005: *The Future of Stem Cells.* (32 pages of articles about stem cells by more than a dozen authors.)

Margulis, Lynn, and Dorian Sagan. *What Is Life?* New York: Simon & Schuster, 1995. (An evolutionary, comparative, and sometimes philosophical look at this age-old question. Well illustrated.)

Sherer, W. F., J. T. Syverton, and G. O. Gey. Studies on the Propagation in Vitro of Poliomyelitis Viruses. IV. Viral Multiplication in a Stable Strain of Human Malignant Epithelial Cells (Strain HeLa) Derived from an Epidermoid Carcinoma of the Cervix. *Journal of Experimental Medicine* 97:695–709, 1953. (The original research paper describing HeLa cells; of historical significance for the especially interested student only.)

Thomas, Lewis. *The Lives of a Cell: Notes of a Biology Watcher.* New York: Viking Press, 1994. (A classic, easy-to-read series of essays.)

## Apply **What You Know**

1. Imagine that you are shown two cells under the microscope. One is small, has lots of mitochondria, and contains numerous glycogen granules. The other is somewhat larger and has only a few mitochondria and no glycogen granules. Which cell do you think is more metabolically active? Explain your reasoning.
2. The sodium-potassium pump is a large protein molecule. Where do you think the sodium-potassium pumps are made in the cell, and how do you think they become inserted into the lipid bilayer of the plasma membrane?
3. Mitochondria resemble a bacterial cell in a number of ways. Some scientists hypothesize that mitochondria evolved from aerobic prokaryotes that were engulfed by anaerobic eukaryotes, and now both have evolved together in a mutually advantageous way. Can you think of an explanation for why it might have been advantageous for both cells to enter into such an arrangement?
4. You have decided that you need to lose a little weight. You have heard a lot about no-carbohydrate and low-carbohydrate diets, and you have decided to use one of these diet plans. Explain how a low-carbohydrate diet works. Can you think of any possible negative side effects of such a diet?
5. Recently a young man from Derby in the United Kingdom entered a contest and drank 26 pints of water in a very short time. He later died of complications due to hypotonic hydration, also known as water intoxication. How were his body's cells affected by the excess water, and how might that have contributed to his death?
6. You have been selected to serve on a jury for a trial involving a young man accused of public intoxication. His defense attorney argues that the alcohol found in his system was the result of natural fermentation; that he had just finished a grueling one-hour workout during which his body could not meet the oxygen demand, and that the excess lactic acid that was produced during the exercise was then converted to alcohol by the process of lactic acid fermentation. Should you believe the defense attorney? Explain why or why not.

*Answers can be found on the Human Biology Place.*

## Internet References

Find links to the following Web sites at the Human Biology Place.

**Cancerquest**
**www.cancerquest.org**
Created to teach the biology of cancer, but also gives a good overview of cell structure and function.

**National Institutes of Health: Stem Cell Information**
**http://stemcells.nih.gov**
This federal agency provides helpful information on stem cells, including a glossary, frequently asked questions, and an overview of U.S. and international research.

# 4 From Cells to Organ Systems

1 What is **homeostasis**, and why is the maintenance of homeostasis so important to multicellular living organisms?

2 **True or False?** When you lose weight you **lose fat cells**.

3 **True or False? Skin** is just a thick layer of dead cells that protects your body from injury and drying out.

4 What is a **controlled variable?**

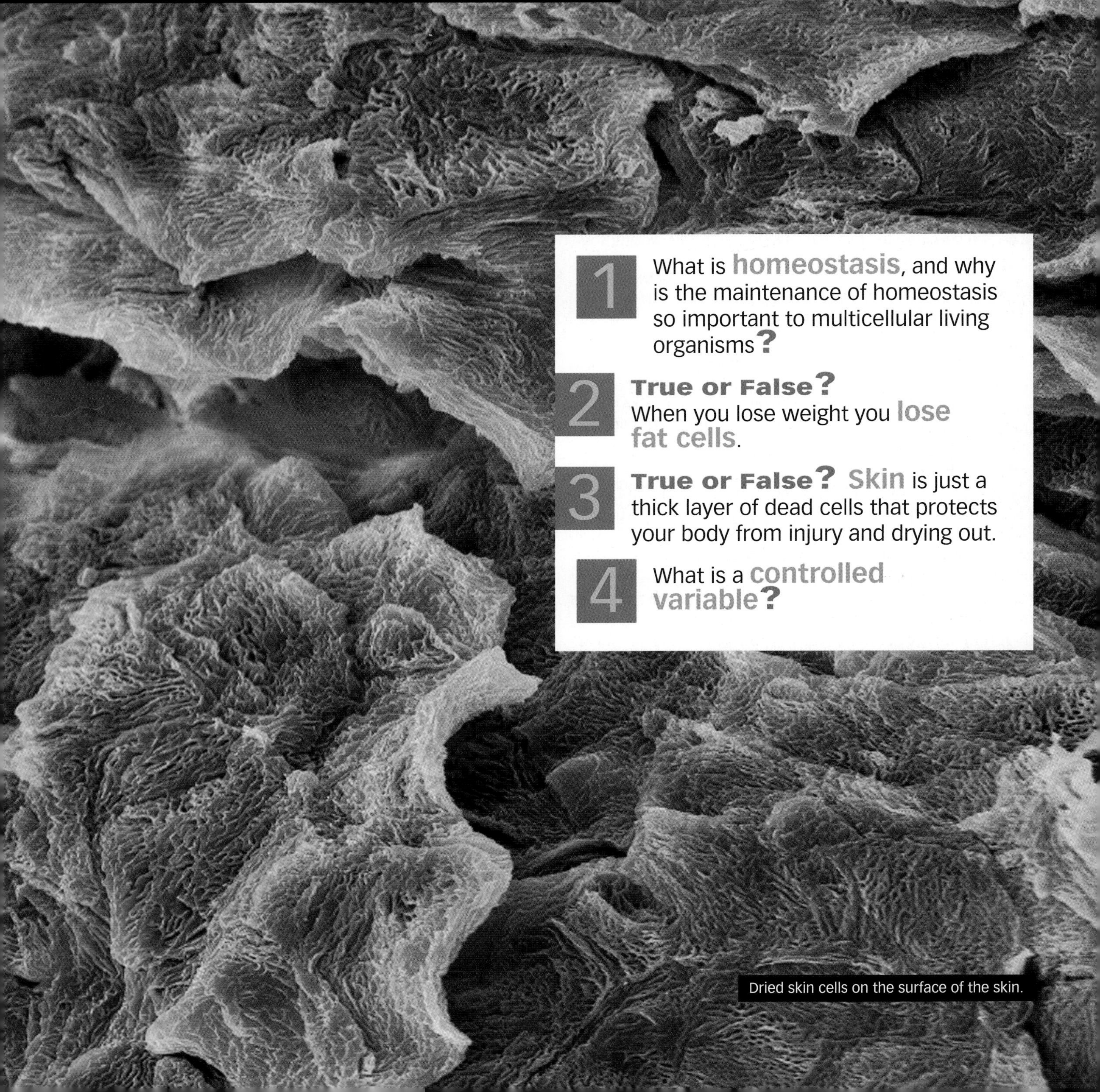

Dried skin cells on the surface of the skin.

**For nearly two-thirds of the history of life,** or more than two billion years, all organisms consisted of just one cell. There are still plenty of single-celled organisms today; in fact they far outnumber multicellular organisms. Theirs is a simple, uncomplicated life. They get their raw materials and energy from the fluid in which they are bathed, they dump their wastes into that same fluid, and they reproduce by dividing in two.

There are, however, disadvantages to being a single cell. The single-celled organism is completely at the mercy of its immediate external environment for every requirement of life. If the pond in which it lives dries up, it will die. If salt levels in the water rise, if the temperature gets too hot, or if its food runs out, it dies. There must be another way!

There is another way, and that is for cells to join together. In this chapter we look at how cells are organized into the tissues, organs, and organ systems that make up your body. We consider the structure and function of your skin as an example of an organ system. And we discuss how your cells, tissues, and organs work together to maintain the health and stability of your body.

## 4.1 Tissues are groups of cells with a common function

A *multicellular organism* consists of many cells that collectively share the functions of life. Advantages to multicellularity include greater size (the better to eat, rather than be eaten) and the ability to seek out or maintain an environment conducive to life.

All cells in a multicellular organism have a specialized function that benefits the organism in some way. However, specialization is not enough. The specialized functions must be organized and integrated if they are to be useful. As an example, the activity of a single cell in your heart is insignificant because the cell is so small. The beating of your heart requires that hundreds of thousands of such cells be arranged end to end, so that their functions are coordinated to produce a single heartbeat.

**Tissues** are groups of specialized cells that are similar in structure and that perform common functions. There are four major types of tissues: epithelial, connective, muscle, and nervous.

## 4.2 Epithelial tissues cover body surfaces and cavities

Most **epithelial tissues** consist of sheets of cells that line or cover various surfaces and body cavities. Two epithelial tissues you know about are your skin and the lining of your mouth. Other epithelial tissues line the inner surfaces of your digestive tract, lungs, bladder, blood vessels, and the tubules of your kidneys.

Epithelial tissues are more than just linings. They protect underlying tissues. Often they are smooth to reduce friction; the smooth epithelial tissue lining your blood vessels helps blood flow more easily through your body, for instance. Some are highly specialized for transporting materials. Epithelial tissues (and cells) absorb water and nutrients across your intestines into your blood. They also secrete waste products across the tubules of your kidneys so that you can eliminate them in urine.

A few epithelial tissues are *glandular epithelia* that form the body's glands. **Glands** are epithelial tissues that are specialized to synthesize and secrete a product. **Exocrine glands** (*exo*- means "outside" or "outward") secrete their products into a hollow organ or duct. Examples of exocrine glands are the glands in your mouth that secrete saliva, sweat glands in your skin, and glands in your stomach that produce digestive acid. **Endocrine glands** (*endo*- means "within") secrete substances called *hormones* into the bloodstream. One endocrine gland is the thyroid gland, which secretes several hormones that help regulate your body's growth and metabolism. We describe various glands throughout the book where appropriate.

### Epithelial tissues are classified according to cell shape

Biologists classify epithelial tissues into three types according to the shapes of the cells (Figure 4.1):

- *Squamous epithelium* consists of one or more layers of flattened cells. (*Squama* means "platelike." Think of

## Answers to Intro Questions

1 Homeostasis is a state of equilibrium (or relative constancy) of the "internal environment" of an organism. The internal environment of an organism includes the fluid that surrounds and bathes all of the organism's cells. Maintenance of homeostasis ensures that each cell is surrounded by a fluid environment that is compatible with life.

2 **False.** Fat cells get smaller when you lose weight, but they never go away.

3 **False.** Only the very outermost part of skin is made up of dead cells. It's easy to take our skin for granted, but as we'll see in this chapter, it is a living organ system that helps us in many crucial ways, including protecting us from injury and drying out.

4 A controlled variable is any chemical or any physical property that must be controlled in order to maintain homeostasis. Blood pressure and blood glucose concentration are examples of controlled variables.

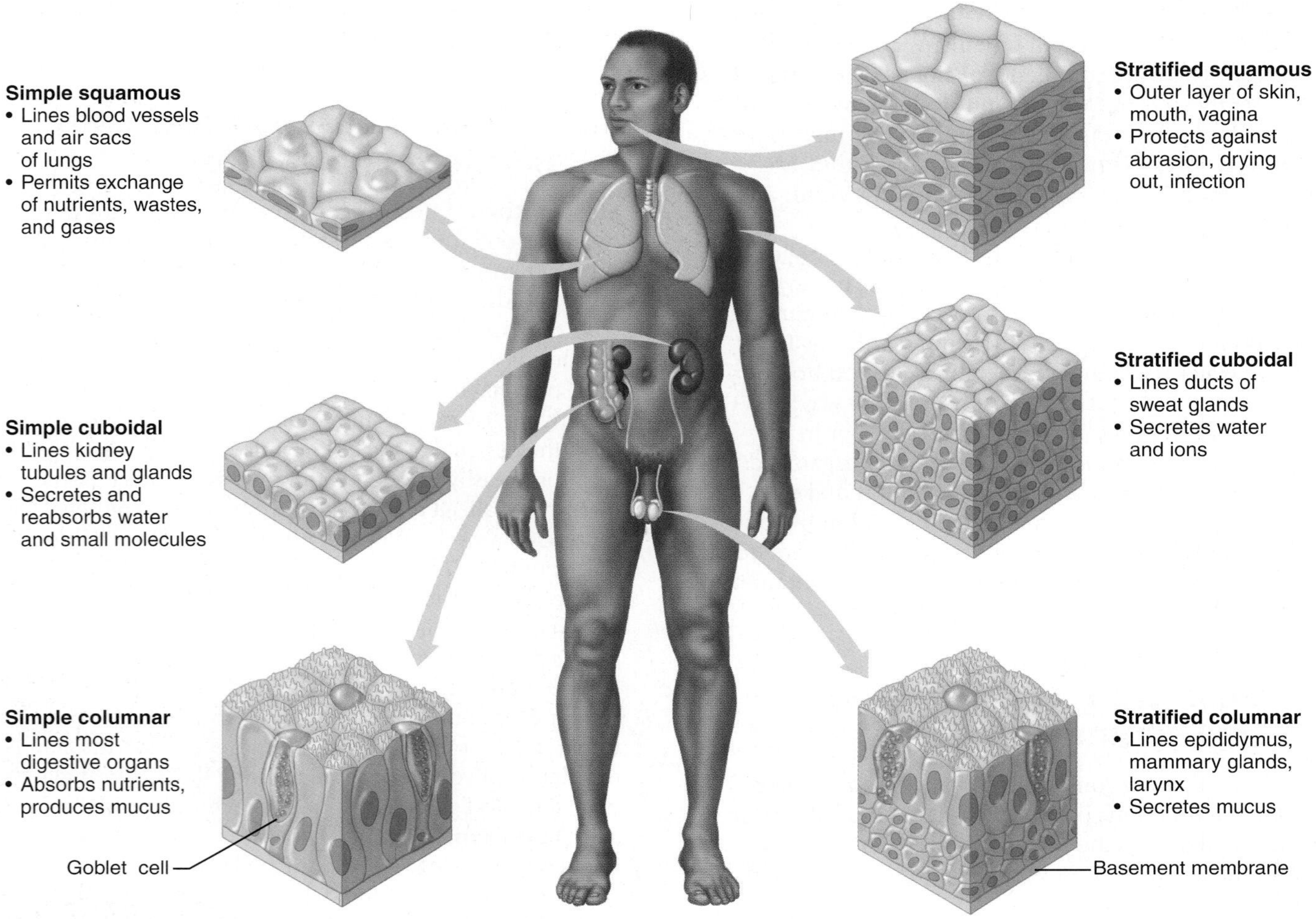


**a) Most epithelial tissues line or cover surfaces or body cavities**

**b) Glandular epithelia secrete a product**

**Figure 4.1 Types of epithelial tissues.**

squamous epithelium as "squashed flat.") Squamous epithelium forms the outer surface of the skin and lines the inner surfaces of the blood vessels, lungs, mouth and throat, and vagina.

- *Cuboidal epithelium* is composed of cube-shaped cells. Cuboidal epithelium forms the kidney tubules and also covers the surfaces of the ovaries.

- *Columnar epithelium* is composed of tall, rectangular (column-shaped) cells. Columnar epithelium lines parts of the digestive tract, certain reproductive organs, and the larynx. Certain cells within columnar epithelium, called *goblet cells,* secrete mucus, a thick fluid that lubricates the tissues and traps bacteria, viruses, and irritating particles.

Epithelial tissues are classified not only by shape but also by the number of cell layers in the tissue. A *simple epithelium* is a single layer of cells, whereas a *stratified epithelium* consists of multiple layers (or strata). Simple epithelium is so thin that molecules can pass through it easily. Stratified epithelium is thicker and provides protection for underlying cells.

### The basement membrane provides structural support

Directly beneath the cells of an epithelial tissue is a supporting noncellular layer called the **basement membrane** (Figure 4.1), and beneath that is generally a layer of connective tissue (described later). You can think of the basement membrane as the mortar that anchors the cells to the stronger connective tissue underneath. The basement membrane is composed primarily of protein secreted by the epithelial cells, and thus although noncellular, it is a cellular product. It should not be confused with the plasma membrane that is a part of every living cell.

In addition to being attached to a basement membrane, epithelial cells may be connected to each other by several types of **cell junctions** made up of various proteins. Three different types of junctions may hold the cells together, depending on the type of epithelial tissue (Figure 4.2):

- *Tight junctions* seal the plasma membranes of adjacent cells so tightly together that nothing can pass between the cells. Tight junctions are particularly important in epithelial layers that must control the movement of substances into or out of the body. Examples include the cells that line the digestive tract (which bring in nutrients) and the bladder (which stores urine), and the cells that form the tubules of the kidneys (which remove waste products from the body).
- *Adhesion junctions,* sometimes called "spot desmosomes," are looser in structure. The protein filaments of adhesion junctions allow for some movement between cells so that the tissues can stretch and bend. Adhesion junctions in the epithelium of your skin, for instance, allow you to move freely.
- *Gap junctions* represent connecting channels made of proteins that permit the movement of ions or water between two adjacent cells. They are commonly found in the epithelial cells in the liver, heart, and some muscle tissues.

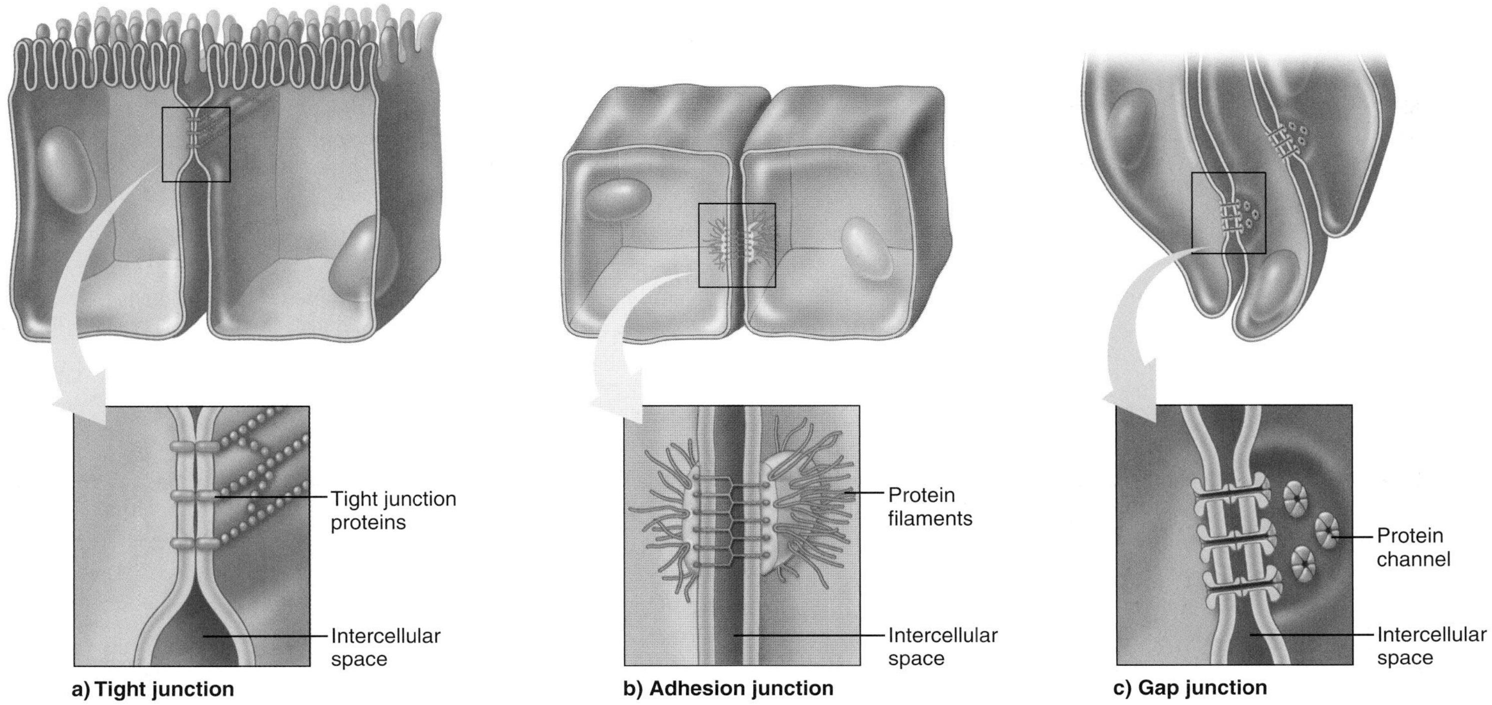


**Figure 4.2 Examples of junctions between cells.** Only one type of junction is generally present in any given tissue. **(a)** Tight junctions form leak-proof seals between cells. **(b)** Adhesion junctions anchor two cells together, yet allow flexibility of movement. **(c)** Gap junctions provide for the direct transfer of water and ions between adjacent cells.

**RECAP**

Epithelial tissues line body surfaces and cavities, and form glands. They are classified according to cell shape (squamous, cuboidal, or columnar) and the number of cell layers (simple or stratified). ■

## 4.3 Connective tissue supports and connects body parts

**Connective tissue** supports the softer organs of the body against gravity and connects the parts of the body together. It also stores fat and produces the cells of blood.

Unlike epithelial tissue, most connective tissues have few living cells. Most of their structure consists of nonliving extracellular material, the *matrix,* that is synthesized by connective tissue cells and released into the space between them. The strength of connective tissue comes from the matrix, not from the living cells themselves. The few living cells rarely make contact with each other, and so direct cell-to-cell junctions are not present.

Connective tissues are so diverse that any classification system is really a matter of convenience (Table 4.1). Broadly, we can divide them into fibrous and specialized connective tissues.

### Fibrous connective tissues provide strength and elasticity

*Fibrous connective tissues* connect various body parts, providing strength, support, and flexibility. Figure 4.3 shows the structural elements of fibrous connective tissue.

As indicated by their name, fibrous connective tissues consist of several types of fibers and cells embedded in a gel-like ground substance. **Collagen fibers,** made of protein, confer strength and are slightly flexible. Most fibrous connective tissues also contain thinner coiled **elastic fibers,** made primarily of the protein *elastin,* which can stretch without breaking. Some fibrous connective tissue also contains thinner fibers of collagen, called **reticular fibers,** that interconnect with each other. The reticular fibers often serve as an internal structural framework for some of the "soft" organs such as the liver, spleen, and lymph nodes.

The various fibers are embedded in a *ground substance* consisting of water, polysaccharides, and proteins that ranges in consistency from gel-like to almost rubbery. The ground substance contains several types of cells, among them fat cells, mast cells, various white blood cells (macrophages, neutrophils, lymphocytes, and plasma cells), and most importantly, **fibroblasts.** The fibroblasts are the cells responsible for producing and secreting the proteins that compose the collagen, elastic, and reticular fibers. The fat cells, of course, store fat, and both the mast

**Table 4.1 Types of connective tissues**

| Type | Structure | Attributes | Locations |
|---|---|---|---|
| *Fibrous Connective Tissue* | | | |
| Loose | Mostly collagen and elastin fibers in no particular pattern; more ground substance | Flexible but only moderately strong | Surrounds internal organs, muscles, blood vessels |
| Dense | Mostly collagen in a parallel arrangement of fibers; less ground substance | Strong | In tendons, ligaments, and the lower layers of skin |
| Elastic | High proportion of elastin fibers | Stretches and recoils easily | Surrounds hollow organs that change shape or size regularly |
| Reticular (lymphoid) | Mostly thin, interconnecting reticular fibers of collagen | Serves as a flexible internal framework | In soft organs such as liver, spleen, tonsils, and lymph glands |
| *Special Connective Tissues* | | | |
| Cartilage | Primarily collagen fibers in a ground substance containing a lot of water | Maintains shape and resists compression | Embryonic tissue that becomes bone. Also the nose, vertebral disks, and the lining of joint cavities |
| Bone | Primarily hard mineral deposits of calcium and phosphate | Very strong | Forms the skeleton |
| Blood | Blood cells, platelets, and blood fluid called plasma | Transports materials and assists in defense mechanisms | Within cardiovascular system |
| Adipose tissue | Primarily cells called adipocytes filled with fat deposits | Stores energy in the form of fat | Under the skin, around some internal organs |

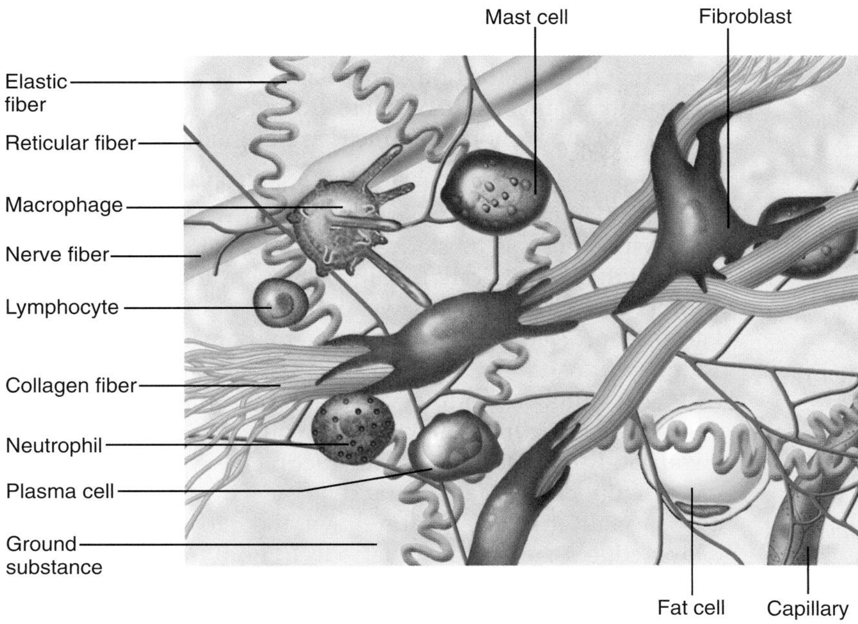


**Figure 4.3 Fibrous connective tissue.** The main elements are three types of fibers (collagen, elastic, and reticular) and a variety of cells (fibroblasts, fat cells, mast cells, and several types of white blood cells) in a ground substance of polysaccharides, proteins, and water. Blood vessels and nerves pass through or are associated with connective tissue. Fibrous connective tissues vary in their relative proportions of cells and fibers, and also in fiber orientation.

cells and white blood cells are involved in the body's immune system (Chapter 9).

Fibrous connective tissues are subclassified according to the density and arrangement of their fiber types:

- *Loose connective tissue* (Figure 4.4a), also called *areolar* connective tissue, is the most common type. It surrounds many internal organs, muscles, and blood vessels. Loose connective tissue contains a few collagen fibers and elastic fibers in no particular pattern, giving it a great deal of flexibility but only a modest amount of strength.
- *Dense connective tissue* (Figure 4.4b), found in tendons, ligaments, and lower layers of skin, has more collagen fibers. The fibers are oriented primarily in one direction, especially in the tendons and ligaments in and around our joints. Dense connective tissue is the strongest connective tissue when pulled in the same direction as the orientation of the fibers, but it can tear if the stress comes from the side. There are very few blood vessels in dense connective tissue to supply the few living cells. This is why, if you strain a tendon or ligament, it can take a long time to heal.
- *Elastic connective tissue* surrounds organs that have to change shape or size regularly. Examples include the stomach, which must stretch to accommodate food; the bladder, which stretches to store urine; and the vocal cords, which vibrate to produce sounds. Elastic connective tissue contains a high proportion of elastic fibers, which stretch and recoil easily.
- *Reticular connective tissue* (also called lymphoid tissue) serves as the internal framework of soft organs such as the liver and the tissues of the lymphatic system (spleen, tonsils, and lymph nodes). It consists of thin, branched reticular fibers (composed of collagen) that form an interconnected network.

**RECAP**

Fibrous connective tissues hold body parts together. Fibrous connective tissues contain extracellular fibers of strong but flexible proteins, a few living cells, and a ground substance of polysaccharides, proteins, and water. ■

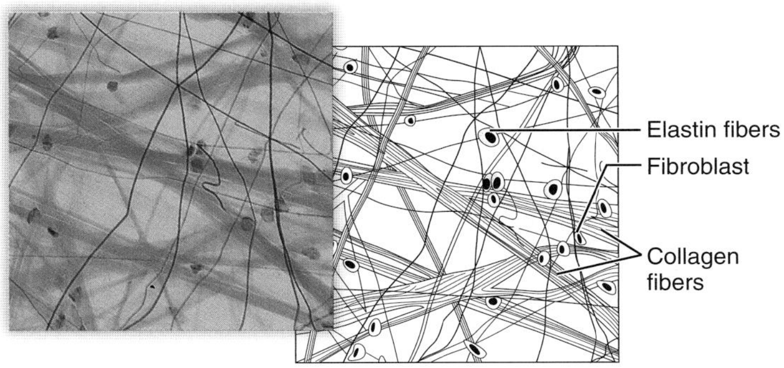


**a) Loose areolar connective tissue** (×160). In loose connective tissue the collagen and elastin fibers are arrayed in a random pattern.

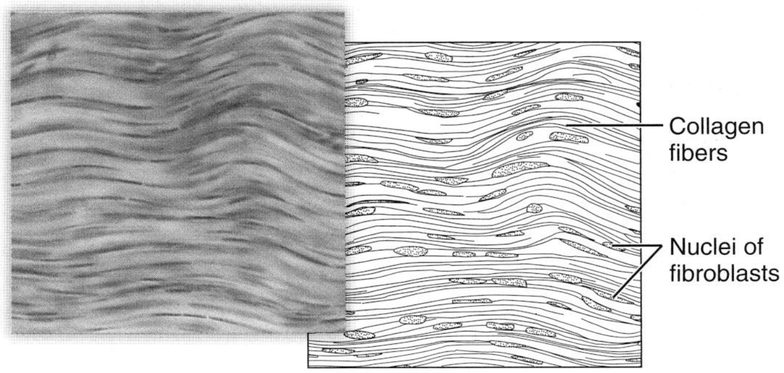


**b) Dense connective tissue** (×160). In dense connective tissue the fibers are primarily collagen fibers. In tendons and ligaments the fibers are oriented all in the same direction, with fibroblasts occupying narrow spaces between adjacent fibers.

**Figure 4.4 Examples of fibrous connective tissues.**

### Specialized connective tissues serve special functions

The so-called *specialized connective tissues* are a diverse group that includes cartilage, bone, blood, and adipose tissue. Each is specialized to perform particular functions in the body.

**Cartilage** **Cartilage** is the transition tissue from which bone develops (Chapter 5). It also maintains the shape of certain body parts (such as the soft tip of your nose) and protects and cushions joints. Disks of cartilage separate and cushion the vertebrae in your backbone, for instance, and cartilage forms the tough, smooth surfaces that reduce friction in some body joints.

Like dense connective tissue, cartilage consists primarily of collagen fibers. The two tissues differ in that the ground substance of cartilage, which is produced by cells called *chondroblasts,* contains a great deal more water. This is why cartilage functions so well as a cushion. As cartilage develops, the cells become enclosed in small chambers called *lacunae* (Figure 4.5a). There are no blood vessels in cartilage, so the mature cells (called *chondrocytes*) obtain their nutrients only by diffusion through the ground substance from blood vessels located outside the cartilage. Consequently, cartilage is slow to heal when injured.

**Bone** Like cartilage, **bone** is a specialized connective tissue that contains only a few living cells. Most of the matrix of bone consists of hard mineral deposits of calcium and phosphate. However, unlike cartilage, bone contains numerous blood vessels, and for this reason it can heal within four to six weeks after being injured. We discuss bone in more detail in Chapter 5 when we discuss the skeletal system.

**Blood** **Blood** consists of cells suspended in a fluid matrix called *plasma.* It is considered a connective tissue because all blood cells derive from earlier cells (called *stem cells*) located within bone. Red blood cells transport oxygen and nutrients to body cells and carry away the waste products of the cells' metabolism. White blood cells function in the immune system that defends the body, and platelets participate in the mechanisms that cause blood to clot following an injury. You will learn more about the functions of blood in Chapter 7.

**Adipose tissue** **Adipose tissue** is highly specialized for fat storage (Figure 4.5b). It has few connective tissue fibers and almost no ground substance. Most of its volume is occupied by **adipocytes** (fat cells). Adipose tissue is located primarily under the skin, where it serves as a layer of insulation. It also forms a protective layer around internal organs such as the kidneys.

The number of adipocytes you have is partly determined by your genetic inheritance. When you eat more food than your body can use, some of the excess energy is stored in your adipocytes as fat (the fat cells get "fatter"). When you lose weight the fat cells slim down, too. However, weight loss reduces the volume of fat cells but not their number. *Lipodissolve* is a controversial technique that disrupts fat cells chemically (see the Current Issue: "Is Lipodissolve a Good Way to Melt Away Fat?" on page 94).

**RECAP**

Among the specialized connective tissues, cartilage and bone provide support, blood transports materials throughout the body, and adipose tissue stores energy in the form of fat. ■

## 4.4 Muscle tissues contract to produce movement

**Muscle tissue** consists of cells that are specialized to shorten, or contract, resulting in movement of some kind. Muscle tissue is composed of tightly packed cells called muscle *fibers.* The fibers are generally long and thin and aligned parallel to

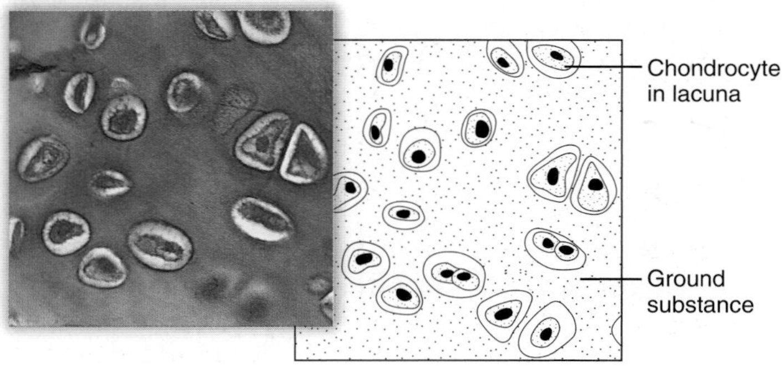


**a) Cartilage from the trachea** (×300). Mature cartilage cells, called chondrocytes, become trapped in chambers called lacunae within the hard, rubbery ground substance. Ground substance is composed of collagen fibers, polysaccharides, proteins, and water.

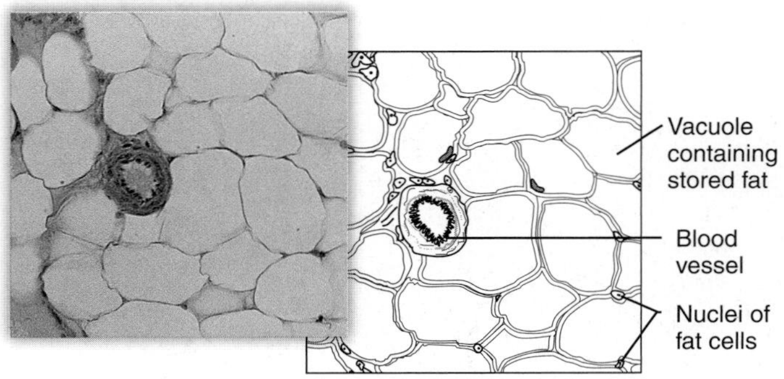


**b) Adipose tissue from the subcutaneous layer under the skin** (×140). Adipose tissue consists almost entirely of fat cells. The fat deposit within a fat cell can become so large that the nucleus is pushed to the side.

**Figure 4.5 Examples of special connective tissues.**

each other (Figure 4.6). The cytoplasm of a muscle fiber contains proteins, which interact to make the cell contract.

There are three types of muscle tissue: *skeletal, cardiac,* and *smooth.* They vary somewhat in body location, structure, and function, but they all do essentially the same thing—when stimulated, they contract. We devote an entire chapter (Chapter 6) to muscles as an organ system. For now, we focus on differences between the three types of muscle tissue.

### Skeletal muscles move body parts

**Skeletal muscle tissue** connects to tendons, which attach to bones. When skeletal muscles contract, they cause body parts to move. The individual fibers are thin cylinders too small to be seen with the naked eye, but they may be as long as the entire muscle (Figure 4.6a). Each muscle fiber has many nuclei, a phenomenon that comes about because many cells fuse end to end during development, producing one long fiber.

A skeletal muscle may contain thousands of individual fibers, all aligned parallel to each other. This parallel arrangement enables them to all pull together, shortening the muscle between its two points of attachment. Skeletal muscle is called *voluntary* muscle because we can exert conscious control over its activity.

### Cardiac muscle cells activate each other

**Cardiac muscle tissue** (Greek *kardia,* the heart) is found only in the heart. The individual cells are much shorter than skeletal muscle fibers, and they have only one nucleus (Figure 4.6b). Like skeletal muscle, the cells are arranged parallel to each other. Cardiac muscle cells are short and blunt-ended, with gap junctions between the ends of adjoining cells. The gap junctions represent direct electrical connections between adjoining cells, so when one cell is activated it activates its neighbors down the line. Because of these gap junctions, the entire heart contracts in a coordinated fashion.

Cardiac muscle is considered involuntary because the heart can contract rhythmically entirely on its own, without any conscious thought on our part and without any stimulation by nerves.

### Smooth muscle surrounds hollow structures

**Smooth muscle tissue** surrounds hollow organs and tubes, including blood vessels, digestive tract, uterus, and bladder. These slim cells are much smaller than skeletal muscle cells and have only one nucleus, like cardiac muscle (Figure 4.6c). The cells are aligned roughly parallel to each other. In blood vessels they are generally aligned in a circular fashion around the vessel. When smooth muscle cells shorten, the diameter of the blood vessel is reduced.

Smooth muscle cells taper at both ends, and there are gap junctions between adjacent cells so that when one contracts, nearby cells also contract. Like cardiac muscle, smooth muscle is involuntary in that we cannot control its contractions consciously.

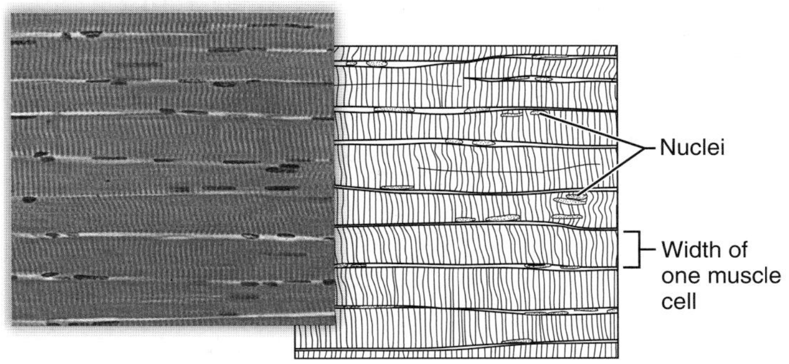


**a) Skeletal muscle** (×100). Skeletal muscle cells are very long and have many nuclei.

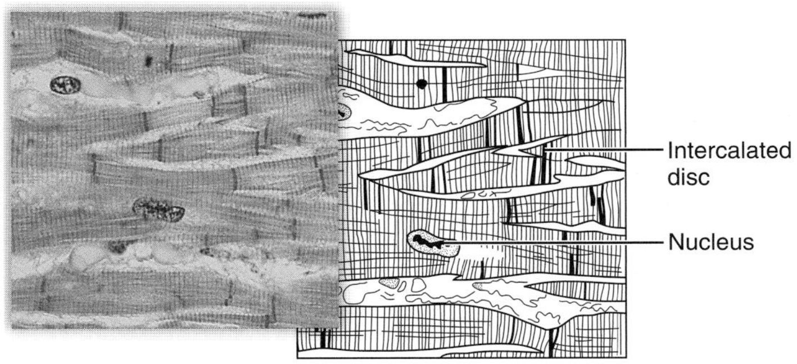


**b) Cardiac muscle** (×225). Cardiac muscle cells interconnect with each other.

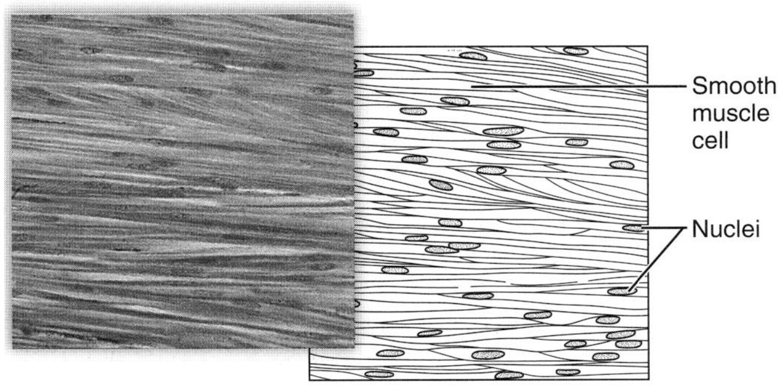


**c) Sheet of smooth muscle** (×250). Smooth muscle cells are thin and tapered.

**Figure 4.6 Muscle tissue.**

## 4.5 Nervous tissue transmits impulses

**Nervous tissue** consists primarily of cells that are specialized for generating and transmitting electrical impulses throughout the body. It forms a rapid communication network for the body. Nervous tissue is located in the brain, the spinal cord, and the nerves that transmit information to and from various organs. Chapter 11 is devoted to the nervous system, so we describe nervous tissue only briefly here.

Nervous tissue cells that generate and transmit electrical impulses are called **neurons** (Figure 4.7). Neurons can be as long as the distance from your spinal cord to the tip of your

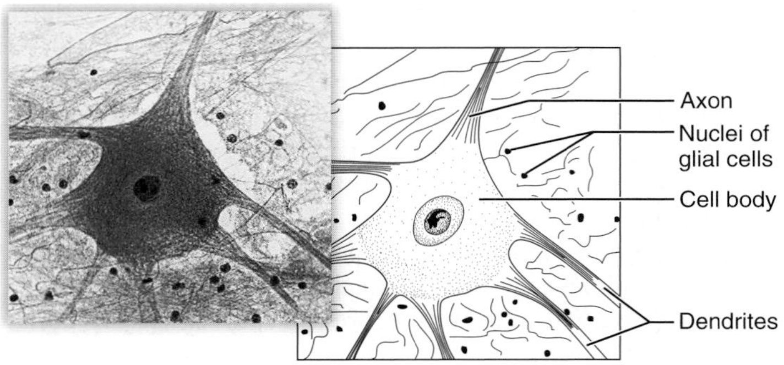


**Figure 4.7 Nervous tissue: a neuron (×170).** The neuron is the functional unit of nervous tissue. The single neuron shown here is surrounded by numerous supporting cells called glial cells. The cell bodies of the glial cells do not stain well, but their nuclei are clearly visible.

toe. Neurons typically have three basic parts: (1) the *cell body* where the nucleus is located; (2) *dendrites,* numerous cytoplasmic extensions that extend from the cell body and receive signals from other neurons; and (3) a long extension called an *axon* that transmits electrical impulses over long distances.

Nervous tissue also includes another type of cell called a **glial cell** that does not transmit electrical impulses. Glial cells play a supporting role by surrounding and protecting neurons and supplying them with nutrients.

**RECAP**

The common feature of all muscle tissues (skeletal, cardiac, and smooth) is that they contract, producing movement. Nervous tissues serve as a communication network by generating and transmitting electrical impulses. ■

## 4.6 Organs and organ systems perform complex functions

Many of the more complex functions of multicellular organisms (such as pumping blood or digesting food) cannot be carried out by one tissue type alone. **Organs** are structures composed of two or more tissue types joined together that perform a specific function or functions.

Your heart is an organ. Most of it consists of cardiac muscle, but there is also smooth muscle in the blood vessels that supply the cardiac muscle. The heart also contains nervous tissue that affects the rate at which the heart beats. It contains some connective tissue, primarily in the heart valves that open and close to control blood flow within the heart, and even a thin layer of epithelial tissue that lines the heart chambers. These tissues function together to pump blood, so together they constitute the organ known as the heart. Some organs have several functions. For example, the kidneys remove wastes and help control blood pressure.

### The human body is organized by organ systems

**Organ systems** are groups of organs that together serve a broad function that is important to survival either of the individual organism (such as respiration, movement, or excretion of wastes), or of the species (reproduction). A good example is the organ system responsible for the digestion of food. Your *digestive system* includes your mouth, throat, esophagus, stomach, intestines, and even your liver, pancreas, and gallbladder. All of these organs must interact and be controlled and coordinated to accomplish their overall function.

The figures on pages 88 and 89 depict the 11 organ systems of the human body. Some organ systems perform several functions and so are discussed in several chapters in this book. For example, the lymphatic system has important functions related to defense against disease, the circulation of certain body fluids, and digestion. Other organ systems are covered in a single chapter.

**RECAP**

An organ consists of several tissue types that join together to perform a specific function. An organ system is a group of organs that share a broad function important for survival. ■

### Tissue membranes line body cavities

Some of the organs and organ systems are located in hollow cavities within the body (Figure 4.8). The large anterior cavity is divided into the thoracic cavity and abdominal cavity by the diaphragm between them. The thoracic cavity is in turn divided into two pleural cavities, each containing a lung, and the pericardial cavity, which encloses the heart. The lower part of the abdominal cavity is sometimes called the pelvic cavity. The smaller posterior cavity consists of the cranial cavity and the spinal cavity (vertebral canal). There are many other smaller cavities as well, such as the synovial cavities in movable joints.

**Tissue membranes** consisting of a layer of epithelial tissue and a layer of connective tissue line each body cavity and form our skin. There are four major types of tissue membranes:

- *Serous membranes.* Line and lubricate body cavities to reduce friction between internal organs.
- *Mucous membranes.* Line the airways, digestive tract, and reproductive passages. Goblet cells within the epithelial layer secrete *mucus,* which lubricates the membrane's surface and entraps foreign particles.
- *Synovial membranes.* Line the very thin cavities between bones in movable joints. These membranes secrete a watery fluid that lubricates the joint.
- *Cutaneous membrane.* Our outer covering. You know it as skin, and it serves several functions discussed later in this chapter.

By now you may have noticed that "membrane" is a general term for a thin layer that covers or surrounds something.

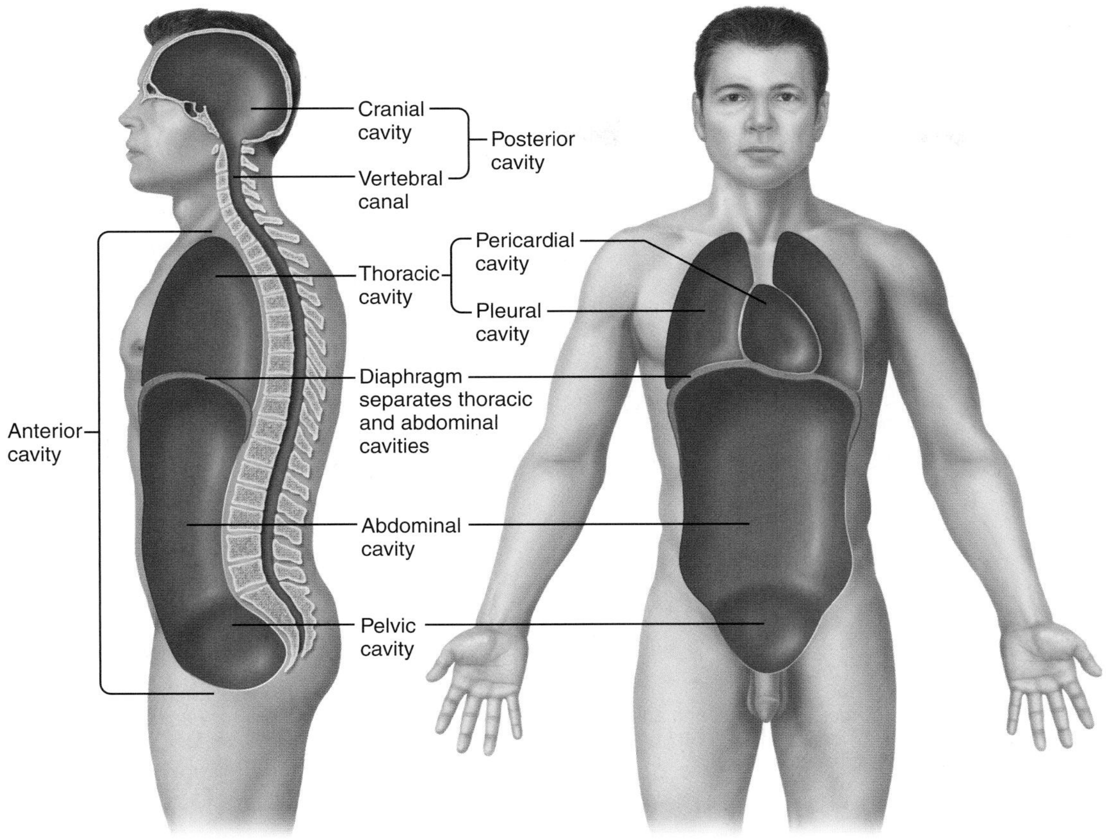


**Figure 4.8 The main body cavities.** The pelvic cavity and the abdominal cavity are continuous (not separated by a membrane).

**RECAP**

The body's hollow cavities are lined by tissue membranes that support, protect, and lubricate cavity surfaces. Locations of cavities and body parts are described relative to three planes (midsagittal, frontal, and transverse), using pairs of directional terms such as "anterior" and "posterior." ■

You have been introduced to three different membranes so far: the *plasma* membrane of phospholipids surrounding every cell, the *basement* membrane of extracellular material on which epithelial tissue rests, and *tissue* membranes consisting of several layers of tissue sandwiched together that cover or surround cavities, organs, and entire organ systems.

### Describing body position or direction

When describing parts of the body, biologists use precise terms to define position and direction. Generally speaking, an organ or even the entire body can be described by three planes known as the *midsagittal, frontal,* and *transverse* planes (Figure 4.9 on page 90). These planes divide the body into left and right, front and back, and top and bottom, respectively. *Anterior* means "at or near the front" and *posterior* means "at or near the back." *Proximal* means "nearer (in closer proximity) to" any point of reference, usually the body trunk, and *distal* means "farther away." For example, your wrist is distal to your elbow. *Superior* means "situated above" or "directed upward," and *inferior* means "situated below" or "directed downward." There are dozens of such terms, each with a precise meaning, defined as they occur in this book.

## 4.7 The skin as an organ system

The proper name for the skin and its accessory structures such as hair, nails, and glands is the **integumentary system** (from the Latin *integere,* meaning "to cover"). We describe the skin here as a representative organ system; other organ systems are covered later in the book.

### Skin has many functions

The skin has several different functions related to its role as the outer covering of the body:

- Protection from dehydration (helps prevent our bodies from drying out)
- Protection from injury (such as abrasion)
- Defense against invasion by bacteria and viruses
- Regulation of body temperature
- Synthesis of an inactive form of vitamin D
- Sensation: provides information about the external world via receptors for touch, vibration, pain, and temperature

### Skin consists of epidermis and dermis

Recall that skin is a tissue membrane, and that tissue membranes contain layers of epithelial and connective tissue. The outer layer of the skin's epithelial tissue is the **epidermis,** and the inner layer of connective tissue is the **dermis** (Figure 4.10 on page 91).

The skin rests on a supportive layer called the *hypodermis* (*hypo-* means "under"), consisting of loose connective tissue containing fat cells. The hypodermis is flexible enough to allow the skin to move and bend. The fat cells in the hypodermis insulate against excessive heat loss and cushion against injury.

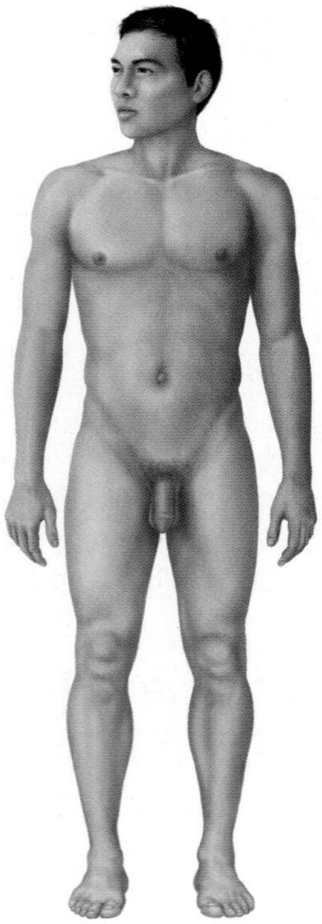

**Integumentary System**
- Protects us from injury, infection, and dehydration
- Participates in temperature control
- Receives sensory input from the external environment

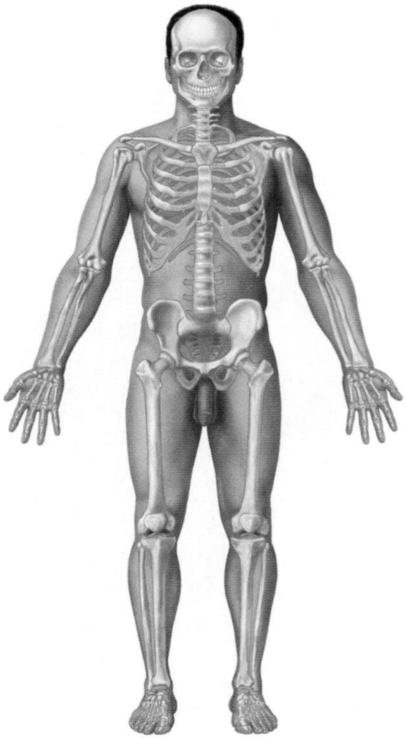

**Skeletal System**
- Protects, supports, and anchors body parts
- Provides the structural framework for movement
- Produces blood cells
- Stores minerals

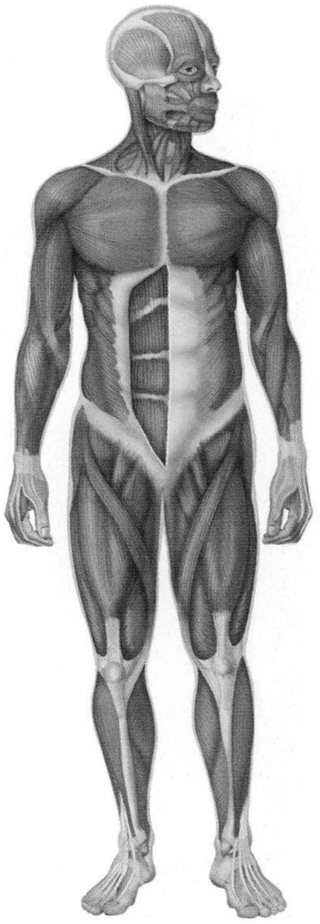

**Muscular System**
- Produces movement or resists movement
- Generates heat

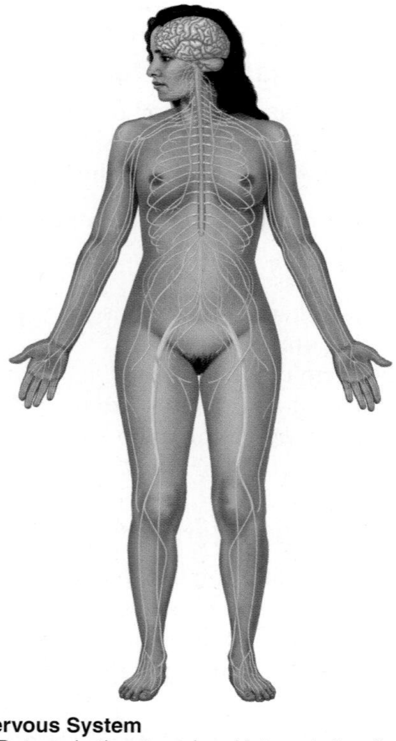

**Nervous System**
- Detects both external and internal stimuli
- Controls and coordinates rapid responses to these stimuli
- Integrates the activities of other organ systems

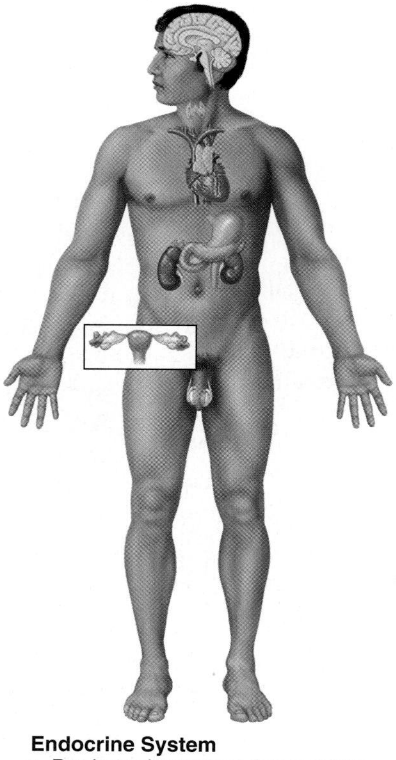

**Endocrine System**
- Produces hormones that regulate many body functions
- Participates with the nervous system in integrative functions

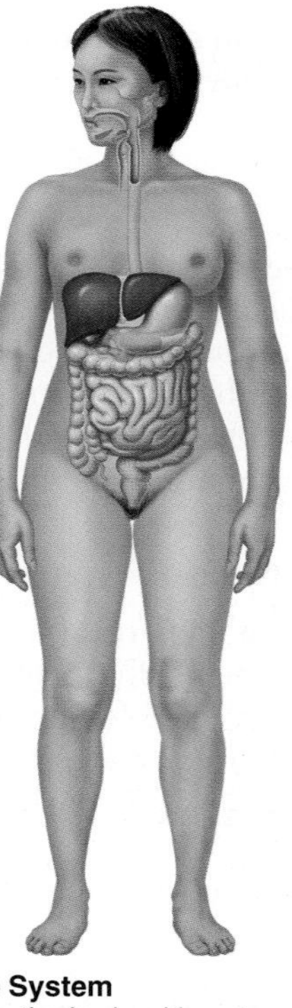

**Digestive System**
- Provides the body with water and nutrients
- (The liver) synthesizes certain proteins and lipids for the body
- (The liver) inactivates many chemicals, including hormones, drugs, and poisons

**The 11 organ systems of the human body.**

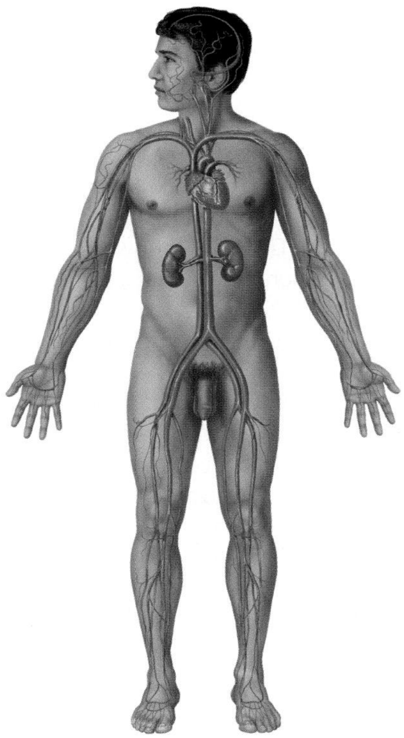

**Circulatory System**
- Transports materials to and from all cells
- Participates in the maintenance of body temperature
- Participates in mechanisms of defense against disease and injury

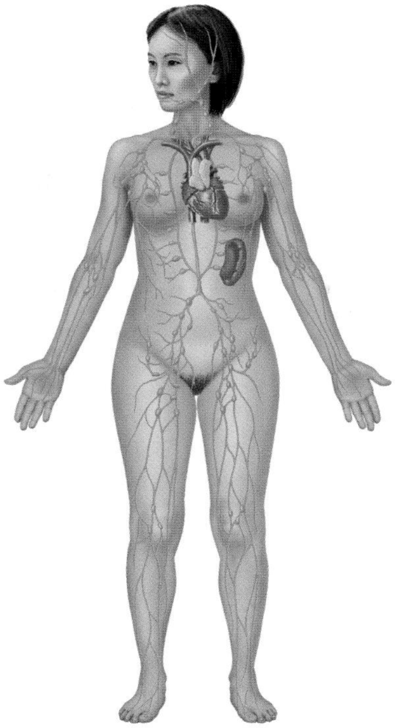

**Lymphatic System**
- Returns excess tissue fluid to the circulatory system
- Participates in both general and specific (immune) defense responses

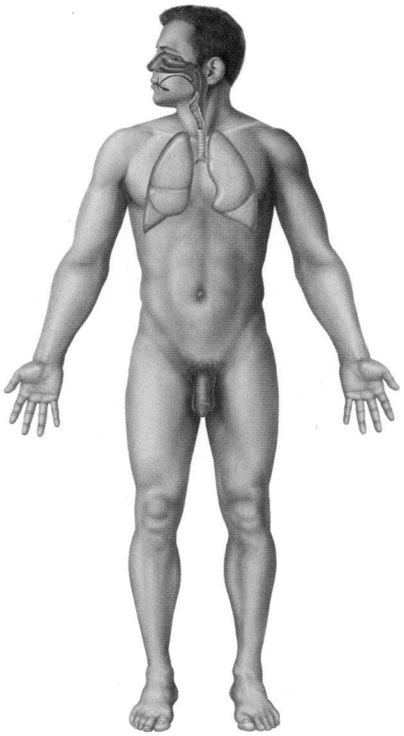

**Respiratory System**
- Exchanges gases (oxygen and carbon dioxide) between air and blood
- Participates in the production of sound (vocalization)

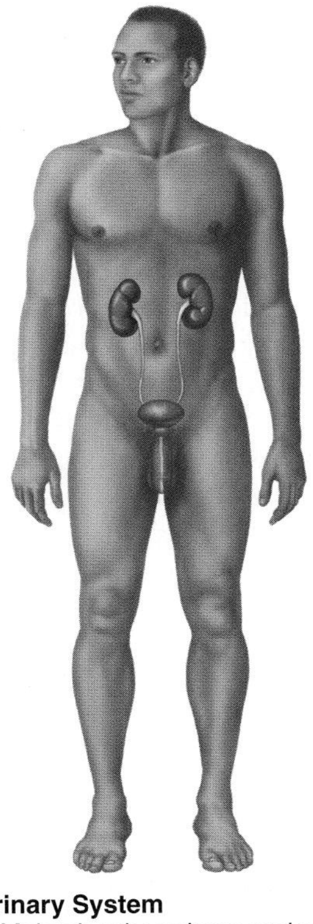

**Urinary System**
- Maintains the volume and composition of body fluids
- Excretes some waste products

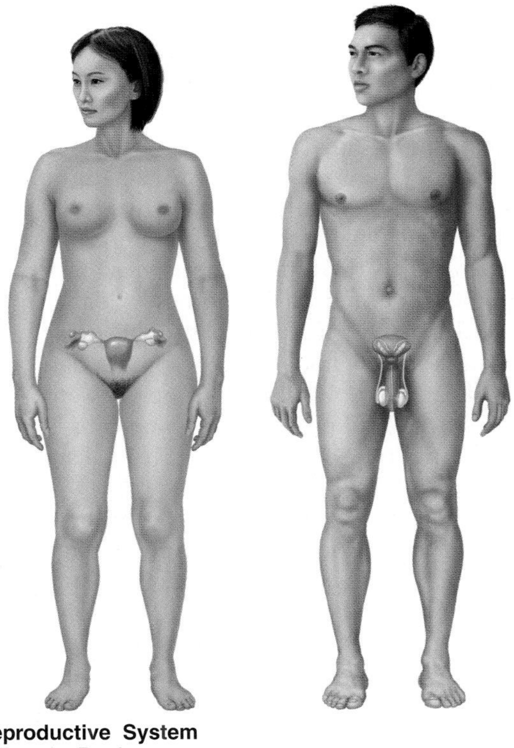

**Reproductive System**
- Female: Produces eggs
- Female: Nurtures the fertilized egg, developing embryo, and fetus until birth
- Male: Produces sperm
- Male: Participates in the delivery of sperm to the female

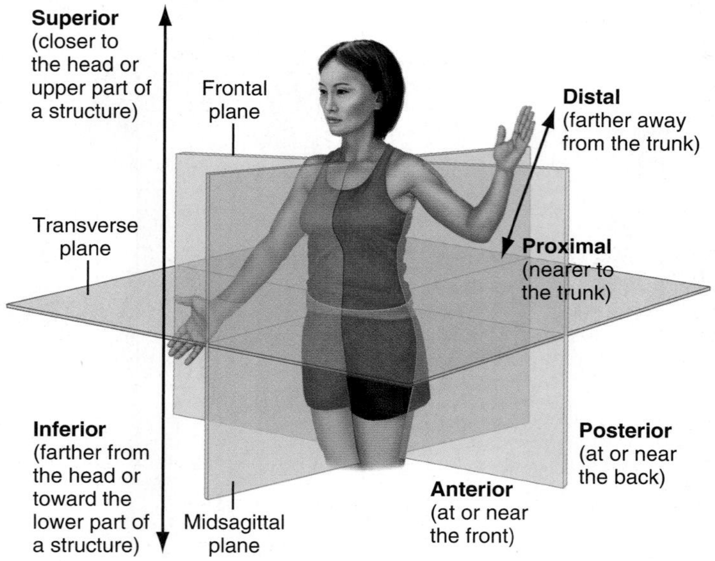


**Figure 4.9 Planes of symmetry and terms used to describe position or direction in the human body.** The frontal plane divides the body into anterior and posterior sections, the midsagittal plane divides it into left and right, and the transverse plane divides it into superior and inferior sections. Proximal and distal refer to points closer to or farther away from a point of reference, usually the trunk.

**Epidermal cells are replaced constantly** The epidermis consists of multiple layers of squamous epithelial cells. A key feature of the epidermis is that it is constantly being replaced as cells near the base of the epidermis divide repeatedly, pushing older cells toward the surface.

Two types of cell make up the epidermis: keratinocytes and melanocytes. The more numerous of the two cell types are **keratinocytes,** which produce a tough, waterproof protein called *keratin.* Actively dividing keratinocytes located near the base of the epidermis are sometimes called *basal cells.* As keratinocytes derived from the basal cells move toward the skin surface, they flatten and become squamous. Eventually they die and dry out, creating a nearly waterproof barrier that covers and protects the living cells below (Figure 4.11). The rapid replacement of keratinocytes allows the skin to heal quickly after injury.

One reason the outer layers of epidermal cells die is that the epidermis lacks blood vessels, so as mature cells are pushed farther from the dermis they can no longer obtain nutrients. The dead cells of the outer layers are shed over time, accounting for the white flakes you sometimes find on your skin or on dark clothing, especially when your skin is dry.

Less numerous cells called **melanocytes** located near the base of the epidermis produce a dark-brown pigment called *melanin.* Melanin accumulates inside keratinocytes and protects us against the sun's ultraviolet radiation. Exposure to sunlight increases the activity of melanocytes, accounting for the ability of some people to develop a suntan. Because all humans have about the same number of melanocytes, racial differences in skin color reflect either differences in melanocyte activity or differences in the rate of breakdown of melanin once it is produced.

**Fibers in dermis provide strength and elasticity** The dermis is primarily dense connective tissue, consisting of collagen, elastic, and reticular fibers embedded in a ground substance of water, polysaccharides, and proteins. The fibers allow the skin to stretch when we move and give it strength to resist abrasion and tearing. Our skin becomes less flexible and more wrinkled as we age because the number of fibers in the dermis decreases.

The surface of the dermis has many small projections called *papillae* that contain sensory nerve endings and small blood vessels. When the skin is rubbed excessively—such as when your shoes are too tight—the epidermis and dermis separate from each other and a fluid-filled blister develops between them.

The most abundant living cells in the dermis are the fibroblasts that produce the various fibers, but there are also mast cells, white blood cells, and occasional fat cells. Other structures in the dermis include:

- *Hair.* Each hair has a *shaft* above the skin's surface and a *root* below the surface. Hair is actually composed of several layers of cells enclosed in an outer layer of overlapping, dead, flattened keratinocytes. The root of a hair is surrounded by a sheath of several layers of cells called the *follicle.* The cells at the very base of the follicle are constantly dividing to form the hair root. As new hair cells are formed at the base, the hair root is pushed upward toward the skin's surface.
- *Smooth muscle.* Attached to the base of the hair follicle, it contracts when you are frightened or cold, causing your hair to become more erect.
- *Sebaceous glands.* Also known as oil glands, these secrete an oily fluid that moistens and softens hair and skin.
- *Sweat glands.* These produce sweat, a watery fluid containing dissolved ions, small amounts of metabolic wastes, and an antibiotic peptide called *dermicidin.* Sweat helps regulate body temperature and protects against bacteria.
- *Blood vessels.* These supply the cells of the dermis and epidermis with nutrients and remove their wastes. The blood vessels also help regulate body temperature. They dilate to facilitate heat loss when we are too hot and constrict to prevent heat loss when we are too cool. The dermis also contains lymph vessels, which drain fluids and play a role in the immune system.
- *Sensory nerve endings.* These provide information about the outside environment. Separate receptors exist to detect heat, cold, light touch, deep pressure, and vibration. You will learn more about these nerve endings in Chapter 12.

As mentioned earlier, the skin synthesizes an inactive form of vitamin D. It is not known which cell type in the skin is responsible. But we do know that a cholesterol-like molecule in the skin becomes an inactive form of vitamin D when it is exposed to the ultraviolet rays of sunlight. The inactive form must then be modified in the liver and kidneys before it becomes active.

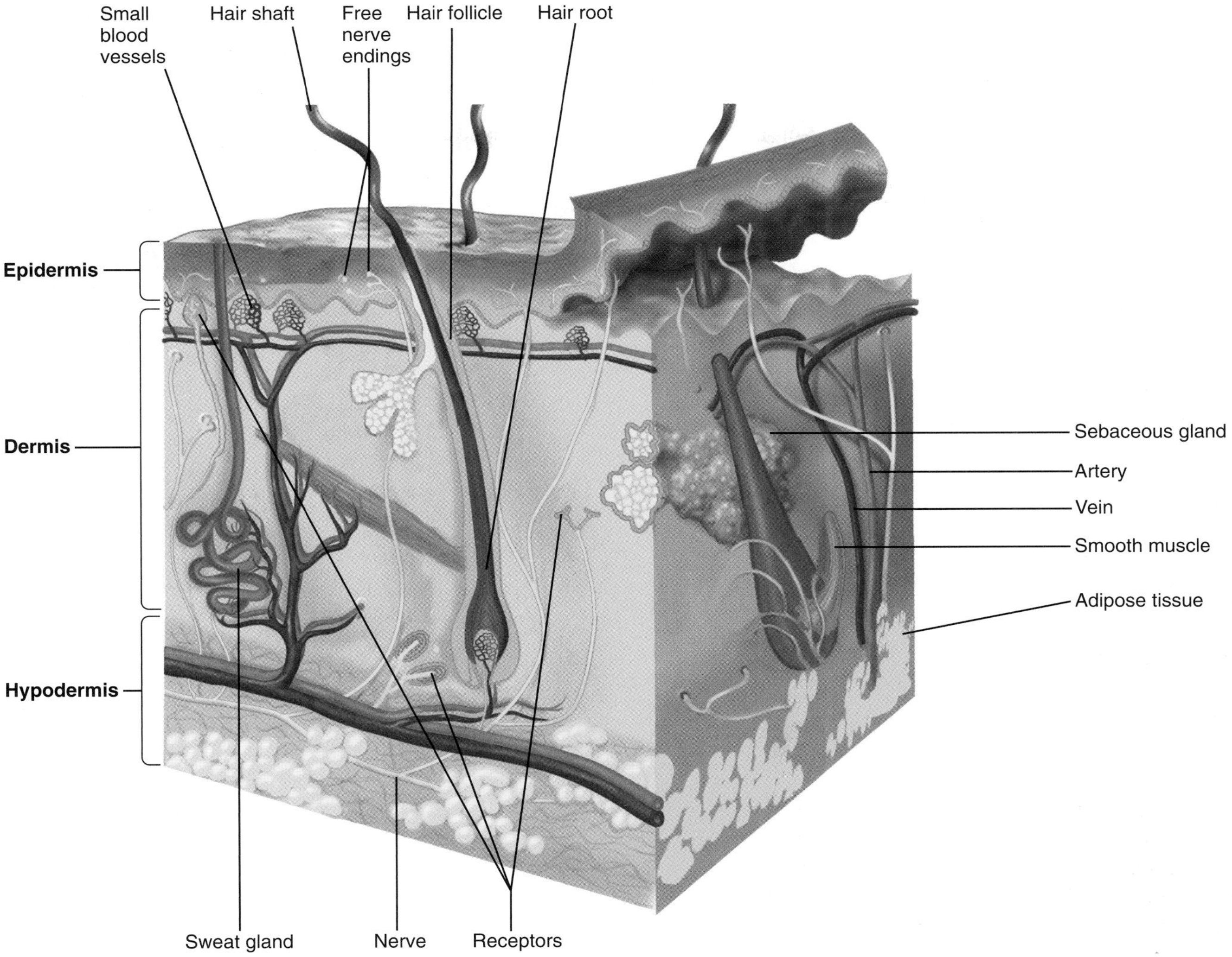


**Figure 4.10 The skin.** The two layers of skin (epidermis and dermis) rest on a supportive layer (hypodermis). Although not part of the skin, the hypodermis serves important functions of cushioning and insulation.

**RECAP**

The skin is an organ because it consists of different tissues serving common functions. Functions of skin include protection, temperature regulation, vitamin D synthesis, and sensory reception. ■

## 4.8 Multicellular organisms must maintain homeostasis

Although multicellularity offers many advantages to organisms, it presents certain disadvantages that must be overcome. For example, cells that are surrounded entirely by other cells can't obtain their nutrients directly from the organism's external environment and are constantly exposed to the waste products of neighboring cells.

The environment that surrounds the cells of a multicellular organism (their external environment) is the **internal environment** of the organism. The internal environment is a clear fluid called the **interstitial fluid** (the Latin noun *interstitium* means "the space between," in this case the space between cells). Every cell gets nutrients from the interstitial fluid around it and dumps wastes into it. In a multicellular organism, the interstitial fluid is the equivalent of the ocean, lake, or tiniest drop of fluid that surrounds and nourishes single-celled organisms.

Because every cell must receive all its requirements for life from the surrounding interstitial fluid, the composition of this fluid must be kept fairly constant to sustain life. In the long run, nutrients consumed by the cell must be replaced and wastes must be removed or the cell will die.

Relative constancy of the conditions within the internal environment is called **homeostasis** (*homeo-* means "unchanging" or "the same," and *-stasis* means "standing"). The maintenance of homeostasis is so important for life that

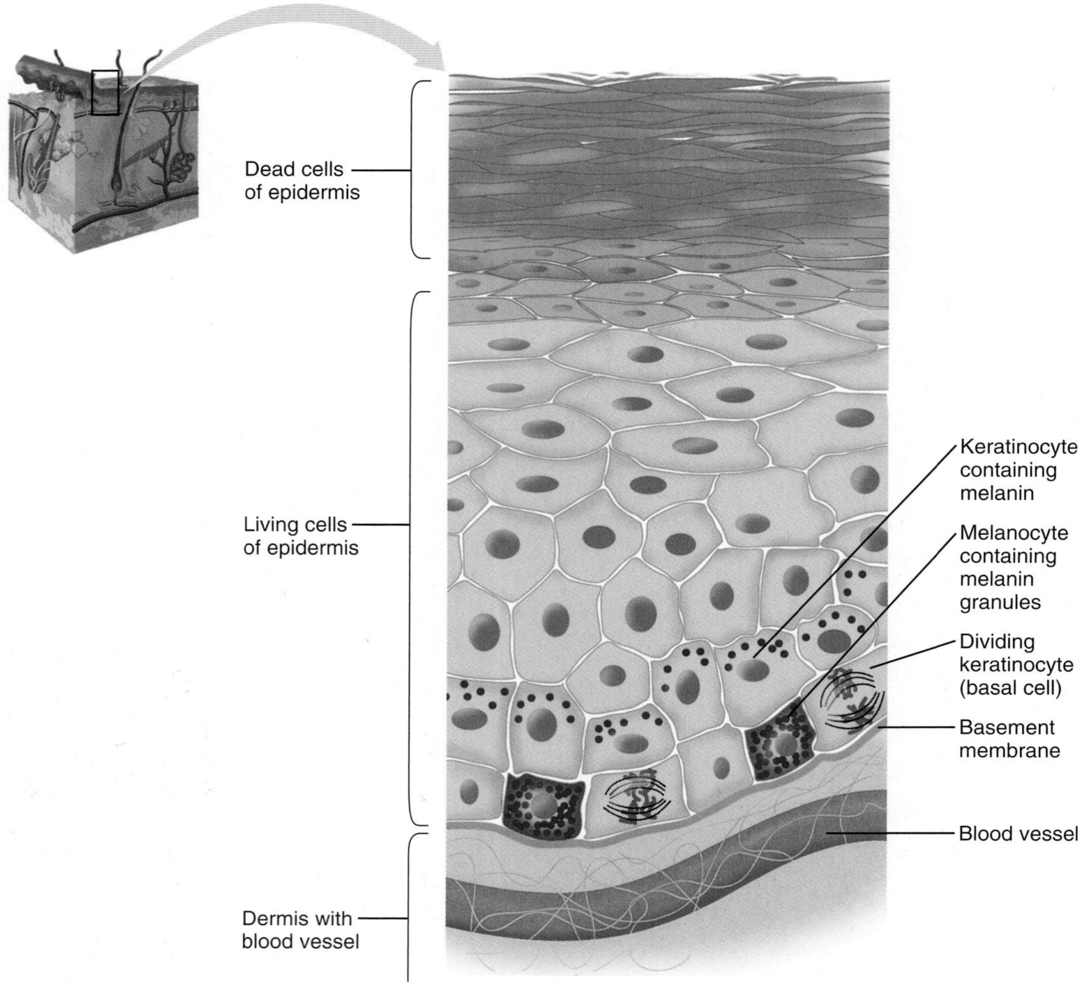


**Figure 4.11 The epidermis.** Living cells near the base of the epidermis divide, pushing more mature cells toward the surface. As cells migrate toward the surface they die and dry out, forming a tough, waterproof barrier. The cells of the epidermis are supplied only by blood vessels located in the dermis.

multicellular organisms, including human beings, devote a significant portion of their total metabolic activities to it. Although small changes in the internal environment do occur from time to time, the activities of cells, tissues, organs, and organ systems are carefully integrated and regulated to keep these changes within acceptable limits.

## Homeostasis is maintained by negative feedback

In living organisms, homeostasis is maintained by **negative feedback** control systems (Figure 4.12 on page 96). Negative feedback control systems operate in such a way that deviations from the desired condition are automatically detected and counteracted. A negative feedback control system has the following components:

- A **controlled variable.** The focal point of any negative feedback control loop is the *controlled variable.* A controlled variable is any physical or chemical property that might vary from time to time and that must be controlled to maintain homeostasis. Examples of controlled variables are blood pressure, body temperature, and the concentration of glucose in blood.
- A **sensor** (or *receptor*). The sensor monitors the current value of the controlled variable and sends the information (via either nerves or hormones) to the control center.
- A **control center.** The control center receives input from the sensor and compares it to the correct, internally set value of the controlled variable, sometimes called the **set point.** When the current value and the set point are not in agreement, the control center sends signals (again, via either nerves or hormones) to an effector.
- An **effector.** The effector takes the necessary action to correct the imbalance, in accordance with the signals it receives from the control center.

The cycle is called *negative* feedback because any change in the controlled variable triggers a series of events that ultimately opposes ("negates") the initial change, returning the variable to its set point. In other words, homeostasis is maintained. (You can demonstrate one instance of negative feedback using the exercise in the Try It Yourself box, page 96)

## Negative feedback helps maintain core body temperature

A prime example of negative feedback is the maintenance of homeostasis of your body temperature. In this case, multiple organ systems participate in maintaining homeostasis (Figure 4.13 on page 97).

The controlled variable is your core temperature, meaning the temperature near the center of your body. Temperature sensors in your skin and internal organs monitor core temperature. These sensors transmit signals via nerves to the control center, located in a region of your brain called the hypothalamus. The control center uses different combinations

# Health Watch

## Suntans, Smoking, and Your Skin

Many of us think suntans are attractive. A suntan indicates we have leisure time to spend basking in the sun, and it gives the skin a healthy-looking "glow." But are suntans really healthy?

The answer is clearly no. Strong light rays, whether from sunlight or tanning beds, can age your skin prematurely and increase your risk for skin cancer. The rays penetrate to the dermis and damage its collagen and elastin fibers. Elastin fibers clump together, leading at first to fine wrinkles and later to a wrinkled, leathery skin texture.

Prolonged exposure to sunlight or tanning lamps can also damage small blood vessels. Sometimes the vessels remain permanently dilated, leading to a condition called *telangiectasis,* or spider veins. Sunlight also damages the keratinocytes and melanocytes in the epidermis. The keratinocytes become rough and thickened and no longer fit together as a smooth interlocking layer. The melanocytes begin to produce melanin unevenly, leading to patches of darker pigmentation known as freckles, age spots, or liver spots.

Perhaps you have heard that ultraviolet (UV) rays combine "good" UVA rays that tan your skin and "bad" UVB rays that cause sunburn. Tanning lotions with high SPF (sun protection factor) numbers are designed to block the UVB rays, which at least prevents the acute damage and pain of a sunburn. However, UVA rays are also bad for you. They penetrate more deeply than the UVB rays and in fact cause most of the long-term changes that age skin prematurely.

What about smoking? Heavy smokers are nearly five times more likely to develop premature wrinkles. Smoking damages and thickens the elastin fibers in the dermis. It also dehydrates keratinocytes in the epidermis, causing the epidermis to develop a rough texture. Finally, smoking narrows blood vessels, reducing blood flow to the skin. As a result the skin of smokers heals more slowly from injury than the skin of nonsmokers.

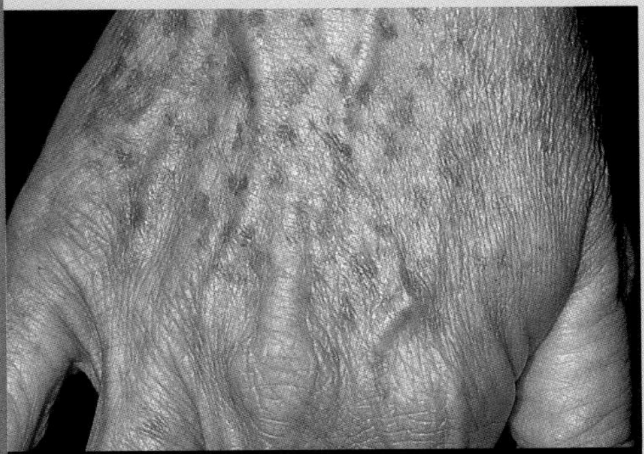

Age spots are more common with advancing age, especially in Caucasians who have had excessive exposure to the sun.

Smoking causes changes in the elastin fibers in the dermis and a loss of water from the cells of the epidermis. The result is dehydrated, wrinkled skin.

of effector mechanisms to raise or lower core temperature as needed.

When your core temperature falls *below* its set point, the hypothalamus:

- Sends more nerve impulses to blood vessels in the skin, causing the blood vessels to constrict. This restricts blood flow to your skin and reduces heat loss.
- Stimulates your skeletal muscles, causing brief bursts of muscular contraction known as shivering. Shivering generates heat.

When your core temperature rises *above* its set point, the hypothalamus:

- Sends fewer nerve impulses to blood vessels in the skin, causing the blood vessels to dilate. This increases blood flow to your skin and promotes heat loss.
- Activates your sweat glands. As perspiration evaporates from your skin, you lose heat.

Even when your core temperature is normal, your hypothalamus is transmitting some nerve impulses to the blood vessels in your skin. Small changes in temperature, then, can be handled effectively just by increasing or decreasing the normal number of signals. Only when the variations in temperature are large is sweating or shivering called into play.

From this example, we can make the following points about negative feedback control:

- Many sensors may be active at once. In this case, sensors throughout the body monitor body temperature.
- The control center integrates all of this incoming information and comes up with an appropriate response.
- There can be multiple effectors as well as multiple sensors, and they may belong to different organ systems.

Both skin and muscles function in returning body temperature to its set point.

# Is Lipodissolve a Good Way to Melt Away Fat?

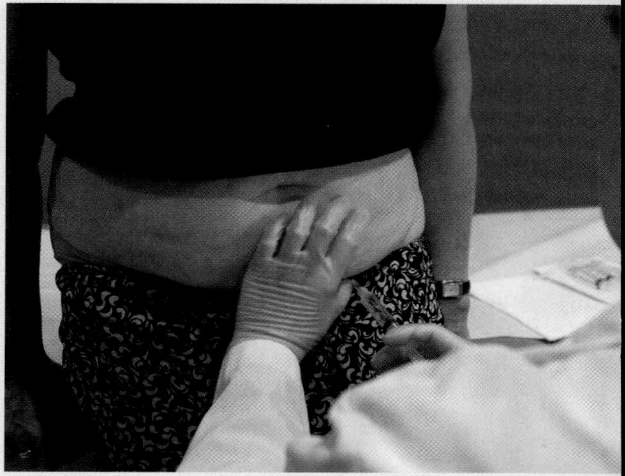

Lipodissolve is injected directly into areas of excess fat.

By now you are familiar with the chemistry of lipids (Chapter 3) and the structure and function of fat cells (this chapter). You understand that when your average daily caloric intake exceeds your average daily caloric expenditure, you gain weight. And yet all this knowledge hasn't helped, because you still have those annoying fat deposits in places where you don't want them! Perhaps you've tried dieting and exercise and still aren't happy with your body shape. Join the tens of millions of Americans in the same boat.

What if you could just melt away that unwanted fat? What if you could kill some of those pesky fat cells once and for all? What if you could sculpt your body into perfect shape without ever having to diet or exercise again? It's a fantasy many of us have indulged in, and it's one of the reasons for the meteoric rise of a controversial cosmetic procedure called Lipodissolve.

## What Is Lipodissolve?

Lipodissolve, also called injection lipolysis, is described by its promoters as a safe, effective, nonsurgical way to sculpt the body into perfect shape. Usually the technique is performed as a series of six treatments two weeks apart, each treatment consisting of injections directly into subcutaneous fat deposits. The injections contain two active ingredients: phosphatidylcholine (a phospholipid) and deoxycholate (a bile acid). The combination of these two drugs, known as PCDC (for phosphotidylcholine deoxycholate), allegedly works by dissolving the bonds between the three fatty acids and the glycerol backbone that comprise a triglyceride molecule, the primary molecular form of stored fat in the body. PCDC also is thought to disrupt the cell membranes of fat cells in the vicinity of an injection, resulting in death of the fat cells themselves.

The process sounds great, at least in theory. The claims for it may even turn out to be true. But as you know, a good theory is not the same as scientific proof. The theory first needs to be stated as a testable hypothesis and then tested by rigorous, scientifically valid experiments. And at the moment, the safety and efficacy of Lipodissolve are not backed by scientific data and it's not approved by the Food and Drug Administration as a fat-reducing therapy. The FDA has called Lipodissolve just another example of "unapproved drugs for unapproved uses."

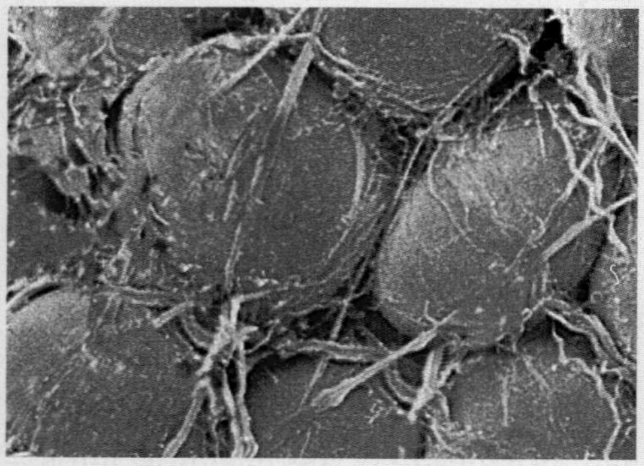

Fat cells located just below the skin's surface are disrupted by Lipodissolve.

## The Rise of an Unapproved Procedure

Even without FDA approval, health clinics and spas can legally administer Lipodissolve because of a loophole in our drug regulatory laws. According to the law, a licensed doctor can legally and ethically formulate and prescribe compounded drugs (drugs made from more than one ingredient) specifically for individual patients, as long as all of the *ingredients* are approved by the FDA and as long as the compound is made by a licensed compounding pharmacy. The intent is to protect the sanctity of the doctor/patient relationship, allowing the doctor to choose what is best for that particular patient. Both of the compounds used in the Lipodissolve technique have been approved by the FDA as ingredients in other drugs, though neither was approved as a fat-dissolving drug.

Health clinics and spas have been quick to capitalize on the loophole, for at nearly $2,000 per treatment they stand to make a lot of money. Most patients who try the technique eventually sign up for treatment of several body parts. Women generally request treatment of their thighs and abdomen, whereas

## the facts...

- A nonsurgical cosmetic procedure for "melting away fat" is being heavily promoted by health clinics and spas.
- The procedure, called Lipodissolve, involves a series of injections of fat-dissolving drugs directly into local fat deposits.
- Lipodissolve is not approved as a fat-reducing therapy by the FDA. Its safety and efficacy are not yet backed by scientific evidence.

men are more likely to choose jaw lines and love handles.

One of the first companies to offer the Lipodissolve technique in this country was Advanced LipoDissolve Center, later renamed fig. (short for figure). Fig.'s "dissolve to your beautiful shape" advertising campaign was so successful that the company grew to 18 body-shaping centers in eight states in just two years. The company went out of business in late 2007, but there are still plenty of other clinics and spas willing to perform the Lipodissolve procedure.

Lipodissolve is not a good way to lose weight overall, but if it works as advertised it could be a way to reduce fat in specific places. One of the distinct advantages of the technique is that because it does not involve surgery there is no recovery period. Not surprisingly, there are persistent rumors on various celebrity-watch web sites that certain celebrities have tried the procedure or are thinking about it.

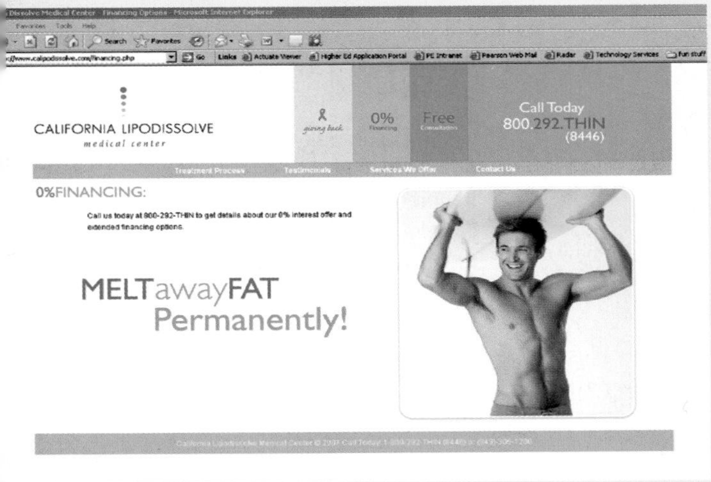


*Companies have been quick to advertise Lipodissolve, even though the effects and safety of the technique have not been tested by the FDA.*

### *Is Lipodissolve Safe and Effective?*

Critics of the Lipodissolve technique argue that the current law covering single doctor/patient relationships was never intended to allow mass marketing by chains of clinics or spas, or mass compounding of the PCDC drug combination. The American Society of Plastic Surgeons, The American Society of Aesthetic Plastic Surgery, and the American Society of Dermatologic Surgery have issued cautionary warnings against the technique, but that's understandable since all three societies represent surgeons who might be financially affected by Lipodissolve's increasing popularity. The Food and Drug Administration is "investigating and evaluating" the situation, but so far it has not interfered with the activities of the clinics.

Is it safe? So far, there are only anecdotal reports of unwanted side effects immediately after Lipodissolve treatment, such as swelling, skin blistering, pain, and blackened skin in some patients. No deaths have been reported. However, because the technique has been performed in this country only since 2004, the long-term consequences of Lipodissolve therapy are still unknown. Some scientists worry that disruption of fat cell membranes at the site of injection might cause a sharp rise in cholesterol in the blood. After all, cholesterol is a normal constituent of cell membranes. In addition, little is known about how the Lipodissolve drugs are metabolized or removed from the body. Nor is it known whether they enter the circulatory system in sufficient quantities to affect other organs or tissues far from the injection site.

Does Lipodissolve work? The jury is still out on this one. Some patients see an improvement in body shape after Lipodissolve, others do not. One possible reason for differences in effectiveness between patients may be that there is no standard dose of Lipodissolve. The procedure is not regulated by the FDA, so physicians are free to try any combination of doses and injection intervals they want.

Faced with the awkward and potentially dangerous situation of having patients flock to an unregulated procedure, the FDA decided to take action. Late in 2007 the FDA approved the first clinical trial of Lipodissolve—a double-blind, placebo-controlled prospective study that will follow patients for up to 46 weeks. The trial, to be conducted by the research arm of the American Society for Aesthetic Plastic Surgery, is expected to provide the first scientifically defensible data on the efficacy and safety of Lipodissolve. The results may not be known for a couple of years. In the meantime the FDA is keeping an eye on the situation. Consumers would be wise to remain skeptical about this procedure until more is known about it.

## *Questions to consider*

**1** *Health clinics sometimes cite retrospective studies to support their claim that the Lipodissolve technique is safe. What is a retrospective study? How is it different from a controlled study?*

**2** *How important is FDA approval and/or scientific evidence of safety to you? If someone were to pay for a Lipodissolve procedure for you, would you try it?*

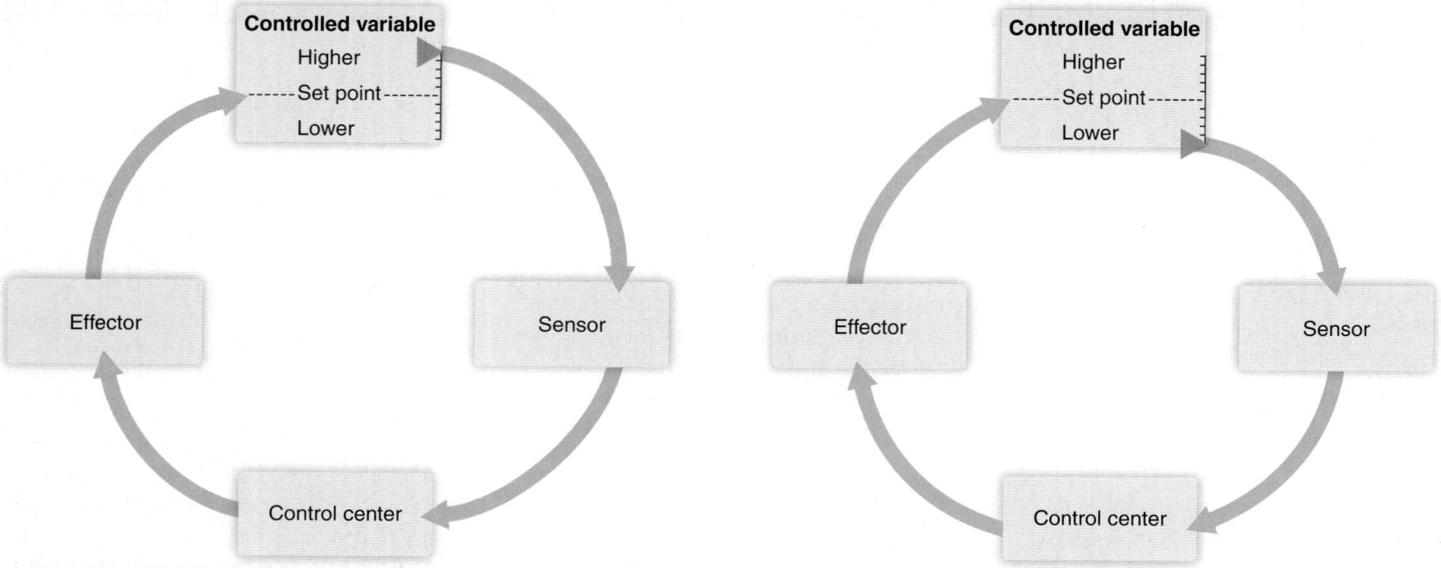


**a) An *increase* in the controlled variable causes events that *lower* the controlled variable toward its set point again.**

**b) A *decrease* in the controlled variable causes events that *raise* the controlled variable toward its set point again.**

**Figure 4.12 Components of a negative feedback control system.** The focal point of the control system is the controlled variable. A sensor monitors the controlled variable and sends signals to a control center, which compares the current value of the controlled variable with its set point. If the controlled variable and set point do not match, the control center sends signals to effectors that take action to reverse the difference between the controlled variable and its set point.

### Positive feedback amplifies events

**Positive feedback** control systems are relatively uncommon in living organisms. In positive feedback, a change in the controlled variable sets in motion a series of events that *amplify* the original change, rather than returning it to normal. The process of childbirth once labor has started is governed by positive feedback mechanisms.

Obviously something must terminate positive feedback events. The contractions of childbirth end when the child is born. The important point is that positive feedback is not a mechanism for maintaining homeostasis.

**try it yourself**

### Negative Feedback Systems

Negative feedback systems keep controlled variables within their acceptable range most of the time. Any variations are so small that we usually do not notice them.

You can demonstrate the small, ongoing changes that occur in controlled variables with the following exercise. In this case, the controlled variables are your balance and your ability to voluntarily control the position of your limbs.

First, stand still and look at a distant point. Everything will look stable, as if your body is not moving at all. Now look at the same point through powerful binoculars, and your field of vision appears unsteady.

The reason is that your body is constantly making small muscular adjustments to keep you upright and hold your hands and arms steady. You become aware of these tiny motions only because the binoculars magnify their effect on your vision.

**RECAP**

All multicellular organisms must maintain homeostasis of their internal environment. In a negative feedback control system, any change in a controlled variable sets in motion a series of events that reverse the change, maintaining homeostasis. ■

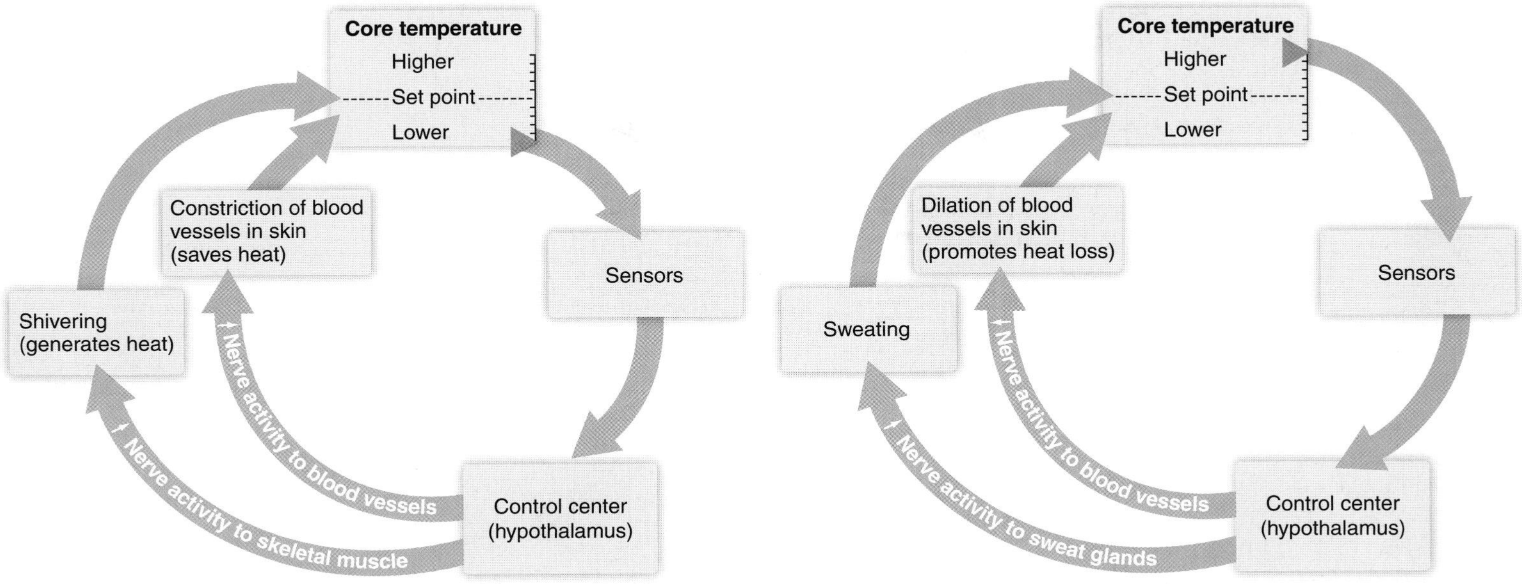


**Figure 4.13 Negative feedback control of core temperature.** Note that different combinations of effector mechanisms may be activated, depending on the direction of the initial change in core temperature.

# Chapter Summary

### Tissues are groups of cells with a common function *p. 79*

- The four types of tissues are epithelial tissue, connective tissue, muscle tissue, and neural tissue.

### Epithelial tissues cover body surfaces and cavities *p. 79*

- Epithelial tissues are sheets of cells that cover or line body surfaces and form the glands.
- Epithelial tissues are supported by a noncellular layer called the basement membrane.

### Connective tissue supports and connects body parts *p. 82*

- Fibrous connective tissues contain several types of extracellular fibers and only a few living cells. They support and connect body parts.
- Cartilage, blood, bone, and adipose tissue are classified as special connective tissues.

### Muscle tissues contract to produce movement *p. 84*

- Muscle tissue is composed of either skeletal, cardiac, or smooth muscle cells.
- Skeletal muscles are attached to bones by tendons.

### Nervous tissue transmits impulses *p. 85*

- Neurons are specialized for conduction of electrical impulses.
- Glial cells surround and protect neurons and supply them with nutrients.

### Organs and organ systems perform complex functions *p. 86*

- The human body is composed of 11 organ systems, each of which has at least one broad function.
- Membranes consisting of layers of epithelial and connective tissues line the body cavities.
- Positions of body parts are described on three planes: midsagittal, frontal, and transverse.

### The skin as an organ system *p. 87*

- The skin functions as a protective barrier, participates in the maintenance of homeostasis, and provides us with sensory information about the external environment.
- Skin has two layers: an outer epithelial layer called the epidermis and an inner connective tissue layer called the dermis.
- Skin also contains nerves, blood vessels, glands, hair follicles, and smooth muscle.

### Multicellular organisms must maintain homeostasis *p. 91*

- In a multicellular organism, the external environment of every cell is the internal environment of the organism.
- Relative constancy of the internal environment is called homeostasis.
- Homeostasis is maintained by negative feedback control systems.

- In a negative feedback control system, a change in the controlled variable sets in motion a sequence of events that tends to reverse (or negate) the initial change.
- In the regulation of body temperature, sensors located throughout the body send information about temperature to the control center, located in the hypothalamus of the brain.
- Possible responses to a change in body temperature include dilating or constricting the blood vessels to the skin, shivering (if temperature is too low), and sweating (if temperature is too high).

## Terms You Should Know

basement membrane, *81*
cell junctions, *81*
connective tissue, *82*
controlled variable, *92*
dermis, *87*
endocrine gland, *79*
epidermis, *87*
epithelial tissue, *79*
exocrine gland, *79*
homeostasis, *91*
internal environment, *91*
muscle tissue, *84*
negative feedback, *92*
nervous tissue, *85*
neuron, *85*
organ system, *86*
set point, *92*

## Concept Review

1. Describe some advantages and disadvantages of multicellularity.
2. Name the four types of tissues in the human body and list their main functions.
3. Describe the functions of the three types of cell junctions.
4. Distinguish between an organ and an organ system.
5. List the 11 organ systems of the body and give at least one function of each.
6. Define *interstitial fluid.*
7. Name the two cavities of the anterior body cavity that are separated from each other by the diaphragm.
8. Compare/contrast positive and negative feedback.
9. Discuss the purpose of *homeostasis* in the body.
10. Describe the function of a control center in a negative feedback control system.

## Test Yourself

### Matching Exercise

_____ 1. Relative constancy of the internal environment
_____ 2. Epithelial tissue composed of flattened cells
_____ 3. Epithelial tissue composed of just one layer of cells
_____ 4. Specialized connective tissue that forms the shape of the nose
_____ 5. Type of muscle found in the walls of the bladder and blood vessels
_____ 6. Pigment-producing cells in the skin

a. simple epithelium
b. cartilage
c. homeostasis
d. squamous epithelium
e. melanocytes
f. smooth

### Fill in the Blank

7. Organized groups of cells with similar types of functions are called ________________.
8. Endocrine glands secrete ________________ into the bloodstream.
9. The ________________ is the outer layer of the skin.
10. The cavity of the body that contains the brain is called the ________________ cavity.
11. Cells of the epidermis that produce the tough waterproof protein called keratin are called ________________.
12. The desired value of a controlled variable is called its ________________.

### True or False?

13. Blood cells are considered to be a specialized connective tissue because they originate from cells in bone.
14. Cardiac muscle is found only in the heart.
15. Both the epidermis and the dermis of the skin have blood vessels.

## References and Additional Reading

Diamond, Jared. Best Size and Number of Human Body Parts. *Natural History* 6:78, 1994. (Why do we have the size and number of organs that we do?)

Gordon, Marsha, and Alice E. Fugate. *The Complete Idiot's Guide to Beautiful Skin.* New York: Alpha Books, 1998. (A practical guide to skin care.)

Maynard-Moody, Steven. *The Dilemma of the Fetus: Fetal Research, Medical Progress, and Moral Politics.* New York: St. Martin's Press, 1995. (A look at the moral politics of fetal tissue research with a focus on the importance of social and political conflict over science.)

The Promise of Tissue Engineering. *Scientific American* 280(4):59, 1999. (A series of five articles on the subject of tissue engineering.)

### Internet References

Find a link to the following Web site at the Human Biology Place.

**The Visible Human Project**
**www.nlm.nih.gov/research/visible**
A project of the National Library of Medicine to provide anatomically detailed three-dimensional views of male and female human bodies.

## Apply **What You Know**

1. Your roommate says that the concept of homeostasis is being violated when the rate of respiration goes up during exercise, because the rate of respiration clearly is not being held constant. Explain to him where his thinking is faulty.
2. What do you think would be some of the problems associated with severe third-degree burns, in which both the epidermis and the dermis are severely damaged or destroyed?
3. Sherlock Holmes, the greatest fictional detective of all time, is talking to a woman in her late 40s, when he suddenly says, "I see, my dear madam, you must have enjoyed your cigarettes and your suntans." The woman is amazed, because she mentioned nothing about these two former favorite activities. What physical characteristics might Mr. Holmes have seen in this woman to indicate she was an avid sun-worshiper and cigarette smoker? And how do these characteristics develop?
4. Dieting is difficult. People who do manage to lose weight can gain it back if they're not careful. Are techniques such as liposuction or lipodissolve a good way to keep the weight off permanently? Why or why not?
5. Fibrous connective tissue consists of ground substance and fibers that provide strength, support, and flexibility. Concrete is used to make tough, durable structures in construction projects. How is a concrete structure like or unlike fibrous connective tissue?
6. By definition, an organ is a structure composed of two or more tissue types that perform a specific function. Performance of that function often requires coordination among many cells. Why is it so important that cardiac muscle cells of the heart be synchronized (coordinated) so that they beat nearly all at once?

*Answers can be found on the Human Biology Place.*

# 5 The Skeletal System

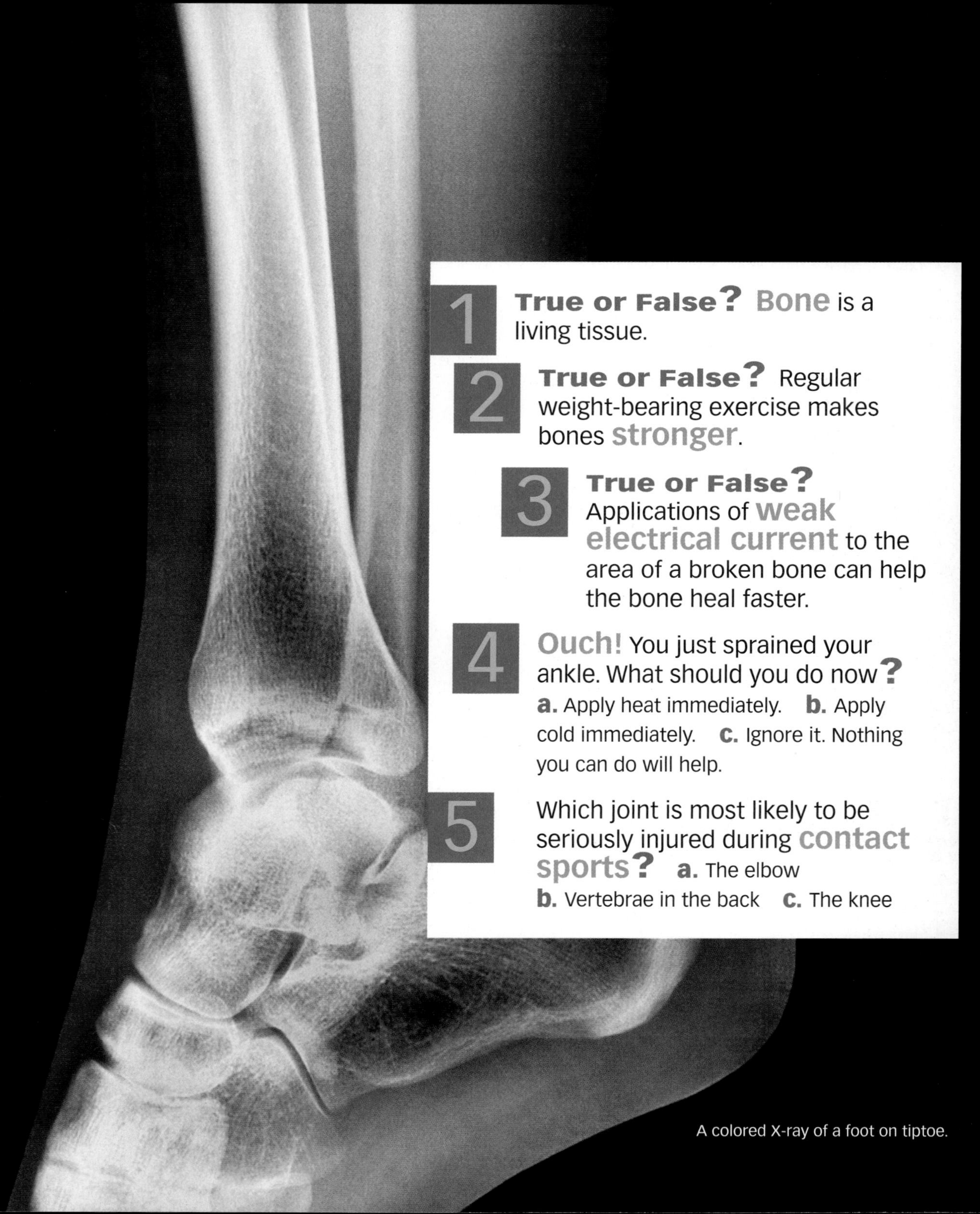

1 **True or False?** Bone is a living tissue.

2 **True or False?** Regular weight-bearing exercise makes bones stronger.

3 **True or False?** Applications of weak electrical current to the area of a broken bone can help the bone heal faster.

4 Ouch! You just sprained your ankle. What should you do now? **a.** Apply heat immediately. **b.** Apply cold immediately. **c.** Ignore it. Nothing you can do will help.

5 Which joint is most likely to be seriously injured during contact sports? **a.** The elbow **b.** Vertebrae in the back **c.** The knee

A colored X-ray of a foot on tiptoe.

**The human body is capable of an awesome array** of physical activities. With training, some individuals can run a mile in less than four minutes or lift more than their own weight. Exquisitely sensitive motor skills allow us to thread a needle, turn our head to focus on a single star, and throw a baseball into the strike zone. Considered individually, any one of these activities may not seem amazing, but for a single structure (the human body) to be capable of all of them is remarkable indeed. From an engineering standpoint it would be like designing a bulldozer that is strong enough to flatten a building, yet delicate enough to pick up a dime.

This chapter describes the skeletal system, the organ system for support, protection, and movement. We examine the structure and development of bones, and the way they remodel and repair themselves. We review how the bones fit together to make the skeleton. We take a look at how joints enable bones and muscles to work together. Finally, we consider what can go wrong with the skeletal system.

## 5.1 The skeletal system consists of connective tissue

The skeletal system comprises three types of connective tissue:

- *Bones,* the hard elements of the skeleton
- *Ligaments,* dense fibrous connective tissue that binds the bones to each other
- *Cartilage,* a specialized connective tissue consisting primarily of fibers of collagen and elastic in a gel-like fluid called ground substance

### Bones are the hard elements of the skeleton

Although most of the mass of **bones** consists of nonliving extracellular crystals of calcium minerals, bones also contain several types of living bone cells, nerves, and blood vessels. Indeed, bones bleed when cut during orthopedic surgery or when they break.

Bones perform five important functions. The first three are the same as the functions of the skeleton, which consists primarily of bone:

- *Support.* Bones form the structure (the skeleton) to which skeletal muscles attach. The skeleton also supports the soft organs.
- *Movement.* Bones support and interact with muscles, making it possible for our bodies to move.
- *Protection.* As the hard elements of the skeleton, bones surround and protect many of our delicate internal organs.
- *Formation of blood cells.* Some bones contain cells that are responsible for producing different types of blood cells.
- *Mineral storage.* Bones store minerals, including calcium and phosphate, that are important to body metabolism and function.

**RECAP**

Bones contribute to support, movement, and protection. They also produce the blood cells and store minerals. ■

### Bone contains living cells

A typical long bone, so called because it is longer than it is wide, consists of a cylindrical shaft (called the *diaphysis*) with an enlarged knob called an *epiphysis* at each end (Figure 5.1). Dense **compact bone** forms the shaft and covers each end. A central cavity in the shaft is filled with *yellow bone marrow.* Yellow bone marrow is primarily fat that can be utilized for energy. Inside each epiphysis is **spongy bone.** Spongy bone is less dense than compact bone, allowing the bones to be light but strong. Spongy bone is a latticework of hard, relatively strong *trabeculae* (from Latin, meaning "little beams") composed of calcium minerals and living cells. In certain long bones, most notably the long bones of the upper arms and legs (humerus and femur, respectively), the spaces between the trabeculae are filled with *red bone marrow.* Special cells called *stem cells* in the red bone marrow are responsible for the production of red and white blood cells and platelets.

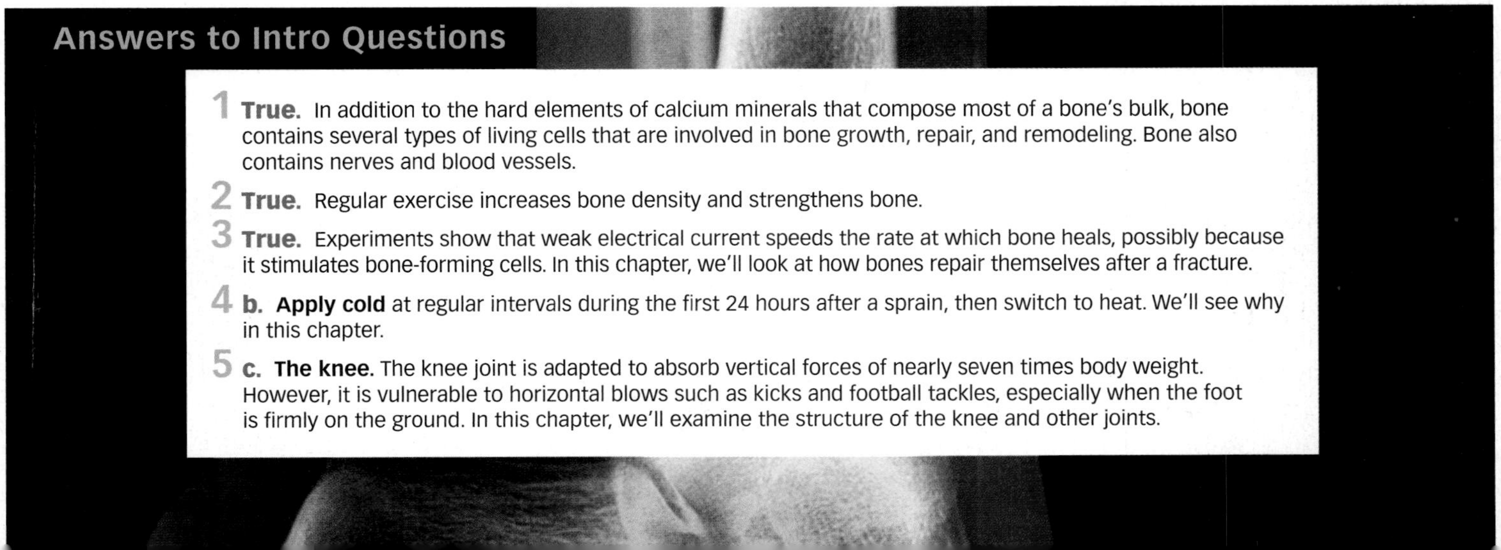

**Answers to Intro Questions**

1 **True.** In addition to the hard elements of calcium minerals that compose most of a bone's bulk, bone contains several types of living cells that are involved in bone growth, repair, and remodeling. Bone also contains nerves and blood vessels.

2 **True.** Regular exercise increases bone density and strengthens bone.

3 **True.** Experiments show that weak electrical current speeds the rate at which bone heals, possibly because it stimulates bone-forming cells. In this chapter, we'll look at how bones repair themselves after a fracture.

4 **b. Apply cold** at regular intervals during the first 24 hours after a sprain, then switch to heat. We'll see why in this chapter.

5 **c. The knee.** The knee joint is adapted to absorb vertical forces of nearly seven times body weight. However, it is vulnerable to horizontal blows such as kicks and football tackles, especially when the foot is firmly on the ground. In this chapter, we'll examine the structure of the knee and other joints.

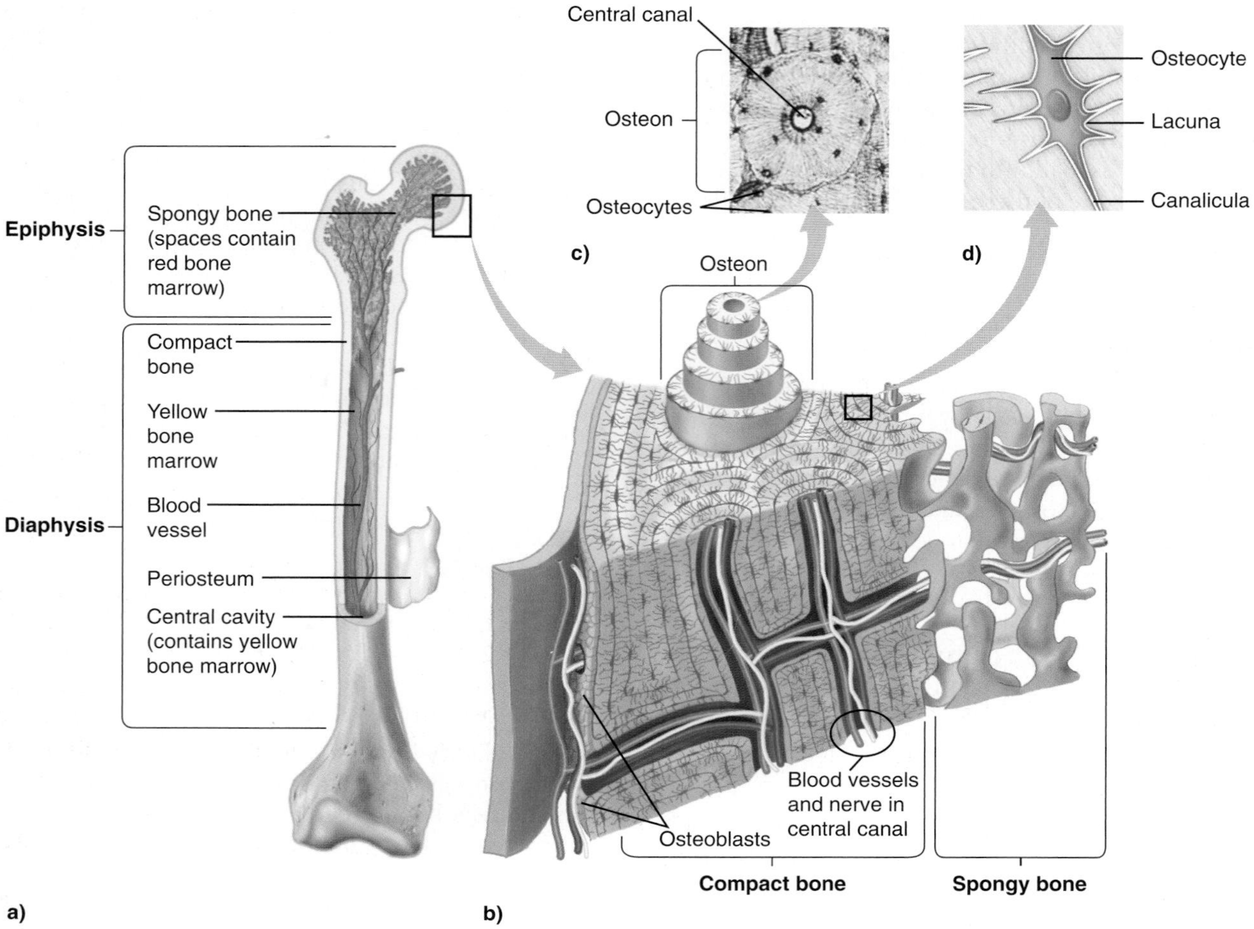


**Figure 5.1 Structure of bone.** **(a)** A partial cut through a long bone. **(b)** A closer view of a section of bone shows that compact bone is a nearly solid structure with central canals for the blood vessels and nerves. **(c)** A photograph of an osteon of compact bone showing osteocytes embedded within the solid structure. **(d)** A single osteocyte in a lacuna. Osteocytes remain in contact with each other by cytoplasmic extensions into the canaliculi between cells.

The outer surface of the bone is covered by a tough layer of connective tissue, the *periosteum*, which contains specialized bone-forming cells. If the end of a long bone forms a movable joint with another bone, the joint surface is covered by a smooth layer of cartilage that reduces friction.

Taking a closer look, we see that compact bone is made up largely of extracellular deposits of calcium phosphate enclosing and surrounding living cells called **osteocytes** (from the Greek words for "bone" and "cells"). Osteocytes are arranged in rings in cylindrical structures called **osteons** (sometimes called *Haversian systems*). As bone develops and becomes hard, the osteocytes become trapped in hollow chambers called *lacunae.* However, the osteocytes remain in contact with each other via thin canals called *canaliculi.* Within the canaliculi, extensions of the cell cytoplasm and the presence of gap junctions between adjacent cells keep the osteocytes in direct contact with each other. Osteocytes nearest the center of an osteon receive nutrients by diffusion from blood vessels that pass through a **central canal** (Haversian canal). These cells then pass nutrients on to adjacent cells via the gap junctions. In this way, all the osteocytes can be supplied with nutrients even though most osteocytes are not located near a blood vessel. Waste products produced by the osteocytes diffuse in the opposite direction and are removed from the bone by the blood vessels.

In spongy bone, osteocytes do not need to rely on central canals for nutrients and waste removal. The slender trabecular structure of spongy bone gives each osteocyte access to nearby blood vessels in red bone marrow.

**RECAP**

Bone may be compact or spongy in appearance. Long bones have a hollow shaft of compact bone filled with yellow marrow; spongy bone with red bone marrow is found in the epiphyses. ■

### Ligaments hold bones together

**Ligaments** attach bone to bone. Ligaments consist of dense fibrous connective tissue, meaning that they are a regular array of closely packed collagen fibers all oriented in the same direction with a few fibroblasts in between. Ligaments confer strength to certain joints while still permitting movement of the bones in relation to each other.

### Cartilage lends support

**Cartilage,** as you already know, contains fibers of collagen and/or elastin in a ground substance of water and other substances. Cartilage is smoother and more flexible than bone. Cartilage is found where support under pressure is important and where some movement is necessary.

There are three types of cartilage in the human skeleton. *Fibrocartilage* consists primarily of collagen fibers arranged in thick bundles. It withstands both pressure and tension well. The intervertebral disks between the vertebrae, and also certain disklike supportive structures in the knee joint called menisci, are made of fibrocartilage. *Hyaline cartilage* is a smooth, almost glassy cartilage of thin collagen fibers. Hyaline cartilage forms the embryonic structures that later become the bones. It also covers the ends of mature bones in joints, creating a smooth, low-friction surface. *Elastic cartilage* is mostly elastin fibers, so it is highly flexible. It lends structure to the outer ear and to the epiglottis, a flap of tissue that covers the larynx during swallowing.

## 5.2 Bone development begins in the embryo

In the earliest stages of fetal development, even before organs develop, the rudimentary models of future bones are created out of hyaline cartilage by cartilage-forming cells called **chondroblasts.** After about two to three months of fetal development, the cartilage models begin to dissolve and are replaced by bone. This process is called *ossification.* Although ossification is slightly different for flat bones and long bones, we will concentrate on the process for long bones.

Figure 5.2 illustrates how ossification occurs in a long bone. After the chondroblasts die, the matrix they produced gradually breaks down inside the future shaft of the bone,

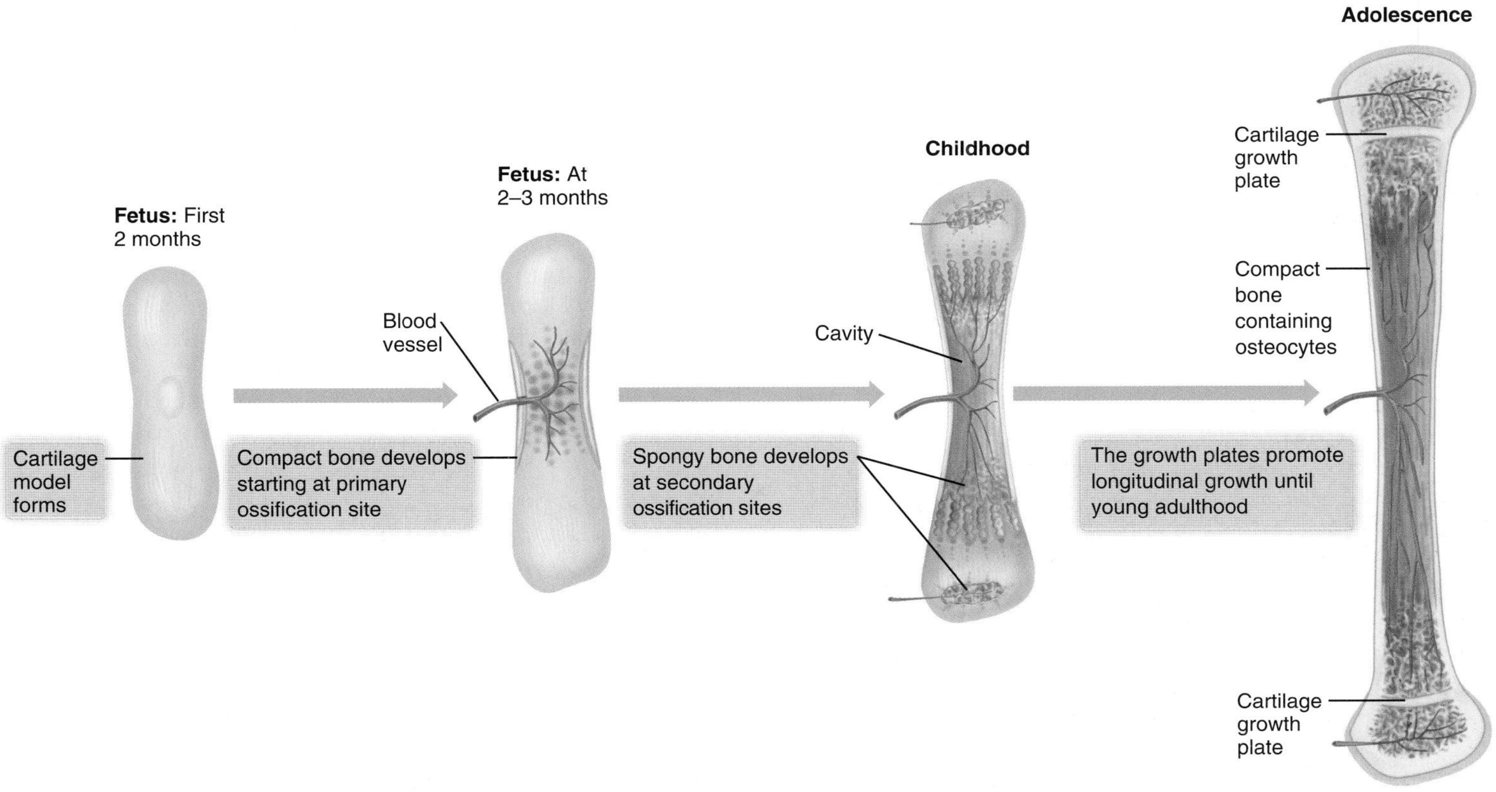


**Figure 5.2 How bone develops.** The first two phases occur in the fetus. Bones continue to grow longer throughout childhood and adolescence because of growth at the growth plates.

making room for blood vessels to develop. The blood vessels carry bone-forming cells called **osteoblasts** (from the Greek words for "bone" and "to build") into the area from the developing periosteum. The osteoblasts secrete a mixture of proteins (including collagen) called *osteoid,* which forms internal structure and provides strength to bone. They also secrete enzymes that facilitate the crystallization of hard mineral salts of calcium phosphate, known as *hydroxyapatite,* around and between the osteoid matrix. As more and more hydroxyapatite is deposited, the osteoblasts become embedded in the hardening bone tissue. In mature compact bone, approximately one-third of the matrix is osteoid and two-thirds is crystals of hydroxyapatite.

Eventually the rate at which osteoblasts produce the osteoid matrix and stimulate the mineral deposits declines, and they become mature osteocytes embedded in their individual lacunae. Mature osteocytes continue to maintain the bone matrix, however. Without them the matrix would slowly disintegrate.

Bones continue to lengthen throughout childhood and adolescence. This is because a narrow strip of cartilage called the **growth plate** (or *epiphyseal plate*) remains in each epiphysis. Chondroblast activity (and hence the development of new cartilage as a model for the lengthening bone) is concentrated on the outside of the plate, whereas the conversion of the cartilage model to bone by osteoblasts is concentrated on the inside of the plate (Figure 5.3). In effect, the bone lengthens as the two growth plates migrate farther and farther apart. Bones also grow in width as osteoblasts lay down more bone on the outer surface just below the periosteum.

The bone development process is controlled by hormones, chemicals secreted by the endocrine glands. The most important hormone in preadolescents is growth hormone, which stimulates the bone-lengthening activity of the growth plate. During puberty the sex hormones (testosterone and estrogen) also stimulate the growth plate, at least initially. But at about age 18 in females and 21 in males these same sex hormones signal the growth plates to stop growing, and the cartilage is replaced by bone tissue. At this point the bones can no longer lengthen, though they can continue to grow in width.

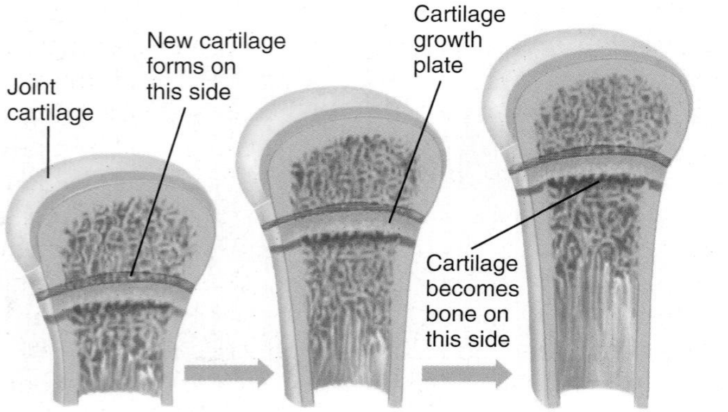


**Figure 5.3 How long bones increase in length.** Chondrocytes produce new cartilage at the outer surface, and cartilage is converted to bone at the inner surface.

**RECAP**

Bone-forming cells called osteoblasts produce a protein mixture (including collagen) that becomes bone's structural framework. They also secrete an enzyme that facilitates mineral deposition within the protein matrix. ■

## 5.3 Mature bone undergoes remodeling and repair

Even though bones stop growing longer, they do not remain the same throughout life. Bone is a dynamic tissue that undergoes constant replacement, remodeling, and repair. Remodeling may be so extensive that there is a noticeable change in bone shape over time, even in adults.

Bone remodeling and repair is in part due to a third type of bone cell called an **osteoclast** (from the Greek words for "bone" and "to break"). Osteoclasts cut through mature bone tissue, dissolving the hydroxyapatite and digesting the osteoid matrix in their path. The released calcium and phosphate ions enter the blood. The areas from which bone has been removed attract new osteoblasts, which lay down new osteoid matrixes and stimulate the deposition of new hydroxyapatite crystals.

Table 5.1 summarizes the four types of cells that contribute to bone development and maintenance.

### Bones can change in shape, size, and strength

Over time, constant remodeling can actually change the shape of a bone. The key is that compression stress on a bone, such as the force of repeated jogging on the legs, causes tiny electrical currents within the bone. These electrical currents stimulate the bone-forming activity of osteoblasts. The compressive forces and the electric currents are greatest at the inside curvature of the long bone undergoing stress (Figure 5.4). Thus, in the normal course of bone

**Table 5.1 Cells involved in bone development and maintenance**

| Type of cell | Function |
|---|---|
| Chondroblasts | Cartilage-forming cells that build a model of the future bone |
| Osteoblasts | Young bone-forming cells that cause the hard extracellular matrix of bone to develop |
| Osteocytes | Mature bone cells that maintain the structure of bone |
| Osteoclasts | Bone-dissolving cells |

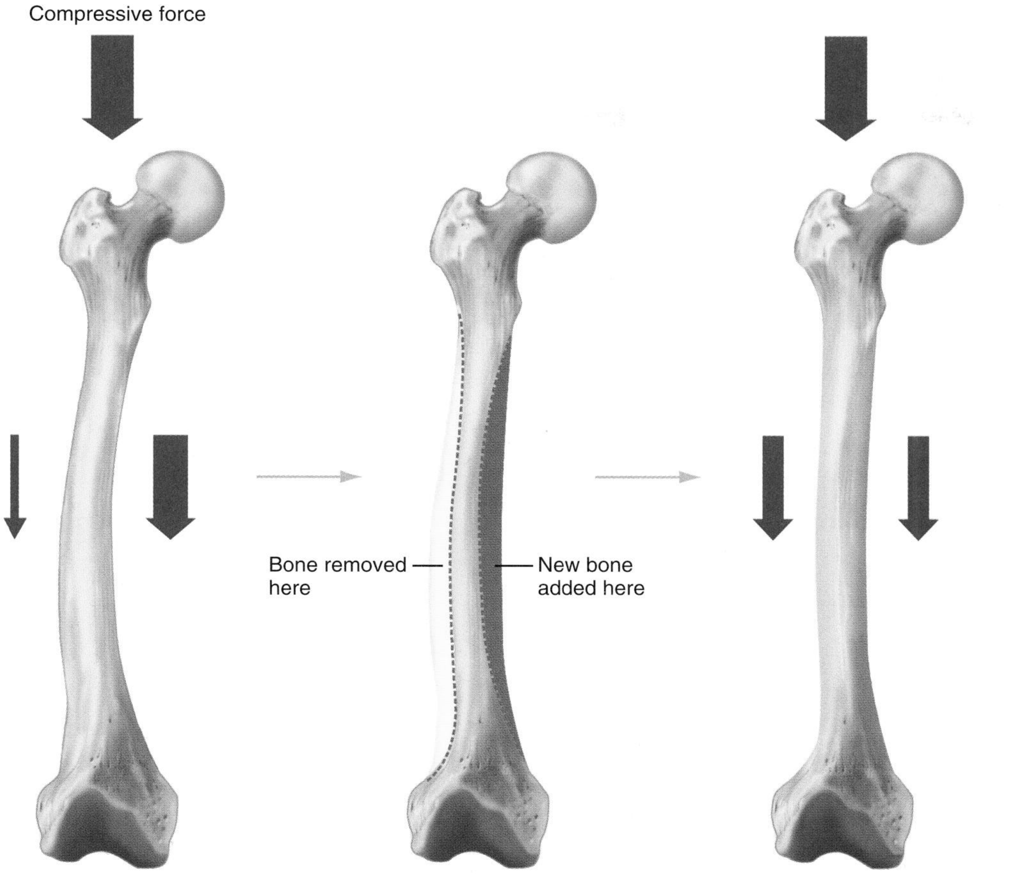


**a) The application of force to a slightly bent bone produces a greater compressive force on the inside curvature. Compressive force produces weak electrical currents which stimulate osteoblasts.**

**b) Over time, bone is deposited on the inside curvature and removed from the outside curvature.**

**c) The final result is a bone matched to the compressive force to which it is exposed.**

**Figure 5.4 Bone remodeling.**

turnover, new bone is laid down in regions under high compressive stress and bone is resorbed in areas of low compressive stress. The final shape of a bone, then, tends to match the compressive forces to which it is exposed.

Weight-bearing exercise increases overall bone mass and strength. The effect is pronounced enough that the bones of trained athletes may be visibly thicker and heavier than those of nonathletes. You don't have to be a professional athlete to get this benefit, however. If you begin a regular program of any weight-bearing exercise, such as jogging or weight lifting, your bones will become denser and stronger as your osteoblasts produce more bone tissue.

The maintenance of homeostasis of bone structure depends on the precise balance of the activities of osteoclasts and osteoblasts. **Osteoporosis** is a common condition in which bones lose a great deal of mass (seemingly becoming "porous") because of an imbalance over many years in the rates of activities of these two types of bone cells.

## Bone cells are regulated by hormones

Like bone growth, the rates of activities of osteoblasts and osteoclasts in adulthood are regulated by hormones that function to maintain calcium homeostasis. When blood levels of calcium fall below a given point, *parathyroid hormone (PTH)* stimulates the osteoclasts to secrete more bone-dissolving enzymes. The increased activity of osteoclasts causes more bone to be dissolved, releasing calcium and phosphate into the bloodstream. If calcium levels rise, then another hormone called *calcitonin* stimulates osteoblast activity, causing calcium and phosphate to be removed from blood and deposited in bone. Although the total bone mass of young adults doesn't change much, it's estimated that almost 10% of their bones may be remodeled and replaced each year. We discuss this and other types of hormonal regulation further in Chapter 13.

## Bones undergo repair

When you break (fracture) a bone, the blood vessels supplying the bone bleed into the area, producing a mass of clotted blood called a *hematoma.* Inflammation, swelling, and pain generally accompany the hematoma in the days immediately after a fracture. The repair process begins within days as fibroblasts migrate to the area. Some of the fibroblasts become chondroblasts, and together they produce a tough fibrocartilage bond called a *callus* between the two broken ends of the bone. A callus can be felt as a hard raised ring at the point of the break. Then osteoclasts arrive and begin to remove dead fragments of the original bone and the blood cells of the hematoma. Finally, osteoblasts arrive to deposit osteoid matrix and encourage the crystallization of calcium phosphate minerals, converting the callus into bone. Eventually the temporary union becomes dense and hard again. Bones rarely break in the same place twice because the repaired union remains slightly thicker than the original bone.

The repair process can take weeks to months, depending on your age and the bone involved. In general, the repair process slows with age. Recently it has been discovered that the application of weak electrical currents to the area of a broken bone can increase the rate of healing. It is thought that electrical current works by attracting osteoclasts and osteoblasts to the area under repair.

**RECAP**

Healthy bone replacement and remodeling depend on the balance of activities of bone-resorbing osteoclasts and bone-forming osteoblasts. When a bone breaks, a fibrocartilage callus forms between the broken ends and is later replaced with bone. ■

## 5.4 The skeleton protects, supports, and permits movement

Now that we have reviewed the dynamic nature of bone tissue, we turn to how all of those bones are classified and organized. Bones can be classified into four types based on shape: long, short, flat, and irregular. So far we have discussed *long bones,* which include the bones of the limbs and fingers. *Short bones* (the bones of the wrists), are approximately as wide as they are long. *Flat bones* (including the cranial bones, the sternum, and the ribs), are thin, flattened, and sometimes curved, with only a small amount of spongy bone sandwiched between two layers of compact bone. *Irregular bones* such as the coxal (hip) bones and the vertebrae include a variety of shapes that don't fit into the other categories. A few flat and irregular bones, including the sternum and the hip bones, contain red bone marrow that produces blood cells.

The 206 bones of the human body and the various connective tissues that hold them together make up the **skeleton** (Figure 5.5). The skeleton has three important functions. First, it serves as a structural framework for support of the soft organs. Second, it protects certain organs from physical injury. The brain, for example, is enclosed within the bones of the skull, and the heart and lungs are protected by a bony cage consisting of ribs, the sternum, and vertebrae. Third, because of the way that the bony elements of the skeleton are joined together at joints, the presence of the skeleton permits flexible movement of most parts of the body. This is particularly true of the hands, feet, legs, and arms.

The skeleton is organized into the *axial skeleton* and the *appendicular skeleton.*

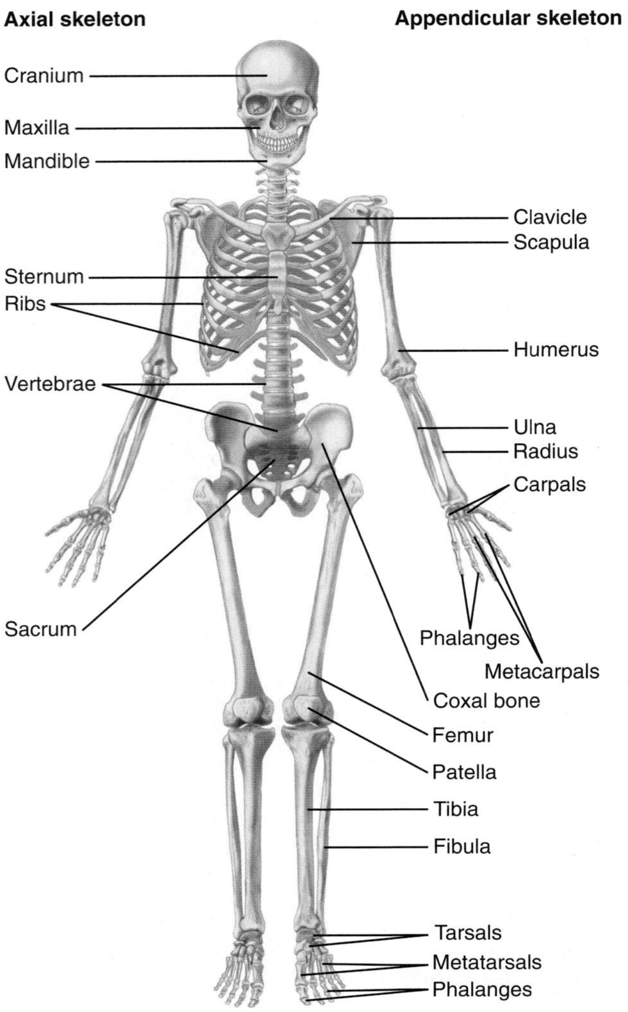


**Figure 5.5 The human skeleton.**

### The axial skeleton forms the midline of the body

The **axial skeleton** consists of the skull, vertebral column, ribs, and sternum.

**The skull: Cranial and facial bones** The human **skull** (cranium) comprises over two dozen bones that protect the brain and form the structure of the face. Figure 5.6 illustrates some of the more important bones of the skull.

The *cranial bones* are flat bones in the skull that enclose and protect the brain. Starting at the front of the skull, the *frontal bone* comprises the forehead and the upper ridges of the eye sockets. At the upper left and right sides of the skull are the two *parietal bones,* and forming the lower left and right sides are the two *temporal bones.* Each temporal bone is pierced by an opening into the ear canal that allows sounds to travel to the eardrum. Between the frontal bone and the temporal bones is the *sphenoid* bone, which forms the back of both eye sockets. The *ethmoid* bone contributes to the eye sockets and also helps support the nose.

Curving underneath to form the back and base of the skull is the *occipital bone.* Near the base of the occipital bone is a large opening called the *foramen magnum* (Latin for "great opening"). This is where the vertebral column connects to the skull and the spinal cord enters the skull to communicate with the brain.

The *facial bones* compose the front of the skull. On either side of the nose are the two *maxilla* (maxillary) bones, which form part of the eye sockets and contain the sockets that anchor the upper row of teeth. The hard palate (the "roof" of the mouth) is formed by the maxilla bones and the two

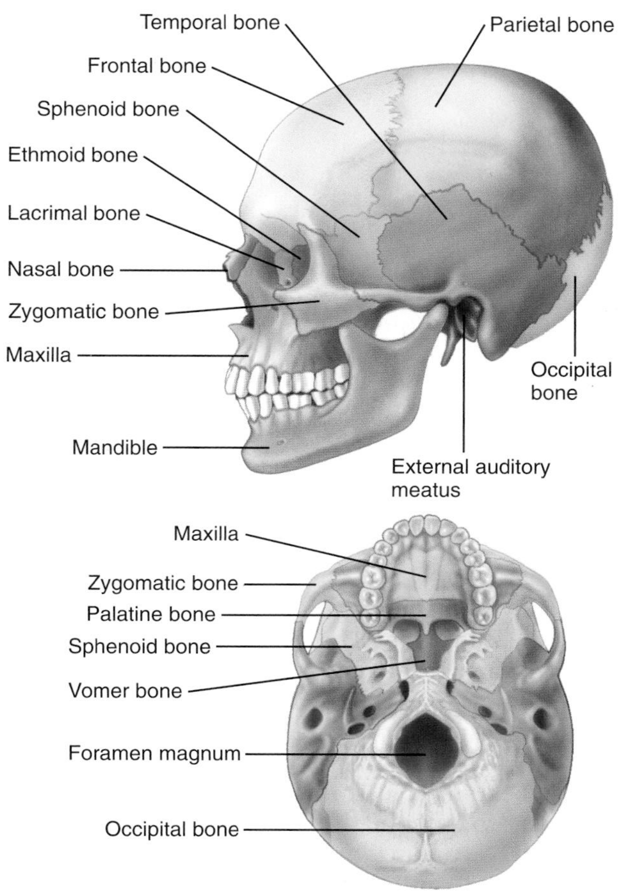


**Figure 5.6 The human skull.** Except for the mandible, which has a hinged joint with the temporal bone, the bones of the skull are joined tightly together. Their function is protection, not movement.

*palatine bones.* Behind the palatine bones is the *vomer bone,* which is part of the nasal septum that divides the nose into left and right halves. The two *zygomatic bones* form the cheekbones and the outer portion of the eye sockets. The two small, narrow *nasal bones* underlie only the upper bridge of the nose; the rest of the fleshy protuberance called the nose is made up of cartilage and other connective tissue. Part of the space formed by the maxillary and nasal bones is the nasal cavity. The small *lacrimal bones,* at the inner eye sockets, are pierced by a tiny opening through which the tear ducts drain tears from the eye sockets into the nasal cavity.

The *mandible,* or lower jaw, contains the sockets that house the lower row of teeth. All the bones of the skull are joined tightly together except for the mandible, which attaches to the temporal bone by a joint that, because it permits a substantial range of motion, allows us to speak and chew.

Several of the cranial and facial bones contain air spaces called **sinuses,** which make the skull lighter and give the human voice its characteristic tone and resonance. Each sinus is lined with tissue that secretes mucus, a thick, sticky fluid that helps trap foreign particles in incoming air. The sinuses connect to the nasal cavity via small passageways through which the mucus normally drains. However, if you develop a cold or respiratory infection, the tissue lining your sinuses can become inflamed and block these passages. Sinus inflammation is called *sinusitis.* If fluid accumulates inside the sinuses, the resulting sensation of pressure may give you a "sinus headache."

**The vertebral column: The body's main axis** The **vertebral column** (the backbone or spine) is the main axis of the body (Figure 5.7). It supports the head, protects the spinal cord, and serves as the site of attachment for the four limbs and various muscles. It consists of a column of 33 irregular bones called *vertebrae* (singular: *vertebra*) that extends from the skull to the pelvis. When viewed from the side the vertebral column is somewhat curved, reflecting slight differences in structure and size of vertebrae in the various regions.

We classify the vertebral column into five anatomical regions:

- Cervical (neck)—7 vertebrae
- Thoracic (the chest or thorax)—12 vertebrae

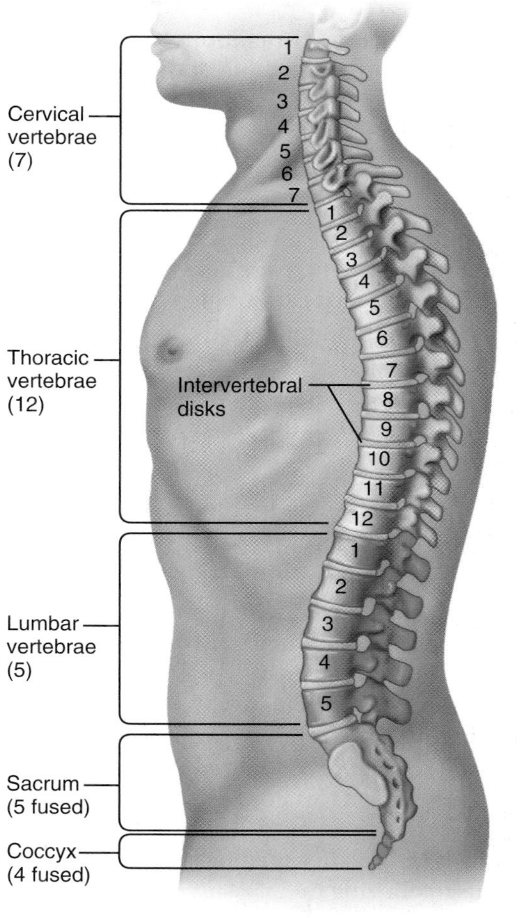


**Figure 5.7 The vertebral column.** Vertebrae are named and numbered according to their location. The vertebral column is moderately flexible because of the presence of joints and intervertebral disks.

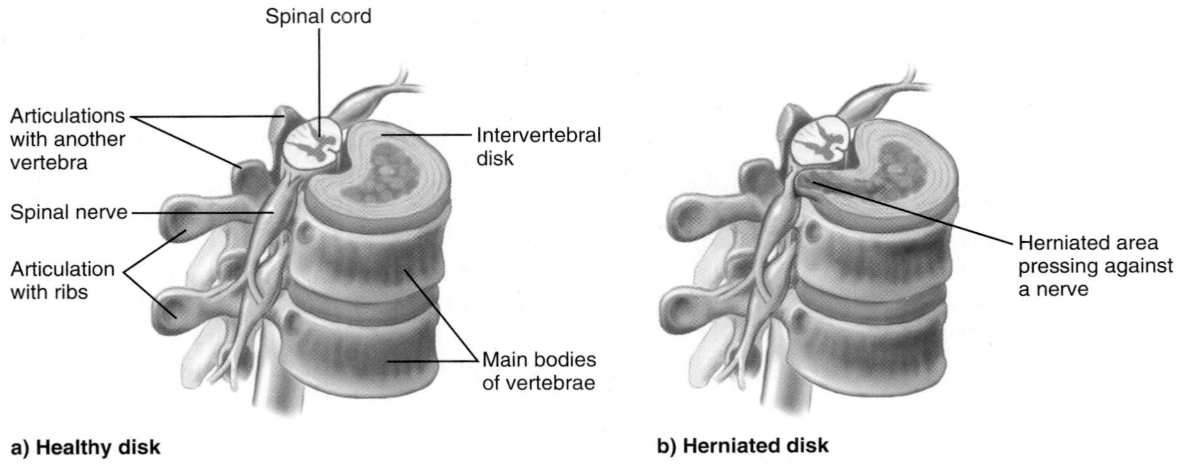


**Figure 5.8 Vertebrae. (a)** Two healthy vertebrae with their intervertebral disks. **(b)** A herniated disk.

- Lumbar (the lower portion or "small" of the back, which forms the lumbar curve of the spine)—5 vertebrae
- Sacral (in the sacrum or upper pelvic region)—In the course of evolution, the 5 sacral vertebrae have become fused.
- Coccygeal (the coccyx or tailbone)—4 fused vertebrae. The coccyx is all that remains of the tails of our ancient ancestors. It is an example of a *vestigial* structure, meaning one that no longer has any function.

A closer look at vertebrae (Figure 5.8) shows how they are stacked on each other and how they are joined. Vertebrae share two points of contact, called *articulations,* located behind their main body. There are also articulations with the ribs. The spinal cord passes through a hollow cavity between the articulations and the main body. Neighboring vertebrae are separated from each other by a flat, elastic, compressible **intervertebral disk** composed of a soft gelatinous center and a tough outer layer of fibrocartilage. Intervertebral disks serve as shock absorbers, protecting the delicate vertebrae from the impact of walking, jumping, and other movements. In conjunction with the vertebral joints, vertebral disks also permit a limited degree of movement. This lends the vertebral column greater flexibility, allowing us to bend forward, lean backward, and rotate the upper body.

An especially strong impact or sudden movement can compress an intervertebral disk, forcing the softer center to balloon outward, press against spinal nerves, and cause intense back pain. This condition is referred to as a "herniated" or "slipped disk" (Figure 5.8b), and it occurs most often in the lumbar vertebrae. Occasionally the disk may rupture, releasing its soft pulpy contents. The pain that accompanies a herniated disk can be alleviated by surgery to remove the damaged disk, relieving the pressure against the nerve. However, surgical correction of a herniated disk reduces spinal flexibility somewhat because the two adjacent vertebrae must be fused together with bone grafts.

Generally the vertebral column does an effective job of shielding the spinal cord. However, injury to the vertebral column can damage the cord or even sever it, resulting in partial or complete paralysis of the body below that point. Persons with suspected vertebral injuries should not be moved until a physician can assess the situation, because any twisting or bending could cause additional, perhaps permanent, damage to the spinal cord. You may have noticed that when athletes are injured on the field, they are instructed to lie absolutely still until a trainer and physician have examined them thoroughly.

**The ribs and sternum: Protecting the chest cavity** Humans have 12 pairs of **ribs** (Figure 5.9). One end of each rib branches from the thoracic region of the vertebral column. The other ends of the upper seven pairs attach via cartilage to the **sternum,** or breastbone, a flat blade-shaped bone composed of three separate bones that fuse during development. Rib pairs 8–10 are joined to the seventh rib by cartilage, and thus attach indirectly to the sternum. The bottom two pairs of ribs are called *floating ribs* because they do not attach to the sternum at all.

The ribs, sternum, and vertebral column form a protective *rib cage* that surrounds and shields the heart, lungs, and other organs of the chest (thoracic) cavity. They also help us breathe, because muscles between the ribs lift them slightly during breathing, expanding the chest cavity and inflating the lungs. The base of the sternum is connected to the diaphragm, a muscle that is important to breathing (see Chapter 10).

**RECAP**

The skull protects the brain, the vertebral column protects the spinal cord and supports the appendicular skeleton, and the rib cage protects the organs of the chest cavity. ■

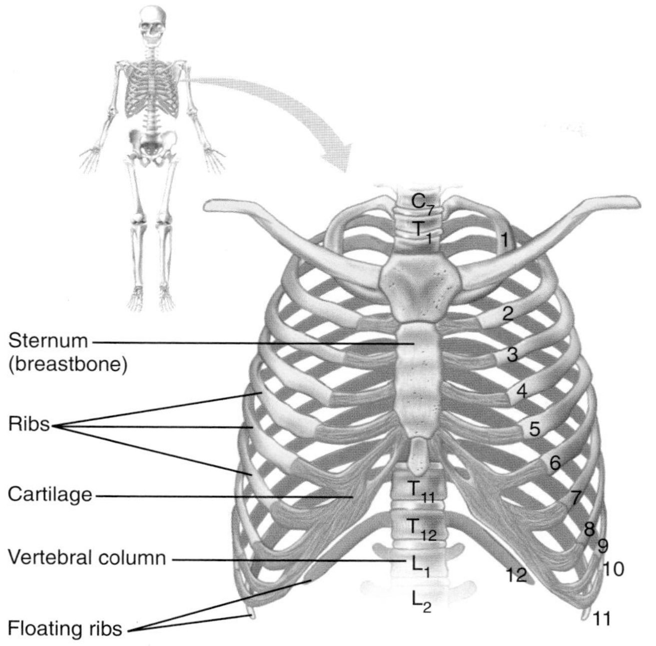


**Figure 5.9 Ribs.** The 12 pairs of ribs are numbered according to their attachment to the thoracic vertebrae. Only the first seven pairs attach directly to the sternum.

## The appendicular skeleton: Pectoral girdle, pelvic girdle, and limbs

Those parts of the body that attach to the axial skeleton are called appendages, from the Latin word meaning "to hang upon." The second division of the human skeleton, the **appendicular skeleton,** includes the arms, legs, and their attachments to the trunk, which are the pectoral and pelvic girdles.

**The pectoral girdle lends flexibility to the upper limbs** The **pectoral girdle,** a supportive frame for the upper limbs, consists of the right and left **clavicles** (collarbones) and right and left **scapulas** (shoulder blades). The clavicles extend across the top of the chest and attach to the scapulas, triangular bones in the upper back.

The arm and hand consist of 30 different bones (Figure 5.10). The upper end of the **humerus,** the long bone of the upper arm, fits into a socket in the scapula. The other end of the humerus meets with the **ulna** and **radius,** the two bones of the forearm, at the elbow. If you've ever hit your elbow and experienced a painful tingling, you know why this area is nicknamed the "funny bone"; you've just struck the ulnar nerve that travels along the elbow.

The lower ends of the ulna and radius meet the *carpal* bones, a group of eight small bones that makes up the wrist. The five *metacarpal* bones form the palm of the hand, and they join with the 14 *phalanges,* which form the fingers and thumb.

The pectoral girdle and arms are particularly well adapted to permit a wide range of motion. They connect to the rest of the body via muscles and tendons—a relatively loose method of attachment. This structure gives the upper body of humans a degree of dexterity unsurpassed among large animals. We can rotate our upper arms almost 360 degrees—a greater range of movement than with any other joint in the body. The upper arm can rotate in roughly a circle, the arm can bend in one dimension and rotate, and the wrist and fingers can all bend and rotate to varying degrees. We also have "opposable thumbs," meaning we can place them opposite our other fingers. The opposable thumb has played an important role in our evolutionary history, as it makes it easier to grasp and manipulate tools and other objects.

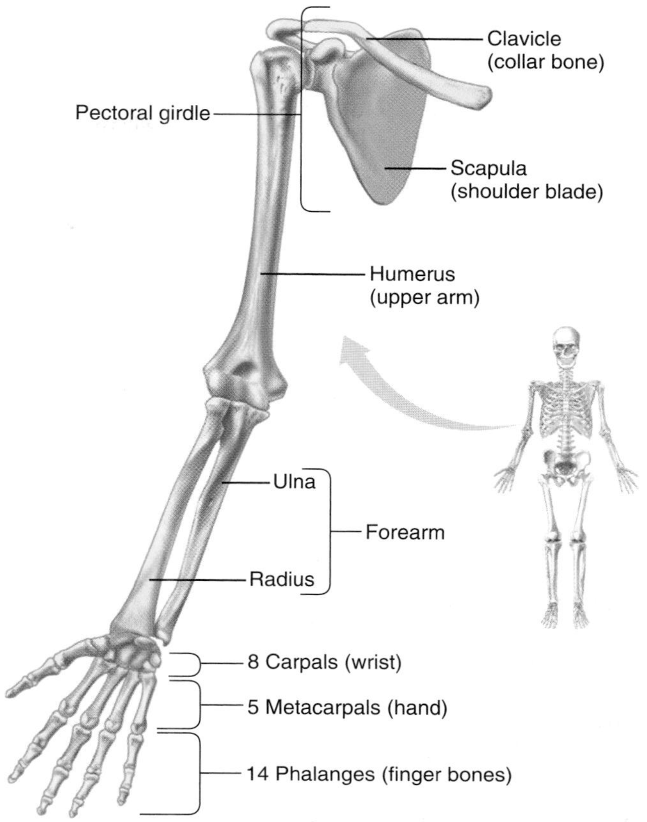


**Figure 5.10 Bones of the right side of the pectoral girdle and the right arm and hand.**

We pay a price for this flexibility, because freedom of movement also means relative instability. If you fall on your arm, for example, you might dislocate your shoulder joint or crack a clavicle. In fact, the clavicle is one of the most frequently broken bones in the body.

Although our upper limbs are well adapted to a wide range of movements, too much of one kind of motion can be harmful. Repetitive motions—performing the same task over and over—can lead to health problems called overuse or repetitive stress syndromes. Depending on the part of the body that is overused, these injuries can take many forms.

A well-known repetitive stress syndrome is *carpal tunnel syndrome,* a condition often due to repetitive typing at a computer keyboard. The carpal bones of the wrist are held together by a sheath of connective tissue. The blood vessels, nerves, and tendons to the hand and fingers pass through the sheath via the "carpal tunnel." Overuse of the fingers and hands produces swelling and inflammation of the tendons, which causes them to press against the nerve supplying the hand. The result may be pain, tingling, or numbness in the wrist and hand. Mild episodes of carpal tunnel syndrome respond to rest and pain relievers. Severe cases can be treated with surgery to relieve the pressure.

**The pelvic girdle supports the body** The **pelvic girdle** consists of the two **coxal bones** and the sacrum and coccyx of the vertebral column (Figure 5.11). The coxal bones attach to the sacral region of the vertebral column in back, then curve forward to meet in front at the *pubic symphysis,* where they are joined by cartilage. You can feel the upper curves of the coxal bones (the iliac region) as your hip bones. Together, these structures form the pelvis.

The primary function of the pelvic girdle is to support the weight of the upper body against the force of gravity. It also protects the organs inside the pelvic cavity and serves as a site of attachment for the legs. The structure of the pelvic girdle reflects a trade-off between dexterity and stability. Partly because the pelvic girdle and lower limbs are larger and more firmly connected to the rest of the body than the pectoral girdle and upper limbs, the lower limbs are less dexterous than the upper limbs.

In adult women the pelvic girdle is broader and shallower than it is in men, and the pelvic opening is wider. This allows for safe passage of a baby's head during labor and delivery. These characteristic differences appear during puberty when a woman's body begins to produce sex hormones. The sex hormones trigger a process of bone remodeling that shapes the female pelvic girdle to adapt for pregnancy and birth.

The **femur** (thighbone) is the longest and strongest bone in the body. When you jog or jump, your femurs are exposed to forces of impact of several tons per square inch. The rounded upper end of each femur fits securely into a socket in a coxal bone, creating a stable joint that effectively supports the body while permitting movement. The lower end of the femur intersects at the knee joint with the larger of the two bones of the lower leg, the **tibia,** which in turn makes contact with the thinner **fibula.** The *patella,* or kneecap, is a triangle-shaped bone that protects and stabilizes the knee joint.

At the ankle, the tibia and fibula join with the seven *tarsal* bones that make up the ankle and heel. Five long bones, the *metatarsals,* form the foot. The 14 bones of the toes, like those of the fingers, are called *phalanges.*

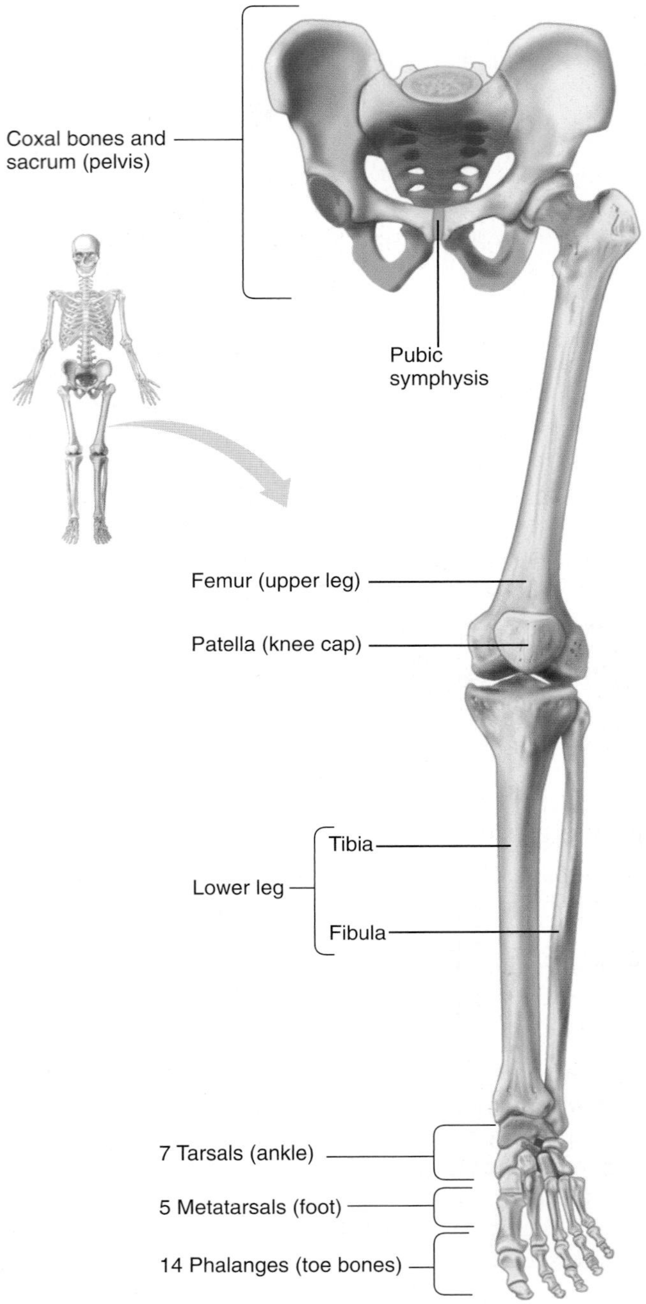


**Figure 5.11 Bones of the pelvic girdle and the left leg and foot.**

**RECAP**

The pectoral girdle and upper limbs are capable of a wide range of motions (dexterous movement). The pelvic girdle supports the body's weight and protects the pelvic organs. The lower limbs are stronger but less dexterous than the upper limbs. ■

## 5.5 Joints form connections between bones

We now turn to the structures and tissues that hold the skeleton together while still permitting us to move about freely: joints, ligaments, and tendons. **Joints,** also called articulations, are the points of contact between bones. Ligaments and tendons are connective tissues that stabilize many joints.

### Joints vary from immovable to freely movable

Joints vary considerably from basically immovable to freely movable. Types of joints include fibrous, cartilaginous, and synovial joints.

*Fibrous joints* are immovable. At birth, the flat bones in a baby's skull are separated by relatively large spaces filled with fibrous connective tissue. These "soft spots," called *fontanels,* enable the baby's head to change shape slightly so that it can squeeze safely through the mother's pelvic opening during childbirth. The presence of joints also allows for brain growth and development after birth. During childhood these fibrous joints gradually harden. By the time we reach adulthood, the joints have become thin lines, or sutures, between skull bones. These immovable joints firmly connect the bones that protect and stabilize the skull and brain.

*Cartilaginous joints,* in which the bones are connected by hyaline cartilage, are slightly movable, allowing for some degree of flexibility. Examples include the cartilaginous joints that connect the vertebrae in the backbone, and those that attach the lower ribs to the sternum.

The most freely movable joints are **synovial joints,** in which the bones are separated by a thin fluid-filled cavity. The two bones of a synovial joint are fastened together and stabilized by ligaments. The interior of the cavity is lined with a *synovial membrane,* which secretes *synovial fluid* to lubricate and cushion the joint. To reduce friction even further, the articulating surfaces of the two bones are covered with a tough but smooth layer of hyaline cartilage. Together, the synovial membrane and the surrounding hyaline cartilage constitute the *joint capsule.*

Different types of synovial joints permit different kinds of movements. A *hinge joint,* such as the knee and elbow, gets its name because it allows movement in one plane like the hinges on a door. Figure 5.12 illustrates a human knee joint. The knee joint is strong enough to withstand hundreds of pounds of force, yet it is flexible enough to swing freely in

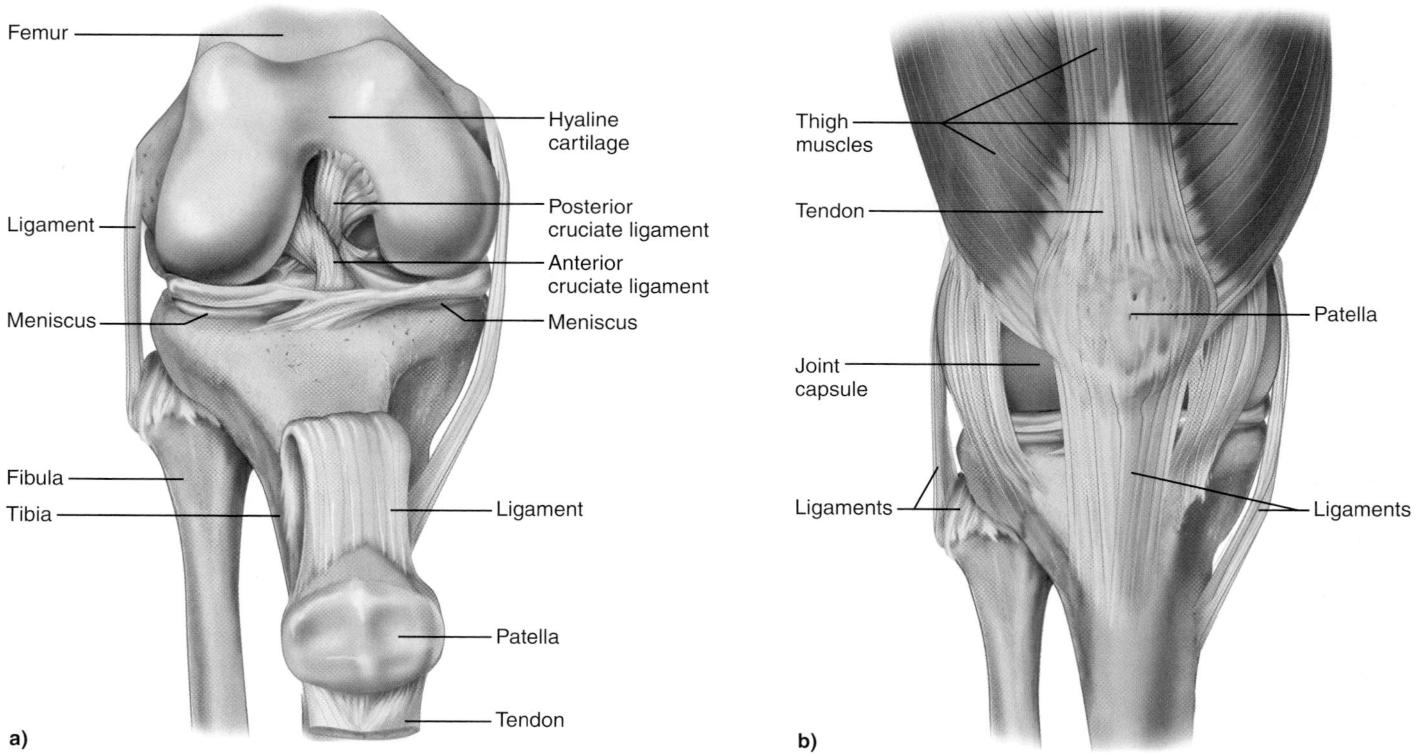


**Figure 5.12 The knee joint is a hinged synovial joint. (a)** A cutaway anterior view of the right knee with muscles, tendons, and the joint capsule removed and the bones pulled slightly apart so that the two menisci are visible. **(b)** A view of the knee with muscles, tendons, and ligaments in their normal position surrounding the intact joint capsule. The combination of ligaments, tendons, and muscles holds the knee tightly together.

one direction. To reduce friction, there are small disks of cartilage on either side of the knee called *menisci* (singular: meniscus). The knee joint also includes 13 small sacs of fluid, called *bursae* (singular: bursa), for additional cushioning. The entire joint is wrapped in strong ligaments that attach bone to bone and tendons that attach bone to muscle. Note the two *cruciate ligaments* that join the tibia to the femur bone. The anterior cruciate ligament is sometimes injured when the knee is hit with great force from the side.

A second type of synovial joint, a *ball-and-socket joint,* permits an even wider range of movement. Examples include the joint between the femur and the coxal bone (Figure 5.11), and between the humerus and the pectoral girdle (Figure 5.10). In both cases, the rounded head of the bone fits into a socket, allowing movement in all planes.

Figure 5.13 illustrates the different types of movements made possible by hinge and ball-and-socket joints. Note that you can rotate your arm and your leg because the shoulder and hip are ball-and-socket joints, but you cannot rotate the hinge joint in your knee.

Thanks to its design, a synovial joint can withstand tremendous pounding day after day, year after year without wearing out. But where does it get its strength? For that we turn to ligaments, tendons, and muscles. As we have seen, the bones of a synovial joint are held tightly together by ligaments. They are stabilized even more by **tendons,** another type of tough connective tissue, which join the bones to muscles. Both ligaments and tendons contain collagen arranged in parallel fibers, making ligaments and tendons as strong and flexible as a twisted rope of nylon. Muscle contraction increases the tension of the tendons, further tightening and strengthening the joint. (See the Try It Yourself box.)

**RECAP**

Joints are the points of contact between bones. Fibrous joints are immovable in adults, cartilaginous joints permit some movement, and synovial joints are highly movable. Synovial joints are held together by ligaments and lubricated by synovial fluid. The structure of a joint determines the type of motion it permits. ■

## 5.6 Diseases and disorders of the skeletal system

In this chapter we have already discussed several health conditions related to the skeletal system, including fractures and carpal tunnel syndrome. Now we look at several more.

### Sprains mean damage to ligaments

A sprain is due to stretched or torn ligaments. Often it is accompanied by internal bleeding with subsequent bruising, swelling, and pain. The most common example is a sprained ankle. Sprains take a long time to heal because the ligaments have few cells and a poor blood supply. Minor sprains, in which the ligaments are only stretched, usually mend themselves with time. If a large ligament is torn completely, it generally does not heal by itself, and surgery may be necessary to remove it. Sometimes the joint can be stabilized with a piece of tendon or by repositioning other ligaments. Torn ligaments in the knee are particularly troublesome because they often leave the knee joint permanently unstable and prone to future injuries.

### Bursitis and tendinitis are caused by inflammation

Bursitis and tendinitis refer to inflammation of the bursae or tendons following injury. We discuss the inflammatory process in Chapter 9. Causes of bursitis and tendinitis may include tearing injuries to tendons, physical damage caused by blows to the joint, and even some bacterial infections. Like ligaments, tendons and the tissues lining the bursae are not well supplied with blood vessels, so they do not heal quickly. Treatment usually involves applying cold during the first 24 hours and heat after that, resting the injured area, and taking pain-relieving medications. "Tennis elbow" is a painful condition caused by either bursitis or tendinitis. Other common locations for pain include the knee, shoulder, and the Achilles tendon that pulls up the back of the heel.

### Arthritis is inflammation of joints

By their nature, joints are exposed to high compressive forces and are prone to excessive wear caused by friction. "Arthritis" is a general term for joint inflammation. The most common type of arthritis is *osteoarthritis,* a degenerative ("wear-and-tear") condition that affects about 20 million Americans, most over age 45. In osteoarthritis the cartilage covering the ends of the bones wears out. With time the bone thickens and may form

**try it yourself**

### Stabilizing a Joint

To appreciate the role ligaments, tendons, and muscles play in stabilizing a joint, try this simple experiment. Sit in a low chair, stretch your leg in front of you with your heel resting on the floor, and relax your muscles. Try to move your kneecap (patella) from side to side gently with your hand. Notice how easily you can shift it out of position. Now, without changing position, tense the muscle of your thigh. Can you still move your patella?

The patella is attached to the tibia by a ligament and to the muscles of the thigh by a tendon. When you contract your thigh muscles the patella remains in position because contraction puts tension on the tendon and the ligament. The increased tension holds the patella firmly in place. If you move your hand to just below the kneecap, you can feel the tightening of the patellar ligament as you alternately contract and relax your thigh muscle.

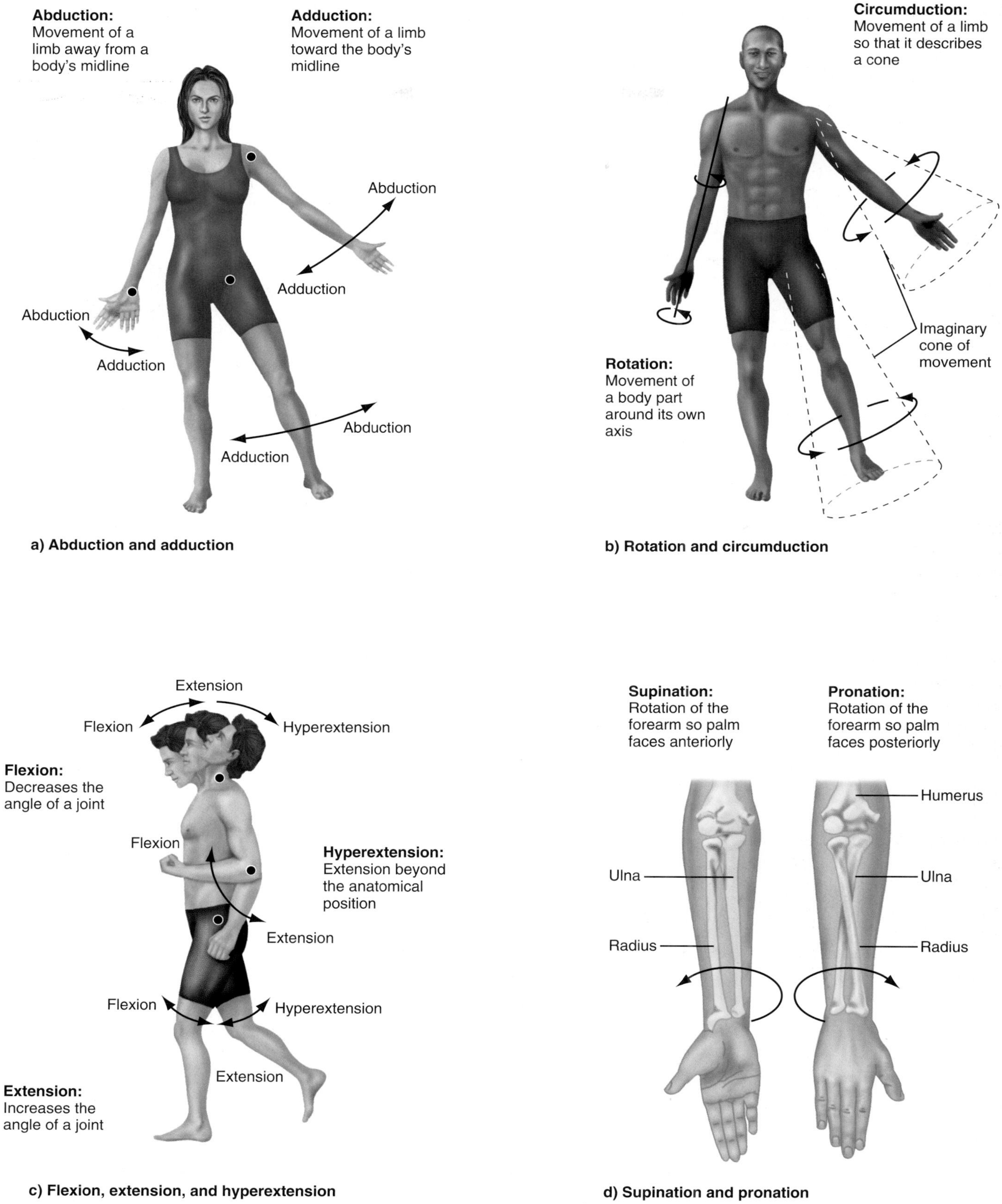


**Figure 5.13** **Types of movements made possible by synovial joints.**

# A Black Market in Human Bones?

Alistair Cooke, famed host of the PBS series *Masterpiece Theatre,* died in 2004 at the age of 95. His body lay in a New York City funeral parlor for a few days awaiting cremation. But before Cooke's body was cremated, it was secretly carved up in a back room, and his bones were removed. Authorities allege that his bones were then sold for a substantial profit, to be transplanted into patients in desperate need of tissue grafts.

Cooke's family, who had not given permission for his body parts to be donated, knew nothing of this until police contacted them after the funeral. Understandably, they were appalled. But there is an even more horrifying side to this story: Cooke died of lung cancer that had spread to his bones. Could his deadly cancer be transmitted to the people who received his bone tissue?

*Alistair Cooke, long-time host of* Masterpiece Theatre. *Cooke's body was subjected to secret, illegal bone harvesting after he died.*

## Human Body Parts: A Legitimate Big Business

The processing of allografts—tissues taken from human corpses to be transplanted into other people—has become a big business. For the most part it's a legitimate industry that serves urgent medical needs. The industry has evolved over the past several decades as harvesting and transplantation techniques have improved. Today it is a $900 million industry that is growing by 10–15% every year. Bones are used to repair fractures and replace cancerous bone. Bone pins and ground bone are used in dental surgery; bone paste plugs holes. Tendons and ligaments repair joints and tissues damaged by sports injuries, transplanted vertebrae relieve back pain, and veins and heart valves are used in heart surgeries. The bones, tendons, veins, and heart valves from just one corpse can be worth over $200,000 to surgeons, hospitals, and recipients.

*Donated bones are cleaned, frozen, and shipped to tissue processing companies.*

Under federal law it is illegal to buy or sell human body parts for a profit—they must first be donated, either by the patient while he or she is still alive or by the family after death. Several hundred legitimate nonprofit tissue banks in the U.S. can receive such donations. (To learn more about organ donations, see Chapter 15.) To avoid transmitting disease,

## the *facts*...

- It is illegal to buy or sell human body parts for a profit. Patients or their families can donate body parts only to nonprofit tissue banks.
- Legitimately donated tissues are tested, sterilized, processed, and transplanted into patients who urgently need them.
- Only 22,000 cadavers are donated annually—not enough to meet the growing legitimate demand for human tissues.
- The supply/demand imbalance may have led one criminal ring to cut up corpses in funeral homes and sell their tissues to unsuspecting medical centers throughout the U.S. and Canada.
- Because of the lack of medical screening and safeguards for these black-market tissues, some patients may have received transplants from people who died of cancer or infectious diseases.

authorities impose strict guidelines that specify what types of tissues may be harvested and how they must be processed. For instance, to prevent any risk of transmitting cancer, federal guidelines prohibit the use of bones from cancer patients for tissue implants. Legitimate tissue-processing companies receive donated tissues and test them for infectious diseases such as HIV (the virus that causes AIDS), syphilis (a sexually transmitted disease), and the viruses that cause hepatitis (inflammation of the liver). Bone tissue is then shaped into usable forms, such as pins and plates. The final products are sterilized and shipped to hospitals and surgeons all over the country, where they are used in more than 600,000 surgical procedures every year. Thousands of patients have benefited from tissues that were legitimately donated and properly processed.

### *Illegal Body Parts Can Enter the Supply Chain*

Unfortunately, only 22,000 cadavers are donated annually—not enough to supply the growing legitimate demand for human tissues. The Alistair Cooke incident is just one example of what may be a thriving black market in human body parts. Prosecutors in New York alleged that an oral surgeon named Michael Mastromarino who had lost his license arranged for a Brooklyn funeral parlor to deliver bodies to a secret operating room. There, prosecutors charge, Mastromarino and his accomplices removed body parts before the bodies were buried or cremated. Authorities say that the men paid the funeral parlor up to $1,000 per body and then sold the harvested tissues for up to $7,000 per body to a legitimate but unsuspecting tissue processing company. In some cases they falsified records indicating the deceased's age and cause of death. Mr. Cooke died of cancer at the age of 95, but his records were falsified to indicate that he died at age 85 of a heart attack. They also allegedly looted body parts from a 43-year-old woman who had died of ovarian cancer; they then forged a signature on a consent form and listed the cause of death as a head injury. When investigators examined the corpse of one grandmother, they found that her leg bones had been removed and replaced with PVC pipes. Prosecutors eventually identified over a thousand corpses from which body parts were taken without permission between 2001 and 2005.

In 2008 Mr. Mastromarino admitted guilt in a plea bargain that could reduce his jail time in exchange for providing information about others who were involved. Nevertheless, he is expected to spend at least 18 years in prison. An assistant will serve eight years. Seven funeral home directors have admitted to lesser charges.

### *Were Patients Put at Risk?*

Implants derived from legitimately harvested and processed human tissue are generally regarded as safe. The chance of contracting a disease is thought to be low because all implants are supposed to be sterilized before use. Nevertheless, at least one patient has died of an infection traced to cartilage used in a knee surgery, and several patients developed hepatitis after receiving organs and tissues from a single infected corpse.

What are the odds of getting cancer from a human tissue implant? For cancer to be transmitted, live cancer cells have to be present in the tissue at the time of surgery. Experts agree that it is unlikely, but to be on the safe side federal guidelines prohibit transplants from cancer patients.

Human bone chips ready for shipment to a hospital.

The lack of medical screening and safeguards for black-market body parts, of course, may increase these risks substantially. Patients who may have received tissue implants from Alistair Cooke or other violated corpses have been notified. Given the broad scope of the transplant network, the investigation could affect thousands of patients who have no idea of the source of their tissue donations. In one Long Island hospital alone, at least 42 patients were warned that they are at risk for HIV, hepatitis, and syphilis from these transplants.

*Michael Mastromarino pled guilty to stealing the bones of Alistair Cooke and other corpses.*

We can hope that the Mastromarino criminal case was an isolated incident and that new safeguards will be put in place to prevent it from happening again. Obviously, there is a large societal demand for human body parts that is not yet being met legitimately. Done properly, the donation of a single cadaver to a legitimate tissue-processing company ultimately benefits several dozen patients. It would be a shame if high-profile cases such as this one caused fewer cadavers to be donated, or fewer potential recipients to use legitimately donated human body parts.

### Questions to consider

**1** *Do you approve of human bones being reshaped into bone products for use in patients, provided the bones are legally obtained?*

**2** *Cancer accounts for nearly one-quarter of all deaths in the U.S. Should the federal government continue to prohibit the use of bones from all cancer patients, regardless of cancer type? Explain your reasoning.*

# Health Watch

## Treating a Sprained Ankle

For a severe sprain, many physicians advise the frequent application of cold to the sprained area during the first 24 hours, followed by a switch to heat. Why the switch, and what is the logic behind the timing of cold versus heat?

The biggest immediate problem associated with a sprain is damage to small blood vessels and subsequent bleeding into the tissues. Most of the pain associated with a sprain is due to the bleeding and swelling, not damage to ligaments themselves. The immediate application of cold constricts blood vessels in the area and prevents most of the bleeding. The prescription is generally to cool the sprain for 30 minutes every hour or 45 minutes every hour and a half. In other words, keep the sprain cold for about half the time, for as long as you can stand it. The in-between periods ensure adequate blood flow for tissue metabolism.

After 24 hours there shouldn't be any more bleeding from small vessels. The damage has been minimized, so now the goal is to speed the healing process. Heat dilates the blood vessels, improves the supply of nutrients to the area, and attracts blood cells that begin the process of tissue repair.

bony spurs, which further restrict joint movement. The result is increased friction between the bony surfaces, and the joint becomes inflamed and painful. Over-the-counter medications can reduce the inflammation and pain, and surgical joint replacements for severe osteoarthritis are fairly routine today. Injections of hyaluronic acid, a component of hyaline cartilage, can also reduce arthritic knee pain. Many physicians advise people with osteoarthritis to exercise regularly, which helps preserve the joints' healthy range of motion. Several promising new treatments to reduce joint inflammation are still in the experimental stage.

Osteoarthritis should not be confused with *rheumatoid arthritis.* Rheumatoid arthritis also involves joint inflammation, but it is caused by the body's own immune system, which mistakenly attacks the joint tissues. We take a closer look at disorders of this type in Chapter 9.

### Osteoporosis is caused by excessive bone loss

Osteoporosis is a condition caused by excessive bone loss over time, leading to brittle, easily broken bones. Symptoms include hunched posture (Figure 5.14), difficulty walking, and an increased likelihood of bone fractures, especially of the spine and hip. Osteoporosis is a major health problem in the U.S. Over 10 million Americans have the condition, and it accounts for more than 1.5 million debilitating fractures every year.

Progressive bone loss occurs whenever a slight imbalance develops between the rates of bone breakdown by osteoclasts and new bone formation by osteoblasts. Over decades, even a small imbalance can lead to a significant reduction in bone density and mass. For example, if you lost just 1% of your bone mass per year, in 30 years your bone mass would be reduced by nearly a third—enough to cause osteoporosis (Figure 5.15). This illustrates why it is so important that homeostatic regulatory systems stay in nearly exact balance.

**Figure 5.14 Osteoporosis.** Osteoporosis can lead to repeated compression fractures of the spine and a permanent change in spine curvature.

Older women have an especially high risk of osteoporosis due to the normal decline in estrogen after menopause. Although the condition is most common in older women, it can affect older men as well. Other risk factors include smoking, a sedentary lifestyle, low calcium intake, and being underweight.

The good news is that osteoporosis can be prevented. Two important strategies: get enough calcium and vitamin D, and maintain a consistent exercise program throughout your life. Calcium is crucial for the formation of new bone

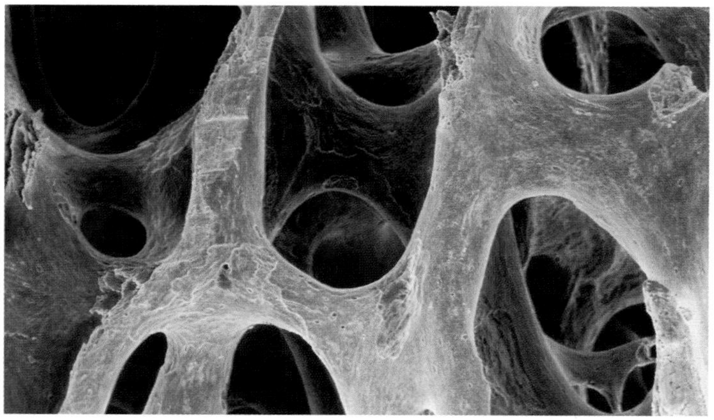

a) Normal bone.

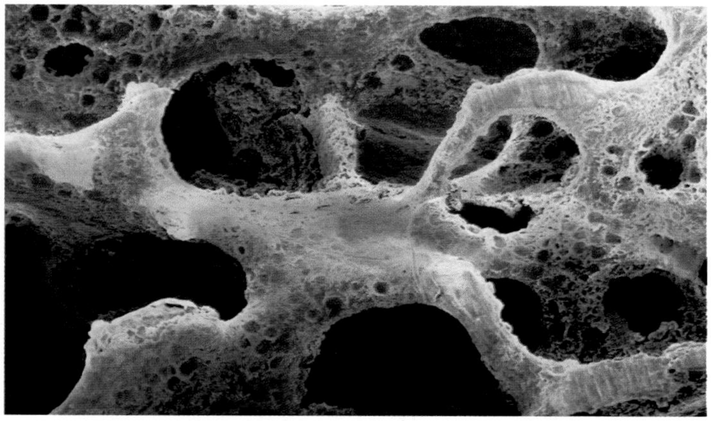

b) Bone showing osteoporosis.

**Figure 5.15 Bone loss in osteoporosis. (a)** A scanning electron micrograph (SEM) of normal bone. **(b)** SEM of a bone showing osteoporosis.

tissue. Current recommendations call for a daily intake of about 1,000–1,500 mg per day for adults, but women who have gone through menopause may benefit from even higher intakes. Both men and women can benefit from weight-bearing exercise (such as walking) and strength training (such as lifting weights), because these activities increase bone mass.

Several medications are now on the market to treat osteoporosis. Estrogen hormones, calcitonin hormones, raloxifene, and biphosphonates (alendronate and risedronate) are drugs that inhibit the bone-resorbing function of osteoclasts. The FDA recently approved a new biphosphonate medication, Boniva Injection, that can be administered intravenously every three months. Teriparatide, a medication that is a fragment of the normal parathyroid hormone molecule, is the first osteoporosis medication that can actually stimulate the activity of the bone-forming osteoblasts.

# Chapter Summary

### The skeletal system consists of connective tissue *p. 101*

- Connective tissues of the skeletal system are bones, ligaments, and cartilage.
- Bone is a living tissue composed of cells and extracellular material.
- Ligaments, composed of dense fibrous connective tissue, attach bones to each other.
- Cartilage forms the intervertebral disks and lines the points of contact between bones.

### Bone development begins in the embryo *p. 103*

- After about two months of fetal development, rudimentary models of bones have been formed from cartilage.
- Throughout the rest of fetal development and on into childhood, bone-forming cells called osteoblasts replace the cartilage model with bone.
- Growth in the length of long bones centers on growth plates in each epiphysis.

### Mature bone undergoes remodeling and repair *p. 104*

- Bone undergoes replacement throughout life.
- Bones can change shape over time, depending on the forces to which they are exposed.
- The process of bone repair includes: (1) the formation of a hematoma, (2) the formation of a fibrocartilage callus that binds the broken ends together, and (3) the eventual replacement of the callus with new bone.

### The skeleton protects, supports, and permits movement *p. 106*

- The axial skeleton is represented by the skull, the vertebral column, the sternum, and the ribs.
- In the vertebral column, intervertebral disks of fibrocartilage absorb shock and permit limited movement.

- The appendicular skeleton includes the pectoral girdle, the pelvic girdle, and the upper and lower limbs.

### Joints form connections between bones *p. 111*

- Three types of joints connect bones: fibrous, cartilaginous, and synovial.
- Synovial joints are designed for movement without friction. They are lined with a synovial membrane and lubricated by synovial fluid.

### Diseases and disorders of the skeletal system *p. 112*

- Sprains are the result of stretched or torn ligaments. Bursitis and tendinitis are caused by injuries to the bursae and tendons.
- Arthritis is a general term for joint inflammation.
- Osteoarthritis is a condition in which the cartilage covering the ends of the bones wears out and joint friction increases.
- Osteoporosis is a condition caused by progressive bone loss over time.

## Terms You Should Know

appendicular skeleton, *109*
axial skeleton, *106*
bone, *101*
cartilage, *103*
central (Haversian) canal, *102*
chondroblast, *103*
compact bone, *101*
growth plate, *104*
intervertebral disk, *108*
joint, *111*
ligament, *103*
osteoblast, *104*
osteoclast, *104*
osteocyte, *102*
osteon, *102*
osteoporosis, *105*
spongy bone, *101*
tendon, *112*

## Concept Review

1. List the five functions of bone.
2. Describe the functions of red and yellow bone marrow.
3. Explain how the two growth plates in a long bone account for the ability of a long bone to lengthen.
4. Explain what might cause a long bone to slowly change shape over many years.
5. Describe the process of bone remodeling and how it can reshape bones to make them stronger.
6. Name the three anatomical regions of the vertebral column that are above the *sacral* and *coccygeal* regions.
7. Explain why it is important not to move someone who may have suffered an injury to the vertebral column until a medical assessment can be made.
8. Describe the features of synovial joints that reduce friction and prevent the joint from wearing out prematurely.
9. Distinguish between *flexion* and *extension.*
10. Define the differences between *osteoarthritis* and *rheumatoid arthritis.*

## Test Yourself

### Matching Exercise

_____ 1. A connective tissue structure that attaches bone to bone
_____ 2. Type of bone that forms the shaft region of a long bone
_____ 3. Region of the bone that produces blood cells
_____ 4. Young bone-forming cell
_____ 5. Bone-resorbing cell
_____ 6. Name for the lower jaw

a. osteoclast
b. compact bone
c. ligament
d. mandible
e. spongy bone
f. osteoblast

### Fill in the Blank

7. Based on shape, bones are classified as either long, short, ____________________, or irregular.
8. During embryonic development, cartilage-forming cells called ____________________ create a cartilage model of the future bones.
9. The ____________________ skeleton forms the midline of the body.
10. The ____________________ girdle anchors the lower limbs.
11. The outer surface of a bone is covered by a layer of connective tissue called the ____________________.
12. The most freely movable type of joint is called a ____________________ joint.

### True or False?

13. Bones continue to lengthen throughout life.
14. In humans, all 12 pairs of ribs attach to the sternum, or breast-bone.
15. The joints between adjacent vertebrae are cartilaginous joints.

## References and Additional Reading

Bone Remodeling and Repair. *Science* 289:1497–1514, September 1, 2000. (A series of five articles on this subject.)

Diamond, J. Building to Code. *Discover,* May 1993, p. 92. (Why are bones and other body parts as strong as they are?)

Rosen, Clifford J. Restoring Aging Bones. *Scientific American,* March 2003, pp. 70–77. (An article about how a better understanding of the molecular basis of bone deposition and loss is leading to improved treatment options for osteoporosis.)

Shipman, P., A. Walker, and D. Bichell. *The Human Skeleton.* Cambridge, MA: Harvard University Press, 1985. (Photographs, fine line drawings, and good written commentary about bones and the human skeleton.)

### Internet References

Find links to the following Web sites at the Human Biology Place.

**Carolyn Csongradi: "The Living Skeleton: A Tour of Human Bones"**
**www.accessexcellence.org/RC/VL/xrays**
This site, part of the National Health Museum web site, has X-ray images of normal bones and bones that are diseased or fractured.

## Apply **What You Know**

1. Compare and contrast swimming and running as forms of exercise training in terms of how they might affect muscle mass, bone mass, and the possibility of injuries to joints.
2. The administration of growth hormone is sometimes used clinically to stimulate growth in unusually short children who are deficient in growth hormone. However, growth hormone is ineffective in unusually short but otherwise normal adults. What accounts for the difference?
3. Although sports are getting more and more competitive at younger and younger ages, in baseball it is not recommended that children learn to throw curveballs at too young an age. What is the problem with throwing a curve ball?
4. You and a friend decide to volunteer to help build houses with Habitat for Humanity over your spring break. Although you have only rarely used a hammer, you take on the task helping to construct the frame of the house. After your break is over and you have returned to campus, you notice a sharp pain in your elbow every time you bend your arm. You seek medical advice, and the doctor tells you that you have tendinitis. What is tendinitis? What might have caused your condition?
5. You just graduated and got your first job as a forensic investigator. Your first case is a skeleton that was discovered in the desert. The pathologist examines the bones and tells you that the skeleton belonged to an adult man. How can the pathologist be certain by examining only the bones? What else might the pathologist be able to tell you by examining the bones of this skeleton?
6. Obesity is a common problem in this country, even among children. What changes would you expect to see in the skeletal system of a person who has been obese for a long time?

*Answers can be found on the Human Biology Place.*

**The eSkeletons Project**
**www.eskeletons.org**
View human bones, study joint movements, and compare human bones with those of a baboon and a gorilla.

**Arthritis Foundation**
**www.arthritis.org**
A national nonprofit organization that provides advocacy, support, and services for people with arthritis and related health conditions.

**National Institute of Arthritis and Musculoskeletal and Skin Diseases**
**www.niams.nih.gov**
A division of the National Institutes of Health, this site offers the latest news on osteoporosis, arthritis, and other skeletal system disorders.

**"Sprains and Strains," MayoClinic.com**
**www.mayoclinic.com/health/sprains-and-strains/DS00343**
An overview of how to cope with these common injuries, including risk factors, symptoms, treatment, self-care, prevention, and when to seek medical help.

**University of Minnesota WebAnatomy: Skeletons and Skulls**
**http://msjensen.cehd.umn.edu/Webanatomy/skeletons_skulls/default.html**
Interactive study aids and self-tests for entry-level students of human anatomy and physiology.

# 6 The Muscular System

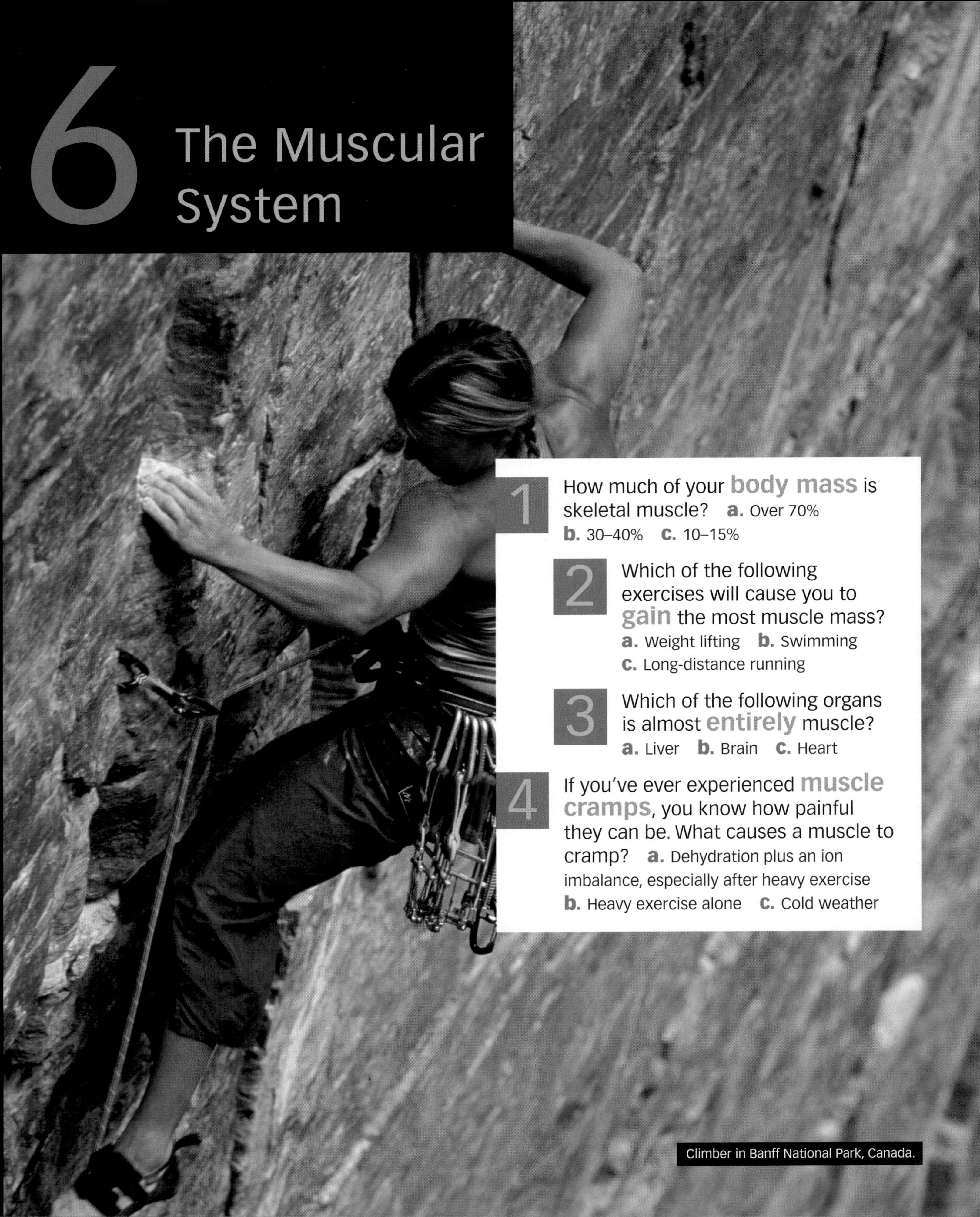

**1** How much of your **body mass** is skeletal muscle? **a.** Over 70% **b.** 30–40% **c.** 10–15%

**2** Which of the following exercises will cause you to **gain** the most muscle mass? **a.** Weight lifting **b.** Swimming **c.** Long-distance running

**3** Which of the following organs is almost **entirely** muscle? **a.** Liver **b.** Brain **c.** Heart

**4** If you've ever experienced **muscle cramps**, you know how painful they can be. What causes a muscle to cramp? **a.** Dehydration plus an ion imbalance, especially after heavy exercise **b.** Heavy exercise alone **c.** Cold weather

Climber in Banff National Park, Canada.

**Muscle cells are found in every organ and tissue** in the body and participate in every activity that requires movement. Together, they constitute nearly half of our body mass. The most obvious are the *skeletal muscles* that attach to the skeleton and give us strength and mobility. Skeletal muscles also sculpt the body and contribute to our sense of attractiveness and well-being. Some of the smallest skeletal muscles control the focus of our eyes; some of the largest are responsible for the shivering that helps keep us warm when it is cold. Nearly 40% of body weight in males and about 32% in females is skeletal muscle.

But there are two other types of muscle in the body besides skeletal muscle. Rhythmic contractions of the *cardiac muscle* of the heart pump blood throughout the body. Powerful intermittent contractions of *smooth muscle* in the walls of the uterus propel the child through the birth canal. Slower waves of smooth muscle contractions push food through the digestive tract and transport urine from the kidney to the bladder. Steady, sustained contractions of smooth muscle in the walls of blood vessels regulate blood flow to every living cell in the body.

How do muscles accomplish all this? In this chapter we examine the structure of muscles, learn how they function, and see how their activity is controlled. Finally, we'll see how muscles can become damaged and describe some diseases of muscle.

## 6.1 Muscles produce movement or generate tension

Some muscle movements are *voluntary*, meaning that we have conscious control over the movements they produce. An example is deliberately picking up an object. Other muscle movements, such as the pumping action of the heart or the maintenance of muscle tone in blood vessels, are *involuntary* in that they are generally beyond our conscious control. You cannot will your heart to stop beating.

We tend to think of muscles as producing movement, but another very important function of many muscles is to *resist* movement. The maintenance of posture while standing is a good example. If you faint, you collapse because you lose control over the muscles that support your upright posture. The maintenance of a constant blood vessel diameter even when blood pressure within the vessel changes is another example of how a muscle resists movement. These are cases where muscles generate a force, or static tension, that exactly opposes an equal but opposite force being applied to a body part.

Besides producing or resisting movement, muscles also generate heat. Under normal circumstances, contraction of our skeletal muscles accounts for over three-quarters of all the heat generated by the body. Heat generated by muscles is important in maintaining homeostasis of our body temperature, because normally our body temperature is higher than that of our surroundings. When we generate too much heat, temperature-control mechanisms are called into play that allow the body to get rid of it. However, if you spend time outdoors on a cold day you may notice that you start to shiver. Shivering occurs because your temperature-control mechanisms cause skeletal muscles to alternately contract and relax so as to generate more heat.

### The fundamental activity of muscle is contraction

All three types of muscle cells have certain fundamental features in common. First, muscle cells are *excitable*, meaning that they contract in response to chemical and/or electrical signals from other organ systems. Second, all muscles have only one basic mechanism of action: they *contract* (shorten), and then they *relax*, returning to their original length. The movements of your limbs, the beating of your heart, and the regulation of the diameters of your blood vessels all depend on muscles.

The muscle type with which you are probably most familiar is skeletal muscle. In this chapter we concentrate on skeletal muscle because skeletal muscle, in conjunction with the skeleton, is responsible for voluntary movement. At the end of this chapter we briefly discuss cardiac and smooth muscle.

**RECAP**

Muscles either produce or resist movement, and generate heat. Muscle tissue is influenced by signals from other organ systems. ■

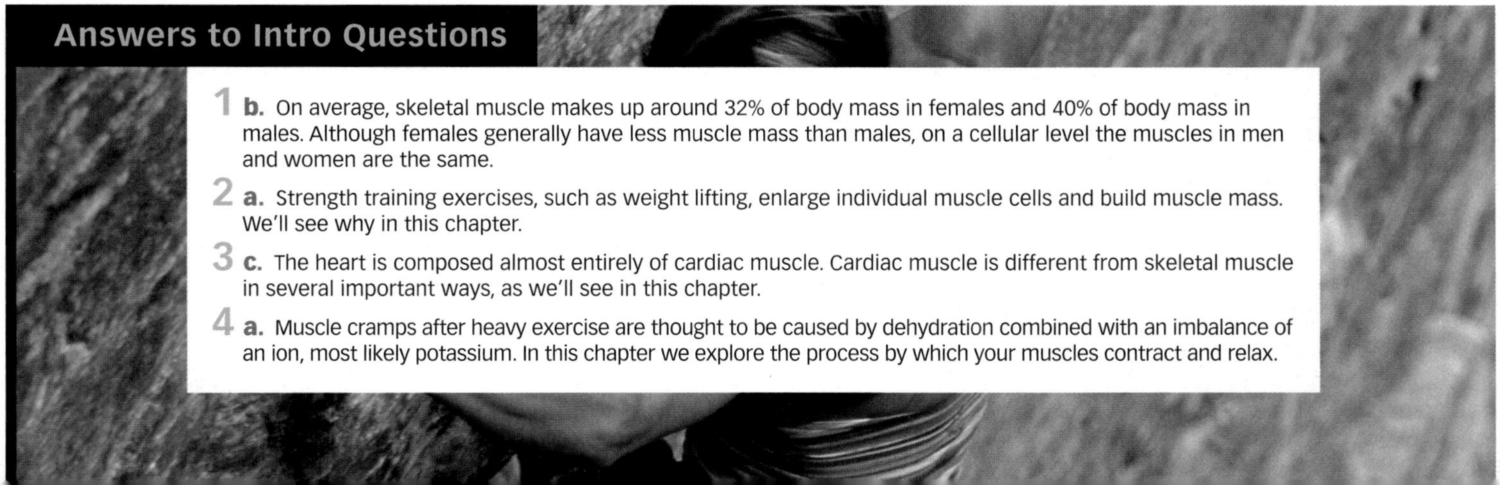

**Answers to Intro Questions**

1 **b.** On average, skeletal muscle makes up around 32% of body mass in females and 40% of body mass in males. Although females generally have less muscle mass than males, on a cellular level the muscles in men and women are the same.

2 **a.** Strength training exercises, such as weight lifting, enlarge individual muscle cells and build muscle mass. We'll see why in this chapter.

3 **c.** The heart is composed almost entirely of cardiac muscle. Cardiac muscle is different from skeletal muscle in several important ways, as we'll see in this chapter.

4 **a.** Muscle cramps after heavy exercise are thought to be caused by dehydration combined with an imbalance of an ion, most likely potassium. In this chapter we explore the process by which your muscles contract and relax.

## Skeletal muscles cause bones to move

Most **skeletal muscles** interact with the skeleton and cause bones to move (or prevent them from moving) relative to each other. All of the tasks accomplished by our skeletal muscles, whether shivering, threading a needle, lifting heavy weights, or even just standing completely still, are performed by skeletal muscles that are either contracting or relaxing. We have more than 600 skeletal muscles, often organized into pairs or groups. Muscle groups that work together to create the same movement are called *synergistic muscles.* Muscles that oppose each other are called *antagonistic muscles.*

Most skeletal muscles are attached to bones via tendons (Figure 6.1a), though a few are attached only to other muscles or to skin (such as the muscles that permit you to smile). Muscles join to the skeleton in such a way that each individual muscle produces a very specific movement of one bone relative to another. The skeleton is a complex set of levers that can be pulled in many directions by contracting or relaxing skeletal muscles. One end of a skeletal muscle, called its **origin,** joins to a bone that remains relatively stationary. The other end of the muscle, called its **insertion,** attaches to another bone across a joint. When the muscle contracts, the insertion is pulled toward the origin. The origin is generally closer to the midline of the body and the insertion is farther away.

Figure 6.1b shows how the two antagonistic muscles of the upper arm, the biceps and triceps, oppose each other to bend (flex) and straighten (extend) the forearm. When the triceps muscle relaxes and the biceps contracts, the combined action pulls on the forearm and flexes it. When the biceps relaxes and the triceps contracts, the combined action pulls the forearm down, extending it again.

Hundreds of muscles, each controlled by nerves and acting either individually or in groups, produce all possible human motions. Figure 6.2 summarizes some of the major muscles of the body and their actions.

**RECAP**

When a muscle contracts (shortens), its insertion is pulled toward its origin. ■

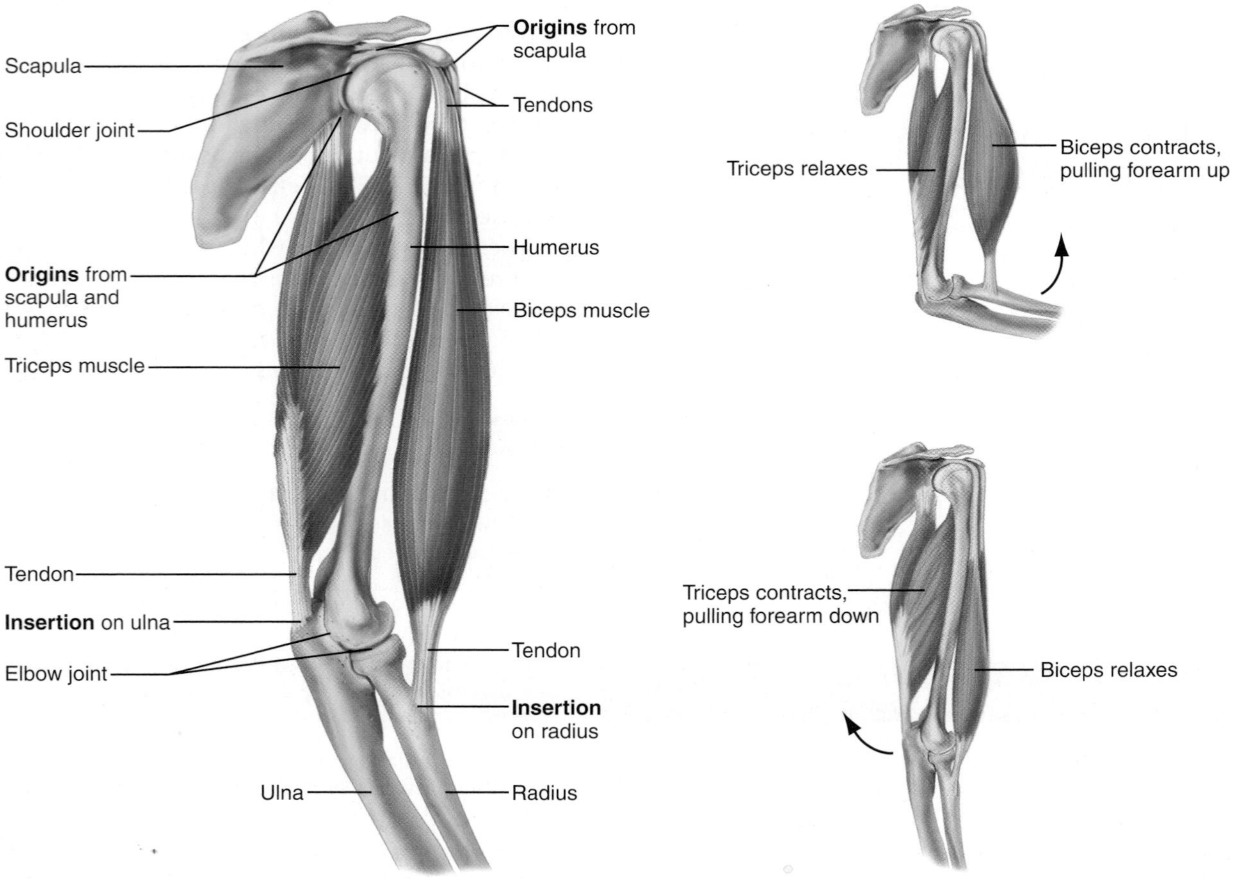


**a) Origin and insertion of skeletal muscle** **b) Movement of the forearm**

**Figure 6.1 Movement of bones. (a)** The point of attachment of a muscle to the stationary bone is its origin; the point of attachment to the movable bone is its insertion. **(b)** Antagonistic muscles produce opposite movements. When the biceps contracts and the triceps relaxes, the forearm bends. The forearm straightens when the biceps relaxes and the triceps contracts.

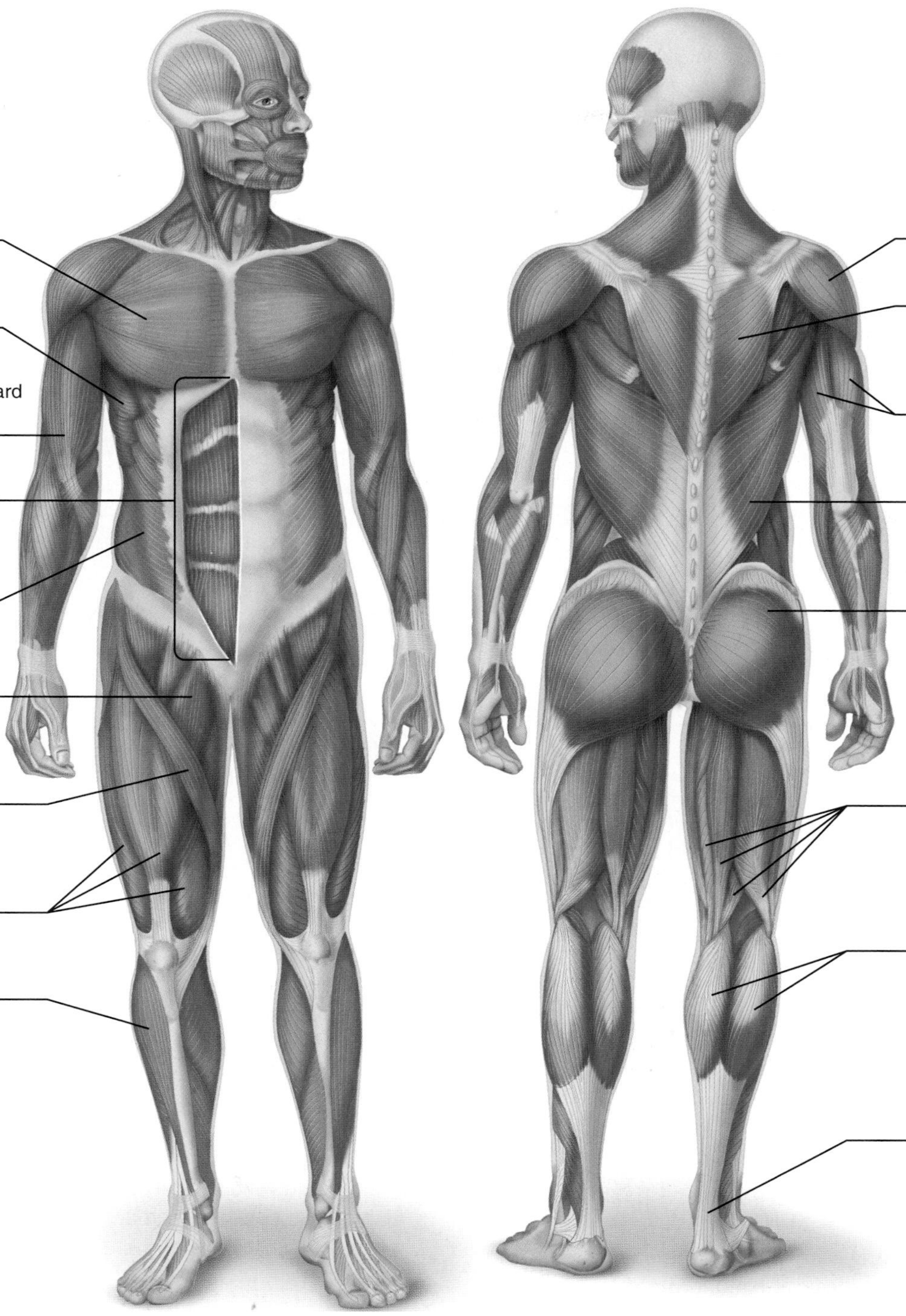


**Figure 6.2 Major skeletal muscle groups and their functions.**

## A muscle is composed of many muscle cells

A single *muscle* (sometimes referred to as a "whole muscle") is a group of individual muscle cells, all with the same origin and insertion and all with the same function. In cross section (Figure 6.3), a muscle appears to be arranged in bundles called *fascicles,* each enclosed in a sheath of a type of fibrous connective tissue called *fascia.* Each fascicle contains anywhere from a few dozen to thousands of individual muscle cells, or *muscle fibers.* The outer surface of the whole muscle is covered by several more layers of fascia. At the ends of the muscle all of the fasciae (plural) come together, forming the tendons that attach the muscle to bone.

Individual muscle cells are tube shaped, larger, and usually longer than most other human cells. Some muscle cells are only a millimeter in length, whereas others may be as long as 30 centimeters—roughly the length of your thigh muscle. Taking a closer look at a single muscle cell (Figure 6.4), we see

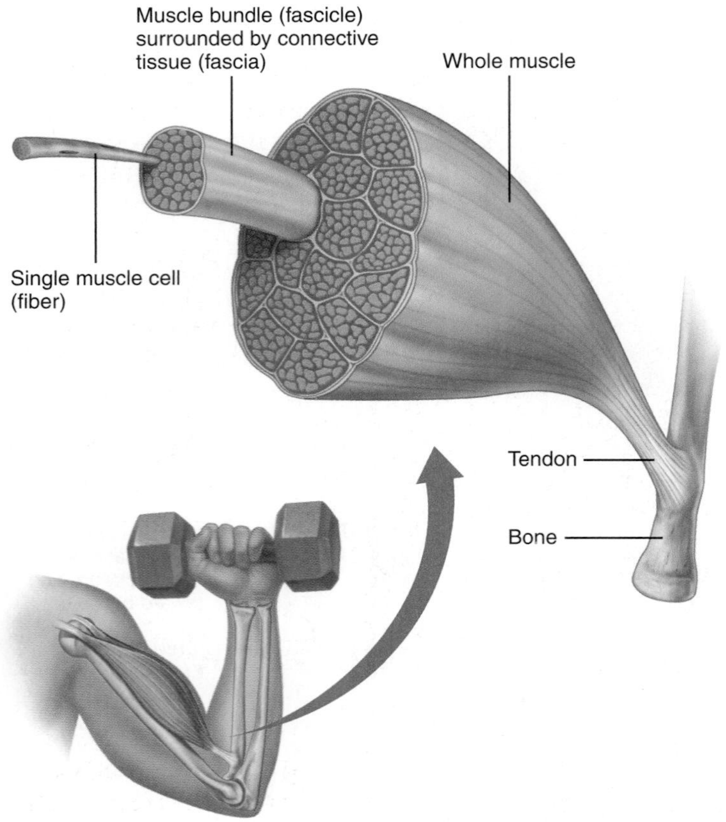


**Figure 6.3 Muscle structure.** A muscle is arranged in bundles called fascicles, each composed of many muscle cells and each surrounded by a sheath of fascia. Surrounding the entire muscle are several more layers of fascia. The fascia join together to become the tendon, which attaches the muscle to bone.

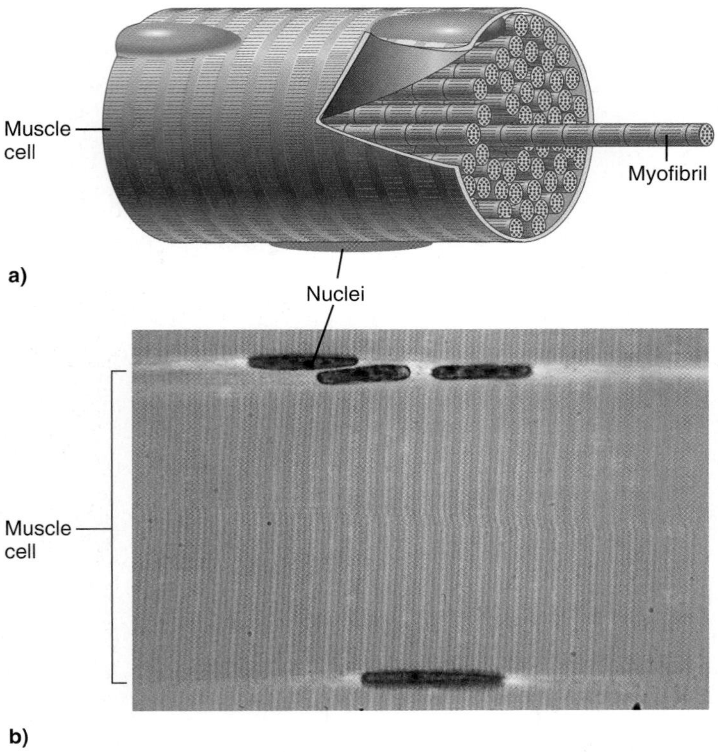


**Figure 6.4 Muscle cells. (a)** A single muscle cell contains many individual myofibrils and has more than one nucleus. **(b)** A photograph (× 2,000) of portions of several skeletal muscle cells.

that each cell contains more than one nucleus. The nuclei are located just under the cell membrane because nearly the entire interior of the cell is packed with long cylindrical structures arranged in parallel, called **myofibrils.** The myofibrils are packed with contractile proteins called *actin* and *myosin,* discussed below. When myofibrils contract (shorten), the muscle cell also shortens.

### The contractile unit is a sarcomere

Looking still closer at a single myofibril, we see a striated (or banded) appearance that repeats at regular intervals. Various elements of the pattern stand out, but the one that is important for our discussion is a dark line called the *Z-line* (Figure 6.5). A segment of a myofibril from one Z-line to the next is called a **sarcomere.** A single myofibril within one muscle cell in your biceps muscle may contain over 100,000 sarcomeres arranged end to end. The microscopic shortening of these 100,000 sarcomeres all at once is what produces contraction (shortening) of the muscle cell and of the whole muscle. Understanding muscle shortening, then, is simply a matter of understanding how a single sarcomere works.

A sarcomere consists of two kinds of protein filaments. Thick filaments composed of a protein called **myosin** are interspersed at regular intervals within filaments of a different protein called **actin.** Notice that the actin filaments are structurally linked to the Z-line and that myosin filaments are located entirely within sarcomeres, stretching between two different actin filaments. As we will see, muscle contractions depend on the interaction between these actin and myosin filaments.

**RECAP**

A muscle is composed of many muscle cells (fibers) arranged in parallel, each containing numerous myofibrils. The contractile unit in a myofibril is called a sarcomere. A sarcomere contains thick filaments of a protein called myosin and thin filaments of a protein called actin. ■

## 6.2 Individual muscle cells contract and relax

During a muscle contraction each sarcomere shortens just a little. Subtle though this action seems, it is also powerful. The contraction of an entire skeletal muscle depends on the simultaneous shortening of the tiny sarcomeres in its cells. There are four keys to understanding what makes a skeletal muscle cell contract and relax:

- A skeletal muscle cell must be activated by a nerve. It does not contract on its own.

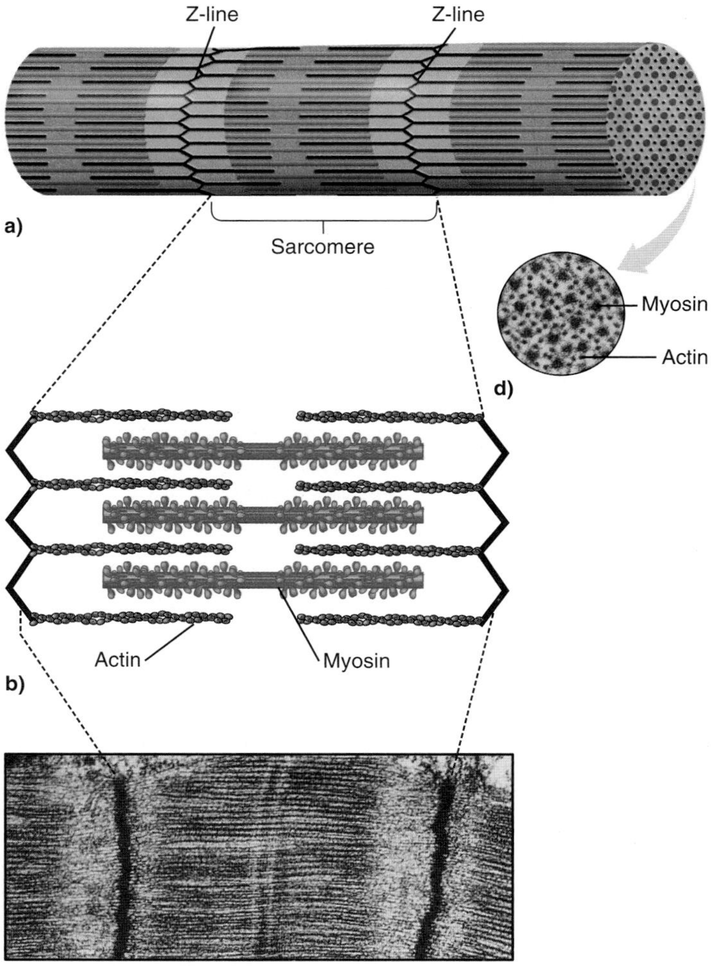


**Figure 6.5 Structure of a myofibril. (a)** A closer view of a section of a myofibril showing that it is composed of sarcomeres joined end to end at the Z-line. **(b)** Sarcomeres contain thin filaments of actin that attach to the Z-lines and thicker filaments of myosin that span the gap between actin molecules. **(c)** An electron micrograph (× 38,000) of a longitudinal section of a sarcomere. **(d)** An electron micrograph cross section of a sarcomere in a region that contains both actin and myosin.

- Nerve activation increases the concentration of calcium in the vicinity of the contractile proteins.
- The presence of calcium permits contraction. The absence of calcium prevents contraction.
- When a muscle cell is no longer stimulated by a nerve, contraction ends.

Let's look at each point in more detail.

## Nerves activate skeletal muscles

Skeletal muscle cells are stimulated to contract by certain nerve cells called **motor neurons.** The motor neurons secrete a chemical substance called *acetylcholine (ACh)*. Acetylcholine is a **neurotransmitter,** a chemical released by nerve cells that has either an excitatory or inhibitory effect on another excitable cell (another nerve cell or a muscle cell). In the case of skeletal muscle, acetylcholine excites (activates) the cells.

The junction between a motor neuron and a skeletal muscle cell is called the **neuromuscular junction.** When an electrical impulse traveling in a motor neuron arrives at the neuromuscular junction, acetylcholine is released from the nerve terminal (Figure 6.6). The acetylcholine diffuses across the narrow space between the neuron and the muscle cell and binds to receptor sites on the muscle cell membrane. The binding of acetylcholine to the receptors causes the muscle cell membrane to generate an electrical impulse of its own that travels rapidly along the cell membrane in all directions. In addition, tubelike extensions of the cell membrane called *T tubules* (the T stands for transverse) transmit the electrical impulse deep into the interior of the cell. The function of the T tubules is to get the electrical impulse to all parts of the cell as quickly as possible.

**RECAP**

Motor neurons stimulate skeletal muscles by releasing acetylcholine at the neuromuscular junction. ■

## Activation releases calcium

As shown in Figure 6.6, T tubules are in close contact with a series of membrane-bound chambers called the **sarcoplasmic reticulum** (*sarco-* is derived from a Greek word for "flesh" or "muscle"). The sarcoplasmic reticulum is similar to every other cell's smooth endoplasmic reticulum except that its shape is different, in part because it must fit into the small amount of space in the cell not occupied by myofibrils. The primary function of the sarcoplasmic reticulum is to store ionic calcium ($Ca^{2+}$).

Inside the muscle cell, an electrical impulse races down the T tubules to the sarcoplasmic reticulum. The arrival of an electrical impulse triggers the release of calcium ions from the sarcoplasmic reticulum. The calcium diffuses into the cell cytoplasm and then comes in contact with the myofibrils, where it sets in motion a chain of events that leads to contraction.

## Calcium initiates the sliding filament mechanism

Muscles contract when sarcomeres shorten, and sarcomeres shorten when the thick and thin filaments slide past each other, a process known as the **sliding filament mechanism** of contraction. Taking a closer look at the arrangement of thick and thin filaments in a single sarcomere (Figure 6.7), we see that every thin filament consists of two strands of actin molecules spiraling around each other. Thick filaments are composed of many individual molecules of myosin. Myosin molecules are shaped somewhat like a golf club, with a long shaft and a rounded head. Myosin shafts form the main part of the thick filaments. The heads stick out to the side, nearly touching the thin filaments of actin. When a muscle is relaxed, the myosin heads do not quite make contact with the thin filaments, however. Contraction occurs when the myosin heads make contact with the thin filaments, forming a *cross-bridge* between the two filaments. The formation of a cross-bridge

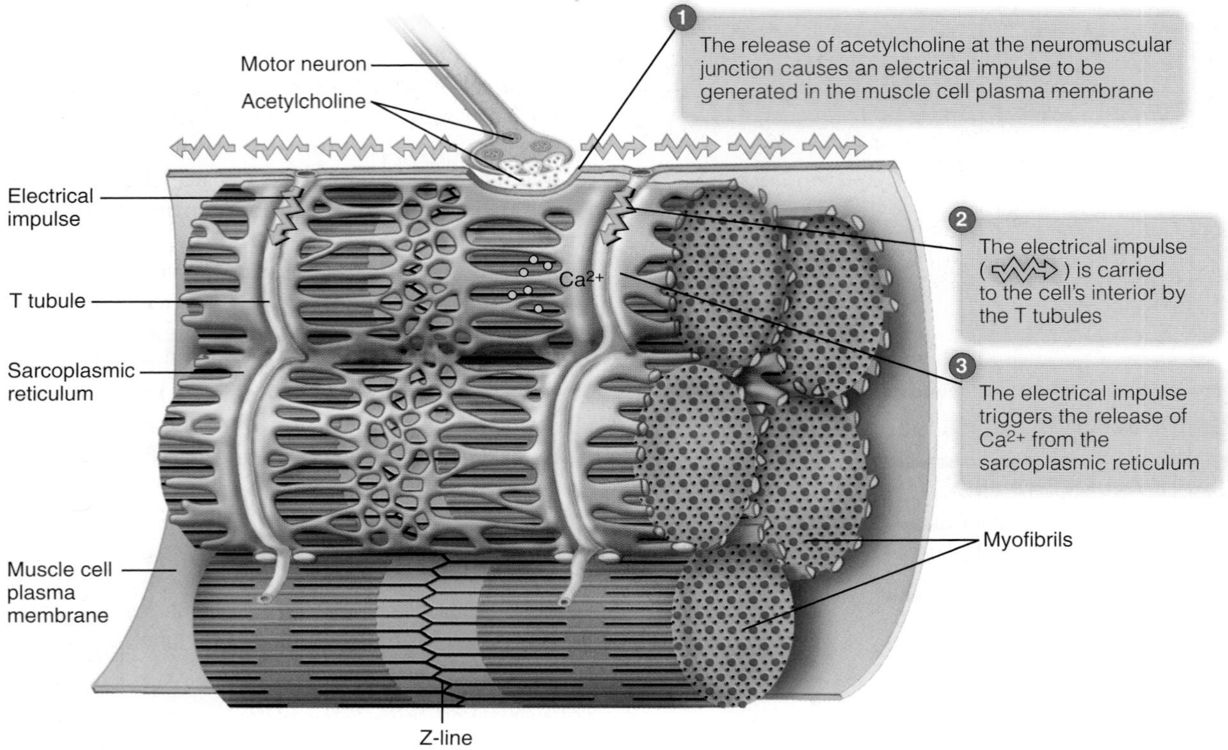


**Figure 6.6 How nerve activation leads to calcium release within a muscle cell.**

causes the head to bend relative to the shaft, pulling the actin molecules toward the center of the sarcomere. The processes of cross-bridge formation and bending (the molecular events of contraction) require energy.

But what initiates the process of contraction? Put another way, what prevents contraction from occurring all the time? The answer is that contraction is inhibited unless calcium is present. An even closer look at a section of myosin and actin (Figure 6.8) shows why. Closely associated with the actin filaments are two other protein molecules called *troponin* and *tropomyosin* that together form the *troponin-tropomyosin protein complex.* In the absence of calcium, the troponin-tropomyosin

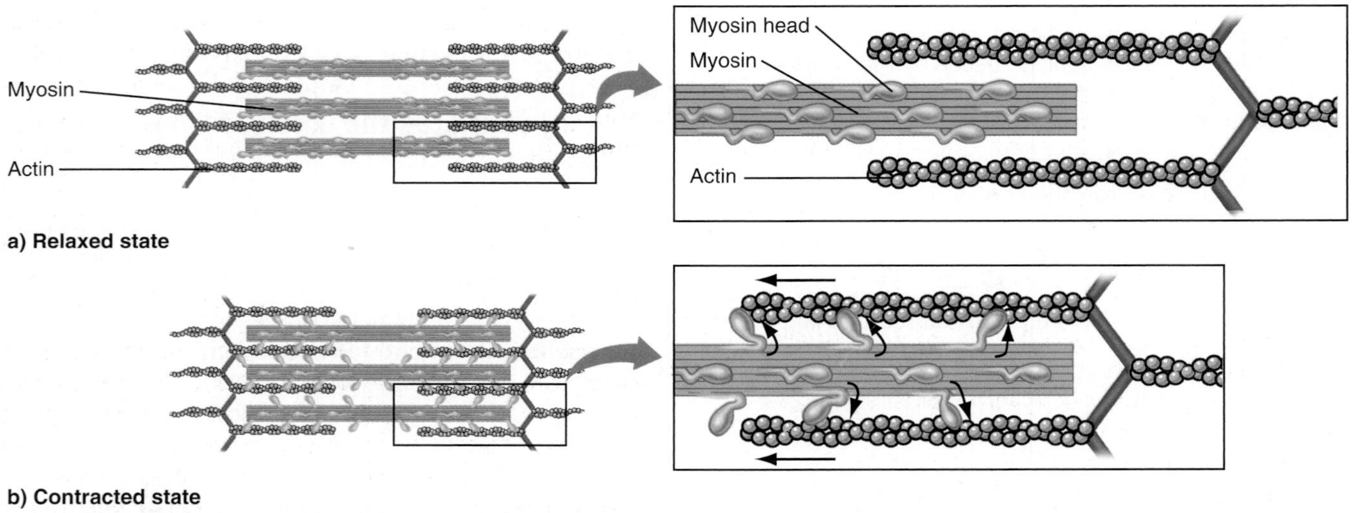


**Figure 6.7 Sliding filament mechanism of contraction. (a)** In the relaxed state the myosin heads do not make contact with actin. **(b)** During contraction the myosin heads form cross-bridges with actin and bend, pulling the actin filaments toward the center of the sarcomere.

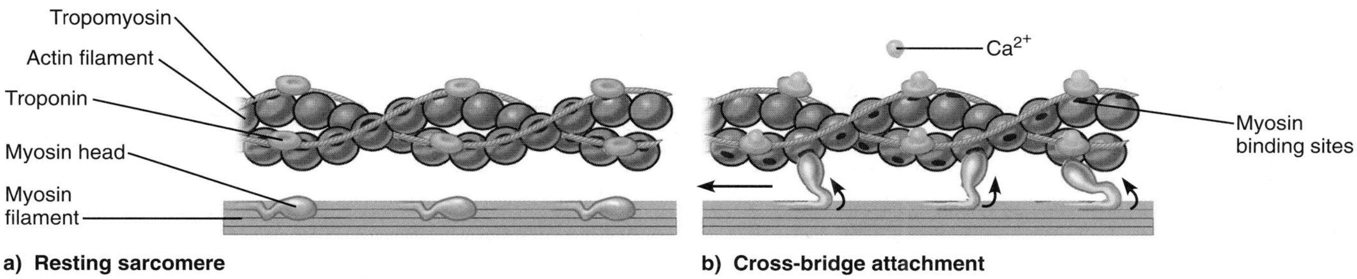


**Figure 6.8 Role of calcium in contraction. (a)** In the absence of calcium the muscle is relaxed because the myosin heads cannot form cross-bridges with actin. **(b)** The binding of calcium to troponin causes a shift in the troponin-tropomyosin complex, allowing cross-bridges to form.

complex interferes with the myosin binding sites on the actin molecule. Following an electrical impulse, calcium released from the sarcoplasmic reticulum binds to troponin, resulting in a shift in the position of the troponin-tropomyosin protein complex that exposes the myosin binding sites and permits the formation of cross-bridges. At this point the myosin heads form cross-bridges with actin, undergo a bending process, and physically pull the actin filaments toward the center of the sarcomere from each end. With thousands of myosin cross-bridges doing this simultaneously, the result is a sliding movement of the thin filaments relative to the thick ones and a shortening of the sarcomere. As hundreds of thousands of sarcomeres shorten, individual muscle cells, and ultimately the whole muscle, shorten as well.

**RECAP**

The release of calcium from the sarcoplasmic reticulum triggers contraction. Calcium allows cross-bridges to form between myosin and actin, which leads to contraction by a sliding filament mechanism. ■

## When nerve activation ends, contraction ends

Relaxation of a muscle cell occurs when nerve activity ends. In the absence of nerve activity, no more calcium is released from the sarcoplasmic reticulum. The calcium released as a result of prior electrical impulses is transported back into the sarcoplasmic reticulum by active transport, which requires energy in the form of ATP. As the calcium concentration in the myofibrils falls, the troponin-tropomyosin complex shifts back into its original position, preventing the binding of the myosin cross-bridges to actin. The sarcomere stretches passively to its original resting length, and the muscle cell relaxes.

Any factor that interferes with the process of nerve activation can disrupt muscle function. In the disorder *myasthenia gravis,* the body's immune system attacks and destroys acetylcholine receptors on the cell membrane of muscle cells. Affected muscles respond only weakly to nerve impulses or fail to respond at all. Most commonly impaired are the eye muscles, and many people with myasthenia gravis experience drooping eyelids and double vision. Muscles in the face and neck may also weaken, leading to problems with chewing, swallowing, and talking. Medications that facilitate the transmission of nerve impulses can help people with this condition.

## Muscles require energy to contract and to relax

Muscle contraction requires a great deal of energy. Like most cells, muscle cells use ATP as the energy source. In the presence of calcium, myosin acts as an enzyme, splitting ATP into ADP and inorganic phosphate and releasing energy to do work. The energy is used to "energize" the myosin head so that it can form a cross-bridge and undergo bending. Once the bending has occurred, another molecule of ATP binds to the myosin, which causes the myosin head to detach from actin. As long as calcium is present, the cycle of ATP breakdown, attachment, bending, and detachment is repeated over and over again in rapid succession. The result is a shortening of the sarcomere.

At the end of the contractile period (when nerve impulses end), energy from the breakdown of ATP is used to transport calcium back into the sarcoplasmic reticulum so that relaxation can occur. However, a second requirement for relaxation is that an intact molecule of ATP must bind to myosin before myosin can finally detach from actin. This last role of ATP is the explanation for *rigor mortis* (Latin, meaning "rigid death"), in which a body becomes stiff during the time period from about four hours to several days after death. Shortly after death, calcium begins to leak out of the sarcoplasmic reticulum, causing muscle contraction. The contractions use up the available ATP, but after death the ATP cannot be replenished. In the absence of ATP, the myosin heads cannot detach from actin, and so the muscles remain "locked" in the contracted state. Eventually the stiffness of rigor mortis decreases as the muscle cells degenerate.

**Muscle cells obtain ATP from several sources** Muscle cells store only enough ATP for about 10 seconds' worth of maximal activity. Once this is used up the cells must produce more ATP from other energy sources, including creatine phosphate, glycogen, glucose, and fatty acids.

An important pathway for producing ATP involves creatine phosphate (creatine-P), a high-energy molecule with an attached phosphate group. Creatine phosphate can transfer a phosphate group and energy to ADP and therefore create a new ATP molecule quickly. This reaction is reversible: if ATP is not needed to power muscle contractions, the excess ATP can be used to build a fresh supply of creatine phosphate, which is stored until needed. In recent years creatine phosphate loading has become common among bodybuilders and athletes, particularly those who need short-term bursts of power. Creatine phosphate also seems to improve muscle performance in certain neuromuscular diseases, such as amyotrophic lateral sclerosis (ALS), also known as Lou Gehrig's Disease.

The combination of previously available ATP plus stored creatine phosphate produces only enough energy for up to 30–40 seconds of heavy activity. Beyond that, muscles must rely on stored glycogen, a complex sugar (polysaccharide) composed of many smaller molecules of glucose. For the first three to five minutes of sustained activity, a muscle cell draws on its internal supply of stored glycogen. Glucose molecules are removed from the glycogen, and their energy is used to synthesize ATP. Part of the process of the breakdown of glucose can happen without oxygen (called anaerobic metabolism) fairly quickly, but it yields only two ATP molecules per glucose molecule and has the unfortunate side effect of producing lactic acid, which can make muscles sore.

The most efficient long-term source of energy is the aerobic metabolism of glucose, fatty acids, and other high-energy molecules such as lactic acid. Aerobic metabolism, as you already know, takes place in mitochondria and requires oxygen. The next time you engage in strenuous exercise, notice that it may take you a few minutes to start breathing heavily. The increase in respiration indicates that aerobic metabolism is now taking place. Until aerobic metabolism kicks in, however, your cells are relying on stored ATP, creatine phosphate, and anaerobic metabolism of glycogen. Weight lifters can rely on stored energy because their muscles perform for relatively short periods. Long-distance runners start out by depending on stored energy, but in less than a minute they are relying almost exclusively on aerobic metabolism. If they could not, they would collapse in exhaustion. Table 6.1 summarizes energy utilization by muscle.

After you finish exercising, note that you continue to breathe heavily for a period of time. These rapid, deep breaths help reverse your body's **oxygen debt,** incurred because your muscles used more ATP early on than was provided by aerobic metabolism. The additional ATP was produced by anaerobic metabolism, with the subsequent buildup of lactic acid. After exercise, you still need oxygen to metabolize the lactic acid by aerobic pathways and to replenish energy stores. The ability of muscle tissue to accumulate an oxygen debt and then repay it later allows muscles to perform at a near-maximal rate even before aerobic metabolism has had a chance to increase. The increase in aerobic metabolism takes several minutes because it requires both an increase in respiration and an increase in blood flow to the tissues.

Muscle **fatigue** is defined as a decline in muscle performance during sustained exercise. The most common cause of fatigue is a lack of sufficient ATP to meet metabolic demands. However, fatigue can also be caused by psychological factors, including discomfort or the boredom of repetitive tasks.

**RECAP**

Energy from the breakdown of ATP is required for contraction and for calcium transport. ATP is produced from metabolism of creatine phosphate and glycogen stores within the muscle, and from glucose and fatty acids obtained from the blood. ■

## 6.3 The activity of muscles can vary

The general functions of muscles are to move body parts or to maintain a certain body position. How well they carry out their functions depends on a number of factors, including whether bones actually move or not, the degree of nerve

**Table 6.1 Energy sources for muscle**

| Energy source | Quantity | Time of use | Comments |
|---|---|---|---|
| Stored ATP | Stored only in small quantities | About 10 seconds | ATP is only direct energy source. It must be replenished by the other energy sources. |
| Stored creatine phosphate | Three to five times amount of stored ATP | About 30 seconds | Converted quickly to ATP. |
| Stored glycogen | Variable; some muscles store large quantities | Primarily used during heavy exercise within the first 3–5 minutes | ATP yield depends on whether oxygen is available. One glucose molecule (derived from stored glycogen) yields only 2 ATP molecules in the absence of oxygen, but 36 ATP molecules in the presence of oxygen. |
| Aerobic metabolism | Not a stored form of energy; oxygen and nutrients (glucose and fatty acids) are constantly supplied by the blood | Always present; increases dramatically within several minutes of onset of exercise, when blood flow and respiration increase | High yield. Complete metabolism of one glucose molecule yields 36 ATP molecules. |

stimulation, the type of muscle fiber, and the degree to which exercise has improved muscle mass and aerobic capacity.

## Isotonic versus isometric contractions: Movement versus static position

Most types of exercise include a combination of two different types of muscle contractions, called isotonic and isometric contractions.

*Isotonic* ("same" + "strength" or "tone") contractions occur whenever a muscle shortens while maintaining a constant force. An example of an isotonic contraction is the generation of enough muscle force to move an object or part of the skeleton. How heavy the object is doesn't matter, as long as parts of the skeleton actually move. It could be just your empty hand, a pencil, a book, or a 100-pound barbell.

In *isometric* ("same" + "length") contractions, force is generated, muscle tension increases, and the muscle may even shorten a little as tendons are stretched slightly, but bones and objects do not move. As a result, isometric contractions do not cause body movement. Examples are tightening your abdominal muscles while sitting still, or straining to lift a weight too heavy to lift. Isometric contractions help to stabilize the skeleton. In fact you contract your muscles isometrically whenever you stand, just to maintain an upright position. If you doubt it, think about how quickly you would fall down if you were to faint and lose control over your skeletal muscles. Isometric contractions are a useful way to strengthen muscles.

## The degree of nerve activation influences force

A single muscle may consist of thousands of individual muscle cells. The individual cells in any muscle are organized into groups of cells that all work together. Each group of cells is controlled by a single nerve cell called a *motor neuron* (because it affects movement). The motor neuron and all of the muscle cells it controls are called a **motor unit** (Figure 6.9). A motor unit is the smallest functional unit of muscle contraction, because when the motor neuron is activated, all the muscle cells in that motor unit are activated together.

Our strength and ability to move effectively depend on how forcefully our muscles contract. The mechanical force that muscles generate when they contract is called **muscle tension.** How much tension is generated by a muscle depends on three factors:

- The number of muscle cells in each motor unit (motor unit size)
- The number of motor units active at any one time
- The frequency of stimulation of individual motor units

Motor unit size can vary widely from one muscle to the next. The number of muscle cells per motor unit is a tradeoff between brute strength and fine control. Larger motor units generate more force but offer less control. In the thigh muscle, where strength is more important than fine control, a single motor unit may consist of as many as a thousand muscle cells. In muscles of the eye, where fine control is essential, a motor unit may consist of only 10 muscle cells.

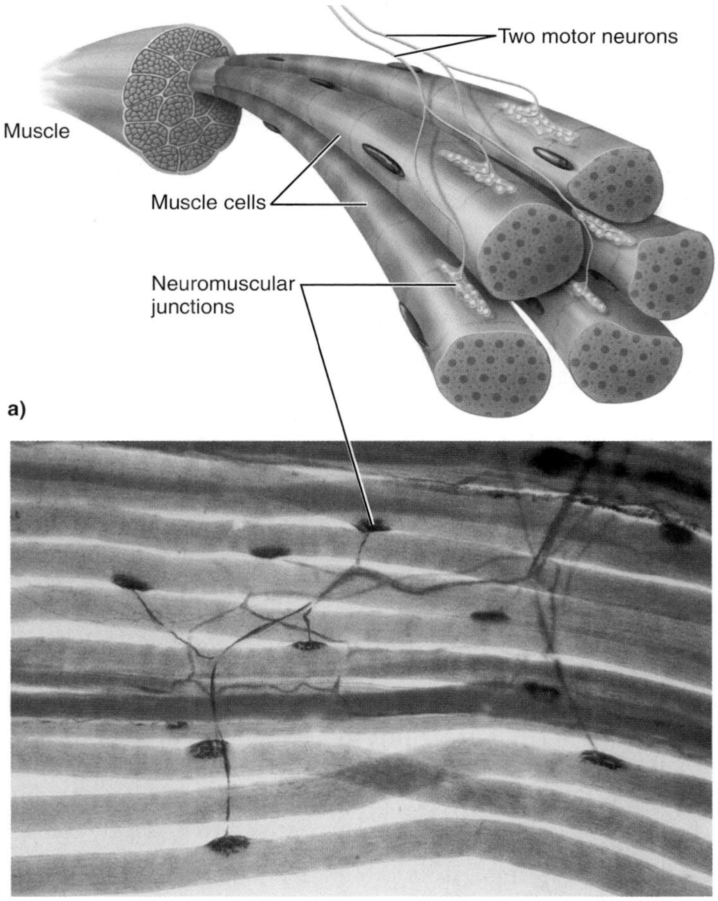


**Figure 6.9 Motor units. (a)** A motor unit consists of a motor neuron and all of the muscle cells it controls. Any one muscle cell is controlled by only one motor neuron, but a motor neuron controls more than one muscle cell. **(b)** A photograph (× 200) of several muscle cells showing branches of the motor neuron and neuromuscular junctions.

According to the **all-or-none principle,** muscle cells are completely under the control of their motor neuron. Muscle cells never contract on their own. For an individual muscle cell, there is no such thing as a half-hearted contraction, and there is no such thing as disobeying an order. Muscle cells always respond with a complete cycle of contraction and relaxation (called a **twitch**) every time they are stimulated by an electrical impulse, called an *action potential,* from their motor neuron. You will learn more about action potentials in Chapter 11. For now you need only understand that they are the stimuli for muscle contraction.

Although individual motor units either are contracting or are relaxed, whole muscles generally maintain an intermediate level of force known as *muscle tone.* Muscle tone exists because, at any one time, some of the muscle's motor units are contracting while others are relaxed. The second factor that affects overall muscle force, then, is the number of motor units active at any one time. Increasing tone (or force) by activating more motor units is called **recruitment.** The maintenance of muscle tone depends on the nervous system.

The third factor that affects force generation by a muscle is the frequency of stimulation of individual motor units. To understand how frequency of stimulation influences force, we need to take a closer look at what happens when a muscle cell is stimulated by its motor neuron. Although we cannot study the contraction of single muscle cells in the laboratory easily, the study of whole muscles has revealed some important findings regarding the timing of the relationship between a stimulus and a twitch. A laboratory recording of muscle activity, called a *myogram,* reveals that the stimulus-twitch relationship has three stages (Figure 6.10):

1. *Latent period* (the time between stimulation and the start of contraction). This is the time it takes for the nerve impulse to travel to the sarcoplasmic reticulum, for calcium to be released, and for the myosin heads to bind to the actin filaments.
2. *Contraction* (the time during which the muscle actually shortens). Actin filaments are pulled toward the center of the sarcomere and myofibrils shorten.
3. *Relaxation* (muscle returns to its original length). Calcium is transported back into the sarcoplasmic reticulum, the troponin-tropomyosin complex shifts back into its original position, and the sarcomere stretches passively to its original length.

A key point is that the contraction/relaxation cycle of the muscle twitch lasts longer than the stimulus that caused the contraction in the first place. If additional stimuli arrive at the muscle before the muscle has had a chance to transport calcium back into the sarcoplasmic reticulum and relax completely, the total force produced becomes greater than the force produced by one twitch alone. In effect, the force becomes greater because more calcium is present. Increasing muscle force by increasing the rate of stimulation of motor units is called **summation.**

There is a limit to summation, however. If stimulation becomes so frequent that the muscle cannot relax at all, it

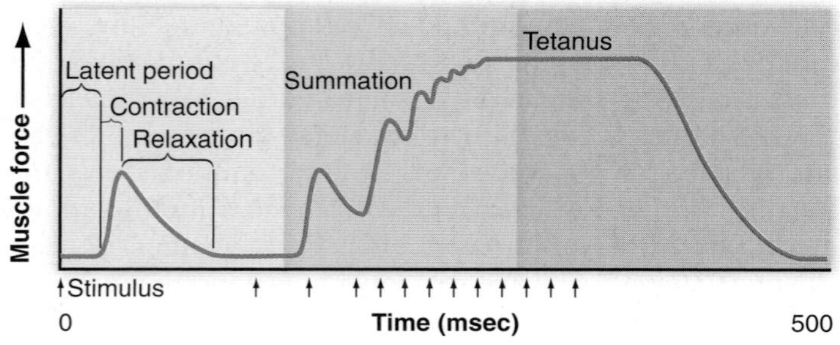


**Figure 6.10 How frequency of stimulation affects muscle contractile force.** A single stimulus produces, after a latent period, a contraction/relaxation cycle called a twitch. More than one stimulus in a short time may produce summation and ultimately a tetanic contraction (tetanus).

will remain in a state of maximum contraction called *tetanus* or a *tetanic contraction.* On a myogram, tetanus appears as a straight horizontal line representing the fusion of the peaks and valleys of individual twitches. A tetanic contraction may lead eventually to muscle fatigue.

Table 6.2 summarizes the mechanism of muscle cell activation and contraction.

**RECAP**

The number of muscle cells in a motor unit varies according to whether the muscle's function is fine control or brute force. Activation of more motor units and/or increased frequency of stimulation of motor units produces greater force. ■

## Slow-twitch versus fast-twitch fibers: Endurance versus strength

As we have seen, all muscle cells can obtain ATP through both aerobic and anaerobic pathways. Humans have two types of skeletal muscle fibers, called slow-twitch and fast-twitch fibers. The distinction is based on how quickly they can utilize ATP to produce a contraction, and whether they use primarily aerobic or anaerobic metabolic pathways. Most muscles contain a mixture of both slow-twitch and fast-twitch fibers. The ratio of fiber types in any one muscle depends primarily on the function of the muscle.

*Slow-twitch fibers* break down ATP slowly, and so they contract slowly. They tend to make ATP as they need it by aerobic metabolism. Slow-twitch fibers contain many mitochondria and are well supplied with blood vessels, so they draw more blood and oxygen than fast-twitch fibers. They store very little glycogen because they can obtain glucose and fatty acids quickly from the blood. They store oxygen, however, in a molecule called myoglobin. The ability to maintain a temporary store of oxygen reduces the slow-twitch fiber's need for oxygen from the bloodstream. This is especially important during the early phases of an increase in activity, before blood flow to the muscle has increased. Myoglobin and the presence of numerous blood vessels make slow-twitch fibers reddish in color, so they are sometimes called "red" muscle.

*Fast-twitch fibers* can contract more quickly than slow-twitch fibers because they break down ATP more quickly. They have fewer mitochondria, fewer blood vessels, and little or no myoglobin compared to slow-twitch fibers, so they're called "white" muscle. Fast-twitch fibers store large amounts of glycogen and tend to rely heavily on creatine phosphate and anaerobic metabolism for quick bursts of high energy. Their contractions are rapid and powerful but cannot be sustained for long. Fast-twitch fibers depend on aerobic mechanisms for any activity that is sustained, but they have the capability of using anaerobic mechanisms for brief periods when bursts of power are needed. During periods of anaerobic activity they tend to accumulate lactic acid, which causes them to become fatigued quickly.

Which type of fiber is better? It depends on the activity. Because slow-twitch fibers offer more endurance, they are most

**Table 6.2 Summary of activation and contraction of skeletal muscle**

| Action | Description | Additional facts |
|---|---|---|
| Motor neuron activation | A brief electrical impulse known as an action potential travels down the motor neuron from the central nervous system. | One motor neuron innervates more than one muscle cell. |
| Neurotransmitter release | At the neuromuscular junctions between a motor neuron and each of its muscle cells, a chemical neurotransmitter called acetylcholine is released. | The acetylcholine is removed quickly, so that stimulation of the muscle cell is short-lived. |
| Muscle cell activation | The release of acetylcholine causes an electrical impulse in the cell membrane of each muscle cell. | The electrical impulse in the muscle cell is similar to the electrical impulse in a nerve. |
| Calcium release | An impulse in the muscle cell membrane causes calcium to be released into the muscle cell cytoplasm from the sarcoplasmic reticulum. | The sarcoplasmic reticulum is a network of membrane-bound storage sacs in the muscle cell. |
| Muscle cell contraction | The presence of calcium allows the thick and thin filaments to attach to each other and to slide past each other. Energy in the form of ATP is required. | Muscle cell contraction lasts longer than neuron activation. |
| Muscle cell relaxation | Calcium is pumped back into the sarcoplasmic reticulum. The thick and thin filaments detach from each other, and the muscle relaxes. | Calcium transport back into the sarcoplasmic reticulum also requires ATP. |

useful for steady activities such as jogging, swimming, and biking. Slow-twitch fibers are also important for maintaining body posture. Many of the muscles of the leg and back, for example, contain a high percentage of slow-twitch fibers because they must contract for long periods to support us when we stand. Fast-twitch fibers are more often used to power brief, high-intensity activities such as sprinting for short distances, lifting weights, or swinging a tennis racquet. Muscles in our hands, for example, contain a high proportion of fast-twitch fibers, allowing the muscles to contract quickly and strongly when necessary.

The percentage of slow- and fast-twitch fibers varies not only from muscle to muscle but from person to person. The percentages are determined in part by inheritance, and they can influence athletic ability. For example, most world-class marathoners have a higher-than-average percentage of slow-twitch fibers in their legs.

**RECAP**

Most muscles contain a combination of slow-twitch and fast-twitch fibers. Slow-twitch fibers rely on aerobic metabolism and are most useful for endurance. Fast-twitch fibers are capable of short bursts of high-intensity work and are most useful where strength is required. ■

## Exercise training improves muscle mass, strength, and endurance

Although part of your athletic potential might be influenced by inheritance, a consistent, planned program of physical exercise (sometimes called *exercise training*) can improve your strength, endurance, and skill at any athletic endeavor (Figure 6.11). Whether primarily strength or endurance is improved by exercise training depends on the type and intensity of training. The two primary types of exercise training are strength (resistance) training and aerobic (endurance) training.

*Strength training* involves doing exercises that strengthen specific muscles, usually by providing some type of resistance that makes them work harder. Strength training is generally short, intense exercise such as weight lifting using free weights or weight machines. It builds more myofibrils, particularly in fast-twitch fibers, and causes the fast-twitch fibers to store more glycogen and creatine phosphate as quick energy sources. This increases the size of individual muscle cells and builds muscle mass and muscle strength, but it does not increase the number of muscle cells.

In general, the heavier the weight used, the more visible the increase in muscle size. However, this does not mean that strength training will necessarily build bulging biceps. The extent of muscle development depends on many factors,

a) Weight lifter

b) Distance runners

**Figure 6.11 The effects of strength training versus aerobic training.**

# Directions in Science

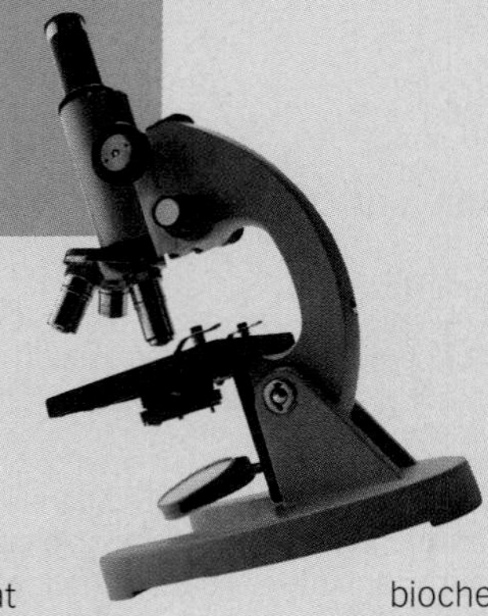

## Science and Sports: Lessons Learned from Lance Armstrong

Covering over 2,000 miles of variable terrain in about 20 stages, the annual Tour de France bicycle race is one of the most grueling athletic events in the world. How could one man dominate this premier sporting event for *seven consecutive years*?

Scientists are interested in that question, too, and now they may have an answer. Researchers who tested Lance Armstrong over the entire period of his record seven consecutive Tour de France wins report that he increased his muscle efficiency by 8% during those years—in other words, his muscles became more efficient at utilizing the same amount of oxygen. At the same time, his average cycling pace during races rose from 85–95 revolutions per minute to about 105–110 rpm.

A physician who studied Armstrong hypothesizes that the process of ATP turnover within his contracting muscle fibers actually became more efficient. Armstrong may also have increased his percentage of slow-twitch muscle fibers from approximately 60% to 80%, an increase similar to those observed previously in other competitive cyclists. Blood tests showed that he had very low levels of lactate, a component of lactic acid—even lower than those of other competitive cyclists. Enhanced muscle efficiency, plus a planned weight loss of 7% before the race, enabled Armstrong to achieve an overall improvement of 18% in what researchers call his "steady-state power per kilogram" output.

This is remarkable, since researchers have long thought that muscle efficiency is genetically determined. Armstrong may have "good genes," but apparently he also trained smarter. How he did it is still under investigation.

Fifty years ago, an aspiring athlete needed only a set of weights, a place to train, and a lot of determination and hard work. Not today. In an era when winning brings big endorsement contracts, sports have gone high-tech. Downhill ski racers and speed skaters are studied in wind tunnels previously used only to test models of airplanes and buildings. Digital video cameras, remote sensors, and computer programs analyze athletes' motion patterns for speed, power, and direction. Researchers in genetics, biochemistry, and exercise training are unlocking the secrets of athletic success (such as Armstrong's) on a cellular level and applying what they learn to young athletes in training.

In the future, a professional athletics "consultant" firm will be able to approach parents of young children with offers of genetic, biochemical, physical, and psychological testing. They'll promise to determine the child's likelihood of success in every sport, and link parents to just the right training facilities and professional trainers. Future Olympic hopefuls will be selected early and trained according to the latest scientifically proven training methods. Unlikely? Listen to the stories of the Olympics winners over the next 20 years and judge for yourself.

including the amount of resistance used, the duration and frequency of exercise, and your own genetic predisposition. However, even low to moderate weights can lead to noticeable improvements in muscle strength.

*Aerobic training* involves activities in which the body increases its oxygen intake to meet the increased demands for oxygen by muscles. Whereas resistance training strengthens muscles, aerobic training builds endurance (see "Directions in Science: Science and Sports: Lessons Learned from Lance Armstrong"). With aerobic training the number of blood capillaries supplying muscle increases. In addition, the number of mitochondria in muscle cells and the amount of myoglobin available to store oxygen both increase. The muscle fibers themselves do not increase much in mass, nor do they increase in number. Aerobic exercise also improves the performance of the cardiovascular and respiratory systems. Less intense than strength training but carried out for prolonged periods, aerobic exercises include jogging, walking, biking, and swimming.

It's a good idea to combine any athletic activity with *stretching exercises.* Gentle stretching before exercise increases your heart rate gradually, pumping additional blood to your muscles and preparing you for more strenuous exertion. This lowers your risk of sprains and pulled muscles. After exercising, let your heart rate and breathing return gradually to normal as you walk slowly and do more stretching. Regular stretching improves joint mobility and range of motion. Whenever you stretch, do it gradually and hold each position for 30 seconds. You should feel a gentle pull in your muscles, but not pain. Try not to bounce, because abrupt stretches could cause your muscles to contract quickly in response, increasing the risk of injury.

**RECAP**

Exercise increases aerobic capacity, muscle mass, and muscle strength but does not increase the number of muscle cells. The type of exercise training determines whether primarily strength or aerobic capacity is improved. ■

## 6.4 Cardiac and smooth muscles have special features

Most of the overall muscle mass of the body is skeletal muscle. Nevertheless, both cardiac and smooth muscle have unique features that suit them ideally for their roles in the body. All three types of muscle tissue are described briefly in Chapter 4. Here we look at some of the special attributes of cardiac and smooth muscle that set them apart from skeletal muscle.

### How cardiac and smooth muscles are activated

Cardiac and smooth muscle are called *involuntary muscle* because we generally do not have voluntary control over them. Both cardiac and smooth muscles can contract entirely on their own, in the absence of stimulation by nerves. Although all cardiac muscle cells are capable of beating spontaneously and establishing their own cycle of contraction and relaxation, those with the fastest rhythm are called *pacemaker cells* because the rest of the cells follow their faster pace. Cardiac muscle cells are joined at their blunt ends by structures called *intercalated discs* (Figure 6.12). The intercalated discs contain gap junctions that permit one cell to electrically stimulate the next one. In effect, the pacemaker cells dictate the rate of contraction of the whole heart because their pace drives the slower cells.

Smooth muscle cells are also joined by gap junctions that permit the cells to activate each other, so that the whole tissue contracts together in a coordinated fashion. In contrast, skeletal muscle cells are activated only by motor neurons. This is why the skeletal muscles of a person with a severed spinal cord are completely paralyzed below the point of injury.

Even though cardiac and smooth muscle cells can contract without signals from the nerves, they do respond to stimulation by nerves as well. In both types of muscle the nerves belong to the autonomic nervous system (Chapter 11). The effect of nerve stimulation may be either inhibitory or stimulatory. Changes in both inhibitory and stimulatory nerve activity to the heart are responsible for the increase in your heart rate when you exercise, for example. Nerve stimulation can also change the contractile force of smooth muscle.

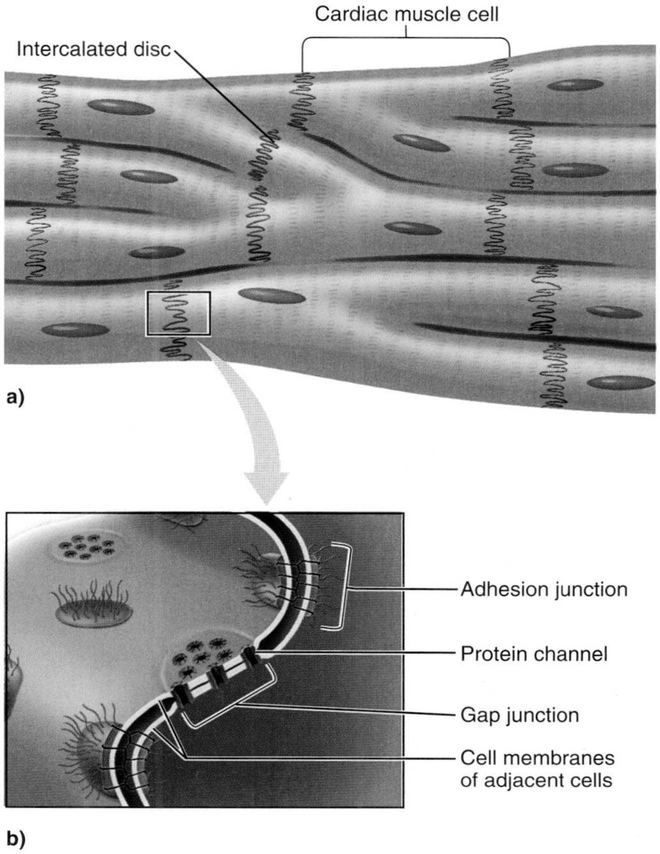


**Figure 6.12 Cardiac muscle cells. (a)** A view of several adjacent cardiac muscle cells showing their blunt shape and the intercalated discs that join them together. **(b)** A closer view showing that intercalated discs are bridged by gap junctions that permit direct electrical connections between cells.

**RECAP**

Unlike skeletal muscle, both cardiac and smooth muscle can contract in the absence of nerve stimulation. However, both also are capable of responding to nerves. ■

### Speed and sustainability of contraction

In terms of speed and sustainability of contraction, skeletal muscle is the fastest, cardiac muscle is of moderate speed, and smooth muscle is very slow.

Cardiac muscle cells go through rhythmic cycles of contraction and relaxation. The relaxation periods are necessary periods of rest so that the muscle doesn't fatigue.

Smooth muscle generally is partially contracted all the time. This makes it ideally suited for situations in which contractions need to be sustained. Nevertheless, it almost never fatigues because it contracts so slowly that its ATP usage is always less than its production capability. Smooth muscle is a key player in the homeostatic regulation of blood pressure because it can maintain the diameter of blood vessels indefinitely, adjusting them slightly as necessary.

# Drug Abuse Among Athletes

Baseball slugger Barry Bonds is under indictment for lying under oath about using performance-enhancing drugs. Sprinter Marion Jones confessed to her drug use and offered a tearful apology, but was stripped of her five Olympic gold medals. High school athletes are routinely being tested for performance-enhancing drugs. What is going on here?

The short answer is that many performance-enhancing drugs do enhance athletic performance. They work in ways that are predictable and understood, based on human physiology. In an environment where just a hundredth of a second can make the difference between an Olympic gold medal and relative obscurity, the temptation to use these drugs is high.

## Anabolic Steroids Build Muscle Mass

Anabolic steroids and related compounds such as dehydroepiandrosterone (DHEA) and androstenedione ("Andro") are the most widely abused drugs in athletics today. Many of them are available over the counter as the result of a 1994 federal law that was written to ensure access to herbal remedies (see the Current Issue in Chapter 1). In general, they are structurally and functionally related to the male sex steroid testosterone, and like the natural hormone, they increase muscle mass. The user finds it easy to "bulk up." Muscle strength improves as well, leading to improved athletic performance in sports that require short bursts of energy. Anabolic steroids also contribute to the development and maintenance of masculine characteristics (an androgenic effect).

Injectible anabolic steroids are illegal without a prescription, and most sports federations and school systems have banned the over-the-counter ones as well. Nevertheless, a study funded by the National Institute on Drug Abuse found that 2.5% of 12th-graders, 1.5% of 10th-graders and 1.1% of 8th-graders had also tried them. Information on anabolic steroid use by college and professional athletes is unreliable because sports federations ban these drugs. A few well-known athletes, including Arnold Schwarzenegger, sprinter Ben Johnson, and wrestler Hulk Hogan, have admitted to using them at one time or another.

Marion Jones after winning the gold in 2000, and in 2007 after admitting to using performance enhancing drugs.

Typically, anabolic steroids are taken in cycles of 6–12 weeks of steadily increasing doses separated by periods of nonuse, a method called "pyramiding." Many users take more than one anabolic steroid at a time, a technique known as "stacking." Because the steroids are not approved and the user typically cannot get good information on how much to take, doses vary widely but can be 10 to 100 times higher than prescription doses.

A recent trend is the increased use of sophisticated "designer drugs" such as THG (tetrahydrogestrinone), designed specifically to avoid detection. THG is known as "the clear" to athletes because allegedly it couldn't be detected. And for years it wasn't detected—until an anonymous tipster sent a sample of the drug to a sport federation for testing. THG is so potent that it doesn't even have to be injected—just a couple of drops under the tongue are enough. After years of angrily and categorically denying

## the facts...

- Performance-enhancing drugs such as anabolic steroids and erythropoietin (EPO) are used by some athletes because they improve certain types of athletic performance.
- Abuse of performance-enhancing drugs can lead to unwanted physical and behavioral side effects, an increased risk of certain chronic diseases, and perhaps even premature death.
- Most sports federations have banned the use of performance-enhancing drugs, but enforcement has proven difficult because newer "designer drugs" are hard to detect.
- Soon it will be possible to use genetic engineering techniques to enhance athletic performance. How this practice could be prevented is not yet known.

that she had ever used performance-enhancing drugs, in 2007 sprinter Marion Jones finally admitted that she started using THG in 1999 as she prepared for the 2000 Olympic games. She stated that she thought it was just flaxseed oil, but nonetheless, she was stripped of her five medals from the 2000 Olympics and banned from participation in the 2008 Olympics in Beijing.

### Risks Associated with Anabolic Steroids

Anabolic steroids have androgenic (masculinizing) effects in both sexes. Side effects in males include gynecomastia (enlargement of the breasts), shrinkage of the testicles, impotence, reduced sperm production, and male-pattern baldness. In females, breast size and body fat decrease and the voice deepens. Women may lose scalp hair but gain body hair. Acne and oily hair and skin may occur in both sexes. Some of these changes, including gynecomastia in males and hair loss in both sexes, are irreversible. Anabolic steroid abuse is also associated with irritability, hostility, and aggressive behavior ("roid rage").

Prolonged anabolic steroid abuse is associated with an increased risk of heart attack, stroke, and severe liver disease, including liver cancer. Although the number of cases of these diseases is fairly low so far, it is likely that the effects of steroid use/abuse are being underestimated because these diseases tend to come later in life. We just don't know what will happen to steroid abusers 30 years later.

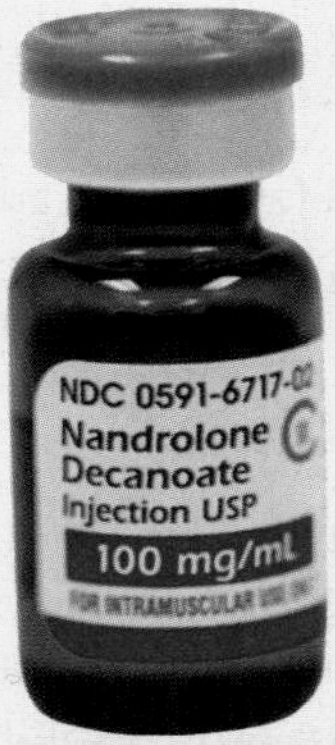


Nandrolone; an anabolic steroid.

### Blood Enhancers Improve Aerobic-Capacity

Marathoners and cyclists aren't interested in muscle mass; they're interested in maintaining a high level of sustained performance over long periods of time. For that, they need increased aerobic capacity. Their (banned) drug of choice is erythropoietin (EPO), a hormone produced by the kidneys that increases the production of red blood cells. EPO is available by prescription only for patients with *anemia* (too few red blood cells in the blood). But it wasn't long before cyclists and marathon runners learned that EPO could reduce their elapsed times. It's all a matter of physiology; EPO produces more red blood cells, which leads to a higher oxygen-carrying capacity, which in turn leads to a higher level of sustainable muscle activity and faster times.

But a health risk is associated with EPO abuse, too. Carried to extremes, excessive production of red blood cells raises the hematocrit (the percentage of the blood that is red cells) to dangerous levels. The blood becomes sludge-like, increasing the risk of high blood pressure, blood clots, and heart attacks. Statistically, one of the most common causes of death among professional cyclists is heart attack, although no deaths have ever officially been listed as having been caused by EPO.

It's hard to test for EPO abuse because EPO disappears from the blood within days of its use, leaving behind an increased hematocrit and an improved endurance that lasts for a month or more. The cycling organizations are only able to curb EPO abuse by setting an upper limit for hematocrit of 50%; above that, EPO abuse is just assumed and the athlete is banned from competition. Some cyclists suspected of using EPO allegedly measure their hematocrit shortly before a race and then remove blood cells to just meet the 50% rule!

### Next Up: Gene Doping

Given the genetic manipulation we are already capable of, it's almost a certainty that within decades, genetic engineering techniques could be used to modify an athlete's genes for improved athletic performance. It's called *gene doping*. Suppose you could tinker with the genes that lead to the production of natural erythropoietin or testosterone, so that an athlete just naturally produces more of these hormones. What if you could alter muscle biochemistry so that muscles used energy more efficiently or more rapidly? What if you could insert genes that caused muscle cells to store up more ATP? These ideas are not so far-fetched. Nearly all experts on the subject are convinced that if gene doping hasn't been tried already, it soon will be. Gene doping will be extremely hard to detect or to prevent.

A young Barry Bonds playing for the Pirates, and years later, a bulkier Barry as the SF Giants' slugger.

Have we lost our perspective for the role that sports should play in our lives? It's something to think about.

## Questions to consider

**1** *Do you think we should continue to try to prevent the use of drugs and genetic engineering in sports? Why or why not?*

**2** *A friend who uses anabolic steroids says that there is no convincing scientific evidence that anabolic steroid use will lead to health problems such as heart disease or cancer later in life. Is he right? What would you say to him?*

### Arrangement of myosin and actin filaments

Like skeletal muscle, cardiac muscle has a regular array of thick and thin filaments arranged in sarcomeres, so it too is called striated muscle. In contrast, the thick and thin filaments in smooth muscle are arranged in bundles that attach at various angles to the cell membrane. When the thick and thin filaments slide past each other, the points of attachment of the filaments are pulled toward each other and the cell gets shorter and fatter (Figure 6.13). Because its filaments are arranged in bundles rather than sarcomeres, smooth muscle lacks the striated appearance of skeletal and cardiac muscle. It is called "smooth" for this reason.

Table 6.3 summarizes important features of the three types of muscle.

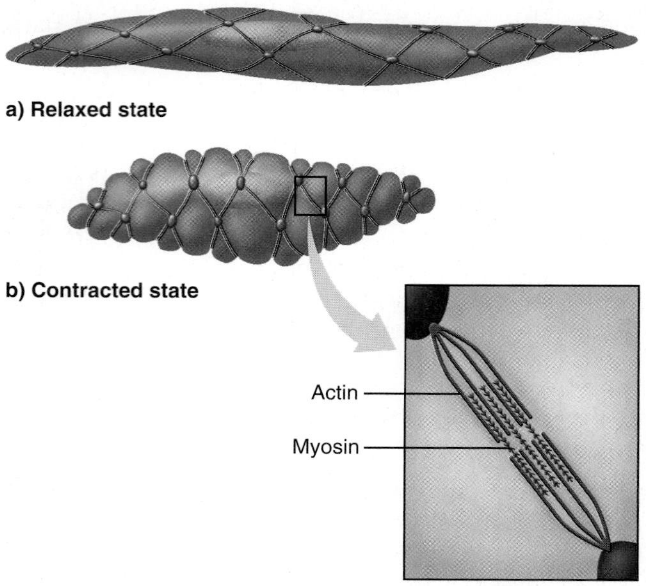


**Figure 6.13 Smooth muscle. (a)** Relaxed state. **(b)** Contracted state. The crisscross arrangement of bundles of contractile filaments causes the cell to become shorter and fatter during contraction. **(c)** A closer view showing how actin filaments are attached to cell membrane proteins.

**RECAP**

Cardiac muscle contracts and relaxes rhythmically, whereas smooth muscle can sustain a contraction indefinitely. Cardiac muscle has thick and thin filaments arranged in sarcomeres, whereas the filaments in smooth muscle are arranged in bundles that crisscross the cell. ■

## 6.5 Diseases and disorders of the muscular system

Throughout this chapter we have discussed a number of musculoskeletal health conditions. We'll finish by looking at several more.

### Muscular dystrophy

Serious diseases of muscle are relatively uncommon, but foremost among them is **muscular dystrophy.** The term actually applies to several different hereditary diseases of muscle (*dystrophy* means "abnormal growth"). In *Duchenne muscular dystrophy,* a single defective gene results in the lack of a particular muscle cell protein. The normal gene, when present, directs the cell to produce a protein called dystrophin that is part of the muscle cell membrane. The function of dystrophin is to limit the inflow of calcium into muscle cells through calcium "leak" channels. People with muscular dystrophy lack dystrophin, and as a result too much calcium leaks into the muscle cell through the leak channels. The high intracellular calcium concentration activates enzymes that damage muscle proteins and ultimately may kill the cell. The result is a loss of muscle fibers and muscle wasting. Eventually much of the muscle mass is replaced with fibrous connective tissue. Many people with muscular dystrophy die before age 30, usually because of failure of the heart muscle or the skeletal muscles used for breathing. At the moment there is no cure; however, it is an area of intense research interest, and progress is being made on several fronts.

### Tetanus

A disease called tetanus is caused by a bacterial infection. Generally the infection is acquired by a puncture wound to a muscle. The bacteria produce a toxin that overstimulates the nerves controlling muscle activity, resulting in tetanic contractions. The toxin affects a variety of skeletal muscles, but especially those of the jaws and neck. Jaw muscles may contract so forcefully that they seem locked shut (the origin of its common name, "lockjaw"). Untreated, tetanus may lead to death due to exhaustion or respiratory failure. The disorder is called tetanus because this is the technical term for a maximal (tetanic) muscle contraction. However, most maximal muscle contractions are not the result of disease.

### Muscle cramps

Muscle cramps are painful, uncontrollable, reflex-mediated muscle contractions. They are thought to be caused by the dehydration and ion imbalances that sometimes occur with heavy exercise. The most likely culprit is a shift in potassium ions between the intracellular and extracellular fluid. Muscle cramps generally can be soothed by increasing the circulation to the affected muscle through gentle stretching and massage.

### Pulled muscles

Pulled muscles, sometimes called torn muscles, result from stretching a muscle too far, causing some of the fibers to tear

# Health Watch

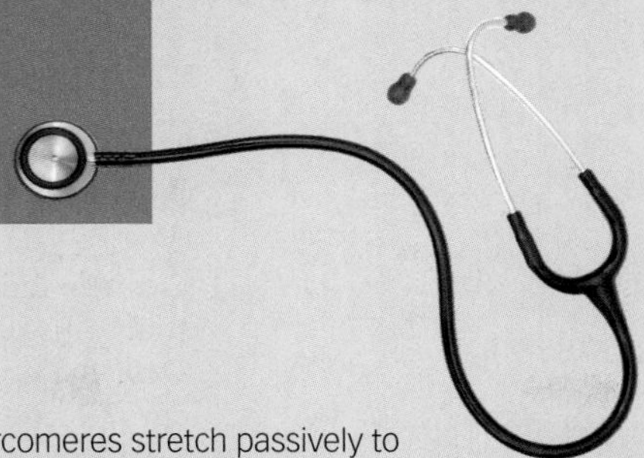

## Muscle Soreness

Most of us are familiar with the feeling of stiffness and soreness that occurs a day or two after an unfamiliar form of exertion. The soreness is actually due to microscopic tears in myofibrils throughout the muscle. It is thought that the damage occurs because in the absence of regular use, some sarcomeres become like old stiff rubber bands, unable to contract as well as they should. During exercise these old or injured sarcomeres stretch passively to the point that the thick and thin filaments no longer overlap, damaging them permanently. The injured sarcomeres disintegrate over several days and are removed as part of the repair process. As they disintegrate, however, they release chemical substances that cause the feeling of soreness. With time, the damaged sarcomeres are removed completely and new sarcomeres take their place.

Once muscles become accustomed to a particular exercise, damage (and the accompanying soreness) no longer occurs. To minimize muscle injury and soreness, undertake any new exercise activity in moderation for the first few days.

apart. Internal bleeding, swelling, and pain often accompany a pulled muscle.

### Fasciitis

Fasciitis involves inflammation of the connective tissue sheath, or fascia, that surrounds a muscle. It is usually caused by straining or tearing the fascia. Most often it affects the sole of the foot (plantar fasciitis), where it is a common cause of heel pain. Like tendons and ligaments, fascia mend slowly. Treatment includes resting the area and protecting it from pressure. Injections of corticosteroid drugs can relieve severe pain.

**RECAP**

Muscular dystrophy is an inherited disease in which the absence of a single protein causes an abnormal leak of calcium into muscle cells. Ultimately the leak of calcium damages muscle cell proteins and kills muscle cells. ■

**Table 6.3 Characteristics of skeletal, cardiac, and smooth muscle**

| Characteristics | Skeletal muscle | Cardiac muscle | Smooth muscle |
|---|---|---|---|
| Location | Attached to bones (skeleton) | Found only in the heart | Found in the walls of blood vessels and in the walls of organs of the digestive, respiratory, urinary, and reproductive tracts |
| Function | Movement of the body<br>Prevention of movement of the body | Pumping of blood | Control of blood vessel diameter. Movement of contents in hollow organs |
| Anatomical description | Very large, cylindrical, multinucleated cells arranged in parallel bundles | Short cells with blunt, branched ends. Cells joined to others by intercalated discs and gap junctions | Small, spindle-shaped cells joined to each other by gap junctions |
| Initiation of contraction | Only by a nerve cell | Spontaneous (pacemaker cells), modifiable by nerves | Some contraction always maintained. Modifiable by nerves |
| Voluntary? | Yes | No | No |
| Gap junctions? | No | Yes | Yes |
| Speed and sustainability of contraction | Fast—50 milliseconds (0.05 second). Not sustainable | Moderate—150 milliseconds (0.15 second). Not sustainable | Slow—1–3 seconds. Sustainable indefinitely |
| Likelihood of fatigue | Varies widely depending on type of skeletal muscle and workload | Low. Relaxation between contractions reduces the likelihood | Generally does not fatigue |
| Striated? | Yes | Yes | No |

# Chapter Summary

### Muscles produce movement or generate tension *p. 121*

- All muscles produce movement or maintain position by contracting (shortening in length).
- The ways in which skeletal muscles attach to the skeleton determine what particular motion they cause.
- Within a single myofibril in a single muscle cell (fiber), thousands of contractile units called sarcomeres are arranged end to end.

### Individual muscle cells contract and relax *p. 124*

- Skeletal muscle cells contract only when activated by their motor nerve.
- Motor nerve activation causes calcium to be released from the sarcoplasmic reticulum of the muscle cell.
- In the presence of calcium, the thick (myosin) and thin (actin) filaments slide past each other, and the sarcomere shortens.
- ATP supplies the energy for the entire contraction/relaxation process.

### The activity of muscles can vary *p. 128*

- An *isotonic contraction* occurs when a muscle shortens while maintaining a constant force; an *isometric contraction* occurs when tension is generated but the bones do not move.
- A motor unit is a single motor neuron and all of the skeletal muscle cells that it controls.
- The force generated by a muscle depends on the number of muscle cells in each motor unit, the number of motor units active at any one moment, and the frequency of stimulation of motor units.
- Muscle strength and endurance depend on the ratio of slow-twitch to fast-twitch fibers in the muscle and on the type and amount of exercise training.

### Cardiac and smooth muscles have special features *p. 133*

- Cardiac and smooth muscles do not attach to bones.
- Both cardiac and smooth muscles can contract spontaneously, and both can be influenced by nerves of the autonomic nervous system.
- Cardiac muscle contracts rhythmically, with a period of relaxation between each contraction. Smooth muscle can maintain at least some contractile force indefinitely.

### Diseases and disorders of the muscular system *p. 136*

- Muscular dystrophy is caused by inheritance of an abnormal gene.
- Pulled (torn) muscles occur when a muscle is stretched too far.

# Terms You Should Know

actin, *124*
all-or-none principle, *129*
fatigue, *128*
motor neuron, *125*
motor unit, *129*
myosin, *124*
neurotransmitter, *125*
oxygen debt, *128*
recruitment, *130*
sarcomere, *124*
sarcoplasmic reticulum, *125*
sliding filament mechanism, *125*
summation, *130*
twitch, *129*

# Concept Review

1. Describe how muscle contraction can resist movement rather than cause movement.
2. Describe how a muscle's origin and insertion determine the specific body movement that will result from muscle contraction.
3. Describe the roles of calcium in muscle contraction.
4. Explain what causes *rigor mortis.*
5. Discuss some possible reasons for muscle fatigue.
6. Define *summation,* and explain why it occurs when a muscle is stimulated rapidly and repetitively.
7. Explain why a spinal cord injury in the neck completely paralyzes the skeletal muscles of the limbs, whereas the cardiac muscle of the heart still beats rhythmically.
8. Compare and contrast how a constant degree of moderate tension, or tone, is maintained by a skeletal muscle that maintains posture versus a smooth muscle that maintains blood vessel diameter.
9. Define a motor unit, and describe how the size and the number of motor units in a muscle affect muscle strength and fine motor control.
10. List the sources of energy that a muscle cell may use to make more ATP, both from within and from outside the cell.

# Test Yourself

### Matching Exercise

_____ 1. Muscle of the upper arm that causes extension of the forearm
_____ 2. Protein in thick filaments in a sarcomere
_____ 3. Most abundant protein in thin filaments in a sarcomere
_____ 4. The contractile unit of a muscle
_____ 5. A type of skeletal muscle fiber capable of explosive bursts of power for short periods of time
_____ 6. Type of muscle found in the walls of blood vessels

a. actin
b. fast-twitch
c. triceps
d. smooth
e. sarcomere
f. myosin

### Fill in the Blank

7. Muscles over which we do not have conscious control are called ________________ muscles.
8. Muscle groups that oppose each other to produce the same movement are called ________________ muscles.
9. A segment of a myofibril from one Z-line to the next is called a(n) ________________.
10. Motor neurons release a chemical neurotransmitter substance called ________________ when a nerve impulse arrives at the neuromuscular junction.
11. The junction between a ________________ neuron and a muscle cell is called the neuromuscular junction.
12. The cells of both cardiac and smooth muscle are joined to each other by ________________ junctions that permit the cells to activate each other.

**True or False?**

13. Release of calcium from the sarcoplasmic reticulum causes muscle relaxation.
14. The time between stimulation of a muscle and the start of a contraction is called the latent period.
15. Strength training can markedly increase the number of muscle cells in a muscle.

## References and Additional Reading

Andersen, Jesper L., Peter Schjerling, and Bengt Saltin. Muscle, Genes and Athletic Performance. *Scientific American*, September 2000, 48–55. (An article about how genetics may influence athletic performance.)

Bahrke, Michael S., and Charles E. Yesalis. *Performance-Enhancing Substances in Sport and Exercise.* Champaign, IL: Human Kinetics, 2002. (A readable and well-referenced text on this subject.)

Coyle, Edward F. Improved muscular efficiency displayed as Tour de France champion matures. *Journal of Applied Physiology* 98:2191–2196, 2005. (The scientific article that documents Lance Armstrong's increase in muscular efficiency.)

McArdle, William D., Frank I. Katch, and Victor L. Katch. *Essentials of Exercise Physiology,* 3rd ed. Baltimore: Lippincott, Williams & Wilkins, 2006. (In-depth coverage for the student interested in exercise and human performance.)

Shermer, Michael. The Doping Dilemma. *Scientific American*, April 2008, 82–89. (An article on why athletes abuse drugs and what could be done about it.)

### Internet References

Find links to the following Web sites at the Human Biology Place.

**SportsInjuryClinic.net**
**www.sportsinjuryclinic.net**
Illustrated guide to common athletic injuries, symptoms, and treatments.

**National Institute on Drug Abuse: Anabolic Steroid Abuse**
**www.steroidabuse.org**
A government information site about anabolic steroid abuse.

## Apply **What You Know**

1. Why do you think it is generally accepted medical practice to get bedridden patients up and walking as soon as possible?
2. In what ways would you expect the training regimen for a sprinter to be different from that of a marathon runner, and why?
3. What would happen to a muscle if one of its tendons were torn? Would the muscle still be able to contract?
4. You and your friend are doing leg presses in the gym one day. As you extend your legs the stack of weights goes up, and when you bend your legs the stack goes down. Your friend says your muscles are actively pushing the weights up. Explain to him where he is wrong in his thinking.
5. You are outside on a cool fall day. You feel cool, but you think little of it until you notice yourself shivering. What is happening at the muscular level, and why is it at least partially effective in helping to maintain body temperature?
6. You have just joined an aerobics exercise class for the first time, and you have calculated your target heart rate. After class you notice that your heart rate remains high for a while and only slowly returns to normal. Explain why this occurs and what is happening at the physiological level. How will this response change over time if you maintain your exercise program consistently?
7. Some weight lifters like to consume various products containing creatine phosphate. Why would this be useful? Why would weight lifters benefit more than marathon runners from creatine phosphate?

*Answers can be found on the Human Biology Place.*

# 7 Blood

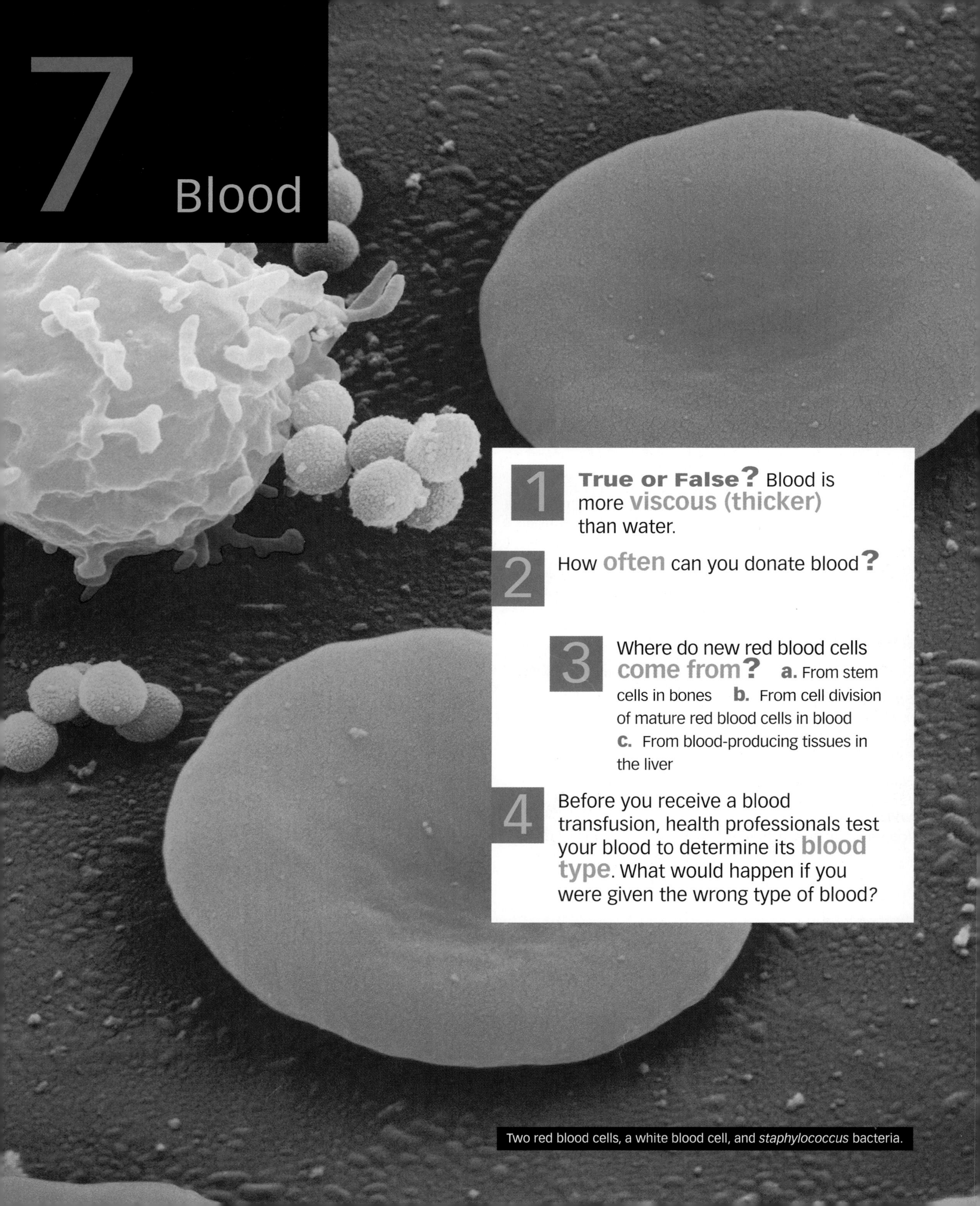

**1** **True or False?** Blood is more **viscous (thicker)** than water.

**2** How **often** can you donate blood**?**

**3** Where do new red blood cells **come from?** **a.** From stem cells in bones **b.** From cell division of mature red blood cells in blood **c.** From blood-producing tissues in the liver

**4** Before you receive a blood transfusion, health professionals test your blood to determine its **blood type**. What would happen if you were given the wrong type of blood?

Two red blood cells, a white blood cell, and *staphylococcus* bacteria.

**All cells in the body must obtain nutrients** and get rid of wastes. How do they do that? Diffusion to and from the fluid that surrounds them is only part of the answer. If every cell drew its nutrients from interstitial fluid and there were no way to replenish them, the cells would soon starve. If every cell dumped its waste into the interstitial fluid and those wastes were not promptly removed, the cells would die in a sea of toxic waste. Cells need a system for keeping the oxygen content, the supply of nutrients, the concentrations of wastes, and the concentrations of every essential molecule and atom within acceptable limits. What they need is a system to maintain homeostasis of the interstitial fluid. In humans, that system is the circulatory system.

The **circulatory system** consists of the heart, the blood vessels, and the blood that circulates through them. As shown in Figure 7.1, the circulatory system plays a central role in supplying all cells with what they need and removing the substances they no longer need. The circulatory system ensures that blood flows throughout the entire body, bringing the necessary raw materials to the interstitial fluid surrounding every living cell and removing the waste. It picks up nutrients from the digestive system, exchanges gases with the respiratory system, and carries wastes and excess water and salts to the urinary system for removal from the body. It also carries some metabolic wastes to the liver for removal. Whenever a substance is transported over any distance within the body, the circulatory system is at work. Closely coupled to the circulatory system—indeed, often considered part of it—is another system of fluid-filled vessels called the *lymphatic system.* We examine the lymphatic system further in Chapter 9 in connection with the immune system.

We discuss the heart and blood vessels as well as the transport functions of the lymphatic system in Chapter 8. In this chapter we concentrate on the composition and crucial functions of blood, the fluid that circulates within the heart and blood vessels.

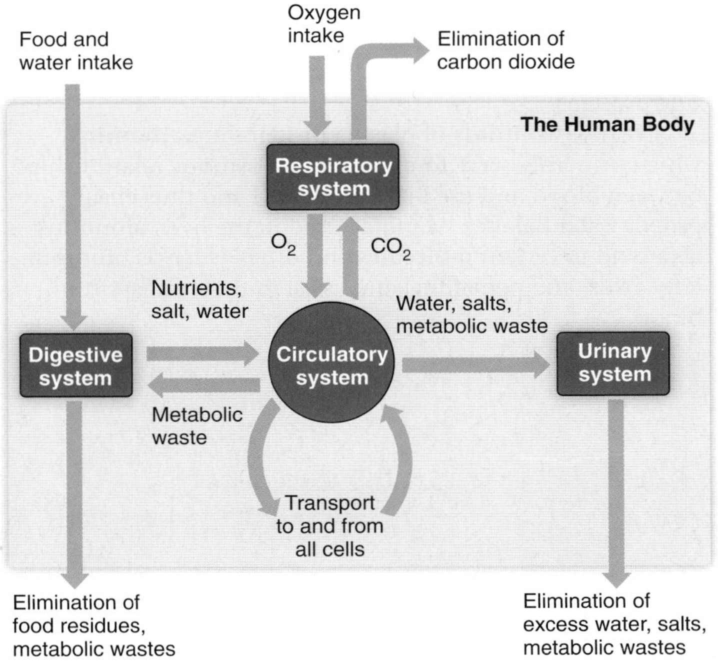


**Figure 7.1 The transport role of the circulatory system.** The cardiovascular system serves homeostasis by transporting nutrients and carrying off wastes from all parts of the body.

## 7.1 The components and functions of blood

As noted in Chapter 4, **blood** is a specialized connective tissue. It consists of specialized cells and cell fragments suspended in a watery solution of molecules and ions. Blood carries out three crucial tasks for the body:

- *Transportation.* Blood transports all substances needed anywhere by the body, including oxygen from the lungs, nutrients from the digestive system, and hormones from the endocrine glands. Blood also transports the products of cell metabolism away from body tissues to organs that eliminate them from the body.
- *Regulation.* Blood helps to regulate body temperature, the volume of water in the body, and the pH of body fluids.
- *Defense.* Blood contains specialized defense cells that help protect against infections and illness, and it has the ability to prevent excessive blood loss through the clotting mechanism.

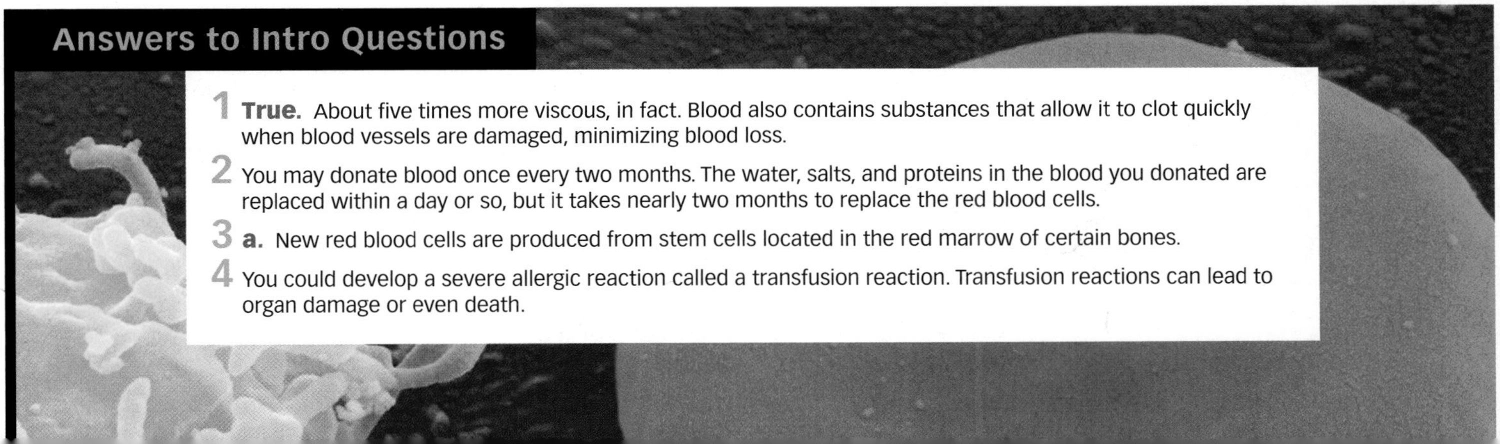

### Answers to Intro Questions

1 **True.** About five times more viscous, in fact. Blood also contains substances that allow it to clot quickly when blood vessels are damaged, minimizing blood loss.

2 You may donate blood once every two months. The water, salts, and proteins in the blood you donated are replaced within a day or so, but it takes nearly two months to replace the red blood cells.

3 **a.** New red blood cells are produced from stem cells located in the red marrow of certain bones.

4 You could develop a severe allergic reaction called a transfusion reaction. Transfusion reactions can lead to organ damage or even death.

Together these functions are crucial for maintaining homeostasis. Blood is so effective at performing these functions that so far scientists' efforts to develop an artificial blood substitute have not been very successful. If someone needs blood, a transfusion of human blood is often the only solution.

Adult men average 5 to 6 liters of blood (about 1.5 gallons), and adult women average 4 to 5 liters. Differences between men and women reflect differences in body size. In general, blood represents approximately 8% of your body weight.

Blood is thicker and stickier than water. This is because some components of blood are denser (heavier) than water and because blood is roughly five times more viscous (viscosity is a measure of resistance to flow). The old saying that blood is thicker than water is true.

Despite its uniform color, blood carries a rich array of components. Table 7.1 summarizes the components of blood and their functions. They fall into two major categories: the liquid component (plasma) and the cellular component or formed elements (*red cells, white cells,* and *platelets*). If you spin a blood sample in a centrifuge (a high-speed rotation device that mimics and magnifies gravitational forces), formed elements sink to the bottom of a test tube because they are denser than plasma (Figure 7.2). Red blood cells (RBCs), representing the bulk of the formed elements, settle to the bottom. White blood cells (WBCs) and platelets appear just above red blood cells in a thin, grayish white layer.

**RECAP**

About 8% of our body weight is blood. Blood maintains homeostasis by (1) transporting nutrients and exporting wastes, (2) regulating temperature and water volume, and (3) carrying molecules that fight disease and promote healing. ■

## Plasma consists of water and dissolved solutes

The top layer of a centrifuged blood sample, representing about 55% of the total volume, consists of a pale yellow liquid called **plasma.** Plasma is the transport medium for blood cells and platelets. About 90% of plasma is water. The rest is dissolved proteins, hormones, more than 100 different small molecules (including amino acids, fats, small carbohydrates, vitamins, and various waste products of metabolism), and ions.

The largest group of solutes in plasma consists of **plasma proteins,** which serve a variety of functions. Important plasma proteins include albumins, globulins, and clotting proteins.

Nearly two-thirds of plasma proteins are **albumins,** which primarily serve to maintain the osmotic relationship between blood and the interstitial fluid and thus ensure proper water balance. Manufactured in the liver, albumins also bind to certain molecules and drugs (such as bilirubin, fatty acids, and penicillin) and assist in their transport in blood.

**Table 7.1 Composition of blood**

| Blood component | Examples and functions |
|---|---|
| *Formed Elements (45%)* | |
| Red blood cells | Transport oxygen to body tissues; transport carbon dioxide away from tissues. |
| White blood cells | Defend the body against invading organisms, abnormal cells. |
| Platelets | Take part in blood clotting as part of the body's defense mechanisms |
| *Plasma (55%)* | |
| Water | The primary constituent of blood plasma. |
| Electrolytes (ions) | Sodium, potassium, chloride, bicarbonate, calcium, hydrogen, magnesium, others. Ions contribute to the control of cell function and volume, to the electrical charge across cells, and to the function of excitable cells (nerve and muscle). All ions must be kept at their normal concentrations for homeostasis to occur. |
| Proteins | Albumins maintain blood volume and transport electrolytes, hormones, and wastes. Globulins serve as antibodies and transport substances. Clotting proteins contribute to blood clotting. |
| Hormones | Insulin, growth hormones, testosterone, estrogen, others. Hormones are chemical messenger molecules that provide information needed to regulate specific body functions. |
| Gases | Oxygen is needed for metabolism; carbon dioxide is a waste product of metabolism. Both are dissolved in plasma as well as carried by RBCs. |
| Nutrients and wastes | Glucose, urea, many others. Nutrients, raw materials, and wastes (including heat) are transported by blood throughout the body. |

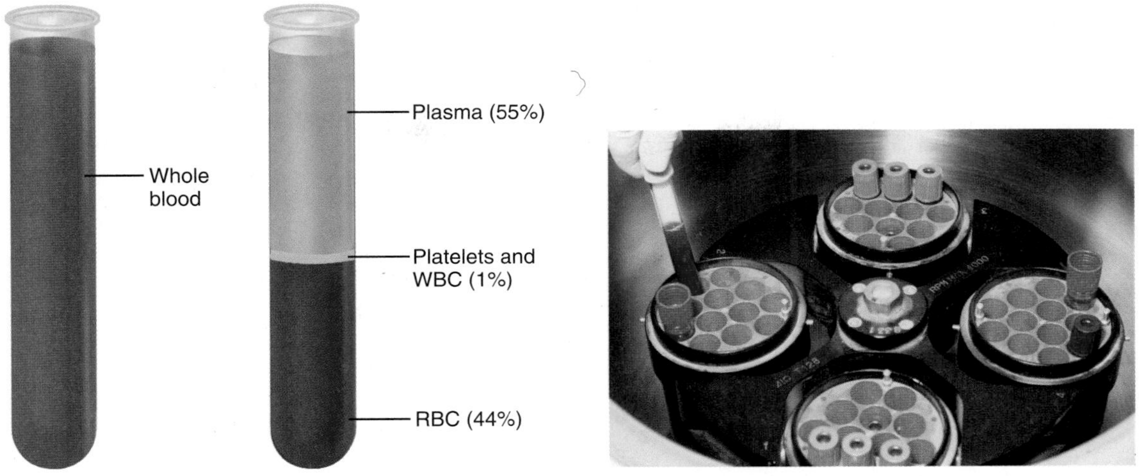


**a) Whole blood** **b) Blood after being spun in centrifuge** **c) A table-top centrifuge**

**Figure 7.2 Blood.** The formed elements sink to the bottom during centrifugation.

**Globulins** (designated alpha, beta, and gamma) are a diverse group of proteins that transport various substances in the blood. Many beta globulins bind to lipid (fat) molecules, such as cholesterol. When a protein attaches to one of these molecules, it creates a complex called a lipoprotein. Two medically important lipoproteins are the low-density lipoproteins (LDLs) and high-density lipoproteins (HDLs), and medical exams often include taking a blood sample to measure their relative proportions. The LDLs are sometimes called "bad cholesterol," because high blood levels of these lipoproteins are associated with increased risk of cardiovascular health problems. High levels of HDLs often indicate a lower risk of cardiovascular disease. We discuss lipoproteins and the health implications of blood cholesterol levels in Chapter 8.

Gamma globulins function as part of the body's defense system, helping to protect against infections and illness. We take a closer look at them in Chapter 9.

*Clotting proteins,* a third group of plasma proteins, play an important role in the process of blood clotting. As we see later in this chapter, blood clotting minimizes blood loss and helps maintain homeostasis after injury.

**Other plasma components** In addition to plasma proteins, plasma transports a variety of other molecules, including ions (also called electrolytes), hormones, nutrients, waste products, and gases. Electrolytes such as sodium and potassium contribute to the control of cell function and cell volume. Hormones, which are chemical "messengers" from the endocrine system, transport information throughout the body. Nutrients such as carbohydrates, amino acids, vitamins, and other substances are absorbed from the digestive tract or produced by cells' metabolic reactions. Waste products in plasma include carbon dioxide, urea, and lactic acid. Gases dissolved in plasma include oxygen, which is necessary for metabolism, and carbon dioxide, a waste product of metabolism.

**RECAP**

About 55% of whole blood consists of plasma. Plasma is mostly water and serves as the medium in which all other blood components are dissolved and transported. Plasma proteins include albumins, globulins, and clotting factors. ■

## Red blood cells transport oxygen and carbon dioxide

Just under half of the volume of whole blood consists of its formed elements. The most abundant are **red blood cells (RBCs),** also called **erythrocytes** ("red cells" in Greek). Red blood cells function primarily as carriers of oxygen and carbon dioxide. Each cubic millimeter of blood contains approximately 5 million red blood cells. They give blood its color and are the major reason why it is viscous.

Red blood cells offer a great example of how structure serves function. Red blood cells are small, flattened, doughnut-shaped disks whose centers are thinner than their edges (Figure 7.3). This is an unusual shape among human cells, but it has several advantages for RBCs. It makes them flexible, so they can bend and flex to squeeze through tiny blood vessels. It also means that no point within an RBC's cytoplasm is ever far from the cell surface, which facilitates the process of gas exchange.

Red blood cells are highly specialized to transport oxygen. Mature RBCs have no nucleus and essentially no organelles. They are essentially fluid-filled bags of plasma membrane, crammed with nearly 300 million molecules of an oxygen-binding protein called **hemoglobin.** Hemoglobin consists of

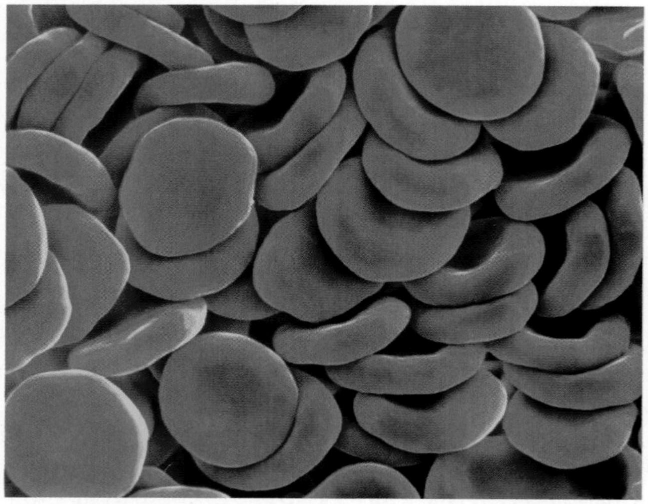

**Figure 7.3 Red blood cells.** Note that their flattened, biconcave shape gives them a sunken appearance (SEM × 1,160).

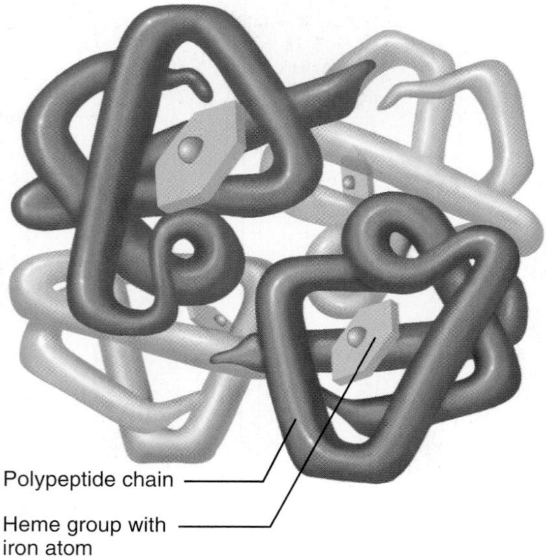


**Figure 7.4 A hemoglobin molecule.** Hemoglobin consists of four polypeptide chains folded together, each with a heme group containing a single iron atom. There are nearly 300 million of these molecules in every red blood cell.

four polypeptide chains, each containing a heme group (Figure 7.4). At the center of each heme group is an iron atom, which can readily form a bond with an oxygen molecule ($O_2$). In total, a single red blood cell can carry up to 1.2 billion molecules of oxygen. RBCs lack mitochondria and generate ATP by anaerobic pathways. So, they don't consume any of the oxygen they carry; they just transport it.

Several factors influence the binding of hemoglobin to oxygen. Hemoglobin binds oxygen most efficiently when the concentration of oxygen is relatively high and the pH is fairly neutral. These are precisely the conditions that prevail in the lungs. In the lungs, oxygen diffuses into blood plasma and then into red blood cells, where it attaches readily to the iron atoms in hemoglobin. The binding of $O_2$ by hemoglobin removes some of the $O_2$ from the plasma, making room for more $O_2$ to diffuse from the lungs into the plasma. Hemoglobin with four oxygen molecules attached, called *oxyhemoglobin,* has a characteristic bright red color.

The bond hemoglobin forms with oxygen must be temporary so that the oxygen can be released to the cells that need it. In body tissues that use oxygen in the course of their metabolic activities, the concentration of dissolved oxygen and the pH are both lower. Under these conditions, hemoglobin readily releases oxygen into body tissues, making it available to cells. Increased body heat also increases the rate at which hemoglobin releases oxygen. Hemoglobin that has given up its oxygen is called *deoxyhemoglobin.* Deoxyhemoglobin is characteristically dark purple, but because venous blood returning from the cells contains a mixture of oxyhemoglobin and deoxyhemoglobin, venous blood generally has a dark red or maroon color that is between red and purple.

Hemoglobin also transports some carbon dioxide ($CO_2$), a waste product of cellular metabolism. In tissues, where carbon dioxide levels are high, about 25% of the $CO_2$ binds to hemoglobin (at different sites than $O_2$). In the lungs, $CO_2$ detaches from hemoglobin and is eliminated through respiration. See Chapter 10 for more about gas transport, including how the rest of the $CO_2$ is transported.

**RECAP**

The ability of RBCs to transport nearly all of the oxygen and some of the carbon dioxide in blood depends on hemoglobin, the primary protein within red blood cells. Each molecule of hemoglobin contains four atoms of iron that can bind reversibly to oxygen. ■

## Hematocrit reflects oxygen-carrying capacity

The percentage of blood that consists of red blood cells is called the **hematocrit.** Hematocrit is an important medical concept because it is a relative measure of the oxygen-carrying capacity of blood.

The normal hematocrit range is 43–49% in men and 37–43% in women. An unusual hematocrit is sometimes a reason for concern. A low hematocrit may signal *anemia* or other disorders of inadequate red blood cell production (see section 7.4). A high hematocrit can also be risky because excessive red blood cells thicken blood and increase the risk of blood clots. In rare cases a high hematocrit could signal *polycythemia,* a disorder of the bone marrow characterized by an overproduction of red blood cells. Polycythemia increases blood volume and blood viscosity, sometimes leading to headaches, blurred vision, and high blood pressure.

Some shifts in hematocrit are normal and temporary. For example, if you visit the mountains on your next vacation and stay for at least several weeks, your hematocrit rises to compensate for lower levels of oxygen in the air you breathe. This is part of the normal homeostatic regulation of the oxygen-carrying capacity of the blood. After you return to your usual altitude, your hematocrit returns to normal.

## All blood cells and platelets originate from stem cells

All blood cells and platelets originate from cells in the red bone marrow. These cells, called **stem cells,** divide repeatedly throughout our lives, continually producing immature blood cells. These immature cells develop into platelets, and the various types of mature red and white blood cells described in Figure 7.5.

## RBCs have a short life span

Some stem cells develop into immature cells called *erythroblasts* ("red" + "immature"). Erythroblasts become filled with hemoglobin and develop into mature RBCs, or erythrocytes, in about a week. As they mature, these cells lose their nucleus and organelles, and so they cannot reproduce. Thus, all new RBCs must originate from dividing stem cells. Because they lack a nucleus and therefore cannot perform many standard cell activities (such as producing new proteins and phospholipids to renew their cell membranes), they wear out rather quickly. Red blood cells live for only about 120 days, but during that time they make nearly 3,000 round trips a day, ferrying $O_2$ from the lungs to the tissues and $CO_2$ from the tissues back to the lungs. Because they live for such a short time, red blood cells must be produced throughout life—at the incredible rate of more than 2 million per second—just to keep the hematocrit constant.

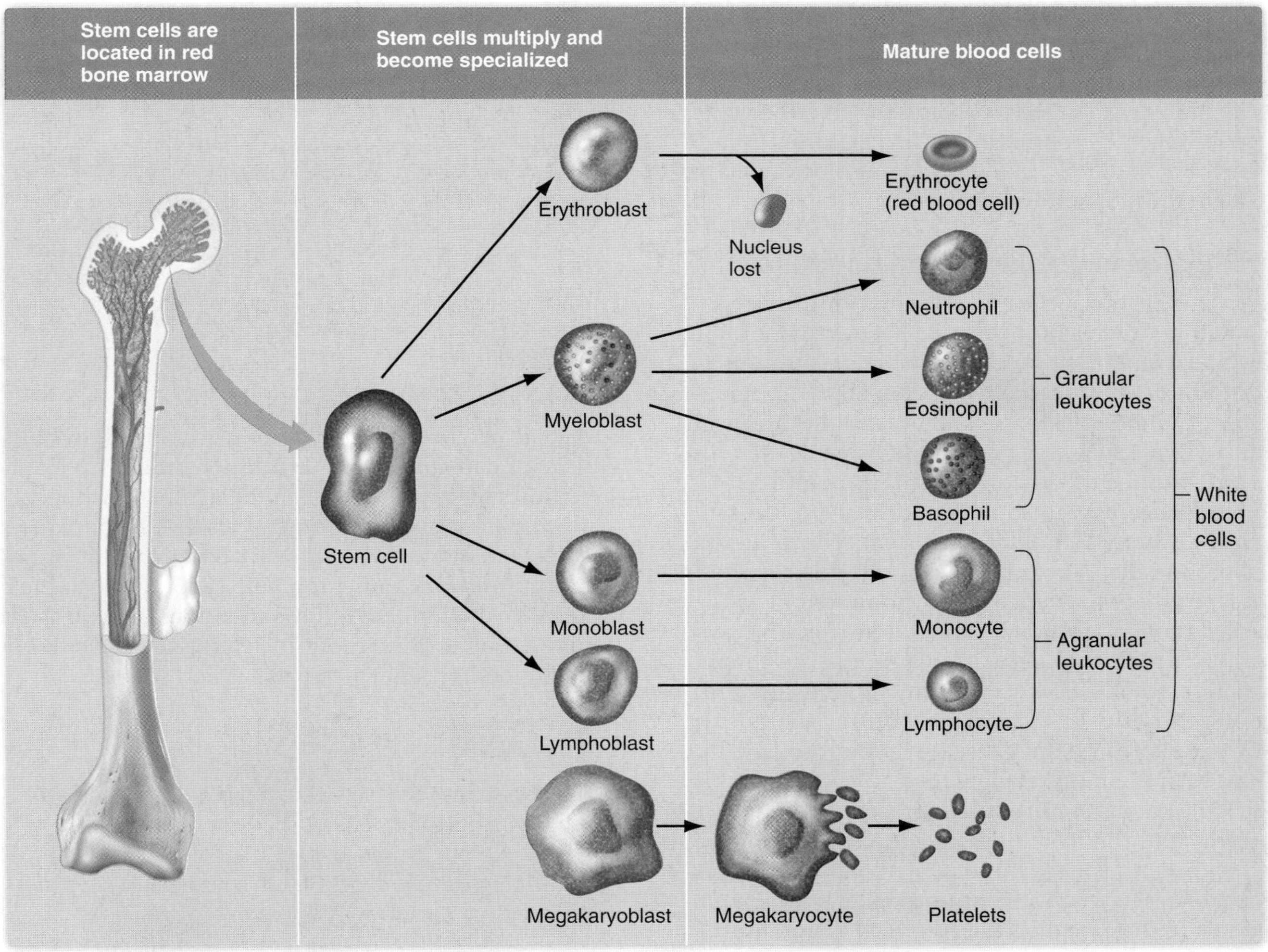


**Figure 7.5 The production of blood cells and platelets.** Blood cells have short life spans and must be continually replaced. Stem cells in the bone marrow continually divide and give rise to a variety of types of blood cells.

Old and damaged RBCs are removed from the circulating blood and destroyed in the liver and spleen by large cells called **macrophages.** Macrophages are derived from *monocytes,* the largest of the white blood cells. Macrophages surround, engulf, and digest the red blood cell. The process is called **phagocytosis.** The four peptide chains of the hemoglobin molecules are then dismantled into their constituent amino acids, and the amino acids are recycled to make new proteins. The iron atoms of the heme groups are returned to the red bone marrow, where they are used again in the production of new hemoglobin for new red blood cells. The heme groups (minus the iron) are converted by the liver to a yellowish pigment called *bilirubin.* If you've ever noticed how a bruise slowly changes color as it heals, from purple to blue to green to yellow, you have observed the chemical breakdown of the heme groups to bilirubin at the site of damage. Under normal circumstances, when hemoglobin is broken down in the liver, bilirubin mixes with bile secreted during digestion and passes into the intestines. This pigment contributes to the characteristic colors of urine and feces.

When the liver fails to secrete bilirubin into the bile properly or when the bile duct from the liver to the intestines is blocked, bilirubin may accumulate in blood plasma. High circulating levels of bilirubin make skin and mucous membranes look yellowish and can turn the whites of the eyes yellow. This condition is called *jaundice* (from *jaune,* French for "yellow"). Jaundice may also be caused by an increase in the rate of RBC breakdown.

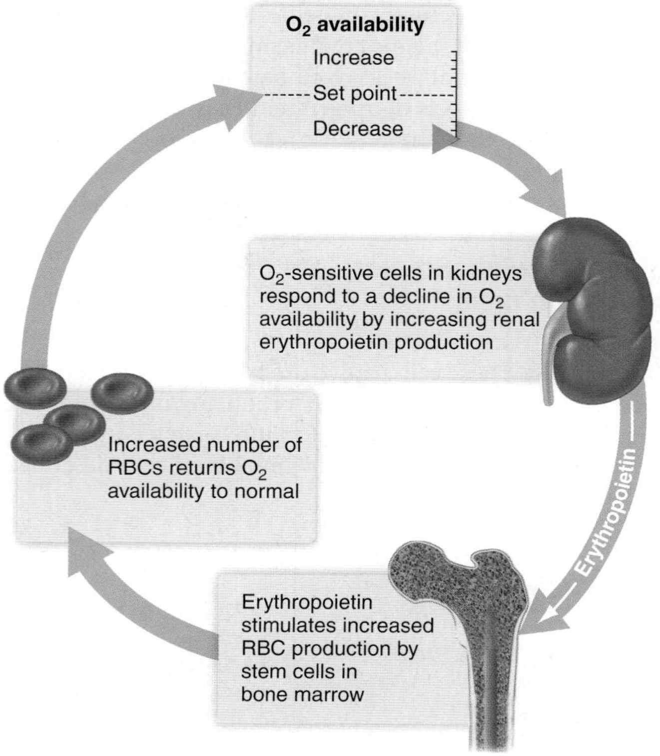


**Figure 7.6 Negative feedback control of the availability of oxygen.** Certain cells in the kidney are sensitive to the amount of oxygen available to them. When oxygen availability falls, these cells produce erythropoietin, a hormone that stimulates the bone marrow to produce red blood cells. The increase in red blood cells returns oxygen availability toward normal, which reduces the stimulus for further erythropoietin secretion. Ultimately, homeostasis of oxygen availability is achieved.

## RBC production is regulated by a hormone

Regulation of RBC production is a negative feedback control loop that maintains homeostasis. The number of RBCs is not regulated (there are no cells capable of counting the number of RBCs), only their effect—their ability to transport oxygen. Certain cells in the kidneys monitor the availability of oxygen. Low oxygen availability signals the cells to secrete a hormone called **erythropoietin.** Once released into the bloodstream, erythropoietin is carried to the red bone marrow, where it stimulates the stem cells to produce more red blood cells. When the oxygen-carrying capacity of blood rises to an appropriate level as monitored by kidney cells, the cells cut back on their production of erythropoietin, and RBC production decreases. Thus, the body maintains homeostasis of oxygen availability by adjusting the production rate of the RBCs that transport it (Figure 7.6).

Some people with kidney disease do not produce enough erythropoietin to regulate their RBC production properly. Fortunately, erythropoietin is now available commercially and can be administered to stimulate red cell production.

Some athletes have abused commercial erythropoietin by injecting it to increase their RBC production and thus their blood oxygen-carrying capacity, a practice called **blood doping.** Three gold medalists at the 2002 Winter Olympics, Spain's Johann Mühlegg and Russia's Larissa Lazutina and Olga Danilova, were disqualified and stripped of their medals because of blood doping. All three skiers tested positive for darbepoetin, an erythropoietin-like drug that is 10 times more powerful than the natural hormone.

Blood doping can have serious health consequences. Excess red blood cells make blood more viscous, and so the heart must work harder to pump blood through the body. The dehydration that follows strenuous exercise can concentrate the blood even more, increasing the risk of blood clots, high blood pressure, heart attack, and stroke.

**RECAP**

All blood cells and platelets are derived from stem cells in red bone marrow. RBCs have a short life span and must be continually replaced. The rate of production of RBCs is stimulated by the hormone erythropoietin, which is produced in the kidneys. ■

## White blood cells defend the body

Approximately 1% of whole blood consists of **white blood cells (WBCs or leukocytes).** Larger than red blood cells, they are also more diverse in structure and function. They have a nucleus but no hemoglobin. Because they are translucent, they are difficult to identify under the microscope unless they have been stained. Each cubic millimeter of blood contains only about 7,000 of them, and there is only one WBC for every 700 RBCs. White blood cells play a number of crucial roles in defending against disease and injury.

Like red blood cells, white blood cells arise from stem cells in the red bone marrow. As shown in Figure 7.5, stem cells produce immature blood cells that develop into the various WBCs. There are two major categories of white blood cells: *granular leukocytes* (granulocytes) and *agranular leukocytes* (agranulocytes). Both types contain granules (actually vesicles) in their cytoplasm that are filled with proteins and enzymes to assist their defensive work. However, the granules of the agranular leukocytes are not visible when the cells are stained for viewing ("a-" "means "without".)

Once produced, most WBCs mature in the red bone marrow. Agranular leukocytes called T lymphocytes are the exception; they travel in the bloodstream to the thymus gland, where they mature. Most WBCs have an even shorter life span than red blood cells. Many granular leukocytes die within a few hours to nine days, probably because of injuries sustained while fighting invading microorganisms. Their agranular cousins usually live longer. Monocytes may survive for several months; lymphocytes for several days to many years. Dead and injured WBCs are continually removed from the blood by the liver and spleen.

Circulating levels of white blood cells rise whenever the body is threatened by viruses, bacteria, or other challenges to health. Each type of WBC seems able to produce chemicals that circulate in blood back to the bone marrow, where they stimulate the production of leukocyte reinforcements.

Red cells remain in the blood, but some white cells leave the vascular system and circulate in the tissue fluid between cells or in the fluid in the lymphatic system. Because they can change their shape, they can squeeze between the cells that form the capillary walls. White blood cells, part of the body's defense system, are discussed in more detail in Chapter 9. Here we only describe the important characteristics of each type.

**Granular leukocytes: Neutrophils, eosinophils, and basophils** The granular leukocytes include neutrophils, eosinophils, and basophils. These names are based on their staining properties:

- **Neutrophils,** the most abundant type of granulocyte, account for about 60% of WBCs. (Their name—which means "neutral-loving"—reflects the fact that their granules do not significantly absorb either a red or blue stain.) The first white blood cells to combat infection, neutrophils surround and engulf foreign cells (Figure 7.7). They especially target bacteria and some fungi, and their numbers can rise dramatically during acute bacterial infections such as appendicitis or meningitis.

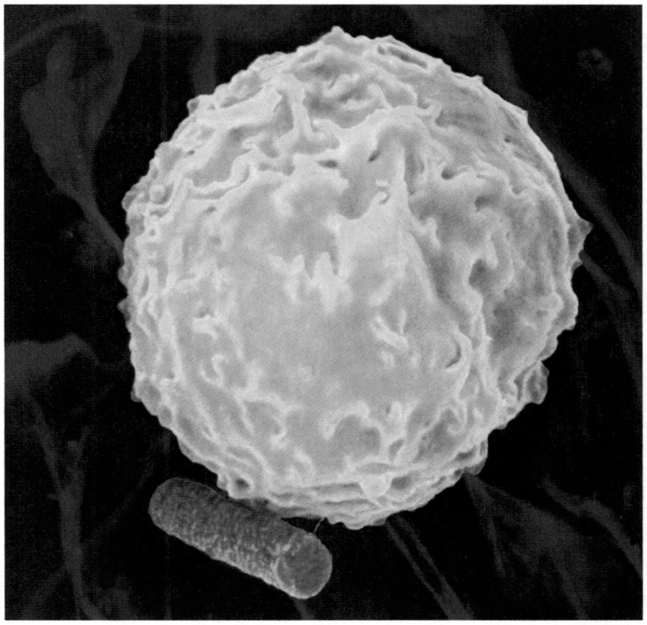

**Figure 7.7 A neutrophil attacks a *Bacillus* bacterium.** In the first stage of phagocytosis, the neutrophil has approached the bacterium using the protuberances on its surface. Next it will engulf and destroy the bacterium (Color SEM × 8,000).

- **Eosinophils** make up a relatively small percentage (2–4%) of circulating white blood cells. (Their name comes from their tendency to stain readily with an acidic red stain called eosin.) Eosinophils have two important functions. The first is to defend the body against large parasites such as worms (hookworms, tapeworms, flukes, and pinworms, among others). These parasites are too big to be surrounded and engulfed through phagocytosis. Instead, clusters of eosinophils surround each parasite and bombard it with digestive enzymes. The second function of eosinophils involves releasing chemicals that moderate the severity of allergic reactions.
- **Basophils,** the rarest white blood cells, account for only 0.5% of leukocytes. (They are named for their tendency to stain readily with basic blue stains.) The granules in the cytoplasm of basophils contain histamine, a chemical that initiates the inflammatory response. When body tissues are injured, basophils secrete histamine, causing adjacent blood vessels to release blood plasma into the injured area. The plasma brings in nutrients, various cells, and chemicals to begin the process of tissue repair. The swelling, itching, and redness associated with inflammation may not feel pleasant, but they are part of the immune system's defenses against molecules that are perceived as threatening.

**Agranular leukocytes: Monocytes and lymphocytes** The agranular leukocytes include monocytes and lymphocytes. The largest WBCs, **monocytes,** make up about 5% of circulating white blood cells. They can filter out of the bloodstream and take up residence in body tissues, where they differentiate into the macrophages that engulf invaders and dead cellular debris by phagocytosis. They also stimulate lymphocytes to defend the body. Monocytes seem especially active during chronic infections, such as tuberculosis, and against viruses and certain bacterial parasites.

**Lymphocytes** total about 30% of circulating white blood cells. They are found in the bloodstream, tonsils, spleen, lymph nodes, and thymus gland. They are classified into two types, *B lymphocytes* and *T lymphocytes* (or B cells and T cells). B lymphocytes give rise to *plasma cells* that produce *antibodies,* specialized proteins that defend against microorganisms and other foreign invaders. T lymphocytes target and destroy specific threats such as bacteria, viruses, and cancer cells. Both play a crucial role in the body's immune system, and we look at them in more detail in Chapter 9.

**RECAP**

White blood cells (leukocytes) defend the body against disease and injury. The activities of various leukocytes include participating in the response to tissue injury, producing antibodies, engulfing entire foreign cells, and releasing enzymes to attack foreign organisms too large to be engulfed whole. ■

### Platelets are essential for blood clotting

Less than 1% of whole blood consists of platelets. **Platelets** are actually small cell fragments, not complete cells, and they play an essential role in the process of blood clotting. Platelets are derived from megakaryocytes, which are large cells derived from stem cells in the bone marrow. However, unlike RBCs and WBCs, megakaryocytes never circulate. Platelets are small pieces of megakaryocyte cytoplasm and cell membrane. Megakaryocytes produce about 200 billion platelets a day; a single cubic millimeter of blood contains anywhere from 250,000 to 500,000 of these tiny cell fragments. Platelets last only about five to nine days. Their production is regulated by a recently discovered hormone called *thrombopoietin,* but how thrombopoietin secretion is regulated is still unknown.

When a blood vessel is injured and leaks blood, platelets play an important role in its repair. We examine this process in the next section.

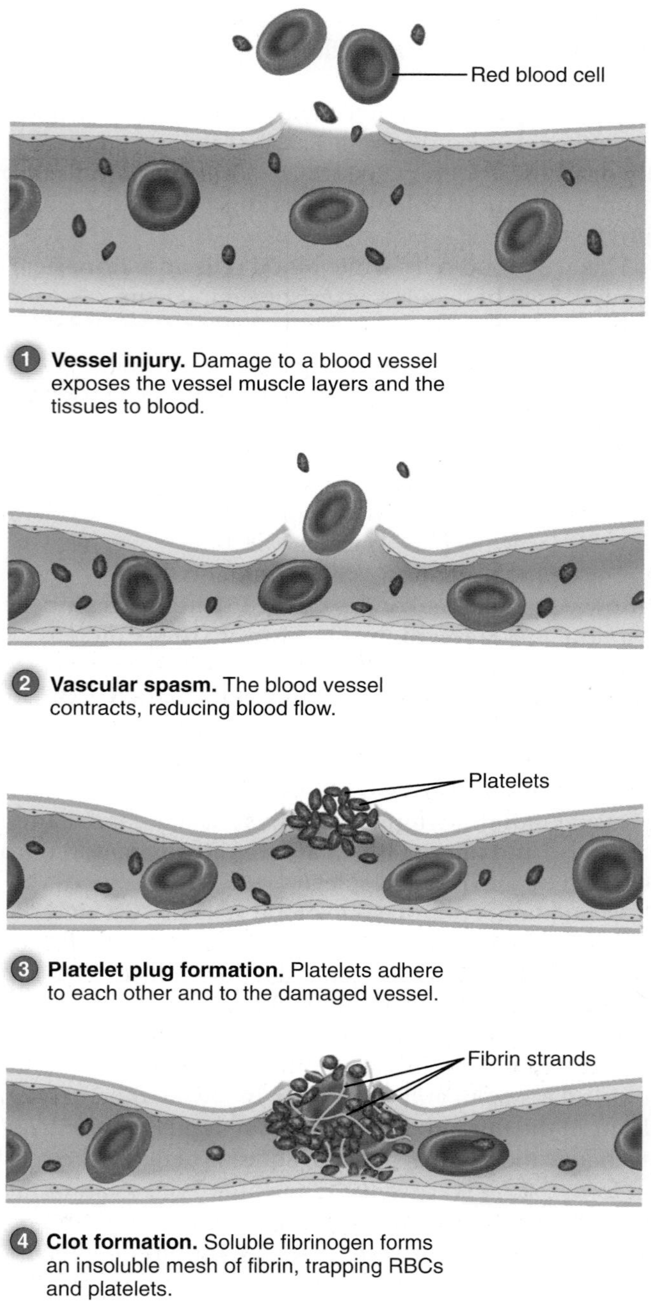


**Figure 7.8 The stages of hemostasis.**

## 7.2 Hemostasis: Stopping blood loss

One of the most important properties of the circulatory system is its ability to limit blood loss following injury. **Hemostasis,** the natural process of stopping the flow or loss of blood, proceeds in three stages: (1) vascular spasm, or intense contraction of blood vessels in the area, (2) formation of a platelet plug, and (3) blood clotting, also called coagulation (Figure 7.8). Once blood loss has stopped, tissue repair can begin.

### Vascular spasms constrict blood vessels to reduce blood flow

When a blood vessel is damaged, smooth muscle in its wall undergoes spasms—intense contractions that constrict the vessels. If the vessels are medium-sized to large, the spasms reduce immediate outflow of blood, minimizing the damage in preparation for later steps in hemostasis. If the vessels are small, the spasms press the inner walls together and may even stop the bleeding entirely. Vascular spasms generally last for about half an hour, long enough for the next two stages of hemostasis to occur.

### Platelets stick together to seal a ruptured vessel

Normally, platelets circulate freely in blood. However, when the lining of a blood vessel breaks, exposing underlying proteins in the vessel wall, platelets swell, develop spiky extensions, and begin to clump together. They also become sticky and start adhering to the walls of the vessel and to each other. More platelets congregate and undergo these same changes. The result is a platelet plug that seals the injured area. If the rupture is fairly small, a platelet plug may be able to close it within several seconds. This may be enough to stop the bleeding. If damage is more severe, blood clotting occurs.

### A blood clot forms around the platelet plug

The third stage in hemostasis is the formation of a blood clot, during which the blood changes from a liquid to a gel. This involves a series of chemical reactions that ultimately produce a meshwork of protein fibers within the blood. At least 12 substances, known as clotting factors, participate in these reactions. We will focus on three clotting factors: prothrombin activator, thrombin, and fibrinogen.

Damage to blood vessels stimulates the vessels and nearby platelets to release *prothrombin activator.* This activates the conversion of *prothrombin,* a plasma protein, into an enzyme called **thrombin.** This reaction requires the presence of calcium ions ($Ca^{2+}$). Thrombin in turn facilitates the conversion of a soluble plasma protein, *fibrinogen,* into long insoluble threads of a protein called **fibrin.** The fibrin threads wind around the platelet plug at the wound site, forming an interlocking net of fibers that traps and holds platelets, blood cells, and various molecules against the opening.

The mass of fibrin, platelets, and trapped red blood cells coalesces into an initial *clot* that reduces the flow of blood at the site of injury (Figure 7.9). This initial fibrin clot can form in less than a minute. Shortly thereafter, platelets in the clot start to contract, tightening the clot and pulling the vessel walls together. Generally the entire process of blood clot formation and tightening takes less than an hour.

If any step in this process is blocked, even a minor cut or bruise can become life threatening. Consider *hemophilia,* an inherited condition caused by a deficiency of one or more clotting factors. People with the most common form of the condition, hemophilia A, lack a protein known as clotting factor VIII. When a vessel is breached, blood clots slowly or not at all. Even if the skin is not broken, severe bruising can spread into joints and muscles (Figure 7.10). Fifty years ago most people with hemophilia did not survive to adulthood, but today many bleeding episodes can be controlled by administering factor VIII. Because clotting factor VIII was initially purified from donor blood, which at that time could not be tested for the HIV virus, in the past some hemophiliacs contracted AIDS. Today all blood is screened for HIV. In addition, the use of donor blood as a source of factor VIII has decreased because genetic engineering techniques have made it possible to produce factor VIII in the laboratory.

Certain medications can also interfere with hemostasis. If you cut yourself after taking aspirin, for example, you may notice that you bleed more than usual. This is because aspirin blocks platelet clumping and slows the formation of a

**Figure 7.9 Magnified view of a developing clot, showing red blood cells trapped in a network of fibrin fibers.**

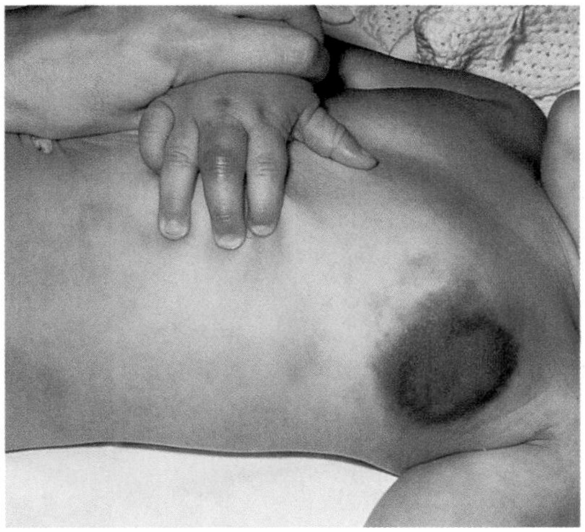

**Figure 7.10 Complications of hemophilia.** People with hemophilia can suffer severe bruising (hemorrhaging) from only minor bumps or scrapes.

platelet plug. If you plan to have surgery, your doctor will probably advise you to avoid taking aspirin for at least 7–10 days before the surgery.

**RECAP**

Damage to blood vessels causes the vessels to spasm (contract) and the nearby platelets to become sticky and adhere to each other, limiting blood loss. In addition, a series of chemical events causes the blood in the area to clot, or coagulate (form a gel). ■

## 7.3 Human blood types

Blood transfusions—the administration of blood directly into the bloodstream of another person—may seem like a miracle of modern medicine, but the concept is not new. For over a century, physicians have tried to counteract severe blood loss by transfusing blood from one living person into another. Sometimes these attempts were successful. More often they were not, resulting in severe illness or even death for the recipient. Why did they save some lives but not others?

Today we know the success of blood transfusions depends largely on **blood type,** based primarily on the ABO blood group system. If you ever donate or receive blood, you will undergo testing to determine your blood type. If you receive blood from someone who does not belong to a compatible blood type, you could suffer a severe reaction.

To understand the concept of blood typing, we must first be familiar with antigens and antibodies. Our cells have certain surface proteins that the immune system can recognize and identify as "self"—in other words, belonging to us. These are like passwords that cause our immune system to ignore our own cells. Foreign cells carry different surface proteins, which the immune system recognizes as "nonself." An **antigen** (*anti* means "against," and the Greek word *gennan* means "to generate") is a nonself cell protein that stimulates the immune system of an organism to defend the organism. As part of this defense, the immune system produces an opposing protein called an **antibody** ("against" + "body").

Produced by lymphocytes, antibodies belong to the class of plasma proteins called gamma globulins, mentioned earlier. Antibodies mount a counterattack on antigens they recognize as nonself. There are many antibodies, each one specialized to attack one particular antigen. This response has been compared to a lock and key: only a specific antibody key can fit a specific antigen lock. Antibodies float freely in the blood and lymph until they encounter an invader with the matching antigen. They bind to the antigen molecule to form an antigen-antibody complex that marks the foreigner for destruction. The formation of an antigen-antibody complex often causes the foreign cells to clump together (Figure 7.11). Some antibodies also inactivate foreign cells by preventing them from entering human cells.

Antigens and antibodies are discussed in more detail in Chapter 9. For now, let's look at how their interactions relate to blood type and blood transfusions.

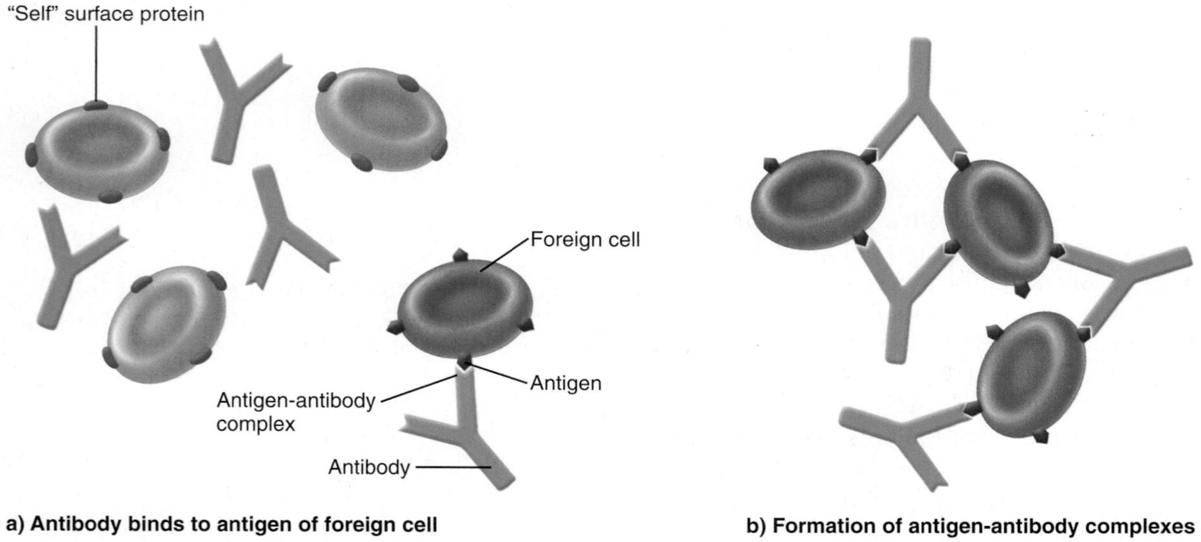


**Figure 7.11 How antibodies recognize and inactivate foreign cells. (a)** Three "self" cells, circulating antibodies, and one foreign cell (indicated by the darker color). The antibody ignores the "self" surface proteins but binds to the antigen of the foreign cell, forming an antigen-antibody complex. **(b)** The formation of antigen-antibody complexes causes foreign cells to clump together, inactivating them.

**RECAP**

Different blood types are determined by the presence of surface antigens on red blood cells and the presence of antibodies to surface antigens other than their own. ■

## ABO blood typing is based on A and B antigens

Like other cells, red blood cells have surface proteins that allow the body to identify them as "self." The interactions between these antigens, and the development of antibodies against the antigens of foreign red blood cells, underlie the reactions that can occur after blood transfusions.

Red blood cells are classified according to the ABO blood group system, in which nearly all individuals belong to one of four types: A, B, AB, or O. Type A blood has A antigens, type B blood has B antigens, type AB blood has *both* A and B antigens, and type O blood has neither (think of the O as a "zero"). In addition, all individuals have circulating antibodies (and the ability to make more antibodies) against any surface antigens different from their own; type A blood has type B antibodies, type B blood has type A antibodies, type O blood has both type A and B antibodies, and type AB blood has neither antibody. Figure 7.12 shows these various blood types and also indicates the relative incidences of each type in various populations. The antibodies appear early in life, regardless of whether a person has ever received a blood transfusion. These antibodies attack red blood cells with foreign antigens, damaging them and causing them to *agglutinate,* or clump together. If agglutination is extreme, the clumps may block blood vessels, causing organ damage or even death. In addition, hemoglobin released by damaged red blood cells can block the kidneys, leading to kidney failure. Any adverse effect of a blood transfusion is called a *transfusion reaction.*

If you have type A blood, you are restricted to receiving transfusions of either type A or type O blood because neither of them has a foreign (type B) antigen. A transfusion of type B or type AB blood would provoke your antibodies to mount an attack against the B antigen of the donated RBCs, causing them to agglutinate. Similarly, if you're type B, you cannot receive any blood with type A antigens (A or AB). People with type AB blood can generally receive transfusions not only from other AB individuals but from all three of the other blood types as well. People with type AB blood, however, can donate only to other type AB individuals. Type O persons can give blood to persons of A, B, or AB type, but they can receive blood only from type O. Notice that it is the antibodies of the recipient that generally cause the transfusion reaction. Though the donor blood may have antibodies against the recipient's RBCs, they rarely cause transfusion reactions because the volume of blood given is generally small compared to the volume of the recipient's blood.

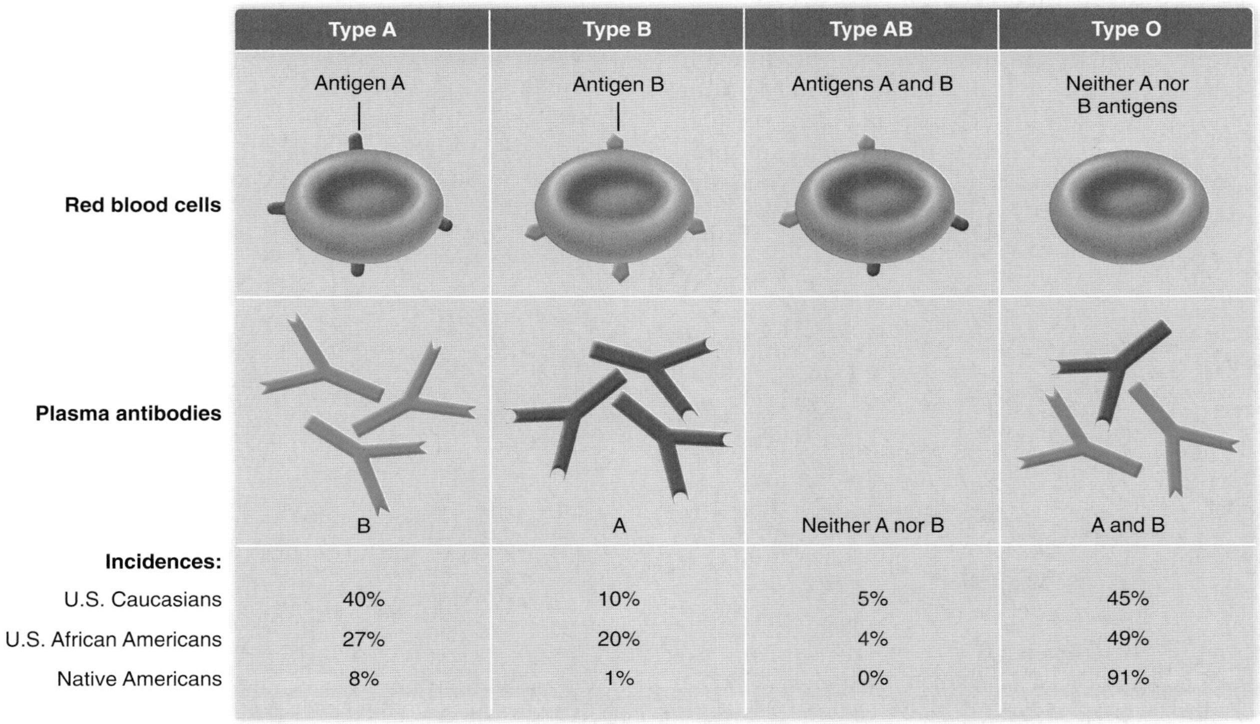


**Figure 7.12 Characteristics of the four major blood types of the ABO typing system, showing their RBC surface antigens, antibodies, and relative incidences among various populations.**

**RECAP**

Types A, B, AB, and O blood are identified by the presence (or absence) of type A and/or type B surface antigens on their red blood cells. ■

## Rh blood typing is based on Rh factor

Another red blood cell surface antigen, called **Rh factor** because it was first discovered in rhesus monkeys, is also important in blood transfusions. Approximately 85% of Americans are *Rh positive,* meaning they carry the Rh antigen on their red blood cells. About 15% are *Rh negative*—they do not have the Rh antigen, and consequently their immune systems respond to any foreign Rh antigen by making antibodies against it.

The Rh factor is a particular concern for Rh negative women who wish to have children. If an Rh negative woman becomes pregnant by an Rh positive man, the fetus may be Rh positive. If some of the fetus's Rh positive blood cells leak into the mother's blood, the mother starts producing anti-Rh antibodies. These maternal antibodies can cross the placenta and attack the fetus's red blood cells. The result may be *hemolytic disease of the newborn (HDN),* a disorder characterized by a reduced number of red blood cells and toxic levels of hemoglobin breakdown products in the newborn. HDN can lead to mental retardation or even death.

The risk of HDN is much higher for the second and all subsequent Rh positive fetuses than for the first (Figure 7.13). This is because it takes days or even weeks for antibodies to be produced after the first exposure to an antigen. Although a few fetal cells may leak across the placenta during a normal pregnancy and so present a slight chance that the first fetus could be affected, the greatest chance of maternal exposure to fetal blood generally occurs right at childbirth, when the placenta detaches from the uterus. The antibodies that develop from maternal exposure during the woman's first delivery come too late to affect the first fetus. But the maternal immune system has learned its lesson, and it is ready and waiting to attack the blood of any subsequent Rh positive fetus (see section 9.7, Immune memory creates immunity).

To prevent this reaction, an Rh negative mother who *may* be carrying an Rh positive child is given an injection of anti-Rh antibodies (RhoGAM) at 28 weeks of gestation, just in case. Then, if the newborn *is* Rh positive, the mother is given a second injection no later than three days after childbirth. The injected antibodies quickly destroy any of the newborn's red blood cells that may have entered the woman's circulation during childbirth, before her immune system has time to react to them. The injected antibodies disappear in a short time.

In addition to its important medical applications, blood typing has many other uses. Because blood types are inherited, anthropologists can track early population migrations by tracing inheritance patterns. Blood typing is also used in criminal investigations to compare the blood of victims and perpetrators, and to eliminate or identify suspects on the basis of matching antigens. DNA tests can be done on blood samples to help determine paternity.

## Blood typing and cross-matching ensure blood compatibility

Blood typing involves determining your ABO type and the presence or absence of the Rh factor. For example, if your blood type is "B-pos" (B+), you are type B and positive for the Rh factor. If you are "O-neg" (O–), you are type O and negative for the Rh factor.

ABO blood typing is done by adding plasma containing small amounts of anti-A and anti-B antibodies to drops of

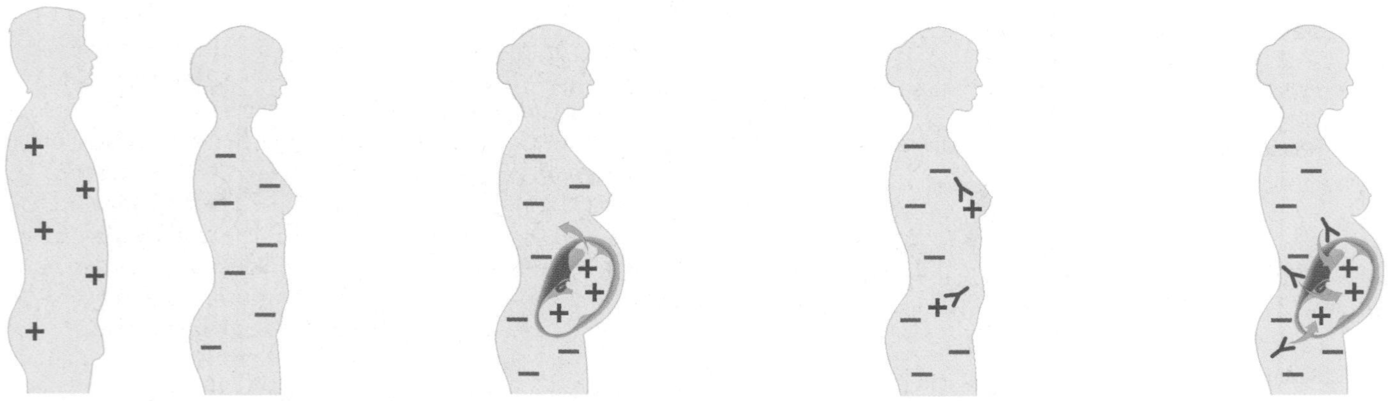

a) When an Rh positive man fathers a child by an Rh negative woman the fetus may inherit the Rh positive antigen.

b) During pregnancy or more commonly at childbirth, a small amount of fetal blood enters the mother's circulation.

c) Over the next several weeks the woman develops antibodies and an immune memory against the Rh antigen.

d) When the woman becomes pregnant with her second Rh positive fetus, her immune system quickly produces antibodies that attack the fetus's red blood cells.

**Figure 7.13 How Rh factor incompatibility can affect a fetus.**

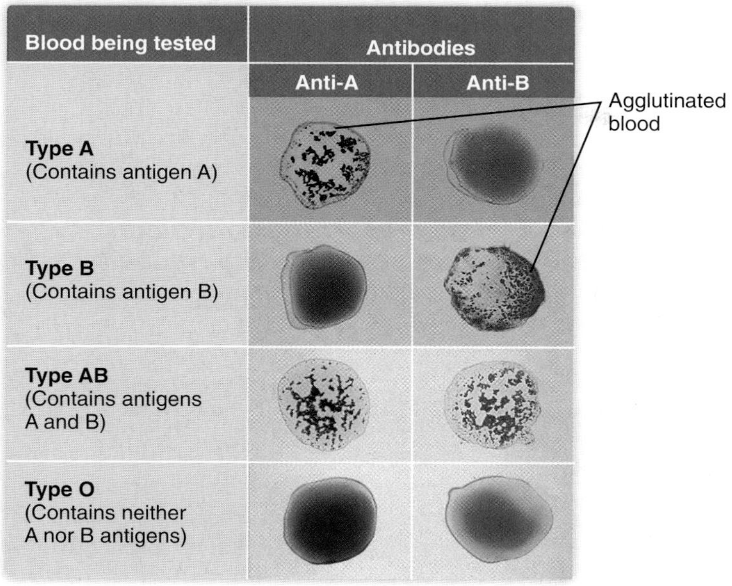


**Figure 7.14 Blood typing for ABO blood types.** Anti-A and Anti-B antibodies are added to diluted samples of blood. If the red blood cells have the surface antigen that matches the antibody, the blood agglutinates. Type O blood does not agglutinate in response to either antibody because it has no surface antigens.

diluted blood. If the blood agglutinates, then it contains the antigens that match the antibodies (Figure 7.14).

AB+ individuals were once called *universal recipients* because they can generally receive blood from any other type. Type O− individuals were formerly called *universal donors* because their blood can usually be donated to any other type. However, because transfusion reactions can occur unexpectedly, the terms are now considered outdated. Why do transfusion reactions occur occasionally even when blood has been adequately typed for ABO blood type and the Rh factor? The reason is that there are over 100 other less common blood antigens in the human population, in addition to the very common A, B, and Rh antigens. Fortunately, most of them are fairly rare. To ensure that blood transfusions are absolutely safe, however, medical laboratories generally do blood typing and *cross-matching.* Cross-matching involves mixing small samples of donor blood with recipient plasma, and recipient blood with donor plasma, and examining both combinations for agglutination. If agglutination does not occur in either combination, the bloods are assumed to be a good match.

**RECAP**

In addition to ABO type, all persons are classified according to the presence or absence of another red blood cell surface antigen called the Rh factor. Rh factor antibodies can cause a serious immune reaction of the mother to her own fetus under certain circumstances. ■

# 7.4 Blood disorders

## Anemia: Reduction in blood's oxygen-carrying capacity

**Anemia** is a general term for reduction in the oxygen-carrying capacity of blood. All causes of anemia produce similar symptoms: pale skin, headaches, fatigue, dizziness, difficulty breathing, and heart palpitations—the uncomfortable feeling that one's heart is beating too fast as it tries to compensate for the lack of oxygen delivery. Major types of anemia include:

- **Iron-deficiency anemia.** Recall that every hemoglobin molecule contains 4 molecules of iron. When the body is deficient in iron, hemoglobin cannot be synthesized properly. The result is fewer hemoglobin molecules per red blood cell, and thus a decreased ability to transport oxygen. Iron-deficiency anemia is the most common form of anemia worldwide. Usually it is due to too little iron in the diet, but it can also be caused by an inability of the digestive tract to absorb iron properly. Generally it can be treated by taking pills that contain iron, or by eating foods rich in iron such as leafy green vegetables and meat.
- **Hemorrhagic anemia.** Anemia due to blood loss (hemorrhage) may be caused by injuries, bleeding ulcers, excessive menstrual flow, and even certain parasites. Treatment includes finding and treating the underlying cause of blood loss, if possible, and making sure one has enough iron in the diet to replenish the lost red blood cells.
- **Pernicious anemia.** Pernicious anemia is caused by a deficiency of vitamin $B_{12}$ absorption by the digestive tract. Vitamin $B_{12}$ is important for the production of normal red blood cells. Pernicious anemia can be treated by injections of $B_{12}$.
- **Hemolytic anemia.** Hemolytic anemia is the result of rupture (lysis) or early destruction of red blood cells. One cause is sickle-cell disease, an inherited disorder in which the red blood cells take on an abnormal sickle shape when the oxygen concentration is low. Because of their abnormal shape, sickled red blood cells become damaged as they travel through small blood vessels. Once damaged, they are destroyed by the body. Sickle-cell anemia is most prevalent in Africans who live near the equator and in African Americans, for reasons discussed in Chapter 7. Another common cause of hemolytic anemia is the parasite that causes malaria.

## Leukemia: Uncontrolled production of white blood cells

**Leukemia** refers to any of several types of blood cancer. Their common characteristic is uncontrolled proliferation of abnormal or immature white blood cells in the bone marrow. Overproduction of abnormal WBCs crowds out the production of normal white blood cells, red cells, and

# Current Issue

## Should You Bank Your Baby's Cord Blood?

When she was 15 and a sophomore in high school, Jaclyn Albanese was diagnosed with acute leukemia. She endured six months of chemotherapy, which made her nauseated and caused her hair to fall out but seemed at first to eradicate the cancer. Soon, however, tiny red bumps appeared all over her body. Testing disclosed cancer cells, which meant that her leukemia had returned. At first Albanese hoped to get a transplant of bone marrow tissue, but none of her relatives was a close enough match. She and her family turned to cord blood from an unrelated donor.

Jaclyn Albanese

### What Is Cord Blood?

During pregnancy, the fetus is cushioned by a temporary organ called the placenta and connected to its mother by the umbilical cord. Blood vessels in the cord and placenta filter out toxic substances, deliver nutrients from the mother, and remove waste products from the fetus. After the baby is delivered, the mother's body expels the placenta and umbilical cord. A health professional cuts the cord, and the baby's circulatory system begins to function on its own.

Until recently, the placenta and cord were discarded after birth. However, these structures still contain about 50 ml of cord blood. In addition to containing the usual components of blood, cord blood is rich in stem cells similar to those found in bone marrow. These stem cells can divide repeatedly to produce immature blood cells, which in turn develop into platelets, red cells, and white cells.

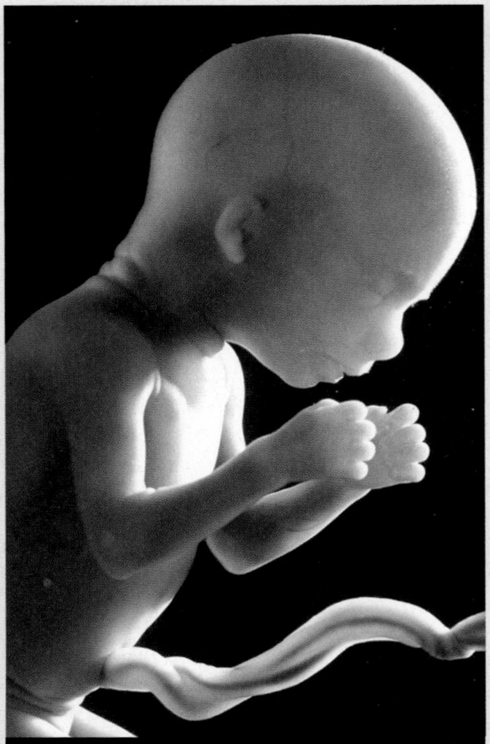

Blood in the umbilical cord contains stem cells similar to those found in bone marrow.

### Bone Marrow, Cord Blood, and Compatibility Issues

Every year, over 20,000 people are diagnosed with diseases, such as leukemia, that can be treated with transfusions of blood stem cells. Traditionally these stem cells have come from bone marrow donated by a family member or an unrelated volunteer whose marrow is compatible. Compatibility is crucial because, as you learned in this chapter, the body's immune cells recognize and attack the antigens of foreign cells.

A good bone marrow transplant match between a donor and a patient involves three key antigens known as HLA-A, HLA-B, and HLA-DR, each of which comes in two forms. The ideal match would be for the patient to have the same six forms as the donor (a 6/6 match). Although a good match is most likely to occur among family members (siblings of the same parents match 25% of the time), only about three of ten patients ever find a good match in their own families. Those who don't find a good match in their families (about 14,000 Americans per year) must rely on stem cells from nonrelated donors. Although the National Marrow Donor Program (NMDP) lists over 7 million potential volunteer bone marrow donors, only about 10% of patients who need a bone marrow transplant actually receive one through the NMDP because of the difficulty of finding a good match between unrelated persons.

### the facts...

- Every year over 20,000 people with cancer or a genetic disorder seek a bone marrow transplant.
- Cord blood—blood remaining in a newborn baby's placenta and umbilical cord—is rich in stem cells similar to those found in bone marrow. Cord blood can benefit many patients who cannot find a suitable bone marrow donor.
- Private cord blood banks urge prospective parents to bank their baby's cord blood solely for their own child's future use. Costs average $1,700 plus an annual fee of about $125.
- The federal government recently authorized funds for a public cord blood network for all Americans.

The odds of finding a match are even worse for members of ethnic minority groups because they have proportionately fewer compatible donors to choose from. African Americans are especially hard-hit because they are more likely than other groups to suffer from sickle-cell anemia, for which the only cure is a blood stem cell transplant. Furthermore, people of African ancestry show greater variation in HLA antigen types and unique combinations of antigens, making compatibility an even bigger challenge.

This is why cord blood has become such a precious commodity. The immune cells in cord blood are less mature than those in bone marrow, so cord blood transplants are less likely to cause transfusion reactions, and even when reactions do occur, they tend to be less severe. As a result, the match between donor and recipient does not need to be a perfect 6/6—matches of 5/6 or even 4/6 are sufficient. This opens a much wider field of possibilities. Jaclyn Albanese could not find a single compatible bone marrow donor, but she was able to locate two units of compatible cord blood. She had a cord blood transplant in 1999 just prior to her junior year in high school, and today she is a college graduate. Jaclyn is one of approximately 6,000 patients who have benefited from cord blood transplants to date.

Cord blood stem cells.

But the potential of cord blood does not stop there. Some scientists think that stem cells in cord blood can develop into other types of cells besides blood cells, such as heart or nerve tissue. If so, perhaps someday they may replace stem cells from human embryos in research and transplantation. This would be good for scientists, for patients, and even for politicians, because the use of stem cells from human embryos is highly controversial. Researchers continue to investigate the potential of cord blood stem cells.

### Banking Privately or Publicly

The issue is whether you should bank your baby's cord blood privately by paying a hefty fee or donate it to a public cord blood bank.

Private blood banks say that banking your baby's cord blood privately is like taking out a medical insurance policy. They argue that you may use your baby's cord blood stem cells to treat a future disease (such as leukemia) in your child or a close family member. By banking your baby's cord blood, you ensure that your child always has access to the "perfect match"—his or her own stem cells. They also point out that scientists are working on stem-cell therapies for a variety of other conditions such as diabetes and heart disease. The implication is that in 30 or 40 years, by the time your newborn is at greater risk of developing these chronic ailments, he or she may be able to use these stem cells for treatments as yet undreamed of. So far they have convinced over 20,000 families to have their baby's cord blood collected, processed, tested, and stored, at an average cost of $1,700 plus an annual storage fee of about $125.

Proponents of public blood banking argue that the likelihood of a baby born to a healthy family ever needing his or her stem cells range from one in 10,000 to one in 200,000. Is such an unlikely event worth hoarding your baby's blood? If you and your family are healthy, you might want to consider helping others by donating your child's cord blood to a public cord blood bank. To support public donations, in 2005 the federal government authorized $79 million in federal funds to collect and store cord blood from ethnically diverse donors, overseen by the NMDP. As a result, the NMDP now lists a national inventory of over 70,000 cord blood units. An inventory of twice that number would give all Americans an 80–90% chance of finding at least a 5/6 antigen match, and about 30% would find a 6/6 match.

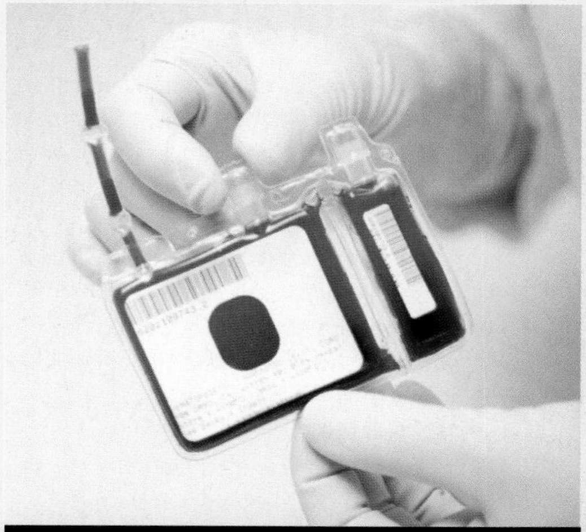

A cord blood collection unit.

Experts agree, however, that if cancer or a genetic disorder that could be treated with stem cells runs in your family, it may be prudent to bank your next child's cord blood privately.

Jaclyn Albanese's parents did not have the choice of banking her cord blood privately when she was born—the technology didn't exist back then. Fortunately, she was able to rely on the generosity of others who donated their baby's cord blood to a public cord blood bank.

## Questions to consider

**1** *Do you agree with the federal government's decision to allocate $79 million (about 40 cents per adult) for a public cord blood collection and storage network?*

**2** *When (or if) you have a child, what will you do with its cord blood? Explain your decision.*

# Health Watch

## Donating and Receiving Blood

A rapid loss of 30% or more of blood volume strains the body's ability to maintain blood pressure and oxygenate tissues. When this happens, survival may depend on receiving blood from others. Approximately 15 million units of blood are given every year, and almost 5 million people receive donated blood. Most people who donate blood get nothing more (and nothing less) than the satisfaction of knowing they have helped someone in need.

To donate blood, you must be at least 17 years old (16 in some states) and weigh at least 110 pounds. You'll be given a physical examination and asked for your health history, including a confidential questionnaire about your sexual history and recent international travel. This is not done to embarrass you, but to ensure that it is safe for you to give blood and that your blood will be safe for others.

The blood withdrawal procedure itself is relatively painless and takes about 10–20 minutes; a needle is inserted into an arm vein. All needles used are brand-new and sterile—you cannot catch AIDS or any other bloodborne disease by donating blood. Afterward you'll be advised to drink and eat something, and avoid rigorous physical exercise for the rest of the day. This is not the best day to go mountain climbing, but just about anything less strenuous is OK.

Most donors are allowed to give only one unit of blood (1 pint, about 10% of your blood volume). This is not enough to affect you adversely. Usually the donated blood volume is replaced within several hours by what you drink and eat. The liver replaces the lost plasma proteins within two days, and the body replaces the lost RBCs in a month or so.

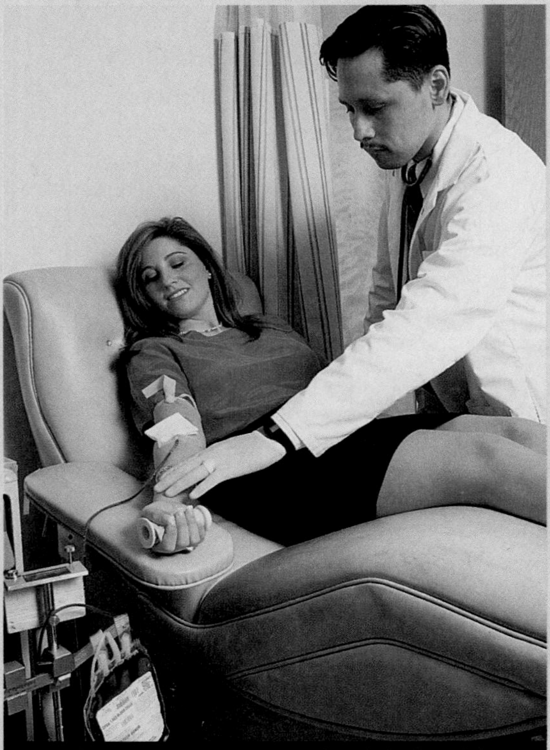

Donating blood. The procedure is relatively painless, takes only a short time, and can save lives.

What happens to the blood you give? Sometimes it is stored as whole blood, but more often it is separated into three components: packed cells, platelets, and plasma. Each may be given to different recipients, meaning that your single "gift of life" can benefit several people.

Receiving blood is also relatively safe, although not as risk-free as donating it. On rare occasions (and getting rarer every day) recipients may contract bloodborne diseases. You may have heard of someone who died as the result of a transfusion, such as the late tennis player Arthur Ashe, who contracted the AIDS virus from donated blood before the screening test for HIV was developed. Today all blood donations undergo extensive testing, including screening for HIV. According to the American Red Cross, the risk of contracting HIV from a blood transfusion is now about one in 676,000. Balance that against the risk of not receiving a blood transfusion that can save your life, and the risk seems small.

To learn more about donating blood, contact the American Red Cross.

platelets. Huge numbers of leukemia cells enter and circulate in the blood, interfering with normal organ function.

There are two major categories of leukemia: acute, which develops rapidly, and chronic. Both are thought to originate in the mutation of a white blood cell (a change in genetic structure) that results in uncontrolled cell division, producing billions of copies of the abnormal cell. Possible causes for the original mutation include viral infection or exposure to radiation or harmful chemicals. Genetic factors may also play a role.

Leukemia can produce a wide range of symptoms. Tissues may bruise easily because of insufficient production of platelets. Anemia may develop if the blood does not contain enough red blood cells. Bones may feel tender because the marrow is packed with immature white blood cells. Some people experience headaches or enlarged lymph nodes.

Treatment can cure leukemia in some cases and prolong life in others. Treatment generally involves radiation therapy and chemotherapy to destroy the rapidly proliferating cancer cells. This kills the normal stem cells as well, so transplants of bone marrow tissue are required to provide new stem cells. Cord blood transplants may be another option (see "Current Issue: Should You Bank Your Baby's Cord Blood?") As with blood transfusions, all tissue must undergo testing to make sure the donor's antigens are compatible with those of the patient.

### Multiple myeloma: Uncontrolled production of plasma cells

Like leukemia, *multiple myeloma* is a type of cancer. In this case, abnormal plasma cells in the bone marrow undergo uncontrolled division. Plasma cells are a type of lymphocyte responsible for making a specific antibody. The proliferating plasma cells manufacture too much of an abnormal, frequently incomplete antibody, impairing production of other antibodies and leaving the body vulnerable to infections. Bones become tender as healthy bone marrow is crowded out by malignant plasma cells. Levels of calcium in the blood soar as bone tissue is destroyed. Treatment includes anticancer drugs and radiation therapy.

**RECAP**

Iron deficiency or hemorrhage, among other factors, can reduce the oxygen-carrying capacity of blood and result in anemia. Leukemia and multiple myeloma are blood cell cancers. They arise as abnormal cells in the bone marrow multiply in huge numbers. ■

### Mononucleosis: Contagious viral infection of lymphocytes

*Mononucleosis* is a contagious infection of lymphocytes in blood and lymph tissues caused by the Epstein-Barr virus, a relative of the virus that causes herpes. Most common during adolescence, "mono" is nicknamed the "kissing disease" because it's frequently spread through physical contact.

Symptoms of mononucleosis can mimic those of flu: fever, headache, sore throat, fatigue, and swollen tonsils and lymph nodes. A blood test reveals increased numbers of monocytes and lymphocytes. The disease is called mononucleosis because many of the lymphocytes enlarge and begin to resemble monocytes. There is no known cure for mononucleosis, but almost all patients recover on their own within four to six weeks. Extra rest and good nutrition help the body overcome the virus.

### Blood poisoning: Infection of blood plasma

Normally blood is well defended by the immune system. Occasionally microorganisms invade the blood, overwhelm these defenses, and multiply rapidly in blood plasma. The organisms may be poisonous themselves, or they may secrete poisonous chemicals as by-products of their metabolism. The result is blood poisoning, also called *septicemia* or toxemia.

Blood poisoning may develop from infected wounds (especially deep puncture wounds), severe burns, urinary system infections, or major dental procedures. To help prevent it, wash wounds and burns thoroughly with soap and water. Consult your doctor immediately if you experience flushed skin, chills and fever, rapid heartbeat, or shallow breathing. Antibiotic drugs are usually effective against blood poisoning.

### Thrombocytopenia: Reduction in platelet number

*Thrombocytopenia* is a reduction in the number of platelets in the blood. Thrombocytopenia can occur for a number of reasons, such as viral infection, anemia, leukemia, other blood disorders, exposure to X-rays or radiation, and even as a reaction to certain drugs. Sometimes platelet levels decline for no apparent reason, in which case they often rise again after several weeks.

Symptoms include easy bruising or bleeding, nosebleeds, bleeding in the mouth, blood in urine, and heavy menstrual periods. Treatment of the underlying cause generally improves the condition. If it persists, surgical removal of the spleen often helps.

**RECAP**

Mononucleosis and blood poisoning are types of blood infection. Thrombocytopenia, a disease of too few platelets, is characterized by easy bleeding or bruising. ■

## Chapter Summary

### The components and functions of blood *p. 141*

- Blood consists of formed elements and plasma. Blood has transport, regulatory, and protective functions.
- Plasma contains numerous plasma proteins involved in transport, regulation of water balance, and protection. It also contains ions, hormones, nutrients, wastes, and gases.
- Erythrocytes (RBCs) are highly specialized for the transport of oxygen, but they also transport some carbon dioxide.
- Hemoglobin is the primary protein in red blood cells and gives blood its oxygen-carrying capacity.
- The formed elements of blood all originate from stem cells in red bone marrow.
- Leukocytes (WBCs) defend the body against disease and the effects of injury.
- RBCs and WBCs have short life spans and must continually be replaced. RBC production is stimulated when the body detects low oxygen levels in the blood.
- Platelets are cell products that participate in blood hemostasis.

### Hemostasis: Stopping blood loss *p. 148*

- Hemostasis is a three-phase process that prevents blood loss through damaged vessels. The phases are (1) vascular spasm, (2) the formation of a platelet plug, and (3) blood clotting.

- During the formation of a blood clot, substances released by damaged blood vessels cause soluble proteins called fibrinogen to become insoluble protein threads called fibrin. The threads form an interlocking mesh of fibers, trapping blood cells and sealing ruptured vessels.

### Human blood types *p. 150*

- Successful transfusion of blood from one person into another depends on compatibility of their blood types, which is determined by antibodies in plasma and surface antigens on red blood cells.
- Blood types are classified primarily on the basis of the ABO system and the presence or absence of the Rh factor.
- Rh factor in particular can affect certain pregnancies adversely.

### Blood disorders *p. 153*

- Anemia is a reduction in blood oxygen-carrying capacity for any number of reasons, including insufficient red blood cell production and excessive blood loss.
- Leukemia is a cancer characterized by uncontrolled production of abnormal leukocytes (white blood cells).
- Mononucleosis is a contagious viral disease of lymphocytes and lymphatic tissue.
- Blood poisoning is a general term for infection of blood plasma by various microorganisms.

## Terms You Should Know

anemia, *153*
blood type, *150*
erythrocyte (RBC), *143*
erythropoietin, *146*
fibrin, *149*
hematocrit, *144*
hemoglobin, *143*
hemostasis, *148*
leukocyte (WBC), *146*
phagocytosis, *146*
plasma, *142*
plasma proteins, *142*
platelet, *148*
Rh factor, *152*
stem cell, *145*

## Concept Review

1. Describe the functions of blood.
2. Describe the role of hemoglobin in the transport of oxygen and carbon dioxide.
3. Explain how the production of red blood cells is regulated to maintain homeostasis of the oxygen-carrying capacity of blood.
4. Define hematocrit, and explain why it is important.
5. Describe how damaged or dead RBCs and the hemoglobin they contain are removed from the blood.
6. Describe the difference between the actions of neutrophils and eosinophils.
7. Describe the mechanism of hemostasis.
8. List the four ABO blood types. For each one, list its red blood cell surface antigen(s) and plasma antibody (antibodies).
9. Describe Rh factor and its implications for pregnancy.
10. Compare and contrast the various causes of anemia.

## Test Yourself

### Matching Exercise

_____ 1. Oxygen-binding protein in RBCs
_____ 2. These help stop bleeding in ruptured blood vessels.
_____ 3. Process whereby white blood cells surround and engulf other cells
_____ 4. Another name for white blood cells
_____ 5. Hormone that regulates the rate of production of red blood cells
_____ 6. Most abundant white blood cells

a. phagocytosis
b. platelets
c. hemoglobin
d. leukocytes
e. neutrophils
f. erythropoietin

### Fill in the Blank

7. Fibrinogen is converted by __________________ into long insoluble threads called fibrin.
8. __________________ is an inherited condition caused by a deficiency of one or more clotting factors.
9. Antibodies attach to cell-surface proteins called __________________.
10. All blood cells originate from __________________ cells.
11. Contraction of blood vessels in a region of damage is called a vascular __________________.
12. Type __________________ blood has neither A nor B surface antigens on its RBCs but both A and B antibodies in its plasma.

### True or False?

13. Type A blood has type A surface antigens on its RBCs and antibodies against type B surface antigens.
14. Rh factor is found only in rhesus monkeys.
15. During clotting, blood changes from a liquid to a gel.

## References and Additional Reading

Becker, R. C. Antiplatelet Therapy. *Scientific American Science & Medicine* 3(4):12, July/August 1996. (An article about how platelet aggregation is controlled.)

Radetsky, P. The Mother of All Blood Cells. *Discover,* March 1995, p. 86. (An article about the apparent isolation of human stem cells and the controversy over who owns the rights to them.)

Thomas, E. D. Hematopoietic Stem Cell Transplantation. *Scientific American Science & Medicine* 2(5):38, September/October 1995. (Discusses the use of stem cells for bone marrow transplants.)

### Internet References

Find links to the following Web sites at the Human Biology Place.

**American Red Cross**
**www.redcross.org**
Information about blood and how to donate it, including profiles of real-life transfusion recipients.

## Apply **What You Know**

1. A 35-year-old white male is sent by his physician for a blood test. The lab results indicate his white blood cell count (number of WBCs per milliliter of blood) is 18,000. The typical WBC count for a man his age is 6,000–9,000, meaning his white blood cell count is considerably higher than normal. What may this mean?
2. One treatment for certain types of leukemia is to try to kill all of the stem cells in bone marrow through radiation and chemotherapy and then to give a bone marrow transplant from another person (a donor). Can just anyone be the donor? Who is most likely to be a good donor? Explain.
3. In the not too distant past, people with type O-negative blood were considered to be universal blood donors, and their blood was sought out during times of need. Explain what was meant by the term universal donor, why O-negative persons were considered to be universal donors, and why "universal blood donor" is now considered an outdated term.
4. The text states that when red blood cells reach actively metabolizing tissues, they release their cargo of oxygen because both the oxygen concentration and the pH are lower in metabolically active tissues than in the general circulation. The oxygen concentration is lower because actively metabolizing tissues are using oxygen at a rapid rate. But what causes the pH to fall? And how might a fall in pH cause the hemoglobin to release oxygen?

   Can you think of any other variables that might also lead to the release of oxygen by hemoglobin?
5. The term has just ended. Over the past three weeks you wrote three term papers, studied for finals, and went to work at your part-time job. You passed all your courses and never missed a day of work. Of course, you spent the last three weeks living on soda, frozen pizza, and Ramen noodles (who has time for real food with all this work?).

   Now that the term is over you notice that you are very tired, your skin is pale, you are experiencing headaches and dizziness, and even your breathing is difficult. You go to your doctor who diagnoses you with anemia. What type of anemia do you most likely have, how is it different from other forms of anemia, and what treatment will your doctor most likely suggest?
6. Coumadin is an anticoagulant drug that is sometimes given to patients who have just suffered a deep vein thrombosis, a pulmonary embolism, or a heart attack, or to patients with artificial heart valves. It helps reduce the chance of future clots and the further risk of embolism. The active ingredient in Coumadin is warfarin, a rat poison. How do you think the same compound can be used for these two very different purposes?

*Answers can be found on the Human Biology Place.*

**Bloodbook.com**
**www.bloodbook.com**
A site devoted to information about blood, including diseases and disorders of blood and blood donation, storage, and safety.

**Blood Typing Game, Nobelprize.org**
**http://nobelprize.org/educational_games/medicine/landsteiner/index.html**
This educational game lets you blood type patients and give them transfusions. Click on *Introduction: blood groups, blood types and blood transfusions* for a quick refresher course on the basic principles.

**The National Heart, Blood, and Lung Institute**
**www.nhlbi.nih.gov**
This division of the National Institutes of Health focuses on blood resources and on diseases of the heart, blood, blood vessels, and lungs.

**Teens Living With Cancer**
**www.teenslivingwithcancer.org**
Informational and inspirational site for adolescents with leukemia and other forms of cancer; includes tutorials, discussion boards, and tips for patients and families on coping with the disease.

**U.S. Anti-Doping Agency**
**www.usantidoping.org**
A nonprofit organization dedicated to the elimination of the practice of doping in sports.

# 8 Heart and Blood Vessels

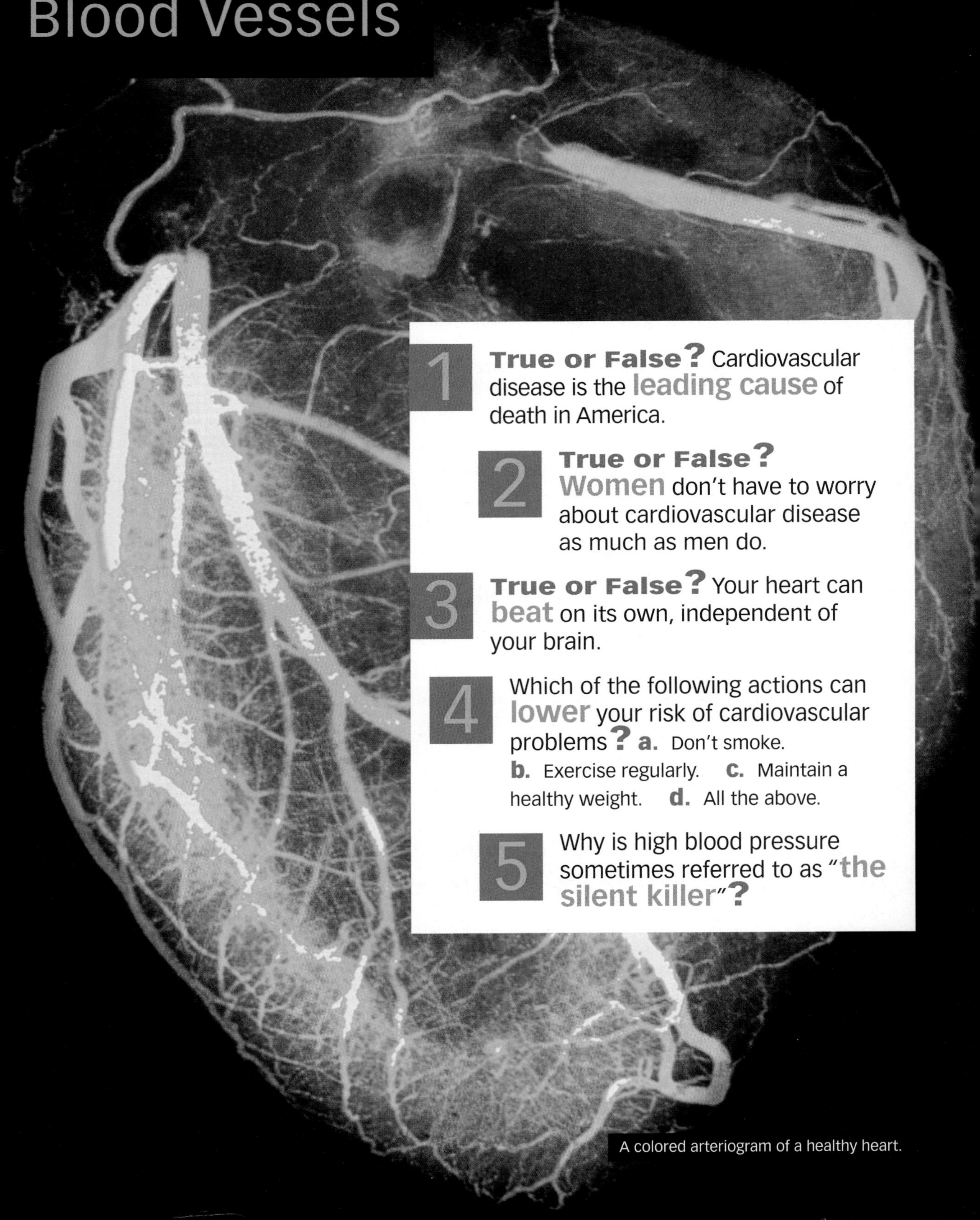

1 **True or False?** Cardiovascular disease is the **leading cause** of death in America.

2 **True or False?** **Women** don't have to worry about cardiovascular disease as much as men do.

3 **True or False?** Your heart can **beat** on its own, independent of your brain.

4 Which of the following actions can **lower** your risk of cardiovascular problems? **a.** Don't smoke. **b.** Exercise regularly. **c.** Maintain a healthy weight. **d.** All the above.

5 Why is high blood pressure sometimes referred to as "**the silent killer**"?

A colored arteriogram of a healthy heart.

**The heart is a pump, but it's a very special pump indeed.** The heart is constructed entirely of living cells and cellular materials, yet it is capable of greater reliability than some of the best pumps ever built by humans. It can easily withstand 80–100 years of continuous service without ever stopping for repairs. Its output is also fully adjustable on demand, over a range of about 5–25 liters of blood per minute.

The heart and blood vessels are known collectively as the **cardiovascular system** (from the Greek *kardia,* heart, and the Latin *vasculum,* small vessel). The heart provides the power to move the blood, and the vascular system represents the network of branching conduit vessels through which the blood flows. The cardiovascular system is essential to life because it supplies every region of the body with just the right amount of blood. It is essential to maintaining homeostasis. We consider the blood vessels first.

## 8.1 Blood vessels transport blood

A branching network of blood vessels transports blood to all parts of the body. The network is so extensive that if our blood vessels were laid end to end, they would stretch 60,000 miles!

We classify the body's blood vessels into three major types: *arteries, capillaries,* and *veins.* Thick-walled arteries transport blood to body tissues under high pressure. Microscopic capillaries participate in exchanging solutes and water with the cells of the body. Thin-walled veins store blood and return it to the heart. Figure 8.1 illustrates the structures of each type of blood vessel, described in more detail below.

### Arteries transport blood away from the heart

As blood leaves the heart it is pumped into large, muscular, thick-walled **arteries.** Arteries transport blood away from the heart. The larger arteries have a thick layer of muscle because they must be able to withstand the high pressures generated by the heart. Arteries branch again and again, so the farther blood moves from the heart, the smaller in diameter the arteries become.

Large and medium-sized arteries are like thick garden hoses, stiff yet somewhat elastic (distensible). Arteries stretch a little in response to high pressure but are still strong enough to withstand high pressures year after year. The ability to stretch under pressure is important because a second function of arteries is to store the blood that is pumped into them with each beat of the heart and then provide it to the capillaries (at high pressure) even between heartbeats. The elastic recoil of arteries is the force that maintains the blood pressure between beats. Think of the arteries as analogous to a city's water system of branching, high-pressure pipes that provide nearly constant water pressure to every home.

The structure of the walls of large and medium-sized arteries is ideally suited to their functions. The vessel wall is a sandwich of three distinct layers surrounding the *lumen,* or hollow interior of the vessel:

1. The thin inner layer, the *endothelium,* is a layer of flattened, *squamous* epithelial cells. It is a continuation of the lining of the heart. The flattened cells fit closely together, creating a slick surface that keeps friction to a minimum and promotes smooth blood flow.
2. Just outside the endothelium is a layer composed primarily of smooth muscle with interwoven elastic connective tissue. In most arteries this is the thickest layer of the three. Tonic contraction of the smooth muscle of large and medium-sized arteries stiffens the arteries and helps them resist the high pressures within, but it does not constrict them enough to alter blood flow. The elastic tissue makes large and medium-sized arteries slightly distensible so they can stretch passively to accommodate the blood that enters with each heartbeat.
3. The outermost layer of large and medium-sized arteries consists of a tough supportive layer of connective tissue, primarily collagen. This sturdy casing anchors vessels to surrounding tissues and helps protect them from injury.

The fact that arteries are constantly under high pressure places them at risk of injury. If the endothelium becomes damaged, blood may seep through the injured area and work its way between the two outer layers, splitting them apart. The result is an *aneurysm,* or ballooning of the artery wall. Some aneurysms cause the smooth muscle and

### Answers to Intro Questions

1 **True.** Cardiovascular disease is the leading cause of death in the U.S. Cancer is number two.

2 **False.** Although it's true that men's risk of cardiovascular disease is much greater than women's before age 45, women's risk rises after menopause.

3 **True.** Specialized cells in your heart initiate an electrical impulse that ripples through your heart muscle and stimulates it to contract. You experience each coordinated series of contractions as a heartbeat.

4 **d.** In this chapter, we'll look at the factors that affect cardiovascular health throughout your life.

5 Left untreated, high blood pressure can damage the heart and blood vessels. Because there are usually no symptoms, millions of Americans have high blood pressure and don't know it.

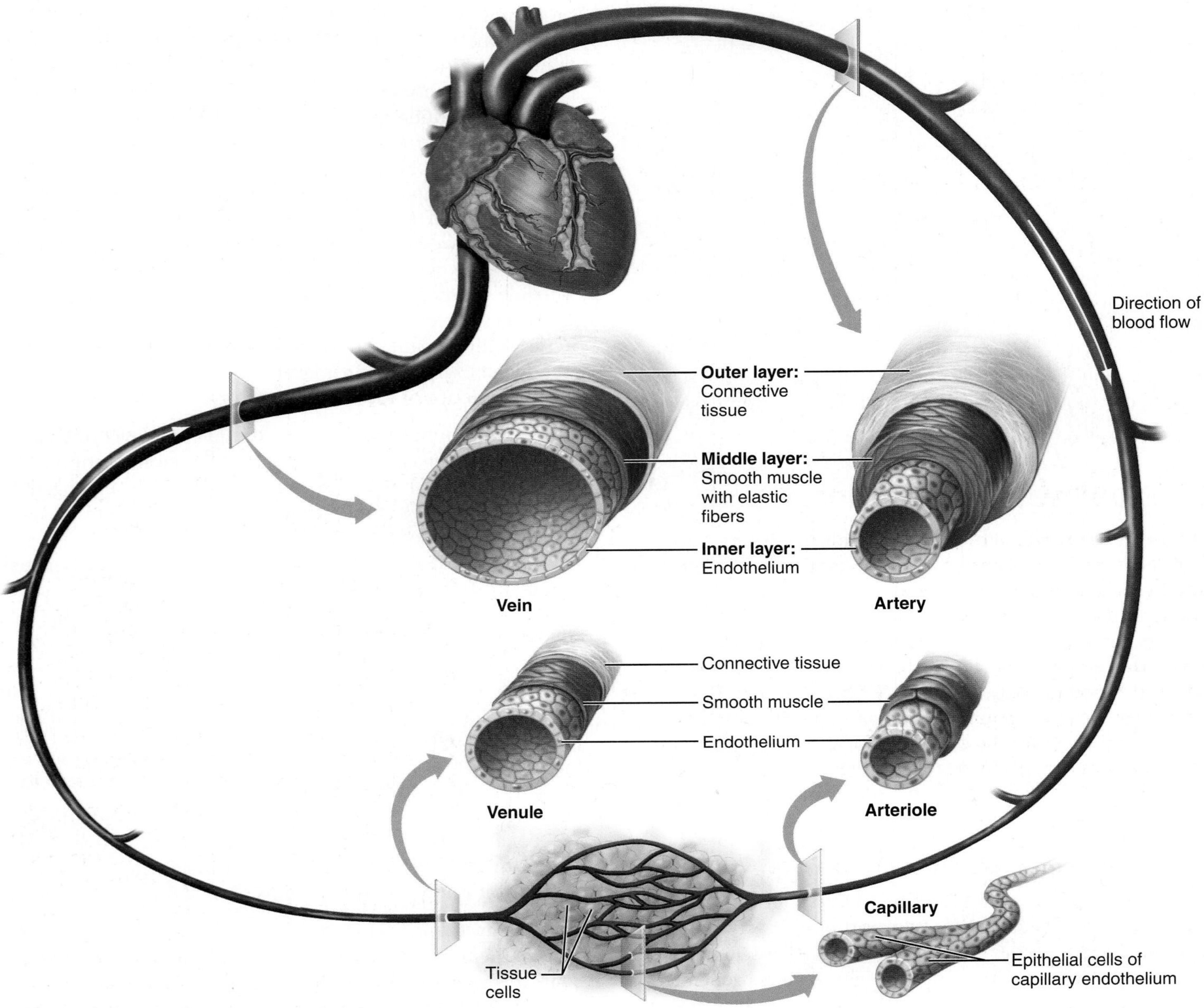


**Figure 8.1 The structures of blood vessels in the human body.**

endothelial layers to bulge inward as they develop, narrowing the lumen enough to reduce blood flow to an organ or region of the body. Others force the outer connective tissue layer to bulge outward. Sometimes aneurysms cause severe chest pain, but in other cases they are completely symptomless until they rupture or "blow out," causing massive internal bleeding and often death. If you've ever seen a water line burst, you know how quickly it can be devastating. Aneurysms of the aorta (see section 8.2) kill an estimated 25,000 Americans every year. Actor John Ritter's sudden death in 2003 was caused by a ruptured aneurysm.

Aneurysms often take years to develop. During this time many can be detected and repaired surgically. Some physicians recommend that anyone with a family history of aneurysm should be examined, even if there are no symptoms. Doctors can sometimes detect inward-bulging aneurysms with a stethoscope (an instrument for listening to sounds inside the body) because flowing blood produces characteristic sounds as it passes through the narrowed area. A computerized tomography (CT) scan may also locate aneurysms before they rupture.

## Arterioles and precapillary sphincters regulate blood flow

Eventually blood reaches the smallest arteries, called **arterioles** (literally, "little arteries"). The largest artery in the body, the *aorta,* is about 2.5 centimeters (roughly 1 inch) wide. In contrast, arterioles have a diameter of 0.3 millimeter or less, about the width of a piece of thread.

By the time blood flows through the arterioles, blood pressure has fallen considerably. Consequently, arterioles can be simpler in structure. Generally they lack the outermost layer of connective tissue, and their smooth muscle layer is not as thick. In addition to blood transport and storage, arterioles have a third function not shared by the larger arteries: they help regulate the amount of blood that flows to each capillary. They do this by contracting or relaxing the smooth muscle layer, altering the diameter of the arteriole lumen.

Right where an arteriole joins a capillary is a band of smooth muscle called the **precapillary sphincter** (Figure 8.2). The precapillary sphincters serve as gates that control blood flow into individual capillaries.

Contraction of vascular smooth muscle is called *vasoconstriction*. Vasoconstriction of arterioles and precapillary sphincters reduces their diameter and so reduces blood flow to the capillaries. Conversely, relaxation of vascular smooth muscle is called *vasodilation*. Vasodilation of arterioles and precapillary sphincters increases their diameter and so increases blood flow to the capillaries.

A wide variety of external and internal factors can produce vasoconstriction or vasodilation, including nerves, hormones, and conditions in the local environment of the arterioles and precapillary sphincters. If you go outside on a cold day, you may notice that your fingers start to look pale. This is because vasoconstriction produced by nerves is narrowing your vessels to reduce heat loss from your body. On the other hand, hot weather will make your skin appear flushed as vasodilation occurs to speed up heat loss and cool you off.

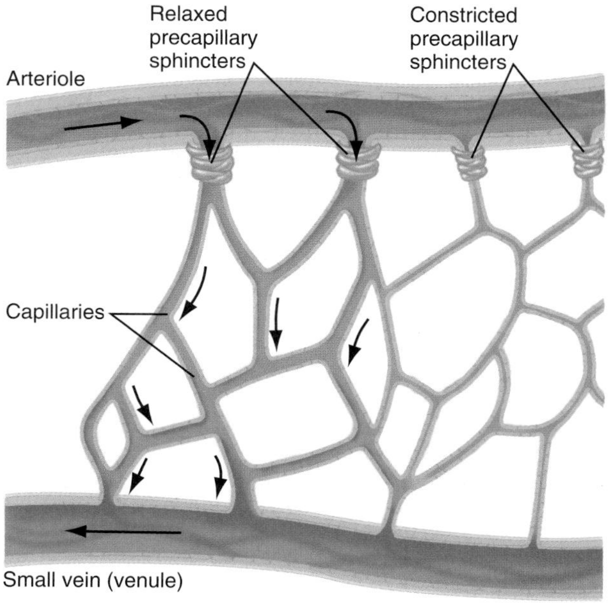


**Figure 8.2 Precapillary sphincters control the flow of blood into individual capillaries.** In this diagram the two precapillary sphincters on the right are vasoconstricted, reducing flow in that region. Arrows indicate direction of blood flow.

Emotions can also have an impact: vasodilation is partly responsible for the surge in blood flow that causes the penis or clitoris to become erect when we are sexually aroused. Later in this chapter we will talk more about how the cardiovascular system is regulated to maintain homeostasis.

**RECAP**

A branching system of thick-walled arteries distributes blood to every area of the body. Arterioles regulate blood flow to local regions, and precapillary sphincters at the ends of arterioles regulate flow into individual capillaries. ■

## Capillaries: Where blood exchanges substances with tissues

Arterioles connect to the smallest blood vessels, called **capillaries.** Capillaries are thin-walled vessels that average only about one-hundredth of a millimeter in diameter—not much wider than the red blood cells that travel through them. In fact, they are so narrow that RBCs often have to pass through them in single file or even bend to squeeze through.

Extensive networks of capillaries, called *capillary beds,* can be found in all areas of the body, which is why you are likely to bleed no matter where you cut yourself. The branching design of capillaries and their thin, porous walls allow blood to exchange oxygen, carbon dioxide, nutrients, and waste products with tissue cells. Capillary walls consist of a single layer of squamous epithelial cells. Microscopic pores pierce this layer, and the cells are separated by narrow slits. These openings are large enough to allow the exchange of fluid and other materials between blood and the interstitial fluid, yet small enough to retain red blood cells and most plasma proteins in the capillary (Figure 8.3). Some white blood cells can also squeeze between the cells in capillary walls and enter the tissue spaces.

In effect, capillaries function as biological strainers that permit selective exchange of substances with the interstitial fluid (the fluid that surrounds every living cell). In fact, capillaries are the *only* blood vessels that can exchange materials with the interstitial fluid.

Figure 8.4 illustrates the general pattern of how water and substances move across a capillary. At the beginning of a capillary, fluid is filtered out of the vessel into the interstitial fluid, accompanied by oxygen, nutrients, and raw materials needed by the cell. The filtered fluid is essentially like plasma except that it contains very little protein because most protein molecules are too large to be filtered. Filtration of fluid is driven by the blood pressure generated by the heart. Waste materials such as carbon dioxide and urea diffuse out of the cells and back into the blood.

Most of the filtered fluid is reabsorbed by diffusion back into the last half of the capillary before it joins a vein. The force for this reabsorption is the presence of protein in

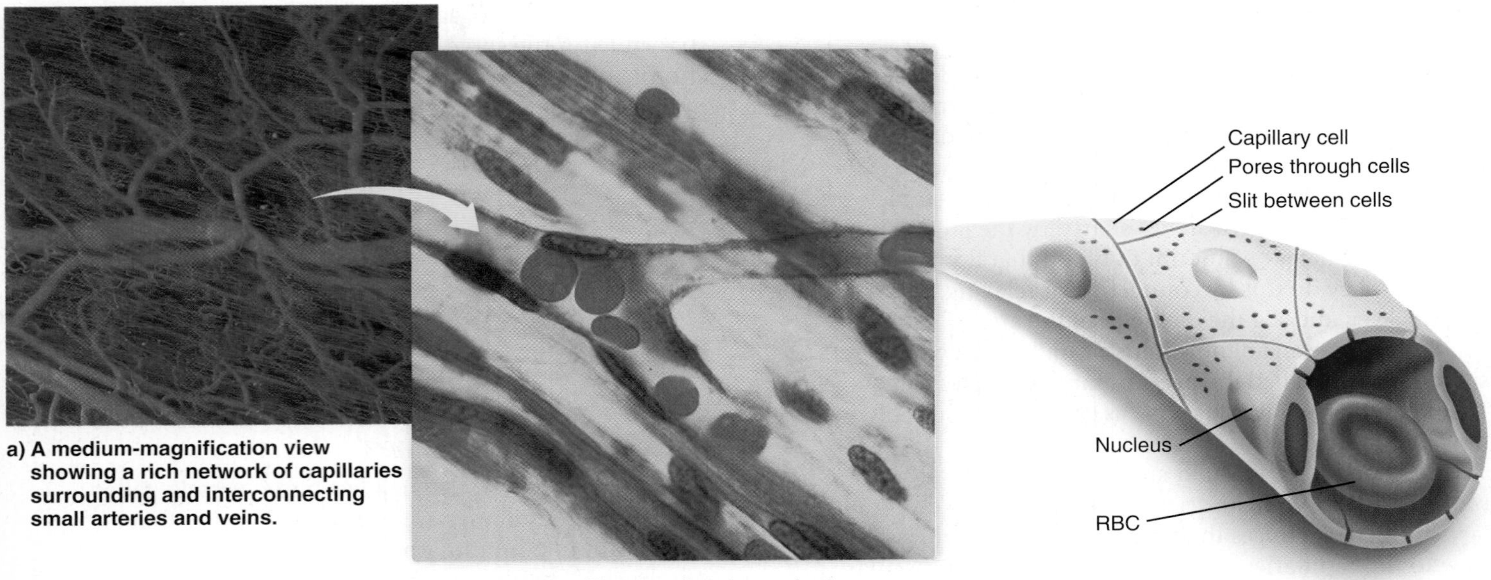


**a) A medium-magnification view showing a rich network of capillaries surrounding and interconnecting small arteries and veins.**

**b) A higher magnification showing a single branching capillary.** Notice the red blood cells travelling single file in the capillary.

**c) The structure of a capillary.**

**Figure 8.3 Capillaries.**

the blood but not in the interstitial fluid. In other words, water diffuses from an area of high water concentration (interstitial fluid) to an area of lower water concentration (blood plasma). However, the diffusional reabsorption of water does not quite match the pressure-induced filtration of water, so a small amount of filtered fluid remains in the interstitial space as excess interstitial fluid.

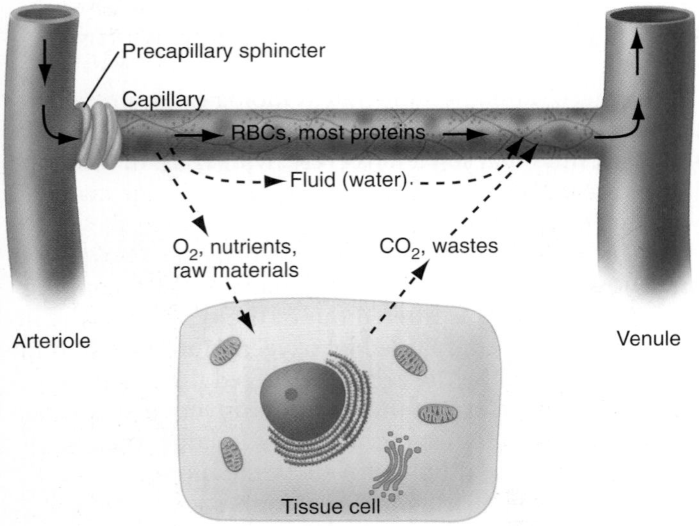


**Figure 8.4 The general pattern of movement between capillaries, the interstitial fluid, and cells.** For simplicity, only a single tissue cell is shown, but a single capillary may supply many nearby cells.

## Lymphatic system helps maintain blood volume

Although the imbalance between the amount of plasma fluid filtered by the capillaries and the amount reabsorbed is not large, over the course of a day it would amount to about two or three liters. This excess plasma fluid must be returned to the cardiovascular system somehow, or soon all the plasma would end up in the interstitial fluid.

The excess plasma fluid is picked up by a system of blind-ended vessels called *lymphatic capillaries,* which branch throughout our body tissues and are part of the *lymphatic system*. The lymphatic system also picks up a few objects in the interstitial fluid that are too large to diffuse into capillaries. These include lipid droplets absorbed during digestion and invading organisms. Lymphatic capillaries transport the excess interstitial fluid and other objects to larger lymphatic vessels, which eventually return the fluid (called *lymph*) to veins near the heart. Along the way the lymphatic system intercepts the invading microorganisms.

We say more about the lymphatic system in Chapter 9 when we discuss the immune system. For now, just be aware that the lymphatic system, though technically not part of the cardiovascular system, plays a vital role in maintaining the proper volumes of blood and interstitial fluid.

**RECAP**

Capillaries consisting of a single layer of cells are the only blood vessels that can exchange materials with the interstitial fluid. The lymphatic system removes excess fluid. ■

### Veins return blood to the heart

From the capillaries, blood flows back to the heart through *venules* (small veins) and **veins.** Like the walls of arteries, the walls of veins consist of three layers of tissue. However, the outer two layers of the walls of veins are much thinner than those of arteries. Veins also have a larger diameter lumen than arteries.

The anatomical differences between arteries and veins reflect their functional differences. As blood moves through the cardiovascular system, the blood pressure becomes lower and lower. The pressure in veins is only a small fraction of the pressure in arteries, so veins do not need nearly as much wall strength (provided by muscle and connective tissue) as arteries. The larger diameter and high distensibility of veins allows them to stretch (like thin balloons) to accommodate large volumes of blood at low pressures.

In addition to their transport function, then, veins serve as a blood volume reservoir for the entire cardiovascular system. Nearly two-thirds of all the blood in your body is in your veins. Thanks to their blood reservoir function, even if you become dehydrated or lose a little blood, your heart will still be able to pump enough blood to keep your blood pressure fairly constant. (See the Try It Yourself box.)

The distensibility of veins can lead to problems in returning blood to the heart against the force of gravity. When you stand upright, blood tends to collect in the veins of your legs and feet. People who spend a lot of time on their feet may develop *varicose veins,* permanently swollen veins that look twisted and bumpy from pooled blood. Varicose veins can appear anywhere, but they are most common in the legs and feet. In severe cases the skin surrounding veins becomes dry and hard because the tissues are not receiving enough blood. Often varicose veins can be treated by injecting an irritating solution that shrivels the vessels and makes them less visible. This should not affect blood flow because surrounding undamaged veins take over and return blood to the heart.

Fortunately, three mechanisms assist the veins in returning blood to the heart: (1) contractions of skeletal muscles, (2) one-way valves inside the veins, and (3) movements associated with breathing. Let's look at each in turn.

**Skeletal muscles squeeze veins** On their path back to the heart, veins pass between many skeletal muscles. As we move and these muscles contract and relax, they press against veins and collapse them, pushing blood toward the heart. You may have noticed that you tire more easily when you stand still than when you walk around. This is because walking improves the return of blood to your heart and prevents fluid accumulation in your legs. It also increases blood flow and the supply of energy to your leg muscles.

**One-way valves permit only one-way blood flow** Most veins contain valves consisting of small folds of the inner layer that protrude into the lumen. The structure of these valves allows blood to flow in one direction only: toward the heart. They open passively to permit blood to move toward the heart and then close whenever blood begins to flow backward. Together, skeletal muscles and valves form what is called the "skeletal muscle pump" (Figure 8.5). Once blood has been pushed toward the heart by skeletal muscles or drained in that direction by gravity, it cannot drain back again because of these one-way valves. The opening and closing of venous valves is strictly dependent on differences in blood pressure on either side.

**Pressures associated with breathing push blood toward heart** The third mechanism that assists blood flow involves pressure changes in the thoracic (chest) and abdominal cavities during breathing. When we inhale, abdominal pressure increases and squeezes abdominal veins. At the same time, pressure within the thoracic cavity decreases, dilating thoracic veins. The result is to push blood from the abdomen into the chest and toward the heart. This effect is sometimes called the "respiratory pump."

**RECAP**

The thin-walled veins return blood to the heart and serve as a volume reservoir for blood. Return of blood to the heart is assisted by (1) contractions of skeletal muscles, (2) one-way valves inside veins, and (3) pressure changes associated with breathing. ■

**try it yourself**

#### Demonstrating That Veins Store Blood

To demonstrate that veins store blood and how the forces of gravity can distend veins, try the following demonstration. (This works best if you have prominent veins on the back of your hand; if you don't, find a friend who does.)

Let your arm hang down by your side, below your waist, for about 30 seconds. Notice that the veins on the back of your hand swell, indicating stored blood. Now raise your hand above your head and hold it there. You can watch the veins almost disappear over the first 10 seconds as the blood in them drains back to the heart.

## 8.2 The heart pumps blood through the vessels

The heart, a muscular, cone-shaped organ slightly larger than your fist, is located in the thoracic cavity between the lungs and behind the sternum (breastbone). As described in Chapter 6, the heart consists mostly of a special type of muscle called cardiac muscle.

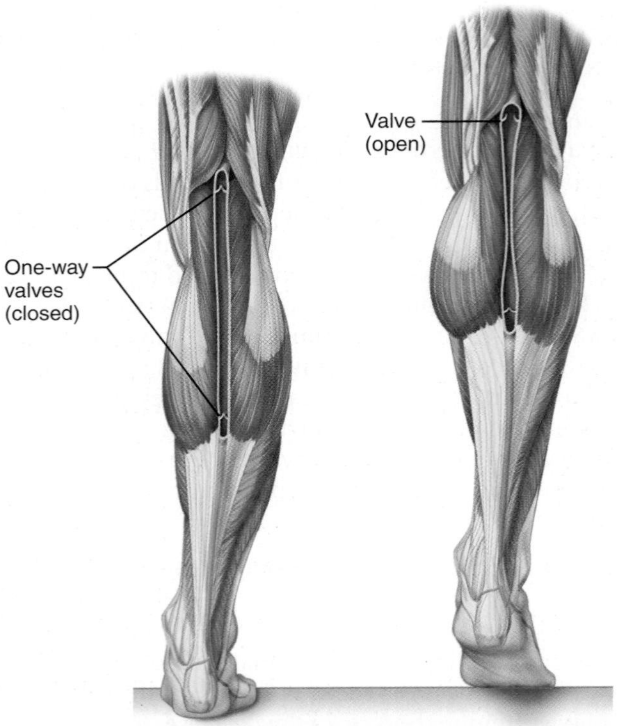


**Figure 8.5 The so-called skeletal muscle pump.** With the calf muscle relaxed, blood accumulates in the vein because of the force of gravity. Backflow is prevented by one-way valves. When the calf muscle contracts, skeletal muscles press on the vein, increasing blood pressure in the vein momentarily and forcing blood toward the heart through the upper one-way valve. The lower one-way valve remains closed, preventing backflow.

Unlike skeletal muscle, cardiac muscle does not connect to bone. Instead, it pumps ceaselessly in a squeezing motion to propel blood through the blood vessels.

Your heart pumps about 75 times every minute—and this does not include the times it speeds up to supply extra blood during exertion or stress. It never rests for more than 2/3 of a second. Over 70 years, this adds up to about 2.8 billion heartbeats, truly an impressive performance for any muscle. Under normal circumstances the heart's rate of pumping is controlled by the brain, but it can also beat on its own without any instructions from the brain at all.

## The heart is mostly muscle

If you were to look at a heart in its natural position within the chest cavity, you would see that it is enclosed in a tough fibrous sac called the *pericardium*. The pericardium protects the heart, anchors it to surrounding structures, and prevents it from overfilling with blood. Separating the pericardium from the heart is a space called the *pericardial cavity*. The pericardial cavity contains a film of lubricating fluid that allows the heart and the pericardium to glide smoothly against each other when the heart contracts.

In cross section we see that the walls of the heart consist of three layers: the epicardium, myocardium, and endocardium (Figure 8.6). The outermost layer, the *epicardium*, is a thin layer of epithelial and connective tissue. The middle layer is the **myocardium.** This is a thick layer consisting mainly of cardiac muscle that forms the bulk of the heart. The myocardium is the layer that contracts every time the heart beats. As noted in Chapter 6, the structure of cardiac muscle cells allows electrical signals to flow directly from cell to cell. An electrical signal in one cardiac muscle cell can spread to adjacent cells, enabling large numbers of cells to contract as a coordinated unit. Every time the myocardium contracts, it squeezes the chambers inside the heart, pushing blood outward into the arteries.

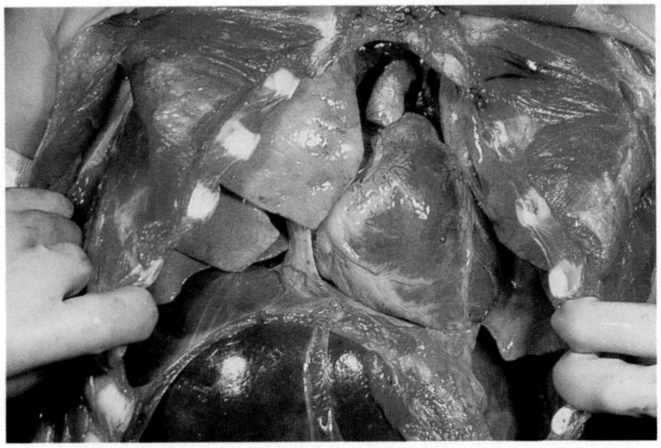

**a) Photograph of a heart in its natural position in the chest.** The pericardium has been cut away.

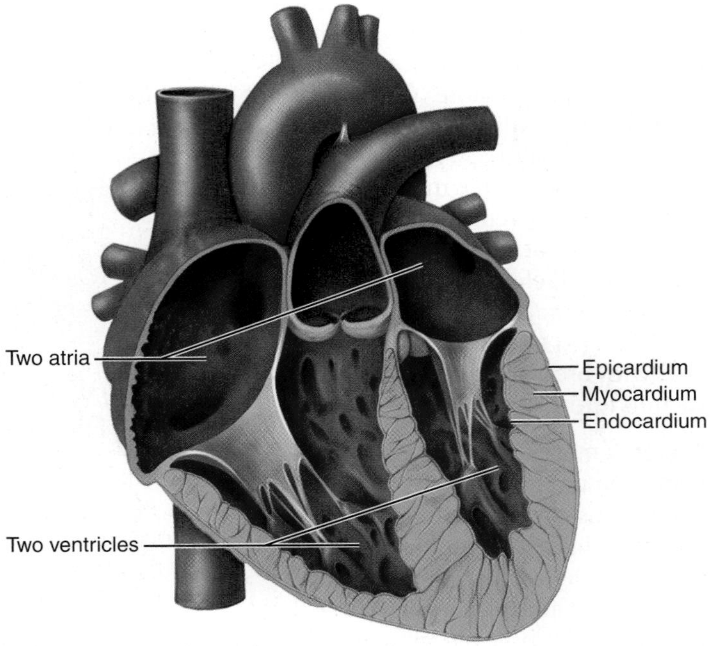


**b)** Schematic cross-section of a heart showing that it is composed of three layers: a thin outer epicardium, a thick layer of muscle called the myocardium, and an inner lining called the endocardium.

**Figure 8.6 The heart.**

The innermost layer of the heart, the *endocardium*, is a thin endothelial layer resting on a layer of connective tissue. The endocardium is continuous with the endothelium that lines the blood vessels.

Occasionally one of the layers of the heart wall becomes inflamed. These conditions are named according to the location of the problem; *-itis* is a suffix that means "inflammation." Thus *pericarditis* refers to inflammation of the pericardium, *endocarditis* to an inflamed endocardium, and so on. A variety of factors can lead to inflammation in or around the heart wall, including infections, cancer, injuries, or complications from major surgery. Depending on the underlying cause, many cases respond well to antibiotic and anti-inflammatory drugs.

**RECAP**

The heart wall consists of three layers. The outer epicardium is a thin layer of epithelial and connective tissue; the middle myocardium consists largely of cardiac muscle and is the layer that contracts. The inner endocardium is a layer of endothelium continuous with the endothelium lining blood vessels. ■

## The heart has four chambers and four valves

Taking a closer look at the details of the structure of the heart, we see that it consists of four separate chambers (Figure 8.7). The two chambers on the top are the **atria** (singular: *atrium*), and the two more-muscular bottom chambers are the **ventricles.** A muscular partition called the **septum** separates the right and left sides of the heart.

Blood returning to the heart from the body's tissues enters the heart at the *right atrium* From the right atrium, the blood passes through a valve into the *right ventricle.* The right ventricle is more muscular than the right atrium because it pumps blood at considerable pressure through a second valve and into the artery leading to the lungs.

Blood returning from the lungs to the heart enters the *left atrium* and then passes through a third valve into the *left ventricle.* The very muscular left ventricle pumps blood through a fourth valve into the body's largest artery, the aorta. From the aorta, blood travels through the arteries and arterioles to the systemic capillaries, venules, and veins and then back to the right atrium again.

The left ventricle is the most muscular of the heart's four chambers because it must do more work than any other chamber. The left ventricle must generate pressures higher than aortic blood pressure in order to pump blood into the aorta (we'll see how high aortic pressure is in a minute). The right ventricle has a thinner wall and does less work because the blood pressure in the arteries leading to the lungs is only about one-sixth that of the aorta.

Four heart valves enforce the heart's one-way flow pattern and prevent blood from flowing backward. The valves open and shut passively in response to changes in the pressure of blood on each side of the valve. The right and left

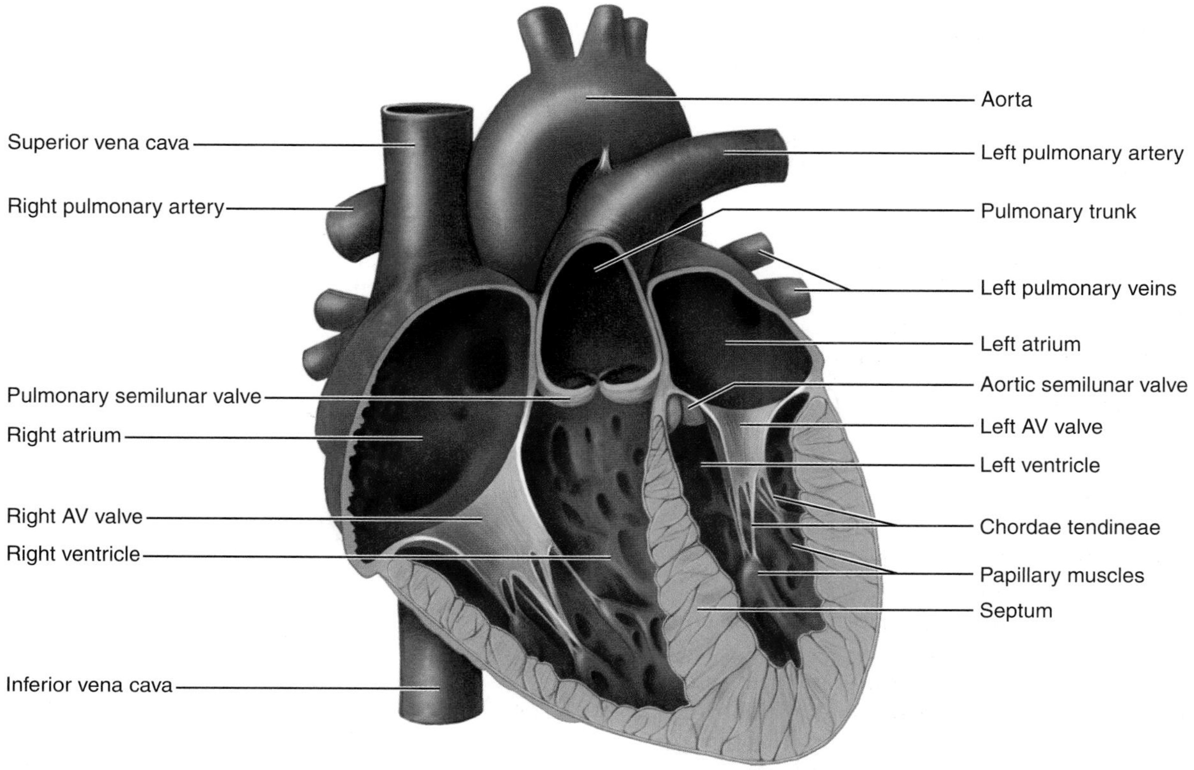


**Figure 8.7 A view of the heart showing major blood vessels, chambers, and valves.**

**atrioventricular (AV) valves** located between the atria and their corresponding ventricle prevent blood from flowing back into the atria when the ventricles contract. The AV valves consist of thin connective tissue flaps (cusps) that project into the ventricles. The right AV valve is called the *tricuspid valve* because it has three flexible flaps. The left AV valve has two flaps, so it is referred to as the *bicuspid* or *mitral valve.* These valves are supported by strands of connective tissue called *chordae tendineae* that connect to muscular extensions of the ventricle walls called *papillary muscles.* Together, the chordae tendineae and papillary muscles prevent the valves from everting (opening backward) into the atria when the ventricles contract.

Two **semilunar valves** (the pulmonary and the aortic) prevent backflow into the ventricles from the main arteries leaving the heart when the heart relaxes. Each semilunar valve consists of three pocketlike flaps. The valves' name reflects the half-moon shape of these flaps (*semi* means "one-half"; *luna* comes from the Latin word for "moon").

Next, let's follow the overall pattern of blood flow through the body.

**RECAP**

The heart is composed primarily of cardiac muscle. It contains four chambers that pump blood to the lungs and the rest of the body simultaneously. Four one-way valves permit blood flow in one direction only. ■

## The pulmonary circuit provides for gas exchange

Figure 8.8 shows the general structure of the entire cardiovascular system. Note that the heart is pumping blood through the lungs (the **pulmonary circuit**) and through the rest of the body to all the cells (the **systemic circuit**) simultaneously. Each circuit has its own set of blood vessels. Let's follow the pulmonary circuit first:

1. When blood returns to the heart from the veins, it enters the right atrium. The blood that returns to the heart is deoxygenated—it has given up oxygen to tissue cells and taken up carbon dioxide.
2. From the right atrium, blood passes through the right atrioventricular valve into the right ventricle.
3. The right ventricle pumps blood through the pulmonary semilunar valve into the pulmonary trunk (the main pulmonary artery) leading to the lungs. The pulmonary trunk divides into the right and left pulmonary arteries, which supply the right and left lungs, respectively.
4. At the pulmonary capillaries, blood gives up carbon dioxide and receives a fresh supply of oxygen from the air we inhale. It is now oxygenated.
5. The freshly oxygenated blood flows into the pulmonary veins leading back to the heart. It enters the left atrium and flows through the left atrioventricular valve into the left ventricle.

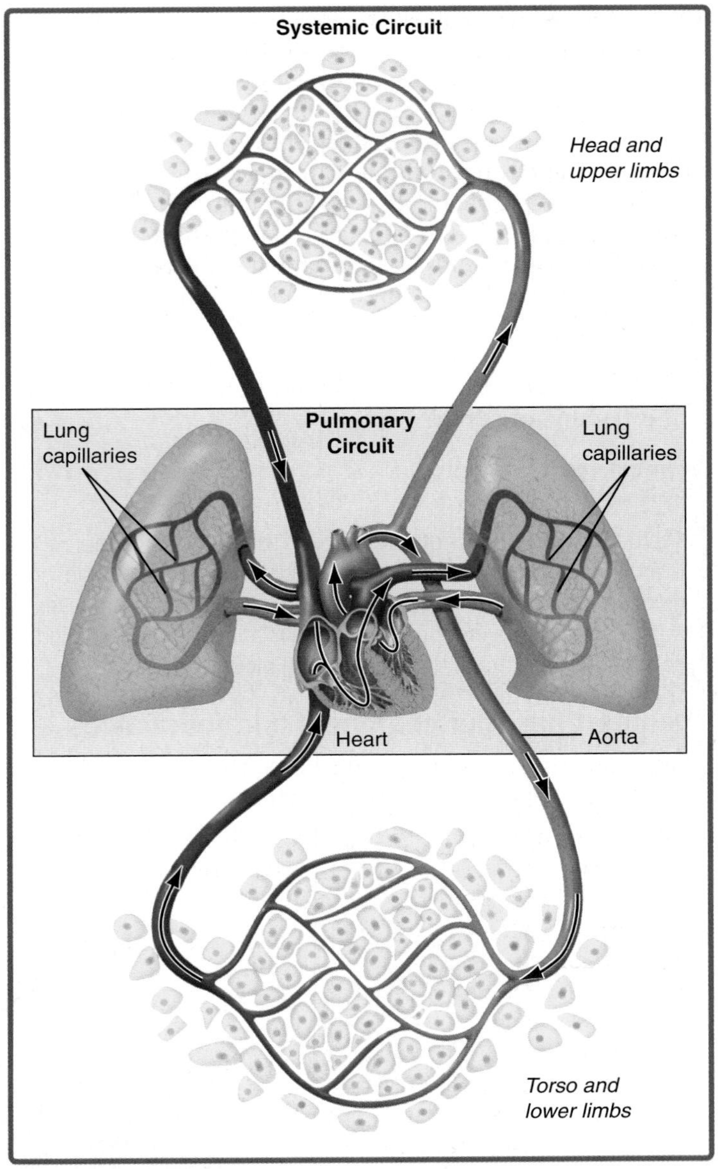


**Figure 8.8 A schematic representation of the human cardiovascular system showing the separate pulmonary and systemic circuits.** The systemic circuit includes the circulations of the head, torso, limbs, and internal organs, including the heart and some tissues in the lungs.

The deoxygenated blood in the right side of the heart never mixes with oxygenated blood in the left. Deoxygenated blood leaving the right side of the heart must pass through the pulmonary circuit (where it picks up oxygen) before it reaches the left side of the heart.

## The systemic circuit serves the rest of the body

When blood enters the left ventricle, it begins the *systemic circuit,* which takes it to the rest of the body.

1. The left ventricle pumps blood through the aortic semilunar valve into the **aorta,** the largest artery.
2. From the aorta, blood travels through the branching arteries and arterioles to the capillaries, where it delivers oxygen and nutrients to all of the body's tissues and organs and removes waste products.
3. From the capillaries, blood flows to the venules, veins, and then back again to the right atrium.

Figure 8.9 shows some of the major arteries and veins of the human body. Arteries and veins serving the same vascular region often (but not always) have the same name and generally are located very near to each other. For example, a common iliac artery supplies blood to each leg, and a common iliac vein returns blood from the leg to the heart. However, carotid arteries supply the head, but jugular veins return the blood from the head.

As you might expect of such a hard-working muscle, the heart requires a great deal of oxygen and nutrients to fuel its own operations. Although the heart represents only about 1/200 of your body's weight, it requires roughly 1/20 of your total blood flow at rest. And although the heart is almost continuously filled with blood, the myocardium is too thick to be served by diffusion of oxygen and nutrients from the blood passing through. Thus the heart has its own set of blood vessels called the **coronary arteries** that supply the heart muscle (Figure 8.10). The coronary arteries branch from the aorta just above the aortic semilunar valve and encircle the heart's surface (the word coronary comes from the Latin *corona,* meaning "encircling like a crown"). From the surface they send branches inward to supply the myocardium. *Cardiac veins* collect the blood from the capillaries in the heart muscle and channel it back to the right atrium.

The coronary arteries are relatively small in diameter. If they become partially or completely blocked, perhaps as a result of atherosclerosis, serious health problems can result. Later in this chapter we will look at what happens when circulation to the heart is impaired.

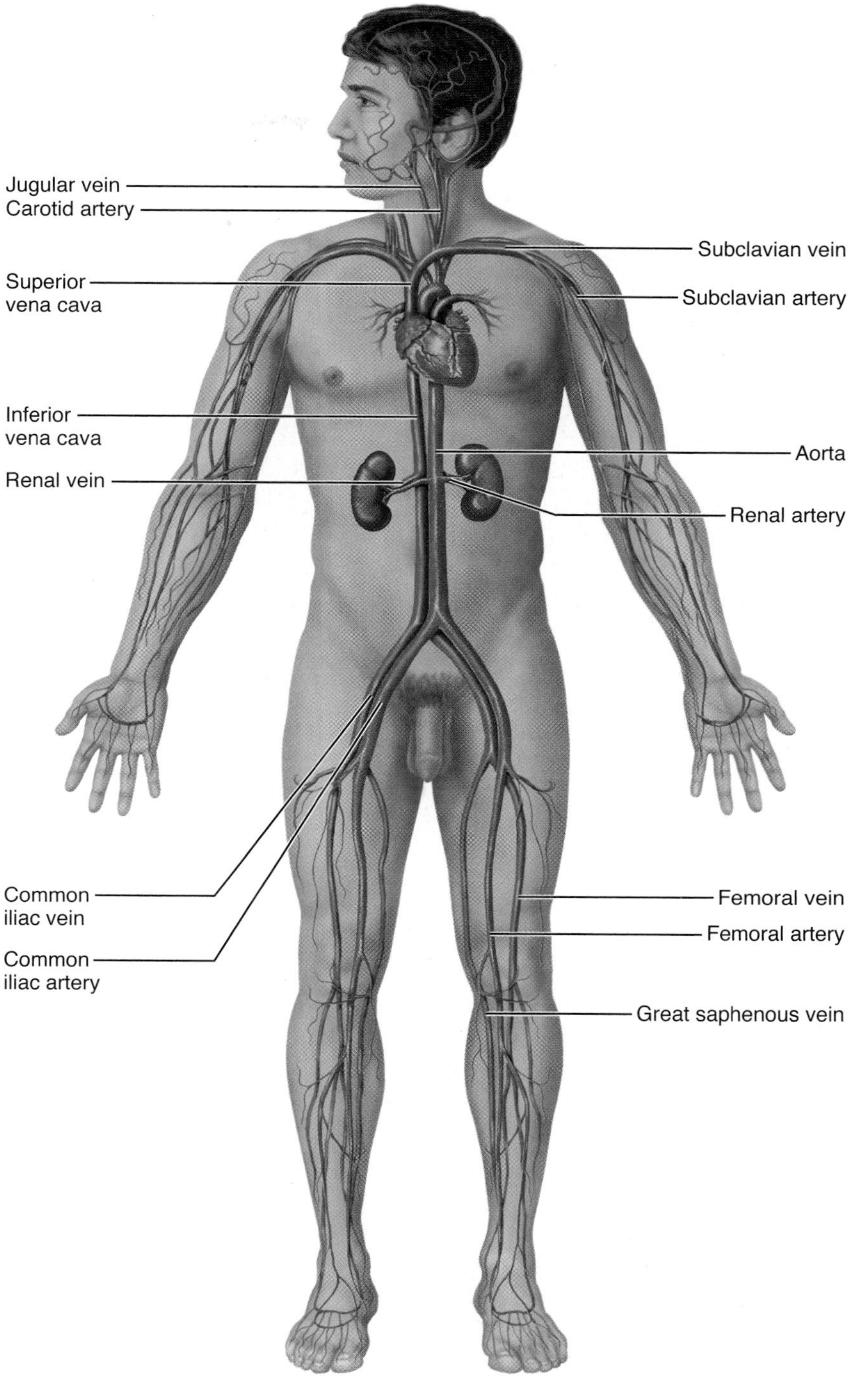


**Figure 8.9 Some of the major arteries and veins in the human body.** For simplicity, the lungs and most of the internal organs have been omitted.

**RECAP**

The right side of the heart (right atrium and right ventricle) pumps blood to the lungs, where blood is oxygenated and carbon dioxide is removed. The left side of the heart (left atrium and left ventricle) pumps blood to the rest of the body, supplying nutrients and removing wastes. ■

## The cardiac cycle: The heart contracts and relaxes

The pumping action of the heart is pulsatile rather than continuous, meaning that it delivers blood in separate and distinct pulses. A complete cardiac cycle involves contraction of the two atria, which forces blood into the ventricles, followed by contraction of the two ventricles, which pumps blood into the pulmonary artery and the aorta, followed by relaxation of the entire heart. The term **systole** refers to the period of contraction and **diastole** refers to the period of relaxation. The entire sequence of contraction and relaxation is called the **cardiac cycle.**

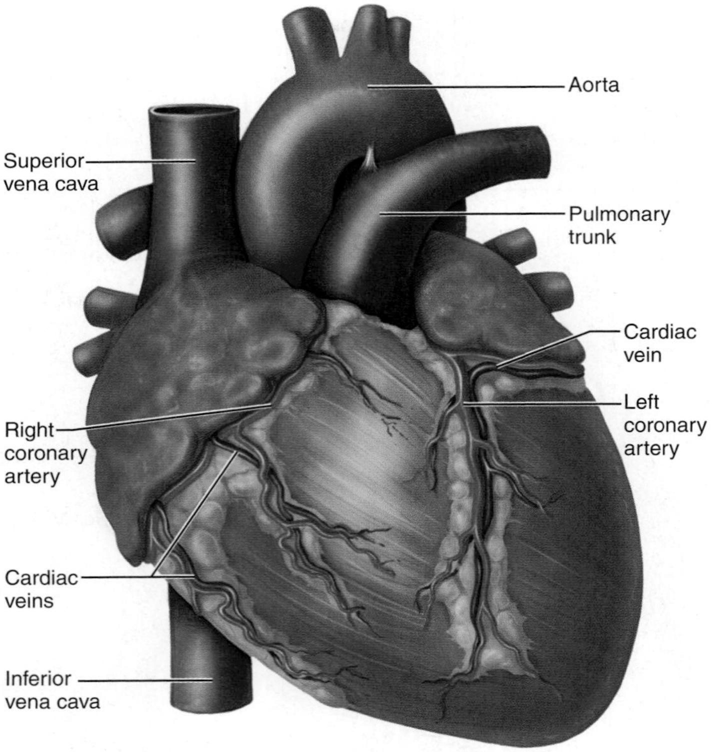


**Figure 8.10 Blood vessels of the heart.**

Every cardiac cycle consists of three steps, as shown in Figure 8.11. Starting with the heart as it first begins to contract:

1. *Atrial systole.* As contraction starts, the heart is already nearly filled with blood that entered the ventricles and atria passively during the previous diastole. Contraction of the heart begins with the atria. During atrial systole, both atria contract, raising blood pressure in the atria and giving the final "kick" that fills the two ventricles to capacity. Atrial systole also momentarily stops further inflow from the veins. Both atrioventricular valves are still open, and both semilunar valves are still closed.
2. *Ventricular systole.* The contraction that began in the atria spreads to the ventricles, and both ventricles contract simultaneously. The rapidly rising ventricular pressure produced by contraction of the ventricles causes the two AV valves to close, preventing blood from flowing backward into the atria and veins. At this time the atria relax and begin filling again. The pressure within the ventricles continues to rise until it is greater than the pressure in the arteries, at which point the pulmonary and aortic semilunar valves open and blood is ejected into the pulmonary trunk and the aorta. With each ventricular systole, about 60% of the blood in each ventricle is forcibly ejected.
3. *Diastole.* Both atria and both ventricles are relaxed throughout diastole. At this point pressure within the ventricles begins to fall. As soon as ventricular pressures

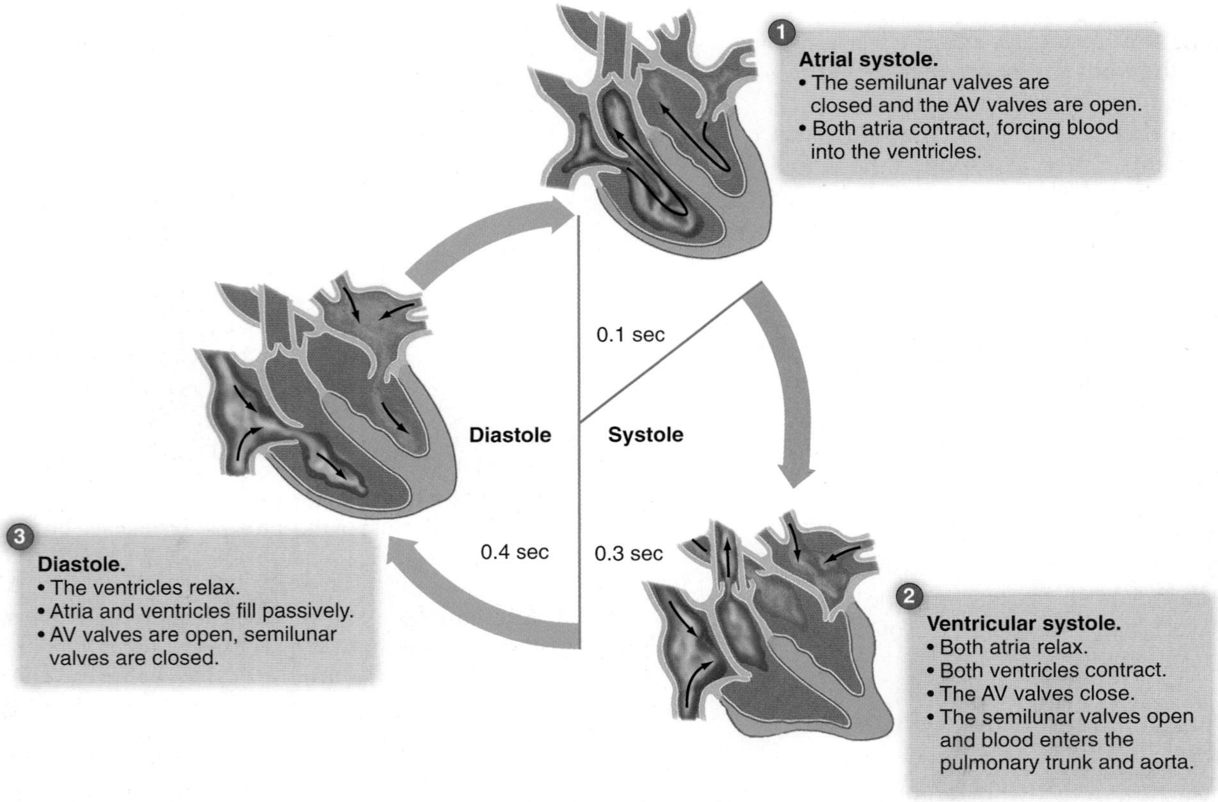


**Figure 8.11 The cardiac cycle.**

fall below arterial pressures during early diastole, the pulmonary and aortic semilunar valves close, preventing backflow of arterial blood. Once ventricular pressure falls below blood pressure in the veins, the AV valves open and blood begins to flow passively into the heart.

A complete cardiac cycle occurs every 0.8 second or so. These cycles repeat, from birth to death, without ever stopping. Atrial systole lasts about 0.1 second; ventricular systole, about 0.3 second. During the remaining 0.4 second, the heart relaxes in diastole.

As each surge of blood enters the arteries during systole, the artery walls are stretched to accommodate the extra volume, and arterial pressure rises. Arteries recoil passively during diastole as blood continues to flow out of them through the capillaries. You can feel this cycle of rapid expansion and recoil in the wall of an artery if it's located close to the skin's surface. This is called a *pulse.* A good place to detect a pulse is the radial artery (inside your wrist, just below the base of the thumb).

The heart is composed primarily of cardiac muscle, and like our skeletal muscles it benefits from regular exercise. During sustained (aerobic) exercise the heart beats more rapidly and more powerfully to sustain blood pressure in the face of increased blood flow to hard-working skeletal muscles. Over time this causes the heart to "bulk up" (hypertrophy) slightly. However, it is important not to overdo any exercise training regimen. If over exercised, the heart itself may become starved for oxygen, and heart muscle may be damaged. The usual guideline for safe but effective exercise training is to perform an activity that raises your heart rate to its "target heart rate" for at least 20 minutes, three times a week or more. (See the Try It Yourself box.)

### Heart sounds reflect closing heart valves

There is probably no more basic rhythm to which humans respond than the familiar "lub-DUB–lub-DUB" of the heart beating. We probably experience it, at least subconsciously, even before we are born. These *heart sounds* reflect events that occur during the cardiac cycle—specifically the closing of the heart valves. The "lub" signals the closure of the two AV valves during ventricular systole. The slightly louder "DUB" occurs when the aortic and pulmonary semilunar valves close during ventricular diastole. The sounds are due to vibrations in the heart chambers and blood vessels caused by the closing of the valves.

Blood flows silently as long as it flows smoothly. However, if blood encounters an obstruction, the disturbed flow can create unusual heart sounds called *murmurs.* Many murmurs result from incomplete closing of the heart valves due to unusually shaped valve flaps or stiffening of the flap tissue. If a valve does not close completely, some blood is forced through it during the cardiac cycle, creating a swishing noise that can be detected through a stethoscope. Murmurs are not necessarily a sign of disease, but physicians can diagnose a variety of heart conditions, including leaking or partially blocked valves, from their sound and timing. Even serious murmurs can often be treated with surgery to replace the defective valve with an artificial valve (Figure 8.12).

**RECAP**

Each cardiac cycle is a repetitive sequence of contraction (systole) and relaxation (diastole). The familiar "lub-DUB" of the heartbeat is caused by the closing of heart valves during the cycle. ■

### Cardiac conduction system coordinates contraction

The coordinated sequence of the cardiac cycle is due to the *cardiac conduction system,* a group of specialized cardiac muscle cells that initiate and distribute electrical impulses throughout the heart. These impulses stimulate the heart muscle to contract in an orderly sequence that spreads from atria to ventricles. The cardiac conduction system consists of four structures: sinoatrial node, atrioventricular node, atrioventricular bundle and its two branches, and Purkinje fibers.

The stimulus that starts a heartbeat begins in the **sinoatrial (SA) node,** a small mass of cardiac muscle cells located near the junction of the right atrium and the superior vena cava. The SA node emits an electrical impulse that travels across both atria like ripples on a pond, stimulating waves of contraction (Figure 8.13). (As noted in Chapter 6 and Figure 6.12, cardiac muscle cells are connected by intercalated discs and gap junctions that let electrical signals flow directly from one cell to the next.) The SA node is properly called the *cardiac pacemaker* because it initiates the heartbeat. However, the cardiac pacemaker can be influenced by the brain to speed up or slow down, as we'll see in a minute.

**try it** *yourself*

### Calculating Your Target Heart Rate

Your target heart rate for aerobic exercise should be 65–85% of your maximum attainable heart rate. The general formula for maximum attainable heart rate (without pushing yourself to the maximum just to find out) is 220 minus your age. To calculate your target heart rate, then, subtract your age from 220 and then multiply the result by 0.65 and 0.85 to find the lower and upper limits of your target range. By these calculations, the target range for a 20-year-old is 130 to 170 beats per minute. When you do aerobic exercise, try to keep your heart rate within the range that is right for you. If you're below the minimum you're probably loafing. If you're above it you could be placing undue strain on your heart and muscles.

Notice that the maximum attainable heart rate and the target heart rate decrease with age. Consult your doctor about the best degree of exertion for your fitness level, particularly if you're new to exercise.

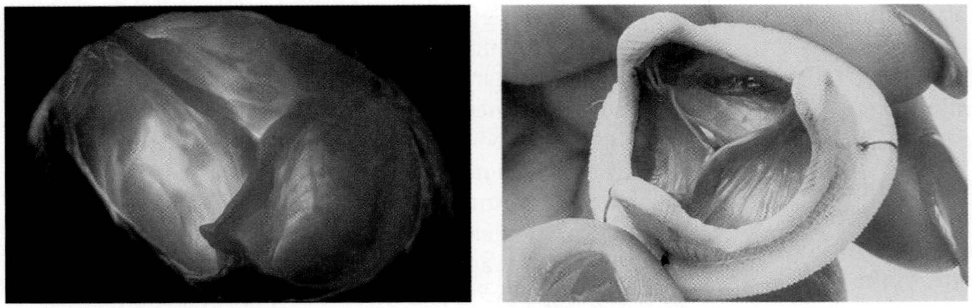

**a)** A pulmonary semilunar valve. **b)** An artificial heart valve.

**Figure 8.12 Heart valves.**

The electrical impulse traveling across the atria eventually reaches another mass of muscle cells called the **atrioventricular (AV) node,** located between the atria and ventricles. The muscle fibers in this area are smaller in diameter, causing a slight delay of approximately 0.1 second, which temporarily slows the rate at which the impulse travels. This delay gives the atria time to contract and empty their blood into the ventricles before the ventricles contract.

From the AV node, the electrical signal sweeps to a group of conducting fibers in the septum between the two ventricles called the **atrioventricular (AV) bundle.** These fibers branch and extend into **Purkinje fibers,** smaller fibers that carry the impulse to all cells in the myocardium of the ventricles. Because the electrical impulse travels down the septum to the lower portion of the ventricles and then spreads rapidly upward through the Purkinje fibers, the lower part of the ventricles contract before the upper part. This lower-to-upper squeezing motion pushes blood into the pulmonary trunk and aorta.

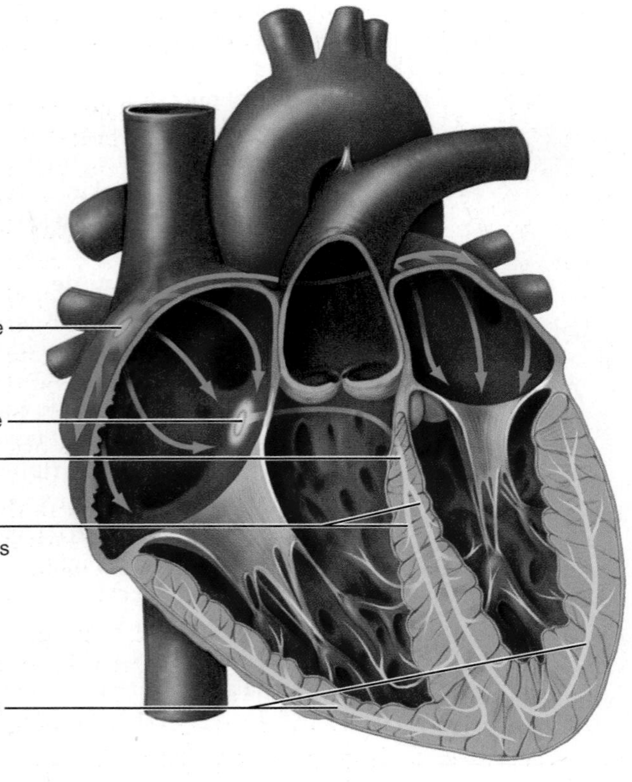


**Figure 8.13 The cardiac conduction system.** Electrical activity of the heart normally starts at the SA node, spreads across the atria to the AV node, and then progresses down the AV bundle and its branches to the Purkinje fibers.

## Electrocardiogram records the heart's electrical activity

Because the body is largely water and water conducts electrical activity well, we can track the electrical activity of the heart as weak differences in voltage at the surface of the body. An **electrocardiogram (ECG** or **EKG)** is a record of the electrical impulses in the cardiac conduction system. An ECG involves placing electrodes on the skin at the chest, wrists, and ankles. The electrodes transmit the heart's electrical impulses, which are recorded as a continuous line on a screen or moving graph.

A healthy heart produces a characteristic pattern of voltage changes. A typical ECG tracks these changes as a series of three formations: P wave, QRS complex, and T wave. First is the small P wave, representing the electrical impulse traveling across the atria. Second is the QRS complex, representing the spread of the electrical impulse down the septum and around the two ventricles in the Purkinje fibers. It occurs just before the ventricles start to contract. Finally, the T wave is the result of the *end* of the electrical activity in the ventricles.

If something goes wrong with the cardiac conduction system or if the heart muscle becomes damaged, abnormal heart electrical impulses and contractions may occur. An abnormality of the rhythm or rate of the heartbeat is called an *arrhythmia.* Arrhythmias take many forms. Occasional skipped heartbeats, for example, are fairly common and usually of no consequence. However, a type of rapid irregular ventricular contraction known as *ventricular fibrillation* (or "V-fib") is very quickly fatal unless treated immediately. Ventricular fibrillation is the leading cause of cardiac death in otherwise healthy people. In a hospital, ventricular fibrillation is treated by "cardioversion," in which a strong electrical current is applied to the chest to eliminate the abnormal fibrillating pattern and restore the normal sinus rhythm.

Arrhythmias produce characteristic ECG tracings, and the ECG is a valuable tool for identifying the cause, type, and location of arrhythmias. Figure 8.14 shows a patient undergoing an ECG, a normal ECG recording, and a recording from a patient in ventricular fibrillation. Arrhythmias less life-threatening than ventricular fibrillation can sometimes be treated with medications. In some cases an artificial pacemaker (a small generating unit that automatically stimulates the heart at set intervals) can be surgically implanted under the chest skin to normalize the heart rate.

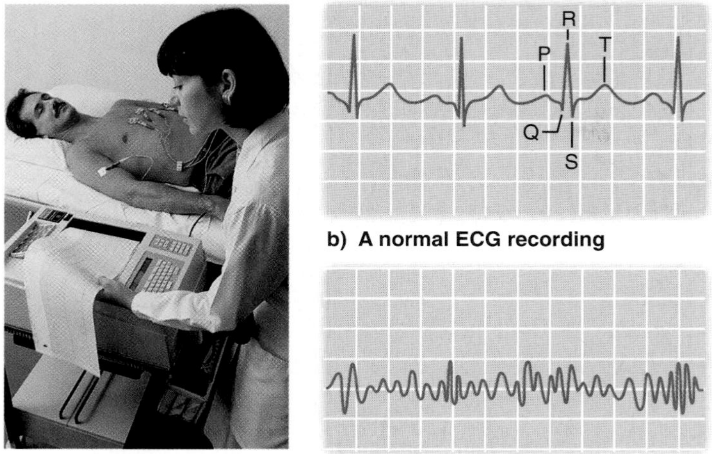


a) An ECG being recorded b) A normal ECG recording c) Ventricular fibrillation

**Figure 8.14 The ECG is a tool for diagnosing heart arrhythmias.**

**RECAP**

Contraction of the heart is coordinated by modified cardiac muscle cells that initiate and transmit electrical impulses through a specialized conduction system. An electrocardiogram (ECG) is a recording of the heart's electrical activity taken from the surface of the body. ■

## 8.3 Blood exerts pressure against vessel walls

**Blood pressure** is the force that blood exerts on the wall of a blood vessel as a result of the pumping action of the heart.

Blood pressure is not the same in all blood vessels. Figure 8.15 compares the pressures in the various segments of the vascular system. You can see from the highs and lows shown here that pressure is pulsatile in the arteries; that is, it varies with each beat of the heart. The highest pressure of the cycle, **systolic pressure,** is the pressure reached during ventricular systole when the ventricles contract to eject blood from the heart. The lowest pressure, **diastolic pressure,** occurs during ventricular diastole when the ventricles relax. Arteries store the energy generated by the heart during systole, and during diastole they use that stored energy to supply blood to the tissues.

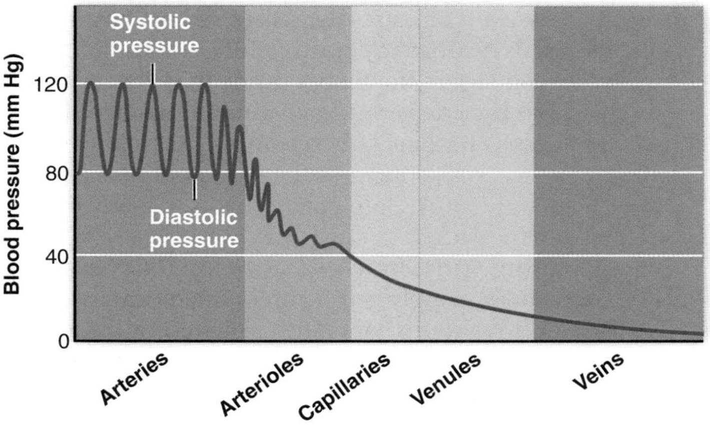


**Figure 8.15 Blood pressure in different segments of the vascular system.**

Maintenance of arterial blood pressure is crucial to drive the flow of blood throughout the body and all the way back to the heart. Recall that fluid always flows from a region of high pressure toward a region of lower pressure. By the time it reaches the capillaries, blood flow is steady rather than pulsatile, and pressure continues to fall as blood flows through venules and veins. The differences in the blood pressure of arteries, capillaries, and veins keep blood moving through the body.

When health professionals measure your blood pressure, however, they are assessing only the pressure in your main arteries. From a clinical standpoint, blood pressure gives valuable clues about the relative volume of blood in the vessels, the condition or stiffness of the arteries, and the overall efficiency of the cardiovascular system. Trends in blood pressure over time are a useful indicator of cardiovascular changes. In young, healthy individuals, systolic pressures of less than 120 mm Hg and diastolic pressures of less than 80 mm Hg are considered desirable. With advancing age there is a slight tendency for systolic blood pressure in particular to increase slightly, as a consequence of age-related stiffening of the arteries.

Blood pressure is measured with a *sphygmomanometer* (*sphygmo* comes from the Greek word for "pulse"; a manometer is a device for measuring fluid pressures). An inflatable cuff is placed over the brachial artery in your upper arm and connected to a pressure-measuring device (Figure 8.16). When the cuff is inflated to a pressure above systolic pressure, blood flow through the brachial artery stops because the high cuff pressure collapses the artery. The cuff is then deflated slowly while a health professional listens with a stethoscope for the sounds of blood flowing in your artery. As soon as pressure in the cuff falls below the peak of systolic pressure, some blood spurts briefly through the artery during the high point of the pressure pulse, making a characteristic light tapping sound that is audible through the stethoscope. The cuff pressure at which this happens is recorded as systolic pressure. As the cuff continues to deflate, eventually blood flow through the artery becomes continuous and the tapping sound ceases. The point where the sound disappears is your diastolic pressure.

This procedure yields two numbers, corresponding to your systolic and diastolic pressures. These represent the high and low points of blood pressure during the cardiac cycle. Blood pressure is recorded as mm Hg (millimeters of mercury, because early equipment used a glass column filled with mercury to measure the pressure).

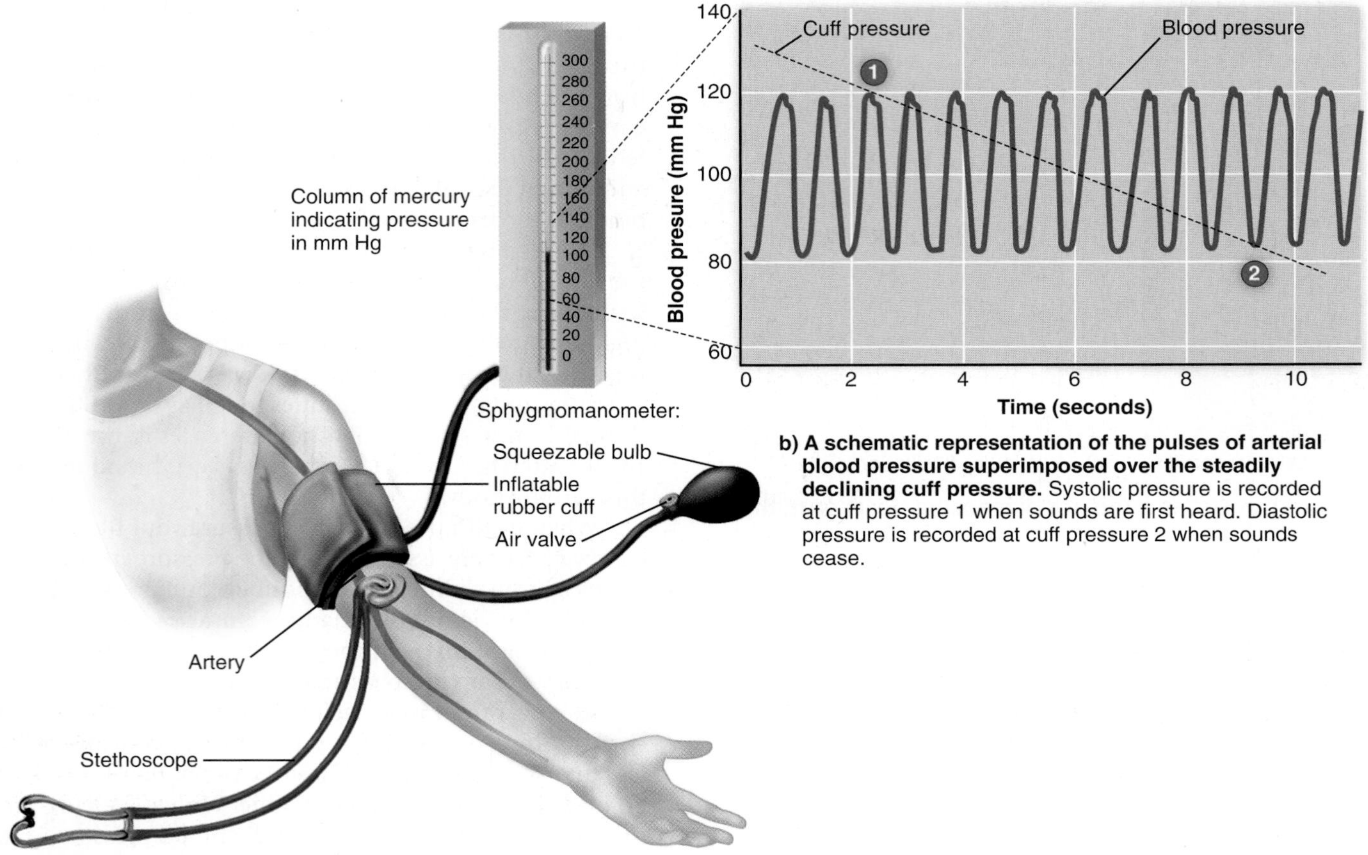


**a) A clinician inflates the cuff with air and then allows the pressure in the cuff to fall gradually while using a stethoscope to listen for the sounds of blood movement through the artery.**

**b) A schematic representation of the pulses of arterial blood pressure superimposed over the steadily declining cuff pressure.** Systolic pressure is recorded at cuff pressure 1 when sounds are first heard. Diastolic pressure is recorded at cuff pressure 2 when sounds cease.

**Figure 8.16 How blood pressure is measured.**

## Hypertension: High blood pressure can be dangerous

Blood pressure higher than normal is called **hypertension** (*hyper* comes from the Greek for "excess"). Table 8.1 presents the systolic and diastolic readings health professionals use to classify blood pressure as normal or hypertensive. Hypertension is a significant risk factor for cardiovascular disease, because the greater the pressure, the greater the strain on the cardiovascular system. Blood vessels react to the pounding by becoming hardened and scarred, which makes them less able to stretch during systole. Hypertension also places a greater strain on the heart, because the work it must do is directly proportional to the arterial pressure against which it must pump.

**Table 8.1 Systolic and diastolic blood pressure**

| Blood pressure category | Systolic (mm Hg) | | Diastolic (mm Hg) |
|---|---|---|---|
| Normal | Less than 120 | and | Less than 80 |
| Prehypertension | 120–139 | or | 80–89 |
| Hypertension, Stage 1 | 140–159 | or | 90–99 |
| Hypertension, Stage 2 | 160 or higher | or | 100 or higher |

*Source:* National Institutes of Health, National Heart, Lung, and Blood Institute, March 2003.

Hypertension is called "the silent killer" because usually it has no symptoms. The American Heart Association estimates that approximately 50 million Americans have hypertension and a third of them don't even realize it. If left untreated, hypertension increases the risk of serious health problems such as heart attack, heart failure, stroke, kidney damage, even damage to the tissues inside the eyes.

What causes hypertension? Many times it happens because blood vessels become narrowed from atherosclerosis. Certain other factors also increase the risk, as summarized in Table 8.2. The only sure way to diagnose it is to have your blood pressure measured.

Blood pressure varies from minute to minute even in healthy individuals. Simply getting up in the morning raises it, as do exercise, emotions, smoking cigarettes, eating, drinking, and many other factors. Even having your blood pressure measured can make you nervous enough for your blood pressure to rise—a situation that health professionals call "white coat hypertension." This is why physicians generally have you sit quietly while measuring your blood pressure.

**Table 8.2 Risk factors for hypertension**

| Risk factor | Comments |
|---|---|
| Heredity | Family history of hypertension raises risk |
| Age | Blood pressure tends to rise throughout life |
| Race | African Americans have twice the incidence found in Caucasian Americans and Asian Americans |
| Sex | Males are more likely than females to develop hypertension |
| Obesity | The heart must pump harder to push blood through vessels |
| High salt intake | In some individuals (but not others) a high salt intake raises blood pressure slightly |
| Smoking | Smoking raises the blood concentration of epinephrine, a hormone that stimulates the heart |
| Sedentary lifestyle | Not well understood. May be due to higher blood lipids or weight gain |
| Persistent emotional stress | Emotional stress activates portions of the nervous system that elevate pressure |
| Diabetes mellitus | Diabetics have a higher incidence of hypertension, for reasons not yet known |
| Heavy alcohol consumption | Mechanisms unknown |
| Oral contraceptives and certain medications | Mechanisms vary by medication |

If hypertension is suspected, your physician will probably measure your blood pressure on at least three different occasions before making a firm diagnosis. True hypertension is a *sustained* elevation in blood pressure above normal levels—a systolic pressure of 140 mm Hg or greater or a diastolic pressure of 90 mm Hg or greater. Even blood pressure that is consistently just below the hypertensive level (prehypertension) may carry a slightly higher risk of health complications.

Generally, if systolic pressure is high, diastolic pressure will be, too. However, sometimes systolic pressure can register at above-normal levels while diastolic pressure remains normal, a condition called *isolated systolic hypertension.* Most common in older adults, it is diagnosed as a systolic pressure of 160 mm Hg or higher with a diastolic reading of less than 90 mm Hg. Like the more common form of hypertension, isolated systolic hypertension is associated with increased health problems.

At the end of this chapter we discuss what you can do to lower your risk of hypertension as well as other cardiovascular problems. If hypertension does develop, however, a number of medical treatments are available to lower blood pressure to a healthy level. It is important for people on antihypertensive drugs to take their medication consistently; even though hypertension has no symptoms, it increases the risk of related health problems.

### Hypotension: When blood pressure is too low

It is also possible for blood pressure to fall below normal levels, a condition called *hypotension* (*hypo* comes from the Greek for "under"). Generally hypotension is a problem only if blood pressure falls enough to reduce blood flow to the brain, causing dizziness and fainting. Drops in blood pressure can follow abrupt changes in position, such as standing up suddenly. Other causes include severe burns or injuries involving heavy blood loss.

**RECAP**

Blood pressure is the force that blood exerts on the wall of a blood vessel. It is measured as two numbers corresponding to systolic and diastolic pressures. Hypertension (high blood pressure) is a serious risk factor for cardiovascular disease and other health problems. ■

## 8.4 How the cardiovascular system is regulated

The overall function of the cardiovascular system is to provide every cell with precisely the right blood flow to meet its needs at all times. This might seem like a complicated process because different types of tissues have different needs, which change according to circumstances. In principle, however, the system is rather simple.

Consider for a minute how your community provides water to every house according to the needs of the occupants. Basically, municipal water systems provide constant water *pressure* to every house. With steady water pressure available, each household simply adjusts the *flow* of water into the house by turning faucets on and off.

The human cardiovascular system is based on similar principles. Consider the following key points:

- Homeostatic regulation of the cardiovascular system centers on *maintaining a constant arterial blood pressure.*
- A constant arterial blood pressure is *achieved* by regulating the heart rate and force of contraction (adjusting flow *into* the arteries) and by regulating the diameters of all the body's arterioles as a whole (adjusting overall flow *out* of the arteries).
- With arterial blood pressure held relatively constant, local blood flows are adjusted to meet local requirements.

As we will see, this overall regulation is achieved with nerves, hormones, and local factors coupled to metabolism.

## Baroreceptors maintain arterial blood pressure

There is probably no more important regulated variable in the entire body than blood pressure. Without a relatively constant blood pressure as the driving force for supplying blood to the capillaries, homeostasis simply would not be possible. Blood pressure does vary, but always within a range consistent with being able to provide blood to all cells.

To regulate blood pressure, the body must have some way of measuring it. In fact, several of the large arteries, including the aorta and the two carotid arteries, have certain regions called **baroreceptors** (the Greek *baro* denotes pressure). The baroreceptors regulate arterial blood pressure in the following manner:

1. When blood pressure rises, arterial blood vessels are stretched passively.
2. Stretch of baroreceptors in the carotid arteries and aorta causes them to send signals via nerves to an area of the brain called the cardiovascular center.
3. The cardiovascular center responds by sending signals via nerves to the heart and blood vessels.
4. The effect on the heart is to lower heart rate and the force of contraction. This reduces **cardiac output,** the amount of blood that the heart pumps into the aorta each minute.
5. The effect on arterioles is vasodilation, an increase in arteriole diameter. Vasodilation increases blood flow through all tissues.
6. The net effect of both reducing cardiac output and increasing flow through the tissues is to return arterial pressure to normal.

Exactly the opposite sequence of events occurs when arterial pressure falls *below* normal. When pressure falls and the arteries stretch less than normal, the baroreceptors send fewer nerve signals to the brain. The brain correctly interprets this as a fall in pressure and sends nerve signals that increase cardiac output and constrict arterioles, raising arterial blood pressure again.

All day long—every time you stand up, sit down, get excited, run for the bus—your blood pressure fluctuates up or down. But it is quickly brought back within normal range by a negative feedback loop initiated by baroreceptors.

**RECAP**

Homeostatic regulation of the cardiovascular system centers on maintaining a relatively constant arterial blood pressure, making blood available to all cells as needed. Arterial pressure is sensed by baroreceptors located in the carotid arteries and aorta. ■

## Nerves and hormones adjust cardiac output

As mentioned before, cardiac output is the amount of blood pumped into the aorta in one minute. We calculate cardiac output by multiplying *heart rate* (number of heartbeats per minute) by *stroke volume* (volume of blood pumped out with each heartbeat). For a healthy adult at rest, the heart rate averages about 75 beats per minute, and the stroke volume averages about 70 milliliters per beat. Resting cardiac output, then, is about 5.25 liters per minute. Since our normal blood volume is only about 5 liters, in essence the entire blood supply passes through the heart every minute.

Regulation of cardiac output is centered in an area of the brain called the *medulla oblongata,* which is where the cardiovascular center is located. The medulla oblongata receives nerve signals from the baroreceptors, from receptors in muscles and joints, and from areas of the brain involved in emotions. In response to the inputs it receives, the cardiovascular center sends nerve signals to the heart in two sets of nerves. *Sympathetic nerves* stimulate the heart and cause it to beat faster, and *parasympathetic nerves* inhibit the heart and cause it to beat more slowly.

The hormones *epinephrine* (also called adrenaline) and *norepinephrine* stimulate the heart as well. Epinephrine and norepinephrine are secreted by the adrenal glands whenever the sympathetic nervous system is activated.

Sympathetic nerves also help to maintain blood pressure by controlling blood vessel diameters. Most blood vessels are under a constant state of partial constriction by the sympathetic nerves. An increase in sympathetic nerve activity further constricts blood vessels and raises blood pressure. Conversely, a decrease in sympathetic nerve activity dilates blood vessels and lowers pressure. Most blood vessels do not have parasympathetic nerves, so activation or deactivation of the parasympathetic nervous system has little effect on overall blood vessel diameters.

## Local requirements dictate local blood flows

With arterial blood pressure held relatively constant, the flow of blood through each precapillary sphincter (and hence each capillary) can be adjusted according to need, just like turning a faucet on or off. How is the flow adjusted? When a particular area is metabolically active, such as when a muscle is contracting, it consumes more oxygen and nutrients. Increased metabolism also raises the production of carbon dioxide and other waste products. One or more of these changes associated with increased metabolism cause precapillary sphincters to vasodilate, increasing flow. Scientists do not yet know the precise mechanisms of this vasodilation or the identity of all the chemical substances that influence blood flow, but we do know that it occurs. Figure 8.17 shows how an increase in cellular metabolism might increase the local blood flow to that region.

Look at the overall process and you can see how together these control mechanisms deliver blood efficiently

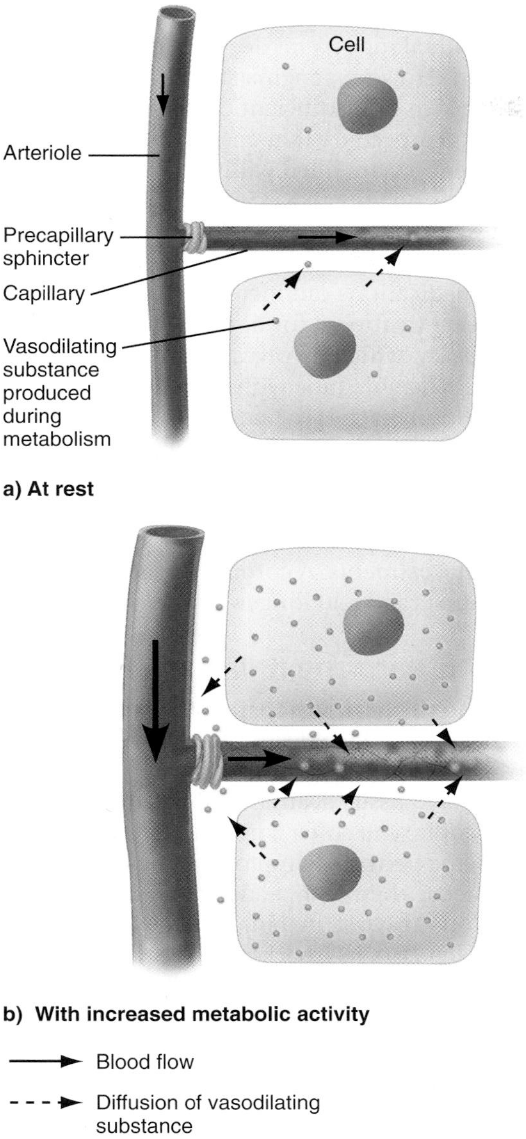


**Figure 8.17 How the increased production of a vasodilating substance during metabolism could regulate local flow.** **(a)** At rest, very little of the vasodilating substance would be produced, and flow would be minimal. **(b)** With increased metabolic activity, the presence of more of the substance in the interstitial space near an arteriole and precapillary sphincter would cause the vessels to vasodilate, increasing flow and washing out the substance.

to all tissues. First, nerves and hormones adjust cardiac output and the rate of blood flow through the vascular system as a whole, in an effort to maintain relatively constant arterial blood pressure. Second, any cell or part of the body that is not receiving enough blood can override the system locally and get exactly what it needs—no more, no less.

Some tissues and organs need a more consistent blood supply than others. That too is taken into account by our control system. Consider what would happen if you lost a substantial volume of blood due to injury, producing a precipitous fall in blood pressure. The negative feedback control of arterial blood pressure would stimulate your heart and constrict your arterioles, reducing flow to most organs in an effort to raise blood pressure. However, organs whose survival depends critically on a constant blood supply (your brain and heart, for example) can override the generalized vasoconstriction with their local control mechanisms. Organs whose metabolic activities are not required for their immediate survival (such as your kidneys and digestive tract) just remain vasoconstricted for a while. In effect, the limited available blood supply is shunted to essential organs.

You may wonder why, if these homeostatic controls are working properly, people ever develop hypertension. Every time blood pressure went up a little, wouldn't feedback mechanisms bring it back to normal? This is the great mystery of hypertension. Although scientists don't fully understand it yet, for some reason the body seems to adjust to high pressure once it has been sustained for a long time. Apparently the feedback system slowly resets itself to recognize the higher pressure as normal. The reason may be that hypertension tends to develop slowly over decades, so there is never a single defining moment when pressure registers as too high.

### Exercise: Increased blood flow and cardiac output

During exercise the metabolic activity of the active skeletal muscles goes up dramatically. As a result the production of vasodilator waste products increases, and the local concentration of oxygen falls. Both of these contribute to dilation of the blood vessels. Consequently, blood flow through the active skeletal muscles increases.

To sustain blood pressure in the face of increased blood flow, the heart must increase its output. From what you know, you might guess that an increase in blood flow to muscle would cause a fall in blood pressure, which in turn would cause a baroreceptor-mediated reflex increase in cardiac output. However, blood pressure doesn't fall very much (if at all) during exercise—if anything, it rises a little. During exercise, the primary cause of increased cardiac output is sensory input from moving muscles and joints. This sensory input signals the cardiovascular center to stimulate the heart and increase cardiac output even before blood pressure can fall very much. In other words, during exercise the body anticipates the need for increased cardiac output and prevents blood pressure from falling in the first place.

In nonathletic people, cardiac output reaches a maximum of about 20–25 liters per minute during heavy exercise. However, trained athletes whose heart muscles have hypertrophied as a result of exercise training can reach cardiac outputs of up to 35 liters per minute, or almost seven times their resting cardiac output.

**RECAP**

Two opposing sets of nerves (sympathetic and parasympathetic) and a hormone (epinephrine) adjust cardiac output and arteriole diameters to maintain arterial blood pressure. Local factors regulate blood flow into individual capillaries by altering the diameters of precapillary sphincters. During exercise, blood pressure is maintained by an increase in cardiac output caused primarily by sensory input from muscles and joints. ■

## 8.5 Cardiovascular disorders: A major health issue

Disorders affecting the cardiovascular system are a major health problem in Western countries. Cardiovascular disorders cause more than 700,000 deaths per year in the U.S. alone. They are the number one killer in the U.S., far ahead of the number two killer, cancer (approximately 550,000 deaths per year).

We have already discussed hypertension and aneurysms, and the Health Watch box on the following page profiles another major cardiovascular disorder, atherosclerosis. In the rest of this chapter we look at several other conditions, including angina pectoris, heart attack, congestive heart failure, embolism, and stroke. Finally, we examine what you can do to reduce your own risk of cardiovascular health problems.

### Angina pectoris: Chest pain warns of impaired blood flow

As a hard-working muscle, the heart requires a constant source of blood. Normally the coronary arteries and their branches provide all the blood the heart needs, even during sustained exercise. However, if these arteries become narrowed (usually because of atherosclerosis), blood flow to the heart may not be sufficient for the heart's demands. This may lead to *angina pectoris* (sometimes called just angina), a sensation of pain and tightness in the chest. Often angina is accompanied by shortness of breath and a sensation of choking or suffocating (*angina* comes from the Latin word for "strangling"; *pectoris* refers to the chest). Many angina episodes are triggered by physical exertion, emotional stress, cold weather, or eating heavy meals, because the heart requires more blood and oxygen at these times.

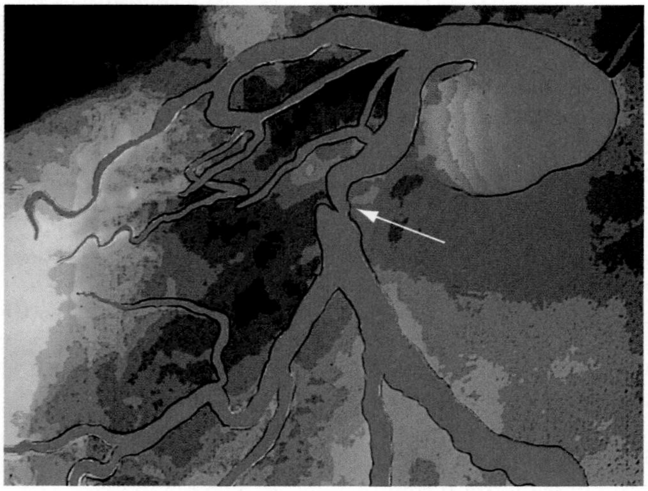

**Figure 8.18 A coronary angiogram.** A contrast medium (similar in function to a dye) is injected into the coronary arteries, causing them to become visible on an X-ray photograph. Note the area of narrowing in the coronary artery indicated by the arrow.

Angina is uncomfortable but usually temporary. Stopping to rest and taking several deep breaths can often relieve the discomfort. However, angina should never be ignored, because it is a sign of insufficient circulation to the heart. *Angiography* is a procedure that enables blood vessels to be visualized after they are filled with a contrast medium (a substance that is opaque to X-rays). Angiography allows health professionals to take X-ray pictures of blood vessels (called *angiograms*) and assess their condition (Figure 8.18).

Certain medications can increase blood flow to the heart muscle. Another treatment for narrowed coronary arteries is *balloon angioplasty,* which involves threading into the blocked artery a slender flexible tube with a small balloon attached. When the balloon reaches the narrowest point of the vessel it is inflated briefly so that it presses against the fatty plaques that narrow the vessel lumen, flattening them and widening the lumen. Balloon angioplasty has a high success rate, although in some cases the vessel narrows again over time, requiring repeat treatments. A coronary artery bypass graft (see the next section) can yield longer-lasting benefits.

### Heart attack: Permanent damage to heart tissue

If blood flow to the heart is impaired long enough, the result is a **heart attack**—sudden death of an area of heart tissue due to oxygen starvation. (The clinical term is *myocardial infarction;* infarction refers to tissue death from inadequate blood supply.) Many people who suffer a heart attack have a previous history of angina pectoris. Symptoms of heart attack include feelings of intense chest pain, nausea, and the sensation of a heavy object on the chest, making it hard to breathe. Pain may radiate to the left arm, jaw, back, or upper abdomen.

By definition, a heart attack means that part of the heart has been permanently injured. Because the body cannot replace cardiac muscle cells, any damage to them can impair the heart's ability to function. Most heart attack fatalities occur because of a serious heart arrhythmia called *ventricular fibrillation.*

Prompt treatment is crucial for recovery from a heart attack. If a heart attack is even suspected, the person should be rushed immediately to a hospital. The diagnosis of a heart attack is generally made on the basis of the ECG and the presence in the blood of certain enzymes that are released from dead and damaged heart cells. Health professionals can often control cardiac arrhythmias and other complications and administer clot-dissolving drugs to unblock vessels. The sooner treatment begins, the more successful it is likely to be.

# Health Watch

## Cholesterol and Atherosclerosis

In Western nations, atherosclerosis—the buildup of fatty deposits on the inner walls of arteries—is a major factor in cardiovascular disease.

As noted in Chapter 2, cholesterol is a lipid, an important component of our body's cells. All cells require a certain amount of it. However, cholesterol can become risky if it adheres to the interior of blood vessels. Over time, fatty deposits of cholesterol snag other substances floating by in the blood—calcium, blood cells, and more cholesterol—forming deposits called plaques that narrow the lumen and reduce blood flow.

Atherosclerotic plaques injure the endothelium that lines blood vessels, and calcium deposits stiffen the vessel walls, increasing arterial resistance to blood flow. Left untreated, atherosclerosis (also called "hardening of the arteries") contributes to heart attacks, strokes, aneurysms, and peripheral vascular disease.

Risk factors for atherosclerosis include factors that raise blood cholesterol (obesity, sedentary lifestyle, and a high-fat diet), smoking, diabetes, hypertension, and a family history of atherosclerosis. Recent evidence indicates that a herpes virus is sometimes involved. Before age 45, men have a 10 times greater risk than women. However, women's risk rises after menopause.

Most cholesterol molecules in the blood are bound to carrier proteins. Together, the protein and cholesterol complex form a lipoprotein. There are two types of lipoproteins, based upon their densities. Low-density lipoprotein complexes (LDLs) are considered "bad" in terms of atherosclerosis because they carry cholesterol to all cells of the body and make it available. LDL cholesterol may

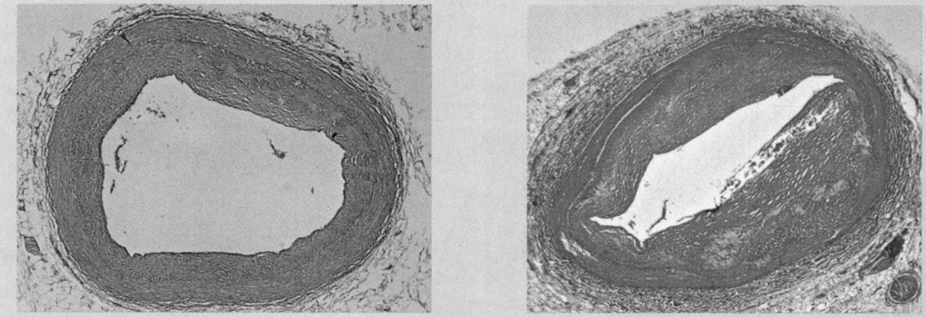

**a) Cross section of a normal coronary artery.**

**b) A coronary artery narrowed by atherosclerotic plaque.**

Atherosclerosis.

also contribute to plaque formation. On the other hand, high-density lipoproteins (HDLs) are considered "good" because they target cholesterol for removal. HDLs in the blood are picked up by the liver. There the cholesterol is detached from the protein, mixed with bile, and secreted into the small intestine. Some of the cholesterol in bile is excreted from the body, although some is reabsorbed to be used again.

Health professionals recommend having your LDL, HDL, and total cholesterol measured periodically. The American Heart Association recommendations (in units of milligrams per deciliter of blood plasma) are:

**LDL:**

| | |
|---|---|
| ■ Less than 100 mg/dl | Optimal |
| ■ 100–129 mg/dl | Near or above optimal |
| ■ 130–159 mg/dl | Borderline high |
| ■ 160–189 mg/dl | High |
| ■ 190 mg/dl and above | Very high |

**HDL:**

| | |
|---|---|
| ■ Less than 40 mg/dl (men) or 50 mg/dl (women) | A major risk factor for heart disease |
| ■ 60 mg/dl and above | Protective against heart disease |

**Total cholesterol:**

| | |
|---|---|
| ■ Less than 200 mg/dl | Desirable |
| ■ 200–239 mg/dl | Borderline high |
| ■ Greater than 240 mg/dl | High |

Optimal or desirable readings mean less risk of atherosclerosis and related cardiovascular problems.

Over time, all of us develop some degree of atherosclerosis. However, lifestyle can make a big difference in how rapidly atherosclerosis develops and whether it becomes severe. Maintaining a healthy weight and getting regular exercise will benefit your blood vessels, as will eating a healthy diet and not smoking. There are also medications available to lower cholesterol levels. At the end of this chapter, we look at what you can do to lower your risk of atherosclerosis and other cardiovascular conditions.

Later (or even before a heart attack has occurred, if the narrowing of coronary vessels has been diagnosed by angiography), a *coronary artery bypass graft (CABG)* can be performed to improve coronary blood flow. In this procedure, a piece of blood vessel is removed from somewhere else in the body (often a leg vein is used) and grafted onto the blocked artery to bypass the damaged region (Figure 8.19). Over time the grafted vein thickens and takes on the characteristics of an artery.

Thanks to these and other treatments, the heart attack survival rate has risen dramatically. Eighty percent of heart attack survivors are back at work within three months.

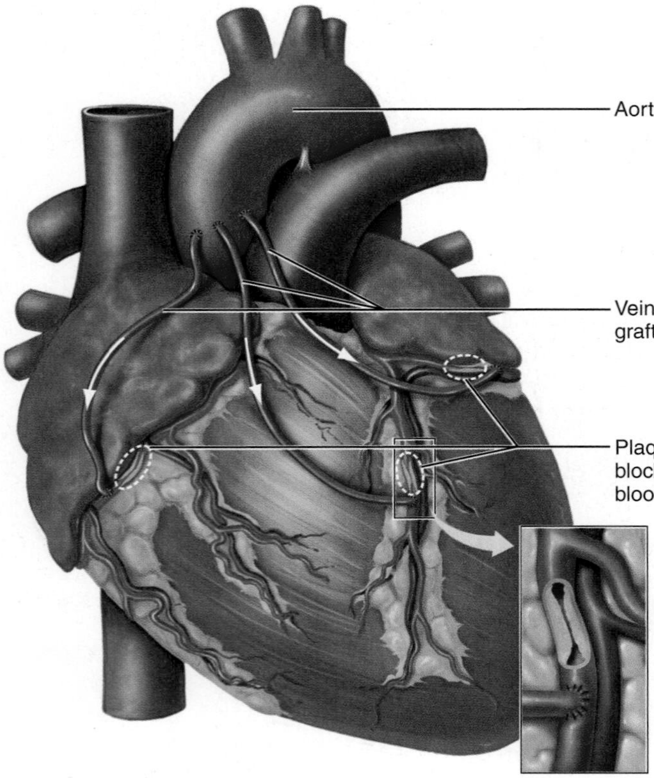


**Figure 8.19 Coronary artery bypass grafts.** This is an example of a "triple CABG," in which three vein grafts have been placed to bypass three areas of atherosclerotic plaque. Arrows indicate additional blood flow to the area beyond the restricted artery.

## Congestive heart failure: The heart becomes less efficient

Generally our bodies maintain adequate arterial pressure because of the tight control mechanisms described earlier. Sometimes, however, the heart becomes weaker and less efficient at pumping blood. When the heart begins to pump less blood, blood backs up in the veins (the venous system) *behind* the failing heart. As a result, pressure in the veins and capillaries rises. Because capillary blood pressure is now higher than usual, more fluid than usual filters out of the capillaries and into the interstitial space. When that happens a person is said to have **congestive heart failure.** ("Congestive" refers to the buildup of interstitial fluid.)

People with congestive heart failure get out of breath when walking or climbing even a short flight of stairs. They may even have trouble breathing while lying down because the horizontal position results in even higher venous pressure and fluid accumulation in the lungs. Other symptoms include swollen ankles and legs, swollen neck veins, and weight gain from the extra fluid.

There are several reasons why a heart might begin to fail. Aging is one factor, but certainly not the only one because older people do not necessarily develop heart failure. Other possible causes include past heart attacks, leaking heart valves, heart valves that fail to open normally, uncontrolled hypertension, or serious arrhythmias. Lung conditions such as emphysema can raise blood pressure in the lungs and strain the heart.

Treatments for congestive heart failure focus on improving cardiac performance and efficiency while preventing the accumulation of interstitial fluid. Regular mild exercise promotes more efficient blood flow, and frequent resting with the feet elevated helps fluid drain from leg veins. Physicians may prescribe diuretics (drugs that help the body get rid of excess fluid), vasodilating drugs to expand blood vessels, or medications to help the heart muscle beat more forcefully.

## Embolism: Blockage of a blood vessel

Embolism refers to the sudden blockage of a blood vessel by material floating in the bloodstream. Most often the obstacle (an *embolus*) is a blood clot that has broken away from a larger clot elsewhere in the body (often a vein) and lodged in an artery at a point where arterial vessels branch and get smaller in diameter. Other possible emboli include cholesterol deposits, tissue fragments, cancer cells, clumps of bacteria, or bubbles of air.

Embolism conditions are named according to the area of the body affected. A *pulmonary embolism* blocks an artery supplying blood to the lungs, causing sudden chest pain and shortness of breath. A *cerebral embolism* impairs circulation to the brain, possibly causing a stroke. These conditions are emergencies that require immediate treatment. An *embolectomy* (surgery to remove the blockage) may be possible. Clot-dissolving drugs may also help.

## Stroke: Damage to blood vessels in the brain

To function normally, the brain requires a steady blood supply—about 15% of the heart's output at rest. Any impairment of blood flow to the brain rapidly damages brain cells. A **stroke** *(cerebrovascular accident)* represents damage to part of the brain caused by an interruption to its blood supply. In effect, it is the brain equivalent of a heart attack. Strokes are the most common cause of brain injury and a leading cause of death in Western nations.

Symptoms of strokes appear suddenly and vary according to the area of the brain affected. They may include weakness or paralysis on one side of the body, fainting, inability to speak or slurred speech, difficulty in understanding speech, impaired vision, nausea, or a sudden loss of coordination.

Immediate medical care is crucial. If the stroke resulted from an embolism, clot-dissolving drugs or an embolectomy can save a life. Eliminating the clot as quickly as possible (within minutes or hours) can limit the area of damage and reduce the severity of the permanent injury. If a ruptured artery is responsible, health providers may be able to surgically drain the excess blood.

Some people recover well from a stroke or suffer only minor effects, but others do not recover completely despite intensive physical therapy over many months. The reason for the poor recovery rate is that the body does not grow new nerve cells to replace damaged ones. However, rehabilitation with skilled health professionals can help many stroke patients improve their ability to function. Recovery involves retraining nerve pathways that already exist so they can take over the functions of damaged nerve cells.

**RECAP**

Cardiovascular disorders are the number one killer in the U.S. Most disorders are caused either by conditions that result in failure of the heart as a pump or by conditions in which damage to blood vessels restricts flow or ruptures vessels. ■

## 8.6 Reducing your risk of cardiovascular disease

Cardiovascular disorders are among the most preventable of chronic health conditions. Although some factors are beyond your control—such as sex, race, age, and genetic inheritance—your lifestyle choices can also affect your risk. Things you can do to reduce your risk include:

- Don't smoke, or if you do, quit. Smokers have more than twice the risk of heart attack that nonsmokers do, and smokers who suffer a heart attack are nearly four times as likely to die from it. Some researchers think secondhand smoke poses a risk as well.
- Watch your cholesterol levels. Cardiovascular risk rises with the blood cholesterol level. There is also evidence that high cholesterol increases risk even more when it is combined with other factors such as hypertension and tobacco smoke.
- Keep moving (Figure 8.20). Regular, moderate exercise lowers the risk of cardiovascular disease. This is not surprising because the heart is, after all, a muscle. Most physicians recommend exercising for at least 20 to 30 minutes, at least three times per week. Physical activity tends to lower blood pressure and cholesterol and makes it easier to maintain a healthy body weight. Always consult your physician before starting an exercise program.
- If your blood pressure is on the high side, seek treatment. As discussed earlier, untreated hypertension damages blood vessels and increases the workload on the heart.

In addition to these major risks, at least three other factors are associated with cardiovascular disease, although the precise link has not yet been determined. This is why doctors recommend the following:

- Maintain a healthy weight. It's not clear how obesity contributes to cardiovascular problems, but overweight people have a higher rate of heart disease and stroke even if they do not have other risk factors. One hypothesis is that increased weight strains the heart. It also has adverse effects on other risk factors such as blood cholesterol and hypertension.
- Keep diabetes under control. Diabetes mellitus is a disorder of blood sugar levels. Untreated diabetes damages blood vessels, but effective treatments reduce cardiovascular damage significantly. (For more on diabetes, see Chapter 13.)
- Avoid chronic stress. Again the mechanism is unclear, but there is an association between a person's perceived stress and behavior patterns and the development of cardiovascular disease. Stress may also affect other risk factors, for example, how much a smoker smokes or whether a person starts smoking.

**RECAP**

You can reduce your risk of developing cardiovascular disease by not smoking, exercising regularly, watching your weight and cholesterol, and avoiding prolonged stress. If you have diabetes and/or hypertension, try to keep these conditions under control. ■

**Figure 8.20 Moderate, regular exercise improves cardiovascular performance and lowers the risk of cardiovascular disease.**

# Merck Versus Users of Vioxx

In 1999 a new drug called Vioxx (rofecoxib) was approved by the FDA for the management of pain in adults and for relief of the symptoms of osteoarthritis. The drug belongs to a new, highly specific class of pain medications called COX-2 inhibitors that were supposed to have fewer side effects than older pain drugs such as Aleve (naproxen) and Advil (ibuprofen). By 2003 Vioxx was a financial winner for drug-maker Merck, with more than 41 million prescriptions filled and over $2.5 billion in sales annually.

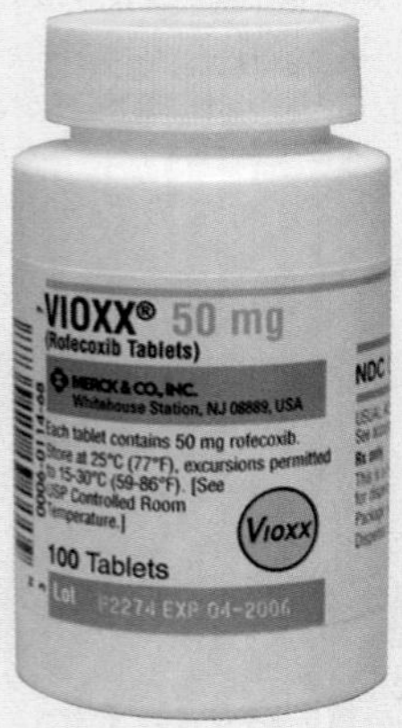


Less than a year later Merck had voluntarily pulled Vioxx off the market because of concerns about possible cardiovascular risks. Ultimately the company was forced to settle over 50,000 lawsuits filed by people who claimed that Vioxx contributed to heart attacks or strokes. To make matters worse, it appears that Merck knew (or should have known) about the cardiovascular risks associated with Vioxx up to four years before it stopped marketing the drug.

### What Did Merck Know, and When?

Did Merck continue to sell a risky product because it was so profitable? Consider the VIGOR controversy.

In 2000 the results of a large clinical trial of Vioxx known as VIGOR (*V*ioxx *G*astrointestinal *O*utcomes *R*esearch) were submitted to the FDA and published in *The New England Journal of Medicine* (NEJM). The goal of the study was to compare the effectiveness and the gastrointestinal side effects of Vioxx and naproxen. The study showed that patients taking Vioxx had fewer gastrointestinal problems (stomach ulcers and bleeding) than those taking naproxen, which, like many pain relievers, can irritate the stomach.

However, the VIGOR study also showed that the patients taking Vioxx had a higher rate of heart attacks than the patients taking naproxen. Merck countered that the VIGOR study actually showed that naproxen had a heart-protective effect compared to Vioxx, but that Vioxx alone was not a risk factor for heart disease. Merck continued its campaign for Vioxx, issuing a press release in May of 2001 entitled "Merck Confirms Cardiovascular Safety Profile of Vioxx."

Merck headquarters in New Jersey. Merck has faced more than 50,000 lawsuits from patients and families of patients who have taken Vioxx.

Meanwhile, the FDA became concerned by Merck's marketing approach. In a warning letter to Merck in September 2001, the director of the FDA's Drug Marketing Division told Merck that their advertisements were minimizing "potentially serious cardiovascular" findings. The FDA also required Merck to send letters to the medical community "to correct false or misleading impressions."

*Vioxx. The popular pain medication was pulled from the market in 2004.*

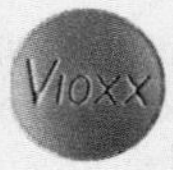


Three independent studies published in 2004 sealed Vioxx's fate. The final blow was a multicenter, randomized, placebo-controlled double-blind study of cancer patients receiving either Vioxx or a similar pain medication called Celebrex (celecoxib). The study had to be terminated early when investigators found that patients taking Vioxx were twice as likely to have a heart attack compared to those taking a placebo. In September 2004 Merck voluntarily took Vioxx off the market.

A few days later, NEJM editors discovered a computer diskette containing early drafts of the VIGOR article published in 2000. Time stamps in the software showed that a table entitled "CV events" (medical shorthand for cardiovascular problems) was deleted from the article two days before it was first submitted for publication.

## the facts...

- Merck's highly profitable pain reliever Vioxx was pulled off the market in 2004 when several studies confirmed that the drug increases the risk of heart attack.
- Critics charged that Merck may have known since 2000 that Vioxx posed an increased risk of heart disease but did nothing about it.
- Merck eventually faced over 50,000 lawsuits related to Vioxx. The company agreed to settle most of the lawsuits for $4.85 billion.
- The case raises the question of how to balance the responsibilities of large companies against the rights of individual patients.

To make matters worse, an internal Merck document surfaced that showed that two of the VIGOR researchers had known about three additional heart attacks but had not included this data in the final article submitted to the NEJM. The patients were all considered at low risk for cardiovascular problems.

### A Climate of Intimidation?

Some Merck critics claim that the company attempted to intimidate and discredit them. One is Dr. Eric Topol, chairman of the cardiovascular medicine department at the Cleveland Clinic, who in 2001 was preparing to publish an article on cardiovascular risks associated with Vioxx. When Dr. Topol contacted Merck to ask for clarification about their data, he received an unprecedented response: a personal visit from Dr. Alise Reicin, the Merck executive who had co-authored the VIGOR study. According to Topol, Reicin told him Merck didn't have access to all the data. After Topol's article was published, Merck sent letters to physicians around the U.S. stating that Dr. Topol's analysis of Vioxx's cardiovascular risks was flawed. In yet another incident, Dr. Gurkirpal Singh, an adjunct clinical professor of medicine at Stanford University, questioned what he saw as missing data related to cardiovascular risks. According to an article in the *Toronto Globe and Mail,* a Merck executive contacted Singh and threatened him with "serious consequences."

### A Multibillion-Dollar Legal Battle

In the aftermath of the withdrawal of Vioxx from the marketplace, over 50,000 lawsuits were filed by Vioxx patients. Many of them sought punitive damages for Merck's apparent concealment of the risks of Vioxx. At first, Merck vowed to fight them, one by one. But when plaintiffs won three of the first five cases and each of the winning plaintiffs was awarded more than $10 million, the company began to have doubts. Most troubling to the company was the suit by relatives of Leonel Garza, a 71-year-old Texas man with a history of heart disease who had taken Vioxx for only a couple of weeks. His family was asking for a total of $1 *billion* in combined damages, including punitive damages. Eventually the Garzas were awarded $32 million by a sympathetic jury, but the amount was reduced to $7.75 million, the maximum under Texas state law.

*Dr. Eric Topol. Merck attempted to discredit his report linking Vioxx to cardiovascular risks.*

Finally, Merck recognized the magnitude of the potential damage the company might be facing. Perhaps the company also finally concluded that it would be at a disadvantage against innocent victims of tragedy, even if the scientific evidence did not always point to Vioxx as the cause of the tragedy. Rightly or wrongly, juries tend to be more sympathetic to "the little guy" than to "the big bad company." So in November of 2007, Merck agreed to a $4.85 billion settlement to cover most of the lawsuits against it. The deal will be finalized only if 85% of the plaintiffs agree to the settlement by October 30 of 2008.

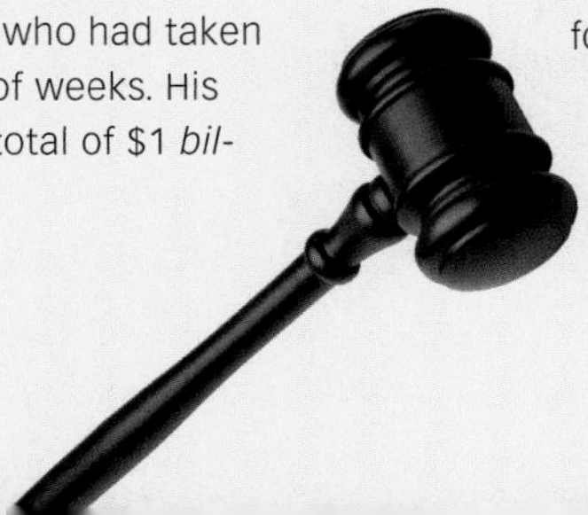

The unfortunate case of Vioxx and its final resolution raise some interesting questions for all of us. For example, what is the best way to punish a big company and not unfairly punish its many good employees? How should we fairly compensate those who have been truly wronged, without having a handful of plaintiffs get huge settlements beyond all reason? How do we assign monetary value to human pain and suffering?

The good news is that many states now recognize these questions as important issues, and some are reviewing and reforming their tort laws. (Tort is the law of civil wrongs, leading to the right to compensation.) Remember Mr. Garza, whose family had asked for $1 billion in damages? A couple of jury awards of that size could bankrupt Merck and put its nearly 60,000 employees out of work.

The human tragedy of Vioxx is nearing a close. Let us hope that Merck has learned a hard lesson. And let us hope that tort reform continues until we find the proper balance between patients' rights and outrageous legal settlements.

### Questions to consider

1 *What do you think would be the fairest way to hold a large drug company responsible for damages done by one of its drugs? Should the company's total financial liability be capped to protect the company's employees?*

2 *Do you think an individual award cap should be placed on personal injury/death lawsuits? If so, who is in the best position to decide the amount?*

# Chapter Summary

### Blood vessels transport blood *p. 161*

- The primary function of blood vessels is to bring blood into close proximity with all living cells.
- Thick-walled arteries transport blood to the capillaries at high pressure.
- Small arterioles and precapillary sphincters regulate the flow of blood into each capillary.
- Thin-walled capillaries are the only vessels that exchange fluids and solutes with the interstitial fluid.
- Distensible venules and veins store blood at low pressure and return it to the heart.

### The heart pumps blood through the vessels *p. 165*

- The heart is composed primarily of cardiac muscle. Structurally, it consists of four separate chambers and four one-way valves. Its primary function is to pump blood.
- The heart pumps blood simultaneously through two separate circuits: the pulmonary circuit, where blood picks up oxygen and gets rid of carbon dioxide, and the systemic circuit, which supplies the rest of the body's cells.
- The heart contracts and relaxes rhythmically. Contraction is called systole, and relaxation is called diastole.
- The coordinated contraction of the heart is produced by a system of specialized cardiac muscle cells that initiate and distribute electrical impulses throughout the heart muscle.
- An electrocardiogram, or ECG, records electrical activity of the heart from the surface of the body. An ECG can be used to diagnose certain cardiac arrhythmias and disorders.

### Blood exerts pressure against vessel walls *p. 173*

- The heart generates blood pressure, and the arteries store the blood under pressure during diastole.
- Systolic and diastolic arterial blood pressures can be measured with a sphygmomanometer.
- High blood pressure, called hypertension, is a major risk factor for cardiovascular disease.

### How the cardiovascular system is regulated *p. 175*

- The most important controlled variable in the cardiovascular system is arterial blood pressure.
- Arterial blood pressure is monitored by stretch receptors located in certain large arteries.
- Cardiac output and the diameters of the arterioles are regulated (controlled) to keep arterial blood pressure relatively constant.
- With pressure held constant, local blood flows can be adjusted according to the metabolic needs of the tissues and cells in that area of the body.

### Cardiovascular disorders: A major health issue *p. 178*

- The heart muscle is always working. Impairment of blood flow to the heart can lead to a sense of pain and tightness in the chest (angina pectoris) and/or permanent damage to heart tissue (myocardial infarction, or heart attack).
- Slowly developing, chronic failure of the heart as a pump can lead to excessive interstitial fluid, a condition known as congestive heart failure.
- An embolism is the sudden blockage of a blood vessel by any object.
- Strokes, also called cerebrovascular accidents, can be caused by either embolisms or rupture of blood vessels. The result is damage to a part of the brain when its blood supply is interrupted.

### Reducing your risk of cardiovascular disease *p. 181*

- Your chances of developing a cardiovascular disorder depend on certain risk factors. Some risk factors you cannot change, whereas others depend on the choices you make in life.

# Terms You Should Know

artery, *161*
atrium, *167*
atrioventricular (AV) valves, *168*
capillary, *163*
diastole, *169*
myocardium, *166*
precapillary sphincter, *163*
pulmonary circuit, *168*
semilunar valves, *168*
sinoatrial (SA) node, *171*
systemic circuit, *168*
systole, *169*
vein, *165*
ventricle, *167*

# Concept Review

1. Why is it so important that the heart always get a consistent and adequate blood supply?
2. Compare and contrast the structures and functions of the three types of blood vessels.
3. Describe how arterial blood pressure is measured by the body.
4. Describe the function of the heart valves.
5. Compare the functions of the pulmonary circuit and the systemic circuit.
6. Describe the cardiac cycle of relaxation and contraction, and explain what causes each of the two heart sounds during the cycle.
7. Describe the function of the SA and AV nodes as they control contraction of the heart.
8. Of what functional value is the distensibility of veins? In other words, why not have them just as thick and stiff as arteries?
9. Name the one hormone that has a stimulatory effect on the heart (increases heart rate).
10. List ways to reduce the risk of cardiovascular disease.

# Test Yourself

### Matching Exercise

_____ 1. Blood vessels that store most of the blood volume in the body
_____ 2. Weakening of an artery that may lead to rupture
_____ 3. Blood vessels that exchange materials with the interstitial fluid
_____ 4. Hormone that can stimulate the heart
_____ 5. The innermost layer of tissue of the heart; it lines the heart chambers
_____ 6. Period of relaxation of all four chambers of the heart

a. epinephrine
b. endocardium
c. aneurysm
d. veins
e. diastole
f. capillaries

**Label** the following components of the heart (7–16):

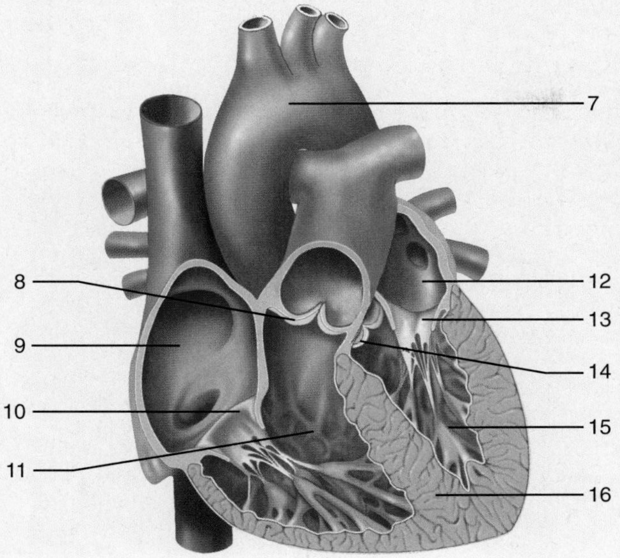


### Fill in the Blank

17. A blood clot that breaks off from a vein in the leg and lodges in a pulmonary artery is called a(n) ________________.
18. Contraction of vascular smooth muscle is called ________________.
19. The amount of blood that the heart pumps every minute is called the ________________.
20. Damage to or blockage of a blood vessel in the brain may lead to a(n) ________________.

## References and Additional Reading

Cabe, Delia K. Saving Hearts That Grow Old. *Scientific American,* June 2000. (An article that discusses some of the latest research findings on the causes of heart disease.)

Dickman, Steven. Mysteries of the Heart. *Discover,* July 1997, pp. 117–119. (A short article discussing the possibility that a virus contributes to coronary artery disease.)

Williams, Paul T. Relationship of Distance Run per Week to Coronary Heart Disease Risk Factors in 8283 Male Runners: The National Runners' Health Study. *Archives of Internal Medicine* 157:191–198, 1997. (A research publication with an alternative view on exercise and cardiovascular disease, written for professionals in the field.)

### Internet References

Find links to the following Web sites at the Human Biology Place.

**American Heart Association**
**www.americanheart.org**
A nonprofit organization offering information for the general public about risk factors, prevention, and treatment of cardiovascular disease and stroke.

**National Heart, Lung, and Blood Institute**
**www.nhlbi.nih.gov**
Gateway to the Web site of the NHLBI, a federal agency that offers information on many cardiovascular health conditions.

**Texas Heart Institute**
**www.texasheart.org**
An online Heart Information Center with patient-friendly descriptions of medical tests, procedures, and other heart-health topics.

## Apply **What You Know**

1. During exercise, arterial blood pressure changes very little. However, cardiac output may double and blood flow to exercising muscle may go up 10-fold, while at the same time the blood flow to kidneys may decline by nearly 50%. Explain possible mechanisms that might account for these very different changes.
2. When a coronary artery bypass graft (CABG) is performed, the vessels used for the bypass grafts are usually veins taken from the patient's legs. Over time the grafted veins take on many of the characteristics of arteries; that is, they become thicker and stiffer. What might this suggest about the possible cause(s) of the structural differences between arteries and veins? Hypothesize what might happen if you took a section of artery and implanted it into the venous circulation.
3. Soldiers have to stand in formation at full attention for long periods of time. Sometimes this can cause otherwise very fit and healthy young people to pass out during long inspections. What would cause this?
4. Workers who spend hours per day standing can develop circulation problems in their legs. A recommended solution is to wear graduated compression stockings. These stockings are tighter around the ankles and less tight higher up on the legs. Why does standing for long periods sometimes lead to circulatory problems, and how can wearing something tight on the legs help prevent this?
5. Inflammation of the pericardium can lead to a condition called pericardial effusion, in which fluids collect in the space surrounding the heart. What effect would this have on the functioning of the heart? How might the condition be treated?
6. Ventricular fibrillation is a potentially fatal condition where the cells of the heart are no longer coordinated in their contractions. Why is it important that contraction of the heart muscle occurs nearly all at once?
7. VSD or ventricular septal defect is a condition that accounts for half of all congenital cardiovascular anomalies. In this condition a hole exists in the septum, the muscular wall between the ventricles, which allows blood from the right and left side of the heart to mix. What sort of problems might this condition cause?
8. Last night you and your roommate were sound asleep when the phone rang. Your roommate, startled awake, jumped from her bed and rushed for the phone across the room. Before she reached the phone she suddenly felt dizzy and had to sit down to avoid fainting. What happened?

*Answers can be found on the Human Biology Place.*

# 9 The Immune System and Mechanisms of Defense

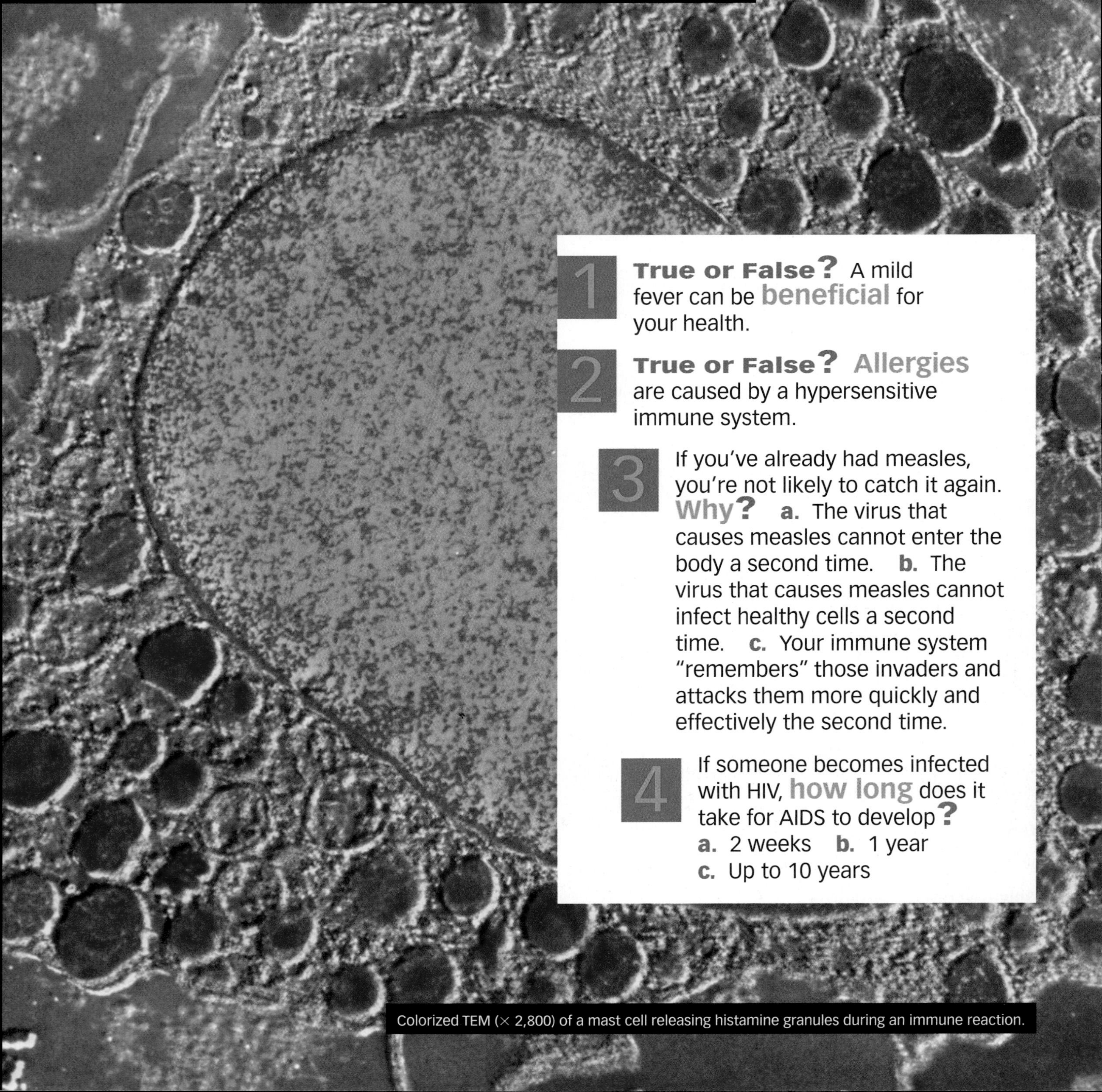

Colorized TEM (× 2,800) of a mast cell releasing histamine granules during an immune reaction.

1 **True or False?** A mild fever can be **beneficial** for your health.

2 **True or False?** **Allergies** are caused by a hypersensitive immune system.

3 If you've already had measles, you're not likely to catch it again. **Why?** **a.** The virus that causes measles cannot enter the body a second time. **b.** The virus that causes measles cannot infect healthy cells a second time. **c.** Your immune system "remembers" those invaders and attacks them more quickly and effectively the second time.

4 If someone becomes infected with HIV, **how long** does it take for AIDS to develop**?**
**a.** 2 weeks **b.** 1 year
**c.** Up to 10 years

**The world is swarming with living organisms** (bacteria) and even some nonliving entities (viruses and prions) too small to be seen with the naked eye. They're found on doorknobs, the money we handle, and our clothes. They're in the food we eat and the air we breathe. Most are harmless—indeed, some are highly beneficial. The ones that cause disease are called **pathogens,** from the Greek *pathos*, disease, plus *gennan*, to produce.

Pathogens come from outside the body. As a group they account for a large fraction of all human disease and suffering. But there are other challenges to our health that come from within. Mutations (alterations to a cell's DNA) may cause some of our own cells to become abnormal and may even lead to cancer. Fortunately, our bodies can recognize cells that become abnormal and dispatch most of them before they ever have the chance to develop further.

What ways do we have to protect ourselves? Our body's immune system and other general defense mechanisms include:

- *Barriers to entry or ways of expelling or neutralizing pathogens before they can do harm.* These include skin, stomach acid, tears, and such actions as vomiting and defecation.
- *Nonspecific defense mechanisms.* Nonspecific defenses help the body respond to generalized tissue damage and many of the more common or obvious pathogens, including most bacteria and some viruses.
- *Specific defense mechanisms.* These enable the body to recognize and kill specific bacteria and other foreign cells and to neutralize viruses. Our specific defense mechanisms employ sophisticated weaponry indeed. The specific defense mechanisms are also the basis of immunity from future disease.

All three mechanisms are operating night and day to protect us. Crucial to the nonspecific and specific defense mechanisms is the **immune system,** a complex group of cells, proteins, and structures of the lymphatic and circulatory systems. However, even the immune system is not perfect; it can only kill or neutralize pathogens or abnormal cells that it can recognize. This has implications for how the human body deals with certain pathogens such as prions.

What is the immune system on alert for? We start by looking at some of the kinds of pathogens that can invade our bodies.

## 9.1 Pathogens cause disease

Pathogens that live in or on our bodies include bacteria, viruses, fungi, a few protozoa, and possibly prions. Larger parasites, including various worms, can also be pathogens, although they are relatively rare in industrialized countries. Because bacteria and viruses are by far the most numerous and problematic pathogens in Western nations, we focus on them as we describe how we protect and defend ourselves. We'll also discuss prions as a newly discovered class of pathogens.

### Bacteria: Single-celled living organisms

As you learned in Chapter 3, **bacteria** (singular: *bacterium*), are single-celled organisms that do not have a nucleus or membrane-bound organelles. All the DNA in most bacteria is contained in just one chromosome, which usually forms a continuous loop that is anchored to the plasma membrane. Their ribosomes are smaller than ours, and they float freely in the cytoplasm. The outer surface of bacteria is a rigid cell wall that surrounds the plasma membrane and gives bacteria their distinctive shapes, which include spheres, rods, and spirals (Figure 9.1).

Judging by their variety and numbers, bacteria are among the most successful organisms on Earth. Although they are smaller than the typical human cell, their small size is actually an advantage. Like all living organisms, bacteria need energy and raw materials to maintain life and to grow and divide. Their small size means that they have a high surface-to-volume ratio, a decided advantage when it comes to getting raw materials and getting rid of wastes by diffusion.

Like our own cells, bacteria use ATP as a direct energy source and amino acids for making proteins. They store energy as carbohydrates and fats. Where do they obtain those raw materials? Anywhere they can. Some bacteria break down raw sewage and cause the decomposition of dead animals and plants, thereby playing an essential role in the recycling of energy and raw materials. Others obtain

### Answers to Intro Questions

**1 True.** Although a high fever is dangerous, a modest fever of 1–2°F may actually help you recover faster from an illness.

**2 True.** Ordinarily the immune system does a superb job of protecting us, but sometimes it overreacts. In this chapter we'll learn more about the immune response.

**3 c.** The immune system's ability to recognize old enemies and mount a swift attack prevents an infection from developing after a second exposure. In fact, your body's second response is so swift that usually you're not even aware of having been infected again.

**4 c.** The average period of time from initial HIV infection to the development of full-blown AIDS is 10 years. During this time, even if HIV-infected people have no symptoms, they can still infect others.

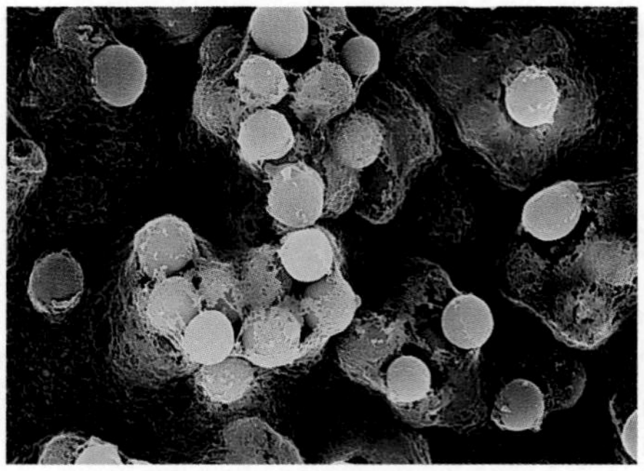

a) SEM (× 2,000) of *Streptococcus*, a spherical bacterium that causes sore throats.

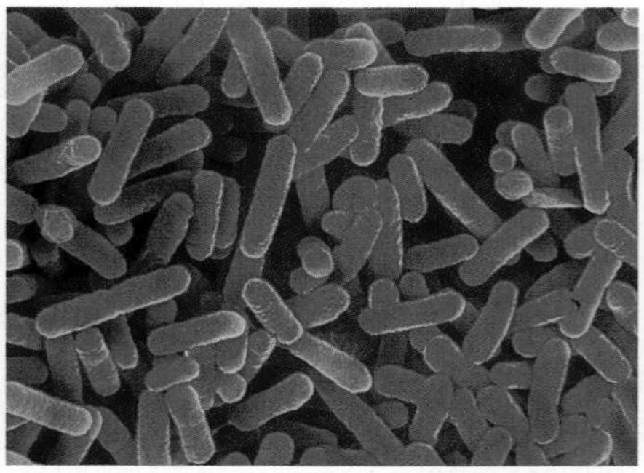

b) SEM (× 2,000) of *Legionella pneumophila*, the rod-shaped bacterium responsible for Legionnaire's disease.

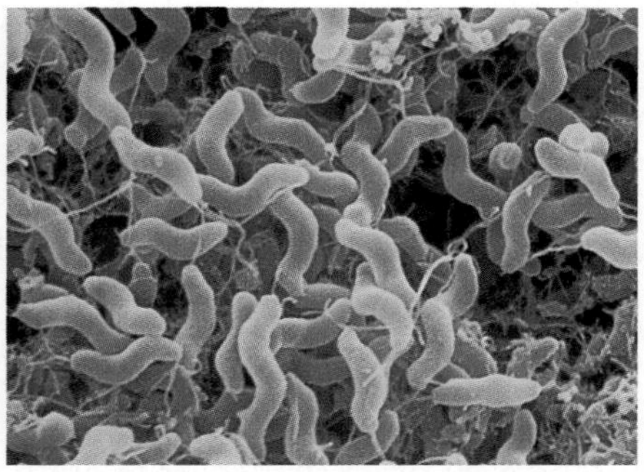

c) SEM (×12,000) of *Campylobacter jejuni*, a spiral-shaped bacterium that causes food poisoning.

**Figure 9.1 Electron micrographs of the three common shapes of bacteria.**

nutrients from the soil and air. Humans have learned to harness bacteria to produce commercial products, including antibiotic drugs, hormones, vaccines, and foods ranging from sauerkraut to soy sauce. Life as we know it would not be possible without these little organisms. Some bacteria even live within our digestive tract, drawing energy from the food we eat in exchange for manufacturing vitamins or controlling the populations of other, more harmful bacteria.

A few bacteria are pathogens. Pathogens rely on living human cells for their energy supply, and in the process they damage or kill the cells. They cause pneumonia, tonsillitis, tuberculosis, botulism, toxic shock syndrome, syphilis, Lyme disease, and many other diseases. Although we concentrate on pathogens in this chapter, do keep in mind that most bacteria are harmless, and many are even beneficial.

Bacterial infections are generally treated with **antibiotics**—chemotherapeutic agents that inhibit or abolish the growth of bacteria, fungi, and protozoa.

**RECAP**

Bacteria are single-celled organisms. Like all cells, they draw their energy and raw materials from their environment. Pathogenic bacteria get the materials they need from living cells, damaging or killing the cells in the process. ■

## Viruses: Tiny infectious agents

**Viruses** are extremely small infectious agents, perhaps one-hundredth the size of a bacterium and one-thousandth the size of a typical human cell (Figure 9.2). Structurally a virus is very simple, consisting solely of a small piece of genetic material (either RNA or DNA) surrounded by a protein coat. They have no organelles of their own, so they don't grow and they can't reproduce on their own.

Are viruses alive? Biologists are divided on this question. Most would say that they are not because they cannot reproduce on their own. Viruses have no observable activity associated with life when they are not in contact with another living cell. However, when they enter a living cell, they take it over and use the cell's organelles to make more viruses.

Viruses have several ways of gaining entry into living cells. Most viruses that infect human cells are taken into the cell cytoplasm by endocytosis; once inside the cell the protein coats are dissolved and the viral genetic material is released for incorporation into the cell's genetic material. Other viruses merge their outer coat with the cell membrane and release their genetic contents into the cell's cytoplasm. Still other viruses attach to the outer surface of the cell membrane and inject just their genetic material into the cell, much as a needle and syringe inject drugs into the body. Regardless of the method of entry, the presence of the viral genetic material causes the cell to begin producing thousands of copies of the virus instead of carrying out its own metabolic activities. Sometimes the newly formed viruses are released by a type of budding from the cell membrane while the cell is still alive. In other cases the cell becomes so packed with viruses that it dies and bursts, releasing a huge number of viruses all at once.

Diseases caused by viruses range from serious—aids, hepatitis, encephalitis, rabies—to annoying—colds, warts, chicken pox. Viral infections can be minor for some people but serious for others. An otherwise healthy person may be ill for only a few days with a viral infection, whereas someone who is very young, very old, or in poor health may die.

Antibiotics generally don't work against viral infections. The best ways to cure a viral infection are either to prevent the viruses from entering living cells, or to stop the host cell from producing more viruses once it's infected.

## Prions: Infectious proteins

In 1986, scientists identified a disease in British cattle that destroyed nerve cells in the animals' brain and spinal cord. They named the disorder bovine spongiform encephalopathy (BSE), because it left the cows' brains riddled with holes, like a sponge. The press nicknamed BSE "mad cow disease," since

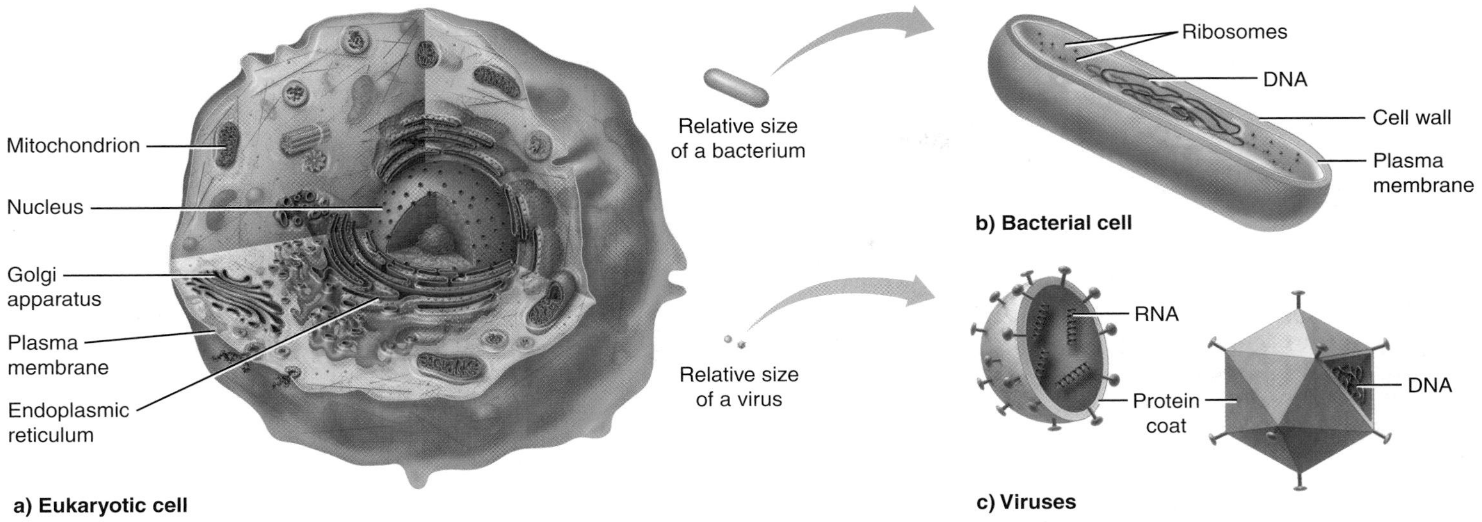


**Figure 9.2 Size and structural differences between a eukaryotic cell, a bacterium (prokaryotic cell), and viruses. (a)** Eukaryotic cells have a membrane-bound nucleus and well-defined membrane-bound organelles. **(b)** Bacteria have a single strand of DNA and free-floating small ribosomes within the cytoplasm. Their plasma membrane is surrounded by a rigid cell wall. **(c)** Viruses consist of a protein coat surrounding either RNA or DNA.

the infected animals staggered, jerked, trembled, and exhibited other bizarre behaviors.

Between 1994 and 1996 twelve Britons, ages 19 to 39, developed signs of Creutzfeldt-Jakob disease (CJD), a fatal neurological disorder with symptoms similar to those of the so-called mad cows. However, typical CJD is rare and occurs later in life (the average age of patients is 65 years), so this sudden outbreak in a younger age group was unprecedented. Also, people with typical CJD usually live for only four to five months after symptoms appear, but these patients lived for approximately 14 months. Researchers named the new illness *variant Creutzfeldt-Jakob disease* (vCJD).

Alarmingly, researchers found that all of the vCJD patients had eaten beef from animals suspected of having mad cow disease. Recent research confirms that vCJD is most likely acquired by consuming BSE-infected meat. The cows originally acquired BSE by eating contaminated feed made from the bones and other waste parts of BSE-infected cattle, sheep, and goats.

There is strong evidence that infectious proteins called **prions** are responsible for both BSE and vCJD. A prion is a misfolded form of a normal brain cell protein. Once prions infect an animal and enter the animal's brain cells, they convert the normal form of a certain brain cell protein to new prions by causing the normal proteins to misfold. (As noted in Chapter 2, protein misfolding can render a protein useless, with devastating effects.) The prions accumulate in brain cells until the cells malfunction or stop working entirely. Eventually the infected cells die and burst, releasing prions to infect other brain cells. The gradual buildup of prions would account for the debilitating neurological symptoms and progressive degeneration seen in both vCJD (in humans) and BSE (in cattle). Some scientists believe that other diseases in which brain cells are destroyed, such as Alzheimer's disease and Parkinson's disease, may also be linked to prions.

Prions are resistant to cooking, freezing, and even drying. There is no known cure for prion infection. Since infection occurs when humans (or cattle) eat prion-infected cattle tissues, the best way to prevent vCJD in humans is to limit the spread of BSE in cattle. Global cooperation is making this possible. In 1994 the European Union banned the use of mammalian meat and bone meal products as cattle feed. Other nations, including the U.S., soon followed suit. Consequently the number of cases of BSE in Great Britain fell from 37,000 in 1992 to only 225 in 2005.

Fortunately, the prion responsible for BSE in cattle is not easily transmitted to humans. From 1986 through 2005 there were 184,000 cases of BSE in cattle in Great Britain but only 156 cases of vCJD in humans. In the U.S. the only known case of vCJD occurred in a Florida patient who was born and raised in the United Kingdom.

**RECAP**

A virus consists of a single strand of DNA or RNA surrounded by protein. Viruses use their DNA or RNA to force a living cell to make more copies of the virus. Prions are infectious proteins that cause normal proteins to misfold. ■

## Transmissibility, mode of transmission, and virulence determine health risk

Some pathogens are clearly more risky to human health than others. Factors that determine the danger of a particular pathogen include transmissibility (how easily it is passed from one person to another), mode of transmission (how it is transmitted), and virulence (how damaging the resulting disease is).

For instance, the viruses that cause the common cold are easily transmitted from hands to mucous membranes, as well as in the fluid particles spread by a sneeze. However, these viruses tend not to be very virulent. The HIV virus that causes AIDS, by contrast, is only moderately transmissible. Its mode of transmission is limited to exchange of body fluids (blood, semen, breast milk, or vaginal secretions). However, the HIV virus is tremendously virulent, and this is what makes it so dangerous.

Imagine what would happen if a disease as transmissible as the flu and as virulent as AIDS were to arise in the human population. In fact, there have been such diseases, and they have caused deadly epidemics. Between 1348 and 1350 **bubonic plague,** a bacterial infection, killed an estimated 25–40% of the European population. A 1918 outbreak of influenza killed more than 20 million people worldwide.

Pathogens continue to challenge human defenses. A prime example is the Ebola virus that arose in Africa in 1976 and still presents a threat today. It is one of the most virulent pathogens known, killing more than 80% of an exposed population in less than two weeks.

## 9.2 The lymphatic system defends the body

As noted in Chapter 8, the **lymphatic system** is closely associated with the cardiovascular system. The lymphatic system performs three important functions:

- It helps maintain the volume of blood in the cardiovascular system.
- It transports fats and fat-soluble vitamins absorbed from the digestive system to the cardiovascular system.
- It defends the body against infection.

In Chapter 8 we briefly described how the lymphatic system helps to maintain blood volume and interstitial fluid volume by returning excess fluid that has been filtered out of the capillaries back to the cardiovascular system. We discuss its role in transporting fats and vitamins when we describe the digestive system, in Chapter 14. In this chapter we turn to the third function: the role of the lymphatic system in protecting us from disease. Most of the cells of the immune system are housed in the lymphatic system, although they can also circulate in blood and enter the interstitial fluid. Here we describe the structural components of the system; in later sections we discuss how specific immune system cells carry out their function.

The basic components of the lymphatic system are a network of lymph vessels throughout the body, the lymph nodes, the thymus gland, the tonsils and adenoids, and the spleen (Figure 9.3).

### Lymphatic vessels transport lymph

The lymphatic system begins as a network of small, blind-ended *lymphatic capillaries* in the vicinity of the cells and blood capillaries. Lymph capillaries have wide spaces between overlapping cells. Their structure allows them to take up substances (including bacteria) that are too large to enter a blood capillary.

The fluid in the lymphatic capillaries is *lymph*, a milky body fluid that contains white blood cells, proteins, fats, and the occasional bacterium and virus. Lymphatic capillaries merge to form the *lymphatic vessels*. Located at intervals along the lymphatic vessels are small organs called **lymph nodes,** described below. Like veins, lymphatic vessels have walls consisting of three thin layers, and they contain one-way valves to prevent backflow of lymph. Also like veins, lymphatic vessels are aided by skeletal muscle contractions and pressure changes in the chest during respiration that help keep the lymph flowing. The lymphatic vessels merge to form larger and larger vessels, eventually creating two major lymphatic ducts: the *right lymphatic duct* and the *thoracic duct*. The two lymph ducts join the subclavian veins near the shoulders, thereby returning the lymph to the cardiovascular system.

### Lymph nodes cleanse the lymph

Lymph nodes remove microorganisms, cellular debris, and abnormal cells from the lymph before returning it to the cardiovascular system. There are hundreds of lymph nodes, clustered in the areas of the digestive tract, neck, armpits, and groin (Figure 9.4). They vary in diameter from about 1 millimeter to 2.5 centimeters. Each node is enclosed in a dense capsule of connective tissue pierced by lymphatic vessels. Inside each node are connective tissue and two types of white blood cells (macrophages and lymphocytes, discussed in greater detail in later sections).

The lymphatic vessels carry lymph into and out of each node. Valves within these vessels ensure that lymph flows only in one direction. As the fluid flows through a node, the macrophages destroy foreign cells by phagocytosis, and the lymphocytes activate other defense mechanisms. The cleansed lymph fluid flows out of the node and continues on its path to the veins.

**RECAP**

The lymphatic system helps protect us from disease. As lymph flows through the lymph nodes, macrophages and lymphocytes within the nodes identify microorganisms and remove them. ■

### The spleen cleanses blood

The largest lymphatic organ, the **spleen,** is a soft, fist-sized mass located in the upper-left abdominal cavity. The spleen is covered with a dense capsule of connective tissue interspersed with smooth muscle cells. Inside the organ are two types of tissue, called red pulp and white pulp.

The spleen has two main functions: it controls the quality of circulating red blood cells by removing the old and damaged ones, and it helps fight infection. The *red pulp* contains macrophages that scavenge and break down microorganisms

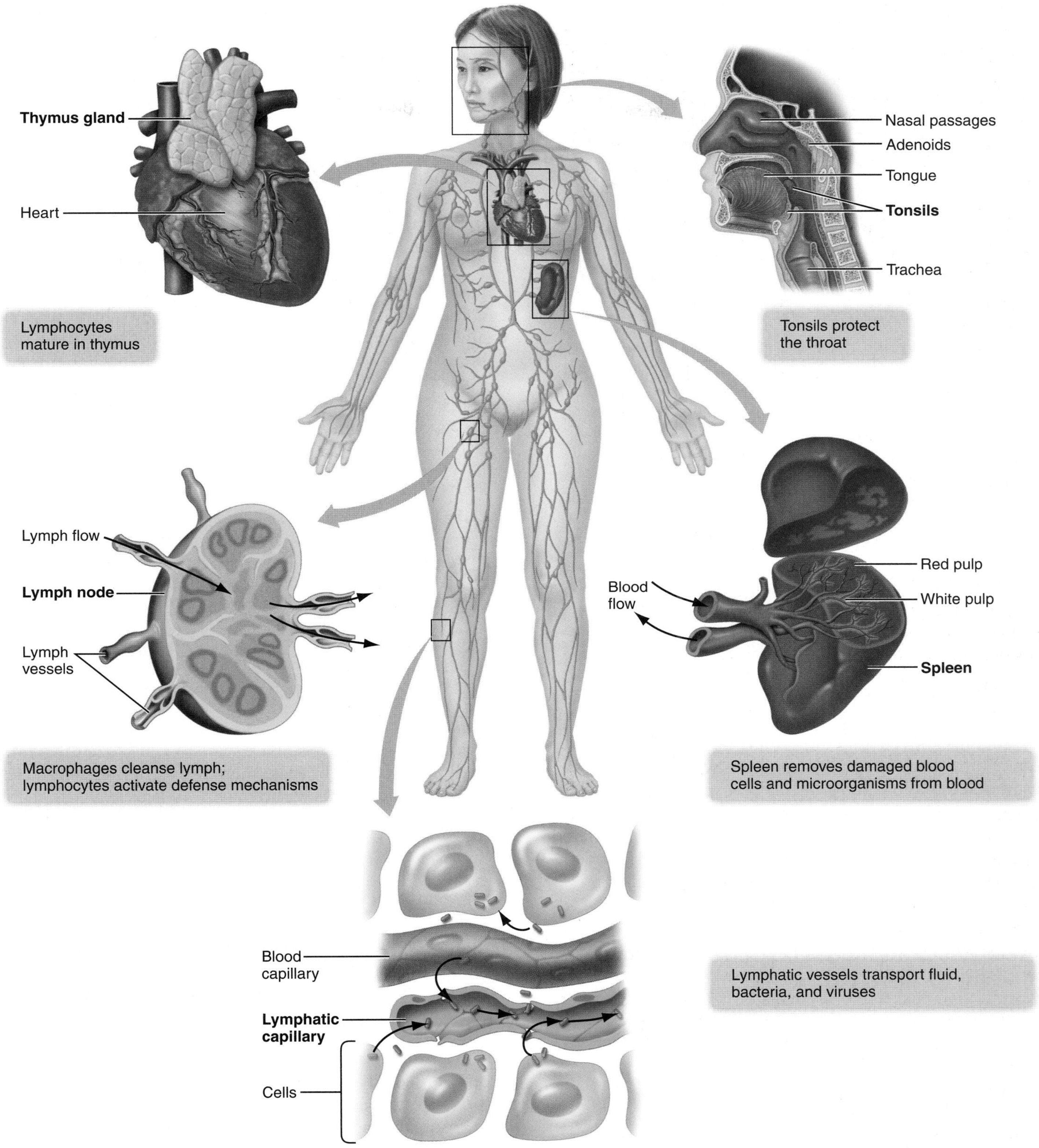


**Figure 9.3** **The lymphatic system.** The lymphatic system consists of a network of lymphatic vessels throughout the body, lymph nodes, the thymus gland, tonsils and adenoids, and the spleen.

**Figure 9.4 Lymph node.** Color scanning electron micrograph (× 1,000) of a section through a lymph node, showing macrophages (pink) and lymphocytes (yellow) lying in wait to attack and destroy foreign and damaged cells. A few red blood cells (red) are also present.

as well as old and damaged red blood cells and platelets. The cleansed blood is then stored in the red pulp. Your body can call on this reserve for extra blood in case of blood loss or a fall in blood pressure, or whenever you need extra oxygen-carrying capacity. The *white pulp* contains primarily lymphocytes. Notice that the main distinction between the spleen and lymph nodes is *which* fluid they cleanse—the spleen cleanses the blood, and the lymph nodes cleanse lymph. Together, they keep the circulating body fluids relatively free of damaged cells and microorganisms.

A number of diseases, such as tuberculosis and leukemia, cause the spleen to enlarge. The swollen spleen can sometimes be felt as a lump in the upper-left abdomen. A strong blow to the abdomen can rupture the spleen, causing severe internal bleeding. In this case surgical removal of the spleen may be necessary to forestall a fatal hemorrhage. We can live without a spleen because its functions are shared by the lymph glands, liver, and red bone marrow. However, people who have had their spleen removed surgically are often a little more vulnerable to infections.

### Thymus gland hormones cause T lymphocytes to mature

The **thymus gland** is located in the lower neck, behind the sternum and just above the heart. Encased in connective tissue, the gland contains lymphocytes and epithelial cells. The thymus gland secretes two hormones, thymosin and thymopoietin, that cause certain lymphocytes called *T lymphocytes* (T cells) to mature and take an active role in specific defenses.

The size and activity level of the thymus gland varies with age. It is largest and most active during childhood. During adolescence it stops growing and then slowly starts to shrink. By that time our defense mechanisms are typically well established. In old age the thymus gland may disappear entirely, to be replaced by fibrous and fatty tissue.

### Tonsils protect the throat

The *tonsils* are masses of lymphatic tissue near the entrance to the throat. Lymphocytes in the tonsils gather and filter out many of the microorganisms that enter the throat in food or air.

We actually have several tonsils, and some are not readily visible. The familiar tonsils at the back of the throat are the largest and most often infected. When they become infected, the resulting inflammation is called *tonsillitis.* If the infection becomes serious, the tissues can be surgically removed.

Lymphatic tissue called the *adenoids* lie at the back of the nasal passages. The adenoids tend to enlarge during early childhood, but in most people they start to shrink after age 5 and usually disappear by puberty. In some cases they continue to enlarge and obstruct airflow from nose to throat. This can cause mouth breathing, a nasal voice, and snoring. Like the tonsils, the adenoids can be surgically removed if they grow large enough to cause problems.

**RECAP**

The spleen removes damaged red blood cells and foreign cells from blood. The thymus gland secretes hormones that help T lymphocytes mature. Cells in the tonsils gather and remove microorganisms that enter the throat. ■

## 9.3 Keeping pathogens out: The first line of defense

Our bodies have several ways to prevent pathogens from entering the body. We also have ways to neutralize them, inhibit their growth, or expel them when they do get in. Here are some of the ways we do that:

### Skin: An effective deterrent

The most important barrier against entry of any pathogen into our bodies is the skin. Skin has four key attributes that make it such an effective barrier: (1) its structure, (2) the fact that it is constantly being replaced, (3) its acidic pH, and (4) the production of an antibiotic by sweat glands.

As described in Chapter 4, the outermost layers of the skin's epidermis consist of dead, dried-out epithelial cells. These cells contain a fibrous protein called keratin, which is also a primary component of fingernails and hair. Once the cells have died and the water has evaporated, the keratin forms a dry, tough, somewhat elastic barrier to the entry of microorganisms. A second key feature of skin is that it is continually being renewed throughout life. Dead cells shed from the surface are replaced by new cells at the base of the epidermis. Any pathogens deposited on the surface are shed along with the dead cells. Third, healthy skin has a pH of about 5 to 6, primarily because of the sweat produced by sweat glands. This relatively low (acidic) pH makes skin a hostile environment for many microorganisms. Finally, sweat glands produce a natural antibiotic peptide called *dermicidin* that can kill a range of harmful bacteria.

For further proof of skin's effectiveness as a barrier to infection, look at what happens when you get a tiny cut or scratch in your skin. If the damage reaches the moist layers of living cells underneath the skin, you may see signs of infection in the area within a few days. One of the most critical problems in treating patients with extensive burns is the infections that often result from the loss of the barrier function of skin.

### Impeding pathogen entry in areas not covered by skin

Most successful pathogens enter the body at places where we do not have skin. They enter through the mucous membranes that line the digestive, urinary, respiratory, and reproductive tracts, where they can take advantage of moist surfaces in direct contact with living cells. They enter around the eyes or in the ears. However, even these areas have ways to impede pathogen entry. Defenses include tears, saliva, earwax, digestive and vaginal acids, and mucus, which impede entry; the ability to remove pathogens by vomiting, urination, and defecation; and even competition created by nonpathogenic bacteria that normally live in (and on) the body.

**Tears, saliva, and earwax** Although we may not think of tears as a defense mechanism, they perform a valuable service by lubricating the eyes and washing away particles. Tears and saliva both contain **lysozyme,** an enzyme that kills many bacteria. In addition, saliva lubricates the delicate tissues inside the mouth so that they do not dry out and crack. It also rinses microorganisms safely from the mouth into the stomach. Earwax traps small particles and microorganisms.

**Mucus** Mucus is a thick, gel-like material secreted by cells at various surfaces of the body, including the lining of the digestive tract and the branching airways of the respiratory system. Microorganisms that come into contact with the sticky mucus become mired and cannot gain access to the cells beneath. In addition, the cells of the airways have tiny hairlike projections, called cilia, that beat constantly in a wavelike motion to sweep mucus upward into the throat. There we get rid of the mucus by coughing or swallowing it. Sometimes we remove mucus and microorganisms by sneezing, which is also one of the primary ways we pass microorganisms to other people (Figure 9.5).

**Digestive and vaginal acids** Undiluted digestive acid is strong enough to kill nearly all pathogens that enter the digestive tract on an empty stomach. Only one strain of bacteria, *Helicobacter pylori,* has actually evolved to thrive in the highly acidic environment of the stomach. *H. pylori* is now known to contribute to many cases of stomach ulcers (see Chapter 14).

**Figure 9.5 Sneezing removes mucus and microorganisms from the body.** Sneezing also promotes the transmission of certain respiratory infections from person to person.

Vaginal secretions are slightly acidic, too, though not nearly as acidic as stomach secretions.

**Vomiting, urination, and defecation** Vomiting, though unpleasant, is certainly an effective way of ridding the body of toxic or infected stomach contents.

Generally speaking, the urinary system does not have a resident population of bacteria. Urine is usually slightly acidic, and in addition the constant flushing action of urination tends to keep bacterial populations low.

Urine pH can vary from fairly acidic to slightly basic, depending on diet. Some physicians advise patients with bladder or urethral infections to drink cranberry juice, which is acidic. The increased acidity of the urine inhibits bacterial growth, and the increased urine volume flushes the bacteria out.

The movement of feces and the act of defecation also help remove microorganisms from the digestive tract. When we become ill, the muscles in the intestinal wall may start to contract more vigorously, and the intestine may secrete additional fluid into the feces. The result is *diarrhea*—increased fluidity, frequency, or volume of bowel movements. Unpleasant though diarrhea may be, mild cases serve a useful function by speeding the removal of pathogens.

**Resident bacteria** Certain strains of beneficial bacteria normally live in the mucous membranes lining the vagina and the digestive tract. They help control population levels of more harmful organisms by competing successfully against them for food. They may also make the body less vulnerable to pathogens. For example, *Lactobacillus* bacteria in the vagina produce a substance that lowers vaginal pH to levels that many fungi and bacteria cannot tolerate.

One might ask how any beneficial bacteria ever get to the small and large intestine if they have to pass through the stomach first. The answer is that following a meal the stomach contents are not so acidic because food both dilutes and buffers the stomach acid, so some bacteria pass through the stomach with the food we eat.

**RECAP**

Various mechanisms create an inhospitable environment for pathogenic microorganisms. Skin is a dry outer barrier. Tears, saliva, earwax, and mucus trap them or wash them away. Acidic conditions kill them or inhibit their growth; urination, defecation, and vomiting forcibly expel them; and resident bacteria compete with pathogens for food. ■

## 9.4 Nonspecific defenses: The second line of defense

If pathogens manage to breach our physical and chemical barriers and start to kill or damage cells, we have a problem of a different sort. Now the body must actively seek out the pathogens and get rid of them. It must also clean up the injured area and repair the damage.

Our second line of defense includes a varied group of defense mechanisms. We refer to them as *nonspecific* because they do not target specific pathogens. Instead, they appear in response to all types of health challenges without discriminating between them. Table 9.1 summarizes nonspecific defenses, which include phagocytes, natural killer cells, the inflammatory response, the complement system, interferons, and fever.

### Phagocytes engulf foreign cells

As noted in Chapter 7, *phagocytes* are white blood cells that destroy foreign cells through the process of **phagocytosis.** As illustrated in Figure 9.6, a phagocyte first captures a bacterium with its cytoplasmic extensions. Then it draws the bacterium in, eventually engulfing it (endocytosis) and enclosing it in a membrane-bound vesicle. Inside the cell, the vesicle containing the bacterium fuses with lysosomes, and the powerful enzymes in the lysosomes dissolve the bacterial membranes. Once digestion is complete the phagocyte jettisons the bacterial wastes by exocytosis.

Recall from Chapter 7 that some white blood cells can filter through the walls of blood vessels into tissue spaces, attracted by substances released by injured cells at the site of infection. Other phagocytes remain in connective tissues of the lymph nodes, spleen, liver, lungs, and brain.

**Neutrophils** are the first white blood cells to respond to infection. They digest and destroy bacteria and some fungi in the blood and tissue fluids. Other white blood cells known as monocytes leave the vascular system, enter the tissue fluids, and develop into **macrophages** (from the Greek for "large eater") that can engulf and digest large numbers of foreign cells, especially viruses and bacterial parasites. Macrophages serve a cleanup function by scavenging old blood cells, dead tissue fragments, and cellular debris. They also release chemicals that stimulate the production of more white blood cells. Technically, macrophages are no longer white blood cells because they are no longer in blood.

When invaders are too big to be engulfed and digested by phagocytosis, other white blood cells called **eosinophils** take action. Eosinophils cluster around large parasites such as flukes and pinworms and bombard them with digestive enzymes. Eosinophils also engulf and digest certain foreign proteins.

When the body is actively fighting an infection, the mortality rate of white blood cells rises dramatically. Tissue fluid, dead phagocytes and microorganisms, and cellular debris accumulate at the infection site, producing a characteristic discharge called *pus.* If pus becomes trapped and cannot drain, the body may wall it off with connective tissue. The result is an *abscess.* Common places for abscesses to form include the breast (mastitis), the gums (dental abscesses), and more rarely the liver or brain. Many abscesses subside after being drained, while others require antibiotic drugs or surgical removal.

**RECAP**

Nonspecific defense mechanisms involve a general attack against all foreign and damaged cells. Neutrophils and macrophages engulf and digest bacteria and damaged cells. Eosinophils bombard larger organisms (too large to be engulfed) with digestive enzymes. ■

### Inflammation: Redness, warmth, swelling, and pain

Any type of tissue injury—whether infection, burns, irritating chemicals, or physical trauma—triggers a series of related events collectively called the inflammatory response, or **inflammation.** Inflammation has four outward

**Table 9.1 The second line of defense: Nonspecific defense**

| Defense | Functions |
|---|---|
| Phagocytes | Neutrophils and macrophages engulf and digest foreign cells. Eosinophils bombard large parasites with digestive enzymes and phagocytize foreign proteins. |
| Natural killer cells | Release chemicals that disintegrate cell membranes of tumor cells and virus-infected cells. |
| Inflammatory response | Four components: redness, warmth, swelling, and pain. Attracts phagocytes and promotes tissue healing. |
| Complement system | A group of proteins that assists other defense mechanisms. Enhances inflammation and phagocytosis, kills pathogens. |
| Interferons | Stimulate the production of proteins that interfere with viral reproduction. |
| Fever | Modest fever makes internal environment less hospitable to pathogens, fosters ability to fight infections. |

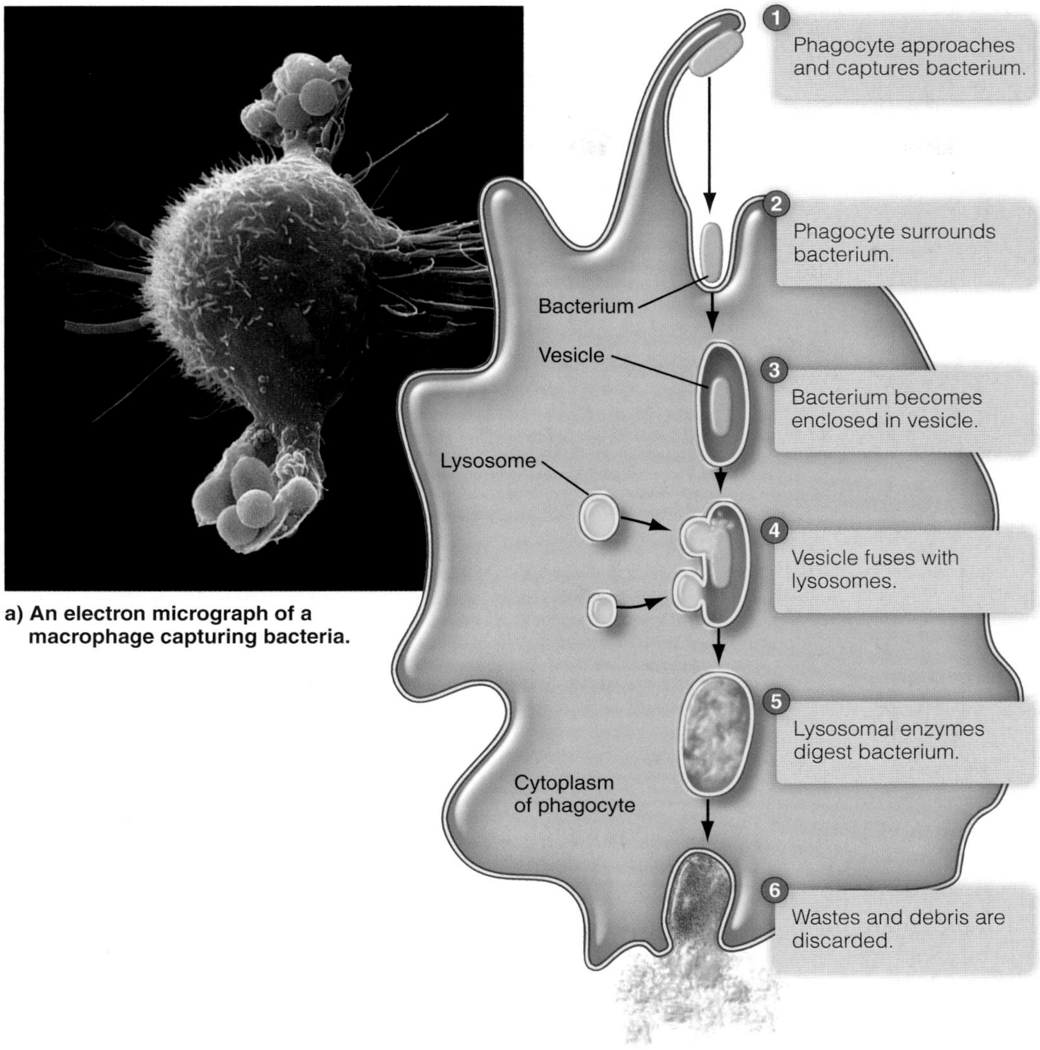


**a) An electron micrograph of a macrophage capturing bacteria.**

**b) Steps in the process.**

**Figure 9.6 Phagocytosis.**

signs: redness, warmth, swelling, and pain. Although these may not sound like positive developments, the events that cause these signs prevent the damage from spreading, dispose of cellular debris and pathogens, and set the stage for tissue-repair mechanisms.

The inflammatory response starts whenever tissues are injured (Figure 9.7). The release of chemicals from damaged cells sounds the alarm for the process to begin. These chemicals stimulate **mast cells,** which are connective tissue cells specialized to release **histamine.** Histamine promotes vasodilation of neighboring small blood vessels. White blood cells called **basophils** also secrete histamine.

Recall that most white blood cells are too large to cross capillary walls. As histamine dilates blood vessels, however, the endothelial cells in vessel walls pull slightly apart, and the vessels become more permeable. This allows additional phagocytes to squeeze through capillary walls into the interstitial fluid. There they attack foreign organisms and damaged cells. After destroying pathogens, some phagocytes travel to the lymphatic system, where their presence activates lymphocytes to initiate specific defense mechanisms, discussed later.

Vasodilation brings more blood into the injured area, making it red and warm. The rising temperature increases phagocyte activity. The increased leakiness of capillary walls allows more fluid to seep into tissue spaces, causing swelling. The extra fluid dilutes pathogens and toxins and brings in clotting proteins that form a fibrin mesh to wall off the damaged area from healthy tissue. As a bonus, the fluid carries in extra oxygen and nutrients to promote tissue healing and carries away dead cells, microorganisms, and other debris from the area.

Swollen tissues press against nearby nerve endings. This swelling, plus the sensitizing effects of inflammatory chemicals, creates the sensation of pain that accompanies inflammation. However, even pain can be positive. The discomfort hinders active movement and forces the injured person to rest, facilitating the healing process.

### Natural killer cells target tumors and virus-infected cells

**Natural killer (NK) cells** are a group of white blood cells (lymphocytes) that destroy tumor cells and cells infected by viruses. NK cells are able to recognize certain changes that take place in the plasma membranes of tumor cells and virus-infected cells. The name "natural killer" reflects the fact that NK cells are nonspecific killers, unlike other killer cells discussed later in this chapter that target only specific enemies.

NK cells are not phagocytes. Instead, they release chemicals that break down their targets' cell membranes. Soon after an NK attack, the target cell's membrane develops holes, and its nucleus rapidly disintegrates. NK cells also secrete substances that enhance the inflammatory response.

### The complement system assists other defense mechanisms

The **complement system,** or *complement,* comprises at least 20 plasma proteins that circulate in the blood and complement, or assist, other defense mechanisms. Normally these

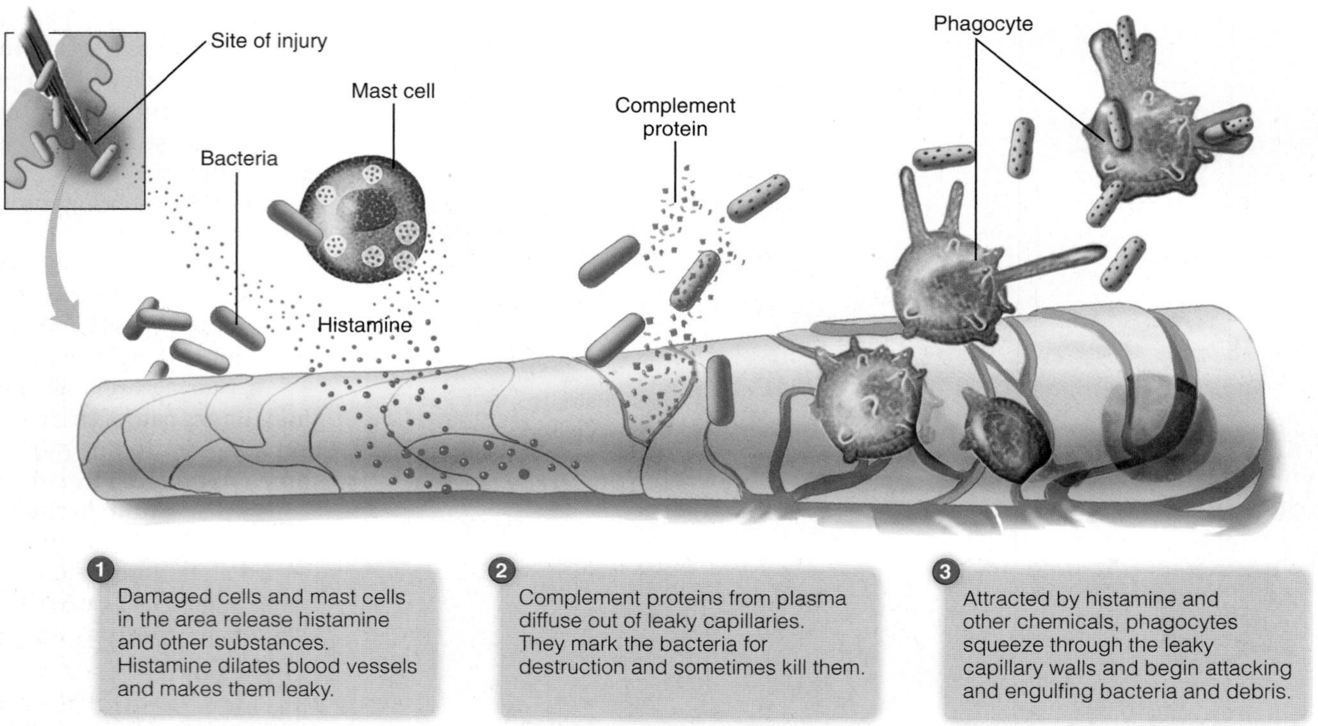


**Figure 9.7 The inflammatory response.**

proteins circulate in an inactive state. When activated by the presence of an infection, however, they become a potent defense force. Once one protein is activated it activates another, leading to a cascade of reactions. Each protein in the complement system can activate many others, creating a powerful "domino effect."

Some activated complement proteins join to form large protein complexes that create holes in bacterial cell walls. Fluids and salts leak in through these holes, until eventually the bacterium swells and bursts (Figure 9.8). Other activated complement proteins bind to bacterial cell membranes, marking them for destruction by phagocytes. Still others stimulate mast cells to release histamine or serve as chemical attractants to draw additional phagocytes to the infection.

## Interferons interfere with viral reproduction

One of the most interesting defense mechanisms is an early warning system between virus-infected and still-healthy cells. As mentioned earlier, viruses cannot reproduce on their own. Instead, they invade body cells and use the cells' machinery to make more viruses.

When a cell becomes infected by viruses, however, it secretes a group of proteins called **interferons.** Interferons diffuse to nearby healthy cells, bind to their cell membranes, and stimulate the healthy cells to produce proteins that interfere with the synthesis of viral proteins, making it harder for the viruses to infect the protected cells.

Interferons are now being produced in pharmaceutical laboratories. At least one interferon protein *(alpha interferon)* has shown promise against certain viral diseases, including genital warts, hepatitis B, and one form of leukemia.

## Fever raises body temperature

A final weapon in our second line of defense is **fever,** an abnormally high body temperature. Your body's "thermostat" is set to approximately 98.6 °F (37 °C), with a normal range of about 97–99 °F (36–37.2 °C). When macrophages detect and attack bacteria, viruses, or other foreign substances, they release certain chemicals into the bloodstream. These chemicals, called *pyrogens,* cause the brain to reset your thermostat to a higher temperature.

There is a tendency to treat all fevers as if they were a problem. But a modest fever may be beneficial because it makes our internal environment less hospitable to pathogens and enhances the body's ability to fight infections. Fever increases the metabolic rate of body cells, speeding up both defense mechanisms and tissue-repair processes. When the infection is gone, the process reverses. Macrophages stop releasing pyrogens, the thermostat setting returns to normal, and your fever "breaks."

However, high fevers can be dangerous. As described in Chapter 2, the chemical bonds that give a protein its shape are relatively weak. Consequently, the shape (and function) of some proteins can be affected by high temperatures. It's a good idea to monitor the course of any fever, particularly in children and older adults. Health professionals recommend seeking medical advice for any fever that lasts longer than two days or rises above 100 °F.

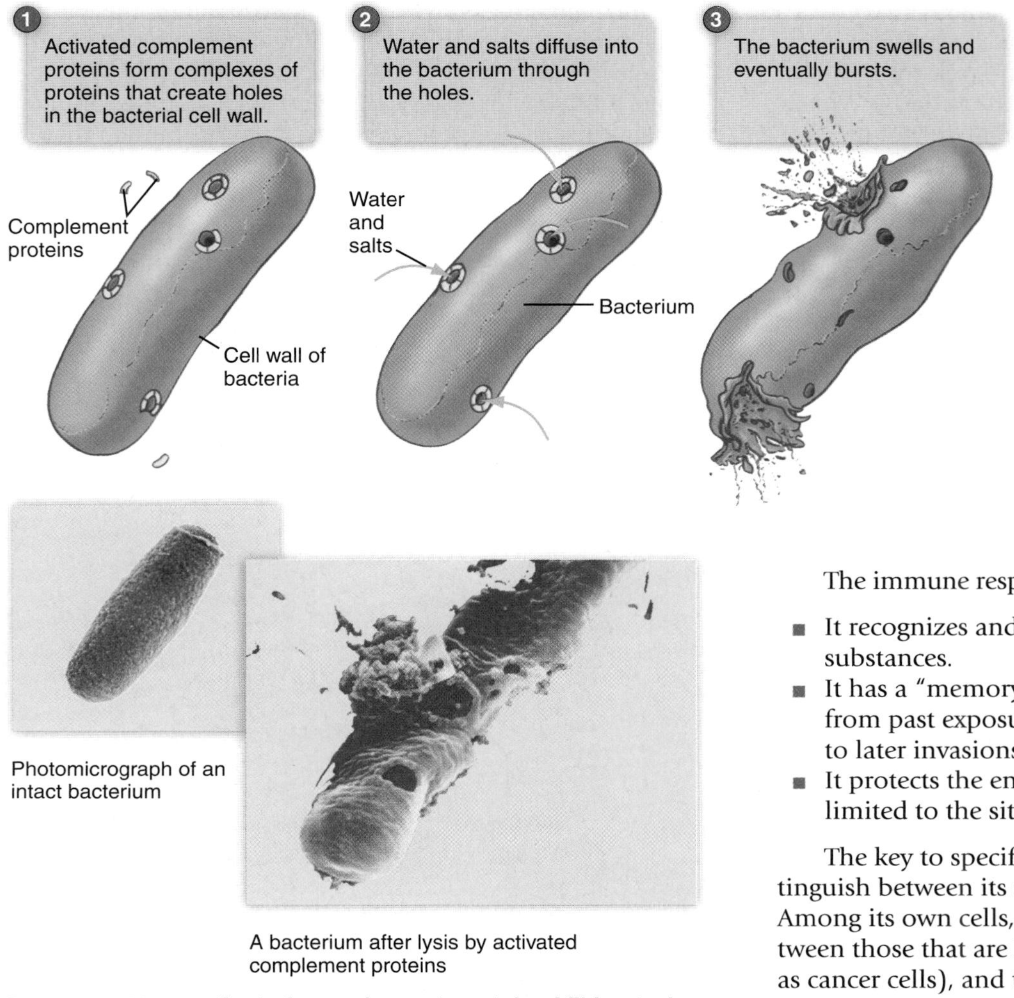


**Figure 9.8** **How activated complement proteins kill bacteria.**

**RECAP**

The inflammatory response attracts phagocytes and promotes tissue healing. Natural killer cells release chemicals that disintegrate cell membranes of tumor cells and virus-infected cells. The complement system assists other defense mechanisms, interferons interfere with viral reproduction, and a modest fever enhances our ability to fight infections. ■

## 9.5 Specific defense mechanisms: The third line of defense

Even if foreign cells manage to bypass physical and chemical barriers and overcome nonspecific defenses, they must still cope with the body's third line of defense, the most sophisticated weapon of all. The *immune system* comprises cells, proteins, and the lymphatic system, all working together to detect and kill particular pathogens and abnormal body cells. The activities of the immune system are collectively called the **immune response.** Because the immune system targets specific enemies, we refer to these operations as *specific defense mechanisms*.

The immune response has three important characteristics:

- It recognizes and targets specific pathogens or foreign substances.
- It has a "memory," the capability to store information from past exposures so that it can respond more quickly to later invasions by the same pathogen.
- It protects the entire body; the resulting immunity is not limited to the site of infection.

The key to specific defenses is the body's ability to distinguish between its own cells and those of foreign invaders. Among its own cells, it must also be able to distinguish between those that are healthy, those that are abnormal (such as cancer cells), and those that are dead or dying.

### The immune system targets antigens

An **antigen** is any substance that mobilizes the immune system and provokes an immune response. Generally antigens are large protein or polysaccharide molecules. In much the same way that a key fits a lock, each antigen has a unique shape, and every bacterium or virus has a different one. The immune system responds to each uniquely shaped antigen by producing specific *antibodies* to attack and inactivate the antigen (and the cell carrying it).

All antigens are located only on the outer surface of a cell or virus. Hence the immune system cannot detect viruses (or viral DNA/RNA) once they are safely inside a living human cell.

Human cells also have surface proteins that can act as antigens under the right circumstances. Your cells have a unique set of proteins on their surfaces that your immune system uses to recognize that the cells belong to you. These *self markers* are known as **major histocompatibility complex (MHC) proteins.** Your MHC proteins are unique to you by virtue of your unique set of genes. Normally they signal your immune system to bypass your own cells. They are a sort of password, the equivalent of a cellular fingerprint. Your immune system "reads" the password and leaves your cells alone.

However, the same MHC proteins that define your cells as belonging to you would be read as *nonself markers* in another person. In other words, your MHC proteins would be antigens in another person. Abnormal and cancerous cells in your own body also have MHC proteins that are not recognized as "self." The immune system targets all antigens, including those on pathogens and foreign and damaged human cells, for destruction.

**RECAP**

An antigen is any substance that provokes an immune response. All cells of an organism have markers called MHC proteins that identify the cells as "self." Nonself MHC proteins are antigens, and as such they activate the immune system. ■

## Lymphocytes are central to specific defenses

Lymphocytes play crucial roles in our specific defense mechanisms. As described in Chapter 7 (see Figure 7.5), lymphocytes are white blood cells originating from stem cells in bone marrow. They are fairly small white blood cells with a single nucleus that fills nearly the entire cell. They total about 30% of circulating WBCs. Lymphocytes are found in the bloodstream, tonsils, spleen, lymph nodes, and thymus gland.

There are two types: B lymphocytes and T lymphocytes, also called **B cells** and **T cells.** (Their names are based on where they mature: B cells mature in bone marrow; T cells in the thymus gland.) Although both types of lymphocytes can recognize and target antigen-bearing cells, they go about this task in different ways.

B cells are responsible for **antibody-mediated immunity.** B cells produce **antibodies**—proteins that bind with and neutralize specific antigens. They release antibodies into the lymph, bloodstream, and tissue fluid, where they circulate throughout the body. Antibody-mediated immunity works best against viruses, bacteria, and foreign molecules that are soluble in blood and lymph.

T cells are responsible for **cell-mediated immunity,** which depends on the actions of several types of T cells. Unlike B cells, T cells do not produce antibodies. Instead, some T cells directly attack foreign cells that carry antigens. Other T cells release proteins that help coordinate other aspects of the immune response, including the actions of T cells, B cells, and macrophages. Cell-mediated immunity protects us against parasites, bacteria, viruses, fungi, cancerous cells, and cells perceived as foreign (including, unfortunately, transplanted tissue—see section 9.8, Tissue rejection: A medical challenge). T cells can identify and kill infected human cells even before the cells have a chance to release new bacteria or viruses into the blood.

## B cells: Antibody-mediated immunity

In adults, B cells mature in the bone marrow. As they mature, they develop unique surface receptors (with the same structure as an antibody) that allow them to recognize specific antigens. Then they travel in the bloodstream to the lymph nodes, spleen, and tonsils, where they remain inactive until they encounter a foreign cell with that particular antigen. When a B cell with just the right surface receptor encounters the appropriate antigen, its surface receptors bind to the antigen (Figure 9.9). This activates the B cell to grow and then multiply rapidly, producing more B cells exactly like the original and bearing the same surface receptors. The

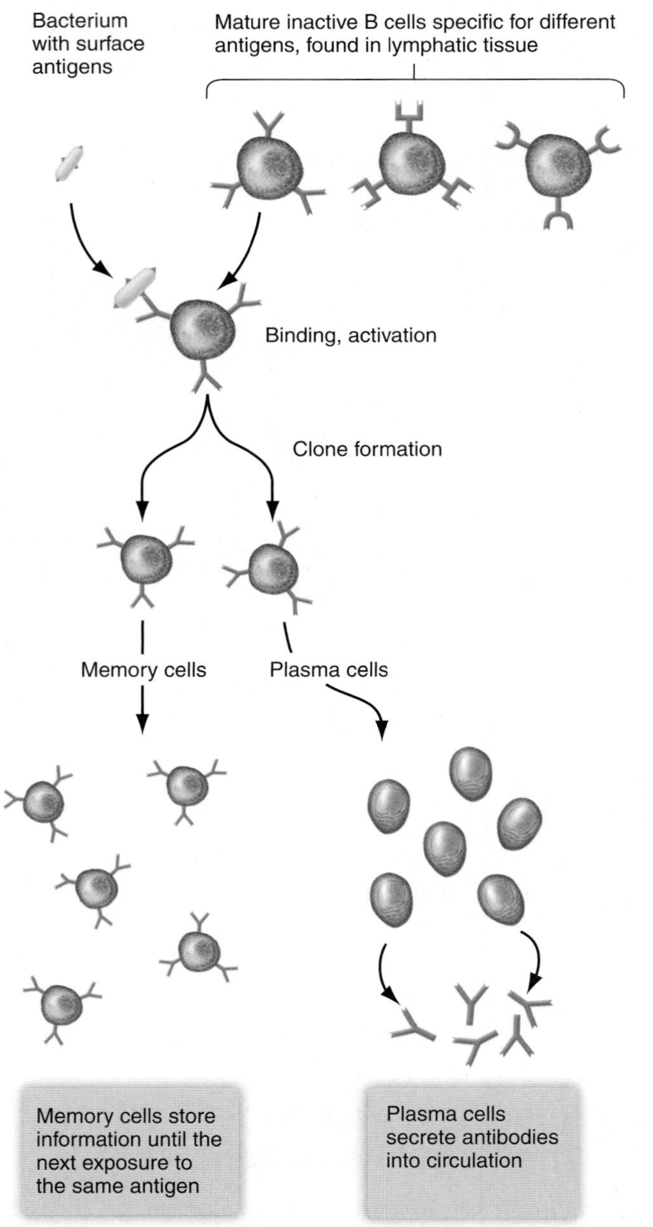


**Figure 9.9 The production of antibodies by B cells.** The surface antigen of a pathogen binds to the matching receptor on a mature, inactive B cell in lymphatic tissue. The B cell becomes activated and grows larger. The enlarged cell begins to divide rapidly, forming a clone. Some of the clone cells become plasma cells; others become memory cells. Plasma cells secrete antibodies into the lymph fluid. Memory cells lie in wait for the next exposure to the antigen.

resulting group of identical cells, all descended from the same cell, is called a *clone.*

Although the B cells themselves tend to remain in the lymphatic system, most of the cells of the clone are called **plasma cells** because they begin to secrete their antibodies into the lymph fluid and ultimately into the blood plasma. A typical plasma cell can make antibody molecules at a staggering rate—about 2,000 molecules per second. A plasma cell maintains this frantic pace for a few days and then dies, but its antibodies continue to circulate in blood and lymph.

When the antibodies encounter matching antigens, they bind to them and create an *antigen-antibody complex.* Antibodies specialize in recognizing certain proteins; thus one particular antibody can bind to one particular antigen (Figure 9.10). The formation of an antigen-antibody complex marks the antigen (and the foreign cell that carries it) for destruction either by activated complement proteins or by phagocytes. Some antibodies also inactivate pathogens by causing the cells to agglutinate, preventing them from entering human cells and causing disease.

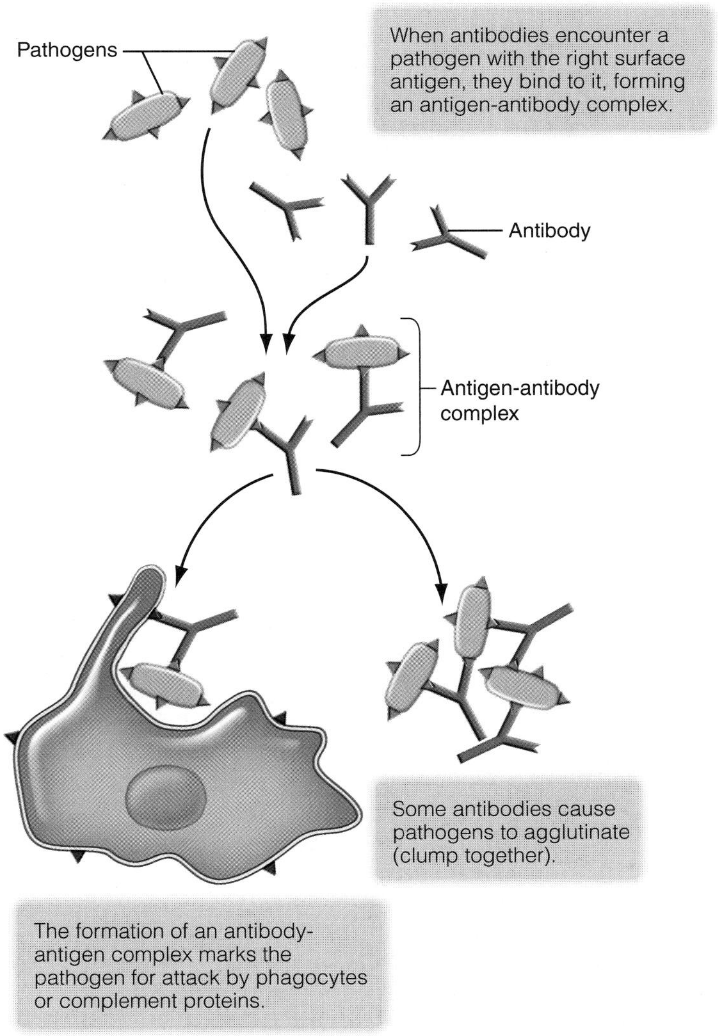


**Figure 9.10 How antibodies inactivate pathogens.**

Some of the clone cells become **memory cells,** long-lived cells that remain inactive until that same antigen reappears in the body at some future date. Memory cells store information about the pathogen; if there is a second exposure, the immune response is even faster than the first time. Upon exposure, these memory cells quickly become plasma cells and start to secrete antibodies. Memory cells are the basis for long-term immunity.

**RECAP**

Lymphocytes called B cells produce antibodies against specific antigens. When activated by first exposure to an antigen, B cells quickly produce a clone of identical antibody-producing B cells called plasma cells. They also produce a few long-lived memory cells that remain inactive until the next exposure to the same antigen. ■

## The five classes of antibodies

Antibodies belong to the class of blood plasma proteins called gamma globulins. Because they play such a crucial role in immunity, the term **immunoglobulin (Ig)** is often used. There are five classes of immunoglobulins, each designated by a different letter: IgG, IgM, IgA, IgD, and IgE. Each type has a different size, location in the body, and function:

- *IgG (75% of immunoglobulins).* This is the most common class. Found in blood, lymph, intestines, and tissue fluid, the long-lived IgG antibodies activate the complement system and neutralize many toxins. They are the only antibodies that cross the placenta during pregnancy and pass on the mother's acquired immunities to the fetus.
- *IgM (5–10%).* IgM antibodies are the first to be released during immune responses. Found in blood and lymph, they activate the complement system and cause foreign cells to agglutinate. ABO blood cell antibodies belong to this class.
- *IgA (15%).* IgA antibodies enter areas of the body covered by mucous membranes, such as the digestive, reproductive, and respiratory tracts. There they neutralize infectious pathogens. They are also present in the mother's milk and are transmitted to the infant during breast-feeding.
- *IgD (less than 1%).* IgD antibodies are in blood, lymph, and B cells. Their function is not clear, but they may play a role in activating B cells.
- *IgE (approximately 0.1%).* The rarest of the immunoglobulins, IgE antibodies are in B cells, mast cells, and basophils. They activate the inflammatory response by triggering the release of histamine. They are also the troublemakers behind allergic responses (covered in section 9.9).

## Antibodies' structure enables them to bind to specific antigens

An antigen provides all the information the immune system needs to know about a foreign substance. Essentially, antigens are the locks on an enemy's doors. The immune system can identify the lock, produce the antibody key, and then send in immune system cells to open the door and neutralize the invader. How does this happen?

All antibodies share the same basic structure, represented by an IgG antibody (Figure 9.11). Each IgG antibody (or surface receptor, if it is attached to a B cell) consists of four linked polypeptide chains arranged in a Y shape. The two larger chains are called "heavy" chains, and the two smaller ones are called "light" chains. Each of the four chains has a constant region that forms the trunk and two branches and a variable region that represents the antigen-binding site. Because it has a unique amino acid sequence, each variable region has a unique shape that fits only one specific antigen.

The constant regions are similar for all antibodies in one class, although they differ from those of other classes. The IgG antibody depicted in Figure 9.10 is a single Y-shaped molecule with two binding sites. Larger antibodies in the IgM class consist of five Y-shaped molecules linked together, with 10 binding sites.

**RECAP**

There are five classes of antibodies (also called immunoglobulins), each with a characteristic size, shape, and function. Within each class, a particular antibody fits only one specific antigen. ■

## T cells: Cell-mediated immunity

There are two basic functional differences between B cells and T cells. First, B cells produce circulating antibodies; T cells either release chemicals that stimulate other cells of the immune system, or they directly attack the foreign cell and kill it. Second, T cell receptors cannot recognize whole antigens—they only react to small fragments of antigens. Thus it is necessary for a certain amount of antigen processing to occur before T cells can do their job. The antigen must be presented to them in a form that they can recognize.

Certain cells—including macrophages and activated B cells—fulfill this role by acting as **antigen-presenting cells (APCs)** that engulf foreign particles, partially digest them, and display fragments of the antigens on their surfaces (Figure 9.12). After an APC engulfs a pathogen, it partially degrades the antigen inside a vesicle. The vesicle containing antigen fragments joins with another vesicle containing MHC molecules, the molecules that become the cell's self markers. The MHC binds to the antigen pieces and moves to the cell surface, to be displayed as an antigen-MHC complex. Essentially, the cell "presents" a fragment of the antigen for T cells to recognize, along with its own cell-surface self marker.

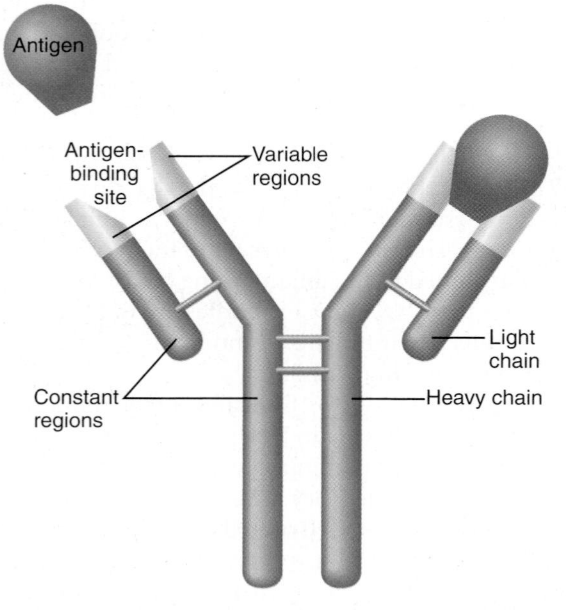


**Figure 9.11 Structure of an antibody (or B cell surface receptor).** An antibody consists of four peptide chains linked together to form a Y shape. Only the lighter-colored ends of each chain vary. These variations determine the specificity of each antibody for only one antigen.

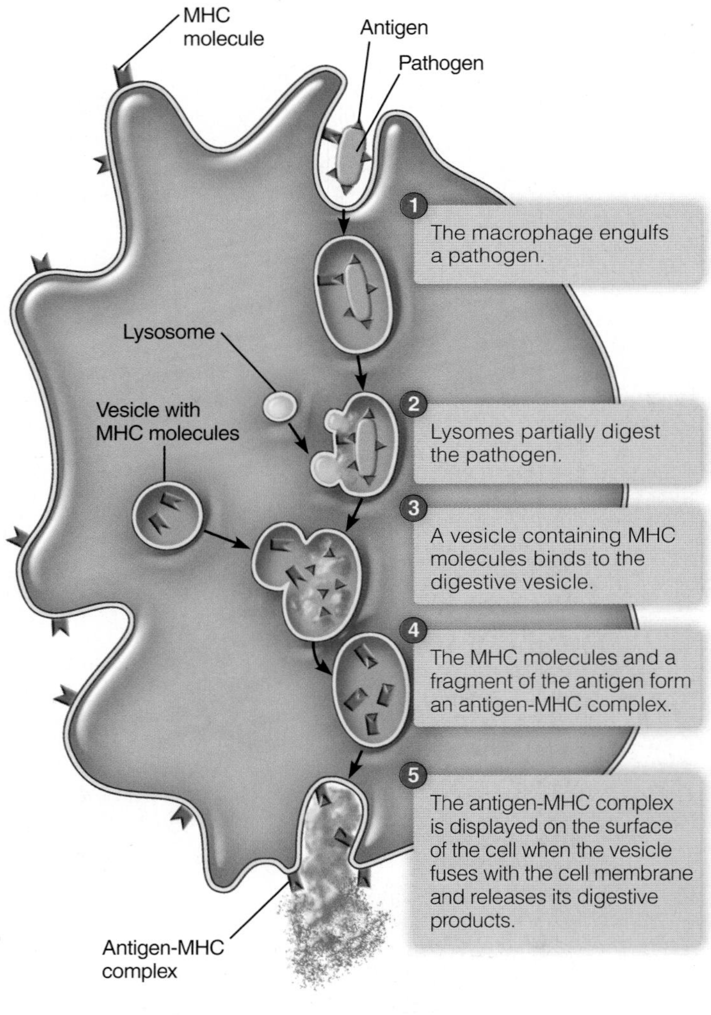


**Figure 9.12 How a macrophage acts as an antigen-presenting cell (APC).**

T cells develop from stem cells in bone marrow but migrate to the thymus gland, where they become mature but remain inactive. During maturation they also develop one of two sets of surface proteins, CD4 or CD8. These proteins determine what type of T cell they will become. CD4 T cells will become helper and memory cells, and CD8 T cells will become cytotoxic and suppressor cells.

**Helper T cells stimulate other immune cells** When a T cell with CD4 receptors encounters an antigen-presenting cell displaying a fragment of an antigen, it differentiates into a **helper T cell.** The new helper T cell undergoes mitosis (see Chapter 17), quickly producing a clone of identical helper T cells (Figure 9.13). Because all the cells in the clone carry the same receptors, they all recognize the same antigen.

Most of the cells in the helper T cell clone begin secreting a class of signaling molecules called **cytokines.** Among them are proteins that stimulate the actions of T cells and macrophages, and substances that promote development of other immune cells. Cytokines released by helper T cells stimulate other immune cells such as phagocytes, natural killer cells, and T cells with CD8 receptors. They also attract other types of white blood cells to the area, enhancing nonspecific defenses. They even activate B cells, creating an important link between antibody-mediated and cell-mediated immunity.

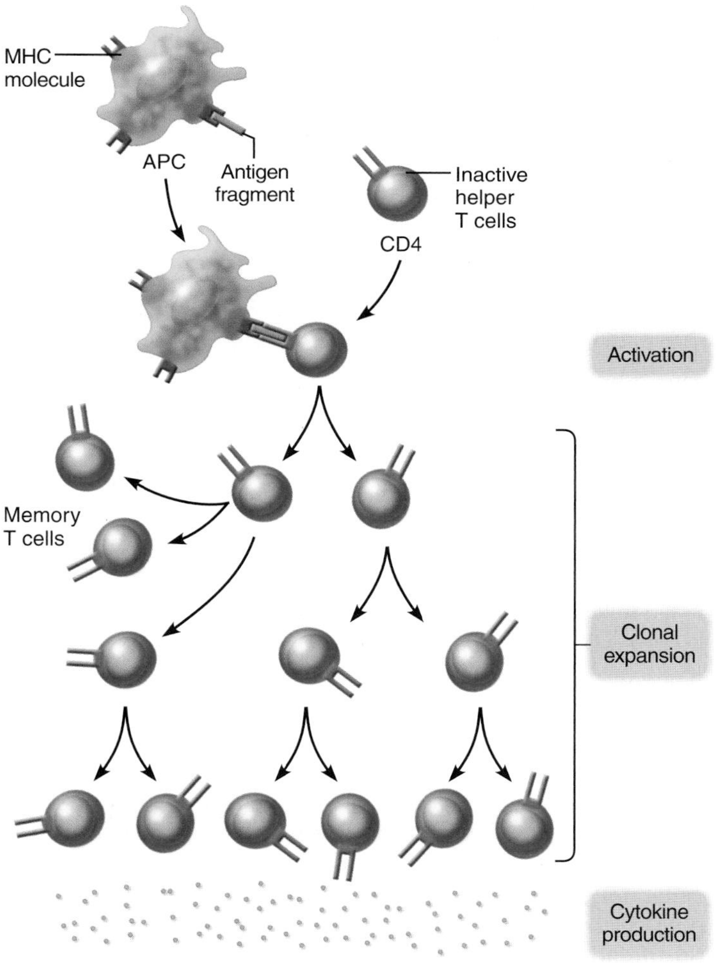


**Figure 9.13 The activation and clonal expansion of helper T cells.** Activation occurs when a mature but inactive helper cell comes in contact with an antigen-presenting cell displaying the appropriate antigen fragment. After clonal expansion, the clones produce cytokines. A few activated clones become memory T cells.

The role of helper T cells and their cytokines in directing the activities of other immune cells is crucial to an effective immune response—without them the immune response would be severely impaired or nonexistent. The reason AIDS is so devastating is that HIV destroys helper T cells, and thus weakens the body's ability to mount a cell-mediated immune response to a wide variety of other diseases. (See section 9.10, Immune deficiency: The special case of AIDS.)

**Cytotoxic T cells kill abnormal and foreign cells** When a mature T cell with CD8 receptors meets an antigen-producing cell that displays an antigen fragment, it begins to produce a clone of **cytotoxic T cells** (also called *killer T cells*). These are the only T cells that directly attack and destroy other cells (Figure 9.14).

Once activated, cytotoxic T cells roam throughout the body. They circulate through blood, lymph, and lymphatic tissues in search of cells that display the antigens they recognize. Or they may migrate to a tumor or site of infection, where they release chemicals that are toxic to abnormal cells.

Figure 9.15 illustrates cytotoxic T cells in action. When a cytotoxic T cell locates and binds to a target cell, secretory vesicles release a protein called perforin into the space between the two cells. The perforin molecules assemble themselves into a pore in the target cell, allowing water and salts to enter. That alone should eventually kill the cell in much the same way that activated complement does (review Figure 9.8). But just to make sure, the cytotoxic T cell also releases granzyme, a toxic enzyme that is small enough to pass through the pore. The cytotoxic T cell then detaches from the target cell and goes off in search of other prey.

Several promising medical treatments involve harnessing the defensive capabilities of a group of cytokines called interferons. Genetically engineered gamma interferon is used to treat the chronic viral disorder hepatitis C. Another type of interferon has been moderately successful for treating multiple sclerosis, and a third is being used to treat certain types of cancer.

**Memory T cells reactivate during later exposures** Some activated T cells become memory cells, retaining receptors for the antigen that originally stimulated their production. If that antigen is presented to them again, the memory cells are reactivated. Some form new helper T cells that multiply quickly to marshal an immune response. Others form a new army of cytotoxic T cells to attack and destroy. Like memory B cells, memory T cells are an important factor

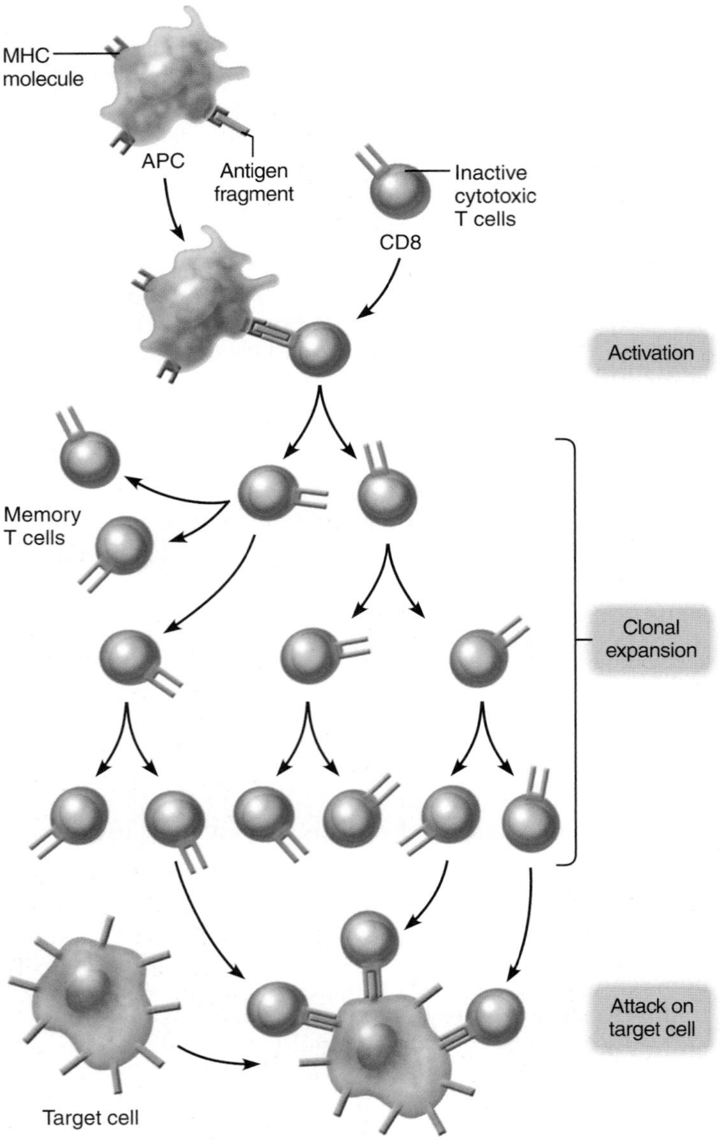


**Figure 9.14 The activation and clonal expansion of cytotoxic T cells.** Following activation and clonal expansion, the clones directly attack and kill cells carrying the antigen fragment they recognize.

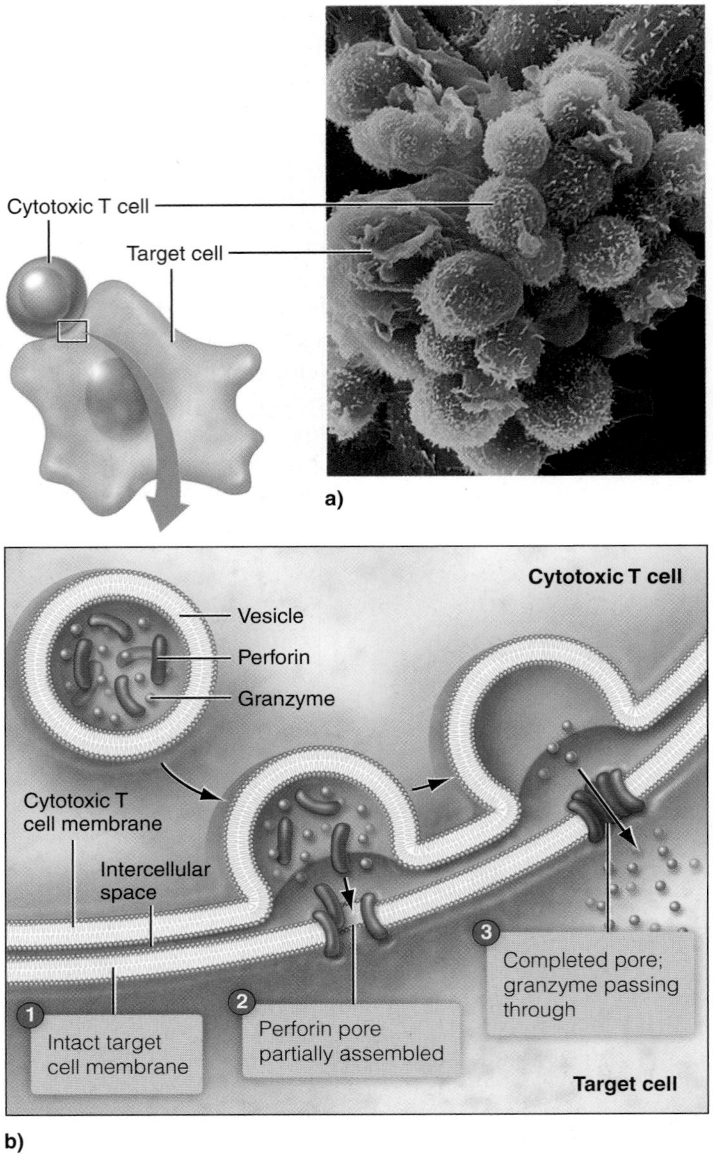


**Figure 9.15 Cell-mediated immunity in action. (a)** Cytotoxic T cells (blue) attaching to a target cell (pink). **(b)** How cytotoxic T cells kill a target cell.

that distinguishes specific defenses from nonspecific defense mechanisms.

Table 9.2 summarizes the various cells and proteins involved in specific defense mechanisms.

**RECAP**

Lymphocytes that mature in the thymus gland become T cells. Helper T cells enhance specific and nonspecific defenses by stimulating other immune cells. Cytotoxic T cells attack abnormal and foreign cells. Memory T cells store information until the next exposure to the same antigen. ■

## 9.6 Immune memory creates immunity

When you are first exposed to an antigen, your immune system protects you with the wealth of defense mechanisms described so far. Your first exposure to a particular antigen generates a *primary immune response.* As we have seen, this involves recognition of the antigen, and production and proliferation of B and T cells.

Typically the primary immune response has a lag time of three to six days after the antigen first appears. During this period B cells specific to that antigen multiply and develop into plasma cells. Antibody concentrations rise, typically reaching their peak about 10–12 days after first exposure. Then they start to level off (Figure 9.16).

**Table 9.2 Cells and proteins involved in specific defenses**

| Cell/Protein | Function |
|---|---|
| ***B cells*** | Mature in bone marrow. Responsible for antibody-mediated immunity. |
| Plasma cells | Produce and secrete specific antibodies. |
| Memory B cells | Store information. Upon subsequent exposure, become plasma cells and secrete antibodies. |
| Immunoglobulins | Five classes of antibodies. Every antibody has a unique shape that fits one specific antigen. |
| ***T cells*** | Mature in thymus. Responsible for cell-mediated immunity. |
| Helper T cells | Produce cytokines. Enhance immune responses by stimulating other immune cells. |
| Cytotoxic T cells | Attack and destroy abnormal cells. |
| Memory T cells | Store information. Upon subsequent exposure, become helper and cytotoxic T cells. |
| Cytokines | A class of signaling molecules that stimulate various immune system activities. |

However, as you have learned, B and T cells create a population of memory cells. The presence of these memory cells is the basis for **immunity** from disease. (The Latin word *immunis* means "safe" or "free from.") Subsequent exposure to the pathogen elicits a *secondary immune response* that is faster, longer lasting, and more effective than the first. Within hours after second exposure to an antigen, memory cells bind to the pathogen. New armies of T and plasma cells form, and within a few days antibody concentrations rise rapidly to much higher levels than in the primary response. Notice that antibody levels remain much higher in the body after second exposure.

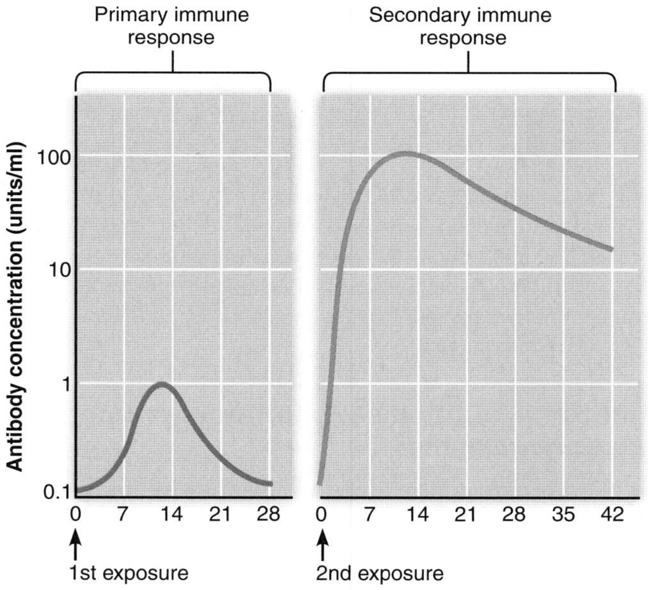


**Figure 9.16 The basis of immunity.** The antibody response to a first exposure to antigen (the primary immune response) declines in about a month. A second exposure to the same antigen results in a response that is more rapid in onset, larger, and longer lasting. On this graph the abscissa scale is broken because it may be months or even years before second exposure. Note that the concentration of antibody during a secondary response may be 100 times higher than the primary response.

Memory cells are long-lived, and many retain their ability to generate a secondary immune response over a lifetime. The secondary immune response can be so effective that you don't even realize you've been exposed to the pathogen a second time. At worst, you may experience only a fleeting sensation of feeling unwell. Other memory cells, such as the ones for the bacterial infection that causes tetanus, need to be reactivated every 10 years or so.

Given this immunity, though, why is it possible to get a cold or the flu over and over, sometimes several times a year? One reason is that there are more than 100 different viruses that can cause colds and flu. Even if your latest respiratory ailment feels like the previous one, it may actually be due to an entirely different pathogen. Furthermore, the viruses that cause colds and flu evolve so rapidly that they are essentially different each year. Their antigens change enough that each one requires a different antibody, and each exposure triggers a primary response. Rapid evolution is their survival mechanism. Our survival mechanism is a good immune system.

**RECAP**

First exposure to a specific antigen generates a primary immune response. Subsequent exposure to the same antigen elicits a secondary immune response that is faster, longer lasting, and more effective. ■

## 9.7 Medical assistance in the war against pathogens

Our natural defenses against pathogens are remarkable. Nevertheless, we humans have taken matters into our own hands by developing the science of medicine. We have been able to conceive of and produce other sophisticated weaponry to help us combat pathogens. Important milestones in human health include the development of active and passive methods of **immunization,** which help the body resist specific pathogens; the production of monoclonal antibodies; and the discovery of antibiotics.

## Active immunization: An effective weapon against pathogens

It is said that an ounce of prevention is worth a pound of cure, and this is certainly true when dealing with pathogens. The best weapon against them is to give the body a dose of the antigen in advance so that the immune system will mount a primary immune response against it. Then, if exposed to that microorganism in the environment, the body is already primed with the appropriate antibodies and memory cells. The immune system can react swiftly with a secondary response, effectively shielding you from the danger of the disease and discomfort of its symptoms.

The process of activating the body's immune system in advance is called **active immunization.** This involves administering an antigen-containing preparation called a **vaccine.** Most vaccines are produced from dead or weakened pathogens. An example is the oral polio vaccine (the Sabin vaccine), made from weakened poliovirus. Other vaccines are made from organisms that have been genetically altered to produce a particular antigen.

Of course, vaccines created from dead or weakened pathogens have their limitations. First, there are issues of safety, time, and expense. Living but weakened pathogens generally make better vaccines because they elicit a greater immune response. However, a vaccine that contains weakened pathogens has a slight potential to cause disease itself. This has happened, although rarely, with the polio vaccine. It takes a great deal of time, money, and research to verify the safety and effectiveness of a vaccine. Second, a vaccine confers immunity against only one pathogen, so a different vaccine is needed for every virus. This is why doctors may recommend getting a flu vaccine each time a new flu strain appears (nearly every year). Third, vaccines are not particularly effective after a pathogen has struck; that is, they do not cure an already existing disease.

Nonetheless, vaccines are an effective supplement to our natural defense mechanisms. Active immunization generally produces long-lived immunity that can protect us for many years. The widespread practice of vaccination has greatly reduced many diseases such as polio, measles, and whooping cough.

In the U.S., immunization of adults has lagged behind that of children. It's estimated that more than 50,000 Americans die each year from infections, including pneumonia, hepatitis, and influenza, that could have been prevented with timely vaccines.

In many countries, vaccines are too costly and difficult to administer: generally they must be injected by a health care worker with some basic level of training. To get around this problem, some researchers are developing potatoes or bananas that are genetically modified to produce vaccines against diseases such as hepatitis B, measles, and the diarrhea-causing Norwalk virus. An oral vaccine against Norwalk virus has already undergone limited testing in humans.

## Passive immunization can help against existing or anticipated infections

To fight an existing or even an anticipated infection, a person can be given antibodies prepared in advance from a human or animal donor with immunity to that illness. Usually this takes the form of a *gamma globulin* shot (serum containing primarily igG antibodies). The procedure is called **passive immunization.** In essence, the patient is given the antibodies that his/her own immune system might produce if there were enough time.

Passive immunization has the advantage of being somewhat effective against an existing infection. It can be administered to prevent illness in someone who has been unexpectedly exposed to a pathogen, and it confers at least some short-term immunity. However, protection is not as long-lasting as active immunization following vaccine administration because the administered antibodies disappear from the circulation quickly. Passive immunization also can't confer long-term immunity against a second exposure, because the person's own B cells aren't activated and so memory cells for the pathogen do not develop.

Passive immunization has been used effectively against certain common viral infections including those that cause hepatitis B and measles, bacterial infections such as tetanus, and Rh incompatibility. Passive immunization of the fetus and newborn also occurs naturally across the placenta and through breast-feeding.

**RECAP**

Active immunization with a vaccine (a preparation of weakened or dead pathogens) produces a primary immune response and readies the immune system for a secondary immune response. Administration of prepared antibodies (passive immunization) can be effective against existing infections but does not confer long-term immunity. ■

## Monoclonal antibodies: Laboratory-created for commercial use

An antibody preparation used to confer passive immunity in a patient is actually a mixture of many different antibody molecules, because a single pathogen can have many different antigens on its surface. **Monoclonal antibodies,** on the other hand, are antibodies produced in the laboratory from cloned descendants of a single hybrid B cell. As such, monoclonal antibodies are relatively pure preparations of antibodies specific for a single antigen. Monoclonal antibodies are proving useful in research, testing, and cancer treatments because they are pure and they can be produced cheaply in large quantities.

Figure 9.17 summarizes a technique for preparing monoclonal antibodies. Typically, B cells are removed from a

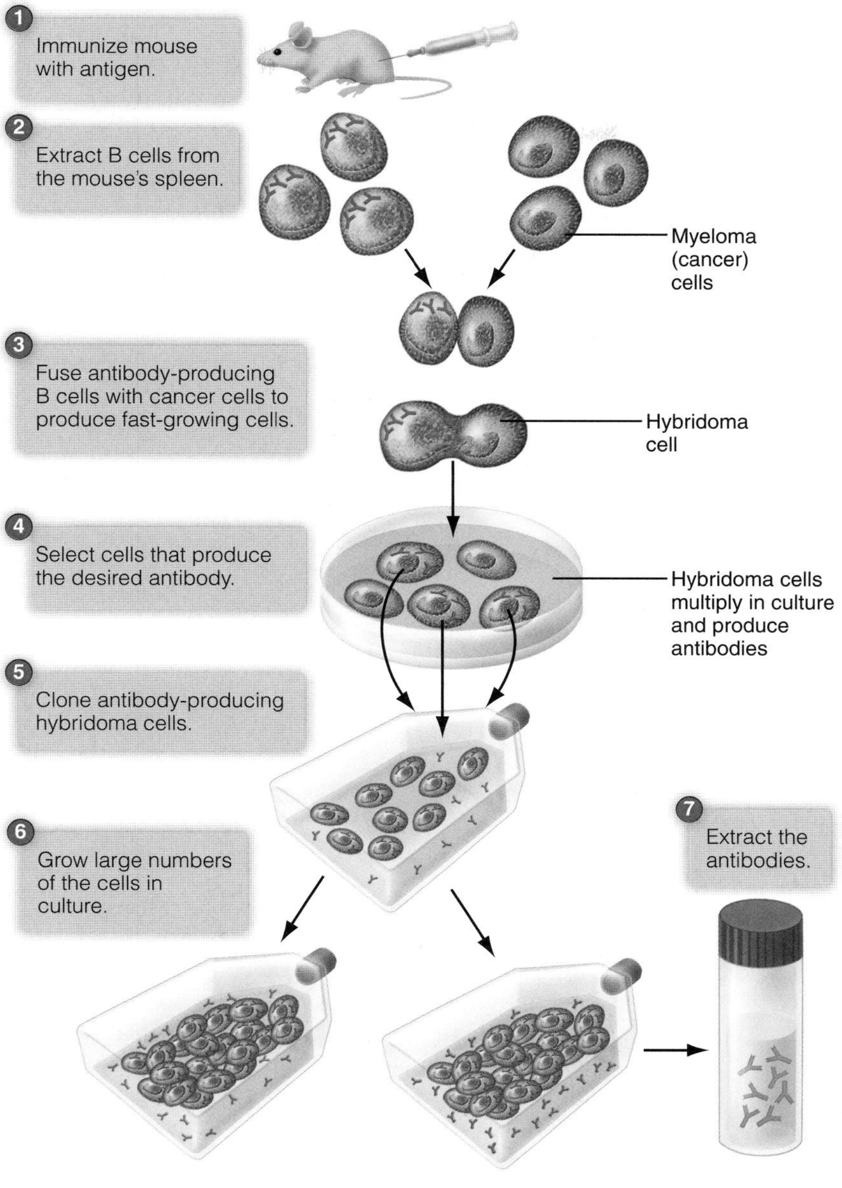


**Figure 9.17 How monoclonal antibodies are produced.**

mouse's spleen after the mouse has been immunized with a specific antigen to stimulate B cell production. The B cells are fused with myeloma (cancer) cells to create *hybridoma* (hybrid cancer) cells that have desirable traits of both parent cells: they each produce a specific antibody, and they proliferate with cancerlike rapidity. As these hybridoma cells grow in culture, those that produce the desired antibody are separated out and cloned, producing millions of copies. The antibodies they produce are harvested and processed to create preparations of pure monoclonal antibodies. (The term *monoclonal* means these antibody molecules derive from a group of cells cloned from a single cell.)

Monoclonal antibodies have a number of commercial applications, including home pregnancy tests, screening for prostate cancer, and diagnostic testing for hepatitis, influenza, and HIV/AIDS. Monoclonal antibody tests tend to be more specific and more rapid than conventional diagnostic tests. In the future it may be possible to use monoclonal antibodies to deliver anticancer drugs directly to cancer cells. The first step would be to bond an anticancer drug to monoclonal antibodies prepared against the cancer. Upon injection into the patient, the antibodies would deliver the drug directly to the cancer cells, sparing nearby healthy tissue.

### Antibiotics combat bacteria

Literally, *antibiotic* means "against life." Antibiotics kill bacteria or inhibit their growth. The first antibiotics were derived from extracts of molds and fungi, but today most antibiotics are synthesized by pharmaceutical companies.

There are hundreds of antibiotics in use today, and they work in dozens of ways. In general, they take advantage of the differences between bacteria and human cells, including these: (1) bacteria have a thick cell wall (our cells do not), (2) bacterial DNA is not safely enclosed in a nucleus (ours is), (3) bacterial ribosomes are smaller than ours, and (4) their rate of protein synthesis is very rapid as they grow and divide. For example, penicillin blocks the synthesis of bacterial cell walls, and streptomycin inhibits bacterial protein synthesis by altering the shape of bacterial ribosomes.

Some antibiotics combat only certain types of bacteria. Others, called *broad-spectrum antibiotics*, are effective against several groups of bacteria. By definition, however, antibiotics are ineffective against viruses. Recall that viruses do not reproduce on their own; they replicate only when they are inside living cells. Using antibiotics to fight viral infections such as colds or the flu is wasted effort and contributes to the growing health problem of bacterial resistance to antibiotics.

**RECAP**

Monoclonal antibodies are laboratory-produced antibody preparations that are specific for a single antigen. Most antibiotics kill bacteria by interfering with bacterial protein synthesis or bacterial cell wall synthesis. ■

## 9.8 Tissue rejection: A medical challenge

Because the goal of the immune system is to protect the body from invasion by nonself cells, it is not surprising that it attacks foreign tissues, even those that are human,

**Health** Watch

## The Benefits of Breast-Feeding

When human infants are born, their immune systems and intestines are not yet fully de-veloped. As a result, newborns are often prone to diarrhea caused by recurring bacte-rial infections.

Breast milk from the newborn's mother may be beneficial. When an infant first begins to suckle, the mother secretes a sort of "pre-milk" called colostrum. Colostrum is rich in antibodies and immune cells, including phagocytes that participate in nonspecific defense mechanisms and lymphocytes of the specific immune system. Together these provide some immunity for the infant until its immune system can develop its own antibodies (about a month after birth). Human milk continues to provide antibodies and immune cells throughout the nursing period, though the concentration of these substances in milk is less than it is in colostrum.

The natural role of human milk in delivering antibodies to the infant has led some immunologists to suggest that mothers should be immunized by vaccination against certain childhood diseases. The mother would then produce specific antibodies for the infant against those diseases. Others have suggested putting antibodies directly into infant formulas or cow's milk for babies who are not breast-fed.

There are other benefits to human milk as well. All of us harbor beneficial bacteria in our digestive systems, and human milk encourages the growth of these good bacteria. Infants can also digest human milk more easily than cow's milk.

However, be aware that certain foods, beverages, and drugs that the mother consumes can also end up in her milk and be transmitted to her infant. Examples include "street drugs," such as heroin and cocaine; prescription medications, such as cimetidine (Tagamet), an anti-ulcer medication; and alcohol and caffeine. HIV (the virus that causes AIDS) can also be transmitted in human milk. With a thorough physical exam and medical history, however, the relatively minor risks of breast-feeding can be kept to a minimum.

with vigor. This phenomenon is called *tissue rejection*. As described in Chapter 7, a type of tissue rejection called a transfusion reaction can be fatal. Red blood cells carry a dozen or so self markers, but most body cells have far more. Therefore, it is even more difficult to match tissues between donor and recipient than it is to match blood types.

Surgical techniques for performing many organ transplants are really not that difficult. Historically, the major stumbling block to widespread transplantation of most organs has been the effectiveness of the recipient's immune response. In the normal immune response, cytotoxic T cells swiftly attack and destroy the foreign cells.

Before a transplant is even attempted, then, the donor's and recipient's ABO and other blood group antigens must first be determined. Next, donor and recipient tissues are tested to compare MHC antigens, because cytotoxic T cells target foreign MHC proteins. The closer the relationship between donor and recipient the better, because their MHC antigens are likely to be similar. Although successful transplants can be done between unrelated people, at least a 75% match between tissues is essential. After surgery the patient must take *immunosuppressive drugs* that block the immune response, such as corticosteroid drugs to suppress inflammation or cytotoxic medications that kill rapidly dividing cells (to block activated lymphocytes).

Immunosuppressive therapy can dramatically prolong the lives of transplant patients, but it brings other risks. An impaired immune system cannot protect the body as effectively against pathogens and abnormal cells, so these patients are vulnerable to infections and certain cancers. The key to a successful transplant is to suppress the immune system enough to prevent rejection while preserving as much immune function as possible. Antibiotic drugs can help control infections as they arise.

In recent years, three factors have made organ transplants more successful than ever before: (1) improvements in immunosuppressive drugs, (2) better techniques for cross-matching (or "typing") tissue, and (3) national sharing of information and donor organs through organ-bank systems. The latter allow patients to receive the best matches possible regardless of where they live. These improvements have made organ transplants a viable option for many people. Still in the development phase are attempts to "mask" foreign antigens so that they do not provoke an immune response.

**RECAP**

The major obstacle to organ transplantation is the recipient's immune response, as cytotoxic T cells usually attack all foreign cells. ■

## 9.9 Inappropriate immune system activity causes problems

Conditions characterized by inappropriate immune system activity include allergies and autoimmune disorders such as lupus erythematosus and rheumatoid arthritis.

### Allergies: A hypersensitive immune system

Many of us—perhaps 10% of North Americans—suffer from allergies. Some are relatively minor; others are quite severe. Examples include hay fever, poison ivy rashes, and severe reactions to specific foods or drugs. Some allergic reactions even require hospitalization.

An **allergy** is an inappropriate response of the immune system to an **allergen** (any substance that causes an allergic reaction). The key is "inappropriate": the allergen is not a dangerous pathogen, but the body reacts as if it were.

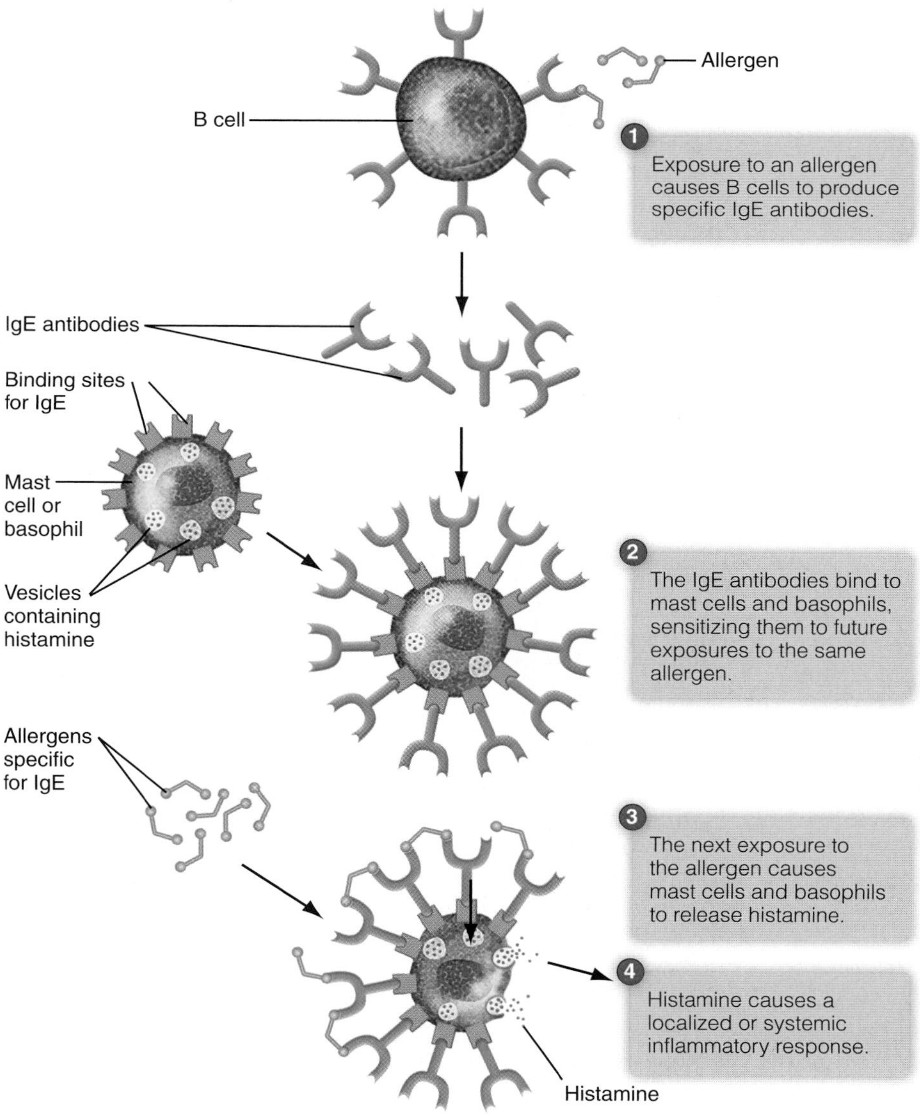


**Figure 9.18 How an allergic reaction develops.**

Recall that there are five classes of immunoglobulins. As shown in (Figure 9.18), the culprits involved in allergic reactions are those in the IgE group. At some point, exposure to an allergen triggers a primary immune response, causing B cells to produce specific IgE antibodies. The IgE antibodies bind to mast cells (found primarily in connective tissue) and to circulating basophils.

When the same allergen enters the body a second time, it binds to the IgE antibodies on mast cells and basophils, causing them to release histamine. The result is an allergic reaction, a typical inflammatory response that includes warmth, redness, swelling, and pain in the area of contact with the allergen. Histamine also increases secretion of mucus in the region. Every time it is exposed to this allergen, the body reacts as if it has an injury or infection, even though it doesn't.

Some allergens, such as poison ivy, affect only the areas exposed. At least 85% of the U.S. population is sensitive to poison ivy. The allergen is a chemical in the plant's sap. Other allergens, including food allergens and bee sting venom, are absorbed or injected into the bloodstream. These substances are carried quickly to mast cells throughout the body, including connective tissue in the respiratory, digestive, and circulatory systems. Such allergens often elicit a *systemic response,* meaning they affect several organ systems. Systemic responses include constriction of smooth muscle in the lungs and digestive system and dilation of blood vessels.

Symptoms of a severe systemic allergic reaction can include difficulty breathing (caused by constricted airways), severe stomach cramps (muscle contractions), swelling throughout the body (increased capillary permeability), and circulatory collapse with a life-threatening fall in blood pressure (dilated arterioles). This is known as *anaphylactic shock*. Anyone who appears to be suffering from anaphylactic shock should be rushed to a hospital, because the reaction can be fatal. The symptoms often begin suddenly, and doctors advise people with a history of strong allergic reactions to carry an emergency kit with them at all times. The kit contains a self-injected hypodermic syringe of epinephrine, a hormone that dilates the airway and constricts peripheral blood vessels, preventing shock.

Most allergies, however, are more annoying than dangerous. Antihistamines—drugs that block the effects of histamine—are often effective treatments for mild to moderate reactions. Allergy shots can help by causing the body to produce large numbers of IgG antibodies, which combine with the allergen and block its attachment to IgE.

**RECAP**

An allergy is an inappropriate inflammatory response. Allergens that produce a systemic response can rapidly affect the ability to breathe and maintain blood pressure. ■

## Autoimmune disorders: Defective recognition of "self"

On rare occasions, the immune system's remarkable ability to distinguish self from nonself fails. When that happens, the immune system may produce antibodies and cytotoxic T cells that target its own cells. Conditions in which this happens are called **autoimmune disorders.**

Approximately 5% of adults in North America, two-thirds of them women, have some type of autoimmune disorder. We don't yet know all the details of how these diseases arise. In some cases, certain antigens simply are never exposed to the immune system as it undergoes fetal development. These antigens were never programmed into the system as self, so when tissue damage exposes them, the mature immune system responds as if they are foreign. In other cases, antibodies produced against a foreign antigen may cross-react with the person's own tissues.

At the moment there are no cures for autoimmune disorders. Treatments include therapies that depress the body's defense mechanisms and relieve the symptoms. Autoimmune conditions include a wide range of diseases, including multiple sclerosis, a progressive disorder of the central nervous system (see Chapter 11), and Type 1 diabetes mellitus, which targets cells in the pancreas (see Chapter 13). Below we look at two more conditions: lupus erythematosus and rheumatoid arthritis.

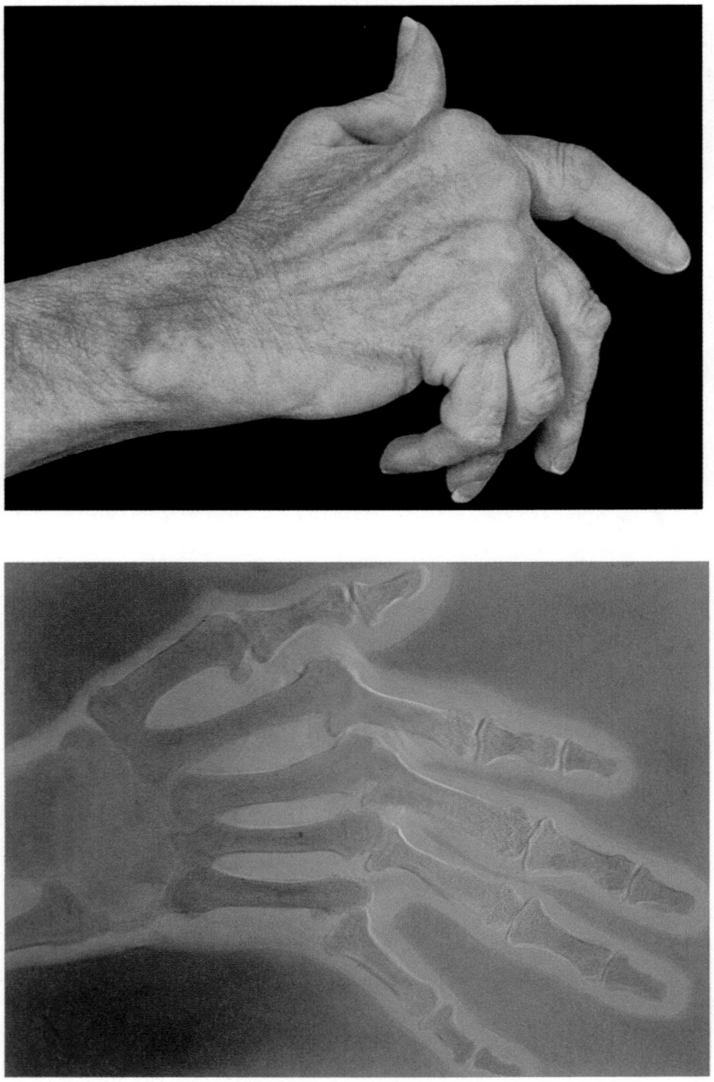

Figure 9.19 **Rheumatoid arthritis.**

**Lupus erythematosus: Inflamed connective tissue** Lupus erythematosus (or *lupus*) is an autoimmune disorder in which the body attacks its own connective tissue. One type of lupus, called discoid lupus erythematosus, primarily affects areas of the skin exposed to sunlight. More serious is systemic lupus erythematosus, which may affect various tissues and organs including the heart, blood vessels, lungs, kidneys, joints, and brain.

Lupus often starts as a red skin rash on the face or head. Other symptoms include fever, fatigue, joint pain, and weight loss. Spreading inflammation can lead to osteoarthritis (see Chapter 5), pericarditis (see Chapter 8), or pleurisy (inflammation of the lining of the lungs).

Lupus affects nine times as many women as men. Typically it occurs during childbearing age and is more common in certain racial groups such as African Americans, West Indians, and Chinese. Medications can reduce the inflammation and alleviate the symptoms.

**Rheumatoid arthritis: Inflamed synovial membranes** Rheumatoid arthritis is a type of arthritis involving inflammation of the synovial membrane that lines certain joints (see Chapter 5). In rheumatoid arthritis, B cells produce antibodies against a protein in the cartilage of synovial membranes. The resulting immune response releases inflammatory chemicals that cause further tissue damage. At first, fingers, wrists, toes, or other joints become painful and stiff. Over time the inflammation destroys joint cartilage and the neighboring bone. Eventually, bony tissue begins to break down and fuse, resulting in deformities (Figure 9.19) and reduced range of motion. The disease is intermittent, but with each recurrence the damage is progressively worse.

Pain-relieving medications can help many people with rheumatoid arthritis, as can regular mild exercise and physical therapy to improve range of motion. Powerful drugs that neutralize chemicals in the inflammatory response can prevent joints from becoming deformed. Surgery to replace damaged joints with artificial joints can restore the ability to move and prevent painful disabilities.

**RECAP**

An autoimmune disorder occurs when the immune system fails to distinguish self from nonself cells and begins to attack the body's own cells. Examples of autoimmune disorders are lupus erythematosus (inflammation of connective tissue) and rheumatoid arthritis (inflammation of synovial membranes). ■

## 9.10 Immune deficiency: The special case of AIDS

*Immune deficiency* is a general term for an immune system that is not functioning properly. One immune deficiency disease is *severe combined immunodeficiency disease (SCID)*. For the rare person who inherits SCID, even a minor infection can become life threatening. People with SCID have too few functional lymphocytes to defend the body against infections.

By far the most common and best-known severe immune deficiency condition is **AIDS (acquired immune deficiency syndrome).** *A syndrome* is a medical term for a group of symptoms that occur together, and *acquired* means that one catches it—in this case by becoming infected with the virus called **HIV (human immunodeficiency virus).**

### HIV targets helper T cells of the immune system

Figure 9.20 shows the structure of HIV. The virus consists of nothing more than single-stranded RNA and enzymes, wrapped in two protein coats and a phospholipid membrane with protein spikes. It has no nucleus and no organelles. Like other viruses, HIV infects by entering a cell and using the cell's machinery to reproduce. HIV targets helper T cells, gaining entry by attaching to CD4 receptors.

HIV belongs to a particular class of viruses called *retroviruses* that have a unique way of replicating (Figure 9.21). Retroviruses first attach to the CD4 receptor of a helper T cell. The attachment fuses the retrovirus's envelope with the cell's membrane, releasing the viral RNA and

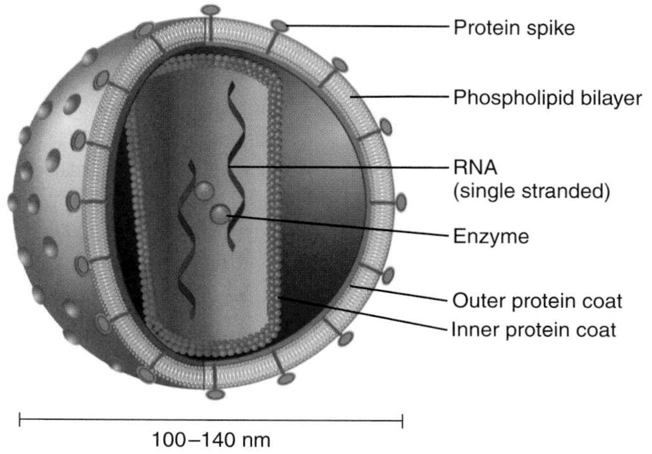


**Figure 9.20 The structure of HIV.**

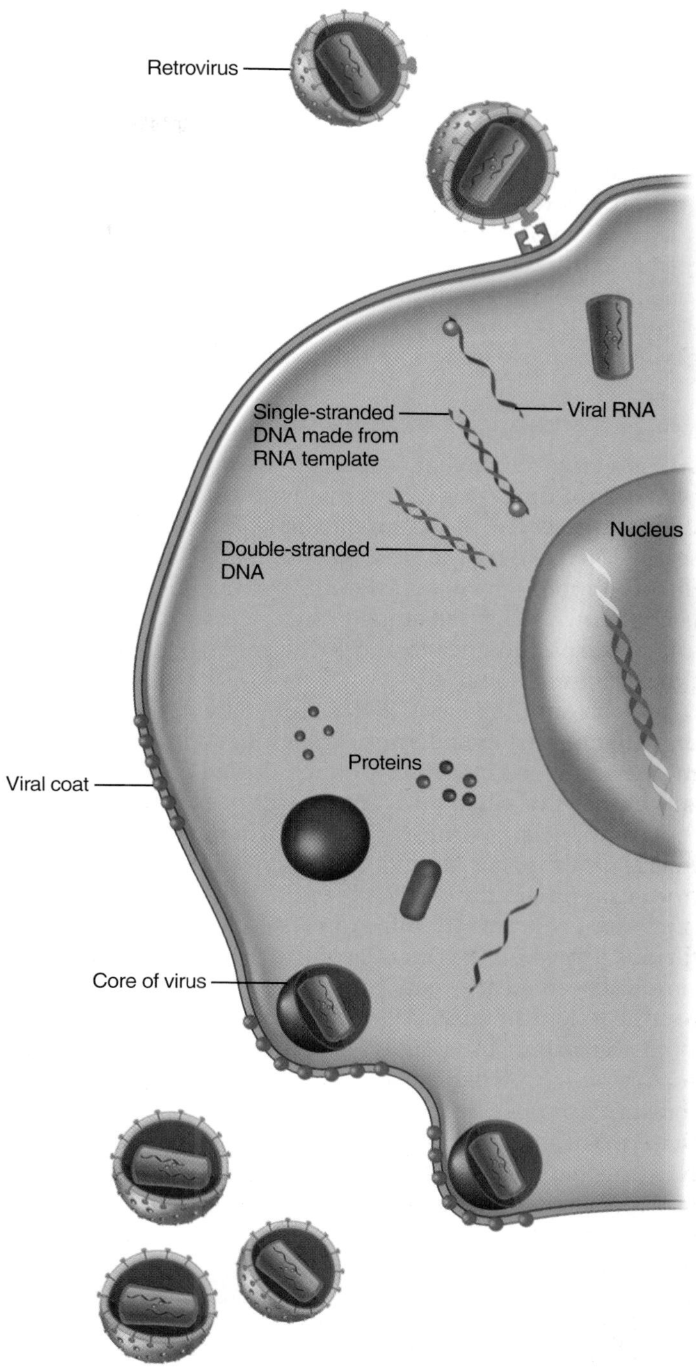


**Figure 9.21 How HIV replicates.** After binding to a helper T cell's CD4 receptor, the virus injects its RNA and enzymes into the cell and uses them to force the cell to make single- and then double-stranded DNA. The DNA is inserted into the cell's own DNA within the nucleus, where it directs the cell to make more protein coat and viral RNA and protein core. The coats and cores join, exiting the cell as new viruses.

enzymes into the cell. Under the influence of the viral enzymes and using the viral RNA as a template (a pattern), the host cell is forced to make a single strand of DNA complementary to the viral RNA, and from it a second strand of DNA complementary to the first. The new double-stranded DNA fragment is then inserted into the cell's DNA. The cell, not recognizing the DNA as foreign, uses it to produce more viral RNA and proteins, which are then assembled into thousands of new viruses within the cell. The sheer magnitude of viral replication so saps the T cell's energy that eventually it dies and ruptures, releasing the viral copies. The new viruses move on to infect yet other helper T cells.

## HIV is transmitted in body fluids

HIV is a fragile virus that cannot survive dry conditions for even a short time. This means that it cannot be transmitted through the air, by casual contact, or by doorknobs or toilet seats. However, HIV can be transmitted in at least four body fluids—blood, semen, breast milk, and vaginal secretions. It is not known to be transmitted by contact with urine, feces, saliva, perspiration, tears, or nasal secretions unless those fluids contain blood.

Most commonly, HIV is transmitted by sexual contact or contaminated hypodermic needles. In addition, infected mothers can pass it to their children during pregnancy, labor and delivery, or when breast-feeding. It has been estimated, for example, that a healthy newborn who is breastfed by an infected mother has about a 20% chance of contracting HIV from its mother's milk. Until the mid-1980s a significant number of cases of HIV infection resulted from blood transfusions. However, the risk of acquiring HIV from a transfusion has been greatly reduced since 1985, when it became routine to test blood for HIV antibodies.

Because transmission of HIV generally requires direct contact with body fluids, HIV is considered relatively hard to transmit from person to person (at least when compared to such common diseases as the flu). However, unlike the flu, HIV is extremely virulent unless it is aggressively treated with an expensive regimen of drugs—over 90% of all U.S. citizens diagnosed with AIDS by 1988 are now dead.

## AIDS develops slowly

The symptoms of HIV infection and the subsequent development of full-blown AIDS progress slowly. The course of the disease falls into three phases (Figure 9.22).

**Phase I** Phase I lasts anywhere from a few weeks to a few years after initial exposure to the virus. There is a brief spike in HIV in the blood, followed by typical flulike symptoms of swollen lymph nodes, chills and fever, fatigue, and body aches. The immune system's T cell population may decline briefly then rebound as the body begins to produce more cells and antibodies against the virus. The presence of antibodies against the virus is the basis for a diagnosis of HIV infection, and a person having these antibodies is said to be "HIV-positive." However, he or she will not yet have the disease syndrome called AIDS.

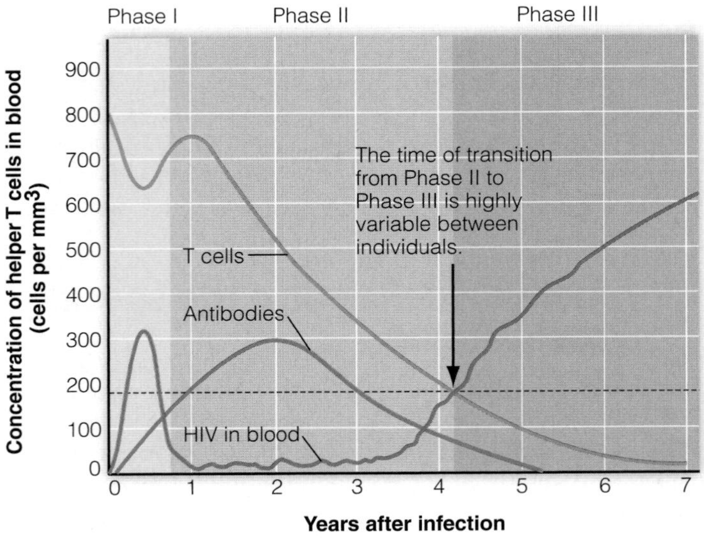


**Figure 9.22 Time course of the progression toward AIDS after HIV infection.** Phase I is characterized by flulike symptoms followed by apparent recovery. There is a brief spike in HIV in the blood. Within six months HIV-specific antibodies appear. In phase II there is a slow decline in the number of T cells. Most of the HIV is harbored inside cells. Phase III (AIDS) is characterized by a T cell count of less than 200 per cubic millimeter of blood, a decline in HIV-specific antibodies, a rise in HIV in blood, opportunistic infections, and certain cancers.

Unless they suspect they have been exposed to HIV, most people would not associate phase I symptoms with HIV infection and so would not think to be tested. The antibodies do not destroy the virus entirely because many of the virus particles remain inside cells, where antibodies and immune cells cannot reach them.

**Phase II** In phase II the virus begins to do its damage, wiping out more and more of the helper T cells. The loss of T cells makes the person more vulnerable to *opportunistic infections*—infections that take advantage of the weakened immune system to establish themselves in the body. During phase II people *may* have persistent or recurrent flulike symptoms, but they may have no symptoms at all if they do not have an opportunistic infection. If they have not been tested for HIV antibodies they may not even know they are infected.

Two-thirds to three-quarters of all people who test positive for antibodies to HIV do not exhibit symptoms associated with AIDS. During phases I and II, many people pass the virus on to others without realizing it. Those they infect may transmit the virus to still others. Phase II can occur within 6 months, but on average it takes about 10 years to progress to phase III. Left untreated, 95% of people in phase II progress to phase III.

**Phase III** Once the number of helper T cells of an HIV-positive person falls below 200 per cubic millimeter of blood *and* the person has an opportunistic infection or type of cancer associated with HIV infection, the person is said to have AIDS. Infections and cancers associated with AIDS include pneumonia,

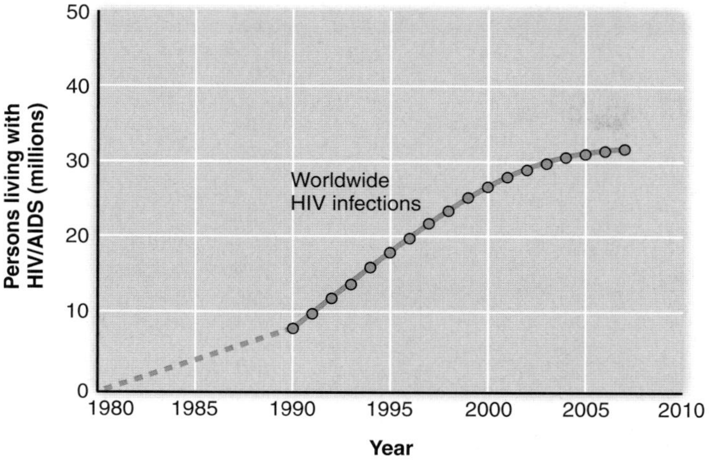


**Figure 9.23 Estimated number of persons living with HIV infections or AIDS worldwide.** Dashed line represents data that are not available.

*Source:* Joint United Nations Programme on HIV/AIDS, 2007.

meningitis, tuberculosis, encephalitis, Kaposi's sarcoma, and non-Hodgkin's lymphoma, among others.

Notice that AIDS may not appear until years after initial HIV infection. Untreated AIDS is nearly always fatal.

## The AIDS epidemic: A global health issue

AIDS was first described in 1981 when the Centers for Disease Control in Atlanta began to notice a disturbing similarity between cases involving a strange collection of symptoms (this illustrates the advantage of having a central clearing-house for information). It is now believed that HIV first infected humans in the 1960s in Africa after "jumping species" from other primates to humans.

The worldwide damage done by HIV so far is truly astonishing. By the end of 1990 there were almost 8 million HIV-infected people worldwide (although accurate numbers are hard to come by). More than 33 million people are currently living with HIV infection or AIDS (Figure 9.23), representing nearly 1% of the adult population worldwide. New infections are occurring at a rate of nearly 7,000 people per day. Fully two-thirds of all HIV-infected people reside in sub-Saharan Africa, where the disease is thought to have originated. The areas of the world where the AIDS epidemic is increasing most rapidly include sub-Saharan Africa, South and Southeast Asia, and Eastern Europe.

So far, more than 25 million people have died of AIDS. In recent years the death toll from AIDS has been hovering around 2 million people per year.

The picture is not much better in the U.S. (Figure 9.24). In this country, the number of newly diagnosed cases of HIV/AIDS is on the rise again. From 2001 to 2004, the last three years for which data are available, the number of newly diagnosed cases of HIV/AIDS rose 8%. The largest percentage increase in diagnosed cases (33%) is among young adults aged 20–24. AIDS is now a leading cause of death among African American women aged 25–44.

The number of deaths from AIDS in the U.S. has stabilized at about 17,000 per year after peaking in 1995 at just over 50,000 per year. Part of the decline in death rates since 1995 is due to new drugs that suppress the HIV infection and

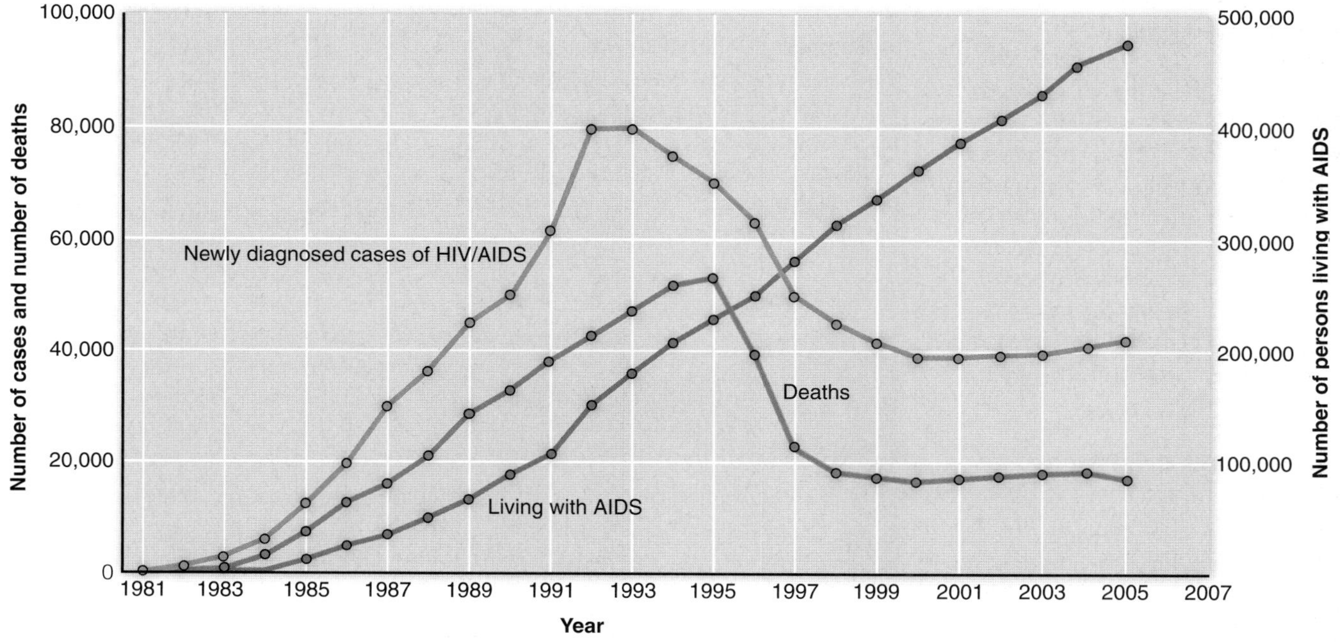


**Figure 9.24 The numbers of newly diagnosed cases of HIV/AIDS, deaths from AIDS, and persons living with HIV/AIDS in the United States for each year since the disease was first reported.**

*Source:* Centers for Disease Control and Prevention, HIV/AIDS Surveillance Report 2005.

# Current Issue

## AIDS: A Crisis in Africa and Asia, a Challenge for the World

Africa and Asia are in the midst of an AIDS epidemic. How bad is it, how will it affect us, and what (if anything) are we willing to do about it?

### In Africa, AIDS Is Out of Control

Approximately two-thirds of the world's HIV-infected people live in sub-Saharan Africa. The United Nations estimates that 22.5 million people there are already infected with HIV. The region accounts for more than three quarters of the world's AIDS deaths.

Patterns of AIDS infection and transmission in Africa differ from those of industrialized countries. In the United States, more men than women are infected with HIV, which is often transmitted via homosexual sex. In Africa, however, an estimated 61% of HIV-infected persons are women who have contracted the virus heterosexually. Studies in several African nations have found that females aged 15–19 are four to five times more likely to be infected than males their age. According to one report, in Africa older HIV-infected men coerce or pay impoverished girls to have sex in the mistaken belief that sex with a virgin will cure AIDS.

The problem of AIDS in sub-Saharan Africa is made worse by political, economic, and social instability. Of the area's 42 nations, almost a third are at war. Many of these economies are weak, sanitation is poor, and even rudimentary medical services are often lacking. Malnutrition and starvation are widespread. Approximately 11 million children in sub-Saharan Africa have already been orphaned by AIDS, war, or famine. Many of them are abandoned and impoverished, fending for themselves without adult supervision.

### In Asia the AIDS Crisis Is Building

Southeast Asia is moving in the same direction. Researchers in India, Vietnam, and Thailand report rapid growth of the AIDS epidemic, which is spreading beyond urban areas to the general population. With a total population of almost 1 billion, the potential impact on India could be overwhelming. The damage is economic as well as medical. AIDS strikes young people in their most productive years, cutting families' earnings and straining government health and social service budgets.

*One-third of these African schoolchildren are orphans whose parents have died of HIV/AIDS.*

What should we do, if anything? There are humanitarian reasons for helping, of course. But there are other reasons for helping, too, including self-interest. According to one scenario, an out-of-control worldwide epidemic would affect our security, the worldwide economy, and even the ability to travel. Like it or not, we live in a global village.

### What Can Be Done?

Any solution to the growing AIDS crisis in other countries must recognize that their problems are different from ours. Possibilities for helping include:

- Providing accurate information on HIV transmission and helping people understand how their sexual practices may contribute to the spread of the disease
- Seeking AIDS treatments and preventive measures that are inexpensive enough to be used effectively in poor countries
- Providing economic assistance and encouraging political stability in other regions
- Improving the delivery of health care

These strategies will not be easy or cheap. For example, improving the delivery of health care

## the facts...

- Two-thirds of the world's HIV-infected people live in sub-Saharan Africa.
- In sub-Saharan Africa, girls aged 15-19 are four to five times more likely to be HIV-infected than boys.
- Attempts to solve the AIDS crisis in Africa are hampered by poor infrastructure, inadequate health care, poor medical record keeping, and educational, political and social issues.
- African and Asian nations cannot afford the high cost of current AIDS treatment drugs.

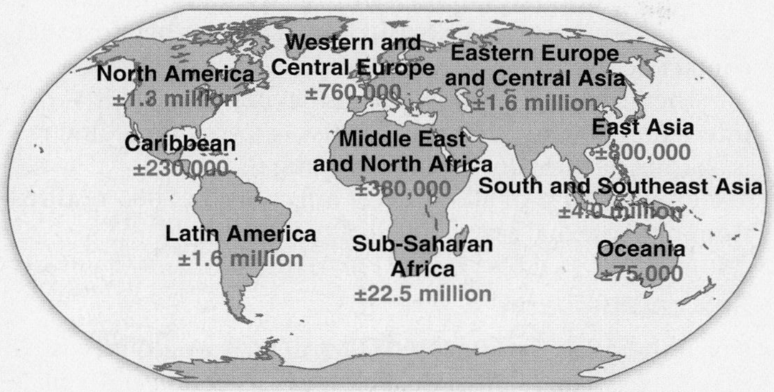


*Over two-thirds of all people living with HIV live in sub-Saharan Africa.*

in sub-Saharan Africa will be difficult in rural areas without roads and bridges and in nations with too few medical personnel. Then there is the problem of identifying AIDS patients in the first place. As discussed in this chapter, people in North America who are suspected of having AIDS generally are tested for HIV, and health professionals maintain careful records documenting their symptoms and treatments. In contrast, African nations do not require that suspected AIDS patients be tested for HIV, and health professionals often can't monitor patients effectively or even pay for the tests to diagnose AIDS. Other health problems rampant in the region, including malnutrition, tuberculosis, and malaria, have symptoms—weight loss, fever, fatigue—that resemble those of AIDS.

What about education? The public information campaigns used in this country may not work in countries with less developed media networks. Furthermore, social norms are different, and misinformation and denial are widespread. Many researchers advocate sex education for both boys and girls, and developing strategies to change men's sexual behavior. Providing male and female condoms at low cost might also help. In Thailand, a national program to promote condom use lowered the prevalence of HIV among 21-year-old military conscripts from 4% in the mid-1990s to less than 1% by 2002.

An HIV caretaker supports an AIDS victim in Ethiopia.

A final hurdle is the cost of treatment. Recent advances in AIDS treatment depend on new drugs that can cost up to $2,500 per month—more than many Africans earn in a year. Pharmaceutical managers point out that a company spends an average of $500 million to develop just one new drug. High prices for new AIDS drugs reflect the enormous research and development costs that are required by U.S. law to ensure drugs' safety and effectiveness. Would we be willing to accept lower development costs (and therefore less assurance of safety and effectiveness in North America) to make drugs more widely available? Should we set a different standard for medicines destined for export than we accept here?

Soaring drug prices are also a consequence of U.S. patent law, which seeks to prevent companies in other countries from copying drugs developed in the U.S. and selling them overseas at lower prices. Foreign firms can manufacture and sell AIDS medicines at one-tenth of the U.S. price because they do not have to recover development costs. In addition to selling the low-cost drugs abroad, they smuggle them into North America. Pharmaceutical firms protest that, by cutting into profits, the knockoffs endanger future research and the development of even better treatments. They have struck back by taking legal action against distributors and purchasers of illegal AIDS medications.

The challenge of AIDS is likely to remain with us for some time. We can deal with it now or deal with an even larger problem later.

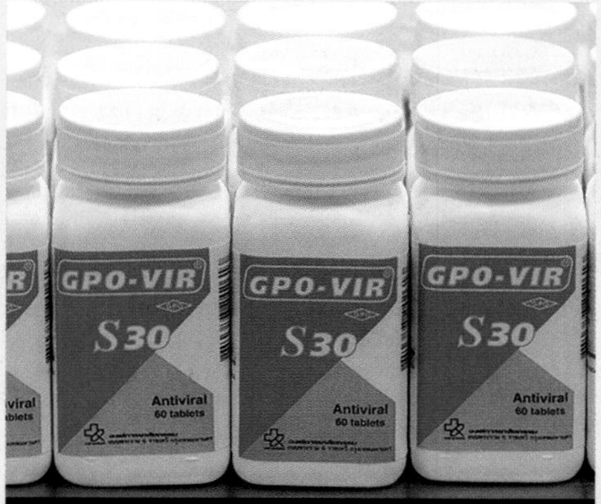


This AIDS drug manufactured in Thailand costs less than $400/year.

## Questions to consider

**1** *What strategies do you think would be most effective in reducing AIDS in sub-Saharan Africa? Explain your reasoning.*

**2** *Should pharmaceutical companies be required to lower the cost of AIDS medicines?*

**3** *As a matter of public health, should governments ensure that AIDS medicines are available at a reasonable cost to those who need them?*

keep infected people alive much longer. Meanwhile, the number of persons living with HIV/AIDS in the U.S. continues to climb because there are over twice as many new diagnoses of HIV/AIDS per year as there are deaths from AIDS.

The stabilization of death rates in the U.S. does not necessarily portend a similar trend in the rest of the world. The treatment of AIDS is very expensive (as much as $10,000–30,000 per person per year), leaving little hope that those currently infected with HIV in Africa or Asia will ever live to see effective treatment.

## Risky behaviors increase your chances of getting AIDS

Because your behavior will ultimately determine your risk for AIDS, it's worth knowing what constitutes "risky behavior" in terms of HIV infection. Table 9.3 shows how HIV is contracted in the U.S. among adults and adolescents (people above 12 years of age).

Nearly three-fourths of all new cases of AIDS in 2005 were men. For men, the most risky behaviors are sharing needles during intravenous drug use or engaging in sex with other males. Some men mistakenly believe that they cannot get AIDS if their only risky behavior is heterosexual sex. They are wrong. The fact that a low percentage of men contract HIV by heterosexual contact may be due to much higher infection rates in men by drug use or homosexual activity, rather than to a low risk of infection by heterosexual contact per se.

The primary risk for women is having sex with HIV-infected men. The other primary risk category for women is sharing needles during injected drug use.

Overall, 19% of all new HIV infections in 2005 resulted from heterosexual sex.

**Table 9.3 AIDS cases in adults and adolescents in 2005, by sex and exposure category**

| Exposure category | Percent of total |
|---|---|
| *Males* | |
| Men who have sex with other men | 48 |
| Injected drug use | 13 |
| Men who have sex with other men and injected drug use | 6 |
| High-risk heterosexual contact: | 10 |
| (Sex with injection drug user) | (1) |
| (Sex with HIV-infected person) | (9) |
| Risk factor not reported or identified | 23 |
| **Male total: 30,956 cases** | **100** |
| *Females* | |
| Injected drug use | 19 |
| High-risk heterosexual contact: | 45 |
| (Sex with injection drug user) | (7) |
| (Sex with bisexual male) | (2) |
| (Sex with HIV-infected person) | (36) |
| Receipt of blood transfusion, blood components, or tissue | 1 |
| Risk factor not reported or identified | 35 |
| **Female total: 10,944 cases** | **100** |

*Source:* Centers for Disease Control and Prevention, HIV/AIDS Surveillance Report, 2005.

## Sex can be safer

Given the risks of contracting HIV/AIDS, it would be wise to make sex as safe as possible. Below are several *safer sex guidelines* and some of the evidence for them. The suggestions do not guarantee complete safety, which is why they are called recommendations for "safer" rather than "safe" sex.

- *Abstain from sex.* Eliminating sexual contact eliminates risk, and some people choose abstinence for ethical as well as practical reasons. However, abstinence may not be considered desirable or practical. In that case, your safest course is to follow as many of the following guidelines as possible.
- *Reduce the number of sexual partners.* Evidence shows that this is particularly effective among homosexual men. The evidence is not yet conclusive regarding the relationship between HIV infection and number of partners in heterosexual transmission, perhaps because the median number of partners is generally lower. Nevertheless, it makes sense that fewer partners translates to less risk.
- *Choose a sexual partner with low-risk behavior.* This is especially important. A partner who has a history of injecting drugs or a man who has sex with other men is a high-risk partner. One study reported that choosing a partner who is not in any high-risk group lowers the risk of AIDS almost 5,000-fold.
- *Avoid certain high-risk sexual practices.* Any sexual behavior that increases the risk of direct blood contact, such as anal-genital sex, should be considered risky. Oral-genital sex is less risky but not risk-free.
- *Use latex or polyurethane condoms or other barriers.* In laboratory tests, latex or polyurethane condoms prevent the passage of HIV. How effective they are in actual use is not certain, but since they are about 90% effective as a birth control method, a reasonable hypothesis (not yet tested) is that they reduce the risk of HIV by about the same amount. Condoms are effective only if used consistently and correctly. Natural skin condoms are not as safe as latex condoms. The use of dental dams is recommended for oral-vaginal sex.
- *Use nonoxynol-9, a spermicidal agent.* In laboratory tests, nonoxynol-9 has been shown to inhibit the growth of HIV. Be aware, however, that the evidence is conflicting

regarding whether nonoxynol-9 offers any protection during sexual contact.

- *Get tested (and have your partner tested).* Notice, however, that the HIV tests currently available are designed to detect the human *antibodies* to HIV, not the virus itself. It can take up to six months after exposure to produce enough antibodies for the antibody test to become positive. For this reason, retesting at least six months after the last possible exposure is a good idea. Evidence shows that close to 90% of HIV-infected persons will have a positive HIV antibody test result within six months. A negative test at six months indicates substantially lower risk, but it does not provide complete assurance. A few individuals may not test positive for three or more years.

### New treatments offer hope

As yet there is no cure for AIDS, but researchers are investigating more than a hundred drugs to treat the condition. Some drugs, such as AZT, inhibit the enzymes the virus needs to replicate inside the cell. Others, such as ritonavir and saquinavir, are protease inhibitors (protease is an enzyme required to assemble viral proteins).

In 2007 the FDA approved maraviroc (brand name Celsentri), the first new oral class of HIV treatment in more than a decade. Developed by Pfizer, miraviroc works by inhibiting the entry of the virus into healthy T cells. If the virus can't enter the T cell it can't take over its metabolic machinery and force it to make more viruses. Maraviroc is expected to be a blockbuster drug for Pfizer, with annual sales of $500 million by 2011.

In addition to treating full-blown AIDS, doctors are starting to treat people who are infected with HIV but don't yet show the symptoms of AIDS. This approach may prevent the widespread destruction of the immune system that precedes the onset of symptoms. Many health professionals advise people to be tested for HIV so that asymptomatic cases can be detected and treated early.

Some researchers believe that safe and effective vaccines offer the only real hope of conquering HIV. Several dozen potential vaccines are already being tested on human volunteers around the world, but so far none has proved effective enough to warrant widespread use.

The production of vaccines is complicated by the fact that HIV mutates rather quickly. There are already several strains of the virus, each of which would need a separate vaccine. In addition, HIV is so dangerous that it is considered too risky to produce vaccines from whole but weakened viruses, the way many other vaccines are produced. Most HIV vaccines are produced from other viruses engineered to contain pieces of the HIV virus, or from pieces of the HIV viral genetic material.

**RECAP**

AIDS (acquired immune deficiency syndrome) is a devastating disorder of the immune system caused by a virus (HIV) that attacks helper T cells. HIV is transmitted in body fluids, typically through sexual contact, blood transfusions, contaminated needles, or breast-feeding. ■

## Chapter Summary

### Pathogens cause disease *p. 187*

- Pathogens include bacteria, viruses, fungi, protozoa, worms, and possibly prions.
- Bacteria have very little internal structure and are covered by a rigid outer cell wall.
- Viruses cannot reproduce on their own. Viral reproduction requires a living host cell.
- Prions are misfolded proteins that replicate by causing a normal protein to misfold.
- The danger from a particular pathogen depends on *how* it is transmitted, how *easily* it is transmitted, and how *damaging* the resulting disease is.

### The lymphatic system defends the body *p. 190*

- The lymphatic system consists of vessels, lymph nodes, the spleen, the thymus gland, and the tonsils.
- The lymphatic system helps protect us against disease.
- Phagocytic cells in the spleen, lymph nodes, and tonsils engulf and kill microorganisms.
- The thymus gland secretes hormones that help T lymphocytes mature.

### Keeping pathogens out: The first line of defense *p. 192*

- Skin is an effective barrier to the entry of microorganisms.
- Tears, saliva, mucus, and earwax trap organisms and/or wash them away.
- Digestive acid in the stomach kills many microorganisms.
- Vomiting, defecation, and urination physically remove microorganisms after entry.

### Nonspecific defenses: The second line of defense *p. 194*

- Phagocytes surround and engulf microorganisms and damaged cells.
- Inflammation has four outward signs: redness, warmth, swelling, and pain.
- Natural killer cells kill their targets by releasing damaging chemicals.
- Circulating proteins of the complement system either kill microorganisms directly or mark them for destruction.
- Interferons are proteins that interfere with viral reproduction.
- Fever raises body temperature, creating a hostile environment for some microorganisms.

### Specific defense mechanisms: The third line of defense *p. 197*

- Cells of the immune system can distinguish foreign or damaged cells from our own healthy cells.

- All cells have cell-surface markers called MHC proteins that identify the cells as "self."
- An antigen is a substance that stimulates the immune system and provokes an immune response.
- B cells produce antibodies against foreign antigens.
- T cells of several types release chemicals that enhance the immune response and kill foreign cells directly.

### Immune memory creates immunity *p. 202*

- Information about an antigen is stored in memory cells after first exposure.
- The second exposure to the antigen produces a much greater immune response than the first.
- The rapidity of the second response is the basis of immunity from disease.

### Medical assistance in the war against pathogens *p. 203*

- Vaccines immunize the body in advance against a particular disease.
- Injected antibodies provide temporary immunity and are of some benefit against an existing infection.
- Monoclonal antibodies are used primarily in medical tests.
- Antibiotics are effective against bacteria, but not against viruses.

### Tissue rejection: A medical challenge *p. 205*

- The phenomenon of tissue rejection is a normal consequence of the body's ability to recognize self from nonself.
- Immunosuppressive drugs, the ability to test for various antigens, and organ donor matching programs have increased the success rate of organ transplantation in humans.

### Inappropriate immune system activity causes problems *p. 207*

- Allergies occur when the immune system responds excessively to foreign particles that are not otherwise harmful.
- Autoimmune disorders develop when a person's immune system attacks the person's own cells as if they were foreign.

### Immune deficiency: The special case of AIDS *p. 209*

- AIDS is caused by a virus (HIV).
- The disease can take years to develop after initial HIV infection, but it is nearly always fatal.
- Worldwide, the number of cases of HIV infection and of AIDS is still rising rapidly.
- The chances of contracting AIDS can be reduced (but never eliminated completely) by practicing "safer" sex.

## Terms You Should Know

active immunization, *204*
AIDS (acquired immune deficiency syndrome), *209*
antibiotics, *188*
antibody, *198*
antibody-mediated immunity, *198*
antigen, *197*
bacteria, *187*
B cell, *198*
cell-mediated immunity, *198*
cytokines, *201*
HIV (human immunodeficiency virus), *209*
immune response, *197*
inflammation, *194*
monoclonal antibodies, *204*
passive immunization, *204*
pathogen, *187*
prion, *189*
T cell, *198*
vaccine, *204*
virus, *188*

## Concept Review

1. Define the term pathogen and give some examples.
2. Describe what is unusual about viruses that causes some people to question whether they are living things.
3. Explain how prions affect human health.
4. Describe the functions of organs of the lymphatic system.
5. List the four components of an inflammatory response.
6. Describe in general terms the distinction between *nonspecific* and *specific* defense mechanisms.
7. Describe the concept of an antigen and how it relates to self and nonself markers.
8. Describe how cells that belong to a particular individual are identified so that the individual's immune system doesn't attack them.
9. Explain how cytotoxic T cells kill target cells.
10. Describe how a vaccine produces immunity from a specific disease.

## Test Yourself

### Matching Exercise

_____ 1. A phagocytic white blood cell best described as a "large eater"
_____ 2. Responsible for cell-mediated immunity
_____ 3. A "self" marker group of proteins found on the surface of every cell
_____ 4. Infectious protein responsible for the disease BSE
_____ 5. A type of cell that secretes histamine
_____ 6. The word for the type of proteins to which antibodies belong

a. mast cell
b. major histocompatibility complex (MHC)
c. immunoglobulins
d. T cells
e. prion
f. macrophage

### Fill in the Blank

7. Ebola kills more than 80% of all those infected, making it one of the most __________________ pathogens in existence.
8. Virus-infected cells secrete a group of proteins called __________________ that improve the ability of nearby cells to resist the viral infection.
9. A substance that causes an allergic reaction is called a(n) __________________.
10. Lymph __________________ cleanse the lymph while the __________________ cleanses the blood.
11. Defective recognition of "self" by the immune system results in a(n) __________________ disorder.
12. Antibodies prepared from a clone of cells derived from a single B cell are called __________________ antibodies.

### True or False?

13. A mild fever may be beneficial in fighting an infection.
14. Passive immunization protects against future infections longer than active immunization.
15. AIDS is so deadly because HIV infection destroys B cells so that antibodies are not produced.

## References and Additional Reading

Garrett, Laurie. *The Coming Plague: Newly Emerging Diseases in a World Out of Balance*. New York: Penguin Books, 1995. 750 pp. (A compelling look at the potential for worldwide epidemics of communicable diseases.)

Newman, Jack. How Breast Milk Protects Newborns. *Scientific American*, December 1995. (Cells and antibodies in breast milk protect newborns until their immune system develops.)

Preston, Richard. *The Hot Zone*. New York: Anchor Books, 1994. 411 pp. (A gripping true account of an outbreak of Ebola, one of the most dangerous viruses in the world.)

Shilts, Randy. *And the Band Played On: Politics, People, and the AIDS Epidemic*. New York: St. Martin's Press, 1987. 630 pp. (The story of the very earliest years of the AIDS epidemic in America.)

### Internet References

Find links to the following Web sites at the Human Biology Place.

**Centers for Disease Control and Prevention, HIV/AIDS Surveillance Reports**
**www.cdc.gov/hiv/topics/surveillance/resources/reports/index.htm**
Started in 1982, these annual reports provide important statistical data on HIV/AIDS in the United States.

**Joint United Nations Programme on HIV/AIDS**
**www.unaids.org/en**
An international coalition that tracks the worldwide epidemic and mobilizes resources.

**World Health Organization Factsheets**
**www.who.int/topics/en**
Factsheets on a variety of health and disease topics, from arsenic to zoonoses, produced by the World Health Organization.

## Apply **What You Know**

1. When you get a minor infection in a small cut in the skin, sometimes soaking it in hot water speeds the healing process. How might the heat help?
2. Explain why antibiotics don't work against viruses.
3. Everyone knows that bacteria can cause disease. Suppose that we could actually remove all bacteria from our bodies all at once. Would that be a good thing or a bad thing?
4. In 1918 a pandemic of a deadly flu strain killed upwards of 30 million people. If that same flu strain were to come around again, would we be better off or worse off than those who were alive in 1918?
5. Researchers have been working on an effective vaccine for gonorrheal infections for some years. One promising vaccine is delivered via a spray into the nasal cavity. This is clearly not the site of gonococcal infection. Why would one administer a vaccine meant to protect the reproductive tract into the nasal cavity?
6. Why is it that most people get the chickenpox only once, but they can get a cold or the flu over and over again throughout a lifetime?
7. The immune system is supposed to defend us from harmful microorganisms. Why doesn't it always work? In other words, why do some people still get sick and die?

*Answers can be found on the Human Biology Place.*

# 10 The Respiratory System: Exchange of Gases

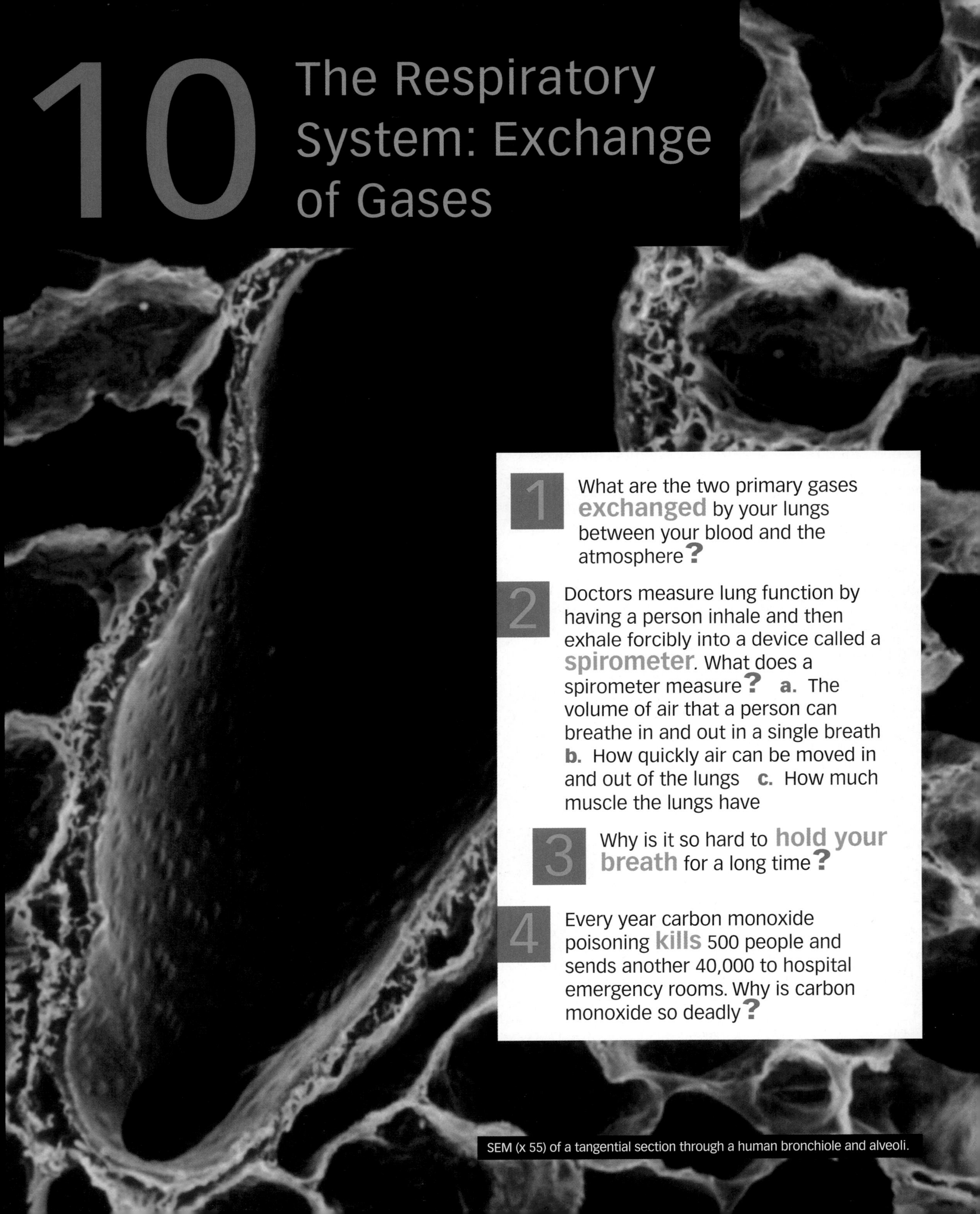

SEM (x 55) of a tangential section through a human bronchiole and alveoli.

1. What are the two primary gases **exchanged** by your lungs between your blood and the atmosphere?

2. Doctors measure lung function by having a person inhale and then exhale forcibly into a device called a **spirometer**. What does a spirometer measure? **a.** The volume of air that a person can breathe in and out in a single breath **b.** How quickly air can be moved in and out of the lungs **c.** How much muscle the lungs have

3. Why is it so hard to **hold your breath** for a long time?

4. Every year carbon monoxide poisoning **kills** 500 people and sends another 40,000 to hospital emergency rooms. Why is carbon monoxide so deadly?

**Your dinner companion is turning blue.** One minute ago he was laughing and drinking and spearing his steak with enthusiasm, and now he can't breathe or talk and is frantically pulling at his collar.

Choking is an emergency, but one that is seldom handled by emergency medical personnel. The victim's fate is almost always decided before professional help can arrive. Unless someone in the immediate vicinity can quickly intervene to relieve the choking, there's a good chance the person won't survive.

We can live for days without nutrients or water, but will die within minutes if denied oxygen. Of all the exchanges of materials between an animal and its environment, the exchange of respiratory gases is almost always the most urgent.

What is the physical basis of this urgency? All cells use energy and certain raw materials in order to survive, grow, and reproduce. To do this, cells rely on aerobic metabolism, meaning that they use up oxygen and create carbon dioxide as a waste product. As discussed in Chapter 3, oxygen is the final electron acceptor in cellular respiration, essential for the production of ATP for most cells. Without oxygen, essential cellular processes cannot continue. Removal of carbon dioxide from the tissues is a pressing concern as well, since its accumulation in the body has many harmful effects.

The primary function of the **respiratory system** is to exchange these gases (oxygen and carbon dioxide) with the air. We extract oxygen from the air we breathe, and when we exhale we get rid of carbon dioxide, the waste product of our metabolism. The oxygen in the air we breathe comes from plants. Plants absorb carbon dioxide through small pores in their leaves and use it in their own energy-producing process called *photosynthesis*. In the process, they produce oxygen for their (and coincidentally our) use. (We consider this and other examples of ecosystems and the delicate balance of life on Earth in Chapters 23 and 24.)

## 10.1 Respiration takes place throughout the body

The term *respiration* encompasses four processes:

- *Breathing* (also called **ventilation**). The movement of air into and out of the lungs.
- *External respiration.* The exchange of gases between inhaled air and blood.
- *Internal respiration.* The exchange of gases between the blood and tissue fluids.
- *Cellular respiration.* The process of using oxygen to produce ATP within cells. Cellular respiration generates carbon dioxide as a waste product.

Breathing is facilitated by the respiratory system and its associated bones, muscles, and nerves. External respiration takes place within the lungs, and internal respiration and cellular respiration take place in the tissues throughout the body.

The respiratory system in humans and most animals has another function in addition to gas exchange, and that is the production of sound (vocalization). The production of sound is an important mechanism that infants use to signal their adult caregivers. Sound production has, of course, also proved valuable in information exchange and cultural development, and thus contributes to the long-term survival of our species.

## 10.2 The respiratory system consists of upper and lower respiratory tracts

The respiratory system (Figure 10.1) consists of (1) a system of passageways for getting air to and from the lungs and (2) the lungs themselves, where gas exchange actually occurs. Also important to respiration are the bones, muscles, and components of the nervous system that cause air to move into and out of the lungs.

### Answers to Intro Questions

1 **Oxygen and carbon dioxide.** Oxygen in the air you breathe is transferred to the blood and carried to all cells, where it helps drive cellular metabolism. Carbon dioxide, a waste product of metabolism, is exhaled by the lungs back into the atmosphere. In this chapter we'll see how gas exchange and gas transport occur.

2 **a and b.** The volume of air that a person can breathe in and out with each breath and the rate at which air can be moved in and out are indicators that help physicians diagnose certain lung diseases, such as asthma.

3 The mechanisms that regulate your body's breathing are so strong that you can't override them for long, even when you want to. If you try to hold your breath indefinitely you'll lose consciousness, at which point the automatic mechanisms take over again.

4 Carbon monoxide reduces the ability of your blood to carry oxygen to body tissues. In this chapter we'll look at how your blood transports oxygen and how carbon monoxide disrupts this life-sustaining process.

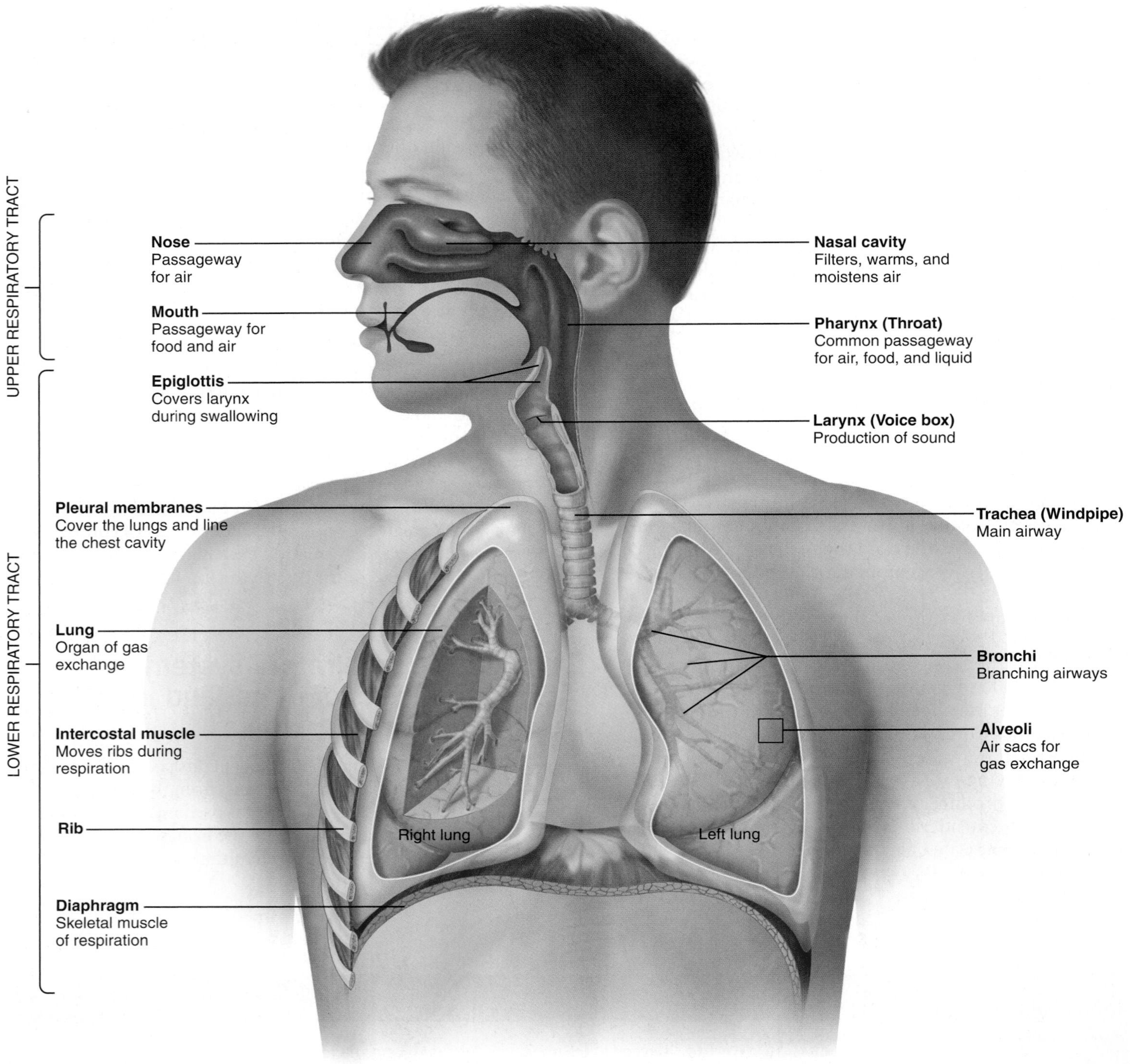


**Figure 10.1 The human respiratory system.** The functions of each of the anatomical structures are included.

For the sake of convenience, the respiratory system can be divided into the upper and lower respiratory tracts. The *upper respiratory tract* comprises the nose (including the nasal cavity) and pharynx—structures above the "Adam's apple" in your neck. The *lower respiratory tract* starts with the larynx and includes the trachea, the two bronchi that branch from the trachea, and the lungs themselves.

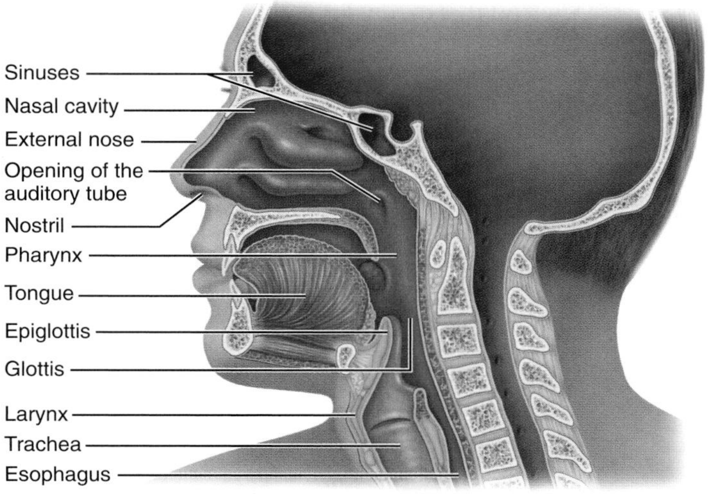


**Figure 10.2 Components of the upper respiratory tract.**

## The upper respiratory tract filters, warms, and humidifies air

When you inhale, air enters through your nose or your mouth (Figure 10.2). Your *nose* is to be appreciated, as it does more than serve as a passageway for respiration. The nose also:

- Contains receptors for the sense of smell
- Filters inhaled air and screens out some foreign particles
- Moistens and warms incoming air
- Provides a resonating chamber that helps give your voice its characteristic tone

The visible portion of the nose is known as the external nose. The internal portion of the nose is called the **nasal cavity.** The external nose consists of cartilage in the front and two nasal bones behind the cartilage. The nose varies in size and shape from person to person, primarily as a result of individual differences in the cartilage tissue.

The external nose and nasal cavity are divided into two chambers by the nasal septum. Air enters through the nostrils, the two openings at the base of the external nose, where it is partially filtered by nose hairs, then flows into the nasal cavity. This cavity is lined with moist epithelial tissue that is well supplied with blood vessels. The blood vessels help to warm incoming air and the epithelial tissue secretes mucus, which humidifies the air. The epithelium is also covered with tiny hairlike projections called cilia.

The mucus in the nasal cavity traps dust, pathogens, and other particles in the air before they get any farther into the respiratory tract. The cilia beat in a coordinated motion, creating a gentle current that moves the particle-loaded mucus toward the back of the nasal cavity and pharynx. There we cough it out, or swallow it to be digested by powerful digestive acids in the stomach. Ordinarily we are unaware of our nasal cilia as they carry on this important task. However, exposure to cold temperatures can slow down their activity, allowing mucus to pool in the nasal cavity and drip from the nostrils. This is why your nose "runs" in cold weather.

As described in Chapter 5, air spaces inside the skull called *sinuses* are also lined with tissue that secretes mucus and helps trap foreign particles. The sinuses drain into the nasal cavity via small passageways. Two tear ducts, carrying fluid away from the eyes, drain into the nasal cavity as well. This is why excess production of tears, perhaps due to strong emotions or irritating particles in your eyes, also makes your nose "runny."

Incoming air next enters the **pharynx** (throat), which connects the mouth and nasal cavity to the larynx (voice box). The upper pharynx extends from the nasal cavity to the roof of the mouth. Into it open the two *auditory tubes* (eustachian tubes) that drain the middle ear cavities and equalize air pressure between the middle ear and outside air. The lower pharynx is a common passageway for both food and air. Food passes through on its way to the esophagus, and air flows through to the lower respiratory tract.

**RECAP**

The respiratory system is specialized for the exchange of oxygen and carbon dioxide with the air. The upper respiratory tract filters, warms, and humidifies the air. ■

## The lower respiratory tract exchanges gases

The lower respiratory tract includes the larynx, the trachea, the bronchi, and the lungs with their bronchioles and alveoli (Figure 10.3).

**The larynx produces sound** The **larynx,** or voice box, extends for about 5 cm (2 inches) below the pharynx. The larynx serves to:

- Maintain an open airway
- Route food and air into the appropriate channels
- Assist in the production of sound

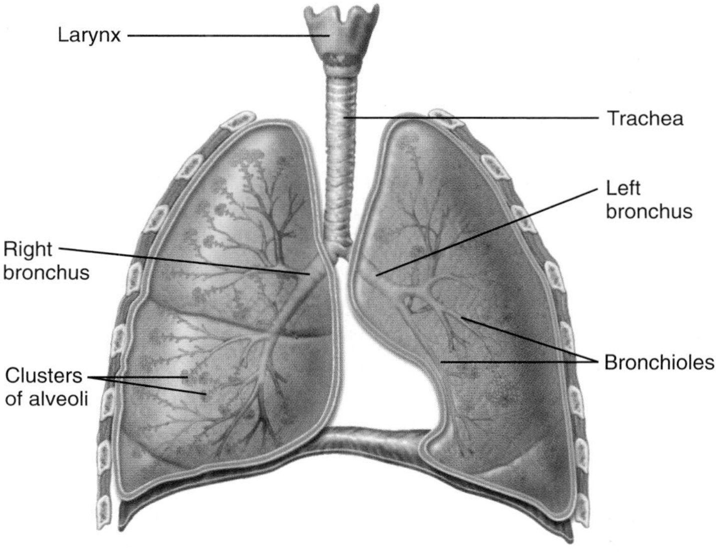


**Figure 10.3 Components of the lower respiratory tract.** Individual alveoli are too small to be seen clearly in this figure.

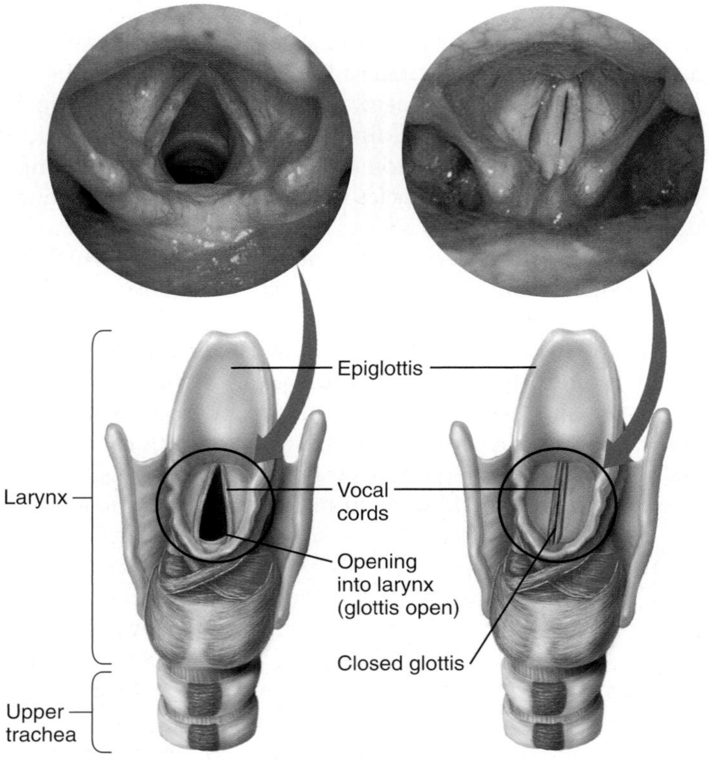


**a) Position of the vocal cords during quiet breathing.**

**b) Position of the vocal cords during sound production.**

**Figure 10.4 Structures associated with the production of sound.**

The larynx contains two important structures: the epiglottis and the vocal cords (Figure 10.4). The **epiglottis** is a flexible flap of cartilage located at the opening to the larynx. When air is flowing into the larynx, the epiglottis remains open. But when we swallow food or liquids, the epiglottis tips to block the opening temporarily. This "switching mechanism" routes food and beverages into the esophagus and digestive system, rather than into the trachea. This is why it is impossible to talk while you are swallowing.

The **vocal cords** consist of two folds of connective tissue that extend across the airway. They surround the opening to the airway, called the **glottis.** The vocal cords are supported by ligaments and enclosed within a cartilaginous structure nicknamed the "Adam's apple."

We produce most sounds by vibration of the vocal cords, although we can also make a few sounds by moving our tongue and teeth. The tone of the sounds produced by the vocal cords depends on how tightly the vocal cords are stretched, which is controlled by skeletal muscle. When we are not talking, the vocal cords are relaxed and open (Figure 10.4a). When we start to talk they stretch tightly across the tracheal opening, and the flow of air past them causes them to vibrate (Figure 10.4b).

Like any string instrument, cords that are relatively short yield higher-pitched tones than longer cords do. Also, the tighter the vocal cords stretch, the higher the tone they produce. Men tend to have deeper voices than women and a more prominent Adam's apple, due to testosterone that causes the larynx to enlarge at puberty. We can exert some control over the volume and pitch of the voice by adjusting the tension on our vocal cords. (You may have noticed that when you're nervous, your voice becomes higher pitched.) The resulting vibrations travel through the air as sound waves.

Most of us can be recognized by the distinctive quality of our voices. In addition to the shape and size of vocal cords, individual differences in voice are determined by many components of the respiratory tract and mouth, including the pharynx, nose and nasal cavity, tongue, and teeth. Muscles in the pharynx, tongue, soft palate, and lips cooperate to create recognizable sounds. The pharynx, nose, and nasal sinuses serve as resonating chambers to amplify and enhance vocal tone.

Speech has played an important role in our evolutionary history and the development of human culture. Although sound production does not play a role in the homeostasis of respiratory gases, animals have evolved to take advantage of the energy available in the moving air to accomplish this important function.

**RECAP**

The larynx maintains an open airway, routes food and air into the appropriate channels, and produces sound. Sound is produced by vibration of the vocal cords as air passes through the glottis. ■

**The trachea transports air** As air continues down the respiratory tract, it passes to the **trachea,** the "windpipe" that extends from the larynx to the left and right bronchi. The trachea consists of a series of C-shaped, incomplete rings of cartilage held together by connective tissue and muscle. As shown in Figure 10.5, each cartilage ring extends only three-quarters of the circumference of the trachea. The rings of cartilage keep the trachea open at all times, but because they are not complete circles they permit the trachea to change diameter slightly when we cough or breathe heavily.

Like the nasal cavity, the trachea is lined with cilia-covered epithelial tissue that secretes mucus. The mucus traps foreign particles and the cilia move them upward, away from the lungs.

If a foreign object lodges in the trachea, respiration is interrupted and choking occurs. If the airway is completely blocked, death can occur within minutes. Choking often happens when a person carries on an animated conversation while eating. Beyond good manners, the risk of choking provides a good reason not to eat and talk at the same time.

Choking typically stimulates receptors in the throat that trigger the *cough reflex*. This is a sudden expulsion of air from the lungs in an attempt to dislodge foreign material (Figure 10.5b). If the object blocks the airway completely before the person has finished inhaling, there may not be much air in the lungs. This will make the obstacle more difficult to remove (see the Health Watch Box on page 226). If the object

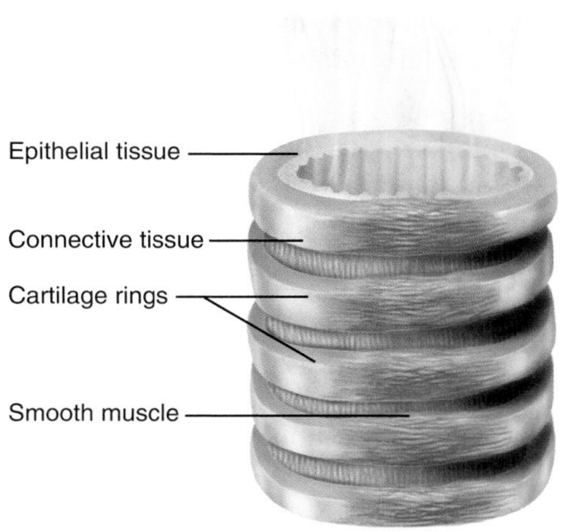


**a) Relaxed state. The maximum diameter facilitates air movement in and out.**

**b) During the cough reflex, the smooth muscle contracts briefly, reducing the diameter of the trachea.** Combined with contraction of the abdominal muscles, this increases the velocity of air movement, forcibly expelling irritants or mucus from the trachea.

**Figure 10.5 The trachea.** The trachea consists of smooth muscle and layers of epithelial and connective tissue held open by tough, flexible C-shaped bands of cartilage.

blocks air flow only partially, it may be possible to dislodge it by inhaling slowly, then coughing.

**Bronchi branch into the lungs** The trachea branches into two airways called the right and left **bronchi** (singular: *bronchus*) as it enters the lung cavity (refer to Figure 10.3). Like the branches of a tree, the two bronchi divide into a network of smaller and smaller bronchi. The walls of bronchi contain fibrous connective tissue and smooth muscle reinforced with cartilage. As the branching airways get smaller and smaller, the amount of cartilage declines. By definition, the smaller airways that lack cartilage are called **bronchioles.** The smallest bronchioles are 1 mm or less in diameter and consist primarily of a thin layer of smooth muscle surrounded by a small amount of elastic connec-tive tissue.

The bronchi and bronchioles have several other functions in addition to air transport. They also clean the air, warm it to body temperature, and saturate it with water vapor before it reaches the delicate gas-exchange surfaces of the lungs. The air is warmed and humidified by contact with the moist surfaces of the cells lining the bronchi and bronchioles. With the exception of the very smallest bronchioles, the bronchi and bronchioles are lined with ciliated epithelial cells and occasional mucus-secreting cells. The thin, watery mucus produced by the mucus-secreting cells traps dust, bacteria, and other small particles. The ciliated cells then sweep the accumulated mucus and trapped material upward toward the pharynx so that it can be swallowed.

Tobacco smoke contains chemicals and particles that irritate the respiratory tract. Mucus production increases in response, but the smoke impairs the activity of the cilia. Continued smoking destroys the cilia, allowing mucus and debris from the smoke to accumulate in the airway. "Smoker's cough" refers to the violent coughing necessary to dislodge the mucus from the airway. Mucus pooling leads to frequent infections because pathogens and irritants remain in the respiratory tract. It also increases the risk of bronchitis, emphysema, and lung cancer (Figure 10.6) (see section 10.6, Disorders of the respiratory system).

From the nose and mouth to the tiniest bronchioles in the lungs, none of the airways we have described so far participate in gas exchange. Essentially, they are all tubes for getting air to the lungs where gas exchange actually occurs.

**RECAP**

The trachea, or "windpipe," branches into the right and left bronchi, which further subdivide into smaller bronchi and then bronchioles. Like other areas of the respiratory tract, the bronchi and bronchioles filter, warm, and humidify the incoming air before it reaches the gas exchange structures in lungs. ■

**The lungs are organs of gas exchange** The lungs are organs consisting of supportive tissue enclosing the bronchi, bronchioles, blood vessels, and the areas where gas exchange occurs. They occupy most of the thoracic cavity. There are two lungs, one on the right side and one on the left, separated from each other by the heart (Figure 10.7). The shape of the lungs follows the contours of the rib cage and the thoracic cavity. The base of each lung is broad and shaped to fit against the convex surface of the diaphragm.

Each lung is enclosed in two layers of thin epithelial membranes called the **pleural membranes.** One of these layers represents the outer lung surface and the other lines the thoracic cavity. The pleural membranes are separated by a small space, called the *pleural cavity*, that contains a very small amount of watery fluid. The fluid reduces friction between the pleural membranes as the lungs and chest wall move during breathing. Inflammation of the pleural membranes, a condition called pleurisy, can reduce the secretion of pleural fluid, increase the friction, and cause pain during

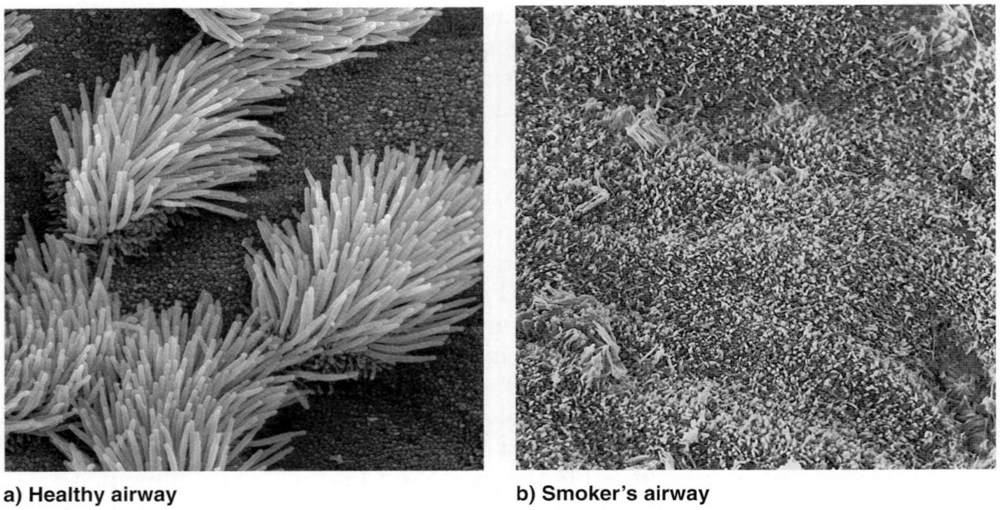


**Figure 10.6 Effects of smoking on the cilia of the airways. (a)** The inner surface of an airway of a healthy person, showing normal ciliated epithelial cells with their clumps of hairlike cilia. The cells without cilia are the mucus-secreting cells. **(b)** The inner surface of an airway of a smoker, showing destruction of the cilia.

breathing. Pleurisy can be a symptom of pneumonia (see section 10.6).

Each lung consists of several lobes, three in the right lung and two in the left. Each lobe contains a branching tree of bronchioles and blood vessels. The lobes can function fairly independently of each other, so it is possible to surgically remove a lobe or two without totally eliminating lung function.

**Gas exchange occurs in alveoli** If you could touch a living lung, you would find that it is very soft and frothy. In fact, most of it is air. The lungs are basically a system of branching airways that end in 300 million tiny air-filled sacs called **alveoli** (singular: *alveolus*). It is here that gas exchange takes place (Figure 10.8). Alveoli are arranged in clusters at the end of every terminal bronchiole, like grapes clustered on a stem. A single alveolus is a thin bubble of living squamous epithelial cells only one cell layer thick. Their combined surface area is nearly 800 square feet, approximately 40 times the area of our skin. This tremendous surface area and the thinness of the squamous type of epithelium facilitate gas exchange with nearby capillaries.

Within each alveolus, certain epithelial cells secrete a lipoprotein called *surfactant* that coats the interior of the alveoli and reduces surface tension. Surface tension is due to the attraction of water molecules toward each other (review Chapter 2). Without surfactant, the force of surface tension could collapse the alveoli. This can occur in infants who are

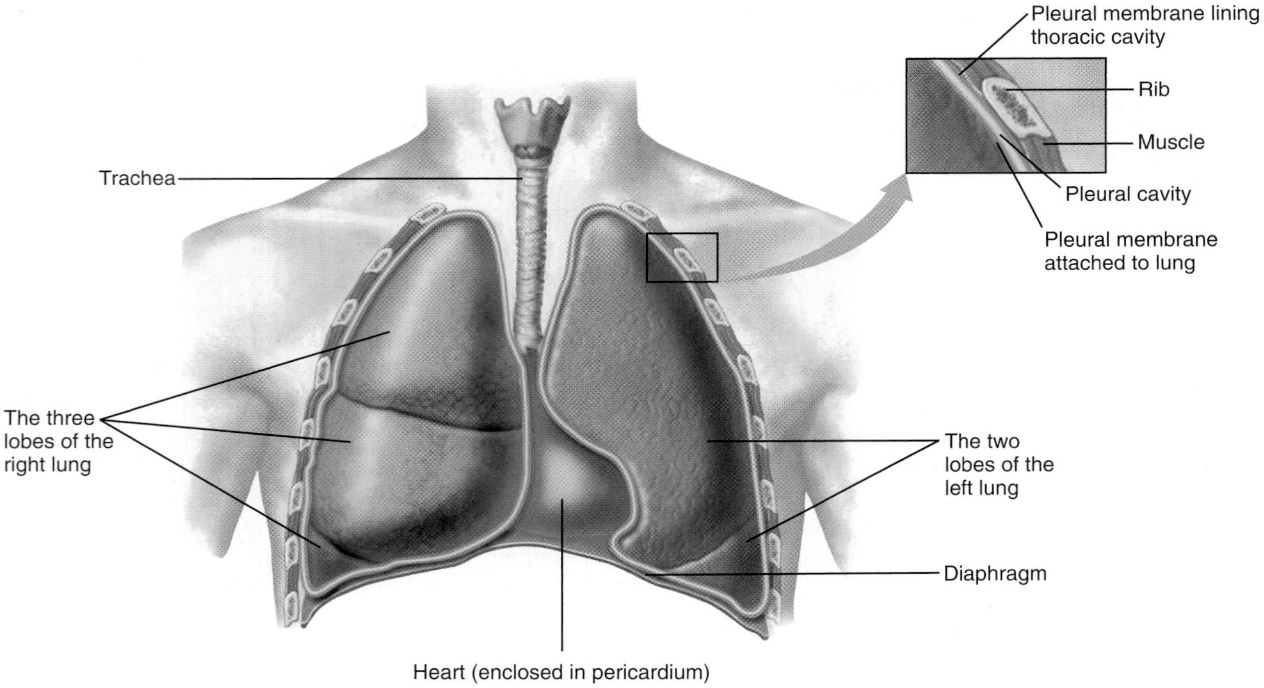


**Figure 10.7 The lungs, pleural membranes, and pleural cavity.** The pleural cavity has been expanded so that it can be seen in the drawing. In reality, it is no more than a very thin, watery space that reduces friction between the two pleural membranes.

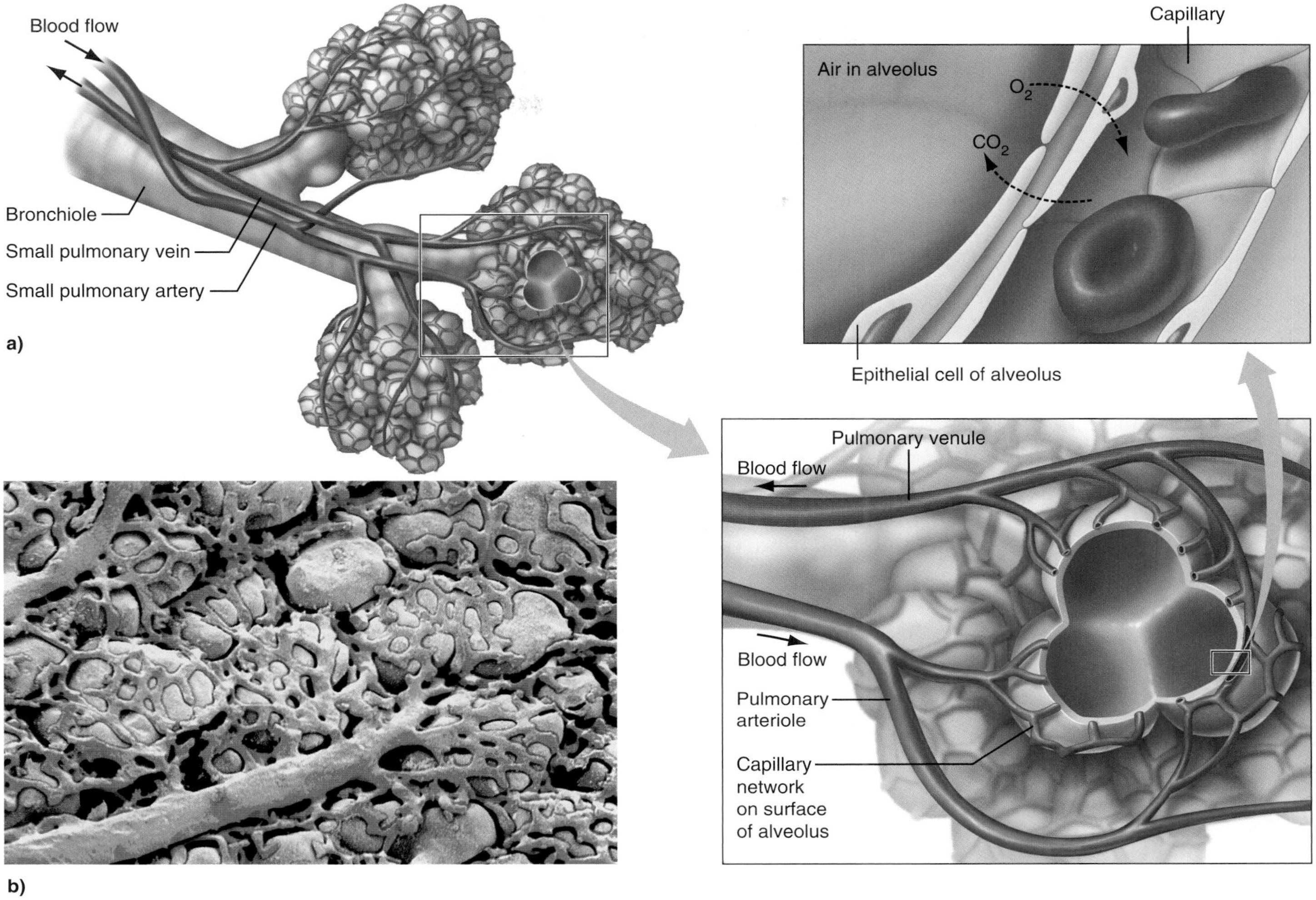


**Figure 10.8 Gas exchange between the blood and alveoli. (a)** Bronchioles end in clusters of alveoli, each surrounded by capillaries. $CO_2$ and $O_2$ are exchanged across the capillary and alveolar walls by diffusion. **(b)** Photo of the surface of alveoli covered with capillaries.

born prematurely, because the surfactant-secreting cells in their lungs are underdeveloped. Called *infant respiratory distress syndrome*, the condition is treated with surfactant replacement therapy.

**Pulmonary capillaries bring blood and air into close contact** As described in Chapter 8, the right ventricle of the heart pumps deoxygenated blood into the pulmonary trunk, which splits into the left and right pulmonary arteries. The pulmonary arteries divide into smaller and smaller arteries and arterioles, eventually terminating in a capillary bed called the *pulmonary capillaries*. In the pulmonary capillaries, blood comes into very close proximity to the air in the alveoli. Only two living cells (the squamous epithelial cell of the alveolus and the cell of the capillary wall) separate blood from air at this point. A series of venules and veins collects the oxygenated blood from the pulmonary capillaries and returns the blood to the left side of the heart. From there it can be transported to all parts of the body.

The close contact between air and blood and the large air surface area of the lungs suggests that the lungs might be useful as an alternative method for delivering medications to the bloodstream. Currently pharmaceutical researchers are experimenting with fine mists or powders that can be inhaled deep into the lungs. The research has begun to pay off. The first inhalable form of insulin (a dry powder) was approved by the Food and Drug Administration in 2006.

**RECAP**

The lungs are organs containing a branching system of bronchi and bronchioles, blood vessels, and 300 million alveoli. Gas exchange occurs between the alveoli and pulmonary capillaries. ■

## Health Watch

# Saving Lives with the Heimlich Maneuver

Every year thousands of people choke to death when a piece of food lodges in the larynx or trachea. Many of these deaths could be prevented by the Heimlich maneuver.

The Heimlich maneuver is a method for dislodging objects that completely block the airway. It is an emergency procedure for saving a life. Do not try it on someone who is having difficulty breathing but is still getting some air in and out—you could shift the obstacle to a position where it blocks the airway completely. People whose airways are completely blocked will appear agitated. They may signal that they are choking by grasping their throat or gesturing with their hands, but they will not be able to speak.

Without startling the person, approach from behind. Make a fist of one hand with your thumb inward, place it below the rib cage but above the navel, and grasp your fist with the other hand. Then pull sharply upward and inward.

The Heimlich maneuver should be done firmly and abruptly to force the obstruction up the trachea. It's best to learn the technique from a qualified instructor, because you need to exert enough force to push the diaphragm and lungs upward, creating air pressure in the lungs to expel the object. A little light pressure won't help. Furthermore, the person may panic and struggle against you. However, if done correctly, the Heimlich maneuver can save a life.

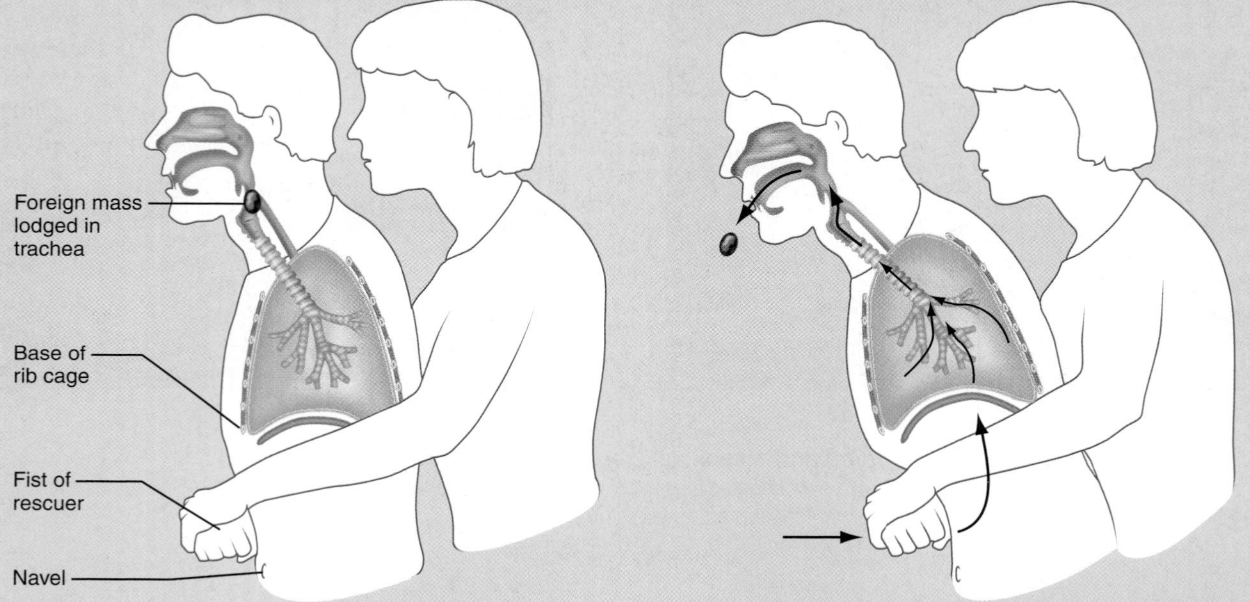


**a) Position of rescuer's hands**

**b) The movement is sharply upward and inward**

## 10.3 The process of breathing involves a pressure gradient

Breathing involves getting air into and out of the lungs in a cyclic manner, and that requires muscular effort. However, the lungs themselves don't have any skeletal muscle tissue. The lungs expand passively because the surrounding bones and muscles expand the size of the chest cavity.

The bones and muscles of respiration include the ribs, the intercostal muscles between the ribs, and the main muscle of respiration, called the **diaphragm,** a broad sheet of muscle that separates the thoracic cavity from the abdominal cavity (review Figure 10.1). The intercostal muscles and the diaphragm are skeletal muscles.

### Inspiration brings in air, expiration expels it

To understand why air moves into and out of the lungs in a cyclic manner, we need to understand some general principles of gas pressure and of how gases move:

- Gas pressure is caused by colliding molecules of gas.
- When the volume of a closed space *increases,* the molecules of gas in that space are farther away from each other, and the pressure inside the space *decreases*.

Conversely, when the volume in a closed space *decreases*, the gas pressure *increases*.

- Gases flow from areas of *higher* pressure to areas of *lower* pressure.

As we have seen, the lungs are air-filled structures consisting almost entirely of bronchioles, alveoli, and blood vessels. Lacking skeletal muscle, they cannot expand (increase in volume) or contract (decrease in volume) on their own. The lungs expand and contract only because they are compliant (stretchable) and because they are surrounded by the pleural cavity, which is airtight and sealed. If the volume of the pleural cavity expands, the lungs will expand with it.

*Inspiration* (inhalation) pulls air into the respiratory system as lung volume expands, and *expiration* (exhalation) pushes air out as lung volume declines again. Let's look at a cycle of inspiration and expiration, starting from the relaxed state at the end of a previous expiration (Figure 10.9):

1. *Relaxed state.* At rest, both the diaphragm and the intercostal muscles are relaxed. The relaxed diaphragm appears dome shaped.
2. *Inspiration.* As inspiration begins, the diaphragm contracts, flattening it and pulling its center downward. At the same time, the intercostal muscles contract, pulling the ribs upward and outward. These two actions of skeletal muscle increase the volume of the pleural cavity and lower the pressure within the pleural space. Because the lungs are elastic and the pressure around them has just fallen relative to the atmosphere, they expand with the pleural cavity. Expansion of the lungs reduces air pressure within the lungs relative to the atmosphere, allowing air to rush in.
3. *Expiration.* Eventually the muscle contractions end. As the muscles relax the diaphragm returns to its domed shape, the ribs move downward and inward, and the pleural cavity becomes smaller. The rest of the process reverses as well. The lungs become smaller, so pressure within the lungs rises relative to the atmosphere and air flows out.

During quiet breathing, inspiration is active (requiring muscular effort) and expiration is passive. When we are under physical or emotional stress, however, we need to breathe more frequently and more deeply. At this point both inspiration and expiration may become active. We can take bigger breaths because additional rib cage muscles raise the rib cage higher. As we exhale deeply, abdominal muscles contract and push the diaphragm even higher into the thoracic cavity, and the inner intercostal muscles contract to pull the rib cage downward. These events combine to increase the speed and force of respiration.

We also exhale forcibly when we sneeze or cough. During sneezing and coughing the abdominal muscles contract suddenly, raising abdominal pressure. The rapid increase in abdominal pressure pushes the relaxed diaphragm upward against the pleural cavity, forcing air out of the lungs.

**RECAP**

Inspiration is an active process (requiring energy) that occurs when the diaphragm and intercostal muscles contract. Normally expiration is passive, but it can become active when we forcibly exhale, cough, or sneeze. ■

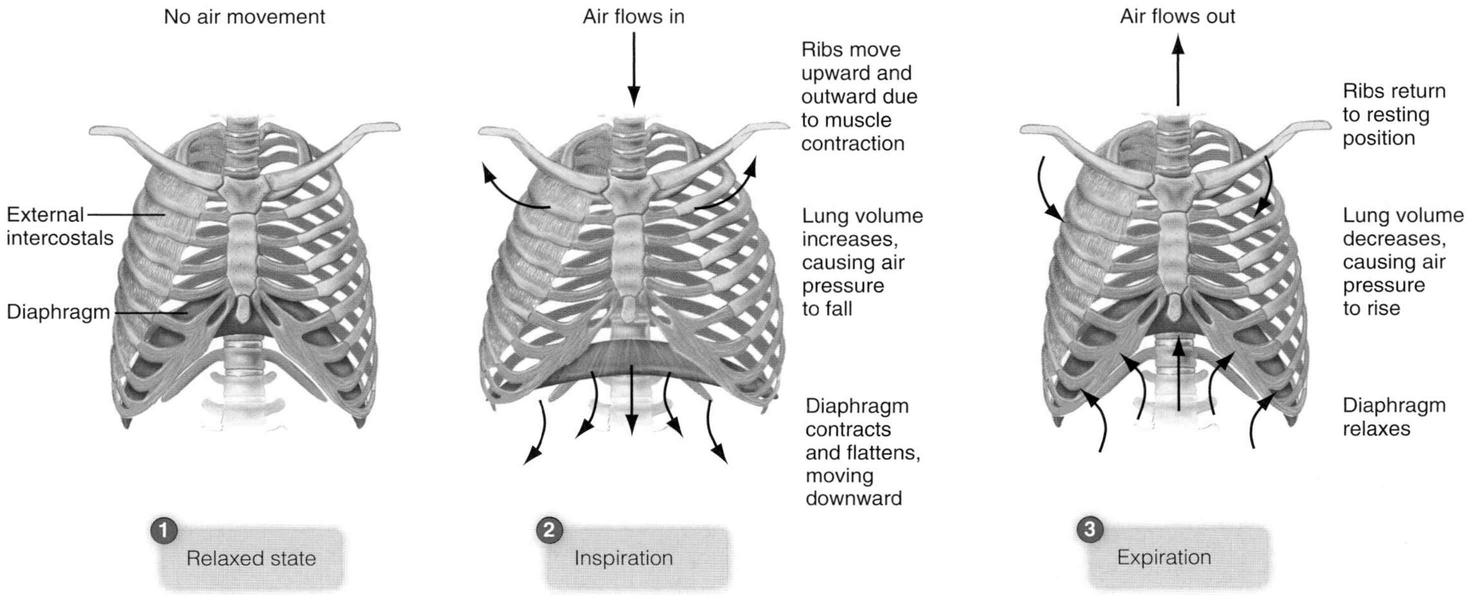


**Figure 10.9 The respiratory cycle.** During inspiration, the ribs move upward and outward, enlarging the thoracic cavity. During expiration, the muscles relax and the ribs return to their relaxed position.

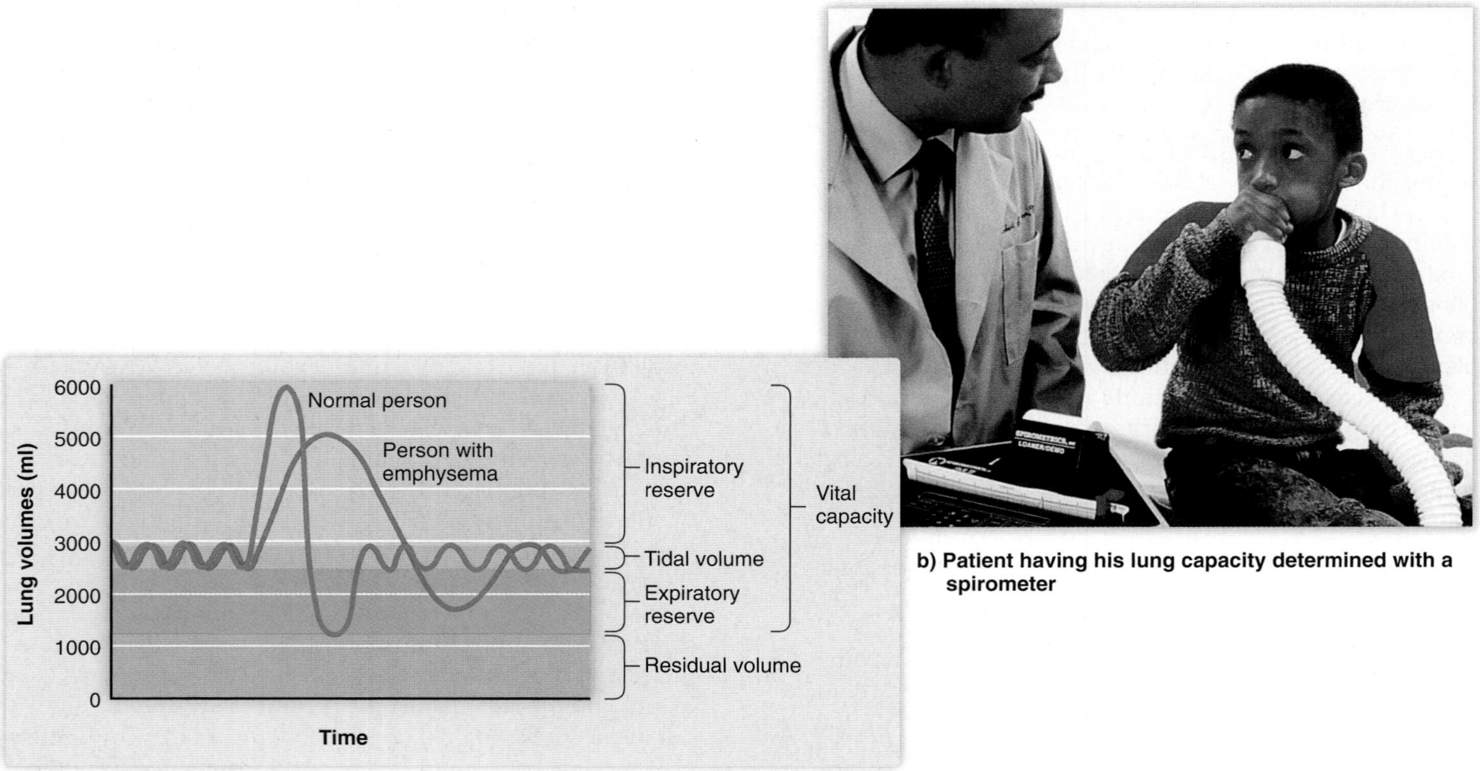


**b) Patient having his lung capacity determined with a spirometer**

**a) A recording of lung capacity**

**Figure 10.10 Measurement of lung capacity.** **(a)** A patient having his lung capacity determined with a spirometer. **(b)** A recording of lung capacity. After several normal breaths, the person inhales and then exhales maximally. The volumes indicated by the green line are for a normal person. The orange line is typical of a patient with emphysema.

## Lung volumes and vital capacity measure lung function

At rest, you take about 12 breaths every minute. Each breath represents a **tidal volume** of air of approximately 500 milliliters (ml), or about a pint (Figure 10.10a). On average, only about 350 ml of each breath actually reach the alveoli and become involved in gas exchange. The other 150 ml remain in the airways, and because it does not participate in gas exchange, this air is referred to as *dead space volume*.

The maximal volume that you can exhale after a maximal inhalation is called your **vital capacity.** Your vital capacity is about 4,800 ml, almost 10 times your normal tidal volume at rest. The amount of additional air that can be inhaled beyond the tidal volume (about 3,100 ml) is called the *inspiratory reserve volume,* and the amount of the air that we can forcibly exhale beyond the tidal volume (about 1,200 ml) is the *expiratory reserve volume*. No matter how forcefully you exhale, some air always remains in your lungs. This is your *residual volume,* approximately 1,200 ml.

A device called a *spirometer* can measure lung capacity (Figure 10.10b). The measurements are made by having a person breathe normally into the device (to measure tidal volume) and then take a maximum breath and exhale it forcibly and as completely as possible (to measure vital capacity). Lung volumes and rates of change of volume are useful in diagnosing various lung diseases. For example, emphysema is a condition in which the smaller airways lose elasticity, causing them to collapse during expiration and impairing the ability to exhale naturally. A spirometer recording of someone with emphysema might show a prolonged period of expiration after a maximum inspiration because of resistance to air outflow.

**RECAP**

Although we normally take breaths of about 500 ml (tidal volume), our vital capacity is about 4,800 ml. Some air, called the residual volume, remains in the lungs even at the end of expiration. ■

## 10.4 Gas exchange and transport occur passively

So far, we have focused on the first process in respiration: breathing. Once air enters the alveoli, gas exchange and transport occur. In this section we review some basic principles governing the diffusion of gases to set the stage for our discussion of external and internal respiration (the second and third processes of respiration). We also describe how the gases are transported by blood. The fourth process of respiration, cellular respiration, is the use of oxygen by cells in the production of energy. Cellular respiration is described in Chapter 3.

## Gases diffuse according to their partial pressures

Earth is surrounded by an atmosphere of gases. Like liquids, gases have mass and are attracted to the earth by gravity. Though it doesn't really feel like we are pressed down by a heavy weight of gases, in fact the atmosphere (air) exerts a total atmospheric pressure at sea level of about 760 mm Hg (millimeters of mercury). A normal atmospheric pressure of 760 mm Hg means that the pressure of the atmosphere will cause a column of mercury in a vacuum to rise 760 mm, or about 2.5 feet. The pressure seems like zero to us because the pressure inside our lungs is the same as atmospheric pressure, at least when we are resting between breaths.

The primary gases of Earth's atmosphere are nitrogen (78%) and oxygen (21%), with a trace amount of carbon dioxide (about 0.04%) and less than 1% of all other gases combined. In a mixture of gases, each gas exerts a **partial pressure** that is proportional to its percentage of the total gas composition. Partial pressure is represented by P and, like atmospheric pressure, it is measured in mm Hg. The pressure of the atmosphere is thus the sum of the partial pressures of each of the gases found in the atmosphere at sea level. Because we know the percentages of each gas in our atmosphere, we can find the partial pressure of each. For example, the partial pressure of oxygen ($P_{O_2}$) in air is about 160 mm Hg (760 mm Hg $\times$ 0.21).

Because partial pressures in a mixture of gases are directly proportional to concentrations, a gas will always diffuse down its *partial pressure gradient*, from a region of higher partial pressure to a region of lower partial pressure. As we shall see, the exchanges of $O_2$ and $CO_2$, both between the alveoli and the blood and between the blood and the tissues, are purely passive. No consumption of ATP is involved; changes in partial pressures are entirely responsible for the exchange and transport of these gases.

## External respiration: The exchange of gases between air and blood

A comparison of the partial pressures of $O_2$ and $CO_2$ in inhaled air, in the alveoli, and in the blood in the lungs illustrates how external respiration takes place (Figure 10.11). As stated above, the partial pressure of the oxygen ($P_{O_2}$) in the air we breathe is about 160 mm Hg. As there is very little $CO_2$ in the air, the partial pressure of inspired $CO_2$ is negligible. The partial pressures of alveolar air are not, however, the same as those of inspired air. This is because only about 1/8 of the air is actually exchanged with each breath, so most of the air in the lungs is actually "old" air that has already undergone some gas exchange. Consequently, the partial pressures of $O_2$ and $CO_2$ in the alveoli average about 104 and 40 mm Hg, respectively.

When venous (deoxygenated) blood with a $P_{O_2}$ of only 40 mm Hg and a $P_{CO_2}$ of 46 mm Hg arrives at the pulmonary capillaries from the pulmonary arteries, $O_2$ diffuses from the alveoli into the capillaries, and $CO_2$ diffuses in the opposite direction. As a result, the $P_{O_2}$ of oxygenated (arterial) blood leaving the lungs rises to 100 mm Hg and the $P_{CO_2}$ falls to 40 mm Hg. The oxygenated blood is carried in the pulmonary veins to the heart and then throughout the body in the arterial blood vessels. The $CO_2$ that diffuses into the alveoli is exhaled, along with some water vapor.

Notice that the definition of venous blood is that it is deoxygenated, not that it happens to be in a vein. The pulmonary arteries transport venous blood to the lungs, and the pulmonary veins transport arterial blood to the heart.

## Internal respiration: The exchange of gases with tissue fluids

The body's cells get their supply of $O_2$ for cellular respiration from the interstitial fluid that surrounds them. Because the cells are constantly drawing oxygen from the interstitial fluid (again, by diffusion), the interstitial fluid $P_{O_2}$ is usually quite a bit lower than that of arterial blood (less than 40 mm Hg). As blood enters the capillaries, then, $O_2$ diffuses from the capillaries into the interstitial fluid, replenishing the $O_2$ that has been used by the cells. $CO_2$ diffuses in the opposite direction: from the cell into the interstitial fluid and then into the capillary blood.

Both external and internal respiration occur entirely by diffusion. The partial pressure gradients that permit diffusion are maintained by breathing, blood transport, and cellular respiration. The net effect of all these processes is that homeostasis of the concentrations of $O_2$ and $CO_2$ in the vicinity of the cells is generally well maintained.

**RECAP**

In a mixture of gases such as air, each gas exerts a partial pressure. Gases diffuse according to differences in their partial pressures. Diffusion accounts for both external and internal respiration. ■

## Hemoglobin transports most oxygen molecules

Our discussion of external and internal respiration brings us to an important aspect of the overall subject of gas exchange, and that is how the gases are transported between the lungs and tissues in the blood. As noted in Chapter 7, an important

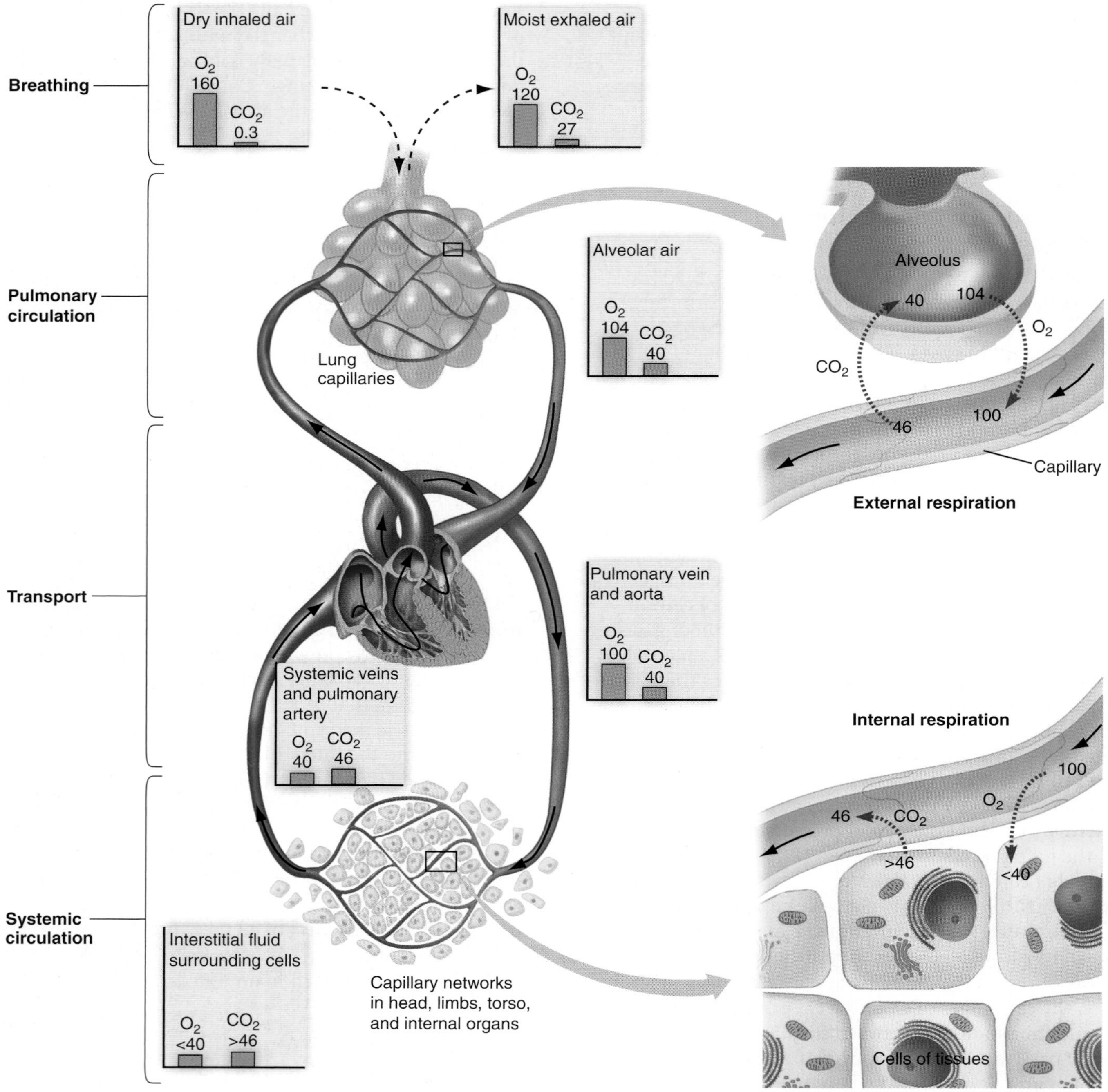


**Figure 10.11 Partial pressures.** All partial pressures are expressed in units of mm Hg. Differences in partial pressures account for the diffusion of $O_2$ and $CO_2$ between the lungs and blood, and between blood and the body's tissues.

function of blood is to carry oxygen from the lungs to body tissues; now we examine how that happens.

Oxygen is transported in blood in two ways: either it is bound to hemoglobin (Hb) in red blood cells, or it is dissolved in blood plasma (Figure 10.12). The presence of hemoglobin is absolutely essential for the adequate transport of $O_2$ because $O_2$ is not very soluble in water. Only about 2% of all $O_2$ is dissolved in the watery component of blood known as blood plasma. Most of it—98%—is taken out of the watery component by virtue of its binding to hemoglobin molecules. Without hemoglobin, the tissues would not be able to receive enough oxygen to sustain life.

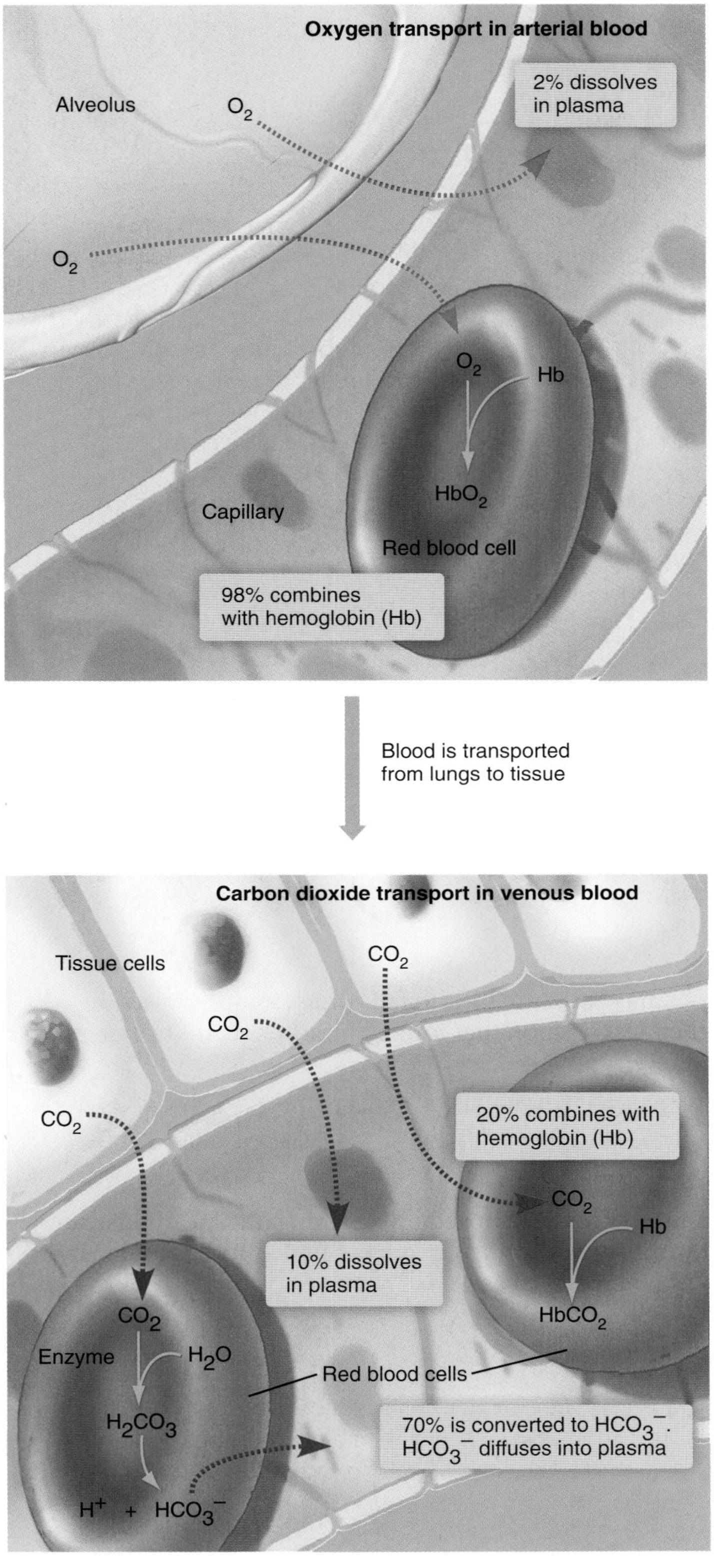


**Figure 10.12 How oxygen and carbon dioxide are transported in blood.** Approximately 98% of all the $O_2$ transported to the tissues by arterial blood is bound to hemoglobin within red blood cells. Most of the $CO_2$ transported to the lungs by venous blood is converted to $HCO_3^-$ within red blood cells and then carried in plasma as dissolved $HCO_3^-$. The rest is either dissolved in plasma as $CO_2$ or transported within the red blood cells bound to hemoglobin.

As described in Chapter 7, *hemoglobin* is a large protein molecule consisting of four polypeptide chains, each of which is associated with an iron-containing heme group that can bind oxygen. Because there are four heme groups, each hemoglobin molecule can bind four oxygen molecules at a time, forming **oxyhemoglobin** ($HbO_2$). We can represent this reaction as:

$$\underset{\text{hemoglobin}}{Hb} + \underset{\text{oxygen}}{O_2} \rightarrow \underset{\text{oxyhemoglobin}}{HbO_2}$$

This reaction is reversible and highly dependent on the partial pressures of $O_2$ in plasma. When the $P_{O_2}$ rises (in the lungs), oxygen attaches to hemoglobin and is transported in arterial blood. When the $P_{O_2}$ falls (at the tissues), oxygen detaches from hemoglobin.

Several other factors affect $O_2$ attachment to hemoglobin as well. Hemoglobin binds $O_2$ most efficiently in conditions of fairly neutral pH and relatively cool temperatures—similar to conditions existing in the lungs. Body regions having warmer temperatures and lowered pH—such as in body tissues—reduce hemoglobin's affinity for binding $O_2$. Consequently, $O_2$ and hemoglobin tend to combine in the lungs, facilitating the transport of oxygen to the tissues, and to detach in body tissues, making $O_2$ available to cells.

Hemoglobin's affinity for oxygen is also greatly reduced by carbon monoxide, a colorless, odorless, highly poisonous gas (see the Health Watch box on page 232).

## Most $CO_2$ is transported in plasma as bicarbonate

Cellular metabolism in body tissues continuously produces carbon dioxide as a waste product. As we learned in Chapter 7, one function of blood is to transport $CO_2$ away from tissues and back to the lungs, where it can be removed from the body.

Because the partial pressure of $CO_2$ is higher in the tissues than it is in blood, $CO_2$ readily diffuses from tissues into the bloodstream. Once in the blood, $CO_2$ is transported in three ways: dissolved in blood plasma, bound to hemoglobin, or in the form of bicarbonate (see Figure 10.12).

Only about 10% of the $CO_2$ remains dissolved in blood plasma. Another 20% binds with hemoglobin to form **carbaminohemoglobin** ($HbCO_2$). This reaction is represented as:

$$\underset{\text{hemoglobin}}{Hb} + \underset{\text{carbon dioxide}}{CO_2} \rightarrow \underset{\text{carbaminohemoglobin}}{HbCO_2}$$

Hemoglobin can transport $O_2$ and $CO_2$ molecules simultaneously because the two gases attach to different sites on the hemoglobin molecule. $O_2$ combines with heme, $CO_2$ with globin.

About 70% of all the $CO_2$ produced by the tissues is converted to bicarbonate prior to transport. When bicarbonate is

## Health Watch

### Carbon Monoxide: An Invisible, Odorless Killer

On January 2, 2006, an explosion roared through the Sago Mine in West Virginia, trapping 13 coal miners 260 feet underground. The men retreated deeper into the mine and, following standard safety guidelines, hung up a fabric barrier that was supposed to block poisonous gases. Rescue workers labored for a day and a half to reach them. Tragically, all but one of them were found dead.

What killed the miners? Not the explosion itself, but a by-product of the combustion called carbon monoxide (CO). It is a colorless, odorless, highly poisonous gas produced by burning carbon-containing substances such as coal, natural gas, gasoline, wood, and oil.

Carbon monoxide has a high affinity for hemoglobin and competes with oxygen for hemoglobin binding sites. CO binds to hemoglobin almost 200 times more tightly than oxygen and, once bound, remains attached for many hours. Even trace amounts significantly reduce the oxygen-transporting capacity of blood. High concentrations reduce the oxygen-carrying capacity of hemoglobin so much that body tissues, including those of the brain, literally starve.

Early symptoms of carbon monoxide poisoning include flushed skin (especially the lips), dizziness, headache, nausea, and feeling faint. Continued exposure leads to unconsciousness, brain damage, and death. The leading cause of accidental poisoning in the U.S., carbon monoxide kills about 500 people and contributes to 40,000 emergency room visits every year. About 2,000 people per year commit suicide by inhaling it. Common sources include industrial pollution, automobile exhaust, furnaces and space heaters, and cigarette smoke.

If you are exposed to carbon monoxide it's vital that you get away from the gas and into fresh air as soon as possible. People with severe cases should be taken to a hospital, where pressurized oxygen or transfusions of red blood cells can be administered to increase blood oxygen levels. Depending on the degree of exposure, survivors can show permanent heart or brain impairment. In one study, almost 40% of CO survivors with heart damage died within seven years, compared to 15% of those without heart damage.

Fortunately, taking a few precautions can prevent CO poisoning. Keep your gas or oil furnace and your car's exhaust system in good repair, and consider installing a carbon monoxide detector in your home. Never run a car's engine in an enclosed space. Don't smoke—cigarette smoke contains measurable amounts of carbon monoxide that are delivered directly to your lungs and blood. As much as possible, avoid spending a lot of time in smoke-filled rooms and high-traffic urban areas.

produced, $CO_2$ combines with water ($H_2O$) to become carbonic acid ($H_2CO_3$). This first reaction is catalyzed by an enzyme called *carbonic anhydrase*. The carbonic acid immediately breaks apart into bicarbonate and hydrogen ions:

$$\underset{\text{carbon dioxide}}{CO_2} + \underset{\text{water}}{H_2O} \rightarrow \underset{\text{carbonic acid}}{H_2CO_3} \rightarrow \underset{\text{bicarbonate}}{HCO_3^-} + \underset{\text{hydrogen}}{H^+}$$

The formation of bicarbonate from $CO_2$ occurs primarily inside red blood cells because this is where the carbonic anhydrase enzyme is located. However, most of the bicarbonate quickly diffuses out of red blood cells and is transported back to the lungs dissolved in plasma.

Some of the hydrogen ions formed along with bicarbonate stay inside the red blood cells and bind to hemoglobin. Their attachment to hemoglobin weakens the attachment between hemoglobin and oxygen molecules and causes hemoglobin to release more $O_2$. This is the explanation for the effect of pH on oxygen binding described above. The overall effect is that the presence of $CO_2$ (an indication that cellular metabolism has taken place) actually enhances the delivery of $O_2$ to the very sites where it is most likely to be needed.

At the lungs, dissolved $CO_2$ diffuses out of the blood and into the alveolar air. The loss of $CO_2$ from the blood plasma causes the $P_{CO_2}$ to fall, which in turn causes the chemical reaction that formed bicarbonate in the first place to reverse:

$$\underset{\text{bicarbonate}}{HCO_3^-} + \underset{\text{hydrogen}}{H^+} \rightarrow \underset{\text{carbonic acid}}{H_2CO_3} \rightarrow \underset{\text{carbon dioxide}}{CO_2} + \underset{\text{water}}{H_2O}$$

Thus, as $CO_2$ is removed by breathing, the bicarbonate and hydrogen ions formed in the peripheral tissues to transport $CO_2$ are removed as well.

**RECAP**

Nearly all of the oxygen in blood is bound to hemoglobin in red blood cells. Most carbon dioxide produced in the tissues is transported in blood plasma as bicarbonate. ■

## 10.5 The nervous system regulates breathing

As mentioned earlier, breathing depends on the contractions of skeletal muscles. Skeletal muscles are activated only by motor neurons, as described in Chapter 5. It follows, then,

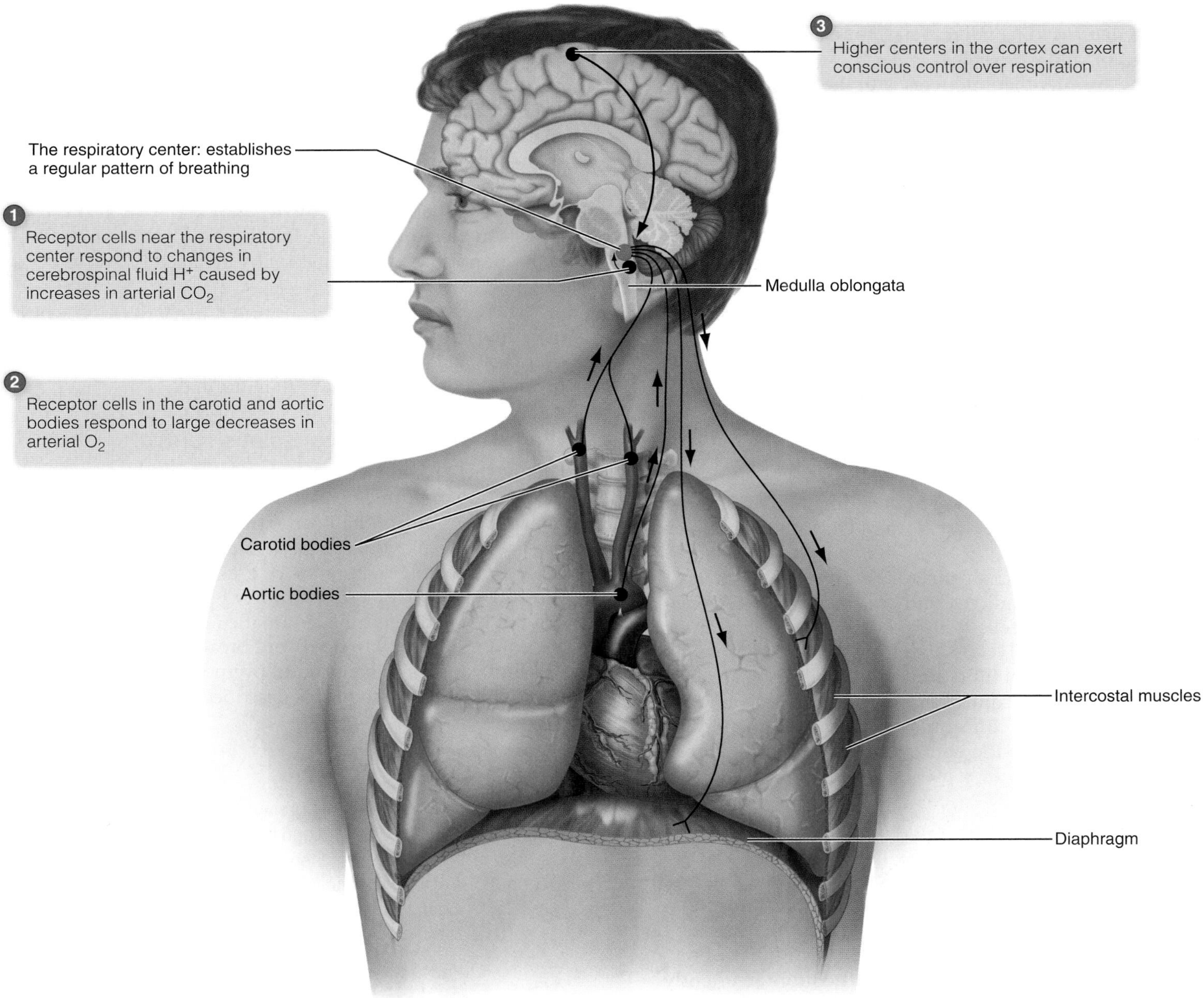


**Figure 10.13 Regulation of breathing.** The basic pattern of breathing is established by a respiratory center within the medulla oblongata. Normally, the rate and depth of respiration are set primarily to regulate blood $CO_2$ levels, but respiration can also be stimulated by a substantial drop in blood $O_2$ levels. In addition, respiration can be controlled (at least for short periods of time) by conscious control.

that respiration is controlled by the nervous system. The nervous system regulates the rate and depth of breathing in order to maintain homeostasis of the concentrations of certain key variables, most notably the concentrations of $CO_2$, $H^+$, and $O_2$. In addition, we can exert a certain amount of conscious control over breathing if we wish.

## A respiratory center establishes rhythm of breathing

The basic cyclic pattern of inspiration and expiration and the rate at which we breathe are established in an area near the base of the brain called the *medulla oblongata* (Figure 10.13). Within this area, called the **respiratory center,** groups of nerve cells automatically generate a cyclic pattern of electrical impulses every 4–5 seconds. The impulses travel along nerves to the diaphragm and the intercostal muscles and stimulate those muscles to contract. As these respiratory muscles contract, the rib cage expands, the diaphragm is pulled downward, and we inhale. As inhalation proceeds, the respiratory center receives sensory input from stretch receptors in the lungs. These receptors monitor the degree of inflation of the lungs and serve to limit inhalation and initiate exhalation. When nerve impulses from the respiratory center to the muscles end, the respiratory muscles relax, the rib cage returns to its original size, the diaphragm moves upward again, and we exhale.

Any disorder that interferes with the transmission of these nerve impulses can affect breathing. Consider amyotrophic lateral sclerosis (ALS; also known as Lou Gehrig's disease, for the famous baseball player who succumbed to it). In ALS the nerves to skeletal muscle become damaged and no longer conduct impulses properly. Over time the skeletal muscles, including the diaphragm and intercostal muscles, weaken and waste away from lack of use. Most ALS patients die within five years of initial diagnosis. Although ALS is not a respiratory condition per se, the immediate cause of death is usually respiratory failure.

### Chemical receptors monitor $CO_2$, $H^+$, and $O_2$ levels

The body modifies, or regulates, the rate and depth of the breathing pattern to maintain homeostasis. Under normal circumstances the regulation of breathing centers on maintaining homeostasis of $CO_2$, $H^+$, and $O_2$, with the main emphasis on $CO_2$.

The sensory mechanisms for detecting changes in $CO_2$ levels are actually indirect. Rather than detecting changes in $CO_2$ levels, certain cells in the medulla oblongata can detect changes in the $H^+$ concentration of the cerebrospinal fluid (the interstitial fluid around the cells in the brain). This is pertinent to control of $CO_2$ because, as you may recall, a rise in $CO_2$ concentration is accompanied by a rise in the hydrogen ion concentration according to the following reaction:

$$CO_2 + H_2O \rightarrow H_2CO_3 \rightarrow HCO_3^- + H^+$$

Thus, when the $P_{CO_2}$ of arterial blood rises, the concentration of $H^+$ in cerebrospinal fluid also rises. Receptor cells detecting an elevated $H^+$ concentration transmit signals to the respiratory center, causing it to increase the rate of the cyclic pattern of impulses and the number of impulses per cycle. As a result, we breathe more frequently and more deeply, exhaling more $CO_2$ and lowering blood levels of the gas back to normal. Our normal arterial $P_{CO_2}$ is maintained at about 40 mm Hg because the normal regulation of respiration keeps it there. Any rise above 40 mm Hg stimulates breathing and any fall below 40 mm Hg inhibits it.

Certain other receptor cells respond to blood $P_{O_2}$ rather than $P_{CO_2}$. These receptors are located in small structures associated with the carotid arteries (the large arteries to the head) and the aorta, called the *carotid* and *aortic bodies*. Normally, $P_{O_2}$ in arterial blood is about 100 mm Hg. If $P_{O_2}$ drops below about 80 mm Hg, these receptors signal the respiratory center to increase the rate and depth of respiration in order to raise blood $O_2$ levels back toward normal. The carotid and aortic bodies also can be stimulated by an increase in the blood concentrations of $H^+$ and $CO_2$ if they are great enough.

It is important to note that the receptors for $O_2$ in the carotid and aortic bodies become activated only when arterial $P_{O_2}$ falls by at least 20%. In contrast, even a 2–3% change in $P_{CO_2}$ stimulates respiration. Under normal circumstances, then, respiration is controlled entirely by the receptors that regulate $CO_2$ by responding to cerebrospinal fluid $H^+$. It just so happens that the regulation of $CO_2$ also keeps $O_2$ within the normal range. In other words, the rate and depth of normal breathing is set by the need to get rid of $CO_2$, not to obtain $O_2$.

There are circumstances, however, when the $O_2$ receptors do come into play. These include certain disease states, drug overdoses, and breathing at high altitudes where the partial pressure of $O_2$ is much lower than normal.

### We can exert some conscious control

Finally, there is another way to regulate breathing, and that is by conscious control. Conscious control resides in higher brain centers, most notably the cortex. The ability to modify our breathing allows us to speak and sing. You can choose to hold your breath for a minute or even to hyperventilate (breathe rapidly) for a short while.

But if you don't think automatic regulatory mechanisms are powerful, just try to hold your breath indefinitely. You will find your conscious control overpowered by the automatic regulatory mechanisms described above.

**RECAP**

The respiratory center in the brain establishes a regular pattern of cyclic breathing. The rate and depth of breathing are then adjusted by regulatory mechanisms that monitor arterial concentrations of $CO_2$, $H^+$, and $O_2$. Conscious control can modify regulatory control but cannot override it completely. ■

## 10.6 Disorders of the respiratory system

Many factors can lead to disorders of respiration. Among them are conditions that reduce air flow or gas exchange, infections by microorganisms, cancer, diseases of other organs such as congestive heart failure, and genetic diseases.

### Reduced air flow or gas exchange impedes respiratory function

Respiration depends on the flow of air between the atmosphere and the alveoli and upon the diffusional exchange of gases across the alveolar and capillary walls. Any factor that impairs these activities impedes respiratory function.

**Asthma: Spasmodic contraction of bronchi** **Asthma** is characterized by spasmodic contraction of bronchial muscle, bronchial swelling, and increased production of mucus. An asthma attack causes partial closure of the bronchi, making breathing difficult. It is a recurrent, chronic lung disorder that affects 17 million people in North America. Its incidence is on the rise both in the U.S. and around the world.

Symptoms of an asthma "attack" include coughing while exercising, shortness of breath, wheezing, and a sense of tightness in the chest. People with asthma often wheeze when they exhale. The symptoms can be triggered by any number of causes, including viruses, air particles, allergies (such as allergies to pollen, house dust, and animal fur), exercise (especially in cold temperatures), tobacco smoke, and air pollution. The symptoms may come and go.

Most asthma attacks are caused by a hyperactive immune system. When a person with asthma breathes in allergens such as pollen or tobacco smoke, the body reacts with excessive production of immunoglobulin E. The IgE stimulates mast cells in the lungs to release chemical weapons such as histamine, leading to excessive inflammation and constriction of bronchiolar smooth muscle.

Drugs are available to dilate the bronchi (bronchodilators), reduce the inflammation (corticosteroids), and restore normal breathing. Treatments also focus on preventing attacks by isolating the cause and avoiding it when possible.

**Emphysema: Alveoli become permanently impaired** **Emphysema** is a chronic disorder involving damage to the alveoli. It begins with destruction of connective tissue in the smaller airways. As a result, the airways become less elastic, do not stay open properly, and tend to collapse during expiration. The high pressures in the lungs caused by the inability to exhale naturally through the collapsed airways eventually damage the fragile alveoli. The result is a permanent reduction in the surface area available for diffusion, and eventually breathlessness and reduced capacity to exchange gases across the lung.

At least one form of emphysema is inherited, but most cases are associated with smoking or long-term exposure to air pollutants. The difference between asthma and emphysema is that asthma is an episodic, recurrent condition of increased airway resistance that largely goes away between episodes, whereas emphysema involves permanent damage to airways that eventually destroys alveoli.

**Bronchitis: Inflammation of the bronchi** **Bronchitis** refers to inflammation of the bronchi, resulting in a persistent cough that produces large quantities of phlegm. Bronchitis may be acute (comes on suddenly and clears up within a couple of weeks) or chronic (persists over a long period and recurs over several years). Both forms are more common in smokers and in people who live in highly polluted areas.

Symptoms include wheezing, breathlessness, and a persistent cough that yields yellowish or greenish phlegm. Sometimes there is fever and a feeling of discomfort behind the sternum. Acute bronchitis can be treated by humidifying the lungs (using a home humidifier or inhaling steam), drinking plenty of fluids, and taking antibiotics if the infection is bacterial in origin. People with chronic bronchitis may need further testing to rule out other health conditions. Bronchodilators can widen the bronchi; oxygen may be prescribed to raise blood oxygen levels.

## Microorganisms can cause lung disease

The lungs are particularly prone to infections. One of the reasons is that they are moist, warm, and covered in a thin layer of fluid, exactly the conditions favored by microorganisms. Besides the common cold and the flu (both caused by viruses), more serious diseases caused by microorganisms include pneumonia, tuberculosis, and botulism.

**Pneumonia: Infection inflames the lungs** In **pneumonia** the lungs become inflamed from an infection, usually caused by viruses or bacteria. The alveoli secrete excess fluid, impairing the exchange of oxygen and carbon dioxide. Symptoms typically include fever, chills, shortness of breath, and a cough that produces yellowish-green phlegm and sometimes blood. Some people experience chest pain when breathing due to inflammation of the membranes that line the chest cavity and cover the lungs.

In North America, pneumonia ranks among the top 10 causes of death, primarily because it is a frequent complication of many serious illnesses. Treatment depends on the microorganism involved. In severe cases, oxygen therapy and artificial ventilation may be necessary. However, most people who develop pneumonia recover completely within a few weeks.

**Tuberculosis: Bacterial infection scars the lungs** **Tuberculosis (TB)** is an infectious disease caused by the bacterium *Mycobacterium tuberculosis*. People pass the infection in airborne droplets by coughing or sneezing. The bacteria enter the lungs and multiply to form an infected "focus." In most cases, the immune system fights off the infection, although it may leave a scar on the lungs. In perhaps 5% of cases, however, the infection spreads via lymphatic vessels to the lymph nodes and may enter the bloodstream. Sometimes the bacteria become dormant for many years, then reactivate later to cause more lung damage.

Major symptoms include coughing (sometimes bringing up blood), chest pain, shortness of breath, fever, night sweats, and appetite and weight loss. A chest X-ray usually reveals lung damage, such as cavities in the lungs or old infections that have healed, leaving scarred lung tissue. A skin test called the tuberculin test can indicate whether someone has been exposed to the infection.

# Smokers' Rights?

It's tough being a smoker these days. First, there's a 39-cent federal excise tax and an average of 80 cents in state taxes on every pack of cigarettes. Then there's that Surgeon General's warning on the pack itself. And to top it off, there are fewer and fewer places where smoking is even permitted. In 2003 only 5 states (California, Connecticut, Delaware, Maine, and New York) had smoke-free workplaces; by 2008 at least 19 states had banned smoking in the workplace. Twenty-five states ban smoking in restaurants as well. Do smokers have any rights?

Smoke-free workplaces force smokers to congregate and smoke outside.

## The Dangers of Secondhand Smoke

We all know that smoking is bad for your health. Cigarette smoke contains a whole host of known or suspected carcinogens. Numerous scientific studies have shown convincingly that smoking is the single leading cause of lung cancer in the world. Hardly anyone would dispute these facts today.

But is the secondhand smoke that comes from a burning cigarette or is exhaled by a smoker also bad for your health? The available scientific evidence is quite convincing but also rather limited in scope; specifically, *women who live with smoking husbands or who work with smokers are at increased risk for lung cancer*. As a result of these findings, the Department of Human Services now officially classifies secondhand smoke (also called environmental tobacco smoke) as a "known human carcinogen." There is also substantial evidence that children who live with smokers are at an increased risk for decreased lung function, increased lung infections, and asthma.

The dilemma we all face is that no one has yet accurately *quantified* the risks of secondhand smoke at all exposure doses. If long-term exposure to a high concentration of secondhand smoke is bad for you, is an occasional whiff of such smoke also bad?

## Emotion Over Science

Smokers argue that an emotional response (fear of cancer) with little or no basis in science is choking off (no pun intended) their right to smoke. Are they correct? Consider the following:

- Of the 19 states that ban smoking entirely in the workplace, not one makes any provision for smokers to smoke in separately ventilated rooms, even though separate rooms could prevent nonsmokers from being exposed to smoke.

*Cigarette smoke has now been classified as a carcinogen.*

- Some anti-smoking laws prohibit smoking closer than 50 feet to a window or door of a building's exterior.
- Thirty-six percent of all respondents to an online poll believe that smoking should be banned in outdoor parks and playgrounds.

## the **facts**...

- Under conditions of heavy or prolonged exposure, secondhand smoke can cause cancer in women and is associated with increased respiratory health risks in children.
- It is not known whether light or occasional exposure to secondhand smoke also poses a health risk.
- Smoking is increasingly being banned in workplaces, in restaurants, and even in public places outdoors.
- Smokers argue that anti-smoking laws take away their right to smoke.

Smokers point out that smoking wouldn't have to affect nonsmokers if buildings were designed with special smoking areas with separate air-circulating systems. After all, our society already provides access to public buildings for the disabled at considerable public expense—where's that same spirit when it comes to accommodating smokers?

Smokers also point out that there is no evidence to suggest that a mere whiff of cigarette smoke is harmful. On that point they are right. The actual scientific evidence is based on fairly heavy exposures to secondhand smoke. There could be a big difference between working or living in an enclosed space with a smoker (there are 28,800 seconds in an 8-hour workday) and catching a whiff of smoke for a few seconds in an outdoor park. Estimates of the health risks (including deaths) from low exposures to secondhand smoke generally are derived by extrapolation—admittedly, not a very convincing scientific technique.

Everyone would probably agree that smoking *should* be banned from places where it might cause harm to others. The question for policy-makers is, just where is that, exactly?

## Questions to Consider

1. *Should smokers have the right to smoke? Why or why not?*
2. *Nonsmokers claim they have a right to smoke-free air. Do you agree?*
3. *Where would you allow smoking, and where would you ban it? On what do you base your opinions?*

A century ago, tuberculosis was a major cause of death worldwide. With the development of antibiotics the incidence of tuberculosis declined precipitously, and most patients in industrialized countries now recover fully. The disease remains a major health problem in undeveloped nations, however, and recently the incidence of tuberculosis has increased in industrialized countries as well. Many authorities attribute this increased prevalence to immigration of people from developing nations. Worldwide, the increased prevalence of AIDS may also be a factor. Furthermore, some strains of tuberculosis are becoming resistant to antibiotics.

**Botulism: Poisoning by bacterial toxin** **Botulism** is a form of poisoning caused by a bacterium, *Clostridium botulinum*, occasionally found in improperly cooked or preserved foods. The bacterium produces a powerful toxin that blocks the transmission of nerve signals to skeletal muscles, including the diaphragm and intercostal muscles.

Symptoms of botulism poisoning usually appear 8 to 36 hours after eating the contaminated food. They can include difficulty swallowing and speaking, double vision, nausea, and vomiting. If not treated, botulism can be fatal because it paralyzes the respiratory muscles.

## Lung cancer is caused by proliferation of abnormal cells

*Cancer* is the uncontrolled growth of abnormal cells. In the lung, cancerous cells crowd out normal cells and eventually impede normal function. Lung cancer can impair not only the movement of air in the airways but also the exchange of gases in the alveoli and the flow of blood in pulmonary blood vessels (Figure 10.14). It accounts for one-third of all cancer deaths in the United States.

Lung cancer takes years to develop and is strongly associated with smoking. More than 90% of lung cancer patients are current or former smokers, and some of those who don't smoke were exposed to secondhand smoke from other people. Two other important causes are radon gas (formed in rock as a breakdown product of uranium, it seeps into uncirculated air in a building's foundation or basement) and chemicals in the workplace, the best known of which is asbestos.

Symptoms of lung cancer include chronic cough, wheezing, chest pain, and coughing up blood. Most people don't go to the doctor for every trivial cough, but any cough that is persistent or accompanied by chest pain—especially coughs that bring up blood—should be checked out immediately. If cancer is caught early it may be possible to remove the cancerous lobe or region of the lung, or to eradicate the tumor with radiation therapy and chemotherapy.

Lung cancer is highly preventable. It is a good idea to not smoke, to know the conditions of your work environment, and, depending on where you live, to have your home inspected for radon gas. For more information on all types of cancer, see Chapter 18.

## Congestive heart failure impairs lung function

In Chapter 8 we discussed *congestive heart failure* as a cardiovascular condition in which the heart gradually becomes less efficient. Even though it starts as a heart disorder, it can end by impairing lung function as well.

Recall that in congestive heart failure the heart begins to fail as a pump. When the left side of the heart fails, blood backs up in the pulmonary blood vessels behind that side of the heart. The result is a rise in blood pressure in the pulmonary vessels. When pulmonary capillary pressure increases, the balance of physical pressure and osmotic forces across the capillary wall favors fluid loss from the capillary. As a result, fluid builds up in the interstitial spaces between capillaries and alveoli and sometimes within alveoli themselves. This increases the diffusional distance and reduces

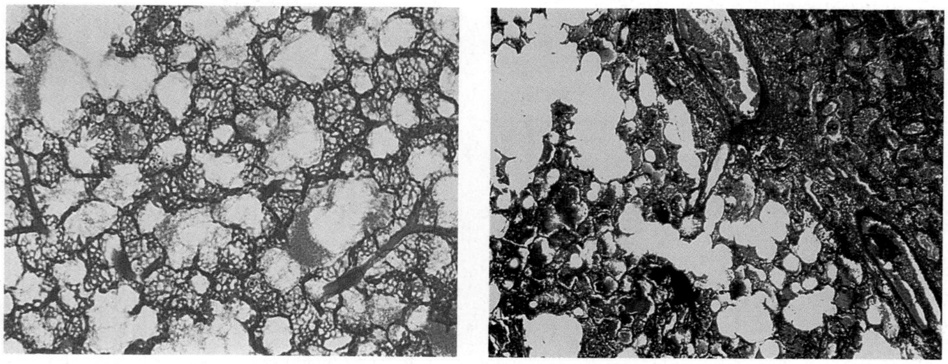

**a) Normal lung** **b) Cancerous lung**

**Figure 10.14 Lung cancer. (a)** Normal lung alveoli and surrounding capillaries. **(b)** A section through a cancerous lung showing alveolar destruction and capillary bleeding (dark red color).

diffusion of gases. Treatments focus on reducing this fluid buildup by helping the body get rid of fluid and improving the heart's pumping action.

### Cystic fibrosis is an inherited disease

Cystic fibrosis is an inherited condition in which a single defective gene causes the mucus-producing cells in the lungs to produce a thick, sticky mucus. The disease affects other organ systems as well. In the lungs, the abnormally thick mucus impedes air flow and also provides a site for the growth of bacteria. People with cystic fibrosis tend to get frequent infections of the airways. Treatment of the disease includes consistent physical therapy to try to dislodge the mucus and keep the airways open. Several promising new drugs are now on the market for this disease. For more on cystic fibrosis, see the Health Watch box in Chapter 19.

**RECAP**

The lungs are prone to damage by environmental pollutants, tobacco smoke, and infections by microorganisms. Cases of both asthma and tuberculosis are on the rise. ■

## Chapter Summary

### Respiration takes place throughout the body *p. 219*

- Respiration encompasses four processes: breathing, external respiration, internal respiration, and cellular respiration.
- External respiration occurs in the lungs; internal respiration and cellular respiration take place in the tissues.

### The respiratory system consists of upper and lower respiratory tracts *p. 219*

- The respiratory system includes the air passageways to the lungs and the lungs themselves.
- Bones and skeletal muscles support the respiratory system and participate in breathing.
- The upper respiratory tract consists of the nose and pharynx. The upper respiratory tract filters, warms, and humidifies the air we breathe.
- The lower respiratory tract consists of the larynx, the trachea, the main bronchi, and the lungs.
- Within the lungs, the bronchi branch many times, becoming smaller airways called bronchioles that end in air-filled sacs called alveoli.
- The tremendous surface area of the alveoli, coupled with the thinness of the respiratory membrane, facilitates gas exchange with the pulmonary capillaries.

### The process of breathing involves a pressure gradient *p. 226*

- Inspiration occurs as the lungs expand due to the action of the diaphragm and the intercostal muscles; expiration occurs when these muscles relax.
- When the lungs expand, the pressure within them falls relative to atmospheric pressure and air rushes in; during expiration, the lungs become smaller and increasing pressure within them forces air out.
- During normal breathing, inspiration is active (requiring energy) and expiration is passive.
- Normally we breathe at about 12 breaths per minute with a tidal volume of 500 ml per breath.
- Vital capacity is the maximum amount of air a person can exhale after a maximal inhalation.

### Gas exchange and transport occur passively *p. 228*

- The diffusion of a gas is dependent on a partial pressure gradient, which is equivalent to a concentration gradient.
- External and internal respiration are both processes that occur entirely by diffusion.
- Nearly all (98%) of the oxygen transported by blood is bound to hemoglobin in red blood cells.
- Although some carbon dioxide is transported as dissolved $CO_2$ or is bound to hemoglobin, most $CO_2$ (70%) is converted to bicarbonate and then transported in plasma.

### The nervous system regulates breathing *p. 232*

- A respiratory center in the medulla oblongata of the brain establishes a regular cycle of inhalation and exhalation.
- Under normal conditions, the rate and depth of breathing is adjusted primarily to maintain homeostasis of arterial blood $P_{CO_2}$.
- Regulation of respiration by $O_2$ comes into play only when the $P_{O_2}$ concentration falls by more than 20%, such as in disease states or at high altitude.
- We can exert some conscious control over breathing.

### Disorders of the respiratory system *p. 234*

- Asthma is episodic, spasmodic contractions of the bronchi that impede air flow.
- Emphysema is a chronic disorder characterized by high resistance to air flow and destruction of alveoli.
- The lungs are prone to infections because their surface is kept moist and warm in order to facilitate gas exchange. Tuberculosis is an infectious disease caused by a bacterium. In pneumonia, infected alveoli secrete excess fluid, impairing gas exchange.
- Lung disease can be a secondary condition resulting from impairment of another organ, as in congestive heart failure.

## Terms You Should Know

alveoli, *224*
asthma, *235*
bronchi, *223*
bronchioles, *223*
bronchitis, *235*
carbaminohemoglobin, *231*
diaphragm, *226*
emphysema, *235*
epiglottis, *222*
glottis, *222*
larynx, *221*
oxyhemoglobin, *231*
partial pressure, *229*
pharynx, *221*
pleural membranes, *223*
respiratory center, *233*
tidal volume, *228*
trachea, *222*
tuberculosis, *235*
ventilation, *219*
vital capacity, *228*
vocal cords, *222*

## Concept Review

1. List at least three functions of your nose.
2. Explain why men's voices are lower than women's.
3. Explain why smokers sometimes have a chronic cough.
4. Distinguish between *bronchi* and *bronchioles*.
5. Explain what happens to gas pressure in a closed container when the size of the container becomes larger and smaller.
6. Describe the sequence of pressure changes that occur during inspiration and expiration.
7. Define *partial pressure* and explain its importance to gas diffusion.
8. Explain why the partial pressure of oxygen in the alveoli is always lower than the partial pressure of oxygen in the air we breathe.
9. Explain (or use a diagram to show) how bicarbonate is formed from dissolved $CO_2$ in the region of metabolizing tissues.
10. Describe how heart failure can lead to a decrease in the ability of $O_2$ and $CO_2$ diffuse between the blood and the alveoli.

## Test Yourself

### Matching Exercise

_____ 1. These have muscle spasms during an asthma attack
_____ 2. The opening between the vocal cords
_____ 3. The air-filled sacs that are the sites of gas exchange between air and blood
_____ 4. Name for the volume of a normal breath at rest
_____ 5. Maximum amount of air we can inhale and then exhale in a single breath
_____ 6. Disease in which a toxin paralyzes respiratory muscles

a. alveoli
b. glottis
c. vital capacity
d. tidal volume
e. bronchi
f. botulism

### Fill in the Blank

7. The flexible flap of cartilage that closes off the airway during swallowing is called the __________.
8. The airway to the lungs begins with the pharynx, then the __________, then the trachea.
9. The space that lies between the outer surface of the lung and the wall of the chest cavity is called the __________ cavity.
10. The __________ establishes a regular, rhythmic cycle of breathing.
11. During inspiration, the dome-shaped __________ contracts and flattens.
12. The __________ and __________ bodies contain sensory receptors that monitor blood $P_{O_2}$.

### True or False?

13. Under normal conditions of quiet breathing at rest, both inspiration and expiration are active processes, requiring contraction of opposing skeletal muscle groups.
14. Under normal conditions, the rate and depth of breathing are adjusted by a homeostatic control mechanism for $CO_2$, not $O_2$.
15. Gas exchange occurs in the bronchiole passageways.

## References and Additional Reading

Buckley, Christopher. *Thank You for Smoking.* New York: HarperPerennial, 1994. 272 pp. (Fiction. A humorous satirical view of smoking from the perspective of a fictional tobacco lobbyist.)

Gibbs, T. W. Breath of Fresh Liquid. *Scientific American,* February 1999, pp. 40–41. (Brief research news article about breathing liquids instead of air.)

Langer, Robert. Where a Pill Won't Reach. *Scientific American,* April 2003, pp. 50–57. (A discussion of newer drug delivery methods, including respiratory inhalation.)

Levitzky, Michael G. *Pulmonary Physiology,* 6th ed. New York: McGraw-Hill, 2003. (A good all-around reference resource for human respiratory system function.)

### Internet References

Find links to the following Web sites at the Human Biology Place.

**American Cancer Society**
**www.cancer.org**
A great resource for information about lung cancer, which kills more Americans every year than any other form of cancer.

**American Lung Association**
**www.lungusa.org**
A nonprofit organization and an excellent resource on respiratory disorders.

**National Heart, Lung, and Blood Institute**
**www.nhlbi.nih.gov**
Interactive tutorials, health assessment tools, and other helpful information on the respiratory and cardiovascular systems.

**National Institute of Allergy and Infectious Diseases**
**www3.niaid.nih.gov**
Contains some useful information about asthma and other allergy and infectious diseases.

## Apply **What You Know**

1. Why would someone administering a Breathalyzer test for alcohol ask the person being tested to give one deep breath rather than many shallow ones?
2. At a murder trial a pathologist is asked whether the dead baby he examined had been alive at the time of birth, or was stillborn. How can the pathologist tell?
3. A lifetime of heavy smoking often leads to destruction of the cilia of the cells that line the bronchi and bronchioles. How does this contribute to an increased chance of lung infections?
4. Laryngitis is an inflammation of the larynx. Why does someone with laryngitis have a hard time speaking?
5. If you take a sharp blow to the stomach you can be said to have the "wind knocked out of you." Why would an unexpected blow to the stomach leave someone unable to breathe for a moment?
6. When a hole is created in the chest wall, the lung collapses, even if the lung is not damaged. A collapsed lung is called a pneumothorax. Why does the lung collapse if it is not damaged? Will the patient be able to breathe?
7. A person who gets overly excited or has an anxiety attack may begin to hyperventilate. This can lead to a feeling of dizziness, light-headedness, and muscle weakness. One remedy is to have the person breathe into a paper bag. Why would this help?

*Answers can be found on the Human Biology Place.*

# 11 The Nervous System: Integration and Control

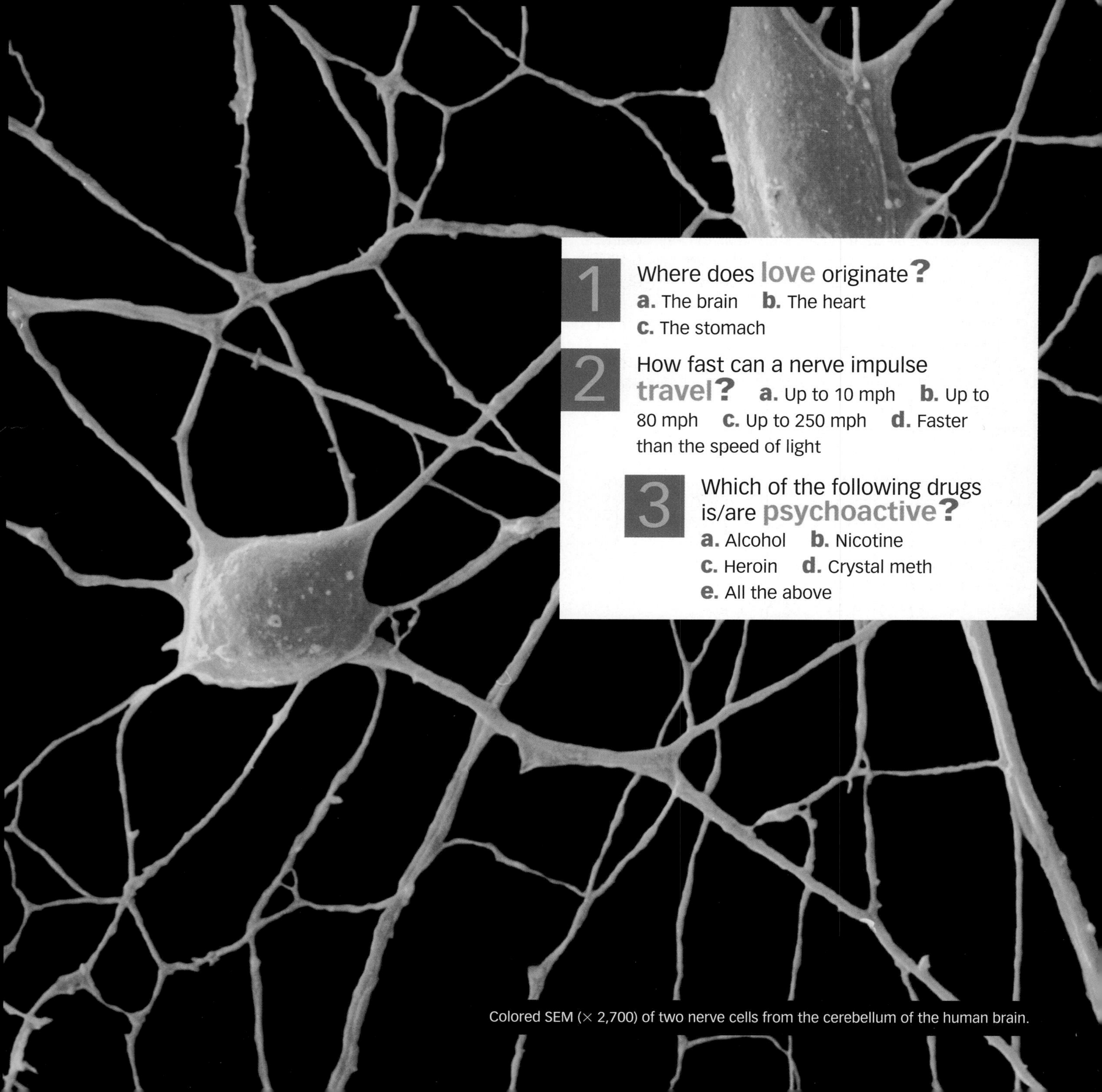

**1** Where does **love** originate**?**
**a.** The brain **b.** The heart
**c.** The stomach

**2** How fast can a nerve impulse **travel?** **a.** Up to 10 mph **b.** Up to 80 mph **c.** Up to 250 mph **d.** Faster than the speed of light

**3** Which of the following drugs is/are **psychoactive?**
**a.** Alcohol **b.** Nicotine
**c.** Heroin **d.** Crystal meth
**e.** All the above

Colored SEM (× 2,700) of two nerve cells from the cerebellum of the human brain.

**You're on your way to class.** It is cold but you are not wearing your coat, and you are hungry. As you cross the street you see a doughnut shop and you smell doughnuts and coffee in the air. Suddenly you hear sounds—the screech of a skidding truck behind you and the blaring of the truck's horn. Quickly you whirl around, glance at the approaching truck, and leap to safety on the sidewalk.

Your nervous system is constantly receiving input from all kinds of sources. There's a huge amount of information to be sorted through, including data in your large memory banks about the probable meaning of all these sounds and other stimuli. The nervous system integrates this seemingly unrelated information quickly and enables you to react in time. How does this happen?

Here are three characteristics of the nervous system:

- The nervous system requires information, which it receives from our senses.
- The nervous system integrates information. Integration is the process of taking different pieces of information from many different sources and assembling the pieces into a whole that makes sense. This process entails sifting through mountains of data and coming up with a plan or course of action.
- The nervous system is very fast. It can receive information, integrate it, and produce a response within tenths of a second. In this chapter we learn about the special properties of the nervous system that give it such speed.

Most of the functions of the nervous system are completely automatic and can be carried on simultaneously without requiring our attention or conscious decision making. However, the nervous system can also bring selected information to the level of conscious awareness. Working with the endocrine system (Chapter 13), the nervous system maintains homeostasis. It also allows us to feel emotions, to be aware of ourselves, and to exert conscious control over the incredible diversity of our physical movements.

## 11.1 The nervous system has two principal parts

The nervous system comprises the **central nervous system (CNS)** and the **peripheral nervous system (PNS).** The CNS consists of the brain and the spinal cord. It receives, processes, stores, and transfers information. The PNS includes the components of the nervous system that lie outside the CNS. The PNS has two functional subdivisions: the sensory division of the PNS carries information to the brain and spinal cord, and the motor division carries information from the CNS (Figure 11.1).

The motor division of the peripheral nervous system is further subdivided along functional lines. The *somatic division* of the PNS controls skeletal muscles, and the autonomic division of the PNS controls smooth muscles, cardiac muscles, and glands. In turn, the *autonomic division* has two subdivisions called the *sympathetic* and *parasympathetic* divisions. In general, the actions of the sympathetic and parasympathetic divisions oppose each other. They work antagonistically to accomplish the automatic, subconscious maintenance of homeostasis.

We examine each of these components in more detail later in this chapter. But first, we discuss the structure and function of neurons and of the neuroglial cells that accompany and support them.

**RECAP**

The nervous system has two major subdivisions: the central nervous system (CNS), consisting of the brain and spinal cord, and the peripheral nervous system (PNS), which includes all parts of the nervous system that lie outside the CNS. The PNS has a somatic division, which controls skeletal muscles, and an autonomic division, which controls smooth muscles, cardiac muscles, and glands. The autonomic division has sympathetic and parasympathetic divisions. ■

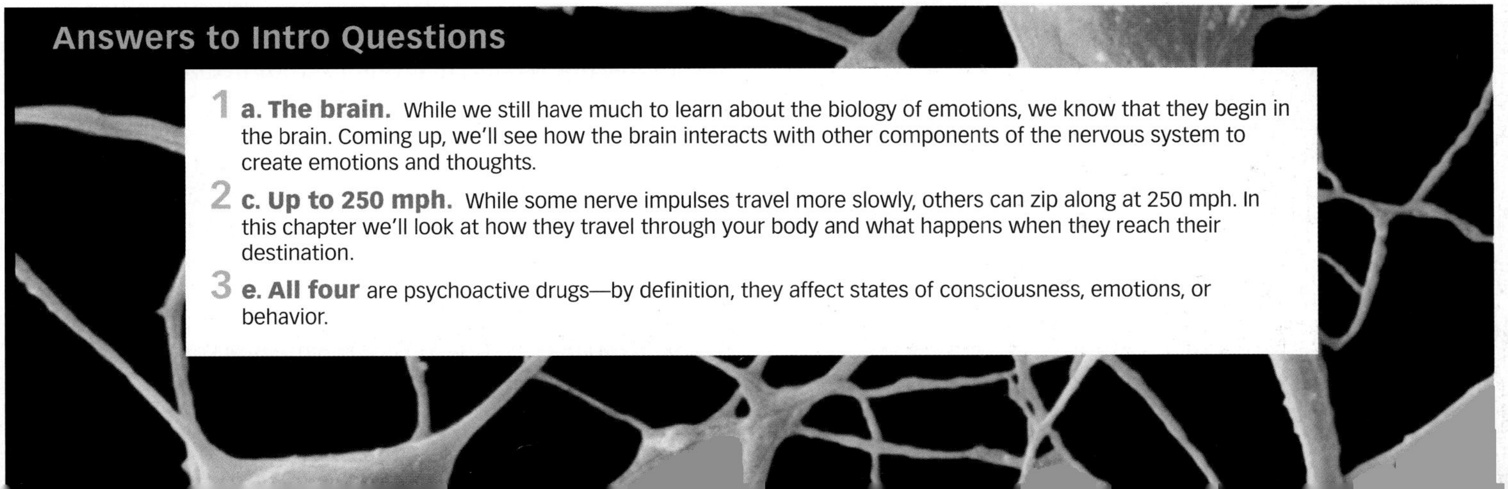

### Answers to Intro Questions

1 **a. The brain.** While we still have much to learn about the biology of emotions, we know that they begin in the brain. Coming up, we'll see how the brain interacts with other components of the nervous system to create emotions and thoughts.

2 **c. Up to 250 mph.** While some nerve impulses travel more slowly, others can zip along at 250 mph. In this chapter we'll look at how they travel through your body and what happens when they reach their destination.

3 **e. All four** are psychoactive drugs—by definition, they affect states of consciousness, emotions, or behavior.

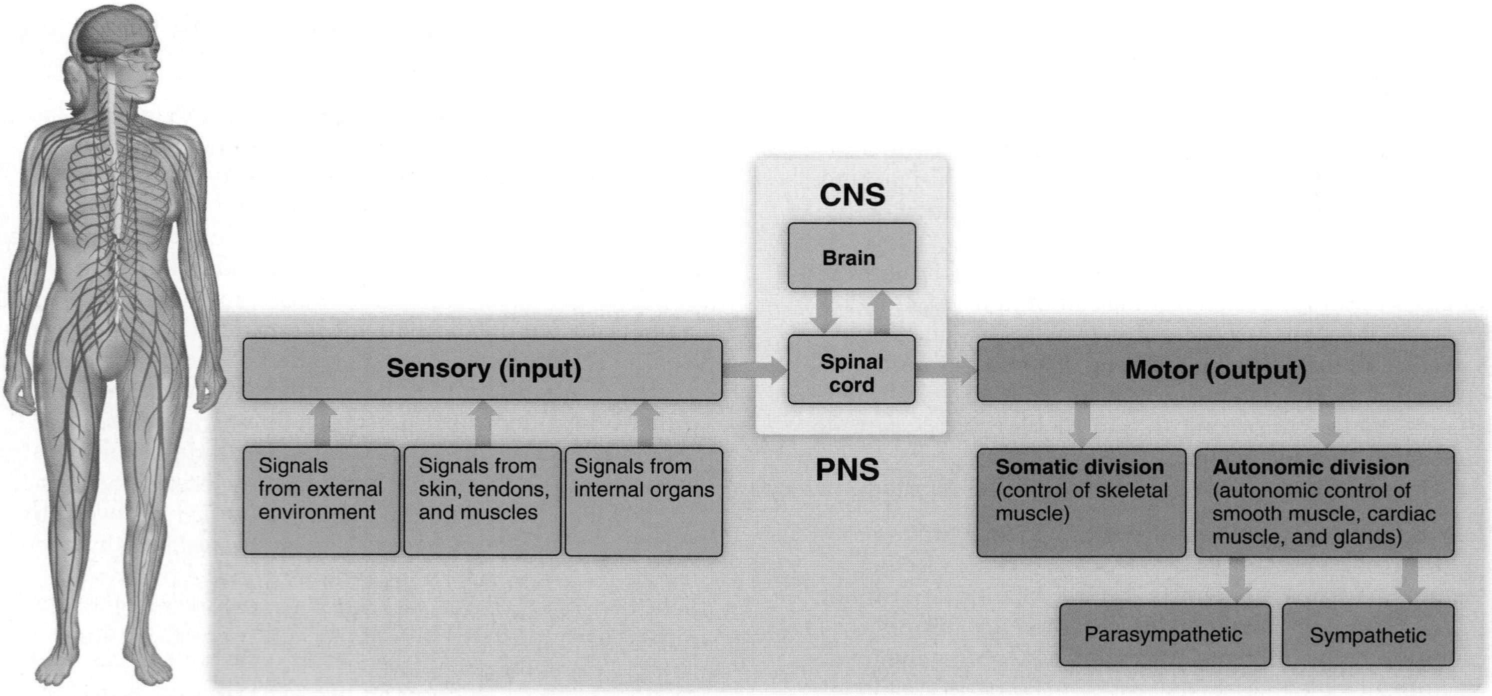


**Figure 11.1 Components of the nervous system.** The CNS receives input from the sensory component of the PNS, integrates and organizes the information, and then sends output to the periphery via the motor components of the PNS.

## 11.2 Neurons are the communication cells of the nervous system

**Neurons** are cells specialized for communication. They generate and conduct electrical impulses, also called *action potentials,* from one part of the body to another. The longest neurons extend all the way from your toes to your spinal cord. These are single cells, remember.

There are three types of neurons in the nervous system, as shown in Figure 11.2.

- **Sensory neurons** of the PNS are specialized to respond to a certain type of stimulus, such as pressure or light. They transmit information about this stimulus to the CNS in the form of electrical impulses. In other words, sensory neurons provide input to the CNS.
- **Interneurons** within the CNS transmit impulses between components of the CNS. Interneurons receive input from sensory neurons, integrate this information, and influence the functioning of other neurons.
- **Motor neurons** of the PNS transmit impulses away from the CNS. They carry the nervous system's output, still in the form of electrical impulses, to all of the tissues and organs of the body.

All neurons consist of a cell body, one or more dendrites, and an axon. The main body of a neuron is called the **cell body.** The nucleus with its content of DNA is located in the cell body, as are the mitochondria and other cell organelles.

Slender extensions of the cell body, called **dendrites,** receive information from receptors or incoming impulses from other neurons. Interneurons and motor neurons have numerous dendrites that are fairly short and extend in many directions from the cell body. Sensory neurons are an exception, for their dendrites connect directly to an axon.

An **axon** is a long, slender tube of cell membrane containing a small amount of cytoplasm. Axons are specialized to conduct electrical impulses. Axons of sensory neurons originate from a dendrite, whereas the axons of interneurons and motor neurons originate from a cone-shaped area of the cell body called the *axon hillock.* At its other end, the axon branches into slender extensions called *axon terminals.* Each axon terminal ends in a small rounded tip called an *axon bulb.*

Typically, an interneuron or motor neuron receives incoming information from other neurons at its dendrites or cell body. If the incoming information is of the right kind and is strong enough, the neuron responds by generating an electrical impulse of its own at its axon hillock. In contrast, in a sensory neuron the impulse is initiated where the dendrite joins the axon. The impulse is then transmitted from one end of the axon to the other, bypassing the cell body entirely. We talk more about different types of receptors in Chapter 12 (Sensory Mechanisms).

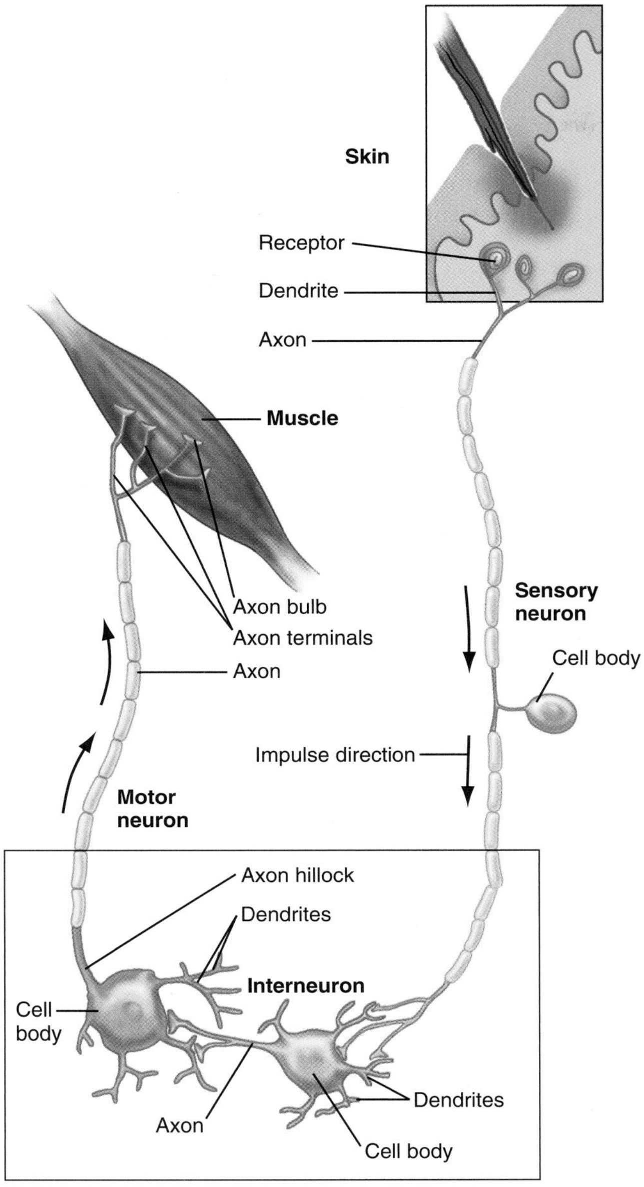


**Figure 11.2 Types of neurons in the nervous system.** The flow of information begins at a receptor near a dendritic ending of a sensory neuron and ends at the axon bulbs of a motor neuron. In this example the receptors are in skin. Interneurons are located entirely within the central nervous system and typically have short axons.

**RECAP**

Neurons generate and transmit electrical impulses from one part of the body to another. Sensory neurons transmit impulses to the CNS. Interneurons transmit impulses between components of the CNS. Motor neurons transmit impulses away from the CNS to muscles and glands. ■

## 11.3 Neurons initiate action potentials

The function of a neuron is to transmit information from one part of the body to another in the form of electrical impulses. Next, we look at how a neuron initiates and conducts an impulse.

### Sodium-potassium pump maintains resting potential

As described in Chapter 3, the sodium-potassium pump is essential to the control of cell volume by virtue of its ability to remove osmotic particles (sodium ions) from the cell. Now we learn that the same sodium-potassium pump is also essential for the development and maintenance of an electrical charge across the cell membrane. How does it help to create and maintain an electrical charge?

Recall that the sodium-potassium pump transports three sodium ions ($Na^+$) out of the cell for every two potassium ions ($K^+$) transported in. Each time the sodium-potassium pump goes through a cycle, the net effect is the removal of one osmotic particle (a $Na^+$ ion) and also one positive charge (because the $Na^+$ ion is positively charged). In other words, the sodium-potassium pump removes both osmotic particles and positive charges from the cell at the same time. As a result of the activity of the sodium-potassium pumps and also the presence of negatively charged protein molecules trapped within the cell, the cell cytoplasm has a slight excess of negative charge compared to the interstitial fluid. The difference in charge results in a small but measurable difference in voltage across the cell membrane, called the *membrane potential.*

In a neuron capable of action potentials but not generating one at the moment, the normal membrane potential at rest is its **resting (membrane) potential.** The resting potential of a neuron is about –70 millivolts (mV), meaning that the inside of the neuron is negatively charged compared to the outside. Figure 11.3 illustrates the role of the sodium-potassium pump and the processes of diffusion of $Na^+$ and $K^+$ (through channels) in maintaining the resting potential.

The concentration of sodium is much higher in the interstitial fluid than it is in the cytoplasm, whereas the inverse is true for potassium. Because sodium is always leaking into the cell and potassium is leaking out by passive diffusion, you might think that the concentration differences between the inside and outside would disappear over time. This doesn't happen because the active transport of sodium and potassium by the pump in the opposite directions exactly balances the rates of leakage. At rest, the ionic concentration differences are maintained and the membrane potential stays at –70 mV, inside negative. As we'll see in a moment, the large concentration differences for sodium and potassium across the axon membrane enable the neuron to generate impulses simply by opening and closing ion channels.

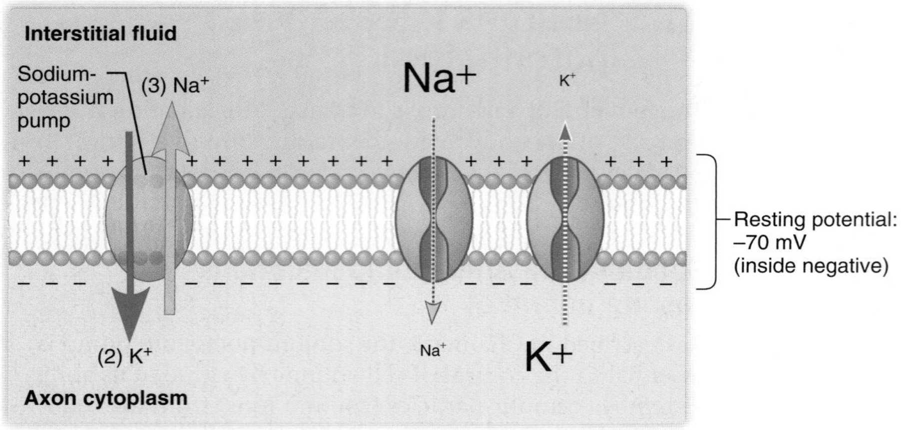


**Figure 11.3 Maintenance of the resting membrane potential.** The sodium-potassium pump actively transports three $Na^+$ ions out of the cell in exchange for two $K^+$ ions. Most of the $K^+$ leaks out again. However, the inward leak of sodium is so slow that the pump effectively is able to exclude most $Na^+$ from the cell. The exclusion of positive ions ($Na^+$) from the cell creates a voltage difference (an electrical potential) across the cell membrane of about –70 mV (inside negative). The relative concentrations of $Na^+$ and $K^+$ in the interstitial fluid and the cytoplasm are indicated by the sizes of the letters associated with the diffusion channels.

## Graded potentials alter the resting potential

The resting potential of a neuron undergoes a change when an impulse arrives from another neuron. Every incoming impulse produces, in a series of steps discussed in a moment, a small transient change in the resting potential in a local area of the membrane. Depending on the type of signal and its strength, the change might be to *depolarize* the membrane (move the voltage closer to zero), or *hyperpolarize* it (make it even more negative). These transient local changes in resting potential are called **graded potentials** because they can vary in size. They occur only at a single region on the membrane, fading away at increasing distances from that region like the ripples made by a raindrop on water. A neuron may receive hundreds of incoming signals from other neurons, so hundreds of these graded potentials may occur at the same time.

A key feature of graded potentials is that they can add up in space and time, meaning that many incoming signals from other neurons produce a bigger change in membrane potential than does one impulse alone. This is known as **summation.**

**RECAP**

A neuron's resting potential of about –70 millivolts is maintained by the constant action of the sodium-potassium pump. Impulses arriving from other neurons can cause small, local changes in the neuron's membrane potential called graded potentials. ■

## An action potential is a sudden reversal of membrane voltage

If the sum of all graded potentials is sufficiently strong to reach a certain triggering membrane voltage called the **threshold,** an action potential results. An **action potential** is a sudden, temporary reversal of the voltage difference across the cell membrane. Once an action potential is initiated, it sweeps rapidly down the axon at a constant amplitude and rate of speed until it reaches the axon terminals.

Figure 11.4 depicts the resting membrane potential, graded potentials and how they summate, and an action potential.

Functionally, an action potential (impulse) is the only form in which information is transmitted long distance by the nervous system. An action potential is like a single monotonic "beep" in a touch-tone phone or a single on-off pulse of current. Its meaning is provided only by where it came from and where it goes—that is, by how the nervous system is wired.

Action potentials occur because the axon membrane contains voltage-sensitive ion channels that open and close sequentially once threshold has been reached. An action potential occurs as a sequence of three events: (1) depolarization, (2) repolarization, and (3) reestablishment of the resting potential (Figure 11.5).

1. *Depolarization: sodium moves into the axon.* When threshold is exceeded, voltage-sensitive $Na^+$ channels in the axon's membrane open briefly and $Na^+$ ions diffuse rapidly into the cytoplasm of the axon. This influx of positive ions causes *depolarization,* meaning that the membrane potential shifts from negative (–70 mV) to positive (about +30 mV).

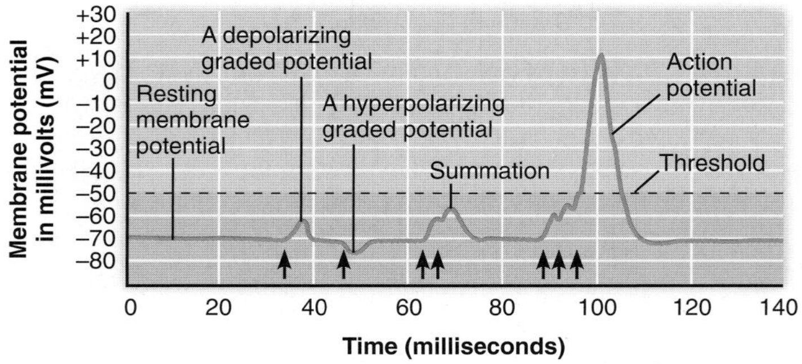


**Figure 11.4 The resting membrane potential, graded potentials, and an action potential in a neuron.** Stimulation by other neurons is indicated by the arrows. Note that graded potentials can either depolarize or hyperpolarize the membrane and that they can summate. If the sum of all graded potentials is sufficient to depolarize the membrane to threshold, an action potential occurs.

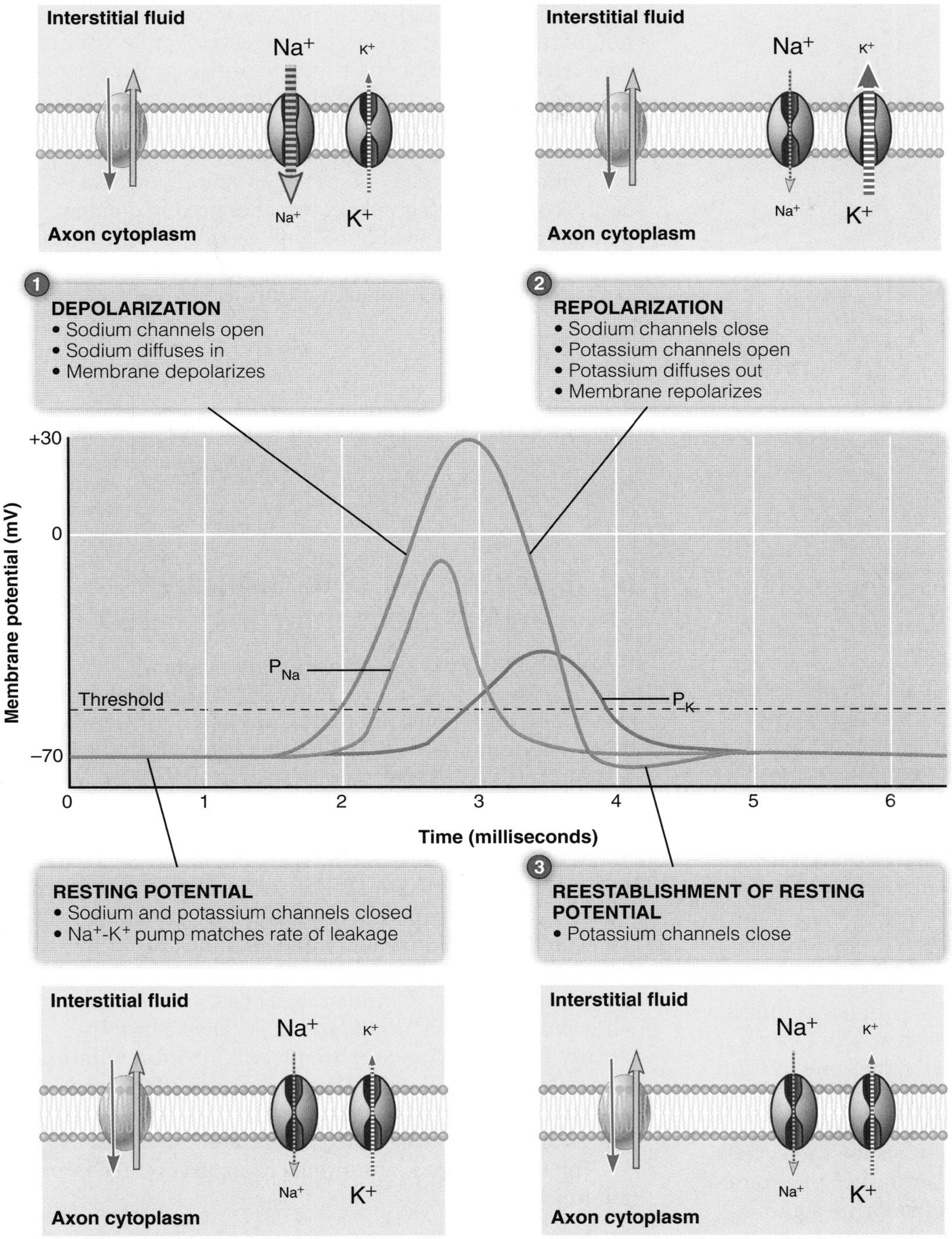


**Figure 11.5 Propagation of an action potential.** This is a graph of changes in potential over time recorded from a single point on the axon. At rest, the sodium-potassium pump transports sodium and potassium, and the sodium and potassium channels are essentially closed. **(1)** *Depolarization*: once threshold is exceeded, voltage-sensitive sodium channels open briefly and the membrane permeability to sodium ($P_{Na}$) increases. Sodium diffuses rapidly into the axon, depolarizing the membrane. **(2)** *Repolarization*: sodium channels close. Potassium channels open and the membrane permeability to potassium ($P_K$) increases. Potassium diffuses outward, repolarizing the membrane. **(3)** *Reestablishment of resting potential*: after a brief hyperpolarization caused by a delay in the full closure of potassium channels, the membrane potential returns to its normal resting value.

2. *Repolarization: potassium moves out of the axon.* After a short delay the $Na^+$ channels close automatically. But the reversal of the membrane polarity triggers the opening of $K^+$ channels. This allows more $K^+$ ions than usual to diffuse rapidly out of the cell. The loss of positive ions from the cell leads to *repolarization,* meaning that the interior of the axon becomes negative again.
3. *Reestablishment of the resting potential.* Because the $K^+$ channels are slow to close, there is a brief overshoot of membrane voltage during which the interior of the axon is slightly hyperpolarized. Shortly after the $K^+$ channels close, the resting potential is reestablished. At this point the axon is prepared to receive another action potential. The entire sequence of three steps takes about 3 milliseconds.

While an action potential is underway, an axon can't generate another action potential. This period is called the *absolute refractory period.* The presence of an absolute refractory period ensures that action potentials always travel in one direction only, because an area of the axon that has just experienced an action potential cannot produce another one right away.

The absolute refractory period is followed by a brief *relative refractory period* during which it is harder than usual to generate the next action potential. In practical terms, this means that by encroaching into the relative refractory period, very strong stimuli can generate more frequent action potentials than relatively weak stimuli can. The absolute and relative refractory periods are shown in Figure 11.6.

Whether or not a neuron is generating action potentials, the

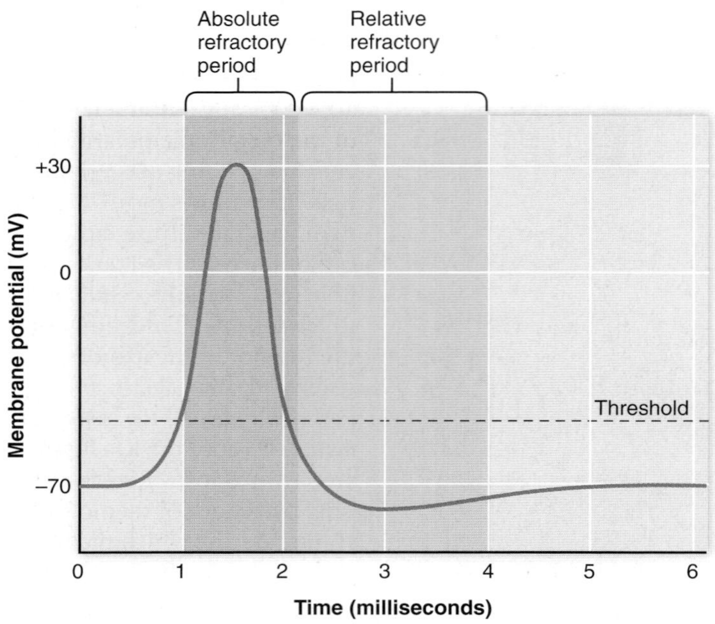


**Figure 11.6 Absolute and relative refractory periods.**

sodium-potassium pumps continue to maintain the normal concentrations of $Na^+$ and $K^+$ and the normal resting potential. The actual number of $Na^+$ and $K^+$ ions that diffuse across the membrane during a single action potential is so small compared to the activity of the sodium-potassium pumps that an axon can transmit many action potentials in a short period of time without adversely affecting the subsequent resting membrane potential.

### Action potentials are all-or-none and self-propagating

As we have seen, an action potential does not occur unless a certain threshold membrane voltage is reached. Once it is triggered, however, it always looks exactly the same in form and voltage. Even if the graded stimulus that causes it is significantly higher than the threshold level, the form and amplitude of the action potential are always the same. Consequently an action potential is an "all-or-none" phenomenon: either it occurs or it does not. It's like firing a gun. A certain amount of pressure—the threshold level—is required to make the gun fire. Pressing the trigger too lightly will not make it fire, and pressing it harder than necessary will not cause the bullet to leave the gun any faster.

An action potential is also a self-propagating event, meaning that it continues to propagate itself in the next region of the axon. This is because the local spread of electrical current forward from the region of the axon that is currently undergoing an action potential brings the next region of the axon to threshold. Thus the action potential is propagated continuously down the axon like a moving wave, at a constant rate of speed and amplitude.

If all action potentials are alike, how does a neuron transmit information about stimulus intensity? Simple, really: it's encoded by the number of action potentials generated and transmitted per unit time, ranging from near zero to perhaps several hundred per second. Stronger stimuli generate more action potentials per unit time, not faster or bigger ones.

Although the speed of travel of an action potential is always constant for a given neuron, the speed in different neurons can vary from about 5 mph up to 250 mph. Action potential speed is greater in larger-diameter axons and in axons covered by an insulating sheath, as we'll see in a minute.

**RECAP**

The sum of all graded potentials may initiate a self-propagating, all-or-none action potential in a neuron. An action potential involves three events: depolarization, repolarization, and reestablishment of the resting potential. ■

## 11.4 Neuroglial cells support and protect neurons

Only about 20% of cells in the human nervous system are neurons. The rest are **neuroglial cells,** which provide physical support and protection to neurons and help maintain healthy concentrations of important chemicals in the fluid surrounding them. (Neuroglia derives from the Greek words for "neuron" and "glue.") Neuroglial cells do not generate or transmit impulses.

In the peripheral nervous system, many neuron axons are enclosed and protected by specialized neuroglial cells called *Schwann cells.* Schwann cells produce a fatty insulating material called *myelin.* During development, individual Schwann cells wrap themselves around a short segment of an axon many times as a sort of insulating blanket, creating a shiny white protective layer around the axon called a **myelin sheath.** Between adjacent Schwann cells are short uninsulated gaps called *nodes of Ranvier* where the surface of the axon is still exposed (Figure 11.7). Neurons that have axons wrapped in a sheath of myelin are called **myelinated neurons.**

The myelin sheath around the axon serves three important functions:

- *It saves the neuron energy.* The insulating layer of myelin prevents some of the slow inward leak of sodium and outward leak of potassium that would otherwise occur. These leaks normally have to be replaced by active transport processes requiring energy (see section 11.3).
- *It speeds up the transmission of impulses.* The myelin sheath prevents nearly all leakage of charged ions across the axon membrane except where the axon is bare (at the nodes of Ranvier). When an action potential occurs at a node of Ranvier, then, the local depolarizing current spreads much farther within the axon—all the way to the next node of Ranvier. The rate of travel of this

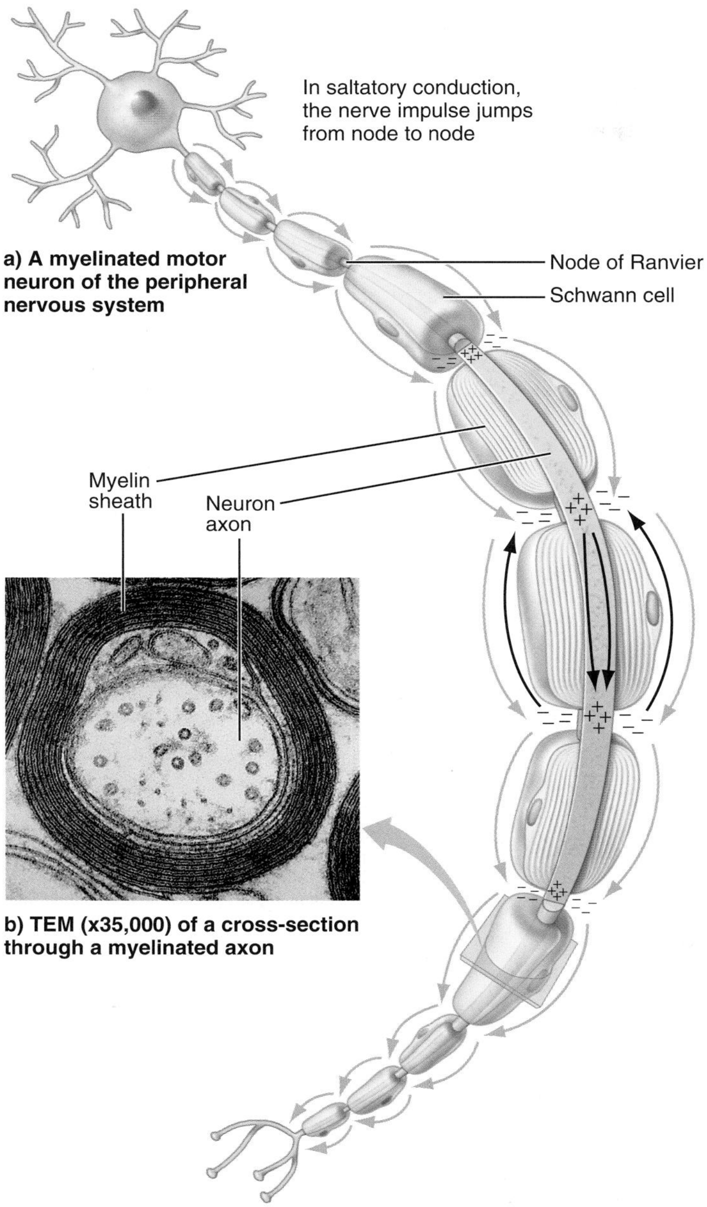


**Figure 11.7 A myelinated motor neuron of the peripheral nervous system.** The axon of the motor neuron is wrapped by individual Schwann cells, which produce an insulating substance called myelin. Between adjacent Schwann cells are uninsulated sections called nodes of Ranvier. In myelinated neurons, electrical impulses appear to jump rapidly from node to node as a result of local current flows both within and outside the neuron (shown by thin black arrows).

local current within the axon is even faster than the rate of travel of a continuously propagated action potential along an unmyelinated axon. At the next node of Ranvier, the local depolarizing current brings the axon membrane to threshold, triggering a new action potential. In effect, a succession of action potentials appear to jump from node to node at a very fast rate. This "leaping" pattern of conduction along myelinated neurons is called **saltatory conduction** (from *saltare,* Latin for "dance"). Continuously propagated action potentials in unmyelinated neurons travel at a speed of only about 5 mph (2.3 meters per second). In contrast, saltatory conduction in myelinated neurons can reach speeds of up to 250 mph (about 110 meters per second).

- *It helps damaged or severed axons of the peripheral nervous system regenerate.* If a neuron axon is severed, the portion of the axon distal to the cell body may degenerate. However, the cut end of the axon still attached to the cell body can regrow through the channel formed by the sheath, eventually reconnecting with the cell that it serves. Depending on the length of the axon, the regeneration process can take anywhere from a few weeks to more than a year. On average, an axon in the peripheral nervous system grows by nearly 1/16 inch (approximately 1.5 millimeters) per day.

In the central nervous system, protective sheaths of myelin are produced by another type of neuroglial cell called an *oligodendrocyte.* Unlike the sheath formed by Schwann cells, however, the sheath formed by oligodendrocytes degenerates once the axon it protects is destroyed. Consequently, neurons of the central nervous system do not regenerate after injury. This is why spinal cord injuries and CNS disorders such as multiple sclerosis result in a permanent change or loss of function (see section 11.13, Disorders of the nervous system).

In the autoimmune disorder *multiple sclerosis* (MS), the sheaths of myelinated neurons in the brain and spinal cord become progressively damaged until they form hardened (sclerotic) scar tissue. These sclerotic areas can no longer insulate the neurons effectively, disrupting and slowing the transmission of impulses. People with MS can experience a variety of symptoms depending on which areas of the CNS are damaged. Common symptoms include muscle weakness, visual impairment, and urinary incontinence. The disease usually appears in people between 20 and 40 years of age. Although the disease is generally progressive, people with MS may experience periods of remission.

A similar but rarer disease is *amyotrophic lateral sclerosis* (ALS). In ALS the sclerotic areas typically begin in regions of the spinal cord involved in the motor control of skeletal muscle. The primary symptom of ALS is progressive weakening and wasting of skeletal muscle tissue, most notably the diaphragm and intercostal muscles. As mentioned in Chapter 10, people with ALS usually die from respiratory failure.

**RECAP**

Neuroglial cells support and protect neurons. Neuroglial cells called Schwann cells (in the PNS) and oligodendrocytes (in the CNS) form myelin sheaths that protect axons and speed transmission of impulses. ■

## 11.5 Information is transferred from a neuron to its target

Once an action potential reaches the axon terminals of a neuron, the information inherent in it must be converted to another form for transmittal to its target (muscle cell, gland cell, or another neuron). In essence, the action potential causes the release of a chemical that crosses a specialized junction between the two cells called a **synapse.** This chemical substance is called a **neurotransmitter** because it transmits a signal from a neuron to its target. The entire process of transmission from a neuron to its target is called synaptic transmission. We describe in Chapter 6 how synaptic transmission occurs between a neuron and skeletal muscle. Now we'll see how it occurs between neurons.

### Neurotransmitter is released

Figure 11.8 illustrates the structure of a typical synapse and the events that occur during synaptic transmission. At a synapse, the *presynaptic membrane* is the cell membrane of the neuron that is sending the information. The *postsynaptic membrane* is the membrane of the cell that is about to receive the information. The small fluid-filled gap that separates the presynaptic and postsynaptic membranes is the *synaptic cleft.*

Each axon terminal of the presynaptic neuron ends in an axon bulb that contains neurotransmitter stored in membrane-bound vesicles. The events that occur during synaptic transmission follow a particular pattern:

1. An action potential arrives at the axon bulb, causing calcium ($Ca^{2+}$) channels in the presynaptic membrane to open. $Ca^{2+}$ diffuses into the axon bulb.
2. The presence of $Ca^{2+}$ causes the vesicles to fuse with the presynaptic membrane and release their contents of neurotransmitter directly into the synaptic cleft. Because the synaptic cleft is so narrow (about 0.02 micrometer, or one-millionth of an inch), the neurotransmitter molecules reach the postsynaptic membrane by diffusion.
3. Molecules of neurotransmitter bind to receptors on the postsynaptic membrane. This causes certain chemically gated channels, such as those for sodium, to open.
4. Sodium ions diffuse inward, producing a graded depolarization of the postsynaptic membrane in the area of the synapse.

Note that graded potentials are caused by the opening of *chemically* sensitive ion channels (the chemical being a neurotransmitter), rather than voltage-sensitive ones.

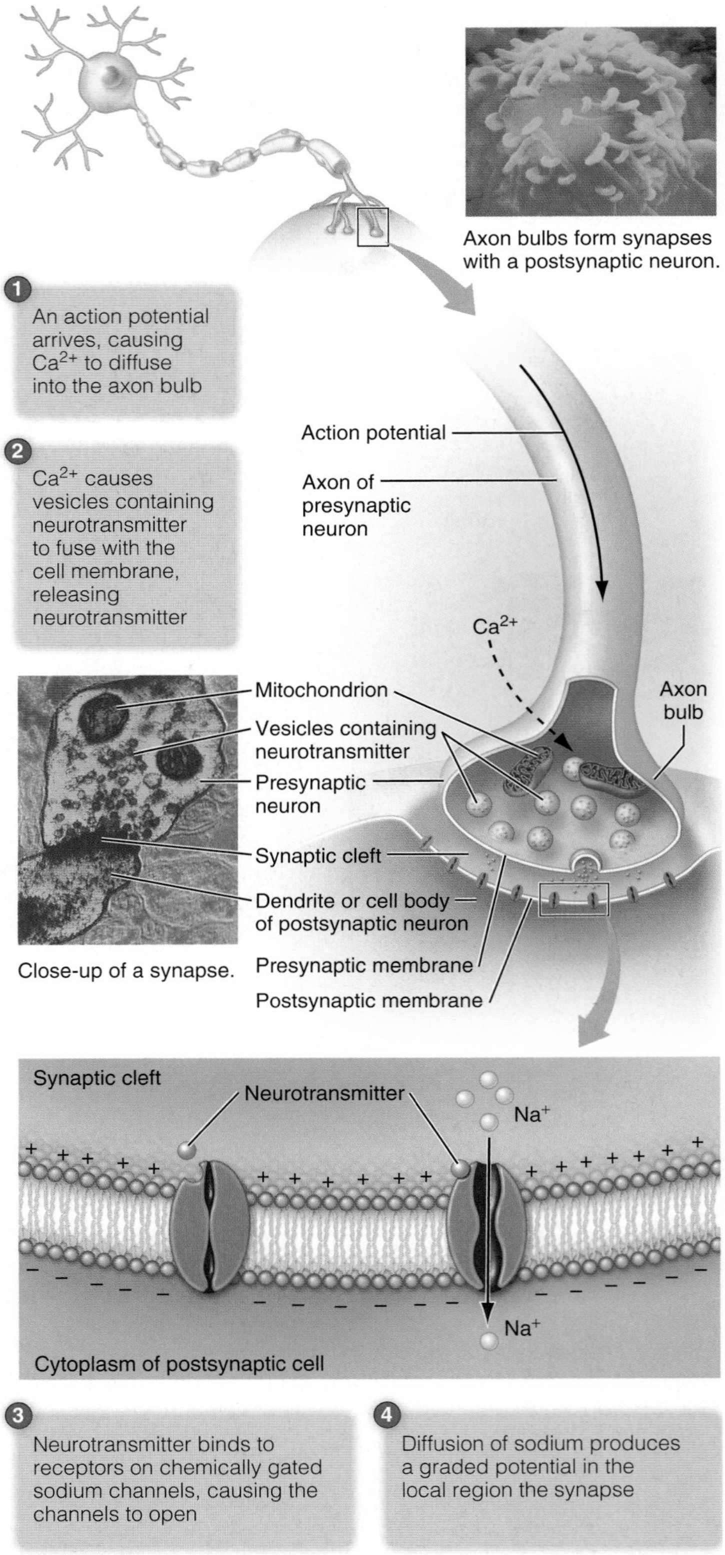


**Figure 11.8 Summary of synaptic transmission.**

### Neurotransmitters exert excitatory or inhibitory effects

The response of the postsynaptic cell to neurotransmitter depends on several factors, including the type of neurotransmitter, its concentration in the synaptic cleft, and the types of receptors and chemically sensitive ion channels in the postsynaptic membrane.

To date, scientists have identified more than 50 chemicals that can function as neurotransmitters. All are stored in vesicles within the axon bulb and released into the synaptic cleft in response to an action potential. All produce a graded potential in the postsynaptic cell, though the effects may be quite different because they can affect different ion channels.

Neurotransmitters are classified as excitatory, inhibitory, or both. Excitatory neurotransmitters depolarize the postsynaptic cell, causing threshold to be approached or exceeded. Therefore, excitatory neurotransmitters encourage the generation of new impulses in the postsynaptic neuron. Inhibitory neurotransmitters cause the postsynaptic cell to hyperpolarize, meaning that the cell's interior becomes even more negative than before. Hyperpolarization makes it harder for threshold to be reached, so inhibitory neurotransmitters tend to prevent the generation of action potentials in the postsynaptic neuron. Some neurotransmitters can be excitatory or inhibitory, depending on the type of receptor to which they bind on the postsynaptic membrane.

Table 11.1 summarizes the actions of several common neurotransmitters.

The effects of neurotransmitters are relatively short-lived because the neurotransmitter remains in the synaptic cleft for only a short time. Prompt removal of neurotransmitter causes neural signals to be terminated almost as rapidly as they are initiated. Only then can the next message be received and recognized. The neurotransmitter may be removed from the synaptic cleft in any or all of three ways: (1) it may be taken back up again by the presynaptic neuron and repackaged into membrane-bound vesicles, to be used again; (2) it may be destroyed by enzymes in the synaptic cleft; or (3) it may diffuse away from the synaptic cleft into the general circulation, where it will ultimately be destroyed.

**RECAP**

A neuron transmits information to another cell across a synapse. At a synapse, neurotransmitter released from a presynaptic neuron diffuses across the synaptic cleft and binds to receptors on the postsynaptic membrane, opening ion channels and causing a graded potential in the postsynaptic cell. ■

## Postsynaptic neurons integrate and process information

The conversion of the signal from electrical (an action potential) to chemical (neurotransmitter) allows the postsynaptic cell to do a lot of integration and information processing. This is because a single all-or-none action potential in the presynaptic neuron does not always cause a corresponding all-or-none action potential in the postsynaptic neuron, as it does in a muscle cell. A single action potential produces only a small graded potential in the postsynaptic neuron, and a lot of these graded potentials generally are required for threshold to be reached.

One way for threshold to be reached in a postsynaptic neuron is for the presynaptic neuron (or a few neurons) to increase their frequency of stimulation, sending lots of action potentials in a short time (hundreds per minute). In addition to stimulus intensity, other factors affecting whether threshold is reached in the postsynaptic neuron include (1) how many other neurons form synapses with it, and (2) whether those synaptic connections are stimulatory or inhibitory. Typically, one neuron receives input from many neurons, a phenomenon known as *convergence*. In turn, its action potential will go to many other neurons, a phenomenon known as *divergence* (Figure 11.9).

Though it would be incorrect to say that neurons "interpret" information—that would imply that a neuron has a brain—the effect of convergence is that neurons may integrate and process thousands of simultaneous incoming stimulatory and inhibitory signals before generating and transmitting their own action potentials. They also reroute the information to many different destinations. Individual neurons do not see, smell, or hear, yet their combined actions allow us to experience those complex sensations.

Consider again the example given at the beginning of this chapter, in which you were able to ignore certain incoming signals—the smell of doughnuts, the sound of your

**Table 11.1 Actions of common neurotransmitters**

| Neurotransmitter | Sites where released | Principal actions |
|---|---|---|
| Acetylcholine | Neuromuscular junctions, autonomic nervous systems, brain | Excitatory on skeletal muscles; excitatory or inhibitory at other sites, depending on receptors |
| Norepinephrine | Areas of brain and spinal cord, autonomic nervous system | Excitatory or inhibitory, depending on receptors; plays a role in emotions |
| Serotonin | Areas of brain, spinal cord | Usually inhibitory; involved in moods, sleep cycle, appetite |
| Dopamine | Areas of brain, parts of peripheral nervous system | Excitatory or inhibitory, depending on receptors; plays a role in emotions |
| Glutamate | Areas of brain, spinal cord | Usually excitatory; major excitatory neurotransmitter in brain |
| Endorphins | Many areas in brain, spinal cord | Natural opiates that inhibit pain; usually inhibitory |
| Gamma-aminobutyric acid | Areas of brain, spinal cord | Usually inhibitory; principal inhibitory neurotransmitter in brain |
| Somatostatin | Areas of brain, pancreas | Usually inhibitory; inhibits pancreatic release of growth hormone |

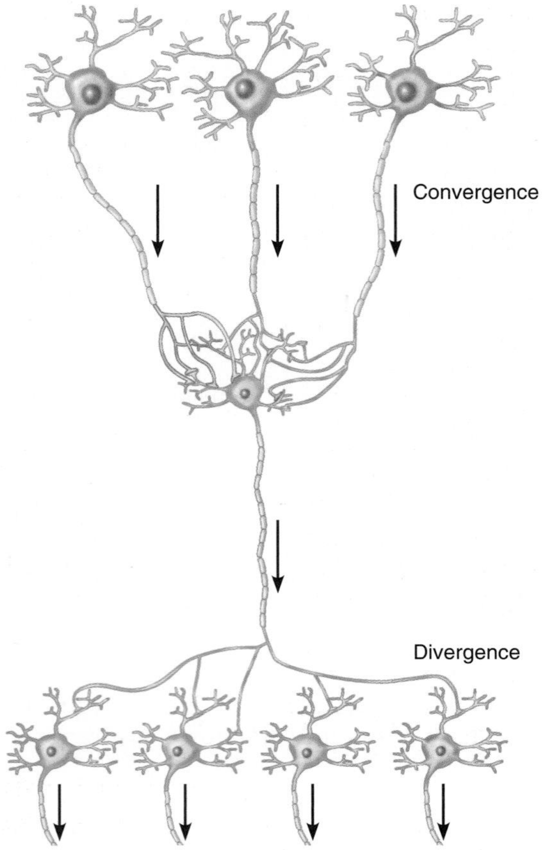


**Figure 11.9 Neural information processing by convergence and divergence.** Convergence occurs when several presynaptic cells form synapses with a single postsynaptic cell. Divergence occurs when one nerve cell provides information to a variety of postsynaptic cells.

shoes on pavement, the sensation of being cold—and focus on others, such as the noises made by the truck and its horn. You tapped your memory banks for the probable meaning of these sounds (danger approaching!), and then coordinated your muscles to turn around, see the truck, and jump out of the way—all in a fraction of a second. This is a complex set of events, and it is all done with neurons, action potentials, and neurotransmitters.

Muscle cells are also target cells of presynaptic neurons. As described in Chapter 6, however, skeletal muscle cells do not process and integrate information. There are two reasons for this. First, a muscle cell receives input from only one neuron. There are no converging neural inputs to process. Second, the neuromuscular junction is quite large, with many points of contact between neuron and muscle cell. Consequently, threshold is reached in a skeletal muscle cell every time the motor neuron sends even a single action potential. Functionally, this means that the nervous system has absolute and final control over the activity of skeletal muscle cells.

**RECAP**

Postsynaptic neurons integrate and process incoming signals. Information processing occurs because of the complex patterns of divergence and convergence between neurons, and because many graded potentials must add up in order to produce an action potential. ■

## 11.6 The PNS relays information between tissues and the CNS

Now that we have seen how neurons generate and transmit action potentials, we look at how this information travels throughout the nervous system. As stated earlier, the nervous system has two major subdivisions: the central nervous system (CNS), which includes the spinal cord and brain, and the peripheral nervous system (PNS), which consists of nerves that transmit information between body tissues and the CNS.

### Nerves carry signals to and from the CNS

A single nerve axon is like a single fiber-optic fiber in that both transmit specific kinds of information from one location to another. By the same token, a nerve is like a large fiber-optic cable strung between two cities. A **nerve** consists of the axons of many neurons, all wrapped together in a protective sheath of connective tissue and all coming from and going to the same place. The function of each nerve depends on where it originates and the organs or tissues to which it travels.

The peripheral nervous system consists of cranial nerves and spinal nerves. The 12 pairs of **cranial nerves** connect directly with the brain. Cranial nerves carry action potentials between the brain and the muscles, glands, and receptors of the head, neck, and thoracic and abdominal cavities.

The 31 pairs of **spinal nerves** connect with the spinal cord. Each spinal nerve attaches to the spinal cord via two short branches of the spinal cord called the dorsal root and the ventral root. The dorsal root contains the sensory neurons that transmit incoming action potentials from body tissues to the spinal cord. The ventral root contains motor neurons that carry action potentials away from the spinal cord to the rest of the body. Thus each spinal nerve carries both sensory and motor (incoming and outgoing) information.

**RECAP**

In the peripheral nervous system, 12 pairs of cranial nerves transmit action potentials between the brain and the head, neck, and thoracic and abdominal cavities. The 31 pairs of spinal nerves transmit action potentials to and from the spinal cord to all regions of the body. ■

### Sensory neurons provide information to the CNS

The nervous system must have good information if it is to take appropriate action. That information arrives at the CNS as action potentials traveling in sensory neurons located throughout the body. Because information provided by sensory neurons to the CNS may affect the motor output of both the somatic and autonomic divisions of the PNS, the sensory (input) component of the PNS cannot be classified as belonging specifically to either the somatic or autonomic motor (output) divisions.

### The somatic division controls skeletal muscles

Recall that the motor (or output) neurons of the peripheral nervous system are organized into the somatic division and the autonomic division. The **somatic division** controls voluntary and involuntary skeletal muscle movement. Somatic motor neurons transmit information from the spinal cord to skeletal muscles.

As described in Chapter 6, a single somatic motor neuron controls several skeletal muscle cells (together they form a motor unit), and every time the neuron sends an action potential down its axon, all the muscle cells of that motor unit experience an action potential and contract. Motor neurons are activated either by conscious control from the brain or by an involuntary response called a *reflex*.

**Spinal reflexes** are involuntary responses that are mediated primarily by the spinal cord and spinal nerves, with little or no involvement of the brain. Figure 11.10 illustrates two such spinal reflexes. Stepping on a sharp object, for example, activates pain receptors, producing action potentials in sensory neurons traveling to your spinal cord. The sensory neurons stimulate interneurons within the spinal cord, which in turn transmit signals to motor neurons in your leg, causing you to flex the appropriate muscles to lift your foot. This is called the *flexor (withdrawal) reflex.* Meanwhile, other interneurons that cross over to the opposite side of the spinal cord are also stimulated by the sensory neuron. These interneurons stimulate motor neurons to extend, rather than flex, certain skeletal muscles in your other leg. After all, it wouldn't do to flex both legs and fall on the sharp object! This second reflex is called a *crossed extensor reflex.*

Notice that these events did not require conscious thought. A simple spinal reflex is processed primarily at the level of the spinal cord, allowing a rather complex series of actions to occur quickly. Some sensory information does ascend to the brain as well, allowing the brain to integrate the sensory information from your foot with all the other information it is receiving and determine your next course of action (such as sitting down and examining your foot). But most of the spinal reflex itself occurs without any involvement of the brain.

Another type of spinal reflex is a *stretch reflex*. In a stretch reflex, stretch receptors in a skeletal muscle stimulate sensory nerves, which carry the signals to the spinal cord. In the spinal cord, motor neurons to the stretched muscle are activated. At the same time, motor neurons to any antagonistic muscles are inhibited so that contraction will be effective. Stretch reflexes play an important role in maintaining upright posture and movement, as they allow

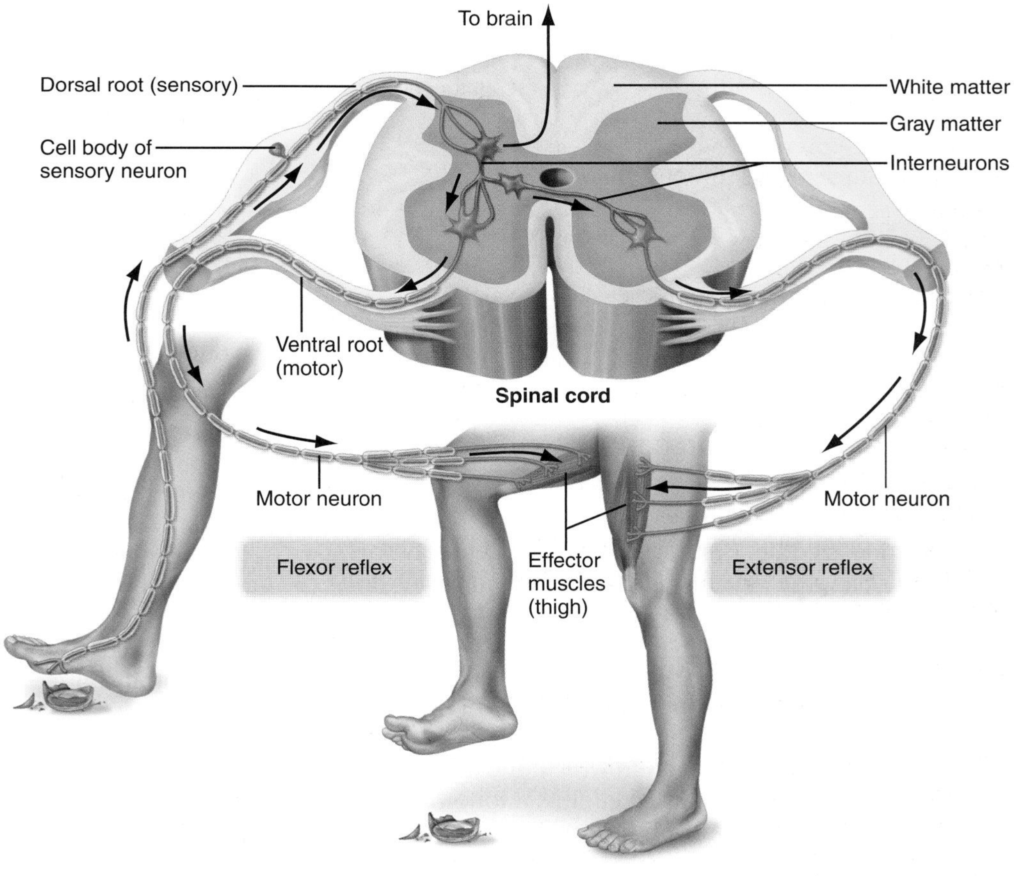


**Figure 11.10 Spinal reflexes.** In this example of withdrawal and crossed extension reflexes, a painful stimulus activates sensory nerves in a foot. Sensory nerves stimulate interneurons within the spinal cord that activate motor neurons to muscles on both sides of the body. Note that the motor effects are different on the two sides of the body: withdrawal (flexion) on the stimulus side and extension on the opposite side. Other interneurons relay the sensory information to the brain.

us to stand and move without having to concentrate on our actions.

Stretch reflexes associated with posture and movement are often modified slightly by signals from higher brain centers. Physicians can test such reflexes to determine whether the spinal cord and areas of the brain involved in stretch reflexes are intact and functioning properly. An example is the well-known knee-jerk reflex. When the patellar tendon is tapped lightly below the kneecap, the resulting slight stretch of the thigh muscles initiates a spinal reflex that ultimately results in contraction of the thigh muscles and an upward movement of the foot and lower leg (Figure 11.11). If the neural pathways are not intact or if the brain is not modifying the reflex properly, the reflex may be either less vigorous or more vigorous than normal.

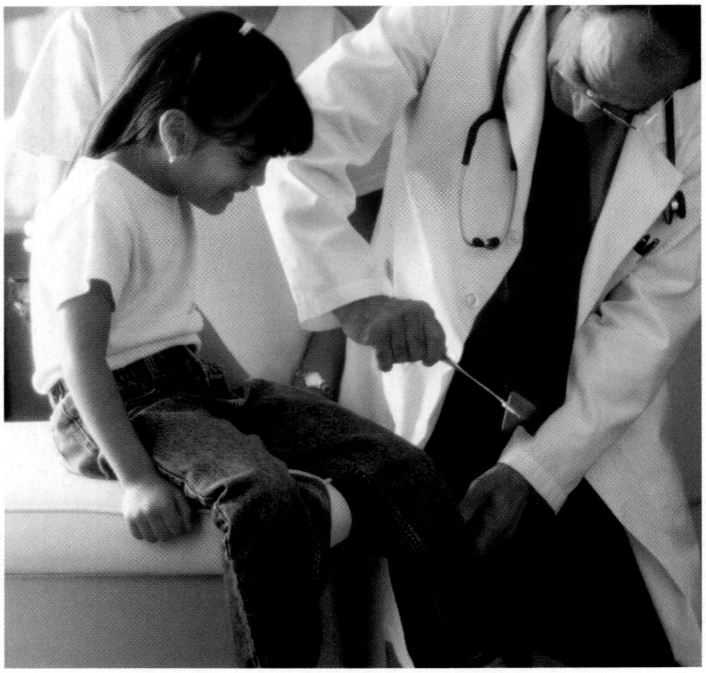

**Figure 11.11 The patellar (knee-jerk) reflex.** The physician tests the integrity of the patellar reflex to verify that certain sensory and motor nerves, the spinal cord, areas of the brain, and skeletal muscle are all functioning normally.

**RECAP**

Sensory neurons provide information (input) to the CNS. The somatic output division of the PNS controls voluntary (conscious) and involuntary (reflex) skeletal muscle movement. ■

## The autonomic division controls automatic body functions

Motor neurons carrying information to smooth or cardiac muscle and to all other tissues and organs except skeletal muscle belong to the **autonomic division** (*autonomic* derives from the Greek words for "self" and "law"). The autonomic division of the peripheral nervous system carries signals from the CNS to the periphery that control "automatic" functions of the body's internal organs. Many of these activities occur without our ever being aware of them.

Unlike the somatic division in which one neuron extends from the CNS to the target cell, the autonomic division requires two neurons to transmit information from the CNS to the target cell. The cell bodies of the first neurons (called *preganglionic neurons*) lie within the central nervous system. The axons of many of these neurons go to structures called *ganglia* (singular: *ganglion*) that lie outside the CNS. Ganglia are clusters of neuron cell bodies of the second neurons (called *postganglionic neurons*). Axons of the postganglionic neurons extend to the far reaches of the body to communicate with internal glands and organs.

## The sympathetic and parasympathetic divisions oppose each other

There are two types of motor neurons in the autonomic division: sympathetic and parasympathetic. Both function automatically, usually without our conscious awareness, to regulate body functions. They innervate smooth muscle, cardiac muscle, glands, the epithelial cells of the kidneys, and virtually every internal organ except skeletal muscle, bone, and the nervous system itself.

In most organs, the actions of the sympathetic and parasympathetic divisions have very opposite effects, as shown in Figure 11.12. Which division predominates at any one time determines what happens in your body. And with two opposing systems active at all times, control can be very precise. It is as if you were driving a car with one foot on the gas pedal and one on the brake—you could speed up by hitting the gas pedal, releasing the brake pedal a little, or both.

**The sympathetic division arouses the body** Preganglionic motor neurons of the **sympathetic division** originate in the thoracic and lumbar regions of the spinal cord. Many of their axons extend to a chain of sympathetic ganglia that lie alongside the spinal cord, where they form synapses with the postganglionic cells. Because these ganglia are connected to each other, the sympathetic division tends to produce a unified response in all organs at once. Axons of the postganglionic neurons branch out to innervate all the organs. The neurotransmitter released by sympathetic postganglionic neurons in the target organs is *norepinephrine.*

The sympathetic division transmits signals that prepare the body for emergencies and situations requiring high levels of mental alertness or physical activity, such as fighting or running away from danger ("fight or flight"), and even play and sexual activity. It increases heart rate and respiration, raises blood pressure, and dilates the pupils—effects that help you detect and respond quickly to changes in your environment. The sympathetic division also reduces blood flow to organs that do not help you cope with an immediate crisis, such as

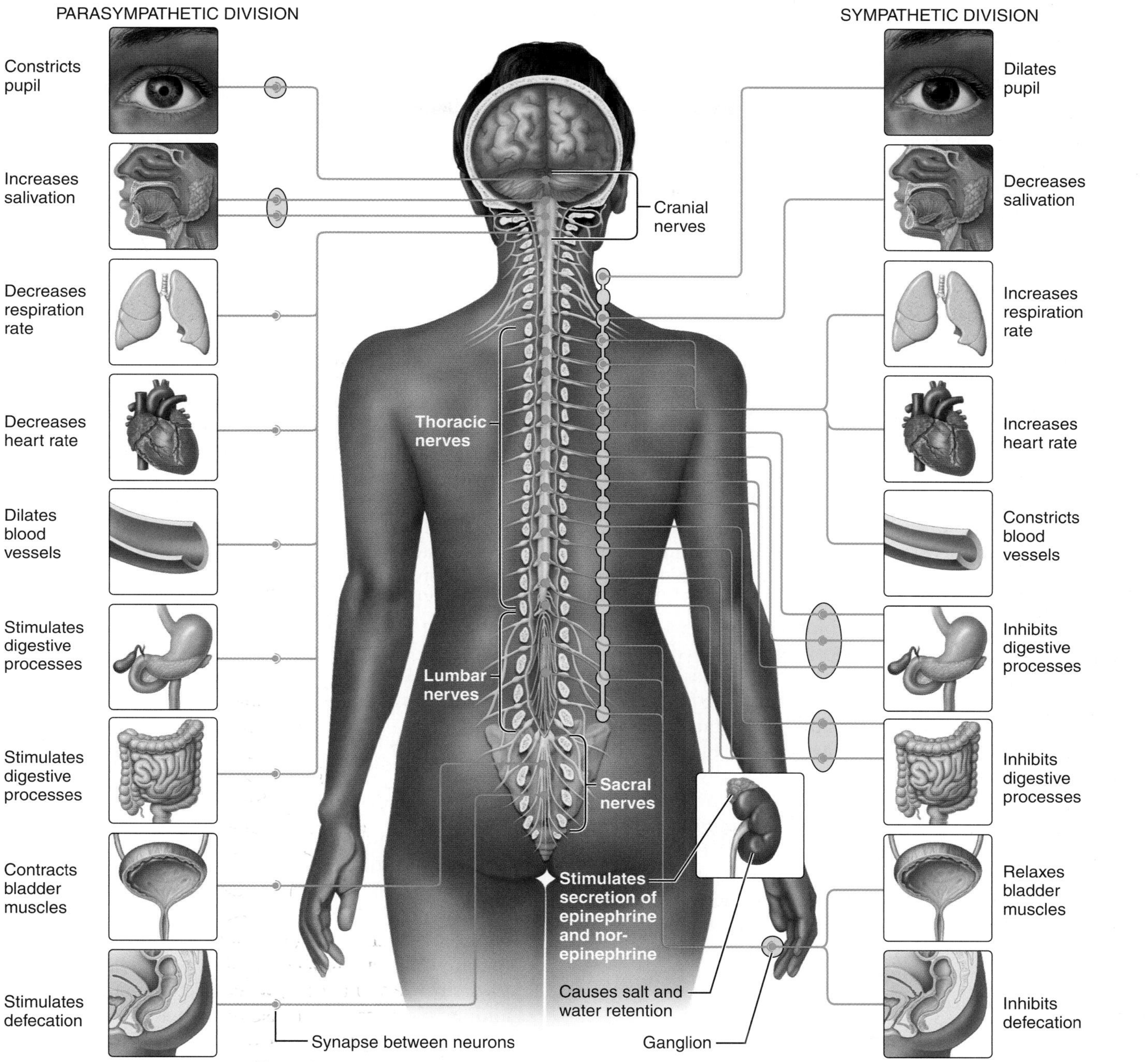


**Figure 11.12 The sympathetic and parasympathetic divisions of the autonomic nervous system.** The sympathetic division is associated with fight-or-flight responses. The parasympathetic division predominates in the body's relaxed state. The nerves of the sympathetic division arise in the thoracic and lumbar segments of the spinal cord, while the nerves of the parasympathetic division arise from cranial and sacral segments. Ganglia (groups of nerve cell bodies) are shown in yellow.

the intestines and kidneys, and inhibits less important body functions such as digestion and production of saliva (this is why your mouth feels dry when you are anxious).

The effects of the sympathetic division are sometimes called the fight-or-flight response, reflecting its association with emergency situations.

**The parasympathetic division predominates during relaxation** Preganglionic neurons of the **parasympathetic division** originate either in the brain, becoming part of the outflow of certain cranial nerves, or from the sacral region of the spinal cord. The ganglia where the preganglionic neurons synapse with the postganglionic neurons is generally some distance from the CNS and may even be in the target organ itself. The neurotransmitter released by parasympathetic postganglionic neurons at their target organs is acetylcholine, the same neurotransmitter used at the neuromuscular junction.

In contrast to the sympathetic division, the parasympathetic division predominates in situations in which you are relaxed. It transmits signals that lower heart rate and respiration, increase digestion, and permit defecation and urination, among other actions. The parasympathetic division exerts calming, restorative effects ("rest and repose") that counteract the fight-or-flight stimulation of the sympathetic division. Parasympathetic nerves are also responsible for the vasodilation that causes erection in males and swelling of the labia and erection of the clitoris in females.

### The sympathetic and parasympathetic divisions work antagonistically to maintain homeostasis

As we have seen, the actions of the sympathetic and parasympathetic divisions oppose each other. They work antagonistically to accomplish the automatic, subconscious maintenance of homeostasis. Both systems are intimately involved in feedback loops that control homeostasis throughout the body.

An example is the control of blood pressure. As described in Chapter 8, certain sensory nerves are activated by baroreceptors. When blood pressure rises, the baroreceptors are activated, and the sensory nerves send more frequent action potentials to the brain. The brain integrates this information with the other information it is receiving. Then it decreases the number of action potentials traveling in sympathetic nerves and increases the number of action potentials traveling in parasympathetic nerves serving the heart and blood vessels. As a result, heart rate slows, blood vessels dilate, and blood pressure falls until it is back to normal.

The sympathetic and parasympathetic divisions can also cause a widespread response, such as arousing the entire body. They can even carry out many localized homeostatic control mechanisms simultaneously and independently. Table 11.2 summarizes the functions of the somatic and autonomic divisions of the PNS.

**RECAP**

The autonomic division of the PNS includes sympathetic and parasympathetic components that serve internal organs and regulate automatic body functions to maintain homeostasis. The sympathetic division predominates in times of high activity or stress, and the parasympathetic division predominates during rest. ■

## 11.7 The brain and spinal cord constitute the CNS

A neuron does not think or love, yet humans do. Scientists are still trying to unravel the biology of emotion and thought, but we do know that they originate in the central nervous system, specifically in the brain.

The central nervous system, consisting of brain and spinal cord, is "central" both in location and action. It is where integration, or processing, of information occurs. It is where information is received and where complex outputs are initiated. It's where billions of action potentials traveling in millions of neurons all come together as a conscious thought. That is not a very satisfactory explanation for "thinking," but it may be the best we can do.

### Bone, meninges, and the blood-brain barrier protect the CNS

The central nervous system is vital to proper functioning of the entire body, so it is no surprise that it is well protected against physical injury and disease.

First, the CNS is protected by bone. The brain is encased in the skull, and the spinal cord is enclosed in a hollow channel within the vertebrae. This shell of bone around the central nervous system helps shield it from physical trauma.

Second, the CNS is enclosed by three membranes of connective tissue, called **meninges,** named (from outermost to innermost layers) the *dura mater*, the *arachnoid*, and the *pia mater*. These three meninges protect the neurons of the CNS and the blood vessels that service them.

**Table 11.2 The somatic and autonomic divisions of the PNS**

| | Somatic division | Autonomic division | |
|---|---|---|---|
| | | *Sympathetic* | *Parasympathetic* |
| **Functions** | Serves skeletal muscles | Fight or flight; arouses body to deal with situations involving physical activity, mental alertness | Relaxes body; promotes digestion and other basic functions |
| **Neurotransmitter** | Acetylcholine | Norepinephrine | Acetylcholine |
| **Number of neurons required to reach the target cell** | One | Two (preganglionic and postganglionic) | Two (preganglionic and postganglionic) |

Third, the CNS is bathed in its own special liquid, called **cerebrospinal fluid,** which fills the space between the arachnoid and the pia mater. In addition to serving as a liquid shock absorber around the brain and spinal cord, cerebrospinal fluid tends to isolate the central nervous system from infections. Inflammation of the meninges due to a bacterial or viral infection is called *meningitis*. Meningitis can be serious because it may spread to the nervous tissue of the CNS.

Cerebrospinal fluid is somewhat similar to the interstitial fluid that bathes all cells, but it does not exchange substances as freely with blood. It is secreted from specialized capillaries into four hollow cavities (called *ventricles*) in the brain. From the ventricles, it flows through a system of fluid-filled cavities and canals, bathing and surrounding the neurons in the brain and spinal cord (Figure 11.13).

Most capillaries in the body are fairly leaky because there are narrow slits between adjacent capillary cells. However, the cells of the capillaries that produce cerebrospinal fluid are fused tightly together. Consequently, substances must pass through the capillary cells rather than between them in order to get from blood to cerebrospinal fluid. Lipid-soluble substances such as oxygen and carbon dioxide can diffuse easily through the lipid bilayer of the cell membrane. Certain important molecules such as glucose are actively transported. However, most charged molecules and large objects, such as proteins, viruses, and bacteria, generally are prevented from entering the cerebrospinal fluid.

This functional barrier between blood and brain is called the **blood-brain barrier.** Thanks to this isolation, bacterial and viral infections of the brain and spinal cord are rare, but when these illnesses occur they are generally serious and difficult to treat. Many of our best antibiotics are not lipid soluble, which means they cannot cross the blood-brain barrier and so are ineffective against CNS infections. Lipid-soluble substances that cross the blood-brain barrier rather easily include alcohol, caffeine, nicotine, cocaine, and general anesthetics.

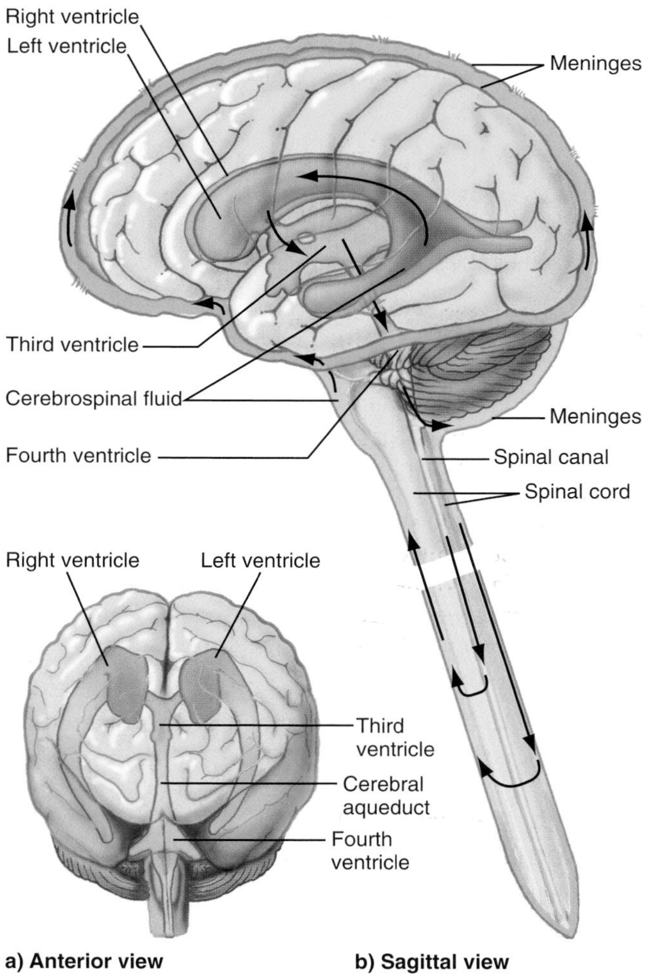


**Figure 11.13 The ventricles of the brain and circulation of cerebrospinal fluid.** Cerebrospinal fluid is secreted into the four brain ventricles (left, right, third, and fourth). From there it flows through a series of cavities, bathing the brain and spinal cord.

**RECAP**

The CNS consists of the brain and spinal cord. It is well protected by bone, the meninges, and cerebrospinal fluid. The capillaries that produce cerebrospinal fluid have special properties that result in a functional blood-brain barrier. ■

## The spinal cord relays information

The **spinal cord** serves as the superhighway for action potentials traveling between the brain and the rest of the body. As we have seen, the spinal cord can also process and act on certain information on its own via spinal reflexes, without necessarily involving the brain. However, its power to act independently is limited, and such actions never reach the level of conscious awareness.

Approximately the diameter of your thumb, the spinal cord extends from the base of the skull to the area of about the second lumbar vertebra, or about 17 inches (Figure 11.14). It is protected by the vertebral column. The outer portions of the spinal cord consist primarily of bundles of axons, which in the CNS are called *nerve tracts* rather than nerves. Because these axons are generally myelinated, giving them a whitish appearance, the areas of the cord occupied by these ascending (sensory) and descending (motor) nerve tracts are called *white matter.* Neurons of the peripheral nervous system enter and leave the spinal cord at regular intervals via the dorsal (sensory) and ventral (motor) horns that fuse to form spinal nerves.

Near the center of the spinal cord is a region occupied primarily by the cell bodies, dendrites, and axons of neurons of the CNS, and also neuroglial cells. These structures are not myelinated, so the area they occupy is referred to as *gray matter*. Within the gray matter, sensory and motor neurons synapse with neurons of the CNS that transmit signals up the spinal cord to the brain.

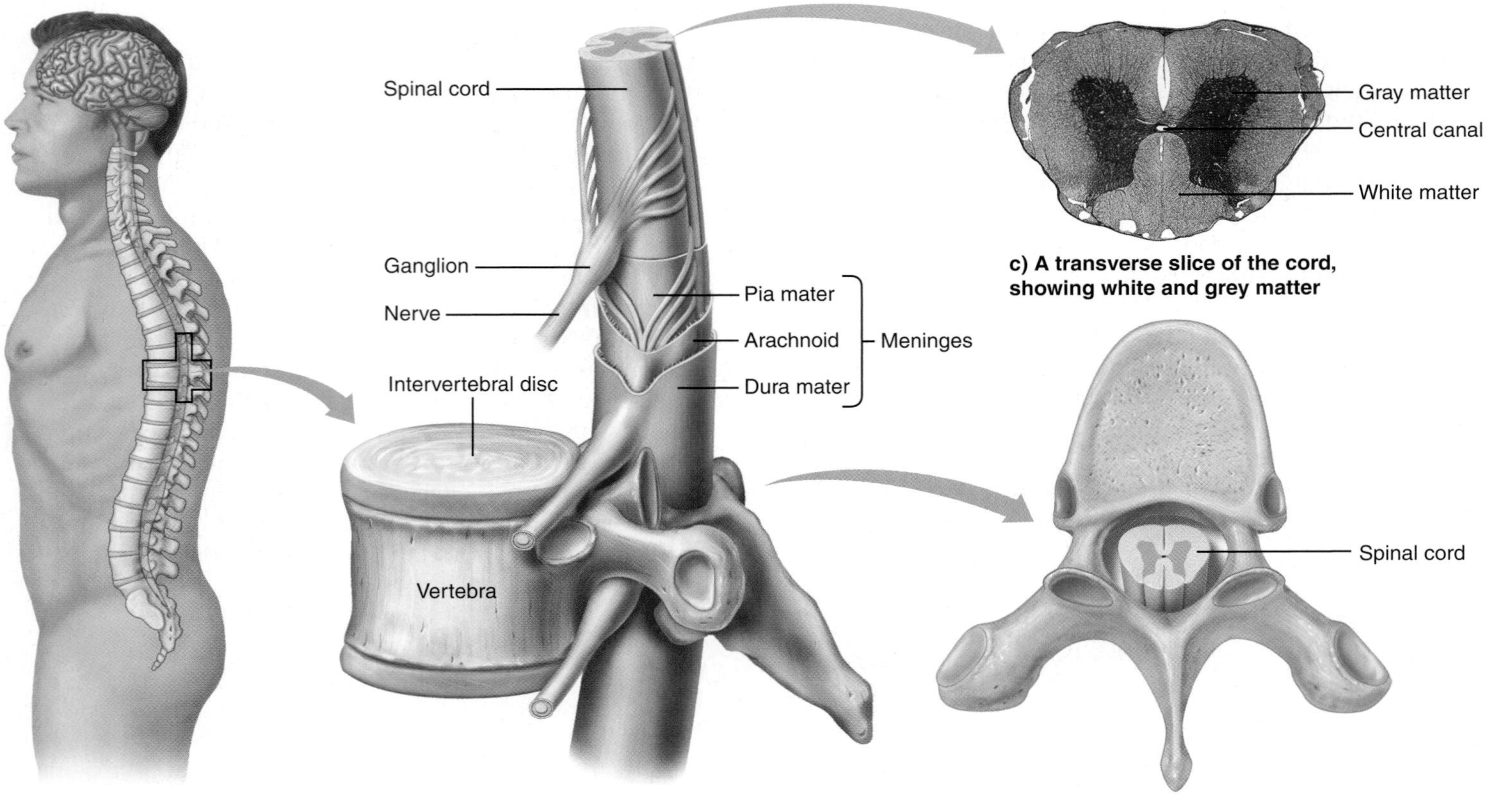


**a) The spinal cord lies within the vertebral column**

**b) A closer look at the spinal cord and its relationship with a vertebra**

**c) A transverse slice of the cord, showing white and grey matter**

**d) Superior view of vertebra**

**Figure 11.14 The human spinal cord.**

**RECAP**

The spinal cord transmits information between the brain and the rest of the body. It contains white matter (myelinated axons) and gray matter (unmyelinated neural structures). ■

## 11.8 The brain processes and acts on information

The **brain** is the command center of the body. The brain receives information in the form of action potentials from various nerves and the spinal cord, integrates it, and generates the appropriate response.

Within the brain, certain areas specialize in integrating different types of information or performing certain motor tasks. Action potentials derived from various receptors, such as light and sound, arrive at the brain in different sensory neurons that specialize in processing those signals. For example, one area of the brain responds to visual stimuli and another area responds to stimuli that help us maintain our balance.

Three major anatomical and functional divisions of the brain have been identified:

- The *hindbrain* coordinates basic, automatic, and vital tasks.
- The *midbrain* helps coordinate muscle groups and responses to sights and sounds.
- The *forebrain* receives and integrates sensory input from the external environment and determines most of our more complex behavior.

Figure 11.15 illustrates these major divisions and their components.

### The hindbrain: Movement and automatic functions

The **hindbrain** is connected to the spinal cord. From an evolutionary standpoint the hindbrain is the oldest, most primitive brain division, and the one most similar among animals. Important components of the hindbrain include the medulla oblongata, the cerebellum, and the pons.

**The medulla oblongata controls automatic functions** The **medulla oblongata** connects to the spinal cord. It contains

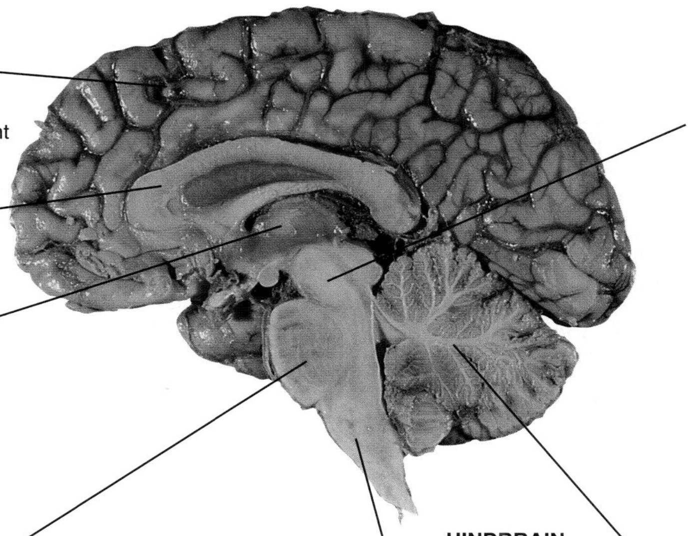


**Figure 11.15 The brain.** A sagittal section (front to back on a vertical plane) of a human brain near the midline.

areas that control vital automatic functions of internal organs. Within the medulla oblongata, the *cardiovascular center* regulates heart rate and blood pressure, and the *respiratory center* integrates information about blood levels of oxygen and carbon dioxide, and adjusts respiration accordingly. Other areas coordinate reflexes such as coughing, vomiting, sneezing, and swallowing.

All information passing between the higher areas of the brain and the spinal cord must pass through the medulla oblongata. An interesting feature of the way the body is "wired" is that the motor nerves from one side of the forebrain cross over to the other side of the body in the medulla oblongata. As a result, the left side of the brain controls the right side of the body, and vice versa.

**The cerebellum coordinates basic movements** Located just behind the medulla oblongata, the **cerebellum** coordinates basic body movements that are below the level of conscious control. For example, the cerebellum ensures that antagonistic muscles do not contract at the same time. The cerebellum also stores and replicates (without our conscious thought) whole sequences of skilled movements, such as tying a shoe, shifting a car, or hitting a home run (hitters sometimes say they just "pull the trigger" and the rest happens automatically). To coordinate these skilled activities, the cerebellum receives sensory input from many sources, including joint and muscle receptors, balance and position receptors in the ear, and visual receptors.

Excessive consumption of alcohol acts on the cerebellum and disrupts its normal functions. This is why people who are drunk can't coordinate their movements or walk a straight line.

**The pons aids information flow** Just above and partially surrounding the medulla oblongata, the *pons* (from the Latin for "bridge") connects higher brain centers and the spinal cord. The pons contains groups of axons that extend from the cerebellum to the rest of the CNS, and is especially important in coordinating the flow of information between the cerebellum and higher brain centers. In addition, the pons aids the medulla oblongata in regulating respiration.

## The midbrain: Vision and hearing

Most functions of the **midbrain** relate to vision and hearing. Visual and auditory sensory inputs pass through the midbrain before being relayed to higher brain centers. The midbrain coordinates movements of the head related to vision and hearing, such as turning toward a sudden sound or flash of light, and it controls movement of the eyes and size of the pupils. The midbrain also monitors the unconscious movement of our skeletal muscles so that their actions are smooth and coordinated.

A group of neurons collectively called the *reticular formation* extends through the medulla oblongata, the pons, and the midbrain. The reticular formation works with the cerebellum to coordinate the skeletal muscle activity that maintains posture, balance, and muscle tone. Neurons in the reticular formation are also responsible for maintaining our level of wakefulness, as explained later in this chapter.

**RECAP**

The brain has three divisions: hindbrain, midbrain, and forebrain. The evolutionarily oldest, more primitive hindbrain controls most automatic functions, and the midbrain functions in vision, hearing, and movement. ■

## The forebrain: Emotions and conscious thought

The **forebrain** determines our most complex behavior, including emotions and conscious thought. Important areas in the forebrain are the hypothalamus and thalamus, limbic system, and cerebrum. It also includes two glands, the pineal and the pituitary, which are described in Chapter 13.

**The hypothalamus and thalamus maintain homeostasis and process information** The **hypothalamus** is a small region at the base of the forebrain that coordinates some automatic functions of the pituitary gland, such as water and solute balance, temperature control, carbohydrate metabolism, and production of breast milk. It plays an important role in regulating homeostasis because it monitors sensory signals relating to sight, smell, taste, noise, and body temperature. A "hunger center" located in the hypothalamus alerts us when we need to eat, and a "thirst center" signals us to drink something when body fluids become too concentrated.

The larger **thalamus**, located just above the hypothalamus, is primarily a receiving, processing, and transfer center. It integrates and relays some outgoing motor activity as well. The thalamus accepts sensory signals from other parts of the body and brain and channels them to the cerebrum to be interpreted. As sensory information—for example, pain, pressure, and temperature changes—arrives at the thalamus, we are conscious of the sensation but cannot identify where it originates. After the information reaches the cerebrum, we become aware of which part of the body is experiencing the sensation.

**The limbic system is involved in emotions and memory** The *limbic system* refers to a group of neuronal pathways that connect parts of the thalamus, hypothalamus, and inner portions of the cerebrum. The limbic system is associated with emotions and memory, and we will look at it in more detail later in this chapter when we discuss memory and behavior.

**The cerebrum deals with higher functions** In humans, the large **cerebrum** is the most highly developed of all brain regions. It deals with many of the functions that we associate with being human: language, decision making, and conscious thought.

The cerebrum (Figure 11.16) consists of left and right cerebral hemispheres joined in the middle by a network of nerve tracts called the *corpus callosum*. The corpus callosum enables the two hemispheres to share sensory and motor information. The outer layer of the cerebrum is called the **cerebral cortex.** The cerebral cortex is primarily gray matter, consisting of CNS neurons with unmyelinated axons and their associated neuroglial cells. It has numerous folds on its

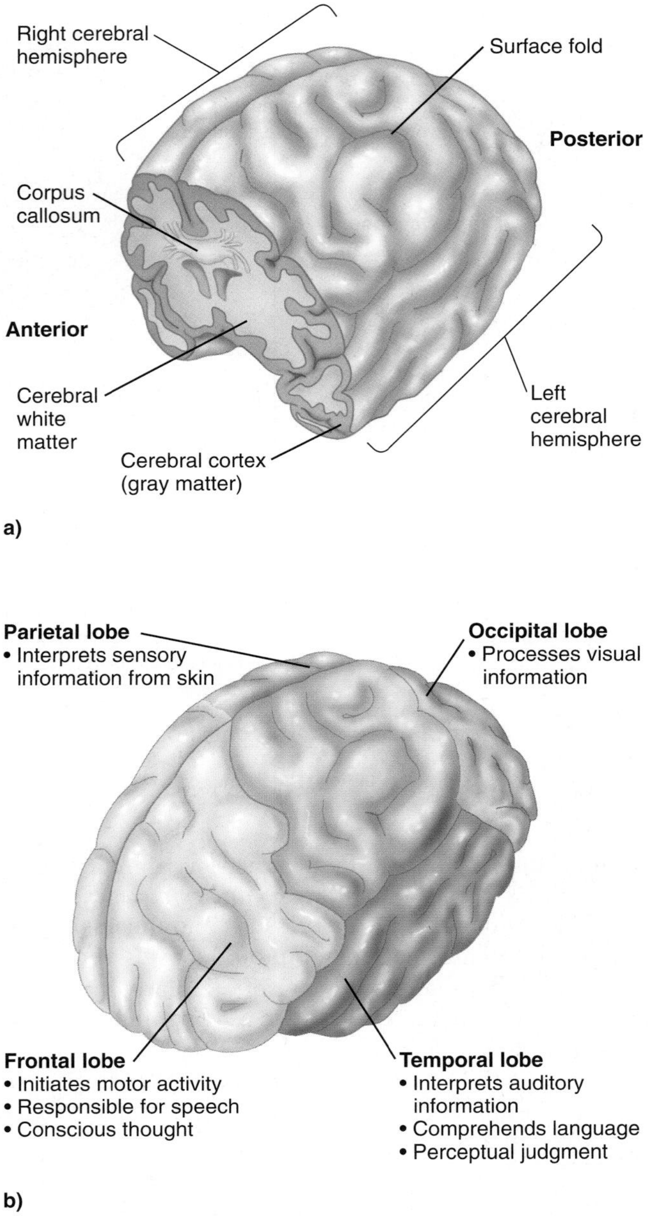


**Figure 11.16 The cerebrum. (a)** Gray matter (the cerebral cortex) consists of interneurons that integrate and process information. White matter consists of ascending and descending nerve tracts. The two separate hemispheres are joined by the corpus callosum. **(b)** The functions of the four lobes of the cerebral cortex are location-specific.

surface, like a walnut. The inner portion of the cerebrum is mostly white matter containing myelinated nerve axons that connect lower brain areas to the cerebral cortex.

The structure of the cerebrum—an inner section of ascending and descending axons and an outer layer of cells—makes it ideally suited to direct incoming information to the proper region of the brain, integrate the information and process it at the highest level, and then route outgoing motor activity to the appropriate areas of the body.

**RECAP**

The forebrain contains the hypothalamus, thalamus, limbic system, and cerebrum. Structures in the forebrain help maintain homeostasis: they receive, process, and transfer information; control emotions and memory; and are responsible for language, decision making, and conscious thought. ■

**A closer look at the cerebral cortex** Although the cerebral cortex is only about 6 millimeters (about 1/4 inch) thick, it contains roughly 50 to 80 billion neuron cell bodies. It is the center for integrating and interpreting sensory information, but it is much more than that. The cerebral cortex is responsible for memory storage, abstract thought, conscious awareness, and conscious control of skeletal muscle.

All of these functions are location-specific. Functionally, the cortex is divided into four lobes (Figure 11.16b). At the back of the brain, the *occipital lobe* processes visual information. The *temporal lobe* interprets auditory information, comprehends spoken and written language, and is responsible for perceptual judgment. The *parietal lobe* receives and interprets sensory information from the skin, such as temperature, touch, pain, and pressure. Finally, toward the front of the cortex is the *frontal lobe*, perhaps the most highly developed of all brain regions. The frontal lobe initiates motor activity and is also responsible for speech and conscious thought. All four lobes are involved in memory storage.

Notice that the region for speech (frontal lobe) is anatomically separate from the region for understanding spoken language (temporal lobe). The reasons for this separation are not known.

Two areas of the brain that have been studied extensively are the region in the parietal lobe that receives sensory input from the skin (called the primary somatosensory area) and the corresponding region of the frontal lobe that initiates motor activity (called the primary motor area). Researchers have found very specific regions within each of these areas corresponding to specific parts of the body (Figure 11.17). Body parts that are extremely sensitive, such as the lips and genitals, involve more neurons and consequently larger portions of the primary somatosensory area, whereas less sensitive body parts involve fewer neurons and smaller portions. Similarly, body parts that can perform intricate and precise movements, such as the fingers, involve more neurons in the primary motor area than do less dexterous regions.

The location-specific nature of information processing explains why damage to different brain regions can cause such varied, seemingly contradictory effects. This is often apparent in stroke victims. One stroke patient might be unable to speak yet still be fully capable of understanding speech. Another could have trouble controlling basic skeletal muscle movements but retain the capacity for abstract thought. Physicians use their understanding of these known location-specific functions to diagnose which areas of the brain have been affected.

**RECAP**

The cerebral cortex is divided into four lobes called the occipital, temporal, parietal, and frontal lobes, each with location-specific functions. For example, the occipital lobe processes visual information, whereas the temporal lobe processes auditory information. ■

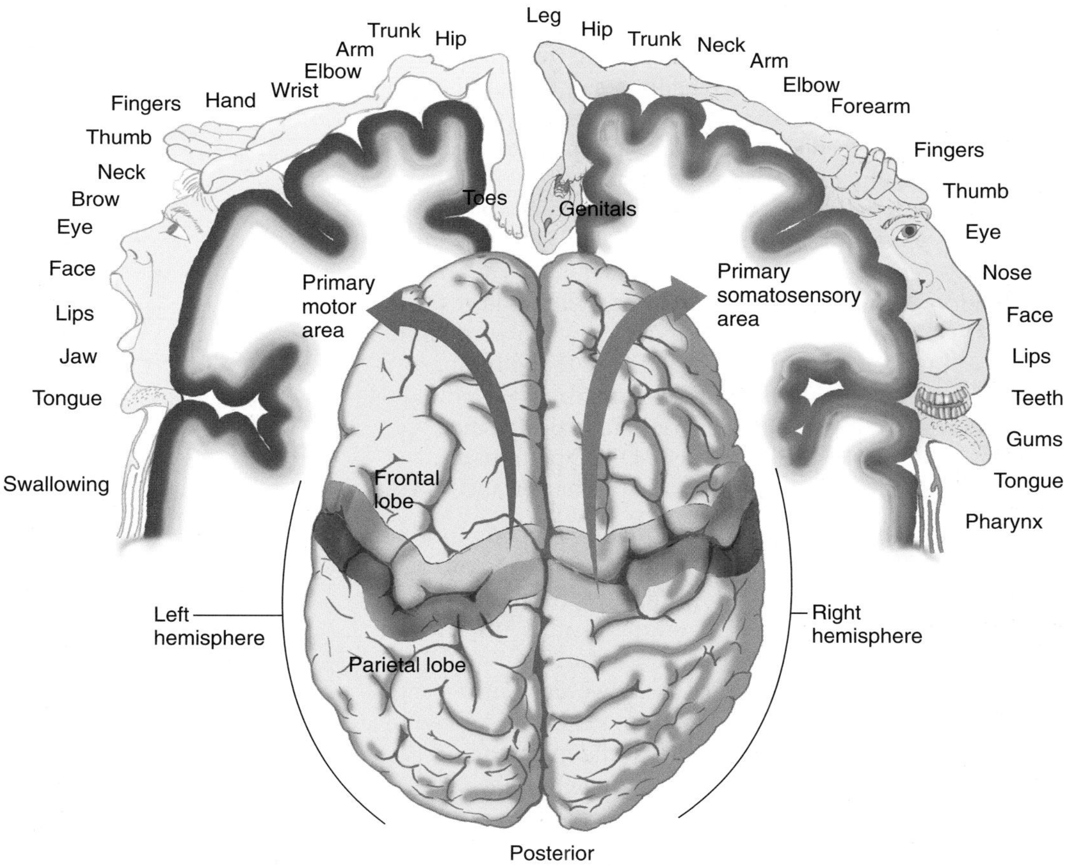


**Figure 11.17 Primary somatosensory and motor areas of the cerebral cortex.** Note the close similarity of the maps of the two areas. The larger the anatomical representation on the diagram, the more precisely controlled or more sensitive the area. The lips, face, and tongue are particularly well represented.

# 11.9 Brain activity continues during sleep

Why do we sleep? This may seem like a simple question, but scientists are still looking for the answer. The obvious hypothesis is that we sleep to get rest. However, brain activity continues even during deep sleep.

Levels of sleep and wakefulness are controlled by the *reticular activating system* (RAS), a group of neurons in the reticular formation. Some neurons of the RAS transmit a steady stream of action potentials to the cerebrum, keeping us awake and alert. A "sleep center" in the RAS releases the neurotransmitter serotonin, which induces sleep by inhibiting the neurons that arouse the brain. Norepinephrine, secreted from another area in the brain, inhibits the effects of serotonin and makes us feel more alert.

We can study what happens to the brain during sleep with *electroencephalograms* (EEGs), recordings of the brain's electrical activity as measured at the body's surface. As Figure 11.18 shows, EEG readings for different states of sleep show characteristic patterns:

- *Stage 1*. Stage 1 is a transitional phase between wakefulness and sleep. The pupils gradually constrict, breathing slows, and heart rate slows. On an EEG, Stage 1 appears as random small waves, only slightly different from wakefulness.
- *Stage 2*. During this phase, skeletal muscles relax, and eye and body movements usually cease. On an EEG, Stage 2 produces sharp waves known as "sleep spindles."
- *Stage 3*. Sleep deepens as heart rate and respiration slow even more. On an EEG, this stage and Stage 4 produce large, slow oscillations, which is why they are sometimes called "slow wave sleep."
- *Stage 4*. Sleepers are difficult to awaken; heart rate and respiration are at their slowest, and body temperature falls.
- *REM (rapid eye movement) sleep*. This is when we dream. Heart rate, respiration, and blood flow to the brain increase. Most of the body's muscles go limp, preventing us from responding to our dreams. Paradoxically, the eyes move rapidly under closed eyelids. EEG patterns show a level of brain activity comparable to that of wakefulness.

Although a typical night's sleep involves cycling through these phases, the length of time spent in each stage can vary. REM sleep returns about every 90 minutes throughout the night and lasts a little longer each time. Toward morning a single REM period may last up to 20 minutes.

Although it is not clear exactly why we sleep, it is clear that we need a certain amount of sleep. Persons deprived of REM sleep become moody, irritable, and depressed and may even suffer hallucinations if deprived long enough.

**RECAP**

The brain remains active even during sleep. Stages of sleep have been correlated with brain wave patterns. The reticular activating system controls levels of sleep and wakefulness. ■

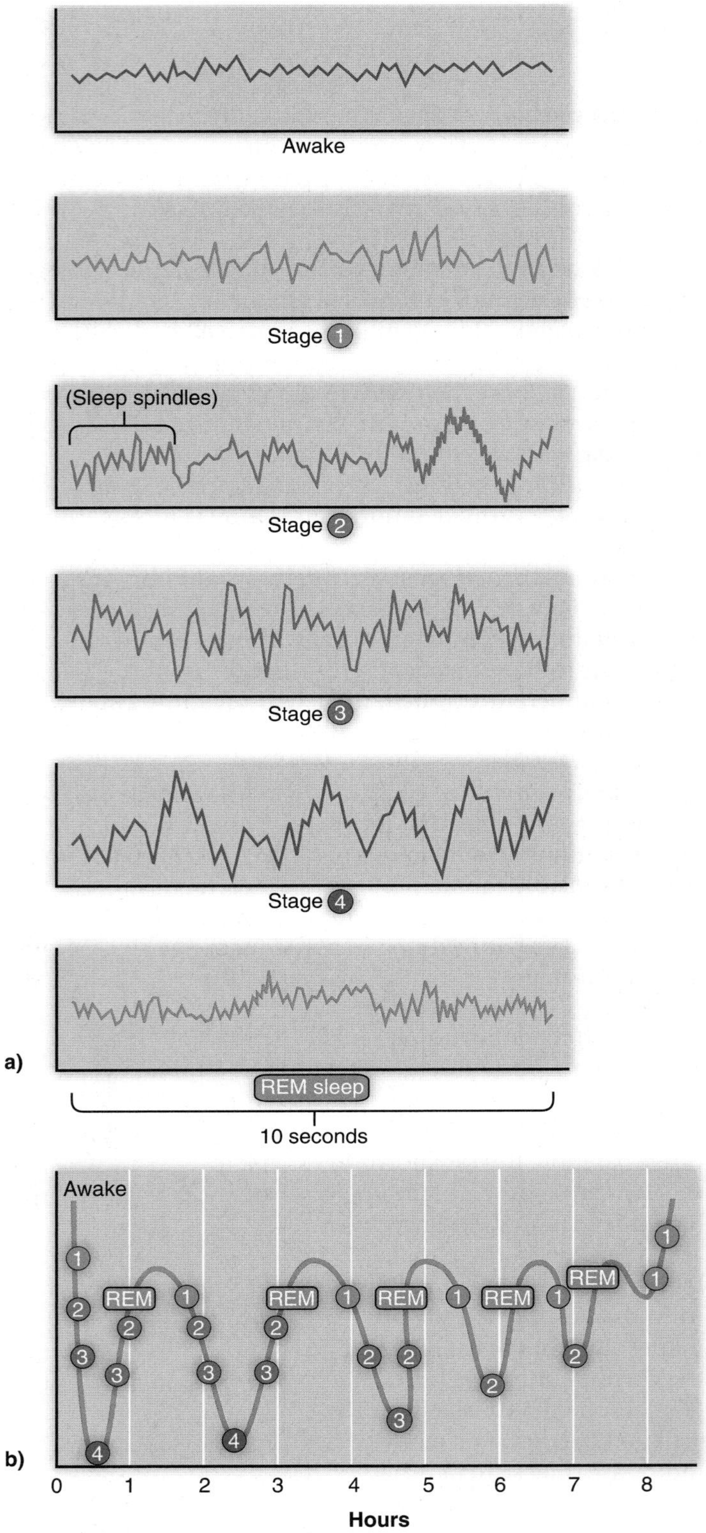


**Figure 11.18 Brain activity patterns during wakefulness and sleep. (a)** EEG recordings in an awake person and during Stages 1–4 and REM sleep. Note the progressively larger waves during Stages 2–4 and the similarity between REM sleep and wakefulness. **(b)** Patterns of sleep.

## 11.10 The limbic system is the site of emotions and basic behaviors

Emotions and basic patterns of behavior originate in the **limbic system** (Figure 11.19). Limbic means "border." The name was originally used to describe those structures that bordered the basal regions of the cerebrum. As we learned about the function of these structures, however, the name came to describe all of the neuronal structures that, together, control emotional behavior and motivational drives. When different areas of the limbic system are stimulated, we experience strong emotions such as fear, anger, sorrow, or love. These reactions, both pleasant and unpleasant, influence our behavior.

You may have noticed that odors have the power to evoke emotions and vivid recollections. This is because pathways for the sense of smell also pass through the limbic system, creating a strong association between olfactory information and memory.

Recall that the hypothalamus monitors and regulates homeostasis of many basic body functions. The hypothalamus also serves as a gateway to and from the limbic system and thus exerts some control over basic self-gratifying behaviors, such as satisfying hunger, thirst, and sexual desire. The thalamus receives and organizes information regarding these behaviors and transmits it to the cerebrum. The cerebrum integrates this information with the other information it is receiving, and then adjusts behavior accordingly.

Thus the intensity with which we feel emotions and the extent to which we act on them depends on modification by the cerebrum. To appreciate the importance of cerebral modification, just imagine what would happen if our most basic urges were no longer influenced by social rules or codes of conduct!

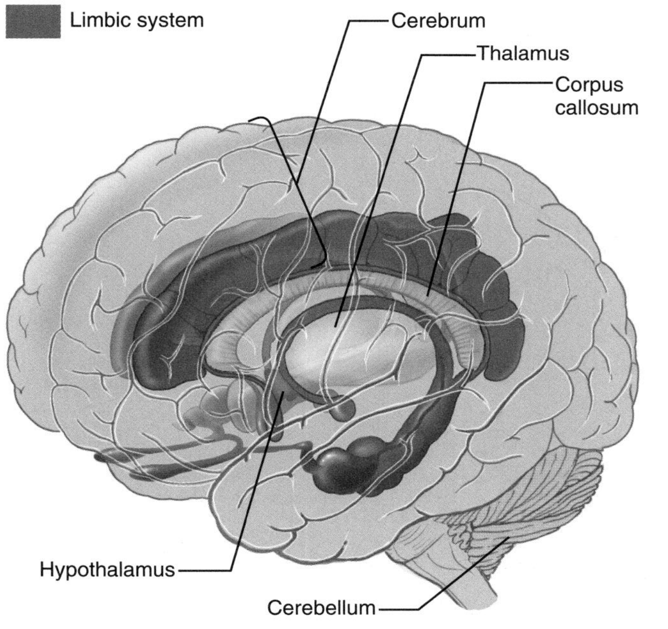


**Figure 11.19 The limbic system.** The limbic system is a collection of neuronal areas near the base of the cerebrum that are involved in emotions, basic behaviors, and short-term memory.

**RECAP**

A collection of structures bordering the cerebrum called the limbic system controls our emotions and behavior. The activities of the limbic system are monitored by the hypothalamus and modified by the cerebrum. ■

## 11.11 Memory involves storing and retrieving information

**Memory** involves storing information and retrieving it later as needed. Memory has two stages: short-term ("working") memory involves retrieval of information that was stored within the past few hours, and long-term memory is the ability to retrieve information days or years later.

There is a clear difference between how the brain manages the two stages of memory. Short-term memory occurs in the limbic system. When you receive new sensory information (such as reading an unfamiliar telephone number), the stimulus triggers a quick burst of action potentials in the limbic system. You can remember the number for a few seconds or minutes, because neurons that have just fired are easier to fire again in the short term. The pathway becomes entrained, if only for a brief time. If the number is not important, you quickly forget it because the enhancement of the limbic pathway is not long lasting. That particular piece of information does not move into long-term memory.

However, if the number is important to you, as evidenced by the fact that you say it out loud several times, write it down and then read it to yourself, or use it repeatedly over several weeks, the information may be transmitted to your cerebral cortex for storage in long-term memory centers. During this process, neurons undergo a permanent chemical or physical change. Evidence from experimental animals suggests that long-term memory storage creates additional synapses between connecting neurons, enabling those circuits to be activated more easily in the future.

**RECAP**

Short-term memory involves quick bursts of action potentials in the limbic system. Long-term memory resides in the cerebral cortex and involves permanent changes in neurons and synapses. ■

## 11.12 Psychoactive drugs affect higher brain functions

A drug is any substance introduced into the body for the purpose of causing a physiological change. Psychoactive drugs are those that affect states of consciousness, emotions, or behavior—in other words, the higher brain functions. Some psychoactive drugs are legal, such as alcohol and nicotine. Others are not legal but have found their way into the fabric of our society.

Most drugs, including psychoactive substances, were originally discovered or designed to treat disease. The non-medical use of drugs is sometimes euphemistically called "recreational" use, but the term "illicit" is certainly a more accurate reflection of the truth.

All psychoactive drugs are able to cross the blood-brain barrier (not all drugs can do so). They work by influencing the concentrations or actions of brain neurotransmitters. Recall that normally the effects of neurotransmitters are short-lived because the neurotransmitter remains in the synaptic cleft for only a brief time. Psychoactive drugs either bind to neurotransmitters or affect their release, action, or reuptake (reabsorption) in some way. This changes normal patterns of electrical activity in the brain.

Depending on which neurotransmitter they influence and where they act, psychoactive drugs can exert a variety of effects. For example, dopamine is one of the most important neurotransmitters in areas of the brain associated with pleasure. Cocaine blocks the reuptake of dopamine back into the presynaptic bulb, leading to too much dopamine in the synaptic cleft and therefore excessive stimulation of postsynaptic neurons. Cocaine initially allows the user to experience pleasurable effects longer than normal.

Psychoactive drugs can lead to *psychological dependence,* meaning that users begin to crave the feelings associated with a drug and alter their behavior to obtain it. Eventually tolerance develops—they need to use more of it, or use it more frequently, to achieve the same effect. Tolerance occurs in part because the liver produces enzymes that detoxify many drugs, and repeated drug use increases circulating levels of these detoxifying enzymes. Soon the original dose is no longer enough to create the desired effect, or sometimes any effect at all. A second reason for tolerance, in the case of cocaine, is that if too much dopamine remains in the synaptic cleft for prolonged periods, the body starts to produce less of it. So with repeated cocaine use, a person needs more and more drug to maintain even a normal amount of dopamine neurotransmitter in the synaptic cleft. Eventually, cocaine addicts become incapable of experiencing pleasure without the drug and cannot even maintain a normal emotional state. At this point, severe anxiety and depression set in.

Tolerance leads to *addiction,* the need to continue obtaining and using a substance despite one's better judgment and good intentions. Essentially, choice is lost. Addiction has serious negative consequences for both emotional and physical health. Eventually, most addicts find it impossible to concentrate and hold a steady job. At the same time, they must spend large amounts of money to support their habit. Personal relationships suffer, and many addicts lose their families, their employment, and their physical health. In addition, they face the probability of *withdrawal,* the symptoms that occur if the drug is removed suddenly.

Cocaine and nicotine are both highly addictive. Alcohol is addictive in some people but not in others, for reasons we do not yet fully understand. One of the most addictive street drugs is crystal methamphetamine (also known as "crank," "ice," "tina" or "glass").

The federal government keeps track of illicit drug use through an annual survey. Figure 11.20 shows past month illicit drug use among persons aged 12 and older. Illicit drug use peaks in 18- to 20-year-olds and then declines with age. The most commonly used illicit drugs in 18- to 25-year-olds are marijuana, prescription pain relievers, cocaine, and hallucinogens (primarily ecstasy, or MDMA), in that order.

Over half of all 18- to 25-year-olds report having used marijuana at least once in their lives. However, only about 15% report having used cocaine or ecstasy, and fewer than 4% have used methamphetamine in the past year.

**RECAP**

Psychoactive drugs work by altering either the concentration or action of brain neurotransmitters. Some lead to psychological dependence, tolerance, and addiction. ■

## 11.13 Disorders of the nervous system

Because the nervous system is so complex and controls so many body functions, disorders of the nervous system can be particularly debilitating. We have already discussed stroke in the context of cardiovascular disease. Here we discuss several classes of disorders that affect the nervous system, including trauma, infections, disorders of neural or synaptic transmission, and brain tumors.

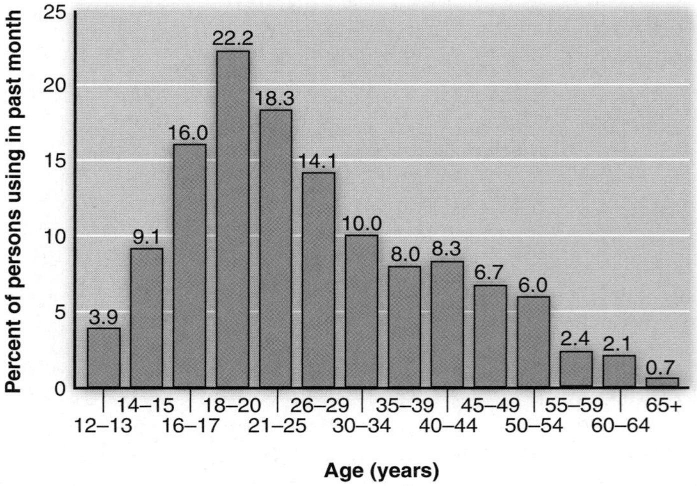


**Figure 11.20 Past month illicit drug use among persons aged 12 and older, 2006.**

*Source:* Substance Abuse and Mental Health Services Administration, 2007. Overview of Findings from the 2006 National Survey on Drug Use and Health.

## Trauma

Trauma (physical injury) to either the brain or spinal cord can be particularly dangerous because the brain controls so many body functions and the spinal cord is the information pathway to virtually all the organs.

**Concussion disrupts electrical activity** A violent blow to the head or neck can cause *concussion,* a brief period of unconsciousness in which electrical activity of brain neurons is briefly disrupted. After the person "comes to," he or she may experience blurred vision, confusion, and nausea and vomiting. Although most concussions are not associated with permanent injury, one of the biggest dangers is a *subdural hematoma,* or hemorrhage (bleeding) into the space between the meninges.

Because the brain is encased in a rigid skull, any bleeding increases pressure within the skull. Eventually the trapped blood presses against healthy brain tissue and disrupts function. Symptoms can include drowsiness, headache, and growing weakness of one side of the body. Depending on how rapidly bleeding occurs, symptoms may take weeks or even months to appear. Sometimes surgeons drill through the skull to drain the hematoma, relieve the pressure, and repair damaged blood vessels.

**Spinal cord injuries impair sensation and function** Violent trauma to vertebrae may press against the spinal cord, tear it, or even sever it completely. Damage to the spinal cord usually impairs sensation and body function below the injured area, so the extent of injury depends on the site of damage. Injuries below the neck can cause paraplegia (weakness or paralysis of the legs and sometimes part of the trunk). Injuries to the neck may lead to quadriplegia (weakness or paralysis of the legs, arms, and trunk). The higher the spinal cord injury, the more likely it is to be fatal. Spinal cord injuries may also cause problems with bladder or bowel control because the autonomic division no longer functions properly.

Researchers are investigating many exciting treatments for spinal cord injuries. For more information, see the Health Watch box, Repairing Spinal Cord Injuries on page 266.

## Infections

The brain and spinal cord are spared most of the infections that affect the rest of the body because of the blood-brain barrier. Nevertheless, certain viruses and bacteria do occasionally infect the brain or spinal cord.

**Encephalitis: Inflammation of the brain** Encephalitis refers to inflammation of the brain, often caused by a viral infection. Frequent sources of encephalitis include the herpes simplex virus (which causes cold sores) and a virus transmitted through mosquito bites. HIV (human immunodeficiency virus) infection is responsible for a growing number of cases.

Symptoms of encephalitis can vary, but often include headache, fever, and fatigue, progressing to hallucinations, confusion, and disturbances in speech, memory, and behavior. Some patients also experience epileptic seizures. Treatment varies depending on the cause, but antiviral drugs may help.

**Meningitis: Inflammation of the meninges** Meningitis involves inflammation of the meninges, usually due to viral or bacterial infection. Symptoms include headache, fever, nausea and vomiting, sensitivity to light, and a stiff neck. Mild cases may resemble the flu. Viral meningitis tends to be relatively mild and usually improves within a few weeks. Bacterial meningitis can be life threatening and requires antibiotics.

**Rabies: Infectious viral disease** Rabies is an infectious viral brain disease of mammals, especially dogs, wolves, raccoons, bats, skunks, foxes, and cats. It is transmitted to humans by direct contact, usually through a bite or a lick over broken skin. The virus makes its way through the sensory neurons in the region of the bite to the spinal cord and then to the brain, where it multiplies and kills cells.

Signs of rabies include swollen lymph glands, painful swallowing, vomiting, choking, spasms of throat and chest muscles, fever, and mental derangement. The symptoms generally appear one to six months after initial infection, followed by coma and death within two to twenty days.

If an animal has bitten you, wash the wound thoroughly and consult a physician. If possible, have the animal tested for rabies. If there is any possibility it could be rabid, your doctor will advise you to be immunized, because untreated rabies may be fatal. The rabies vaccine is most effective if administered within a few days after the bite, but it may still work when given weeks or months later.

## Disorders of neural and synaptic transmission

The nervous system depends on action potentials traveling in neurons and the chemical transfer of signals from one neuron to another across a synapse. It should come as no surprise, then, that problems involving neural or synaptic transmission can cause disease. The symptoms of these disorders depend on which nerves and/or neurotransmitters are affected.

**Epilepsy: Recurring episodes of abnormal electrical activity** Epilepsy is a disorder characterized by transient, recurring bouts of abnormal brain cell activity. Fatigue, stress, or patterns of flashing lights may trigger epileptic attacks, known as seizures. Seizures vary widely, because virtually any activity controlled by the brain may be affected. Some epileptic seizures are almost not noticeable: perhaps a short episode of staring or nonpurposeful movements, a shaking limb, or repeated hand rubbing. Some seizures result in changes in the way things smell, taste, or sound to the patient or cause temporary speech disturbances. These seizures end quickly without causing any loss of consciousness. Other seizures affect larger areas of the brain and thus have more noticeable symptoms, such as sudden collapse, convulsions (stiffening and shaking of the extremities or the entire body), or temporary loss of consciousness, from which the person recovers fully after a short time. Epilepsy usually appears during childhood or

# Health Watch

## Repairing Spinal Cord Injuries

On September 7, 2007, Buffalo Bills football player Kevin Everett suffered a fracture and dislocation of the cervical spine while making a tackle during a game against the Denver Broncos. As he was taken off the field, Kevin moved only his eyes. The next day, Kevin's doctors relieved the pressure on his spinal cord and repaired the bone damage to his third and fourth vertebrae with a bone graft and metal rods. But two days after the accident Kevin still could barely feel or move his arms and legs. Doctors gave him a "statistically very small" chance of ever walking again.

Two hundred fifty thousand Americans are living with spinal cord injuries, and 11,000 new cases occur every year—one every 49 minutes. Most spinal cord patients are young males, with an average age of 32. The major causes of these injuries are car accidents (38.5%), violence (30%), falls (19%), and sports injuries (8%).

Injuries like Kevin Everett's generally crush the spinal cord axons rather than actually severing the cord. This initiates a series of events that ultimately cause most of the resulting damage. First, normal blood flow is disrupted, depriving spinal tissues of vital oxygen. Then, bleeding at the injury site causes swelling, which further compresses and damages the axons. The injured cells emit chemical signals that can damage neighboring neurons and expand the affected area, sometimes even doubling the size of the original injury. Macrophages migrate to the area to clean up the debris, but their actions may destroy healthy neurons as well.

Several weeks after the initial injury, fluid-filled cysts develop at the site. Scar tissue forms around these cysts, creating permanent cavities in the tissue that block the conduction of nerve signals. Oligodendrocytes die and axons lose their myelination, further disrupting communication between the brain and the rest of the body. The most common outcomes of spinal cord injuries are paralysis of both legs and the lower part of the body (*paraplegia:* 52% of patients), or paralysis of all four limbs (*quadriplegia:* 46%).

Until recently it was believed that damaged neurons could not regenerate. However, researchers are investigating a number of exciting possibilities for helping spinal cord patients recover lost function. Since the damage occurs in stages, it may be possible to intervene at various points in the sequence. Current areas of research or treatment include:

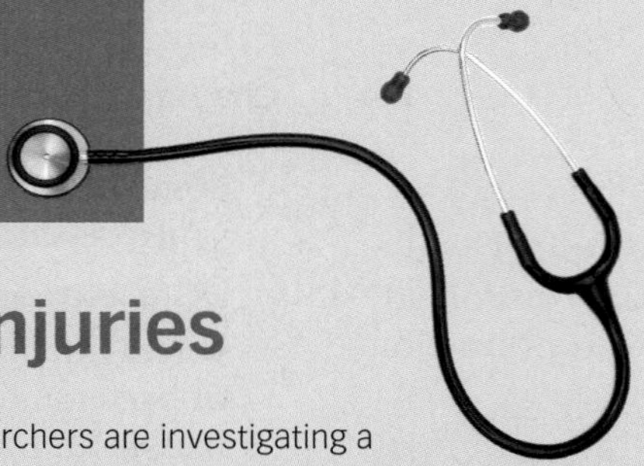

- *Limiting cell injury and death.* At least three mechanisms of cell injury and death are involved. Researchers are exploring ways to block these injury and death pathways to preserve as many neurons and oligodendrocytes as possible.
- *Controlling inflammation.* Ironically, the inflammatory process, which normally promotes healing, makes matters worse by causing secondary damage to cells that were not injured initially. Anti-inflammatory drugs such as *methylprednisolone* can help, especially if given within eight hours of the injury.
- *Blocking factors that prevent regeneration.* The CNS of adult mammals contains inhibitory factors that block neurons from continually growing and dividing inappropriately in healthy adults. After an injury, however, they become an obstacle to tissue repair. One lab is developing ways to neutralize these molecules.
- *Stimulating axons to grow.* Some researchers are working with growth factors and guidance molecules to stimulate damaged axons to "sprout" new extensions across the injured area.
- *Replacing lost cells with new tissue.* Stem cells, which have the potential to differentiate into many types of cells, might be stimulated to develop into neurons and neuroglial cells for transplant. See the Current Issue box in Chapter 3 for a detailed discussion of stem cell research.
- *Bridging the injury site or removing barriers to regrowth.* Some researchers are using artificial materials to support and guide neurons as they regenerate across an injured area. Other groups are experimenting with grafts of neural tissue, or even proteins that can assemble into nanofibers much smaller than a human hair. Still others are experimenting with enzymes that dissolve scar tissue and allow neurons to grow through the affected area.

Kevin Everett suffered a fracture of the spine on September 7, 2007. He was walking again just five months later.

- *Stimulating muscles electronically.* Computer-controlled functional electrical stimulation (FES) systems help patients move by activating their muscles with electrodes.

Does any of this work? Ask Kevin Everett. He attended the Superbowl on January 31, 2008 and was able to walk under his own power during an appearance on the *Oprah* show that same day. Today, 90% of people with spinal cord injuries survive and live a near-normal life span. Unfortunately, fewer than half are able to return to the workforce. Perhaps with further advances that number will rise.

adolescence. Some cases result from infections (such as meningitis or encephalitis), head injuries, brain tumors, or stroke, but often the cause is not known.

**Parkinson's disease: Loss of dopamine-releasing neurons** Parkinson's disease is a progressive, degenerative disorder that strikes nearly 50,000 people a year in North America, most over age 55. Symptoms include stiff joints and muscle tremors in the hands and feet. Eventually people with Parkinson's lose mobility; they may also become mentally impaired and depressed.

We now know that Parkinson's disease is caused by degeneration of dopamine-releasing neurons in the area of the midbrain that coordinates muscle movement. The shortage of dopamine impairs the ability to perform smooth, coordinated motions. The symptoms can be improved by taking L-dopa, a drug that the body converts into dopamine, but this does not slow the loss of neurons. As the disease progresses, even L-dopa becomes ineffective.

However, there is an experimental and highly controversial treatment for patients with Parkinson's disease that might replace lost cells: receiving transplants of fetal neurons directly into the brain. Experiments with animals have shown that transplanted fetal neurons will survive and grow in the recipient animal. In humans, the fetal cells would come from aborted fetuses, which is why the technique generates such controversy. For an in-depth discussion of stem cell research and related social and ethical issues, see the Current Issue in Chapter 3.

**Alzheimer's disease: Shortage of acetylcholine** In contrast to Parkinson's disease, which affects primarily physical activity, Alzheimer's disease is a disorder of mental impairment, especially impairment of memory. One in every ten people over age 65 has the disorder.

Alzheimer's disease begins with memory lapses and progresses to severe memory loss, particularly of recent events; long-term memory is affected more slowly. Patients can also become disoriented, demented, and develop personality changes. Eventually they can no longer function independently.

The disease primarily affects neurons in the limbic system and frontal lobe, which use acetylcholine as their neurotransmitter. As the disease progresses, the supply of acetylcholine becomes insufficient for normal neurotransmission. The study of affected brains has revealed definite anatomical changes, including abnormal, tangled neurons and unusually large deposits of an abnormal protein called *beta amyloid.* Along with these anatomical changes, metabolic activity in the frontal and temporal lobes declines, as do levels of the enzyme that produces acetylcholine (Figure 11.21). Drugs that enhance the brain's production of acetylcholine can slow the progression of the disease, but as yet there is no cure.

The cause of Alzheimer's is still unknown, but possibilities include infections and impaired circulation to the brain.

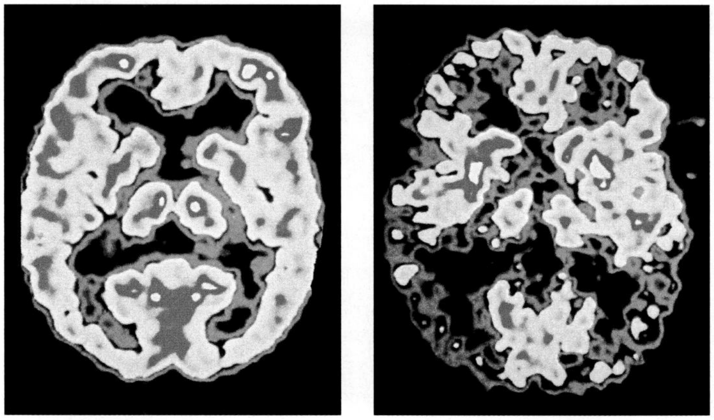

a) Healthy brain b) Brain with Alzheimer's

**Figure 11.21 Changes in brain metabolic activity in Alzheimer's disease.** A positron emission tomography (PET) scan reveals differences in metabolic activity of tissue. Reds and yellows represent high metabolic activity, blues and greens represent lower activity. **(a)** A PET scan of a healthy brain. **(b)** A PET scan of a patient with Alzheimer's disease. Note the decreased activity and the irregular pattern.

There appears to be a genetic component, as a family history of the disease increases the risk. Recent studies suggest that an abnormal gene on chromosome 21 for the beta amyloid precursor protein may be involved.

## Brain tumors: Abnormal growths

A brain tumor is an abnormal growth in or on the brain. Brain tumors are not necessarily cancerous, but even noncancerous growths can cause problems if they press against neighboring tissue and increase pressure within the skull. Over time, the rising pressure disrupts normal brain function. Depending on the location and size of the tumor, symptoms include headache, vomiting, visual impairment, and confusion. Some people also experience muscle weakness, difficulty speaking, or epileptic seizures.

Some brain tumors originate from the brain itself, but most are seeded by cancer that spreads from other parts of the body. For more information on cancer, see Chapter 18.

Some brain tumors can be surgically removed. If tumors are inaccessible or too large to be removed, radiation and chemotherapy treatments may shrink them or limit their growth.

**RECAP**

Disorders of the nervous system are often serious because of the central role of the nervous system in regulating other body systems. Common disorders include physical trauma and infections, as well as acquired or genetic diseases that disrupt neural transmission in some way, such as epilepsy, Parkinson's disease, and Alzheimer's disease. ■

# Current Issue

## Medically Induced Coma: Risks and Tradeoffs

Ariel Sharon, former prime minister of Israel, suffered a massive stroke and deteriorated rapidly. Randal McCloy, the sole survivor of a West Virginia mining accident (see the Health Watch box in Chapter 10), was close to death from carbon monoxide poisoning when he was rescued. Minutes after Mexican boxer Ruben Contreras stopped fighting in the sixth round of a scheduled eight-round bout, he had a seizure and collapsed. One month after being bitten by a bat, Wisconsin teenager Jeanna Giese almost died from rabies, a viral infection.

Jeanna Giese was placed in a coma after contracting rabies. She leaves the hospital as the first unvaccinated victim in the world to survive the disease.

Boxer Ruben Contreras throws a punch in a match against Brian Viloria. Contreras suffered a seizure after the match and was placed in a coma during his treatment.

What do these people have in common? While their circumstances were different, each suffered some type of injury to the nervous system. And in each case, they were placed in a medically induced coma.

As we saw in this chapter, an injury to the brain can lead to swelling within the skull, cutting off blood flow and reducing oxygen delivery. The result is that brain cells may begin to die within minutes.

Treatment for brain injury generally centers on limiting the extent of initial brain damage as quickly as possible by limiting the degree of swelling and oxygen deprivation. The patient is rushed to a hospital, where a breathing tube is inserted into the airway so that a respirator can take over the breathing function. Physicians may inject a drug called *mannitol* to reduce brain swelling, or cool the patient's body to 90°F to lower the metabolic rate. Sometimes part of the skull is removed surgically to give brain tissue room to swell.

Medically induced coma is a treatment of last resort. Physicians administer a large dose of a barbiturate or sedative drug, which induces the coma. An EEG shows flat waves with no brain activity at all, and the person literally appears to be dead. EEG monitoring continues, and drug levels are adjusted accordingly to ensure that the brain stays "asleep."

Theoretically, medically induced coma allows the brain to rest, reducing the brain's consumption of oxygen and glucose and lowering blood flow. The reduction in blood flow, in turn, should reduce the movement of fluid into brain tissue and reduce brain swelling. In effect, medically induced coma is used to protect the brain from the aftermath of injury, which is often more damaging than the original injury.

Admittedly, medicating an already critically ill individual into a coma is risky. An immobilized patient may develop pneumonia. Complete inactivity may lead to blood clots that can be fatal if they migrate to the lungs. Some patients develop persistent muscle weakness or paralysis that can linger for weeks even after they come out of the coma. Furthermore, it is impossible for physicians to assess the extent of brain damage until the person is aroused.

And yet, there are success stories. The physicians who placed Jeanna Giese in a coma for eight days in a last-ditch gamble to save her from rabies were able to see her return to high school. Today Giese is the first unvaccinated person to have survived symptomatic rabies. Randal McCloy survived his mining accident and has returned home. As for Ruben Contreras, less than four months after his seizure and subsequent coma he was well enough to attend a boxing match.

### Questions to consider

**1** *If someone you love were to suffer a severe head injury, would you want that person placed in a medically induced coma? Would you want to be placed in one yourself? Why or why not?*

**2** *What would you ask the physician in order to help you make an informed decision?*

### the facts...

- Medically induced coma is used to reduce brain metabolism and blood flow in certain patients in an effort to limit or prevent brain damage.
- Physicians induce the coma by administering drugs that essentially put the brain to sleep.
- Medically induced coma remains a risky, last-ditch choice: while it can buy time for the brain to recover, it may lead to unrelated medical complications.

# Chapter Summary

### The nervous system has two principal parts *p. 243*

- The central nervous system receives, processes, and stores information, and the peripheral nervous system provides sensory input and motor output.
- The PNS has somatic and autonomic divisions.
- The autonomic division of the PNS has sympathetic and parasympathetic divisions.

### Neurons are the communication cells of the nervous system *p. 244*

- Neurons generally consist of a cell body, several short extensions called dendrites, and a long, thin extension called an axon.

### Neurons initiate action potentials *p. 245*

- Incoming signals from other neurons produce short-lived graded potentials in a neuron that alter its resting potential slightly.
- If the sum of all graded potentials exceeds threshold, voltage-sensitive sodium channels open briefly and an action potential is initiated.
- The three components of an action potential are (1) depolarization, in which sodium channels open briefly and then close, (2) repolarization, in which potassium channels open briefly and then close, and (3) reestablishment of the resting potential by the continuous action of the sodium-potassium pump.

### Neuroglial cells support and protect neurons *p. 248*

- Schwann cells produce myelin, an insulating material that increases conduction velocities in neurons.
- Multiple sclerosis is a disease in which the myelin sheath of neurons becomes damaged.

### Information is transferred from a neuron to its target *p. 250*

- An action potential in a presynaptic neuron causes ion channels for $Ca^{2+}$ to open in the membrane of the axon bulb.
- $Ca^{2+}$ diffuses into the axon bulb and causes a chemical neurotransmitter to be released into the synaptic cleft.
- The neurotransmitter binds to receptors on the postsynaptic cell membrane, causing a graded potential in the postsynaptic cell.
- Information processing depends on differences in stimulus intensity and on converging and diverging neural connections.

### The PNS relays information between tissues and the CNS *p. 252*

- The peripheral nervous system consists of 12 pairs of cranial nerves and 31 pairs of spinal nerves. Each nerve may contain a mixture of sensory, somatic motor, and autonomic motor nerve axons.
- The somatic motor division of the peripheral nervous system controls skeletal muscle.
- The autonomic motor division of the peripheral nervous system controls automatic functions and helps to maintain homeostasis.

### The brain and spinal cord constitute the CNS *p. 256*

- The brain and spinal cord are protected by bone, by three layers of connective tissue called meninges, and by cerebrospinal fluid.
- The spinal cord consists of ascending (going to the brain) and descending (coming from the brain) nerve tracts, plus neurons and neuroglial cells of the CNS.

### The brain processes and acts on information *p. 258*

- The brain receives sensory information, integrates and stores it, and generates the appropriate response.
- The medulla oblongata contains areas that control blood pressure and respiration.
- The cerebellum coordinates basic and certain skilled body movements.
- The hypothalamus coordinates certain automatic functions and participates in the maintenance of homeostasis.
- The cerebrum is involved in language, decision making, and conscious thought. It is also the site of long-term memory storage.

### Brain activity continues during sleep *p. 262*

- The brain exhibits characteristic cyclic patterns of activity during sleep.
- The functional importance of sleep is unknown.

### The limbic system is the site of emotions and basic behaviors *p. 263*

- The limbic system is the center of emotions such as fear, anger, sorrow, and love and basic behaviors such as seeking food or sexual gratification.

### Memory involves storing and retrieving information *p. 263*

- Short-term memory resides in the limbic system. Long-term memory involves permanent changes to neurons in the cerebral cortex.

### Psychoactive drugs affect higher brain functions *p. 263*

- Psychoactive drugs act either by altering the concentrations of brain neurotransmitters or by altering the responses of postsynaptic neurons to them.
- Addiction to psychoactive drugs is characterized by the compulsion to use the drug, often at increasing doses, despite good intentions and negative consequences.

### Disorders of the nervous system *p. 264*

- Head trauma can be dangerous because any bruising or bleeding within the confined space of the skull presses against the brain.
- Spinal cord injury can interrupt neural signals traveling up and down the spinal cord, resulting in a loss of sensation and paralysis of muscle.
- Rabies is an infectious viral disease that is transmitted by the bite of an infected animal. The virus travels to the spinal cord and brain via the axon of a sensory nerve.
- Alzheimer's disease is characterized by a decline in the amount of the neurotransmitter acetylcholine in the limbic system and frontal lobe. Although the cause of Alzheimer's is unknown, the disease is associated with deposits of an abnormal protein in the brain.

## Terms You Should Know

action potential, *246*
autonomic division, *254*
axon, *244*
blood-brain barrier, *257*
central nervous system (CNS), *243*
cerebellum, *259*
cerebral cortex, *260*
cerebrospinal fluid, *257*
cerebrum, *260*
dendrite, *244*
forebrain, *260*
graded potential, *246*
hindbrain, *258*
interneuron, *244*
midbrain, *259*
motor neuron, *244*
myelin sheath, *248*
nerve, *252*
neuroglial cell, *248*
neuron, *244*
neurotransmitter, *250*
parasympathetic division, *255*
peripheral nervous system (PNS), *243*
resting potential, *245*
sensory neuron, *244*
somatic division, *253*
synapse, *250*
sympathetic division, *254*

## Concept Review

1. Distinguish between the central nervous system and the peripheral nervous system.
2. Explain what is meant by summation of graded potentials and explain how summation may lead to an action potential.
3. Describe, in terms of the opening and closing of ion channels and the subsequent diffusion of ions, how the depolarization and repolarization phases of an action potential take place.
4. Describe the functions of neuroglial cells.
5. Describe the role of neurotransmitters in the function of neurons.
6. List the three major divisions of the brain and identify their general functional roles.
7. Explain what is meant by the statement that the functions of the cerebral cortex are "location-specific."
8. Define REM sleep and indicate the physiological changes that might be observed during REM sleep.
9. Describe why a subdural hematoma is so much more dangerous than a hematoma in a muscle (known commonly as a bruise).
10. Explain why an injury to the spinal cord may impair sensations and motor movement below, but not above, the point of injury.

## Test Yourself

### Matching Exercise

_____ 1. Type of neuron providing information to the central nervous system
_____ 2. Type of neuron that integrates information and influences the activity of other neurons
_____ 3. A small change in membrane potential caused by the opening of chemically gated ion channels
_____ 4. The difference in voltage across the cell membrane of a resting cell
_____ 5. An all-or-none, self-propagating electrical impulse
_____ 6. Short uninsulated region of an axon not covered by myelin

a. action potential
b. interneuron
c. node of Ranvier
d. sensory neuron
e. graded potential
f. resting potential

### Fill in the Blank

7. Axons branch into slender extensions called ______________, each of which ends with an axon bulb.
8. Approximately 80% of the cells of the nervous system are ______________ cells, which provide support and protection to neurons.
9. Neurotransmitters are released into the ______________ between two neurons.
10. The ______________ nervous system consists of the brain and spinal cord.
11. Activation of the ______________ division of the autonomic nervous system raises heart rate; activation of the ______________ division lowers heart rate.
12. The ______________ system of the brain deals with emotions.

### True or False?

13. Myelinated axons conduct action potentials more slowly than unmyelinated axons.
14. The repolarization phase of an action potential is due entirely to the sodium-potassium pump.
15. Sensory nerves provide input to the central nervous system only in the form of action potentials.

## References and Additional Reading

Pinker, Steven. *How the Mind Works.* New York: Norton, 1997. 660 pp. (A modern examination of the human mind by a leading cognitive scientist. Difficult but informative reading.)

Willoughby, Rodney E., Jr. A Cure for Rabies? *Scientific American,* April 2007, pp. 88–95. (An article by one of the physicians who treated Jeanna Giese, the first nonimmunized person to survive rabies.)

Wolfe, Michael S. Shutting Down Alzheimer's. *Scientific American,* May, 2006, pp. 72–79. (A recent article about what may be causing this disease and what might be done about it.)

### Internet References

Find links to these Web sites at the Human Biology Place.

**The Christopher and Dana Reeve Foundation**
**www.christopherreeve.org**
Founded by actor Christopher Reeve, this nonprofit organization funds research and works to improve quality of life for the disabled.

**International Spinal Research Trust**
**www.spinal-research.org**
A British charity that raises research funds and international awareness of spinal cord injuries.

**Mayo Clinic**
**www.mayoclinic.com**
Affiliated with the well-known medical center; a helpful site with practical guidelines on health and fitness. Discusses disorders of all body systems.

**National Institute of Neurological Disorders and Stroke**
**www.ninds.nih.gov**
One of the 27 institutes that form the National Institutes of Health, the NINDS is a good source of information about disorders of the brain and nervous system.

## Apply **What You Know**

1. Explain in terms of brain anatomy and function how it would be possible for people to remember whole events in the distant past yet not be able to recall what they had for breakfast.
2. What do you suppose would happen to a person's behavior and emotional expression if the neural connections between the limbic system and the cerebral cortex were severed?
3. A friend is washing dishes one evening and gets a deep cut from a sharp knife hidden in the soap suds. Several weeks after the visit to the ER, the stitches are removed. Your friend mentions that one part of his finger is numb; he cannot feel anything when he touches one spot. Will this numbness ever go away?
4. You're feeding a semi-wild cat outside the campus cafeteria when it accidentally nips you, drawing blood. Your friends advise you to report to the campus medical center immediately for a rabies vaccination. Should you go for the vaccination?
5. Overnight, your roommate develops a high fever. She says she has a severe headache and complains of neck stiffness. An hour later she seems confused. You take her to the hospital and the physician recommends a spinal tap—a test in which a sample of cerebrospinal fluid is removed and analyzed. What might the physician be looking for?
6. Some states still administer the death penalty by lethal injection. The injection may contain an anesthetic (for pain) combined with a high dose of potassium to stop the heart. Why would a large dose of potassium stop the heart?
7. At a party someone offers you an ecstasy pill. Aside from the legal issues involved, what are the short-term and long-term effects of trying it just one time?
8. Certain bacteria, such as those that cause botulism or tetanus, produce toxins that interfere with neuromuscular transmission. From what you know of neuromuscular transmission, how might such toxins work?

*Answers can be found on the Human Biology Place.*

# 12 Sensory Mechanisms

1 How are you able to tell the **positions** of your hands and fingers even when your eyes are closed?

2 How many different **taste sensations** are there?

3 Why does a dark red car look **black** in dim light?

4 Why do many older people need bifocals or reading glasses to **focus** on near objects?

Colorized SEM (× 52) of the surface of the tongue showing papillae (pointing toward the back of the tongue) and a taste bud.

**Look around you at the complex and colorful world you inhabit.** Then, after reading this paragraph, close your eyes and concentrate for a moment on what you can hear. Identify the sources of any sounds you hear and try to judge their direction and distance from you. Describe any odors that you smell, and make a guess at the temperature in the room. Now concentrate on your own body. Move your arms and legs about, and then identify what type of clothing you are wearing. Finally, visualize in your mind the precise position of every part of your body, right down to your fingers and toes.

Your body's sensory mechanisms are constantly providing the brain with detailed information about the world around you, and even about the body itself. In this chapter we learn how different kinds of sensory information are received by the body, how that information is converted to nerve impulses, and how the nerve impulses are transmitted to the brain in such a way that the brain can make sense of it all.

## 12.1 Receptors receive and convert stimuli

Sensory input that causes some change within or outside the body is called a **stimulus** (plural: *stimuli*). The stimulus is often a form of physical energy such as heat, pressure, or sound waves, but it can also be a chemical. A **receptor**—a structure specialized to receive certain stimuli—accepts the stimulus and converts its energy into another form.

Some receptors are evolved from the dendritic structures of a sensory neuron. They convert the stimulus into a graded potential that, if it is powerful enough, initiates an impulse within the sensory neuron. Other receptors are parts of cells that produce graded potentials and release a neurotransmitter, stimulating a nearby sensory neuron. In the end, the effect is the same—generation of an impulse in a sensory neuron.

When the central nervous system receives these impulses, we often experience a **sensation,** meaning that we become consciously aware of the stimulus. A sensation is different from **perception,** which means understanding what the sensation means. As an example, hearing the sound of thunder is a sensation; the belief that a storm is approaching is a perception.

**RECAP**

Receptors receive a physical or chemical stimulus and ultimately cause nerve impulses to be generated in sensory neurons. A sensation is the conscious awareness of a stimulus. ■

### Receptors are classified according to stimulus

Receptors are classified according to the type of stimulus energy they convert:

- **Mechanoreceptors** respond to forms of mechanical energy, such as waves of sound, changes in fluid pressure, physical touch or pressure, stretching, or forces generated by gravity and acceleration.
- **Thermoreceptors** respond to heat or cold.
- **Pain receptors** respond to tissue damage or excessive pressure or temperature.
- **Chemoreceptors** respond to the presence of chemicals in the nearby area.
- **Photoreceptors** respond to light.

Many of these receptors contribute to sensations, although some (such as joint receptors) contribute no more than a general sense of where our limbs are located. Table 12.1 lists examples of each type of receptor and the sensations they give us.

A few receptors are "silent" in the sense that we are not consciously aware of their actions. These receptors function in negative feedback loops that maintain homeostasis inside the body. They include stretch receptors for monitoring and regulating blood pressure and fluid volumes, and chemoreceptors for regulating the chemical composition of our internal environment. They aren't discussed in detail here, as we discuss most of them in the context of the homeostatic control of various organ systems.

### Answers to Intro Questions

1 Your brain is constantly receiving information from receptors in your skin, muscles, and joints that allow you to know your body's position. You are sometimes aware of the skin receptors, but you really can't "feel" the receptors in your muscles and joints.

2 At least four (sweet, salty, sour, and bitter), and some people would say five (umami). But combined with over 1,000 different receptors for smell, we can actually distinguish about 10,000 different taste/smell combinations.

3 The receptors in your eyes that allow you to see in color are not nearly as sensitive to light as the receptors for black-and-white vision. They just don't work well in dim light. Therefore in very dim light you're essentially seeing only in black and white.

4 With aging, the lens of the eye becomes stiffer and less elastic. Consequently it may not be able to change shape sufficiently to allow a person to focus on near objects.

**Table 12.1 Types of receptors**

| Type of receptor | Examples | Sensation |
|---|---|---|
| *Mechanoreceptors* | | |
| Touch, pressure | Unencapsulated dendritic endings, Meissner's corpuscles, Pacinian corpuscles, Ruffini endings, Merkel disks | Touch and pressure on skin or body hair |
| Vibration | Pacinian corpuscles | Vibration on skin |
| Stretch | Muscle spindles | Muscle length |
| | Tendon receptors | Tendon tension |
| | Joint receptors | Joint position |
| Hearing | Hair cells in cochlea of the inner ear | Vibration of fluid originating from sound waves |
| Balance | Hair cells in semicircular canals of the inner ear. Hair cells in the utricle and saccule of the inner ear | Rotational movement of the head. Static position and linear acceleration and deceleration of the head |
| *Thermoreceptors* | | |
| Temperature | Receptors in unencapsulated dendritic endings in skin | Heat or lack of heat (cold) |
| *Pain Receptors* | | |
| Pain | Receptors in unencapsulated dendritic endings in skin and internal organs | Pain caused by excessive pressure, heat, light, or chemical injury |
| *Chemoreceptors* | | |
| Taste | Taste receptors in taste buds | Salty, sweet, sour, and bitter tastes |
| Smell | Olfactory receptors of nasal passages | Over a thousand different chemical smells |
| *Photoreceptors* | | |
| Vision | Rods of the retina | Light (highly sensitive black-and-white vision) |
| | Cones of the retina | Light (color vision) |

**RECAP**

Receptors are classified according to the type of stimulus they convert. The five classes of receptors are mechanoreceptors, thermoreceptors, pain receptors, chemoreceptors, and photoreceptors. ■

## The CNS interprets nerve impulses based on origin and frequency

How can cells in the central nervous system (CNS) interpret some incoming impulses as images and others as sounds? How do they distinguish a loud sound from a soft one and bright lights from dim?

As described in Chapter 11, nerve impulses are transmitted from receptors to specific brain areas. For example, impulses generated by visual stimuli travel in sensory neurons whose axons go directly to brain regions associated with vision. All incoming impulses traveling in these neurons are interpreted as light, regardless of how they were initiated. This is why, when you are hit in the eye, you may "see stars." The blow to your eye triggers impulses in visual sensory neurons. When these signals arrive in the visual area of the brain, they are interpreted as light.

Stronger stimuli activate more receptors and trigger a greater frequency of impulses in sensory neurons. In effect, the central nervous system gets all the information it needs by monitoring where impulses originate and how frequently they arrive.

## Some receptors adapt to continuing stimuli

The central nervous system can ignore one sensation to concentrate on others. For example, you ignore the feel of your clothing when you are more interested in other things. Some sensory inputs are ignored after a while because of **receptor adaptation,** in which the sensory neuron stops sending impulses even though the original stimulus is still present. To demonstrate, try touching a few hairs on your forearm. Notice that the initial feeling of light pressure goes away within a second or so, even though you maintain the same amount of pressure.

Receptors in the skin for light touch and pressure adapt rather quickly. This confers a survival advantage, because they can keep the central nervous system informed of *changes* in these stimuli, without constantly bombarding it with relatively unimportant stimuli. Olfactory (smell) receptors also adapt rapidly. Olfactory adaptation can be hazardous to people if they are continually exposed to low levels of hazardous chemicals that they can no longer smell.

Other receptors—pain receptors, joint and muscle receptors that monitor the position of our limbs, and essentially all of the silent receptors involved in homeostatic feedback control loops—adapt slowly or not at all. Lack of adaptation in these receptors is also important to survival. Persistent sensations such as pain alert us to possible tissue damage from illness or injury and prompt us to take appropriate action. Persistent activity of silent receptors is essential to our ability to maintain homeostasis.

**RECAP**

Sensations are transmitted to specific brain areas. Stronger stimuli activate more receptors and trigger a greater frequency of action potentials in sensory neurons. Some receptors adapt rapidly; others adapt slowly or not at all. ■

### Somatic sensations and special senses provide sensory information

The sensations (or senses) provided by receptors are categorized as either somatic or special. The **somatic sensations** originate from receptors present at more than one location in the body (*soma* is the Greek word for "body"). The somatic sensations include temperature, touch, vibration, pressure, pain, and awareness of body movements and position. The five **special senses** (taste, smell, hearing, balance, and vision) originate from receptors that are restricted to particular areas of the body, such as the ears and eyes. The special senses deliver highly specialized information about the external world.

We look at the somatic sensations first and then discuss the five special senses in detail.

## 12.2 Somatic sensations arise from receptors throughout the body

The somatic sensations of temperature, touch, pressure, vibration, pain, and awareness of body movements and position are essential to help us coordinate muscle movements, avoid danger, and maintain body temperature. Some somatic sensations contribute to pleasurable feelings as well, such as our response to the gentle touch of a loved one.

Receptors that detect the somatic sensations are located throughout the body in skin, joints, skeletal muscles, tendons, and internal organs. Sensory neurons linked to these receptors send their impulses to the brain, specifically to the primary somatosensory area of the parietal lobe of the cerebral cortex (review Figure 11.17). As you already know, body parts with the greatest sensory sensitivity, such as the mouth and fingers, involve more neurons in the somatosensory area, whereas less sensitive body parts involve fewer neurons.

The somatosensory area processes the information and sends it to the nearby primary motor area in the frontal lobe. If necessary, impulses are then generated in motor (output) neurons of the peripheral nervous system to cause body movement.

### Mechanoreceptors detect touch, pressure, and vibration

Receptors for sensing touch, pressure, and vibration are called mechanoreceptors. Though they may take several different forms, all mechanoreceptors are the modified dendritic endings of sensory neurons. Any force that deforms the plasma membrane of the dendritic ending produces a typical graded potential. If the graded potential (or the sum of multiple graded potentials) is large enough to exceed threshold, the sensory neuron initiates an impulse.

The various receptors for touch, pressure, and vibration differ in their locations, the intensity of the stimulus that must be applied in order to generate an impulse (pressure is a stronger mechanical force than light touch), and the degree to which they adapt. Vibration-sensitive receptors adapt so quickly that it takes a rapidly changing physical deformation (many on-and-off cycles per second) to keep them stimulated. Vibration-sensitive receptors are particularly useful for providing information about potentially harmful flying insects because they respond to the kinds of vibrations generated by insects' wings.

Figure 12.1 depicts the skin with several types of receptors for detecting somatic sensations. They are:

- **Unencapsulated dendritic endings.** Naked dendritic endings of sensory neurons around hairs and near the skin surface signal pain, light pressure, and changes in temperature.
- **Merkel disks.** Detect light touch and pressure. Merkel disks are modified unencapsulated dendritic endings.
- **Pacinian corpuscles.** Several kinds of dendritic endings are encapsulated (enclosed) in epithelial or connective tissue. The best known, called Pacinian corpuscles, are encapsulated receptors located in the dermis that respond to either deep pressure or high-frequency vibration. The encapsulation structure of the Pacinian corpuscle permits the mechanoreceptor to adapt rapidly, even to a continuously applied stimulus (Figure 12.2).
- **Meissner's corpuscles.** Encapsulated touch receptors located closer to the skin surface than Pacinian corpuscles. They detect the beginning and the end of light pressure and touch.
- **Ruffini endings.** Encapsulated receptors that respond continually to ongoing pressure.

**RECAP**

Somatic sensations include temperature, touch, pressure, vibration, pain, and awareness of body movements and position. Mechanoreceptors that detect touch, pressure, and vibration include a variety of unencapsulated and encapsulated dendritic endings. ■

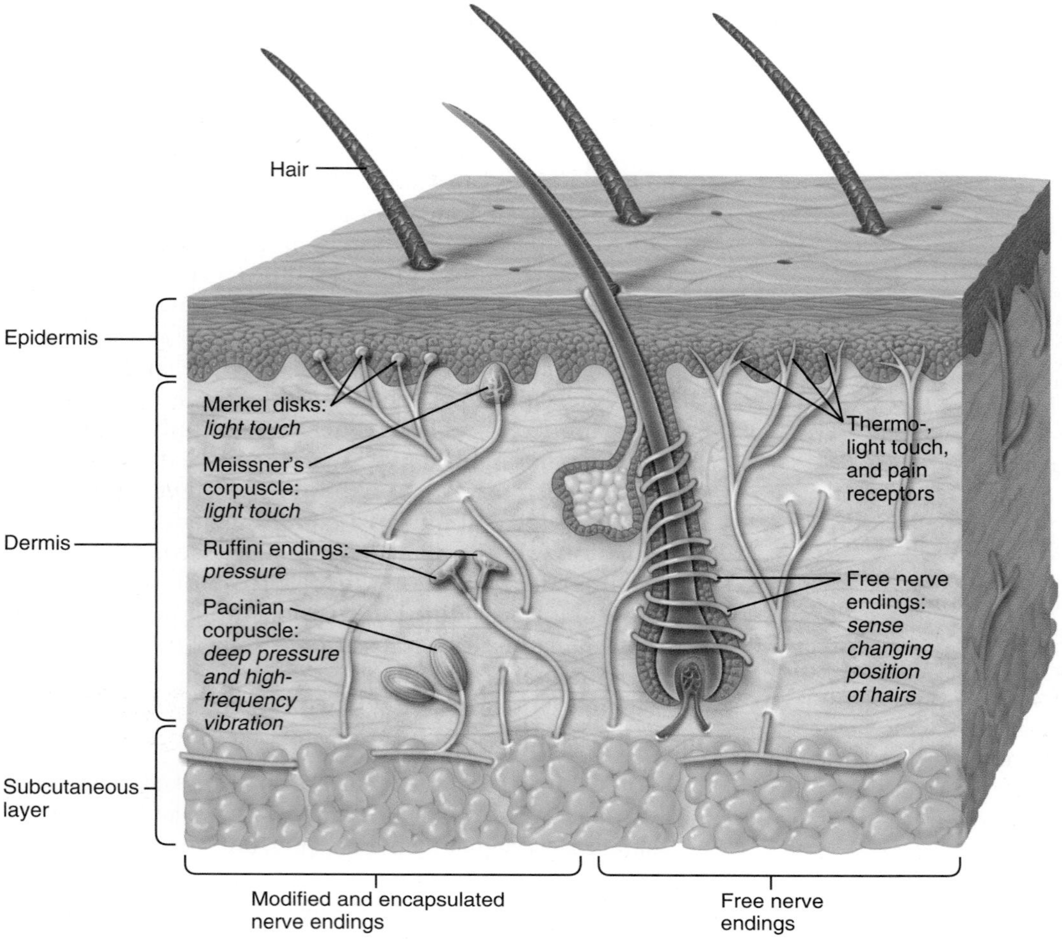


**Figure 12.1 Sensory receptors in skin.** Thermoreceptors, some of the receptors for light touch, and the receptors for pain are the free endings of sensory neurons. Other receptors for touch, pressure, and vibration are modified or encapsulated endings of sensory neurons.

## Mechanoreceptors indicate limb position, muscle length, and tension

With your eyes closed, try to describe the positions of your arms and legs. You can probably describe their position rather well. You may even be able to tell which muscle groups are contracting. You do this with a variety of mechanoreceptors in joints (for joint position), in skeletal muscles (for muscle length), and in tendons (for tension). Perhaps the best known of these mechanoreceptors are the specialized structures for monitoring muscle length, called **muscle spindles.** For most joints, muscle length determines joint position because of the way the muscle is attached to the bones.

A muscle spindle is a small bundle of modified skeletal muscle cells located within a skeletal muscle (Figure 12.3). Muscle spindles are innervated by sensory nerves whose dendritic endings are mechanoreceptors that respond to stretch (lengthening). One type of dendritic ending wraps around the middle of a muscle spindle cell. Another has several branches that attach nearer the end of the muscle spindle cell. When the whole muscle is stretched, the receptors attached to the muscle spindle cells are stretched as well. Mechanical distortion of the mechanoreceptors produces local graded potentials in the dendritic endings and (if threshold is passed) an action potential.

This is exactly what happens in the classic patellar stretch reflex, described in Chapter 11. When a physician taps your patellar tendon (at the front of your knee) with a hammer, the patellar tendon and quadriceps (thigh) muscle are stretched, stretching the muscle spindle as well. Stretch of the muscle causes sensory neurons innervating the muscle spindle to transmit action potentials to the spinal cord. Within the cord, motor nerves to the quadriceps are activated, causing the quadriceps to contract. All this occurs in a fraction of a second.

Tendons, which connect muscle to bone, also have mechanoreceptors. Tendon receptors respond to tension, but they cannot distinguish between tension produced by passive stretch and tension produced by active muscle contraction. Tendon receptors may play a protective role in preventing injury by extremely high tensions. For example, if you were to fall out of a tree but land on your feet, the impact when you hit the ground would produce high levels of tension, activating your tendon stretch receptors. The sensory information they provide inhibits muscle contraction, so you would crumple to the ground rather than stay upright. This reflex-induced collapse protects your muscles from tearing and your bones from breaking.

**RECAP**

Mechanoreceptors in skeletal muscle, tendons, and joints respond to changes in muscle length, tendon tension, and joint position. They provide information about the position of our limbs and the amount of tension on muscles. ■

## Thermoreceptors detect temperature

Thermoreceptors for heat and cold near the skin's surface provide useful information about the external environment.

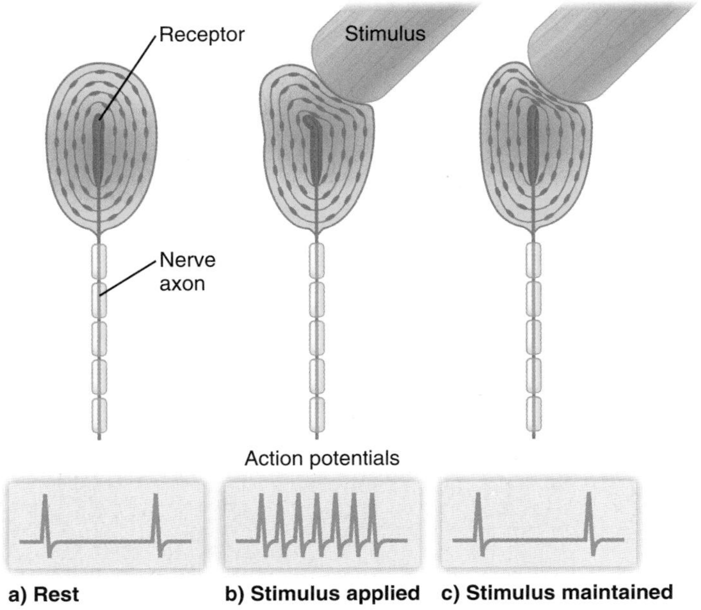


**Figure 12.2 The Pacinian corpuscle.** **(a)** At rest. **(b)** The initial application of a stimulus deforms the encapsulation layers and bends the receptor ending of the nerve, producing more action potentials in the nerve axon. **(c)** With continuous application of the stimulus, the layers of encapsulation slide past each other and come closer together, permitting the receptor ending to return to its initial shape.

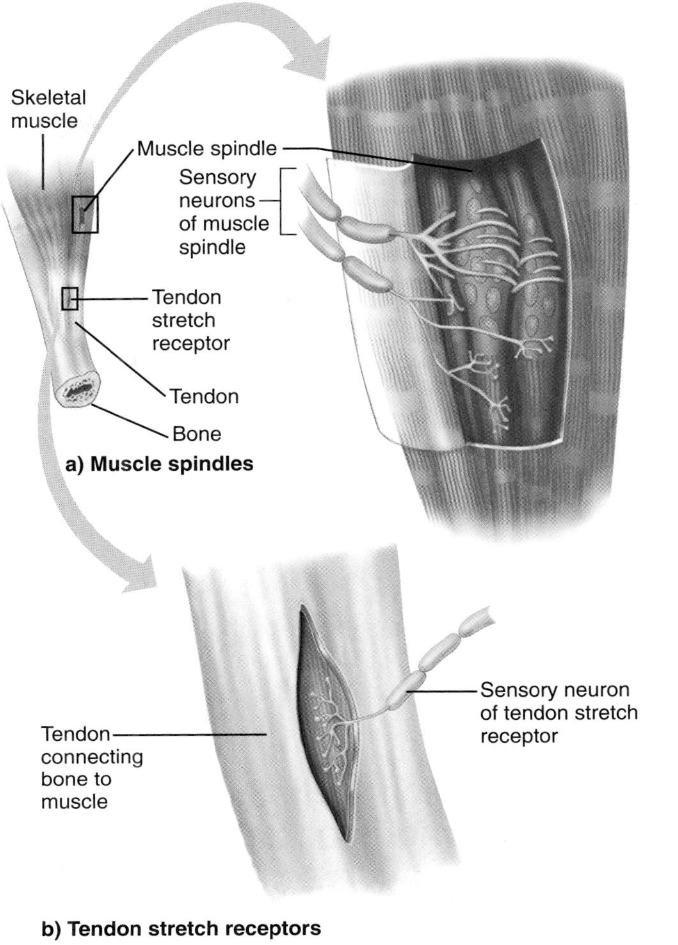


**Figure 12.3 Muscle spindles and tendon receptors.** **(a)** Muscle spindles are a group of modified muscle cells that are innervated by sensory neurons. Passive stretch of a muscle stretches the muscle spindle, stimulating mechanoreceptors in the nerve endings of the sensory neurons. Conversely, muscle contraction shortens the muscle spindle and reduces muscle spindle mechanoreceptor stimulation. **(b)** Tendon stretch receptors respond to tension in tendons. When a muscle contracts and also when it is stretched passively, tension on the tendon increases, activating the tendon stretch receptors.

These receptors adapt quickly, allowing us to monitor changes in temperature accurately and yet adjust sensory input so it becomes more bearable. For example, when you step into a hot shower the water may seem uncomfortably warm at first, but you soon become used to it.

Other thermoreceptors located in abdominal and thoracic organs throughout the body monitor internal temperature (also called core temperature). In keeping with their role in maintaining homeostasis, these thermoreceptors do not adapt rapidly.

**RECAP**

Thermoreceptors near the skin surface monitor the temperature of the external environment. Thermoreceptors in internal organs maintain homeostasis of body temperature. ■

## Pain receptors signal discomfort

As much as we dislike pain, the ability to perceive pain is essential for survival. Pain warns us to avoid certain stimuli and informs us of injuries. Pain receptors are unencapsulated endings that respond to injury from excessive physical pressure, heat, light, or chemicals. Pain is described as either fast or slow, depending on its characteristics.

Fast pain, also called sharp or acute pain, occurs as soon as a tenth of a second after the stimulus. Receptors for fast pain generally respond to physical pressure or heat and usually are located near the surface of the body. They inform us of stimuli to be avoided—for example, stepping on a nail or touching a hot burner on the stove. The reflex withdrawal response to fast pain is rapid and strong.

In contrast, slow pain generally arises from muscles or internal organs. Slow pain, which may not appear until seconds or even minutes after injury, is due to activation of chemically sensitive pain receptors by chemicals released from damaged tissue. Slow pain from internal organs is often perceived as originating from an area of the body completely removed from the actual source. This phenomenon, called **referred pain,** happens because action potentials from internal pain receptors are transmitted to the brain by the same spinal neurons that transmit action potentials from pain receptors in the skin and skeletal muscles. The brain has no way of knowing the exact source of the pain, so it assigns the pain to another location.

Referred pain is so common that physicians use it to diagnose certain disorders of internal organs. For example, a heart attack usually manifests itself as pain in the left shoulder and down the left arm. Figure 12.4 shows where pain from internal organs may be felt. The close association between areas of referred pain from the heart and esophagus is why it can be difficult, by sensations alone, to distinguish a heart attack from the less serious problem of esophageal spasm.

Pain receptors generally do not adapt. From a survival standpoint this is beneficial, because the continued presence of pain reminds us to avoid doing whatever causes it. However, it also means that people with chronic diseases or disabilities can end up experiencing constant discomfort.

**RECAP**

Fast pain arises from receptors near the body surface, while slow pain originates in muscles or internal organs. Pain is important to survival because it warns us of injury. ■

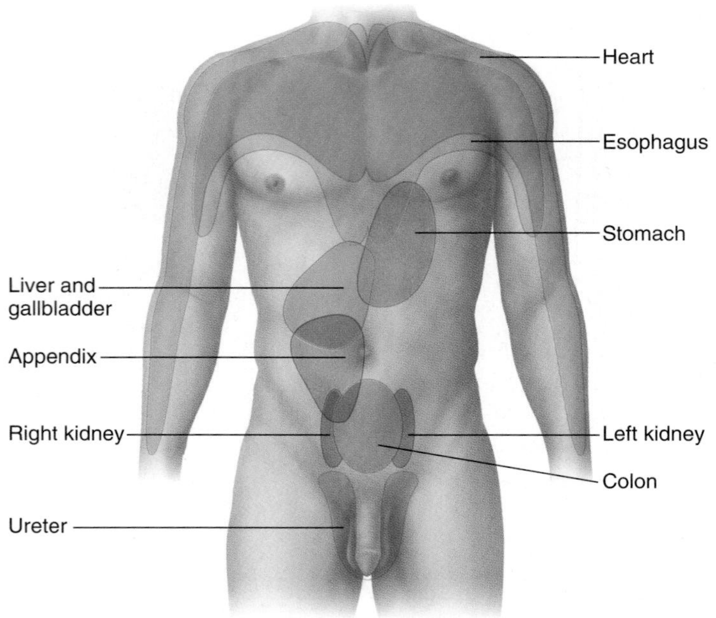


**Figure 12.4 Locations of referred pain from various internal organs.** Note that the areas of overlap for esophageal and heart pain are so extensive that it is often difficult to tell them apart by location.

## 12.3 Taste and smell depend on chemoreceptors

We turn now to the five special senses: taste, smell, hearing, balance, and vision. As mentioned earlier, these senses originate from receptors located in special areas of the body.

The first senses we consider, taste and smell, are both due to the action of chemoreceptors. The rich fragrance of a rose, the less pleasing odor of a skunk, the tart taste of an orange—all depend on our ability to convert a chemical stimulus into the only language the central nervous system can understand: action potentials.

### Taste: Chemoreceptors bind with dissolved substances

The tongue has a rough texture because its surface is composed of numerous small projections, called papillae, surrounded by deep folds (Figure 12.5). About 10,000 **taste buds** are located at the surface of many of these folds. A taste bud is a cluster of about 25 taste cells and 25 supporting cells that separate the taste cells from each other.

The exposed tip of a taste cell has hairs that project into the mouth. The hairs contain chemoreceptors that are specific for certain chemicals (called *tastants*). When we eat

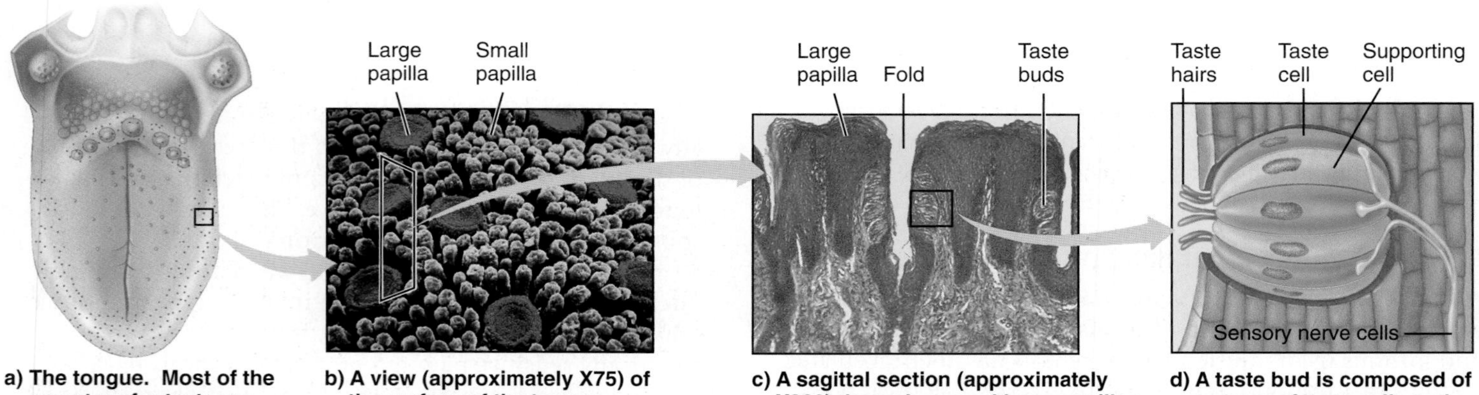


a) The tongue. Most of the receptors for taste are located at the edges and at the front and back of the tongue.

b) A view (approximately X75) of the surface of the tongue showing that it is covered with large and small papillae.

c) A sagittal section (approximately X200) through several large papillae showing the location of the taste buds along their sides, just beneath the tongue's surface.

d) A taste bud is composed of a group of taste cells and supporting cells. Each taste cell connects to a sensory neuron.

**Figure 12.5 The structure of the receptors for taste.**

# Directions in Science

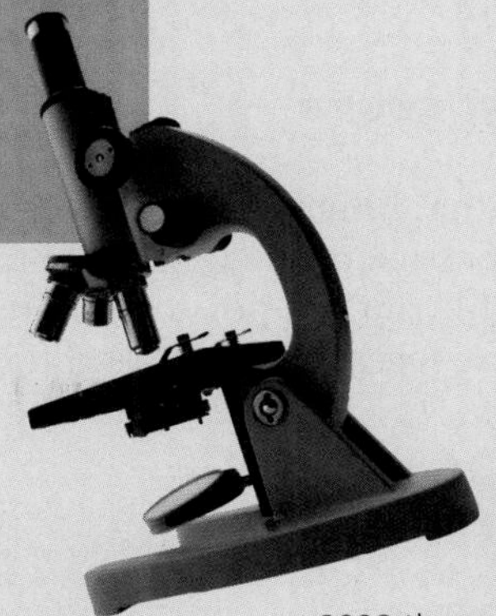

## The Discovery of Umami

How many basic taste qualities are there? In ancient Greece, scholars identified seven: sweet, salty, sour, bitter, spicy, astringent, and sandy. In ancient India, yogic principles identified eight. A Chinese medical text written around 1000 B.C.E. described five.

Rigorous application of the scientific method beginning several centuries ago reduced the number of proven taste qualities to just four: sweet, sour, salty, and bitter. To be considered a basic taste quality there had to be evidence of specific receptors on the tongue that responded primarily to specific chemicals, such as sugar (sweet taste), sodium (salty taste), hydrogen ion (sour taste), and certain toxic plant chemicals (bitter taste).

Then in 1908 Kikunae Ikeda, a chemistry professor at the Imperial University of Tokyo, hypothesized that there was a fifth taste and set out to prove it. Ikeda noted that the dominant flavor of dashi, a Japanese soup base, was mild but distinctly different from the four known tastes, and thus might exemplify this mysterious fifth quality. The seaweed *Laminaria japonica* is a major ingredient of dashi, so Ikeda attempted to isolate the chemical source of *Laminaria*'s flavor. In a series of painstaking chemical procedures, he extracted and removed other ingredients until eventually he had crystallized glutamic acid (glutamate), the most common amino acid in proteins. In 1909 Ikeda published an article in a Japanese journal in which he announced that there was indeed a fifth taste that involved the detection of glutamate. Ikeda named his discovery *umami,* a term derived from the Japanese word *umai* (delicious).

Many Asians were receptive to the concept of umami. In fact, commercial production of monosodium glutamate (MSG), a seasoning agent that adds the sensation of umami to food, began the same year that Ikeda published his article.

However, scientists in the U.S. and Europe remained skeptical. One reason may have been that Ikeda's article was published in Japanese, so many of his foreign peers were unable to read his original work. In the 1950s the U.S. FDA classified umami as a flavor enhancer, not a taste. Around 1980 scientists began to investigate whether laboratory animals could detect glutamate. The research was not entirely convincing to the skeptics because different species, and even different strains of lab mice, showed a variety of responses to the chemical. Although an international symposium accepted umami as the fifth basic taste in 1990, many U.S. researchers remained unconvinced.

The development of molecular biology techniques for sequencing and identifying specific proteins provided new tools for studying sensory receptors. Using these techniques, two groups of researchers reported in 2002 the existence of human glutamate taste receptors. Further research showed that a common form of glutamate (L-glutamate) activates these receptors and elicits the sensation of umami. These findings provide powerful independent confirmation of the pioneering work of Dr. Ikeda a century ago.

Research continues into the molecular basis of taste in general and umami in particular. Some scientists are seeking to block molecular activity at glutamate receptors; if this also blocks the perception of umami, the finding would support the link between the two. Other researchers are exploring the paths by which signals travel from glutamate receptors to the brain, to determine whether umami truly is a single taste or a combination of other taste sensations.

Whether or not you accept that umami is an elusive "fifth taste," it is clear that MSG and umami-rich foods can add depth and richness to recipes. Foods said to be high in umami include Parmesan cheese, shiitake mushrooms, scallops, chicken, soy sauce, and Worcestershire sauce.

or drink, tastants dissolve in our saliva and bind to the chemoreceptor. The binding of tastant to chemoreceptor causes the taste cell to release a neurotransmitter, which stimulates a nearby sensory neuron to produce action potentials. Note that the taste cell itself is not a sensory neuron. It takes two cells (the taste cell and a sensory neuron) to convert the chemical stimulus into a nerve impulse, but the ultimate effect is the same as if it were one cell.

The four commonly accepted primary taste qualities are sweet, sour, salty, and bitter. Recently scientists have also accepted a fifth taste known as *umami* (see the Directions in Science box). Although an individual taste receptor and its associated sensory neuron seem to be "tuned" to respond most strongly to only one of the taste qualities, they do respond weakly to the other taste qualities as well.

Most of the taste receptors are located around the edges and at the front and back of the tongue. Although all receptor types can be found in each of these regions, there is some evidence that their distribution is not entirely even. The tongue is slightly more sensitive to sweet tastes on the tip, sour on the sides, salty on the tip and sides, and bitter toward the back (the distribution of umami receptors is not yet well documented). Therefore, to gain the maximum taste sensation, we move food around in our mouth before swallowing. The combined sensitivities of our taste receptors allow us to distinguish hundreds of different flavors, far beyond the basic five qualities. On the other hand, if we don't want to taste something, we pass it over the center of the tongue and swallow quickly.

It is probably no accident that bitter taste receptors are heavily concentrated at the very back of the tongue. Bitterness is often a sign of an inedible or even poisonous substance, and the location of these receptors makes it difficult to bypass them.

**RECAP**

Taste buds contain chemoreceptor cells that bind dissolved chemicals. The five currently accepted basic taste qualities are sweet, salty, sour, bitter, and umami. ■

### Smell: Chemoreceptors bind with odorants

The sense of smell also relies on a chemoreceptor mechanism. There are two fundamental differences between taste and smell: (1) The receptors for smell are located on true sensory neurons, and (2) there are receptors for over 1,000 different "odorant" chemicals, as opposed to just four tastant classes. With these 1,000 different receptor types and our sense of taste we can distinguish as many as 10,000 taste and smell sensations. Odors are detected by **olfactory receptor cells** located in the upper part of the nasal passages. The receptor cells are sensory neurons, each with a modified dendritic ending that branches to become several olfactory hairs (Figure 12.6). The olfactory hairs extend into a layer of mucus covering the surface of the nasal passages. The mucus, produced by nearby olfactory glands, keeps these hairs from drying out.

Gaseous and airborne odorants enter the nasal passages, become dissolved in the mucus, bind to chemoreceptors located on the olfactory hairs, and cause the olfactory receptor cell to generate impulses. Olfactory receptor cells synapse with olfactory neurons in a nearby area of the brain called the olfactory bulb, where information is partially integrated and then passed to higher brain centers.

Our sense of smell complements our sense of taste because when food is chewed it releases chemicals that come into contact with olfactory receptors. The combined sensations create an effect that is interpreted at higher brain levels (Figure 12.7). When we have a cold, most foods taste less appetizing. In part this is because increased production of mucus prevents odorant molecules from reaching olfactory receptors, impairing our sense of smell.

**RECAP**

Our sense of smell augments and complements our sense of taste, allowing us to experience over 10,000 combinations of taste and smell. ■

## 12.4 Hearing: Mechanoreceptors detect sound waves

Sounds are waves of compressed air. Sound intensity is a physical property of sound that refers to the energy of the sound, whereas loudness refers to our subjective interpretation of sound. Both intensity and perceived loudness are related to the amplitude of the sound waves, and both are measured in units called decibels (dB). The threshold of human hearing (barely audible) is set at 0 dB. A 10-dB increase represents a 10-fold increase in sound intensity (sound energy), but only a doubling of perceived loudness. In other words, a sound of 30 dB has 100 times more energy than a 10-dB sound, but humans would perceive it as only four times as loud. Hearing loss can result from exposure to sounds louder than 85 dB. Table 12.2 lists the decibels associated with some common sounds.

The tone or pitch of a sound is determined by its frequency, the number of wave cycles that pass a given point per second (cycles/sec). Frequency is expressed in *hertz* (Hz). Higher tones are those of a higher frequency (Figure 12.8). The frequency range for normal human hearing is from 20 to 20,000 Hz.

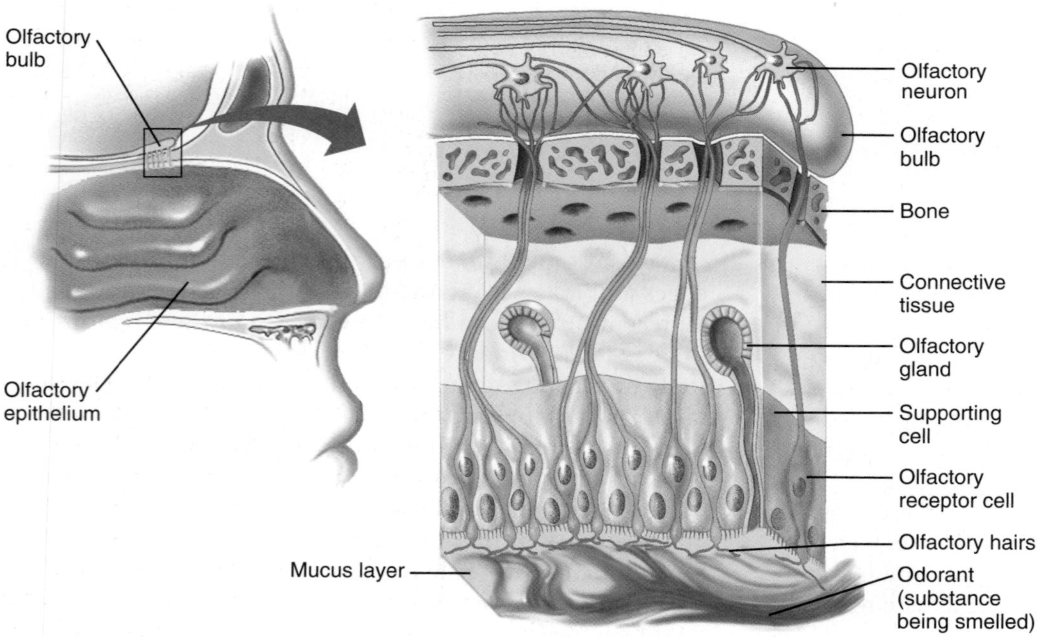


**Figure 12.6 Olfactory receptors and the mucus-producing olfactory glands.** Odorants become trapped in mucus and then bind to the olfactory hairs of receptor cells.

**Figure 12.7 Smell.** Over 1,000 different olfactory receptors contribute to our sense of smell and taste.

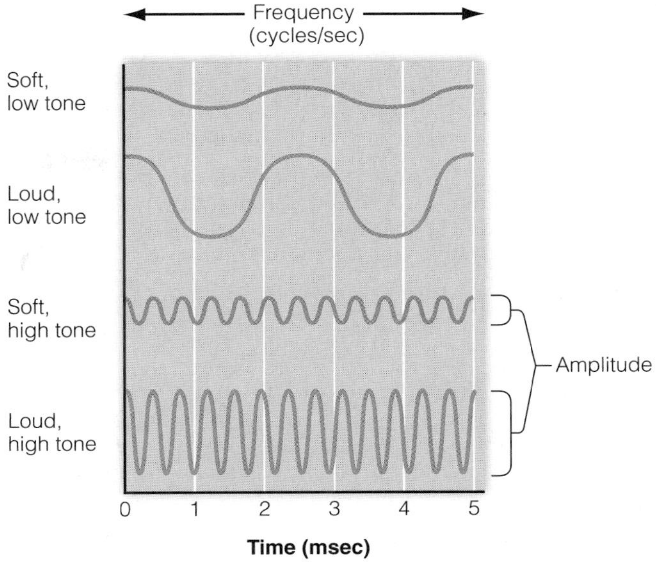


**Figure 12.8 Properties of sound waves.** Intensity (loudness) is determined by sound wave amplitude. Tone is determined by sound wave frequency.

When waves of sound strike the ear they cause vibration-sensitive mechanoreceptors deep within the ear to vibrate. The vibration causes the production of impulses that travel to the brain for interpretation.

## The outer ear channels sound waves

The human ear consists of three functionally different regions: the outer, middle, and inner ear (Figure 12.9).

The **outer ear** consists of the pinna, or visible portion of the ear, and the auditory canal. Sound waves arrive at the pinna and are directed into the auditory canal, which channels them to the **tympanic membrane (eardrum)**. The tympanic membrane serves as a partition between the outer and middle ears.

**Table 12.2 Common noises and your hearing**

| Sound | Decibels | How it affects your hearing |
|---|---|---|
| Rustling leaves | 20 | Does not cause hearing loss |
| Normal conversation | 50–60 | Does not cause hearing loss |
| Vacuum cleaner | 70 | Does not cause hearing loss |
| Power lawn mower | 85–100 | Cumulative exposure causes hearing loss; newer mowers may be quieter |
| Live rock concert | 110–130 | Definite risk of permanent hearing loss |
| Jackhammer | 120–150 | Definite risk of permanent hearing loss |
| Shotgun | 140 | One exposure likely to cause permanent hearing loss |
| Jet engine | 150 | One exposure likely to cause permanent hearing loss |

## The middle ear amplifies sound

The **middle ear** consists of an air-filled chamber within the temporal bone of the skull, bridged by three small bones called the malleus ("hammer"), incus ("anvil"), and stapes ("stirrup"). When sound waves strike the tympanic membrane, it moves back and forth slightly (vibrates). Vibration of the tympanic membrane makes the malleus, incus, and stapes vibrate. The stapes touches a smaller membrane, called the **oval window,** causing it to vibrate too.

All the vibrating force of the much larger tympanic membrane is now concentrated on the smaller oval window. In effect, the middle ear amplifies the sound waves severalfold. Amplification is essential because the oval window must vibrate with sufficient force to produce pressure waves in the watery fluid of the inner ear.

The air-filled middle ear is kept at atmospheric pressure by the **auditory tube** (eustachian tube), a narrow tube that runs from the middle ear chamber to the throat. Although the tube is normally held closed by the muscles along its sides, it opens briefly when you swallow or yawn to equalize air pressure in the middle ear with that of the surrounding atmosphere. When you change altitude quickly, your ears "pop" as the auditory tube opens briefly and air pressures are suddenly equalized. When you have a cold or allergy, inflammation and swelling may prevent the auditory tube from equalizing pressures normally, which is why airplane trips

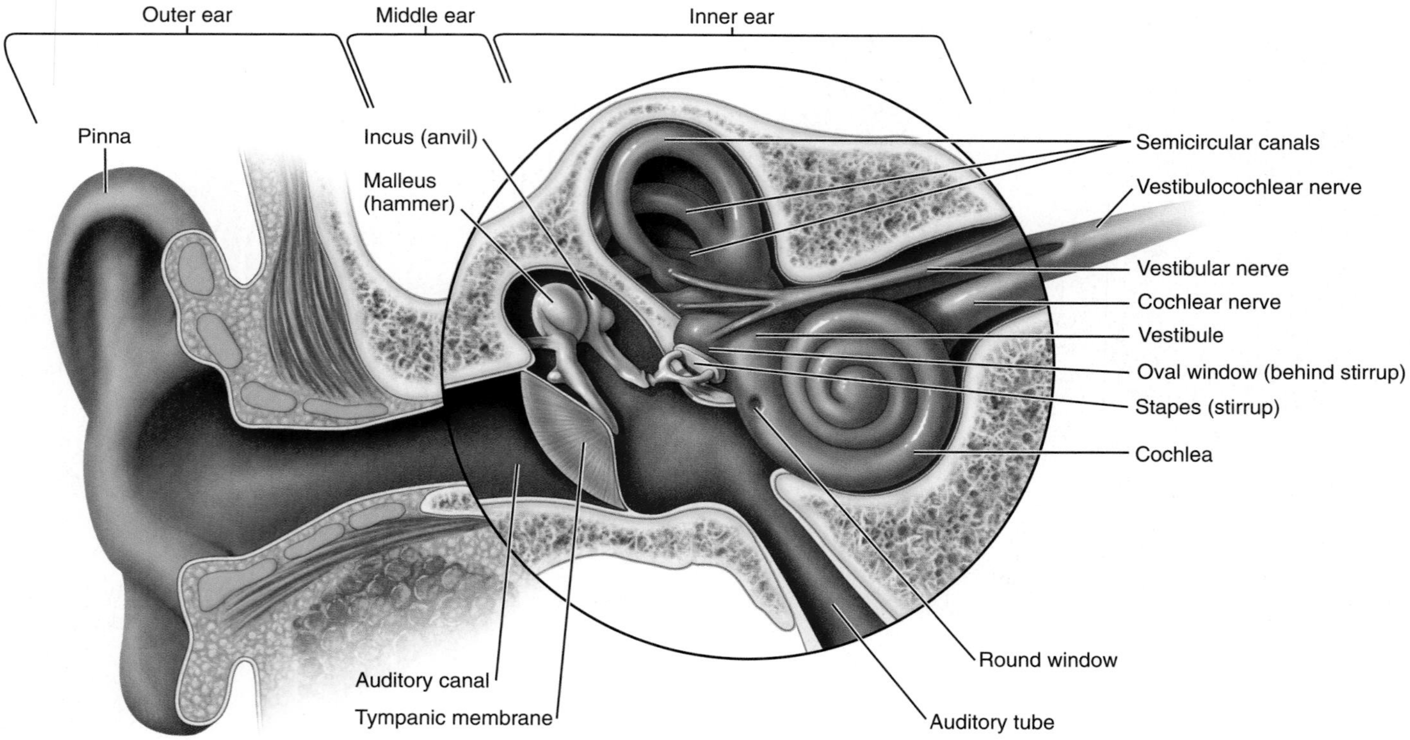


**Figure 12.9 Structure of the human ear.** The outer ear receives and channels sound, the middle ear amplifies sound, and the cochlea of the inner ear converts the sound to action potentials. The vestibule and the three semicircular canals are responsible for balance.

can be painful when you have a cold or allergies. Children tend to get a lot of earaches (middle ear infections) via the auditory tube until the skull elongates, changing the angle of the tube to the ear.

## The inner ear sorts and converts sounds

The **inner ear** sorts sounds by tone and converts them into impulses. It consists of the **cochlea,** where sound is converted, and the vestibular apparatus consisting of the vestibule and the three semicircular canals, which does not contribute to hearing at all. We will discuss the vestibular apparatus later in connection with the sense of balance.

The cochlea is a coiled structure shaped a bit like a snail. Figure 12.10a shows what the cochlea would look like if it were uncoiled. It is a tapered tube containing two interconnected outer canals called the vestibular canal and the tympanic canal, surrounding a third, closed fluid-filled space called the cochlear duct. The base of the cochlear duct is formed by the **basilar membrane.** The basilar membrane supports a population of about 15,000 **hair cells,** the mechanoreceptor cells of the ear. Hair cells have hairlike projections that are embedded in an overhanging structure called the **tectorial membrane** (the Latin word for "roof" is *tectum*), which is composed of a firm, gelatinous, noncellular material. Together, the hair cells and the tectorial membrane are called the organ of Corti, the organ that converts pressure waves to impulses.

When sound waves strike the oval window, it generates pressure waves in the watery fluid in the vestibular canal. These waves travel around the cochlea to the tympanic canal. Eventually the waves strike another membrane called the round window, which bulges inward and outward in synchrony with the oval window, dissipating some of the pressure.

Some of the pressure waves take a shortcut from the vestibular canal to the tympanic canal via the cochlear duct. These pressure waves cause the basilar membrane to vibrate like the strings of a musical instrument. The slight movement of the basilar membrane causes the hair cells above the membrane to vibrate as well. Because the hairs of the hair cells are embedded in the less movable tectorial membrane, vibration of the basilar membrane causes the hairs to bend. This physical movement of the hairs causes the hair cells to release more or less neurotransmitter, depending on which way the hairs are bent. The release of neurotransmitter in turn generates impulses in nearby sensory neurons (Figure 12.11). The impulses travel in neurons of the auditory nerve, which joins the vestibular nerve to become the vestibulocochlear nerve leading to the brain.

Vibrations of fluid in the vestibular and tympanic canals are of the same frequency as the original sound waves, which may be of many different tones at once. But because the fibers of the basilar membrane are different

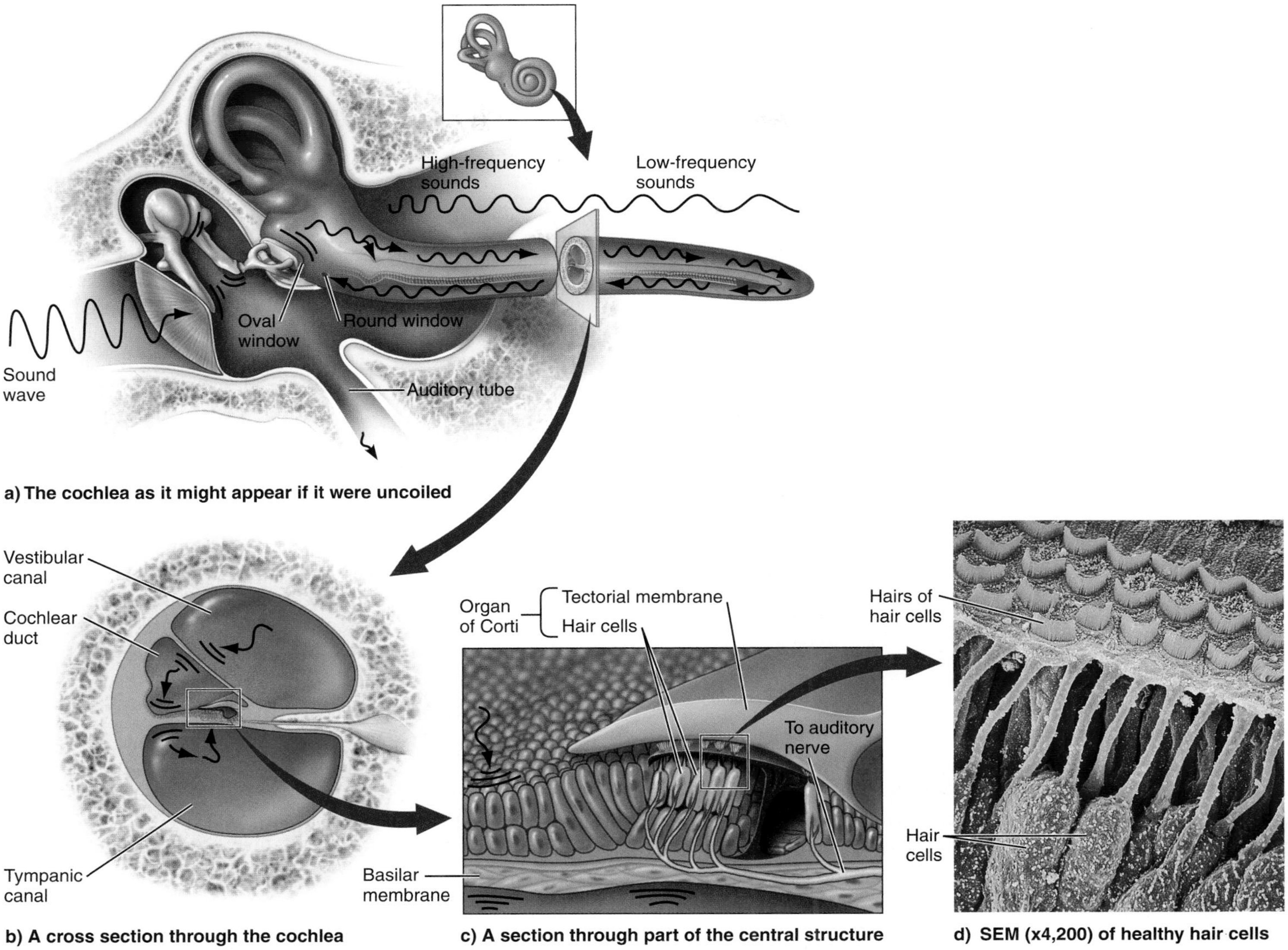


**Figure 12.10 Structure and function of the cochlea. (a)** The cochlea as it might appear if it were uncoiled. Higher-frequency sounds are converted to impulses nearer the oval window, whereas lower-frequency sounds are converted near the tapered tip. **(b)** A cross section through the cochlea, showing how pressure waves passing from vestibular canal to tympanic canal through the cochlear duct cause the basilar membrane to vibrate. **(c)** A section through part of the central structure shows the hair cells with their hairs embedded in the tectorial membrane. Vibration of the basilar membrane bends the hairs, ultimately generating impulses in sensory neurons **(d)** Healthy hair cells (SEM × 4,200).

lengths at different regions of the cochlea, sound waves are converted to vibrations of the basilar membrane in a location-specific manner according to tone. High-pitched tones vibrate the basilar membrane closer to the base of the cochlea (near the oval and round windows), whereas low-pitched tones vibrate the basilar membrane closer to the cochlear tip. The identical impulses generated in sensory neurons at these different locations are interpreted by the brain as sounds of specific tones on the basis of where they originated on the basilar membrane. This is yet another example of the location-specific nature of information processing by the brain.

**RECAP**

The outer ear receives and directs sound to the middle ear. The three bones of the middle ear amplify the sound and pass it to the cochlea. Vibrations of fluid in the cochlea cause the hairs of receptor hair cells to bend, generating action potentials in nearby neurons. ■

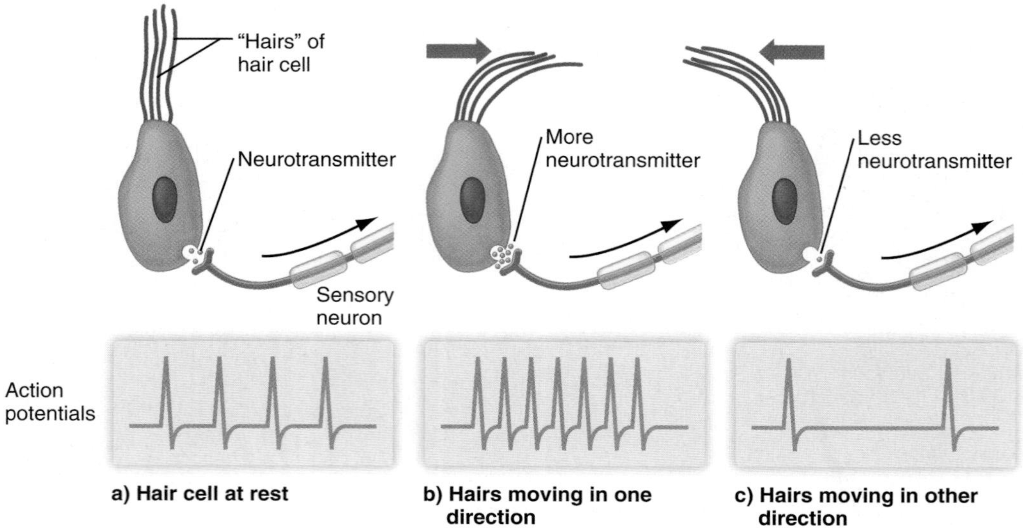


**Figure 12.11 How hair cells function as mechanoreceptors.** The hairs are actually modified cilia or microvilli.

## 12.5 The inner ear plays an essential role in balance

Maintaining your balance against gravity requires integration of multiple sensory inputs. Those sensory inputs include signals from the joint receptors, muscle spindles, and tendon receptors previously described as well as special structures associated with the inner ear. Even visual input is involved. The inner ear structures, described next, provide information about rotational movement, position, and linear acceleration of the head.

Looking again at the inner ear (Figure 12.12a), we see that next to the cochlea is the **vestibular apparatus,** a system of fluid-filled canals and chambers. The vestibular apparatus consists of three *semicircular canals* for sensing rotational movement of the head and body, and an area called the *vestibule,* which senses static (nonmoving) position and linear acceleration and deceleration.

The semicircular canals and the vestibule have mechanoreceptor-type hair cells embedded in a gel-like material. When the head moves or changes position, the gel also moves, although a bit more slowly because of inertia. The movement of the gel bends the hairs, which causes the hair cells to release a neurotransmitter that ultimately generates impulses in sensory neurons of the vestibular nerve.

### Sensing rotational movement

The three semicircular canals are fluid-filled tubes of bone. Near the end of each canal is a bulging region called the *ampulla* containing a soft, gel-like dome called the *cupula* (Figure 12.12b). Hairs of mechanoreceptor sensory neurons are embedded in the cupula.

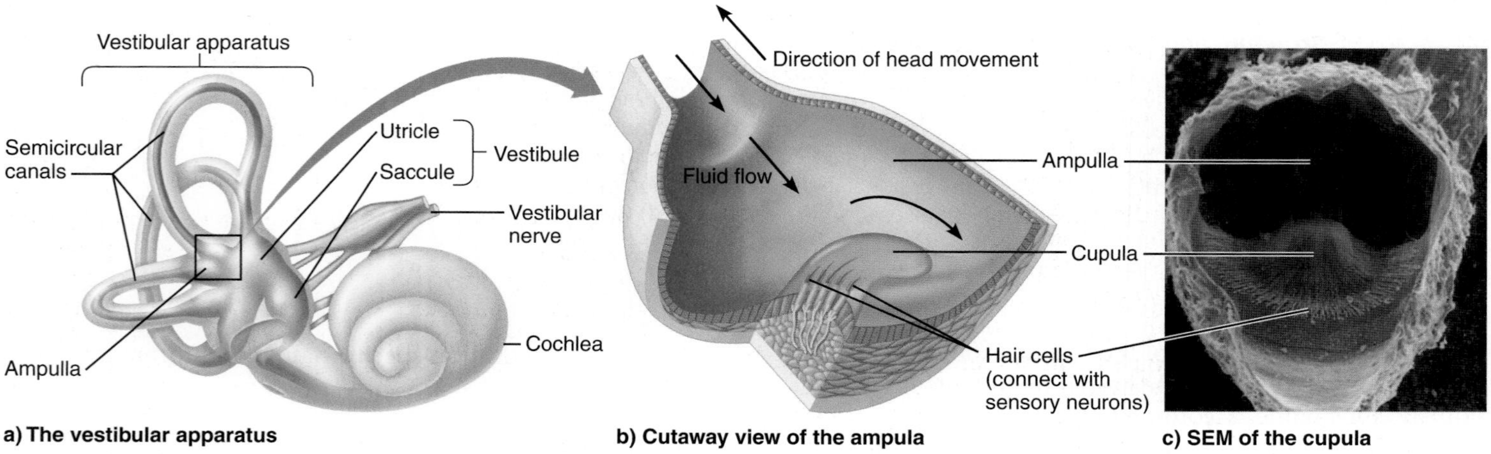


**Figure 12.12 The vestibular apparatus. (a)** The vestibular apparatus (the organ of balance) is part of the inner ear, which also includes the cochlea. **(b)** Cutaway view of the ampulla of a semicircular canal, showing the hair cells embedded in the base of the gel-like cupula. Rotational movement of the head causes fluid movement in the opposite direction in the semicircular canal. The fluid pushes against the cupula, bending it and activating the mechanoreceptor hairs of the hair cells. The hair cells release a neurotransmitter that stimulates sensory neurons of the vestibular nerve. **(c)** SEM of the cupula.

When you turn your head, the fluid in your semicircular canal moves more slowly than your head because of inertia. (See the Try It Yourself box on page 286.) The shifting position of the fluid bends the soft cupula and the hairs within it, producing impulses. The structure of the hairs enables them to detect the direction of the movement, in addition to movement in general. Because there are three semicircular canals and each is oriented on a different plane, together they can detect any and every possible rotational movement of the head.

### Sensing head position and acceleration

To sense the position of the head relative to the Earth, we need a mechanism that is sensitive to gravity. The two fluid-filled chambers of the vestibule, called the **utricle** and the **saccule,** each contain mechanoreceptor hair cells, gel, and hard crystals of bonelike material called **otoliths** (literally, "ear stones") (Figure 12.13).

The otoliths are embedded in the gel near the gel's surface, unattached to the bone wall of the vestibule. The otoliths are indeed like little rocks, and they are considerably heavier than the gel itself. When the head tips forward, for instance, the otoliths slide toward the center of the gravitational pull, causing the gel to slip and bending the hairs of hair cells (Figure 12.13a, b). Again, this produces impulses in nearby sensory neurons that are transmitted to the brain for interpretation.

The utricle and saccule respond to linear acceleration and deceleration as well as static position. When you are in a car that is accelerating rapidly, you feel like you are being pushed backward in your seat. This is the force of acceleration acting against your own inertia. Likewise, your otoliths are being pushed backward, causing the hair cells to bend (Figure 12.13c). The otoliths respond only to acceleration and deceleration (a change in linear velocity), and not to a constant rate of speed in one direction.

The unpleasant sensation we call "motion sickness" represents a physiological response to abnormal body motion and visual experience. Motion sickness may be due to conflicting sensory inputs from the vestibular apparatus, the eyes, and various receptors in muscles, tendons, and joints throughout the body. The CNS is unable to integrate these conflicting signals into an understandable whole, producing the characteristic symptoms of nausea, cold sweats, hyperventilation, and headache.

Table 12.3 summarizes the structures and functions of the ear.

**RECAP**

Rotational movement of the head is sensed as the result of movement of fluid in the three semicircular canals of the inner ear. Head position and linear acceleration are sensed as the result of movement of otoliths (ear stones) in the utricle and saccule of the inner ear. ■

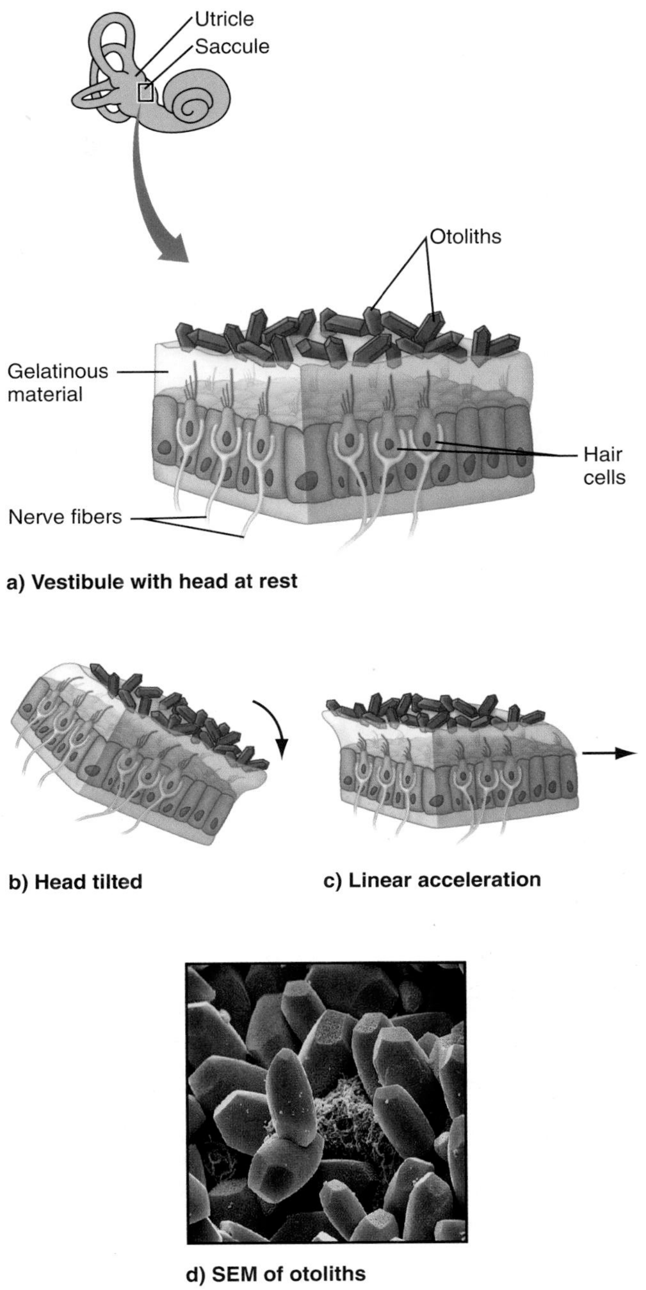


**Figure 12.13 How the utricle and saccule sense static head position and linear acceleration. (a)** A cutaway view of the vestibule with the head at rest. **(b)** A change of head position causes a shift in position of crystals of bonelike material called otoliths, which ultimately stimulates hair cells. **(c)** Linear acceleration also causes otoliths to shift position. **(d)** SEM of otoliths.

## 12.6 Vision: Detecting and interpreting visual stimuli

Light is a form of electromagnetic radiation that travels in waves at a speed of 186,000 miles per second. Our eyes allow us to receive and process light. They enable us to detect light from objects both nearby and distant and from

**Table 12.3 Structures and functions of the ear**

| Region of ear | Functions | Structures | |
|---|---|---|---|
| **Outer Ear** | Receives and channels sound | Pinna | |
| | | Auditory canal | |
| **Middle Ear** | Amplifies sound | Eardrum | Stapes |
| | | Malleus | Oval window |
| | | Incus | Auditory tube |
| **Inner Ear** | Sorts sounds by tone and converts them into impulses | Cochlea | Hair cells |
| | | Vestibular canal | Tectorial membrane |
| | | Tympanic canal | Organ of Corti |
| | | Cochlear duct | Round window |
| | | Basilar membrane | |
| | Senses rotational movements and converts them into impulses | Semicircular canals | Cupula |
| | | Ampulla | Hair cells |
| | Senses static (nonmoving) position and linear acceleration and deceleration; converts them into impulses | Vestibule | Otoliths |
| | | Utricle | Hair cells |
| | | Saccule | |

sources either dim or bright, from the candle in your hand to a star light-years away. But first we must collect and focus light onto specialized cells in our eyes called photoreceptors.

## Structure of the eye

The structure and functional components of the eye are illustrated in Figure 12.14 and summarized in Table 12.4. A tough outer coat known as the sclera, or "white of the eye," covers the outer surface except in the very front, where it is continuous with the clear **cornea.**

Light passes through the cornea and a space filled with fluid called *aqueous humor* that nourishes and cushions the cornea and lens. Light then either strikes the **iris,** a colored, disk-shaped muscle that determines how much light enters the eye, or passes through the **pupil,** the adjustable opening in the center of the iris. Light that passes through the pupil strikes the **lens,** a transparent, flexible structure attached by connective tissue fibers to a ring of circularly arranged smooth muscle called the *ciliary muscle.*

After passing through the main chamber of the eye filled with *vitreous humor,* light encounters the layers at the back and sides of the eye. This is the **retina,** comprising primarily photoreceptor cells, neurons, and a few blood vessels. Between the retina and the sclera at the back of the eye lies the choroid, consisting of pigmented cells and blood vessels. The pigmented cells absorb light not sensed by photoreceptors so that the image does not become distorted by reflected light, and the blood vessels nourish the retina. At the back of the eyeball is the **optic nerve,** which carries information to the thalamus, to be forwarded to the visual cortex for interpretation. Finally, skeletal muscles surround the eye and control its movements, so we can choose exactly where to look.

Two particular sites on the retina deserve special mention. The **fovea** is a small, funnel-shaped pit where the concentration of photoreceptors is higher than anywhere else in the eye. When we look directly at an object, we are focusing the image directly on the fovea. The **optic disk** is the area where the axons of the optic nerve exit the eye, so there are no photoreceptors there at all. The optic disk leaves us with a "blind spot" in each eye. (See the Try It Yourself box on page 289.)

**try it yourself**

### A Model of Fluid Movement in the Semicircular Canals

You can easily demonstrate the principle of fluid movement in the semicircular canals relative to movement of the head. Fill a glass half-full with water and place a few objects in it, such as peppercorns or peas. Now twist the glass a half-turn or so. Notice that the objects (and the water) move more slowly than the glass, especially if the movement of the container is rapid. The water and the objects appear to be flowing in the opposite direction from the container, but in fact they are just slow to get started. When you stop rotation of the glass, the opposite happens. The water and the objects are now in motion and so they continue to spin for a short time.

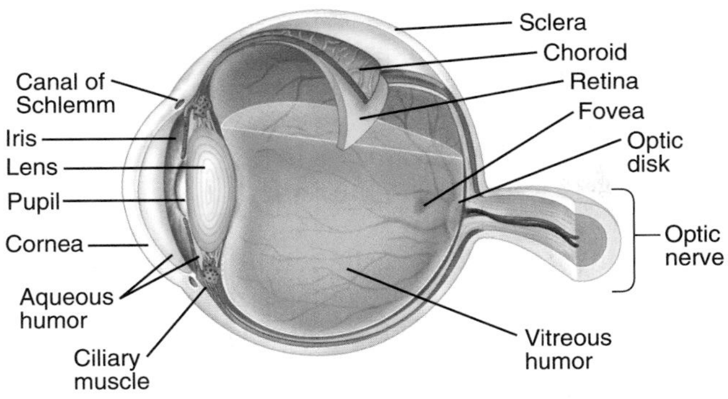


**Figure 12.14 Structure of the eye.** Light enters through the transparent cornea and passes through aqueous humor, the pupil, the lens, and vitreous humor before striking the retina at the back of the eye. The fovea is the area of the retina with the highest visual acuity. The nerves and blood vessels exit the eye through the optic disk.

**RECAP**

Light passes through the clear cornea, the adjustable opening in the iris called the pupil, the lens, and the aqueous fluid of the eye before striking the photoreceptors in the retina. ■

## Regulating the amount of light and focusing the image

The iris adjusts the amount of light entering the eye with two sets of smooth muscle. When bright light strikes the eye, contraction of muscle arranged circularly around the pupil causes the pupil to contract. Otherwise, the intensity of daylight would overwhelm our photoreceptors and temporarily blind us. In dim light, contraction of smooth muscle arranged radially around the pupil causes the pupil to dilate.

Nerves control each set of muscles. When examining an unconscious or injured person, a physician may shine a light in each eye. The pupils should contract in response to light and dilate when the light is removed. Pupils that are "fixed" (unresponsive to light) are a bad sign, possibly indicating more widespread failure of the nervous system.

Light entering the eye is focused by the cornea and the lens. The cornea, which is curved, is actually responsible for bending most of the incoming light. However, the curvature of the cornea is not adjustable. Our ability to regulate the degree to which incoming light is bent, and therefore our ability to change focus between near and far objects, is accomplished solely by adjusting the curvature of the lens. This is done by the ciliary muscle.

When the ciliary muscle contracts, the inner radius of the muscle shrinks, reducing the tension on the fibers attached to the lens. This allows the lens to bulge, and we focus on a near object. When the ciliary muscle relaxes, the ring of muscle increases the tension on the lens, stretching and flattening it and bringing more distant objects into focus (Figure 12.15). **Accommodation** refers to the adjustment of lens curvature so we can focus on either near or far objects.

**Table 12.4 Parts of the eye and their functions**

| Eye structure | Functions |
|---|---|
| Sclera | Covers and protects eyeball |
| Cornea | Bends incoming light (focuses light) |
| Aqueous humor | Nourishes and cushions cornea and lens |
| Iris | Adjusts amount of incoming light |
| Lens | Regulates focus |
| Ciliary muscle | Adjusts curvature of the lens |
| Vitreous humor | Transmits light to retina |
| Retina | Absorbs light and converts it into impulses |
| Rods | Photoreceptors responsible for black-and-white vision in dim light |
| Cones | Photoreceptors responsible for color vision and high visual acuity |
| Fovea | Contains greatest concentration of photoreceptors |
| Optic disk | "Blind spot" where optic nerve exits eye |
| Optic nerve | Transmits impulses to the brain |
| Choroid | Nourishes retina and absorbs light not absorbed by retinal photoreceptors |

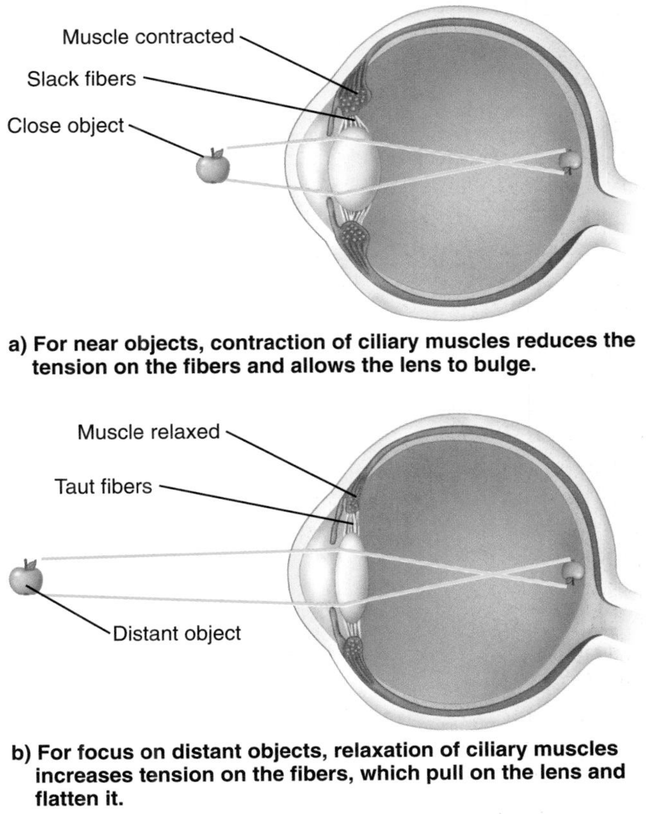


**Figure 12.15 Accommodation.** Notice that the images created on the retina are upside down.

The light rays from each point of an object are bent and focused so that the image created on the retina is inverted (upside down). However, the brain interprets the image as right side up.

As we get older, the lens tends to stiffen and cannot resume a bulging shape even when the ciliary muscles are maximally contracted. The result is *presbyopia,* the inability to focus on nearby objects, which generally appears after age 40. People with presbyopia must hold reading material farther away to see the print clearly. Reading glasses can easily correct presbyopia.

## Eyeball shape affects focus

Differences in the shape of the eyeball can affect the ability to focus properly (Figure 12.16).

*Myopia* is a common inherited condition in which the eyeball is slightly longer than normal (more rarely, myopia occurs when the ciliary muscle contracts too strongly). Even when the lens is flattened maximally, distant objects focus in front of the retina. People with myopia can see nearby objects, but distant objects are out of focus, which is why it is called nearsightedness. Concave lenses, which bend incoming light so it focuses on the retina, can correct nearsightedness.

Less common is the opposite condition, *hyperopia* (farsightedness), which occurs when the eyeball is too short and nearby objects focus behind the retina. Farsighted people can see distant objects clearly, but nearby objects are out of focus. Convex lenses correct farsightedness.

*Astigmatism* refers to blurred vision caused by irregularities of the shape of the cornea or lens. The result is that light is scattered and may not focus evenly on the retina. Astigmatism can be corrected with specially ground lenses that exactly compensate for the irregularities of the cornea and lens.

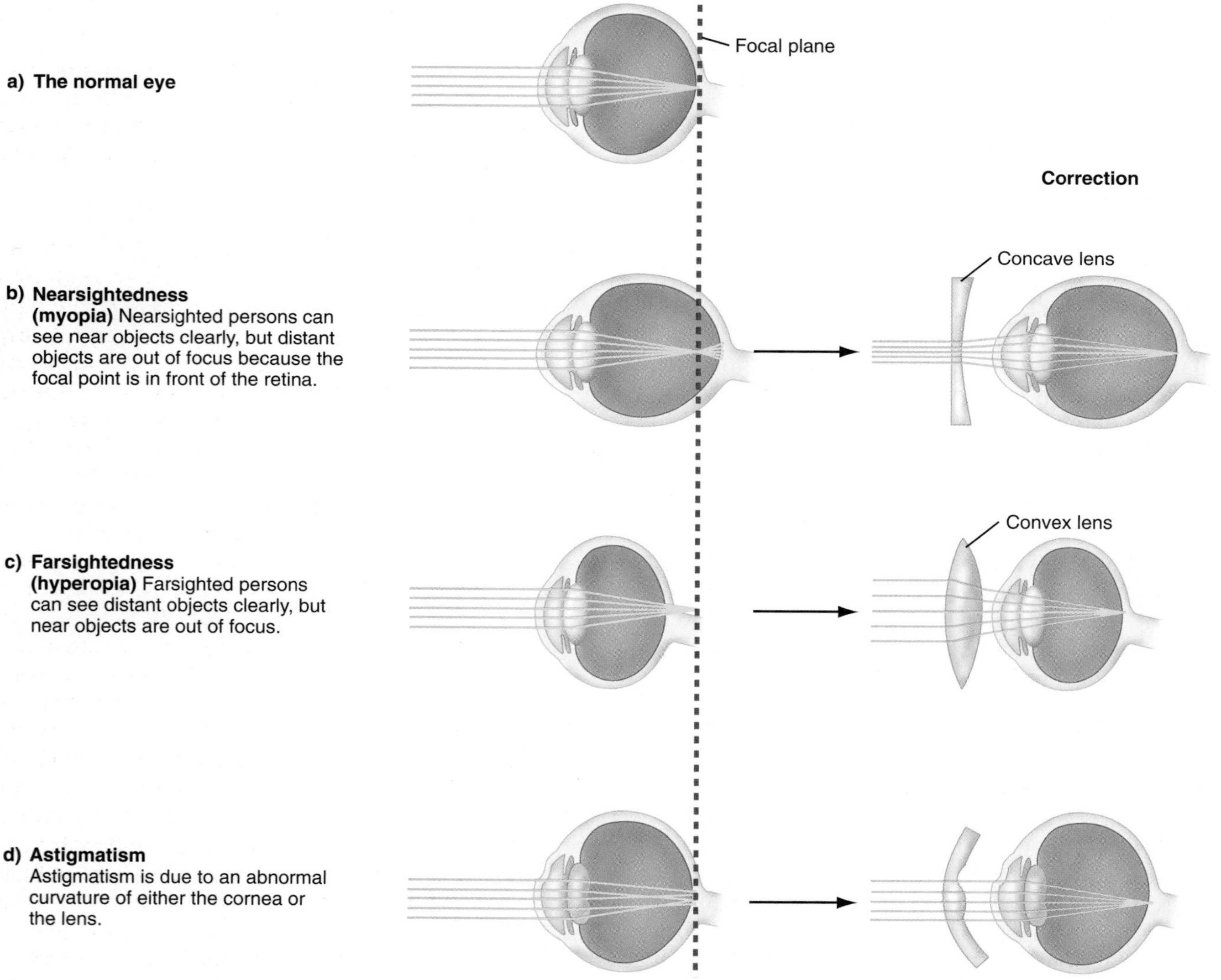


**Figure 12.16 Examples of abnormal vision.** All three types of abnormal vision are correctable.

**RECAP**

The iris regulates the amount of light entering the eye, and the cornea and the lens adjust the focus. Problems that affect the ability to focus include presbyopia, nearsightedness, farsightedness, and astigmatism. ■

## Light is converted into action potentials

Like other sensory organs, the eyes convert a stimulus (light) into impulses. In the eye this process occurs in the retina. The unique structure of the retina allows us to see in color, adapt to varying light intensities, and perceive images of the world around us.

Figure 12.17 shows a close-up of the retina, which consists of four layers:

1. The outermost layer consists of pigmented cells that, along with the choroid, absorb light not captured by the photoreceptor cells.
2. Next is a layer of photoreceptor cells called **rods** and **cones** because of their shapes.
3. The rods and cones synapse with the third layer, a layer of neurons called bipolar cells. Bipolar cells partially process and integrate information and then pass it on to the fourth layer.
4. The innermost layer consists of ganglion cells. Ganglion cells are also neurons. Their long axons become the optic nerve going to the brain.

Notice that light must pass through the third and fourth layers to reach the photoreceptor cells, but this does not significantly hinder the ability of the photoreceptor cells to receive and convert light.

## Rods and cones respond to light

Figure 12.18 takes a closer look at the photoreceptor cells, rods and cones. One end of the cell consists of a series of flattened disks arranged to form either a rod- or cone-shaped structure, as the names imply. The flattened disks contain numerous molecules of a particular light-sensitive protein called a *photopigment.*

A photopigment protein undergoes a change of shape when it is exposed to energy in the form of light. The change in photopigment molecule shape causes the photoreceptor (rod or cone) to close some of its sodium channels and reduce the amount of neurotransmitter it normally releases. Because the neurotransmitter released by rods or cones normally inhibits the bipolar cells, light ultimately increases the activity of the bipolar cells, which in turn activate the ganglion cells.

There are approximately 120 million rods and 6 million cones, but only 1 million ganglion cells with axons going to the brain. Clearly, a great deal of convergence and summation of signals occurs at each level of neuron transfer.

## Rods provide vision in dim light

Rods all have the same photopigment, called **rhodopsin.** As we have seen, there are about 20 times more rods than cones. If we imagine that all 120 million rods converge on only half of the ganglion cells (one-half million), there would be 240 rods converging on a single ganglion cell. This means that the ganglion cells supplied by rods are highly sensitive to dim light. However they cannot detect color and they do not give us detailed images.

Rods function in dim light, but they do not detect color or detailed images. They give us only black-and-white vision, which is why objects appear less colorful and images are not as sharp in dim light.

Rods and cones are not distributed evenly on the retina. Regions of the retina farthest away from the fovea have the highest ratio of rods to cones. If you want to see a dim star at night, don't look directly at it—look off to the side just a little.

## Cones provide color vision and accurate images

Not all animals perceive color, but humans do. We are able to see colors because we have three different kinds of cones: red, green, and blue. Each contains a photopigment that absorbs the energy of red, green, or blue light particularly well.

Our ability to distinguish a variety of colors is due to the way the brain interprets the ratios of impulses coming from the ganglion cells connected to the three types of cones. When all three types are activated by all different wavelengths, we perceive white light. The perception of black is no light at all.

Cones also are responsible for visual acuity (accurate and detailed vision). However, cones require stronger light to be activated because the cone photopigments are much less sensitive to light than the rhodopsin in rods. This is why your ability to distinguish between colors declines in dim light and it becomes difficult to tell whether a dark-colored car is green or red. In dim light you are seeing primarily with your rods, which can detect only black and white.

**try it yourself**

### Find Your Blind Spot

You can locate the blind spot in each eye with the following demonstration. Cover your left eye and hold this page 4 inches in front of your face. Focus on the square with your right eye, then move the book slowly away until the circle disappears. The circle disappears because at this distance from your eye, its image is striking the blind spot of your right eye.

Try the same demonstration with your left eye by focusing on the circle with your right eye closed. In this case the square disappears when the image strikes the blind spot of your left eye.

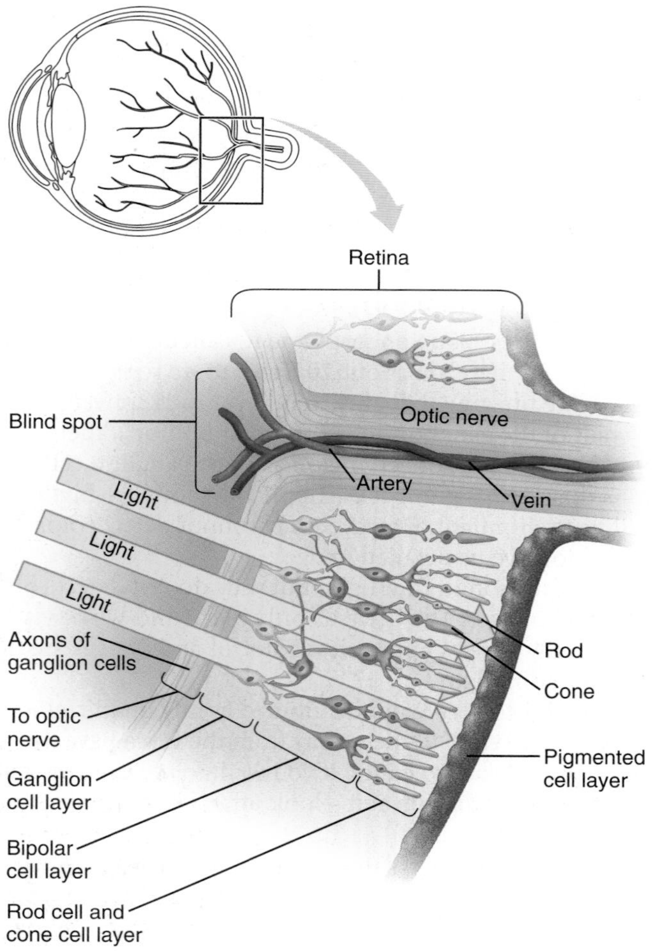


**Figure 12.17 Structure of the retina.** Light must pass between the axons of the ganglion cells and through the ganglion and bipolar cell layers to reach the photoreceptor cells, the rods and cones.

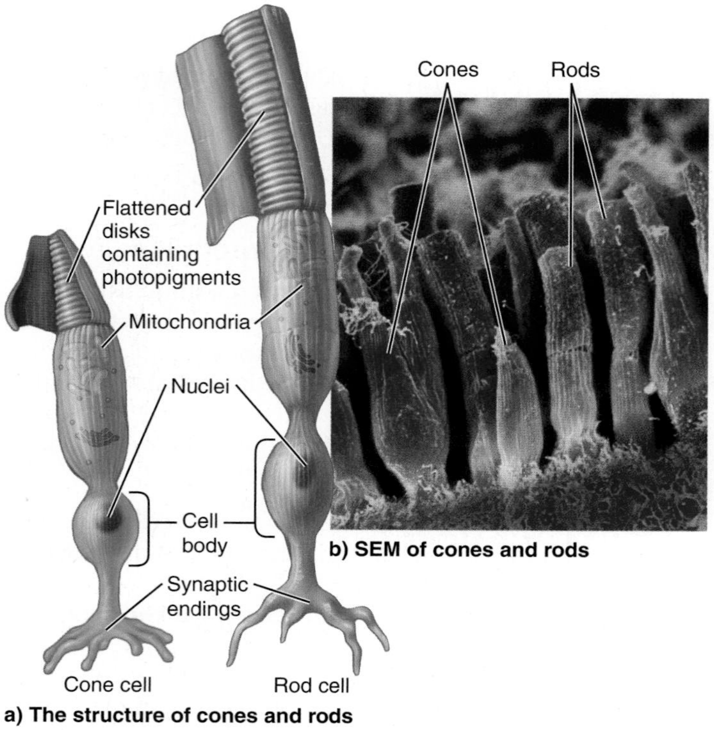


**Figure 12.18 The photoreceptor cells, cones and rods.** **(a)** The structure of cone and rod cells. The photopigments in the flattened disks are sensitive to light. **(b)** SEM of cones and rods.

## Visual receptors adapt

From your own experience you know that vision adapts to changing light conditions over several seconds or minutes. Adaptation seems to take longer when going from bright to dim light than it does in the opposite direction. Adaptation depends on rapid adjustment of the pupil by the iris and on adaptation by the rods.

The absorption of light by rhodopsin "uses up" the photopigment temporarily. Light energy actually breaks the rhodopsin into two molecules. These molecules can be resynthesized into rhodopsin again, but only over a period of minutes.

When you have been out in bright light, most of the rhodopsin in the light-sensitive rods has been broken down. Then, when you enter a dim room and the cones no longer are functioning, there is not enough intact rhodopsin for good vision in dim light. With time (5–15 minutes) the rhodopsin is resynthesized and available again.

Conversely, when you go out into sunlight from a dimly lit room, the light seems very bright because you have the maximal amount of photopigment available in both rods and cones. Most of the rhodopsin in the rods is quickly used up, however, and you revert to using primarily cones in bright light.

**RECAP**

Light energy alters the structure of photopigments—rhodopsin in rods, and red, blue, or green photopigments in cones. Rods provide vision in dim light. Cones are responsible for color vision and detailed images. ■

# 12.7 Disorders of sensory mechanisms

## Disorders of the ears

**Deafness: loss of hearing** Deafness can have many causes. Deafness caused by damage to hair cells (Figure 12.19) is called **nerve deafness** because sounds cannot be converted into impulses in sensory nerves. Nerve deafness is generally the result of frequent exposure to loud sounds. Damage to the tympanic membrane or the bones of the middle ear, on the other hand, is called **conduction deafness.** In conduction deafness sound waves simply are not transferred to the inner ear at all. Conduction deafness is frequently due to arthritis of the middle ear bones.

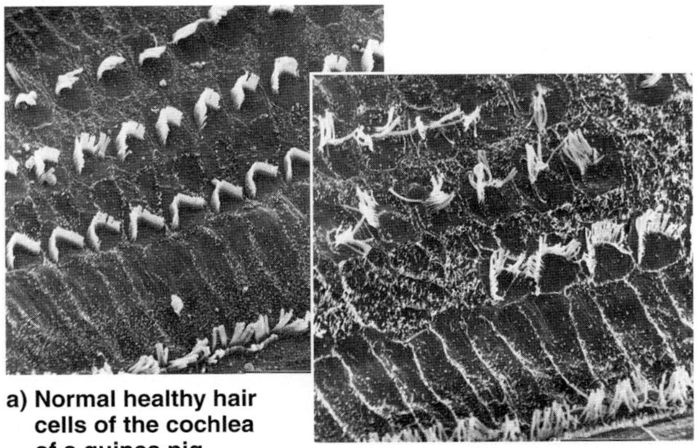

a) Normal healthy hair cells of the cochlea of a guinea pig.

b) Hair cells after 24 hours of exposure to loud sounds.

**Figure 12.19 Damage to hair cells in the ears.**

Some types of hearing loss may be partially corrected with a hearing aid, which amplifies incoming sounds, but even amplification won't be very effective if hair cells are missing. Some people with nerve deafness benefit from a cochlear implant, a tiny implanted microprocessor that converts sound waves into electrical signals.

**Otitis media: Inflammation of the middle ear** A common cause of earache is *otitis media,* or inflammation of the middle ear. Usually this results from an upper respiratory tract infection that extends up the auditory tube. The tube may become blocked and trap fluid in the middle ear. Otitis media usually responds to antibiotics.

**Ménière's syndrome: Inner ear condition impairs hearing and balance** Ménière's syndrome is a chronic condition of the inner ear. The cause is unknown, but it may be due to excess fluid in the cochlea and semicircular canals. Symptoms include repeated episodes of dizziness and nausea accompanied by progressive hearing loss. Balance is usually affected to the point that patients find it difficult to stay upright. Mild cases can be treated with motion sickness medications. Severe cases may benefit from surgery to drain excess fluid from the inner ear.

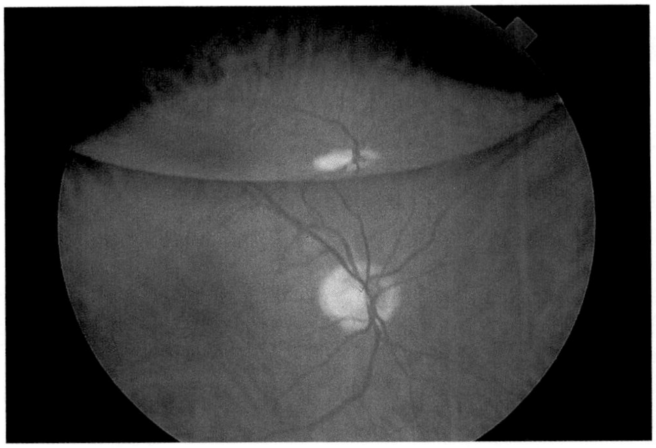

**a) Retinal detachment.** In this ophthalmoscope view of a patient's eye the retina has peeled away from the choroid (upper third of the eye). At lower center is the yellow optic disk, through which the blood vessels travel.

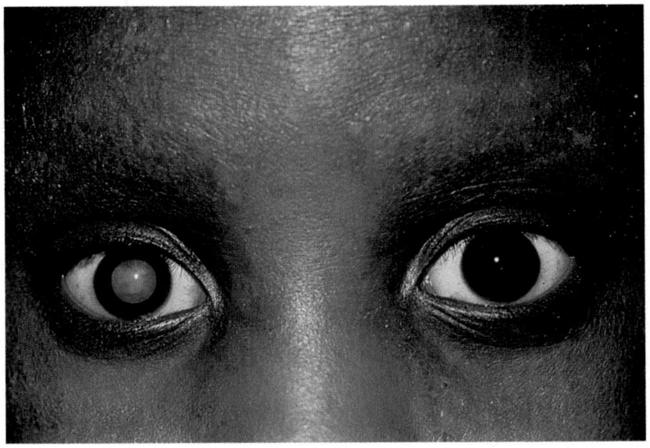

**b) Cataracts.** The cataract in this person's right eye was caused by a chronic inflammatory disease process.

**Figure 12.20 Common eye disorders.**

## Disorders of the eyes

**Retinal detachment: Retina separates from choroid** If the thin retina is torn, the vitreous humor may leak through the tear and peel the retina away from the choroid, like peeling wallpaper from a wall (Figure 12.20a). The most common cause of retinal detachment is a blow to the head. The detached region of the retina loses most of its blood supply and its ability to focus an image properly. Symptoms include flashes of light, blurred vision, or loss of peripheral vision. Retinal detachment is an emergency, but prompt surgery can usually repair the damage.

**Cataracts: The lens becomes opaque** Cataracts are a decrease in the normal transparency of a lens (Figure 12.20b). Normally, the lens contains a particular kind of protein folded in such a way that it is transparent. If the delivery of nutrients to the lens is not sufficient, these proteins may denature, or clump, making the lens opaque. Some cataracts are congenital, but most are age-related or secondary to diabetes or other diseases. The treatment, which is usually successful, involves removing the lens surgically and replacing it with an artificial lens.

**Glaucoma: Pressure inside the eye rises** As mentioned previously, a clear fluid called aqueous humor fills the chamber between the cornea and the lens. Capillaries located near the ciliary muscles of the eye produce aqueous humor, which brings nutrients and oxygen to the lens and cornea and carries away wastes. Normally, aqueous humor is drained from the eye and returned to the venous blood by a vessel called the canal of Schlemm (review Figure 12.14). Glaucoma is a condition in which this drainage vessel becomes blocked. The excess fluid increases pressure inside the eye and compresses blood vessels supplying the retina. Cells of the retina or optic nerve may eventually die, impairing vision and ultimately leading to blindness. The impairment of vision often starts as a loss of peripheral vision (Figure 12.21).

Glaucoma generally develops slowly and painlessly over several years, without

a) Normal vision.

b) Same scene as it might be viewed by a person with glaucoma.

**Figure 12.21 Glaucoma.**

any outward symptoms. Most patients do not realize they have it until they have already lost some vision. Less commonly, glaucoma develops acutely (within hours) with symptoms of blurred vision and red, swollen, sometimes painful eyes. Acute glaucoma is a medical emergency that requires immediate attention by an eye doctor.

Both chronic (slow-onset) and acute glaucoma can be detected with a simple test that measures the pressure in the eye. If it is detected early enough, glaucoma can be controlled with drugs or surgery before any permanent damage is done. However, any vision that has already been lost cannot be restored. This is why a test of pressure in the eye is usually included in any comprehensive eye examination.

**Color blindness: Inability to distinguish the full range of colors** Color blindness is a general term for the inability to distinguish the full range of colors. Most forms of color blindness are caused by deficient numbers of particular types of cones. Less common are conditions in which one of the three cones is completely missing.

People with red-green color blindness, the most common form, are deficient in either red cones or green cones. They have trouble distinguishing between red and green, or they perceive them as the same color. The color they see is red or green, depending on which type of cone is missing.

The inability to perceive any color at all is quite rare in humans because it occurs only when two of the three cones are completely missing.

Color blindness is often inherited. Red-green color blindness is an X-linked recessive trait that is more common in men than in women (see Chapter 19). It affects approximately 8% of Caucasian males but only 1% of Caucasian females, and is less common in other races. Traffic lights always have the red ("stop") light at the top and the green ("go") light at the bottom so that color-blind people can tell them apart by position. Color blindness is easily tested with a series of colored test plates (Figure 12.22).

**RECAP**

Earaches are most often caused by infections of the middle ear. A detached retina is a retina that has separated from the underlying choroid. Glaucoma is a condition in which fluid pressure inside the eye rises, constricting the blood vessels that normally supply the living cells. ■

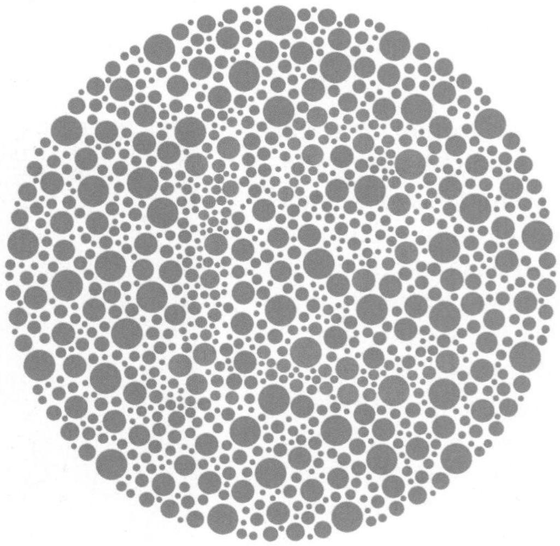

**Figure 12.22 Test plate for diagnosing color blindness.** A person with red-green color blindness would not be able to see the number 12 in this test plate. The original plate should be used for accurate testing of color blindness.

**Current Issue**

# Do Portable Music Players Endanger Your Hearing?

Do you enjoy taking your music with you? Join the club: portable music players, like the Discman, and MP3 players, such as the iPod, are more popular than ever. Apple has sold more than 150 million iPods. However, some music fans have sued the company, claiming that the iPod's design endangers listeners' hearing by exposing them to loud noise levels.

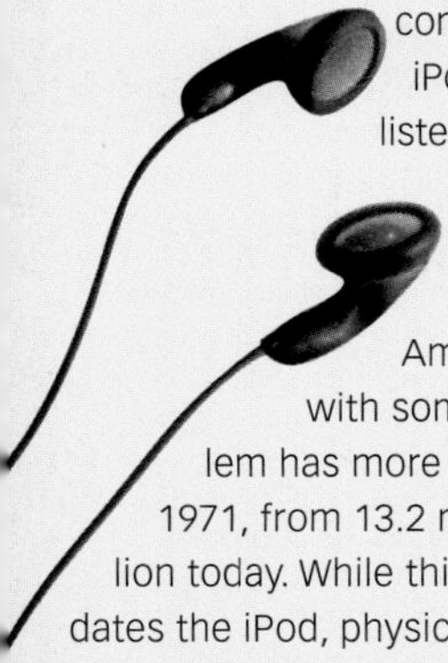

The number of Americans age 3 and older with some type of hearing problem has more than doubled since 1971, from 13.2 million to about 30 million today. While this trend obviously predates the iPod, physicians worry that the widespread popularity of portable music devices such as the iPod will only accelerate the trend.

### Loud Sounds Damage or Kill Hair Cells

Sound is measured in decibels (see Table 12.2). According to the Occupational Safety and Health Administration (OSHA), sustained noise over 85 decibels may be enough to produce at least some hearing loss. Louder sounds produce damage in a shorter time. For example, music played at 100 decibels may produce hearing loss after just two hours; 115 decibels can cause damage in less than 10 minutes.

Loud sounds cause excessive vibration of the hair cells of the ear's cochlea, breaking the delicate hairs embedded in the tectorial membrane. Although some temporary loss of hearing due to damage to the hairs is reversible, repeated or excessive damage can kill the entire hair cell. Hair cells are not replaced, so when you lose them they are gone forever. Often the loss of hair cells occurs so slowly over time that people do not notice it until the damage is fairly advanced.

### Are Portable Music Devices a Problem?

A few countries now limit the maximum amplitude permitted from portable music devices. Apple was forced to redesign its iPods sold in France because the devices exceeded the allowable limit of 100 decibels. However, more powerful iPods are still sold in the U.S. The first lawsuit against Apple charges that iPods sold in the U.S. are "inherently defective in design" because they can generate more than 115 decibels. The plaintiffs also charge that Apple's support literature includes such phrases as "crank up the tunes," encouraging listening at excessive volume. Apple counters that each iPod sold carries a warning that "permanent hearing loss may occur if earphones or headphone are used at high volume."

Some audiologists claim that the widespread use of earbuds instead of headphones only compounds the problem. Earbuds position the sound less than an inch from the eardrum. If you turn up the volume to try to compensate for the background noise of a busy street or a subway, you have a recipe for trouble.

Of course, portable music devices may be popular with consumers precisely because they can deliver high-volume sound without signal distortion, anywhere, any time. As a result, people are listening longer and at higher volumes than in the past. Is that Apple's fault or just a sign of their success?

### Protecting Your Hearing

What can you do to protect your hearing? Brian Fligor, director of diagnostic audiology at Children's Hospital in Boston, recommends a listening limit of one hour per day at 60% of maximum volume. This should be easily audible but still below the 85 decibel level at which hearing damage begins.

Some experts recommend replacing those earbuds with earphones that work like earplugs to block out ambient noise. Alternatively, consider noise-canceling headphones that actively remove background noise. Noise-canceling headphones aren't cheap and they aren't likely to be popular with active, image-conscious teenagers, but they allow the listener to reduce the music's volume to a safer level. And if you ever notice that you suffer a temporary change in hearing after playing music, turn down the volume next time.

### Questions to consider

**1** *Should portable music devices come with information about decibel levels achieved at each volume setting?*

**2** *Whose responsibility is it to turn down (or limit) the volume? If users do suffer hearing loss, should they be able to sue the manufacturers?*

### the facts...

- Some portable music players can reach sound levels of 115 decibels, a level that can lead to permanent hearing loss.
- Earbuds channel loud music directly to the eardrum, increasing the risk of hearing loss.
- A safe guideline is to limit listening to one hour per day at 60% of maximum volume.

# Chapter Summary

### Receptors receive and convert stimuli *p. 273*

- Receptors convert the energy of a stimulus into impulses in sensory neurons.
- The brain interprets incoming impulses on the basis of where the sensory neurons originate.
- Some types of receptors adapt to continuous stimulation, whereas others (most notably pain receptors) do not.
- The somatic senses (temperature, touch, vibration, pressure, pain, and awareness of body position and movements) arise from receptors throughout the body.
- The five special senses (taste, smell, hearing, balance, and vision) arise from only certain specialized areas of the body.

### Somatic sensations arise from receptors throughout the body *p. 275*

- The skin contains receptors for heat, cold, vibration, pressure, light touch, and pain. Receptors for temperature and for pain are also located in some internal organs.
- Receptors in joints sense joint position.
- Muscle spindles sense muscle length, and tendon receptors sense tendon (and muscle) tension.

### Taste and smell depend on chemoreceptors *p. 278*

- Chemoreceptors for taste are located in structures called taste buds, most of which are on the tongue.
- The receptors for smell (called olfactory receptors) are located in the nasal passages. Humans have over 1,000 different olfactory receptor types.

### Hearing: Mechanoreceptors detect sound waves *p. 280*

- The outer ear channels sound waves to the tympanic membrane, the middle ear amplifies the sound waves, and the cochlea of the inner ear converts sound waves to impulses.
- Sound waves of different tones are converted to impulses at different locations in the cochlea.

### The inner ear plays an essential role in balance *p. 284*

- The vestibular apparatus of the inner ear consists of three semicircular canals and the vestibule.
- The semicircular canals are structures that sense rotational movement of the head on three planes.
- Structures of the vestibule sense static (nonmoving) head position and linear acceleration.

### Vision: Detecting and interpreting visual stimuli *p. 285*

- The eye is the organ of vision, with structures for moving the eye (muscles), regulating the amount of light entering the eye (iris), focusing the visual image (lens), and converting light to impulses (retina).
- The photoreceptor cells in the retina are called rods and cones.
- Rods are 20 times more numerous than cones. They give us vision in dim light, but not in color and not with the highest detail.
- The three types of cones have different photopigments, so each type responds best to a different wavelength (color) of light. Cones are most effective in bright light, and they give us color vision and the sharpest image.
- Photoreceptors adapt to conditions of varying light intensities (brightness). It takes about 15 minutes to fully adapt to very dim light.

### Disorders of sensory mechanisms *p. 290*

- Inflammation of the middle ear is a common cause of earache.
- Common eye disorders include retinal detachment, cataracts, glaucoma, and color blindness.

# Terms You Should Know

accommodation, *287*
auditory tube, *281*
basilar membrane, *282*
cochlea, *282*
cones, *289*
cornea, *286*
hair cell, *282*
iris, *286*
lens, *286*
muscle spindle, *276*
olfactory receptor cell, *280*
photoreceptor, *273*
receptor adaptation, *274*
retina, *286*
rhodopsin, *289*
rods, *289*
somatic sensations, *275*
special senses, *275*
taste bud, *278*
tympanic membrane (eardrum), *281*
vestibular apparatus, *284*

# Concept Review

1. List the five classifications of receptors in terms of types of stimulus they convert.
2. Describe how receptor adaptation works.
3. Describe what information the somatic sensations provide.
4. Name the five special senses.
5. Compare and contrast fast pain, slow pain, and referred pain.
6. Describe the overall function of the three bones (the malleus, the incus, and the stapes) of the middle ear.
7. The eye contains both skeletal muscle and smooth muscle. Describe where each is located and indicate their functions.
8. Compare and contrast rods and cones.
9. Explain why it may take up to 15 minutes to become fully adapted to very dim light conditions.
10. Explain what causes glaucoma.

# Test Yourself

### Matching Exercise

_____ 1. A structure specialized to receive a certain stimulus
_____ 2. A cluster of about 50 receptor and supporting cells for taste
_____ 3. Becoming consciously aware of a stimulus received by the central nervous system
_____ 4. Understanding the meaning of a stimulus received by the central nervous system
_____ 5. Hard crystals of bonelike material that are important to our ability to sense position of the head
_____ 6. A protein in the photoreceptor cells of the eye that changes shape when exposed to light

a. taste bud
b. sensation
c. receptor
d. perception
e. photopigment
f. otoliths

### Fill in the Blank

7. Both taste and smell depend on the class of receptors called ____________________.
8. The four (or five) primary taste qualities are ____________________, ____________________, ____________________, ____________________, and (____________________).
9. Acute pain or ____________________ pain is typically caused by physical pressure or heat.
10. The hairs of hair cells that convert sound waves to nerve impulses are embedded in the ____________________ membrane.
11. The photoreceptor cells of the eye are called ____________________ and ____________________.
12. Light is bent and focused on the retina by the cornea and the lens, but only the ____________________ has an adjustable curvature.

### True or False?

13. Visual and auditory sensory input are both received by the brain in exactly the same form—as action potentials (impulses).
14. Rotational movement of the head is sensed by the three semicircular canals of the inner ear.
15. Rods contain a photopigment called rhodopsin.

## References and Additional Reading

Smith, David V., and Robert F. Margolskee. Making Sense of Taste. *Scientific American*, March 2001, pp. 32–39. (An in-depth review of how taste receptors and taste neurons work.)

### Internet References

Find links to the following Web sites at the Human Biology Place.

**Anatomy, Physiology & Pathology of the Human Eye**
**www.tedmontgomery.com/the_eye**
Developed by an optometrist, this site includes exercises and quizzes to test your knowledge of the eye.

**hear-it**
**www.hear-it.org**
A noncommercial site with good information on hearing loss, hearing loss prevention, hearing aids, and living with impaired hearing.

**National Eye Institute**
**www.nei.nih.gov**
This member of the National Institutes of Health contains up-to-date information on eye health and eye diseases.

**National Institute on Deafness and Other Communication Disorders**
**www.nidcd.nih.gov**
A good site for information on hearing, ear infections, and deafness.

## Apply What You Know

1. With the eyes closed, would an astronaut in outer space be able to detect lateral movement of the head (would the semicircular canals be functioning normally)? Would the astronaut be able to detect static head position (would the utricle and saccule be functioning normally)? Explain.
2. Why do you suppose that you are not normally aware of the blind spot in each eye?
3. Our sense of smell is closely linked to our feelings and emotions. Bad odors usually evoke negative feelings, whereas pleasant odors give us a general sense of well-being or may be associated with good memories (perfume makers know this). The house of a pet owner can have an odor that a guest finds objectionable but the owner may not even be aware of. With a long enough visit even the guest may not notice the pet odors. Why is this?
4. Walk into any drugstore and you'll find dozens of over-the-counter products for reducing pain. Why is the experience of pain so common and so problematic?
5. An amateur boxer reported on an online forum that he saw lights flash before his eyes after being hit on the top of the head. This was unusual since he's normally hit in the chin or ear and knows what it's like to brownout during a knockout blow. Once the lights faded he was able to continue the fight. What happened when he was hit on the top of the head?
6. Try taking a really, really deep breath. If done correctly there should be a moment of sharp pain in your chest. What's causing this?
7. What do you think might cause motion sickness, the combination of nausea and dizziness that some people get after a roller-coaster ride or when riding in a boat or a car? And why don't gymnasts get motion sick when they're performing?

*Answers can be found on the Human Biology Place.*

# 13 The Endocrine System

1 What is a **hormone**?

2 Hormones can take anywhere from **30 seconds** to **several years** to exert their effect—very long times compared to nerves. Why so long?

3 If a hormone circulates in blood everywhere at the same concentration, why does it affect only **certain** tissues?

4 What causes **diabetes**?

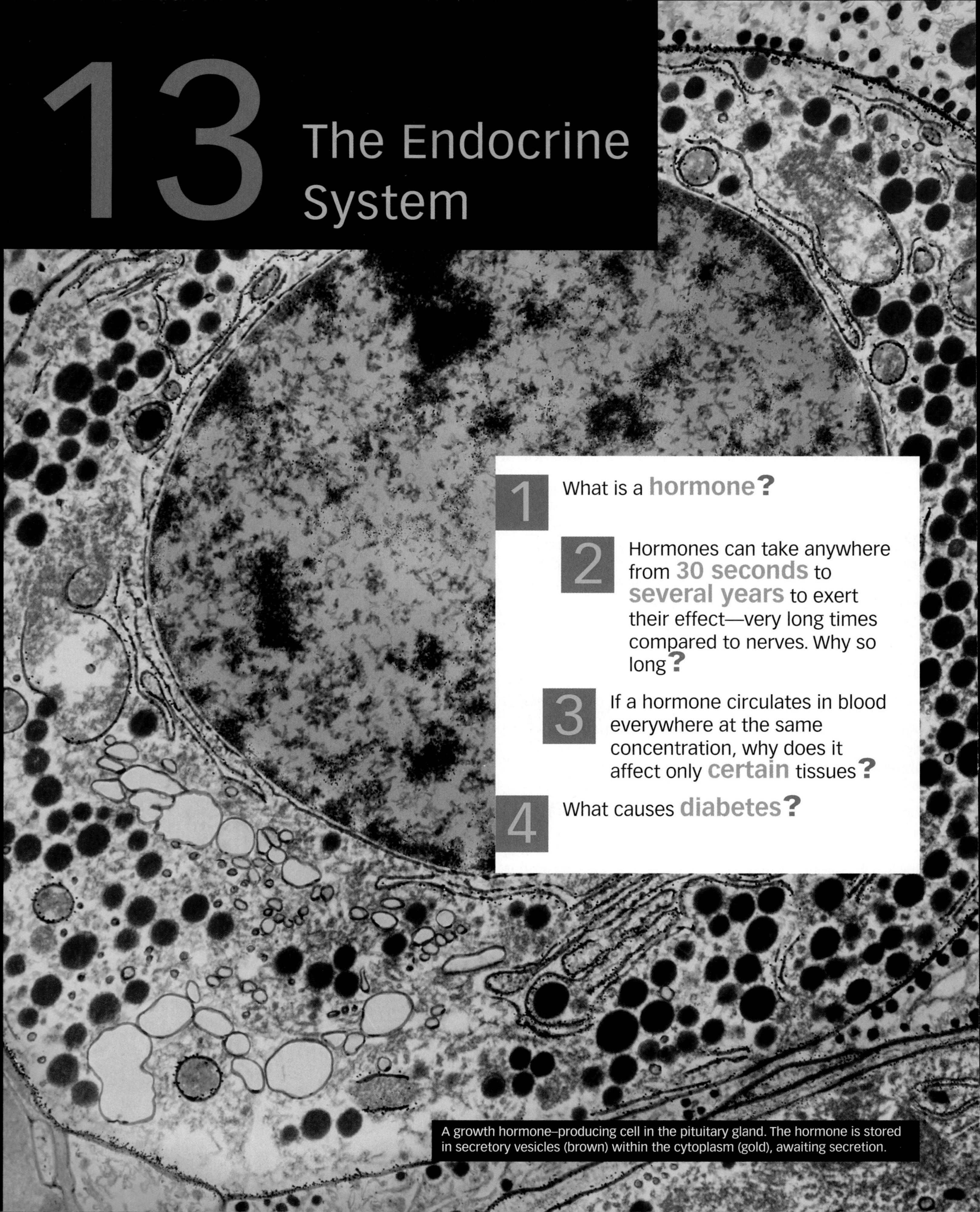

A growth hormone–producing cell in the pituitary gland. The hormone is stored in secretory vesicles (brown) within the cytoplasm (gold), awaiting secretion.

**At about ages 11–13,** something strange and wonderful happens to the human body and mind. The body grows rapidly, and secondary sex characteristics develop. Many boys get interested in girls, and many girls get interested in boys with an intensity that sometimes seems to border on obsession, when only months before they couldn't care less. At that age, neither sex can articulate why it happens. It just does.

Welcome to the endocrine system, an internal system of powerful chemicals that controls a host of body functions. In addition to sexual maturation and sexual desire, the endocrine system regulates salt and water balance, blood pressure, stress responses, digestion, cellular metabolism, the production of red blood cells, and overall organ growth and development.

## 13.1 The endocrine system produces hormones

The **endocrine system** is a collection of specialized cells, tissues, and glands that produce and secrete circulating chemical messenger molecules called **hormones.** Hormones are secreted by **endocrine glands**—ductless organs that secrete their products into interstitial fluid, lymph, and blood (*endocrine* means "secreted internally"). In contrast, **exocrine glands** secrete products such as mucus, sweat, tears, and digestive fluids into ducts that empty into the appropriate sites. Approximately 50 known hormones circulate in the human bloodstream, and new ones are still being discovered.

Hormones are bloodborne units of information, just as nerve impulses are units of information carried in nerves. Some hormones participate in feedback control loops regulating various body functions. We need these hormones to maintain homeostasis. Other hormones produce specific effects, such as contraction of the uterus at birth, growth during childhood, and the development of sexual characteristics at puberty. We need specific hormones to carry out each of these very specific functions.

Figure 13.1 shows the various tissues and organs that make up the endocrine system and the most important hormones they secrete. The many functions of these hormones are discussed in this chapter or in other chapters where appropriate.

The endocrine system has certain characteristics that set it apart from the nervous system as a communications system:

1. *Hormones of the endocrine system reach nearly every living cell.* This attribute gives the endocrine system a distinct advantage over the nervous system. Delivery of hormones to nearly all cells occurs because hormones circulate in the blood, and almost every cell in the body is near a blood vessel. (An exception is the central nervous system, which is effectively isolated from exposure to most systemic hormones by the blood-brain barrier.) With the endocrine system there is no need for the direct connections (the hard wiring, so to speak) required by the nervous system.
2. *Each hormone acts only on certain cells.* As all hormones circulate together in the same well-mixed blood, how can one hormone specifically regulate red blood cell production while another regulates blood calcium concentration? The answer is that each hormone acts only on a certain group of cells, called its **target cells,** because only the hormone's target cells have the appropriate receptor to fit it. When a hormone binds to a receptor on its target cell, a change occurs within the cell. The cell may grow, divide, or change its metabolism in some way. All other cells of the body fail to respond to the hormone because they lack the appropriate receptor. As an analogy, consider that your car is a cell, the car's ignition switch is the receptor, and the car key is the hormone. Your car key fits only your car (the "target" car) and no other. Fitting your key into the ignition and turning it causes the car to start. Gas is consumed, engine parts rotate, and heat is generated.
3. *Endocrine control tends to be slower than nervous system control.* There is a price for using the cardiovascular

### Answers to Intro Questions

1. A hormone is a chemical messenger molecule released by an endocrine gland and dispersed throughout the body by the blood. Each hormone carries information specific to certain cells and tissues throughout the body.
2. At a minimum, blood takes 30 seconds to transport newly released hormones to their targets. In addition, some hormones are released very slowly and others stimulate activities that just take a long time to occur, such as growth and sexual maturation.
3. Only cells with specific receptors for a particular hormone are able to respond to that hormone. Cells in female breast tissue have numerous receptors for estrogen, whereas heart muscle cells have very few.
4. Diabetes usually starts with an inability of cells and tissues to respond properly to the hormone insulin, followed later by a decline in insulin production. It may have a genetic component, but it also seems to be strongly affected by diet—too many high-fat, high-sugar calories too often.

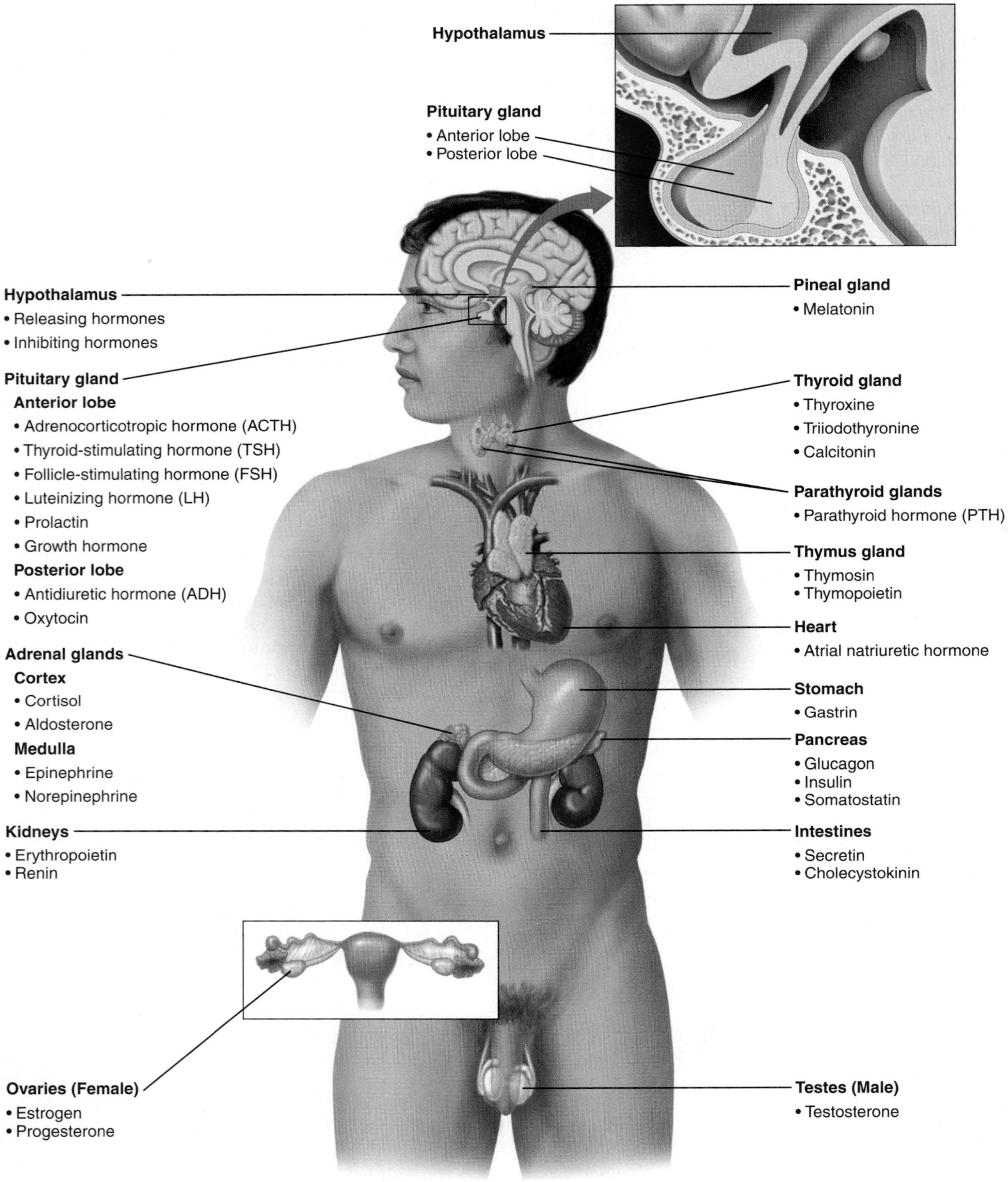


**Figure 13.1 Components of the human endocrine system.** Note that some organs with nonendocrine primary functions (the heart, stomach, intestines, and kidneys) produce and secrete hormones as secondary functions.

system as the message delivery system, and that is a reduction in speed—a lengthening of the response time. Nerve impulses can travel from head to toe in a fraction of a second. It takes longer to secrete a hormone into the bloodstream, have the hormone circulate to its target, and exert its effect. At the very fastest, this takes 20 seconds or so.

Given this difference in speed, it is not surprising that reflexes that prompt us to avoid a hot flame are controlled by the nervous system and not the endocrine system. On the other hand, endocrine communication is highly effective for longer-term controls, such as regulation of blood pressure, production of red blood cells, and onset of puberty.

4. *The endocrine and nervous systems can (and often do) interact with each other.* The timing of growth and sexual maturation, for example, involves a complex sequence of changes in both neural and endocrine signals, and the release of some hormones depends on input from sensory neurons.

**RECAP**

Hormones secreted by glands of the endocrine system act only on target cells with appropriate receptors. Hormones reach their targets via the circulatory system, making endocrine system control slower than nervous system control. The two systems frequently interact. ■

## 13.2 Hormones are classified as steroid or nonsteroid

Hormones are classified into two basic categories based on their structure and mechanism of action. **Steroid hormones** are structurally related to cholesterol, and all are lipid soluble. **Nonsteroid hormones,** because they are structurally related to proteins, are lipid insoluble. The differences in lipid solubility of steroid and nonsteroid hormones explain the differences in their mechanisms of action. Steroid hormones enter the cell, bind to an intracellular receptor, and activate genes that produce new proteins. Nonsteroid hormones bind to receptors on the cell's surface, initiating a series of events that ultimately alters cellular activity in some way, even though the hormone never entered the cell at all.

### Steroid hormones enter target cells

Recall that the cell membrane is primarily composed of a bilayer of phospholipids. Because steroid hormones are related to cholesterol and therefore are lipid soluble, they can easily diffuse right across both the cell membrane and the nuclear membrane. Once inside the cell, steroid hormones bind to specific hormone receptors, forming a hormone-receptor complex either within the nucleus (Figure 13.2) or within the cytoplasm (not shown). If the hormone-receptor complex was formed in the cytoplasm, it too can diffuse into the nucleus.

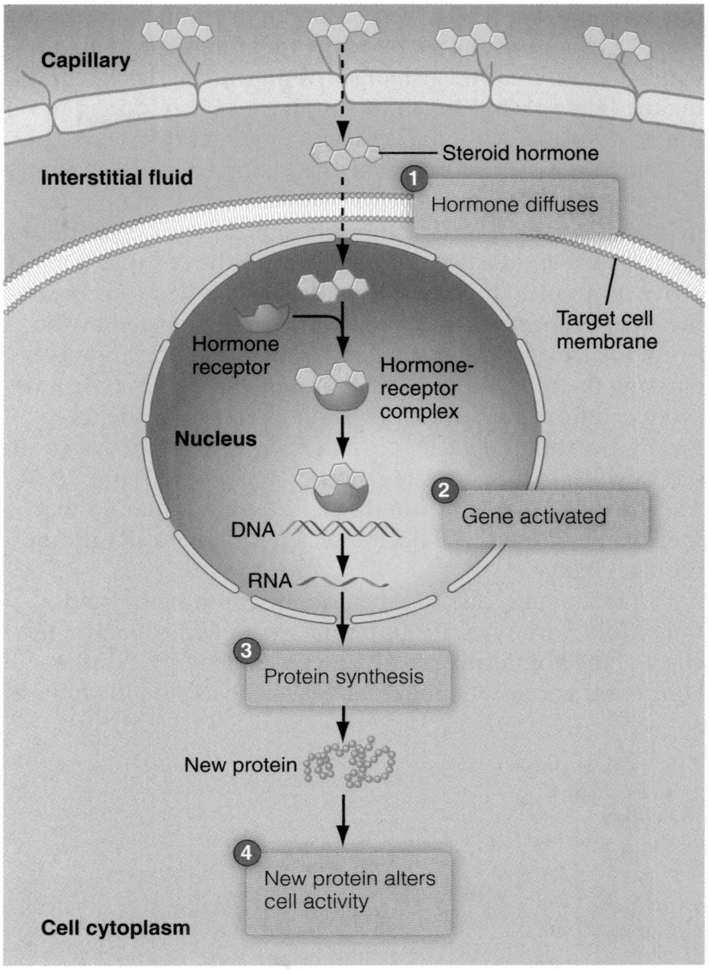


**Figure 13.2 Mechanism of steroid hormone action on a target cell.** Lipid-soluble steroid hormones diffuse across the cell and nuclear membranes into the nucleus, where they bind to hormone receptors that activate genes. Gene activation results in the production of a specific protein.

Once inside the nucleus, the hormone-receptor complex attaches to DNA, activating specific genes. Gene activation causes the formation of messenger RNA, which then leaves the nucleus and directs the synthesis of certain proteins. The proteins then carry out the cellular response to the hormone, whatever it might be.

Steroid hormones tend to be slower acting than nonsteroid hormones. Starting from the time the steroid hormone first enters the cell, it can take minutes or even hours to produce a new protein.

### Nonsteroid hormones bind to receptors on target cell membranes

Nonsteroid hormones cannot enter the target cell because they are not lipid soluble. Instead they bind to receptors located on the outer surface of the cell membrane. The receptors are generally associated with, or are part of, protein molecules floating in the phospholipid bilayer of the cell membrane (Chapter 3).The binding of hormone to receptor causes a change in the shape of the membrane protein, which in turn initiates a change within the cell. It's like turning the lights on in a room by flipping a switch located in the hall outside, without ever having to enter the room.

Some nonsteroid hormones cause ion channels in the cell membrane to open or close, similar to the action of a neurotransmitter. More commonly, hormone-receptor binding converts an inactive molecule within the cell into an active molecule. The activated molecule is called a **second messenger,** because it carries the message provided by the hormone (the "first messenger") without the hormone ever entering the cell. A common second messenger is cyclic AMP, produced from ATP when the hormone binds to the receptor. Cyclic AMP then activates an enzyme, which activates another, which in turn activates another, and so on (Figure 13.3). At each successive activation the effect is amplified, so that even a small amount of hormone can produce a significant cellular change.

In fact, amplification is the norm for both steroid and nonsteroid hormones. If a hormone were a lighted match, the effect of the hormone would be the equivalent of a bonfire. Hormones start something small (a change in protein synthesis or activation of an enzyme), but the final effect can be as dramatic as the development of secondary sexual characteristics.

Most nonsteroid hormones tend to be faster-acting than steroid hormones because they activate enzymes that already exist within the cell in inactive form. An entire cascade of existing enzymes can be activated within seconds or minutes.

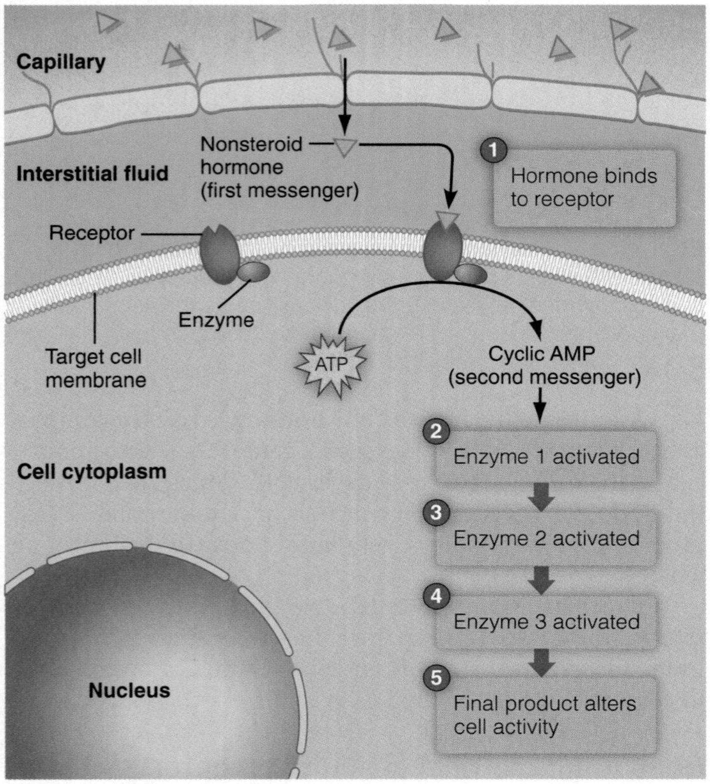


**Figure 13.3 Mechanism of nonsteroid hormone action on a target cell.** Nonsteroid hormones bind to receptors in the cell membrane, leading to the conversion of ATP to cyclic AMP (the second messenger) within the cell. Cyclic AMP initiates a cascade of enzyme activations, amplifying the original hormonal signal and generating a cellular response.

## Hormones participate in negative feedback loops

As messenger molecules, some hormones participate in internal homeostatic control mechanisms and control vital physiological processes. It is essential to regulate carefully the rate at which each hormone is secreted, so that its concentration in blood is just right to carry out its function.

As described in Chapter 4, homeostasis is generally maintained by a negative feedback control loop. In a negative feedback loop involving a hormone, the endocrine gland is the control center, the hormone represents the pathway between the control center and the effectors, and the effectors are the hormone's target cells, tissues, or organs (Figure 13.4). As the figure shows, a negative feedback loop involving an endocrine gland and a hormone is a stable, self-adjusting mechanism for maintaining homeostasis of the controlled variable, because any change in the controlled variable sets in motion a response that reverses that change. (Figure 7.6 shows an example of a hormonal negative feedback loop.)

Not all negative feedback loops involving hormones are quite as simple as the one depicted in Figure 13.4. In some cases the real control center is the brain, which activates an endocrine gland via nerves. Nevertheless the effect is the same—reversal of the initial change in the controlled variable.

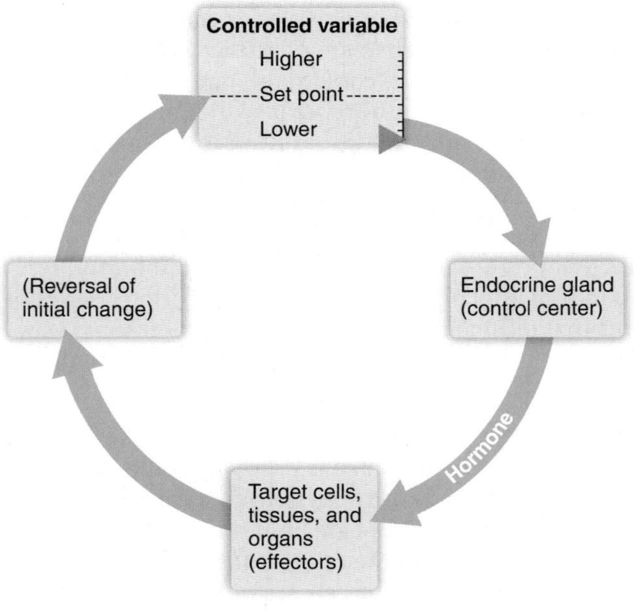


**Figure 13.4 A negative feedback loop involving a hormone.** In response to a change in the controlled variable, the endocrine gland releases a hormone that acts on target cells to return the controlled variable to its normal state.

A few hormones are secreted in response to specific environmental cues or for specific purposes, such as to avoid danger or to initiate puberty. This type of secretion is not part of a negative feedback loop.

We turn now to specific endocrine glands and their hormones.

**RECAP**

Many hormones participate in negative feedback loops that maintain homeostasis of certain controlled variables. Steroid hormones enter the target cell, activate specific genes, and cause the production of new proteins. Nonsteroid hormones bind to a cell membrane receptor that either opens or closes ion channels or activates a second messenger within the cell. ■

## 13.3 The hypothalamus and the pituitary gland

As described in Chapter 11, the **hypothalamus** is a small region in the brain that serves as a homeostatic control center. It is an important link between the nervous system and the endocrine system. It receives neural input about certain internal environmental conditions such as water and solute balance, temperature, and carbohydrate metabolism. The hypothalamus produces two hormones of its own, and it monitors and controls the hormone secretions of the pituitary gland, located directly beneath it and connected to it by a thin stalk of tissue (review Figure 13.1).

The **pituitary gland** is sometimes called the "master gland" because it secretes eight different hormones that in turn regulate many of the other endocrine glands (Table 13.1). It consists of two lobes: a posterior lobe that appears to be a bulging extension of the connecting stalk, and a larger, more distinct anterior lobe (Figure 13.5).

### The posterior pituitary stores ADH and oxytocin

The interaction between the hypothalamus and posterior lobe of the pituitary gland is an example of the close working relationship between the nervous and endocrine systems. Cells in the hypothalamus called **neuroendocrine cells** essentially function as both nerve cells and endocrine cells, because they can generate nerve impulses and secrete hormones into blood vessels.

Figure 13.5 illustrates the posterior pituitary lobe and its connections to the hypothalamus. Neuroendocrine cells with cell bodies in the hypothalamus have axons that extend down the stalk connecting to the posterior pituitary. The neuron cell bodies make either antidiuretic hormone (ADH) or oxytocin in the hypothalamus and then transport the hormones down the axon for storage in axon endings in the posterior pituitary.

When the hypothalamus is stimulated to release the hormones, the neuroendocrine cells send impulses down the axon, causing hormone to be secreted into nearby capillaries. The hormones circulate to their target cells.

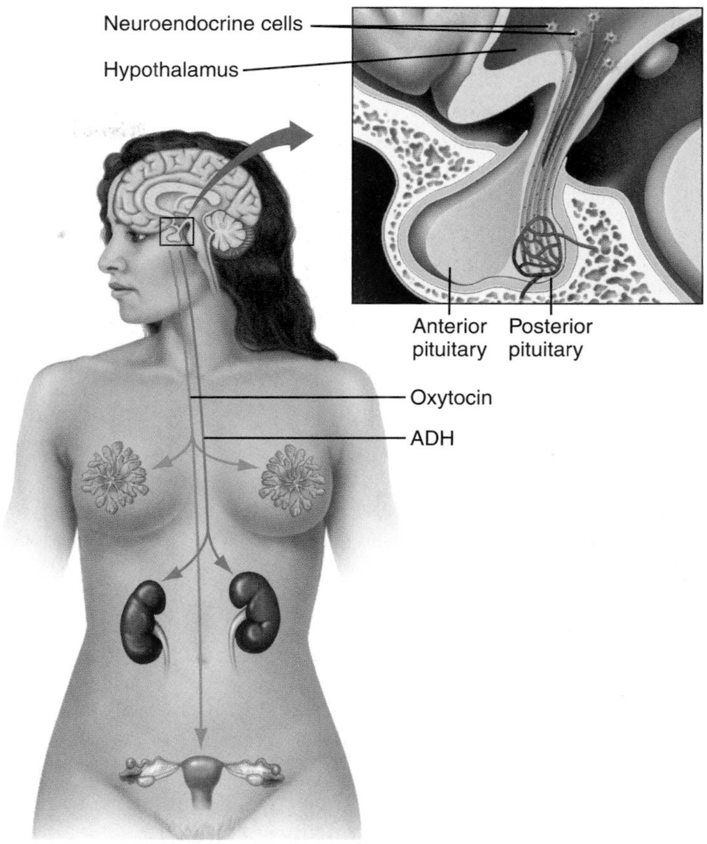


**Figure 13.5 Posterior pituitary lobe and hypothalamus.** Individual neuroendocrine cells of the hypothalamus and the posterior pituitary secrete either ADH or oxytocin. The hormones enter the blood supply of the posterior pituitary and make their way to the general circulation. ADH acts on the kidneys to regulate water balance in the body. Oxytocin primarily acts on the mammary glands and uterus muscles of lactating and pregnant women, respectively.

**ADH regulates water balance** Antidiuretic hormone reduces the amount of water lost in urine, helping to regulate the body's overall water balance. The primary target cells for ADH are in the kidneys, where it causes changes in cell permeability to water as part of the mechanism for conserving water (Chapter 15).

When the hypothalamus detects low concentrations of water (equivalent to a high concentration of solute particles) in the blood, neuroendocrine cells release ADH from the posterior pituitary. ADH circulates in blood to the kidneys, where it stimulates the reabsorption of water. When water concentrations rise to normal levels, the hypothalamus is no longer stimulated to release ADH, and ADH secretion declines.

**Oxytocin causes uterine contractions and milk ejection** The primary target cells for oxytocin are in the uterus and the mammary glands (breasts) of pregnant and lactating females, respectively. Oxytocin is secreted at high concentrations during childbirth and also when an infant nurses at its

**Table 13.1 Hormones of the pituitary gland**

| Hormone | Abbrev | Main targets | Primary actions |
|---|---|---|---|
| ***Posterior Pituitary*** | | | |
| Antidiuretic hormone | ADH | Kidneys | Reduces amount of water lost in urine |
| Oxytocin | — | Uterus | Induces uterine contractions |
| | | Mammary glands | Induces ejection of milk from mammary glands |
| ***Anterior Pituitary*** | | | |
| Adrenocorticotropic hormone | ACTH | Adrenal cortex | Stimulates adrenal cortex to release glucocorticoids |
| Thyroid-stimulating hormone | TSH | Thyroid gland | Stimulates synthesis and secretion of thyroid hormones |
| Follicle-stimulating hormone | FSH | Ovaries | In females, stimulates egg maturation and the secretion of estrogen |
| | | Testes | In males, stimulates the formation of sperm |
| Luteinizing hormone | LH | Ovaries | In females, stimulates ovulation (egg release) and the secretion of progesterone |
| | | Testes | In males, stimulates testosterone secretion |
| Prolactin | PRL | Mammary glands | Stimulates the development of mammary gland cells and production of milk |
| Growth hormone | GH | Most cells | Stimulates growth in young individuals; plays multiple roles in cell division, protein synthesis, and metabolism in adults |

mother's breast (Figure 13.6). It stimulates contractions of the uterus during childbirth and ejection of milk into the ducts of the mammary glands during suckling.

The stimulation of oxytocin secretion by nursing is an example of a *neuroendocrine reflex,* in which a nervous system stimulus (activation of sensory mechanoreceptors in the mother's breast) is responsible for secretion of a hormone. When a baby suckles, sensory receptors in the nipple are stimulated. Impulses are transmitted to neuroendocrine cells in the hypothalamus, which release oxytocin from the posterior pituitary. The hormone circulates to breast tissue, binds with receptors, and causes contractions of smooth muscle that eject milk.

Oxytocin is also present in males. In both sexes it is thought to play a role in sexual arousal and the feeling of sexual satisfaction after orgasm.

**RECAP**

ADH acts on the kidneys to regulate water balance. Oxytocin stimulates uterine contractions and milk ejection in pregnant and lactating females, respectively. In both sexes, oxytocin contributes to feelings of sexual satisfaction. ■

## The anterior pituitary produces six key hormones

The anterior lobe of the pituitary gland produces six key anterior pituitary hormones:

- Adrenocorticotropic hormone (ACTH), also called corticotropin
- Thyroid-stimulating hormone (TSH), also called thyrotropin
- Follicle-stimulating hormone (FSH)
- Luteinizing hormone (LH)
- Prolactin (PRL)
- Growth hormone (GH)

Each anterior pituitary hormone is produced and secreted by a separate cell type, and each hormone is regulated by separate mechanisms. The first four hormones (ACTH, TSH, FSH, and LH) act by stimulating the release of yet other hormones from other endocrine glands.

The secretion of anterior pituitary hormones depends partly on the hypothalamus, but the mechanism differs from that of the posterior pituitary. The connection between the hypothalamus and anterior pituitary is endocrine, not neural; it relies on specific releasing and inhibiting hormones secreted by neuroendocrine cells in the hypothalamus (Figure 13.7). These releasing and inhibiting hormones, in turn, alter the secretion of the six anterior pituitary hormones. Releasing and inhibiting hormones are produced in minuscule quantities. However, they are secreted directly into a special blood supply that runs directly between the hypothalamus and anterior pituitary (called the pituitary portal system), so their concentrations are sufficient to regulate anterior pituitary hormone secretions.

**ACTH stimulates the adrenal cortex** The names of hormones generally offer a clue to their function or site of action. The target cells for ACTH are located in the outer layer, or cortex, of the adrenal gland (in *adrenocorticotropic* the suffix *-tropic* means "acting upon").

ACTH stimulates the adrenal cortex to release another group of hormones called glucocorticoids, which are steroid

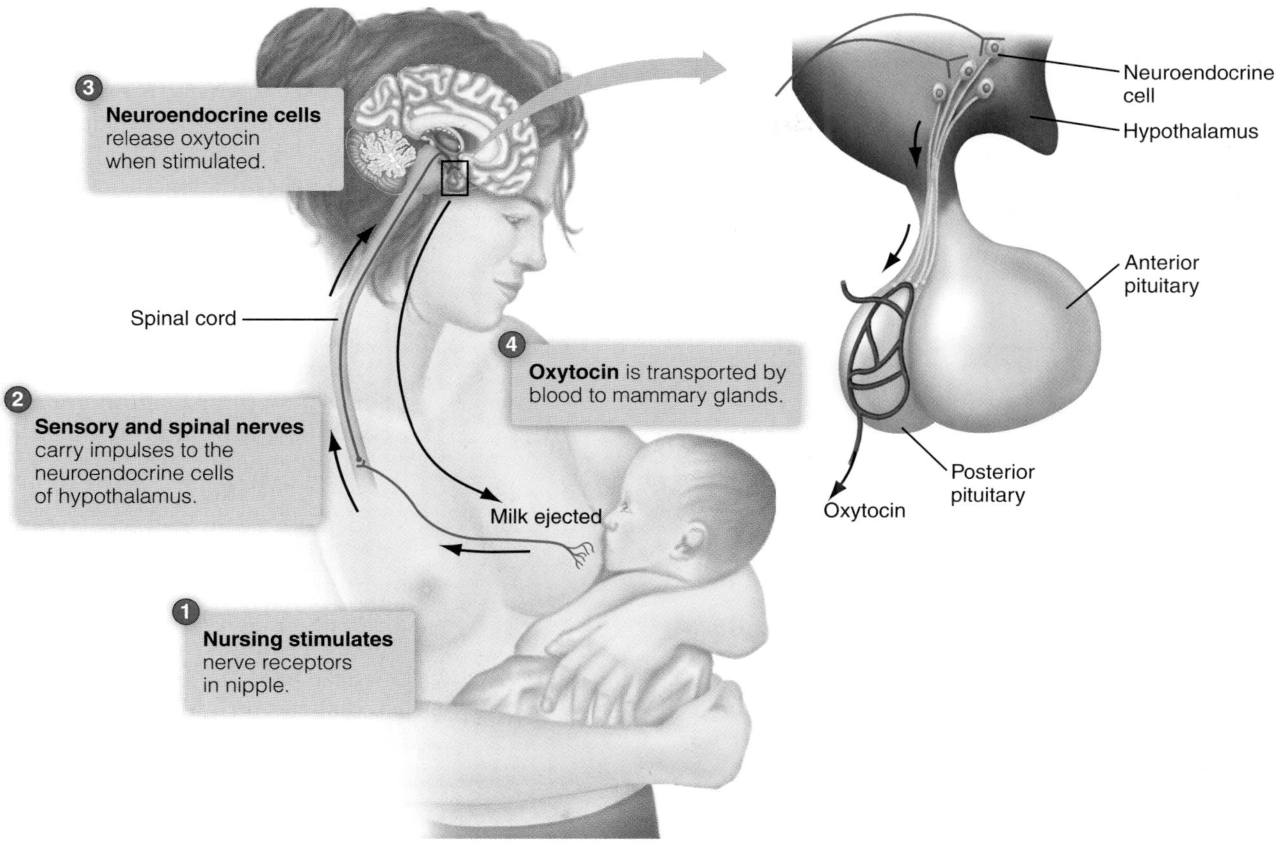


**Figure 13.6 The control of oxytocin secretion by nursing.** The act of suckling triggers a series of events that ultimately eject milk from the nipple.

hormones involved in stress-related conditions and the control of glucose metabolism (see section 13.5). ACTH secretion is regulated by a negative feedback loop involving a releasing hormone from the hypothalamus and the concentration of glucocorticoids in blood.

**TSH acts on the thyroid gland** TSH stimulates the thyroid gland to synthesize and release thyroid hormones. There is a TSH-releasing hormone from the hypothalamus, mentioned earlier.

**FSH and LH stimulate the reproductive organs** FSH and LH are called "gonadotropins" because they stimulate the growth, development, and function of the reproductive organs (gonads) in both males and females. In females, FSH induces egg development, LH promotes ovulation (egg release), and both hormones stimulate the secretion of the ovarian hormone estrogen. In addition, LH stimulates the secretion of the ovarian hormone progesterone after ovulation. In males, FSH induces sperm development and LH stimulates the production of the hormone testosterone by the testes.

FSH and LH are essentially absent until about age 10–13. A major increase in the production of these two hormones is what initiates sexual maturation and the development of secondary sex characteristics (puberty).

**Prolactin (PRL): Mammary glands and milk production** Prolactin's primary function is to stimulate the development of mammary gland cells and the production of milk. Prolactin is present in males but its function is unknown. In females, the prolactin concentration in blood rises toward the end of pregnancy because estrogen stimulates the hypothalamus to step up production of *prolactin-releasing hormone,* one of those releasing hormones mentioned earlier. When estrogen levels decline after birth, prolactin-releasing hormone and prolactin levels are kept high by a sensory neural reflex associated with nursing.

When a woman is not in late pregnancy or breast-feeding, prolactin secretion is suppressed by *prolactin-inhibiting hormone,* another of those releasing/inhibiting hormones from the hypothalamus. It is now thought that prolactin-inhibiting hormone is actually identical to the neurotransmitter, dopamine.

**Growth hormone (GH): Widespread effects on growth** The effects of growth hormone are so widespread that it is difficult to define a specific target cell or action. The effects of GH are most obvious in bone and muscle. In general, GH influences cells in ways that promote growth. Specific actions include stimulating protein synthesis and cell division, and using body fat as a source of energy.

GH is present throughout life, but most of its growth-promoting effects occur during childhood and adolescence. At these

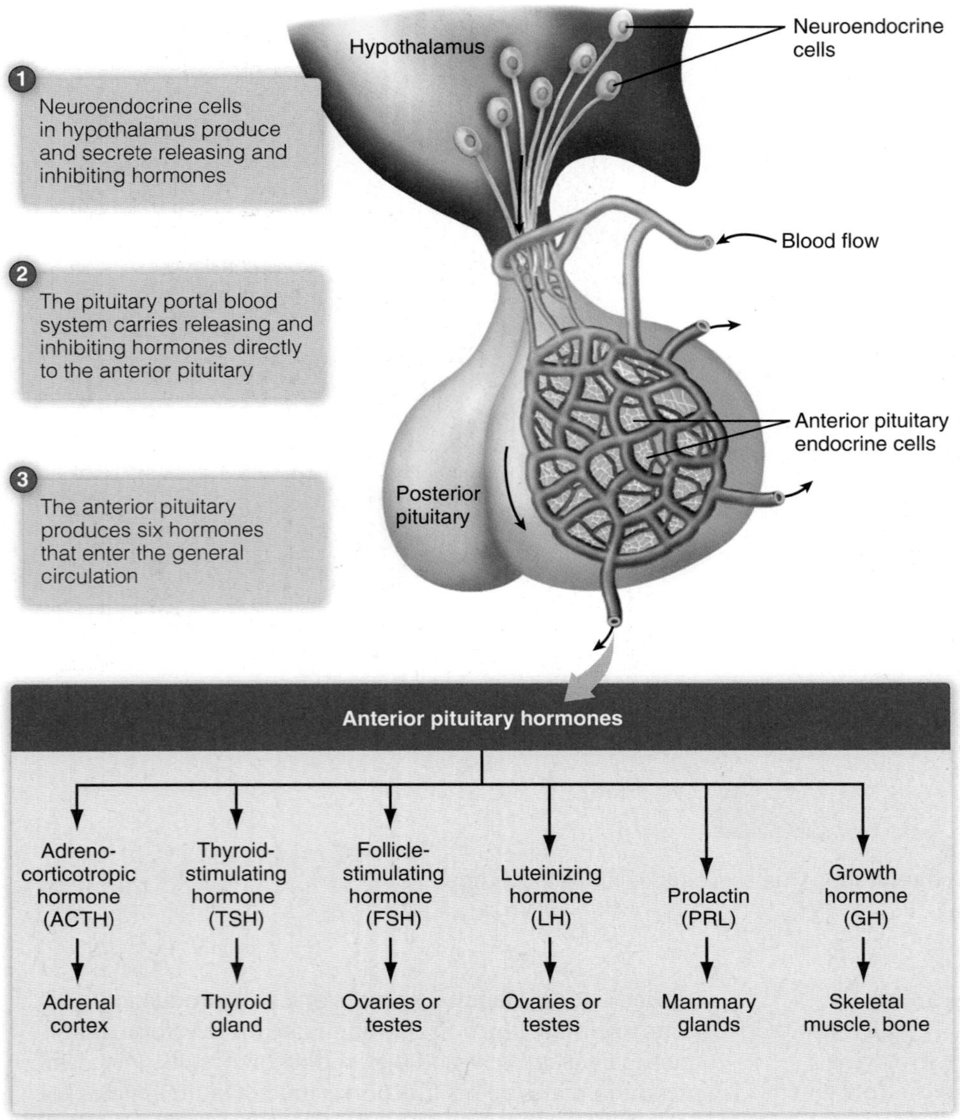


**Figure 13.7 The relationship between the hypothalamus and the anterior pituitary gland.** Neuroendocrine cells in the hypothalamus secrete releasing hormones and inhibiting hormones into a system of capillaries that goes directly to the anterior pituitary. Specific hypothalamic hormones inhibit or stimulate each anterior pituitary hormone.

times it causes a dramatic increase in the mass and length of muscles and bones. Abnormal GH concentrations during development can lead to permanent changes in the final height of an adult. In adults it continues to help regulate metabolism by promoting the utilization of fats and amino acids as cellular fuel and by helping to maintain blood glucose levels.

**RECAP**

The six hormones produced by the anterior pituitary are ACTH, TSH, FSH, LH, prolactin (PRL), and GH. The release of each hormone is controlled in part by a releasing or inhibiting hormone from the hypothalamus. ■

## Pituitary disorders: Hypersecretion or hyposecretion

As you might guess, maintaining just the right quantities of hormones in the blood is a delicate balance that can sometimes go awry. Many diseases and disorders are chronic conditions of too much hormone (hypersecretion) or too little hormone (hyposecretion). Some are inherited. To illustrate the types of things that can go wrong we focus on hyposecretion of one posterior pituitary hormone (ADH) and both hyposecretion and hypersecretion of an anterior pituitary hormone (GH).

ADH affects maintenance of water balance by the kidneys. Hyposecretion of ADH causes the kidneys to lose too much water, leading to a disorder called *diabetes insipidus*. Symptoms include excessive urination, dehydration, thirst, headache, and dry mouth. Some cases of diabetes insipidus are caused by head trauma or brain surgery that disrupts the normal production of ADH.

Even when ADH hormone levels are normal, diabetes insipidus can still occur if the kidney cells that normally respond to ADH are lacking the specific ADH receptors. As a general rule, then, an endocrine control loop can be disrupted either by lack of a hormone or by lack of target cell receptors for that hormone. Either way, the system does not function effectively. Endocrine disorders due to defects in target cell receptors are quite common and are often inherited.

Growth hormone has much longer-acting effects than ADH. Recall that in children, growth hormone stimulates the bone-lengthening activity of the growth plate, so that bones grow longer along with the child's overall growth. It is not surprising, therefore, that abnormalities of growth hormone secretion are most damaging when they occur before puberty. Hyposecretion of growth hormone during childhood can result in *pituitary dwarfism*. Conversely, hypersecretion of growth hormone during childhood and adolescence produces *gigantism* (Figure 13.8).

Dwarfism can be prevented if children are diagnosed early and treated with growth hormone throughout childhood. However, once adulthood is reached, dwarfism cannot be overcome by administering growth hormone. The reason is that during puberty the sex steroid hormones cause the cartilaginous growth plates at the ends of long bones to be replaced by bone. After that time, bones cannot grow longer.

**Figure 13.8 Effect of growth hormone on body growth.** The tall person exhibits the traits of gigantism caused by excessive secretion of growth hormone during childhood. The short person has pituitary dwarfism, the result of too little growth hormone during childhood.

Excessive production of growth hormone in adults over long periods produces a condition called *acromegaly.* The features of acromegaly are quite different from gigantism, because bones can no longer lengthen in adults. Instead, under the influence of growth hormone there is gradual thickening of the bones in the face, hands, and feet. The most notable visible effect is a change in facial features (Figure 13.9). Excessive production of growth hormone in adults usually results from a tumor of either the pituitary or the hypothalamus. Acromegaly is no longer common because growth hormone-secreting tumors are now usually diagnosed and treated early enough to prevent the development of the condition. Excessive growth hormone secretion is diagnosed by measuring growth hormone levels.

## 13.4 The pancreas secretes glucagon, insulin, and somatostatin

The **pancreas** is both an endocrine gland (secreting hormones into the blood) and an exocrine gland (secreting enzymes, fluids, and ions into the digestive tract to aid in digestion). In this chapter we deal with its endocrine function.

**Figure 13.9 Effect of excessive growth hormone as an adult.** This woman developed acromegaly as a result of too much growth hormone as an adult. She was symptom-free at 16.

The endocrine cells of the pancreas are located in small clusters of cells scattered throughout the pancreas called the *islets of Langerhans* (an islet is a little island), or just the pancreatic islets. The pancreatic islets contain three types of cells and produce three hormones, all of them having to do with the regulation of blood sugar (glucose). One hormone raises blood sugar, the second lowers it, and the third inhibits the secretion of the other two hormones. Specifically:

1. Alpha cells secrete **glucagon,** which raises blood sugar. As blood glucose levels decline between meals, glucagon is secreted into the bloodstream. In the liver, glucagon causes the breakdown of glycogen (a stored form of sugar) to glucose, raising blood glucose levels. Glucagon is particularly important between meals for increasing the supply of glucose to cells that need it.
2. Beta cells secrete **insulin,** which lowers blood sugar. After a meal, blood glucose levels rise as sugars are absorbed from the digestive tract. The high glucose concentration stimulates the beta cells to secrete insulin into the blood, where it does the opposite of glucagon. Insulin promotes the uptake of glucose by cells of the liver, muscle, and fat tissue. It also promotes the conversion of glucose into glycogen in the liver, both glycogen and proteins in muscle, and fats in adipose tissue.
3. Delta cells secrete somatostatin. The physiological significance of pancreatic somatostatin is not well understood, though it appears to inhibit the secretion of both glucagon

and insulin. Somatostatin is also secreted by the hypothalamus, where it is the inhibitory hormone for growth hormone secretion, and the digestive tract, where it helps regulate several digestive secretions. The example of somatostatin reinforces the principle that the function of a hormone in any particular tissue or organ depends on the types of target cells present in those locations.

Figure 13.10 illustrates how the pancreas might respond to a meal. In actual fact, insulin and glucagon are both secreted in modest amounts all of the time. Adjusting the blood sugar is just a matter of altering the relative secretion rates of these two hormones—more insulin and less glucagon when blood sugar is high, and the inverse when blood sugar is low.

**RECAP**

Hormones secreted by the pancreas include glucagon, insulin, and somatostatin. Glucagon raises blood glucose levels by increasing production of glucose from glycogen. Insulin lowers glucose levels by facilitating glucose uptake and storage. Somatostatin inhibits the secretion of both glucagon and insulin. ■

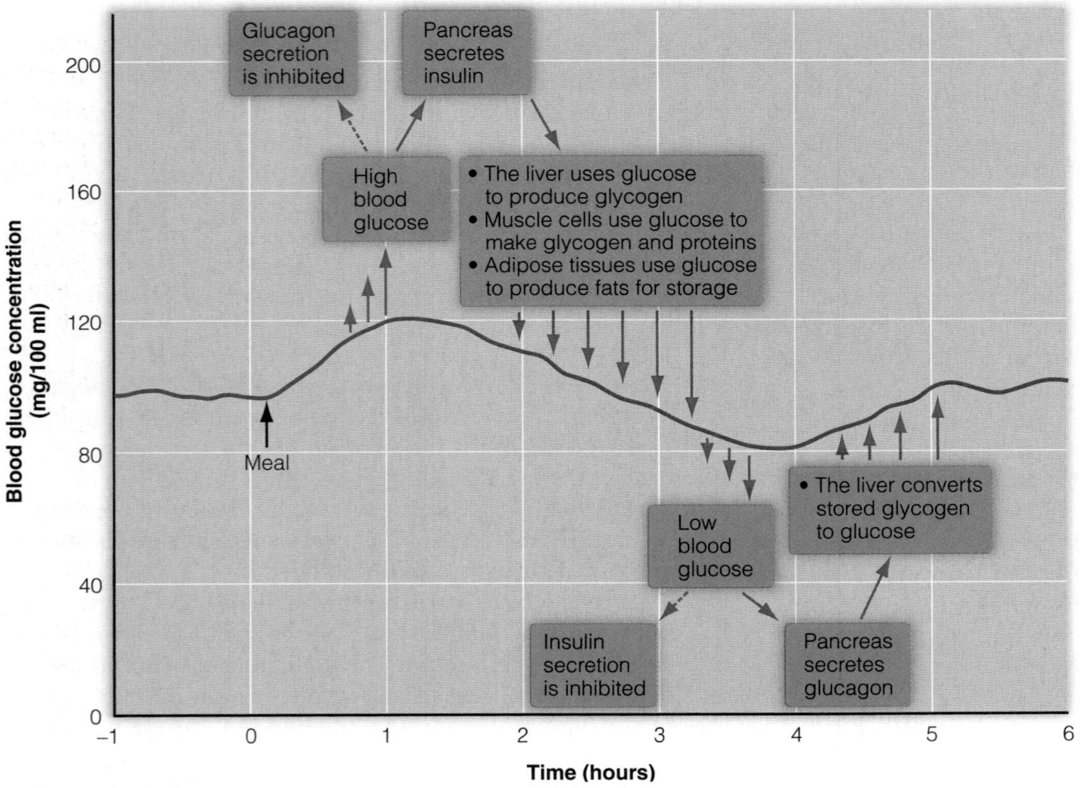


**Figure 13.10 How the pancreas responds to a meal.** The normal range for blood glucose concentration is 80–120 mg/100 ml. As blood glucose concentration rises, the secretion of insulin increases and the secretion of glucagon decreases, promoting the uptake and storage of glucose. If glucose concentration falls to near its normal lower limit, the secretion of glucagon increases and the secretion of insulin is inhibited. In the steady state, both hormones are secreted in modest amounts.

## 13.5 The adrenal glands comprise the cortex and medulla

The **adrenal glands** are two small endocrine organs located just above the kidneys. Each gland has an outer layer called the adrenal cortex, and an inner core called the adrenal medulla. The cortex and medulla function as two separate endocrine glands. (**Cortex** and **medulla** are general terms for outer and inner regions; you'll hear the terms again in the context of the kidneys and you're already aware of the cerebral cortex of the brain.)

### The adrenal cortex: Glucocorticoids and mineralocorticoids

The adrenal cortex produces small amounts of the sex hormones estrogen and testosterone (most of the sex hormones are produced by the ovaries and testes, discussed later) and two classes of steroid hormones called glucocorticoids and mineralocorticoids. Their names give a clue to their functions: glucocorticoids help regulate blood glucose levels, and mineralocorticoids help regulate the minerals sodium and potassium.

**Glucocorticoids: Cortisol** The adrenal cortex produces a group of glucocorticoids with nearly identical structures. **Cortisol** accounts for approximately 95% of these glucocorticoids. During prolonged fasting, cortisol assists in maintaining blood glucose levels by promoting the utilization of fats and by increasing the breakdown of protein to amino acids in muscle. The free amino acids are then converted to new glucose by the liver. In addition to its role in controlling blood glucose, cortisol is also important in suppressing inflammatory responses that occur following infection or injury.

Cortisol secretion is controlled by a typical feedback loop. A releasing factor from the hypothalamus stimulates the secretion of ACTH from the anterior pituitary gland, which in turn stimulates the adrenal cortex to secrete cortisol. When cortisol reaches its upper limit of normal blood level, it inhibits further secretion of the releasing hormone from the hypothalamus and of ACTH from the anterior pituitary.

A fall in blood glucose concentration can override the

normal feedback control mechanism and increase cortisol secretion significantly. So, too, can physical injury and emotional stress. All of these stimuli act at the level of the hypothalamus, which secretes more releasing hormone, ultimately raising both ACTH and cortisol. The elevated cortisol concentration helps to restore the blood glucose concentration to normal and makes more amino acids available to repair damaged tissues. It also reduces inflammation by decreasing fluid loss from capillaries.

Cortisol and cortisol-like drugs can be administered topically to treat inflammation or injury. When used for prolonged periods, however, these drugs suppress the immune system.

**Mineralocorticoids: Aldosterone** The other hormones produced by the adrenal cortex are the mineralocorticoids, the most abundant of which is **aldosterone.** Aldosterone is the hormone primarily responsible for regulating the amounts of sodium and potassium in the body. With ADH, it helps maintain body water balance.

Adrenal secretion of aldosterone increases whenever the total amount of sodium and water in the body is too low or when too much potassium is present (see Chapter 15 for the details). In turn, aldosterone acts on cells in the kidneys to promote sodium reabsorption and potassium excretion, precisely what you would expect it to do if it were part of a homeostatic control loop for these ions.

### The adrenal medulla: Epinephrine and norepinephrine

The **adrenal medulla** produces the nonsteroid hormones **epinephrine** (adrenaline) and **norepinephrine** (noradrenaline). These hormones play roles in metabolism and controlling blood pressure and heart activity.

Epinephrine and norepinephrine are mentioned in Chapter 11 (the nervous system) because they are also neurotransmitters. Function, not structure, determines whether they act as neurotransmitters or hormones. When norepinephrine and epinephrine are released into the blood and act on distant target cells, they function as hormones.

Like the hypothalamus and the posterior pituitary, the adrenal medulla is really a neuroendocrine organ. Epinephrine and norepinephrine are synthesized and stored in specialized cells called chromaffin cells in the adrenal medulla that are innervated by sympathetic nerves. When sympathetic nerves are activated, the chromaffin cells secrete epinephrine and norepinephrine (Figure 13.11).

Once released, the two hormones participate in a wide range of actions that are essentially like the fight-or-flight responses of the sympathetic division. They raise blood glucose levels, increase heart rate and force of contraction, increase respiration rate, and constrict or dilate blood vessels in many organs, all actions that prepare the body for emergency activity.

You may have noticed that approximately 30 seconds to a minute after you are frightened by a dangerous situation such as avoiding an auto accident, your heart starts to pound, you breathe faster, and you feel "pumped up," alert, and a little shaky. These changes may occur even though the danger has already passed. You are experiencing an "adrenal rush" due to intense and rapid stimulation of your adrenal glands by the sympathetic nervous system. The adrenal hormonal response occurs about half a minute after the event, because it takes that long for the two hormones to be released, circulate to all tissues, bind to receptors on their target cells, and initiate the appropriate intracellular cascade of events. The response is also short-lived, lasting only a couple of minutes at most. Norepinephrine and epinephrine from the adrenal glands enhance the action of the sympathetic nervous system because the hormones reach more cells and are released in large amounts.

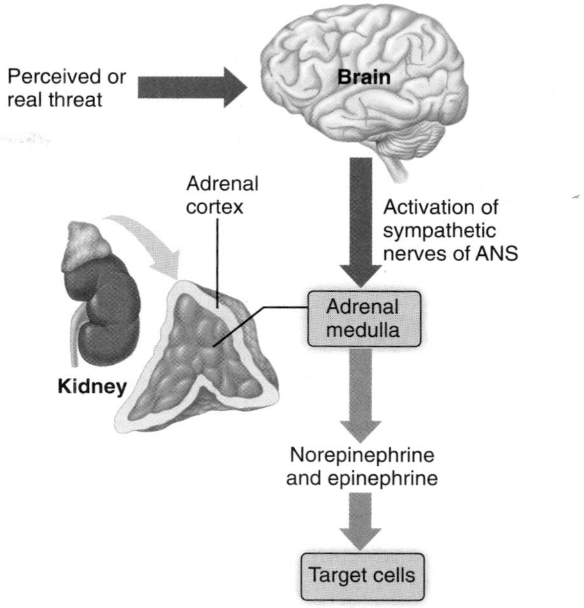


**Figure 13.11 Secretion of norepinephrine and epinephrine by the adrenal medulla.** The secretion of these two hormones is closely linked with the activity of the sympathetic division of the autonomic nervous system (ANS). Neural pathways are noted in red; hormonal pathways, in orange.

**RECAP**

The main secretory products of the adrenal cortex are cortisol and aldosterone. Cortisol raises blood glucose levels and suppresses inflammatory responses, and aldosterone regulates water balance by promoting sodium reabsorption. The hormones secreted by the adrenal medulla (epinephrine and norepinephrine) contribute to the fight-or-flight response initiated by the sympathetic nervous system. ■

## 13.6 Thyroid and parathyroid glands

The thyroid and parathyroid glands are anatomically linked. The **thyroid gland** is situated just below the larynx at the front of the trachea, and the two lobes of the thyroid gland wrap part of the way around the trachea (Figure 13.12). The four small **parathyroid glands** are embedded in the back of the thyroid.

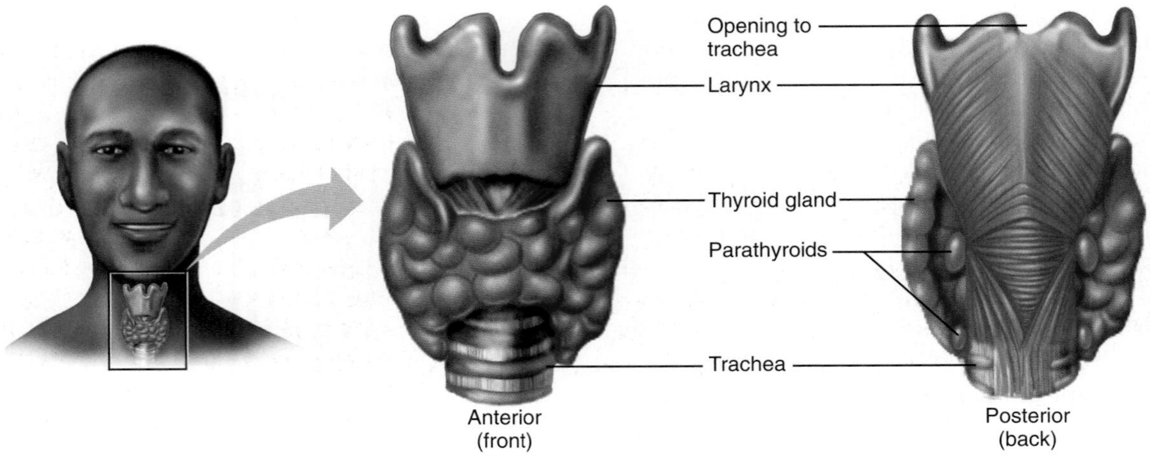


**Figure 13.12 The thyroid and parathyroid glands.**

The thyroid and parathyroid glands are also functionally linked; both help to regulate calcium balance. In addition, the thyroid has a separate and important role in controlling metabolism.

The two main hormones produced by the thyroid gland are thyroxine and calcitonin. The parathyroid glands produce parathyroid hormone.

## The thyroid gland: Thyroxine speeds cellular metabolism

The thyroid gland produces two very similar hormones called **thyroxine** ($T_4$) and triiodothyronine ($T_3$). Thyroxine and triiodothyronine are identical except that thyroxine contains four molecules of iodine (hence the abbreviation $T_4$) whereas triiodothyronine contains only three. Because they are so similar we consider them together as thyroxine.

Structurally, thyroxine is not a steroid hormone. Nevertheless, it acts like a steroid because it is lipid soluble. It crosses the cell and nuclear membranes, binds to nuclear receptors, and activates genes as its mode of action. Those genes carry the code for the various enzymes that regulate our metabolic rate.

Thyroxine increases the production and use of ATP from glucose in nearly all body cells. When thyroxine concentration increases, the basal metabolic rate (BMR) also increases (see section 14.11). Conversely, decreasing the blood concentration of thyroxine reduces energy utilization and BMR.

The basal rate of thyroxine secretion is regulated by a typical negative feedback loop (Figure 13.13). Any fall in thyroxine concentration would increase the secretion of the hypothalamic releasing hormone for TSH, which would increase pituitary TSH concentration, ultimately increasing thyroxine secretion and driving thyroxine concentration back toward normal. Superimposed on this normal feedback loop, conditions that increase the body's energy requirements (such as exposure to cold temperatures) can stimulate the hypothalamus and raise the steady-state concentrations of *all* hormones in the loop.

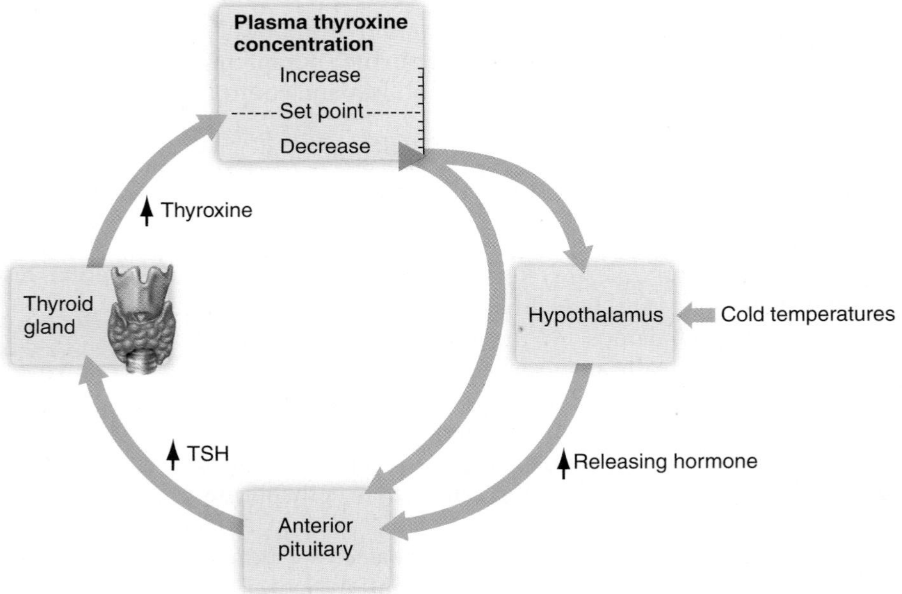


**Figure 13.13 Negative feedback control of thyroxine secretion.** A fall in plasma thyroxine concentration causes the hypothalamus and anterior pituitary to increase their secretion of the releasing hormone and TSH. The increase in TSH stimulates thyroid gland production and secretion of thyroxine, returning the plasma concentration to normal. Conversely, a rise in thyroxine causes a fall in the releasing hormone and TSH. Cold temperatures alter the feedback loop (raise plasma thyroxine concentration) by increasing hypothalamic secretion of the releasing hormone.

**Figure 13.14 A goiter caused by dietary iodine deficiency.**

**Iodine deficiency can cause goiter** Production of active thyroid hormones requires iodine. In fact, the main reason we need iodine in our diet is to ensure adequate production of thyroxine. Iodine deficiency can result in a thyroid-deficiency disease. When thyroxine is absent or abnormally low, the normal feedback inhibitory controls on the hypothalamus and pituitary are missing, so the hypothalamus and pituitary continue to secrete large quantities of the releasing hormone and TSH unchecked.

The high TSH levels stimulate the thyroid gland to grow to enormous size in an effort to get the thyroid to make more hormone, which it cannot do because it lacks iodine. An enlarged thyroid, as a result of iodine deficiency or other factors, is called a goiter (Figure 13.14). Goiter is less common today in industrialized nations because iodine is added to table salt. However, it is still a public health problem in certain areas of the world, most notably in Africa, China, and mountainous regions where rain has leached iodine from the soil.

**Calcitonin promotes bone growth** **Calcitonin,** the other main hormone of the thyroid gland, is produced by a separate group of thyroid cells. Calcitonin decreases the rate of bone resorption by inhibiting the activity of osteoclasts. It also stimulates the uptake of calcium by bone. These two actions tip the normal balance of bone deposition/resorption toward deposition, which over time increases bone mass. Calcitonin is part of a negative feedback control mechanism for calcium in which high blood calcium levels stimulate calcitonin release and low blood calcium levels inhibit its release.

Calcitonin is particularly important for the growth and development of bones in children. Once adulthood is reached, bone responsiveness to calcitonin declines. In adults, calcitonin is not essential for the normal regulation of blood calcium concentration. However, calcitonin may play a role in protecting the skeleton when calcium demand is high, such as during pregnancy.

### Parathyroid hormone (PTH) controls blood calcium levels

The parathyroid glands produce only one hormone, **parathyroid hormone (PTH)**, which:

1. Removes calcium and phosphate from bone
2. Increases absorption of calcium by the digestive tract
3. Causes the kidneys to retain calcium and excrete phosphate

Together these actions tend to raise the blood calcium concentration (and coincidentally lower blood phosphate concentration). As you might expect for a negative feedback control system, the secretion of PTH is stimulated by low blood calcium levels and inhibited by high blood calcium levels. Figure 13.15 shows the overall regulation of blood calcium concentration.

The effect of PTH on calcium absorption by the digestive tract is actually indirect, through vitamin D. Vitamin D is required for calcium absorption by the intestines. However, vitamin D circulates in an inactive form until it is activated by a biochemical alteration that occurs in the kidneys. PTH is required for the renal activation step. An increase in PTH concentration increases the renal activation of vitamin D, which in turn enhances calcium absorption from the digestive tract.

As mentioned previously, calcitonin plays little or no role in the normal maintenance of blood calcium concentration once adulthood is reached. In adults, the primary regulator of blood calcium concentration is PTH.

**RECAP**

Production of the thyroid gland hormones ($T_4$ and $T_3$) requires iodine. $T_3$ and $T_4$ speed cellular metabolism and have widespread effects on growth in children and basal metabolic rate (BMR) in adults. Calcitonin (from the thyroid) lowers blood calcium levels and PTH (from the parathyroids) raises blood calcium. ■

## 13.7 Testes and ovaries produce sex hormones

The human gonads are the testes of males and the ovaries of females. These organs are responsible for the production of sperm and eggs, respectively. Both organs are also endocrine glands in that they produce the steroid sex hormones.

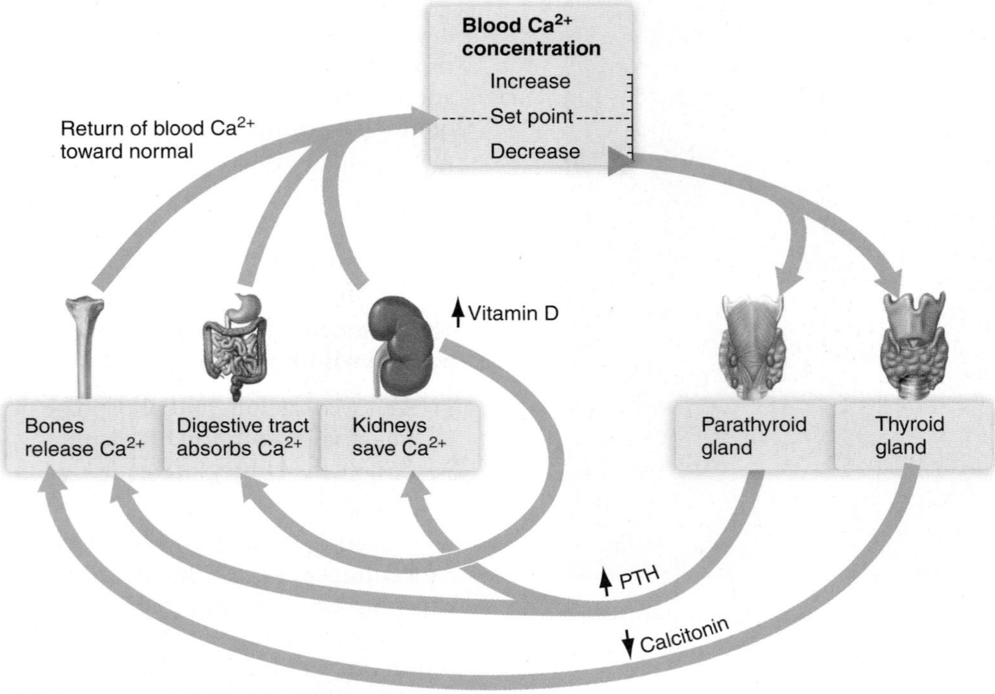


**a) Responses to a fall in blood calcium.**

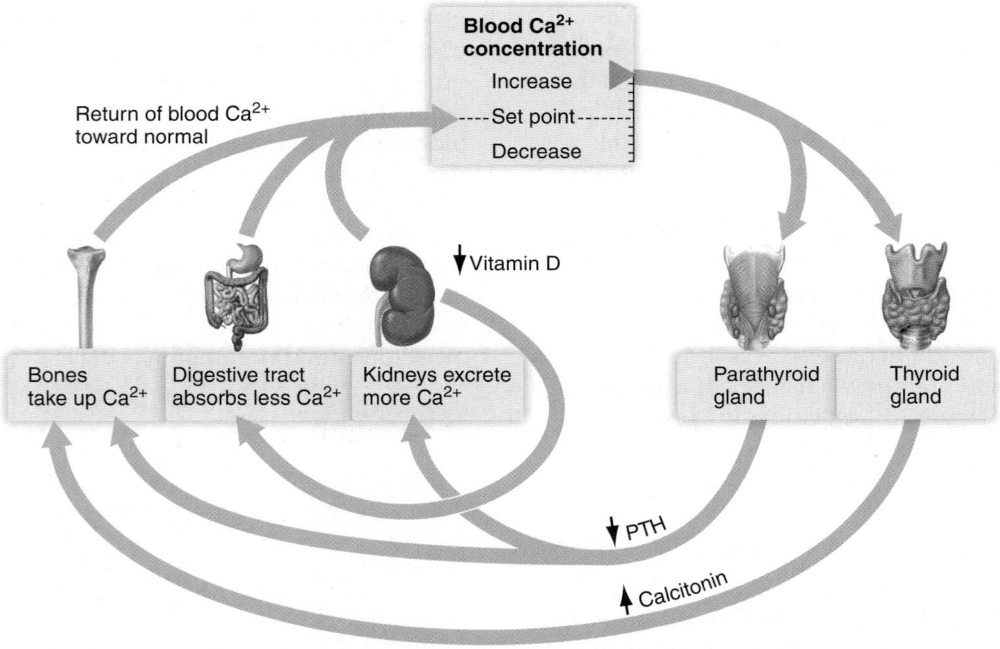


**b) Responses to a rise in blood calcium.** The importance of calcitonin is greatest in children, declining once adulthood is reached.

**Figure 13.15 The homeostatic regulation of blood calcium concentration.**

## Testes produce testosterone

The testes, located in the scrotum, produce androgens, the male sex hormones. The primary androgen produced by males is testosterone.

Before birth, testosterone production by the fetal testes is responsible for the development of the external male genitalia. Testosterone production declines essentially to zero between birth and puberty. During puberty the anterior pituitary gland begins to release luteinizing hormone (LH), which stimulates the testes to resume testosterone production.

In males, testosterone regulates the development and normal functioning of sperm, the male reproductive organs, and male sex drive. It is also responsible for the spurt of bone and muscle growth at puberty and the development of male secondary sex characteristics such as body hair and a deepening voice. LH, FSH, and testosterone continue to maintain the male reproductive system after puberty.

The adrenal glands in both sexes produce a small amount of a testosterone-like androgen called dihydroepiandrosterone (DHEA). DHEA has no demonstrable effect in males because they have an abundance of the more powerful testosterone. In females, DHEA from the adrenal glands is responsible for many of the same actions as testosterone in males, including enhancement of female pubertal growth, the development of axillary (armpit) and pubic hair, and the development and maintenance of the female sex drive.

### Ovaries produce estrogen and progesterone

The ovaries, located in the abdomen, produce the female sex hormones known collectively as estrogens (17b-estradiol, estrone, and estriol), and also progesterone. The estrogens are often commonly referred to just as estrogen.

During puberty, the anterior pituitary starts to release luteinizing hormone (LH) and follicle-stimulating hormone (FSH). These hormones stimulate the ovaries to begin secreting estrogen and progesterone.

Estrogen initiates the development of female secondary sex characteristics such as breast development, widening pelvis, and distribution of body fat. Both estrogen and progesterone regulate the menstrual cycle, the monthly changes in the tissue of the uterus that prepare the female body for pregnancy. Release of LH, FSH, estrogen, and progesterone continues throughout a woman's reproductive years.

We discuss male and female hormones and reproductive systems in greater detail in Chapter 16.

## 13.8 Other glands and organs also secrete hormones

In addition to the glands described so far there are several lesser endocrine glands, and also organs with glands within them whose functions are described in other chapters. Among these are the thymus and pineal glands, the heart, the digestive system, and the kidneys.

### Thymus gland hormones aid the immune system

The **thymus gland** is located between the lungs, behind the breastbone and near the heart. Sometimes it is considered part of the lymphatic system. For years the function of the thymus gland went unrecognized because its removal in an adult has little effect.

We now know that the thymus gland secretes several peptide hormones that assist in the development of lymphocytes into mature T cells. The thymus is relatively important in children, but it shrinks and reduces its secretion in adults, especially after age 30.

### The pineal gland secretes melatonin

The **pineal gland** is a pea-sized gland located deep within the brain, in the roof of the third ventricle. Its name derives from the fact that it is shaped like a small pine cone (*pineas* in Latin). More than 200 million years ago the pineal gland of our ancestors was a photosensitive area, or "third eye," located near the skin's surface. Although it is now shielded from light by the skull, it still retains its photosensitivity because it receives input indirectly from the eyes via the optic nerve and nerve pathways in the brain.

The pineal secretes the hormone **melatonin** (not to be confused with the skin pigment, melanin) in a cyclic manner, coupled to the daily cycle of light and dark. Melatonin is sometimes called the "hormone of darkness" because its rate of secretion rises nearly 10-fold at night and then falls again during daylight. Its secretion appears to be regulated by the absence or presence of visual cues. During the day, nerve impulses from the retina inhibit its release.

We are just beginning to understand what melatonin does. Researchers believe that it may be important in synchronizing the body's rhythms to the daily light/dark cycle (the *circadian cycle*). Some scientists suggest that declining sensitivity to melatonin may contribute to the onset of puberty; evidence in favor of this hypothesis is that destruction of the pineal gland by disease is associated with early puberty. Other proposed roles include inducing sleep, slowing the aging process, and enhancing immunity.

Melatonin is readily available over the counter as a pill. Some people take it as a natural sleep aid, although its effectiveness is controversial.

Table 13.2 lists all of the primary endocrine organs other than the hypothalamus and the pituitary, and summarizes their targets and hormonal actions.

### Endocrine functions of the heart, the digestive system, and the kidneys

The heart, the digestive system, and the kidneys all have functions unrelated to the endocrine system. Nevertheless, all three of these organs secrete at least one hormone. The hormones they secrete and the functions of the hormones are listed below and summarized in Table 13.3.

- *Atrial natriuretic hormone (ANH)* is a peptide (nonsteroid) hormone secreted by the atria of the heart that helps regulate blood pressure. When blood pressure rises, ANH increases the rate at which sodium and water are excreted in urine. This decreases blood volume and lowers blood pressure. We discuss how ANH acts on the kidneys in Chapter 15.
- *Gastrin, secretin,* and *cholecystokinin* are all hormones secreted by the digestive system. They have effects on the stomach, pancreas, and gallbladder (see Chapter 14).

**Table 13.2 Hormones of endocrine glands other than the hypothalamus and pituitary**

| Gland | Hormone(s) | Main targets | Primary actions |
|---|---|---|---|
| Pancreas | Glucagon | Liver | Raises blood sugar levels |
| | Insulin | Liver, muscle, adipose tissue | Lowers blood sugar levels |
| | Somatostatin | Pancreas, hypothalamus, digestive tract | Inhibits release of glucagon, insulin, growth hormone, and digestive secretions |
| Adrenal cortex | Glucocorticoids (including cortisol) | Most cells | Raise blood glucose levels and promote breakdown of fats and proteins; suppress inflammation |
| | Mineralocorticoids (including aldosterone) | Kidneys | Regulate body water balance by promoting sodium reabsorption, potassium excretion |
| Adrenal medulla | Epinephrine and norepinephrine | Liver, muscle, adipose tissue | Raise blood sugar; increase heart rate and force of contraction; dilate or constrict blood vessels, increase respiration |
| Thyroid | Thyroxine ($T_4$) and triiodothyronine ($T_3$) | Most cells | Regulate the rate of cellular metabolism; affect growth and development |
| | Calcitonin | Bone | Lowers blood calcium levels |
| Parathyroid glands | Parathyroid hormone (PTH) | Bone, digestive tract, kidneys | Raises blood calcium levels |
| Testes | Testosterone | Most cells | Development of sperm, male secondary sex characteristics, and reproductive structures |
| Ovaries | Estrogen, progesterone | Most cells | Development of female secondary sex characteristics and reproductive structure; regulate menstrual cycle |
| Thymus | Thymosin, thymopoietin | Lymphocytes | Help lymphocytes mature, especially in children |
| Pineal | Melatonin | Many cells | Synchronizes body rhythms; may be involved in onset of puberty |

- *Erythropoietin* and *renin* are secreted by the kidneys. Erythropoietin stimulates the production of red blood cells in bone marrow (see Chapter 7). Renin ultimately stimulates aldosterone secretion and constricts blood vessels (Chapter 15).

## 13.9 Other chemical messengers

Some chemical messengers can function in ways similar to hormones but are not considered hormones because they are not secreted into the blood. Their actions are primarily local (near their site of release). You already know about neurotransmitters, one group of chemical messengers that act on nearby cells.

Such nonhormonal chemical messengers include histamine, prostaglandins, nitric oxide, and various growth factors and growth-limiting factors, plus dozens of other molecules about which we still know very little (Table 13.4). Most of these substances are short-lived because they are either quickly destroyed or taken back up by the cells that produced them.

### Histamine is important in inflammation

**Histamine** is discussed in Chapter 9. Mast cells release histamine into the local interstitial fluid in response to tissue

**Table 13.3 Hormones of the digestive tract, kidneys, and heart**

| System or organ | Hormone(s) | Main targets | Primary actions |
|---|---|---|---|
| Digestive tract | Gastrin, secretin, cholecystokinin | Stomach, pancreas, gallbladder | Stimulate activities of the stomach, pancreas, and gallbladder |
| Kidneys | Erythropoietin | Bone marrow | Stimulates red blood cell production |
| | Renin | Adrenal cortex, blood vessels | Stimulates aldosterone secretion, constricts blood vessels |
| Heart | Atrial natriuretic hormone (ANH) | Kidney, blood vessels | Increases sodium excretion, dilates blood vessels |

**Table 13.4 Other chemical messengers**

| Messenger(s) | Primary actions |
|---|---|
| Histamine | Important in inflammatory response; increases secretion of mucus, dilates blood vessels, increases leakiness of capillaries |
| Prostaglandins | Control local blood flow; constrict blood vessels, dilate blood vessels, contribute to inflammatory response and blood clotting |
| Nitric oxide (NO) | Regulates local blood flow, controls penile erection, regulates smooth muscle contraction in digestive tract, acts as a "chemical warfare" agent against bacteria, interferes with clotting mechanisms, acts as a neurotransmitter in brain |
| Growth factors | Modulate growth of tissues at local level |

injury or the presence of an allergen. In turn, the histamine increases local secretion of mucus by mucus-secreting cells, dilates blood vessels, and increases the leakiness of capillaries, all part of a constellation of symptoms called inflammation.

Histamine is largely responsible for the runny nose of a cold and the nasal congestion of allergies. This is why over-the-counter drugs for colds and allergies generally contain an antihistamine compound.

### Prostaglandins: Local control of blood flow

**Prostaglandins** are a group of chemicals derived from a fatty acid precursor. Their name comes from the fact that they were first discovered in semen and were thought to originate from the prostate gland, but they have since been found in nearly every tissue in the body.

Prostaglandins have a variety of functions, including local control of blood flow. Some prostaglandins constrict blood vessels; others dilate blood vessels. They also contribute to the inflammatory response and are involved in blood clotting at the site of an injury.

### Nitric oxide has multiple functions

Nitric oxide (NO) is a gas that has only recently received attention as a chemical messenger. NO was originally called "endothelial-derived relaxing factor" because an extract of the endothelial cells lining blood vessels caused blood vessels to relax, or dilate. We now know that NO is produced in many other tissues as well.

Nitric oxide functions include regulating local blood flow in many tissues of the body, controlling penile erection, and regulating smooth muscle contraction in the digestive tract. Macrophages use it as a "chemical warfare" agent against bacteria, and it also interferes with clotting mechanisms. It even functions as a neurotransmitter in the brain.

### Growth factors regulate tissue growth

Chemical messenger molecules called growth factors modulate development of specific tissues at the local level. The list includes nerve growth factor, epidermal growth factor, fibroblast growth factor, platelet-derived growth factor, tumor angiogenesis growth factors, insulin-like growth factor, and many more. Growth factors influence when a cell will divide and even in what direction it will grow. For example, nerve growth factors help to determine the direction of neuron axon growth so that nerves develop properly.

**RECAP**

Various chemical messengers (histamine, prostaglandins, nitric oxide, and growth factors) act primarily locally. Among their actions are regulating local blood flows, participating in local defense responses, and regulating growth of specific types of tissue. ■

## 13.10 Disorders of the endocrine system

Because the endocrine system is one of the two primary systems for controlling body functions, any disruption to it can have dramatic and widespread effects on the body. We have already discussed several endocrine disorders earlier in this chapter. Here we look at several more.

### Diabetes mellitus: Inadequate control of blood sugar

Diabetes mellitus means "a high flow of urine with a sweet taste." Called diabetes for short, it is a disease of sugar regulation. The common feature of the several types of diabetes is an inability to get glucose into cells where it can be used. The result is an abnormally high glucose concentration in the blood—so high that it overwhelms the kidney's ability to reabsorb all that is filtered. Glucose and excessive water appear in the urine (hence the name of the disease), causing dehydration and thirst. In addition to these symptoms, many diabetics experience fatigue, frequent infections, blurred vision, cuts that are slow to heal, and tingling in the feet or hands.

Without the ability to metabolize glucose properly, the body turns to the metabolism of fat and proteins. The abnormal metabolism of glucose, fats, and proteins causes most of the other medical problems associated with diabetes, including cardiovascular and neural diseases, renal failure, blindness, and damage to small blood vessels that may lead to the need for amputations. There are two types of diabetes:

- *Type 1 diabetes* (5–10% of all cases) is caused by the failure of the pancreas to produce enough insulin. It is called insulin-dependent diabetes because the person depends on

# Dealing with Diabetes

According to the World Health Organization (WHO), in 1985 30 million people worldwide had diabetes. In 2000 it was up to 171 million, and by 2030 it is estimated to be a whopping 366 million. In the U.S. one-third of all children born five years ago are projected to develop diabetes during their lifetime, according to the U.S. Centers for Disease Control and Prevention (CDC). What is going on?

### Why Is Diabetes on the Rise?

Most of this rise in diabetes is due to an increase in Type 2 diabetes. The major risk factors for Type 2 diabetes are obesity, unhealthy diets, and insufficient exercise. All these risk factors are on the rise around the world, including in countries considered less industrialized. Basically, the human body is not well suited for a sedentary lifestyle combined with a steady diet of high-calorie, high-sugar foods.

Humans evolved from prehuman ancestors over several hundred thousand years. Over most of that time, humans existed only as small bands that traveled widely in search of food and shelter. Abundant food was a rare event, and finding food and obtaining shelter was often hard physical work. Under such conditions it was entirely appropriate, when high-calorie foods rich in carbohydrates were available, for a burst of insulin from the pancreas to help the body's cells take up the glucose quickly so that it could be used or converted to storage products for future use.

In just the last few centuries, food has become readily available to most people in the world. With glucose always in abundance and the body's glucose and fat storage depots chronically stuffed to capacity, our cells slowly develop a *resistance to insulin* to slow down the influx of glucose into cells. This raises blood glucose levels. In response, the pancreas secretes *more* insulin to overcome the resistance and lower the blood glucose to normal. Eventually, however, the ability of the pancreas to produce insulin begins to decline. Decreased insulin production, coupled with increased insulin resistance, result in the body's inability to control blood glucose properly on its own.

Genetics may also play a role, but it cannot account for the recent rise, because genes do not mutate that quickly. More than 250 genes have been identified that affect appetite, insulin resistance, obesity, and fat storage, but so far no "diabetes gene" has been identified. Nevertheless, certain human populations—South and East Asians, Hispanics, Africans, Native Americans, and Pacific Islanders—seem at greater risk than other groups.

It may seem counterintuitive, but an increased life expectancy can also raise the prevalence of diabetes within a population. When more people escape death from accidents, war, and infectious disease, they live long enough to develop the diseases that take time to appear, such as diabetes. In the U.S. and Europe, people are living longer and populations are aging.

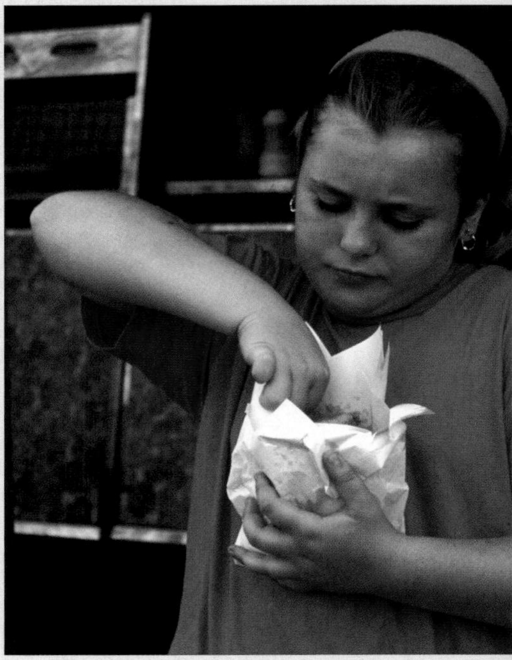

*The easy availability of high-sugar, high-fat foods places children and adults alike at increased risk for diabetes.*

## the **facts...**

- Diabetes is on the rise around the globe, from 30 million people in 1985 to over 171 million today.
- Many cases of diabetes could be prevented by lifestyle changes that include a healthy diet, moderate weight loss, and exercise.
- Early detection and disease management would reduce the economic, social, and medical impact of diabetes dramatically.
- Our health care system focuses on the long-term complications of diabetes because this is more profitable. Hospitals actually lose money on preventive care.

## Prevention Is the Key

Health experts agree that even a modest change in lifestyle dramatically reduces the risk of Type 2 diabetes. In a study published in the *New England Journal of Medicine,* over 2,000 nondiabetic subjects who were considered at risk for the disease because their blood sugar was in the high-normal range were randomly assigned to either a control group or a lifestyle modification group. Persons in the lifestyle modification group were asked to lose approximately 7 pounds and keep it off by eating a healthy low-fat, low-calorie diet and exercising regularly but moderately (such as walking 150 minutes per week). In less than three years the lifestyle-modification group had reduced their risk of diabetes by 58% compared to the control group.

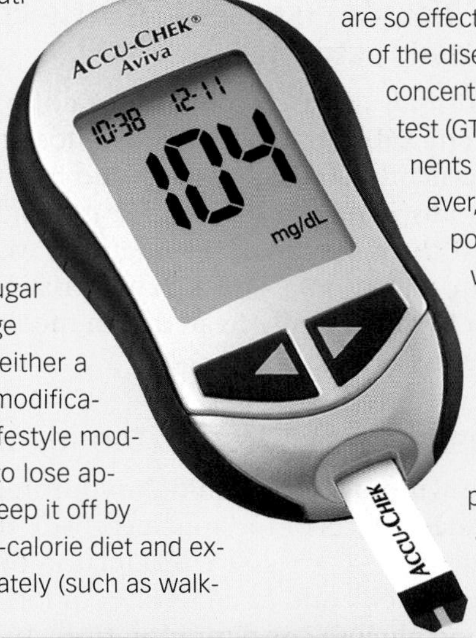


People with diabetes use a glucometer to check their blood glucose levels.

## Early Detection and Management Would Help

For both types of diabetes, early detection and careful management can reduce the social, economic, and health impacts of the disease. It's not the high blood sugar itself that is the problem, at least early on. Rather, it's the complications that arise from sustained high blood sugar over time. Untreated diabetes can lead to a host of other debilitating problems, including cardiovascular disorders, kidney failure, blindness, and neural diseases.

For example, in the U.S. approximately 40,000 diabetics develop kidney disease each year. Many of them progress to kidney failure, at which point they require treatment at a cost of over $50,000 per year (assuming the treatment, called *dialysis,* is available to them). Their lives and the lives of their families begin to revolve around managing their disease as they spend several half-days a week in a hospital or dialysis unit. Eventually they may need a kidney transplant, which can cost $100,000 or more. Because of devastating long-term complications like this, the total cost of treating diabetes in the U.S. is estimated to be $130 billion/year—the equivalent of $1,000 for every U.S. taxpayer.

Because early detection and management are so effective in limiting the ultimate cost of the disease, a fasting blood glucose concentration and a glucose tolerance test (GTT) are now standard components of most medical workups. However, early detection may not be possible in areas of the world where basic health care is not readily available. Over a third of all diabetics do not even know they have the disease.

Even when the diagnosis is made early, motivating patients to rigorously monitor and control their blood sugar can be a problem. It's hard to convince a newly diagnosed diabetic of the need to make major lifestyle changes when such devastating long-term complications are still in the future. Nobody wants to stick a finger several times a day and draw blood to measure glucose levels. And who among us is willing to give up sweets, lose 5–10 pounds (and keep it off), and start exercising nearly every day? But for a diabetic, lifestyle changes such as these become life-and-death issues.

## Shortcomings in Our Health Care System

A concerted effort by health professionals and governments aimed at promoting healthy lifestyles, combined with early detection and effective management of those who do develop high blood sugar levels, may be the best ways to combat this disease in the long run. Unfortunately, the U.S. health care reimbursement system does not take this into account. A short example will show you why.

Hospitals, doctors, and health care centers make their money through payments from government sources (such as Medicare and Medicaid) and private insurers. At current reimbursement rates, they generally lose money on preventive care and disease management but make money every time a diabetic is hospitalized for a major complication such as a kidney transplant or an amputation. For example, one recent study estimated that New York health care centers lost $40–$55 every time a diabetic met with a diabetes educator to learn how to monitor blood sugar properly or administer insulin or other treatment, and another $40–$55 when the patient met with a nutritionist to discuss controlling blood sugar through weight loss and a proper diet. In contrast, hospitals earned $1,500 to over $10,000 for every amputation, depending on the type of amputation and its complications. Is it any wonder that hospitals are more likely to hire a surgeon and promote their center as a surgical center of excellence, rather than add nutritionists or health educators to their staff?

Something needs to be done. The question is: what?

## Questions to consider

**1** *Would you be in favor of government-supported screening of all people for high blood sugar? Should it be mandatory?* **2** *What should be the government's role in paying for education, counseling, and follow-up of patients with diabetes? What about private insurance companies?*

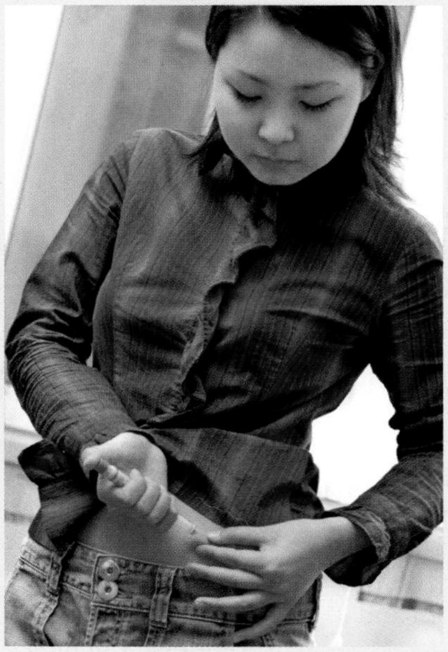

*Some diabetics must inject themselves with insulin daily.*

daily injections of insulin to allow glucose to enter the cells. It is thought to be caused by a virus that triggers the body's immune system to attack the beta cells of the pancreas. Typically it appears in childhood or adolescence.

- *Type 2 diabetes (non-insulin-dependent diabetes)* represents 90–95% of all cases. Its hallmark is *insulin resistance*—cells fail to respond adequately to insulin even when it is present. Type 2 diabetes usually occurs in adults beyond the age of 40; however, in recent years it has been occurring more frequently and at younger ages (see the Current Issue box). Type 2 diabetes may have a genetic component, but lifestyle factors are thought to be the major determinants.

Some Type 2 diabetics and "prediabetics" whose blood sugars are just approaching the diabetic range can control the disease entirely through lifestyle changes—maintaining a healthy weight, eating a nutritious diet, and exercising regularly. Others take insulin, especially to supplement their lifestyle changes when necessary. Other treatments include oral drugs that stimulate the pancreas to secrete more insulin, drugs that improve the action of the body's natural insulin, and drugs that increase the uptake of glucose by liver and muscle cells. More permanent solutions, such as implanting an artificial pancreas or transplanting human pancreatic cells, are under investigation.

### Hypothyroidism: Underactive thyroid gland

Hypothyroidism refers to underactivity of the thyroid gland (hyposecretion of thyroid hormones). Mild cases of hypothyroidism may not have any signs, but more severe deficiencies can cause a variety of symptoms.

In children, insufficient thyroxine production for any reason can slow body growth, alter brain development, and delay the onset of puberty. Left untreated, this deficiency can result in cretinism, a condition of mental retardation and stunted growth.

In adults, insufficient thyroxine can lead to myxedema, a condition characterized by edema (swelling) under the skin, lethargy, weight gain, low BMR, and low body temperature. Hyposecretion of the hormone can be treated with thyroxine pills.

### Hyperthyroidism: Overactive thyroid gland

Hyperthyroidism involves an overactive thyroid gland and hypersecretion of thyroid hormones. Too much thyroxine increases BMR and causes hyperactivity, nervousness, agitation, and weight loss.

The most common form of hyperthyroidism is Graves' disease, an autoimmune disorder in which a person's antibodies stimulate the thyroid to produce too much thyroxine. Graves' disease is often accompanied by protruding eyes caused by fluid accumulation behind the eyes.

### Addison's disease: Too little cortisol and aldosterone

Addison's disease is caused by failure of the adrenal cortex to secrete sufficient cortisol and aldosterone. Lack of cortisol lowers blood glucose levels, and lack of aldosterone lowers blood sodium. Addison's disease tends to develop slowly, with chronic symptoms of fatigue, weakness, abdominal pain, weight loss, and a characteristic "bronzed" skin color. It can be successfully treated with medications that replace the missing hormones.

### Cushing's syndrome: Too much cortisol

The symptoms of Cushing's syndrome are due to the exaggerated effects of too much cortisol, the main effects of which are (1) excessive production of glucose from glycogen and protein, and (2) retention of too much salt and water. Blood glucose concentration rises, and muscle mass decreases because of the utilization of protein to make glucose. Some of the extra glucose is converted to body fat, but only in certain areas of the body, including the face, abdomen, and the back of the neck (Figure 13.16). Symptoms

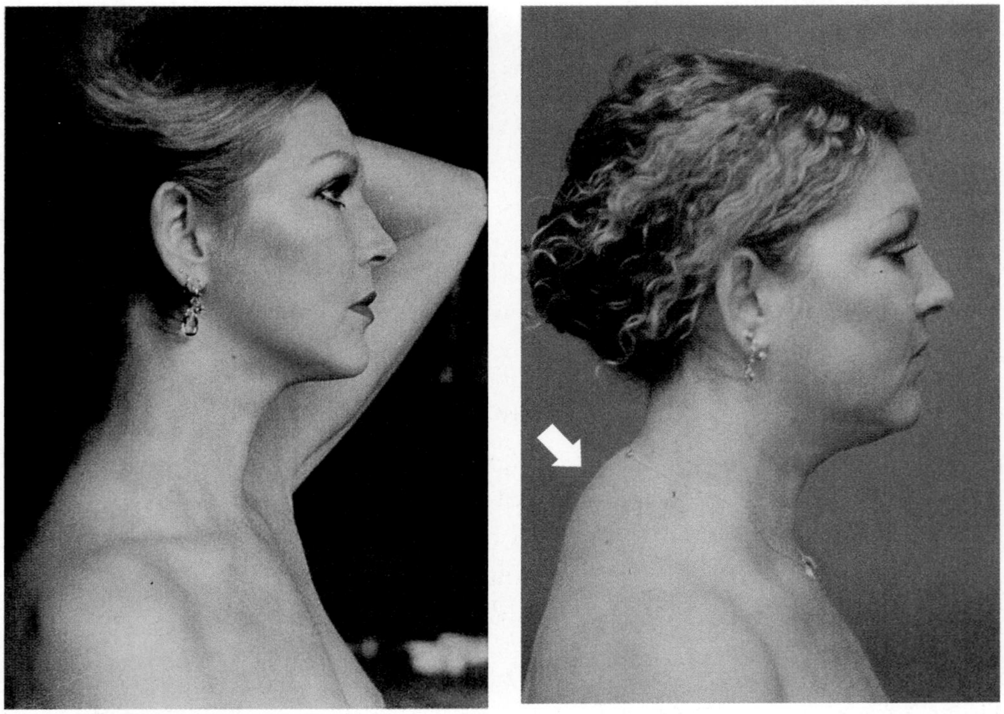

**a) Before the disease.**

**b) During the disease a characteristic hump of fat develops at the back of the neck.**

**Figure 13.16 Cushing's syndrome.**

of Cushing's syndrome include muscle weakness and fatigue, edema (swelling due to too much fluid), and high blood pressure. The disease can be caused by tumors of the adrenal gland or the ACTH-secreting cells of the pituitary. It can also be due to excessive use of cortisol and cortisol-like drugs (cortisone, prednisone, dexamethasone, and others) to control chronic inflammatory conditions such as allergies and arthritis.

## Chapter Summary

### The endocrine system produces hormones *p. 297*

- The endocrine system is a collection of glands that secrete hormones into the blood.
- Hormones are chemical messengers secreted by the endocrine system that circulate in the blood and act on specific target cells.

### Hormones are classified as steroid or nonsteroid *p. 299*

- Steroid hormones are lipid soluble; they enter the target cell in order to function.
- Nonsteroid hormones generally are not lipid soluble. They bind to receptors on the outer surface of the cell membrane of the target cell.

### The hypothalamus and the pituitary gland *p. 301*

- The hypothalamus of the brain and the pituitary gland of the endocrine system link the nervous and endocrine systems.
- The posterior lobe secretes two hormones (ADH and oxytocin) that are produced by the hypothalamus.
- The anterior lobe of the pituitary produces and secretes six hormones (ACTH, TSH, FSH, LH, PRL, and GH). The first four stimulate the release of other hormones from other endocrine glands.
- Abnormalities of ADH secretion lead to disorders of water balance.
- Hypersecretion of growth hormone in a child leads to gigantism; hyposecretion causes dwarfism. In an adult, hypersecretion of growth hormone causes acromegaly.

### The pancreas secretes glucagon, insulin, and somatostatin *p. 305*

- Within the pancreas, clusters of cells called the pancreatic islets produce and secrete three hormones (glucagon, insulin, and somatostatin).
- Glucagon raises blood glucose levels, insulin lowers blood glucose levels, and somatostatin appears to inhibit the secretion of glucagon and insulin.

### The adrenal glands comprise the cortex and medulla *p. 306*

- The outer zone of the adrenal gland, called the cortex, secretes steroid hormones that affect glucose metabolism (glucocorticoids) and salt balance (mineralocorticoids).
- The inner zone of the adrenal gland, called the medulla, is actually a neuroendocrine organ. The adrenal medulla secretes epinephrine and norepinephrine into the blood.

### Thyroid and parathyroid glands *p. 307*

- The thyroid gland produces thyroxine ($T_4$), triiodothyronine ($T_3$), and calcitonin.
- The four small parathyroid glands produce PTH, which, along with calcitonin, is responsible for the regulation of blood calcium concentration.

### Testes and ovaries produce sex hormones *p. 309*

- The primary male sex hormone is testosterone, produced by the testes.
- The ovaries produce the two female sex hormones, estrogen and progesterone.

### Other glands and organs also secrete hormones *p. 311*

- The thymus gland produces two hormones (thymosin and thymopoietin) that help lymphocytes mature into T cells.
- Melatonin from the pineal gland synchronizes the body's daily rhythms to the daily light/dark cycle.
- The heart secretes atrial natriuretic hormone, the kidneys secrete renin and erythropoietin, and the digestive tract secretes gastrin, secretin, and cholecystokinin.

### Other chemical messengers *p. 312*

- Some substances not defined as hormones (because they are not specifically secreted into the bloodstream) nevertheless serve as chemical messengers.
- Most of these chemical messengers tend to act locally, near their site of secretion. They include histamine, prostaglandins, nitric oxide, and growth factors.

### Disorders of the endocrine system *p. 313*

- Because the endocrine system controls so many body functions, disruptions can have widespread effects.
- Hypothyroidism can lead to cretinism (stunted growth and mental retardation) in children and myxedema in adults. Graves' disease is the most common form of hyperthyroidism.
- Insufficient cortisol and aldosterone can cause Addison's disease, and hypersecretion of cortisol results in Cushing's syndrome.

## Terms You Should Know



## Concept Review

1. List the functions of the six hormones secreted by the anterior lobe of the pituitary gland.
2. Explain the characteristics of the endocrine system that make its reactions different from those of the nervous system.
3. Compare and contrast the mechanisms by which steroid and nonsteroid hormones act.
4. Define when you would call norepinephrine a neurotransmitter and when you would call it a hormone.
5. Explain why a 30-year-old short person cannot be made taller by taking growth hormone.
6. Describe the function of the two hormones from the thymus gland. Why is this function likely to be more important in children than in adults?
7. Explain how the pineal gland can be sensitive to light, even though it is located deep within the brain.
8. Describe why substances such as histamine and nitric oxide, although they are chemical messengers, are not considered true hormones.
9. Name the hormone that is released from the posterior pituitary of lactating females when the infant nurses.
10. Describe the role of the pineal gland in the circadian cycle.

## Test Yourself

### Matching Exercise

_____ 1. A hormone that regulates water balance
_____ 2. A hormone that contributes to the increase in bone and muscle mass during childhood and adolescence
_____ 3. Sometimes functions as a second messenger within a cell
_____ 4. Pituitary hormone associated with feelings of sexual satisfaction
_____ 5. A glucocorticoid produced by the adrenal cortex
_____ 6. One of two hormones from the kidneys

a. cyclic AMP
b. cortisol
c. ADH
d. erythropoietin
e. oxytocin
f. growth hormone

### Fill in the Blank

7. Neuroendocrine cells in the hypothalamus make ______________ and ______________, which are transported to and released by the posterior pituitary.
8. A (steroid/nonsteroid) hormone binds to a receptor on the target cell's cell membrane.
9. The two anterior pituitary hormones that stimulate the reproductive organs in both men and women are ______________ and ______________.
10. The primary mineralocorticoid hormone produced by the adrenal cortex is ______________.
11. The hormone ______________ is released after a meal to lower blood sugar levels.
12. The hormone properly called ______________ is also commonly known as adrenaline.

### True or False?

13. Calcitonin is produced and secreted by the anterior pituitary gland.
14. Insulin and glucagon are produced and secreted by different types of cells in the pancreas.
15. The pineal gland secretes melatonin, a hormone that increases at night.

## References and Additional Reading

Duncan, David E. The Covert Plague: Have You Got It? *Discover,* December 2005 (An article on the recent rise of Type 2 diabetes.)

Hadley, M.E. *Endocrinology.* 5th ed. Prentice Hall, 2000. (A standard textbook of endocrinology.)

Lacy, Paul E. Treating Diabetes with Transplanted Cells. *Scientific American,* July 1995, pp. 50–58. (A discussion of recent advances and future directions in the treatment of Type 1 diabetes.)

### Internet References

Find links to the following Web sites at the Human Biology Place.

**American Diabetes Association**
**www.diabetes.org**
A leading nonprofit organization for diabetes research, information, and advocacy.

**UpToDate Patient Information**
**www.uptodate.com**
Sponsored by several professional medical organizations, this table of contents links to information on a variety of health conditions.

**The Endocrine Society**
**www.endo-society org**
An international professional organization of endocrinologists; contains information for the general public as well as professionals.

**National Institute of Diabetes and Digestive and Kidney Diseases**
**www2.niddk.nih.gov**
This institute of the National Institutes of Health contains health information about diabetes and other endocrine and metabolic disorders.

## Apply **What You Know**

1. If the biological effectiveness of a hormone were greatly reduced because its target cells lacked the appropriate receptors, would you expect the hormone concentration to be high, normal, or low? Explain. (*Hint:* It may help to draw the components of a negative feedback loop.)
2. Explain why an injection of epinephrine to combat an acute immune reaction (such as an allergic response to a bee sting) has an almost immediate effect, whereas an injection of a steroid hormone can take hours to have an effect.
3. From what you read in section 13.5, draw the negative feedback control loop for cortisol secretion. Then indicate on your diagram how stress or injury would affect the feedback loop. Check your diagram with a classmate or your teacher—if you can draw it and explain it, you understand it!
4. When a pregnant woman goes into labor, a series of strong muscle contractions force the baby from the uterus through the birth canal. Labor can be painful. Normally, such pain would initiate a negative feedback loop that would inhibit muscle contractions to prevent such pain, but that doesn't happen during labor. Why not?
5. Diabetics have to be particularly careful about sugar intake. Some are able to control the condition through careful diet. What sorts of foods should diabetics avoid, what foods should they try to get more of, and what can they do if they make a mistake?
6. A student finishes up the fall semester with several term papers and a number of big exams. After the semester she goes home for the holidays and comes down with a bad cold. The following year the same thing happens; she's sick for the holidays. During her senior year the fall semester isn't too bad, but applications to graduate school are due and she spends most of her semester break filling out forms and nervously worrying about what she will do next year. She's again sick for the beginning of the next term. Is this student just unlucky, or is something else at work?

*Answers can be found on the Human Biology Place.*

# 14 The Digestive System and Nutrition

1 What are the main **functions** of your stomach?

2 Where in the digestive tract are nutrients and water **absorbed** into the body?

3 Which of the following foods or food products is likely to contain ***trans* fats**?

**a.** A red meat steak **b.** Fish, especially sardines **c.** Commercial baked goods, such as crackers **d.** Olive oil

4 What percentage of the U.S. population is **obese**? **a.** Under 5% **b.** Around 30% **c.** Over 50%

5 Which of the following legumes contains **all** of the amino acids required by humans?

**a.** Peanuts **b.** Soybeans **c.** Black-eyed peas **d.** Lima beans

Colored SEM (× 20) of the lining of the stomach. The large folds flatten out when the stomach is full. The small indents are gastric pits.

**Stop for a moment and make a list** of what you ate for lunch—a hamburger, fries, and a soft drink? Pizza and bottled water? A salad, apple, and milk?

All cells need **nutrients**—substances in food that are required for growth, reproduction, and the maintenance of health. Quite simply, the cells of your body must live on whatever you choose to eat. Right now the nutrients in your last meal (as well as nutrients stored in your body from previous meals) are being used to fuel cellular activities, build cell components, and serve other vital functions. Your cells draw these nutrients from your blood, and your blood obtains them from your digestive system or from nutrient storage pools.

In many ways the digestive system is a highly efficient disassembly line. It takes in food and processes it, breaking it into small pieces and digesting the fragments with enzymes and strong chemicals. Then it passes the mixture down the line, absorbing its nutrients along the way, and stores the leftover waste until it can be eliminated from the body.

Does what you eat matter? Yes! Poor nutrition is associated with diseases ranging from cancer to cavities. Good nutrition, on the other hand, improves overall health and lowers the risk of health problems. In this chapter we follow the digestive process and the fate of your food. Then we discuss how you can apply this information to promote a healthy diet and body weight.

## 14.1 The digestive system brings nutrients into the body

The **digestive system** consists of all the organs that share the common function of getting nutrients into the body. It includes a series of hollow organs extending from the mouth to the anus: the mouth, pharynx, esophagus, stomach, small intestine, large intestine, rectum, and anus. These organs form a hollow tube called the **gastrointestinal (GI) tract** ("gastric" is the adjective for stomach). The space within this hollow tube—the area through which food and liquids travel—is called the *lumen.*

The digestive system also includes four accessory organs—the salivary glands, liver, gallbladder, and pancreas. Figure 14.1 summarizes the functions of the organs and accessory organs of the digestive system.

### The walls of the GI tract are composed of four layers

From the esophagus to the anus, the walls of the GI tract share common structural features (Figure 14.2). The walls of the GI tract consist of four layers of tissue:

1. **Mucosa.** The innermost tissue layer (the mucous membrane in contact with the lumen) is the mucosa. All nutrients must cross the mucosa to enter the blood.
2. **Submucosa.** Next to the mucosa is a layer of connective tissue containing blood vessels, lymph vessels, and nerves, called the submucosa. Components of food that are absorbed across the mucosa enter the blood and lymph vessels of the submucosa.
3. **Muscularis.** The third layer of GI tract tissue, called the muscularis is responsible for motility or movement. The muscularis consists of two or three sublayers of smooth muscle. In general, the fibers of the inner sublayer are oriented in a circular fashion around the lumen, whereas those in the outer sublayer are arranged lengthwise, parallel to the long axis of the digestive tube. The exception is the stomach, which has a diagonal (oblique) sublayer of muscle inside the other two.
4. **Serosa.** The outermost layer of the GI tract wall, or serosa, is a thin connective tissue sheath that surrounds and protects the other three layers and attaches the digestive system to the walls of the body cavities.

Some of the organs of the GI tract are separated from each other by thick rings of circular smooth muscle called *sphincters.* When these sphincters contract they can close off the passageway between organs.

### Answers to Intro Questions

1 The stomach stores food after a meal, mixes the contents with acid and protein-digesting enzymes, and delivers the partially digested food to the small intestine over the next four hours or so.

2 In the small and large intestines. Most are absorbed in the small intestines—only the last 10% or so is absorbed in the large intestine.

3 **c.** *Trans* fats are found in solidified vegetable oils such as margarine and in many baked goods. They are thought to increase the risk of heart disease.

4 **b.** Approximately 30% of Americans are obese, according to U.S. government statistics.

5 **b.** Of these legumes, only soybeans contain all of the essential amino acids. Because so many plant foods are missing one or more of the essential amino acids, vegetarians need to be especially careful of the combination of foods they eat if they are to achieve a balanced amino acid intake.

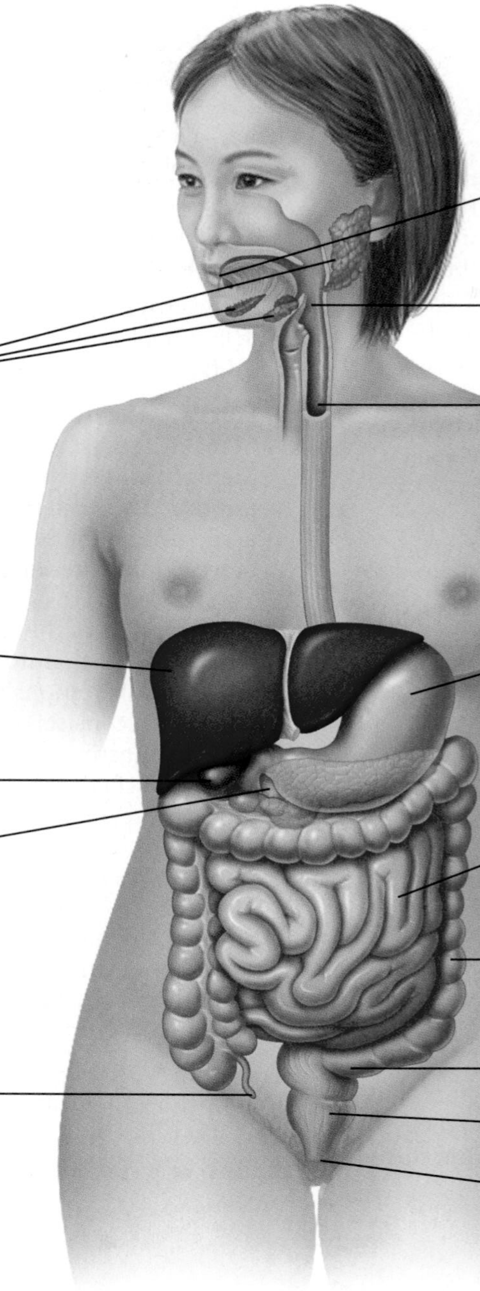


**Figure 14.1 Organs and accessory organs of the digestive system and their functions.**

**RECAP**

The digestive system consists of organs and accessory organs that share the function of bringing nutrients into the body. The wall of the GI tract consists of four tissue layers: the mucosa, the submucosa, the muscularis, and the serosa. ■

## Five basic processes accomplish digestive system function

In practical terms, the digestive system is a huge disassembly line that starts with huge chunks of raw material (we call it food) and takes them apart so that the nutrients in food can

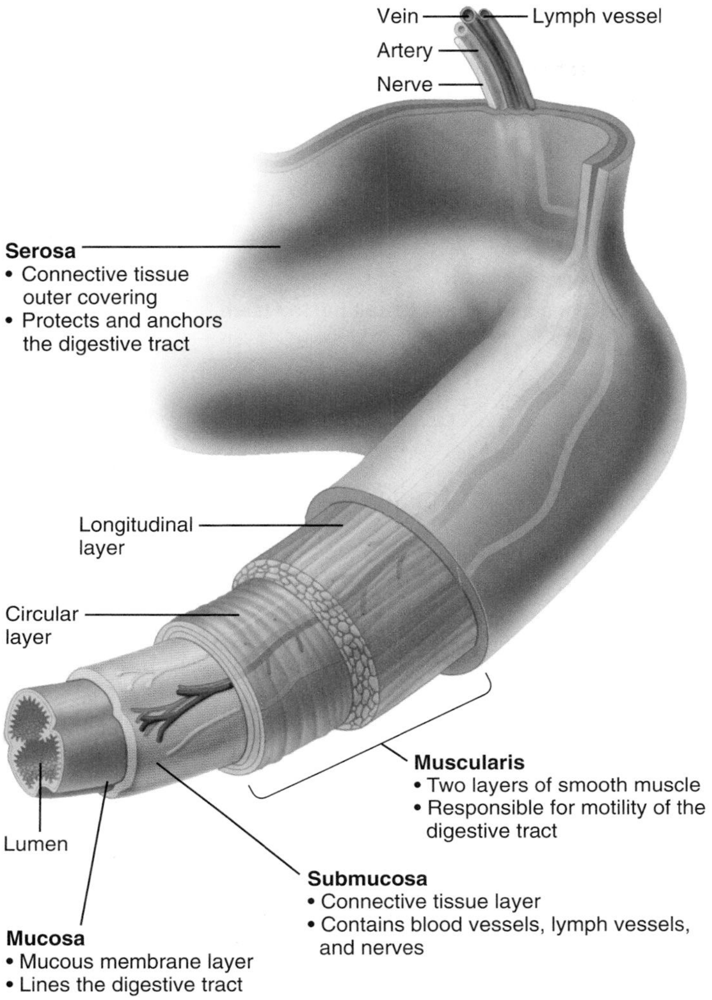


**Figure 14.2 The four tissue layers of the GI tract wall.**

be absorbed into the body. The digestive system accomplishes this task with five basic processes:

1. *Mechanical processing and movement.* Chewing breaks food into smaller pieces, and two types of movement (motility) mix the contents of the lumen and propel it forward.
2. *Secretion.* Fluid, digestive enzymes, acid, alkali, bile, and mucus are all secreted into the GI tract at various places. In addition, several hormones that regulate digestion are secreted into the bloodstream.
3. *Digestion.* The contents of the lumen are broken down both mechanically and chemically into smaller and smaller particles, culminating in nutrient molecules.
4. *Absorption.* Nutrient molecules pass across the mucosal layer of the GI tract and into the blood or lymph.
5. *Elimination.* Undigested material is eliminated from the body via the anus.

## Two types of motility aid digestive processes

The smooth muscle of the GI tract produces two kinds of motility, called peristalsis and segmentation. The functions of peristalsis and segmentation are quite different.

**Peristalsis** propels food forward (Figure 14.3a). Peristalsis begins when a lump of food (called a bolus) stretches a portion of the GI tract, causing the smooth muscle in front of the bolus to relax and the muscle behind it to contract. The contractions push the food forward, stretching the next

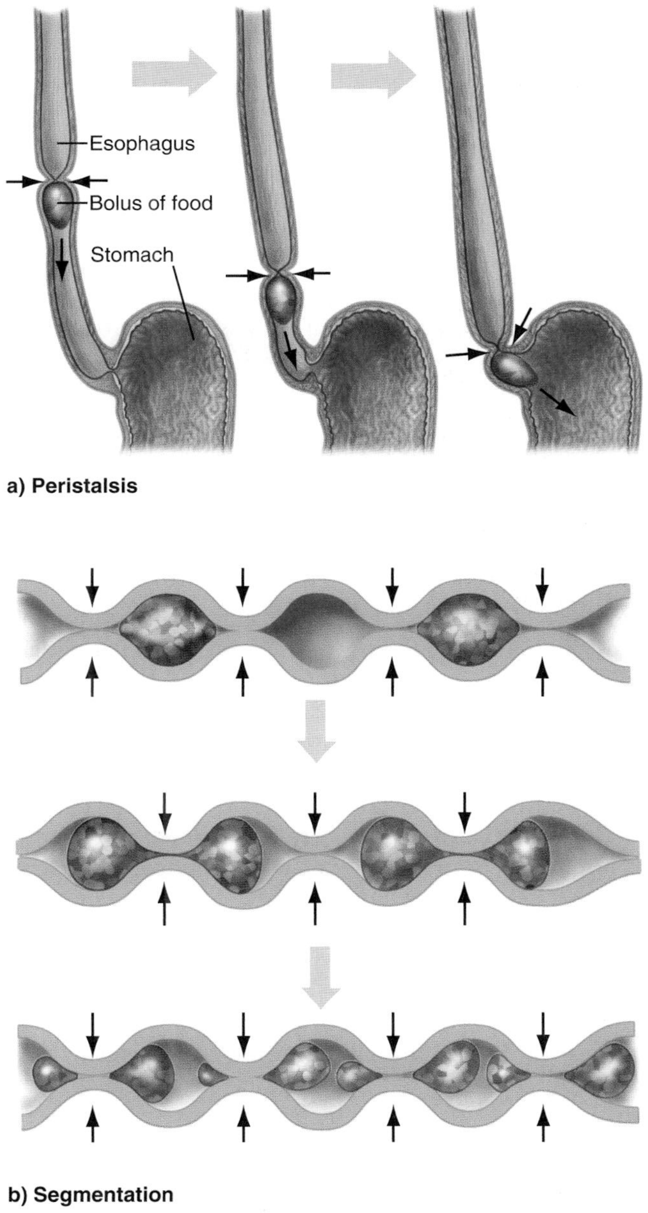


**Figure 14.3 Motility of the gastrointestinal tract. (a)** Peristalsis in the esophagus. The three sequential diagrams show how peristalsis moves the contents of the lumen onward. **(b)** Segmentation in the small intestine. Segmentation mixes the contents of the lumen.

part of the tube and causing muscle relaxation in front and contraction behind. The peristaltic wave of contraction ripples through the organs of the GI tract, mixing the contents of the stomach and pushing the contents of the esophagus and intestines forward. Peristalsis occurs in all parts of the GI tract, but is especially prevalent in the esophagus, where it transports food rapidly to the stomach.

**Segmentation** mixes food (Figure 14.3b). In segmentation, short sections of smooth muscle contract and relax in seemingly random fashion. The result is a back-and-forth mixing of the contents of the lumen. Food particles are pressed against the mucosa, enabling the body to absorb their nutrients. Segmentation occurs primarily in the small intestine as food is digested and absorbed.

## 14.2 The mouth processes food for swallowing

The mouth, or oral cavity, is the entrance to the GI tract. Digestion begins in the mouth with the process of chewing, which breaks food into smaller and smaller chunks. Essentially, the mouth functions as an effective food processor.

### Teeth bite and chew food

The teeth chew food into pieces small enough to swallow. There are four types of teeth, each specialized for a different purpose (Figure 14.4a). The sharp-edged incisors cut food and the pointed canines tear it. The flat surfaces of the premolars and molars are well adapted to grinding and crushing food.

Children have only 20 teeth. They develop by about age 2 and are gradually replaced by permanent teeth. Permanent teeth usually develop by late adolescence, except for the wisdom teeth (third molars), which generally appear by age 25. Most adults have 32 permanent teeth.

Each tooth (Figure 14.4b) consists of a visible region called the crown and a region below the gum line called the root. The crown is covered by a layer of enamel, an extremely hard nonliving compound of calcium and phosphate. Beneath the enamel is a bonelike living layer called dentin. The soft innermost pulp cavity contains the blood vessels that supply the dentin, as well as the nerves that cause so much pain when a tooth is infected or injured. The entire tooth sits in a socket in the jawbone that is lined with periodontal membrane.

Our mouths contain large numbers of bacteria that flourish on the food that remains between the teeth (Figure 14.4c). During their metabolism these bacteria release acids that can dissolve enamel, creating cavities or *dental caries.* If not treated, cavities deepen, eroding the dentin and pulp cavity and causing a toothache. Tooth decay may inflame the soft gum tissue (gingiva) around the tooth, causing *gingivitis.* Decay that inflames the periodontal membrane leads to *periodontitis.* However, good dental hygiene—including regular exams and teeth cleaning—can prevent most dental problems from becoming serious.

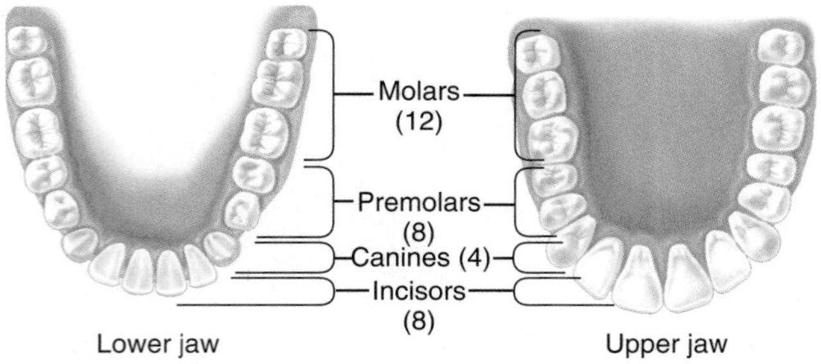


**a) Locations and types of adult human teeth.**

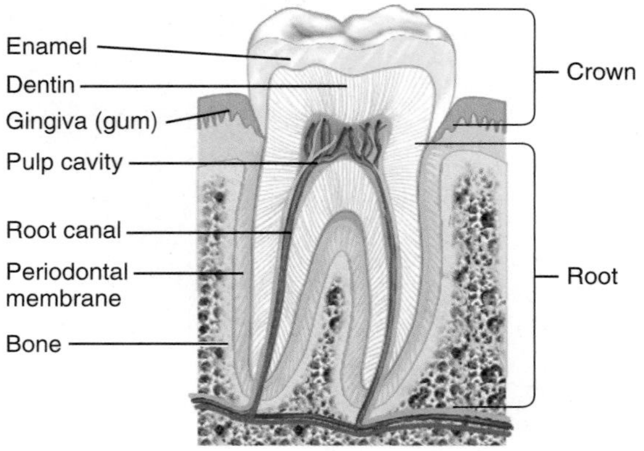


**b) Anatomy of a tooth.**

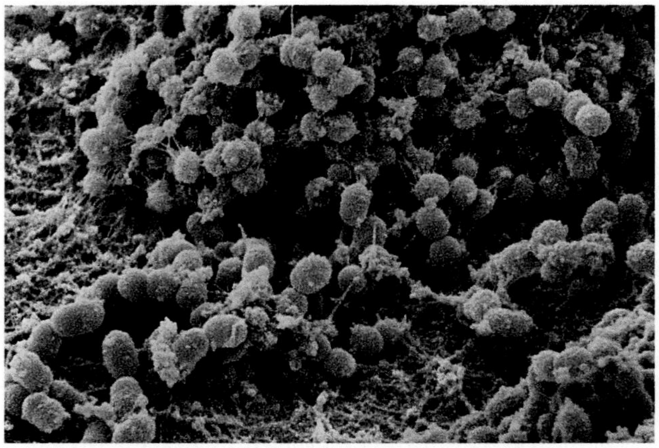

**c) Bacteria on a tooth's surface (approx. ×8,000).**

**Figure 14.4 Teeth.**

### The tongue positions and tastes food

Chewing would be inefficient without the muscular tongue, which positions food over the teeth and mashes it against the roof of the mouth. The tongue consists of skeletal muscle enclosed in mucous membrane, so we have voluntary control over its movements. The tongue contributes to the sense of taste (Chapter 12) and also is important for speech.

### Saliva begins the process of digestion

Three pairs of **salivary glands** produce a watery fluid called saliva. The parotid gland lies near the back of the jaw, and

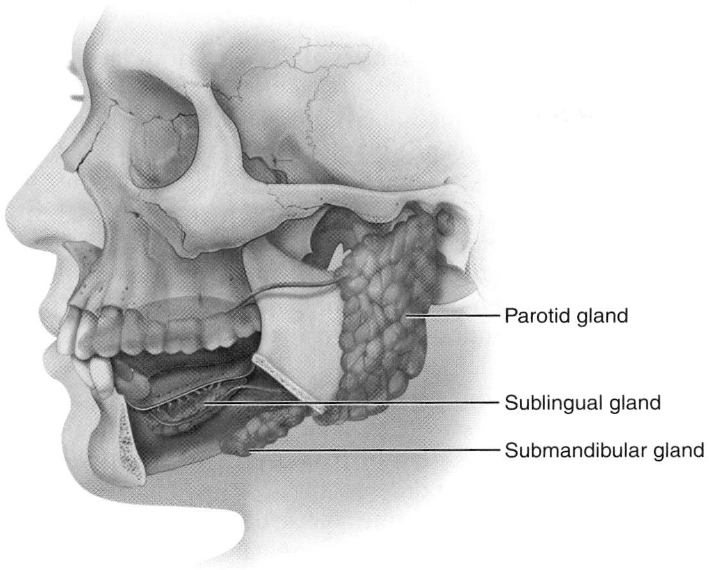


**Figure 14.5 The salivary glands.** The three pairs of glands deliver saliva to the mouth via salivary ducts.

the smaller submandibular and sublingual glands are located just below the lower jaw and below the tongue, respectively (Figure 14.5). All three glands connect to the oral cavity via ducts.

Saliva moistens food, making it easier to chew and swallow. Saliva contains four main ingredients, each with important functions. One is *mucin,* a mucuslike protein that holds food particles together so they can be swallowed more easily. An enzyme called *salivary amylase* begins the process of digesting carbohydrates. *Bicarbonate* ($HCO_3^-$) in saliva maintains the pH of the mouth between 6.5 and 7.5, the range over which salivary amylase is most effective. Salivary bicarbonate may also help protect your teeth against those acid-producing bacteria. Saliva also contains small amounts of an enzyme called *lysozyme* that inhibits bacterial growth.

**RECAP**

The four kinds of teeth (molars, premolars, canines, and incisors) mechanically digest chunks of food. Salivary glands secrete saliva, which moistens food, begins the chemical digestion of carbohydrates, maintains the pH of the mouth, and protects the teeth against bacteria. ■

## 14.3 The pharynx and esophagus deliver food to the stomach

After we have chewed our food and mixed it with saliva, the tongue pushes it into the **pharynx,** or throat, for swallowing. The act of swallowing involves a sequence of events that is coordinated with a temporary halt in breathing.

First, voluntary movements of the tongue and jaws push a bolus of food into the pharynx. As described in Chapter 10, the pharynx is a common passageway for food and air (Figure 14.6a). The presence of the food stimulates receptors in the pharynx that initiate the second, involuntary phase, the "swallowing reflex." The soft palate rises to close off the passageway into the nasal cavities and the larynx rises slightly. The epiglottis bends to close the airway to the trachea temporarily, so we do not inhale the food. Meanwhile, the tongue pushes the food back even farther, sliding it past the epiglottis and into the esophagus (Figure 14.6b). Once started, the swallowing reflex is involuntary and cannot be stopped. The initiation of swallowing is the last voluntary act in the process until defecation.

Just beyond the pharynx is the **esophagus,** a muscular tube consisting of both skeletal and smooth muscle that connects the pharynx to the stomach. The lining of the esophagus produces lubricating mucus that helps food slide

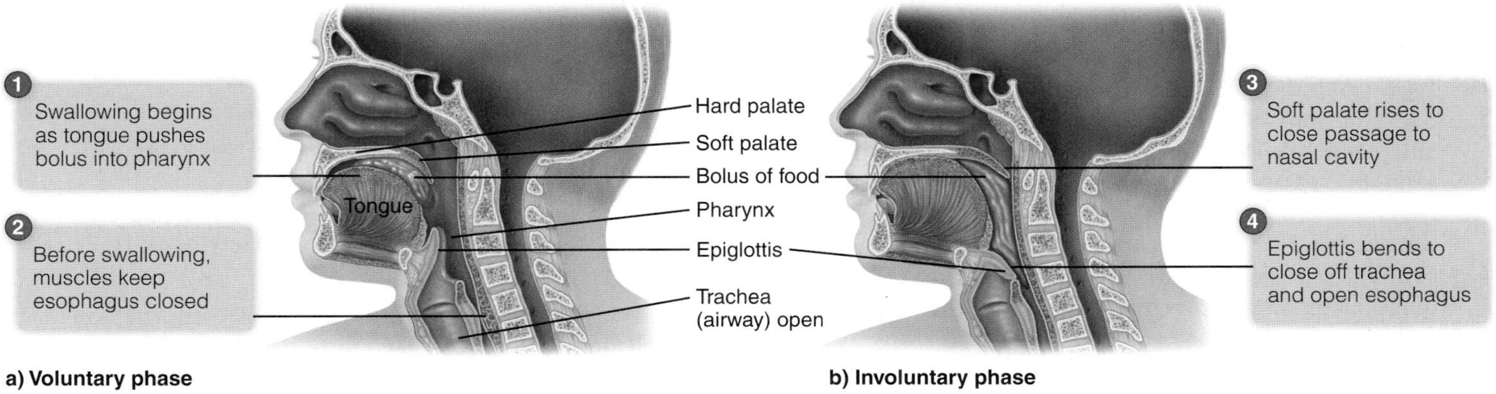


**Figure 14.6 Swallowing. (a)** During the voluntary phase the tongue pushes a bolus of food back against the soft palate. **(b)** During the involuntary (reflex) phase the force of the tongue causes the soft palate to rise, closing off the nasal passage. The epiglottis bends to close off the airway and the bolus slides past the epiglottis and into the esophagus.

easily. The presence of a bolus of food in the esophagus initiates peristaltic contractions of smooth muscle that push the bolus to the stomach. Occasionally thick foods like mashed potatoes or peanut butter stick briefly to the mucosa of the esophagus, causing a painfully strong reflex contraction behind the food. If the contraction does not dislodge the food, drinking liquid may help.

Gravity assists peristalsis in propelling food. However, peristaltic contractions enable the esophagus to transport food even against gravity, such as when we are lying down.

The lower esophageal sphincter, located at the base of the esophagus, opens briefly as food arrives and closes after it passes into the stomach. The sphincter prevents reflux of the stomach's contents back into the esophagus. Occasionally this sphincter malfunctions, resulting in the backflow of acidic stomach fluid into the esophagus. This condition, known as *acid reflux,* is responsible for the burning sensation known as "heartburn." Acid reflux becomes more common with weight gain, pregnancy, and age. Occasionally it indicates a *hiatal hernia,* a condition in which part of the stomach protrudes upward into the chest through an opening (hiatus) in the diaphragm muscle. Mild or temporary acid reflux is usually not serious and often improves with weight loss. However, prolonged acid reflux may cause esophageal ulcers because stomach acid can erode the mucosa of the esophagus.

**RECAP**

Swallowing begins with voluntary movements of the tongue; the presence of food initiates an involuntary swallowing reflex. Peristalsis and gravity transfer food through the esophagus to the stomach. ■

## 14.4 The stomach stores food, digests protein, and regulates delivery

The **stomach** is a muscular, expandable sac that performs three important functions:

- *Food storage.* Humans tend to eat meals several times a day. The stomach stores the food until it can be digested and absorbed. The stomach shrinks when empty, then expands to 1–3 liters of capacity when we eat.
- *Digestion.* The stomach is more than a storage bag, however. It also digests proteins, using strong acid and protein-digesting enzymes. The strong acid also kills most bacteria. Muscle contractions mix these secretions with food, assist in mechanically breaking apart food particles, and push the mixture into the small intestine.
- *Regulation of delivery.* The stomach regulates the rate at which food is delivered to the small intestine.

### Gastric juice breaks down proteins

The walls of the stomach consist of the usual four layers: mucosa, submucosa, muscularis, and serosa (Figure 14.7a). A closer look at the mucosal layer reveals millions of small openings called gastric pits that lead to gastric glands below the surface (Figure 14.7b, c). Some of the cells lining the glands secrete either hydrochloric acid (HCl) or mucus, but most secrete pepsinogen, a large precursor molecule that becomes a protein-digesting enzyme called **pepsin** once it is exposed to acid in the stomach. Collectively, the HCl, pepsinogen, and fluid that are secreted into the glands are known as gastric juice.

Typically the stomach produces 1–2 liters of gastric juice per day, most of it immediately after meals. The pepsin and acid in gastric juice dissolve the connective tissue in food and digest proteins and peptides into amino acids so they can be absorbed in the small intestine. The acid in gastric juice gives the stomach an acidic pH of approximately 2. The watery mixture of partially digested food and gastric juice that is delivered to the small intestine is called **chyme.** Between the stomach and the small intestine is the pyloric sphincter, which regulates the rate of transport of chyme into the small intestine.

If gastric juice is powerful enough to digest proteins, why doesn't it digest the stomach too? The reason is that some of the cells lining the stomach and the gastric glands continuously produce a protective barrier of mucus. Normally the stomach contents are in contact with mucus, not living cells. If the mucus layer becomes damaged, however, this leaves the underlying tissue vulnerable. An open (sometimes bleeding) sore called a **peptic ulcer** (from the Greek word *peptein,* digest) may form. Peptic ulcers occasionally occur in the esophagus and upper part of the small intestine as well.

In addition to pepsinogen, HCl, and mucus, some mucosal cells secrete *intrinsic factor,* a protein that binds to vitamin $B_{12}$ so that it can be absorbed in the small intestine. Finally, certain cells in the gastric glands secrete a hormone called *gastrin* into the bloodstream. We talk about gastrin when we discuss the regulation of the digestive process.

**RECAP**

The stomach stores food, digests it, and regulates its delivery to the small intestine. Gastric juice dissolves connective tissue, large proteins, and peptides in food. ■

### Stomach contractions mix food and push it forward

While your stomach is empty, tonic muscle contractions keep it small. When you eat a meal, tonic contractions cease and the stomach relaxes and stretches to accommodate the food. Stretching signals peristalsis to increase.

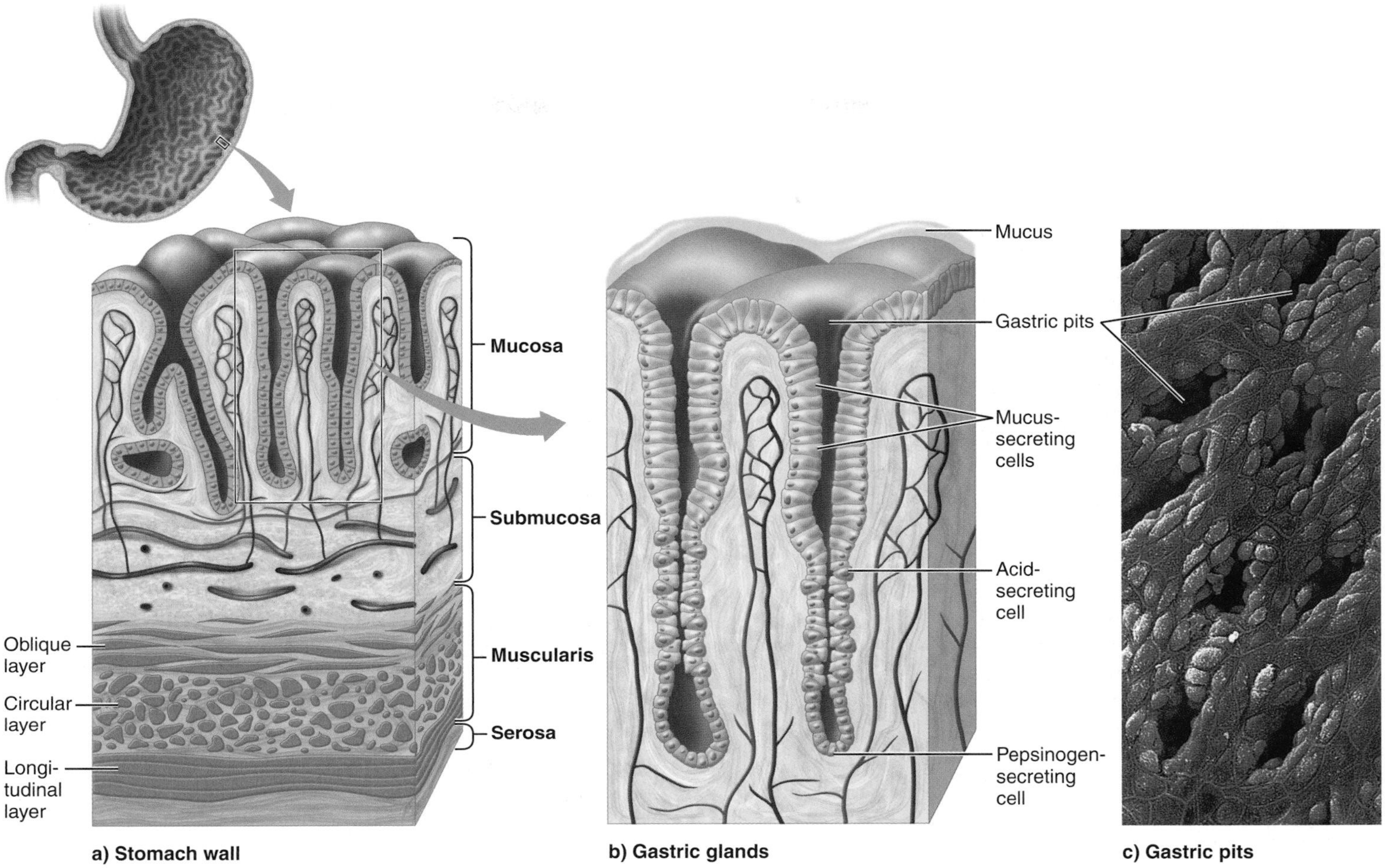


**Figure 14.7 The stomach.**

Each wave of peristalsis starts at the lower esophageal sphincter and moves toward the pyloric sphincter, becoming stronger as it proceeds. The peristaltic wave pushes the chyme forward and then, when there is nowhere else for it to go, backward again in a squeezing, mixing motion (Figure 14.8). Each contraction propels about a tablespoon of chyme into the small intestine before the pyloric sphincter closes momentarily. A peristaltic contraction occurs every 15–25 seconds. Have you ever noticed your stomach gurgling at this rate after a meal? You're hearing peristalsis in action.

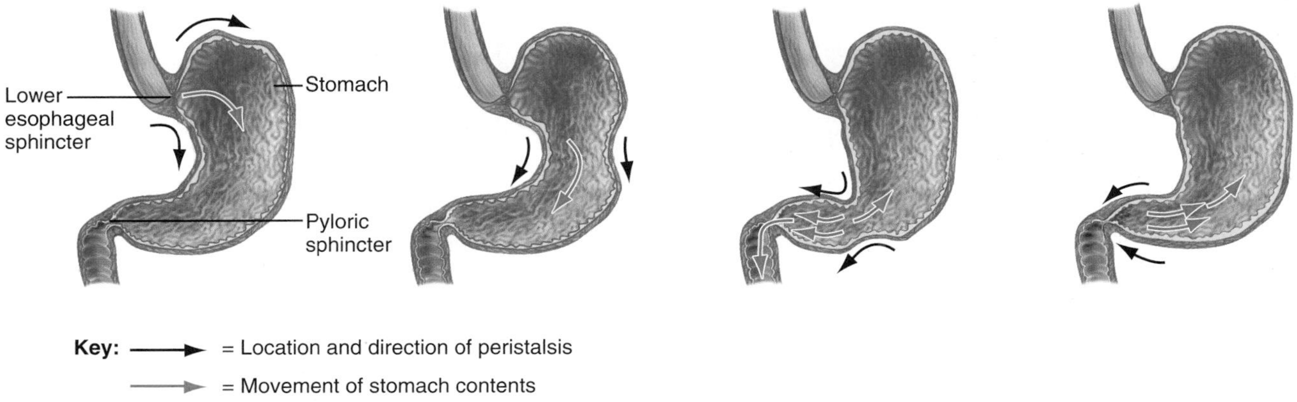


**Figure 14.8 Peristalsis of the stomach.** A peristaltic wave of contraction occurs in the stomach approximately every 15–25 seconds. Peristalsis mixes the contents of the stomach and forces a small amount of chyme into the small intestine with each contraction.

# Directions in Science

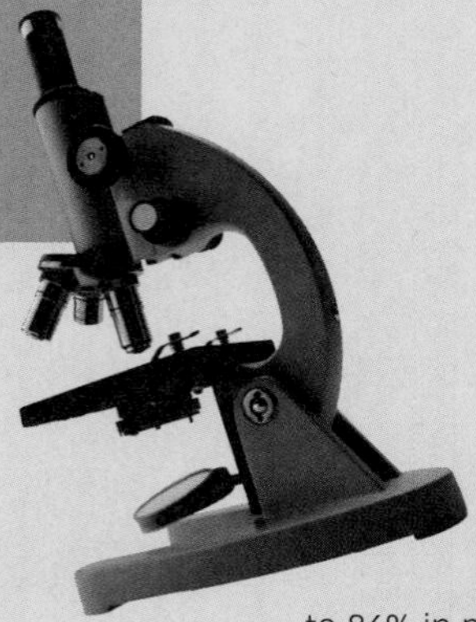

## Treating Peptic Ulcers

Peptic ulcers afflict 4 to 5 million Americans each year. Until the early 1980s doctors believed that peptic ulcers were caused by excess production of stomach acid, triggered by stress, diet, alcohol, and smoking. Many sufferers had to undergo surgery, and research focused on developing drugs that block gastric acid production. By the mid-1990s two drugs, cimetidine (Tagamet) and ranitidine (Zantac), were prescribed for nearly 90% of all peptic ulcer patients, generating huge profits for the pharmaceutical companies that held their patents.

By the time the two drugs had been in use for 15 years, ulcer surgeries had declined by nearly 60%—an astounding success by any measure. There was just one problem: neither Tagamet nor Zantac prevented the recurrence of ulcers. Relapse rates were as high as 95% over two years, meaning that patients had to treat new ulcers over and over again.

Meanwhile, in 1982 two Australian medical researchers, J. Robin Warren and Barry Marshall, discovered that the mucosal lining of ulcer patients' stomachs was infected with a previously unknown bacterium, which they named *Helicobacter pylori.* Warren and Marshall proposed that *H. pylori* actually causes peptic ulcers and that antibiotics would cure them.

So why did it take until 1995 for an antibiotic treatment for *H. pylori* to be approved? Some researchers point to the pharmaceutical industry, which at first showed little interest in the bacterium. This may be because the drugs required to treat it, a combination of bismuth and two antibiotics, were already available and relatively inexpensive (less than $200 per person). Another reason for the delay was healthy scientific skepticism. The *H. pylori* theory represented a major departure from the status quo, and the scientific community expects any new discovery to be repeated and confirmed by other researchers.

Recent research does confirm the *H. pylori* hypothesis. One study reports that peptic ulcers recur in only 8% of ulcer patients treated with antibiotics that eradicate *H. pylori,* compared to 86% in patients not receiving the antibiotics. Indeed, the antibiotic regimen could well cure ulcers *and* save $600 to $800 million per year in total health care costs!

Researchers have also found that *H. pylori* infection is surprisingly common. About 50% of U.S. adults have the organism in their stomachs. Older age groups have higher rates of infection than younger age groups. However, only 10–15% of those infected ever experience any symptoms.

Despite initial resistance, the importance of Warren's and Marshall's discovery was duly recognized. In 2005 they received the ultimate vindication of their work—the Nobel Prize for medicine and physiology. Ultimately the process of science worked.

And what about stomach acid, so long believed to be the culprit in peptic ulcers? We now know that although stomach acid is required for ulcers to form, it alone does not cause them. In fact, most ulcer patients have only a normal level of stomach acid. Tagamet and Zantac help ulcer patients because they reduce stomach acid and soothe existing sores, but continuing *H. pylori* infection allows ulcers to redevelop.

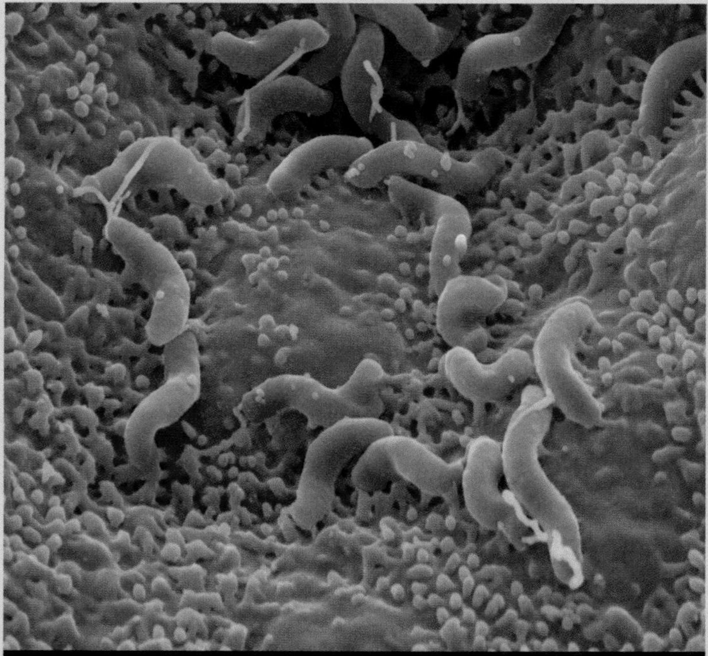

*H. pylori*, the bacterium that causes peptic ulcers.

It takes two to six hours for the stomach to empty completely after a meal. Most forceful when the stomach is full, peristalsis declines as the stomach empties. Chyme with a high acid or fat content stimulates the release of hormones that slow stomach peristalsis, giving the small intestine more time to absorb the nutrients.

The stomach does not absorb nutrients because it lacks the required cellular transporting mechanisms and because its inner lining is coated with mucus. Exceptions to this rule are alcohol and aspirin, both of which are small lipid-soluble substances that can cross the mucus barrier and be absorbed into the bloodstream directly from the stomach. Nevertheless, this is not the primary absorptive pathway for alcohol; most alcohol is absorbed in the intestine along with the nutrients.

**RECAP**

The presence of food stretches the stomach and increases peristalsis. Peristaltic contractions mix the chyme and push it gradually into the small intestine. ■

## 14.5 The small intestine digests food and absorbs nutrients and water

The process of digestion continues in the small intestine, so named because it is smaller in diameter than the final segment of the digestive tract, the large intestine. The small intestine has two major functions:

1. *Digestion.* The stomach partially digests proteins to smaller peptides, under the influence of strong acids and pepsin. Protein digestion continues in the small intestine, but here we also digest carbohydrates and lipids. Digestion of proteins, carbohydrates, and lipids in the small intestine involves neutralizing the highly acidic gastric juice and adding additional digestive enzymes from the intestine and pancreas.
2. *Absorption.* Eventually the proteins, carbohydrates, and lipids in food are broken down to single amino acids, monosaccharides, fatty acids, and glycerol, which are small enough to be transported across mucosal cells into the blood. Nearly 90% of the absorbable nutrients and water is absorbed in the small intestine.

### The small intestine has a large surface area for absorption

The small intestine consists of three different regions. The first region, the **duodenum,** is only about 10 inches long, but it is here that most of the digestion takes place. The products of digestion are absorbed primarily in the other two segments, the *jejunum* and the *ileum,* which together are about 10 feet long.

The structure of the small intestine wall makes it well suited for absorption (Figure 14.9). The mucosa contains large folds covered with microscopic projections called **villi** (singular: *villus*). Each epithelial cell of the villi has dozens of even smaller, cytoplasmic projections called microvilli. The microvilli give the mucosal surface a velvety appearance, which is why they are sometimes called the "brush border." Combined, the folds, villi, and microvilli enlarge the surface area of the small intestine by more than 500 times, increas-

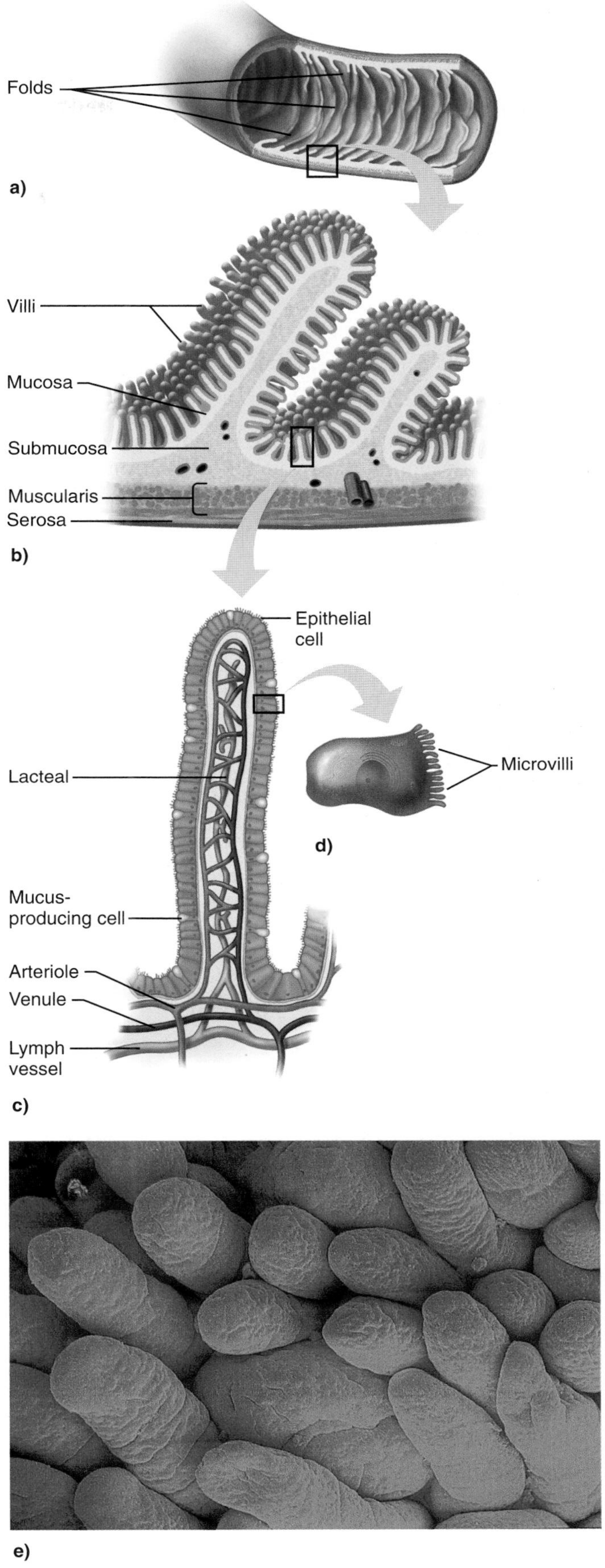


**Figure 14.9 The wall of the small intestine. (a)** The wall of the small intestine contains numerous folds that increase its surface area. **(b)** Each fold is covered with smaller folds called villi. **(c)** A close-up view of a villus showing the single layer of mucosal cells covering the surface and the centrally located lymph vessel (lacteal) and blood vessels. **(d)** A single cell with its outer membrane of microvilli. **(e)** Human intestinal villi (× 270).

ing its ability to absorb nutrients. At the center of each villus are capillaries and a small lymph vessel called a lacteal, which transport nutrients to larger blood vessels and lymph vessels.

**RECAP**

The small intestine has two major functions: a. digesting proteins, carbohydrates, and lipids; and b. absorbing approximately 90% of the nutrients and water we consume. Projections called villi in the mucosa increase the small intestine's surface area for absorption. ■

## 14.6 Accessory organs aid digestion and absorption

As mentioned earlier, the digestive system has four accessory organs: salivary glands, pancreas, gallbladder, and liver. We have already discussed the salivary glands. Before discussing absorption in more detail, let's look at the roles of the other three accessory organs.

### The pancreas secretes enzymes and $NaHCO_3$

The **pancreas,** an elongated organ that lies just behind the stomach, has both endocrine and exocrine functions (Figure 14.10). In Chapter 13 we saw that as an endocrine gland it secretes hormones that regulate blood glucose levels. In this chapter we focus on its exocrine role. The pancreas produces and secretes:

- *Digestive enzymes.* Pancreatic enzymes include *proteases* (enzymes that digest proteins), such as trypsin, chymotrypsin, and carboxypeptidase; *pancreatic amylase,* which continues the digestion of carbohydrates only partially accomplished by salivary amylase; and *lipase,* a lipid-digesting enzyme.

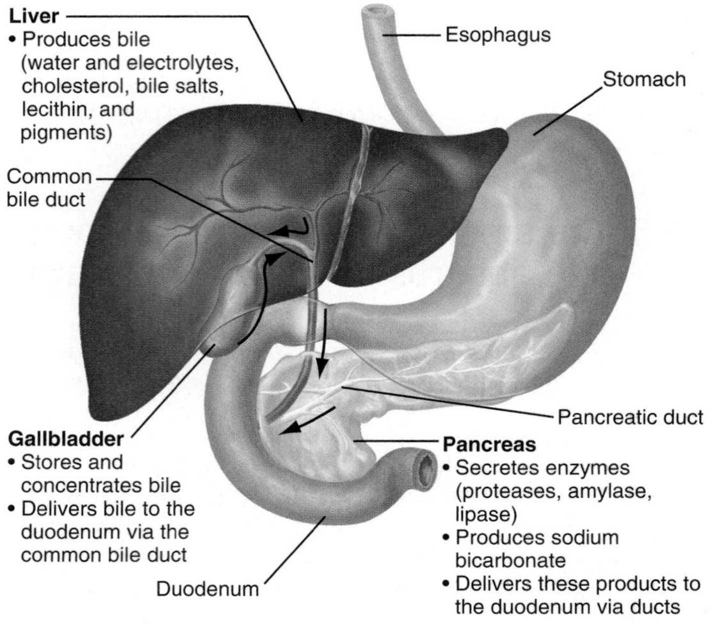


**Figure 14.10 Locations and digestive functions of the liver, gallbladder, and pancreas.** These three accessory organs are connected to the small intestine via ducts. The common bile duct joins one of the two pancreatic ducts just before it enters the duodenum. Arrows indicate direction of movement of secretory products.

- *Sodium bicarbonate* ($NaHCO_3$). Unlike pepsin, which is effective in acid conditions, pancreatic enzymes work best at a more neutral pH. $NaHCO_3$ functions to neutralize stomach acid.

Two pancreatic ducts deliver these secretions to the duodenum, where they facilitate the process of digestion. Table 14.1 lists major digestive enzymes in the gastrointestinal tract.

**Table 14.1 Major enzymes of digestion**

| Enzyme | Source | Where active | Substance digested | Breakdown products |
|---|---|---|---|---|
| ***Carbohydrate Digestion*** | | | | |
| Salivary amylase | Salivary glands | Mouth | Polysaccharides | Disaccharides |
| Pancreatic amylase | Pancreas | Small intestine | Polysaccharides | Disaccharides |
| Intestinal enzymes | Small intestine | Small intestine | Disaccharides | Monosaccharides (e.g., glucose) |
| ***Protein Digestion*** | | | | |
| Pepsin | Stomach | Stomach | Proteins | Peptides |
| Trypsin | Pancreas | Small intestine | Proteins | Peptides |
| Chymotrypsin | Pancreas | Small intestine | Proteins | Peptides |
| Carboxypeptidase | Pancreas | Small intestine | Peptides | Amino acids |
| Intestinal enzymes | Small intestine | Small intestine | Peptides | Amino acids |
| ***Lipid Digestion*** | | | | |
| Lipase | Pancreas | Small intestine | Triglycerides | Free fatty acids, monoglyceride |

**RECAP**

The pancreas assists digestion by producing (1) digestive enzymes and (2) sodium bicarbonate to neutralize stomach acid and make enzymes more effective. ■

## The liver produces bile and performs many other functions

The liver is a large organ located in the upper right abdominal cavity. The liver performs many significant functions, some of which are associated with digestion.

The liver's primary digestive function is to facilitate the digestion and absorption of lipids by producing **bile.** Bile is a watery mixture containing electrolytes, cholesterol, bile salts derived from cholesterol, a phospholipid called lecithin, and pigments (primarily bilirubin) derived from the breakdown of hemoglobin. The bile salts emulsify lipids in the small intestine; that is, they break them into smaller and smaller droplets. Eventually the droplets are small enough to be digested by lipases (lipid-digesting enzymes) from the pancreas.

An important feature of the vascular anatomy of the GI tract is the **hepatic portal system** (Figure 14.11). In general terms, a *portal system* carries blood from one capillary bed to another: we have seen a portal system before, in the vascular connection between the hypothalamus and the anterior pituitary gland. In the digestive system the hepatic portal system carries nutrient-rich blood directly from the digestive organs to the liver (*hepatos* is the Greek word for "liver") via the hepatic portal vein. Therefore, the liver is ideally located to begin processing and storing nutrients for the body just as soon as digestion and absorption have begun. After passing through the liver the blood is returned to the general circulation.

The liver serves a number of other functions that maintain homeostasis. The liver:

- Stores fat-soluble vitamins (A, D, E, and K) and iron
- Stores glucose as glycogen after a meal, and converts glycogen to glucose between meals
- Manufactures plasma proteins, such as albumin and fibrinogen, from amino acids
- Synthesizes and stores some lipids
- Inactivates many chemicals, including alcohol, hormones, drugs, and poisons
- Converts ammonia, a toxic waste product of metabolism, into less toxic urea
- Destroys worn-out red blood cells

Because of its central role in so many functions, liver injury can be particularly dangerous. Overexposure to toxic chemicals, medications, or alcohol can damage the liver because it takes up these substances to "detoxify" them, killing some liver cells in the process. Long-term exposure, such as prolonged alcohol abuse, can destroy enough cells to permanently impair liver function, a condition known as *cirrhosis.*

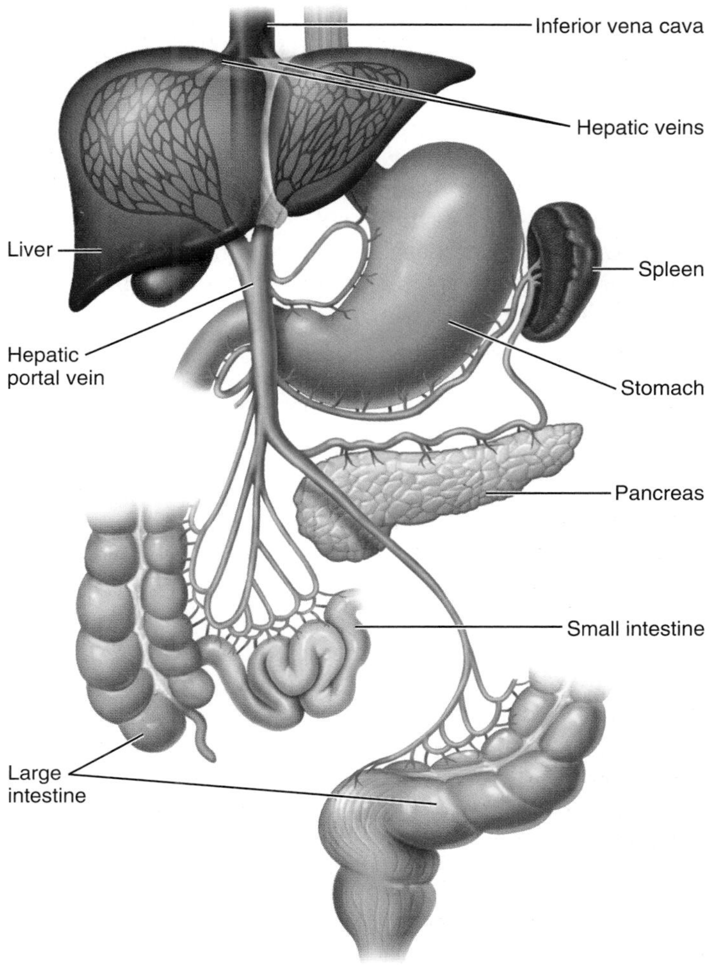


**Figure 14.11 The hepatic portal system.** The hepatic portal system carries nutrient-rich venous blood from the stomach, intestines, pancreas, and spleen directly to the liver before the blood is returned to the general circulation. Only the first part of the large intestine is shown.

## The gallbladder stores bile until needed

The bile produced by the liver flows through ducts to the **gallbladder.** The gallbladder concentrates bile by removing most of the water and stores it until after a meal, when it is secreted into the small intestine via the bile duct, which joins the pancreatic duct.

**RECAP**

Bile is produced by the liver and stored in the gallbladder until after a meal. The liver also produces plasma proteins; inactivates toxic chemicals; destroys old red blood cells; stores vitamins, iron, and certain products of metabolism; and performs other functions important for homeostasis. ■

## 14.7 The large intestine absorbs nutrients and eliminates wastes

By the time the contents of the digestive tract reach the large intestine, most of the nutrients and water have been absorbed. The **large intestine** absorbs most of the remaining nutrients and water and stores the now nearly solid waste material until it can be eliminated.

Although the large intestine is larger in diameter than the small intestine, it is only about half as long. It begins at a pouch called the cecum, which receives the chyme from the small intestine (Figure 14.12). A small fingerlike pouch, the **appendix,** extends from the cecum. The appendix has no known digestive function, but we become acutely aware of its presence if it becomes inflamed or infected, a condition called appendicitis.

Most of the large intestine consists of four regions collectively called the **colon.** The ascending colon rises along the right side of the body (the left side of Figure 14.12, viewed from the front), the transverse colon crosses over to the left side, and the descending colon passes down the left side to the short final segment, the sigmoid colon. Feces are stored in the sigmoid colon until defecation, when they pass through the rectum to the anus.

In addition to indigestible material, the feces contain about 5% bacteria by weight. Many strains of bacteria thrive on the leftover material in the colon that we cannot digest. Some of these bacteria release by-products that are useful to us, such as vitamin K, which is important for blood clotting. They also produce less helpful substances such as intestinal gas, a by-product of their metabolism as they break down food.

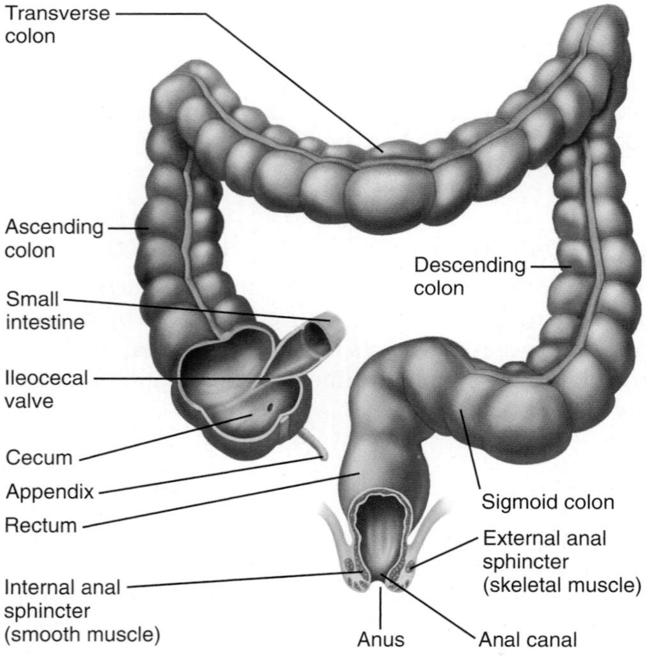


**Figure 14.12 The large intestine.** The large intestine begins at the cecum and ends at the anus.

Defecation is controlled by neural reflex. Normally the anus is kept closed by tonic contraction of a ring of smooth muscle called the *internal anal sphincter*. But when feces enter the rectum and the rectum is stretched, a neural reflex causes the internal anal sphincter to relax and the rectum to contract, expelling the feces.

We can prevent defecation by voluntarily contracting the *external anal sphincter,* a ring of skeletal muscle under our conscious control. "Potty training" of children involves learning to control the external anal sphincter. Until they learn how to control it consciously, children defecate whenever the defecation reflex occurs.

**RECAP**

The large intestine absorbs the last of the water, ions, and some nutrients and stores feces until defecation occurs. ■

## 14.8 How nutrients are absorbed

Once food has been digested, how does your body absorb the nutrients? The mechanism depends on the type of nutrient.

### Proteins and carbohydrates are absorbed by active transport

In the small intestine, enzymes from the pancreas and enzymes secreted by the mucosal layer of the stomach and from the small intestine itself break down proteins into amino acids, completing the digestion of proteins that began in the stomach. The amino acids are then actively transported into the mucosal cells. Eventually they move by facilitated diffusion out of the mucosal cells and make their way into the capillaries (Figure 14.13).

Carbohydrate digestion begins in the mouth, where salivary amylase breaks down polysaccharides into disaccharides (review Table 14.1). It is completed in the small intestine with the addition of pancreatic amylase and enzymes from the small intestine. Together these enzymes break down the remaining carbohydrates into monosaccharides (simple sugars such as glucose). Monosaccharides follow transport pathways that are similar to those for amino acids. However, they use different active transport proteins.

**RECAP**

Proteins and carbohydrates are absorbed from the lumen of the small intestine by active transport processes, then move by facilitated diffusion into capillaries. ■

### Lipids are broken down, then reassembled

Recall that bile salts emulsify lipids into small fat droplets, which are then digested by pancreatic and intestinal lipases. The products of lipid digestion are fatty acids and

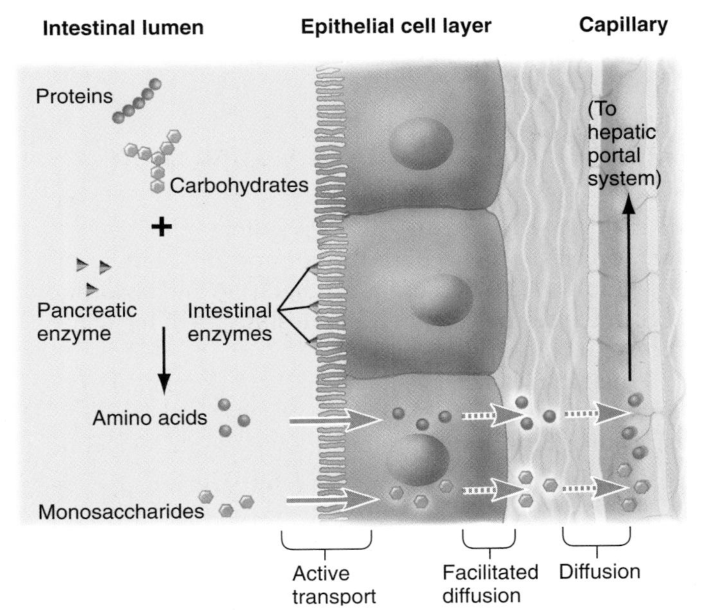


**Figure 14.13 Digestion and absorption of proteins and carbohydrates in the small intestine.** Digestion depends on enzymes from the pancreas and enzymes attached to the surface of the epithelial cells of the intestine. The amino acid and carbohydrate products of digestion cross the epithelial cell layer of the mucosa and enter a capillary for transport to the liver.

monoglycerides. Because they are nonpolar, the fatty acids and monoglycerides quickly dissolve in *micelles*—small droplets composed of bile salts and lecithin that have a polar outer surface and a nonpolar inner core. The function of micelles is to transport fatty acids and monoglycerides to the outer surface of the mucosal cells so that they can be absorbed into the cells (Figure 14.14).

Once inside the cells, the fatty acids and monoglycerides recombine into triglycerides. Clusters of triglycerides are then coated with proteins to form water-soluble droplets called *chylomicrons.* Chylomicrons are released from the cell by exocytosis. However, they are too large to enter the capillaries directly. Instead, they enter the more permeable lacteals and travel in the lymph vessels until the lymph is returned to the venous blood vessels near the heart.

## Water is absorbed by osmosis

As nutrients are absorbed in the small intestine (or when you drink pure water), the concentration of the water in the intestinal lumen becomes higher than in the intestinal cells or in the blood. A higher concentration of water in the lumen represents a strong driving force for the diffusion of water through the epithelial layer of cells of the small intestine and into the blood. The capacity for water absorption by the small intestine is nearly limitless, which explains why you do not experience diarrhea every time you drink a lot of fluid.

Water absorption continues in the large intestine, but here the capacity is limited. Conditions that cause the small intestine to deliver too much food residue to the large intestine or that speed up the rate of movement through the large intestine can lead to diarrhea (watery feces). A common cause of diarrhea is a bacterial infection in the small intestine.

The opposite problem is constipation, in which the food residue, now called feces, remains in the large intestine and colon so long that too much water is absorbed. The feces become dry and hard, making defecation difficult. Constipation can result from stress, lack of exercise, or insufficient fiber (indigestible material) in the diet.

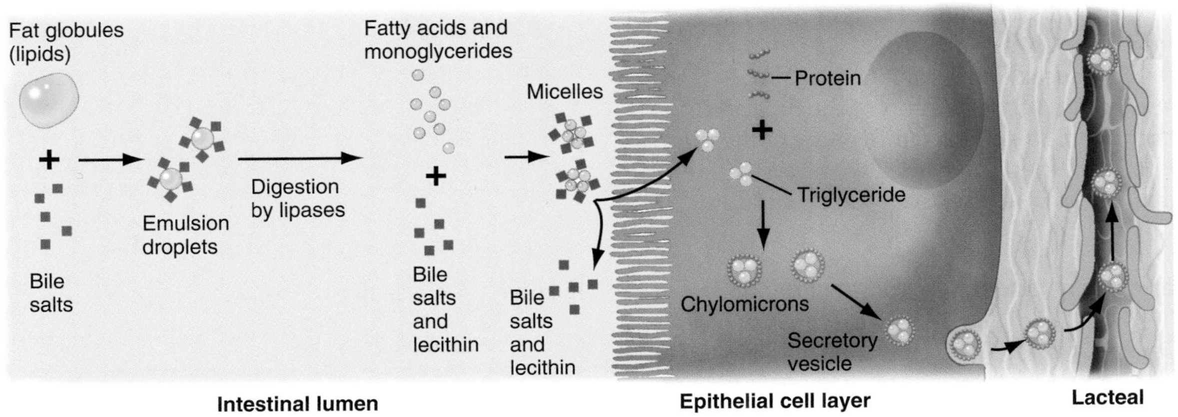


**Figure 14.14 Digestion and absorption of fats in the small intestine.** Bile salts emulsify large fat droplets into smaller droplets so that lipases can digest the fats into fatty acids and monoglycerides. The fatty acids and monoglycerides dissolve in micelles composed of bile salts and lecithin. Micelles near the cell's surface release their fatty acids and monoglycerides, which then diffuse across the cell membrane. In the cell the fatty acids and monoglycerides are resynthesized to triglycerides and coated with protein. The protein-coated triglycerides are called chylomicrons. Chylomicrons exit the cell by exocytosis and enter a lacteal for transport to the circulation.

### Vitamins and minerals follow a variety of paths

How vitamins are absorbed depends on whether they are fat soluble or water soluble. Fat-soluble vitamins dissolve in the micelles and are absorbed by diffusion across the lipid membrane of the mucosal cell layer, just like the components of lipids. Water-soluble vitamins are absorbed either by active transport or diffusion through channels or pores. Minerals (ions) such as sodium, potassium, calcium, phosphate, sulfate, and magnesium are electrically charged and hence not lipid soluble. These are either actively transported or are absorbed by diffusion via specific transport proteins, pores, or channels.

In addition to the nutrients we ingest in our food, the body digests and reabsorbs the components of the digestive secretions themselves. Nearly 9 liters of gastric juice, pancreatic juice, digestive enzymes, and bile are produced every day. The water and minerals in the digestive secretions are reabsorbed by the normal mechanisms for these nutrients. Enzymes are digested to their component amino acids, and the amino acids are then reabsorbed. Bile salts are reabsorbed, returned to the liver, and used again.

**RECAP**

The components of lipid digestion are transported to the mucosa in micelles, diffuse into the cell, and recombine into lipids within the cell. Then they are coated with protein to become chylomicrons that enter the lymph. The digestive system also absorbs water, vitamins, minerals, and digestive secretions. ■

## 14.9 Endocrine and nervous systems regulate digestion

The digestive system is most active when food or chyme is present and fairly inactive when it is not. Regulation involves altering the motility and secretions of various organs so that each operates as efficiently as possible.

Most regulatory mechanisms operate to maintain a constant internal environment. Regulation of the digestive system, on the other hand, promotes rapid, efficient digestion and absorption of whatever is delivered to the system, regardless of homeostasis. The digestive process actually alters the internal environment temporarily because all those absorbed nutrients enter the blood in a relatively short time—a few hours.

### Regulation depends on volume and content of food

The endocrine system and nervous system regulate digestion according to both the volume and content of food (Table 14.2). Because most digestion and absorption occur in the stomach and small intestine, most regulatory processes involve those organs.

When the stomach stretches to accommodate food, neural reflexes increase stomach peristalsis and secretion of gastric juice. Stretching and the presence of protein stimulate the stomach to release the hormone **gastrin,** which triggers the release of more gastric juice.

When chyme arrives at the small intestine, stretching of the duodenum increases segmentation to mix the chyme. The duodenum also secretes two hormones into the bloodstream: secretin and cholecystokinin. Acid in chyme triggers release of **secretin,** which stimulates the pancreas to secrete water and bicarbonate to neutralize acid. Fat and protein stimulate release of **cholecystokinin (CCK),** which signals the pancreas to secrete more digestive enzymes. CCK and stretching of the duodenum also stimulate the gallbladder to contract and release bile.

Secretin, CCK, and stretching of the small intestine inhibit stomach motility and stomach secretions. In other words, if chyme flows too quickly from the stomach, the small intestine will slow stomach activity accordingly.

Gastrin and a neural reflex involving stretching of the stomach increase motility of the large intestine after eating. This is why people often feel the urge to defecate after their first meal of the day.

**RECAP**

The endocrine and nervous systems regulate digestion based on content and volume of food. Regulatory mechanisms include neural reflexes involving organ stretching and release of the hormones gastrin, secretin, and cholecystokinin. ■

**Table 14.2 Nervous and endocrine systems' regulation of the digestive processes**

| Organ | Nervous system | Endocrine system |
|---|---|---|
| Stomach | Stretching increases peristalsis and secretion of gastric juice | Stretching and protein trigger release of gastrin, which stimulates gastric glands |
| Small intestine | Stretching increases segmentation<br>Stretching inhibits stomach motility and stomach secretions | Acid stimulates release of secretin, which stimulates pancreas to secrete bicarbonate, neutralizing acid. Fat and protein stimulate release of CCK, which stimulates pancreas to secrete enzymes and the gallbladder to release bile. CCK and secretin inhibit stomach motility and stomach secretions |
| Large intestine | Stomach stretching increases motility | Gastrin increases motility |

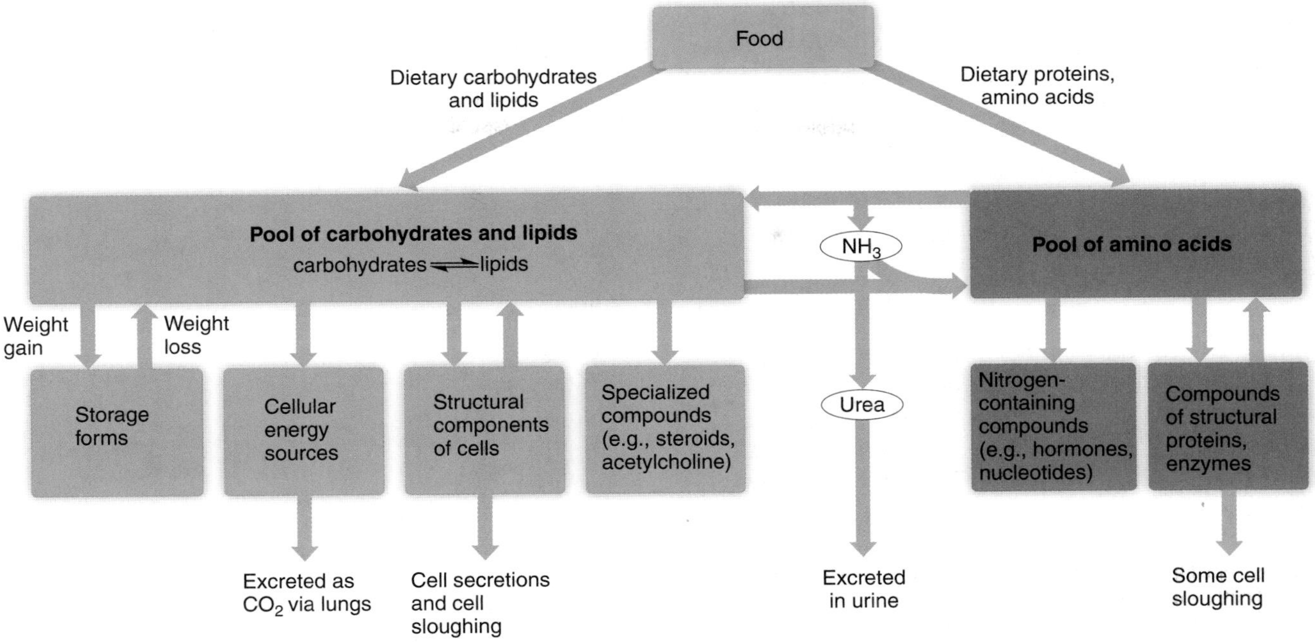


**Figure 14.15 The pathways of organic metabolism.** When nutrient intake is greater than utilization, the excess is stored, often as fat. When nutrient intake is less than utilization, the storage forms are used to produce structural compounds and additional energy.

### Nutrients are used or stored until needed

Once all those nutrients have been absorbed, the body must use them. Will they be consumed for immediate energy, stored until later, or combined with more nutrients to create other molecules? Regulation of organic metabolism involves interactions between virtually all organs in the body. Key organs are the pancreas with its two main endocrine secretions (insulin and glucagon) and the liver with its multiple roles in overall metabolism.

Figure 14.15 summarizes how the body utilizes organic molecules. Three concepts are evident from this figure:

1. Depending on which molecules are in short supply and which are in excess at the moment, there can be a great deal of interconversion of one to another. We first introduced this concept in connection with cellular metabolism in Chapter 3. Lipids, carbohydrates, and proteins can all be converted to storage forms of lipid or carbohydrate, then recycled according to the body's needs.
2. When we consume more energy-containing nutrients than we use, our bodies store the excess for future use. Over time, these mounting reserves can increase body weight.
3. When we consume fewer energy-containing nutrients than we use, the body draws on these storage forms of energy to make up the difference. If we do this on a regular basis, we lose weight.

In the rest of this chapter we discuss nutrition, energy balance, and healthy body weight.

**RECAP**

Lipids, carbohydrates, and amino acids can all be converted to storage forms of lipid or carbohydrate. They can be recreated from stored forms according to the body's needs at that moment. ■

## 14.10 Nutrition: You are what you eat

Nutrition is the interaction between an organism and its food. Because nearly all nutrients enter the body through the digestive system, it is fair to say that "you are what you eat." What nutrients do we actually need, and why?

### MyPyramid plan offers a personalized approach

Figure 14.16 presents one answer to these questions. Developed by the Center for Nutrition Policy and Promotion at the U.S. Department of Agriculture (USDA), *MyPyramid* is a comprehensive, personalized approach that includes physical activity as well as healthy nutrition. MyPyramid divides foods into six groups and shows the recommended consumption of each. The recommended amounts in Figure 14.16 apply to a daily diet of 2,000 Calories, a standard estimate that is often used as a basis of comparison. For instance, the Nutrition Facts label on a food package, which gives the percentage of daily values for various nutrients in that food, is also based on 2,000 Calories per day.

A 2,000-Calorie-per-day plan isn't right for everyone, but no problem: MyPyramid provides many options to help you

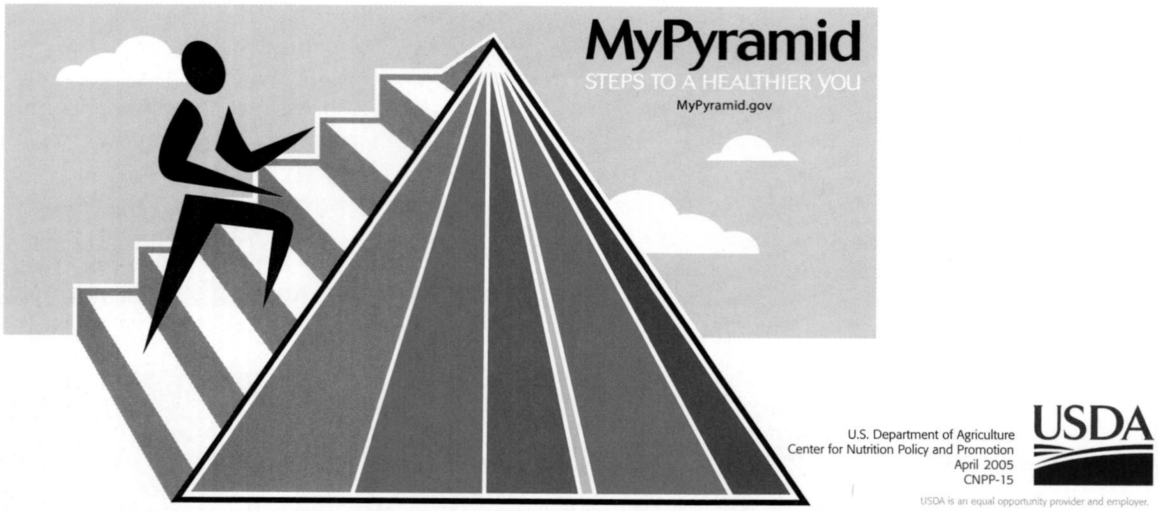


| GRAINS<br>Make half your grains whole | VEGETABLES<br>Vary your veggies | FRUITS<br>Focus on fruits | MILK<br>Get your calcium-rich foods | MEAT & BEANS<br>Go lean with protein |
|---|---|---|---|---|
| Eat at least 3 oz. of whole-grain cereals, breads, crackers, rice, or pasta every day<br><br>1 oz. is about 1 slice of bread, about 1 cup of breakfast cereal, or 1/2 cup of cooked rice, cereal, or pasta | Eat more dark-green veggies like broccoli, spinach, and other dark leafy greens<br><br>Eat more orange vegetables like carrots and sweet potatoes<br><br>Eat more dry beans and peas like pinto beans, kidney beans, and lentils | Eat a variety of fruit<br><br>Choose fresh, frozen, canned, or dried fruit<br><br>Go easy on fruit juices | Go low-fat or fat-free when you choose milk, yogurt, and other milk products<br><br>If you don't or can't consume milk, choose lactose-free products or other calcium sources such as fortified foods and beverages | Choose low-fat or lean meats and poultry<br><br>Bake it, broil it, or grill it<br><br>Vary your protein routine—choose more fish, beans, peas, nuts, and seeds |
| For a 2,000-calorie diet, you need the amounts below from each food group. To find the amounts that are right for you, go to MyPyramid.gov. | | | | |
| Eat 6 oz. every day | Eat 2 1/2 cups every day | Eat 2 cups every day | Get 3 cups every day; for kids aged 2 to 8, it's 2 | Eat 5 1/2 oz. every day |

**Find your balance between food and physical activity**

- Be sure to stay within your daily calorie needs.
- Be physically active for at least 30 minutes most days of the week.
- About 60 minutes a day of physical activity may be needed to prevent weight gain.
- For sustaining weight loss, at least 60 to 90 minutes a day of physical activity may be required.
- Children and teenagers should be physically active for 60 minutes every day, or most days.

**Know the limits on fats, sugars, and salt (sodium)**

- Make most of your fat sources from fish, nuts, and vegetable oils.
- Limit solid fats like butter, margarine, shortening, and lard, as well as foods that contain these.
- Check the Nutrition Facts label to keep saturated fats, trans fats, and sodium low.
- Choose food and beverages low in added sugars. Added sugars contribute calories with few, if any, nutrients.

**Figure 14.16 MyPyramid.** MyPyramid is a visual representation of the recommended dietary guidelines of the Center for Nutrition Policy and Promotion at the United States Department of Agriculture (USDA). The pyramid indicates the recommended consumption of foods from six different groups, taking into account both nutritional needs and concerns about the effects of diet on nutrition-related disease. The steps indicate the importance of regular physical activity. MyPyramid is designed to be highly interactive.

prepare a personalized nutrition plan. The system includes food plans appropriate to 12 Calorie levels of food intake, based on the latest *Dietary Guidelines for Americans* issued by the USDA and the Department of Health and Human Services. If you enter your age, gender, and activity level on the MyPyramid Web site, the system will match you with the best plan for your needs. It will suggest how many Calories you need per day and recommend specific amounts of each food group as well as discretionary Calories such as alcohol and added sugar. You can print worksheets to help you set nutrition goals and monitor your progress. The feature, MyPyramid Tracker, lets you compare your current eating and physical activity patterns to recommendations in the *Dietary Guidelines* and track them for up to a year to follow your progress.

Recommendations for a healthy diet include:

- Eat a variety of foods.
- Maintain a healthy weight.
- Eat plenty of fruits, vegetables, and whole-grain products.
- Choose a diet low in cholesterol and saturated fat.
- Use sugar only in moderation.

- Consume salt and sodium in moderation (less than 2,300 milligrams, or about 1 teaspoon of salt per day).
- If you drink alcoholic beverages, do so in moderation. How much is "moderate"? The equivalent of up to one drink per day for women and up to two drinks per day for men.

We consider the three basic nutrient groups first—carbohydrates, lipids, and proteins—before discussing vitamins, minerals, and the importance of fiber.

**RECAP**

Good nutrition includes maintaining a healthy weight while consuming a variety of foods. Eat plenty of fruit, vegetables, and whole grains; cut back on saturated fat; and use sugar, salt, and alcohol only in moderation. ■

## Carbohydrates: A major energy source

**Carbohydrates** are one of the body's main sources of energy, and many nutritionists recommend that approximately 45–65% of our Calorie intake come from carbohydrates. (A Calorie is a measure of energy, discussed in more detail in section 14.11.)

Carbohydrates may be either simple or complex (see Table 14.3). Simple carbohydrates (sugars) are found in many natural foods such as fruit and honey. Refined sugars, such as granulated sugar and corn syrup, have had most other nutrients removed, so they are less nutritious than their natural counterparts. Complex carbohydrates, such as starch or glycogen, consist of many sugar units linked together. Whole foods containing complex carbohydrates are better for us than refined sugars because they release sugars more slowly and also contribute fiber, vitamins, and minerals. In the body, stored starch and glycogen are broken down to glucose, one of the premier sources of energy.

**Table 14.3 Good sources of natural carbohydrates**

| Simple carbohydrates | Complex carbohydrates |
|---|---|
| Fruit | Starchy vegetables |
| Citrus | Potatoes |
| Berries | Corn |
| Melons | Peas |
| | Beans |
| Unsweetened fruit juice | |
| Honey | Grains |
| | Whole-grain breads and cereals |
| | Whole-grain pasta |
| | Rice |
| | Oatmeal |
| | Wheat bran |

It is difficult to tell exactly how much refined sugar we eat because so much is disguised on food labels as "corn sweeteners," "dextrose," or "fructose" (levulose). The USDA estimates the average North American consumes more than 142 pounds of sweeteners and refined sugar annually—almost 3 pounds each week.

**RECAP**

Carbohydrates are a good source of energy. Natural sugars and complex carbohydrates are the best sources. ■

## Lipids: Essential cell components and energy sources

Lipids (including fats) are essential components of every living cell. Phospholipids and cholesterol make up most of the cell membrane. Cholesterol also forms the backbone of steroid hormones and is used to synthesize bile. Fat stores energy, cushions organs, insulates the body under the skin, and stores several vitamins. Most of the fats in food are triglycerides, which consist of three fatty acids attached to a glycerol molecule. Recall from Chapter 2 that fats are classified according to the ratio of hydrogen to carbon atoms in their fatty acids:

- *Saturated fats.* Saturated fats have two hydrogen atoms for every carbon atom in their fatty acid tails. They tend to be solids at room temperature. Saturated fats are found primarily in meat and dairy products and in a few plant sources such as coconut and palm kernel oil. They tend to raise blood levels of LDL cholesterol, the "bad" cholesterol that is associated with atherosclerosis and heart disease (Chapter 8).
- *Unsaturated fats.* Unsaturated fats are missing one or more pairs of hydrogen atoms in their fatty acid tails. Every missing pair of hydrogen atoms leads to a double bond between adjacent carbons and a kink, or bend, in the tail, making it more difficult for adjacent molecules to form bonds with each other. Consequently, unsaturated fats are liquids (oils) at room temperature. In general, unsaturated fats are considered healthier than saturated fats because they tend to lower LDL cholesterol levels. Olive, canola, safflower, and corn oils are all unsaturated fats derived from plants. Certain cold-water fish (salmon, trout, and sardines) are rich in omega-3 fatty acids, polyunsaturated fatty acids that have been linked to a reduced risk of heart disease.

Vegetable oils can be turned back into solids at room temperature by partial hydrogenation of the fatty acid tails. However, the process of partial hydrogenation reconfigures the positions of some of the remaining unpaired hydrogen atoms, producing *trans* fats. *Trans* fats were once very popular with fast-food restaurants as a deep-frying oil because they increase the shelf-life and flavor stability of foods. *Trans* fats are used in commercial baked goods (cookies, crackers, and snacks) and are also found in vegetable shortening and margarine.

However, like saturated fats, *trans* fats tend to raise LDL cholesterol and thus may increase the risk of cardiovascular disease. Food manufacturers now list the percentage of *trans* fats in the Nutrition Facts panel on product labels, and many fast-food restaurants no longer use *trans* fats in their deep-fryers.

The liver can synthesize cholesterol and most of the lipids the body needs, but it cannot produce every last one of them. The few fatty acids that our bodies cannot make, called *essential fatty acids,* must be consumed as food. Two examples are linoleic and linolenic acids, present in corn and olives, both of which contribute to proper cell membrane structure. A teaspoon of corn or olive oil, or its equivalent in food, is enough to satisfy our daily requirements.

Although lipids are essential to human health, most of us consume far more than we need. Nutritionists recommend that lipids account for no more than 20–35% of Calories consumed per day. In addition to watching the amount of fat we eat, though, it's important to pay attention to the type. Diets high in saturated fat, cholesterol, and *trans* fats place us at risk for cardiovascular disease and certain cancers. Less than 10% of Calories consumed daily should come from saturated fats, with less than 300 milligrams per day of cholesterol and as little *trans* fat as possible.

**RECAP**

Saturated fats are found mostly in meat and dairy products, and *trans* fats are found in many snacks and processed foods. Unsaturated fats, which include plant and fish oils, are a healthier choice. Some essential fatty acids must be consumed to meet the body's nutritional requirements. ■

## Complete proteins contain every amino acid

Like lipids, **proteins** are vital components of every cell. They make up the enzymes that direct metabolism, they serve as receptor and transport molecules, and they build our muscle fibers. A few are hormones.

Despite their variety, all proteins are composed of just 20 different amino acids. The body can make 12 of these amino acids. The eight that the body cannot produce (isoleucine, leucine, lysine, methionine, phenylalanine, threonine, tryptophan, and valine) are called **essential amino acids** because they must be ingested in food. Two more that the body can make (histidine and arginine) are sometimes considered essential in children because their rapidly growing bodies cannot synthesize them fast enough.

A **complete protein** contains all 20 of the amino acids in proportions that meet our nutritional needs. Most animal proteins are complete, but nearly all plant proteins (with the exception of soybeans) lack one or more of the essential amino acids. Vegetarians must be careful to choose the right combinations of plant-based foods to obtain all amino acids. A combination of foods from any two of the three rightmost columns of Figure 14.17 will provide the necessary balance of all essential amino acids. Foods such as trail mix (roasted soybeans and nuts), hummus (chick peas and sesame seeds), a bean burrito in a corn tortilla, and red beans and rice do just that.

Approximately 15% of our Calories should come from protein. In many parts of the world protein deficiency is a serious health problem. Every enzyme has a unique amino acid sequence, so if even one amino acid is missing in the diet, the body may be unable to produce crucial enzymes at the proper time in development. Protein deficiencies during pregnancy and childhood can retard growth and alter physical and mental performance. Unfortunately, foods with complete proteins such as meat and milk are often expensive in poor societies, and many people remain uninformed about ways to achieve a balanced diet of plant proteins.

**RECAP**

The body needs 20 amino acids but cannot synthesize eight of them, called essential amino acids. Complete proteins contain all 20 amino acids. Most animal proteins are complete, but most plant proteins are incomplete. ■

| Complete proteins | Incomplete proteins: low in lysine | Incomplete proteins: low in methionine | Incomplete proteins: low in tryptophan |
|---|---|---|---|
| **Legumes:**<br>Soybean<br>Tofu<br>Soy milk | **Legumes:**<br>Peanuts | **Legumes:**<br>Beans (dried)<br>Black-eyed peas<br>Chickpeas<br>Lentils<br>Lima beans<br>Mung beans<br>Peanuts | **Legumes:**<br>Beans (dried)<br>Garbanzos<br>Lima beans<br>Mung beans<br>Peanuts |
| **Cereal grains:**<br>Wheat germ | **Cereal grains:**<br>Barley<br>Corn<br>Oats<br>Rice<br>Rye<br>Wheat | **Fresh vegetables:**<br>Asparagus<br>Broccoli<br>Green peas<br>Mushrooms<br>Potatoes | **Fresh vegetables:**<br>Green peas<br>Mushrooms<br>Swiss chard |
| **Dairy products:**<br>Milk<br>Cheeses<br>Yogurt<br>Eggs<br>Meats | **Nuts, seeds:**<br>Almonds<br>Cashews<br>Coconut<br>English walnuts<br>Hazelnuts<br>Pecans<br>Sunflower seeds<br>Sesame seeds | **Nuts, seeds:**<br>Hazelnuts | **Nuts, seeds:**<br>Almonds<br>English walnuts |

**Figure 14.17 Getting the essential amino acids.** Most plants are low in one or more of the essential amino acids. A vegetarian should choose a combination of foods from any two of the three rightmost columns to ensure an adequate intake of all essential amino acids.

## Vitamins are essential for normal function

In addition to carbohydrates, lipids, and proteins, humans need **vitamins,** a group of at least 13 chemicals that are essential for normal functioning. The body can produce only a few vitamins; our skin synthesizes vitamin D when exposed to sunlight, and bacteria living in the colon manufacture vitamins K, $B_6$, and biotin. We must obtain all others from our food and absorb them in the digestive tract. Table 14.4 lists the 13 vitamins along with their sources, functions, and signs of deficiency or excess.

Vitamins fall into two groups: fat soluble and water soluble. The distinction affects how a vitamin is absorbed and stored and how steady a supply of it you need. Fat-soluble

**Table 14.4 Vitamins**

| Vitamin | Common sources | Primary functions | Signs of severe, prolonged deficiency | Signs of extreme excess |
|---|---|---|---|---|
| ***Fat-Soluble Vitamins*** | | | | |
| A | Fortified dairy products, egg yolk, liver, yellow fruits, yellow and dark green leafy vegetables | Synthesis of visual pigments and the development of bones and teeth | Night blindness, dry scaly skin, increased susceptibility to infections | Damage to bone and liver, blurred vision |
| D | Fish oil, fortified milk, egg yolk; also produced by skin | Promotes absorption of calcium, required for healthy bones and teeth | Bone deformities in children, bone weakening in adults | Calcium deposits in tissues, leading to cardiovascular and kidney damage |
| E | Vegetable oils, nuts, whole grains | Thought to be an antioxidant that prevents cell membrane damage | Damage to red blood cells and nerves | Generally nontoxic |
| K | Green vegetables, also produced by bacteria in colon | Formation of certain proteins involved in blood clotting | Defective blood clotting, abnormal bleeding | Liver damage and anemia |
| ***Water-Soluble Vitamins*** | | | | |
| $B_1$ (thiamine) | Whole grains, legumes, eggs, lean meats | Coenzyme in carbohydrate metabolism | Damage to heart and nerves, pain | None reported |
| $B_2$ (riboflavin) | Dairy products, eggs, meat, whole grains, green leafy vegetables | Coenzyme in carbohydrate metabolism | Skin lesions | Generally nontoxic |
| Niacin | Nuts, meats, grains, green leafy vegetables | Coenzyme in carbohydrate metabolism | Causes a disease called pellagra (damage to skin, digestive tract, and nervous system) | Skin flushing, potential liver damage |
| $B_6$ | High-protein foods in general; also made by colonic bacteria | Coenzyme in amino acid metabolism | Muscle, skin, and nerve damage, anemia | Poor coordination, numbness in feet |
| Folic acid | Green vegetables, nuts, grains, legumes, orange juice | Coenzyme in nucleic acid and amino acid metabolism | Anemia, digestive disturbances | Masks vitamin $B_{12}$ deficiency |
| $B_{12}$ | Animal products | Coenzyme in nucleic acid metabolism | Anemia, nervous system damage | Thought to be nontoxic |
| Pantothenic acid | Widely distributed in foods, especially animal products | Coenzyme in glucose metabolism, fatty acid and steroid synthesis | Fatigue, tingling in hands and feet, intestinal disturbances | Generally nontoxic except occasional diarrhea |
| Biotin | Widely distributed in foods; also made by colonic bacteria | Coenzyme in amino acid metabolism, fat and glycogen formation | Scaly skin (dermatitis) | Thought to be nontoxic |
| C (ascorbic acid) | Fruits and vegetables, especially citrus fruits, cantaloupe, broccoli, and cabbage | Antioxidant; needed for collagen formation; important for bone and teeth formation; improves iron absorption | A disease called scurvy, poor wound healing, impaired immune responses | Digestive upsets |

vitamins are absorbed more readily if there is fat in the diet. They tend to be absorbed along with the components of fat, and they are stored in fat tissue and released as needed. Body stores of some fat-soluble vitamins may last for years, so it is rarely necessary to take supplements.

Water-soluble vitamins are absorbed more readily than fat-soluble vitamins, but they are stored only briefly and rapidly excreted in urine. Thus we need to consume foods containing water-soluble vitamins on a regular basis.

## Minerals: Elements essential for body processes

**Minerals** are the atoms of certain chemical elements that are also essential for body processes. They are the ions in blood plasma and cell cytoplasm (sodium, potassium, chloride, and many others). They represent most of the chemical structure of bone (calcium, phosphorus, and oxygen). They also contribute to the activity of nerves and muscles (sodium, potassium, and calcium), among many other functions. Twenty-one minerals are considered essential for animals. Nine of the twenty-one (arsenic, chromium, cobalt, manganese, molybdenum, nickel, selenium, silicon, and vanadium) are called trace minerals because they represent less than 0.01% of your body weight. Table 14.5 lists the 12 most important minerals.

How much do we need of each vitamin and mineral? The National Research Council publishes the current best estimate, the **Recommended Dietary Allowance (RDA).** Most healthy people can achieve the RDA without taking supplements if they eat a balanced diet of whole foods.

**Table 14.5 Major minerals in the human body**

| Mineral | Common sources | Primary functions | Signs of severe, prolonged deficiency | Signs of extreme excess |
|---|---|---|---|---|
| Calcium (Ca) | Dairy products, dark green vegetables, legumes | Bone and teeth formation, nerve and muscle action, blood clotting | Decreased bone mass, stunted growth | Kidney damage, impaired absorption of other minerals |
| Chloride (Cl) | Table salt | Role in acid-base balance, acid formation in stomach, body water balance | Poor appetite and growth, muscle cramps | Contributes to high blood pressure in susceptible people |
| Copper (Cu) | Seafood, nuts, legumes | Synthesis of hemoglobin, melanin | Anemia, bone and blood vessel changes | Nausea, liver damage |
| Fluoride (F) | Fluoridated water, tea, seafood | Maintenance of teeth and perhaps bone | Tooth decay | Digestive upset, mottling of teeth |
| Iodine (I) | Iodized salt, marine fish and shellfish | Required for thyroid hormone | Enlarged thyroid (goiter), metabolic disorders | Goiter |
| Iron (Fe) | Green leafy vegetables, whole grains, legumes, meats, eggs | Required for hemoglobin, myoglobin, and certain enzymes | Iron-deficiency anemia, impaired immune function | *Acute:* shock and death. *Chronic:* liver and heart failure |
| Magnesium (Mg) | Whole grains, green leafy vegetables | Coenzyme in several enzymes | Nerve and muscle disturbances | Impaired nerve function |
| Phosphorus (P) | Meat, poultry, whole grains | Component of bones, teeth, phospholipids, ATP, nucleic acids | Loss of minerals from bone, muscle weakness | Depressed absorption of some minerals, abnormal bone deposition |
| Potassium (K) | Widespread in the diet, especially meats, grains | Muscle and nerve function; a major component of intracellular fluid | Muscle weakness | *Acute:* cardiac arrhythmias and death. *Chronic:* muscle weakness |
| Sodium (Na) | Table salt; widespread in the diet | Muscle and nerve function; major component of body water | Muscle cramps | High blood pressure in susceptible people |
| Sulfur (S) | Meat, dairy products | Component of many proteins | None reported | None reported |
| Zinc (Zn) | Whole grains, meats, seafood | Component of many enzymes | Impaired growth, reproductive failure, impaired immune function | *Acute:* nausea, vomiting, diarrhea. *Chronic:* anemia and impaired immune function |

That's a big "if" for some of us, considering our diets. Scientific studies suggest that supplements may also benefit certain groups, such as newborns, the elderly, or people taking medications that interfere with nutrient absorption. Calcium is advised for postmenopausal women to prevent the bone loss of osteoporosis.

Never take massive doses of any vitamin or mineral unless prescribed by your doctor. As the "excess" columns show, more is not always better.

### Fiber benefits the colon

**Fiber**—found in many vegetables, fruit, and grains—is indigestible material. Even though our bodies cannot digest it, we need a certain amount in our diet. Fiber is beneficial because it makes feces bulky and helps them pass more efficiently through the colon.

A low-fiber diet can lead to chronic constipation, *hemorrhoids* (swollen veins in the lining of the anus, often caused by straining during defecation), and a disorder called *diverticulosis* (see section 14.12). A low-fiber diet has also been associated with a higher risk of colon cancer, perhaps because cancer-causing substances remain in the colon longer (see Chapter 18). Doctors recommend eating 20–35 grams of fiber every day—considerably more than the average 12–17 grams that most North Americans consume.

**RECAP**

All minerals and nearly all vitamins must be obtained from food. For most healthy people, a balanced diet, including adequate fiber, is the best way to achieve the RDA. ■

## 14.11 Weight control: Energy consumed versus energy spent

The body requires energy to fuel metabolic processes and other activities. When we digest nutrients, we can put the energy they contain to use.

Energy is measured in units called calories. Technically, a calorie is the amount of energy needed to raise the temperature of 1 gram of water by 1° Celsius. Because this is not much energy in biological terms, scientists use a kilocalorie (1,000 calories) to measure the nutrient content of food and the energy used to perform biological activities. A kilocalorie is commonly referred to as a **Calorie** with a capital "C." When people "count calories" they really mean the big Calories, and that is the unit we use in this chapter.

### BMR: Determining how many Calories we need

If we want to maintain a stable body weight, the number of Calories we consume must equal the number we use. So how do we determine the number of Calories we use?

You can estimate your daily energy needs by determining your **basal metabolic rate (BMR),** the energy your body needs to perform essential activities such as breathing and maintaining organ function. (See the Try It Yourself box to estimate your BMR.) Factors that influence the BMR include:

- *Gender and body composition.* BMR is higher in males. Muscle tissue consumes more energy than fat tissue; because men generally have more muscle than women, they have a higher BMR. Also, highly muscular men and women have a faster BMR than their less muscular counterparts.
- *Age.* BMR declines over time.
- *Health.* Some health conditions (such as fever, infections, and hyperthyroidism) increase BMR. Other conditions (such as hypothyroidism) lower it.
- *Stress.* Norepinephrine and epinephrine raise BMR.
- *Food intake.* Eating increases the metabolic rate, whereas fasting and extreme dieting decrease it. This is why crash diets often fail to lower body weight permanently. Although weight may fall temporarily, a slower BMR makes it difficult to keep the pounds from returning.
- *Genetics.* Rates of metabolism vary between individuals, independent of the factors listed above. Genetics plays a strong role in determining your BMR, although precisely how has not been fully determined.

Of course, your body performs many activities in addition to basic metabolic functions. However, the BMR accounts for a surprisingly large proportion of Calories used, as much as two-thirds of daily utilization. The rest go to fuel physical activity.

### Energy balance and body weight

Healthy weight control involves balancing energy intake against energy expenditure.

**try it yourself**

### Calculate Your BMR

1. Calculate your weight in kilograms: Divide the number of pounds by 2.2 = ______
2. If you are male:
   Multiply your weight × 1.0 = ______
3. If you are female:
   Multiply your weight × 0.9 = ______
4. This number approximates the number of Calories you consume per hour. Multiply this number by 24 to estimate how many Calories you need each day to support basic metabolic functions =______

For example:

- A 200-pound man (91 kg) has a BMR of 91 Calories/hour. His metabolic activities consume approximately 2,184 Calories per day.
- A 130-pound woman (59 kg) has a BMR of 53 Calories/hour. Her metabolic activities consume approximately 1,272 Calories per day.

Notice that the three classes of nutrients have quite different Caloric contents. Fat contains about 9 Calories per gram, but carbohydrates and proteins contain only 4. Thus, although fat is a good energy source, a high-fat diet can easily contain more Calories than we need. This is one reason why controlling fat intake is so important.

When we eat more Calories than we use, the excess energy is stored in specialized cells as fat. The number of fat cells a person has is largely determined by the time he or she is an adult. This may be why some people find losing weight so difficult and others do not. Research suggests that overweight people have two to three times more fat cells than normal-weight individuals, so when they diet and shrink their fat reserves in each cell, their bodies respond as if they are starving. Dieting is difficult for chronically overweight persons because they are constantly fighting the body's own weight-control system, which responds as if their excess weight were normal.

**RECAP**

Weight control involves balancing energy consumed in food against energy spent. Calculating your BMR helps you estimate how many Calories you need each day. ■

### Physical activity: An efficient way to use Calories

Although the BMR stays fairly constant, the amount of exercise we get can dramatically change the total number of Calories we burn each day. Table 14.6 compares the number of Calories spent per hour by a 100-, 150-, or 200-pound person performing various types of exercise. Note that heavier people do more work per hour for the same level of activity. To lose one pound of fat, we must use up about 3,500 Calories.

**Table 14.6 Approximate number of Calories burned per hour by various activities**

| Activity | 100-lb Person | 150-lb Person | 200-lb Person |
|---|---|---|---|
| Bicycling, 6 mph | 160 | 240 | 312 |
| Bicycling, 12 mph | 270 | 410 | 534 |
| Jogging, 5.5 mph | 440 | 660 | 962 |
| Jogging, 10 mph | 850 | 1,280 | 1,664 |
| Jumping rope | 500 | 750 | 1,000 |
| Swimming, 25 yds/min | 185 | 275 | 358 |
| Swimming, 50 yds/min | 325 | 500 | 650 |
| Walking, 2 mph | 160 | 240 | 312 |
| Walking, 4.5 mph | 295 | 440 | 572 |
| Tennis (singles) | 265 | 400 | 535 |

*Source:* American Heart Association

The best approach to weight loss is a gradual one. Nutritionists recommend reducing caloric intake by a small amount each day while gradually increasing physical activity.

Of course, exercise has many benefits in addition to weight loss. It improves cardiovascular health, strengthens bones, tones muscles, and promotes a general sense of well-being. Your best strategy is a healthful diet combined with moderate exercise.

### Healthy weight improves overall health

Why do we worry about caloric intake and body weight, anyway? A primary reason is that there is a link between obesity and health status. According to the federal Economic Research Service, nutrition-related health conditions cost the U.S. $80 billion annually in medical expenses and lost productivity. Numerous studies reveal a direct correlation between obesity and the incidence of heart disease, diabetes (see the Chapter Current Issue), cancer, arthritis, and other health problems. The connection is strong enough that government groups and insurance companies regularly publish charts that use a person's height and weight to define **body mass index (BMI).** Read your own BMI from the chart in Figure 14.18.

According to the government, a BMI of between 18.5 and 25 is considered healthy, 25 to 30 is considered overweight, and 30 or higher represents obesity. These numbers should be considered a general guide only because they are based on population statistics and do not take into account such factors as bone structure, fitness, or gender. BMI may overestimate the amount of body fat in individuals who are very muscular or have a heavy bone structure. It may also underestimate the amount of body fat in people who have lost muscle mass. Thus, BMI charts do not provide definitive information about the appropriate weight status for any one individual. Within each range, the higher weights generally apply to men and the lower weights to women.

**RECAP**

Increasing physical activity is an efficient way to increase Calorie expenditure. The best strategy for losing weight combines a healthful diet with moderate regular exercise. ■

## 14.12 Disorders of the digestive system

Although common, many digestive problems are not necessarily life threatening. One of the most common conditions worldwide is *food poisoning,* caused by food and beverages contaminated with bacteria or their toxic products. Diarrhea and vomiting often accompany food poisoning. *Food allergies* can also cause diarrhea, vomiting, and generalized allergic responses throughout the body. Common food allergens include shellfish, wheat, peanuts, and eggs.

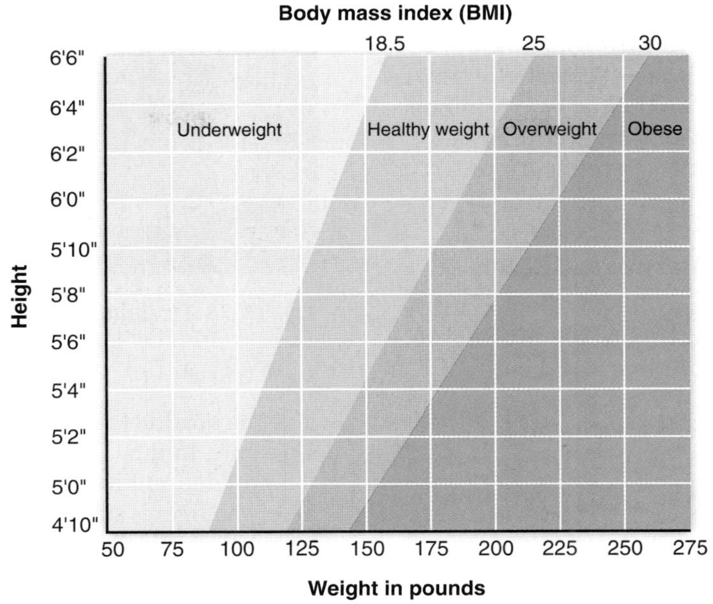


**Figure 14.18 Find your BMI.** Find your height in the left column of the chart and read right to find your weight, shown at the bottom. The government's weight categories (Underweight, Healthy weight, Overweight, or Obese) are indicated by colors. Their corresponding BMI ranges are shown at the top of the chart. The weight categories are government definitions based on large population groups. They are not a good measure of an individual's health or fitness.

## Disorders of the GI tract

**Lactose intolerance: Difficulty digesting milk** Human infants are born with the enzyme lactase in their small intestines for digesting lactose, the primary sugar in milk. However, many adults gradually lose the enzyme, and with it their ability to digest lactose. The result is lactose intolerance. Symptoms of lactose intolerance include diarrhea, gas, bloating, and abdominal cramps after ingesting milk products. Diarrhea occurs because the undigested lactose causes fluid to be retained in the digestive tract. The gas, bloating, and abdominal cramps are due to bacterial fermentation of the lactose, which produces gases.

Lactose-intolerant people can eat cheese or yogurt because the lactose in these milk products has already been digested. Lactose-free milk is also available.

**Diverticulosis: Weakness in the intestinal wall** Diverticulosis gets its name from its characteristic diverticula (small sacs produced when the mucosal lining of the large intestine protrudes through the other layers of the intestinal wall). Most people with diverticulosis do not experience discomfort, but sometimes the diverticula become infected or inflamed. Antibiotics usually resolve the problem.

Diverticulosis is relatively common in Western countries, perhaps as a result of inadequate dietary fiber. A low-fiber diet produces smaller feces, narrowing the colon and making its contractions more powerful. This increases the pressure on colon walls, forcing weak areas outward and forming diverticula.

**Colon polyps: Noncancerous growths** A polyp is a noncancerous growth that projects from a mucous membrane. Polyps can develop in many areas of the body, including the colon. The majority of colon polyps do not become cancerous, but because most colon cancers start as polyps, doctors recommend removing them. Polyps can be detected and removed in a *colonoscopy,* an outpatient procedure in which a flexible fiber-optic scope is inserted into the colon through the anus.

## Disorders of the accessory organs

**Hepatitis: Inflammation of the liver Hepatitis** refers to inflammation of the liver, generally caused by viruses or toxic substances. Researchers have identified at least five viruses that cause hepatitis. The most common are hepatitis A, B, and C.

Hepatitis A is transmitted by contaminated food or water and causes a brief illness from which most people recover completely. A vaccine is available for hepatitis A. Although the vaccine is not considered necessary for most residents of industrialized nations, it may be a good idea for travelers to underdeveloped countries.

Hepatitis B travels in blood or body fluids, so it is usually passed via contaminated needles, blood transfusions, or sexual contact with infected individuals. Approximately 300,000 new cases are diagnosed each year. If not treated, hepatitis B can lead to liver failure. Symptoms include jaundice (the skin takes on a yellowish color due to accumulated bile pigments in the blood), nausea, fatigue, abdominal pain, and arthritis. A vaccine is available for hepatitis B. Federal law requires all health care workers to be vaccinated.

Hepatitis C is also transmitted in infected blood, usually through contaminated needles or blood transfusions. By 1992 U.S. blood banks began routine testing for hepatitis C, so the risk of contracting it from transfusions has fallen. However, researchers estimate that as many as 4 million Americans may already be infected, and many of them have no symptoms. Hepatitis C may remain dormant for years but still damage the liver. Severe cases can lead to chronic hepatitis, cirrhosis, or liver cancer. Doctors recommend testing for anyone who has had kidney dialysis (Chapter 15) or an organ transplant before 1992. Also at risk are those who have injected drugs or had sexual contact with a hepatitis C carrier.

**Gallstones can obstruct bile flow** The gallbladder normally concentrates bile about 10-fold by removing about 90% of the water. Excessive cholesterol in the bile may precipitate out of solution with calcium and bile salts, forming hard crystals called gallstones (Figure 14.19). Only about 20% of gallstones ever cause problems, but if the crystals grow large enough they can obstruct bile flow and cause intense pain, especially after a meal. Treatments include drugs to dissolve the crystals, ultrasound vibrations or laser treatments to break the stones apart, or surgery to remove the gallbladder.

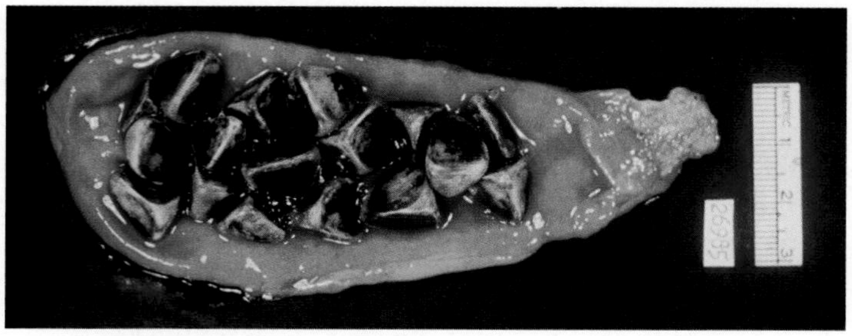

**Figure 14.19 Gallstones.**

## Malnutrition: Too many or too few nutrients

Malnutrition refers to conditions in which human development and function are compromised by an unbalanced or insufficient diet. Malnutrition can be caused either by overnutrition or undernutrition. Overnutrition can lead to obesity. Worldwide, however, undernourishment is far more common. The United Nations estimates that 800 million people, or about 13% of the world's population, are undernourished.

Deficiencies of one or more nutrients can produce specific effects. For example, years of vitamin A deficiency lead to eye damage and night blindness. In children, undernutrition stunts growth and increases susceptibility to infection. Severe undernutrition, or starvation, is still the leading cause of malnutrition worldwide. Nearly 20 million people, most of them children, die every year of starvation or related diseases.

## Obesity: A worldwide epidemic?

Estimates of the prevalence of obesity vary depending on how it's defined and how the data are collected. Nevertheless, the World Health Organization calls obesity a global epidemic. In the U.S., obesity has increased from 12.6% of the population in 1990 to 34% in 2006. Figure 14.20 compares the figures state by state. Obesity is rising even in some less industrialized countries: 5% of women in Papua New Guinea are obese today, compared to none in 1980.

Body weight is determined by both internal factors (such as genetic makeup) and environmental factors (such as activity level and availability of food). There's a lot of interest in genetic factors these days, such as "fat genes" that might make it harder to maintain a healthy weight. But genetics cannot account for an entire population's weight gain, because genes don't evolve that fast. It took us millions of years to become what we are, and our collective gene pool cannot change in just 20 years.

We must look to the environment to explain this global rise in obesity. Modernization has produced an environment

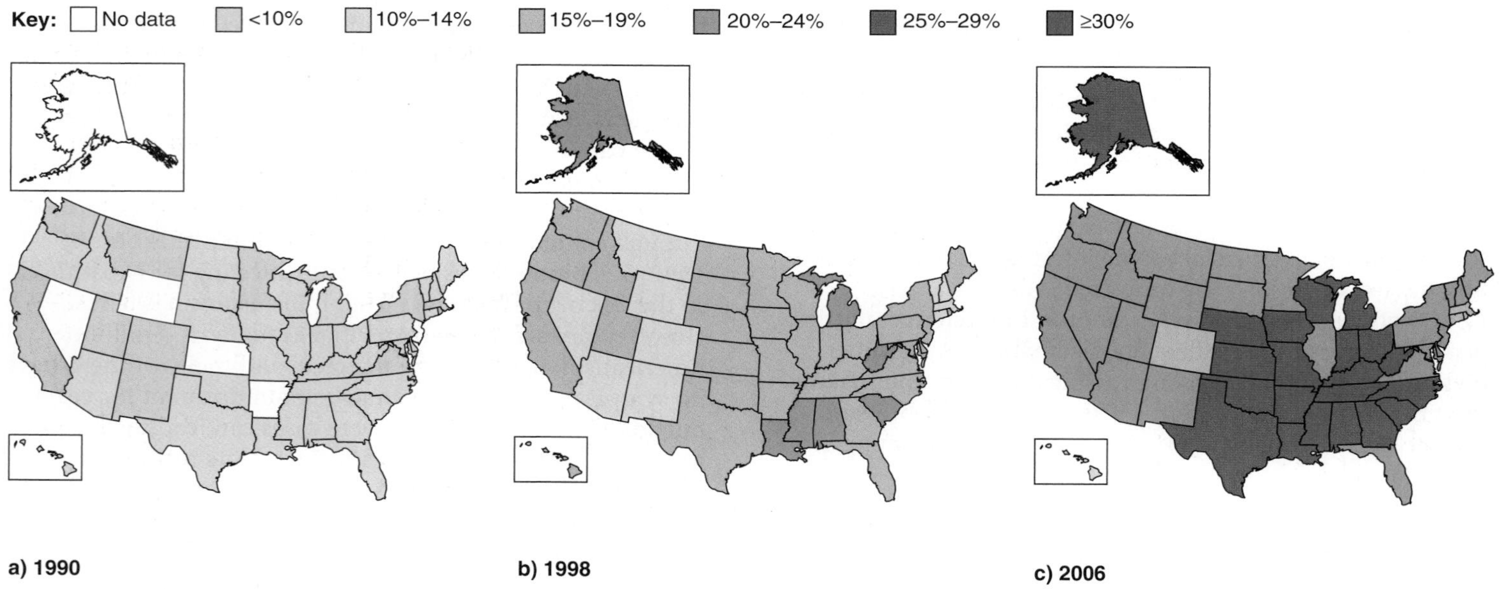


**Figure 14.20 Obesity trends among U.S. adults, 1990, 1998, and 2006.** These maps show the percentage of the population classified as obese in each state. Obesity is defined as a body mass index greater than 30.

*Source:* Behavioral Risk Factor Surveillance System, Centers for Disease Control.

that favors an imbalance between caloric intake and expenditure. Computers, television, cars, desk jobs—all combine to produce a more sedentary lifestyle. At the same time, food has become relatively cheap and available, which has apparently encouraged us to eat and drink more. In 1970 Americans consumed an average of 2,234 Calories per day; by 2003 this had risen to 2,757 Calories daily. Additional fats and oils account for 42% of the increase, or an extra 216 Calories per person each day.

**RECAP**

Disorders of the GI tract and accessory organs include lactose intolerance, diverticulosis, colon polyps, gallstones, and hepatitis. Malnutrition can be caused by over- or undernutrition. Whereas starvation is the leading cause of malnutrition in underdeveloped countries, obesity is increasing in industrialized nations. ■

## 14.13 Eating disorders: Anorexia nervosa and bulimia

Several conditions involving digestion and nutrition are really not digestive disorders at all but eating disorders involving the nervous system. Although eating disorders occur around the world, they are most common in women living in industrialized Western countries. Two examples are anorexia nervosa and bulimia.

**Anorexia nervosa** is a condition in which a person diets excessively or stops eating altogether, even to the point of starvation and death (Figure 14.21). Symptoms include:

- Refusal to maintain healthy body weight; people with anorexia often weigh less than 85% of their ideal weight.
- Intense fear of gaining weight, even though underweight.
- Distorted perception or preoccupation with body weight or shape.

**Figure 14.21 Anorexia nervosa.** Anorexia nervosa is a form of starvation based on an intense fear of gaining weight.

- In premenopausal women, the absence of at least three consecutive menstrual cycles. Severe undernutrition interferes with the hormonal cycles of menstruation. Male anorexics also experience hormonal abnormalities.

**Bulimia** is a binge-and-purge condition in which someone eats and deliberately vomits or takes other steps to minimize the Calories ingested. Symptoms of bulimia are:

- Recurrent episodes of binge eating. An episode of binge eating involves both (1) eating large amounts of food and (2) feeling a lack of control over eating.
- Taking recurrent inappropriate steps to prevent weight gain, such as self-induced vomiting; misusing laxatives, diuretics, enemas, or other medications; fasting; or exercising excessively.
- Binge eating and compensatory behaviors that occur, on average, at least twice a week for three months.
- Preoccupation with body shape and weight. However, unlike anorexics, some bulimics maintain a normal weight.

Both anorexia and bulimia play havoc with the body and mind. Anorexics become malnourished and suffer insomnia, hair loss, fatigue, and moodiness. Over time, they lose bone mass and develop osteoporosis. Repeated trauma to a bulimic's digestive system leads to ulcers, chronic heartburn, and rectal bleeding. Recurrent vomiting damages gums, erodes tooth enamel, and makes salivary glands swell, giving a chipmunklike appearance.

Doctors are not sure what causes eating disorders, but there appear to be deep-rooted psychological and cultural factors. Young women with a history of extreme dieting are 18 times more likely to develop eating disorders than those who do not have a history of dieting. Many people with eating disorders also suffer from depression and anxiety. Because these conditions are complex, multidisciplinary treatment seems most effective, with a team of professionals who can address the patient's medical, psychiatric, dental, psychological, and nutritional needs.

# Current Issue

## Is "Overweight" Overstated?

If you have a body mass index (BMI) of greater than 25 but under 30, then you're officially considered overweight by the federal government. The government believes that your health may be at risk and it's out to save you. You're likely to feel like you're being targeted by a concerted campaign to get you to eat better, exercise more, and above all, slim down! It's all very well-meaning, of course, but there's a problem: some of the statements made about the dangers of being overweight are based on poor science, weak statistics, and sloppy grammar.

On the other hand, several recent books have challenged the conventional wisdom that too much body fat is bad for your health. Generally they have very little data to back their claims up—they're just telling us what we want to hear. It's time for a little scientific skepticism.

Regardless of her BMI, 2008 U.S. Open Champion Serena Williams would best be described as "fit."

### Too Much Body Fat Is Bad

The hard fact is that nearly every scientific study conducted on the relationship between body fat and health risk has found a positive association between BMIs above the normal range and the risk of certain diseases. Those diseases include hypertension, type 2 diabetes, coronary heart disease, stroke, gallbladder disease, osteoarthritis, several types of cancers, among others. Being slightly overweight is *sometimes* a risk factor, but being obese generally *always* is.

The question becomes, then, "How much body fat is too much for *me*?" That's where the truth is unknown and misinformation begins. The answer depends on the specific disease you're concerned about and upon your lifestyle and genetic risk factors, and not just on your BMI. To understand this, we need to understand the BMI scale; what it's useful for and what it's not.

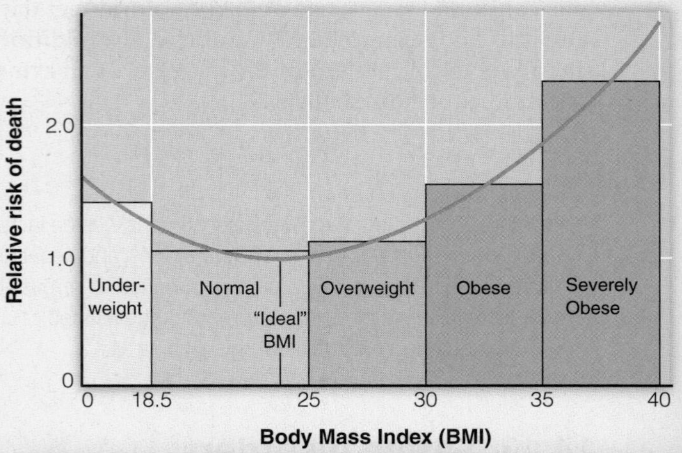


A representation of the typical J-shaped relationship between BMI and relative risk of death in a large population. The lowest risk of death is at a BMI of 24.

### BMI and the Definition of "Overweight"

You and I tend to judge our fatness by getting on a bathroom scale. BMI is a bit more precise because height is taken into account. It is the simplest comparative measure of fatness. Its value is that it is easy to obtain, even as a self-report over the phone or on a questionnaire.

Before 1980 the BMI scale was primarily used by life insurance companies to predict mortality risk (risk of death). It came into widespread use within the industry because insurance companies learned that there is a normal, predictable U- or J-shaped relationship between risk of death and BMI (see figure above). Compared to people at an "ideal" BMI, which turns out to be 24 for mortality, people with very high and very low BMIs have a greater relative risk of dying in a given year.

It wasn't long before medical researchers began to use the BMI scale to tease out the health risks associated with specific diseases within large populations. Literally hundreds of studies, some well-done and some not, came to the same conclusion—that there is a positive relationship between BMI and certain chronic diseases: the higher the BMI the greater the risk.

## the facts...

- According to government statistics, over 64% of the U.S. adult population is either overweight or obese.
- Government statements about our national weight problem tend to lump overweight and obesity together as one problem.
- Obesity increases the risk of mortality and of certain chronic diseases. The health risk of being just slightly overweight is less severe.
- BMI is not particularly useful in assessing one's individual health.

But then the government got into the act, for it soon became clear that hundreds of thousands of people were dying or suffering from disease needlessly. If only everyone were at that ideal BMI of 24, imagine all the lives that would be saved! It wasn't long before the government declared that women with a BMI of 27 and men with a BMI over 28 were officially classified as "overweight," and a concerted educational campaign was begun to get us to eat better, exercise more often, and above all, lose that weight. The over-zealous authors of one study even declared that "adults should try to maintain a BMI between 18.5 and 21.9 to minimize their risk of disease."

But the average weight of the U.S. adult population kept rising, and government concern rose with it. In 1998 the federal government changed its definition of overweight to include everyone over a BMI of 25. Overnight, another 29 million Americans were labeled overweight. And that's why by 2000, over 64% of the U.S. population was overweight or obese.

### BMI Is an Imperfect Measure of Health and Fitness

The BMI simply does not work as a measure of an individual's level of fitness or health. People who have a high muscle mass or are just genetically built with larger body frames are likely to be labeled overweight or even obese by the BMI scale. The BMI is a useful tool for epidemiologists and public policy makers as they study whole populations, but it should not be used to make a recommendation about your personal lifestyle.

### Hyperbole and Half-Truths about Overweight

Consider these statements from a National Institutes of Health study entitled *Clinical Guidelines on the Identification, Evaluation, and Treatment of Overweight and Obesity in Adults: The Evidence Report,* published in 1998:

> An estimated 97 million adults in the United States are overweight or obese. . . . Higher body weights are also associated with increases in all-cause mortality. . . . As a major contributor to preventive death in the United States today, overweight and obesity pose a major public health challenge.

Or this statement, from the same report:

> All overweight and obese adults (age 18 years or older) with a BMI of ⩾25 are considered at risk for developing associated morbidities or diseases such as hypertension, high blood cholesterol, type 2 diabetes, coronary heart disease, and other diseases.

Or this, from a Department of Health and Human Services news report in 2001:

> Approximately 300,000 deaths per year currently are associated with obesity and overweight (compared to more than 400,000 deaths a year associated with cigarette smoking).

The statements above pose two problems. First, they lump overweight and obesity together as one health problem, as if the risks are the same. And second, the second statement assigns the risk to individuals, when the data were derived only from population studies.

### Overweight and Obese Are Not the Same

Look again at the graph depicting mortality versus BMI. Clearly, there *is* a positive correlation between mortality and BMI above a BMI of 25, so that statement is true. However, it is also true that as a group, the overweight category is not that different from all normals. Nearly all of those 300,000 deaths allegedly associated with being obese or overweight must be associated with obesity alone.

To be fair, a population with a BMI in the overweight range *is* at increased risk for some of those specific diseases listed previously. But as you might expect, the risks are not as great as the risks associated with obesity. It's a matter of degree.

### National versus Personal Risk

Is the government right to worry that obesity continues to rise in this country and to try to do something about it through public education? The answer is a resounding "yes." If every U.S. adult could somehow magically lose 10 pounds, would the incidence of hypertension, diabetes, and mortality go down? The answer again is "yes." But if you are in the overweight category, would losing 10 pounds reduce your risk by the same amount? The answer is probably not. It depends on whether you have any of the risk factors for those diseases in the first place. If you exercise regularly and eat properly and your blood pressure and cholesterol are normal, then don't worry too much about your personal BMI. Lose 10 pounds if you want to, but don't do it because you think you'll live longer.

### Questions to consider

**1** *Do you agree with the government's definition of overweight as BMIs above 25? Why or why not?*

**2** *What do you think is government's proper role (if any) when it comes to noncommunicable health risks such as obesity?*

*According to the BMI scale Sylvester Stallone is classified as obese.*

# Chapter Summary

### The digestive system brings nutrients into the body *p. 321*

- The digestive system consists of the gastrointestinal (GI) tract and four accessory organs: the salivary glands, liver, gallbladder, and pancreas.
- The five basic processes of the digestive system are motility, secretion, digestion, absorption, and excretion.
- Two types of motility in the GI tract are peristalsis, which propels food forward, and segmentation, which mixes the contents.

### The mouth processes food for swallowing *p. 324*

- The 32 teeth of adults include incisors, canines, premolars, and molars. Teeth cut, tear, grind, and crush food.
- Saliva moistens food, begins the digestion of starch, and helps to protect against bacteria.

### The pharynx and esophagus deliver food to the stomach *p. 325*

- Swallowing is a reflex that is initiated by voluntary movements of the tongue. Once started, swallowing is involuntary.
- The sole function of the esophagus is to get food from the mouth to the stomach.
- The lower esophageal sphincter prevents reflux of stomach contents.

### The stomach stores food, digests protein, and regulates delivery *p. 326*

- The stomach stores ingested food until it can be delivered to the small intestine.
- Glands in the mucosa of the stomach secrete gastric juice into the lumen, beginning the process of protein digestion.
- Peristalsis of the stomach mixes the food and pushes it toward the small intestine.

### The small intestine digests food and absorbs nutrients and water *p. 329*

- Digestion occurs primarily in the first part of the small intestine, called the duodenum.
- The jejunum and ileum of the small intestine absorb most of the products of digestion.
- The small intestine has a very large surface area because of its many folds, villi, and microvilli.

### Accessory organs aid digestion and absorption *p. 330*

- The pancreas secretes fluid containing bicarbonate and digestive enzymes into the small intestine.
- The liver produces bile and participates in homeostasis in a variety of ways.
- All of the venous blood from the GI tract is routed directly to the liver.
- The gallbladder stores bile from the liver and concentrates it by removal of most of the water.

### The large intestine absorbs nutrients and eliminates wastes *p. 332*

- The large intestine absorbs most remaining nutrients and water, and vitamin K produced by bacteria. It also stores wastes.
- Defecation is generally controlled by a neural reflex, but it can be overridden by conscious control.

### How nutrients are absorbed *p. 332*

- Amino acids and simple sugars are actively transported into the mucosal cells that line the small and large intestines.
- The products of fat digestion enter the mucosal cells by diffusion, then re-form into triglycerides. Triglycerides are coated with protein and move into lymph vessels for transport to the blood.
- Water is absorbed by osmosis.
- Vitamins and minerals follow a variety of specific pathways.

### Endocrine and nervous systems regulate digestion *p. 334*

- The volume and content of food play a large part in regulating digestive processes.
- Stretching of the stomach increases stomach peristalsis and the secretion of gastric juice.
- Stretching of the small intestine inhibits gastric motility, increases intestinal segmentation, and causes the secretion of two digestive enzymes, secretin and cholecystokinin.
- Acid in the small intestine triggers the secretion of pancreatic juice containing bicarbonate.

### Nutrition: You are what you eat *p. 335*

- Good nutrition requires a variety of foods weighted toward fruits, vegetables, and whole-grain products.
- The human body needs certain nutritional components that it cannot make, including a few fatty acids, eight amino acids, 13 vitamins, and all essential minerals.

### Weight control: Energy consumed versus energy spent *p. 341*

- The basal metabolic rate (BMR) represents the daily energy needs of the body for all essential activities except physical activity.
- Fat contains over twice as many Calories per gram as carbohydrate or protein.
- A person must use 3,500 Calories more than he or she ingests to lose a pound of body fat.

### Disorders of the digestive system *p. 342*

- Lactose intolerance is caused by the lack of the enzyme (lactase) that normally digests lactose.
- Hepatitis, or inflammation of the liver, can be caused by several different viruses.
- Starvation is the most common form of malnutrition in the world. However, the incidence of obesity is rising in the U.S. and other industrialized nations.

### Eating disorders: Anorexia nervosa and bulimia *p. 345*

- Two serious eating disorders are anorexia nervosa, in which the person diets excessively or stops eating entirely, and bulimia, a binge-and-purge condition in which the person eats and deliberately vomits or takes other steps to minimize caloric intake.
- The most effective treatments are multidisciplinary, addressing medical, psychiatric, dental, psychological, and nutritional needs.

## Terms You Should Know

anorexia nervosa, *345*
basal metabolic rate (BMR), *341*
bile, *331*
bulimia, *345*
Calorie, *341*
cholecystokinin (CCK), *334*
chyme, *326*
colon, *332*
complete protein, *338*
esophagus, *325*
essential amino acids, *338*
gallbladder, *331*
gastrin, *334*
gastrointestinal (GI) tract, *321*
hepatic portal system, *331*
hepatitis, *343*
large intestine, *332*
mucosa, *321*
muscularis, *321*
nutrient, *321*
pancreas, *330*
pepsin, *326*
peptic ulcer, *326*
peristalsis, *323*
Recommended Dietary Allowance (RDA), *340*
salivary gland, *324*
secretin, *334*
segmentation, *324*
serosa, *321*
submucosa, *321*
villus, *329*
vitamin, *338*

## Concept Review

1. Describe the organs of the GI tract including the four accessory organs.
2. Name the five basic processes associated with carrying out the function of the GI tract.
3. Describe the role saliva plays in initiating the digestive process.
4. Compare and contrast *peristalsis* and *segmentation.*
5. Indicate how many teeth adult humans have.
6. Describe the events that occur in the stomach that contribute to the digestive process.
7. Indicate where in the GI tract most of the absorption of nutrients occurs.
8. Rank the major nutrient groups (carbohydrates, lipids, or proteins) according to Calories per gram.
9. Indicate what fraction of our daily caloric expenditure is accounted for by our basal metabolic rate (BMR).
10. Explain why it is harder to get an adequate supply of all amino acids from a vegetarian diet than from meat.

## Test Yourself

### Matching Exercise

_____ 1. Neutralizes acid in the duodenum, allowing pancreatic enzymes to function
_____ 2. Protein-digesting enzyme
_____ 3. Mineral element needed for the production of hemoglobin
_____ 4. One of two hormones secreted by the small intestine
_____ 5. Hormone secreted by the stomach
_____ 6. A fat-digesting enzyme

a. pepsin
b. secretin
c. bicarbonate
d. iron
e. lipase
f. gastrin

### Fill in the Blank

7. The ____________________ is responsible for removing bilirubin from the blood.
8. The four types of adult teeth are incisors, ____________________, premolars, and molars.
9. Glycogen and starch belong to the nutrient group known as ____________________.
10. Calcium, sodium, and potassium belong to the nutrient group known as ____________________.
11. In order to maintain a constant body weight, our energy ____________________ must exactly balance our energy expenditure.
12. ____________________ intolerance is caused by an inability to break down the main sugar in milk.

### True or False?

13. The pancreas secretes digestive enzymes and bicarbonate into the small intestine.
14. Only the large intestine absorbs water.
15. The gallbladder concentrates bile by removing water from it.

## Apply What You Know

1. A meal containing a lot of fat takes longer to be emptied out of the stomach than a low-fat meal. Why?
2. Procter & Gamble produces a calorie-free fat substitute called Olean (olestra) that is used to deep-fry foods such as potato chips. Olestra is a fat-soluble molecule that is neither digested nor absorbed. There is a concern that eating too much olestra might lead to certain vitamin deficiencies. What types of vitamins do you think would be affected by the use of olestra, and how might they be affected?
3. Other side effects of the consumption of too much olestra include gas, diarrhea, and a sudden need to defecate. What could be a cause of these?
4. Many prescription medications are supposed to be taken with a meal. Others are only to be taken on an empty stomach. Why would there be such differences?
5. Sometimes, the cure for gallstones is to surgically remove the gallbladder. What effect would removal of the gallbladder have on digestion?
6. People with lactose intolerance cannot digest the common dairy sugar lactose. Besides being careful not to eat dairy foods, is there anything else a lactose intolerant person can do?
7. Cholera is a dangerous infectious disease that is common in places that do not have a steady supply of clean drinking water. Severe untreated cholera can be fatal within a matter of days. Cholera is caused by a bacterial toxin that causes severe diarrhea. What do you think might cause death from cholera, if the only symptom is diarrhea?

*Answers can be found on the Human Biology Place.*

## References and Additional Reading

Kiberstis, Paula A., and Jean Marx, editors. Regulation of Body Weight. *Science* 280:1363–1390, 1998. (A compilation of four news articles and five research articles presenting some of the latest information on this subject.)

Scientific American Special Issue: Feast or Famine. *Scientific American* 297(3):54–117, September 2007. (A compilation of nine articles on dieting, fitness, and world obesity, and hunger)

U.S. Department of Health and Human Services and U.S. Department of Agriculture. *Dietary Guidelines for Americans 2005.* 6th ed. Washington, D.C.: U.S. Government Printing Office, January 2005. (The U.S. government dietary guide, published every five years.)

### Internet References

Find links to the following Web sites at the Human Biology Place.

**MyPyramid.gov**
**www.mypyramid.gov**
USDA Web site that offers dietary guidelines, information about food groups, and personalized tools for assessing diet and physical activity.

**American Dietetic Association**
**www.eatright.org**
Largest U.S. association of food and nutrition professionals; nutrition fact sheets, food news, and recipes.

**WebMD Health**
**www.webmd.com**
Information on eating disorders, fitness, weight loss, and many other health topics.

**National Institutes of Health**
**www.nih.gov**
An A–Z index of health topics, including eating disorders, obesity, exercise/physical fitness, nutrition, and teen health.

# 15 The Urinary System

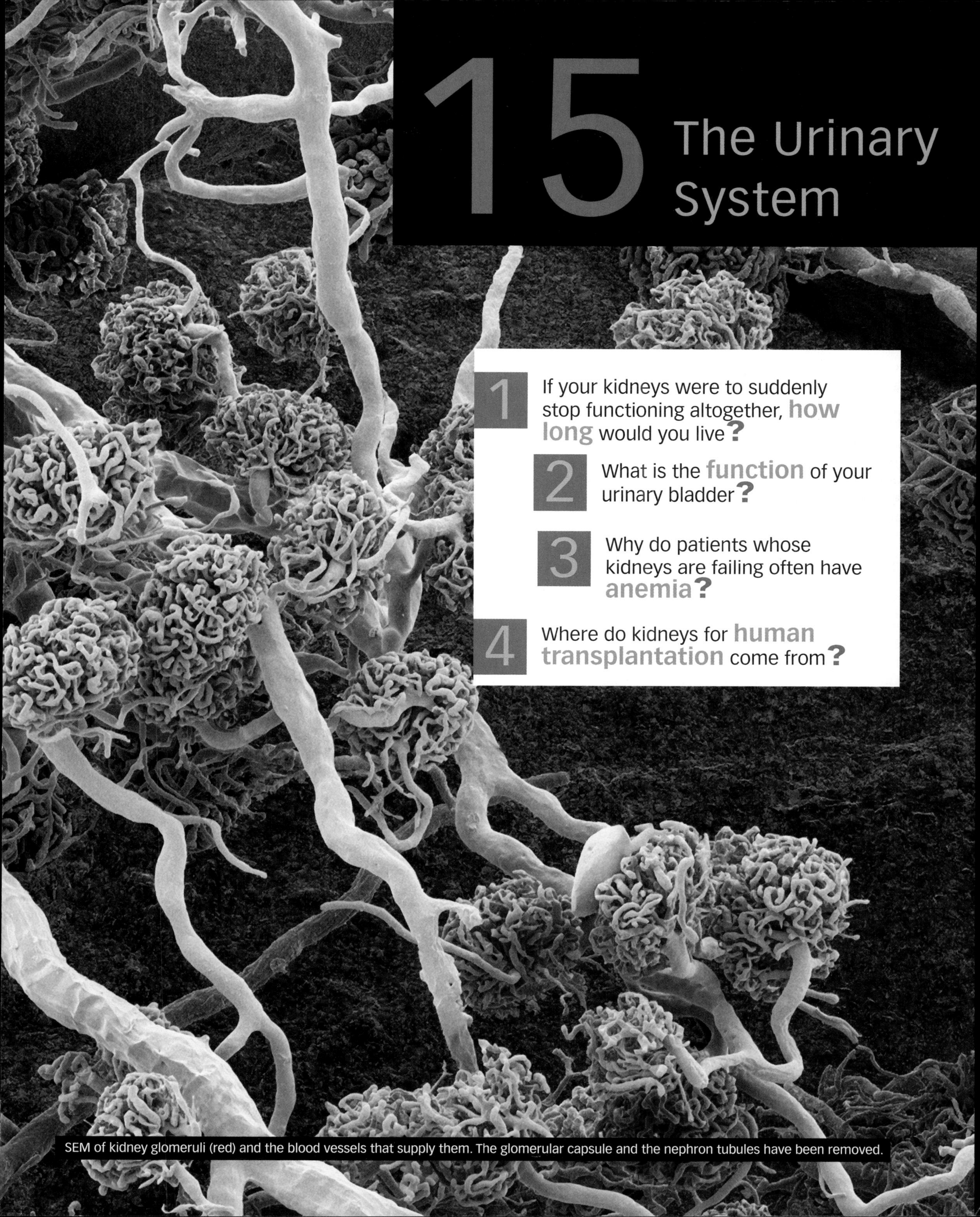

1. If your kidneys were to suddenly stop functioning altogether, **how long** would you live?
2. What is the **function** of your urinary bladder?
3. Why do patients whose kidneys are failing often have **anemia**?
4. Where do kidneys for **human transplantation** come from?

SEM of kidney glomeruli (red) and the blood vessels that supply them. The glomerular capsule and the nephron tubules have been removed.

**Drop by drop—slowly but steadily,** the kidneys go about the business of making urine. Minutes or even hours pass as the urinary bladder slowly fills. Finally, although you hadn't been thinking about it before, the thought comes to your mind that you need to find a bathroom, and soon. Before long you can think of little else.

We are aware of our heartbeat, consciously develop muscle tone, and are often preoccupied by our stomach. But do we ever give our kidneys a second thought? They are forgotten organs, tucked away at the back of the abdominal cavity. With urine as their primary product, the kidneys may not seem to serve a very glamorous function, but they play a vital role in maintaining the constancy of the internal environment. Urine itself serves no purpose; it is simply the end product of the regulation of the internal environment, the waste that is discarded.

As a recurrent theme in physiology, we have discussed homeostasis in terms of regulating body temperature, blood pressure, blood gases, and many other controlled variables in connection with the functions of other organ systems. This chapter describes the central role of the urinary system in maintaining the constancy of the composition and volume of the body fluids.

## 15.1 The urinary system contributes to homeostasis

**Excretion** refers to processes that remove wastes and excess materials from the body. Let's briefly review the excretory organs and systems involved in managing metabolic wastes and maintaining homeostasis of water and solutes (Figure 15.1). The digestive system provides the body with nutrients and water, and excretes food residues. The lungs take in oxygen and excrete carbon dioxide gas. The skin gets rid of heat and is also a site of water and salt loss, especially when we get rid of heat quickly. The liver destroys or inactivates numerous substances, some of which are excreted as bile in the feces. But the key organs in maintaining homeostasis of body fluids are the kidneys.

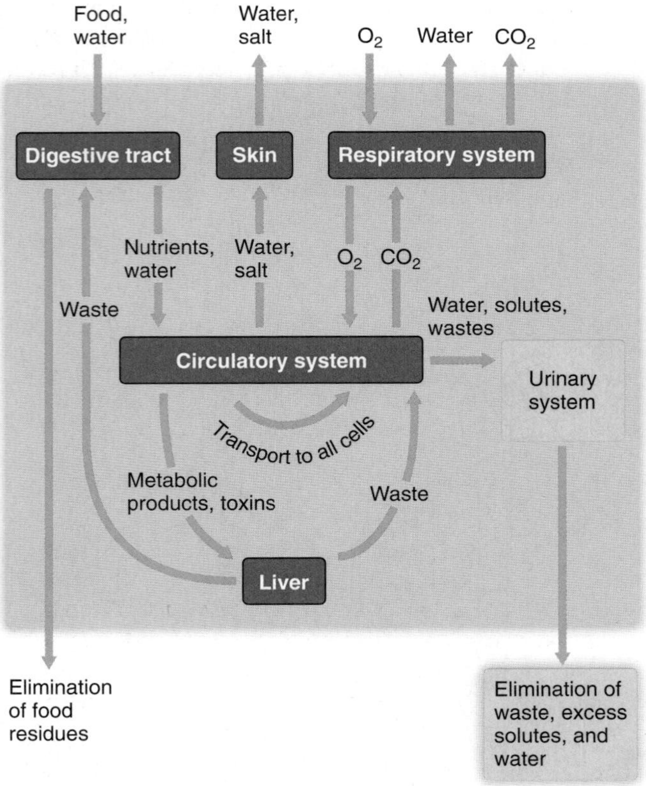


**Figure 15.1 Organ systems involved in removing wastes and maintaining homeostasis of water and solutes.** With the large tan box representing the body, this diagram maps the inflow and outflow of key compounds we consume. The kidneys of the urinary system are the organs primarily responsible for the maintenance of homeostasis of water and solutes and for the excretion of most waste products.

The **urinary system** consists of the kidneys, the ureters, the bladder, and the urethra. The two **kidneys** produce urine. The other components of the urinary system just transport and store urine until it is eliminated from the body.

Urine is primarily waste water and waste solutes. Among the solutes are various ions, drugs, vitamins, toxic chemicals,

### Answers to Intro Questions

1 You'd probably live for a week or more. The kidneys are constantly working to maintain homeostasis of the internal body fluids, and that's a slow and continuous (but essential) process. In practical terms, this is why patients with failed kidneys only need dialysis treatments several times a week.

2 The bladder is just a bag for storing urine. It does not make urine—that is the role of the kidneys.

3 The kidneys are the source of a hormone (erythropoietin) that stimulates the production of red blood cells in bone marrow. In patients with kidney failure the production of erythropoietin declines, so fewer red blood cells are produced.

4 About 45% come from live donors (often relatives of the patient), and the rest come from deceased donors. There is a severe shortage of both live and deceased donors in this country. More than 20 people die every day while waiting for a kidney.

and virtually every small waste molecule produced anywhere in the body. But the kidneys do much more than just get rid of liquid garbage. They also carefully regulate how much water and salt are excreted in order to maintain homeostasis of fluid volume and blood pressure. Finally, they retain within the body all three classes of nutrients (carbohydrates, lipids, and proteins), leaving their management to other organs.

### The kidneys regulate water levels

Water is the most abundant molecule in your body, representing about 60% of body weight. Normally you exchange about 2 $^1/_2$ liters of water per day with the external environment (Table 15.1). We consume most of our water in food and beverages, but we also produce about 300 milliliters as part of cellular metabolism. Meanwhile, we lose water steadily through evaporation from lungs and skin (not counting sweat), and through defecation.

Homeostasis is maintained only when water intake equals water output, as it does in Table 15.1. But you know from experience that water intake can vary tremendously, and so can loss through sweat. When you take in a lot of water or when you become severely dehydrated on a hot day, it's up to the kidneys to excrete the excess water or to conserve as much water as possible. The kidneys have a tremendous capacity to adjust water excretion as necessary, from a minimum of about 1/2 liter per day to nearly 1 liter per hour.

### The kidneys regulate nitrogenous wastes and other solutes

The primary solutes excreted by the kidneys are nitrogenous wastes, excess ions, and trace amounts of other substances, as described below.

The normal metabolism of proteins leaves us with excess nitrogenous wastes, which must be excreted by the kidneys. The metabolism of protein initially liberates ammonia ($NH_3$). Ammonia is toxic to cells, but the liver quickly detoxifies it by combining two ammonia molecules with a molecule of carbon dioxide to produce **urea** ($H_2N$-CO-$NH_2$) plus water. Most of the urea is excreted by the urinary system.

Dozens of different ions are ingested in excess with food or liberated from nutrients during metabolism. The most abundant ions in the body are sodium ($Na^+$) and chloride ($Cl^-$), both of which are important in determining the volume of the extracellular fluids, including blood. The volume of blood, in turn, affects blood pressure. Other important ions include potassium ($K^+$), which maintains electrical charges across membranes; calcium ($Ca^{2+}$), important in nerve and muscle activity; and hydrogen ($H^+$), which maintains acid-base balance. The kidneys regulate the urinary excretion of these ions in order to maintain homeostasis of each one.

Trace amounts of many other substances are excreted in direct proportion to their daily rate of production. Among them are creatinine, a waste product that is produced during the metabolism of creatine phosphate (an energy source in muscle), and various waste products that give urine its characteristic yellow color.

**Table 15.1 Sources of water gain and loss per day**

| Water gain (ml/day) | | Water loss (ml/day) | |
|---|---|---|---|
| Drinking fluids | 1,000 | Urine | 1,500 |
| Water in food | 1,200 | Evaporative loss (lung) | 500 |
| Metabolic production | 300 | Evaporative loss (skin) | 350 |
| | | Feces | 150 |
| **Total** | **2,500** | **Total** | **2,500** |

**RECAP**

The urinary system maintains a constant internal environment by regulating water balance and body levels of nitrogenous wastes, ions, and other substances. It filters metabolic wastes from the blood and excretes them in urine. The major nitrogenous waste product is urea. ■

## 15.2 Organs of the urinary system

Table 15.2 lists the four organs of the urinary system and their principal functions. In the following discussion, function will be covered after anatomy.

### Kidneys: The principal urinary organs

The kidneys are located on either side of the vertebral column, near the posterior body wall (Figure 15.2a). Each kidney is a dark reddish-brown organ about the size of your fist and shaped like a kidney bean. A renal artery and a renal vein connect each kidney to the aorta and inferior vena cava, respectively (*renal* comes from the Latin word *ren,* "kidney").

**Table 15.2 Functions of organs in urinary system**

| Organ | Functions |
|---|---|
| Kidneys | Excrete metabolic wastes, especially urea |
| | Maintain water and salt homeostasis |
| | Help regulate acid-base balance |
| | Help regulate blood pressure (produce renin, a hormone) |
| | Control red blood cell production (produce erythropoietin, a hormone) |
| | Activate vitamin D |
| Ureters | Transport urine to bladder |
| Urinary bladder | Stores urine until excretion |
| Urethra | Transports urine to outside |

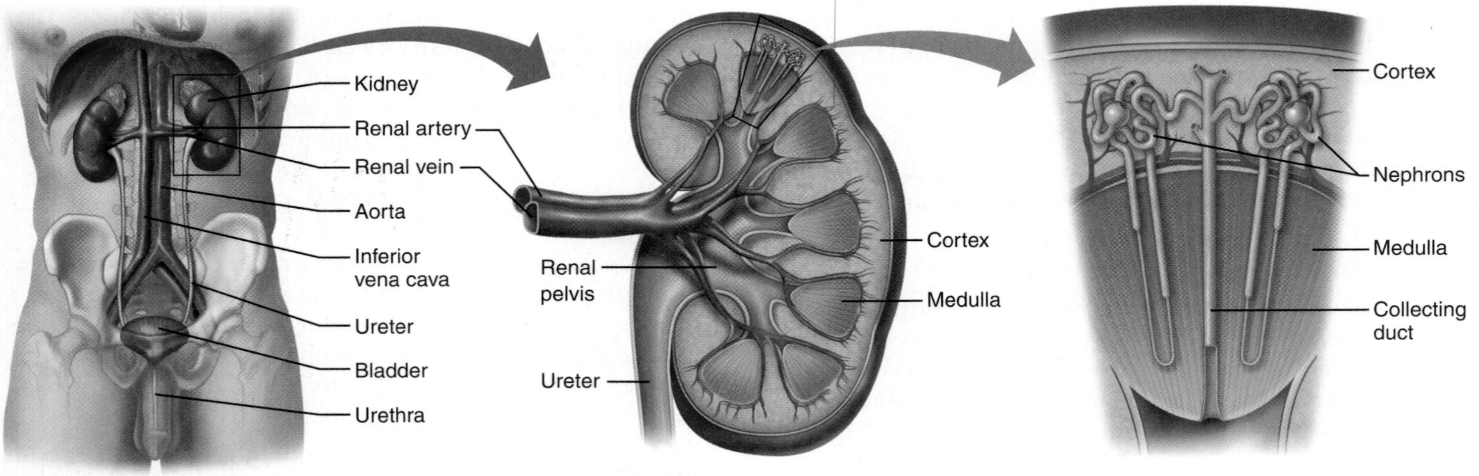


**a) The components of the urinary system.** **b) Internal structure of the kidney.** **c) The cortex and medulla of the kidney are composed of numerous nephrons.**

**Figure 15.2 The human urinary system.**

Seen in a longitudinal section (Figure 15.2b), each kidney consists of inner pyramid-shaped zones of dense tissue (called renal pyramids) that constitute the **medulla,** and an outer zone called the **cortex.** At the center of the kidney is a hollow space, the **renal pelvis,** where urine collects after it is formed.

A closer look at a section of the renal cortex and medulla reveals that it contains long, thin, tubular structures called nephrons (Figure 15.2c). Nephrons share a common final section called the collecting duct, through which urine is delivered to the renal pelvis.

Besides being the primary organs of the urinary system, the kidneys have many other functions related to maintaining homeostasis, which are discussed later in this chapter.

## Ureters transport urine to the bladder

The renal pelvis of each kidney is continuous with a **ureter,** a muscular tube that transports urine to the bladder. Peristaltic waves of smooth muscle contraction, occurring every 10–15 seconds, move urine along the 10-inch length of the ureters to the bladder.

## Urinary bladder stores urine

The **urinary bladder** stores urine. The bladder consists of three layers of smooth muscle lined on the inside by epithelial cells. Typically the bladder can hold about 600–1,000 ml of urine, though volumes that large may feel uncomfortable. Women generally have a smaller bladder capacity than men because their bladders are slightly compressed by the nearby uterus (Figure 15.3).

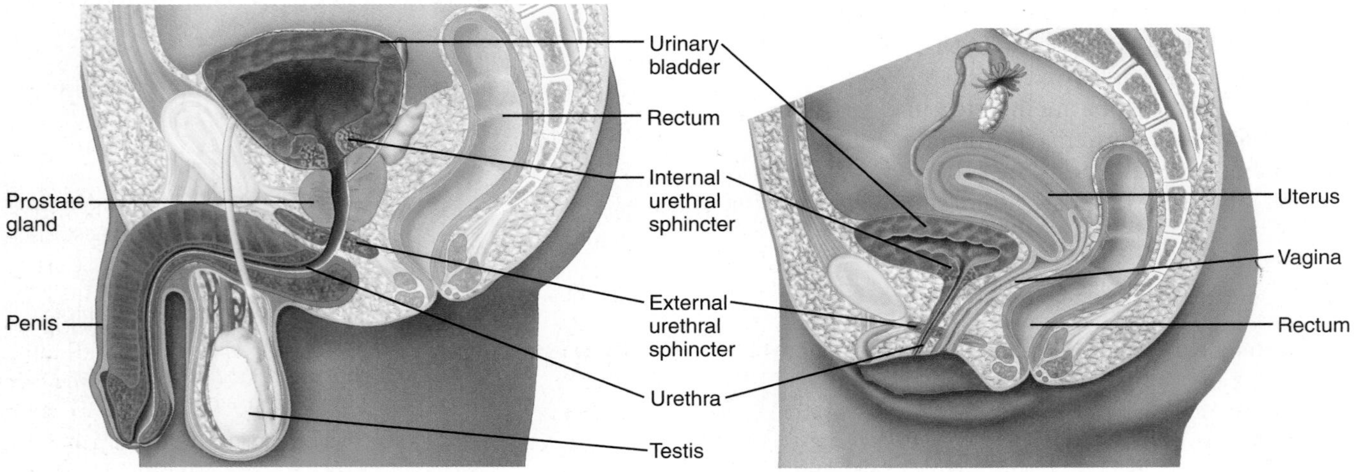


**a) The male** **b) The female**

**Figure 15.3 The positions of the bladder, the urethra, and associated organs in males and in females.**

### Urethra carries urine from the body

During urination, urine passes through the **urethra,** a single muscular tube that extends from the bladder to the body's external opening. Until then the bladder is prevented from emptying by the internal urethral sphincter, where the bladder joins the urethra, and the external urethral sphincter farther down the urethra. The urethra is about 8 inches long in men and about 1.5 inches long in women.

**RECAP**

Organs of the urinary system include the kidneys, ureters, bladder, and urethra. The kidneys are the principal urinary organs, although they have several homeostatic functions as well. The ureters transport urine to the bladder, where it is stored until carried by the urethra to the body's external opening. ■

## 15.3 Nephrons produce urine

Each kidney contains approximately a million small functional units called **nephrons** (from the Greek word for kidney, *nephros*). An individual nephron consists of a thin hollow tube of epithelial cells, called a tubule, plus the blood vessels that supply the tubule. The function of the nephron is to produce urine. However, nephrons don't just pick the waste molecules out of blood and excrete them. Instead, they remove about 180 liters of fluid from the blood every day (about $2^1/_2$ times your body weight) and then return almost all of it to the blood, leaving just a small amount of fluid behind in the tubule to be excreted as urine. If you took a similar approach to cleaning your room, you would take everything out of the room and then put it all back except for the dust and waste paper you wanted to discard.

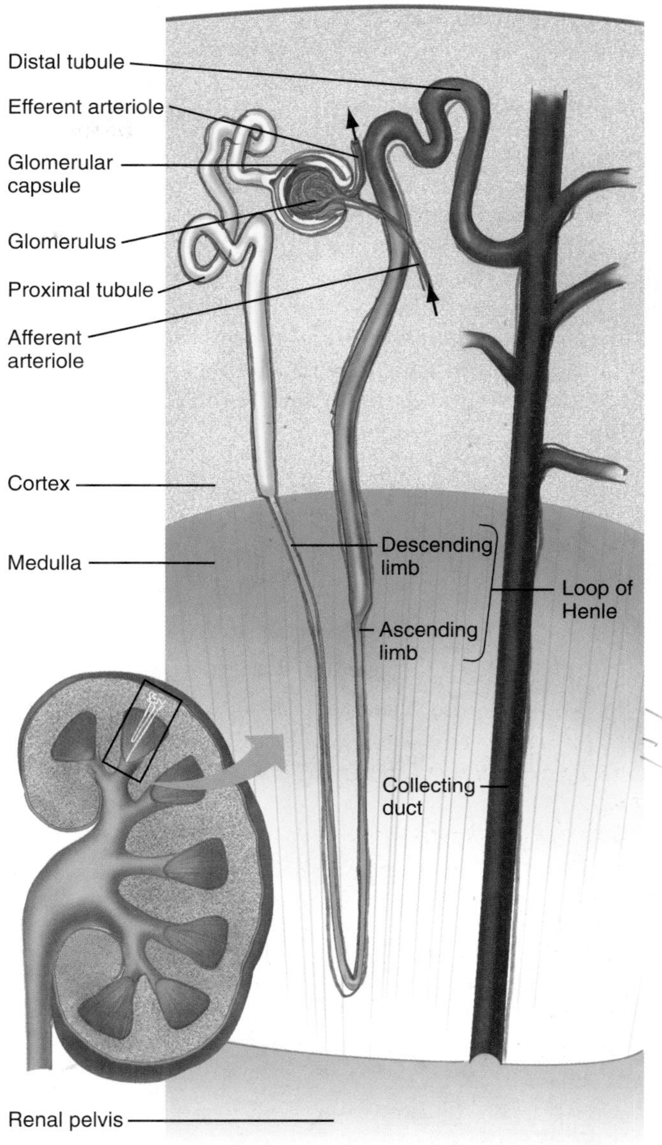


**Figure 15.4 Tubular regions of a nephron.** A portion of the glomerular capsule has been cut away to expose the blood vessels (the glomerulus) enclosed by the capsule. The proximal tubule begins at the glomerular capsule and ends where the tubule narrows and enters the medulla. The loop of Henle consists of descending and ascending limbs; it ends where the tubule passes the glomerular capsule. The distal tubule connects to a collecting duct, which is shared by many nephrons.

### The tubule filters fluid and reabsorbs substances

Figure 15.4 shows the tubular portion of a nephron. The nephron begins with a cup of tissue that looks like a deflated ball with one side pushed in, called the **glomerular capsule** (sometimes called Bowman's capsule). The glomerular capsule surrounds and encloses a network of capillaries called the **glomerulus,** which is part of the blood supply of the nephron.

The process of urine formation begins when plasma fluid is filtered out of the capillaries of the glomerulus and into the space between the two layers of the glomerular capsule. From the glomerular capsule the tubule continues as a long, thin tube with four distinct regions: proximal tubule, loop of Henle, distal tubule, and collecting duct. The **proximal tubule** (*proximal* means nearest to) starts at the glomerular capsule and ends at the renal medulla. The hairpin-shaped **loop of Henle** (loop of the nephron) extends into the medulla as the *descending limb* and then loops back up to the vicinity of the glomerular capsule as the *ascending limb.* After it passes the glomerular capsule, the tubule is called the **distal tubule** (*distal* means more distant from). Finally, the distal tubules of up to a thousand nephrons join to become a **collecting duct.** The collecting duct extends from the cortex to the renal pelvis, where the urine is finally deposited.

As we will see, the tubule and collecting duct are not just passive conduits. As urine flows through the tubule and collecting duct, their cells modify the urine content substantially by reabsorbing water and ions. Reabsorption prevents the loss of valuable substances from the body and adjusts the composition of blood and body fluids.

## Special blood vessels supply the tubule

Figure 15.5 provides a closer look at the blood vessels serving the nephrons. The renal artery supplying a kidney branches many times to serve those million nephrons. Ultimately, every nephron is supplied by a single arteriole, called the **afferent arteriole** (*afferent* means "directed toward"). The afferent arteriole enters a glomerular capsule and then divides many times to become the network of capillaries that constitutes the glomerulus. Here plasma fluid and solutes are filtered from the blood into the capsular space.

The glomerular capillaries rejoin to become the **efferent** ("directed away") **arteriole,** which carries filtered blood from the glomerulus. The efferent arteriole divides again into another capillary network that surrounds the proximal and distal tubules in the cortex, called the **peritubular capillaries** (*peri-* means "around"). The peritubular capillaries remove water, ions, and nutrients, which are reabsorbed by the proximal and distal tubules. The efferent arterioles of a few nephrons descend into the medulla and divide into long thin capillaries called the **vasa recta** (Latin for "straight vessels") that supply the loop of Henle and collecting duct. Eventually the filtered blood flows into progressively larger veins that become the single renal vein leading to the inferior vena cava.

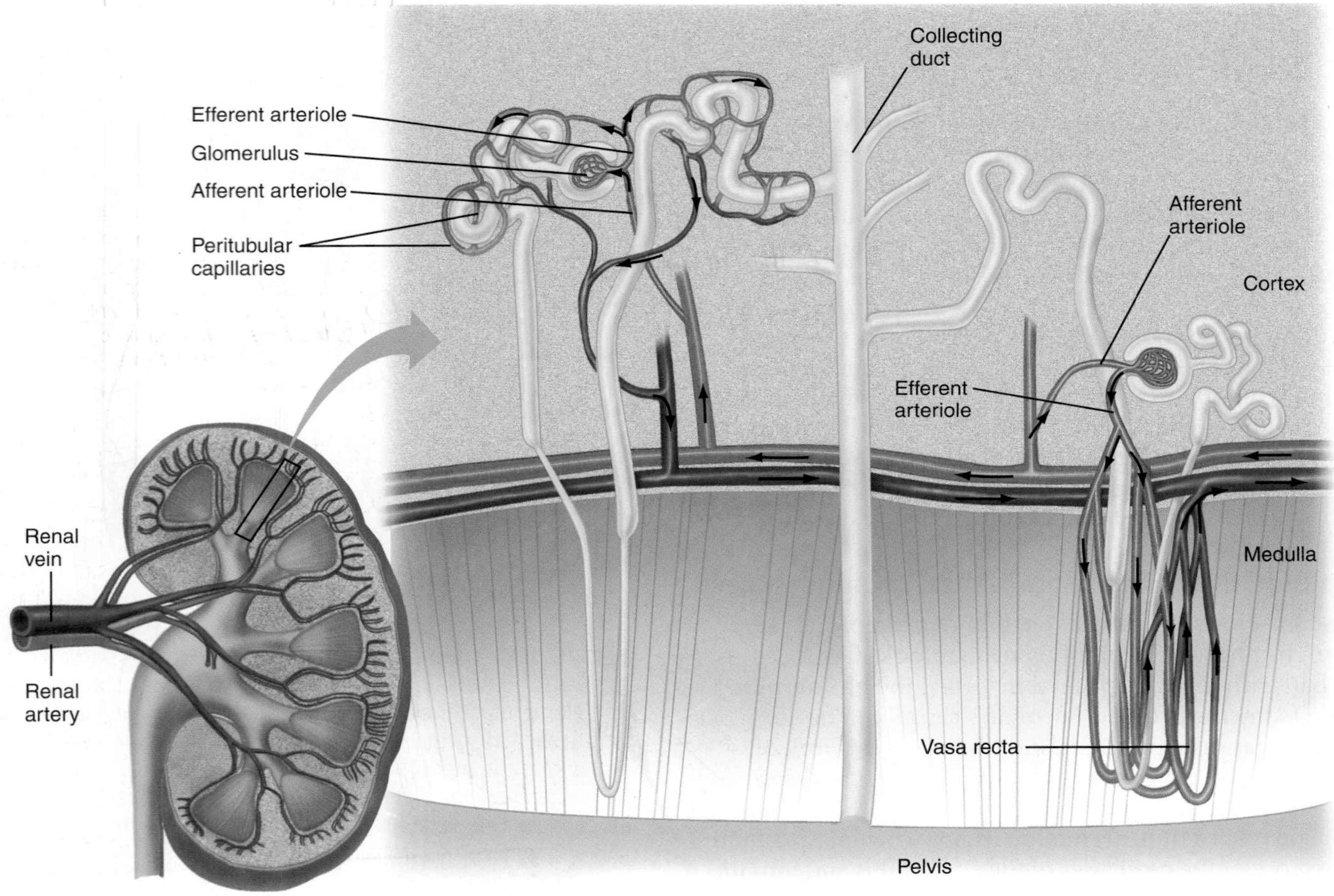


**a) Main blood vessels in the kidney**

**b) Most post-glomerular blood vessels perfuse tubular structures in the cortex; a few perfuse medullary structures.**

**Figure 15.5 Relationships between the tubular and vascular components of nephrons.** **(a)** The renal artery and renal vein branch many times to deliver blood to each glomerulus. **(b)** The efferent arteriole of most nephrons, such as the one shown here on the left, divide to become the peritubular capillaries, which supply proximal and distal tubules in the cortex. In some nephrons, such as the one on the right, the efferent arteriole descends into the medulla to become the vasa recta, which supply loops of Henle. Nephrons are so closely packed together that these two nephron tubules would actually share peritubular capillaries and vasa recta.

**RECAP**

A nephron is the functional unit of a kidney. A nephron tubule consists of a glomerular capsule, where fluid is filtered, and four regions in which the filtrate is modified before it becomes urine: proximal tubule, loop of Henle, distal tubule, and collecting duct. Blood flows to the glomerulus via the renal artery and afferent arterioles. Peritubular capillaries carry the blood to the proximal and distal tubules, and vasa recta supply the loops of Henle and collecting ducts. ■

## 15.4 Formation of urine: Filtration, reabsorption, and secretion

As we have noted, the urinary system regulates the excretion of water and ions to achieve homeostasis of fluid volume and composition. It excretes certain wastes while retaining precious nutrients. How do the kidneys select what to retain and what (and how much) to excrete in urine?

The formation of urine involves three processes:

1. *Glomerular filtration.* The movement of a protein-free solution of fluid and solutes from the glomerulus into the space within the glomerular capsule.
2. *Tubular reabsorption.* The return of most of the fluid and solutes back into the peritubular capillaries or vasa recta.
3. *Tubular secretion.* The addition of certain solutes from the peritubular capillaries or vasa recta into the tubule.

The fluid and solutes that remain in the tubule constitute the urine, which is eventually excreted. Figure 15.6 summarizes the relationship between these three processes. As the figure indicates, the amount of any substance excreted in urine is equal to the amount filtered, minus the amount reabsorbed back into the blood, plus the amount secreted into the tubule.

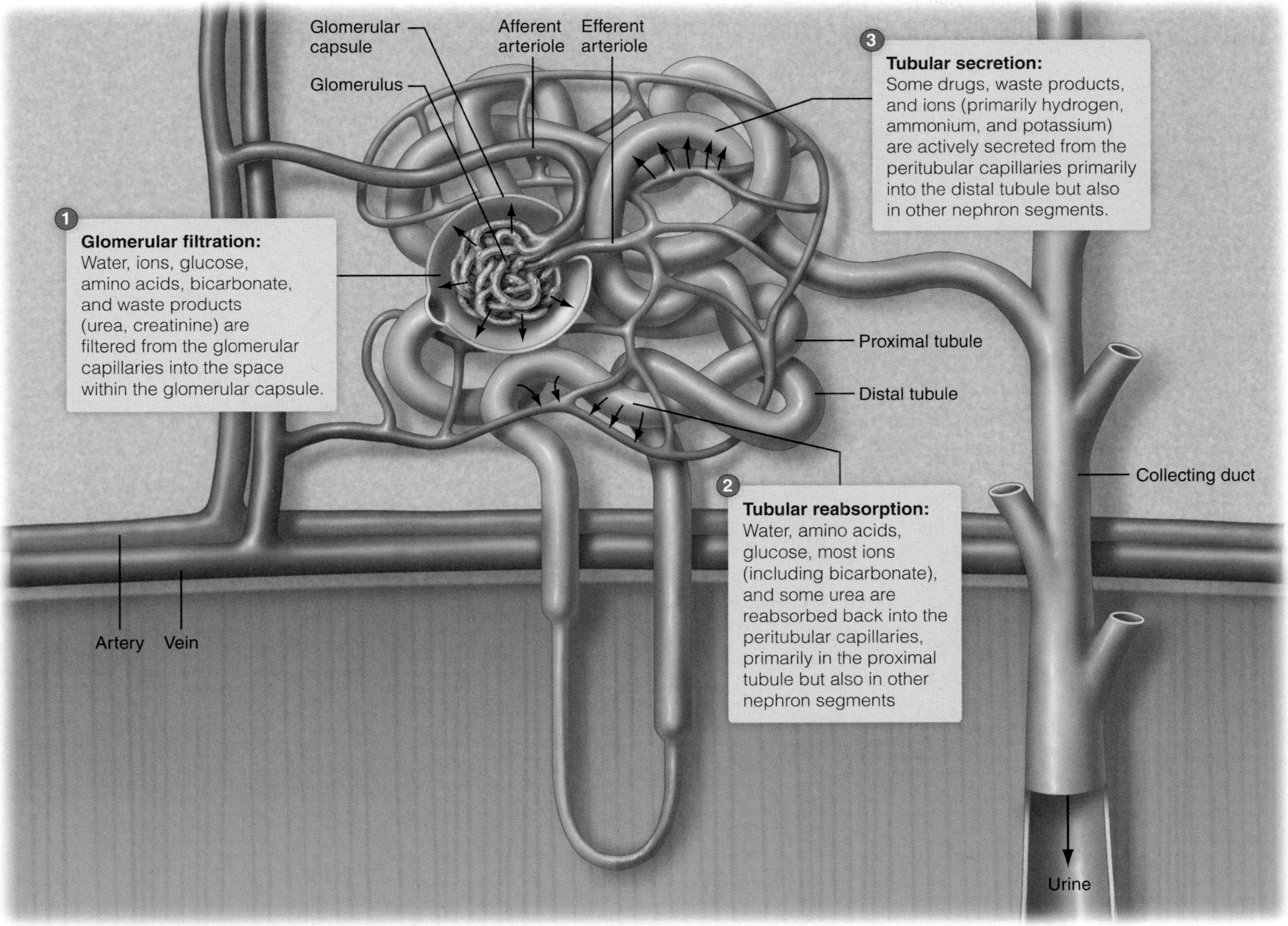


**Figure 15.6 The three processes that contribute to the formation of urine.**

## Glomerular filtration filters fluid from capillaries

Urine formation starts with **glomerular filtration,** the process of filtering a large quantity of protein-free plasma fluid from the glomerular capillaries into the glomerular space. The filtration barrier consists of two cell types: modified epithelial cells called **podocytes** that cover and surround the outside surface of the capillaries, and the capillary cells themselves. Fluid first passes through pores in the capillary cells (Figure 15.7b), and then through tiny slits between cytoplasmic extensions of the podocytes in order to enter the glomerular space.

The podocytes and the glomerular capillary cells are highly specialized for filtration of a large volume of fluid. Together, they are nearly 100 times more permeable to water and small solutes than the capillaries in most other vascular beds. However, they are also highly selective; they are *less* permeable than other capillaries to large proteins and whole cells. As a result, the filtered fluid, called the glomerular filtrate, contains water and all of the small solutes in the same concentrations found in blood plasma, but it contains no large proteins or blood cells.

Together, the two kidneys produce about half a cup of glomerular filtrate per minute, a whopping 180 liters per day. Contrast that amount with the daily urine excretion of about 1.5 liters, and you can see how efficient the kidneys are at reabsorbing substances that are filtered.

Glomerular filtration is driven by high blood pressure in the glomerular capillaries. As described in Chapter 8, the filtration of fluid out of capillaries is driven by the capillary blood pressure. Usually the inward and outward movements of fluid are nearly equal because the blood pressure is opposed by similar osmotic pressure generated by the proteins in blood. The difference is that the blood pressure in the glomerular capillaries is about twice that in any other capillary. This high pressure forces large amounts of glomerular filtrate into the glomerular space. The kidneys themselves do not have to expend energy to produce the filtrate.

The rate of filtration is regulated in two ways:

- Under resting conditions, pressure-sensitive cells in the arterioles and flow-sensitive cells in the tubule walls can release chemicals to adjust the diameter of the afferent arterioles. These feedback mechanisms maintain a relatively constant rate of glomerular filtration, allowing the kidneys to carry out their regulatory functions.

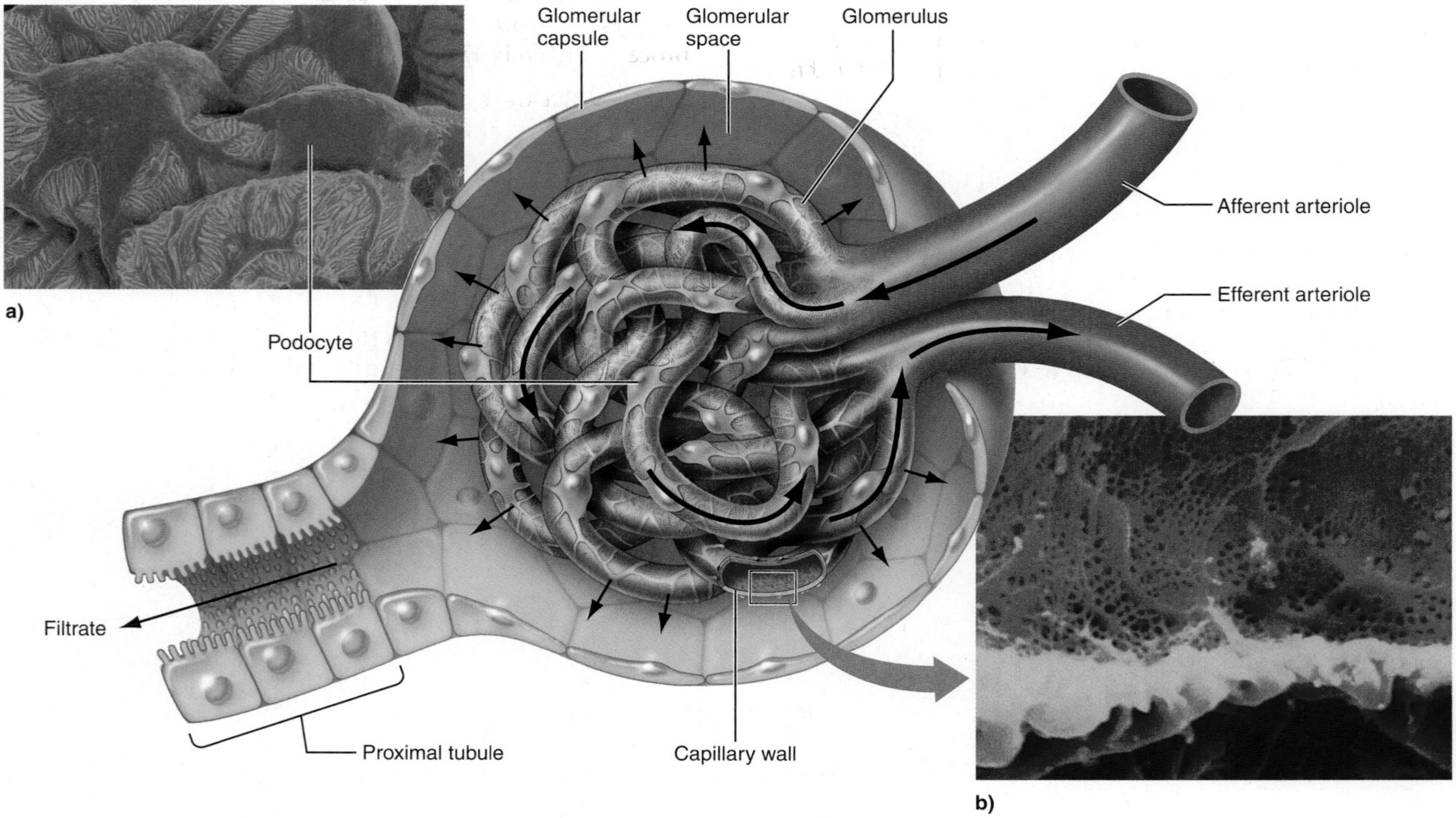


**Figure 15.7 Glomerular filtration. (a)** A view of the outer surface of several glomerular capillaries as seen from within the glomerular space. Glomerular capillaries are covered with modified tubular cells called podocytes that contribute to the filtration barrier. **(b)** A highly magnified view of the inner surface (blood side) of a single glomerular capillary, revealing its porous sieve-like structure.

- During times of stress (such as after an injury or while running a marathon), blood flow to the kidneys falls substantially as blood is redistributed to more critical organs. The sympathetic division of the autonomic nervous system constricts afferent and efferent arterioles, reducing blood flow and the rates of glomerular filtration and urine formation. The kidneys are unharmed because they do not need a high blood flow to survive, and the body can cut back on urine production temporarily without ill effects.

If the delicate sievelike structure of the glomerular capillaries is disrupted, proteins may cross the filtration barrier into the tubule fluid. This is *proteinuria,* the appearance of protein in urine. Persistent proteinuria is a sign of glomerular damage, perhaps by toxins or sustained high blood pressure. However, temporary proteinuria can occur after strenuous exercise, even in healthy people. The reason for this is unknown, but it may be that reduced renal blood flow during exercise allows blood to remain in contact with the glomerular barrier longer, letting more plasma proteins leak through. Exercise-induced proteinuria is not dangerous and goes away within a day or so.

**RECAP**

Glomerular filtration separates plasma fluid and small solutes from larger proteins and blood cells. High blood pressure in the glomerular capillaries drives this process. ■

## Tubular reabsorption returns filtered water and solutes to blood

**Tubular reabsorption,** the second step in urine formation, returns filtered water and solutes from the tubule into the blood of the peritubular capillaries or vasa recta. As filtrate flows through the tubule, major nutrients are almost completely reabsorbed—all of the filtered glucose, amino acids, and bicarbonate, and more than 99% of the water and sodium. About 50% of the urea is also reabsorbed. The final product—urine—contains just enough water and sodium to balance the daily net gain from all other sources, the equivalent of all the urea produced in one day's metabolism, and trace amounts of other ions and wastes. Some waste products, such as creatinine, are not reabsorbed at all once they are filtered (Table 15.3).

Most tubular reabsorption occurs in the proximal tubule, leaving the fine-tuning and regulation of reabsorption to the more distal regions. A good example is water. The proximal tubule always reabsorbs about 65–70% of the water, and the loop of Henle reabsorbs another 25%, both completely unregulated. The distal tubule and collecting duct together reabsorb less than 10%, yet it is here that water excretion is effectively regulated.

To be reabsorbed, substances must cross the layer of epithelial cells of the tubules to reach blood capillaries. Like the epithelial cells of the digestive tract, the cell membrane on the lumen side of proximal tubular cells has a "brush border" of microvilli to increase the surface area for reabsorption (Figure 15.8). The process of reabsorption begins in the proximal tubule with the active transport of sodium from inside the cell toward the peritubular capillaries that surround the tubule. This is an active process that requires energy in the form of ATP. Other steps in the reabsorptive process, shown in Figure 15.9, follow from this one event:

1. The active transport of sodium out of the tubular cell decreases the intracellular concentration of sodium, setting up a driving force for sodium to diffuse into the cell by facilitated transport.
2. Because sodium is a positively charged ion, its movement drives the diffusion of chloride across the tubular cell (negative charges must follow positive ones to maintain electrical neutrality).
3. The transport of solutes ($Na^+$ and $Cl^-$) across the tubular cell creates a concentration gradient for the diffusion of

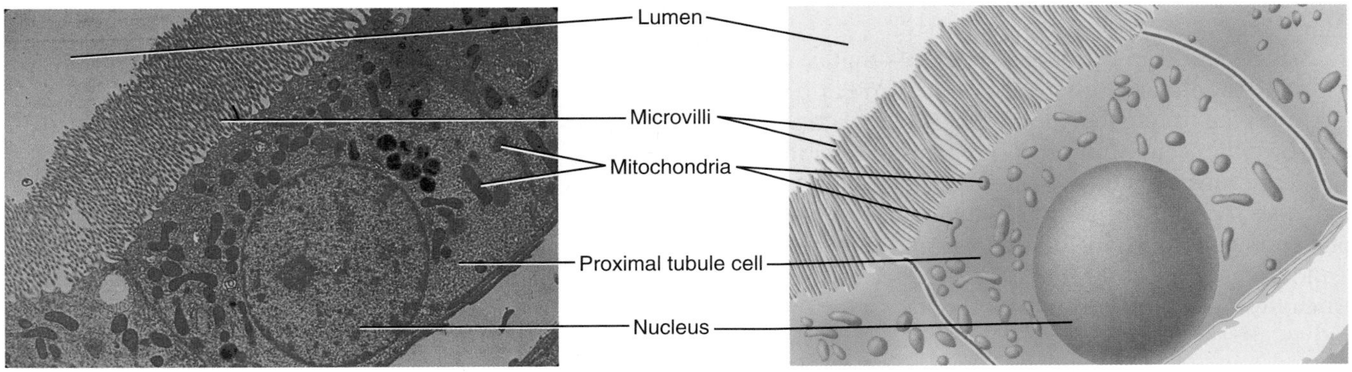


**a) TEM (×19,000) of a section of a proximal tubule, showing the microvilli that form the brush border of the inner (luminal) surface.**

**b) A diagram showing the major features of the photograph.**

**Figure 15.8 The proximal tubule.**

**Table 15.3 Amounts of various substances filtered and excreted or reabsorbed**

| Substance | Amount filtered per day | Amount excreted in urine per day | Proportion reabsorbed |
|---|---|---|---|
| Water | 180 L | 1–2 L | 99% |
| Sodium ($Na^+$) | 620 g | 4 g | 99% |
| Chloride ($Cl^-$) | 720 g | 6 g | 99% |
| Potassium ($K^+$) | 30 g | 2 g | 93% |
| Bicarbonate ($HCO_3^-$) | 275 g | 0 | 100% |
| Glucose | 180 g | 0 | 100% |
| Urea* | 52 g* | 26 g | 50% |
| Creatinine* | 1.6 g* | 1.6 g | 0 |

*The plasma concentrations of these substances and the amounts filtered per day vary with diet, age, and level of physical activity.

water, so water is also reabsorbed. Water reabsorption occurs through special water channels in membrane proteins called **aquaporins.**

4. The facilitated transport of sodium inward across the luminal cell membrane provides the energy for the secondary active transport of glucose and amino acids into the cell. Once inside the cell, the glucose and amino acids diffuse into the interstitial fluid and eventually into the peritubular capillaries.

Note that the reabsorption of water, salt, glucose, and amino acids in the proximal tubule all depend on just one metabolic energy-using process: the primary active transport of sodium out of the tubular epithelial cell. Reabsorption in the more distal regions of the tubule, although less in amount, also relies on the active transport of sodium as the energy-utilizing step.

## Tubular secretion removes other substances from blood

A few substances undergo **tubular secretion**—that is, they move from the capillaries (either peritubular capillaries or vasa recta) into the tubule to be excreted. Tubular secretion may occur by either active transport or passive diffusion, depending on the substance being secreted.

Tubular secretion is critical for removing or regulating levels of certain chemicals, including toxic and foreign substances and drugs. The list of substances secreted into the tubule includes penicillin, cocaine, marijuana, many food preservatives, and some pesticides.

Some substances that occur naturally in the body are secreted just to maintain normal homeostatic levels. The proximal tubule secretes hydrogen ($H^+$) and ammonium ($NH_4^-$) to regulate the body's acid-base balance, and the distal tubule secretes potassium ($K^+$) to maintain healthy levels of that mineral.

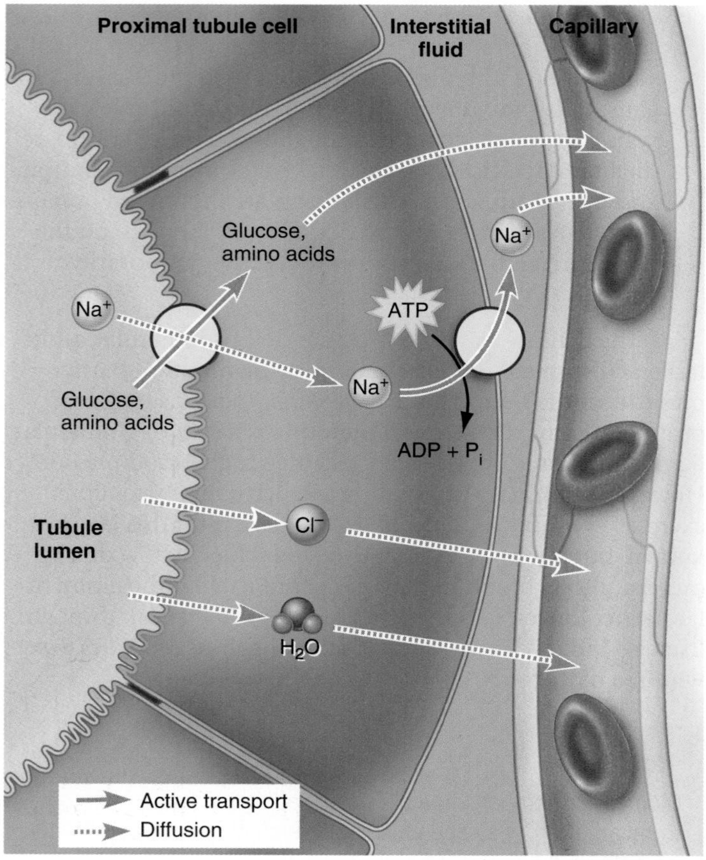


**Figure 15.9 Basic mechanisms of reabsorption in the proximal tubule.** The key to the entire process is the active transport of sodium ($Na^+$) across the tubular cell membrane on the capillary side of the cell. This step requires energy in the form of ATP. The active transport of sodium keeps the intracellular sodium concentration low, which permits sodium to diffuse into the cell from the luminal side. Negatively charged chloride ions follow in order to maintain electrical neutrality, and water follows because the reabsorption of sodium and chloride produces an osmotic driving force for the diffusion of water. Finally, the facilitated diffusion of sodium across the luminal membrane is used as an energy source for the reabsorption of glucose and amino acids.

**RECAP**

During tubular reabsorption, nearly all the filtered water and sodium and all the major nutrients are reabsorbed from the nephron tubule. The process begins with the active transport of sodium across the cell membrane located on the capillary side of the tubular cell. Tubular secretion removes toxic, foreign, and excess substances from the capillaries. It is essential to the regulation of acid-base balance, potassium balance, and the excretion of certain wastes. ■

# 15.5 The kidneys can produce dilute or concentrated urine

Your kidneys are capable of producing urine that is either more dilute or more concentrated than plasma. In other words, the kidneys can conserve water when it is in short supply and get rid of it when there is too much. The ability to do this depends on a high concentration of solutes in the renal medulla, coupled with the ability to alter the collecting ducts' permeability to water.

## Producing dilute urine: Excreting excess water

If you drink a large glass of water quickly, the water is absorbed by your digestive system and enters your blood, increasing your blood volume and decreasing the concentration of ions in blood and body fluids. Most of the water enters your cells. To prevent osmotic swelling and damage to cells, the kidneys adjust the process of urine formation so that you reabsorb less water and produce dilute urine. Figure 15.10 illustrates this process.

The process of forming dilute urine begins at the descending limb of the loop of Henle. The descending limb is highly permeable to water. Because the solute concentration is higher in the interstitial fluid than in the lumen, water diffuses out of the loop, into the interstitial fluid, and eventually into the blood. As a result, the remaining fluid becomes more concentrated.

When fluid turns the hairpin corner of the loop, however, the permeability characteristics of the tubule change. The first part of the ascending limb is permeable to NaCl and urea but not to water. Because so much water was removed in the descending limb, sodium concentration in the ascending limb is now higher than in the interstitial fluid of the medulla. With the change in permeability, NaCl can now diffuse out of the ascending limb and into the interstitial fluid of the medulla.

Meanwhile, urea diffuses into the ascending limb of the loop from the interstitial fluid. The concentration of urea in the deepest (innermost) portion of the medulla is actually quite high because urea is being reabsorbed from the collecting duct. In other words, urea recycles—from collecting duct, to ascending limb of the loop of Henle, and back to the collecting duct again. Because of this recycling pattern, urea concentrations can become much higher in medullary interstitial fluid than in blood plasma.

The final portion of the ascending limb of the loop of Henle becomes impermeable to salt and urea as well as water, so no passive diffusion occurs. However, this region of the ascending limb actively transports sodium and chloride into interstitial fluid by a process that requires energy in the form of ATP. Consequently the interstitial fluid gains solutes while the fluid remaining in the tubule becomes more dilute.

The process of active salt reabsorption without the reabsorption of water continues in the distal tubule and collecting duct. By the time the urine reaches the end of the collecting duct it is a very dilute solution of a lot of water, a little urea, and very little salt. You may need to urinate frequently when you are forming a very dilute urine because your kidneys are producing over a liter of urine per hour.

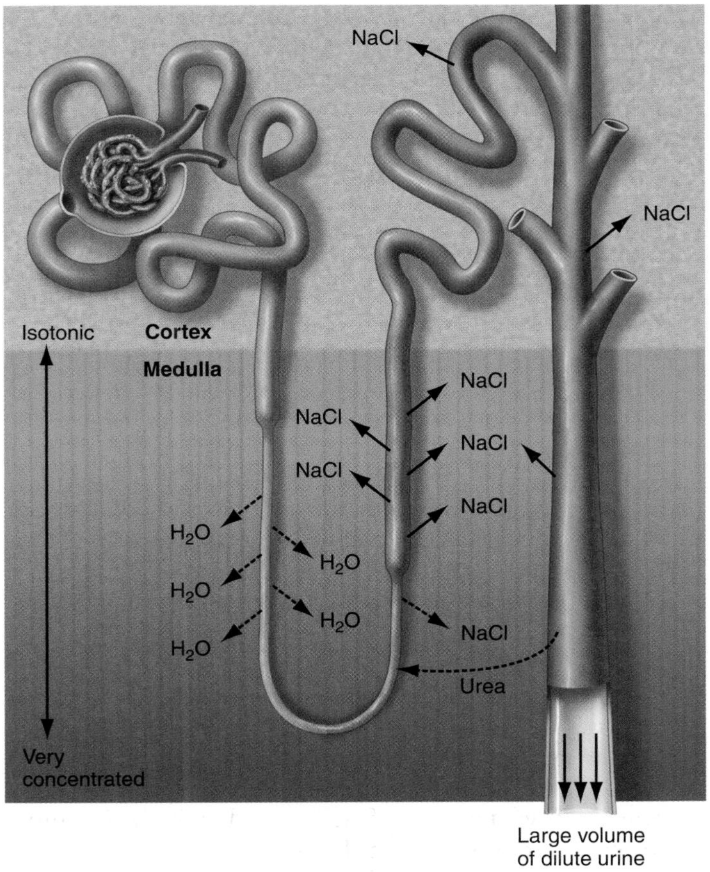


**Figure 15.10 The formation of a high volume of dilute urine.** Urine volume is regulated by controlling the water permeability of the collecting duct. In the absence of antidiuretic hormone (ADH) the distal tubule is impermeable to water. The tubular fluid has been diluted by the active reabsorption of salt, and this fluid passes through the medulla in the collecting duct without being reabsorbed. The result is a high urine flow rate and a very dilute urine.

**RECAP**

Production of dilute urine requires the reabsorption of salt without the concurrent reabsorption of water in the ascending limb of the loop of Henle, the distal tubule, and the collecting duct. ■

## Producing concentrated urine: Conserving water

Sometimes our problem is too little water, perhaps due to perspiration or living in an arid climate. Less water in the blood means lower blood volume, declining blood pressure, and a risk of dehydration for body cells. Again your kidneys compensate, this time by reabsorbing more water. The result is a more concentrated urine.

We urinate less when we are dehydrated because the kidneys are reabsorbing more of the glomerular filtrate water than usual. The process of reabsorbing water is regulated by **antidiuretic hormone (ADH)** from the posterior pituitary gland (see Chapter 13). ADH increases the permeability of the collecting duct to water. The formation of concentrated urine follows a process similar to that just described for the formation of dilute urine until the urine reaches the collecting duct. In the presence of ADH, more water is reabsorbed because it diffuses out of the collecting duct toward the higher solute concentration in the medulla. Consequently only a small volume of highly concentrated urine is excreted (Figure 15.11).

The production of concentrated urine depends on a **countercurrent exchange mechanism.** Because of the hairpin arrangement of the loops of Henle, fluid flows in opposite directions in the two sides of the loop (*countercurrent* flow). The countercurrent direction of flow and the close anatomical association between the two sides of the loop allow events happening on one side of the loop to influence conditions on the other, and even for water and solutes to be *exchanged* between the two sides if permitted by permeability characteristics of the tubule. Countercurrent exchange is critical to the development of the high concentration gradient of the inner medulla because it permits a small difference in composition between the tubular fluid and the medullary interstitial fluid to be multiplied severalfold along the length of the loop (from the top of the medulla to the bottom). Countercurrent flow and exchange in the vasa recta is also important, because it removes solutes and water from the medulla without dissipating the medullary solute concentration from top to bottom (Figure 15.12).

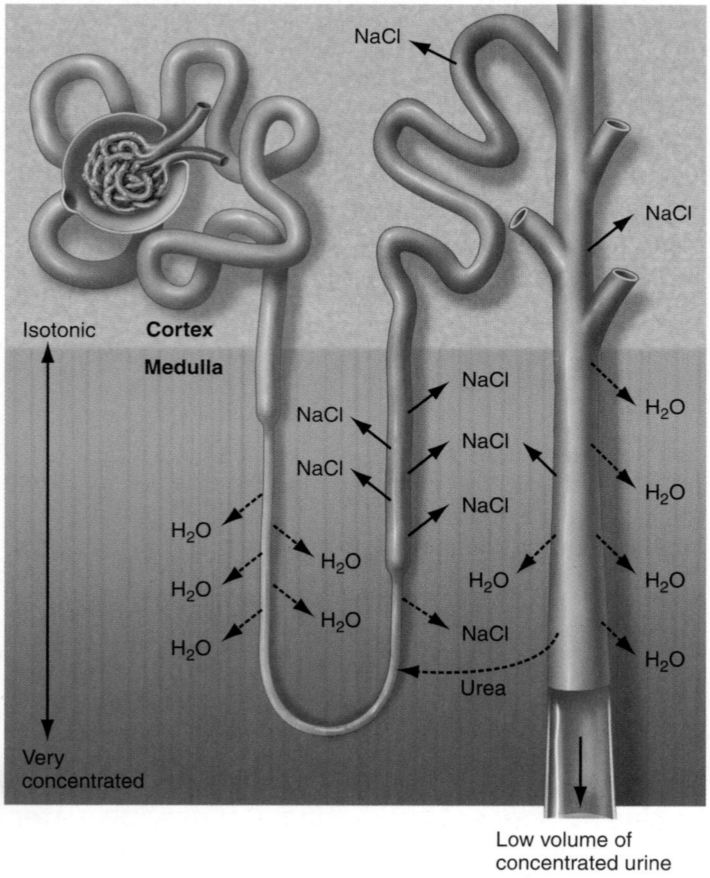


**Figure 15.11 The formation of a low volume of concentrated urine.** In the presence of the hormone ADH the collecting duct becomes permeable to water. Consequently most of the water in the collecting duct is reabsorbed by passive diffusion as the fluid passes through the medulla with its high solute concentration.

**RECAP**

The formation of concentrated urine requires antidiuretic hormone (ADH). In the presence of ADH, most of the water is reabsorbed from the collecting duct, leaving a small volume of concentrated urine to be excreted. ■

## 15.6 Urination depends on a reflex

Urination depends on a neural reflex called the *micturition reflex*. This involves the two urethral sphincters and the bladder. The internal urethral sphincter, which consists of smooth muscle, is an extension of the smooth muscle of the bladder. It remains contracted unless the bladder is emptying. The external urethral sphincter is skeletal muscle and therefore under voluntary control.

Normally the external urethral sphincter is kept closed by tonic activity of somatic motor neurons controlled by the brain. As the bladder fills with a cup (roughly 250 ml) or more of urine, it starts to stretch. Stretching stimulates sensory nerves that send signals to the spinal cord. Nerves in the spinal cord initiate an involuntary (parasympathetic autonomic) reflex that contracts the smooth muscle of the bladder and relaxes the internal urethral sphincter. Stretch receptor input also goes to the brain, which decreases the activity of somatic motor neurons to the external urethral sphincter, allowing it to relax so that urine can flow through.

Humans don't usually have the opportunity to urinate whenever the urge strikes. Fortunately the brain can voluntarily override the micturition reflex by increasing the activity of the somatic nerves that control the external urethral sphincter. This delays urination, for extended periods if necessary. When we finally decide to urinate, the somatic nerve activity is shut off, the external urethral sphincter relaxes, and urination occurs. Voluntary prevention of urination becomes increasingly difficult as the bladder approaches maximum capacity.

**RECAP**

Urination depends on the neural micturition reflex; bladder stretching initiates involuntary relaxation of the internal urethral sphincter. The brain can override the reflex by voluntary contraction of the external urethral sphincter. ■

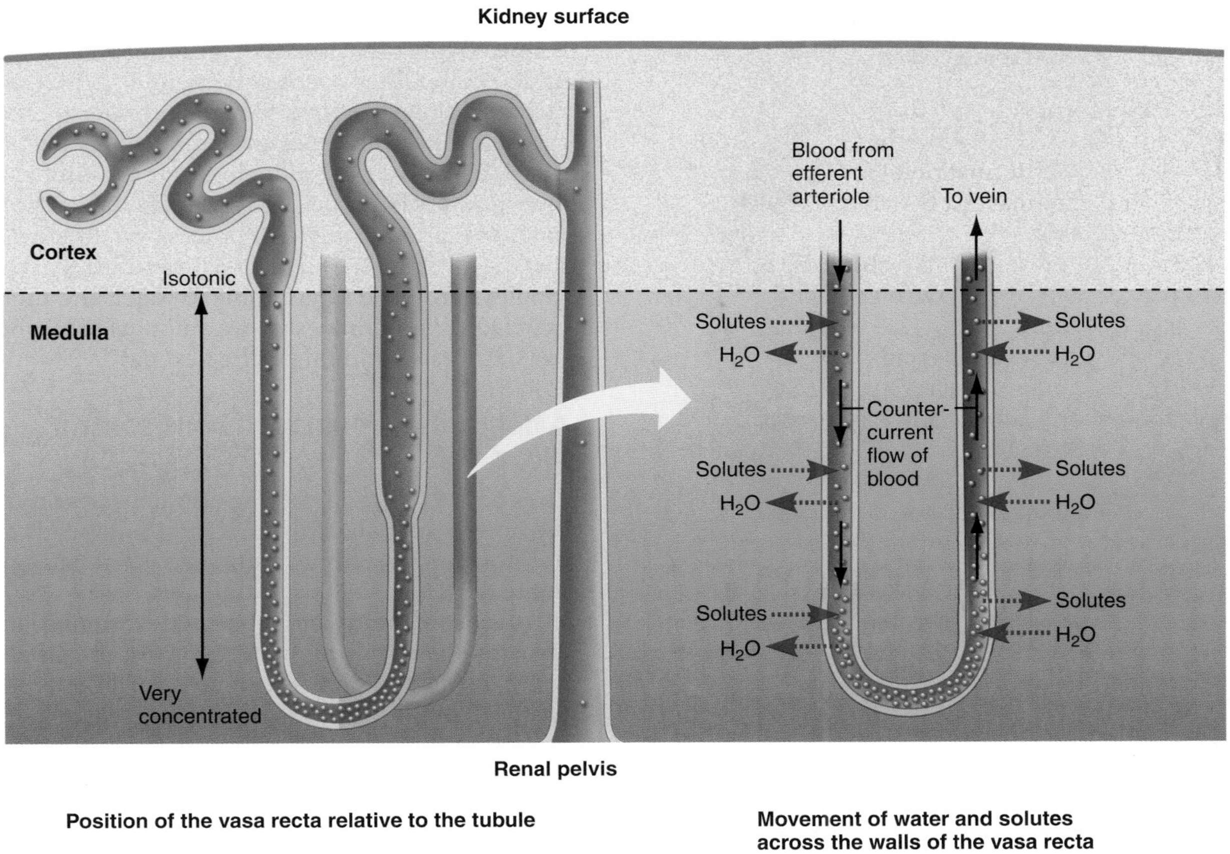


**Figure 15.12 Countercurrent exchange in the vasa recta.** The vasa recta are closely associated with the tubular segments in the medulla. The vasa recta remove the water and solutes that accumulate in the medulla as a result of reabsorption from the loop of Henle and the collecting duct. Like most capillaries, the vasa recta are highly permeable to water and solutes and rapidly equilibrate with their surrounding fluid. The countercurrent flow of blood in the two parallel vessels of the vasa recta permits the rapid exchange of water and solutes by diffusion, at the same time preserving the medullary concentration gradient from top to bottom.

## 15.7 The kidneys maintain homeostasis in many ways

The kidneys are much more than simply the organs that make urine. As mentioned earlier, they play other important roles in the body as well. The kidneys help to:

- Maintain water balance, which adjusts blood volume and blood pressure
- Regulate salt balance, which also controls blood volume
- Maintain acid-base balance and blood pH
- Control production of red blood cells
- Activate an inactive form of vitamin D

The kidneys are responsible for maintaining homeostasis (by excretion) of virtually every type of ion in the body, considering that ions cannot be created or destroyed by metabolic processes. Because the kidneys secrete hormones, they are also endocrine organs. And by chemically altering the vitamin D molecule so that it can function as a vitamin, they play a role in metabolism as well. The common theme in these activities is the maintenance of homeostasis.

### Water balance determines blood volume and blood pressure

As mentioned earlier, blood volume is determined in part by how we retain or excrete water. Increases in blood volume raise blood pressure, and decreases in blood volume lower it, so it is critical to maintain blood volume (and water volume).

The kidneys, the hypothalamus of the brain, and the posterior pituitary gland of the endocrine system share the function of maintaining water balance. This balance is achieved by a negative feedback loop that regulates the solute concentration of the blood (Figure 15.13).

When the concentration of blood solutes rises (too little water compared to the amount of solutes in the blood), the ADH-producing neurons in the hypothalamus cause ADH

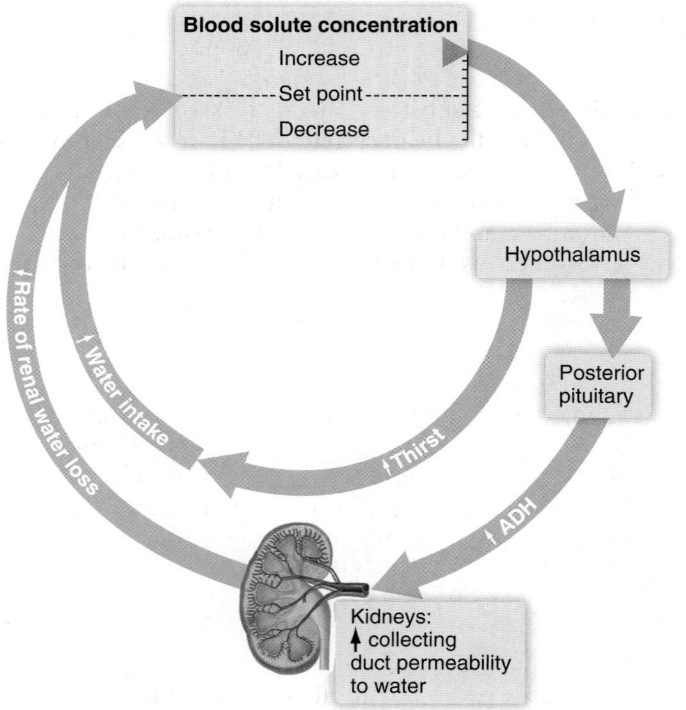


**Figure 15.13 Negative feedback loop for the control of blood solute concentration.** A rise in blood solute concentration triggers thirst and increases ADH secretion. ADH causes the kidneys to form a more concentrated urine and decrease their excretion of water. An increase in water intake coupled with a reduction in water loss from the kidneys dilutes the blood and returns blood solute concentration toward normal. Although only the responses to an increased solute concentration are shown here, the control loop responds equally well (with opposite responses) to a fall in blood solute concentration.

to be secreted from the posterior pituitary into the blood. ADH circulates to the kidney, where it increases the permeability of the collecting duct to water. This allows more water to be reabsorbed, reducing the amount of water excreted in the urine.

In addition to its effect on ADH, a rise in the blood solute concentration triggers a sensation of thirst, encouraging us to drink more water. The increased water intake combined with the reduced loss of water in the urine lowers the blood solute concentration toward normal again.

Normally some ADH is present in the blood. This allows the control mechanism to respond to excess water, too. When there is too much water and blood solute levels fall, the hypothalamus signals the posterior pituitary to reduce its secretion of ADH. The fall in ADH concentration makes the renal collecting duct less permeable to water, and so the excess water is excreted. We also feel less thirsty when we already have more than enough water.

The term *diuresis* refers to a high urine flow rate. A *diuretic* is any substance that increases the formation and excretion of urine. Diuretic drugs, such as furosemide (Lasix), are prescribed to reduce blood volume and blood pressure in certain patients, such as people with congestive heart failure or hypertension.

Caffeine is a mild diuretic because it inhibits sodium reabsorption, and as sodium is excreted it takes water with it. Alcohol is also a diuretic, although by a different mechanism: it inhibits ADH release. The result is that the renal tubules become less permeable to water, and more water is excreted. If you drink excessive amounts of alcohol you may feel dehydrated and thirsty the next day.

## Aldosterone, renin, and ANH control blood volume

The control of blood volume also depends on maintaining the body's salt balance, which in turn depends on three hormones: aldosterone, renin, and atrial natriuretic hormone (ANH).

**Aldosterone,** a steroid hormone from the adrenal gland, increases the reabsorption of $Na^+$ across the distal tubule and collecting duct. High concentrations of aldosterone cause nearly all of the filtered sodium to be reabsorbed, so that less than 50 milligrams (0.05 gram) per day appears in the urine. Low levels of the hormone allow as much as 20–25 grams of sodium to be excreted each day. When we consider that the average North American consumes about 10 grams of sodium daily, we see that aldosterone provides more than enough control over sodium excretion.

Given what aldosterone does, we might think its concentration is controlled by blood sodium levels. This is only partly true, for sodium concentration is only a weak stimulus. The strongest stimulus for aldosterone secretion is a decrease in blood volume (or blood pressure), and in particular how a change in blood volume affects another hormone, *renin*.

**Renin** is technically an enzyme that functions like a hormone. It is secreted by a group of afferent arteriole cells that are part of a structure located very near the glomerulus called the **juxtaglomerular apparatus** (Figure 15.14), the region where the afferent and efferent arterioles are in close contact with the distal tubule.

Figure 15.15 on page 366 illustrates the negative feedback mechanism for the control of blood volume. The steps in this mechanism are as follows:

1. Decreases in blood volume or pressure stimulate the juxtaglomerular apparatus within the kidneys to secrete renin.
2. In the blood, renin cleaves a small peptide of 10 amino acids called *angiotensin I* from a large inactive protein molecule, *angiotensinogen,* produced by the liver. Angiotensin I loses two more amino acids to become *angiotensin II* a highly active and important regulatory hormone.
3. Angiotensin II stimulates the adrenal cortex to secrete aldosterone.

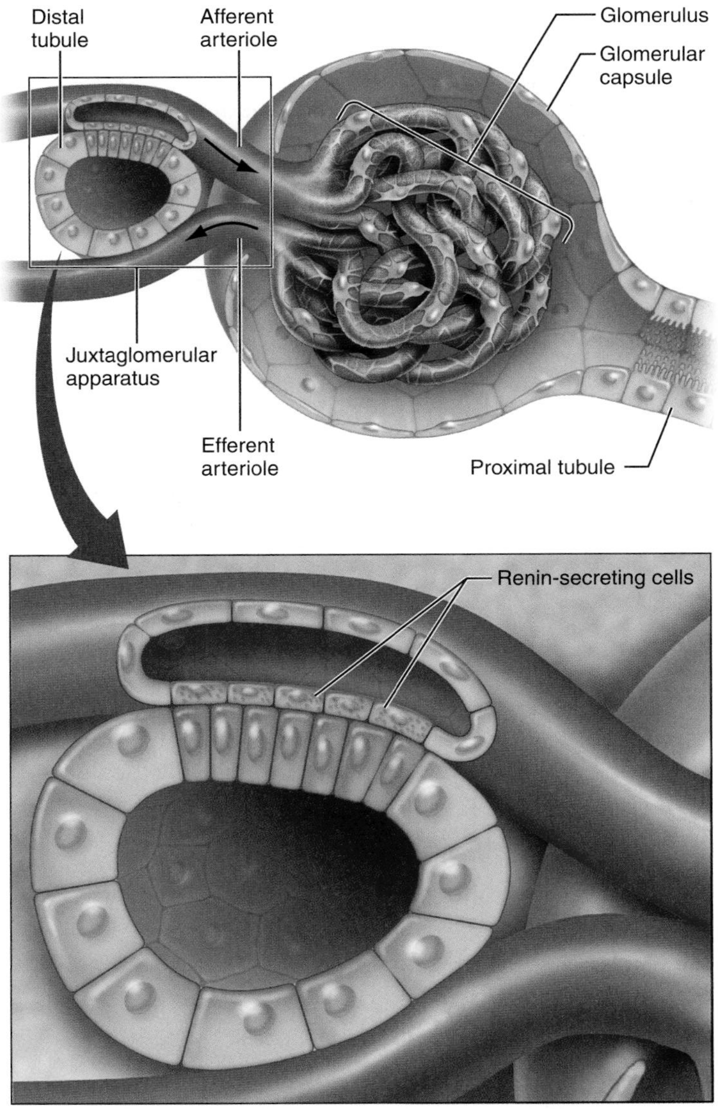


**Figure 15.14 The juxtaglomerular apparatus.** The juxtaglomerular apparatus is a region of contact between the afferent arteriole, the efferent arteriole, and the distal tubule. The afferent arteriolar cells of the juxtaglomerular apparatus synthesize and secrete renin.

4. Aldosterone increases the rate of sodium reabsorption by the distal tubules and collecting ducts.
5. As blood sodium levels rise, water is retained and blood volume rises. Water is retained along with sodium because of ADH and its control over solute concentrations, as discussed previously. Thus renin and aldosterone (and ADH) all interact to control blood volume and blood pressure.

Renin regulates blood pressure in another way as well: angiotensin II is a potent vasoconstrictor that narrows the diameter of blood vessels. An increase in renin secretion can raise arterial blood pressure within minutes, long before it has influenced aldosterone secretion and blood volume.

There is yet another controller of sodium excretion, a peptide hormone called *atrial natriuretic hormone (ANH)*. (A "natriuretic" is a substance that increases the excretion of $Na^+$.) The atria of the heart secrete ANH in response to being stretched (which indicates increased blood volume). After circulating to the kidneys, ANH inhibits $Na^+$ reabsorption in the distal tubule and collecting duct, increasing $Na^+$ excretion. Essentially, ANH has an effect opposite to that of renin and aldosterone.

**RECAP**

The solute concentration of blood is maintained by a feedback loop involving ADH. Renal excretion of sodium is regulated largely by aldosterone, which in turn is controlled by the secretion of renin in response to changes in blood volume or blood pressure. The hormone ANH stimulates sodium excretion. ■

## Kidneys help maintain acid-base balance and blood pH

Recall that *acids* are molecules that can donate hydrogen ions ($H^+$) and *bases* are molecules that can accept a hydrogen ion. Many of the body's metabolic reactions generate $H^+$. If not eliminated, these acids would accumulate—a dangerous situation, because blood pH must remain in a relatively narrow range of 7.35 to 7.45. Any change in blood pH by more than a few tenths of a unit beyond this range could be fatal.

The kidneys participate in the maintenance of acid-base balance, a role they share with various buffers in the body and with the lungs. The kidneys do this in two ways (Figure 15.16):

- *Reabsorption of filtered bicarbonate.* Kidney tubular cells secrete $H^+$ into the tubular lumen. Most of the secreted $H^+$ combines with bicarbonate ($HCO_3^-$) filtered by the glomerulus, creating carbon dioxide ($CO_2$) and water. The $CO_2$ and water are then reabsorbed back into the cell, where they dissociate into $H^+$ and $HCO_3^-$ again. The $H^+$ is secreted once again, but the $HCO_3^-$ diffuses into the blood capillary. In effect, the secretion of $H^+$ is a mechanism for reabsorbing, or recovering, nearly all of the $HCO_3^-$ that is filtered. When nearly all of the filtered $HCO_3^-$ is recovered as $CO_2$, any additional $H^+$ that is secreted is buffered by negatively charged ions in the urine (phosphate and sulfate) and eventually excreted in the urine.
- *Renal excretion of acid as ammonium.* Kidney tubule cells produce ammonium ($NH_4^+$) and $HCO_3^-$ as part of their normal metabolism of the amino acid glutamine within the cell. The $NH_4^+$ is transported into the tubule lumen and then excreted in the urine. The new $HCO_3^-$ diffuses

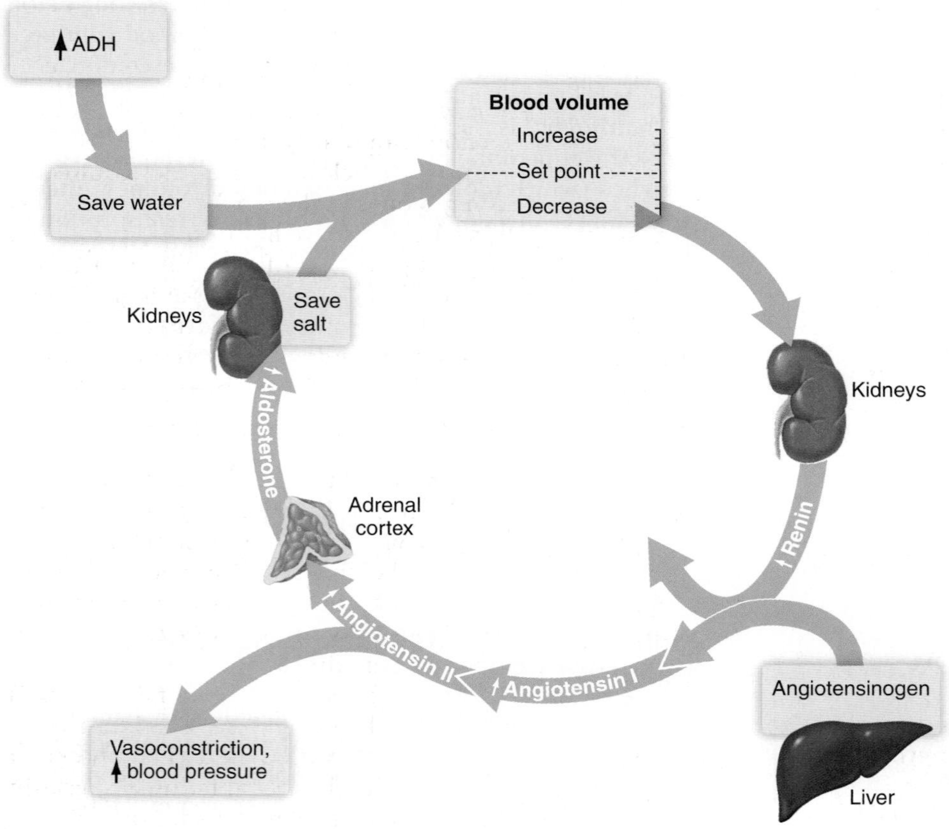


**Figure 15.15 Regulation of blood volume by renin, aldosterone, and ADH.** A decline in blood volume causes the kidneys to secrete renin. Renin activates a cascade of events that ultimately causes the kidneys to save salt and water, returning blood volume to normal.

When certain cells scattered throughout the kidneys sense a fall in the amount of oxygen available to them, they release erythropoietin, which then stimulates the bone marrow to produce more red blood cells. The presence of more red blood cells increases the oxygen-carrying capacity of the blood. Once oxygen is again being delivered normally, the cells stop activating erythropoietin, and RBC production slows. The activation of erythropoietin by certain kidney cells constitutes a negative feedback loop for controlling oxygen availability to all cells, because it keeps the oxygen-carrying capacity of the blood within normal limits.

## Kidneys activate vitamin D

Vitamin D is important for absorbing calcium and phosphate from the digestive tract and developing healthy bones and teeth. We absorb some vitamin D from food, but the body also manufactures it in a three-step process involving the skin, liver, and kidneys.

Vitamin D synthesis begins when ultraviolet rays in sunlight strike a steroid molecule in skin that is similar to cholesterol, producing an inactive form of

into the blood to replace a $HCO_3^-$ lost from the lung during respiratory control of $CO_2$ concentration.

Ordinarily our diets provide us with a small amount of excess $H^+$ that must be excreted if we are to stay in balance. Most of our daily production of $H^+$ results from the creation of $CO_2$ during metabolism, which is handled by the lungs. The renal excretion of $H^+$ with sulfate, phosphate, and ammonia exactly offsets the excess acid intake per day.

## Erythropoietin stimulates production of red blood cells

As mentioned in Chapter 7, the kidneys regulate the production of red blood cells in the bone marrow. They do this by secreting a hormone, **erythropoietin.**

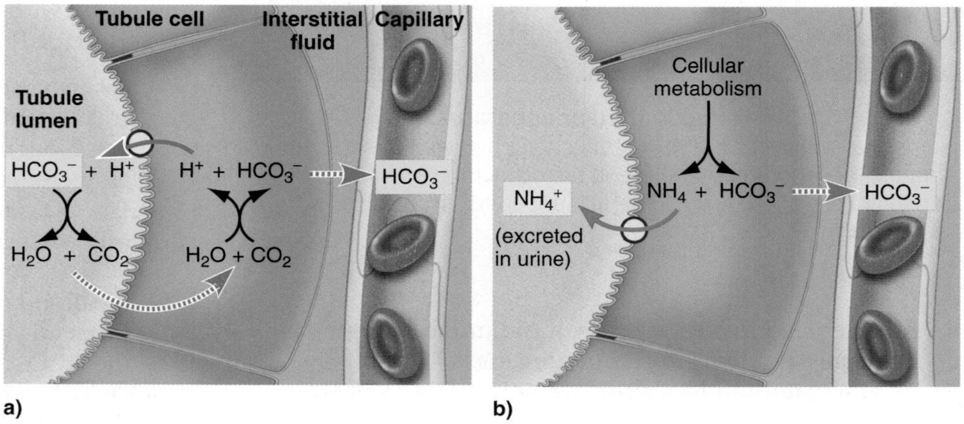


**Figure 15.16 Renal maintenance of acid-base balance. (a)** Reabsorption of filtered bicarbonate. Hydrogen ions within the cell are secreted into the lumen, where they combine with filtered bicarbonate to form $CO_2$ and water. The $CO_2$ and water diffuse into the cell and dissociate back into hydrogen ion and bicarbonate. The hydrogen ion is secreted again, but the bicarbonate diffuses from the cell back into the blood. **(b)** Excretion of ammonium. Kidney cells produce ammonium and bicarbonate during cellular metabolism of glutamine. The ammonium is secreted into the tubule and is excreted in the urine, but the new bicarbonate diffuses into the blood.

vitamin D. The inactive vitamin D is transported to the liver where it is chemically altered, then carried to the kidneys where it is converted to its active form under the influence of parathyroid hormone (PTH) from the parathyroid gland. During kidney failure this final step may not occur. This is why people with long-standing kidney failure often suffer from vitamin D deficiency.

**RECAP**

The kidneys help maintain the body's acid-base balance and blood pH by reabsorbing all filtered bicarbonate and by excreting H+. Decreased oxygen delivery to the kidneys triggers the release of erythropoietin, which stimulates the production of red blood cells by bone marrow. Synthesis of vitamin D involves the skin, liver, and kidneys. ■

## 15.8 Disorders of the urinary system

The good news about urinary system disorders is that the kidneys have an enormous reserve of function. You can survive quite nicely on one kidney, and even on one kidney that is functioning only half as well as it should. Nevertheless, sometimes urinary system problems do occur. They include kidney stones, urinary tract infections, and renal failure.

### Kidney stones can block urine flow

Sometimes minerals in urine crystallize in the renal pelvis and form solid masses called *kidney stones.* Most stones are less than 5 millimeters (1/5 inch) in diameter and are excreted in urine with no trouble. Others may grow larger and obstruct a ureter, blocking urine flow and causing great pain. Kidney stones can be removed surgically or crushed with ultrasonic shock waves, after which the pulverized fragments can be excreted with less pain.

### Urinary tract infections are often caused by bacteria

A *urinary tract infection (UTI)* refers to the presence of microbes in urine or an infection in any part of the urinary system. Symptoms include swelling and redness around the urethral opening, a burning sensation or pain while urinating, difficulty urinating, bed-wetting, low back pain, and sometimes visible blood and pus in urine.

Most UTIs are caused by bacteria that make their way up the urethra from the body surface. Although men can get UTIs, they are more common in women because women's urethras are shorter, allowing organisms to reach the bladder more easily. From the urethra and bladder, microbes can travel up the ureters to the kidneys. This is why it is important to treat all urinary tract infections immediately. Most cases can be cured with antibiotics.

### Acute and chronic renal failure impair kidney function

Kidney impairments that are short term and possibly correctable are called *acute renal failure.* Conditions that might impair kidney function temporarily include sustained decreases in blood pressure to below the pressure required for filtration, large kidney stones in the renal pelvis, infections, transfusion reactions, burns, severe injuries, and toxic drugs or chemicals. A surprising number of common medications are toxic to the kidneys if taken too long or at high doses. The kidneys are particularly vulnerable because of their reabsorptive efficiency, which tends to concentrate harmful substances in the urine. The toxicity problem may be prevented by drinking lots of water and excreting a more dilute urine.

*Chronic renal failure,* also known as "end-stage renal disease" (ESRD), is defined as long-term irreversible damage leading to at least a 60% reduction in functioning nephrons and failure of the kidneys to function properly. People with chronic renal failure may have less than 10% of the normal filtering capacity of the kidneys, and some essentially have no renal function at all.

Any of the factors that cause acute renal failure can, if not corrected, progress to chronic failure. In addition, approximately 40% of people with Type 1 (insulin-dependent) diabetes eventually develop renal failure, especially if the diabetes has not been well controlled. Approximately 13 million Americans have some form of chronic renal failure.

**RECAP**

The kidneys have a huge reserve of function. However, acute or chronic renal failure can result from prolonged changes in blood pressure, disease, large kidney stones, transfusion reactions, burns, injuries, toxic substances, and other conditions such as diabetes. ■

### Dialysis cleanses the blood artificially

The body cannot replace irreparably damaged nephrons. This leaves two options for people with severe renal failure: dialysis or a kidney transplant.

**Dialysis** attempts to duplicate the functions of healthy kidneys. A dialysis technique that can be done at home without a kidney machine is called *continuous ambulatory peritoneal dialysis (CAPD).* In this procedure, dialysis fluid (a fluid similar to extracellular fluid) is placed directly into the peritoneal cavity through an access port permanently implanted in the abdominal wall. The fluid is left in the peritoneal cavity for several hours, during which time it exchanges wastes and ions with the capillaries. Then the fluid is drained and discarded. If done on a regular basis, CAPD can be modestly effective. It is convenient and allows freedom of movement. However, there is a risk of infection

# How Should We Allocate Scarce Organs?

For years now a serious imbalance has been developing between the numbers of organs available for transplant and the number of patients needing them. Where do organs for transplant come from, and who decides who gets an organ when one becomes available?

About 45% of all donated organs come from living donors. A living donor may donate a kidney or part of a lung or liver to a specific patient, but he or she cannot sell it. Patient and donor must have the same blood type and be tested for six key tissue antigens that determine the closeness of the immunological match. Living donors are usually close relatives, but even among close relatives the chances of a perfect match are not all that good. Matches between unrelated donors are rare. *The responsibility for finding a living donor rests with the patient*.

If you cannot find your own living donor or if you need a heart or a pancreas, the only source is from a deceased person (a cadaver). Organs may be harvested from a cadaver only when permission has been granted by the deceased or the deceased's relatives. Persons who wish to donate their organs after death can make their wishes known by signing and carrying a uniform donor card available through most state motor vehicle departments or on the Web (see the Internet References for this chapter). Fewer than a third of all adults have signed an organ donor card.

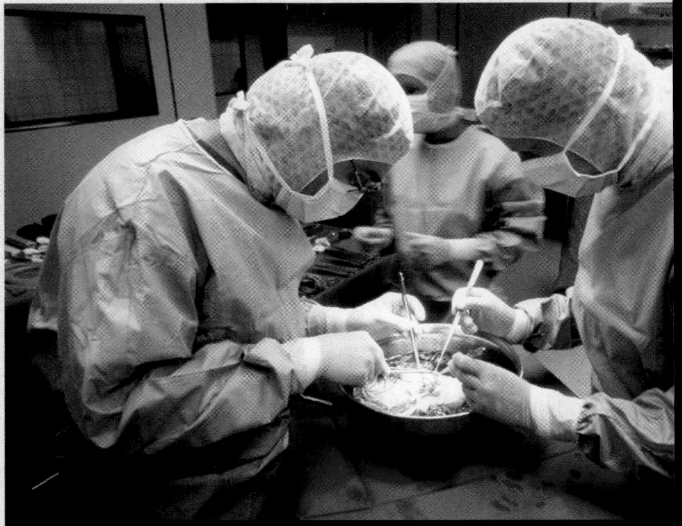

A human kidney being prepared for shipment. Over 98,000 patients waiting for organ transplants each year, and how organs are allocate a matter of life and death.

## How Are Cadaver Organs Currently Allocated?

The United States is divided into 11 geographic regions, each of which has its own Organ Procurement Organization (OPO) that is responsible for obtaining cadaveric organs and coordinating transplant allocations within that area. The United Network for Organ Sharing (UNOS), a private nonprofit corporation, links the regional OPOs together and maintains the national waiting lists of potential transplant recipients. UNOS and the OPOs operate according to federal rules established by the Department of Health and Human Services (DHHS). In essence, the system is operated by the private sector but watched over by the government.

According to current DHHS rules, patients who need a cadaveric organ place themselves on the transplant list of a regional OPO, generally in the region where they live. When a cadaveric organ becomes available in a particular region it is tested for blood type and (for some organs) the six antigens. Perfect matches—the same blood type and the same six antigens—are so rare that a patient anywhere in the country has first priority for a perfectly matched organ.

For all partial matches, the organ is first made available to all patients in the OPO that procured the organ. Only if none of the patients in that region is considered suitable is the organ made available to patients in other OPOs. A patient's income is not supposed to be a consideration, but people who are willing to pay for the transplant themselves can put themselves on the transplant lists of several OPOs simultaneously (insurance generally pays for a transplant only in the patient's primary OPO).

Is the current allocation system fair? Critics point out that the current system results in disparities in waiting times between the various regions. In addition, organs do not always go to the patients who need them the most (the sickest first) because they must be offered first to *all* possible patients in the OPO that

*A kidney that has been transported arrives at a hospital for transplant.*

## the facts...

- Human organs may not be bought or sold.
- There are not enough donated cadaveric organs to meet the growing need for organ transplants.
- Under current federal allocation rules, where you live affects your chances of receiving a cadaveric organ.
- The responsibility for finding a living donor rests with the patient.
- Some patients are using Web sites to locate living unrelated donors.

procured the organ. The current system may also discriminate against minorities and the poor because they live in regions that have lower rates of organ donation.

The DHHS has proposed that organs be allocated according to common criteria of *medical need*, not geographical location. This suggestion has sparked fierce opposition, particularly from smaller OPOs with higher rates of organ donation. The smaller OPOs argue that with geography no longer a factor, the country's largest hospitals and transplant centers would sign up the most patients on their waiting lists. They would then get most of the donated organs (and make the most money doing transplants). Smaller transplant centers might close. In the long run this could reduce competition, which would not be in patients' best interests. They also argue that organ donations might decline when people realized that their organs would not be used for patients in their region.

## Should People Be Able to Sell Organs?

Studies show that in deaths where organ donation is possible and is requested of a family, only about 50% of families give their consent. The American Medical Association has suggested that families who donate cadaveric organs from a loved one should be compensated in some way. The DHHS is also considering proposals to compensate live donors, such as people who donate a kidney.

It is highly likely that financial incentives would increase the supply of organs available for transplant. Yet many people oppose the idea on ethical grounds. In addition, UNOS officials worry that that payment might actually discourage donations, because families would no longer view the action as a substantial gift of life.

Madolena (right) chose to give one of her kidneys to a total stranger, Tracy (center). Here they meet for the first time.

## Developments to Watch

U.S. law requires evidence of donor or family consent before an organ can be used for transplantation. A legal change to "presumed consent" would dramatically increase organ donations. Under presumed consent, it would be presumed that organs are available unless the donor (or family) explicitly states otherwise. In Belgium, the number of kidney donations doubled in the first three years after the passage of a presumed consent law. At least 21 countries now have presumed consent laws, and although citizens in these countries can still opt out of donation, only 2% have chosen to do so. The U.S. does not yet have a presumed consent law.

In the meantime, some patients are finding their own unrelated living donors by turning to the Internet. The first commercial Web site to match living organ donor volunteers with potential patients was MatchingDonors.com. Patients who need an organ make an appeal on the site, and potential donors read through them and choose a patient to help, provided the immunological match is good. Donors receive no financial rewards for their donation, but perhaps money can't buy the ultimate gift. As one donor put it, "I wanted to do something nice for somebody."

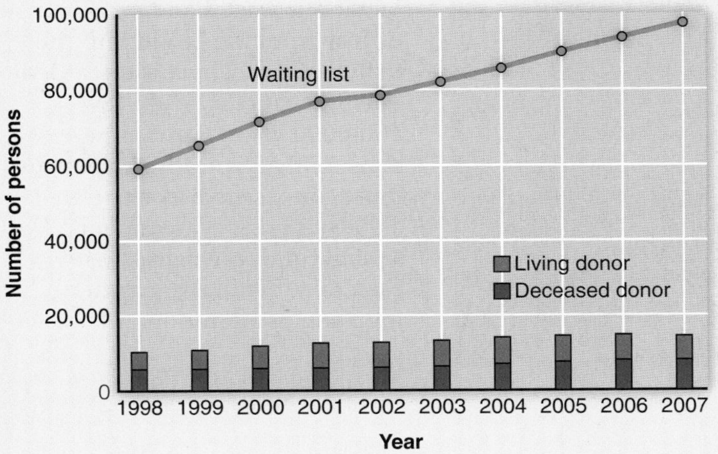


And yet, some doctors and ethicists aren't so sure this is a good idea. They point out that when matches are made on sites such as MatchingDonors.com, organs are more likely to go to patients with the best story or the best picture, not the sickest patients. That may well be true, but the fact is that there is no national registry for living unrelated donors in the U.S., and in the meantime the commercial sites on the Internet fill that void.

In an interesting twist, at least five states (Kentucky, Louisiana, Oklahoma, South Carolina, and Wisconsin) have passed laws mandating that organs donated in their states must be offered first to in-state patients. Whether these laws will stand up under challenge is an open question. The battle for scarce organs continues.

## Questions to consider

**1** *How do you think we should allocate cadaveric organs? What improvements, if any, would you suggest to the present system?*

**2** *Would you be willing to donate your organs after death? Have you completed a donor card?*

**3** *Should the government set up a national registry to match living donors with unrelated patients? Why or why not?*

# Directions in Science

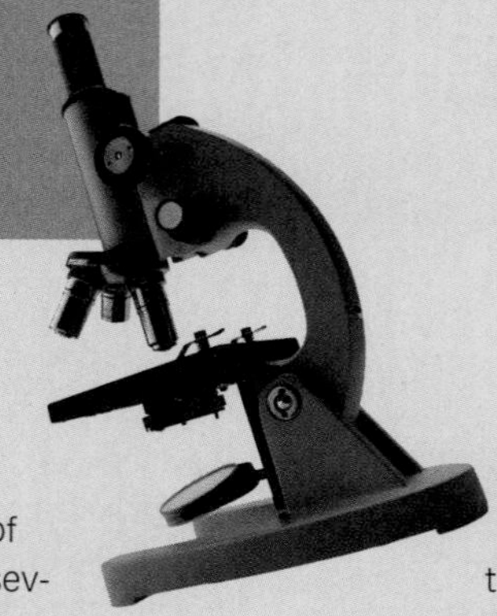

## Is It Safe to Donate a Kidney?

The 66,300 people waiting for kidney transplants almost certainly have parents, siblings, and/or children. Relatives make the best donors because they are genetically closer than unrelated individuals. One of the most difficult decisions those relatives will ever have to make is whether to donate one of their kidneys if it turns out to be a good match.

The question that any potential donor would ask, of course, concerns safety. The surgery itself is very safe, but what about the long-term consequences—is it possible to live a long and healthy life with just one kidney? The answer has changed several times since live kidney donations became possible, an example of how our knowledge has progressed over time.

During the 1960s, when renal transplants were first performed, donating a kidney seemed perfectly safe. After all, the reasoning went, we can function on as little as 25% of normal renal capacity. Furthermore, when one kidney is removed, the remaining organ grows substantially, and within a year renal function achieves 60–75% of the function of two kidneys. For several years, nearly all transplanted kidneys came from living, related donors.

In the 1980s the story changed dramatically. A prominent group of researchers from Harvard University questioned the long-term safety of donating a kidney. Based on findings in rats, they proposed that reducing the kidney mass might, under poor dietary conditions (such as a very high-protein diet), cause renal damage and a slow decrease of renal function over time. As the debate raged in academic circles, kidney transplants from living donors came to a virtual halt.

To resolve the controversy, scientists needed reliable long-term data on people with only one kidney. Researchers began to comb the country for past donors, but finding and convincing them to be examined wasn't the only problem. The other was that transplants had been performed for only about 20 years, a relatively short time. To address the time issue, some researchers studied people who had had a kidney removed in childhood.

Since the 1990s, multiple studies have shown that people retain good renal function after losing a kidney. In addition, they do not show increased rates of high blood pressure or other kidney-related diseases. Today we again believe (based on more data than we had originally) that kidney donation is safe. Consequently, the number of living kidney donations is again on the rise.

Were the Harvard researchers "wrong"? Absolutely not! They conducted valuable experiments in rats that caused them to formulate an important hypothesis about the possible risks of kidney donation in humans. Thanks to their efforts and follow-up from other researchers, today's kidney donors can enjoy greater confidence than ever.

because of the access port through the abdominal wall.

In another type of dialysis, called *hemodialysis,* the patient's blood is circulated through an artificial kidney machine consisting of semipermeable membranes in contact with a large volume of clean fluid (Figure 15.17). Metabolic wastes and excess ions diffuse from the blood into the dialysis fluid, which is discarded. The procedure is costly (over $50,000 per year) and time consuming. Typically the patient must go to a medical site called a dialysis unit for treatment several times each week, with each treatment taking a whole morning or afternoon.

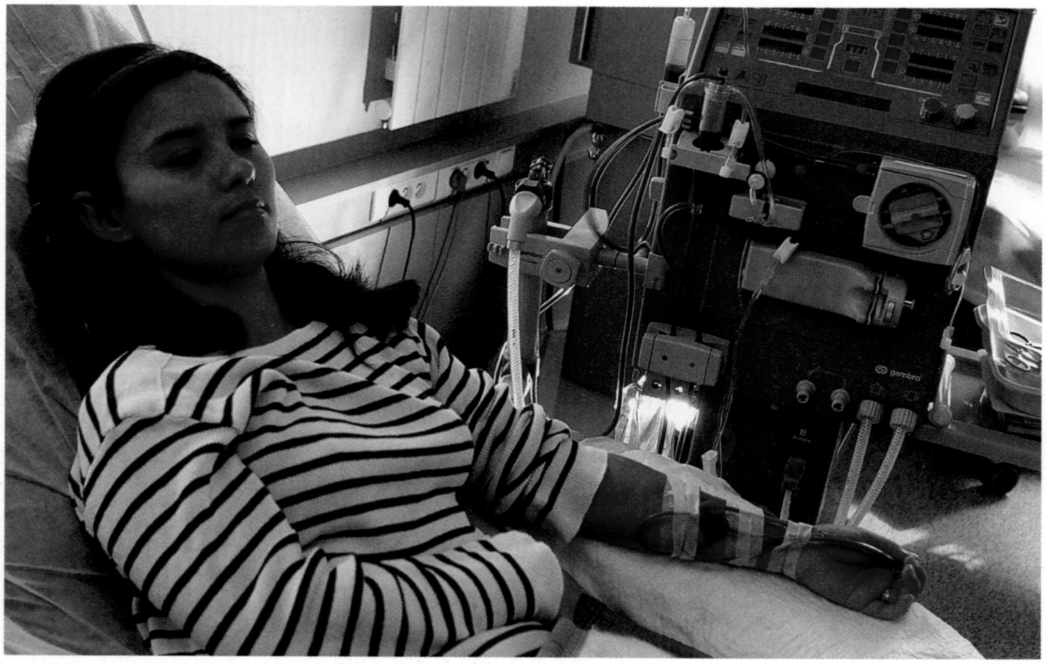

**Figure 15.17 A patient undergoing hemodialysis.**

### Kidney transplants are a permanent solution to renal failure

Most people currently on renal dialysis will remain on dialysis for the rest of their lives. Although dialysis is a life-saving technique, it is not the perfect solution. It is difficult, if not impossible, to achieve complete homeostasis of all ions and wastes by artificial means. Furthermore, dialysis does not replace the renal hormones. The best hope for many chronic renal failure patients is to receive a living kidney from another person, but over 65,000 people are on waiting lists to get a kidney transplant.

When kidney transplants began in the 1960s, the biggest challenge was to find a good immunological match so that the recipient's body would not reject the foreign kidney. Often close relatives were asked to consider donating a kidney. With the advent of better drugs to suppress the immune system, improved tissue-matching techniques, national data banks of patients awaiting kidneys, and rapid jet transport, it is now feasible for the donor kidney to come from a cadaver. The main bottleneck now is that not enough people have offered to donate their organs after death. Thousands of people currently on waiting lists will die before they can receive a kidney.

What can you do to help? Specify your willingness to make an anatomical gift by completing a uniform donor card. In many states, driver's licenses have a donor card on the back. You can also download a card from the Internet (see Internet References at the end of this chapter).

**RECAP**

CAPD is an at-home dialysis technique in which fluid is placed in the peritoneal cavity and replaced at regular intervals. Hemodialysis cleanses the blood by means of an artificial kidney machine consisting of a semipermeable membrane and clean fluid. Kidney transplants are the best hope for people in renal failure. Currently there is a severe shortage of kidneys available for transplant. ■

## Chapter Summary

### The urinary system contributes to homeostasis *p. 352*

- The kidneys, the lungs, the liver, and the skin all participate in the maintenance of homeostasis.
- The kidneys are the primary regulators of water balance and most excess solutes, especially inorganic ions and urea.

### Organs of the urinary system *p. 353*

- The urinary system consists of those organs that produce, transport, store, and excrete urine. The urinary system includes the kidneys, the ureters, the bladder, and the urethra.
- Functions of the kidneys include regulation of the volume and composition of body fluids, excretion of wastes, regulation of blood pressure, regulation of the production of red blood cells, and the activation of vitamin D.

### Nephrons produce urine *p. 355*

- The functional unit of the kidneys is the nephron. Each nephron consists of a tubular component and the blood vessels that supply it.
- The tubular components of a nephron are the glomerular capsule, proximal tubule, loop of Henle, distal tubule, and collecting duct. The collecting duct is shared by many nephrons.
- A tuft of capillaries called the glomerulus is enclosed within each glomerular capsule. Peritubular capillaries supply proximal and distal tubules, and vasa recta supply loops of Henle and collecting ducts.

### Formation of urine: Filtration, reabsorption, and secretion *p. 357*

- The formation of urine involves three processes: glomerular filtration, tubular reabsorption, and tubular secretion.
- Approximately 180 liters per day of protein-free plasma fluid is filtered across the glomerulus and into the glomerular space. Filtration is driven by high blood pressure in the glomerular capillaries.
- Ninety-nine percent of all filtered water and salt and all of the filtered bicarbonate, glucose, and amino acids are reabsorbed in tubular reabsorption. The active transport of sodium provides the driving force for the reabsorption of nearly all other substances.
- Tubular secretion is a minor process relative to reabsorption but is critical for the regulation of acid-base balance and for the removal of certain toxic wastes.

### The kidneys can produce dilute or concentrated urine *p. 361*

- The ability of the kidneys to form either dilute or concentrated urine depends on the high solute concentration in the renal medulla and the ability to alter the permeability of the collecting duct to water.
- Dilute urine is formed in the absence of the hormone ADH. In the absence of ADH, reabsorption of salt without reabsorption of water continues in the collecting duct.
- Concentrated urine is formed when ADH increases the collecting duct's permeability to water, allowing water to diffuse toward the high solute concentration in the medulla.
- The ability of the kidneys to produce concentrated urine is dependent upon a countercurrent mechanism that exists in the hairpin arrangements of the loops of Henle and the vasa recta.

### Urination depends on a reflex *p. 362*

- Urination is caused by the micturition reflex, a neural reflex initiated when the bladder is stretched.
- Urination can be prevented by higher (voluntary) neural signals from the brain.

### The kidneys maintain homeostasis in many ways *p. 363*

- Water balance is maintained by a negative feedback loop involving ADH. The main stimulus for the secretion of ADH is an increase in the solute concentration of the blood.
- Blood volume is regulated by maintenance of the body's salt balance, which is controlled primarily by a negative feedback loop influenced by two hormones: renin from the kidney and aldosterone from the adrenal cortex.
- The kidneys secrete (and excrete) $H^+$ and $NH_4^+$ in amounts equal to the net gain of acid per day (other than as $CO_2$). They also secrete $H^+$ as part of the mechanism for the reabsorption of all filtered $HCO_3^-$.
- The kidneys synthesize and secrete erythropoietin, the hormone responsible for the regulation of red blood cell production.
- The kidneys are required for the activation of vitamin D.

### Disorders of the urinary system *p. 367*

- The kidneys are vulnerable to damage by toxic substances, infections, sustained decreases in blood pressure, or blockage of urinary outflow.
- Nephrons that are damaged beyond repair are not replaced.
- Hemodialysis is an artificial procedure for cleansing the blood of wastes and excess solutes.
- Renal transplantation is technically easy and usually quite successful, but there is a shortage of donor kidneys.

## Terms You Should Know

antidiuretic hormone (ADH), *362*
collecting duct, *355*
countercurrent exchange mechanism, *362*
dialysis, *367*
distal tubule, *355*
glomerular capsule, *355*
glomerular filtration, *358*
glomerulus, *355*
loop of Henle, *355*
nephron, *355*
peritubular capillary, *356*
proximal tubule, *355*
renin, *364*
tubular reabsorption, *359*
tubular secretion, *360*
urea, *353*
ureter, *354*
urethra, *355*
vasa recta, *356*

## Concept Review

1. Describe in general terms the kidneys' role in maintaining homeostasis.
2. Describe the function of each of the organs of the urinary system.
3. Give the names and functions of each of the tubular sections of the nephron.
4. Indicate where vasa recta are located, and list the two tubular regions of the nephron they serve.
5. Describe the driving force responsible for filtration of fluid from the glomerular capillaries into the glomerular space.
6. Name the one region of the tubule where water permeability is *regulated.*
7. Indicate the primary stimulus for the secretion of the hormone ADH.
8. Describe the function of the hormone aldosterone.
9. Describe how chronic renal failure differs from acute renal failure.
10. Discuss the treatment options available to someone in chronic renal failure (end-stage renal disease).

## Test Yourself

### Matching Exercise

_____ 1. Blood vessel that leads directly to either peritubular capillaries or vasa recta
_____ 2. Carries urine from hundreds of distal tubules into the renal pelvis
_____ 3. Tuft of capillaries where filtration occurs
_____ 4. Structure that transports urine from a kidney to the bladder
_____ 5. Structure that transports urine from the bladder to the exterior of the body
_____ 6. Blood vessel that carries blood into a glomerulus

a. ureter
b. urethra
c. glomerulus
d. collecting duct
e. afferent arteriole
f. efferent arteriole

### Fill in the Blank

7. The secretion of the hormone ____________________ is stimulated by a drop in oxygen delivery to the kidney.
8. ____________________ is a hormone-like enzyme secreted by afferent arteriole cells of the juxtaglomerular apparatus.
9. The primary nitrogenous waste excreted in the urine is ____________________.
10. The loop of ____________________ has both a descending and an ascending limb.
11. The active transport of ____________________ out of the renal tubular cell is ultimately responsible for the tubular reabsorption of sodium, chloride, water, and all amino acids and monosaccharides.
12. An increase in the production of the hormone ADH will lead to an (increase/decrease) in the reabsorption of water.

### True or False?

13. The interstitial fluid in the renal medulla has the same solute concentration as interstitial fluid in the renal cortex.
14. The kidneys cannot contribute to acid-base balance because they do not excrete $CO_2$.
15. Urinary tract infections are more common in women than men due to differences in urethra length.

## References and Additional Reading

Koeppen, Bruce M., and Bruce A. Stanton. *Renal Physiology,* 4th ed. St. Louis: Mosby, 2006. 248 pp. (A standard text of renal function and the maintenance of body fluids.)

Munson, Ronald. *Raising the Dead: Organ Transplants, Ethics, and Society.* Oxford University Press, 2004. (Recent coverage of this subject at an understandable level.)

Smith, Homer W. *From Fish to Philosopher.* Boston: Little, Brown, 1953. 264 pp. (A classic book in renal physiology that describes the evolution of the vertebrate kidney.)

Veatch, Robert M. *Transplantation Ethics.* Georgetown University Press, 2002. (A systematic analysis of ethical issues in transplantation.)

## Apply **What You Know**

1. Do your kidneys have to work harder (expend more metabolic energy) to get rid of the extra salt and water after you binge on salty snacks and liquid beverages? Explain your reasoning.
2. Explain the mechanism for why you feel thirsty after heavy exercise accompanied by sweating.
3. What does the production of a low volume of dark yellow urine indicate?
4. The kidneys filter a large volume of fluid, putting it on a path to ultimate disposal, and then reabsorb nearly all of it back into the body. Only a few waste products are actively secreted into the tubule. Why are the kidneys set up in this way? Wouldn't it be easier and more energetically efficient to selectively secrete only the waste molecules and the exact right amount of excess water and ions directly into an excretory tube or the bladder?
5. Why aren't children already "potty trained"—able to hold urination and defecation as well as adults can—when they are born?
6. A possible complication of a strep throat infection is post-streptococcal glomerulonephritis. In this disease, antibodies produced against the streptococcus invader also cause inflammation of glomeruli in the kidneys and damage to the glomerular filtration barrier. What might be the symptoms of damage to the glomerular filtration barrier, and what effect would you expect this to have on kidney function?

*Answers can be found on the Human Biology Place.*

## Internet References

Find links to the following Web sites at the Human Biology Place.

**United Network for Organ Sharing**
**www.unos.org**
Organization that assists doctors, patients, and the general public in procuring and allocating organs in the U.S.; good source for transplant information and statistics.

**National Kidney Foundation**
**www.kidney.org**
Organization that works to prevent diseases of the kidney and urinary tract, and to promote the health and well-being of people affected by them.

**Coalition on Donation**
**www.donatelife.net**
A not-for-profit alliance of national and local organizations that promotes organ and tissue donations; you can check your state's requirements for becoming a donor and download a uniform donor card.

**National Institute of Diabetes and Digestive and Kidney Diseases**
**www2.niddk.nih.gov**
A division of the National Institutes of Health that sponsors clinical research and offers information for professionals and patients.

# 16 Reproductive Systems

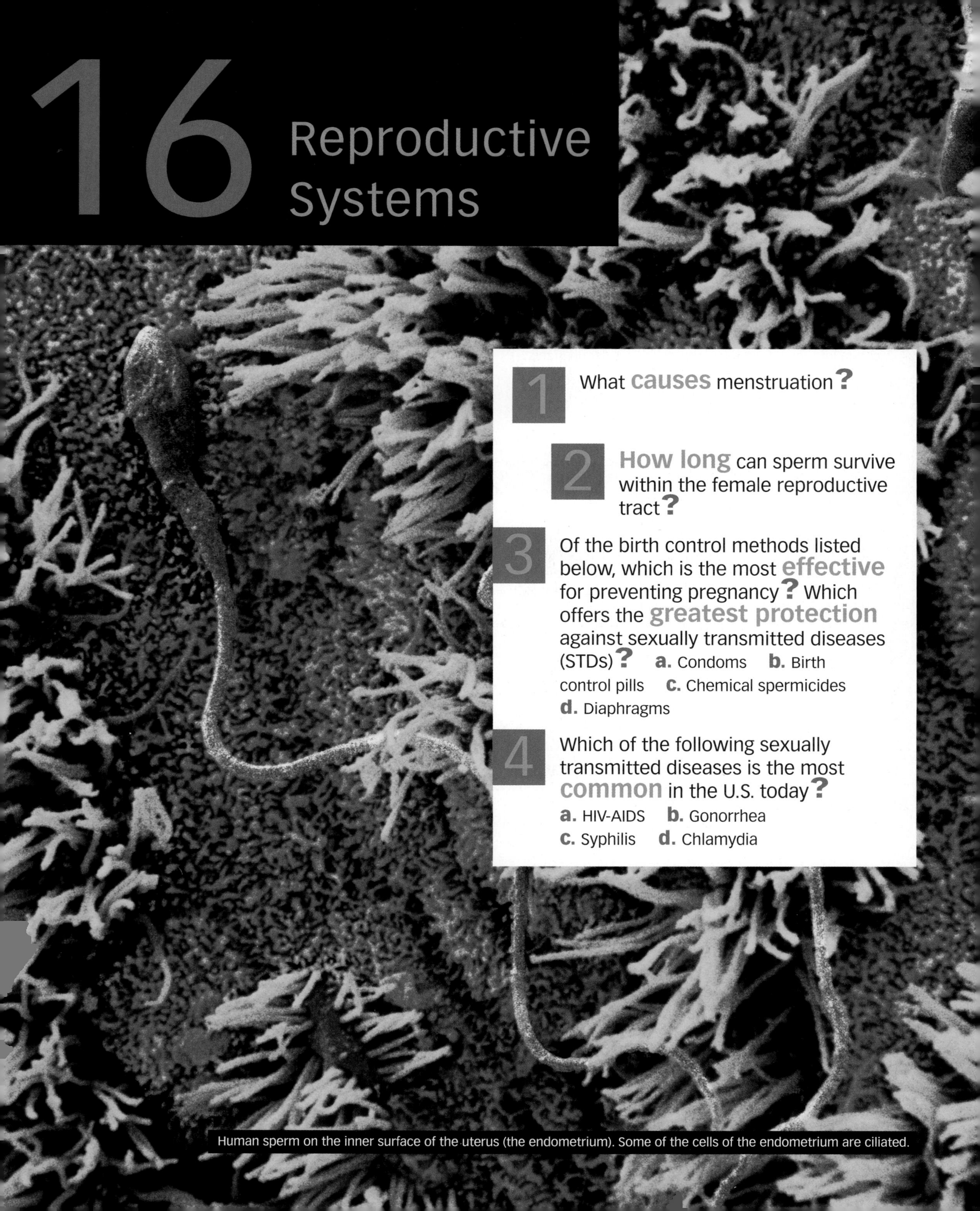

1 What **causes** menstruation?

2 **How long** can sperm survive within the female reproductive tract?

3 Of the birth control methods listed below, which is the most **effective** for preventing pregnancy? Which offers the **greatest protection** against sexually transmitted diseases (STDs)? **a.** Condoms **b.** Birth control pills **c.** Chemical spermicides **d.** Diaphragms

4 Which of the following sexually transmitted diseases is the most **common** in the U.S. today? **a.** HIV-AIDS **b.** Gonorrhea **c.** Syphilis **d.** Chlamydia

Human sperm on the inner surface of the uterus (the endometrium). Some of the cells of the endometrium are ciliated.

**Most of the organ systems** we have considered so far in this book are not exactly hot topics in popular media. How many songs have you heard praising the urinary system or the digestive process? Certainly some of the subjects in this chapter, such as differences in male and female anatomy and in patterns of sexual arousal, get more than their share of attention—in songs, books, movies, even Web sites. The beauty and mystery of sex are a source of endless fascination to us.

On a practical level, sexual attractiveness and sexual arousal are normal events in the human reproductive process—a process that requires the **reproductive systems.** The male and female reproductive systems consist of the tissues and organs that participate in creating a new human being. At first glance, it may seem that the male and female reproductive systems are completely dissimilar. After all, the external and internal structures look different from each other. Even secondary sexual characteristics, such as body form, muscle mass, hair patterns, and distribution of body fat, aren't the same. From an evolutionary standpoint, there must have been a tremendous advantage to having the male and female reproductive systems evolve in this manner.

However, there are many similarities between male and female reproductive systems. Both systems consist of primary reproductive organs, accessory glands, and ducts. Both men and women experience similar phases of sexual desire. Each system has highly specific functions that allow it to complement the other perfectly. And ultimately, both systems share the same goal: to join a sperm and an egg in an environment (the woman's body) that enables the fertilized egg to become an individual.

## 16.1 The male reproductive system delivers sperm

Figure 16.1 illustrates the organs of the male reproductive system. The male reproductive system evolved to deliver the male reproductive cells, called **sperm,** to the female. As we will see, the chance of any one sperm fertilizing a female reproductive cell (an **egg**) is extremely low. The reproductive strategy of the male, then, is to deliver huge numbers of sperm at a time to improve the odds that one will reach the egg.

### Testes produce sperm

The sites of sperm production in the male are the paired **testes** (singular: *testis*). Shortly before birth the testes descend into the **scrotum,** an outpouching of skin and smooth muscle. The scrotum regulates the temperature of the developing sperm within the testes, for sperm develop best at temperatures a few degrees cooler than body temperature. When the temperature within the scrotum falls below about 95°F the smooth muscle of the scrotum contracts, bringing the testes closer to the warmth of the body. When the temperature warms to above 95°F the smooth muscle relaxes and the scrotum and testes hang away from the body.

Each testis is only about 2 inches long, but it contains over 100 yards of tightly packed **seminiferous tubules,** where the sperm are produced. The seminiferous tubules join to become the **epididymis,** a single coiled duct just outside the testis. The epididymis joins the long **ductus (vas) deferens,** which eventually joins the duct from the seminal vesicle to become the **ejaculatory duct.** The newly formed sperm are not fully mature (they cannot yet swim) when they leave the seminiferous tubules. Their ability to swim develops in both the epididymis and the ductus deferens. The epididymis and the ductus deferens also store the sperm until ejaculation.

When the male reaches sexual climax and ejaculates, rhythmic contractions of smooth muscle propel the sperm through the short ejaculatory duct and finally through the urethra, which passes through the penis. (As described in Chapter 15, the urethra is a pathway for urine as well.)

The **penis** is the male organ of sexual intercourse. Its function is to deliver sperm internally to the female, safely away from the harsh external environment. The penis contains erectile tissues that permit **erection**—an increase in length, diameter, and stiffness of the penis that facilitates its entry into the vagina.

### Accessory glands help sperm survive

Sperm must endure the rapid journey from epididymis to vagina and then continue to live within the woman for

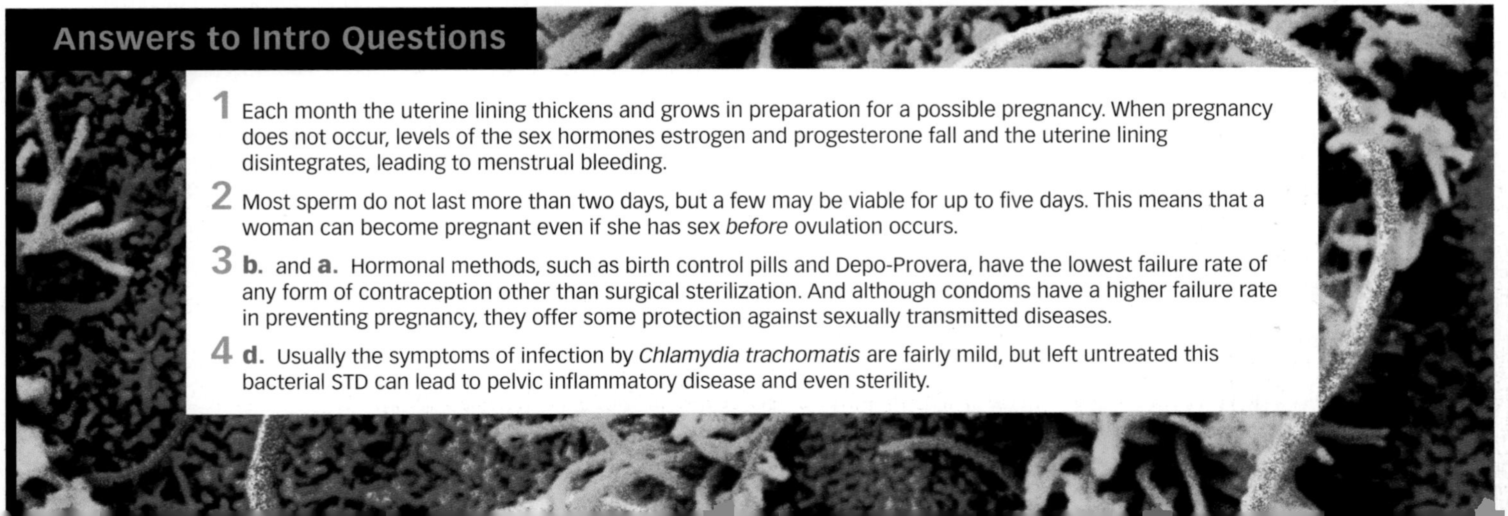

**Answers to Intro Questions**

1 Each month the uterine lining thickens and grows in preparation for a possible pregnancy. When pregnancy does not occur, levels of the sex hormones estrogen and progesterone fall and the uterine lining disintegrates, leading to menstrual bleeding.

2 Most sperm do not last more than two days, but a few may be viable for up to five days. This means that a woman can become pregnant even if she has sex *before* ovulation occurs.

3 **b.** and **a.** Hormonal methods, such as birth control pills and Depo-Provera, have the lowest failure rate of any form of contraception other than surgical sterilization. And although condoms have a higher failure rate in preventing pregnancy, they offer some protection against sexually transmitted diseases.

4 **d.** Usually the symptoms of infection by *Chlamydia trachomatis* are fairly mild, but left untreated this bacterial STD can lead to pelvic inflammatory disease and even sterility.

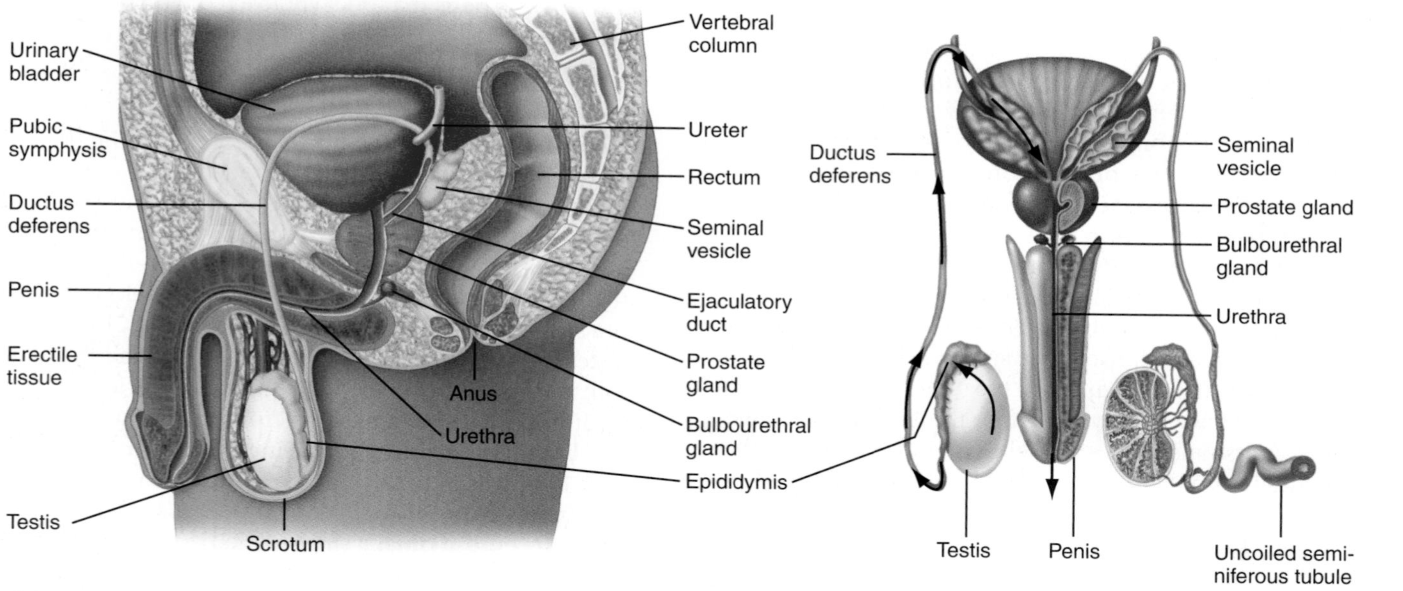


**a) A sagittal cutaway view**

**b) A posterior view of the reproductive organs and bladder**

**Figure 16.1 The male reproductive system.**

many hours. To improve their chances of survival, the male delivers sperm in a thick, whitish mixture of fluids called **semen.** In addition to sperm, semen contains secretions from the seminal vesicles, the prostate gland, and the bulbourethral gland.

The **seminal vesicles** produce seminal fluid, a watery mixture containing fructose and prostaglandins that represents about 60% of the volume of semen. Fructose, a carbohydrate, provides the sperm with a source of energy. The prostaglandins are thought to induce muscle contractions in the female reproductive system that help sperm travel more effectively. The **prostate gland** contributes an alkaline fluid. The vagina is generally fairly acid (pH 3.5–4.0), which helps prevent infections but is too acid for sperm. The prostate secretions temporarily raise the vaginal pH to about 6, optimal for sperm. Finally, the **bulbourethral glands** secrete mucus into the urethra during sexual arousal. The mucus washes away traces of acidic urine in the urethra before the sperm arrive and also provides lubrication for sexual intercourse. The sperm are not mixed with seminal and prostate fluids until the moment of ejaculation.

Table 16.1 summarizes the organs and glands of the male reproductive system.

**RECAP**

The male reproductive system consists of the testes where sperm are produced, a series of ducts and accessory glands, and the penis. Semen consists of sperm and three glandular secretions that provide energy and the proper pH environment for the sperm and also lubrication for sexual intercourse. ■

## Sperm production requires several cell divisions

Let's take a closer look at the process of sperm production. As mentioned, it takes place in the seminiferous tubules within each testis (Figure 16.2). Toward the outer surface of each tubule are undifferentiated cells (cells that have not yet become any kind of specialized cell) called

**Table 16.1 Summary of the male reproductive organs and glands**

| Organ | Function |
|---|---|
| Testis (2) | Produces sperm, testosterone, and inhibin |
| Scrotum | Keeps the testes at the proper temperature |
| Epididymis (2) | Site of sperm maturation and storage |
| Ductus deferens (2) | Duct for sperm maturation, storage, and transport |
| Ejaculatory duct (2) | Duct for transporting sperm and glandular secretions |
| Penis | Erectile organ of sexual intercourse |
| ***Accessory Glands*** | |
| Seminal vesicle (2) | Secretes fructose and most of the seminal fluid |
| Prostate gland | Secretes watery alkaline fluid to raise vaginal pH |
| Bulbourethral gland (2) | Secretes lubricating mucus |

*spermatogonia* (singular: *spermatogonium*). Spermatogonia are *diploid* cells, meaning they have 46 chromosomes, the normal human number.

The formation of both sperm and eggs involves a series of cell divisions called *mitosis* and *meiosis*. In Chapter 17, we discuss meiosis and mitosis in more detail. The important point to remember here is that in order to produce the **gametes** (sperm and eggs), the diploid number of chromosomes must be halved. Gametes are called *haploid* cells (from the Greek *haploos*, "single") because they contain only 23 chromosomes. This ensures that when a sperm and egg unite, the embryo will have the proper (diploid) number of chromosomes again.

Spermatogonia divide several times during the course of sperm development (Figure 16.2b). The first division, by mitosis, ensures a constant supply of *primary spermatocytes*, each with the diploid number of chromosomes. Primary spermatocytes then undergo two successive cell divisions during meiosis to become *secondary spermatocytes* and finally *spermatids*. Spermatids, which are haploid cells, mature slowly to become the male gametes, or sperm. The entire process of sperm formation and maturation takes about 9–10 weeks. During this time the cells are surrounded and nourished by the large **Sertoli cells** that make up most of the bulk of the seminiferous tubules.

A mature sperm has a head, midpiece, and tail (Figure 16.2d). The head contains the DNA, organized into chromosomes. The head is covered by an *acrosome*, a cap containing enzymes that help the sperm penetrate the egg. The sperm's whiplike tail moves it forward, powered by energy produced by mitochondria in the midpiece.

Tens of millions of sperm are produced every day after puberty in young men. A typical ejaculation may contain 100–300 million sperm, but only one sperm, if it is lucky, will fertilize an egg.

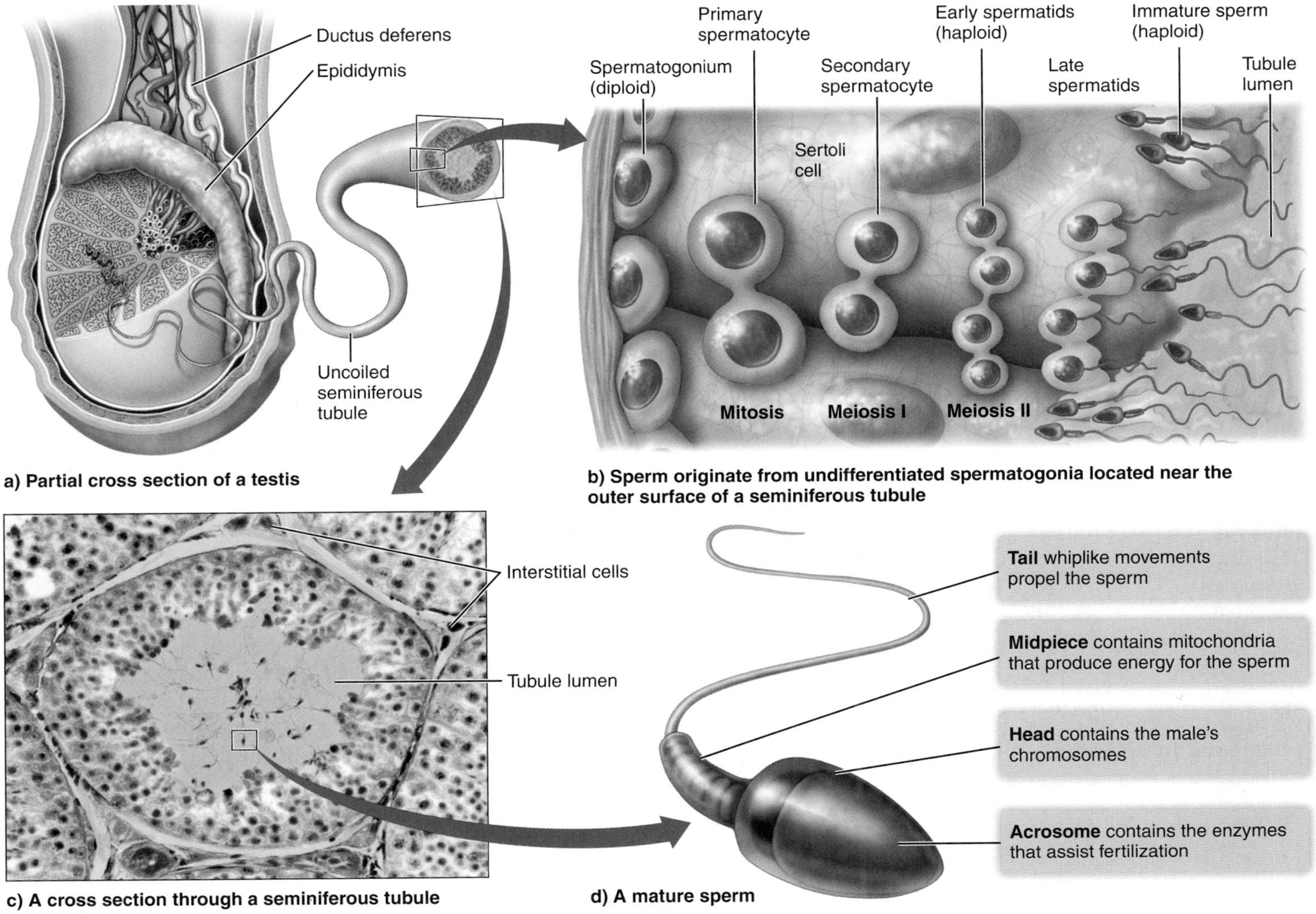


**Figure 16.2 Sperm formation in a seminiferous tubule (a)** Partial cross-section of a testis showing the coiled seminiferous tubules. **(b)** The production of sperm is supported by Sertoli cells. **(c)** A cross-section through a seminiferous tubule (×100) showing the location of the testosterone-producing interstitial cells between the tubules. Mature sperm are visible within the lumen of tubule. **(d)** Illustration of a sperm, showing the head, midpiece, and tail.

**RECAP**

The haploid sperm form continuously in the seminiferous tubules from undifferentiated diploid cells called spermatogonia. Millions of sperm form every day throughout a man's life, and a typical ejaculate contains up to 300 million. ■

### Testosterone affects male reproductive capacity

Male reproductive capacity depends on **testosterone,** a steroid hormone produced by **interstitial cells** located between the seminiferous tubules within the testes (Figure 16.2c). Testosterone controls the growth and function of the male reproductive tissues, stimulates aggressive and sexual behavior, and causes the development of secondary sexual characteristics at puberty, such as facial hair and deepening voice. Within the testes, testosterone stimulates the undifferentiated spermatogonia to begin dividing and the Sertoli cells to support the developing sperm, and thus it determines the rate of sperm formation.

The production and secretion of testosterone depends on three hormones: **gonadotropin-releasing hormone (GnRH)** from the hypothalamus, and luteinizing hormone (LH) and follicle-stimulating hormone (FSH) from the anterior pituitary gland. (As described in Chapter 13, LH and FSH are called gonadotropins because they stimulate the reproductive organs—the gonads.) Historically, the names for LH and FSH came from their functions in the female, but they are active hormones in the male as well.

Negative feedback loops involving the hypothalamus, the pituitary, and the testes maintain a fairly constant blood concentration of testosterone, and thus a consistent rate of sperm production (Figure 16.3). When blood concentrations of testosterone fall, the hypothalamus secretes gonadotropin-releasing hormone (GnRH), which stimulates the anterior pituitary gland to release LH and FSH. LH stimulates the secretion of testosterone by the interstitial cells. The role of FSH is less clear, but it seems to enhance sperm formation indirectly by stimulating the Sertoli cells.

Excessively high concentrations of testosterone inhibit the secretion of GnRH and also LH and FSH. In addition, when Sertoli cells are highly active they secrete a hormone called **inhibin** that directly inhibits the secretion of FSH.

**RECAP**

Testosterone stimulates the growth and function of the male reproductive system, aggressive and sexual behavior, and development of secondary sexual characteristics. Blood levels of testosterone are regulated by a negative feedback loop involving GnRH from the hypothalamus and LH and FSH from the anterior pituitary. ■

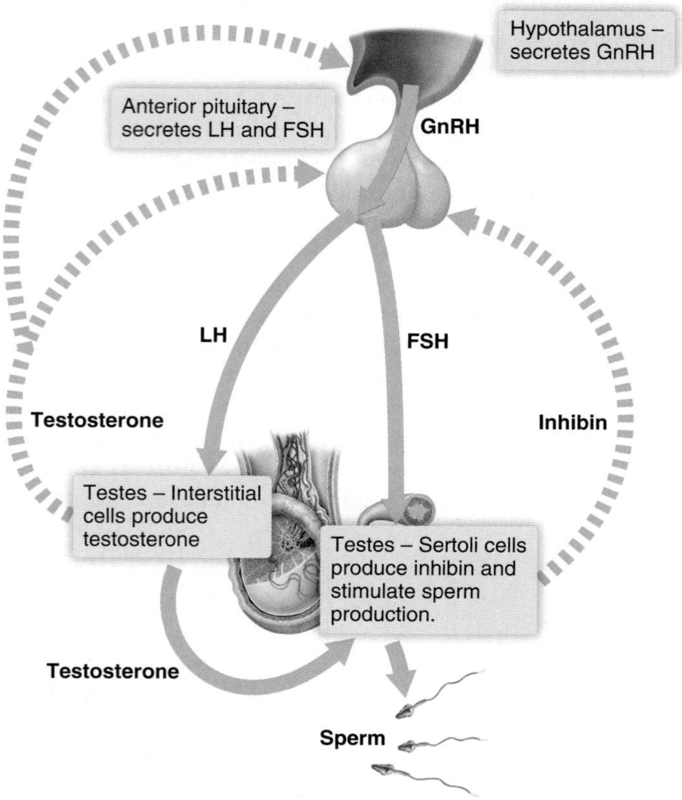


**Figure 16.3 Feedback control of blood testosterone concentration and sperm production.** Negative feedback control loops effectively maintain testosterone concentration (and hence sperm production) relatively constant over time. Negative feedback control occurs at both the hypothalamus and the anterior pituitary.

## 16.2 The female reproductive system produces eggs and supports pregnancy

The female reproductive system evolved to perform more functions than that of the male. Eggs are precious, so the system releases only one or two every month. In addition, because it can never be known for certain if an egg will be fertilized, the female reproductive system must go through cyclic changes every month just to prepare for the possibility of fertilization. If fertilization does occur, the female system adapts to pregnancy and supports the developing fetus.

### Ovaries release oocytes and secrete hormones

Figure 16.4a illustrates the organs of the female reproductive system. The primary female reproductive organs are the two **ovaries,** which release the female gametes, immature eggs called *oocytes,* at regular intervals during the reproductive years. The ovaries also secrete the female sex steroid hormones **estrogen** and **progesterone.** (As mentioned in Chapter 13, the term estrogen is commonly used to refer to three hormones known collectively as *estrogens*—17β-estradiol, estrone, and estriol.)

Once released, the oocyte is swept into the open end of an **oviduct** (also called a Fallopian tube), which leads from the ovary to the uterus. The open end of the oviduct has fingerlike projections called fimbriae that help move the oocyte into the oviduct. If fertilization by a sperm occurs, it usually takes place in the upper third of the oviduct. The unfertilized oocyte or fertilized egg moves down the oviduct over the course of about 3–4 days to the uterus.

## The uterus nurtures the fertilized egg

The **uterus** is a hollow pear-shaped organ where the fertilized egg grows and develops. The walls of the uterus comprise two layers of tissue (Figure 16.4b).

The inner layer of the uterus, the **endometrium,** is a lining of epithelial tissue, glands, connective tissue, and blood vessels. A fertilized egg attaches to the endometrium in a process called implantation. After implantation, the endometrium helps to form the *placenta,* a common tissue between the uterus and the fetus. The placenta provides nourishment to the developing fetus and also provides for waste removal and gas exchange.

The outer layer of the uterus, or **myometrium,** consists of thick layers of smooth muscle. The myometrium stretches during pregnancy to accommodate the growing fetus. It also provides the muscular force to expel the mature fetus during labor.

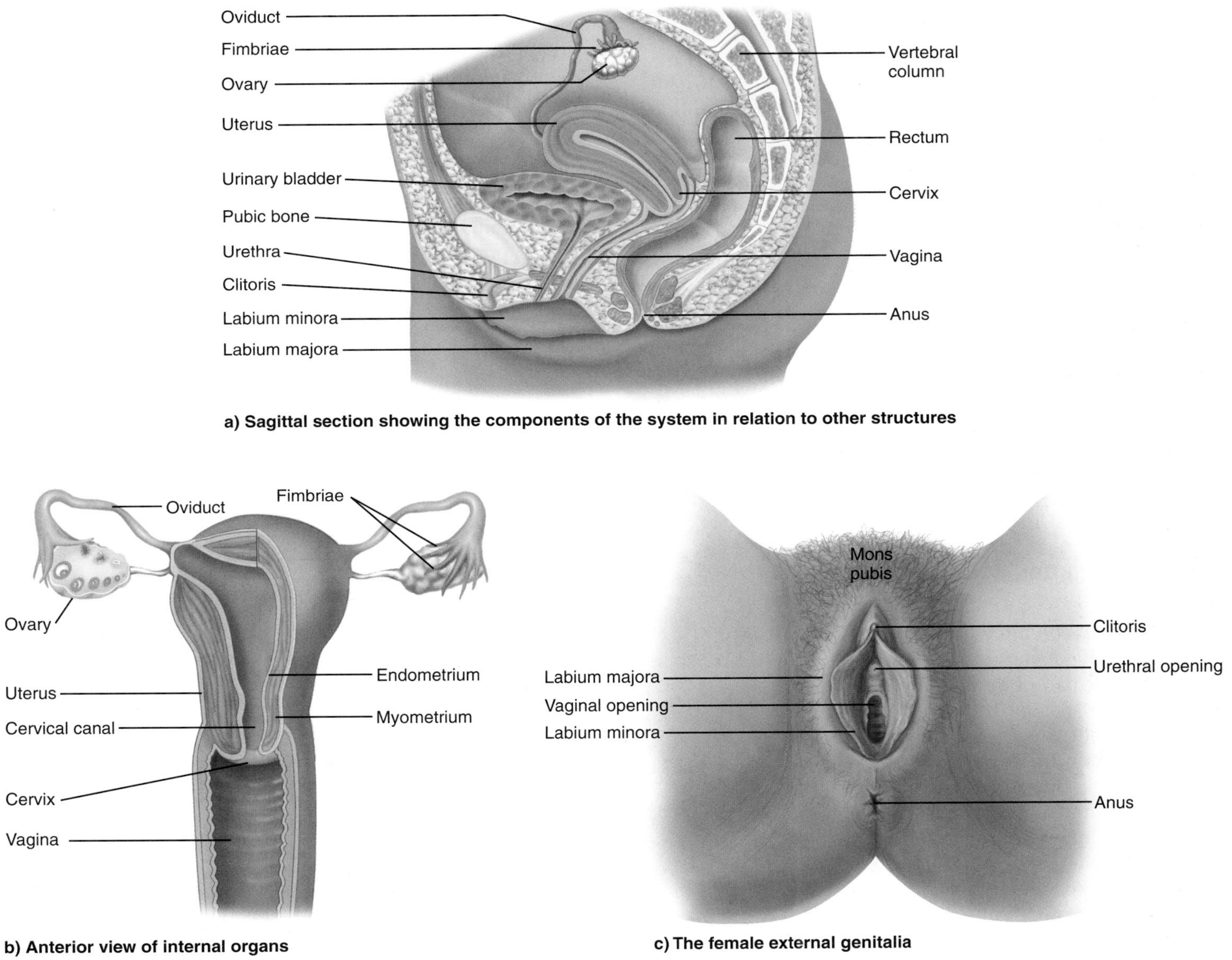


**Figure 16.4 The female reproductive system.** The labia have been pulled to the sides to expose the vaginal and urethral openings.

The narrow lower part of the uterus is the **cervix.** An opening in the cervix permits sperm to enter the uterus and allows the fetus to exit during birth.

**RECAP**

The ovaries secrete estrogen and progesterone, store immature oocytes, and release generally one oocyte at a time at intervals of about 28 days. The oocyte travels through the oviduct to the uterus, where implantation occurs if the egg has been fertilized. ■

## The vagina: Organ of sexual intercourse and birth canal

The cervix joins the **vagina,** a hollow muscular organ of sexual intercourse and also the birth canal. Glands within the vagina produce lubricating secretions during sexual arousal. A thin ring of tissue called the *hymen* may partially cover the opening to the vagina. The hymen is ruptured by the first sexual intercourse, or sometimes by the insertion of tampons or vigorous physical activity.

The vagina is continuous at the body surface with the female external genitalia, collectively called the **vulva** (Figure 16.4c). An outer, larger pair of fat-padded skin folds called the **labia majora** (in Latin, "major lips") surround and enclose the **labia minora** (singular: *labium*), a highly vascular but smaller pair of folds. The **clitoris,** a small organ partly enclosed by the labia minora, is important in the female sexual response. The clitoris and the penis originate from the same tissue during early development, and like the penis, the clitoris contains erectile tissue that is highly sensitive to stimulation. Between the clitoris and the vaginal opening lies the urethral opening. Table 16.2 summarizes the main components of the female reproductive system.

**Table 16.2 Summary of the components of the female reproductive system**

| Component | Function |
|---|---|
| Ovary (2) | Site of storage and development of oocytes |
| Oviduct (2) | Duct for transporting oocyte from ovary to uterus; also site of fertilization if it occurs |
| Uterus | Hollow chamber in which embryo develops |
| Cervix | Lower part of the uterus that opens into the vagina |
| Vagina | Organ of sexual intercourse; produces lubricating fluids; also the birth canal |
| Clitoris | Organ of sexual arousal |

## Mammary glands nourish the infant

Human breasts contain **mammary glands,** modified sweat glands that technically are part of the skin, or integumentary system. Though breasts are not required to produce a viable fetus, they undergo developmental changes during puberty in women and they support the infant's development, so we consider them here.

A *nipple* at the center of each breast contains smooth muscles that can contract, causing the nipple to become erect in response to sexual stimulation, cold temperatures, or a nursing infant. Surrounding the nipple is the pigmented *areola.* Internally, the breasts contain the mammary glands, which are specialized to produce milk (Figure 16.5). The mammary glands consist of hundreds of small milk-producing lobules. Contractile cells around each lobule allow the milk to be released, and ducts deliver it to the nipple. Most of the breast consists of adipose tissue, so breast size does not indicate the potential for milk production. A network of fibrous connective tissue supports the glands and adipose tissue.

At puberty, female mammary glands enlarge under the control of the hormone estrogen. Both estrogen and progesterone prepare the glands for **lactation,** or the production of milk, late in pregnancy. At birth, prolactin stimulates lactation and oxytocin stimulates the contractions that release milk during nursing. In males the mammary glands are *vestigial,* meaning that they have no function.

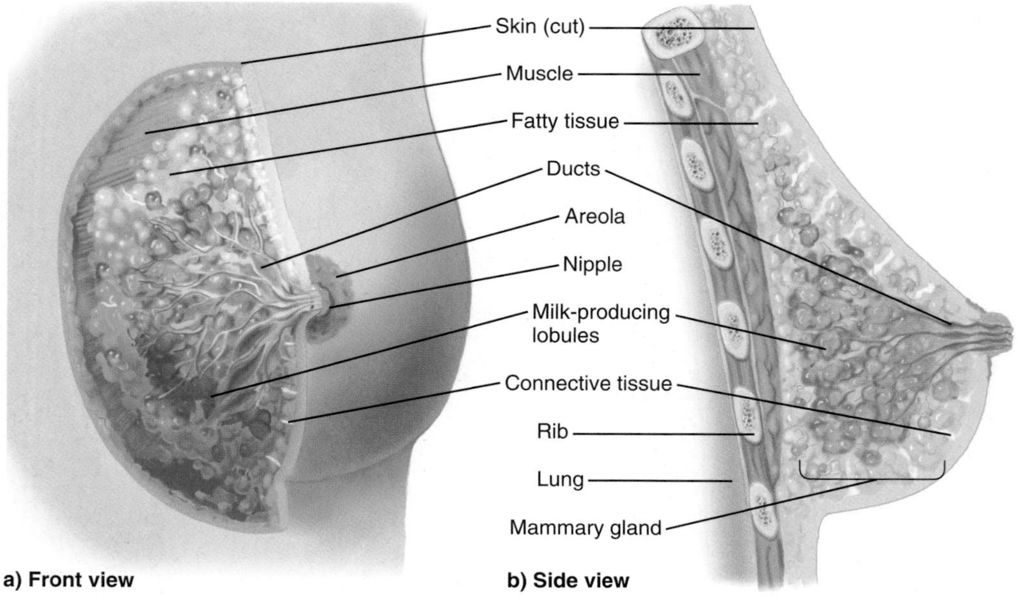


**Figure 16.5 The female breast.** Anatomical relationships between the milk-producing mammary glands, adipose tissue, and muscle.

**RECAP**

The vagina is the female organ of sexual intercourse and the birth canal; around its opening are the structures of the vulva. Mammary glands are accessory organs that produce and store milk. ■

## 16.3 Menstrual cycle consists of ovarian and uterine cycles

Every month, the ovaries and uterus go through a pattern of changes called the **menstrual cycle.** The menstrual cycle lasts about 28 days and is controlled by hormones. Menstrual cycles begin at puberty and generally continue throughout the reproductive years, except during pregnancy.

A complete menstrual cycle consists of two linked cycles, the *ovarian cycle* and the *uterine cycle.* Together, they periodically release oocytes and prepare the uterus to receive a fertilized egg.

### The ovarian cycle: Oocytes mature and are released

The **ovarian cycle** is a regular pattern of growth, maturation, and release of oocytes from the ovary. At birth, a female has approximately one million *primary oocytes* already formed and stored in each ovary, and no more are ever produced. Each primary oocyte has already developed partway through meiosis at birth, but at birth all further development halts until after puberty. By puberty 85% of them have been resorbed, leaving only about 300,000 in both ovaries.

Each month perhaps a dozen primary oocytes start the development process, but typically only one completes it. Only about 400 to 500 oocytes are released during a woman's lifetime, a number that contrasts sharply with the 100–300 million sperm released in a single ejaculation.

Figure 16.6 illustrates the events of the ovarian cycle.

1. A primary oocyte is surrounded by a layer of *granulosa cells* that nourish it. Together, a primary oocyte and its granulosa cells constitute an immature **follicle.** At the beginning of the ovarian cycle, an increase in GnRH from the hypothalamus slowly increases the secretion of FSH and LH by the anterior

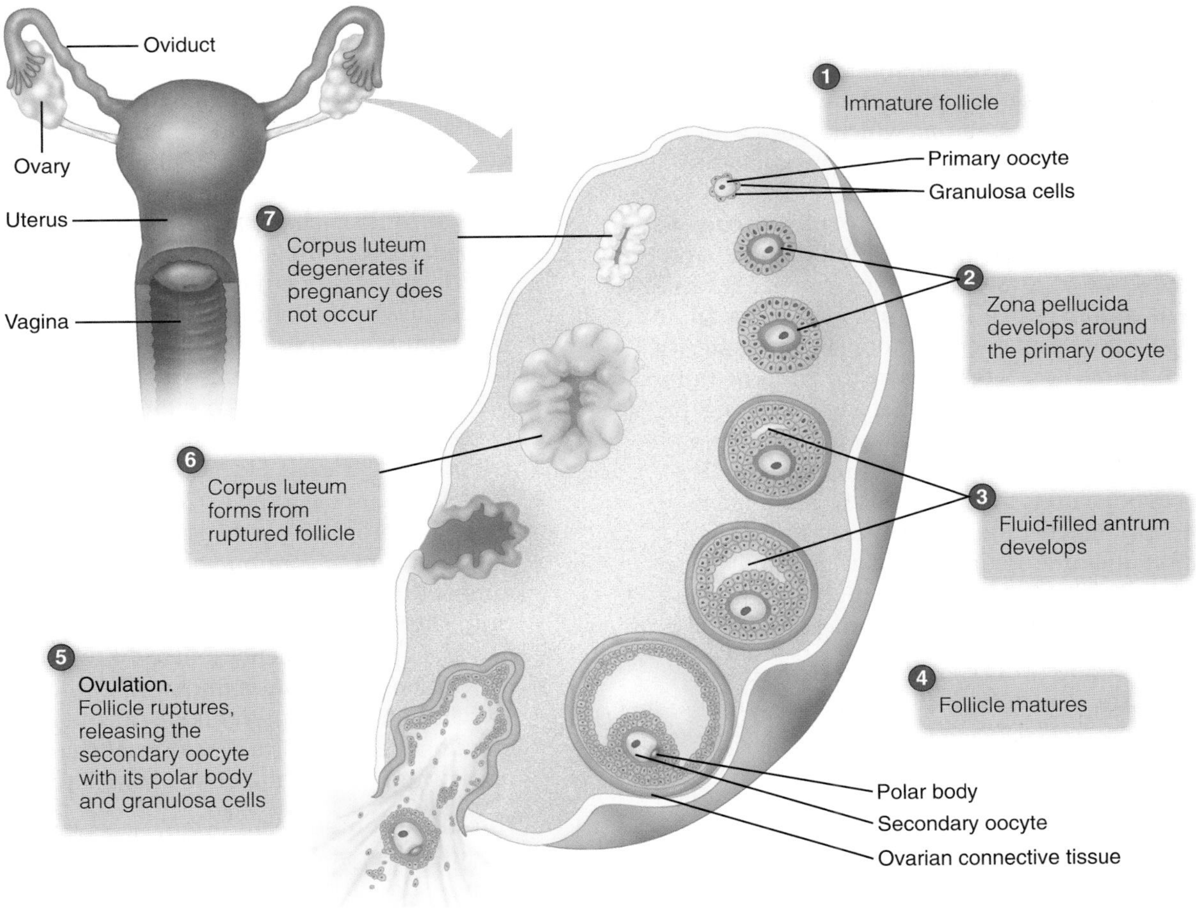


**Figure 16.6 The ovarian cycle.** Approximately a dozen primary follicles start this process each month, but generally only one completes it. For any particular primary follicle the events take place in one location, but for clarity the events are shown as if they migrate around the ovary in a clockwise fashion.

pituitary. These two hormones stimulate the follicle to grow, enlarge, and change form. FSH and LH also stimulate the follicle (and surrounding ovarian cells) to secrete estrogen.
2. The granulosa cells begin to divide and to secrete a sugary material (glycoproteins) that becomes the *zona pellucida*, a noncellular coating around the oocyte.
3. A fluid-filled space called the *antrum* develops within the follicle, and some of the granulosa cells begin to secrete estrogen and progesterone.
4. The primary oocyte completes stage I of meiosis to yield a *secondary oocyte* and a nonfunctional *polar body*. The mature follicle, sometimes called a Graafian follicle, consists of a secondary oocyte, a polar body, and numerous granulosa cells, all surrounded by ovarian connective tissue cells.
5. Several days before the midpoint of the ovarian cycle, rising levels of estrogen produced by the follicle and surrounding ovarian cells stimulate the pituitary to release a surge of LH. The LH surge triggers **ovulation** at the midpoint of the cycle—the follicle wall balloons outward and ruptures, releasing the secondary oocyte with its polar body, zona pellucida, and surrounding granulosa cells into the extracellular fluid.

   At this point the secondary oocyte enters the oviduct and is swept toward the uterus (and toward any sperm that may be swimming toward it) by peristaltic contractions of the oviduct. If fertilization occurs, the secondary oocyte quickly goes through the second stage of meiosis to produce a mature egg, or *ovum*, which unites with the sperm. Chapter 21 discusses the developmental events that follow the union of sperm and egg.
6. But the ovarian cycle is not over yet. A **corpus luteum** forms from what is left of the ruptured follicle (the name "luteinizing hormone" comes from the fact that LH causes the corpus luteum to form). The corpus luteum has an important function: it secretes large amounts of progesterone and estrogen. These hormones prepare the endometrium of the uterus for the possible arrival of a fertilized egg that would need the proper environment for further development. The high levels of progesterone and estrogen also signal the hypothalamus to inhibit FSH secretion, temporarily preventing other follicles from developing.
7. If fertilization does not occur, the corpus luteum degenerates in about 12 days. At this point estrogen and progesterone levels fall rapidly, and the ovarian cycle starts again.

If pregnancy does occur, a layer of tissue derived from the embryo called the *chorion* begins to secrete a hormone called *human chorionic gonadotropin (hCG)*. Home-use pregnancy test kits work by detecting hCG in urine. The presence of hCG signals the corpus luteum to produce progesterone and estrogen for another 9–10 weeks. By 10 weeks the developing placenta secretes enough progesterone and estrogen to support the pregnancy, and the corpus luteum degenerates. The high levels of estrogen and progesterone that are maintained throughout pregnancy ensure that ovulation does not occur during pregnancy. Pregnancy and fetal development are discussed further in Chapter 21.

**RECAP**

During the ovarian cycle, a primary oocyte within a developing follicle divides once to form a secondary oocyte. The follicle ruptures, releases the oocyte, and forms the corpus luteum that secretes progesterone and estrogen. ■

## The uterine cycle prepares the uterus for pregnancy

The **uterine cycle** is a series of structural and functional changes that occur in the endometrium of the uterus as it prepares each month for the possibility that a fertilized egg may arrive. The uterine cycle is linked to the ovarian cycle. Because the beginning of the cycle is defined as the first day of menstruation, we begin there. Note that although a complete cycle generally lasts about 28 days, many women have cycles that are shorter or longer. Figure 16.7 summarizes the ovarian, uterine, and hormonal events of a single menstrual cycle of 28 days.

- *Days 1–5: Menstrual phase.* If no fertilized egg from the previous cycle has arrived, body levels of estrogen and progesterone decline precipitously. Without these hormones the uterus cannot maintain its endometrial lining, which has thickened to prepare for a potential pregnancy. **Menstruation** is the process by which the endometrial lining disintegrates and its small blood vessels rupture. The shed tissue and blood pass through the vagina and are excreted. The period of visible menstrual flow, which lasts about 3–5 days, is called the *menstrual period.*
- *Days 6–14: Proliferative phase.* Triggered primarily by rising levels of estrogen from the next developing follicle, the endometrial lining begins to proliferate. It becomes thicker, more vascular, and more glandular. In addition, the lining of the cervix produces a thin, watery mucus that facilitates the passage of sperm, if present, into the uterus from the vagina.
- *Ovulation.* Ovulation occurs midway through the cycle, around the 14th day.
- *Days 15–28: Secretory phase.* Production of estrogen and especially progesterone by the corpus luteum causes the endometrium to continue proliferating, until it becomes almost three times thicker than it was after menstruation. Uterine glands mature and begin producing glycogen as a potential energy source for the embryo. The cervical mucus becomes thick and viscous, forming a "cervical plug" that prevents sperm and bacteria from entering the uterus. These structural changes in the endometrium prepare the uterus for a developing embryo.

If fertilization does not occur, degeneration of the corpus luteum at about 12 days after ovulation results in declining estrogen and progesterone levels, and another menstrual cycle begins.

The menstrual cycle is not a pleasant experience for some women, to put it mildly. It involves rapid hormonal and physical changes that can sometimes cause pain or mood changes.

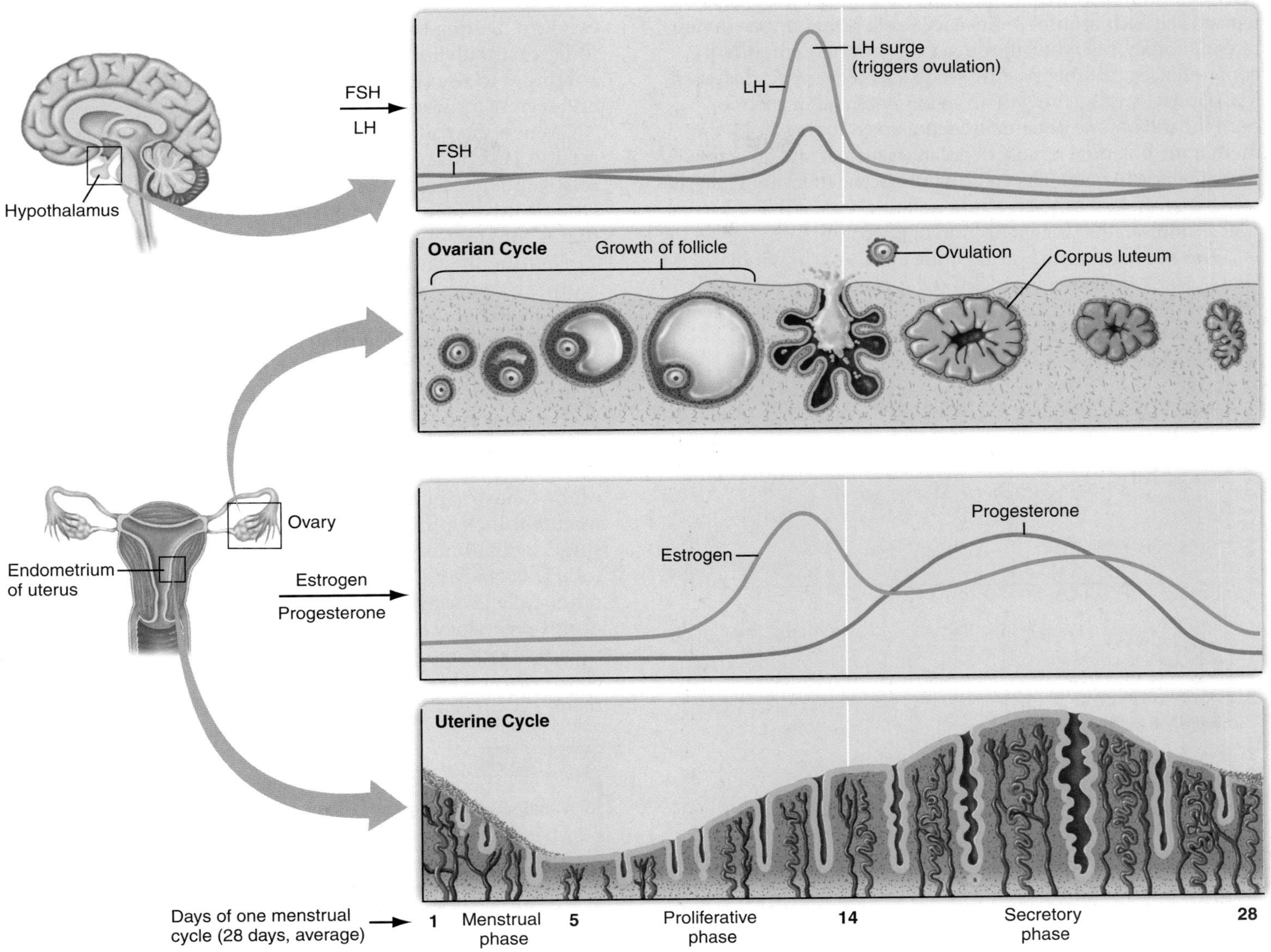


**Figure 16.7 The menstrual cycle.** The menstrual cycle consists of linked ovarian and uterine cycles. The ovarian cycle is a series of changes associated with oocyte maturation, which depends on the blood levels of FSH and LH. The uterine cycle involves changes in the endometrial lining of the uterus, which depend on the blood levels of estrogen and progesterone.

*Premenstrual syndrome (PMS)* is a group of symptoms often associated with the premenstrual period, including food cravings, mood swings, anxiety, back and joint pain, water retention, and headaches. It generally develops in the second half of the cycle, after ovulation, and lasts until menstruation begins. Exercise and medications that reduce pain and water retention can help.

Painful menstruation is known as *dysmenorrhea.* The endometrium of the uterus produces prostaglandins, which can trigger contractions and cramping of the uterine smooth muscle. Aspirin and ibuprofen may offer some relief from dysmenorrhea because these drugs inhibit prostaglandin formation. Although ovulation itself is usually not uncomfortable, some women experience a brief sharp pain when the follicle ruptures.

**RECAP**

Rising levels of estrogen cause the endometrium to proliferate. If pregnancy does not occur, hormone levels fall and the endometrial layer disintegrates and is shed, a process known as menstruation. ■

## Cyclic changes in hormone levels produce the menstrual cycle

The ovarian and uterine cycles are regulated by cyclic changes in hormone levels. Normally a typical negative feedback control loop controls the hormonal cycles most of the time. But there is a single *positive feedback* event just before the midpoint of the cycle that ultimately triggers ovulation and causes the cycle to repeat itself each month. Positive feedback regulatory events are rare in biology, but when they do occur they have important consequences. Another positive feedback mechanism, discussed in Chapter 11, is the firing of an action potential in a nerve—once the membrane potential is depolarized to threshold, the membrane potential rapidly depolarizes further and an action potential is generated. The cyclic nature of the menstrual cycle is somewhat analogous to an action potential except that it occurs over a month rather than a fraction of a second.

The key regulatory events of the cycle are shown in Figure 16.8. At the beginning of the cycle, LH rises slowly,

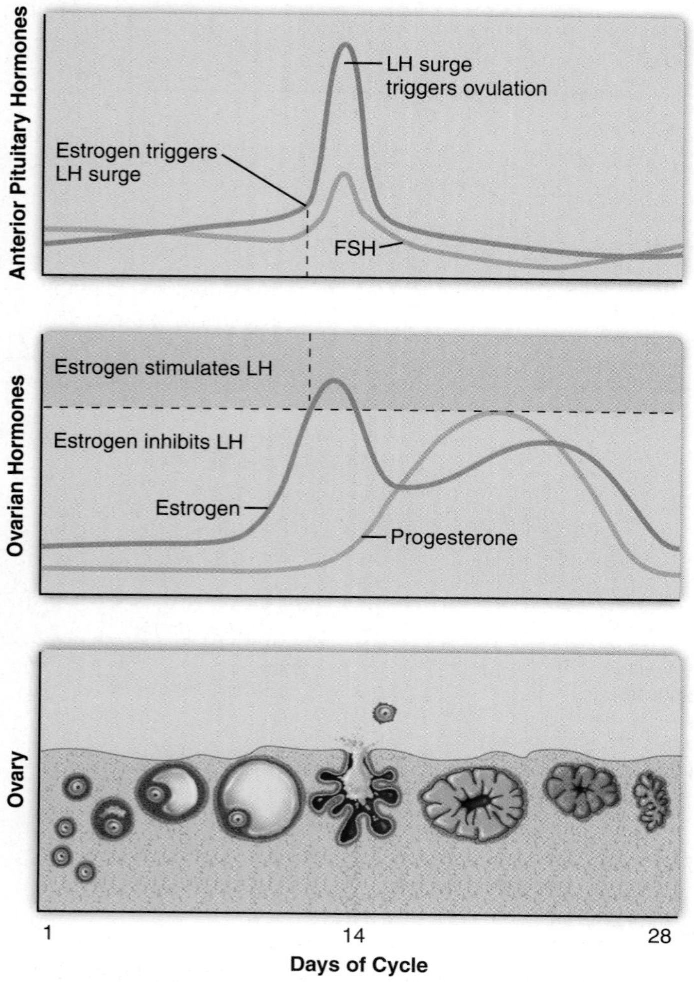


**Figure 16.8 Regulation of the menstrual cycle.** During the first half of the cycle LH and FSH stimulate follicular growth and development. The growing follicle secretes estrogen, which partially inhibits LH secretion. Shortly before the midpoint of the cycle estrogen from the mature follicle triggers the LH surge, which in turn triggers ovulation. In the second half of the cycle, estrogen and progesterone from the corpus luteum again inhibit LH and FSH secretion, preventing maturation of another follicle until it is determined (by regression of the corpus luteum and a decline in estrogen and progesterone concentrations) that pregnancy has not occurred. Then the cycle can begin again.

stimulating an immature follicle to develop and secrete estrogen. During this time estrogen from the developing follicle partially inhibits LH secretion, but LH nevertheless continues to rise slowly and the follicle continues to grow and secrete more estrogen.

When the follicle nears maturity and its estrogen secretion is sufficiently high, a threshold concentration of estrogen is reached at which it now *stimulates* LH release (the positive feedback event). This results in the LH surge that ultimately triggers ovulation at about day 14.

During the latter half of the menstrual cycle, the system returns to typical negative feedback control. The LH surge is short-lived because high but steady levels of estrogen and progesterone from the corpus luteum inhibit LH and FSH secretion. Without LH and FSH, the next follicle does not develop. This prevents a second ovulation until the cycle is complete and estrogen and progesterone return to low levels again.

From a functional standpoint, hormonal regulation of the menstrual cycle makes perfect sense. Because only a mature follicle produces enough estrogen to trigger the LH surge, ovulation is triggered at the precise moment that the follicle is ready. And once ovulation occurs, the start of another cycle is delayed until the body determines whether or not pregnancy has taken place. If there is no pregnancy, then estrogen and progesterone return to low levels within about two weeks and the cycle begins again with a slowly rising LH concentration.

**RECAP**

Ovulation is triggered by a surge of LH, which in turn is caused by the positive feedback effect of a high concentration of estrogen from the maturing follicle. During the second half of the menstrual cycle, sustained high levels of estrogen and progesterone inhibit further ovulation. ■

## 16.4 Human sexual response, intercourse, and fertilization

The human sexual response is a series of events that coordinate sexual function to accomplish intercourse and fertilization. The response can have up to four phases in both men and women:

1. *Excitement.* Increased sexual awareness and arousal
2. *Plateau.* Intense and continuing arousal
3. *Orgasm.* The peak of sexual sensations
4. *Resolution.* The abatement of arousal

### The male sexual response

In men, excitement is accompanied by pleasurable sensations from the penis and by an erection. Erection occurs when neural activity relaxes (dilates) arterioles leading

# Health Watch

## Erectile Dysfunction and Viagra Abuse

Healthy, young adult men generally do not have any difficulty achieving and sustaining an erection sufficient for sexual intercourse, except on rare occasions. But as they get older, many men find that it takes longer to become erect, more stimulation is needed, and the penis becomes less rigid than when they were younger. The occasions when an erection cannot be achieved or sustained may become more common. This is fairly normal; some decline in sexual function is expected with age.

True erectile dysfunction, on the other hand, is a medical condition. Formerly called impotence, *erectile dysfunction* is defined as the *repeated* inability to develop and maintain an erection sufficient for satisfactory sexual intercourse or activity. By that measure, erectile dysfunction is rare in 20-year-olds, reaches a prevalence of about 5% in 40-year-olds, and rises to 15–25% after age 65.

Until 1998, many of the standard treatments for erectile dysfunction were almost worse than the condition. They included vascular surgery, penile implants, vacuum devices to pull blood into the penis, and injections (with a needle and syringe) of a muscle-relaxing drug (alprostadil) into the base of the penis to enhance blood flow right before intercourse.

But then in 1998 Viagra (sildenafil) came on the market, followed by Levitra and Cialis. Although all three drugs were developed to treat a medical condition common only in older men, suddenly men of all ages were being diagnosed with erectile dysfunction. Physicians and health care officials are concerned that an increasing number of men are trying these drugs in the belief that they have "recreational" value.

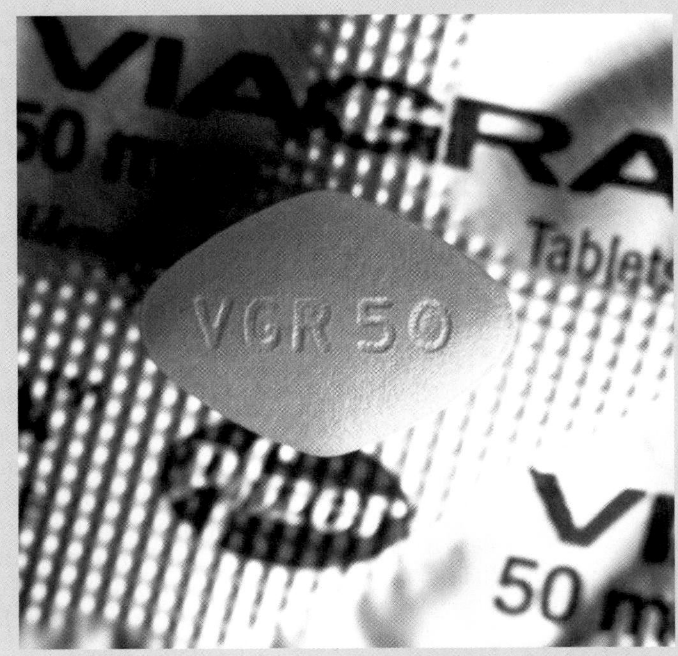


All three drugs work by enhancing the effects of the chemical messenger nitric oxide (NO). Recall from Chapter 13 that NO regulates local blood flow in many tissues. By relaxing vascular smooth muscle in the penis, NO promotes blood inflow to the penis and increases the chances that sexual stimulation will produce an erection.

Note that these drugs do not automatically *cause* an erection—they *allow* one to occur following normal sexual stimulation. They are not aphrodisiacs, and they won't turn a normal erection into one of mythic proportions. Furthermore, like all medications, they have side effects. Some men have experienced sudden vision loss from blocked blood flow to the optic nerve. Because they enhance the vasodilating action of NO, the drugs can cause a drop in blood pressure. This is especially true if they are taken with cardiovascular medications or street drugs such as ecstasy, methamphetamines, and ketamine.

The bottom line: Viagra is not a recreational drug. If you don't need it, don't take it. A drug that increases blood flow to the penis is not the only, or perhaps even the best, way to improve your sex life.

into vascular compartments within the penis. The compartments fill with blood, and as they fill they press on the veins draining the penis and reduce the rate of venous outflow. As more blood enters the penis and less blood leaves it, the penis swells, lengthens, and stiffens. Heart rate and breathing increase, as does the tone of skeletal muscle. Sights, sounds, memories, and other psychological stimuli; kissing or other physical contact; and especially physical contact with the penis all contribute to excitement. Arousal continues during the plateau phase, which can last for a few seconds or many minutes.

At some point sexual arousal becomes so great that **orgasm** occurs. An orgasm is a brief, intensely pleasurable reflex event that accomplishes **ejaculation,** or the expulsion of semen. During ejaculation, sympathetic nerve activity contracts smooth muscle in the seminal vesicles, epididymis, bulbourethral glands, and prostate to move glandular secretions into the urethra. The internal urethral sphincter closes tightly to prevent urine from leaking into the urethra, and the skeletal muscles at the base of the penis contract rhythmically, forcing semen out of the urethra in several spurts. In a typical ejaculation, the male expels about 3–4 ml (a teaspoon or more) of semen.

During the resolution phase, the erection subsides and breathing and heart rate return to normal. Generally a refractory period follows, during which another erection and orgasm cannot be achieved. The refractory period may last from several minutes up to several hours.

### The female sexual response

Women experience the same four phases of the sexual response. As in men, the excitement phase is triggered by sights, sounds, psychological stimuli, and physical stimulation, especially of the clitoris and breasts. Stimulation initiates neural reflexes that dilate blood vessels in the labia, clitoris, and nipples. During arousal the vagina and the area around the labia secrete lubricating fluids. Without these lubricating fluids intercourse can be difficult and sometimes painful for both partners.

The female orgasm, like that of the male, consists of rhythmic and involuntary muscular contractions. Contractions of the uterus and vagina are accompanied by intense feelings of pleasure and sensations of warmth and relaxation. The rate of orgasm is more variable in females than in males. Some women do not experience orgasms frequently, whereas others experience multiple orgasms within one period of sexual contact. Female orgasm is not required for fertilization or pregnancy, nor is arousal for that matter.

**RECAP**

Women and men experience the same four phases of sexual responsiveness. Sexual arousal in the male results in penile erection that leads to orgasm and ejaculation. Females experience sexual arousal and pleasurable orgasms marked by rhythmic muscular contractions. ■

### Fertilization: One sperm penetrates the egg

During ejaculation, the male may deposit several hundred million sperm inside the vagina, near the cervix. The sperm have a long way to go, however, before one of them encounters an egg. Random swimming takes some sperm through the cervical opening, through the uterus, and up the two oviducts. The journey can take hours or even a day or more. Fertilization occurs when a sperm encounters an oocyte in an oviduct and penetrates the zona pellucida (Figure 16.9). Some sperm may be viable for up to five days in the female reproductive tract, although most do not last more than two days.

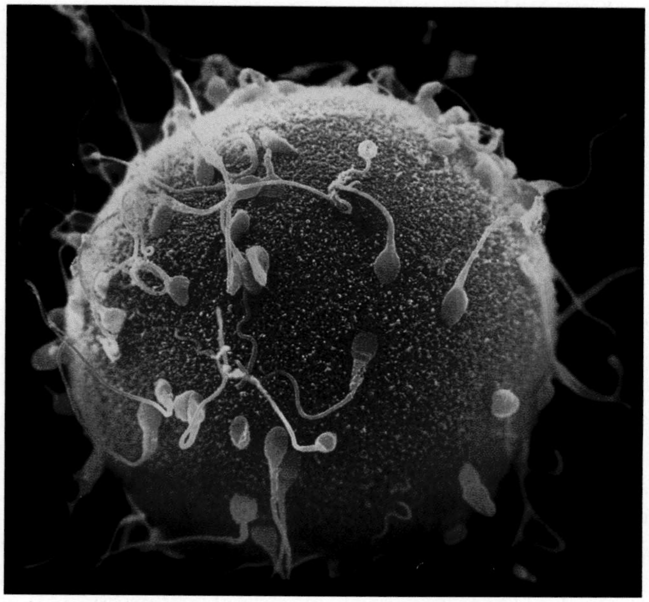

**Figure 16.9 Colored SEM (× 900) of sperm in contact with an egg.** Only one sperm will fertilize the egg.

**RECAP**

During ejaculation, the male deposits several hundred million sperm in the vagina. Fertilization of the egg by a single sperm occurs within five days, if it occurs at all. ■

## 16.5 Birth control methods: Controlling fertility

There are many reasons why couples or individuals might choose to control fertility, and many ways to do it. Birth control (contraceptive) methods vary widely in effectiveness (Table 16.3). Some methods reduce the chance of pregnancy from just a single intercourse; others virtually eliminate the chances of pregnancy for a lifetime. An understanding of the advantages and the limitations of each method will help you make an informed choice, should you choose to control your own fertility for any period of time.

### Abstinence: Not having intercourse

The only completely effective method of birth control is to not have sexual intercourse at all. Abstinence, as it is called, works for many people for short periods of time, and throughout life for others. Abstinence is natural in that no intervention or artificial method is employed. When abstinence is not the option of choice, there are still many ways to reduce the probability of pregnancy.

### Surgical sterilization: Vasectomy and tubal ligation

Both men and women may opt for surgical sterilization (Figure 16.10). Male surgical sterilization is called *vasectomy.* It can generally be performed in a doctor's office under local anesthesia. The doctor makes small incisions in the scrotum, locates each ductus deferens, and ties them in two places. The segments between the two ties are then removed, preventing sperm from reaching the urethra.

After a vasectomy the testes continue to produce testosterone and sperm, and sexual interest and all secondary sexual characteristics remain

**Table 16.3 Approximate failure rates of various contraceptive methods**

| Contraceptive method | Average failure rate[a] |
|---|---|
| None attempted | 85–90 |
| Spermicide alone | 20–50 |
| Withdrawal | 20–30 |
| Periodic abstinence | 20 |
| Diaphragm or cervical cap with spermicide | 15–20 |
| Male or female condoms | 10–20 |
| Hormonal contraceptives | |
| Oral contraceptives | 1–2 |
| Skin patch | 1 |
| Vaginal contraceptive ring | 1 |
| Injected hormonal contraceptives | Less than 1 |
| Intrauterine devices | Less than 1 |
| Vasectomy or tubal ligation | Less than 1 |
| Abstinence | 0 |

*Note:* The numbers should not be taken as absolutes since effectiveness will vary with the degree of proper use. The list should be viewed as an approximate rank order in terms of effectiveness.

[a]Annual pregnancies per 100 women.

*Source:* Adapted from *Birth Control Guide.* © 2003 U.S. Food and Drug Administration.

unchanged. With no access to the urethra, however, the sperm eventually are resorbed, just as they are if ejaculation never takes place. Generally it is impossible to detect a change in semen volume per ejaculation. If done properly, surgical male sterilization is close to foolproof. However, to be on the safe side, the surgeon will probably recommend doing a sperm count several months after the operation.

Female sterilization involves a *tubal ligation*. The doctor makes a small incision in the woman's abdominal wall, locates each oviduct, and ties (ligates) each at two sites. The sections between the ties are cut away, leaving the oocyte no way to reach the uterus or sperm to reach the oocyte. In a newer version of a tubal ligation, called a *hysteroscopy,* a flexible tube is inserted through the vagina and uterus and into the oviduct. The tube emits electrical current that seals shut the oviduct. Both tubal ligation and hysteroscopy are highly effective but require surgery that is slightly more difficult than in the male. In addition, tubal ligation may leave two small but possibly visible scars.

A drawback to surgical sterilization in both men and women is that although it *may* be possible to reverse, sterilization generally is permanent. Sterilization should be carefully considered before it is chosen as a method of birth control.

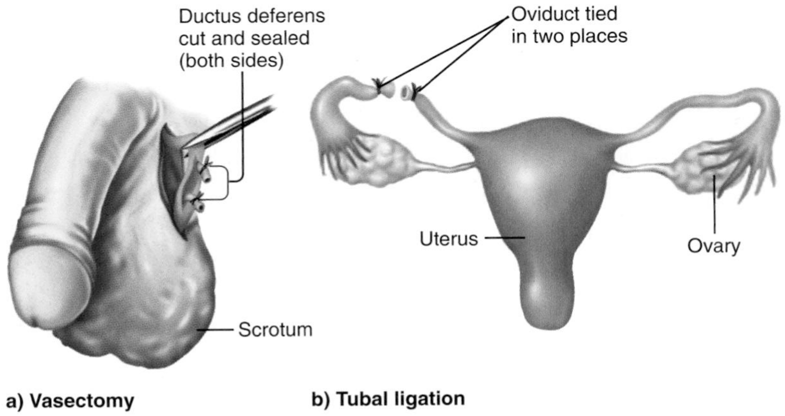


**Figure 16.10 Surgical sterilization. (a)** In a vasectomy, small incisions are made in the scrotum, and each ductus deferens is tied in two places. **(b)** In a tubal ligation, an incision is made in a woman's abdominal wall, the two oviducts are located, and each is tied in two places.

## Hormonal methods: Pills, injections, patches, and rings

Manipulation of hormone levels provides reasonably effective and safe methods of birth control. The most common is oral contraceptives, or *birth control pills.* Although the exact mix of hormones in the pills varies, they all administer synthetic progesterone and estrogen in amounts that inhibit the release of FSH and LH. That way, follicles do not mature and ovulation does not take place. It is important to take a pill at the same time every day; if pills are not taken regularly, ovulation (and pregnancy) may occur.

Most birth control pills are taken for three weeks and then replaced with placebo pills for a week so that normal menstrual periods occur each month. However, many physicians have questioned the need for regular monthly periods. In 2003 the FDA approved the first *continuous birth control pill (Seasonale)* that reduces the number of menstrual periods to only four per year. In 2007 the FDA approved a pill that eliminates all periods for a full year (*Lybrel*). Continuous birth control pills are particularly attractive to women who routinely suffer from PMS.

Roughly a third of all women in the U.S. use birth control pills for at least some period of their lives. Oral contraceptives have several side effects, some beneficial and others harmful. Some women report that oral contraceptives reduce cramps and menstrual flow, and they may offer some protection against cancers of the ovaries and uterus. On the negative side, oral contraceptives can cause acne, headaches, fluid retention, high blood pressure, or blood clots. Women who smoke have a greater risk of blood clots and vascular problems from birth control pills.

To avoid the drawbacks of taking—or forgetting to take—a daily pill, some women opt for hormone injections, skin patches, vaginal rings, or implants. *Depo-Provera* is a progesterone injection that lasts three months; *Lunelle* is a monthly injection of progesterone and estrogen. *Ortho Evra* is a patch that slowly releases hormones through the skin into the bloodstream. The user applies a fresh patch every week for three weeks straight, followed by one week with no patch, during which she menstruates. *NuvaRing,* a flexible ring about 2 inches in diameter, is inserted into the vagina, where it slowly releases hormones. The ring remains in place for three weeks, then is removed for one week to allow menstruation. Injections, patches, and rings can all have side effects similar to those of hormone pills, including weight gain, headaches, and irregular menstrual periods. The latest in contraception is *Implanon,* a matchstick-size rod containing synthetic progesterone that is implanted under the skin. Implanon provides effective contraception for up to three years.

Hormonal methods of contraception have the advantage of not interfering with sexual activity or foreplay in any way. However, none of them protect against sexually transmitted disease.

A variety of contraceptive methods is shown in Figure 16.11.

**RECAP**

Abstinence and male or female surgical sterilization are highly effective methods of birth control. Hormonal methods—pills, injections, patches, and rings—are also relatively effective but can have side effects. ■

### IUDs are inserted into the uterus

*Intrauterine devices,* or *IUDs,* are small pieces of plastic or metal that are inserted into the uterus by a health care provider. They should be removed only by a health care provider.

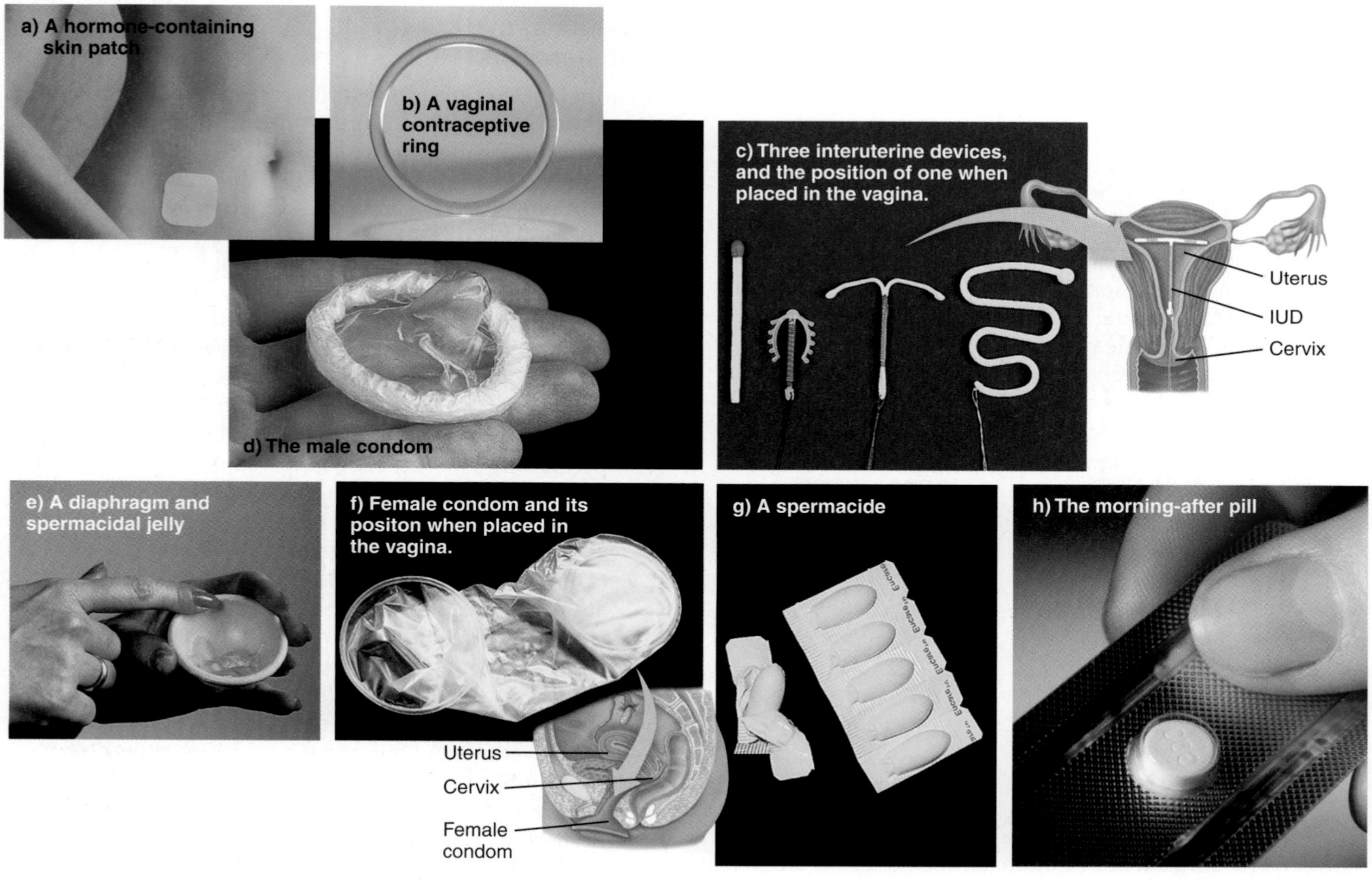


**Figure 16.11 Some birth control methods.**

IUDs create a mild chronic inflammation that prevents either fertilization or implantation of the fertilized egg in the uterine wall. On the positive side, they are relatively effective and, like hormonal methods, do not interfere with sexual activity. However, risks include uterine cramping and bleeding, infection, and possible damage to the uterus. IUDs offer no protection from sexually transmitted diseases.

An IUD called Mirena contains small amounts of a progesterone-like steroid. The steroid decreases the possibility of conception and also reduces menstrual flow, a significant benefit to women who normally experience heavy bleeding during their periods. Mirena is effective for up to five years.

### Diaphragms and cervical caps block the cervix

*Diaphragms* and *cervical caps* are latex devices that a woman inserts into her vagina. They cover the cervical opening and prevent sperm from entering the uterus.

Both types of devices must be fitted initially to the user's cervix. A disadvantage is that they must be inserted shortly before intercourse and then removed sometime later, making sexual activity less spontaneous. However, they are fairly effective, especially if inserted correctly and used with chemical spermicides. Diaphragms and cervical caps do not protect against sexually transmitted disease.

### Chemical spermicides kill sperm

Chemical *spermicides,* which destroy sperm, are available in a wide variety of forms—foams, creams, jellies, and douches. Their effectiveness varies; all reduce the risk of pregnancy, but none are 100% effective. Most are inserted into the vagina shortly before intercourse, except douches, which are used after intercourse (and are less effective). Some kill organisms that cause sexually transmitted diseases; others do not.

### Condoms trap ejaculated sperm

Despite their decidedly low-tech approach (a condom is just a balloon, really), *condoms* remain one of the most popular forms of birth control. They are fairly effective if used properly. Combining them with a chemical spermicide makes them even more effective. They also offer some protection against sexually transmitted diseases.

The male condom is a soft sheath, made of latex or animal membrane, that encloses the penis and traps ejaculated sperm. There is also a female condom that is essentially a polyurethane liner that fits inside the vagina. Condoms made of latex (but not animal membrane) have the tremendous advantage of offering some protection against disease, including AIDS.

**RECAP**

Physical barriers (diaphragms, cervical caps, and condoms) and chemical spermicides are moderately effective, and a few afford some protection against disease. IUDs, although more effective against pregnancy, are also more risky. ■

### Withdrawal and periodic abstinence

Two other methods, withdrawal and periodic abstinence, are not very effective in preventing pregnancy. In fact, for a sexually active couple they are so ineffective in the long run that some people believe they should not be classified as birth control at all. Couples who are serious about preventing pregnancy should consider more effective techniques.

In principle, the *withdrawal* method means that the man withdraws his penis from the vagina at just the right moment before ejaculation, so that ejaculation occurs outside the vagina. In practice, it takes skill and commitment on the part of the male and a lot of trust on the part of the female. In addition, some sperm can be flushed into the ejaculatory duct even before ejaculation, so there is a possibility of fertilization even if the man does not ejaculate.

People who practice *periodic abstinence* (sometimes called the *rhythm method*) rely on the fact that fertilization is possible for only a limited time in each menstrual cycle, defined by the life span of sperm and the time during which an oocyte can be fertilized after ovulation. As its name suggests, periodic abstinence requires the woman to avoid intercourse for about an eight-day span every month in the middle of her cycle, from approximately five days before ovulation to three days after ovulation. It is possible to determine the day of ovulation by carefully monitoring body temperature, because the temperature rises slightly—several tenths of a degree—at ovulation and stays elevated for about three days. However, it is difficult to determine which five days *precede* ovulation, because obviously it has not yet occurred.

**RECAP**

Withdrawal and periodic abstinence are not effective forms of birth control in the long term. ■

### Pills that can be used after intercourse

When intercourse has occurred in the absence of any birth control method, couples have several options that may either prevent pregnancy or terminate it early on. A product called *Preven* is a series of four pills that, if started within 72 hours *after* intercourse, may prevent a pregnancy entirely. Available only by prescription, Preven contains high doses of progesterone and estrogen. It is thought to work by preventing ovulation if it has not already occurred. It may also prevent fertilization even after ovulation, but this is not well documented. Another postcoital pill, *Plan B,* contains progesterone only. Both Plan B and Preven are commonly called "emergency contraception" or "morning after" pills. Plan B is now available without a prescription to those over 18.

More controversial is *Mifeprex* (mifepristone, formerly called RU-486), a drug that *blocks* the action of progesterone. By blocking the action of progesterone, Mifeprex can prevent the endometrial lining from proliferating. If taken in the first few days after intercourse, it can prevent pregnancy by preventing implantation of the pre-embryo in the uterine lining. However, Mifeprex is more commonly prescribed *after* a pregnancy has been identified, because its main advantage is that it is effective up to seven weeks after pregnancy. By causing the endometrial lining to regress to the point that it can no longer nourish the fetus, Mifeprex essentially causes a very early-stage chemical abortion. For this reason, Mifeprex has generally been labeled an "abortion pill" rather than an emergency contraception. Although it has been available in Europe for many years, concern over its mode of action caused so much controversy in the U.S. that it was not approved for sale until 2000.

### Elective abortion

An *elective abortion* is an elective termination of a pregnancy. In common usage the term "elective" is generally understood without being stated. Aside from the very early-stage use of Mifeprex, an abortion can be performed in several ways, including vacuum suctioning of the uterus, surgical scraping of the uterine lining, or infusion of a strong saline solution that causes the fetus to be rejected. Sometimes abortions are performed in cases of incest or rape, or when continuing the pregnancy would endanger the mother's health. Some women choose to have an abortion if medical tests reveal a nonviable fetus.

Abortions are highly controversial. Some people support a woman's right to choose her own reproductive destiny, whereas others support an embryo's right to life. The beliefs on both sides are often based on strongly held moral and religious convictions.

**RECAP**

Pills can be taken after intercourse to forestall ovulation or prevent a pregnancy from continuing. Abortion is a controversial procedure that terminates a pregnancy electively. ■

### The future in birth control

Several new forms of birth control are still in the research and development stage. Possibilities include a male birth control pill that reduces sperm production, and several vaccines for women. For instance, a vaccine is being developed to immunize women against human chorionic gonadotropin, the hormone that maintains the corpus luteum so implantation can occur. Also under development is a vaccine against sperm.

As it stands today, women have most of the choices. It's worth knowing what the options are so that one's choices can be well-informed (Figure 16.12).

**Figure 16.12 Controlling reproduction.** Women have many options for choosing when (or if) to have a baby. Good information can be obtained from a variety of sources, including health care professionals and counselors.

## 16.6 Infertility: Inability to conceive

If both partners are healthy, pregnancy is usually not difficult to achieve. As Table 16.3 shows, the annual pregnancy rate without any birth control averages 85–90%. Timing can improve the odds. For example, if a couple wants to increase their chance of having a child, they might have intercourse near the middle of the menstrual cycle, around the time of ovulation.

But some couples find it difficult to become pregnant. Next we describe conditions that can impair fertility and solutions that are available.

### Infertility can have many causes

A couple is considered infertile if they fail to achieve pregnancy after a year of trying. By this definition, about 15% of all couples in the U.S. are infertile. Infertility is about equally attributable to men and women.

Male infertility is the insufficiency or lack of normal, healthy sperm. The chance of any one sperm achieving reproductive success is so low that men whose sperm count is below 60 million per ejaculation are, for all practical purposes, infertile. Reasons for a low sperm count include low testosterone levels, immune disorders that attack the sperm, radiation, certain drugs such as anabolic steroids, and diseases such as mumps and gonorrhea.

Sperm function best at temperatures slightly cooler than body temperature. One simple measure that may raise the viable sperm count is to switch from tight-fitting underwear, which hold the testicles close to the body, to looser-fitting boxer shorts.

Causes of female infertility are more variable. One of the most common reasons is *pelvic inflammatory disease (PID)*, a general term for any extensive bacterial infection of the internal female reproductive organs. PID that involves the oviducts can result in scar tissue that seals the oviducts shut, preventing passage of either eggs or sperm (Figure 16.13). Abnormal production of LH or FSH may limit the development of oocytes into follicles. Irregular menstrual cycles can make it difficult to time the period of ovulation. Some women produce strongly acid vaginal secretions or thick cervical mucus that damage sperm or make it difficult for sperm to move toward the egg. Uterine tumors may interfere with implantation.

Some women (1–3%) develop *endometriosis*, a condition in which endometrial tissue migrates up the oviduct during a menstrual period and implants on other organs such as the ovaries, the walls of the bladder, or the colon. There it grows, stimulated each month by the normal hormonal cycle. Endometriosis can cause pain and infertility, but can sometimes be corrected by surgery, drugs, or hormone therapy.

Female reproductive capacity is more affected by age than male reproductive capacity. By the mid 40s, women begin to run out of oocytes. In addition, the ovaries become less responsive to LH and FSH, leading eventually to menopause and the end of menstrual cycles. Oocytes ovulated later in life are also more likely to have been damaged by years of exposure to radiation, chemicals, and disease.

A common cause of failure to achieve reproductive success even when the couple is fertile is spontaneous abortion, or *miscarriage*, defined as the loss of a fetus before it can survive outside the uterus. Perhaps as many as one-third of all pregnancies end in miscarriages, some of them so quickly that a woman has no idea she ever conceived.

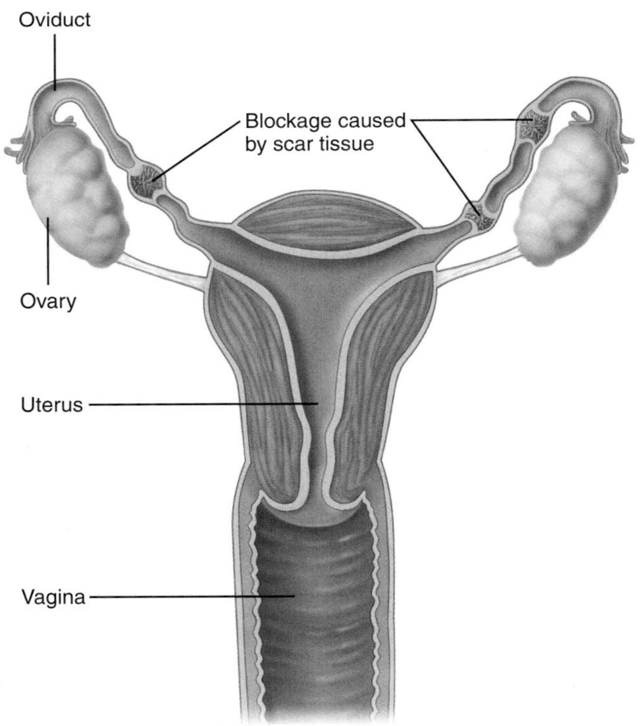


**Figure 16.13 Pelvic inflammatory disease can make women sterile.** Bacteria that migrate from the vagina into the oviducts can inflame the oviducts, leading to scarring and either partial or complete closure of the oviduct.

**RECAP**

Male infertility is an insufficiency or lack of sperm. Causes of female infertility are variable and include failure to ovulate, damage to oviducts, pelvic inflammatory disease, secretions that impair sperm function, uterine tumors, endometriosis, age-related changes, and miscarriages. ■

## Enhancing fertility

Several options are available for infertile couples who wish to have a child. None guarantee success and most are expensive. It is not unusual for couples to spend tens of thousands of dollars, even $200,000 or more, to conceive a child. Techniques include artificial insemination, *in vitro* fertilization, gamete intrafallopian transfer, and fertility-enhancing drugs. Some couples choose to hire a surrogate mother.

**Artificial insemination** By far the easiest, most common, and least expensive technique is *artificial insemination:* sperm are placed with a syringe into the vagina or uterus, as close to the time of ovulation as possible. Artificial insemination is the method of choice when the man's sperm count is low, because his sperm can be collected over a period of time and all delivered at once. It is also a good option for men who produce no sperm, in which case the woman may receive sperm from an anonymous donor who has sold his semen to a "sperm bank," and for single women who make the personal choice to become a parent. Over 20,000 babies are born in the U.S. each year as a result of artificial insemination.

***In vitro* fertilization** *In vitro fertilization (IVF)* essentially means fertilization in a test tube, outside the body (*vitreus* is Latin for "glass"). A clinician uses a needle, guided by ultrasound, to harvest immature eggs from the woman. The eggs mature in laboratory glassware under sterile conditions, and then sperm are added. Two to four days later, when it is clear that fertilization has occurred because cells are dividing (Figure 16.14), the embryo is inserted into the woman's uterus through her cervix. If the embryo implants in the endometrium, pregnancy and fetal development are generally normal.

IVF is effective when infertility results from damaged oviducts or female secretions that prevent contact between sperm and egg. If the woman cannot produce viable eggs because of an ovarian problem, IVF can be done with an egg

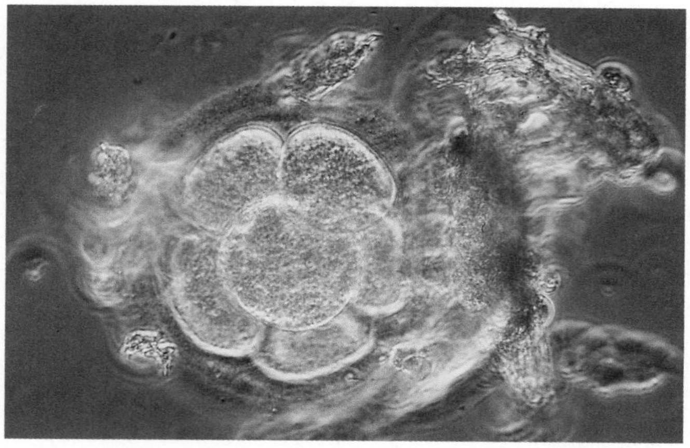

**Figure 16.14 A human embryo at the eight-cell stage, approximately 2-1/2 days after *in vitro* fertilization.**

donated by another woman. It is even possible to freeze embryos so they can be used later, without having to collect new eggs and start over again.

IVF results in a live birth only about 20% of the time, so some couples try it several times before achieving pregnancy. To improve the chances of pregnancy, some women elect to have three or more embryos transferred at once. Consquently, multiple births are common among women undergoing IVF.

**GIFT and ZIFT** *Gamete intrafallopian transfer (GIFT)* attempts to simplify the IVF procedure and improve the odds of success. In GIFT, unfertilized eggs and sperm are placed directly into an oviduct (Fallopian tube) through a small incision in the woman's abdomen. In a variation of this method, *zygote intrafallopian transfer (ZIFT)*, the egg is fertilized outside the woman's body and then inserted in the same way (a *zygote* is a fertilized egg).

**Fertility-enhancing drugs** Medications are available to boost the production of developing eggs. Sometimes these drugs are tried before IVF, or given to women who are preparing for IVF so that several eggs may be harvested at once. Occasionally multiple pregnancies can occur as a result of the medications themselves. When you hear news reports of multiple births of four or more babies, the mother was almost certainly taking fertility-enhancing drugs.

**Surrogate motherhood** Some couples choose to pay another woman, called a *surrogate mother*, to become pregnant and bear a baby for them. The prospective parents may contribute sperm, eggs, or both.

Surrogate motherhood raises a number of difficult legal issues that the couple and mother should explore before entering into an agreement. The surrogate must confirm legally that she will give up the baby for adoption to the parents. However, there have not yet been enough court cases to define legal precedents should conflicts arise between the surrogate mother and the prospective parents.

**RECAP**

A variety of methods are available to improve fertility; the choice varies according to the cause of the infertility. Options include artificial insemination, in vitro fertilization, gamete intrafallopian transfer, zygote intrafallopian transfer, fertility-enhancing drugs, and surrogate motherhood. ■

## 16.7 Sexually transmitted diseases: A worldwide concern

Disorders of the reproductive systems fall into four classes: (1) infertility, (2) complications of pregnancy, (3) cancers and tumors of the reproductive organs, and (4) sexually transmitted diseases. We have already considered infertility and approaches to overcoming it. We discuss potential complications of pregnancy in Chapter 21, and we cover cancer in detail in Chapter 18. In the rest of this chapter, we focus on sexually transmitted diseases.

**Sexually transmitted diseases (STDs)** are transmitted by sexual contact, whether genital, oral-genital, or anal-genital. STDs are on the rise worldwide, apparently because young people are becoming sexually active earlier, and birth control reduces the fear of pregnancy. In the U.S. alone, over 12 million people contract an STD each year. A quarter of them are teenagers.

STDs are not just a social embarrassment. Some cause serious organ damage, and a few are deadly. Many don't actually affect the reproductive organs, even though they are transmitted sexually. Some STDs are difficult if not impossible to cure, so an ounce of prevention is definitely worth a pound of (attempted) cure.

Now that we have studied the human reproductive systems, you can see why STDs are so common. Most disease organisms cannot live long outside a warm, moist environment. That's why their most common sites of entry are those that are warm and moist, such as the digestive tract, respiratory tract, and, of course, the reproductive organs. Some organisms, such as the virus that causes AIDS, travel in body fluids. Others, like the pubic lice known as "crabs," simply take the opportunity afforded by intimate contact to hop from one human to another.

STD-causing organisms include viruses, bacteria, fungi, protozoa, and even arthropods. Table 16.4 summarizes common STDs, including causes, symptoms, potential complications, and treatments.

### Bacterial STDs: Gonorrhea, syphilis, and chlamydia

**Gonorrhea** Caused by the bacterium *Neisseria gonorrhoeae*, gonorrhea is easily transmitted—roughly 50% of women and 20% of men contract it after a single exposure. It can be

**Table 16.4 Sexually transmitted diseases**

| Disease | Organism | Symptoms | Complications | Comments |
|---|---|---|---|---|
| Gonorrhea | *Neisseria gonorrhoeae* bacterium | Men: Pus from penis, painful urination<br>Women: Painful urination, vaginal discharge | Men: Inflamed testicles and sterility<br>Women: Pelvic inflammatory disease, scarring, sterility | May be asymptomatic, or symptoms may disappear even though disease remains; can be treated with antibiotics |
| Syphilis | *Treponema pallidum* bacterium | Primary: Chancre at infection site | Secondary: Non-itchy rash, hair loss, gray areas of infection on mucous membranes<br>Tertiary: Widespread damage to cardiovascular and nervous systems, blindness, skin ulcers | Symptoms may disappear spontaneously between phases; can be treated with antibiotics |
| Chlamydia | *Chlamydia trachomatis* bacterium | Men: Discharge from penis, burning during urination<br>Women: Vaginal discharge, burning, and itching | Pelvic inflammatory disease, urethral infections, sterility, complications of pregnancy | Can be treated with antibiotics |
| AIDS (also see Chapter 9) | Human immunodeficiency virus (HIV) | Fatigue, fever, chills, night sweats, swollen lymph nodes or spleen, diarrhea, loss of appetite, weight loss | Infections, pneumonia, meningitis, tuberculosis, encephalitis, cancer | Asymptomatic phase can last for years, even though disease is still contagious; no cure |
| Hepatitis B (also see Chapter 14) | Hepatitis B virus | Nausea, fatigue, jaundice, abdominal pain, arthritis | Cirrhosis, liver failure | Preventable with a vaccine |
| Genital herpes | Herpes simplex virus types 1 and 2 | Genital blisters, painful urination, fever, swollen lymph nodes in groin | Symptoms disappear during remission, then reappear; contagious during active phases | Drugs available to control active phase |
| Genital warts | Human papillomavirus (HPV) | Warts on penis, labia, anus, or in vagina or cervix | Risk factor for cancers of cervix or penis | Warts can be removed by surgery, freezing, or drugs. Preventable with a vaccine |
| Yeast infections | *Candida albicans* | Men: Discharge from penis, painful urination<br>Women: Vaginal pain, inflammation, cheesy discharge | Can develop in women without sexual contact, but is transmitted sexually to men | Can be treated with antifungal drugs |
| Trichomoniasis | *Trichomonas vaginalis* protozoan | Men: Discharge from inflamed penis<br>Women: Frothy, foul-smelling vaginal discharge | Recurrent urethral infections | Can be treated with drugs |
| Pubic lice | *Phthirus pubis* | Intense itching, skin irritation in pubic area; lice are small but visible | Can also be transmitted through infected sheets, clothing | Can be treated with drugs |

transmitted to the mouth and throat by oral-genital contact, or to the mouth or eyes through hand contact. An infected mother can pass gonorrhea to her child during birth, causing a potentially blinding eye infection.

In men, early symptoms include discharge of pus from the penis and painful urination, but the symptoms may disappear even though the disease remains. Women may experience a burning sensation during urination and vaginal discharge that may not appear particularly abnormal. However, nearly 20% of infected men and up to 80% of infected women show no symptoms, at least for periods of time, and so do not seek medical advice. Left untreated, gonorrhea can lead to inflammation, scarring, and sterility.

Gonorrhea is far less common than it was just 20 years ago (Figure 16.15). Although gonorrhea generally responds to antibiotics, in recent years antibiotic-resistant strains have emerged.

# Directions in Science

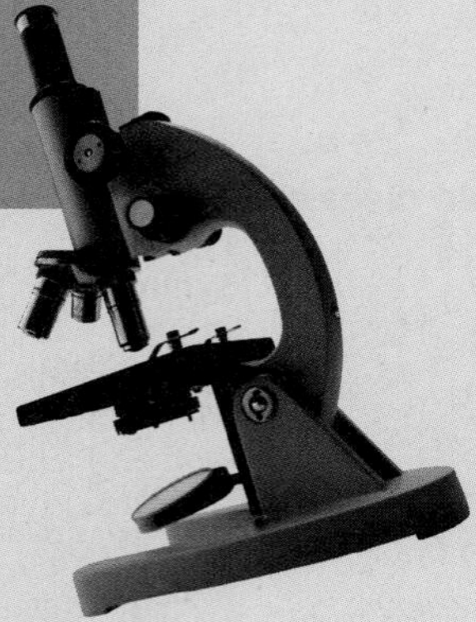

## Assisted Reproductive Technologies

July 25, 1978, is the birthday of Louise Joy Brown, the first human being ever conceived *in vitro,* or outside the human body. Her parents and the two British physicians who performed the procedure had been trying for nearly a decade to accomplish the feat. The announcement of the birth of the first "test-tube baby" changed reproductive choices forever and created a new industry called assisted reproductive technologies (ART).

The birth of Louise Joy Brown came less than 10 years after a Harris poll reported that the majority of Americans thought that techniques like *in vitro* fertilization were "against God's will." The media paid the feat a great deal of attention, and the subject of *in vitro* fertilization was debated by ethicists, physicians, and religious leaders. The outcry from strong lobbyist groups caused the federal government to ban the use of federal dollars for ART research. The ban still stands today. However, the government stopped short of declaring *in vitro* fertilization illegal.

Public outcry soon died down, and as infertile couples began clamoring for the technology, the private sector took up the call. The first *in vitro* fertilization procedure in the U.S. took place in 1982 in Norfolk, Virginia. Today there are approximately 422 ART clinics (or fertility clinics, as they are more commonly known) in the U.S. where couples go for *in vitro* fertilization, gamete intrafallopian transfer (GIFT), and zygote intrafallopian transfer (ZIFT). Since ART clinics do not receive federal support, infertile couples may spend tens of thousands of dollars in the process of having a child. The user pays, not the taxpayer.

Some scientists argue that the government's hands-off approach has caused the U.S. to lag behind other countries in reproductive technologies, because the fledgling ART clinics have had to develop and advance the technologies themselves. This is debatable, given the ultimate success of the private clinics.

In the end the government did have to get involved. With a rapidly increasing number of private clinics performing ART, legislators recognized a need to regulate the industry. The U.S. Congress passed the Fertility Clinic Success Rate and Certification Act in 1992, which requires that the Centers for Disease Control and Prevention (CDC) publish pregnancy success rates for all ART clinics in the U.S. The CDC lists the names and locations of every clinic and publishes their individual success rates, broken down by type of procedure.

According to the CDC, the 422 reporting ART clinics performed 134,260 ART cycles (pregnancy attempts) in 2005, the most recent year for which data have been compiled. The average age of the female client was 36. The result was 52,041 babies in one year — up from just one in 1978. Artificial reproductive technologies have gone from experimental to highly practical in just 25 years.

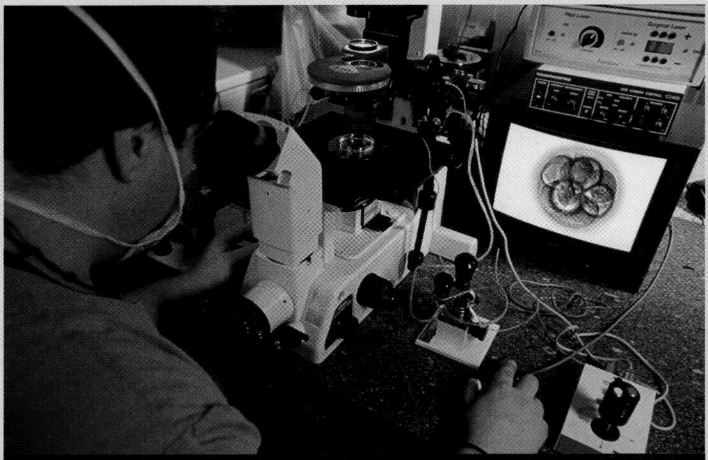

A technician examines an early-stage human embryo prior to transfer

British tabloids announce the birth of the first "test-tube baby."

DAILY Mirror

THERE'S More TO THE Mirror IF IT'S FUN YOU'RE AFTER

TEST-TUBE BABY GIRL

STEEL IS QUIZZED ON SCOTT

DAILY EXPRESS

THE VOICE OF BRITAIN

PLAY TIME EXPRESS See Page 20

Born safe—the world's first test-tube baby weighs in at 5lb 12oz and mother's delighted

By Harry Pugh

IT'S A GIRL! THE WORLD'S FIRST TEST-TUBE BABY WAS BORN LATE LAST NIGHT. SHE CAME INTO THE WORLD NEAR MIDNIGHT. BOTH MOTHER AND BABY ARE WELL.

IT'S A GIRL

Steptoe's obsession

First tes and med a mother

IT'S

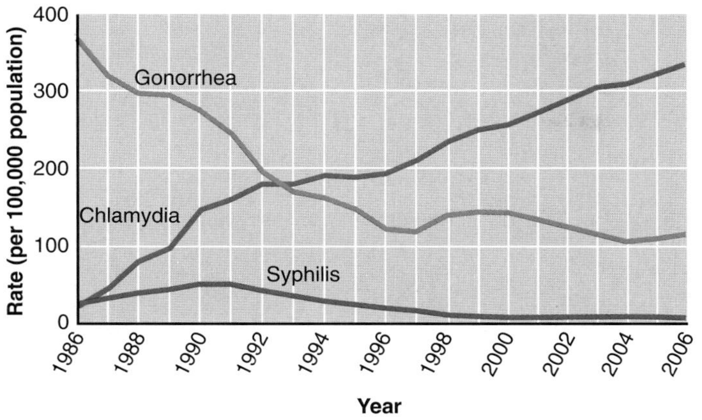


**Figure 16.15 Relative rates of infection for the three most common bacterial STDs.** Data are expressed in terms of numbers of infection per 100,000 population per year in the U.S., since 1986. Syphilis rates refer to primary and secondary syphilis.

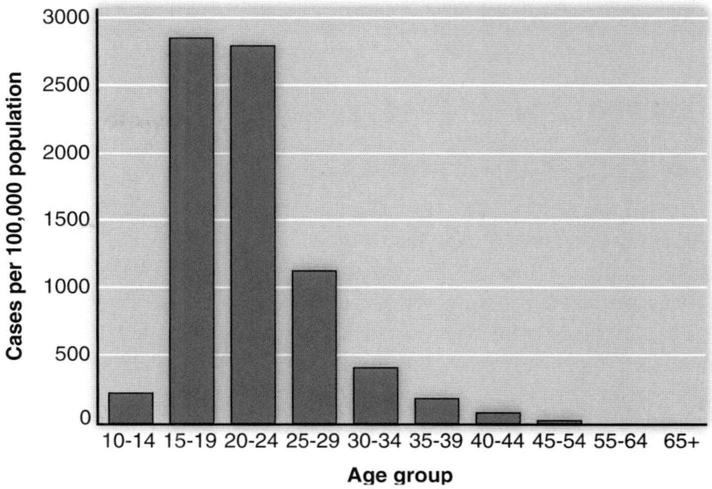


**Figure 16.16 Rates of chlamydia infection in women, by age.** Young women ages 15–24 are particularly likely to contract chlamydia.

**Syphilis** The bacterium *Treponema pallidum* causes syphilis, one of the most dangerous STDs if left untreated. Fortunately it is no longer very common. Syphilis develops in three phases, often separated by periods in which the disease seems to disappear. One to eight weeks after infection, the disease enters its *primary phase.* A hard, dry, bacteria-filled sore, called a *chancre,* appears at the infection site. The chancre is not painful and disappears spontaneously after several weeks; infected women may not even notice it.

During the *secondary phase,* which can last several years, the bacteria invade lymph nodes, blood vessels, mucous membranes, bones, and the nervous system. Symptoms include a widespread but non-itchy rash, hair loss, and gray patches representing areas of infection on mucous membranes. Again the symptoms may disappear, and sometimes the symptoms end there. However, some people progress to the *tertiary phase* characterized by widespread damage to the cardiovascular and nervous systems, blindness, skin ulcers, and eventual death. A child of a syphilis-infected woman can be born blind, malformed, or dead because the bacteria cross the placenta into the developing fetus. Syphilis can be treated with penicillin.

**Chlamydia** Chlamydia is a bacterial infection caused by *Chlamydia trachomatis.* Although it is easily cured with antibiotics, it often goes undiagnosed and untreated because the symptoms are so mild. Men may experience a discharge from the penis and a burning sensation during urination, and women may have a vaginal discharge and a burning and itching sensation.

Women are diagnosed with chlamydia three times as often as men, leading health officials to suspect that most men, and even most women, go undiagnosed. Women between 15 and 24 years old are especially at risk, with reported rates of infection nearly 10 times that of the general population (Figure 16.16).

The eventual health consequences for women can be severe despite the apparent mildness of the symptoms. If left untreated, chlamydia can cause pelvic inflammatory disease, permanent scarring of the fallopian tubes, complications of pregnancy, and sterility. It can also infect a newborn's eyes and lungs at birth, leading to pneumonia. Health officials recommend that all sexually active women under the age of 26 be tested for chlamydia every year.

**RECAP**

Major bacterial STDs include gonorrhea, syphilis, and chlamydia. If not treated, gonorrhea and chlamydia can cause inflammation and sterility; syphilis can cause widespread damage to body systems and eventual death. ■

## Viral STDs: HIV, hepatitis B, genital herpes, and HPV

The government does not keep accurate statistics on most of the viral STDs. Some of them are very dangerous; others are just very common.

**HIV** Human immunodeficiency virus (HIV), the virus that causes *acquired immune deficiency syndrome (AIDS),* is one of the most dangerous STDs of our time. One of the most dangerous features of AIDS is that it can be transmitted from person to person long before symptoms of the disease appear.

HIV slowly destroys the immune system over a period of years. Early symptoms include fatigue, fever and chills, night sweats, swollen lymph nodes or spleen, diarrhea, loss of appetite, and weight loss. As the immune system grows weaker, patients experience numerous infections and complications that lead eventually to death. There are drugs that can keep it in remission, but it cannot be cured. AIDS and its global impact were discussed in detail in Chapter 9.

# Current Issue

## Would You Like a Boy or a Girl?

Your parents probably did not know whether you were a boy or a girl until the very moment you were born. Prenatal diagnostic tests were generally advised only when there was a definite risk of genetic disease. Ultrasound, typically done between 18 to 26 weeks of pregnancy, could detect gender only about 80% of the time.

Today, expectant parents may be able to discover the gender of a fetus as early as five weeks. They may even be able to select gender (and several other genetic traits) ahead of time. If you were going to have a child, would you want to know whether it's a boy or a girl ahead of time?

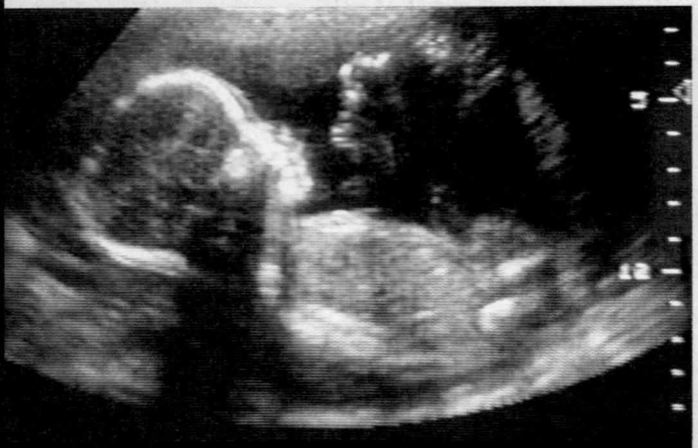

Ultrasound can detect the gender of a fetus

### Determining the Gender of the Fetus

A biotech company called Acu-Gen Biolab, Inc. now offers a gender testing service and kit called Baby Gender Mentor™. According to the company, Baby Gender Mentor can determine the gender of an unborn child with 99.9% accuracy as early as five weeks after fertilization. For $275, the service analyzes a small blood sample from the mother and provides confidential results via e-mail, generally within 48 hours. Baby Gender Mentor is based on the principle that a small amount of fetal DNA is generally present in the mother's blood plasma. The presence of Y-chromosomal material in the mother's blood plasma indicates a boy; the presence of only X-chromosomal material indicates a girl. (We discuss the X and Y chromosomes in Chapter 19.)

A word of caution is due here. Baby Gender Mentor is not regulated by the FDA, and the company won't release the "scientific information" on which their 99.9% accuracy is based. Blog sites are reporting that the test is not nearly as accurate as claimed by the company.

Early gender detection can be a wonderful tool that helps expectant parents begin bonding emotionally with their baby. But note that detection at five weeks also allows sufficient time for an elective abortion if the parents strongly desire a particular gender and the fetus turns out to be the "wrong one." Does this sound far-fetched? In South and East Asia, where there is a strong cultural preference for male children, the growing availability of prenatal testing has increased the selective abortion of female fetuses. In India, prenatal testing and selective abortions are thought to be responsible for a deficit of over 500,000 girls every year. In nature, births average a ratio of 105 boys for every 100 girls, but in some parts of China the ratio is closer to 120 boys for every 100 girls, again due to selective abortion and infanticide. It's estimated that up to 100 million "missing women" in Asia have resulted from the ability to detect gender before birth.

### Improving the Odds by Selecting the Right Sperm

Some parents prefer to maximize the odds of choosing their child's sex before pregnancy, not after. A procedure called *sperm sorting* is based on the fact that the X (female) chromosome is larger and carries more DNA than the Y (male) chromosome. First, the sperm in a semen sample from the would-be father are labeled with a fluorescent dye that attaches to

*Parents can now select the gender of their children.*

## the facts...

- It is now possible to determine the gender of a fetus by five weeks after fertilization with a simple home testing kit.
- The ability to determine gender early in pregnancy may lie behind millions of elective abortions worldwide each year based on fetal gender alone.
- Sperm sorting can improve the odds of having a child of the desired gender. *In vitro* fertilization and pre-implantation testing can virtually guarantee it.
- As our ability to specify gender and other genetic traits develops, so does the possibility of being able to "customize" children genetically.

DNA. Because sperm with the female (X) chromosome have more DNA, they fluoresce more brightly than sperm with the male (X) chromosome. The sperm are then sorted on the basis of light intensity by a machine called a *flow cytometer.* After sorting, either the "female-enriched" or the "male-enriched" sperm sample is inserted into the mother using artificial insemination. For couples who want a girl, sperm sorting results in an average of 88% X-bearing sperm in a sample, with 91% of the resulting babies being female. The odds of successfully producing a boy are somewhat lower but still better than average: 73% Y-bearing sperm in a sample and a male birth rate of 76%.

Do you think gender selection is discriminatory? Some would say yes—after all, by definition it values one sex over the other. In some Asian countries, these decisions may be based on economics: male children are viewed as an extra pair of helping hands while female children may be seen as a financial liability. But why do Western parents prefer one gender over the other? One U.S. couple reportedly wanted a girl so they could buy little dresses; another man preferred to leave his business to a son rather than a daughter. A couple in the United Kingdom desperately wanted a girl because one of their daughters had died. Do you think these motivations are valid? Are they any more or less valid than Asian families' desire for sons? How should we feel about using the power we already have over reproduction for purposes of vanity or personal preference?

In some countries there is a strong cultural preference for male babies.

### Beyond Gender Selection: Customizing Our Kids?

Molly Nash was born with Franconi's anemia, a rare incurable disease in which the bone marrow does not produce blood cells normally. Typically people with this condition die by their early 20s. Franconi's anemia is a genetic disorder; although Molly's parents do not have the disease themselves, both carry the gene that causes it.

In a desperate attempt to save their daughter, Molly's parents turned to preimplantation genetic diagnosis (PGD), an experimental procedure that is combined with *in vitro* fertilization to screen embryos for specific genetic conditions. Eggs were harvested from the mother's uterus, fertilized, and tested for the Franconi gene. The embryos that lacked the fatal gene had further testing to screen for those that would be a safe donor match for Molly, and were then implanted in the mother's uterus. After four IVF attempts, the mother gave birth to a healthy boy whom they named Adam. Blood from Adam's umbilical cord was infused into Molly shortly after his birth, and apparently it cured her (see the Current Issue in Chapter 7). Today both children are healthy, and Molly has started school.

When the Nash story first hit the press it caused a firestorm of controversy. The media labeled Adam the "savior sibling" and predicted dire effects on his future mental health from knowing that he had been brought into being to save his sister. Molly's parents insisted that they wanted more children anyway, so this procedure enabled them to have a healthy child and also save their daughter's life. However, many people questioned whether it is ethical to have a child for the purpose of being a tissue donor. And of course there is always the issue of what happens to all the embryos not selected by Molly's parents because they were not a good match for Molly.

PGD can also be performed to select embryos on the basis of gender, virtually guaranteeing a child of the desired sex. While the American Society of Reproductive Medicine does not endorse PGD for sex selection, a number of fertility clinics perform it for this purpose. Sometimes gender selection is advertised as selecting against prostate cancer by choosing female embryos, or against breast cancer by opting for males.

There's no doubt that as medical technology improves, so will our ability to predetermine gender and other genetic traits. We already know that genes determine physical characteristics such as hair, skin, and eye color. Scientists are also investigating the genetic basis of intelligence, musical ability, even personal qualities such as shyness. Should we be able to pick and choose from a menu of specific traits for our offspring? Do we want to?

*The Nash family. Linda and Jack Nash used genetic selection to choose an embryo that could donate umbilical cord blood to their daughter upon birth.*

### Questions to consider

1. *If you and your partner decided to have a child together, would you want to know its gender before it is born?*
2. *Would you try to select the gender of your next child by one of the methods described here? Explain why or why not.*
3. *Would you be willing to select a second child specifically to help an earlier child, as the Nashes did?*

**Hepatitis B** Several viruses can cause *hepatitis* (inflammation of the liver). The hepatitis B virus is transmitted in blood or body fluids during unprotected sex. It is more contagious than HIV but not as deadly. A vaccine for hepatitis B became widely available in 1991, and since that time the incidence of hepatitis B has declined. The government requires all health care workers to be vaccinated against hepatitis B because of their risk of being stuck with a needle on the job.

**Genital herpes** Genital herpes is caused by *herpes simplex* viruses. Generally it is caused by herpes simplex virus type 2 (HSV-2) as a result of sexual contact or skin-to-skin contact. Less commonly, the type 1 virus (HSV-1) that causes cold sores or blisters around the mouth may be spread to the genital area during oral sex.

Although the government does not keep accurate statistics on genital herpes, it is thought that over 8% of the population is infected. Most infected people have no or minimal symptoms. The primary symptoms are blisters around the genitals or rectum which eventually break, leaving painful sores that are slow to heal (Figure 16.17). The blisters may recur from time to time, but usually their number and frequency decrease over a period of years. The virus can stay in the body indefinitely.

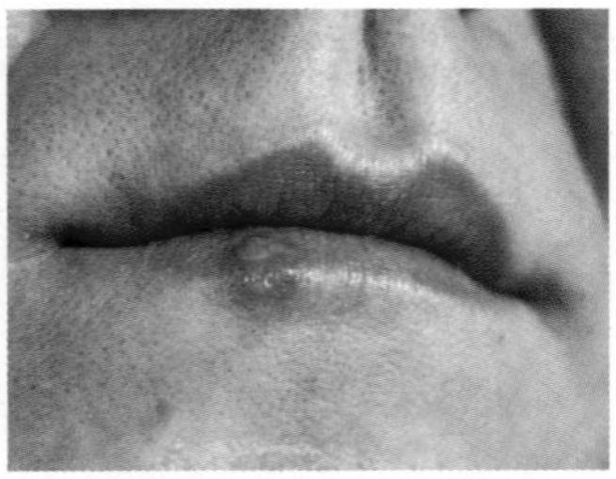

**a) Oral herpes: Cold sores (also called fever blisters) are most often caused by HSV-1.**

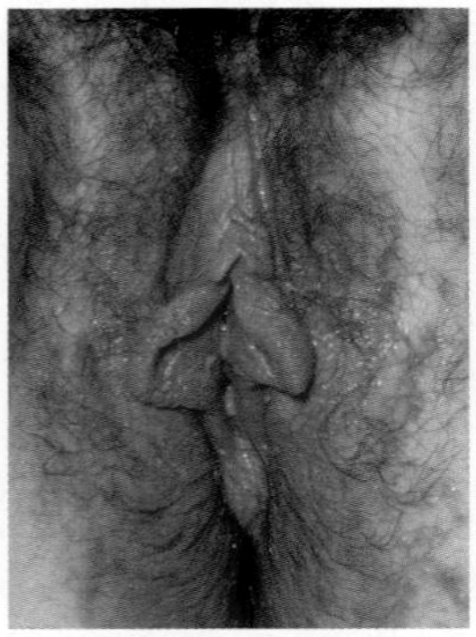

**b) Genital herpes, shown here on the external genitalia of a female, is usually caused by HSV-2.**

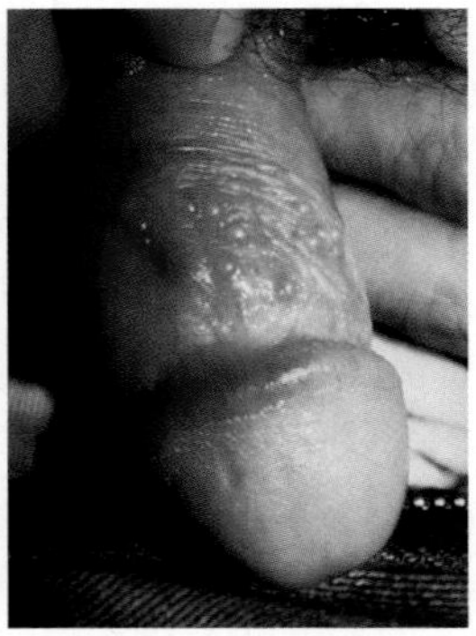

**c) Genital herpes, shown here on the penis of a male, is usually caused by HSV-2.**

**Figure 16.17 Herpes simplex virus. (a)** Cold sores on the lips generally are caused by HSV-1. Rarely, HSV-1 can be transmitted to the genitals. **(b)** Genital herpes on the external genitalia of the female. Genital herpes is generally caused by HSV-2. **(c)** Genital herpes on the penis of the male.

There is no cure for genital herpes, but drug treatments are available that can suppress the active (and contagious) phase. Like so many STDs, genital herpes can infect infants' eyes during birth and cause blindness if not treated.

**Human Papillomavirus (HPV)** Infection with one of about 30 HPV viruses can cause **warts** in the genital area, including the penis, the vulva (the area outside the vagina), around the anus, and in the vagina or cervix. Genital warts can be removed by several methods including laser surgery, freezing with liquid nitrogen, or certain drugs, but they have a tendency to reappear.

HPV is so common that most women have been infected with HPV by the time they are 50. The infection generally goes away on its own. Most people who are infected will have no symptoms at all (fewer than 5% will get warts), so they don't worry about it much. However, it is now known that certain strains of HPV increase the risk of cancers of the cervix or the penis.

In 2006 the FDA approved Gardasil, a vaccine against the strains of HPV that cause cervical cancer. To be effective, however, Gardasil must be given *before* infection. Doctors and the CDC (Centers for Disease Control) strongly recommend that all girls be vaccinated with Gardasil at about age 11 or 12, before their first sexual contact. The recommendation has sparked controversy in some circles, but the fact remains that if most girls were vaccinated, cervical cancer would be nearly eliminated over the next 50 years.

**RECAP**

The most dangerous viral STD is HIV. Hepatitis B can be prevented by a vaccine. Genital herpes is irritating but not particularly deadly. HPV can cause warts and is a risk factor for cervical cancer—it, too, can be prevented by a vaccine. ■

## Other STDs: Yeast infections, trichomoniasis, and pubic lice

**Yeast infections** *Candida albicans* is a yeast (a type of fungus) that is always present in the mouth, colon, and vagina. Normally it is kept in check by competition from other organisms. Sometimes, however, the *Candida* population may grow out of control in the vagina, leading to pain, inflammation, and a thick, cheesy vaginal discharge. A woman with an active yeast infection can pass it to her partner. Infected men sometimes develop a discharge from the penis accompanied by painful urination. It is easily treated by antifungal drugs.

**Trichomoniasis** Another condition that can cause *vaginitis* (inflammation of the vagina) is *trichomoniasis,* caused by the protozoan *Trichomonas vaginalis*. In women it causes a frothy, foul-smelling vaginal discharge; in men it inflames the penis and causes a discharge. Trichomoniasis can be transmitted even when there are no symptoms, and reinfection is common if partners are not treated simultaneously. It is treatable with drugs.

**Pubic lice** Pubic lice are tiny arthropods related to spiders and crabs (Figure 16.18). Commonly called "crabs," pubic lice live in hair but especially prefer pubic hair, jumping from one host to the next during sexual contact. They can also be transmitted by infected bed sheets or clothes. The adult lice lay eggs near the base of the hair, and the eggs hatch in a few days. Pubic lice nourish themselves by sucking blood from their host, causing intense itching and skin irritation; the adults are very small but visible with the naked eye. They can be killed with antilice treatments, but all clothes and bedding should be thoroughly washed in hot water to prevent reinfestation.

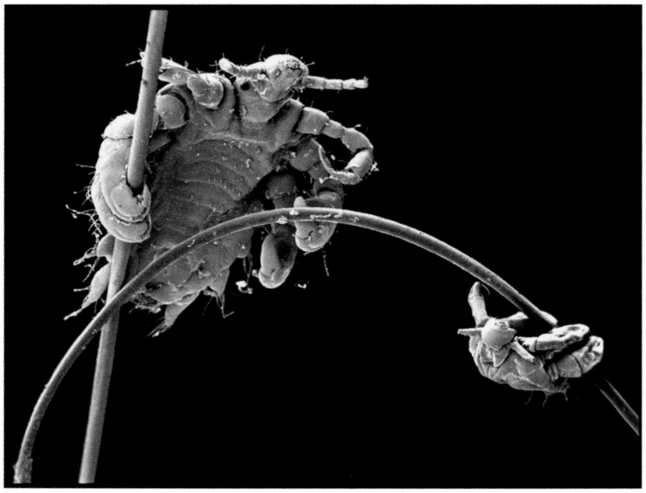

**Figure 16.18 The pubic louse, *Phthirus pubis*.** (Approximately × 30)

**RECAP**

Yeast, normally present in the vagina, can multiply and cause a yeast infection; trichomoniasis results from infection by the protozoan *Trichomonas vaginalis*. Pubic lice are tiny arthropods that are transmitted during intimate contact or by contact with clothes or bedding. ■

## Protecting yourself against STDs

We've just reviewed a group of diseases with symptoms ranging from painful urination to brain damage and outcomes ranging from full recovery to death. The good news is that you can probably avoid contracting an STD, but you need to know what to do and, more importantly, be willing to do it.

In Chapter 9 we present a number of safer-sex recommendations that can lower your risk of STDs. Many of them are commonsense precautions:

- Select your partner wisely. A monogamous relationship with someone you know and trust is your best defense.
- Communicate with your partner. If you have questions or concerns, share them, and be willing to do the same yourself.
- Use suitable barriers, depending on the sexual activity in which you engage. Be aware, though, that barrier methods of birth control are not a cure-all for risky behavior. For example, condoms are only marginally effective in preventing the transfer of HIV, HPV, and genital herpes, and they will not protect at all against pubic lice.

Finally, know your own health. If you or your partner think you are at risk for or may have a certain disease, get tested. It's confidential, it's not difficult, and it can save you a lot of embarrassment. It may even save your life.

**RECAP**

You can reduce your risk of contracting an STD with a little effort. Choose your partner wisely, use a barrier method of birth control, and, if you suspect you have a disease, get tested promptly. ■

# Chapter Summary

### The male reproductive system delivers sperm *p. 375*

- Sperm are produced in the male reproductive organs, called the testes, and stored in the epididymis and ductus deferens.
- Semen contains sperm and the secretions of three glands: the seminal vesicles, the prostate gland, and the bulbourethral glands.
- Tens of millions of sperm are formed every day throughout the male's adult life. The production of sperm is under the control of three hormones: testosterone, LH, and FSH.

### The female reproductive system produces eggs and supports pregnancy *p. 378*

- The female reproductive organs (the ovaries), produce mature oocytes and release them one at a time on a cyclic basis.
- Fertilization of the oocyte (if it occurs) takes place in the oviduct.
- The fertilized egg makes its way to the uterus, where it implants and begins to develop into a fetus.
- The vagina contains glands that produce lubricating fluid during sexual arousal.
- The hormone estrogen causes the mammary glands to enlarge at puberty.

### Menstrual cycle consists of ovarian and uterine cycles *p. 381*

- The cyclic changes in the female reproductive system are called the menstrual cycle. The menstrual cycle consists of an ovarian cycle that produces mature oocytes, and a uterine cycle in which the uterus prepares for pregnancy.
- The menstrual cycle is controlled by the hormones estrogen, progesterone, LH, and FSH. A surge in LH secretion triggers ovulation.

### Human sexual response, intercourse, and fertilization *p. 384*

- Both males and females are aroused by certain stimuli and respond in ways that facilitate intercourse and ejaculation. In males, the penis swells and hardens. In females, glandular secretions provide lubrication.
- Both males and females experience a pleasurable reflex event called an orgasm. Orgasm is accompanied by ejaculation, or the expulsion of semen, in the male.
- Sperm deposited in the vagina during intercourse make their way through the cervix and uterus and migrate up the oviducts to the egg. Only one fertilizes the egg.

### Birth control methods: Controlling fertility *p. 386*

- The most effective methods of preventing pregnancy are abstinence and female or male surgical sterilization. Sterilization should be considered permanent, though it may be reversible.
- Other effective methods of birth control include intrauterine devices (IUDs) and manipulation of hormone levels with pills, patches, injections, or vaginal rings.
- Moderately effective methods of birth control include condoms, cervical caps and diaphragms, and various spermicides. The "natural" methods (withdrawal and periodic abstinence) are the least effective.
- Morning-after pills are now available to be used as emergency contraceptives up to 72 hours after intercourse.

### Infertility: Inability to conceive *p. 390*

- Infertility is defined as the failure to achieve a pregnancy after a year of trying. Nearly 15% of all couples are infertile.
- For male infertility, the primary option is artificial insemination. When the male has a low sperm count but still some viable sperm, the sperm can be concentrated before insemination. In many cases, donor sperm are used.
- Female infertility may be overcome by several methods. In *in vitro* fertilization, egg and sperm are combined under laboratory conditions. The fertilized egg is allowed to develop for several days and then inserted into the uterus. In GIFT, the egg and sperm are inserted directly into an oviduct immediately after collection. In ZIFT, the egg and sperm are combined first, and then the fertilized egg is inserted into the oviduct.

### Sexually transmitted diseases: A worldwide concern *p. 392*

- The common feature of sexually transmitted diseases (STDs) is that they are transmitted during sexual contact. Their disease effects are not necessarily on the reproductive system.
- Bacterial STDs include gonorrhea, syphilis, and chlamydia. Syphilis is the most dangerous; chlamydia, the most common. All are treatable with antibiotics.
- Viral STDs include HIV (the virus that causes AIDS), hepatitis B, genital herpes, and genital warts (HPV). HIV is particularly deadly, and there is as yet no cure. There are now vaccines for hepatitis B and HPV.
- Avoiding the diseases caused by STDs is a matter of reducing your risk of exposure and paying attention to (and taking responsibility for) your own health.

# Terms You Should Know

cervix, *380*
clitoris, *380*
corpus luteum, *382*
ductus (vas) deferens, *375*
egg, *375*
endometrium, *379*
epididymis, *375*
erection, *375*
estrogen, *378*
follicle, *381*
gametes, *377*
menstrual cycle, *381*
menstruation, *382*
orgasm, *385*
ovarian cycle, *381*
ovary, *378*
oviduct, *379*
ovulation, *382*
penis, *375*
progesterone, *378*
semen, *376*
sperm, *375*
testes, *375*
testosterone, *378*
uterine cycle, *382*
uterus, *379*
vagina, *380*

# Concept Review

1. Name the three accessory glands of the male reproductive system.
2. Describe the development of a sperm cell.
3. Explain where fertilization takes place in the female reproductive system.
4. Describe the phases of the uterine cycle.
5. Describe what is happening in the uterus that leads to menstruation, and explain why menstruation does not occur during pregnancy.

6. Compare and contrast the male and female sexual responses.
7. Describe how in vitro fertilization is done.
8. Name three viral STDs.
9. Describe birth control options, and list those that afford at least some protection against STDs.
10. Describe the various STDs of worldwide concern.

## Test Yourself

### Matching Exercise

_____ 1. The primary reproductive organs in males
_____ 2. The primary reproductive organs in females
_____ 3. Rupture of the follicle and release of the oocyte
_____ 4. A sexually transmitted disease caused by human papillomavirus
_____ 5. Pituitary hormone that stimulates the secretion of testosterone in males
_____ 6. The other hormone secreted by the corpus luteum, besides estrogen

a. ovaries
b. LH
c. testes
d. progesterone
e. genital warts
f. ovulation

### Fill in the Blank

7. Each testicle has over 100 yards of __________ tubules where sperm are produced.
8. The __________ glands in the male secrete mucus into the urethra to provide lubrication for intercourse.
9. The inner lining of the uterus, called the __________, undergoes a monthly cycle of growth and then disintegration and shedding each month.
10. After ovulation, the remainder of the follicle becomes the __________, which continues to produce estrogen and progesterone during the second half of the ovarian cycle.
11. The __________ is a small organ that contributes to the female sexual response. It originates from the same tissue as the penis early in fetal development.
12. In females, the hormone __________ causes a primary follicle to begin to grow and mature.

### True or False?

13. An LH surge is the trigger for ovulation.
14. Pelvic inflammatory disease can lead to female infertility.
15. Sperm and the eggs are diploid cells, like all other body cells.

## References and Additional Reading

*2005 Assisted Reproductive Technology Success Rates: National Summary and Fertility Clinic Reports.* Centers for Disease Control and Prevention, December 2007. (The official report on the U.S. fertility clinics.)

Crooks, R., and K. Baur. *Our Sexuality.* 10th ed. Thomson International, 2008. (An introduction to human sexuality.)

Kaplan, Lawrence J., and Rosemarie Tong. *Controlling Our Reproductive Destiny: A Technological and Philosophical Perspective.* Cambridge, MA: MIT Press, 1996. (An interdisciplinary look at birth control and fertility enhancement, including scientific, ethical, legal, and social implications.)

Steptoe, P. C., and R. G. Edwards. Birth after the reimplantation of a human embryo. *Lancet* 2:366, 1978. (Brief announcement of the birth of the first test-tube baby.)

### Internet References

Find links to these Web sites at the Human Biology Place.

**American Society for Reproductive Medicine**
**www.asrm.org**
A nonprofit organization specializing in infertility, reproductive medicine, and biology.

**Birth Control Guide, U.S. Food and Drug Administration**
**www.fda.gov**
Factual evaluation of each contraceptive method with description, failure rate, health risks, protection from sexually transmitted diseases, and availability.

**World Health Organization**
**www.who.int/en**
This international agency unites 192 nations in providing health information and working to promote good health around the world.

## Apply What You Know

1. Male sexual responsiveness and secondary sex characteristics remain unchanged after a vasectomy. Explain why this is so.
2. What keeps the ovarian and uterine cycles always exactly in phase with each other, even though the length of the menstrual cycle can vary slightly?
3. Why is it important for a new mother to breastfeed her baby immediately after birth if she wishes to breastfeed the baby once she gets home?
4. What provides the force that pushes the baby out of the uterus during childbirth?
5. Both women and men can have an STD and not have any symptoms. What might be the long-term consequences of an untreated STD?
6. If a woman does not have an intact hymen does that mean she's not a virgin?

*Answers can be found on the Human Biology Place.*

# 17 Cell Reproduction and Differentiation

1 Where did all of the **specialized** cells of your body come from?

2 **True or False?** **Mistakes** are made as DNA is copied.

3 Why is a fetus more **vulnerable** to genetic damage than an adult?

4 **True or False?** Adult humans have already been **cloned**.

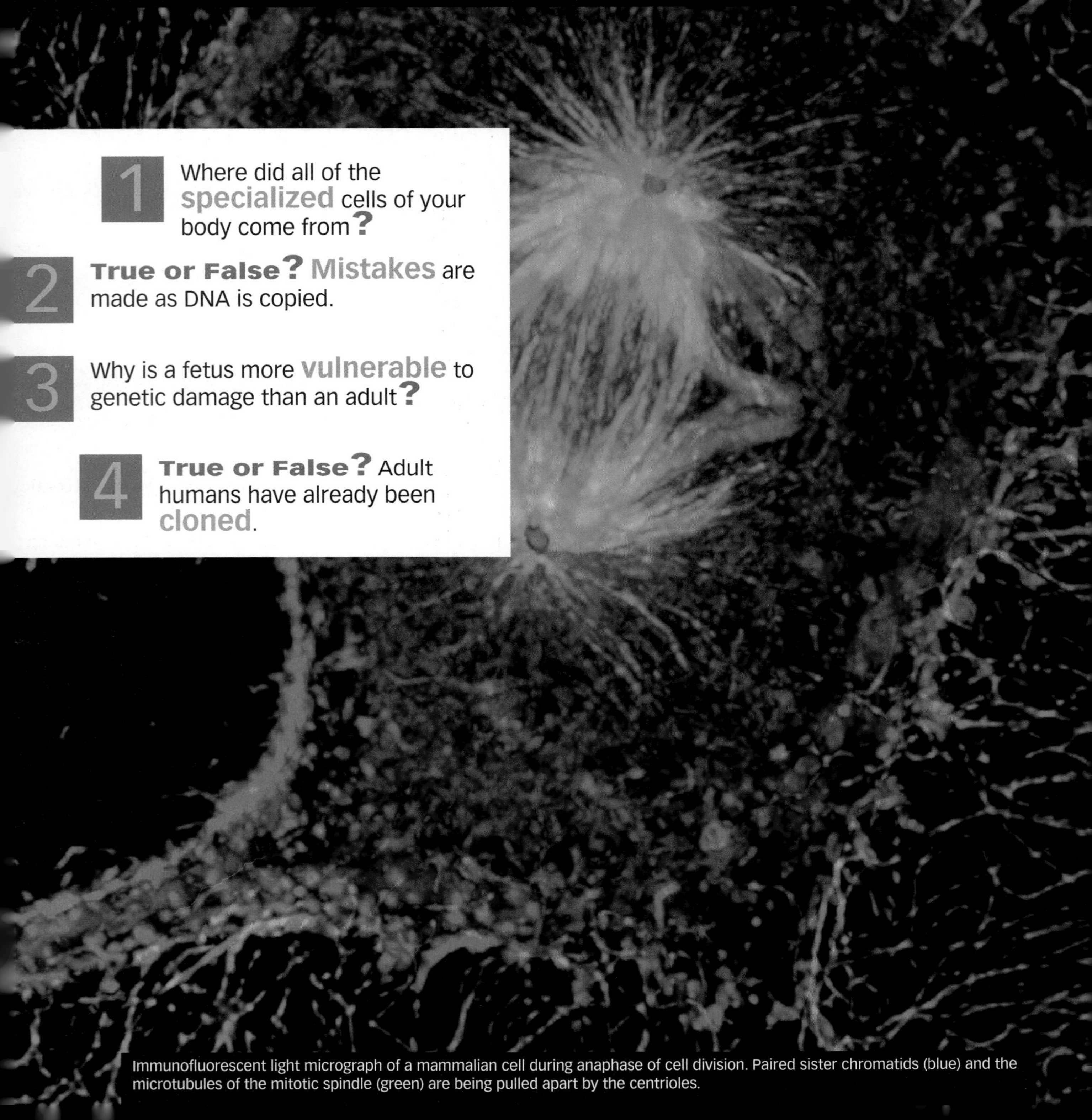

Immunofluorescent light micrograph of a mammalian cell during anaphase of cell division. Paired sister chromatids (blue) and the microtubules of the mitotic spindle (green) are being pulled apart by the centrioles.

**Cells reproduce by dividing in two.** Indeed, cell division (cell reproduction) is one of the defining features of life. For single-celled organisms, cell division is the equivalent of organism reproduction. For multicellular organisms, cell division and growth allow the organism to grow in size.

You started life as just a single cell created by the union of your father's sperm and your mother's egg. By the time you were born you were already composed of over 10 trillion cells, each created by cell division. Cell division continues throughout childhood and adolescence as the body grows and matures. Even after adulthood, some cells continue to divide in order to replace cells that die or become damaged. For instance, your 25–30 trillion red blood cells are completely replaced every 120 days, which works out to an astonishing 175 million cell divisions every minute.

The mechanisms of cell division are the same in all eukaryotes (organisms with cell nuclei) regardless of organism size. In this chapter we see how the cell's genetic material is copied to prepare for cell division, how the cell divides in two, and how cell growth and division are regulated. Finally, we discuss how cells differentiate to take on special forms and functions.

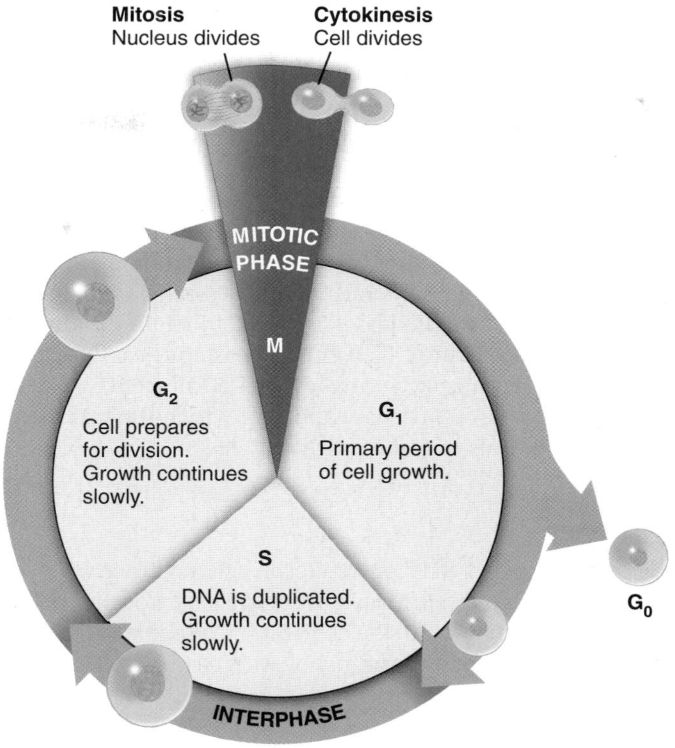


**Figure 17.1 The cell cycle.** The cell grows throughout all three phases of interphase, though most of the growth is in $G_1$. During the short mitotic phase, first the nucleus divides (mitosis) and then the cell divides (cytokinesis).

## 17.1 The cell cycle creates new cells

The creation of new cells from existing cells involves a repetitive sequence of events known as the **cell cycle** (Figure 17.1). The cell cycle consists of two distinct periods, called *interphase* and the *mitotic phase.*

**Interphase** is a long growth period during which the cell grows and DNA is duplicated in preparation for the next division. Interphase is divided into three subphases:

- **$G_1$ phase.** The cell cycle begins with $G_1$ ("first gap"), the period between the last cell division and DNA synthesis. At the start of $G_1$ the cell is at its smallest size. $G_1$ is a period of very active cell growth.
- **S phase.** The S stands for "synthesis" of DNA. During the S phase the cell's chromosomes are duplicated. Growth continues throughout the S phase, although at a slower pace.
- **$G_2$ phase.** During $G_2$ ("second gap"), the cell continues to grow slowly as it prepares for cell division.

The **mitotic phase** is a much shorter period during which first the nucleus and then the cytoplasm divide. The mitotic phase consists of (1) *mitosis,* during which the duplicated DNA is divided into two sets and the nucleus divides, and (2) *cytokinesis,* when the cytoplasm divides and two new cells, called "daughter" cells, are formed. The two new cells are called daughter cells regardless of the person's sex. This cycle repeats itself over and over.

### Answers to Intro Questions

1 All of the cells of your body came from just one cell: the fertilized egg. How your cells came to be so numerous and so different from each other is the subject of this chapter.

2 **True,** and it's not surprising since 6 billion DNA nucleotide molecules must be faithfully strung together each time a cell divides—the equivalent of all the letters, numbers, and symbols in 3,300 copies of this book! Most of the mistakes are caught and repaired before the cell divides again.

3 Damage to undifferentiated fetal cells early in fetal development can affect many different future cell and tissue types later in development. In this chapter we look at some substances that may disrupt fetal development.

4 **False.** Although it hasn't been done yet, it's now technically feasible. Someone is likely to do it sooner or later, whether we approve of it or not. Coming up, we talk about scientific, social, ethical, and political issues related to cloning.

In mammals, a complete cell cycle takes about 18–24 hours if the cells are actively dividing. (Cell cycles as short as 2 hours have been recorded in some nonmammalian species.) DNA replication during the S phase in mammalian cells takes about 7–8 hours. Mitosis and cytokinesis generally take only about 30–45 minutes.

Most of the cells in your body eventually enter a nongrowing, nondividing state called $\mathbf{G_0}$. In tissues that do not need a steady supply of new cells, $G_0$ is a healthy condition that stops cells from proliferating unnecessarily. Cells in some tissues can be called back from $G_0$ to begin dividing again, but others cannot. Neurons and osteocytes, for example, generally remain in $G_0$ forever after adolescence.

In Chapter 18 we discuss cancer, in which the process of cell division spirals out of control.

**RECAP**

Cell reproduction is required for growth and to replace cells throughout life. The cell cycle consists of a long growth phase (interphase), during which the cell's DNA is replicated, and a shorter phase (mitotic phase), during which first the nucleus and then the cell cytoplasm divide. ■

## 17.2 Replication, transcription, and translation: An overview

As described in Chapter 2, **DNA (deoxyribonucleic acid)** is a double-stranded string of nucleotides intertwined into a helical shape. Three billion base pairs of human DNA are packed onto 46 separate structures called **chromosomes** that organize and arrange the DNA within the nucleus. Chromosomes also contain proteins called *histones* that confer a certain structure to the chromosome molecule. The number of chromosomes varies among species of organisms, but it is always the same for all the individuals of a species. Humans have 46 chromosomes in their cell nuclei.

Throughout most of the cell cycle the chromosomes are not visible because they are so long and thin. During interphase they appear only as a diffuse, grainy substance known collectively as *chromatin* material. However, just before the nucleus divides, the duplicated chromosomes condense briefly into a shorter, compact shape that can be seen under the microscope (Figure 17.2). Chromosomes are moved around a lot during nuclear division, and their compactness at this stage helps prevent the delicate chromatin strands from breaking. Each visible duplicated chromosome consists of two identical *sister chromatids* held together by a *centromere.*

Mitochondria also contain a very small amount of DNA. The single human mitochondrial DNA molecule is not organized into a chromosome and contains only 37 genes, about 5% of the genes needed for mitochondrial function. Scientists believe that mitochondrial DNA is a holdover from a time in evolutionary history when mitochondria were independent organisms. At some point, mitochondria were incorporated into eukaryotic cells and became dependent on them.

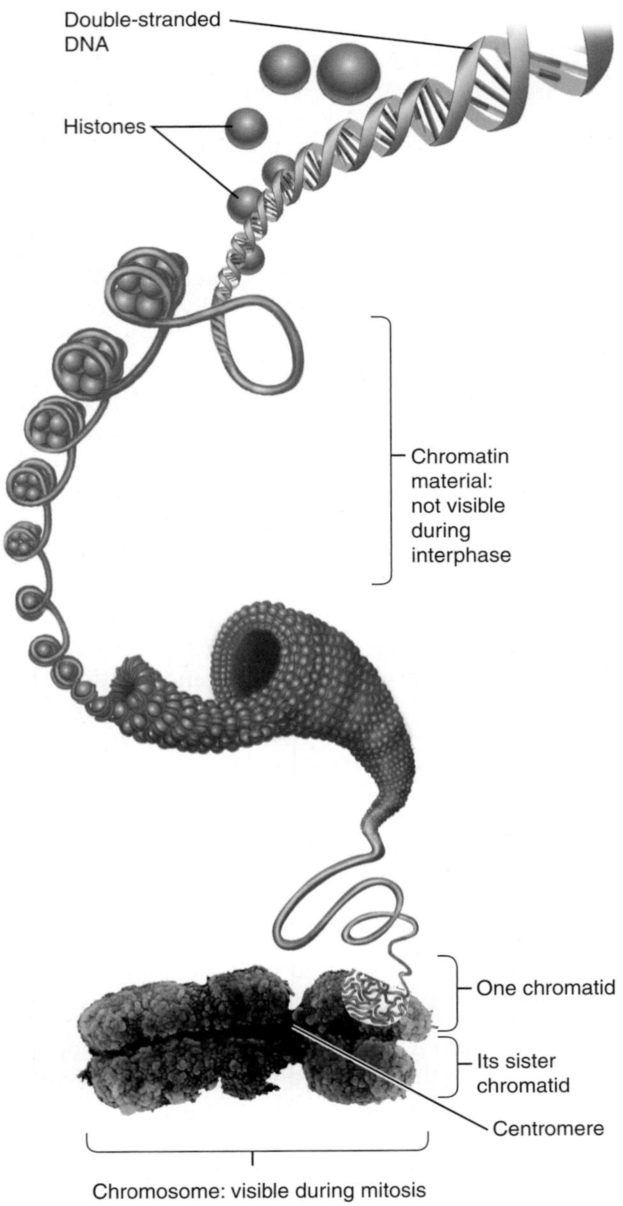


**Figure 17.2 The structure of a chromosome.** DNA combines with histone proteins to become long, thin strands of chromatin material. During most of the cell cycle the chromatin material of a chromosome is not visible within the cell. During mitosis the chromatin material condenses and the duplicated chromosome becomes visible as two identical sister chromatids held together by a centromere. The two sister chromatids separate during nuclear division.

Because DNA represents essentially all instructions for life, every cell in the organism must contain exactly the same set of DNA. It follows that the DNA must be duplicated every time a cell divides. DNA **replication** is the process of copying the DNA prior to cell division.

A **gene** is a short segment of DNA that contains the code, or recipe, for one or more proteins. A single gene is the smallest functional unit of DNA. There are approximately 20,000 genes on the 46 chromosomes, each one located at a precise position on a particular chromosome. The chromosomes are too large to pass through the nuclear pores, so they remain within the nucleus. For a gene to be useful to the cell, its code must first be converted to a form that can leave the nucleus and enter the cytoplasm. This is the function of single-stranded **ribonucleic acid (RNA),** more specifically a certain form of RNA called **messenger RNA (mRNA),** described in more detail later.

**Transcription** is the process by which the DNA code of a single gene is converted into a complementary single strand of mRNA. Messenger RNA is small enough to pass through the nuclear pores and enter the cytoplasm. In the cytoplasm, mRNA is used as a template to create a precise sequence of amino acids that constitute one particular protein. The process of converting the mRNA template code into one or more proteins is called **translation**.

Figure 17.3 summarizes replication, transcription, and translation. We now look more closely at these three processes.

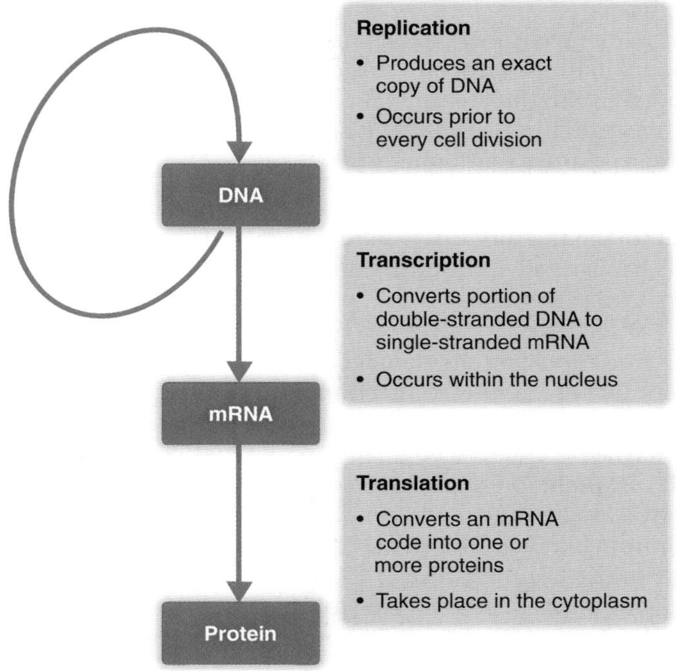


**Figure 17.3 Replication, transcription, and translation.** DNA is replicated before every cell division. Within the nucleus the genetic code for a protein is first transcribed into RNA. RNA transfers the code to the cytoplasm, where it is translated into the correct sequence of amino acids for one or more proteins.

**RECAP**

Human DNA is organized and arranged on 46 chromosomes within the cell nucleus. A gene is the smallest functional unit of DNA. Before a cell divides, its DNA is duplicated during the process of replication. ■

## Replication: Copying DNA before cell division

Before a cell can divide, its DNA must be duplicated so that the two new cells resulting from the division each have an identical set of genes. This process, called replication, begins with the uncoiling of the DNA helices. As described in Chapter 2, the nucleotides in each strand of the double-helical DNA molecule consist of a sugar group, a phosphate group, and one of four bases (adenine, thymine, guanine, or cytosine). The double helix is formed as the bases pair up, thymine with adenine and guanine with cytosine. This precise pairing facilitates the replication of DNA, because upon the uncoiling and "unzipping" of the two strands, each single strand can serve as a template for the creation of a new complementary strand. The precise nature of the base pairing of the nucleotides (T–A and G–C) ensures that the new complementary strand is exactly like the original complementary strand (Figure 17.4a). The new nucleotides are positioned and linked together by enzymes called *DNA polymerases.*

The "unzipping" of the DNA strands does not proceed linearly from one end of the DNA molecule to the other. Instead, the DNA strands become detached from one another at multiple locations along the length of the molecule. Were this not so, replication would take too long, considering the huge number of nucleotides involved. Because there are 3 billion nucleotide pairs in the human set of DNA, 6 billion nucleotides have to be added to the unzipped single strands in order to replicate the DNA entirely. Even if the cell replicated all 46 DNA molecules simultaneously, it would have to add an average of 5,000 nucleotides per second to each developing new strand of DNA to get the job done during the 7–8 hours of the S phase. That is an incredibly fast rate of unzipping and complementary base pairing—too fast when accuracy is essential.

What actually happens during replication is much more efficient. Certain enzymes bind at various points along the DNA molecule and gently unwind and "unzip" a portion of the DNA, creating a "replication bubble" in the two strands. New complementary strands begin to form at these bubbles. Replication proceeds outward in opposite directions in each strand until the expanding replication bubbles join (Figure 17.4b). Because replication occurs at thousands of sites along the molecule at once, it can conclude much more quickly.

Once replication is complete the two identical sister chromatids remain attached at a single point called the *centromere* (refer back to Figure 17.2). The centromere holds the sister chromatids together until they are physically pulled apart during mitosis. Figure 17.5 illustrates how the structure of a chromosome changes during the various stages of the cell cycle.

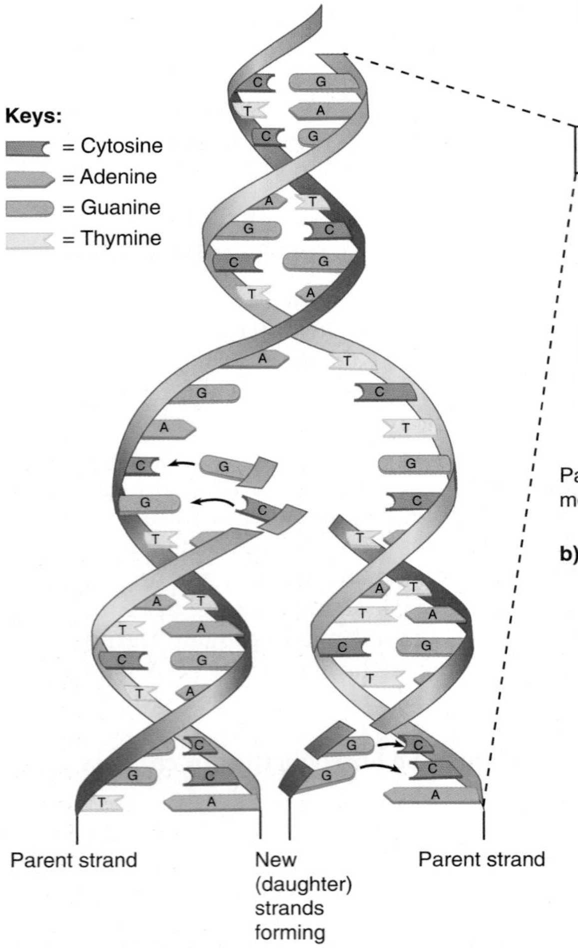


**a) The double-stranded DNA unwinds, and each single strand serves as a template for a new complementary strand.**

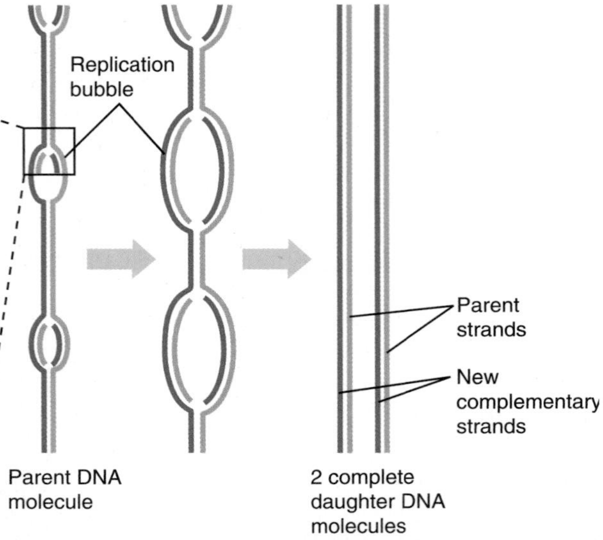


**b) The unwinding and the formation of new strands occur simultaneously at many sites on the DNA molecule.** The sites of replication expand outward until they join. For simplicity the two strands are shown as parallel in (b), but in actuality they form a helical shape as shown in (a).

**Figure 17.4 How DNA replicates.**

**RECAP**

During replication, the two strands of DNA unwind and separate from each other. Each strand serves as a template to form a new complementary strand. Enzymes called DNA polymerases add new nucleotides to each of the old strands in order to build two complete molecules of DNA from one. ■

**Mutations can be helpful or harmful** Considering that DNA spells out the instructions for building all the proteins of a complex organism, you might think that it is essential for every copy of it to be perfect. It turns out, though, that changes in DNA are necessary in order for evolution to occur. Changes in the DNA of the cells that produce sperm and eggs may be passed to future generations.

Alterations in DNA, called **mutations,** create the differences between individuals and species. Generally speaking, heritable mutations occur very slowly. The DNA of humans and chimpanzees, for example, differ by only about 1% even though our evolutionary paths diverged over 5 million years ago. Two humans differ by perhaps one base pair in a thousand, but that is still 3 million base pair differences, more than enough to account for all our individual variations.

Mutations may result from mistakes in DNA replication. In addition, chemicals or physical forces can damage a segment of DNA before it is replicated. Unless these errors are detected and corrected before the next replication, they may be passed on to future cells or could even prevent the DNA from being copied at all. In other words, the DNA needs to be in as good a shape as possible before it is replicated.

When DNA is severely damaged, it may not be possible to repair all the errors. In this case, substantial mutations and even life-threatening cancers may result. For example, skin cancer can be caused by damage to DNA from excessive exposure to sunlight.

**Mechanisms of repair** DNA repair mechanisms play a crucial role in the survival of an organism and its species. These mechanisms are quite efficient unless they are overwhelmed by massive damage.

DNA repair involves recognizing the errors, cutting out and replacing the damaged section or incorrect nucleotide base, and reconnecting the DNA backbone. The process utilizes numerous *DNA repair enzymes.* Typically one enzyme might recognize certain types of damage and cut out the impaired nucleotide, another might insert the correct nucleotide, and yet another might reconnect the adjoining ends of the DNA. The repair process is most active in the hour between DNA replication and the beginning of mitosis. Repair prior to cell division ensures that the best possible copy of DNA is passed on to each daughter cell.

DNA repair mechanisms are directed by certain genes that code for the repair enzymes. Thus the genetic code plays a vital role in repairing itself. If the damaged genes are the ones that control the repair process, DNA errors may accumulate more quickly than normal. Researchers now know that mutations of certain genes that direct DNA repair are associated with an increased risk of several cancers, including forms of colon and breast cancer.

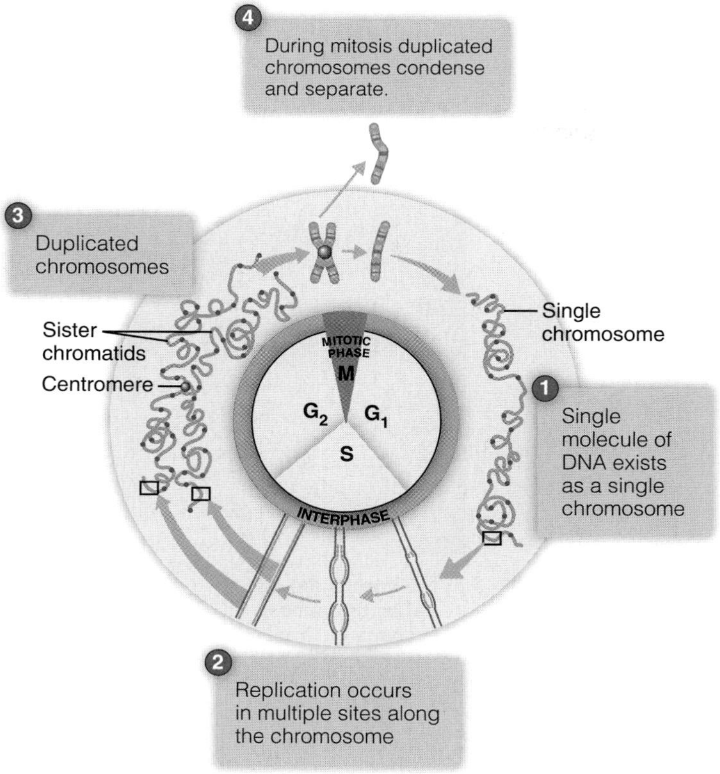


**Figure 17.5 The structure of DNA throughout the cell cycle.** **(1)** During $G_1$ the DNA molecule exists as a long, thin chromosome that cannot be seen distinctly under the microscope. **(2)** During the S phase the two strands of the DNA molecule unwind and replicate. **(3)** After the DNA has been replicated, the duplicated chromosome consists of sister chromatids held together by a centromere. **(4)** At the beginning of the mitotic phase, the duplicated chromosome condenses and becomes visible. During mitosis the duplicates are pulled apart, with one going to each daughter cell. When mitosis is complete, the single chromosome again takes on the more dispersed form and is no longer visible.

**RECAP**

Mutations may result from mistakes in DNA replication or from physical or chemical damage. Repair mechanisms remove and replace damaged DNA, if possible, before replication. ■

## Transcription: Converting a gene's code into mRNA

A gene is "expressed" when it is called into action and the protein for which it codes is produced. An essential step in this process is to make a complementary single strand of mRNA. Transcription involves converting the DNA code of a single gene into a complementary single strand of mRNA.

Transcription is similar to the process of DNA replication, with these exceptions:

- Only the segment of DNA representing a single gene unwinds, as opposed to the entire molecule.
- RNA is single stranded, so that only one of the two strands of DNA actually carries the genetic code specifying the synthesis of RNA.
- One of the four complementary base pairs of RNA is different from those of DNA: uracil replaces thymine.
- The sugar group of RNA is ribose rather than deoxyribose.

Once it is fully transcribed the RNA molecule is released from the DNA strand and the two DNA strands entwine around each other again. Figure 17.6a illustrates the process of transcription.

How is the specific gene to be transcribed identified on the chromosome? A unique base sequence called the *promoter* marks the beginning of every gene. An enzyme called **RNA polymerase** attaches to the promoter, starts the DNA unwinding process, and assists in attaching the appropriate RNA nucleotides to the growing chain. The process ends at another base sequence that identifies the end of the gene.

The RNA molecule first transcribed from DNA, called the *primary transcript,* is not yet functional because most of the DNA base sequences of a gene do not code for anything at all. The primary transcript is "edited" by enzymes that snip out the sections that do not carry any useful genetic information, called **introns,** leaving only the sequences that do carry genetic information, called **exons** (Figure 17.6b–c). The importance of the introns is unclear, though there is now some evidence that they may allow the exon fragments to be joined in different ways so that a single gene could code for different mRNA molecules in different cells. The RNA molecule produced from the primary transcript is called "messenger" RNA (mRNA) because it contains a message, in the form of a template, that can be "translated" into a specific sequence of amino acids that constitute a particular protein.

The message is encrypted as a *triplet code,* so called because three successive bases of mRNA, called a **codon,** each code for one of the 20 amino acids. Because there are four possible nucleotide bases and the code is a triplet code, there are precisely 64 different possible codons ($4 \times 4 \times 4$). We know exactly which amino acids are specified by the 64 possible codons of mRNA (Figure 17.7). Note two important points:

1. Several different codons can specify the same amino acid because there are more possible codons than there are amino acids. For example, both the UUU and UUC codons code for the same amino acid, phenylalanine (Phe).
2. The codon AUG specifies a "start" code and three others specify "stop" codes. These are needed to specify where to begin and end the gene.

**RECAP**

Transcription converts short segments of DNA representing single genes into a readable and transportable mRNA code. Only a portion of the DNA molecule unwinds, and only one strand is used to make single-stranded RNA. In the final edited mRNA molecule, three successive bases, called a codon, encode for a particular amino acid. ■

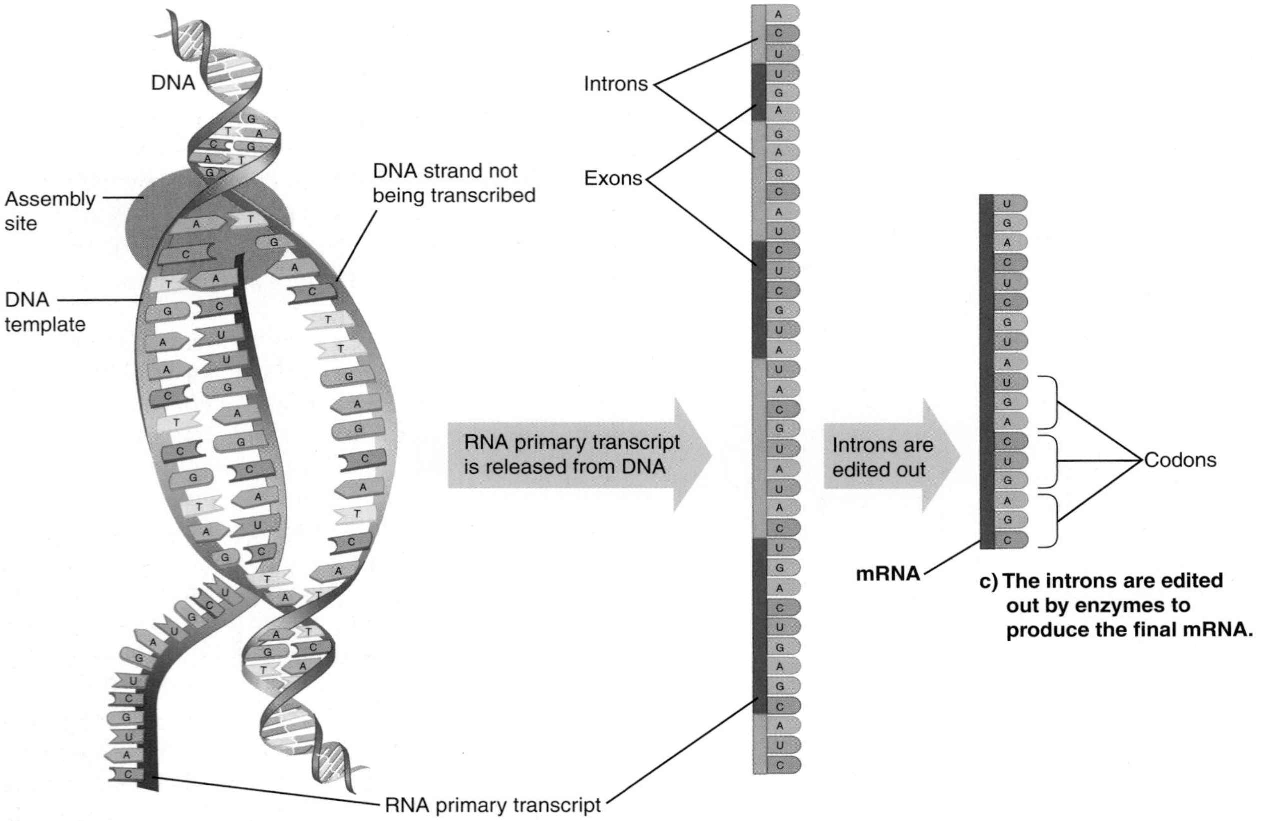


**a) The portion of the DNA molecule corresponding to the gene unwinds temporarily, and a complementary strand of RNA is produced from the DNA strand.**

**b) The strand of the RNA released from DNA is called a primary transcript.** It contains sections that carry genetic information, called exons, and sections that are apparently useless, called introns.

**c) The introns are edited out by enzymes to produce the final mRNA.**

**Figure 17.6 Transcription of a gene into mRNA.** Transcription takes place in the nucleus.

## Translation: Making a protein from RNA

Translation is the process of using mRNA as a template to convert, or "translate," the mRNA code into a precise sequence of amino acids that compose a specific protein.

The genes of DNA actually produce three different kinds of RNA, each with a specific role in the production of proteins. Only mRNA carries the recipe for a new protein. The other two kinds of RNA are called *transfer RNA* and *ribosomal RNA*. Each has an important role in protein synthesis.

**Transfer RNA (tRNA)** molecules are small molecules that carry the code for just one amino acid. They also carry an **anticodon,** a base triplet that is the complementary sequence to a codon of mRNA. The function of tRNA is to capture single amino acids and then bring them to the appropriate spot on the mRNA chain.

Once they have been captured and brought to the mRNA molecule, the amino acids must be connected together into one long chain in order to become a protein. This is the function of a ribosome. A **ribosome** consists of two subunits composed of **ribosomal RNA (rRNA)** and proteins. A ribosome has binding sites for both mRNA and tRNA. It also contains the enzymes that connect the amino acids together. The function of a ribosome, then, is to hold the mRNA and tRNA in place while joining the amino acids.

Translation occurs in three steps, as illustrated in Figure 17.8:

1. *Initiation.* A particular initiator tRNA binds to the smaller of two ribosome subunits and to the mRNA molecule. The tRNA and the ribosome subunit move along the mRNA until they encounter a "start" (AUG) codon. At this point they are joined by a larger ribosomal subunit to form the intact ribosome, which holds the mRNA in place while the tRNAs bring amino acids to it.
2. *Elongation.* The chain of amino acids lengthens one amino acid at a time. A tRNA molecule carrying the next appropriate amino acid binds to the ribosome and to mRNA. As the mRNA passes between the two ribosomal subunits, the ribosome catalyzes the formation of the bond between the newest amino acid and the previous amino acid in the growing chain. The tRNA molecule is then released to find another amino acid.

| First position | Second position U | Second position C | Second position A | Second position G | Third position |
|---|---|---|---|---|---|
| U | UUU Phe | UCU Ser | UAU Tyr | UGU Cys | U |
| U | UUC Phe | UCC Ser | UAC Tyr | UGC Cys | C |
| U | UUA Leu | UCA Ser | UAA Stop | UGA Stop | A |
| U | UUG Leu | UCG Ser | UAG Stop | UGG Trp | G |
| C | CUU Leu | CCU Pro | CAU His | CGU Arg | U |
| C | CUC Leu | CCC Pro | CAC His | CGC Arg | C |
| C | CUA Leu | CCA Pro | CAA Gln | CGA Arg | A |
| C | CUG Leu | CCG Pro | CAG Gln | CGG Arg | G |
| A | AUU Ile | ACU Thr | AAU Asn | AGU Ser | U |
| A | AUC Ile | ACC Thr | AAC Asn | AGC Ser | C |
| A | AUA Ile | ACA Thr | AAA Lys | AGA Arg | A |
| A | AUG Met/start | ACG Thr | AAG Lys | AGG Arg | G |
| G | GUU Val | GCU Ala | GAU Asp | GGU Gly | U |
| G | GUC Val | GCC Ala | GAC Asp | GGC Gly | C |
| G | GUA Val | GCA Ala | GAA Glu | GGA Gly | A |
| G | GUG Val | GCG Ala | GAG Glu | GGG Gly | G |

**Figure 17.7 The genetic code of mRNA.** Three successive bases represent a codon, and all but three codons encode for an amino acid. The letters correspond to the four RNA bases: uracil (U), cytosine (C), adenine (A), and guanine (G). To read the chart, start with the letter in the left column, then move across to one of the letters in the four center columns, then down the final column to the appropriate letter. AUG is the "start" codon and the only codon for the amino acid methionine; there are three "stop" codons.

3. *Termination.* There is no tRNA anticodon corresponding to a "stop" codon on mRNA. When a "stop" mRNA codon is encountered, the ribosomal subunits and the newly formed peptide chain detach from the mRNA.

To use a cooking analogy, the mRNA brings the recipe, the tRNAs find and deliver the ingredients, and the ribosome is the cook who creates the final product. What happens next to the newly formed peptide chain depends on its function. Some enter the endoplasmic reticulum for further processing, packaging, and shipping, whereas others remain in the cytoplasm. Many become parts of new structural units, organelles, cell membrane components, and enzymes that the cell will need as it grows and then divides into two new cells.

**RECAP**

Translation is a three-step process (initiation, elongation, and termination) by which proteins are assembled according to an mRNA code. In the process, tRNA molecules are used to capture the amino acids in the cytoplasm specified by each mRNA codon. The amino acids are connected together on a ribosome, which binds both mRNA and tRNA. ■

## 17.3 Cell reproduction: One cell becomes two

Let's review what we have learned so far about the preparations for cell division. DNA is replicated during the S phase of the cell cycle so there are two complete copies. The genes of DNA are used to produce specific proteins. These proteins in turn direct the cell's activities and form many of its structural units as the cell grows.

We turn now to the mitotic phase of the cell cycle, when first the nucleus and then the cell cytoplasm divide. The division of the nucleus is called **mitosis.** It is followed by **cytokinesis,** the division of the cytoplasm.

### Mitosis: Daughter cells are identical to the parent cell

Mitosis is the process of nuclear division in which the sister chromatids of each duplicated chromosome are separated from each other. Following mitosis, each daughter cell has a complete set of DNA and is identical to the parent cell. Mitosis ensures that all cells of a complex organism have the same set of DNA.

Mitosis (Figure 17.9) includes a sequence of phases that compose most of the mitotic phase of the cell cycle. The phases are defined by the structural changes taking place in the cell as the DNA divides and two new nuclei form. Although each stage has a name and certain defining characteristics, mitosis is really a seamless series of events.

**Prophase** In late $G_2$ of the interphase, the strands of replicated DNA and associated proteins begin to condense and coil tightly. Eventually they become visible as a duplicated chromosome consisting of sister chromatids held together by the centromere. **Prophase** is defined as the point at which the duplicated chromosomes first become visible.

Recall that the cell has a cytoskeleton that helps hold it together. During prophase the tubular elements of the cytoskeleton come apart and are reassembled between the pairs of centrioles. This newly formed parallel arrangement of microtubules, called the *mitotic spindle,* will become the structure that causes the two identical sets of DNA to divide. The pairs of centrioles drift apart and the mitotic spindle lengthens between them. The nuclear membrane dissolves, and the centrioles move to opposite sides of the cell. This allows the mitotic spindle to cross through the middle of the cell. The centromere in each duplicated chromosome develops into two separate structures (one for each of the duplicate DNA molecules) that attach to microtubules originating from opposite sides of the cell. Forces within the mitotic spindle draw the duplicated chromosomes toward the center of the cell.

**Metaphase** During **metaphase,** the duplicated chromosomes align on one plane at the center of the cell. Cells often seem to rest at this stage, and metaphase can occupy as much as 20 minutes of the entire one-hour process of mitosis. In fact, the

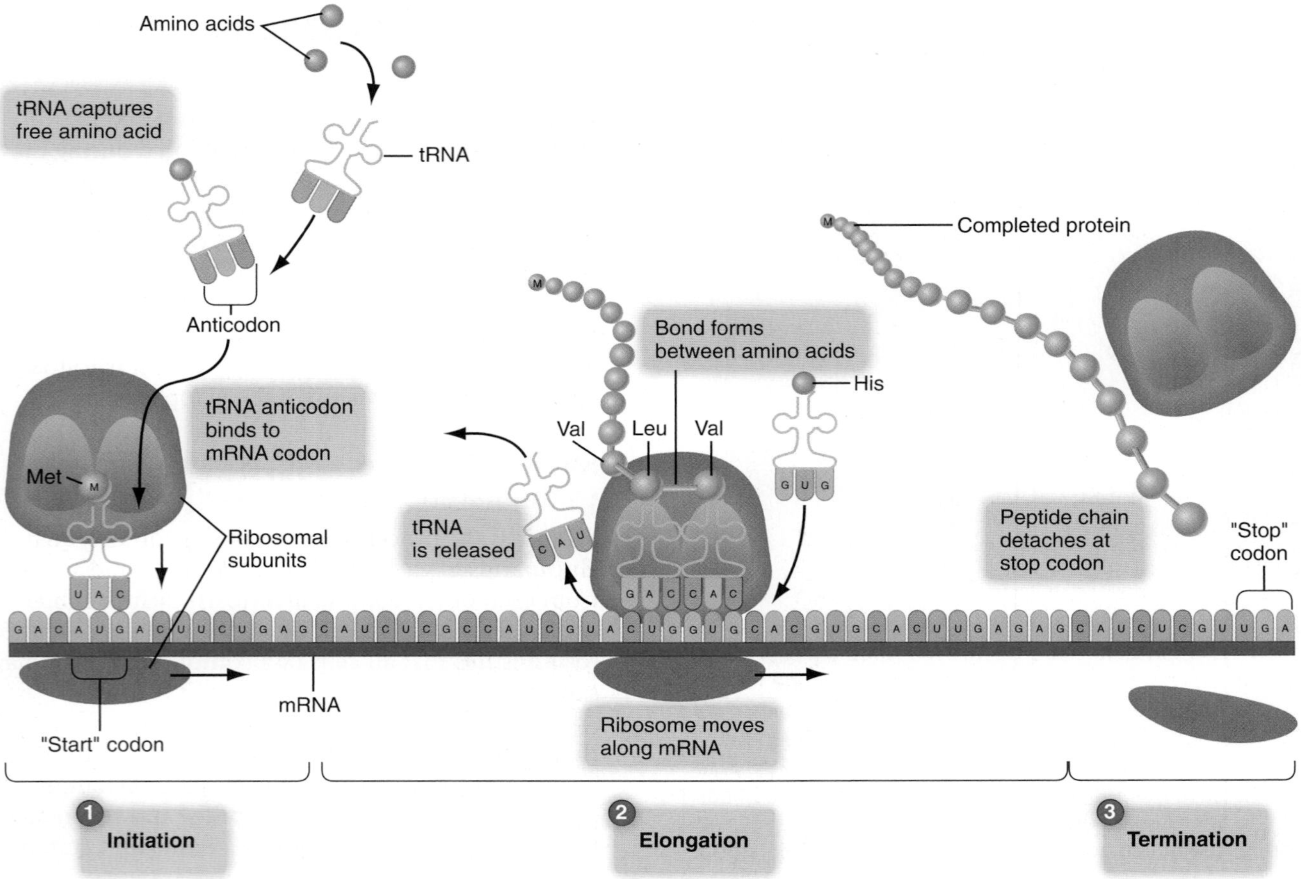


**Figure 17.8 The three steps of translation. (1)** Initiation. A tRNA carrying the "start" anticodon binds to the smaller ribosomal subunit and to the "start" codon of mRNA. The larger ribosomal subunit joins them. **(2)** Elongation. tRNA molecules capture free amino acids and bring them to the appropriate codon on the mRNA. As mRNA passes between the two ribosomal subunits, the ribosome binds to the tRNA and catalyzes the formation of the bond between successive amino acids. The tRNA is then released to find another amino acid. **(3)** Termination. When a stop codon is reached, the ribosomal subunits and the newly formed protein detach from the mRNA.

duplicate DNA molecules are being pulled in opposite directions by equal forces (like a tug-of-war), but no separation occurs because they are still held together by the centromeres.

**Anaphase** During **anaphase,** the duplicate DNA molecules separate and move toward opposite sides of the cell. It is the shortest phase of mitosis, lasting only a minute or so. The centromere abruptly comes apart, and the now separated DNA molecules are pulled in opposite directions by the microtubules to which they are attached. The process of separation requires energy in the form of ATP and utilizes certain proteins that act as "motors" to tow the microtubules in opposite directions. Cytokinesis usually begins at this time.

**Telophase** **Telophase** begins when the two sets of chromosomes arrive at opposite poles of the cell. At this point the mitotic spindle comes apart, and new nuclear membranes form around the chromosomes. The chromosomes uncoil and revert to the extended form in which they are no longer visible under a microscope.

**RECAP**

Mitosis is the process by which the cell nucleus containing duplicated chromosomes divides in two. During mitosis, the sister chromatids of a duplicated chromosome are separated, resulting in two daughter cells with complete sets of DNA. The duplicated chromosomes become visible in prophase, align along the center of the cell in metaphase, are pulled apart in anaphase, and move to opposite sides of the cell and become surrounded by new nuclear membranes in telophase. ■

## Cytokinesis divides one cell into two identical cells

Cytokinesis is the process by which a cell divides to produce two daughter cells. Certain physical properties of the cell

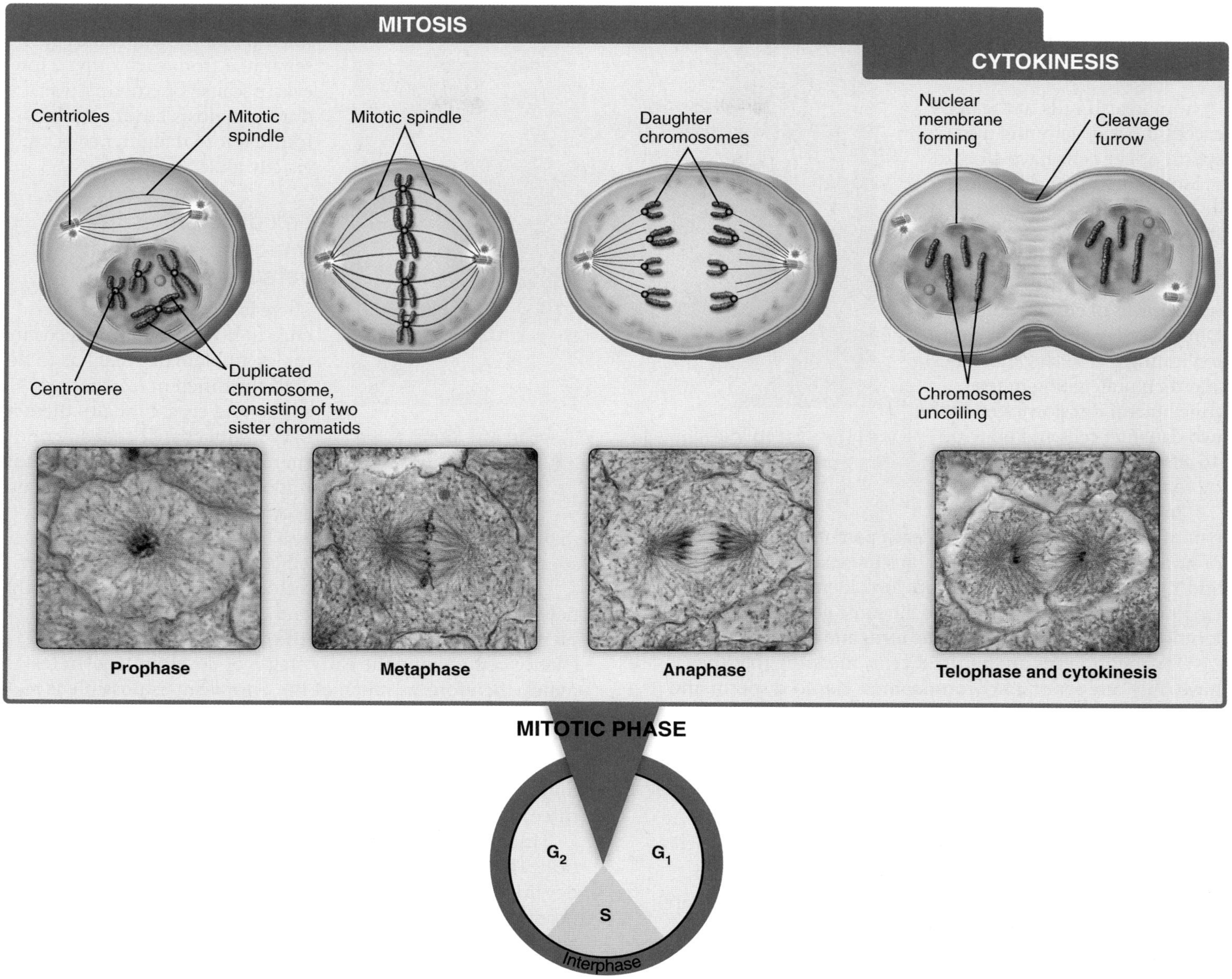


**Figure 17.9 Mitosis.** Mitosis accounts for most of the mitotic phase of the cell cycle, overlapping slightly with cytokinesis, the division of the cell into two cells. The duplicated chromosomes become visible in prophase, line up in metaphase, are pulled apart in anaphase, and uncoil and become surrounded by nuclear membranes in telophase.

facilitate this process. A contractile ring of protein filaments of the same type found in muscle forms just inside the cell membrane. The contractile ring tightens, forming a cleavage furrow and then pinching the cell in two (Figure 17.10). The ring is perpendicular to the long axis of the mitotic spindle, which ensures that one nucleus is enclosed in each of the daughter cells.

Cytokinesis is an example of the resourcefulness and efficiency of life's processes. The contractile ring is assembled just before it is needed from the remnants of the cytoskeleton that dissolved during mitosis. After the cell divides, the ring itself is disassembled, presumably to form new cytoskeletons for the daughter cells. In effect, cells use a "just-in-time" materials delivery system coupled to an efficient recycling system. Living cells were doing it long before the business community invented a name for it.

**RECAP**

During cytokinesis, a contractile ring of microfilaments pinches the cell into two cells. Each daughter cell contains a nucleus identical to that of the parent. ■

### Mitosis produces diploid cells and meiosis produces haploid cells

In humans, all cells in the body except those developing into sperm or egg cells have 46 chromosomes. Human cells with 46 chromosomes are called **diploid** cells (in Greek, *diploos* means "twofold") because the 46 chromosomes actually represent 23 *pairs* of chromosomes. Diploid cells reproduce by first replicating the 46 chromosomes and then undergoing mitosis (one nuclear division), so that the two daughter cells end up with 46 chromosomes that are identical to those of the parent cell.

In diploid cells, one of each pair of chromosomes came from each parent. There are 22 pairs of **homologous chromosomes** plus the sex chromosomes X and Y. Homologous chromosomes look identical under the microscope, and they have copies of the same genes in the same location (*homologous* means "same form and function").

Sperm and eggs are **haploid** cells, meaning that they have only one set of 23 chromosomes. Haploid sperm and eggs are created by **meiosis,** a sequence of two successive nuclear divisions in which the human genes are mixed, reshuffled, and reduced by half. Once fertilization occurs, the fertilized egg and all subsequent cells have the diploid number of chromosomes again.

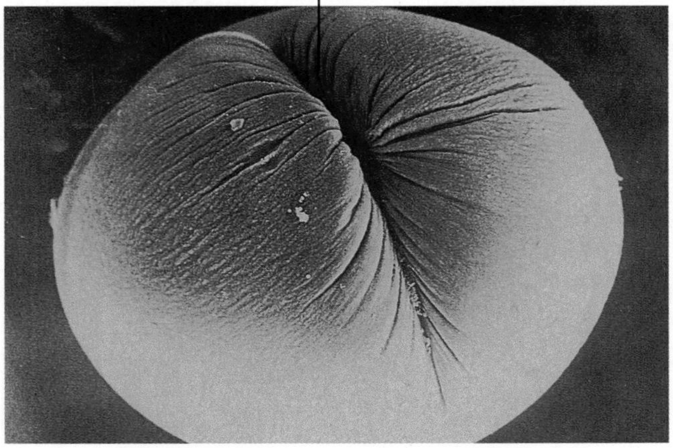


**Figure 17.10 Cytokinesis.** A cleavage furrow forms as the ring of contractile filaments in the cell tightens.

### Meiosis: Preparing for sexual reproduction

The two successive nuclear and cell divisions of meiosis are called *meiosis I* and *meiosis II.* Both meiosis I and II can be subdivided into four stages: prophase, metaphase, anaphase, and telophase. Figure 17.11 illustrates the events that occur in each stage.

**Meiosis I** Before meiosis begins, the precursor cell undergoes a typical S phase of interphase in which the DNA is replicated and the 46 chromosomes are duplicated. But then something very different happens, compared to mitosis:

1. During prophase of meiosis I the duplicated homologous chromosomes pair up and swap sections of DNA (genes) by a process called **crossing-over.** Consequently, the homologous chromosomes now contain a recombination of the genes of both of the person's parents.
2. During the rest of meiosis I (metaphase through telophase), the homologous pairs of chromosomes are separated from each other, rather than the duplicates of each pair.

**Meiosis II** Meiosis II proceeds like mitosis except that the chromosomes are not duplicated again. During meiosis II, the 23 duplicated chromosomes line up and the duplicates are separated from each other. However, because of crossing-over during meiosis I, none of the four haploid daughter cells are exactly alike.

### Sex differences in meiosis: Four sperm versus one egg

There is a fundamental difference in how meiosis proceeds in males and females that has to do with the different functions of sperm and eggs. In males there is only a slim chance that any one sperm will ever reach an egg. It is important, therefore, that lots of sperm be produced. Meiosis in males produces four equal-sized but genetically different sperm from every precursor cell (Figure 17.12 on page 414).

In females, each egg is precious. If fertilized, an egg will need a lot of energy to grow and develop. A large egg with plenty of cytoplasm and lots of organelles has a better chance of surviving the early stages of development. In females, therefore, as much of the cytoplasm as possible is reserved for only one daughter cell at each cell division. The smaller cell produced at each division is called a *polar body.* The polar body produced during meiosis I may or may not divide again during meiosis II, but in any event the two (or three) polar bodies eventually degenerate.

In females, meiosis II is not completed until fertilization. The secondary oocyte released from the ovary stops development at metaphase of meiosis II. Once fertilization occurs the secondary oocyte quickly completes meiosis II and the sperm and egg nuclei then unite.

**RECAP**

Meiosis is a two-step process in which the nucleus and cell divide twice, producing sperm or eggs with the haploid number of chromosomes. Crossing-over ensures that sperm (and eggs) are genetically different from each other because they contain a mixture of genes from each parent. ■

## 17.4 How cell reproduction is regulated

Although division is the norm for most cell types, not all cells in the body divide at the same rate. Some groups of cells divide rapidly throughout life, whereas others stop after adolescence. Still others reproduce at highly variable speeds, increasing or decreasing their rates of cell division in response to

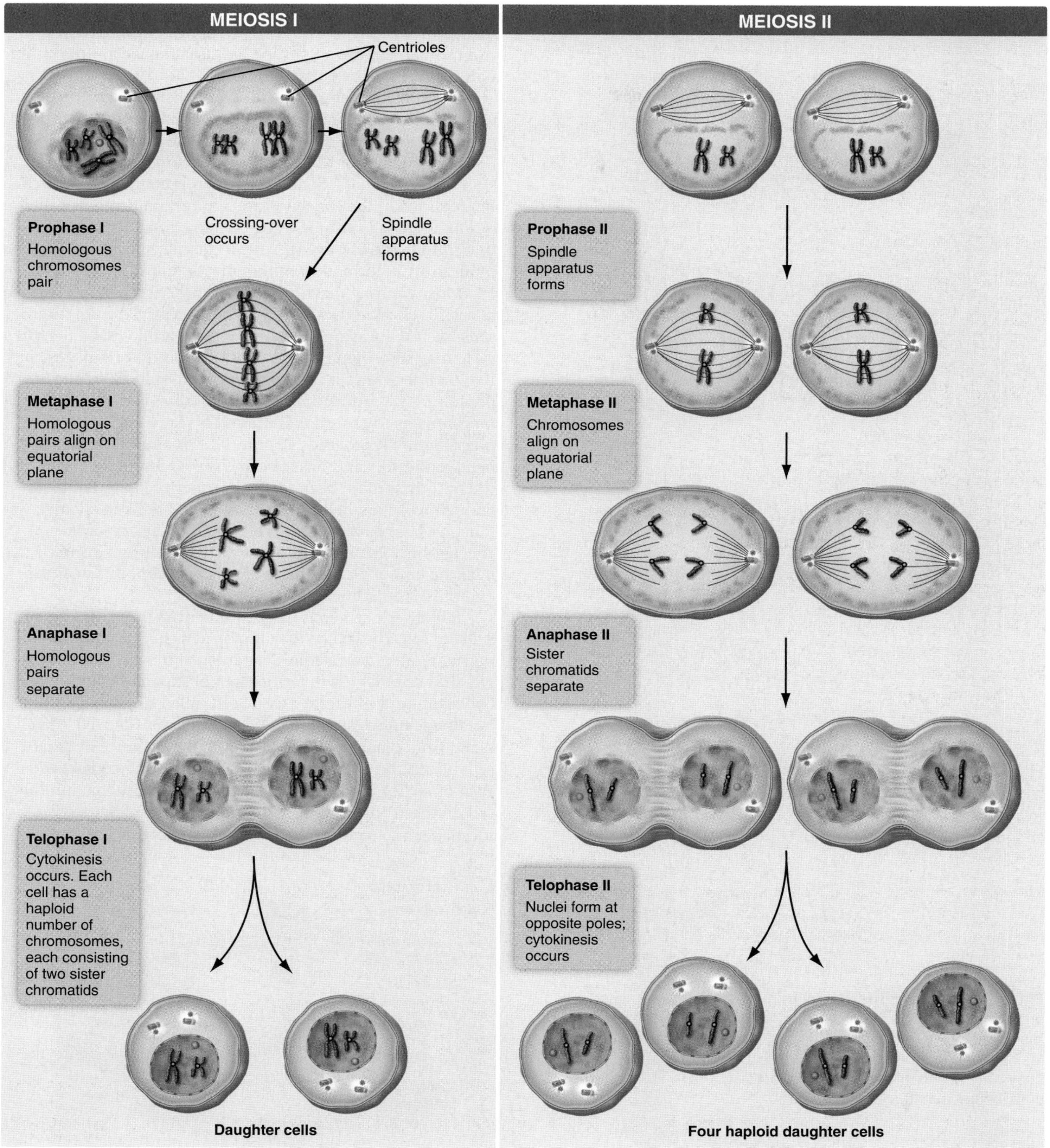


**Figure 17.11 Meiosis.** Meiosis is a process of two nuclear divisions in which the chromosomal material is reshuffled and reduced by half during the formation of sperm and eggs. The blue and purple colors indicate homologous chromosomes that were inherited from each of the person's parents. During prophase of meiosis I, pairs of duplicated homologous chromosomes pair up and exchange sections of DNA by a process known as crossing-over. During the rest of meiosis I, the homologous pairs are separated from each other. In meiosis II the duplicates of each chromosome are separated from each other, just as they are in mitosis. The result is four daughter cells, none of which are alike.

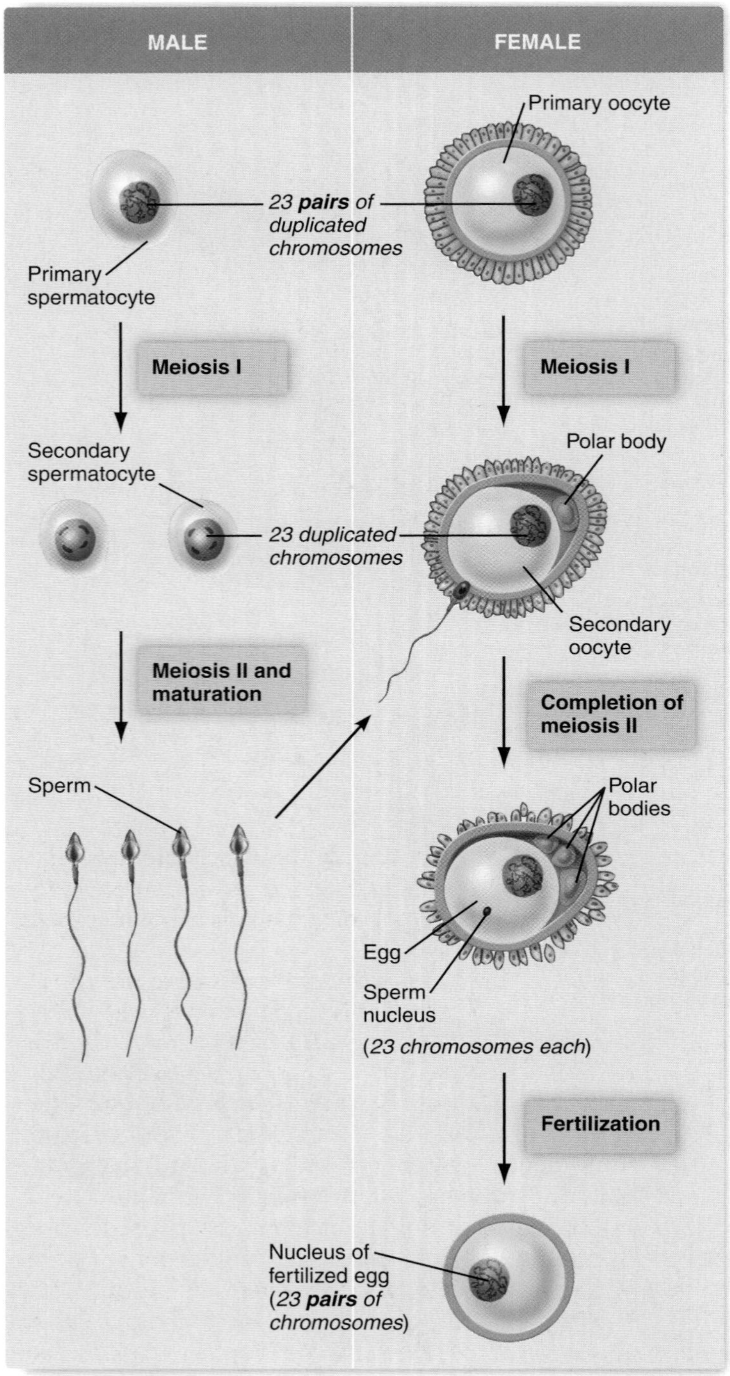


**Figure 17.12 Sex differences in meiosis.** In males, meiosis produces four different small sperm. In females, nearly all of the cytoplasm is reserved for the future egg at each stage of meiosis. Meiosis I in females thus results in a secondary oocyte and a polar body. Meiosis II is not completed in females until fertilization. The polar bodies eventually disintegrate.

regulatory signals. Table 17.1 lists examples of variations in the rates of cell division.

What causes such different and sometimes changing rates of cell divisions? Although we do not yet have all the answers, we do know that cells have an internal control mechanism that undergoes cyclic changes, and that the control mechanism can be stopped at certain checkpoints by signals from inside or outside the cell.

Consider a washing machine or a dishwasher. Once a wash cycle is started, a whole sequence of timed events occurs until the entire cycle is finished. The same thing happens in a living cell. Under normal circumstances, progression through the $G_1$, S, and $G_2$ phases is controlled by cyclic fluctuations in the concentrations of certain proteins called *cyclins*. Cyclins in turn activate certain regulatory proteins that initiate specific events within the cell, such as DNA replication or formation of the mitotic spindle.

Most washing machine control devices can stop the cycle at certain checkpoints, based on input received from internal sensors. If the washing machine does not fill with water, the cycle may stop right before agitation would normally begin. If a load of clothes is out of balance, the spin cycle may stop prematurely. Cells also have internal surveillance and control mechanisms to ensure that the cell is ready for the next phase before it proceeds (Figure 17.13). Has all of the DNA been replicated, and has it been checked for errors? Has the mitotic spindle been formed properly? Is the cell large enough to be divided in two? Unless the cell surveillance system gives the go-ahead, the cell may stop at one of several checkpoints. The most important checkpoint seems to be near the end of $G_1$, but there are also checkpoints near the end of $G_2$ and at metaphase of mitosis.

Finally, the cell cycle can be influenced by conditions outside the cell. The cell cycle may stop at a checkpoint if certain nutrients are not available, if a particular hormone is not present, or if certain growth factors are not supplied by other cells. For example, a connective tissue cell called a fibroblast will not divide unless *platelet-derived growth factor* (derived, obviously, from platelets) is present. Even the presence of other cells affects the cell cycle. When cells come into contact with each other, for instance, they release a substance that inhibits cell division. This inhibition is an effective negative feedback mechanism to regulate tissue growth and organ size.

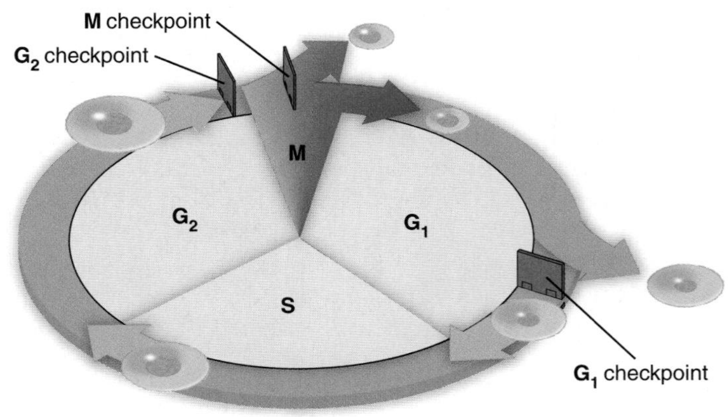


**Figure 17.13 Cell cycle checkpoints.** The cell cycle stops at several well-defined checkpoints unless the cell is ready for the next phase.

**Table 17.1 Variation in rates of cell division by human cells**

| Rate of division | Cell type | Comments |
|---|---|---|
| Divide constantly and rapidly throughout life | Skin cells | Skin is continually being formed from deep layers. The outermost layer of skin is composed of dead cells; they are constantly being sloughed off. |
| | Most epithelial cells | Epithelial cells line the inner surfaces of body organs such as the digestive tract and the lungs. These cells are exposed to frequent damage and must be replaced. |
| | Bone marrow cells | Precursor cells in the bone marrow produce red blood cells (RBCs) and white blood cells (WBCs) throughout life. RBCs live only about 120 days. The rate of WBC production can be increased as part of the immune response. |
| | Spermatogonia (after puberty) | Spermatogonia divide to produce sperm throughout life in the adult male, though the rate may decline some in old age. |
| Do not normally divide but can be stimulated to divide under the right circumstances | Liver cells | Liver cells don't normally divide in adulthood but will do so if part of the liver is removed. |
| | Epithelial cells surrounding the egg | Called granulosa cells, they are quiescent for most of adult life. They begin to divide as the follicle matures prior to ovulation. |
| Do not divide in adulthood | Most nerve cells | Most human nerve cells apparently do not divide in adulthood, although recently it has been shown that neurons in the hippocampus do. |
| | Osteocytes | Mature bone cells called osteocytes become trapped within the hard crystalline matrix of bone, with no room for growth or division. Only immature bone cells (osteoblasts) divide. |
| | Most muscle cells | The commonly held view is that muscle cells do not divide in adulthood. There is some disagreement about this. |

**RECAP**

An internal cyclic control mechanism regulates the cell cycle. The cycle can be stopped at certain checkpoints by internal surveillance systems and is influenced by conditions outside the cell. ■

## 17.5 Environmental factors influence cell differentiation

All of the cells in your adult body originated from a single cell, the fertilized egg, and all of those cells (except those destined to become your sperm or eggs) have exactly the same set of DNA. Yet your body is composed of lots of different kinds of specialized cells. If all your cells have the same exact set of genes, why don't all your cells stay identical, like identical twins? What causes the cells to change form and function?

**Differentiation** is the process by which a cell becomes different from its parent or sister cell. At various developmental stages of life, cells differentiate because they begin to express different genes. The examples below show that differentiation is probably due to environmental influences.

### Differentiation during early development

Let's examine the earliest stage of human development, starting from a fertilized egg. The fertilized egg is a relatively large cell. Soon after fertilization it begins to divide, becoming two cells, then four, then eight. During these early divisions, up to about 16 or 32 cells, the cells do not grow. Consequently each cell gets progressively smaller as a ball of identical cells develops (Figure 17.14).

Up to about eight cells, each cell is exposed to the same environment—the surrounding fluid plus contact with cells just like themselves. Once they form a tight ball of many cells, however, the situation changes, for now only the cells at the outer surface of the ball are exposed to the surrounding fluid. The rest are exposed only to the extracellular fluid between the cells. At this point the environment that surrounds a cell at the center of the ball becomes different from the environment of a cell at the surface. Cells at the center may be exposed to a lower $O_2$ content, higher levels of $CO_2$, or a different pH, or they may be influenced by products secreted by the other cells. Any one of these or other environmental factors could activate different genes, leading to different developmental pathways for the cells at the center versus the cells at the surface.

Notice that no "thought" or feedback control mechanisms are needed to account for early differentiation; it can be accounted for solely by differences in the physical and chemical environment of individual cells. Cell differentiation begins long before homeostatic feedback mechanisms ever develop in the organism.

Scientists have known for some time that it is possible to clone (make copies of) an organism by "embryo splitting"; that is, by splitting the eight-cell ball that develops from a fertilized egg into eight separate cells. At that stage, all eight cells are equally capable of becoming complete organisms,

# Should We Clone Humans?

In 1997 researchers announced they had cloned a sheep named Dolly. Since then, cloning experiments have produced dogs, pigs, mice, rats, cattle, horses, goats, cats, and monkeys.

Should we allow human cloning? If you and your partner were infertile, would you want to clone one of you? Could we stop human cloning now even if we wanted to? The answer to the first question is a societal decision, up to all of us. The answer to the second question would be a personal choice, but whether you will have that choice depends on how society answers the first question. And the answer to the third question is a political and law-enforcement issue.

In the broadest sense, a clone is a copy. The popular media generally think of a clone as a copy of an adult organism, but scientists use the term cloning to describe the copying of cells, genes, and molecules as well. Using genetic engineering techniques, scientists now routinely insert human genes into bacteria, yeast, and even large animals to produce cloned human hormones in large quantities. Human erythropoietin (to treat anemia), insulin (for diabetes), and growth hormone (for endocrine disorders) are produced this way. Human cells can also be cloned to produce specialized tissues. Scientists who grow layers of skin cells to treat badly burned patients are practicing a form of cloning.

Cloning an entire organism generally involves one of two techniques: *embryo splitting* or *somatic cell nuclear transfer*.

## *Embryo Splitting*

Recall that until the eight-cell stage of development, all cells in a fertilized egg are undifferentiated. At this stage it is possible to separate the cells, implant each into a different mother, and create up to eight identical clones of the organism that would have resulted from the original fertilized egg (Figure 1). It is fairly commonplace to produce cloned offspring of valuable farm animals in this manner.

There are, however, limitations to this technology. In embryo splitting, the eight clones are made *after* the union of sperm and egg. Clones produced by embryo splitting, while identical to each other, are not exact copies of either parent. In other words, a prized adult animal cannot be copied exactly, and humans produced in this manner would be no more than identical siblings (up to octuplets).

## *Somatic Cell Nuclear Transfer*

A *somatic cell* is any cell in the body except a germ (sex) cell. Every somatic cell has the same set of DNA, so in theory any body cell could be used to produce a new adult identical to the original. But until the birth of Dolly the sheep it was considered impossible to make a

*The first cloned horse (foreground) with her identical twin and surrogate mother.*

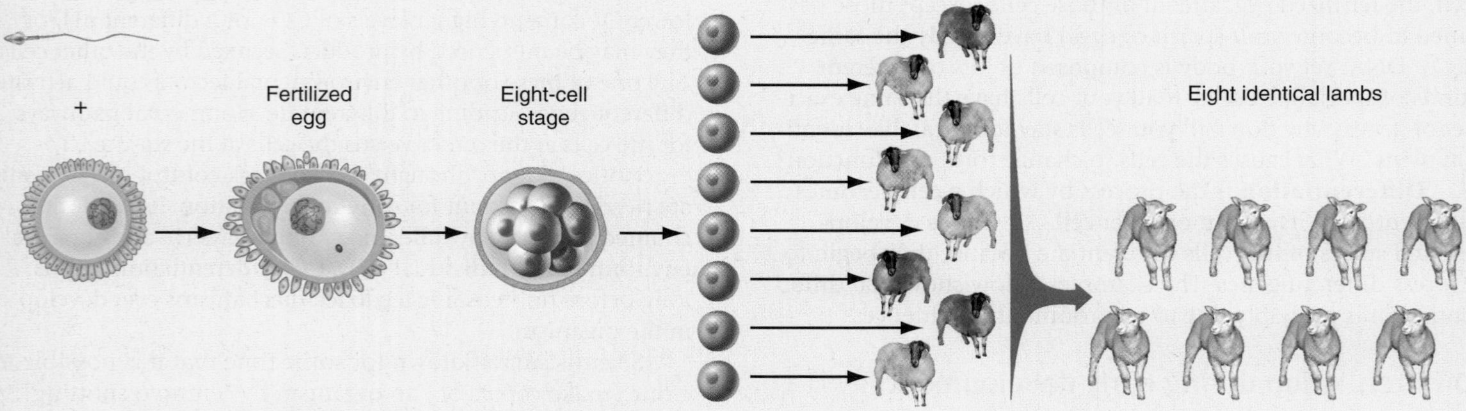


**Figure 1 An example of embryo splitting.** The resulting clones are not exact copies of either parent, but identical twins.

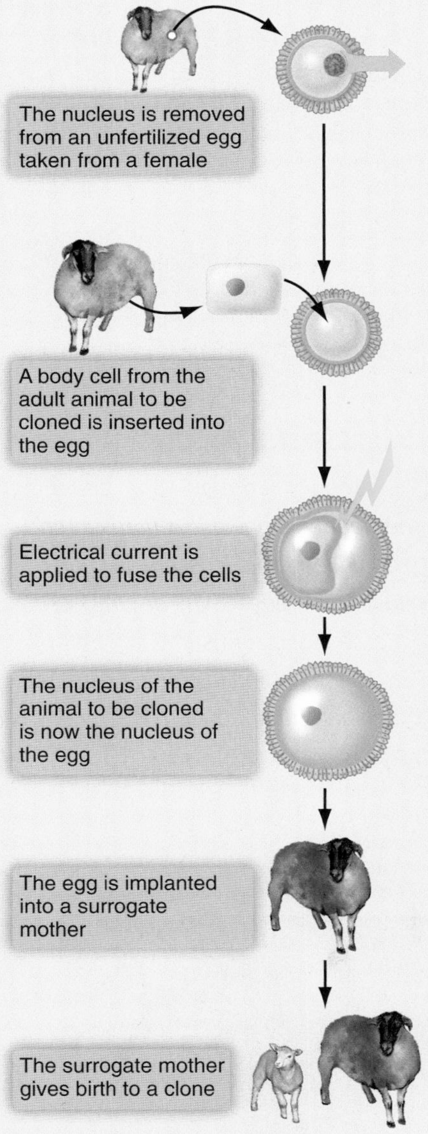


**Figure 2 Somatic cell nuclear transfer.** The clone is a copy of the animal providing the body cell.

somatic cell "start over" and differentiate as if it were a fertilized egg. Dolly was created when a somatic cell (from the udder) of an adult sheep was fused with another sheep's egg after the egg's nucleus had been removed (Figure 2). The egg, now containing the DNA of the udder cell, developed into Dolly. In essence, Dolly was a twin of the sheep providing the udder cell.

### Biological Issues

With sexual reproduction, sperm or eggs with damaged chromosomes generally don't survive. This eliminates potentially harmful mutations from the human gene pool before fertilization takes place. With cloning by somatic cell nuclear transfer, however, any defects in the cell used for cloning would be passed on to the clone. Indeed, some cloned animals show genetic and developmental abnormalities and have poor survival rates. Dolly, the famous sheep who started it all, had to be euthanized at age 6 after developing early arthritis and a lung tumor. Scientists are unsure whether such problems are due to accumulated mutations, unstable donor cells, or errors in the cloning procedure itself. Better information will probably come from further experiments with animals.

British embryologist Professor Ian Wilmut with "Dolly," the first cloned sheep.

### Therapeutic Versus Reproductive Cloning

Ethical and political discussions of human cloning often center on the distinction between therapeutic cloning and reproductive cloning. **Therapeutic cloning** is the cloning of cells from an embryo for the purpose of producing human stem cells, with the ultimate goal of treating human diseases. In therapeutic cloning, a somatic cell from a person would be fused with an enucleated egg by nuclear transfer, and then once the embryo had begun to develop, stem cells would be harvested from it, grown into tissues and organs, and transplanted back into the patient. The need for organ donations and problems with tissue rejection would be things of the past. It's easy to imagine that therapeutic cloning could transform medical treatment in the future, though a lot of basic research still needs to be done before it becomes routine.

Human **reproductive cloning,** on the other hand, would be cloning an adult human cell with the intent of producing a human baby.

(continued on page 418)

## the *facts*...

- Researchers routinely clone (make exact copies of) molecules, genes, and cells.
- Whole animals can be cloned either by embryo splitting or by somatic cell nuclear transfer.
- Some cloned animals show signs of poor health and shortened lifespans.
- Therapeutic cloning has the potential to transform medical care. Reproductive cloning raises fundamental biological, ethical, legal, and social issues. The techniques required for both types of cloning are essentially the same.

*Snuppy, the first successfully cloned Afghan hound, sits with his genetic father.*

In reproductive cloning, the embryo derived from the cloned adult cell would be allowed to develop naturally inside a woman's womb into a full-term baby. A reproductive clone would be an identical twin of the adult from which the cell was taken. The adult and its clone would look and act like twins separated by a big age difference, because individuals are shaped by their experiences and their environments as well as by their genes. Except for the novelty factor of actually accomplishing human reproductive cloning for the first time, human reproductive cloning is likely to be of little practical value in the near future. It's easy enough to produce babies the natural way or by IVF techniques.

The political and ethical problem for all of us is that the techniques used to create cloned early-stage human embryos are essentially the same, regardless of whether the goal is therapeutic or reproductive. Which, if either, of these two types of cloning should we endorse? If we choose to endorse only therapeutic cloning, can we create laws and safeguards that would prevent reproductive cloning? Many people worry that it will be hard to prevent reproductive cloning if we endorse therapeutic cloning—someone is likely to try it just to see if they can.

Reproductive cloning raises especially difficult issues. There is a very real possibility that the first human clones would be born with birth defects. Who would be responsible and how would we react if a substantial number of human clones were created that required expensive medical care? Is some risk worth taking in order to achieve future success?

### Political and Legal Issues

When Dolly was born in 1997 there were no laws specifically addressing human cloning because they weren't considered necessary. That changed quickly. Under current U.S. law, federal funds may not be used for the creation of human embryos for research purposes. The government does, however, allow the use of federal funds for research using human stem cell lines that were already in existence at the time of the ban (see the Current Issue box in Chapter 3). Human cloning research has not been banned altogether, leaving the door open (at least for now) for research conducted with private funds. Nevertheless, the official view of the U.S. mission to the United Nations is that all human cloning should be banned. Not everyone agrees, however. The National Academy of Sciences endorses basic cloning research to produce human stem cells but recommends that human reproductive cloning be banned.

The political and ethical debate has had a chilling effect on cloning research in the U.S., but research continues in other nations where it is legal and regulated, such as Singapore, China, Japan, and the United Kingdom. Recently researchers in South Korea made global headlines with the announcement that they had grown human embryos to the stage where stem cells could be extracted. While this claim later proved fraudulent, investigators found that the South Korean team had successfully produced human blastocysts in about 10% of their cloning attempts. Researchers in the U.K. have achieved a comparable track record. Near successes such as these are a warning sign that regulation and oversight are sorely needed.

Can successful human reproductive cloning be far off? The time to deal with the issue is now, not later.

### Questions to consider

**1** *Do you think the potential benefits of therapeutic cloning justify research that could lead to successful human reproductive cloning? Why or why not?*

**2** *Some U.S. scientists worry that the U.S. is falling behind in cloning research. Do you share their concern? Why or why not?*

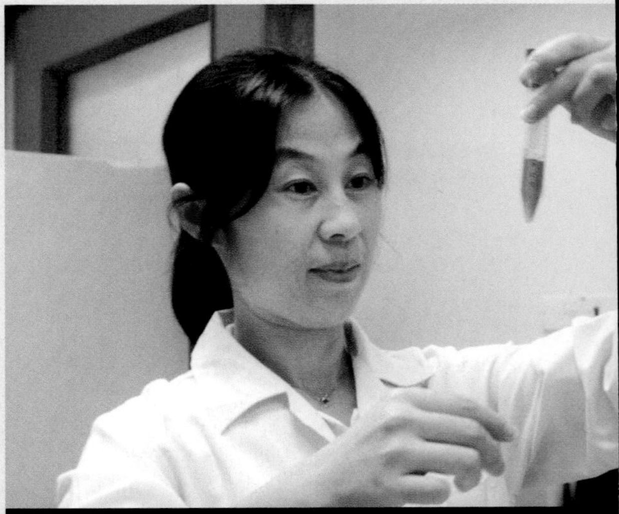

Dr. Li Tin, of the National University of Singapore, looks at a sample of embryos that were cloned for their stem cells.

presumably because they have not yet differentiated. After about 16 cells, however, cloning by embryo splitting no longer works.

**RECAP**

Differentiation is the process whereby cells become different from each other. During early development, environmental influences trigger differentiation. ■

## Differentiation later in development

Differentiation at later stages is similar in principle to that at earlier stages. Each cell is shaped by two factors: the developmental history of the cells that came before it and its local environment. Genes are turned on at certain stages of development and then turned off, some never to be used again.

For example, early in development some cells begin to express the genes that cause them to become epithelial cells. Others become connective tissue, nerves, or muscle cells. Those that are destined to become muscle tissue differentiate even further, becoming either skeletal, smooth, or cardiac muscle.

In the end, even cells that are closely related in function and structure can differ in hundreds of ways. Each difference in gene expression, added to those that occurred before, eventually results in a very specialized cell. For example, your smooth and skeletal muscle cells differ in their metabolic pathways (how they use energy), speed and strength of contraction, shape and size, and internal arrangement of muscle fibers. They got that way by an ever-increasing cascade of selective gene expressions.

The mechanisms of differentiation explain why the developing fetus is more vulnerable to genetic damage than an adult. Alteration of a gene that plays a critical role in early development can be so disruptive to embryonic differentiation that the embryo may not survive. Later in development the embryo may be able to survive the damage but be left with marked physical deformities. In an adult, alteration of a single gene may be similarly dangerous, or it could have little or no visible effect. It all depends on what the proteins coded by the gene do.

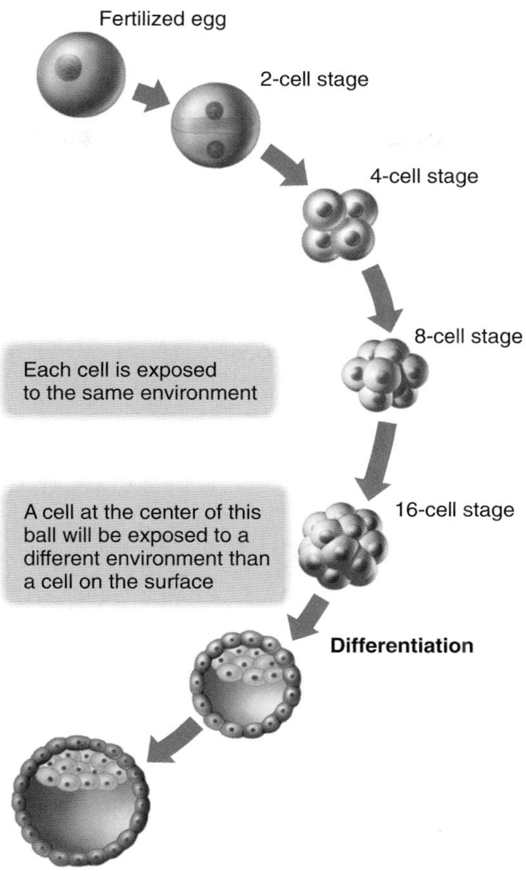


**Figure 17.14 How early differentiation might occur.** Beyond about the eight-cell stage, the cells begin to be exposed to different environments. Differences in environments may trigger different gene expressions, leading to differentiation.

These are some substances that can harm a fetus:

- Cigarette smoke. Smoking can retard fetal growth and may contribute to spontaneous abortions.
- Alcohol. Babies born to mothers who abuse alcohol may have fetal alcohol syndrome. These babies may have heart defects, limb abnormalities, and delays in motor and language development.
- Prescription and over-the-counter medications. If a woman becomes pregnant, she should review with her physician all the drugs she takes.
- Illegal drugs. Cocaine and heroin use during pregnancy can kill a fetus or cause abnormalities. The use of marijuana is associated with poor fetal weight gain and behavioral abnormalities in the newborn.
- Chemicals in air, water, and soil. Examples include lead, mercury, pesticides, and industrial solvents such as polychlorinated biphenyls (PCBs) and toluene.
- Radiation, for instance, from radon gas or pelvic irradiation during cancer treatment. Video display terminals and natural radiation from cosmic rays are not thought to pose any risk.

Intrauterine infections can also be dangerous. The most damaging are HIV infection, syphilis, and rubella (German measles).

**RECAP**

Some genes are expressed only at certain stages of development; for this reason, genetic mutations during early development can be particularly damaging. Later in development hundreds of different genes may be expressed by various types of cells. Agents that can harm a fetus include cigarette smoke, alcohol, legal and illegal drugs, chemicals, radiation, and bacterial and viral infections. ■

# Chapter Summary

### The cell cycle creates new cells *p. 403*

- Cells reproduce by a repetitive cycle called the cell cycle in which one cell grows and then divides in two.
- The cell cycle has two primary phases: interphase and the mitotic phase. During interphase the cell grows and the DNA is replicated. During the mitotic phase, first the nucleus and then the cell divide in two.

### Replication, transcription, and translation: An overview *p. 404*

- Human DNA is packed into 46 separate molecules called chromosomes.
- A gene is the smallest functional unit of a chromosome. A gene contains the code for making a specific protein.
- DNA replication is a process in which the two strands of DNA separate and a new complementary copy is made of each strand.
- DNA is repaired when it is damaged and is checked for errors after it is replicated.
- For a gene to be expressed, the strand of DNA with that gene must be transcribed to create a complementary strand of mRNA. The mRNA leaves the nucleus, attaches to a ribosome, and serves as the template for protein synthesis.
- Translation is the process of making a polypeptide chain (protein) using the mRNA as a template. Three successive bases of mRNA, called a codon, code for a particular amino acid.
- The amino acid building blocks for the polypeptide chain are captured in the cytoplasm by tRNA, brought to the mRNA, and attached to each other by ribosomal enzymes.

### Cell reproduction: One cell becomes two *p. 409*

- Mitosis is a sequence of events in which the replicated chromosomes are separated to form two new genetically identical nuclei.
- Cytokinesis is the process whereby the cell divides into two new cells, each with one of the new nuclei produced by mitosis and roughly half of the cell's organelles and mass.
- Meiosis is a sequence of two cell divisions that produces haploid cells. Meiosis occurs only in cells destined to become sperm or egg. Crossing-over during meiosis mixes the genes of homologous chromosomes, and subsequent cell divisions reduce the number of chromosomes by half.

### How cell reproduction is regulated *p. 412*

- Cell reproduction is regulated in part by selective gene expression. Selective gene expression is controlled by regulatory genes.
- The cell cycle may be influenced by the physical and chemical environments both inside and outside the cell.

### Environmental factors influence cell differentiation *p. 415*

- Differentiation is the process by which cells become different from each other, acquiring specialized forms and functions.
- Because all cells have the same set of genes, differentiation in the early embryo must be triggered by environmental influences.
- Cell differentiation later in development can be influenced by environmental cues, but it also depends on the developmental history of the cells that preceded it.

# Terms You Should Know

anaphase, *410*
cell cycle, *403*
chromosome, *404*
codon, *407*
cytokinesis, *409*
differentiation, *415*
diploid, *412*
gene, *405*
haploid, *412*
homologous chromosomes, *412*
interphase, *403*
metaphase, *409*
mitosis, *409*
mutation, *406*
prophase, *409*
replication, *404*
ribosomal RNA (rRNA), *408*
ribosome, *408*
telophase, *410*
transcription, *405*
transfer RNA (tRNA), *408*
translation, *405*

# Concept Review

1. Describe how DNA is replicated before cell division.
2. Compare and contrast the processes of transcription and translation.
3. Explain what mutations are and the role of DNA repair mechanisms.
4. Name the four phases of mitosis and describe briefly what is happening to the chromosomes during each phase.
5. Explain why only one large egg is formed during meiosis in the female, whereas four sperm are formed during meiosis in the male.
6. Describe what is meant by *selective gene expression* and why it is important to how a cell functions.
7. Explain how factors present in the environment can influence cell differentiation.
8. Describe how ribosomes contribute to the formation of a protein.
9. Compare and contrast the roles of introns and exons.
10. Describe how the cell cycle is regulated.

# Test Yourself

### Matching Exercise

_____ 1. The process of making a protein using the mRNA code as a template
_____ 2. The process of making a single strand of RNA from a short segment of DNA
_____ 3. Enzyme copies from and produces new double stranded DNA molecules
_____ 4. Copies from DNA and produces a primary transcript
_____ 5. mRNA base triplet representing the code for a particular amino acid
_____ 6. tRNA base triplet that binds to the base triplet of mRNA

a. translation
b. codon
c. DNA polymerase
d. anticodon
e. transcription
f. RNA polymerase

### Fill in the Blank

7. The first phase of mitosis is called ________________.
8. A short segment of DNA representing the code for a particular protein is called a(n) ________________.
9. Small molecules of RNA called ________________ bind to specific amino acids and bring them to the ribosomes, where protein synthesis takes place.
10. The process whereby a cell becomes different from its parent or sister cell is called ________________.
11. The process of cell division is called ________________.
12. A pair of chromosomes that look alike and have the same genes at the same locations are called ________________ chromosomes.

### True or False?

13. Human cells (except those developing into sperm or eggs) have 23 pairs of chromosomes.
14. Sperm and eggs are haploid cells.
15. Roughly 32 clones can be produced by embryo splitting.

## Apply What You Know

1. Recall that the base pairing in DNA is always A–T and C–G. Suppose that during a DNA replication a C is accidentally paired with a T. Explain why it is important that the error be detected and corrected before the cell divides again, by illustrating what would happen at the next cell division if the error were not corrected.
2. The RNA code is a "triplet code," meaning that three bases code for a single amino acid. Would a "doublet code" be sufficient? Explain.
3. Are gene mutations that occur during fetal development always fatal? Why or why not?
4. Why do so many commercials for various pharmaceutical drugs contain warnings for women who are pregnant or are trying to become pregnant?
5. Mitochondria contain their own DNA that is inherited independently of nuclear DNA. From which parent did you inherit your mitochondrial DNA?
6. Bacteria can reproduce by simple cell division. Sexual reproduction is far more complicated and difficult; success is not guaranteed. What is the main advantage of sexual reproduction?

*Answers can be found on the Human Biology Place.*

## References and Additional Reading


Becker, Wayne M., Lewis J. Kleinsmith, and Jeff Hardin. *The World of the Cell.* 7th edition. San Francisco: Benjamin Cummings, 2009. (A comprehensive textbook of cell and molecular biology, for advanced reference only.)

McGee, Glenn, and Arthur Caplan, editors. *The Human Cloning Debate.* Albany, CA: Berkeley Hills Books, 2006. (A collection of essays by 25 contributors.)

Persaud, T.V.N. *Environmental Causes of Human Birth Defects.* Springfield, IL: Charles C Thomas, 1990. 182 pp. (A good summary, with references to the literature for specific substances that cause birth defects.)

Silver, Lee M. *Remaking Eden: Cloning and Beyond in a Brave New World.* New York: Avon Books, 1997. (A provocative account suggesting that cloning will be driven by our desire for new reproductive technologies.)

Watson, James D. *The Double Helix: A Personal Account of the Discovery of the Structure of DNA.* New York: Atheneum, 1968. 226 pp. (A readable and entertaining account of the discovery of the structure of DNA by the Nobel laureate.)


### Internet References

Find links to these Web sites at the Human Biology Place.

**National Center for Biotechnology Information**
**www.ncbi.nlm.nih.gov**
This national agency conducts research, builds public databases, and distributes information relating to genes and human health.

**CRS Report for Congress: Human Cloning**
**http://italy.usembassy.gov/pdf/other/RL31358.pdf**
A report to Congress summarizing the United States' position on human cloning.

**Genomic Resource Centre, World Health Organization: News and Events**
**www.who.int/genomics/news/en**
An international perspective on recent developments in genetics, cloning, stem cell research, and related topics.

**"Cloning and Stem Cell Research," American Society for Reproductive Medicine**
**www.asrm.org/Patients/topics/cloning.html**
Links to resources and information on these topics, on the ASRM Web site and other sites.

# 18 Cancer: Uncontrolled Cell Division and Differentiation

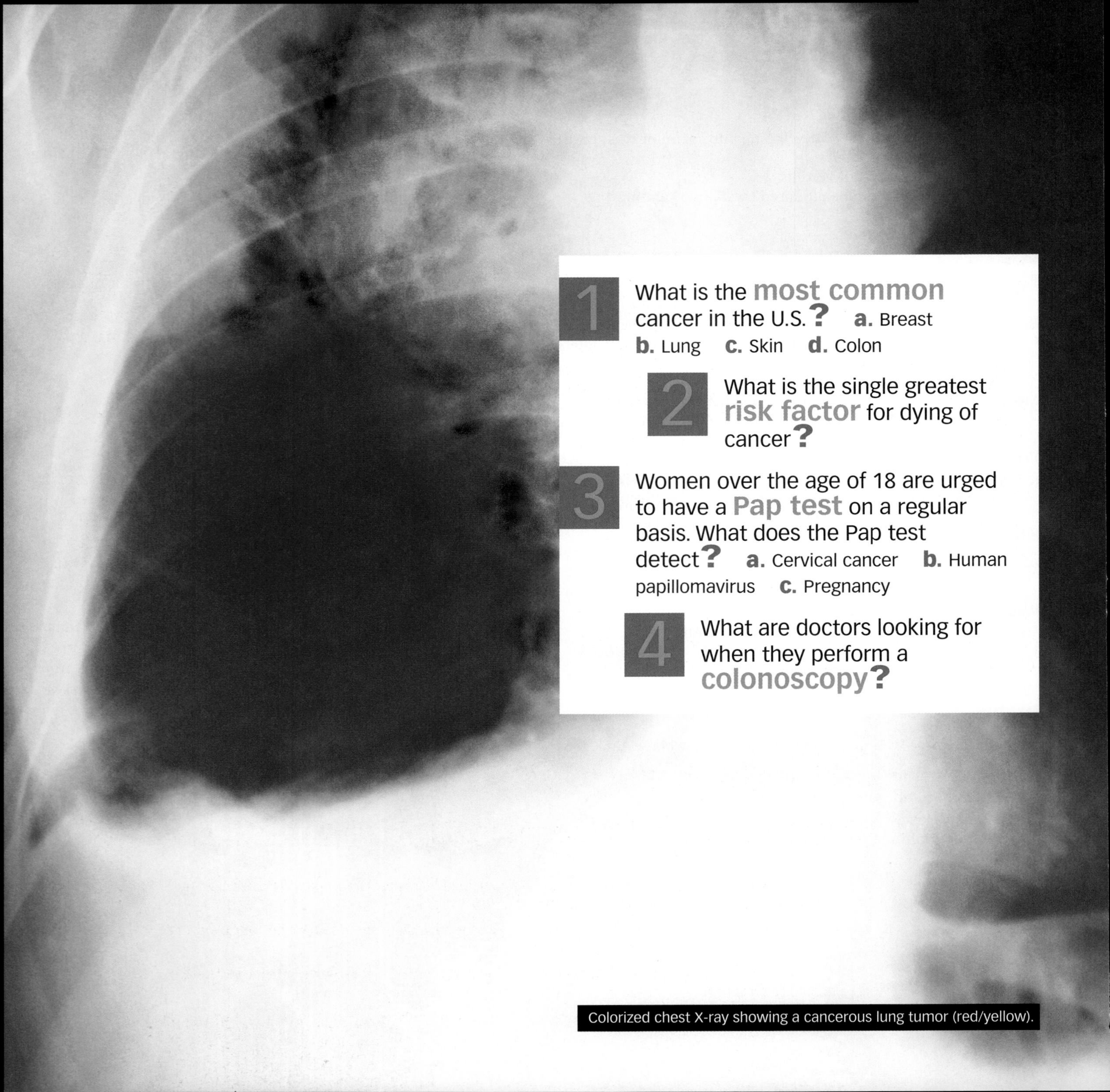

**1** What is the **most common** cancer in the U.S.? **a.** Breast **b.** Lung **c.** Skin **d.** Colon

**2** What is the single greatest **risk factor** for dying of cancer?

**3** Women over the age of 18 are urged to have a **Pap test** on a regular basis. What does the Pap test detect? **a.** Cervical cancer **b.** Human papillomavirus **c.** Pregnancy

**4** What are doctors looking for when they perform a **colonoscopy**?

Colorized chest X-ray showing a cancerous lung tumor (red/yellow).

**The word *cancer* may conjure up images of pain,** suffering, and lingering death. We may associate the word with visits to the hospital with our parents when we were children; we may recall years of long-term care of a grandparent at home; we may remember a friend or loved one no longer with us. A diagnosis of cancer sounds like a death sentence.

And yet, people do recover from cancer. There are known risk factors for most types of cancers and things we can do to reduce our risk. There are treatments for many cancers, some of which work rather well. The death rate from some cancers is even declining as we learn more about the disease.

We know of at least 100 different types of cancers, but all are the same in one respect—they all are diseases of cell division and differentiation. Once that is understood, cancer makes some sense. In this chapter we examine the biological basis for how cancer develops and spreads. Then we discuss how cancer is diagnosed and look at new advances in treatment and prevention.

To understand how cancer develops we must first understand two key characteristics of normal cells:

- Normal cells have regulatory mechanisms that keep their rates of cell division appropriately in check. They may divide more frequently at some times than at others, but their rates of cell division are carefully controlled by regulatory mechanisms that may involve an internal clock and various hormones. In addition, their rates of division are generally inhibited by signals from nearby cells.
- Normal cells generally remain in one location throughout their lifetime because they adhere to their nearby neighbors. (Blood cells are an exception, because they must travel throughout the body to carry out their normal function.)

## 18.1 Tumors can be benign or cancerous

Sometimes even normal cells increase their rate of cell division as part of their normal physiological function. Examples are the growth of the lining of the uterus during the menstrual cycle and the growth of breast tissue during pregnancy. In general, any substantial increase in the rate of cell division is called **hyperplasia** ("increased" plus Greek *plasis*, "formation").

In the progression toward cancer of normal cells, however, hyperplasia is not necessarily a normal event. Instead, it may signal a loss of control over cell division. Eventually, these rapidly dividing cells will develop into a discrete mass called a **tumor,** or *neoplasm* (meaning literally "new growth").

Not all tumors are cancers. Tumors that remain in one place as a single well-defined mass of cells are *benign tumors* (from the Latin *benignus*, "well disposed") (Figure 18.1). The cells in a benign tumor still have most of the structural features of the cells from which they originated, and in particular they stay together and may be surrounded by a layer of connective tissue. Benign tumors tend to threaten health only if they become so large that they crowd normal cells, which can happen sometimes in the brain. In most cases surgery can easily remove benign tumors because they are so well contained. Many moles on the skin are a form of benign tumor so inconsequential that usually we don't bother to remove them. Occasionally, a previously benign tumor may change into something more damaging. For example, certain moles have the potential to develop into melanoma, a form of skin cancer.

## 18.2 Cancerous cells lose control of their functions and structures

If and when cells progress toward cancer, in addition to dividing more frequently than normal they also undergo a series of structural changes. The nucleus often becomes larger, there is less cytoplasm, and the cells lose their specialized functions and structures. An abnormal structural change is called **dysplasia** (from *dys*, abnormal, plus *plas*, growth.) Figure 18.2 shows how dysplasia may lead to cancer.

Doctors have learned to recognize characteristic patterns of changes that cells typically go through as they get more and more out of control. Dysplasia is often a sign that tumor cells are "precancerous," meaning they are altering in ways

### Answers to Intro Questions

1 **c.** More than a million Americans are diagnosed with skin cancer every year. Too much sun is the likely cause. Except for melanomas, most skin cancers are not very dangerous, but they should still be removed just to be safe.

2 **Smoking.** Lung cancer kills more people per year than the next four most deadly cancers combined, and we now understand that most cases of lung cancer are due to smoking.

3 **a.** It detects cervical cancer. A regular Pap test is important because the survival rate for cervical cancer is high (over 90%) if the cancer is detected early.

4 **Polyps** in the rectum and colon. Polyps are benign precancerous growths that are easily removed before they become colon cancer.

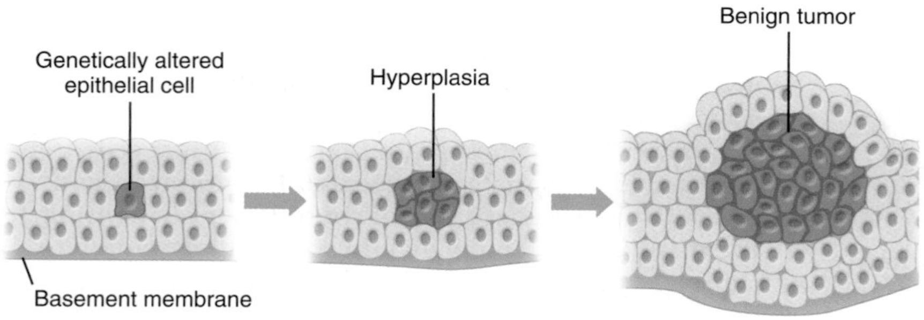


**Figure 18.1 Development of a benign tumor.** A benign tumor begins when a cell (in this case an epithelial cell) becomes genetically altered and begins to divide more frequently than normal. The mass enlarges but stays well contained, generally by a capsule of normal cells.

that may herald the possibility of cancer. The tumor itself becomes more and more disorganized as cells pile on top of each other in seemingly random fashion.

An example of a precancerous skin lesion is *actinic keratosis* (Figure 18.3). Actinic keratoses generally appear as dry, scaly, or rough skin lesions on areas of the skin exposed to the sun. Often they are felt more easily than seen, although sometimes they appear as reddish patches. They may grow slowly and then even disappear for a time, only to return later. Only 10–20% of all actinic keratoses ever become cancerous. Fortunately they are easily removed by chemical peeling, freezing, or scraping.

A tumor is defined as a **cancer** when at least some of its cells completely lose all semblance of organization, structure, and regulatory control. As long as the entire tumor remains in one place it is known as an ***in situ* cancer.** *In situ* cancers can often be successfully removed surgically if they are detected early enough.

If cancer cells go through additional changes that cause them not to adhere to each other in the normal fashion, the result may be **metastasis**—the spread of cancer to another organ or region of the body. Metastasis occurs when cancer cells break away from the main tumor, travel via the blood or lymph, and develop into new colonies of cancer cells at distant sites. Cancers that *metastasize* and cancers that invade normal tissues until they compromise organ function are called **malignant tumors** (from the Latin *malignus,* "ill-disposed"). Table 18.1 compares benign, *in situ*, and malignant tumors.

A malignant, metastasizing tumor is like a forest fire that is out of control and throwing off sparks. The sparks start new fires in sometimes distant locations, which also spread uncontrollably. Metastasizing cancer continues to spread until it completely overruns the functions of tissues, organs,

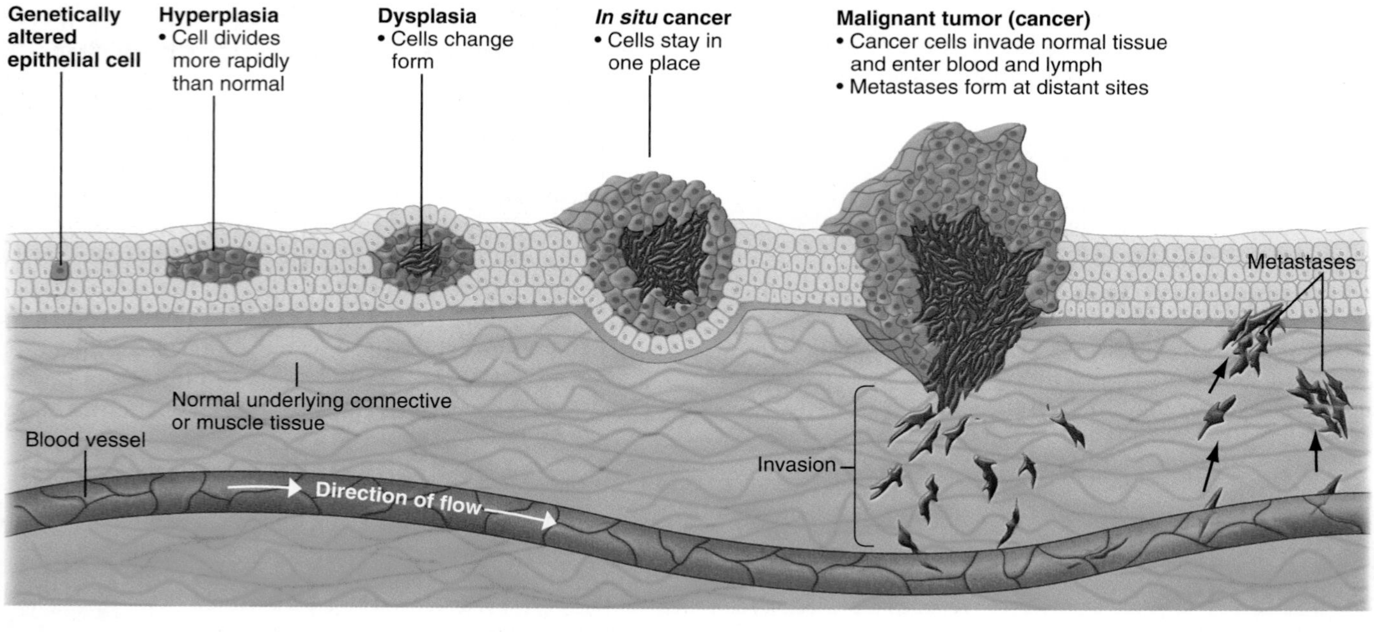


**Figure 18.2 The development of a malignant tumor (cancer).** A genetically altered cell begins to divide more frequently than normal, resulting in an increased number of cells (hyperplasia). Additional genetic alterations cause some cells to change form (dysplasia) and to lose all semblance of organization or control over cell division and function. As long as the mass stays in one place it is called an *in situ* cancer. However, additional changes in the cells may cause them to break away from the tumor and invade normal tissues or enter the blood or lymph. These invading cells may set up new colonies of cancer (called metastases) at distant sites. A cancer that invades and metastasizes is called a malignant tumor.

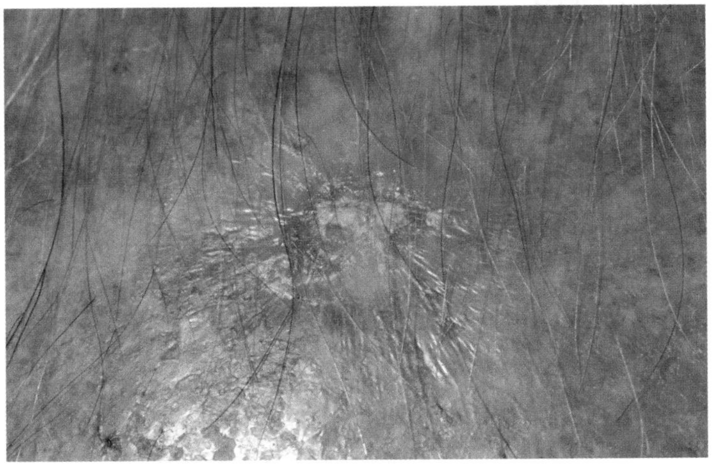

**Figure 18.3 Actinic keratosis.** Actinic keratosis is a precancerous skin lesion caused by repeated exposure to sunlight. Actinic keratosis lesions usually do not progress to cancer.

and organ systems. Ultimately it may kill the entire organism, just as a forest fire may not die out until it has consumed the whole forest.

Cancer is extremely difficult to treat, for obvious reasons. One in three people in the United States will experience cancer in their lifetime, and one in four will die of it. Cancer ranks second only to heart disease as a cause of death. The good news is that most incidences of cancer could be prevented, and later in this chapter we discuss how you can lower your risk.

**RECAP**

Some tumors are benign, but when tumor cells change form dramatically and divide uncontrollably, the tumor is called cancer. Cancer becomes malignant when cells invade and metastasize, starting new tumors at distant sites. ■

## 18.3 How cancer develops

For cancer to develop, at least two things must happen simultaneously:

- The cell must grow and divide uncontrollably, ignoring inhibitory signals from nearby cells to stop dividing.
- The cell must undergo physical changes that allow it to break away from surrounding cells. These events begin when some of the cell's genes become abnormal and no longer function properly.

### Mutant forms of proto-oncogenes, tumor suppressor genes, and mutator genes contribute to cancer

Several types of genes control the various activities of a cell. *Structural genes* code for the proteins necessary for cell growth, division, differentiation, and even cell adhesion (the adherence of cells in the same tissue to each other). *Regulatory genes,* on the other hand, code for proteins that either activate or repress the expression of these structural genes.

Some regulatory genes code for proteins secreted by cells in order to influence nearby cells. These proteins are called *growth factors* or *growth inhibitors,* depending on which it is that they do. Growth inhibitors are especially important in regulating cell division because they influence cells in a particular tissue to stop dividing when enough cells are present.

Under normal circumstances, two classes of regulatory genes control the cell's activities: proto-oncogenes and tumor suppressor genes. **Proto-oncogenes** are normal regulatory genes that *promote* cell growth, differentiation, division, or adhesion (*proto,* "first"; *onco-* means "mass, bulk," that is, a tumor). Mutated or damaged proto-oncogenes that contribute to cancer are called **oncogenes.** Some oncogenes drive the internal rate of cell growth and division faster than normal. Others produce damaged protein receptors that fail to heed inhibitory growth signals from other cells. However, it is important to recognize that one oncogene alone is not sufficient to cause cancer. Because so many cellular processes

**Table 18.1 A summary of the characteristics of benign tumors and cancers**

| | Benign tumor | *In situ* tumor (cancer) | Malignant tumor (cancer) |
|---|---|---|---|
| **Frequency of cell division** | More rapid than normal | Rapid and completely out of control | Rapid and completely out of control |
| **Cell structure and function** | Slightly abnormal | Increasingly abnormal | Very abnormal |
| **Tumor organization** | A single mass generally surrounded by a capsule | Still a single mass, but increasingly disorganized and not always surrounded by a capsule | Some cells break away to invade underlying normal tissues or to enter the blood or lymph. New tumor colonies (metastases) become established at distant sites |

must be disrupted at once and each process may be controlled by multiple genes, cancer develops only when multiple oncogenes are present.

**Tumor suppressor genes** are regulatory genes that under normal conditions apply the brakes to unchecked cell growth, division, differentiation, or adhesion. They tend to *inhibit* these cell activities when cells are stressed or when conditions are not right for cell division. When they become damaged, tumor suppressor genes contribute to cancer because then the cell activities they normally regulate are likely to continue unchecked.

One tumor suppressor gene, called p53, has received a lot of attention lately. The p53 gene codes for a protein found in most tissues that prevents damaged or stressed cells from dividing. In fact its primary role may be to inhibit division by cells that already show cancerous features. If the p53 gene itself becomes damaged, a variety of cancers may develop more easily. To date, mutated p53 genes have been identified in tumors of the cervix, colon, lung, skin, bladder, and breast.

A third class of gene may also contribute to cancer. In their unmutated form, **mutator genes** are involved in DNA repair during DNA replication. When these genes mutate, the cell becomes increasingly prone to errors in DNA replication. As a result, the cell may accumulate mutations in other genes at a faster rate than normal.

**RECAP**

Proto-oncogenes and tumor suppressor genes normally control the rate of cell division. Mutator genes are involved in DNA repair. Mutations of any of these genes may contribute to cancer. ■

## A variety of factors can lead to cancer

A car analogy demonstrates how a cell progresses toward cancer. At first your new car runs very well. As time goes on a few parts wear out, but you manage to keep it in good repair with regular service checkups. But as the car gets older, the need for repairs gets more frequent, and you aren't always able to keep up with them. Now the suspension needs replacing, the tires are worn out, the accelerator pedal sticks occasionally, and the brakes are thin. No single defect is enough to cause an accident, but together they spell trouble. There may come a moment when you may not be able to control the car, and you'll have an accident.

The same sort of progression occurs within cells. In fact, the single most important factor in the development of cancer may be age. Skin cancer is uncommon before adulthood, even though most severe sunburns occur during childhood. Recall from Chapter 4 that the outer layers of your skin are continually being replaced by basal cells located at the base of the epidermis. The basal cells of a child's skin haven't been through very many cell divisions yet—they are still in good repair. But decades later, after thousands more cell divisions and a few more sunburns, those same basal cells are about worn out. Cellular repair mechanisms fail more frequently; mechanisms controlling cell division become less effective. First there's dysplasia, then cancer. The cells are out of control.

In addition, your parents may carry a few of the cancer-promoting mutations that have accumulated in the precursor cells to human eggs and sperm during the course of human evolution. These rare heritable mutations may not be enough to guarantee cancer, but they do increase your *heritable susceptibility*. If six mutations are required to produce cancer, for example, you could inherit five mutations and still be cancer free. This is why, even in families with a history of cancer, some siblings develop the disease and others do not.

The multigene basis of cancer also explains why it is possible to develop cancer even if there is no family history. Remember that we all inherit a slightly different combination of our parents' genes, and if you happen to get mutated genes from both parents, you could be at greater risk than either of them. (We discuss genetic inheritance in more detail in Chapter 19.)

The process of transforming a normal cell into a cancerous one is called *carcinogenesis*. A **carcinogen** is any substance or physical factor that causes cancer. The word *carcinogen* comes from the recognition by early physicians that certain skin cancers had a crablike appearance (Greek *karkinos*, "crab"; *genein*, "to produce"). Some of the factors that contribute to the probability that a normal cell will progress toward cancer are described below.

**Viruses and bacteria** Some viruses and bacteria may contribute to certain cancers. As described in Chapter 9, viruses reproduce by inserting their DNA into the host's DNA. If the viral sequence of DNA impairs the function of a normal gene, perhaps by preventing a regulatory gene from being turned off after it is turned on, this will increase the cancer risk.

Viruses thought to contribute to cancer include:

- Human papillomavirus (HPV; cancers of the cervix and penis)
- Hepatitis B and hepatitis C viruses (liver cancer)
- HIV (Kaposi's sarcoma, non-Hodgkin's lymphoma)
- Epstein-Barr virus (Hodgkin's disease and non-Hodgkin's lymphoma)
- Human T-cell leukemia/lymphoma virus (HTLV-1; T-cell non-Hodgkin's lymphoma)

The *Helicobacter pylori* bacterium, which causes ulcers, may contribute to stomach cancer as well. Although this list may sound frightening, viruses and bacteria probably account for fewer than 15% of all cancers.

**Chemicals in the environment** Some chemical carcinogens damage DNA directly. Others do not themselves damage DNA, but their presence increases the potency of still other carcinogens. The list of chemical carcinogens in the environment includes many chemicals used in (or produced by) industrial processes, such as coal tar, soot, asbestos, benzene, vinyl chloride, and some pesticides and dyes (Figure 18.4).

**Figure 18.4 Environmental carcinogens.** This agricultural worker is wearing protective clothing and an air-filtering mask while spraying.

Table 18.2 lists examples of viral, chemical, and radiation carcinogens, ranked by likelihood of exposure.

**Tobacco** About 2% of all cancers are thought to be caused by industrial pollutants. In contrast, tobacco is by far the single most lethal carcinogen in the U.S., accounting for over 30% of all cancer deaths. Smoking dramatically increases your risk of cancer of the lungs, mouth, pharynx, pancreas, and bladder. Smokers are not the only ones at risk; passive smoking (inhaling secondhand smoke) can cause lung cancer too.

Smokeless tobacco (chewing tobacco or snuff) is also a carcinogen. It is a major risk factor for cancers of the mouth, pharynx, and esophagus.

**Radiation** Sources of radiation include the sun and radioactive radon gas, which is released by rocks, soil, and groundwater at intensities that vary in different geographic areas. Cellular telephones, household appliances, and electric power lines also emit trace amounts of radiation.

From time to time, the carcinogenic potential of radiation receives a great deal of media attention. In truth, all sources of radiation combined cause only about 2% of all cancer deaths, and most of these are due to skin cancer caused by the sun's ultraviolet rays.

The high-frequency ultraviolet B rays in sunlight cause over 80% of all skin cancers, including a particularly dangerous cancer of the melanin-producing cells of the skin called **melanoma.** Frequent sunburns, especially during childhood, increase the risk of melanoma. Fair-complexioned people who sunburn quickly are more vulnerable than those who tan easily (Figure 18.5). However, cumulative exposure to ultraviolet radiation, even without burning, raises the risk of skin cancer. Ultraviolet radiation from sunlamps and tanning booths is just as dangerous as radiation from natural sunlight.

**Diet** How much does diet contribute to cancer? Although difficult to define precisely, its role appears substantial. Dietary factors may be involved in up to 30% of cancers, rivaling smoking. In particular, red meat and saturated animal fat raise the risk of cancers of the colon, rectum, and prostate gland.

**Table 18.2 Examples of carcinogens**

| Carcinogen | Source of exposure or types of persons exposed | Type of cancer | Exposure of general population |
|---|---|---|---|
| Tobacco (smoking and smokeless) | Smokers, chewers, people exposed to secondhand smoke | Lung, bladder, mouth, pharynx, pancreas | Common |
| Diesel exhaust | Buses and trucks, miners, railroad yard workers | Lung | Common |
| Benzene | Paints, dyes, furniture finishes | Bone marrow (leukemias) | Common |
| Pesticides | Agricultural workers | Lung | Common |
| Ultraviolet light | Sunlight | Skin cancers | Common |
| Ionizing radiation | Radioactive materials, medical and dental procedures | Bone marrow (leukemias) | Common |
| Human papillomaviruses | Sexually transmitted | Cervix, penis | Common |
| Hepatitis B virus | Sexually transmitted | Liver | Less common |
| HIV | Sexually transmitted | Kaposi's sarcoma | Less common |
| Hydrocarbons in soot, tar smoke | Firefighters, chimney cleaners | Skin, lung | Uncommon |
| Asbestos | Shipyard, demolition, and insulation workers, brake linings | Lung, epithelial linings of body cavities | Uncommon |
| Radon | Mine workers, basements of houses | Lung | Uncommon |

Obesity in general is a risk factor for several types of cancer, and a high salt intake may contribute to stomach cancer. Excessive consumption of alcohol is associated with breast, rectal, colon, and liver cancer.

Certain fungi and plants produce carcinogens. One such carcinogen is *aflatoxin,* a by-product of a fungus that infects ground nuts. Aflatoxin may be present in raw peanut butter. Commercial peanut butters are processed to eliminate the fungus.

**Figure 18.5 Risky behavior.** Persons who were often sunburned as children have an increased risk for skin cancer later in life. Persons with lighter complexions are at greater risk.

In recent years researchers have become interested in what might be *missing* from the diet that could contribute to cancer. Recent evidence suggests that fruits and vegetables in particular may be mildly protective. A compound in broccoli sprouts has received a lot of attention lately as a cancer risk-reducing agent. Dietary analysis is complicated because there are literally thousands of compounds in the foods we eat.

**Internal factors** It is difficult to estimate how significant internal factors might be to the development of cancer. In theory, errors introduced during DNA replication and damage caused by certain chemicals within the body could contribute to the disease.

In particular, scientists are studying the effects of *free radicals,* highly reactive fragments of molecules that are produced by the body's biochemical processes. Free radicals are a normal by-product of cellular metabolism, and ordinarily they are detoxified by peroxisomes. However, if detoxification processes become less efficient for any reason, free radicals may accumulate in the body and damage other molecules, including DNA. Some researchers believe that free radicals play a role in the aging process as well.

Certain vitamins known as *antioxidants* appear to neutralize free radicals, although the mechanism by which they do this is still controversial. In particular, vitamins A, C, and E seem to exert antioxidant benefits. Whether antioxidants affect the development of cancer or the aging process, however, is still an open question.

**RECAP**

Aside from heritable susceptibility, factors that may contribute to the development of cancer include viruses and bacteria, environmental chemicals, tobacco, radiation, dietary factors, and alcohol. Free radicals created during cellular metabolism may also contribute to cancer. ■

### The immune system plays an important role in cancer prevention

Under normal circumstances, the immune system plays a critical role in defending against damaged or defective cells, including cancer cells. Recall that all cells display proteins that identify them as "self" so that the immune system leaves them alone. As cells change in ways that make them cancerous they may stop displaying "self" proteins, or they may display completely different proteins that mark them as abnormal. This makes them subject to attack and destruction by the immune system, at least as long as it is functioning normally.

Suppression of the immune system by drugs, viruses such as HIV, or even mental states of anxiety, stress, or depression may allow certain cancers to develop more easily. Some cancers apparently can suppress the immune system, and others may have mechanisms for disguising themselves from attack by the immune system. Figure 18.6 presents an overview of how cancer develops.

**RECAP**

The immune system normally protects us from cancer cells by killing them before they spread. Immune system suppression allows cancers to develop more easily. ■

## 18.4 Advances in diagnosis enable early detection

In 1971 President Nixon signed into law the National Cancer Act, declaring "war" on cancer. At that time many researchers hoped we could overcome cancer with early diagnosis and better treatments.

The sobering fact is that the overall death rate from all cancers has decreased only 6% in the past 55 years. The main reason has been a dramatic increase in lung cancer in older Americans. These were the teens and young adults of the 1940s and 1950s, when smoking was popularized and even encouraged (Figure 18.7). We are now paying the price with cancer rates in the over-65 age groups four to seven times the rate more than 50 years ago. As these older generations are replaced with generations who grew up with anti-smoking campaigns, lung cancer rates may begin to decline.

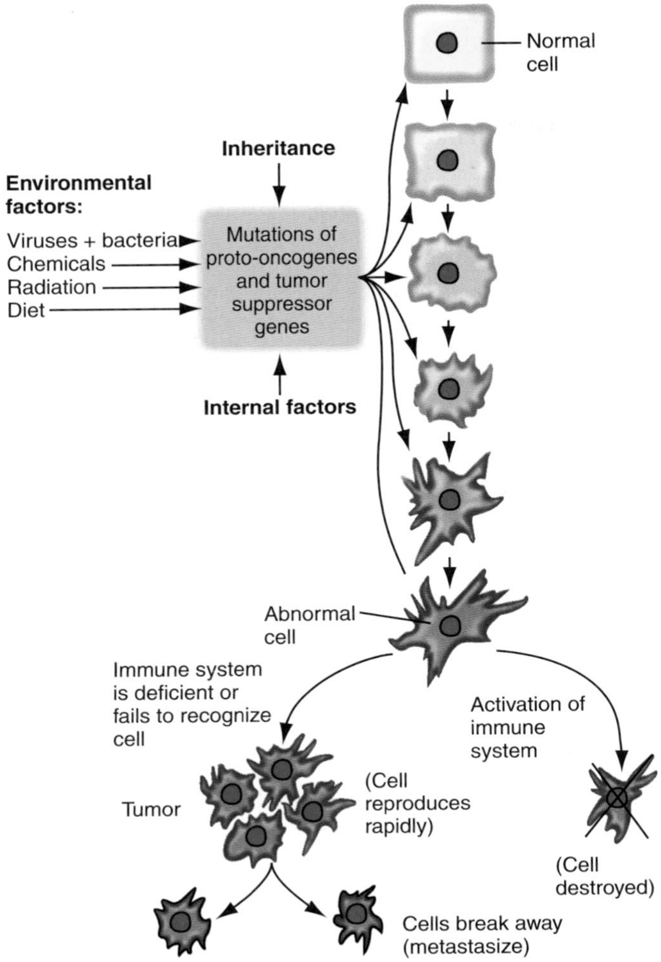


**Figure 18.6 Overview of the development of cancer.** The progression to cancer requires multiple genetic changes in regulatory genes, some of which may be inherited and some of which may be caused by environmental or internal factors. A cancer cell reproduces rapidly (develops into a cancer) and may invade and colonize distant tissues (metastasize). Suppression of the immune system appears to be involved in many cancers.

**a) Ads promoting smoking were common in the 1940s and 1950s.**

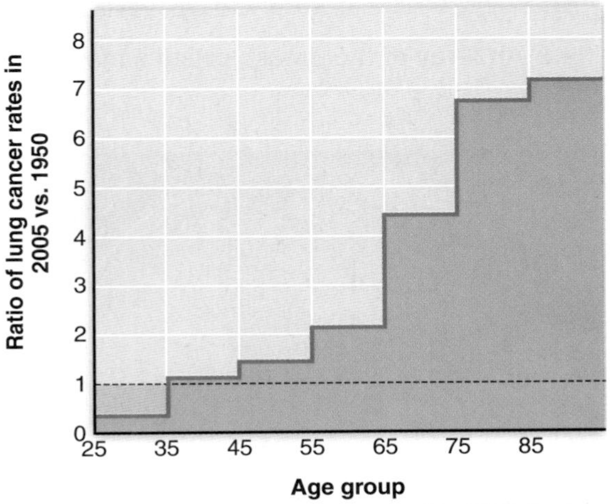


**b) Lung cancer rates in 2005 compared to 1950, by age group.** A ratio greater than 1 indicates that the rate of cancer was higher in 2005 than in 1950.

**Figure 18.7 Smoking and lung cancer.**

Although we have made significant progress against certain types of cancer, much more remains to be done. Early detection (diagnosis) of cancer is an important key to success. Early detection means that therapy can begin sooner, hopefully before the disease has had a chance to metastasize. Prompt treatment can even cure some cancers.

## Tumor imaging: X-rays, PET, and MRI

The classic approach to diagnosing a tumor is to view its image, either on an X-ray (Figure 18.8) or with a newer method. Computer-enhanced imaging is now able to detect changes that visual imaging may miss. Advanced imaging techniques such as *positron-emission tomography (PET)* and *magnetic resonance imaging (MRI)* show physiological differences between tissues in places that cannot be diagnosed effectively with X-rays.

PET scans employ radioactive substances to create three-dimensional images showing the metabolic activity of body structures. In addition to diagnosing cancer, PET scans are used to study blood flow, heart function, and brain activity.

MRI scans use short bursts of a powerful magnetic field to produce cross-sectional images of body structures. For example, MRI detects differences in water and chemical composition between tissues on the basis of changes in magnetic fields. MRI can detect tumors because tumors often have a slightly different consistency and composition than normal tissue. It can detect tumors even when they are hidden behind bone, such as tumors of the brain (Figure 18.9). Unlike X-rays, MRI is not itself an added risk factor for cancer.

## Genetic testing can identify mutated genes

As we learn more about which human characteristics are transmitted by specific genes, genetic testing for diseases, including cancers, becomes a real possibility. Already hundreds of new genes and their mutated counterparts have been identified, and tests are being devised to detect them.

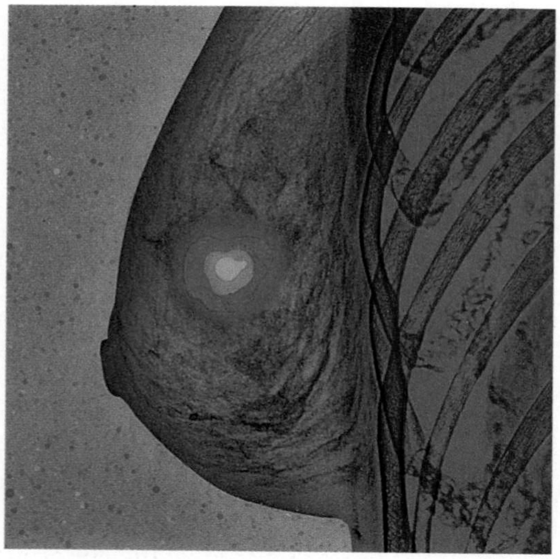

**Figure 18.8 An X-ray of the breast, called a mammogram.** A tumor is clearly visible in this X-ray.

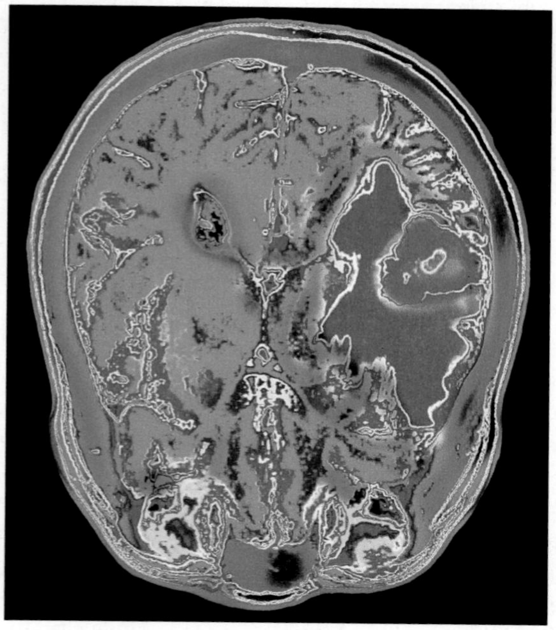

**Figure 18.9 An MRI of the brain.** The magenta and red area to the right is a brain tumor.

Such tests are highly controversial, however, and society will have to choose how to use them. One of the concerns about genetic testing is that it may be possible to test for mutated genes that have no cure. Some people believe that such knowledge may not be in the patient's best interest. In addition, it is difficult to convince people that in many cases a mutated gene is nothing more than a risk factor. It does not guarantee development of a disease.

### Enzyme tests may detect cancer markers

An enzyme called *telomerase* is rarely found in normal cells but is present in nearly all cancer cells. Some researchers propose that a sensitive test for telomerase in body fluids could detect early stages of cancer. An enzyme test could also be used to screen large populations or monitor the progression of the disease in known cancer patients. Researchers are exploring other potential cancer markers as well.

**RECAP**

Early diagnosis and prompt treatment of cancer are vital. Diagnostic techniques include X-rays, positron-emission tomography, magnetic resonance imaging, genetic testing, and enzyme markers. ■

## 18.5 Cancer treatments

Many cancers are treatable, especially if discovered early. Although some forms of the disease have higher survival rates than others, current treatments cure approximately 50% of all cancer cases.

### Conventional cancer treatments: Surgery, radiation, and chemotherapy

Classic treatments for cancer include surgery, radiation, chemotherapy, or a combination of two or more of these. Better imaging techniques have benefited the surgical treatment of cancer, and techniques for focusing external sources of radiation directly onto the cancer have improved as well. These focused sources of intense radiation are designed to damage and kill cancer cells in a specific location. It is sometimes possible to implant radioactive materials in the region of a tumor.

Healthy cells recover from radiation more readily than cancer cells, but radiation therapy generally does injure or kill some normal tissue, too. A drawback of both surgery and radiation is that they may miss small groups of metastasized cells, allowing the cancer to reappear later.

**Chemotherapy** is the administration of cytotoxic (cell-damaging) chemicals to destroy cancer cells. Chemotherapy addresses some of the limitations of surgery and radiation. Some chemotherapeutic drugs act everywhere in the body, and for that reason they must inflict only acceptable amounts of damage to normal cells. Some chemotherapy chemicals stop cells from dividing by interfering with their ability to replicate DNA. Chemicals that inhibit cell division act primarily on cancer cells because cancer cells divide very rapidly. But such chemicals also damage or kill many normal cells that divide rapidly, such as bone marrow cells and cells lining the digestive tract. Damage to cells in the digestive tract is the reason so many chemotherapy patients experience nausea.

In addition to nausea and vomiting, common side effects of chemotherapy include hair loss, anemia (a reduction in the number of red blood cells), and an inability to fight infections (due to fewer white blood cells). A major problem is that many tumors become resistant to chemotherapeutic drugs, just as bacteria become resistant to antibiotics. Treatment then becomes a battle of trying to destroy abnormal cells with stronger and stronger chemicals without killing the patient in the process. Sometimes combination therapy, in which surgery is followed by radiation and combinations of chemotherapeutic drugs, works best.

### Magnetism and photodynamic therapy target malignant cells

To avoid the side effects of standard radiation and chemotherapy, researchers are developing techniques to target malignant cells more precisely while sparing healthy tissue. Promising developments include:

- *Magnetism:* Positioning a powerful magnet at the tumor site and injecting tiny metallic beads into the patient's bloodstream. The magnet pulls the beads, which have been coated with a chemotherapy drug, into the tumor where they kill the cancer cells. Magnetism is undergoing clinical trials in liver cancer patients.
- *Photodynamic therapy:* Targeting cancer with light-sensitive drugs and lasers. The patient takes light-sensitive drugs that are drawn into the rapidly dividing cancer cells. Laser light of a particular frequency is focused on the tumor, where it triggers a series of chemical events that kill malignant cells. Photodynamic therapy has been approved for several years to treat tumors in the esophagus and lung, and new refinements in lasers make it promising for other cancers too (Figure 18.10).

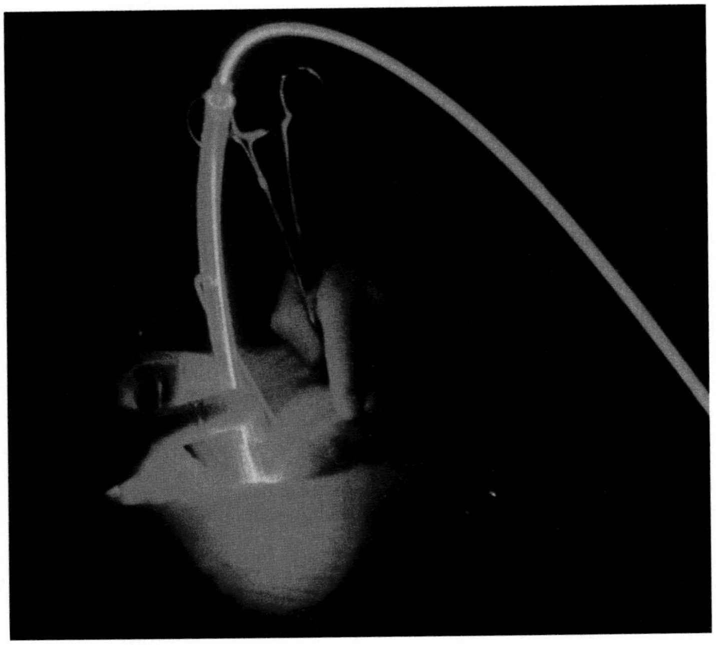

**Figure 18.10 Photodynamic therapy.** Before surgery, this patient was injected with a light-sensitive drug that is taken up by cancer cells. During surgery to remove the cancer, laser light (seen here traveling in a fiber-optic cable) is aimed directly at cells in the region of the excised cancer. Activation of the drug by laser light leads to a toxic reaction that kills any remaining cancer cells, but not any normal cells.

### Immunotherapy promotes immune response

**Immunotherapy** attempts to boost the general responsiveness of the immune system so that it can fight cancer more effectively. Recent efforts have focused on finding specific antigen molecules that are present on cancer cells but not on normal cells, and using them to produce antibodies that target cancer cells for destruction by the immune system. This approach is showing particular promise. Taking it one step further, researchers are working to attach radioactive molecules or chemotherapeutic drugs to the antibodies so that treatments can be delivered only to cancer cells and spare normal cells. Researchers are working to create vaccines that prevent specific cancers.

Researchers are also testing other vaccines created from a patient's own cancer cells. When injected into the patient, the modified cancer cells appear to stimulate the person's immune defenses to recognize and combat the abnormal cells.

### "Starving" cancer by inhibiting angiogenesis

Tumors grow and divide rapidly, so they require a great deal of energy. We now know that enlarging tumors promote the growth of new blood vessels (called *angiogenesis*) to serve their energy needs. Without angiogenesis, the tumor would reach about the size of a pea and stop growing. At least a dozen proteins stimulate angiogenesis, some of which are released by tumor cells, and several other proteins are known to inhibit angiogenesis. Interest is very high in antiangiogenic drugs, which literally starve tumors by limiting their blood supply. Several drugs are already in clinical trials (the early stages of testing in humans).

### Molecular treatments target defective genes

Sophisticated molecular strategies target the defective genes that lead to cancer. Some researchers are attempting to inactivate specific genes, or the proteins they encode, to slow the runaway cell division. Future techniques may include *gene therapy,* in which defective genes are repaired or replaced with their normal counterparts. A key target for gene therapy is the p53 tumor suppressor gene that, when defective, contributes to many cancers.

**RECAP**

The mainstays of cancer treatment are surgery, radiation, and chemotherapy. Recent advances include magnetism, photodynamic therapy, immunotherapy, drugs to inhibit angiogenesis, and molecular treatments that focus on specific defective genes. ■

## 18.6 The 10 most common cancers

Table 18.3 ranks the 10 most common cancers by incidence. Each has its own risk factors, warning signs, methods of detection, treatments, and (most important of all) survival rate.

**Table 18.3 The top 10 cancers ranked by estimated incidence (numbers of new cases per year)**

| Cancer | New cases per year | Deaths per year |
|---|---|---|
| Skin (melanoma and nonmelanoma) | >1,000,000[a] | 11,200 |
| Lung | 215,000 | 161,800 |
| Prostate | 186,000 | 28,700 |
| Breast | 182,000 (women) | 40,900 (women) |
| | 2,000 (men) | 450 (men) |
| Colon and rectum | 149,000 | 50,000 |
| Lymphoma | 74,000 | 20,500 |
| Urinary bladder | 69,000 | 14,100 |
| Kidney | 54,000 | 13,000 |
| Uterus | 51,000 | 11,300 |
| Leukemia | 44,000 | 21,700 |

*Source:* American Cancer Society, Cancer Facts & Figures 2008, American Cancer Society, Inc.; 2008.

[a]Estimate—nonmelanoma cases are often not reported.

In both men and women, the most frequent cancers are those of the skin, lung, and colon and rectum. In addition, prostate cancer is common in men and breast cancer is common in women.

The most deadly cancers—in terms of the number of deaths—are lung, colon and rectum, and breast cancer. Lung cancer kills more people than the next top four cancers combined.

## Skin cancer: Look for changes in your skin

Skin cancers are generally classified as either melanoma or nonmelanomas (all other skin cancers). Although most of the nonmelanomas are not particularly deadly if detected early, they should still be removed as soon as they are detected. In contrast, melanoma can be very serious.

- The most common of the nonmelanomas is *basal cell* carcinoma (cancer). Recall that basal cells located at the base of the epithelium divide throughout life to produce the squamous epithelial cells that form the outer layer of the skin. Basal cell cancer occurs when the basal cells begin to divide out of control. Basal cell cancer usually appears as a pink or flesh-colored bump with a smooth texture. Sometimes the bump bleeds or crusts. Basal cell cancer rarely metastasizes but should still be removed. If not treated it can eventually spread to underlying tissues.
- *Squamous cell* cancer arises from the epithelial cells produced by the basal cells. It consists of pink scaly patches or nodules that may ulcerate and crust. Squamous cell cancer can metastasize, although slowly.
- *Melanoma* is the least common of the three main skin cancers, but it is also the deadliest because it is likely to metastasize fairly quickly. It arises from abnormal melanocytes, the cells that produce the dark-brown pigment called melanin. Look for dark spots or patches on your skin and evaluate them according to the "ABCD" rule (Figure 18.11): A = *Asymmetry*—the two halves of the spot or patch don't match; B = *Border*—the border is irregular in shape; C = *Color*—color varies or is intensely black; and D = *Diameter*—diameter is greater than 6 millimeters, or about the size of a pea. Itchiness, scaliness, oozing, or bleeding may also be significant signs.

Early detection of skin cancers is important. Both basal and squamous cell cancers have a better than 95% cure rate if removed promptly because they metastasize slowly, if at all. Early detection is especially important for melanomas;

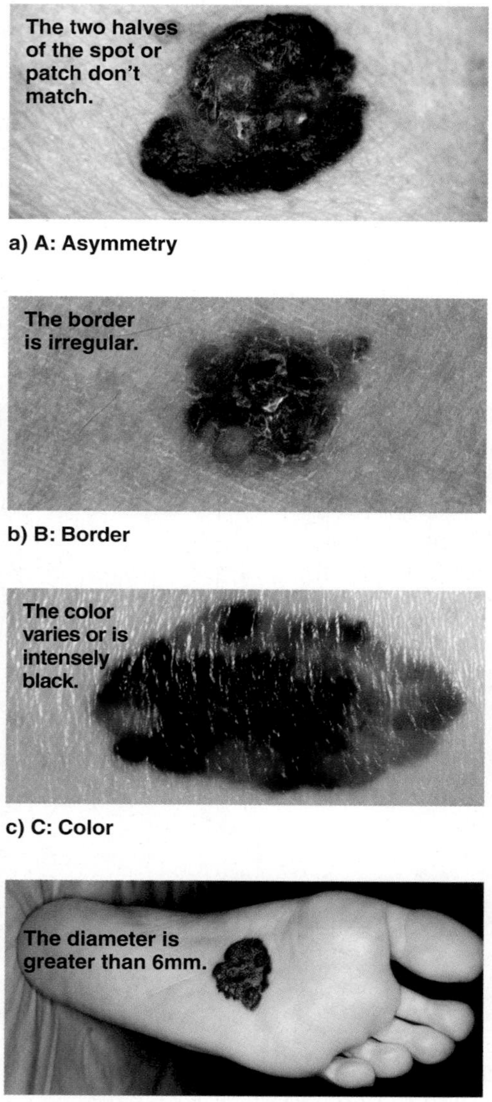


a) A: Asymmetry

b) B: Border

c) C: Color

d) D: Diameter

**Figure 18.11 Melanoma.** Melanomas generally are diagnosed by the ABCD rule.

the five-year survival rate (percentage of persons diagnosed who are still alive after five years) is 98% if the melanoma is detected while it is still localized, but only 16% if it has already metastasized.

## Lung cancer: Smoking is leading risk factor

Most cases of lung cancer are preventable, because by far the greatest risk factor is cigarette smoking. All other risk factors, which include exposure to smoke, radiation, and industrial chemicals such as asbestos, are relatively minor by comparison.

Unfortunately there is no simple screening test for lung cancer, and so it is generally not detected early. Most of the symptoms of lung cancer (persistent cough, recurrent pneumonia or bronchitis, voice change) are relatively non-specific, by the time blood appears in the sputum and the patient experiences chest pain, the cancer may already be at an advanced stage. Early detection improves the odds, but the one-year survival rate for all stages of diagnosis is still only 41%, and the overall five-year survival rate is only 15%.

Treatment options depend on when the cancer is detected. When the cancer is detected early and is still localized, surgery is the treatment of choice. However, in most cases the disease has already spread by the time it is detected. For the more advanced stages, radiation therapy and chemotherapy, sometimes combined with surgery, are the only options.

Current research efforts are directed at finding earlier, more effective detection methods. A large clinical trial is currently underway to determine whether screening high-risk individuals with low-dose computed tomography (CT) scans can reduce lung cancer deaths. Such scans are not cheap, however. Other research is aimed at finding molecular markers for lung cancer in sputum so that inexpensive screening tests could detect the disease at an earlier stage.

## Prostate cancer: Most common after age 50

Symptoms of prostate cancer include difficulty urinating or inability to urinate, blood in the urine, and pain, usually in the pelvic area.

The biggest risk for prostate cancer is advancing age. Physicians recommend yearly testing for men aged 50 and older (Table 18.4). The cancer can be diagnosed by digital rectal exam or by the PSA (prostate-specific antigen) test, which detects elevated blood levels of a protein produced by the prostate gland.

Treatment options include surgery, radiation therapy, and hormones. Treatment in older men is controversial because prostate cancer generally grows so slowly that it is unlikely to be the cause of death. The five-year survival rate is now almost 99%, up from 69% just 25 years ago. The dramatic improvement is due to earlier diagnoses and improved treatments.

## Breast cancer: Early detection pays off

Breast cancer is almost exclusively a cancer of women (but note that it can occur in men; approximately 2,000 new cases of male breast cancer are diagnosed each year). Breast cancer is usually first diagnosed by a mammogram (an X-ray of breast tissue) or when the patient or health care provider detects an abnormal lump during a physical exam.

Recent research suggests that there are at least two inherited susceptibility genes for breast cancer. A major risk factor is age; only one in 200 women will get breast cancer before age 40, but one out of 26 will get breast cancer in her 60s. Other risk factors include early onset of menstruation or late onset of menopause, obesity after menopause, use of oral contraceptives, and hormone replacement therapy after menopause.

Environmental and dietary factors may also play a role. Early detection dramatically increases the chance of survival: the 5-year survival rate for breast tumors that have not yet metastasized is 98%, but it falls to 27% for women who have distant metastases at diagnosis. Overall, the 10-year survival rate for all diagnoses is now 80%.

## Cancers of colon and rectum: Tests can detect them early

An obvious worrisome sign is blood in the stool or rectal bleeding, though bleeding can also result from noncancerous causes. Risk factors include sedentary lifestyle, obesity, smoking, a family history of colorectal cancer, and a low-fiber, high-fat diet with not enough fruits and vegetables.

Most colorectal tumors start as **polyps,** small benign growths that develop from the colon lining (Figure 18.12). The majority of colon polyps never turn malignant, and even

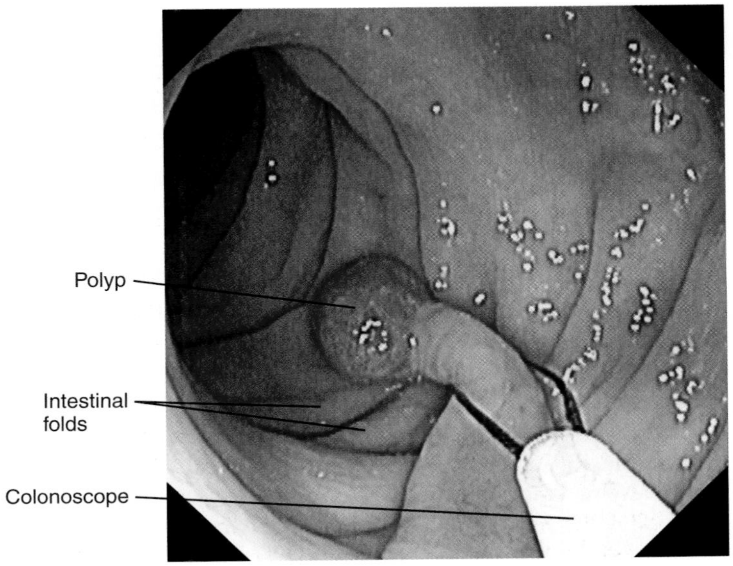


**Figure 18.12 Polyps.** A polyp in the colon being removed with a wire snare.

**Table 18.4 Recommendations for cancer screening**

| Cancer | Gender | Test | Age and frequency | Description |
|---|---|---|---|---|
| All | Men and women | Cancer-related checkup | 20–40: Every 3 years<br>40+: Every year | General exam by health professional that includes health counseling and screening as appropriate for malignant and nonmalignant diseases |
| Colon and Rectum | Men and women | Fecal occult blood test | 50+: Every year | Checks for hidden blood in feces |
| | | Digital rectal exam | 50+: Every 5 years | Physical exam by health professional |
| | | Flexible sigmoidoscopy | Every 5 years | Examining interior of rectum and sigmoid colon with flexible fiber-optic scope |
| | | Colonoscopy | 50+: Every 10 years | Examining interior of colon with flexible fiber-optic scope |
| Breast | Women | Self-examination | 20+: Once per month | See Health Watch box |
| | | Clinical examination | 20–40: Every 3 years<br>40+: Every year | Physical exam by health professional |
| | | Mammogram | 40+: Every year | X-ray of breast tissues |
| Cervix and Endometrium | Women | Pelvic exam | 18+ and all sexually active women: Every year | Physical exam by health professional |
| | | Pap test | 18+ and all sexually active women: Every year | Smear of cells taken from cervix by health professional |
| Endometrium | Women | Endometrial tissue sample | At menopause. Women who have any risk factors should be screened every year starting at age 35 | Sample of uterine tissue taken by health professional |
| Prostate | Men | Digital rectal exam | 50+: Every year. Men who have any risk factors should be screened every year starting at age 45 or earlier | Physical exam by health professional |
| | | PSA (prostate-specific antigen) | 50+: Every year | Blood test that detects elevated levels of PSA |
| Testicles | Men | Self-examination | Men who have any risk factors: Once per month after puberty | See Health Watch box |

*Note:* People who have one or more risk factors for any cancers should begin screening at earlier ages and have tests done more often. Consult your physician for advice.
Data based on American Cancer Society Prevention and Detection Guidelines.

when they do, the process usually takes years. This underscores the importance of regular exams to detect polyps and remove them before they can become dangerous. For everyone over age 50, the American Cancer Society recommends a *colonoscopy* (examining the interior of the complete colon with a flexible fiber-optic scope) every 10 years. People who have any risk factors should begin screening earlier and undergo testing more often. Polyps can generally be removed rather easily with a small wire snare or by electrocautery (electric heat).

The five-year survival rate for all cases of colorectal cancer has improved to 64%, largely because of early detection and treatment. For people with distant metastases at the time of diagnosis, the five-year survival rate drops to just 10%. Here is another case where early detection is extremely beneficial. However, fewer than 40% of colorectal cancers are detected at an early stage because rates of screening are still low.

## Lymphoma: Cancers of lymphoid tissues

**Lymphoma** is the general term for cancers of the lymphoid tissues, which include Hodgkin's disease and non-Hodgkin's lymphoma. Symptoms include enlarged lymph nodes, intermittent fever, itching, weight loss, and night sweats.

## Health Watch

# Examining Yourself for Breast Cancer

Breast cancers can sometimes be detected at an early stage through self-examination techniques. Self-examination is quick, easy, private, and free.

Examine your breasts at the same time each month. Lie down with a pillow or folded towel under your right shoulder (see illustration). Using the first three fingers of your left hand, press firmly to check the right breast in every possible location. Press hard enough that you can feel the underlying tissue.

Establish a regular pattern of pressure (patterns 1, 2, and 3 in the figure) and use it consistently so you become familiar with how your breast feels. Then examine the left breast by placing the pillow under your left shoulder and using your right hand. Repeat the process while standing in the shower.

Finally, stand in front of a mirror, first with your arms on your hips and then behind your head. Look for any changes in the appearance of your breasts, such as swelling, dimpling, redness, or changes in the nipples.

If you find anything suspicious, consult your physician immediately. The good news is that many breast lumps turn out to be noncancerous upon further testing.

Of course, self-examination should not take the place of regular exams by a health professional. However, when done correctly it can save your life.

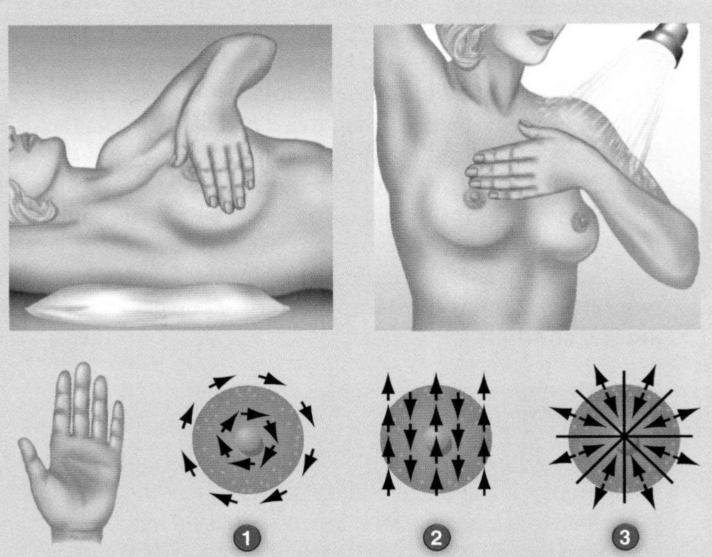


**a) Use the pads of the first three fingers of the hand opposite to each breast.** Establish a regular and complete pattern of pressure (1, 2 or 3) that works for you. Do the exam while lying down and again in the shower, when your hands are soapy and glide easily over the skin.

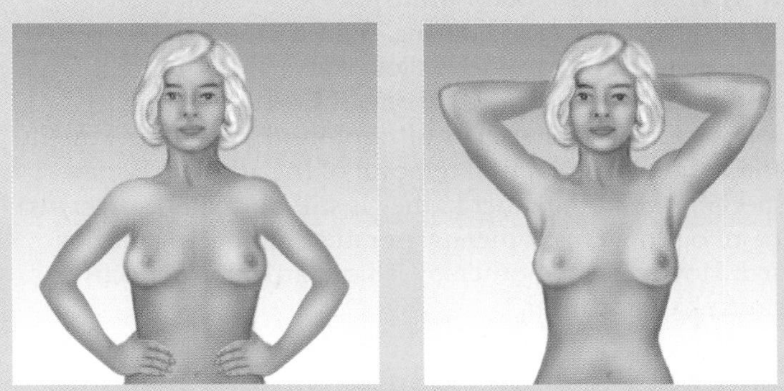

**b) It is also a good idea to examine your breasts visually while standing in front of a mirror.**

**Breast self-examination.**

Risk factors are not entirely clear but seem to relate to altered immune function. People at risk include organ transplant recipients, those with HIV or human T-cell leukemia/lymphoma virus-1 (HTLV-1) infection, and perhaps workers with high occupational exposure to herbicides. Treatments generally are radiation or chemotherapy. Treatments involving specific antibodies to lymphoma cells can be effective. Bone marrow transplant may be necessary after high-dose radiation therapy.

### Urinary bladder cancer: Surgery is often successful if done early

Blood in the urine is an important sign, although there may be other reasons for it. Smoking doubles the risk of bladder cancer. Living in an urban area, exposure to arsenic in the water supply, or occupational exposure to rubber, leather, or dye are also risks. Bladder cancer is usually diagnosed by microscopic examination of cells in the urine, and by direct visualization of the bladder wall with a cytoscope (a thin tube with a lens) inserted into the bladder via the ureter.

Surgery combined with chemotherapy is almost always successful if the cancer is detected early (94% five-year survival rate), but the survival rate declines dramatically if the cancer has already metastasized to distant sites (6% five-year survival rate).

### Kidney cancer: Detected during examination for a renal-related problem

Risk factors for kidney (renal) cancer include heritable gene mutations, smoking, and exposure to certain toxic agents such as asbestos and cadmium. Indeed, cancer-causing agents and toxic chemicals are more likely to affect the kidneys than many other organs because as the kidneys concentrate the urine, they also concentrate the toxic agents in it. Other risk factors that you can do nothing about are age (renal cancer occurs primarily after middle age) and gender (males are twice as likely as females to get it).

There are no blood or urine tests to screen for renal cancer. It is usually detected during examination for a suspected renal-related problem such as low back pain or blood in the urine, and then confirmed by one of several imaging techniques, such as a CT scan or ultrasound. The main treatment for renal cancer is surgical removal of the affected kidney, especially when the other kidney is still normal. If surgery is not an option, chemotherapy or radiation therapy may be used. However, chemotherapy is not particularly effective against kidney cancer.

### Cancer of the uterus: Unusual uterine bleeding is major symptom

Uterine cancer includes cancers of the endometrium and cervix. The primary symptoms of endometrial cancer are abnormal bleeding or spotting. Pain is a late manifestation of the disease. High lifetime exposure to estrogen is the major risk factor for endometrial cancer. Reasons for high exposure include early onset of menstrual periods, late menopause, obesity, not having children, and/or estrogen replacement therapy after menopause (progesterone added to estrogen is thought to offset the risk related to estrogen alone). Pregnancy and the use of oral contraceptives seem to offer some protection from endometrial cancer.

Cervical cancer, in contrast, is strongly correlated to sexually transmitted infection with the human papillomavirus (HPV). Women who have had many sexual partners (or whose partners have had many sexual partners) are at higher risk for cervical cancer. Cigarette smoking also increases the odds. Cervical cancer is usually detected by a Pap test (examination of a smear of cervical cells; the name comes from Papanicolaou, the doctor who devised the test). The Pap test is not very effective at detecting cancer of the endometrium, which is generally detected by a pelvic exam.

Treatments for both endometrial and cervical cancer include surgery, radiation, hormones, or chemotherapy. The one-year survival rate is 92% for endometrial cancer and 88% for cervical cancer.

Cervical cancer may be one of the first cancers to be largely preventable by a vaccine. In clinical trials in more than 17,000 girls and women the vaccine, called Gardasil, was nearly 100% effective in blocking the strains of the human papillomavirus that cause most cases of cervical cancer and genital warts.

### Leukemia: Chemotherapy is often effective

**Leukemias** are cancers of immature white blood cells within bone marrow. In its more advanced stages the bone marrow becomes completely filled with cancerous cells. Eventually the production of normal blood cells declines, leading to anemia and a reduced resistance to infections. The causes of leukemia are largely unknown, but may be linked to Down syndrome, excessive exposure to ionizing radiation, and benzene. Certain leukemias are caused by the HTLV-1 virus.

Although leukemia is commonly thought of as a childhood disease, more adults than children develop leukemias. The symptoms of leukemia are fairly general (fatigue, weight loss, increased incidence of infections), and as a result leukemias are not always diagnosed early. A firm diagnosis is made with a blood test and a bone biopsy.

The standard treatment for leukemias is chemotherapy. Sometimes chemotherapy is followed by a bone marrow transplant to replace the normal blood-forming stem cells eliminated by chemotherapy. The survival rates for certain types of leukemias have improved over the years, especially among children.

**RECAP**

Cancers vary widely in terms of incidence, ease of detection and treatment, and death rate. For any cancer the probability of survival is much higher if the disease is detected early, before it metastasizes. ■

## 18.7 Most cancers can be prevented

Some cancers are linked to the genes we inherit from our parents, such as the BRCA genes that increase the risk of breast and ovarian cancer. For heritable cancers, early detection is not only vital but increasingly possible. Early detection of risk factors will allow treatment options to begin earlier. However, true prevention of heritable cancers will have to wait for advances in gene therapy and vaccines.

Nevertheless, most incidences of cancer are thought to be preventable. At least 60% of all cancer cases other than non-melanoma skin cancers are thought to be caused by just two factors—smoking and poor diet. In addition, most non-melanoma skin cancers could be prevented by reducing our exposure to the sun.

If we really want to make a dent in the cancer death rate, we need to work on public education: encouraging people to exercise, control their weight, eat a healthy diet, limit

# Voluntary Breast and Ovary Removal—Could You Do It?

Would you choose to have your breasts and ovaries removed surgically (called prophylactic mastectomy and oophorectomy) in order to avoid breast and ovarian cancer and perhaps live longer? Some women are making that very difficult decision.

The dilemma these women face is a direct consequence of our increased understanding of the risk factors for cancer. It is now known that mutations in at least two genes, called BRCA1 (short for breast cancer 1) and BRCA2, are strongly associated with breast and ovarian cancer. In their normal forms these two genes function to suppress cell growth; only the mutated forms increase the risk of cancer.

Renee Syler, former anchorwoman of CBS's The Early Show, had both breasts removed and reconstructed in 2007 as a preemptive strike against breast cancer.

Mutated forms of BRCA genes are relatively rare—only 0.5% of all women have one—but for those who do, the risk of cancer goes up dramatically. For all women the lifetime risk of developing breast cancer is 13%. For women with a mutated BRCA gene the risk of breast cancer is 36–85%. For ovarian cancer the lifetime risk is 1.7% for all women, 16–60% for women with a mutated BRCA gene.

Testing for mutated forms of BRCA1 and BRCA2 genes is relatively easy, requiring only a blood sample. That means that women can learn whether they are at high risk before cancer might develop. Should you be tested? That depends on whether, if you did have a mutated gene, you would really want to know. Would you opt for surgery if you had a mutated gene? If you were convinced that you could never have your breasts and ovaries removed while you were still healthy, then perhaps you would be better off not knowing. It might also depend on whether you think you are at especially high risk. Although fewer than 0.5% of all women have a mutated BRCA gene, your chances of having a mutated gene go up five- to tenfold if you have a family history of women who developed breast or ovarian cancer. Like all genes, these can be inherited from your parents (the BRCA genes are also associated with slightly increased risks of breast and prostate cancer in men).

If you inherited a mutated BRCA gene, couldn't you just wait to see if cancer ever developed in a breast or ovary, and then (and only then) have it removed? After all, if you're still of reproductive age you may want to have children. The problem is that ovarian cancer is particularly deadly. There is no easy screening test for it and there are generally no symptoms in the early stages, so it may not be diagnosed until it is already in an advanced stage. The five-year survival rate after a diagnosis of ovarian cancer is still under 40%.

How effective is the surgery? The risk of developing ovarian cancer essentially disappears. The risk of developing breast cancer drops by 90%, but not completely to zero. There is still a very small risk of developing breast cancer even after surgical breast removal because breast tissue is located diffusely and it is nearly impossible to get all the tissue. There are other treatment options, too, but they're not quite as effective as surgery. Some physicians recommend a drug called tamoxifen for women at high risk who choose not to have surgery—it reduces the cancer risk by about 50%.

We've been talking about probabilities of cancer and even death in an impersonal way, as if this were a game of numbers. But this is not a game, and there lies the lesson for all of us. Each of us may have to make difficult choices for ourselves or for a loved one some day. We'll be forced to balance personal feelings and preferences against impersonal odds.

## Questions to consider:

**1** *Blood tests for BRCA1 and BRCA2 are readily available. Are you planning to be tested? Why or why not?* **2** *If you knew that you had a mutated BRCA gene, would it change what you do or how you live?* **3** *Guys: What would you want your wife/girlfriend to do if it she had a mutated BRCA gene?*

## the facts...

- Heritable mutations of two genes known as BRCA1 and BRCA2 are strongly associated with breast and ovarian cancer.
- Ovarian cancer often goes undetected until it is too late. The five-year survival rate is still under 40%.
- Some women who have mutated BRCA genes are opting for prophylactic breast and ovary removal while they are still healthy.

**Health** Watch

## Examining Yourself for Testicular Cancer

Testicular cancer is *the* most common cancer among men aged 20–35. It is also one of the most curable cancers if caught early. Testicular self-examination has not been studied enough to know whether it is effective in lowering the death rate among men without any known risk factors. Nevertheless, the American Cancer Society recommends testicular self-examination for men who do have risk factors, such as cryptorchidism (an undescended testicle), a family history of testicular cancer, or a past episode of cancer in a testicle. Some physicians recommend monthly self-exams for all men, regardless of whether they have any risk factors. Since it's easy to do and costs nothing, why not try it?

The best time to examine your testicles is after a warm shower when the skin of the scrotum is fully relaxed. Place the index and middle fingers of both hands gently underneath one testicle and your thumbs on top (see figure). Roll each testicle gently between your thumbs and fingers, feeling for unusual pea-sized lumps on the front or sides. Be aware that it is not unusual for one testicle to be slightly larger than the other, and do not confuse the cordlike epididymis located on the top and back of the testicle with a lump.

Consult your physician immediately if you find anything suspicious. Many testicular lumps turn out to be noncancerous, but play it safe.

Of course, in addition to doing self-exams you should also have regular examinations done by a health professional. However, some patients do find their own cancers first, and early detection is always a plus.

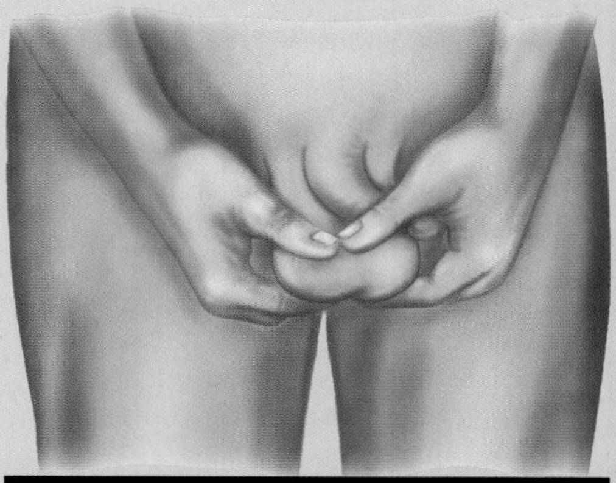

Testicular self-examination. Roll each testicle gently between your thumb and fingers, feeling for unusual lumps.

alcohol, avoid too much sun, and above all, not smoke. Researchers are studying what constitutes a healthy diet and why certain dietary components are harmful or beneficial.

What can you do to reduce your own risk of cancer?

- Know your family history. Because cancer generally involves multiple genetic defects, you may have inherited one or more risk factors. Of course, this does not guarantee you will develop cancer. However, until we know of and can test for all such defects, you can at least assess your potential by examining your family's history of cancer and discussing it with your physician.
- Get regular medical screenings for cancer. As we've seen, early detection is best, and some slow-growing cancers can be cured if caught early. Your physician may suggest other tests based on your family history, gender, and age, in addition to those described in Table 18.4, page 434.
- Learn self-examination techniques. Women can examine their breasts, and men their testicles, to check for lumps. All of us should be on the lookout for changes in the skin that might represent skin cancer (refer to Figure 18.11). While self-examination is not a substitute for regular checkups by a health professional, many cancers are detected early by the patients themselves. The American Cancer Society provides information on self-examination techniques.
- Avoid direct sunlight between 10 a.m. and 4 p.m., wear a broad-brimmed hat, and apply sunscreen with an SPF (sun protection factor) of 15 or greater. Also avoid sunlamps and tanning salons.
- Watch your diet and your weight. There are no absolutes here, but the general recommendation is a diet high in fruits, vegetables, legumes (peas and beans), and whole grains, and low in saturated fats, red meat, and salt. Unsaturated fats, such as fish and olive oil, appear to be beneficial.
- Don't smoke. Here is a personal choice you can make that will dramatically lower your risk. Smoking is considered *the* single largest preventable risk factor for cancer. It accounts for fully 85% of all lung cancers and also contributes to cancers of the bladder, mouth, colon, cervix, pancreas, and pharynx. Ultimately, we may save more lives by persuading people not to smoke than by any amount of early detection.
- If you consume alcohol, drink in moderation. One to two alcoholic beverages per day *may* reduce the chance of cardiovascular disease, but the trade-off is

that alcohol consumption appears to raise the risk of certain cancers. It is particularly risky when combined with smoking.

- Stay informed. There's a wealth of information on cancer in general, on specific types of cancer, and on the effects of nutrition and diet. Good resources include your physician, the American Cancer Society, the National Cancer Institute, or any good library.

**RECAP**

Most cancers could be prevented; smoking is by far the leading preventable risk factor. Other prevention strategies include knowing your family history, getting regular medical screenings, learning self-examination techniques, avoiding sunlight and sunlamps, watching your diet and weight, drinking alcohol in moderation if at all, and staying informed. ■

# Chapter Summary

### Tumors can be benign or cancerous *p. 423*

- Normal cells have two key characteristics: (1) their rates of division are kept under control, and (2) most remain in one location in the body.
- A mass of cells that is dividing more rapidly than normal is called a tumor. Some tumors are benign.

### Cancerous cells lose control of their functions and structures *p. 423*

- Cancer develops when cells divide uncontrollably, undergo physical changes, and no longer adhere to each other.
- Eventually some cancer cells invade nearby tissues. Others metastasize, colonizing distant sites.
- Cancer is the second leading cause of death in the U.S.

### How cancer develops *p. 425*

- Mutations of proto-oncogenes, tumor suppressor genes, and/or mutator genes may contribute to cancer.
- Inheritance of one or more mutated genes from your parents may increase your risk of developing certain cancers.
- Known carcinogens include some viruses and bacteria, environmental chemicals, tobacco, radiation, and dietary factors including alcohol consumption. Internal factors, such as faulty DNA replication and internally produced chemicals, can also contribute to cancer.
- Cancer is a multifactorial disease. Perhaps six or more mutations may need to be present before a cell becomes cancerous.

### Advances in diagnosis enable early detection *p. 428*

- Most cancers are diagnosed when a tumor is detected by imaging techniques such as X-rays, PET, or MRI.
- Enzyme tests may also identify cancer.
- Genetic testing can determine the presence of a specific known mutated gene, but the presence of the mutated gene does not necessarily mean that cancer will develop.

### Cancer treatments *p. 430*

- Many cancers are treatable; early diagnosis is important.
- Conventional treatments for cancer include surgical removal of the tumor, radiation, and chemotherapy.
- Newer treatments include magnetism and photodynamic therapy to target malignant cells precisely, immunotherapy to activate the patient' immune system, drugs to inhibit angiogenesis and cut off the tumor's blood supply, and molecular treatments that target specific genes.

### The 10 most common cancers *p. 431*

- In both sexes, the most frequently occurring cancer is cancer of the skin.
- In addition, prostate cancer is common in men; breast cancer is common in women.
- Lung cancer causes more deaths than any other type of cancer.

### Most cancers can be prevented *p. 436*

- Some cancers will occur despite our best efforts because we cannot control inherited risk factors.
- However, most cancers could be prevented. The single most effective way to reduce cancer deaths is to reduce the rate of smoking.
- A healthy diet will also decrease your cancer risk. Eat lots of fruits, vegetables, legumes, and grains; reduce your intake of saturated fat, red meat, and salt.
- Other preventive strategies include knowing your family's health history, examining yourself for cancer and getting regular medical screenings, maintaining a healthy weight, avoiding direct sunlight and sunlamps, drinking alcohol in moderation if at all, and staying informed.

# Terms You Should Know

cancer, *424*
carcinogen, *426*
chemotherapy, *430*
dysplasia, *423*
hyperplasia, *423*
immunotherapy, *431*
leukemia, *436*
lymphoma, *434*
malignant tumor, *424*
melanoma, *427*
metastasis, *424*
mutator gene, *426*
oncogene, *425*
proto-oncogene, *425*
tumor, *423*
tumor suppressor gene, *426*

# Concept Review

1. Compare and contrast a benign tumor and a malignant tumor.
2. Describe the key changes in cancer cells that allow them to metastasize.
3. Describe the impact a carcinogen has on a cell.
4. Explain why we have not yet made much progress against lung cancer, compared to other types of cancer.

5. Explain what causes most skin cancers.
6. List two dietary factors associated with an increased risk of cancers of the colon and rectum.
7. Describe the role the immune system plays in preventing different types of cancer.
8. Describe how tumors are diagnosed.
9. Describe how antibodies against cancer cells could improve the delivery of chemotherapeutic drugs.
10. List the things one can do to help prevent cancer.

## Test Yourself

### Matching Exercise

_____ 1. A change for the worse in cell structure
_____ 2. An increase in cell number as a result of increased cell division
_____ 3. Regulatory genes that limit cell growth and division
_____ 4. Tumors that remain in place and don't spread
_____ 5. Mutated or damaged genes that contribute to cancer
_____ 6. Tumors that spread to other parts of the body

a. dysplasia
b. oncogenes
c. hyperplasia
d. malignant
e. benign
f. tumor suppressor genes

### Fill in the Blank

7. __________________ is the least common form of skin cancer but also the most likely to be fatal.
8. The three standard methods of treating cancer are __________________, __________________, and __________________.
9. The three cancers that cause the most deaths per year are cancers of the __________________, __________________, and __________________.
10. A cancer-producing substance is called a(n) __________________.
11. Cancer of immature white blood cells in bone marrow is called __________________.
12. A discrete mass of cells is called a tumor or a __________________.

### True or False?

13. Smoking is a risk factor for cancer of the urinary bladder.
14. Over 20% of all cancers are caused by industrial environmental pollutants.
15. Human papillomavirus can cause cancer of the cervix.

## Apply What You Know

1. Why do you suppose that the death rate from lung cancer has increased much more in women than in men over the past 35 years? What information would you like to have that might support or disprove your hypothesis?
2. If you can't do anything about the genes you inherit, does it do any good to know your family history for particular cancers? Explain your reasoning.
3. The overall death rate from cancer dropped only 6% between 1950 and 2005. Why do you think we seem to have made so little progress against cancer?
4. From time to time we hear stories in the press that cell phones may cause certain types of brain cancer. Then someone else says the evidence is not yet clear. From what you know of the scientific method, why do you think this issue has been so hard to resolve?
5. Common therapies for cancer include chemotherapy and radiation treatments. How effective are these therapies, and why do they both have such serious side effects?
6. The first cancer that can be nearly completely prevented by a vaccine is cervical cancer. How does the vaccine work? And if a vaccine can be developed against cervical cancer, why hasn't someone developed a vaccine against the number one cancer killer—lung cancer?

*Answers can be found on the Human Biology Place.*

## References and Additional Reading

Cancer Facts & Figures 2008. (A yearly fact booklet published by the American Cancer Society.)

Cavenee, W. K., and R. L. White. The Genetic Basis of Cancer. *Scientific American*, March 1995, pp. 72–79. (Discusses the role of multiple genes in causing cancer.)

Gibbs, W. Wayt. Untangling the Roots of Cancer. *Scientific American*, July 2003. (New theories of what causes cells to become cancerous.)

Radetsky, P. Magic Missiles. *Discover*, March 1993. (Describes the use of antibodies to fight cancer.)

What You Need to Know About Cancer. *Scientific American Special Issue*, September 1996. (An entire issue devoted to the subject of cancer, serving as an excellent review.)

## Internet References

Find links to these Web sites at the Human Biology Place.

**American Cancer Society**
**www.cancer.org**
A leading advocacy group for cancer patients, survivors, and family members.

**National Cancer Institute**
**www.cancer.gov**
Federal agency that funds research and distributes information.

**OncoLink**
**www.oncolink.upenn.edu**
This University of Pennsylvania site offers information about specific cancers, new treatments, and research advances.

**Canadian Cancer Society**
**www.cancer.ca**
Cancer encyclopedia and glossary, plus news on prevention, treatments, and living with cancer.

# 19 Genetics and Inheritance

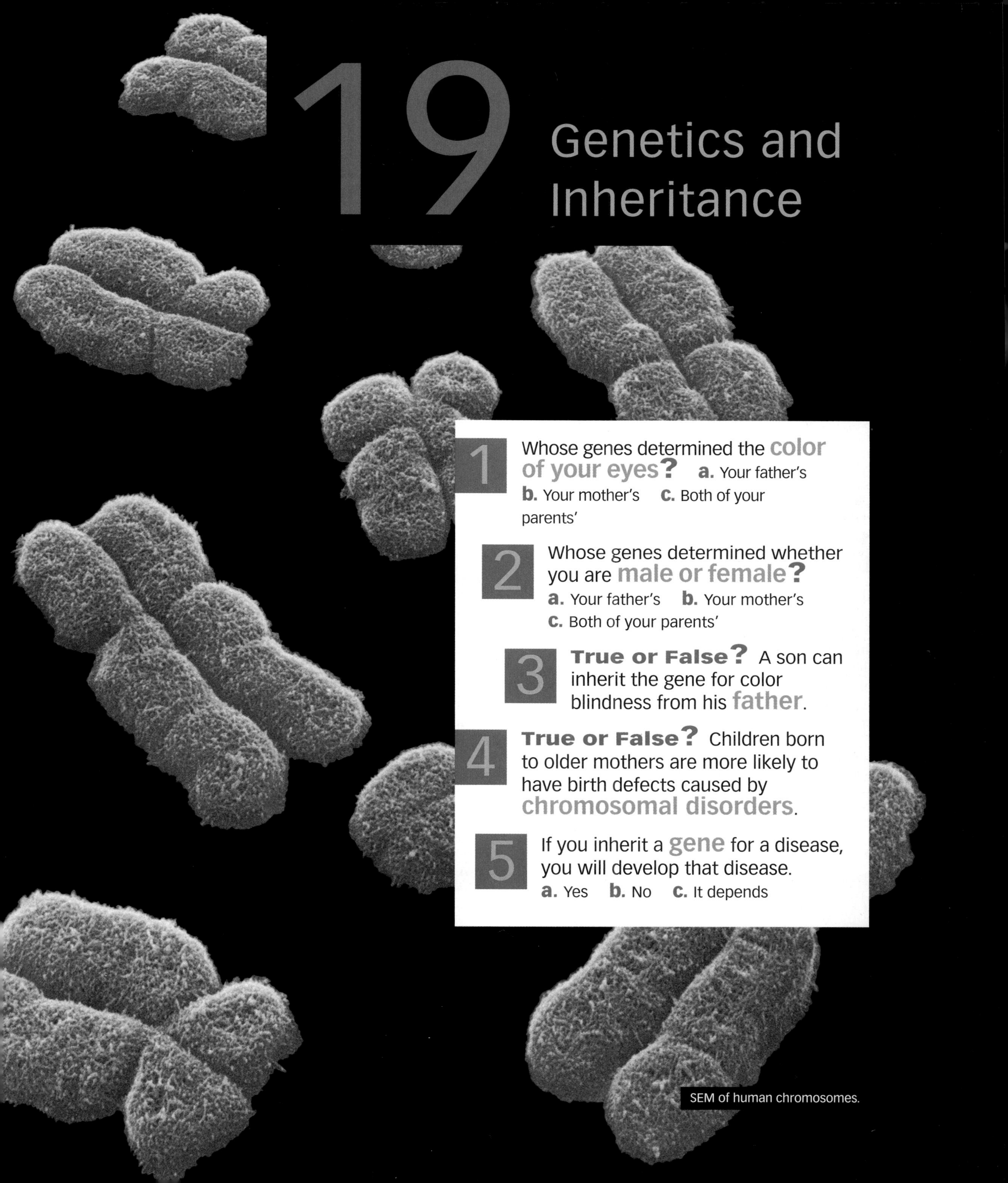

SEM of human chromosomes.

**1** Whose genes determined the **color of your eyes?** **a.** Your father's **b.** Your mother's **c.** Both of your parents'

**2** Whose genes determined whether you are **male or female?** **a.** Your father's **b.** Your mother's **c.** Both of your parents'

**3** **True or False?** A son can inherit the gene for color blindness from his **father**.

**4** **True or False?** Children born to older mothers are more likely to have birth defects caused by **chromosomal disorders**.

**5** If you inherit a **gene** for a disease, you will develop that disease. **a.** Yes **b.** No **c.** It depends

**As we have seen,** the information necessary for the development of a new human being is contained in the DNA within the nucleus of the fertilized egg. This information is found in the form of **genes,** DNA sequences that code for one or more specific proteins. An organism's **genome** is the sum total of all of its DNA, even though not all of that DNA codes for proteins. **Genetics** is the study of genes and their transmission from one generation to the next.

The word **inheritance** often conjures up notions of money or possessions. The broader definition of inheritance, however, is something received from an ancestor or another person. In terms of genetics, each of us inherits one complete set of genes from our mother and one set from our father. Although everyone inherits two complete sets of genes, the sets vary slightly from individual to individual. Those variations help to account for the differences between us. In this chapter, we explore how genes are passed from generation to generation, and how genes affect our traits, or distinguishing features, such as our appearance, health, and possibly even our thoughts and actions.

**Table 19.1 Key concepts in genetics**

| Term | Definition |
|---|---|
| Gene | A DNA sequence that codes for one or more proteins |
| Genome | The complete sequence of DNA found in an organism's chromosomes |
| Locus (plural Loci) | The site on a chromosome where a specific gene is located |
| Homologous chromosomes | A pair of chromosomes that contain the same genes at the same loci |
| Alleles | Alternate versions of a single gene |
| Homozygous | Refers to an individual who possesses two identical alleles for a given gene |
| Heterozygous | Refers to an individual who possesses two different alleles for a given gene |
| Mutation | A change in an individual's DNA sequence that can be passed to future generations |
| Genotype | The set of alleles that an individual possesses |
| Phenotype | The traits that an individual exhibits |

## 19.1 Your genotype is the genetic basis of your phenotype

As described in Chapter 17, chromosomes are partially composed of DNA, and genes are DNA sequences that contain instructions for building proteins. Humans have 22 pairs of **homologous chromosomes** called *autosomes*—both males and females have two copies of each autosome—plus a pair of sex chromosomes, which determine the gender of the individual. Homologous chromosomes look alike, and they each have a copy of the same gene at the same location, or **locus** (Table 19.1). Humans inherit one of each pair of homologous chromosomes from each parent, and thus inherit two copies of each gene in the genome.

While two homologous chromosomes may look alike, closer inspection reveals that they are not completely identical. Small differences in DNA sequence may exist between two homologous chromosomes. These sequence differences may occur within genes, and when they do, they produce, alternative versions of genes called **alleles.** As the DNA sequence differs between alleles, they code for slightly different proteins that may have slightly different structures. As discussed in Chapter 2, alterations in protein structure can affect how the protein functions. For example, the ability to roll your tongue is influenced by a single gene, but there are two alleles for that gene: one allele enables you to curl your tongue, the other allele does not.

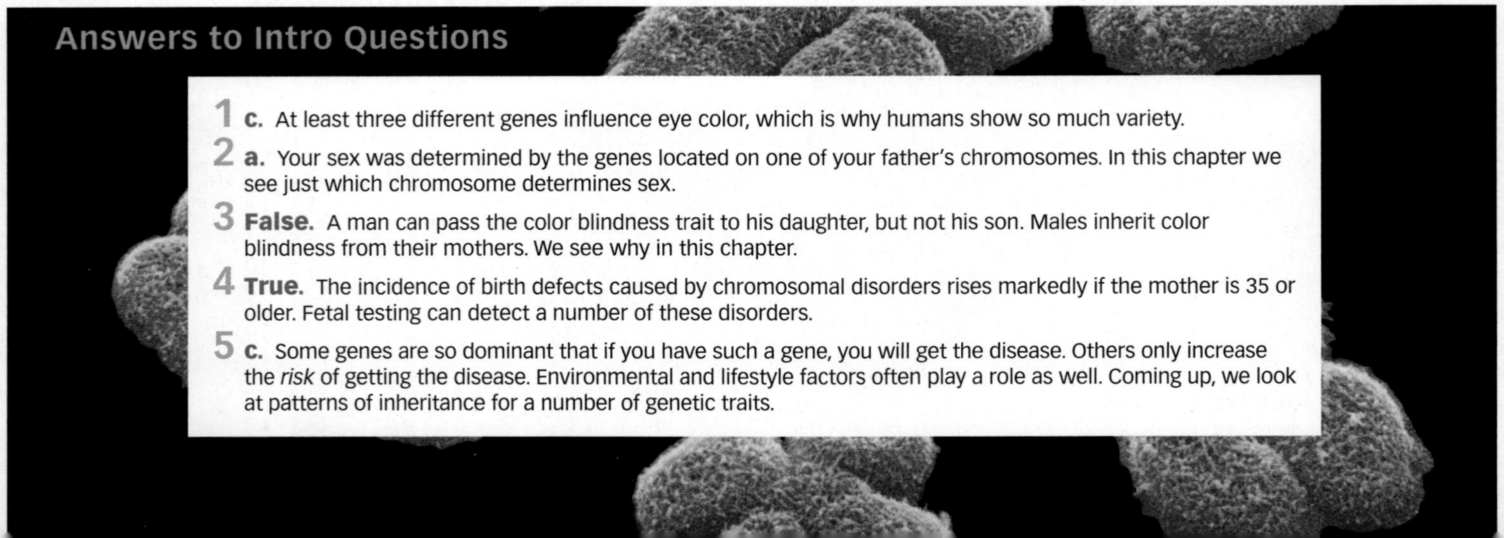

### Answers to Intro Questions

1 **c.** At least three different genes influence eye color, which is why humans show so much variety.

2 **a.** Your sex was determined by the genes located on one of your father's chromosomes. In this chapter we see just which chromosome determines sex.

3 **False.** A man can pass the color blindness trait to his daughter, but not his son. Males inherit color blindness from their mothers. We see why in this chapter.

4 **True.** The incidence of birth defects caused by chromosomal disorders rises markedly if the mother is 35 or older. Fetal testing can detect a number of these disorders.

5 **c.** Some genes are so dominant that if you have such a gene, you will get the disease. Others only increase the *risk* of getting the disease. Environmental and lifestyle factors often play a role as well. Coming up, we look at patterns of inheritance for a number of genetic traits.

If an individual possesses two identical alleles of a particular gene, the person is said to be **homozygous** for that gene (*homo-* means "same," and *zygous* means "yoked," or joined together). A person who has two different alleles of a gene is **heterozygous.** In many cases there are more than two alleles of a particular gene in the human population, although a given individual can inherit only two of them. For example, there are three alleles for blood type: the A, B, and O alleles.

So where did these different alleles come from? Most likely, different alleles resulted from millions of years of **mutations,** or random changes to the DNA sequence, of cells destined to become sperm or eggs. Since those mutations were not corrected before cell division and meiosis, and since they did not cause the sperm or egg to be nonviable, they were passed on to the next generation as slight variations of the original gene, and they remain in the human population to this day. Collectively, all the various genes and their alleles in the human population are known as the *human gene pool.* There are enough different alleles among our approximately 22,000 genes to account for the uniqueness of each individual.

Your complete set of alleles is called your **genotype.** Your genotype has a profound influence on your **phenotype,** or the observable physical and functional traits that characterize you. Among your phenotypic traits are your hair, eye, and skin color; your height and body shape; and your ability (or inability) to curl your tongue. Many phenotypic traits, such as blood type and susceptibility to disease, are less observable. Your phenotype is determined not only by the alleles you inherit from your parents (your genotype), but also by environmental factors and lifestyle choices such as how much you are exposed to the sun, whether you exercise, and how much and what you eat.

**RECAP**

We inherit two alleles of every gene; these alleles may be identical or slightly different. The sum of our alleles is our genotype, and the physical and functional expression of those alleles is our phenotype. ■

## 19.2 Genetic inheritance follows certain patterns

### Punnett square analysis predicts patterns of inheritance

One easy way to designate two alleles of the same gene is to assign them uppercase (such as A) and lowercase (a) letters. Recall that people with the same two alleles of a gene (either aa or AA) are homozygous for that gene and people with different alleles (Aa) are heterozygous.

A **Punnett square** provides a simple way to represent patterns of inheritance of alleles and to predict the probability that a particular genotype will be inherited (Figure 19.1).

To create a Punnett square, place the possible alleles of the male gametes (produced during meiosis, Chapter 17) on one axis and the possible alleles of the female gametes on the other. Bear in mind that although the parents are diploid—they contain two copies of each chromosome—they will each donate *only one* of each chromosome to their offspring. By combining the letters for the sperm and egg in the appropriate squares, which represent the possible combinations that might occur during fertilization, we can see all of the possible genotypes of the offspring and the ratios of each possible genotype. (See the Try It Yourself box.)

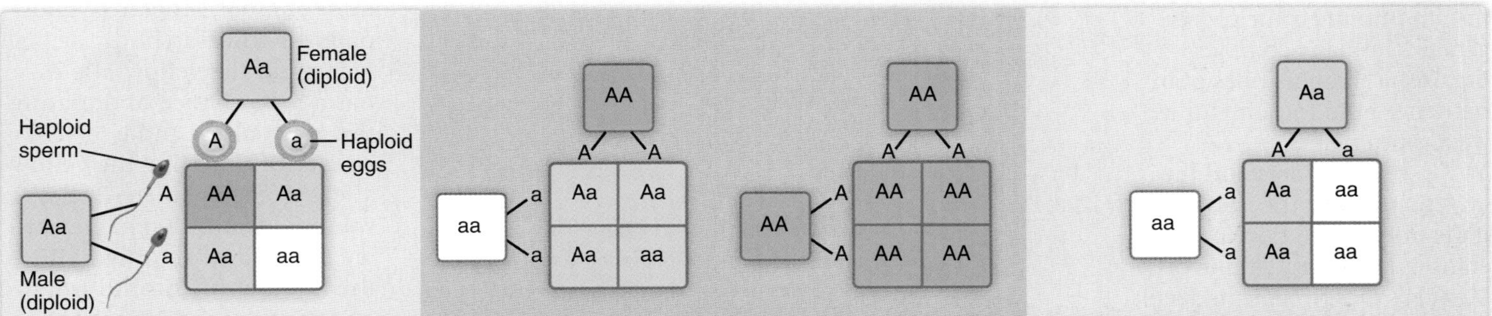


**a) In a Punnett square, the possible combinations of male and female gametes are placed on two axes, and then the possible combinations of the offspring are plotted in the enclosed squares.** This square shows that in a cross between two heterozygotes only half the offspring will be heterozygotes.

**b) A cross between two homozygotes produces offspring that are all the same genotype as each other, but not necessarily the same genotype as their parents.**

**c) A cross between a homozygote and a heterozygote produces an equal number of offspring of each parent's genotype.**

**Figure 19.1 Punnett squares.** Punnett squares are used to predict the outcomes of a particular combination of parental alleles.

## Mendel established the basic principles of genetics

In the 1850s, Gregor Mendel, a university-educated Austrian monk who specialized in natural history, described many of the fundamental principles of inheritance through a number of experiments involving controlled breeding of garden peas. He chose pea plants as a "model" organism because they were cheap and easy to grow, and matings between plants could be set up easily. Many biologists use model organisms to investigate the fundamental principles of biology because they can do experiments such as setting up matings that would be unethical to do with human subjects. Mendel followed the inheritance of traits such as flower color, pea color, pea texture, and plant height from one generation to the next. He collected an extensive set of data over a seven-year period, and proposed that there were discrete "factors" of heredity that united during fertilization and then separated again in the formation of sperm and eggs. He concluded that pea plants inherit two units of each factor, one unit from each parent. Today, we call these factors genes and we know that they are found on chromosomes. Even though Mendel knew nothing about chromosomes, DNA, or meiosis, his pioneering studies with pea plants provided great insight into the principles of genetics in many complex organisms, and his rules of inheritance hold for humans as well as pea plants.

To better understand the laws that govern the passage of traits from generation to generation, let's consider one of Mendel's experiments in detail. In this experiment, Mendel performed a one-trait cross, where he followed the inheritance of a single trait: pea color. Pea plants can produce either green or yellow peas; when Mendel mated, or crossed, a plant with green peas to a plant with yellow peas, he found that all of the offspring produced yellow peas. These peas were identical to those produced by the parent with yellow peas; it seemed that the green pea trait had disappeared completely in these offspring. But was the green trait really gone? To check, Mendel crossed two of these yellow pea–producing offspring together. To his surprise, Mendel found that only about 75% of this second group of offspring produced yellow peas, while the remaining 25% of these offspring produced green peas. Thus, the green pea trait hadn't disappeared; it was as if the green trait had simply "skipped" a generation. Mendel deduced that the information needed to produce green peas was still present in the first group of yellow pea–producing offspring but was somehow hidden. Based on this and other experiments, Mendel reasoned that each pea plant must have two alleles of the gene for pea color, and that each parent contributes only one allele of the gene to the offspring (Figure 19.2).

This is now known as Mendel's first rule of inheritance, the *law of segregation:* when gametes are formed in the parents, the alleles separate from each other so that each gamete gets only one allele of each gene. Importantly, which allele a parent contributes to a gamete is determined in a completely random manner; a heterozygous parent harboring both the green and the yellow alleles has a 50% chance of donating the green allele and a 50% chance of donating the yellow allele to each gamete. Today we understand that gametes are haploid, with only half the number of chromosomes and genes of the parent (review the process of meiosis, Chapter 17).

Mendel's law of segregation doesn't apply only to pea plants; it applies to many complex diploid organisms, including humans. For example, let's consider hairlines (Figure 19.3). Human hairline

**try it yourself**

### Calculating the Probability of Inheriting a Dominant Trait

Can you curl your tongue into a U shape? Can your parents do it? The ability to curl (or roll) the tongue is due to the presence of a dominant allele, so we can calculate the probability that a child will have this phenotype if we know the parents' genotype. Draw a Punnett square to illustrate the combinations of alleles that would result if both parents are heterozygous (Tt) for this trait:

| | |
|---|---|
| | |

On average, what percentage of these parents' offspring should be able to curl their tongues, and what percentage should be unable to? Able: ______ Unable: ______.

In another family, the father is heterozygous for this trait but the mother cannot curl her tongue. Draw a Punnett square to show the probable genotypes of their children:

| | |
|---|---|
| | |

Do you know your parents' tongue-curling ability? If so, draw Punnett squares to illustrate the possibilities for the genotypes of their children (you and any full siblings). (Actual percentages within your family may not match the predicted percentages because the sample size is so small.)

| | |
|---|---|
| | |

| | |
|---|---|
| | |

| | |
|---|---|
| | |

As far as we know, tongue-curling ability confers no evolutionary advantage at all. The recessive allele remains in the human gene pool because it does not affect our chances of survival.

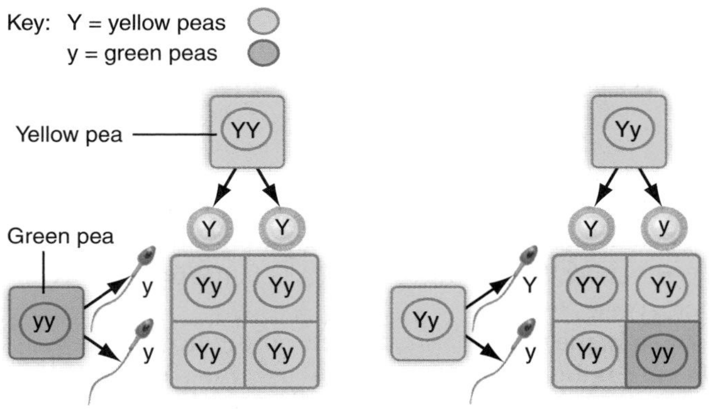


**a) Mendel's first cross between a homozygous plant with yellow peas (YY) and a homozygous plant with green peas (yy).**

**b) Mendel's second cross between two of the offspring of his first cross.**

**Figure 19.2 One-trait crosses in pea plants. (a)** All of the offspring were heterozygotes (Yy) with the dominant yellow phenotype. **(b)** In Mendel's second cross, 25% of the offspring were homozygous dominant (YY), 50% of the offspring were heterozygous (Yy), and 25% of the offspring were homozygous recessive (yy). Only the homozygous recessive genotype shows the recessive green phenotype.

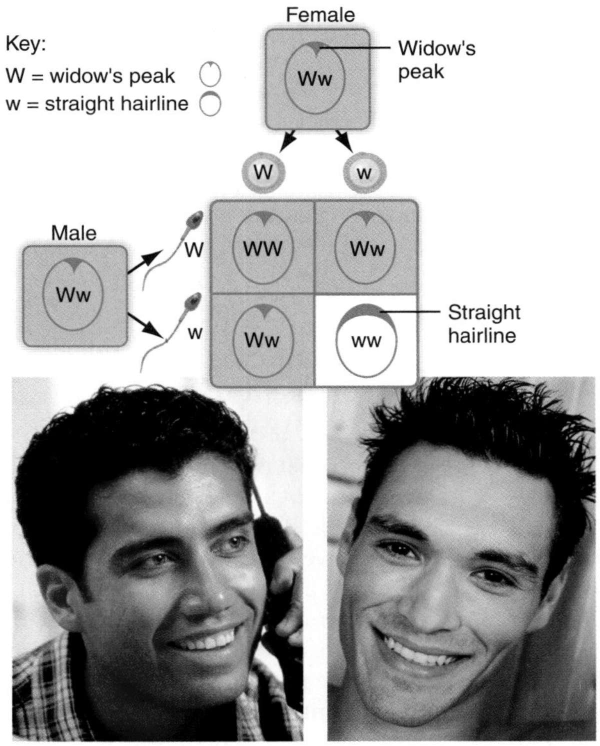


**Figure 19.3 One-trait crosses in humans.** The allele for the widow's peak (W) is dominant. A mating between two parents heterozygous (Ww) for the widow's peak trait can produce homozygous dominant (WW), heterozygous (Ww), and homozygous recessive children (ww). Only the homozygous recessive genotype will have the straight hairline phenotype.

pattern is controlled by a single gene that has two alleles. One allele causes a person to have a widow's peak, while the other allele causes people to have straight hairlines. If two people heterozygous for the hairline pattern gene have a child, each parent has a 50% chance of donating the widow's peak allele to the child and a 50% chance of donating the straight hairline allele to the child. Mendel's law of segregation, or the fact that the parents randomly donate one allele of each gene to their sperm or egg cells, is a major reason that so much phenotypic variation exists among individuals in the human population.

**RECAP**

A Punnett square is a useful method for predicting the ratios of possible offspring genotypes from a particular mating. Gregor Mendel worked out the fundamental principles of genetics. Mendel's law of segregation holds that when sperm and eggs form, the alleles separate from each other so that each sperm or egg receives only one allele of each gene. ■

## Dominant alleles are expressed over recessive alleles

In the experiment described above, Mendel observed that the green pea trait "skipped" a generation. Why did this happen? Mendel reasoned that the yellow allele behaves in a **dominant** manner with respect to the green allele; when both alleles are present in the same plant, the plant will only show the yellow phenotype. The green allele is thus **recessive** to the yellow allele, and is only visible when no yellow alleles are present. Figure 19.2 shows the inheritance pattern of pea color that Mendel observed. It is customary to denote the dominant allele by an uppercase letter (in this case, Y) and the recessive allele by a lowercase letter (y).

Many human genes have dominant and recessive alleles as well. The hairline pattern gene has a dominant allele (W) that produces the widow's peak phenotype, and a recessive allele (w) that causes the straight hairline phenotype. If a person homozygous for the widow's peak allele were to have children with a person homozygous for the straight hairline allele, all of their children would be heterozygous for the gene, and would show the dominant widow's peak phenotype. But, if one of these heterozygous children were to mate with another person heterozygous for the hairline pattern gene, as shown in Figure 19.3, the recessive straight hairline phenotype could reappear in their offspring. It would appear that the straight hairline trait had skipped a generation, just like the green pea trait in Mendel's experiment.

Most recessive alleles do not confer a distinct advantage or disadvantage to the homozygous recessive person. Many of them—such as the allele for a straight hairline, another for attached earlobes, or another for the inability to curl the tongue (Figure 19.4)—probably originated as mutations at some point in our evolutionary history. They remain in the human gene pool because they do no harm.

However, some recessive alleles result in the absence of a functionally important protein. An example is cystic fibrosis (see Health Watch box), which afflicts only homozygous recessive individuals. These alleles no longer code for a specific essential protein because their nucleotide sequence has been altered slightly from the dominant form. In principle, the frequency of truly harmful recessive alleles in a population is kept in check by the occasional premature death of homozygous recessives, but the allele can persist in the population in heterozygotes.

Finally, the term dominant refers only to how an allele behaves in combination with a recessive allele in a heterozygote. Dominance has nothing to do with the frequency in which an allele is found in a population; in fact, some dominant alleles are quite rare. Consider the number of human fingers and toes. Most people are homozygous recessive (pp) for the gene controlling the number of fingers and toes, and they have four fingers and a thumb on each hand and five toes on each foot. But some people possess a dominant allele (Pp or PP), and the presence of this allele causes them to have extra fingers and toes on each hand and foot (Figure 19.5a), a condition known as polydactyly. Even though this allele behaves in a dominant fashion with respect to the allele for the normal number of fingers and toes, it is extremely rare in the population. Interestingly, there is a dominant allele in cats that causes affected individuals to have extra toes, as well (Figure 19.5b).

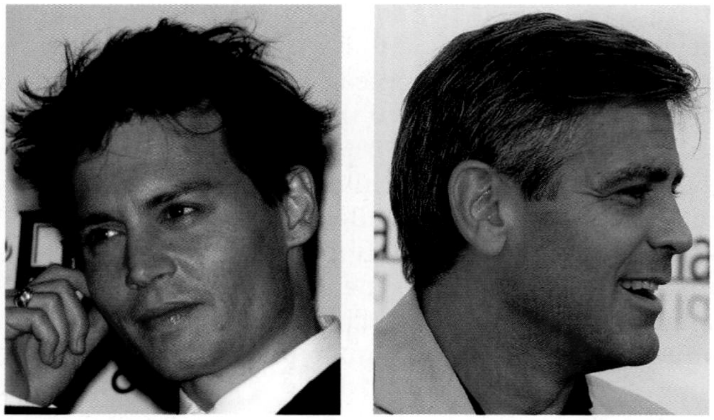

**a) Attached earlobes (Johnny Depp, left) and unattached earlobes (George Clooney, right).**

**b) Tongue-curling ability**

**Figure 19.4 Harmless dominant/recessive traits and alleles.** **(a)** The allele for unattached earlobes is dominant over that for attached earlobes. Johnny Depp is homozygous for the recessive allele, while George Clooney is either homozygous for the dominant allele or heterozygous. **(b)** The daughter in this family photo inherited the dominant allele for tongue-curling from her father. Her mother has two of the recessive alleles and cannot curl her tongue, so the daughter must be heterozygous for this trait.

**RECAP**

Where two alleles of a particular gene exist in the human gene pool, one is often dominant over the other and controls the phenotype of a heterozygote. Harmless alleles are more likely to remain in the population than harmful ones. Dominant alleles are not always common in the human population; some are extremely rare. ■

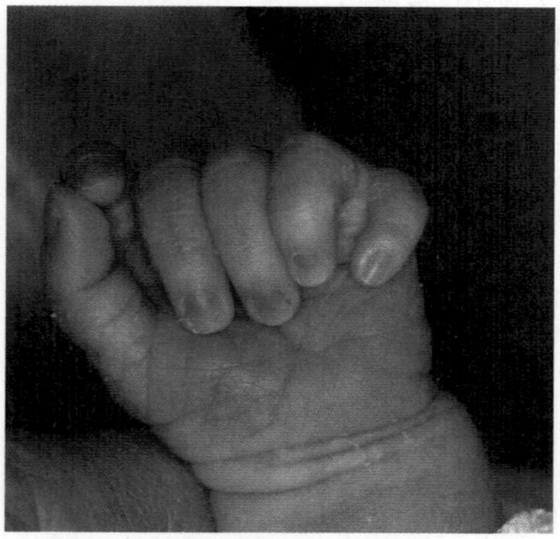

**a) A human infant with polydactyly.**

**b) A polydactyl cat.**

**Figure 19.5 Dominant alleles are not always common in a population.** Polydactyly, or the presence of extra digits, is an uncommon phenotype in both humans and cats caused by a dominant allele.

## Two-trait crosses: Independent assortment of genes for different traits

So far we have followed the inheritance patterns of single genes throughout multiple generations. But what happens when we follow *two* genes? Are they inherited as a set, or can they be inherited independently of each other? To answer this question, let's consider the human hairline pattern gene and a second gene that controls whether a person's earlobes hang freely or are attached (Figure 19.6). For the earlobe gene, the allele for free earlobes (E) is dominant over the allele for attached earlobes (e). If a person with a widow's peak and free earlobes who is homozygous dominant for both genes (EEWW) mates with a person with a straight hairline and

## Health Watch

# Cystic Fibrosis

Cystic fibrosis (CF), the most common fatal genetic disease in North America today, is caused by a recessive allele of a gene on chromosome 7. Because it is recessive, parents may have no idea that they are both carriers for cystic fibrosis until they have a child with the disease. Approximately 1 in 23 Caucasians carries the recessive allele and about 1 Caucasian child in 2,000 has the disease. Among African Americans, only 1 child in 17,000 is born with the disease.

The recessive allele produces a defective version of a protein that normally aids the transport of chloride across the cell membrane of epithelial cells. Impaired chloride transport affects the secretion of salt and water across cells that line the ducts in several organs. As a result, organs that normally produce a thin, watery mucus secrete a thick, sticky mucus instead.

In the lungs, the thick mucus clogs the bronchioles and leads to chronic inflammation and infections that can be fatal. In the pancreas, the mucus blocks ducts and prevents pancreatic enzymes from reaching the intestines. The sweat glands are also affected, but ordinarily this does not cause major problems.

Typical symptoms of cystic fibrosis include persistent coughing, wheezing or pneumonia, excessive appetite but poor weight gain, and foul-smelling, bulky feces. The disease is usually diagnosed by age 3 by testing for high salt levels in perspiration. A DNA-based blood test can screen for variations on the gene responsible.

Management of cystic fibrosis focuses on reducing the damage caused by the symptoms, often a constant battle throughout life. Regular, vigorous chest physical therapy helps to dislodge mucus in the lungs, and antibiotics are often needed to treat lung infections. In addition, a small hand-held mucus clearance device called the Flutter® has been developed to help dislodge mucus.

Several drugs are useful in treating the condition. High doses of the pain reliever *ibuprofen* may slow down the deterioration of the lungs, especially in children ages 5 to 13. *Pulmozyme* (dornase alfa) thins pulmonary mucus and reduces the number of respiratory infections. *Tobramycin* is an inhalant antibiotic that delivers a concentrated dose directly to the lungs. We now know that the defective sodium chloride transport protein gets trapped deep within the cell, so it is never inserted into the cell membrane properly. Drugs to help the transport protein move to the cell membrane are in the early stages of clinical trials. Other researchers are working on gene therapy techniques that insert copies of the normal gene into viruses, such as those that cause colds, and then deliver the modified viruses to the airway. (For more on gene therapy, see Chapter 20.)

Improved treatments and better understanding of the disease have increased the average life expectancy for patients with cystic fibrosis from just 5 years to over 35 years. In addition, genetic testing can now identify couples who at are at risk of having a child with the disease. Do not be surprised if cystic fibrosis is cured in our lifetime, or at least treated so effectively that patients live long and healthy lives.

**Cystic fibrosis.** This child with cystic fibrosis is receiving vigorous percussion therapy ("clap therapy") to loosen mucus in the lungs.

attached earlobes who is homozygous recessive for both genes (eeww), all of their children will be heterozygous for both genes (EeWw), and will have a widow's peak and free earlobes (Figure 19.6a).

But what happens if two people heterozygous for both genes were to mate? Would their children have either both dominant or both recessive phenotypes, or are other combinations possible? As shown in Figure 19.6b, a mating between two heterozygotes for both genes can indeed produce children with both dominant traits and children with both recessive traits, but other combinations are also possible. Some offspring may have the dominant widow's peak and the recessive attached earlobe phenotypes, and others may have the recessive straight hairline and the dominant free earlobe phenotypes.

When predicting the results of a two-trait cross, remember that each parent donates only one allele of each gene, and that the genes for different traits assort independently of each other during the formation of sperm and egg. That is, a parent can donate a dominant hairline pattern allele and a dominant earlobe allele, a recessive hair pattern allele and a recessive earlobe allele, or a mixture of the two. Each of these outcomes is equally probable because the hairline pattern and earlobe alleles are donated to egg and sperm independently of each other. The outcome of a two-trait cross can be predicted by

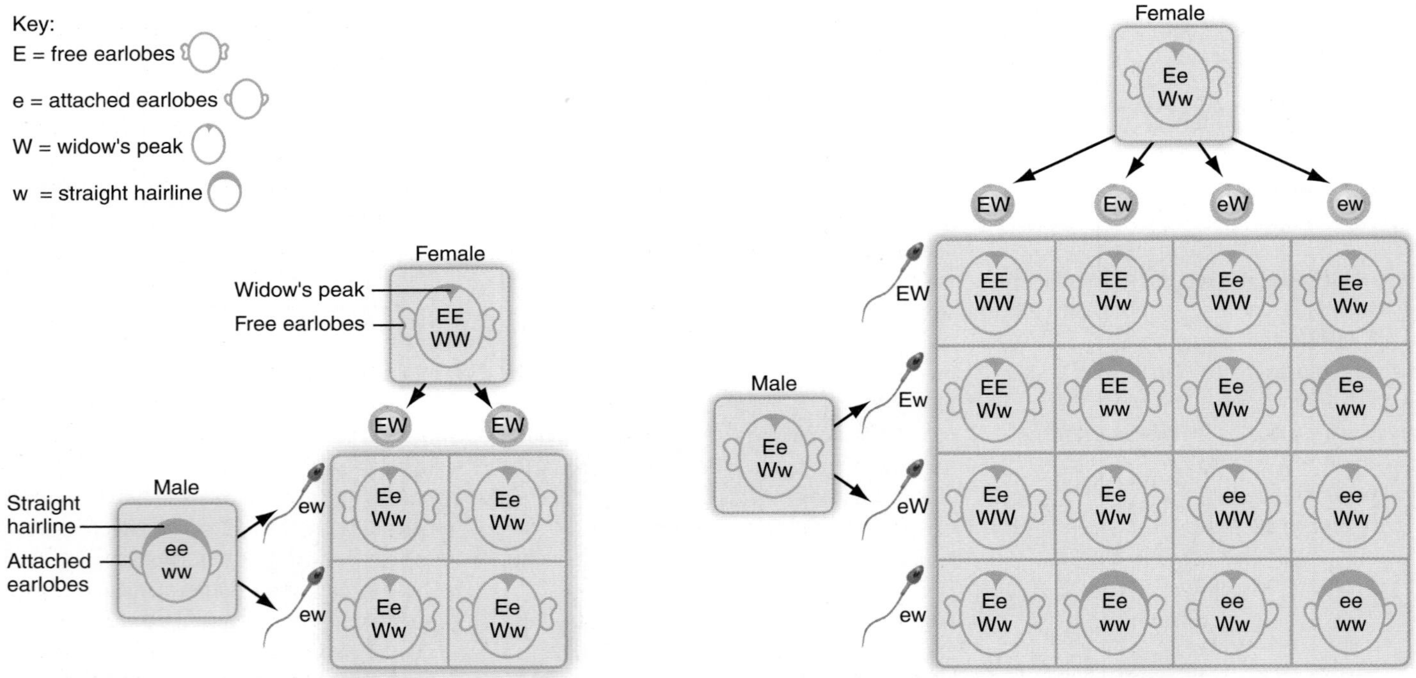


**a) A mating between a homozygous person with a widow's peak and free earlobes (EEWW) and a homozygous person with a straight hairline and attached earlobes (eeww).**

**b) A mating between two heterozygous people with widow's peaks and free earlobes (EeWw).**

**Figure 19.6 A two-trait cross showing independent assortment of alleles for different traits. (a)** Remember that diploid organisms have two alleles of each gene, so we must consider four alleles in this example. From this mating, all of the offspring will have the dominant widow's peak and free earlobes phenotypes. **(b)** Note that because the alleles for the two traits assort independently of each other, some of the offspring show one dominant and one recessive trait.

using either a large Punnett square as shown in Figure 19.6b, or by considering each gene independently and simply multiplying the ratios from small Punnett squares as shown in Figure 19.7.

Mendel saw similar results in pea plants when performing two-trait crosses, and he formulated his *law of independent assortment,* which states that the alleles of different genes are distributed to egg and sperm cells independently of each other during meiosis. But, on this point Mendel was only partly right. Recall that he knew nothing about chromosomes or meiosis. We now know that the 22,000 genes in the human genome do not simply float around independently of each other in the cell's nucleus. Instead, genes are structurally part of the 23 pairs of chromosomes found in the cell's nucleus. Only genes that are located on different chromosomes always assort truly independently. Alleles located on the same chromosome, called linked alleles, may or may not be inherited together, as discussed later in this chapter.

**RECAP**

During meiosis, alleles for different traits are distributed independently of each other to egg and sperm cells, provided those alleles are located on different chromosomes. Punnett squares can be used to predict the outcomes of two-trait crosses. ■

## Incomplete dominance: Heterozygotes have an intermediate phenotype

Some alleles do not follow the dominant/recessive pattern described above. In **incomplete dominance,** the heterozygous genotype results in a phenotype that is intermediate between the two homozygous phenotypes. An example of incomplete dominance in Caucasian humans is the trait of having straight, wavy, or curly hair (Figure 19.8). Another is *familial hypercholesterolemia.* People homozygous for familial hypercholesterolemia may have blood cholesterol concentrations more than six times the normal level. The homozygous condition is quite rare (around one in a million people) because most homozygous individuals have heart attacks in childhood or adolescence and die by age 20. In contrast, the heterozygous condition is fairly common (about one in 500 people). People heterozygous for the disease may have blood cholesterol concentrations that are two to three times the normal level. With diagnosis and treatment, most can live fairly normal, healthy lives.

## Codominance: Both gene products are equally expressed

In **codominance** the products of both alleles are expressed equally. One important example of codominance is the gene for blood type. There are three alleles for this gene: A, B, and O. The

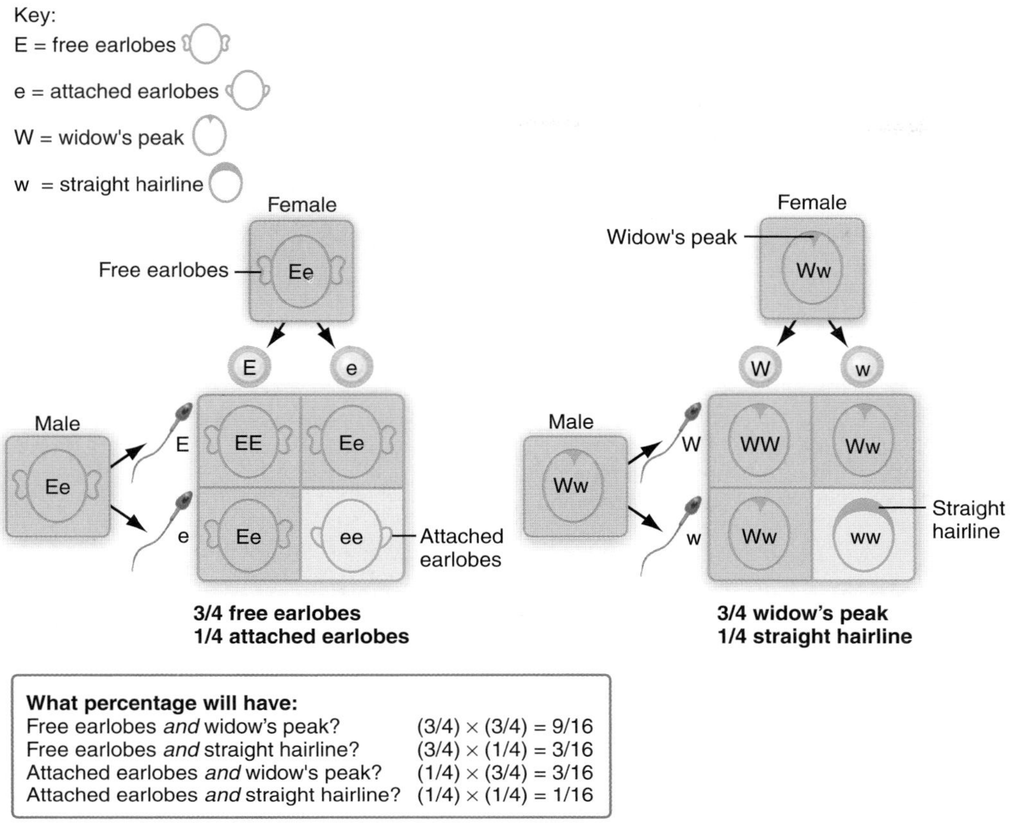


**Figure 19.7 Another method of calculating phenotypic ratios from two-trait crosses.** Instead of drawing the large Punnett square in Figure 19.6b, each trait can be considered individually. The phenotypic ratios obtained can then be multiplied together to get the same results shown in Figure 19.6b.

O allele is recessive; when combined in a heterozygous person with either the A allele or the B allele, the person will have A or B blood type. But the A and B alleles are codominant. If an individual is heterozygous with an A allele and a B allele, that person will have type AB blood with *both* A and B antigens on his or her red blood cells, rather than a mixed or intermediate antigen. (See Figure 19.9 and the Try it Yourself box on page 451.) Blood phenotype has important implications for which types of blood can be given to which patients, as seen in Chapter 7.

Another example of codominance is **sickle-cell anemia.** Sickle-cell anemia is a disease caused by one of two alleles involved in the production of hemoglobin for red blood cells. One of the two alleles codes for a hemoglobin molecule (designated $Hb^S$) that differs from the normal hemoglobin molecule (designated $Hb^A$) by just one amino acid. People homozygous for *sickle-cell anemia* ($Hb^SHb^S$) have only $Hb^S$ hemoglobin in their red blood cells, whereas heterozygous individuals, who are said to have *sickle-cell trait* ($Hb^AHb^S$), have equal amounts of each type of hemoglobin. As shown in Figure 19.10a, a mating between two individuals with sickle-cell trait can result in children who are phenotypically normal ($Hb^AHb^A$), children with sickle-cell trait ($Hb^AHb^S$), and children with sickle-cell anemia ($Hb^SHb^S$).

In people with sickle-cell anemia, breathing air with even slightly lower oxygen concentrations than normal can cause the $Hb^S$ hemoglobin to crystallize within the red blood cells. When this happens their red blood cells take on a crescent, or sickle, shape (Figure 19.10b). Sickled cells rupture easily because they are more fragile than normal red blood cells. They are also less flexible, so they tend to clog small blood vessels and block blood flow, and they carry less oxygen. The resultant oxygen deprivation of tissues and organs produces symptoms of fatigue, chest pain, bone and joint pain, swollen hands and feet, jaundice, and visual problems due to retinal damage. If sickle-cell anemia is left untreated, long-term complications can include stroke, blindness, pneumonia, and other health problems. Many people with sickle-cell anemia do not live into their 30s. In contrast,

**Figure 19.8 Incomplete dominance.** Wavy hair (Hh) is an intermediate phenotype between straight (HH) and curly (hh) hair because neither allele is dominant.

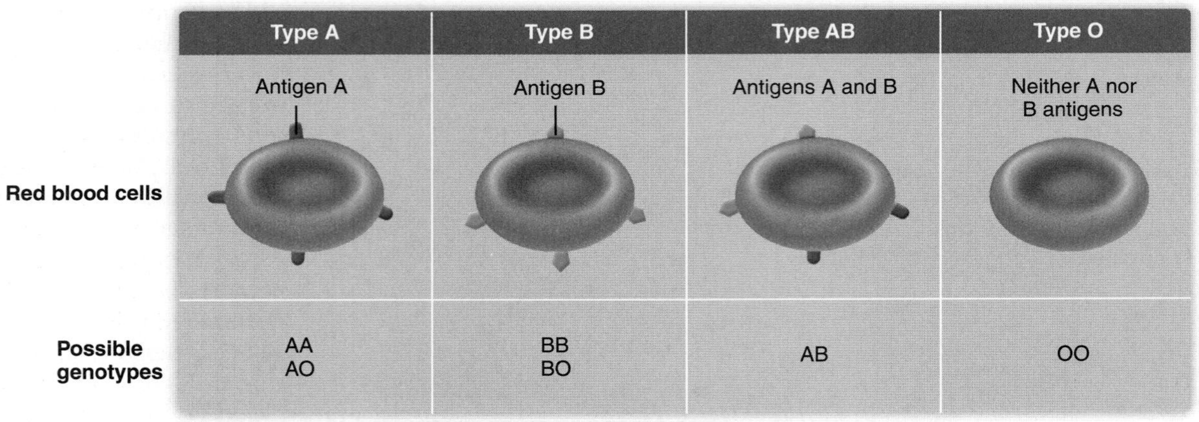


**Figure 19.9 Blood type: An example of codominance.** Characteristics of the four major blood types are shown, including their surface antigens and the genotypes that cause each blood type phenotype.

people with sickle-cell trait rarely suffer from any symptoms. The half of their hemoglobin that is normal is generally sufficient for them to lead normal lives. However, they may have mild episodes of red blood cell sickling when oxygen concentrations are lower than normal, such as at high altitudes or in airplanes in flight.

Sickle-cell anemia affects primarily Africans (and their descendants on other continents) and Caucasians of Mediterranean descent. In East Africa, sickle-cell anemia is fairly common and nearly 40% of the black population have sickle-cell trait. In contrast, only about one in 500 African Americans is born with sickle-cell anemia and only 8% have sickle-cell trait. Why the big difference?

It turns out that the sickle-cell allele protects against malaria, a deadly parasitic disease common in tropical climates. The malaria parasite spends part of its life cycle in humans (in the liver and in red blood cells) and the other part in mosquitoes. When the malaria parasite enters the red blood cell of a person with sickle-cell trait or sickle-cell disease, the cell sickles and eventually ruptures, killing the parasite before it can reproduce.

Malaria kills one million people every year worldwide. Where malaria exists, having sickle-cell trait (but not sickle-cell anemia) is a distinct advantage. Were it not for malaria, we could surmise that sickle-cell anemia and sickle-cell trait would become rare in Africa, just as they are becoming rarer in the United States.

Because our phenotype includes all of our unique characteristics from our physical appearance to our biochemical makeup, the definition of an inheritance pattern as either incompletely dominant or codominant depends on the context. At the biochemical level, sickle-cell trait is an example of codominance because both the normal hemoglobin ($Hb^A$) and the sickle cell hemoglobin ($Hb^S$) are produced in equal amounts. However, at the level of the whole person, sickle-cell trait is an example of incomplete dominance, because the person with sickle-cell trait exhibits a disease pattern that is intermediate between the two homozygous conditions. Understanding the concept is more important than an argument over whether sickle-cell trait is one or the other.

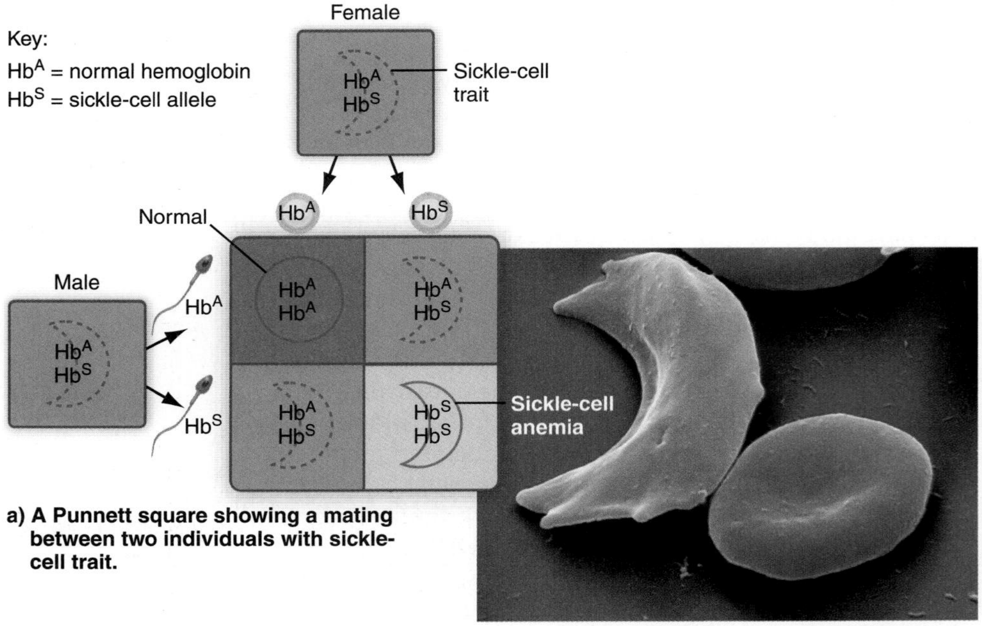


**a) A Punnett square showing a mating between two individuals with sickle-cell trait.**

**b) A sickled red blood cell next to a normal red blood cell**

**Figure 19.10 Sickle-cell anemia: an example of codominance.** If two people who have sickle-cell trait have children, each child will have a 25% chance of being phenotypically normal, a 50% chance of having sickle-cell trait, and a 25% chance of having sickle-cell anemia.

**RECAP**

People heterozygous with incompletely dominant alleles have a phenotype that is intermediate between the phenotype of either homozygous genotype. People heterozygous with codominant allele express the products of both alleles equally. In AB blood type both A and B antigens are expressed in an AB heterozygote. In sickle-cell anemia, two forms of hemoglobin are equally expressed in the heterozygote. ■

## Polygenic inheritance: Phenotype is influenced by many genes

Many traits result from not just one pair of genes, but many genes acting simultaneously. Inheritance of phenotypic traits that depend on many genes is called **polygenic inheritance.** Eye color, for example, is controlled by at least three genes, yielding a range of different eye color phenotypes from nearly black to light blue (Figure 19.11). Both skin and eye color are determined by the amount of a light-absorbing pigment called melanin in the skin and iris. The striking differences in eye color occur because in people with relatively low amounts of melanin we see different wavelengths of light (green, gray, or blue) reflected from the iris.

Physical characteristics such as height, body size, and shape are also examples of polygenic inheritance. Traits governed by polygenic inheritance generally are distributed in the population as a continuous range of values, with more people at the middle (or median) and fewer people at the extremes. As an example of a trait influenced by multiple genes, let's consider height. We will simplify matters and assume that height is influenced by only three genes, each of which has two alleles. Each gene has a tall allele (A, B, or C) that behaves in an incompletely dominant manner with respect to the short alleles (a, b, or c). In this example, an individual homozygous for tall alleles for all three genes (AABBCC) would be very tall, while an individual homozygous for short alleles for all three genes (aabbcc) would be very short. Heterozygotes for all three genes (AaBbCc) would have an intermediate phenotype and would be of medium height. Now, consider a cross between individuals of medium height. Most of their offspring would be similar in height to their parents, inheriting a mix of tall and short alleles, but by random chance, some offspring might inherit mostly tall or mostly short alleles, and a few might be very tall or very petite (Figure 19.12). This phenotypic distribution occurs throughout the human population, and a plot of the numbers of individuals at each value for the trait typically forms a normal (bell-shaped) curve.

We are just beginning to understand that many health conditions may be caused or at least influenced by polygenic inheritance. Examples include cancer, high blood pressure, heart disease, and stroke.

**try it yourself**

### Predicting Blood Type

The gene for blood type has three alleles: A, B, and O. The A and B alleles are both dominant over the O allele, so we can calculate the probability that a child will have a certain blood type if we know the genotype of the parents. What are the genotypes of a heterozygous man with A blood type, and a heterozygous woman with B blood type?

Male:______ Female:______

If these two were to have children, what blood types are possible, and in what frequencies? Draw a Punnett square to illustrate the possible genotypes that would result from this mating:

| | |
|---|---|
| | |

In another family, the father has AB blood, while the mother's blood type is O. What are their genotypes?

Male:______ Female:______

Draw a Punnett square to show the possible genotypes and phenotypes that could result from a mating between these two individuals:

| | |
|---|---|
| | |

Do you know your blood type? If so, what possible genotypes could give you your blood type?

Possible genotypes:______________

Do you know your parents' blood types? If so, draw Punnett squares to illustrate the possibilities for the genotypes of their children. Remember that there may be more than one genotype responsible for a certain blood type, so you may have to draw several alternate Punnett squares.

| | |
|---|---|
| | |

| | |
|---|---|
| | |

| | |
|---|---|
| | |

## Both genotype and the environment affect phenotype

Phenotype is determined in part by our genotype and in part by environmental influences (Figure 19.13). A prime example of an environmental influence is the effect of diet on height and body size. Analysis of human populations reveals a clear trend toward increased height and weight in certain populations, particularly in developed countries. The changes in height and weight have sometimes occurred within one generation, much too short a time to be due to changes in the gene pool. The trend is primarily due to improvements in diet and nutrition, especially early in childhood.

Except for a few rare genetic diseases such as Huntington disease (more on this later in the chapter), our genotype is not the sole determinant of whether we will actually develop a heritable disease (that is, have the disease

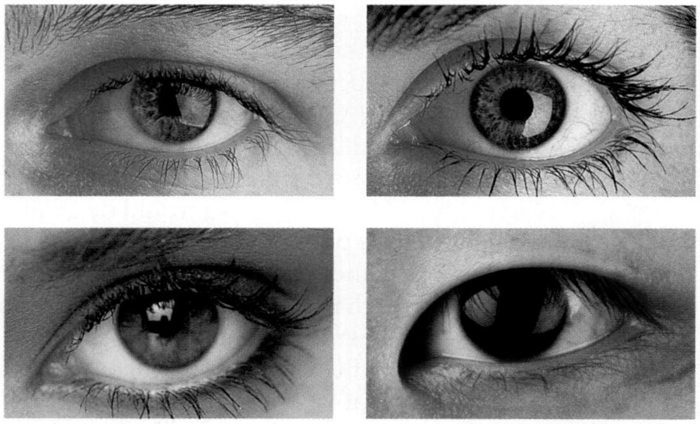

**Figure 19.11 Polygenic inheritance.** Eye color is determined by at least three genes, not just one. Different combinations of the alleles of the genes account for a range of eye colors.

phenotype). Usually we inherit only a slightly increased *risk* of developing the disease, with those risks modifiable by environmental factors and our own actions. If you know that certain heritable conditions or diseases run in your family, it would be prudent to reduce any environmental risk factors associated with that disease. For example, if your family has a history of skin cancer, limit your exposure to the sun. If your family has a history of heart disease due to high cholesterol, have your cholesterol measured regularly and change your diet or begin other corrective measures if your cholesterol levels are above normal.

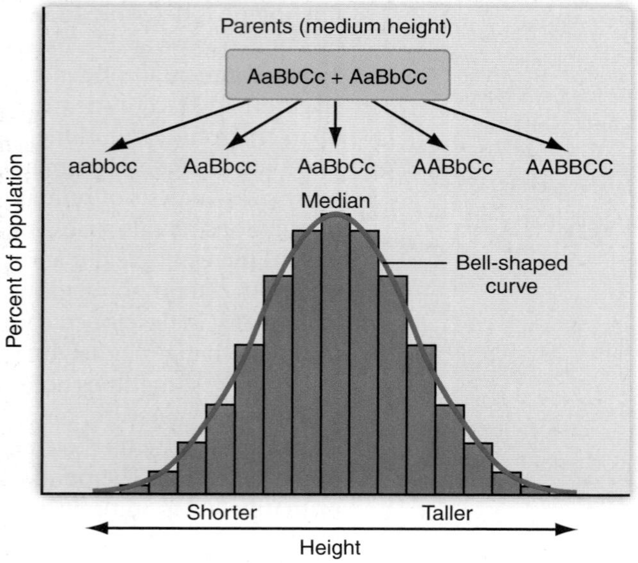


**Figure 19.12 Continuous range of variation in traits governed by polygenic inheritance.** Polygenic traits, such as height, appear in the population as a continuous range of phenotypes, with more people in the middle than at either extreme. In this hypothetical example, three genes influence height. Heterozygotes for all three genes have an intermediate (average) height, and can produce a wide range of heights among their offspring, depending on how many tall alleles and short alleles each child inherits.

This is really the old nature-versus-nurture question: Are we the way we are because of our genes or because of our environment? The answer is both. Your genes carry the instructions for all your proteins, but the environment can influence how genes are expressed and how they contribute to your phenotype. There is no one answer to the nature-versus-nurture dichotomy. But since you cannot change your genes, your best defense against any possible future disease is to take proper care of yourself.

**RECAP**

In polygenic inheritance, many different genes influence a single phenotype, such as height or eye color. In addition, some phenotypes can be influenced by environmental factors such as diet. ■

## Linked alleles may or may not be inherited together

As previously mentioned, alleles of different genes are distributed to egg and sperm cells independently of each other during meiosis. But, because humans have only 23 pairs of chromosomes, it doesn't always work this way. Many alleles for different traits are often inherited together because they are physically joined on the same chromosome. These alleles are called **linked alleles,** and the closer they are located to each other on the chromosome the more likely are they to be inherited together. However, they are not *always* inherited together because of crossing-over, which partially reshuffles

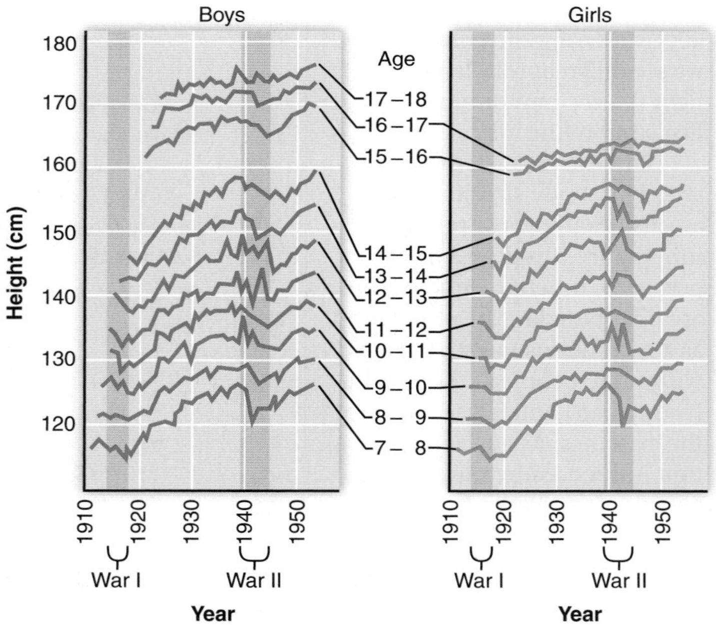


**Figure 19.13 Environmental factors may influence phenotype.** Sudden changes in environmental factors can cause changes in phenotype over a very short period of time. The average height of schoolchildren in Stuttgart, Germany, aged 7–18 increased slowly between World Wars I and II. During the Second World War, however, nutrition was often inadequate and average height decreased significantly.

alleles across homologous chromosomes during meiosis (review meiosis in Chapter 17). How often two linked alleles are inherited together is directly proportional to how close together they are and inversely proportional to how often crossing-over occurs (the more that crossing-over occurs, the less likely the linked alleles will be inherited together).

To get a feel for how often linked alleles might be inherited together, consider that the average pair of homologous chromosomes may have 2,000 or more genes, and that crossing-over occurs approximately 30 times per pair of chromosomes. Alleles located close to each other, then, may be inherited together quite often. Scientists have learned that they can map the positions of genes by studying how often particular linked alleles are inherited together, a technique called *linkage mapping*.

Adding it all up, there are three major sources of genetic variability as a result of sexual reproduction:

- Independent assortment of alleles located on different chromosomes
- Partial shuffling of linked alleles as a result of crossing-over between homologous chromosomes
- Random fertilization of an egg by a sperm

**RECAP**

Alleles located close together on the same chromosome are inherited together, except when crossing-over occurs. ■

## 19.3 Sex-linked inheritance: X and Y chromosomes carry different genes

Chromosomes are identifiable in cells only just before cell division. At this time each chromosome can be identified by its characteristic size, centromere location, and distinct banding pattern. A composite display of all the chromosomes of an organism is called a **karyotype.**

The karyotype shown in Figure 19.14 shows the 23 pairs of human chromosomes. Of these, 22 are matched pairs (autosomes). The last pair of chromosomes, however, do not look alike and do not match up. These are the sex chromosomes, X and Y. The sex chromosomes are not a homologous pair. They look different from each other, and they function differently because they carry different genes. They represent a pair only in that you get one from each parent as a consequence of meiosis. As seen in Figure 19.15, the sperm from the father determines the gender of the offspring. Females have two X chromosomes and will donate one of them to the offspring, while males have an X and a Y chromosome, only one of which is donated to the offspring. If the male donates an X chromosome, the fertilized egg will have two X chromosomes and will develop into a female. If the male donates a Y chromosome, the fertilized egg has an X and a Y chromosome and will develop into a male.

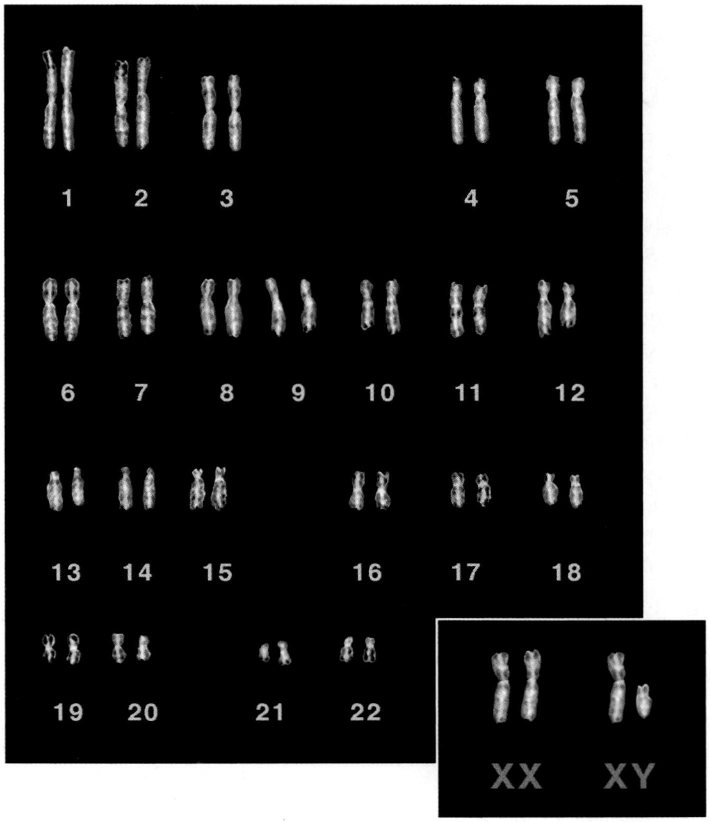


**Figure 19.14 The human karyotype.** Chromosomes are identified and paired according to their size, centromere location, and characteristic banding patterns. A numbered arrangement of all 23 pairs of human chromosomes is called the human karyotype. The sex chromosomes are shown in boxes; females are XX and males are XY. Note that the sex chromosomes (X and Y) are quite different from each other.

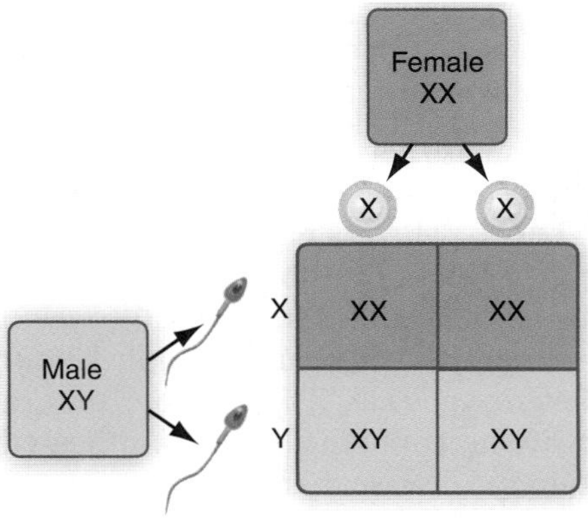


**Figure 19.15 Sex determination in humans.** The sex of the embryo is determined by the male's sperm, about 50% of which carry an X chromosome and 50% of which carry a Y chromosome. Maleness is determined by the inheritance of a Y chromosome.

### Sex-linked inheritance depends on genes located on sex chromosomes

Gender determination by inheritance of sex chromosomes is not without cost, especially to males. The advantage of having two homologous chromosomes is that each has a second copy—a backup file, if you will. If something goes wrong with one copy, the other can still carry out its function.

In sexually reproducing animals in which the Y chromosome determines maleness, females have a homologous pair of X chromosomes but males do not. This means that males have a greater susceptibility for diseases associated with recessive alleles on the sex chromosomes.

**Sex-linked inheritance** refers to inheritance patterns that depend on genes located on the sex chromosomes. Sex-linked inheritance is *X-linked* if the gene is located only on the X chromosome and *Y-linked* if the gene is located only on the Y chromosome. There are plenty of examples of X-linked inheritance because many of the genes on the X chromosome are not related to sex determination at all. However, there are relatively few well-documented examples of Y-linked inheritance. The reason is that the Y chromosome is relatively small and many of its genes relate to "maleness." Genes on the Y chromosome apparently influence differentiation of the male sex organs, production of sperm, and the development of secondary sex characteristics, but not much else.

In the female, X-linked inheritance behaves just like inheritance of homologous chromosomes with paired genes. Not so in the male, because he inherits only one X chromosome. In the male, X-linked genotype and phenotype are both determined solely by the single X chromosome he inherited from his mother.

The best known example of an X-linked disease is hemophilia, also known as bleeder's disease. Hemophiliacs lack a blood-clotting factor that is encoded by an X-linked gene with two alleles. The recessive allele ($X^h$) is a mutant that cannot produce the clotting factor, whereas the dominant allele ($X^H$) produces the clotting factor. Individuals have the disease only if they do *not* have at least one normal dominant allele (that is, if they are an $X^hX^h$ female or an $X^hY$ male).

The inheritance of hemophilia and other X-linked recessive diseases follows this pattern:

- Many more males have the disease than females. Females can be protected by inheriting at least one normal allele ($X^H$) out of two, whereas males inherit only one allele because they inherit only one X chromosome.
- The disease is passed to sons solely through their mothers even though the mothers may only be *carriers*. Carriers are heterozygous ($X^HX^h$); therefore, they can pass on the recessive hemophilia allele even though they do not suffer from the disease themselves. Statistically, half of the sons of carrier mothers will have the disease and half of the daughters will be carriers.
- A father cannot pass the disease to a son, but his daughters will all be carriers (unless the mother is also a carrier or has the disease, in which case the daughters may also have the disease).

The inheritance pattern of a genetic disorder can be followed through many generations by using a pedigree chart to map out a family's lineage. Figure 19.16 shows a pedigree following the hemophilia trait. Muscular dystrophy and red-green

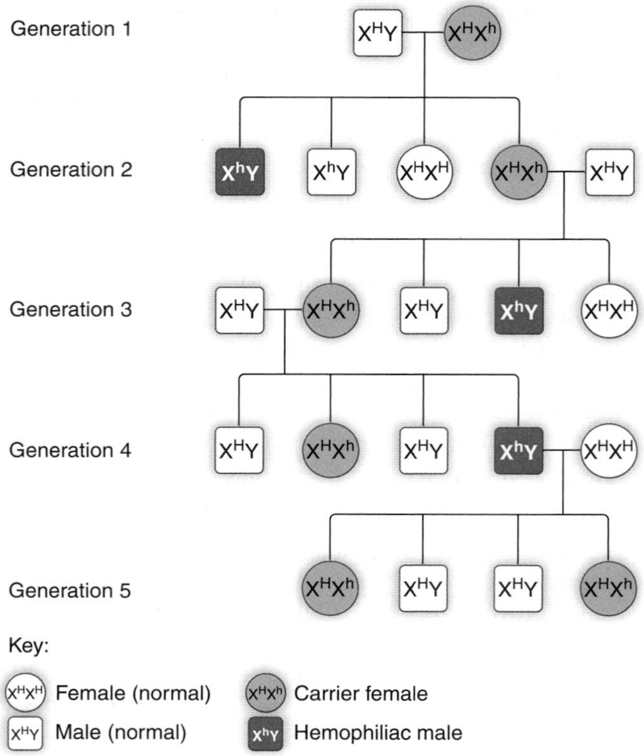


**a) A pedigree chart following the passage of hemophilia for five generations**

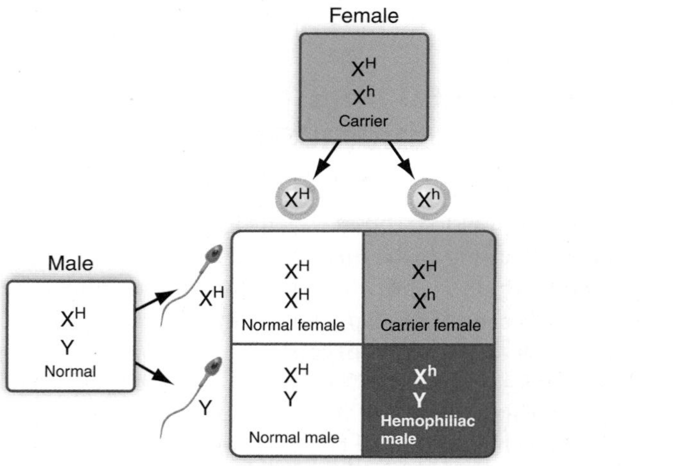


**b) A Punnett square showing the possible outcomes of the mating in generation 1**

**Figure 19.16 A typical inheritance pattern for an X-linked recessive disease.** The example depicted here is hemophilia. **(a)** The normal ($X^H$) and hemophilia ($X^h$) alleles are located on the X chromosome. Note that female carriers (genotype $X^HX^h$) pass the hemophilia allele to half their daughters and the disease to half their sons. Males with the disease pass the hemophilia allele to all of their daughters (if they survive long enough to have children), but never pass the allele to their sons. **(b)** The mating of a normal male and a carrier female in generation 1 can result in a normal female, carrier female, normal male, or hemophiliac male.

color blindness (see Try It Yourself: Estimating the Probability of Inheriting an X-Linked Trait) are also X-linked recessive conditions that follow this inheritance pattern. Nearly all X-linked diseases are caused by a recessive allele rather than a dominant one.

**RECAP**

In humans, the sex chromosome carried by the male sperm determines the gender of the fertilized embryo. Males receive only one X chromosome, and are more susceptible to sex-linked recessive diseases than females are. Sex-linked inheritance refers to patterns of inheritance that depend on genes located on the sex chromosomes. ■

### Sex-influenced traits are affected by actions of sex genes

A few genes that you might suspect are located on the sex chromosomes are actually located on one of the 22 autosomal pairs of chromosomes. A good example is a gene that influences baldness. The normal allele ($b^+$) and the allele for baldness (b) can be present in both men and women. However, the baldness allele is recessive in women. Women must be (bb) and probably have other baldness genes or factors as well before their hair loss is significant. Men become very bald if they are (bb) and develop significant pattern baldness even if they are heterozygous ($bb^+$).

Why the difference between men and women? Testosterone strongly stimulates the expression of the baldness allele, in effect converting it from a recessive to a dominant allele in males. This is an example of a *sex-influenced* phenotype, one not inherited with the sex chromosomes but influenced by the actions of the genes on the sex chromosomes. In fact, a number of genes influence the presence and pattern of hair on the head in addition to this particular baldness gene.

## 19.4 Chromosomes may be altered in number or structure

During mitosis of diploid cells and meiosis of the precursor cells of sperm and eggs, duplicated chromosomes must separate appropriately into two different cells. Just as duplication of DNA is not always perfect, neither is separation of the chromosomes.

Failure of homologous chromosomes or sister chromatids to separate properly is called **nondisjunction.** Sometimes both sister chromatids go to one of the two cells formed during mitosis. Occasionally homologous chromosomes or sister chromatids fail to separate during meiosis (Figure 19.17), resulting in an alteration in chromosome number of sperm or egg cells. Very rarely, a piece of a chromosome may break off and be lost, or it may reattach to another chromosome where it doesn't belong.

For the most part we never see these chromosomal alterations. If mitosis goes awry, the two daughter cells probably just die and their place is taken by other dividing cells. Alterations that arise during meiosis are more serious because they have at least the potential to alter the development of an entire organism. However, it appears that we never see most of these either because so many of the genes on the chromosomes are essential for embryonic development. Any sperm, egg, or developing embryo with errors as great as an extra or missing chromosome is unlikely to survive. Most die early in embryonic development before we are even aware of their presence.

### Down syndrome: Three copies of chromosome 21

A few alterations of autosomal chromosome number do result in live births. The most common alteration of autosomal chromosome number is *Down syndrome.* There are actually three types of Down syndrome, but the overwhelming majority (95% of all cases) are caused by having three copies of chromosome 21 (trisomy 21) (Figure 19.18). Other disorders resulting from altered autosomal chromosomal number are Edwards syndrome (trisomy 18) and Patau syndrome (trisomy 13).

People with Down syndrome are typically short with round faces and other distinctive physical traits; most are friendly, cheerful, and affectionate. They generally are slow to develop mentally and are prone to respiratory complications or heart defects that can lead to death at a young age. However, with improved care many now live well into their adult years.

**try it yourself**

### Estimating the Probability of Inheriting an X-Linked Trait

Recall from Chapter 12 that people with red-green color blindness, the most common form of color blindness, have trouble distinguishing between red and green. The color they perceive is either red or green, depending on whether their eyes are deficient in red cones or green cones. We can designate the normal color vision trait as $X^B$ and the red-green color blind trait as $X^b$.

Suppose that a male has normal color vision but a female carries an allele for red-green color blindness on one of her X chromosomes. What is this man's genotype? ______ What is this woman's genotype? ______

Draw a Punnett square to illustrate the probable genotypes of their offspring.

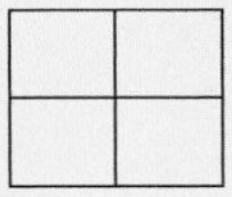

How do the genotypes of the sons compare to the genotypes of the daughters? How do their phenotypes compare? Do you think their mother has any problems with color vision?

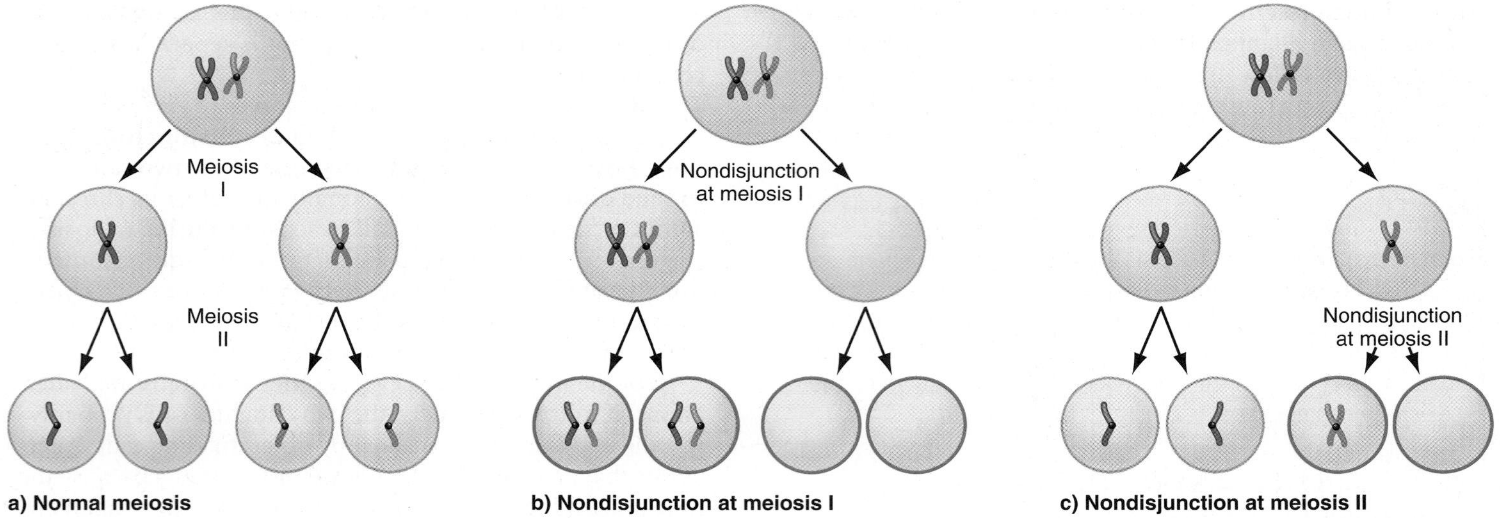


**Figure 19.17 Nondisjunction during meiosis.** **(a)** During normal meiosis, duplicated homologous chromosomes separate during meiosis I, sister chromatids separate during meiosis II. **(b)** When nondisjunction occurs during meiosis I, the duplicated homologous chromosomes fail to separate from each other. **(c)** When nondisjunction occurs during meiosis II, sister chromatids fail to separate from each other. In either case, some gametes (sperm or egg) will have an altered number of chromosomes. Abnormal gametes have red outlines. This figure shows just one of the 23 pairs of human chromosomes.

Down syndrome affects approximately one in every 1,000 live births in the United States. The risk of a woman giving birth to a Down syndrome baby rises markedly with increasing age. The chance is around one in 1,300 for mothers under 30, one in 100 at age 40, and one in 25 for mothers over age 45. Recent evidence suggests that paternal age may also be a factor when both parents are 35 or older.

Some pregnant women elect to undergo fetal testing to detect Down syndrome and other disorders. In amniocentesis, a sample of amniotic fluid containing fetal cells is withdrawn and tested. Another option is chorionic villi sampling, in which a small sample of fetal tissue is suctioned from the placenta for examination. Fetal cells are then examined for the presence of third copies of chromosome 21 (Down syndrome), third copies of chromosomes 18 and 13, and for alterations of sex chromosome number. Chromosomal damage can also sometimes be detected.

**RECAP**

Nondisjunction leads to altered numbers of chromosomes in daughter cells. Down syndrome is usually caused by inheriting three copies of chromosome 21. ■

## Alterations of the number of sex chromosomes

Nondisjunction of the sex chromo-somes can produce a variety of combinations of sex chromosome number, several of which are fairly common in the human population. In general, an individual with at least one Y chromosome will be essentially a male phenotype. An individual lacking a Y chromosome will be a female phenotype, regardless of the number of X chromosomes. The four most common alterations of sex chromosome number are the following:

**XYY—Jacob syndrome** XYY individuals are males who tend to be tall but otherwise fairly normal, except that some show impaired mental function. At one time it was thought that XYY males had a tendency toward violent criminal behavior, but careful study has shown this is not true. Whether their

**Figure 19.18 A person with Down syndrome.** Down syndrome is caused by inheriting an extra copy of chromosome 21. Note that alterations in chromosome number can happen for any of the chromosomes, but most alterations are not seen in the population because they are lethal during fetal development.

rate of minor, nonviolent criminality tends to be higher than normal is still a disputed issue.

**XXY—Klinefelter syndrome** People with Klinefelter syndrome are also tall male phenotype. They are sterile, may show mild mental impairment, and may develop enlarged breasts because of the extra X chromosome (Figure 19.19a).

**XXX—Trisomy-X syndrome** Trisomy-X syndrome individuals are female phenotype. Typically they are nearly normal except for a tendency toward mild mental retardation.

**XO—Turner syndrome** Individuals with only one X chromosome (XO) are phenotypically female. However, they tend to be short with slightly altered body form and small breasts (Figure 19.19b). Most are not mentally retarded and can lead normal lives, though they are sterile and may have shortened life expectancies. Turner syndrome is relatively rare compared to the other three because the XO embryo is more likely to be spontaneously aborted.

Table 19.2 summarizes the most common alterations of chromosomal number and gives their frequencies of occurrence.

**Table 19.2 Some common alterations of chromosome number**

| Chromosome genotype | Sexual phenotype | Common name | Approximate frequency among live births |
|---|---|---|---|
| Trisomy 21 | Male or female | Down syndrome | 1/1,000 |
| Trisomy 18 | Male or female | Edwards syndrome | 1/6,000 |
| Trisomy 13 | Male or female | Patau syndrome | 1/5,000 |
| XYY | Male | Double-Y syndrome | 1/2,000 |
| XXY | Male | Klinefelter syndrome | 1/2,000 |
| XXX | Female | Trisomy-X syndrome | 1/2,000 |
| XO | Female | Turner syndrome | 1/10,000 |

## Deletions and translocations alter chromosome structure

A **deletion** occurs when a piece of chromosome breaks off and is lost. In general we cannot afford to lose genes, and therefore nearly all deletions are lethal to the sperm, egg, or embryo. There are a few rare conditions in which a chromosome deletion results in a live birth. An example is *cri-du-chat* (French, meaning "cat-cry") syndrome, caused by a deletion from chromosome 5. Babies born with this syndrome are often mentally and physically retarded, with a characteristic kittenlike cry due to a small larynx.

**Translocation** occurs when a piece of a chromosome breaks off but reattaches at another site, either on the same chromosome or another chromosome. Conceptually you might think that translocations are not a problem because all of the genes are still present, just in different locations. However, translocations result in subtle changes in gene expression and therefore their ability to function. For instance, translocation appears to increase the risk of certain cancers, including one form of leukemia.

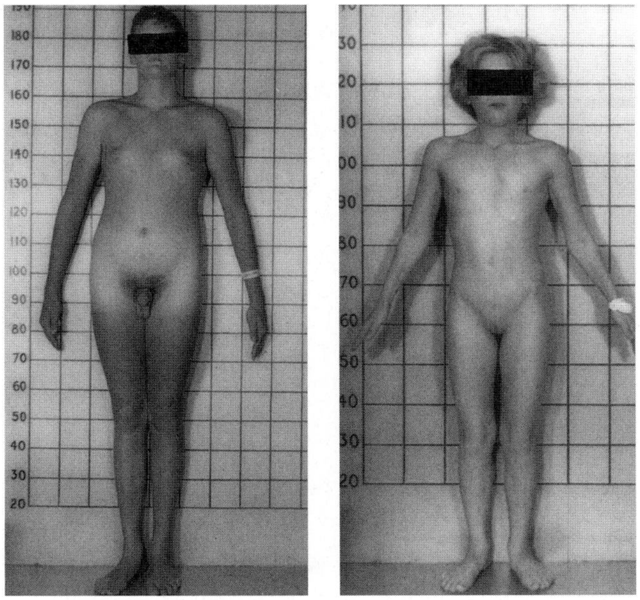

**a) Klinefelter syndrome (XXY).** **b) Turner syndrome (XO).**

**Figure 19.19 Alterations of sex chromosome number.**

**RECAP**

Alterations of sex chromosome number occur when the sex chromosomes fail to separate during meiosis. In general, people with at least one Y chromosome are male phenotype, and people without a Y chromosome are female phenotype. A deletion occurs when part of a chromosome is lost; it rarely results in a live birth. ■

# 19.5 Many inherited genetic disorders involve recessive alleles

People express inherited genetic disorders caused by recessive alleles only if they inherit two of the defective alleles. People who inherit only one defective allele can pass the gene to their children, but they do not get the disease themselves because their good allele is dominant. For this reason, recessive disease-causing alleles are likely to remain in a population more readily than dominant ones.

Current Issue

# The Promises and Perils of Genetic Testing

Jeremy is having trouble in school, so his mother takes him to the doctor. A genetic test reveals that he has fragile X syndrome, an inherited form of mental retardation. His mother's insurance company promptly cancels Jeremy's health coverage on the grounds that since he has had the disorder all his life, this is a preexisting condition. After trying desperately to find an insurance company that will insure both of them, his mother quits her job so that she can become eligible for Medicaid.

Scientists are making exciting progress toward understanding how genes interact to influence human health. The potential benefits of this knowledge are tremendous. So, too, are the potential pitfalls, as evidenced by Jeremy's situation. The possibility of widespread genetic testing raises crucial social, ethical, and legal issues.

## What Is Genetic Testing?

*Genetic testing* refers to the analysis of an individual's genetic material to determine predisposition to a particular health condition or confirm a diagnosis of genetic disease. Already, over 1,200 genetic tests are performed in clinical settings, and more than 200 additional tests are being developed. Most detect mutations associated with rare genetic disorders that involve dominant or recessive traits. Examples include cystic fibrosis and Huntington disease. Other tests look for mutations that involve more complex inheritance patterns. Although certain genes appear to increase the risk of breast, ovarian, or colon cancer, for example, people with those genes do not always develop cancer.

Genetic testing revealed that folk singer Arlo Guthrie would not suffer from Huntington disease as his father Woody Guthrie did.

## Genetic Testing Offers Many Benefits

DNA-based tests provide undeniable benefits. They can confirm a diagnosis before symptoms appear, enabling patients to start treatment early. They can also rule out other health conditions with similar symptoms. An accurate diagnosis ensures that patients are treated for the condition they actually have, which prevents unnecessary surgery and side effects from the wrong medications.

Genetic testing can promote healthy childbirth. Couples can be tested to determine whether they are carriers of recessive disorders, enabling them to make an informed decision about whether to have a child. Prenatal genetic testing can also examine the cells of the fetus to screen for approximately 40 genetic defects.

As mentioned earlier, some tests look for genes that do not necessarily cause a disease but are associated with a higher risk of it. Suppose you learn that you carry a gene that predisposes you to colon cancer. The American Cancer Society recommends that most people have their first colonoscopy at age 50. Given your genes, you might decide to have one at 35 instead. Earlier testing could save your life.

*Tests are now available for many potential genetic disorders.*

## Social and Ethical Issues

Genetic testing can provide a wealth of information, but many questions arise about the best ways to use it.

## the facts...

- DNA-based tests screen for genetic disorders or predict increased risk of disease.
- Over 1,200 genetic tests are already available, and more than 200 additional tests are in development.
- Genetic testing offers many benefits: confirming a diagnosis, promoting healthy childbirth, and helping people prevent future health problems.
- It also raises difficult questions of privacy, psychological harm, and the potential for genetic discrimination.

**Privacy** Who owns your genetic data—you? your physician? the company that performed the test? the insurance company that paid for it? Consider your existing medical records, which are probably available to your insurance company, all physicians you have ever consulted, and all hospitals you have ever used, including clinical and clerical personnel. Should your genetic data become part of this record?

**Eligibility for health insurance** Seven-year-old Bobby is healthy, but genetic testing shows that he carries a gene that predisposes him to future heart problems. Bobby starts taking medicine to lower his risk, but his parents' insurance company refuses to insure him. As in Jeremy's case, the company labels this a preexisting condition.

Many health insurance policies exclude preexisting conditions. If your test reveals a gene that might increase your risk of cancer or heart disease later in life, it is conceivable that an insurer might deny you coverage entirely or refuse to cover any expenses related to your test finding. This could exclude any cardiovascular or cancer-related test—a significant financial burden that might discourage you from visiting a doctor as often as you should. If you did become ill, even many years after your genetic test, could insurers refuse to pay for treatments?

Before we blame the insurers, consider that under the U.S. system they are private companies that must make a profit to survive. The cost of health care is soaring, and many insurers attempt to control their costs by restricting coverage. If the insurance companies go bankrupt, no one will have health insurance.

**Potential for employment discrimination** Managers at the Burlington Northern Santa Fe Railroad became concerned about employees' high rate of insurance claims for carpal tunnel syndrome. Managers instructed company-paid physicians to secretly test employees for a rare genetic condition that can cause the syndrome. Employees were not informed that their DNA was being tested, and managers threatened to fire one staff member who refused the test.

In another case a social worker mentioned at work that her mother died of Huntington disease. One week later she was fired, despite a recent outstanding performance review.

These true stories demonstrate the potential for employment discrimination. When you apply for a job or promotion, does the company have the right to take your genetic information into account? An employer might not want to invest time and money in training someone who carries the gene for Huntington disease, since this person is likely to become ill before age 40. An employee with sickle-cell anemia or even sickle-cell trait might be viewed as a poor risk because of the potential for medical problems. Employees who take sick leave and require many medical services make a company less productive and raise its health insurance premiums.

**Potential for ethnic or racial discrimination** Sickle-cell anemia is most common in people of African heritage. Tay-Sachs disease occurs most frequently in Ashkenazi Jews. People of Northern European descent are most likely to develop hemochromatosis, a genetic disorder that causes the body to absorb excess iron. Does this mean we should test all African Americans for sickle-cell anemia, all Jews for Tay-Sachs, or all Northern Europeans for hemochromatosis? Should we require members of high-risk groups to be tested if they are getting married or considering having children? Where do we draw the line between individual privacy and public health?

**Psychological and emotional impact** So far, we have explored how other people might react to the results of genetic testing. What about the person who undergoes the test? Discovering a genetic predisposition for colon cancer might motivate you to take preventive steps, but suppose you discover a gene that codes for an unpreventable condition such as Alzheimer's disease. Could this knowledge harm you psychologically and emotionally? Many researchers counsel against widespread genetic testing because that knowledge could do more harm than good if a test reveals a disorder over which we have no control. Nonetheless, genetic testing is becoming ever more accessible. Consider the home testing kit sold by DNADirect.com; the company analyzes cells scraped from the inside of a person's cheek and e-mails a personalized genetic risk assessment.

**Genetic testing and the law** In 2008 the Genetic Information Nondiscrimination Act (GINA) took effect. This law prevents insurers from setting higher insurance premiums or denying coverage to healthy people based on the results of genetic tests. GINA also makes it illegal for employers to use genetic information in making decisions about hiring or firing a person. However, GINA does not address other privacy issues, such as a genetic testing company selling genetic information to outside parties, such as other companies and academic researchers. Also, there is always the potential for noncompliance with the law by employers and insurance providers, which may make some people reluctant to undergo genetic testing.

The science of genetic testing is progressing far more rapidly than our solutions for the social and ethical challenges that it raises. Expect continued debate on these issues in the future.

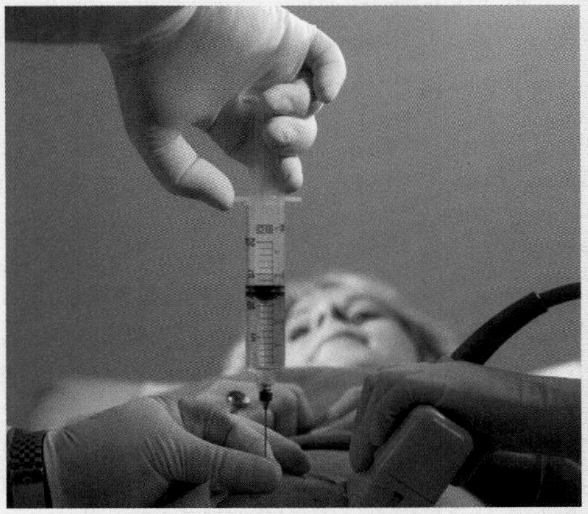

*Fetal cells harvested during amniocentesis can now be tested for over 40 inherited genetic disorders.*

## Questions to consider

**1** *If you carried a gene for an unpreventable condition such as Alzheimer's disease, would you want to know? Why or why not?*

**2** *Should employers have the right to test employees for potential genetic disorders and refuse future health care coverage for that disorder, even if the employee does not yet have the disease?*

In some cases more than one gene pair may contribute to a disease. Hypertension and heart disease are examples of diseases that apparently have a heritable component but aren't associated with any single gene pair.

One of the better known recessive genetic disorders is cystic fibrosis, discussed in the Health Watch box on page 447. In this section we discuss two other genetic disorders caused by recessive alleles (phenylketonuria and Tay-Sachs disease), as well as one (Huntington disease) that is caused by a dominant allele.

### Phenylketonuria is caused by a missing enzyme

Phenylketonuria (PKU) is a human inherited disease in which homozygous recessive individuals are unable to make an enzyme that is needed for the normal metabolism of phenylalanine, an amino acid. If phenylalanine accumulates, some of it is used in other metabolic pathways, including one in which excess phenylalanine is converted to phenylpyruvic acid instead. Phenylpyruvic acid is toxic at high concentrations and can lead to mental retardation, slow growth rate, and early death.

Phenylketonuria occurs in about one in 12,000 births in Caucasians, so it is considerably less prevalent than cystic fibrosis. The disease is caused by mutation of the gene on chromosome 1 that is responsible for producing the enzyme phenylalanine hydroxylase.

Fortunately, people homozygous for the recessive allele are not affected before birth because the mother's enzymes metabolize phenylalanine for the fetus. After birth, the blood level of phenylalanine is very much dependent upon the amount of phenylalanine in the diet. Given the seriousness of mental retardation, all states now require that newborns be tested for PKU by a simple blood test called the Guthrie test that detects excess phenylalanine in the blood.

Treatment of PKU requires limiting the dietary intake of phenylalanine. This is not easy because most proteins contain phenylalanine, but it can be done for about $5,000 per year by substituting a carefully controlled mixture of amino acids for most protein. In addition, individuals with phenylketonuria cannot use the artificial sweetener NutraSweet because it contains aspartame, a chemical consisting of just two amino acids, phenylalanine and aspartic acid, linked together. When aspartame is broken down, people with PKU may experience a dangerous increase in phenylalanine.

### Tay-Sachs disease leads to brain dysfunction

Tay-Sachs disease is another enzyme deficiency disease, this one caused by a recessive gene located on chromosome 15. Individuals homozygous for the recessive allele are unable to make an enzyme that is responsible for the metabolism of a particular type of lipid, called a sphingolipid, found primarily in the lysosomes of brain cells. Without this enzyme, the sphingolipid accumulates in brain cells, causing cerebral degeneration. Infants seem unaffected at birth, but by 4–8 months of age motor function and brain function begin to decline. The child gradually develops seizures, becomes blind and paralyzed, and usually dies by age 3 or 4. There is no known cure or treatment.

Tay-Sachs disease is rare in the general population. However, it is fairly common among Ashkenazi Jews of Central European descent, with about 1 in 3,500 children having the disease. Carriers of the disease remain unaffected because they have sufficient enzyme activity for normal function. Tests are available to determine whether either member of a couple is a carrier of the disease.

### Huntington disease is caused by a dominant-lethal allele

Huntington disease is marked by progressive nerve degeneration leading to physical and mental disability and death. Afflicted individuals begin to show symptoms only in their 30s, and most die in their 40s or 50s.

Huntington disease follows the simple rules of inheritance of a single pair of alleles, one or both of which may be the dominant (HD) or recessive (hd) form. However, in this case it is the *dominant* allele (HD) that causes Huntington disease. Anyone with even one HD allele will ultimately develop the disorder. The disease is fatal, and there is no known cure at the moment. For this reason HD is called a **dominant-lethal** allele.

Dominant-lethal alleles are by their nature uncommon because they tend to eliminate themselves from the population, especially if they cause disease before the affected individual's reproductive years. Huntington disease is unusual in this regard. The disease remains in the human population because in the past, individuals who carried the HD allele had no way of knowing they would develop Huntington disease, and so they would pass the allele on to half their children before they knew for sure. Today there is a test for the HD allele. Here is an example where genetic testing and counseling could have a dramatic effect on the prevalence of a disease in the future. (See the Current Issue box in this chapter for a discussion of the biological, social, and ethical issues raised by genetic testing.)

Genetic testing for Huntington disease and other inherited disorders is one of the great benefits of the *Human Genome Project.* Engaging scientists from around the world, this massive endeavor involved locating each of the approximately 22,000 genes in the human genome and identifying their functions. Researchers have already successfully identified the genes responsible for several disorders, including forms of breast cancer, skin cancer, and osteoporosis. This information holds promise for developing ways to prevent new cases of genetic diseases and treating existing cases with new technologies. One possibility might be to correct genetic defects with *gene therapy.* We discuss gene therapy in more detail in Chapter 20.

**RECAP**

Recessive alleles such as those for phenylketonuria and Tay-Sachs disease cause disease only if the individual is homozygous recessive. Dominant disease-causing alleles are unusual because they tend to be eliminated from the population. Huntington disease is a rare example of a dominant-lethal disease. ■

## 19.6 Genes code for proteins, not for specific behaviors

Genes represent the set of instructions for a human being. The actions of genes can be very specific, such as determining hair patterns or earlobe shape. In terms of behavior, the logical conclusion might be that specific genes determine specific behaviors. Indeed, we read in the popular press of a heritable "schizophrenia gene." We hear of studies that show certain groups of criminals may share a common genetic defect; that some people may have a gene that predisposes them to depression; that there may even be a "happiness gene." Is any of this true?

The bottom line is that genes code for specific proteins. Specific genes code for proteins that give you curly hair or freckles. Other genes (and their protein products) may strongly *influence* whole patterns of behavior or moods, such as a tendency toward anxiety or aggression. However, genes do not necessarily cause *specific* behaviors. They do not lead to specific thoughts, and there is no one gene that causes you to turn to the left and another one that causes you to turn to the right. Nor are there any genes that cause people to commit specific crimes, as far as we know.

The key to understanding how genes influence behaviors lies in understanding the many roles of proteins. Proteins may act as hormones, neurotransmitters, enzymes, or intracellular messengers. They make up many of the structural components of cells, and they control cell functions. Some proteins influence a broad range of other genes and proteins; others have very specific effects within only certain target cells. Together, groups of genes and their protein products apparently do influence broad patterns of behavior, such as feeding, mating, or learning. They may also influence moods. Nevertheless, there is no evidence that specific genes or their protein products cause depression, lead to complete happiness, or produce specific physical behaviors.

**RECAP**

Genes influence patterns of behavior. They do not cause specific behaviors. ■

# Chapter Summary

### Your genotype is the genetic basis of your phenotype *p. 442*

- The DNA we inherit from both parents represents the complete set of instructions for creating a human being.
- The two copies of every gene (one from each parent) can differ very slightly because of mutations. Different copies of a gene are called alleles.
- Our genotype is the complete set of alleles that we inherit; our phenotype refers to the physical and functional expression of those alleles.

### Genetic inheritance follows certain patterns *p. 443*

- A Punnett square can be used to show patterns of inheritance for one or two pairs of alleles.
- A common pattern of phenotypic inheritance is one in which one allele exerts complete dominance over the other.
- Other phenotypic inheritance patterns include incomplete dominance, where heterozygotes exhibit an intermediate phenotype; codominance, where heterozygotes express both phenotypes equally; and polygenic inheritance, where multiple genes influence a single trait.
- More than two alleles for any given gene may exist in the human gene pool, as seen with the alleles for blood type. However, any one individual can inherit only two of them, one from each parent.
- Independent assortment of alleles on different chromosomes, crossing-over between homologous chromosomes, and random fertilization of eggs by sperm all contribute to the genetic diversity of the human population.
- Our phenotype is determined both by our genotype and by our environment.
- Alleles located on the same chromosome that may be inherited together are called linked alleles.

### Sex-linked inheritance: X and Y chromosomes carry different genes *p. 453*

- Maleness is determined early during development by genes on the Y (male) sex chromosome. In the absence of this chromosome, the individual becomes a female.
- Sex-linked inheritance refers to inheritance of genes located on the sex chromosomes. Most of these genes have nothing to do with sex determination.
- Diseases associated with sex-linked inheritance include hemophilia, color blindness, and muscular dystrophy.

### Chromosomes may be altered in number or structure *p. 455*

- Nondisjunction refers to the failure of homologous chromosomes or sister chromatids to separate properly during mitosis or meiosis; this causes altered chromosome number in the daughter cells

- Down syndrome is a condition usually caused by the inheritance of three copies of chromosome 21. The primary risk factors are the age of the parents, especially the mother.
- Deletion of even part of a chromosome is usually fatal to a sperm, egg, or embryo. Translocation of a chromosome segment may alter a gene's ability to function properly.

### Many inherited genetic disorders involve recessive alleles *p. 457*

- Most autosomal heritable genetic diseases are caused by recessive alleles.
- Phenylketonuria, Tay-Sachs disease, and cystic fibrosis are diseases caused by recessive alleles.
- Huntington disease is caused by a dominant-lethal allele. It has persisted in the human population because people who inherit it do not show symptoms until after reaching reproductive age.

### Genes code for proteins, not for specific behaviors *p. 461*

- Genes influence only general patterns of behavior or mood. They do not determine specific behaviors.

## Terms You Should Know

allele, *442*
codominance, *448*
deletion, *457*
dominant, *445*
genotype, *443*
heterozygous, *443*
homozygous, *443*
incomplete dominance, *448*
inheritance, *442*
karyotype, *453*
mutation, *443*
nondisjunction, *455*
phenotype, *443*
polygenic inheritance, *451*
Punnett square, *443*
recessive, *445*
sex-linked inheritance, *454*
sickle-cell anemia, *449*
translocation, *457*

## Concept Review

1. Where do we get the two copies we have of every gene?
2. What is the difference between a gene and an allele?
3. Distinguish between genotype and phenotype.
4. Describe the contributions of Mendel to the field of genetics.
5. Explain how alterations of chromosome number and structure can occur.
6. Distinguish between the concepts of dominance, incomplete dominance, and codominance.
7. Describe how genetic variability is accomplished via sexual reproduction.
8. Describe what is meant by sex-linked inheritance.
9. Explain why lethal diseases caused by dominant alleles are so rare.
10. Explain how genes affect mood or behavior.

## Test Yourself

### Matching Exercise

_____ 1. Sickle-cell anemia is a disease caused by this pattern of genetic inheritance
_____ 2. Characteristics such as body height and eye color result from this pattern of genetic inheritance
_____ 3. Familial hypercholesterolemia is caused by this pattern of genetic inheritance
_____ 4. Composite display of all chromosomes of an organism.
_____ 5. A condition caused by having three copies of chromosome 21
_____ 6. An X-linked disease

a. polygenic inheritance
b. incomplete dominance
c. codominance
d. hemophilia
e. karyotype
f. Down syndrome

### Fill in the Blank

7. A(n) _____________ is a DNA sequence coding for one or more proteins.
8. A(n) _____________ occurs when a piece of a chromosome breaks off and reattaches at another site.
9. A(n) _____________ square is used to represent patterns of inheritance of alleles.

## Apply What You Know

1. What fraction of the offspring of two wavy-haired Caucasians would have wavy hair? Explain using a Punnett square. Hint: The allele for curly hair exhibits incomplete dominance over the allele for straight hair.
2. Why is it that the range of resting blood pressures of humans is best represented by a bell-shaped curve covering a continuous range rather than by two populations, one with high blood pressure and one with normal blood pressure?
3. How is it that each parent is able to contribute only a single allele of each gene to his/her offspring, rather than both alleles?
4. Geneticists often study patterns of gene transfer in a variety of model organisms, including plants, fruit flies, and even worms. If they're really interested in patterns of inheritance in humans, why don't they use humans or at least larger animals more similar to humans, like pigs or even primates?
5. Can a father who is blood type A and a mother who is blood type B have a child who is blood type O?
6. Hemophilia is a sex-linked trait that mothers pass on to male offspring. Is it possible for females to have hemophilia too? How would such a thing happen?
7. Nondisjunction during meiosis can lead to the formation of gametes (sperm or eggs) with extra copies of one or more chromosomes. Normally, fertilizations involving extra copies of chromosomes simply do not result in a live birth because too many developmental events are altered in some way. The most common extra-chromosomal condition that *does* lead to live births is Down syndrome (trisomy 21). Why do you suppose that trisomy 21 is more common than other trisomies?

*Answers can be found on the Human Biology Place.*

10. If the alleles at a particular gene locus are different, the person is ____________________ for that allele.
11. The physical and functional expression of the alleles you inherit is your ____________________.
12. The complete set of alleles you inherit is your ____________________.

### True or False?

13. An individual with an X and Y chromosome will be female.
14. In polygenic inheritance, phenotypic traits depend on the interactions of many genes.
15. In incomplete dominance, the heterozygous genotype results in a phenotype that is identical to the mother's phenotype.

## References and Additional Reading

Jessee, Jennifer. Y? *Discover*, November 1997, pp. 88–93. (A short and entertaining account of the evolution and function of the Y chromosome.)

Russell, Peter J. i*Genetics*. San Francisco: Benjamin Cummings, 3rd ed. 2010. (A standard textbook of genetics: for reference or advanced study only.)

Sapolsky, Robert. A Gene for Nothing. *Discover*, October 1997, pp. 40–46. (A general-interest article about what genes do and don't do.)

Skloot, Rebecca. Putting the Gene Back in Genealogy. *Popular Science*, January 2004. (An account of how the ability to test your DNA may offer some clues to your ancestry.)

## Internet References

Find links to these Web sites at the Human Biology Place.

**National Down Syndrome Society**
**www1.ndss.org**
Advocacy group for people with Down syndrome and their families.

**Human Genome Project Information**
**www.ornl.gov/sci/techresources/Human_Genome/home.shtml**
Information about genetics in general and the Genome Project in particular; a Genome Primer discusses basic concepts, health applications, and social and legal issues.

**National Center for Biotechnology Information**
**www.ncbi.nlm.nih.gov**
This national agency conducts research, builds public databases, and distributes information relating to genes and human health.

**Genomic Resource Centre, World Health Organization: News and Events**
**www.who.int/genomics/news/en**
An international perspective on recent developments in genetics, genetic diseases, and related topics.

**1** **True or False?** Human DNA can be inserted into bacteria.

**2** **True or False?** You have already eaten genetically modified foods.

**3** **True or False?** It is much harder to produce transgenic animals than transgenic plants.

**4** DNA fingerprinting is an important tool for: **a.** identifying a particular individual. **b.** determining a person's age. **c.** determining a person's race.

**5** **True or False?** Most human genetic disorders can now be cured by gene therapy.

These genetically modified thale cress plants can act as natural Geiger counters, changing colors when exposed to radioactive concentration.

**Knowledge for the sake of knowledge** alone has never been enough for humans—we have always felt the need to put our knowledge to good use. The technical application of biological knowledge for human purposes is called **biotechnology.**

The recent explosion of knowledge regarding DNA and the human genome has spawned a new field of biotechnology called **recombinant DNA technology.** As the phrase implies, we now know how to take DNA apart, analyze its structure, and recombine it in new ways, producing molecules of DNA that did not exist previously in nature. We also know how to cut and splice genes into bacteria, plants, and animals, causing them to make proteins they never made before. We are even beginning to understand how to insert, alter, or replace genes in humans to correct certain genetic diseases and treat cancer. Manipulation of the genetic makeup of cells or whole organisms, including humans, is known as **genetic engineering.** Genetic engineering is still in its infancy, but it holds great promise for the future.

As with all new technologies, biotechnology comes with new risks and new responsibilities. If we tinker with the structure of DNA, could we accidentally produce harmful organisms? How will we even know what the potential risks are until something happens? What kinds of oversight and regulation are needed for these new technologies? It would be tempting to prohibit or at least limit some of these new techniques because of their possible risks, but their potential benefits are just too great to ignore.

In this chapter we discuss technical and practical aspects of the new technologies so that we may make better judgments regarding their application. First, we look at how researchers determine the sequence of a piece of DNA. Then we look at how DNA can be combined in new ways and how to make more of it. We discuss how genes are located and identified and how they are being used to alter living organisms. Finally, we discuss the promises and pitfalls of genetic engineering.

## 20.1 DNA sequencing reveals structure of DNA

Biologists have known for some time how to purify the DNA from a cell. But how do they discover the precise sequence of the base pairs that make up individual strands of DNA?

First, they place millions of identical copies of a short single-stranded piece of DNA to be sequenced into a test tube. Then they add short single-stranded pieces of DNA called **primers** that bind to one end of the strands. The primer serves as the beginning point for synthesis of a new strand of DNA complementary to the first. They also add a mixture of the four nucleotides (T, A, G, and C) that normally constitute DNA, plus a mixture of four altered nucleotides (designated T*, A*, G*, and C*) that have been modified in two ways: (1) all four have been labeled with different fluorescent markers that can be identified easily, and (2) they have been modified so that as soon as one of them is added to the growing DNA chain, further chain synthesis stops. Finally, biologists add an enzyme called **DNA polymerase** that facilitates the addition of the nucleotides one by one to the growing strand. Synthesis of DNA begins.

During synthesis, either a normal or a modified nucleotide appropriate for that point in the chain is added, one by one. But because synthesis always stops as soon as a modified (labeled) nucleotide is added, the final result is a mixture of pieces of DNA of varying lengths, each ending with a single labeled nucleotide (Figure 20.1, step 1).

Next, the pieces are placed on a column (or a flat slab) of gel and subjected to a process called **gel electrophoresis.** Gel electrophoresis creates an electrical field that causes the DNA pieces to migrate through the gel. Smaller pieces move more quickly through the gel than larger pieces. A laser connected to a computer detects the four different fluorescent labels as they come off the gel (Figure 20.1, step 2). The result is a graphic display of the nucleotides in the pieces, arranged in order by the size of the pieces

### Answers to Intro Questions

1 **True.** Human genes are routinely inserted into bacteria, turning the bacteria into tiny factories that can make at least some human proteins. Insulin is an example.

2 **Probably true.** Over half of the prepared foods in U.S. supermarkets are thought to contain traces of genetically modified plant products. Are genetically modified foods safe? We examine that question later in this chapter.

3 **True.** The techniques are more difficult, only a few eggs are available at a time, and large-animal gestation and maturation times are long. Nevertheless, genes that encode for certain human proteins have been inserted into goats, sheep, and cows.

4 **a.** DNA fingerprinting is currently used to establish paternity in paternity suits and identify suspected criminals in criminal cases. It cannot identify age or race.

5 **False.** A few diseases may be treatable by gene therapy in the near future, but the technique is still largely experimental.

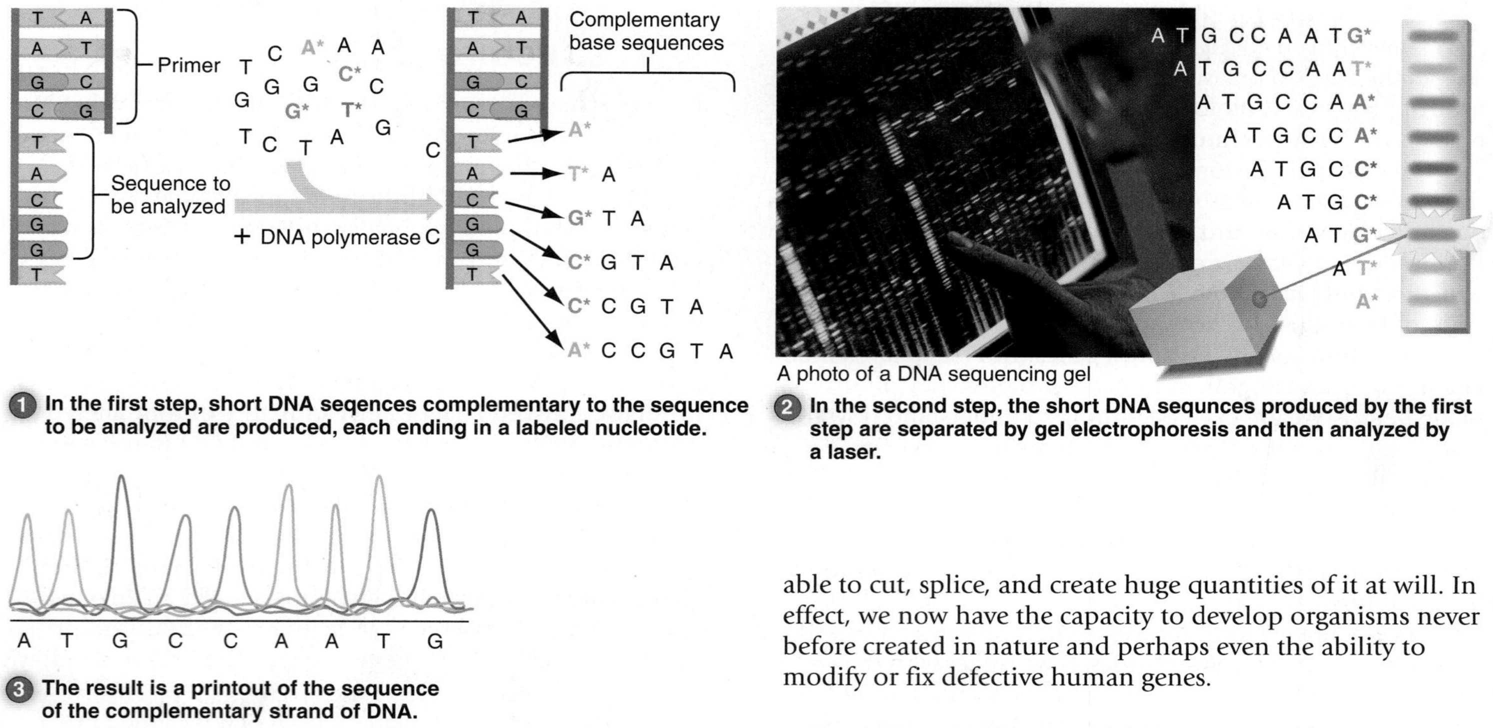


**Figure 20.1 DNA sequencing.**

(Figure 20.1, step 3). This represents the sequence of a single strand of DNA complementary to the original fragment of DNA. The sequence of the original unknown fragment of DNA can then be easily calculated on the basis of the known complementary base pairing in DNA.

**RECAP**

DNA sequencing can determine the nucleotide sequence of short pieces of DNA. Gel electrophoresis separates DNA segments by length. ■

## 20.2 DNA can be modified in the laboratory

For billions of years nature has been recombining DNA every time an organism reproduces. For thousands of years humans have been domesticating and selectively breeding plants and animals to induce nature to recombine DNA in ways useful to us. In just the last few decades we have learned enough about DNA to be able to cut, splice, and create huge quantities of it at will. In effect, we now have the capacity to develop organisms never before created in nature and perhaps even the ability to modify or fix defective human genes.

### Recombinant DNA technology: Cutting, splicing, and copying DNA

Cutting, splicing, and copying (cloning) DNA and the genes it contains requires specialized tools and components, including restriction enzymes, DNA ligases, plasmids, and bacteria.

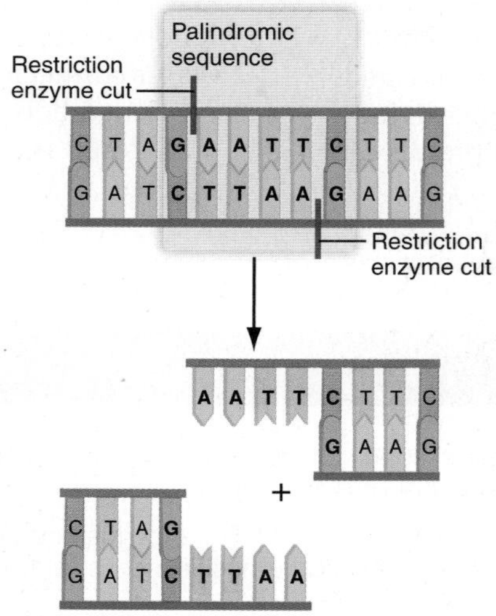


**Figure 20.2 Cutting DNA with restriction enzymes.** Restriction enzymes are used to cut DNA only at particular palindromic sequences, leaving single-stranded cut ends that are complementary to each other.

**Restriction enzymes** are enzymes that break the bonds between specific base pairs in a DNA strand. In nature they protect bacteria from viral invasion by cutting up—restricting—the DNA of the invading virus, but they will cut DNA from any source. They are like specialized scissors that cut a line of text only after a specific word. There are many different restriction enzymes in nature, but the most useful for recombinant DNA technology are those that make their cut in a **palindromic** DNA nucleotide sequence. A palindromic sequence is one that reads the same from left to right on one DNA strand as it does from right to left on the other, such as GAATTC (Figure 20.2). A cut in a palindromic sequence leaves two short single-stranded ends that are complementary to each other and to any other DNA that is cut with the same enzyme.

**DNA ligases** are enzymes that bind fragments of DNA back together after the restriction enzymes have cut them.

**Plasmids** are small, circular, self-replicating DNA molecules found in

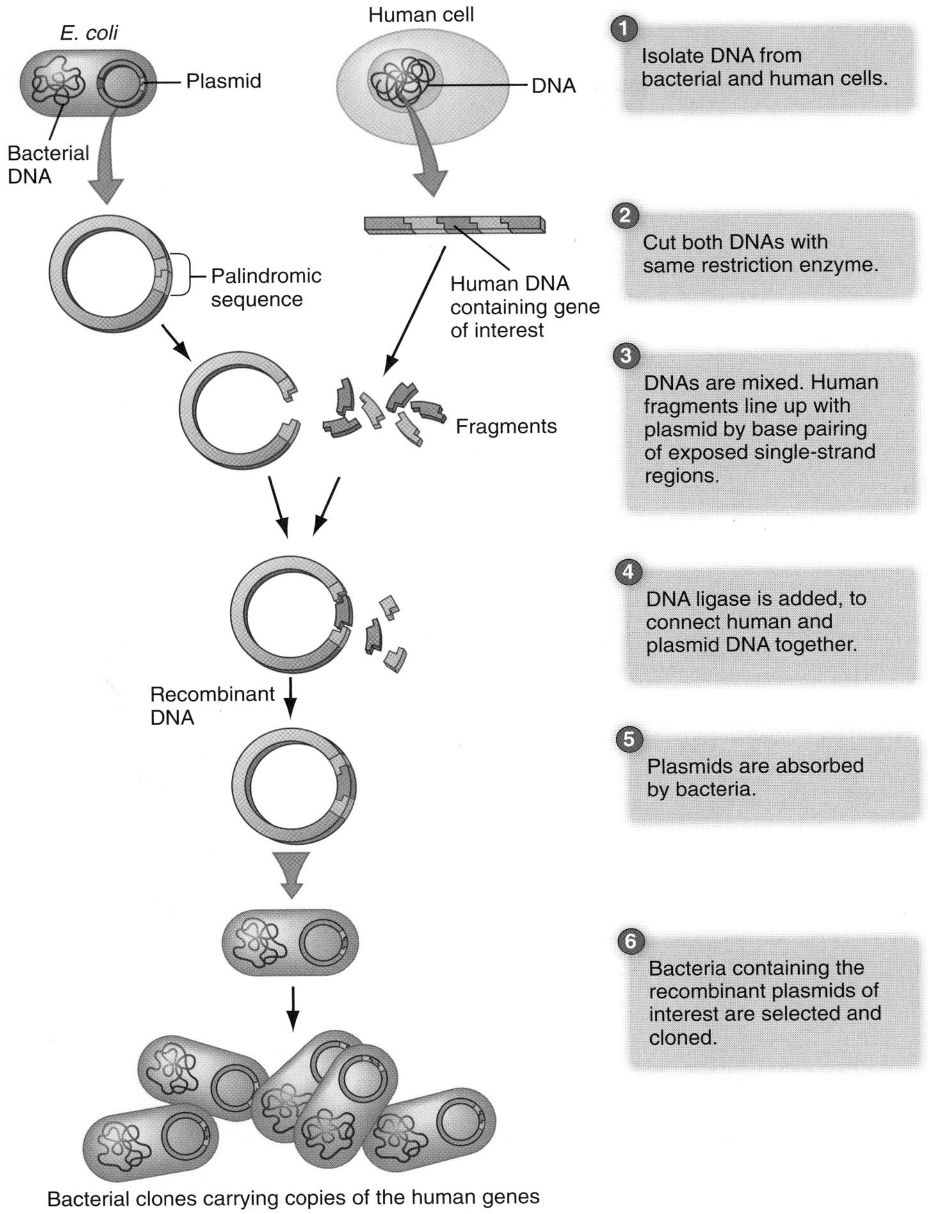


**Figure 20.3 Recombinant DNA technique for producing clones of a gene or the protein product of a gene.**

bacteria. They are not part of the normal bacterial chromosome, but they are important to the bacterium because they contain certain genes needed for bacterial replication. Plasmids are useful because they can be made to incorporate a foreign piece of DNA. Once the plasmid is reinserted into a bacterium, it is copied every time the bacterium reproduces. By reproducing the bacteria in the laboratory, then, scientists can manufacture unlimited copies of a recombinant DNA plasmid.

Figure 20.3 illustrates the technique for producing recombinant DNA using human DNA:

1. **Isolate DNA plasmids and the human DNA of interest.** The DNA of interest is first isolated and purified from a sample of tissue. DNA plasmids are also prepared from bacteria.
2. **Cut both DNAs with the same restriction enzyme.** The restriction enzyme cuts the DNA of interest and the plasmid DNA only at specific palindromic nucleotide sequences, leaving single-stranded ends that will match up with each other.
3. **Mix the human DNA fragments with the cut plasmids.** The DNA fragments begin to join together with the plasmids by complementary base pairing of the single-stranded cut ends of the fragments.
4. **Add DNA ligase to complete the connections.** DNA ligase joins the plasmid and human DNA strands together. The circular bacterial plasmid now contains human DNA.
5. **Introduce the new plasmid into bacteria.** Relatively harmless bacteria such as *E. coli* generally are used for this purpose.
6. **Select the bacteria containing the human DNA of interest and allow them to reproduce.** Many different plasmids will have been formed by the technique described above, each containing a different fragment of human DNA. Therefore the bacteria that are carrying the human fragments of interest must first be identified and isolated before cloning the bacteria (and their human genes) in large numbers. Generally this is done by adding labeled antibodies against the protein expressed by the DNA to small colonies of bacteria. If the gene (and its protein product) are present in the bacterial colony, the antibody will bind to the protein and the bacterial colony of interest can be identified.

This, in essence, is the technique for cloning genes. Taking it one step further, if you can get the bacteria to express (activate) the gene located in the DNA fragment, the bacteria may churn out virtually limitless quantities of a particular protein.

If the goal is to make millions of copies of a specific small fragment of DNA very rapidly, a different technique is the **polymerase chain reaction (PCR).** The polymerase chain reaction is particularly useful for amplifying a small sample of DNA (such as might be found at a crime scene) so it can be identified accurately. However, it is not a useful technique for cloning functional genes and the proteins they produce, because copies of DNA produced by PCR lack the regulatory genes and proteins required to activate genes.

# Directions in Science

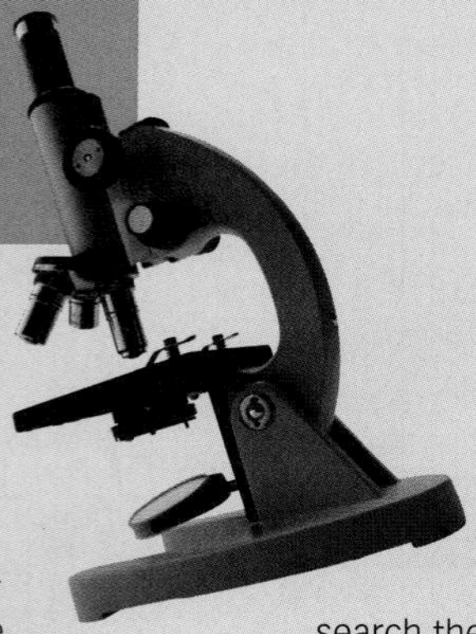

## DNA Fingerprinting

Dermal fingerprints (prints of the tips of a person's fingers) have been used since the 1800s to identify specific individuals. An exciting new development in science is **DNA fingerprinting,** a sophisticated technique for identifying human beings, whether living or dead, from only a few strands of their DNA. DNA fingerprinting is the modern sequel to dermal fingerprinting.

The usefulness of DNA fingerprinting as a form of identification relies on the following facts:

- The genome of every person consists of the same genes located at the same places on the same chromosomes. The actual nucleic acid sequences of functional genes vary only slightly between individuals.
- Located between the useful genes in DNA are long repeating sequences of nucleic acids that do not code for anything at all. Over millions of years of evolution, the lengths of these repeating sequences of "junk" DNA have become quite variable—much more variable than the sequences of the functional genes themselves.
- Enzymes called restriction enzymes can be used to slice DNA at particular nucleic acid sequences.
- Because the lengths of the repeating junk sequences of DNA vary between individuals, the sizes of the DNA pieces that result from treatment with restriction enzymes are different for each individual.

In practice, here's how the technique works. A small sample of DNA is sliced into smaller pieces using restriction enzymes. The pieces of DNA are labeled so that they can be visualized after separation. Next they are placed on a sheet of porous paper and subjected to electrophoresis, which separates them according to size. The pattern of the location of DNA fragments on the paper after electrophoresis is called an *electropherogram*, or DNA fingerprint. It is essentially unique for each person except for identical twins.

Despite its widespread use today and its alleged accuracy, DNA fingerprinting continues to be controversial. Legal hearings about DNA evidence can take weeks, cost taxpayers millions of dollars, and still not settle the issues of reliability and uniqueness. In the 1994 trial of ex-football player O.J. Simpson for the murder of his wife and her friend, the defense document challenging the DNA data was over 100 pages long. Simpson was acquitted in a criminal trial but was later convicted in a civil trial.

Several countries are building databases of DNA samples from known criminals, with the goal of solving crimes more quickly. The United Kingdom has a database of almost 3 million profiles, and the probability of identifying a suspect by checking against this database is estimated to be greater than 40%. In one case, a DNA sample from a man arrested for a recent traffic violation linked him to a murder committed in 1968; he was subsequently convicted.

A new twist to DNA database searches is raising real questions of privacy. California intends to search their criminal database for "partial matches" with a DNA sample from a crime scene. If a known criminal is a partial match, it would mean that he or she did not commit the crime, but that one of his or her relatives probably did. That would make all of the close relatives possible suspects, even if there is no other reason for linking them to the crime. Imagine, for example, that your brother once committed a crime and is already in the DNA database, and now your cousin's DNA is found at a crime scene and is linked as a partial match to your brother. You and your cousin could both become suspects. Privacy advocates are concerned by this new development, calling it "genetic surveillance" of people for crimes they did not commit. It will be interesting to follow the politics of this issue.

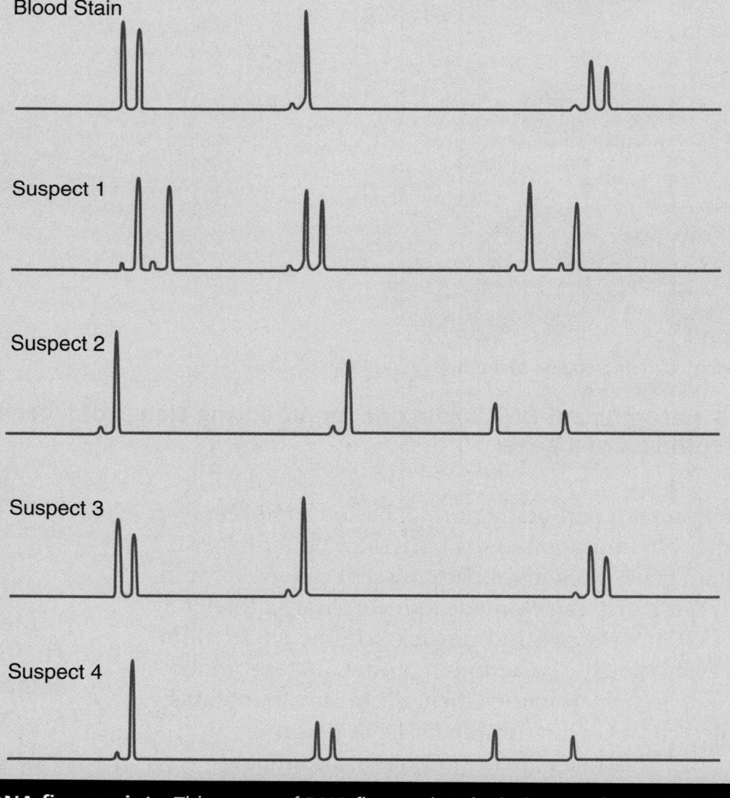


**DNA fingerprints**. This group of DNA fingerprints includes one from a blood sample found at a crime scene and four from different people. Can you identify the match?

Conceptually, PCR is fairly straightforward (Figure 20.4). First the two strands of the DNA sample are unwound by gentle heating. Then they are mixed with (1) primers that are complementary to one end of each strand, (2) nucleotides, necessary to create the new complementary strands of DNA, and (3) DNA polymerase, the enzyme that catalyzes the attachment of nucleotides to the growing complementary DNA strand. When the mixture is cooled slightly, the primers bind to the ends of the two single strands. The primers represent the starting point for replication of each strand. The nucleotides then attach to the growing complementary chain in sequence, assisted by DNA polymerase. Once both strands of DNA are completely replicated, the heating and cooling sequence is repeated again. Each heating and cooling cycle doubles the amount of the desired DNA sample. Repeat the reaction just 20 times and you have over a million identical copies of the original DNA.

**RECAP**

Recombinant DNA technology is used to cut and splice DNA into new combinations and make multiple copies of DNA fragments. Copies of DNA fragments can be produced by bacteria or the polymerase chain reaction (PCR) technique. ■

## 20.3 Genetic engineering creates transgenic organisms

The ability to produce **transgenic** organisms—organisms that have been genetically engineered so that they carry one or more foreign genes from a different species—has spawned a new frontier for life scientists. Next, we describe some of the exciting applications of genetic engineering techniques in the twenty-first century.

### Transgenic bacteria have many uses

In the past few decades we have created new strains of transgenic bacteria specifically for our own purposes. Bacteria are rapidly becoming the workhorses of the genetic engineering industry because they readily take up plasmids containing foreign genes, and because their reproductive cycles are so short. Once a gene that codes for a desirable protein is introduced into bacteria by recombinant DNA techniques, it is only a matter of selecting those bacteria that express the gene (and thus make the protein) and then reproducing them endlessly to obtain nearly a limitless supply of the protein.

One of the very first applications of transgenic bacteria involved the manufacture of essential human proteins, most notably hormones. Recall that hormones are signaling molecules produced in very small amounts only by specific endocrine organs. The lack of a single hormone can be devastating, even life threatening. Take insulin, for example. People with insulin-dependent diabetes mellitus need to inject this hormone daily just to survive. Prior to genetic

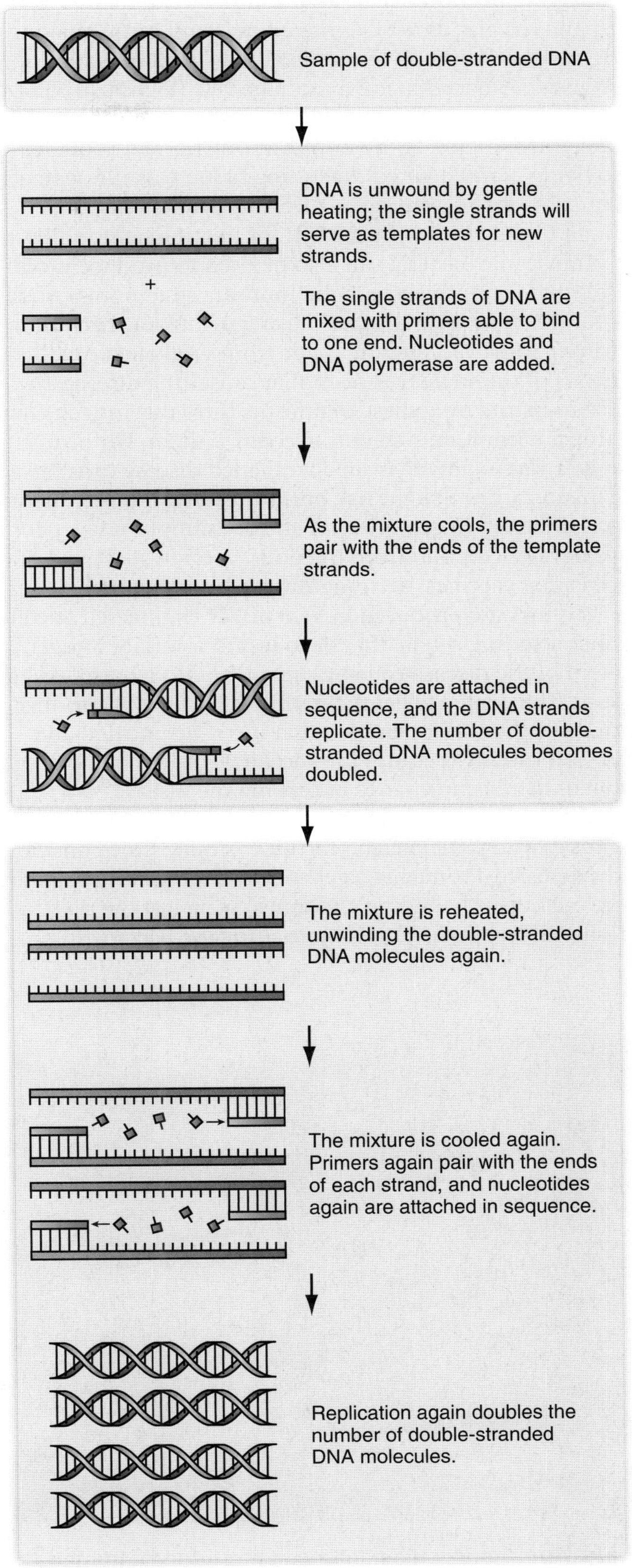


**Figure 20.4 The polymerase chain reaction (PCR) for amplifying a small sample of a segment of DNA.**

engineering, insulin had to be purified by extraction from the pancreas glands of slaughtered pigs and cattle, making it expensive and difficult to obtain. Today, insulin is produced by transgenic bacteria grown in huge vats (Figure 20.5). Transgenic bacteria also produce human growth hormone and erythropoietin. Some nonhormone human proteins are also being manufactured, including tissue plasminogen activator (tPA) for preventing or reversing blood clots, and human blood clotting factor VIII for treating hemophilia.

Transgenic bacteria can also be used to produce vaccines. Recall that vaccines prepare the immune system for a possible future attack by a disease-causing organism (bacterium or virus). Most vaccines are made from weakened or killed versions of the same organism that causes the disease, because in nature only these organisms carry the antigens that enable the immune system to recognize them. Unfortunately, a vaccine made from a weakened disease-causing organism carries a slight risk of transmitting the very disease it was designed to protect against. For example, a few people have developed polio from the polio vaccine. A second drawback is that vaccines are sometimes in short supply.

Vaccines are produced in genetically engineered bacteria by first inserting a gene that encodes for a surface antigen protein of the disease-causing organism into a harmless bacterium. The goal is to get the harmless bacteria to produce enough of the surface antigen that it can be purified and used as a vaccine. Because the vaccine is only the purified antigen, there is no chance of causing the disease.

Although producing a vaccine by genetic engineering sounds easy in principle, in practice it is quite time-consuming and expensive. Producing a genetically engineered vaccine requires successfully finding and transferring just the right gene into harmless bacteria, and then getting the bacteria to produce the desired protein in large amounts. To complicate matters, some disease-causing organisms evolve so rapidly that a vaccine produced one year may not work the next. Nevertheless, a genetically engineered vaccine against hepatitis B is now on the market and several other vaccines are under investigation, including one against malaria. However, work on several potential vaccines against HIV had to be halted recently because the vaccines just didn't prevent HIV infection. Successful production of vaccines by genetic engineering will continue to be a challenge.

Current practical uses of transgenic bacteria include producing enzymes in industrial quantities (for example, amylase to break down starch to glucose), manufacturing citric acid and ethanol, and producing drugs for human use. Transgenic bacteria are also used to clean up toxic wastes and oil pollutants, remove sulfur from coal, and even monitor hazardous waste sites (Figure 20.6).

**RECAP**

Bacteria are useful for genetic engineering because they readily take up plasmids containing foreign DNA and their reproductive cycles are short. Transgenic bacteria can produce human proteins, human hormones, and even vaccines. ■

## Transgenic plants: More vitamins and better resistance

It is somewhat more difficult to create transgenic plants than transgenic bacteria. Typically, the DNA of interest is inserted

**Figure 20.5 Transgenic bacteria can produce a human hormone.** These vats are producing human insulin using *E. coli* bacteria.

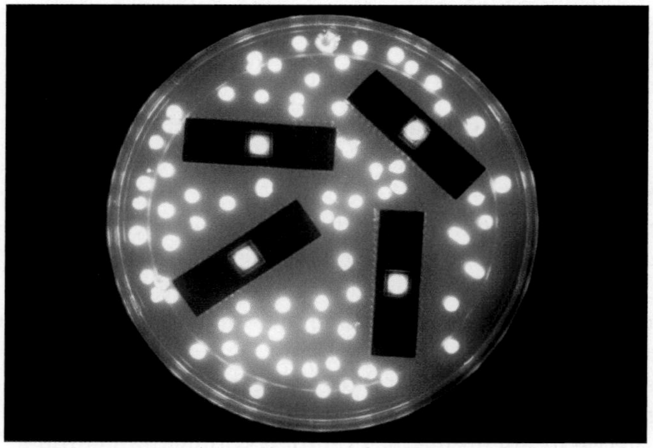

**Figure 20.6 "Critters on a chip."** The *Pseudomonas fluorescens* bacteria in this photo have been genetically engineered to emit light when they eat and digest naphthalene, a potential environmental pollutant. Some of the bacteria have been grown on small silicon chips (black rectangles) that are designed to convert the light to electrical current and send it to an electronic receiver. Bacteria and microelectronic devices such as this could be used to monitor hazardous waste sites.

into a plasmid in a particular bacterium that infects plants. When the bacterium is incubated with embryonic plant cells, a few of the plant cells may take up the DNA-laced plasmid, and a few of those may incorporate the recombinant DNA into their own genetic material. Other techniques include shocking plant cells with high voltage in the presence of recombinant DNA, and shooting the recombinant DNA into plant cells at high velocity. Once the individual plant cells with the desired DNA are identified, they are used to regenerate entire plants with the desired traits.

Despite the difficulties, genetic engineering has already produced tomato plants that resist freezing, tomatoes that last longer on the shelf, corn and cotton plants resistant to insect pests (Figure 20.7), soybean and cotton plants resistant to a commonly used herbicide, and "golden rice" that contains high levels of beta-carotene (Figure 20.8). Beta-carotene is converted to vitamin A in the human body, and vitamin A is in short supply in the diets of many people, especially in Latin America and Asia. Researchers are also developing plants that mature earlier, produce larger leaves for better photosynthesis,
develop more extensive root systems for better drought resistance, and have short, stiff stems to better resist being blown down by the wind.

Transgenic plants are also being used to produce edible vaccines against infectious diseases. Researchers have already produced a hepatitis B vaccine in raw potatoes, and they are investigating bananas as a source of vaccines against hepatitis B, cholera, and viruses that cause diarrhea. Bananas containing edible vaccines would be of great value because they are palatable to children, do not require cooking, and are easy to grow in tropical and subtropical climates.

Transgenic plants can even be made to incorporate human genes and produce human proteins. For example,

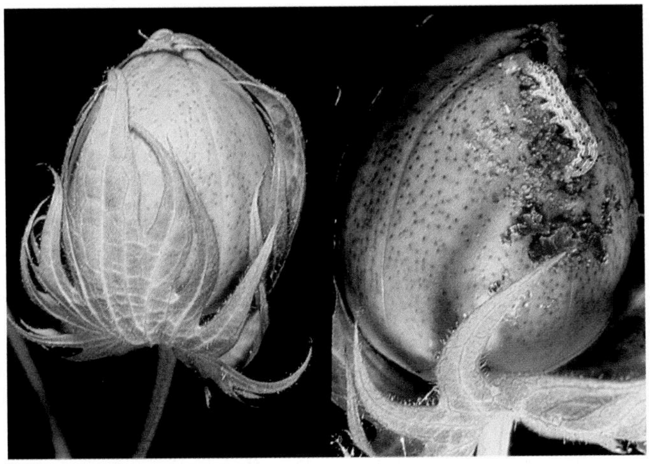

Figure 20.7 **Genetically engineered cotton.** The cotton boll on the left is from a plant genetically engineered for resistance to the boll weevil. On the right is a boll weevil on a normal cotton boll.

Figure 20.8 **Transgenic plants can improve human nutrition.** The golden rice on the right is high in beta-carotene, a nutrient in short supply in many areas of the world.

efforts are currently underway to produce commercially viable quantities of human serum albumin in potatoes and tobacco plants. Serum albumin is an essential component of fluid replacement therapy.

Some people are concerned about the safety of transgenic plants, particularly when the development of new plants seems to be happening so quickly compared to their regulation and safety testing. Protests against so-called Frankenfoods are becoming more commonplace, especially in Europe. Look for genetic engineering of plants to come under increased political scrutiny and public debate in the future.

Aside from the issue of safety, there is concern that the widespread use of genetically engineered food crops could lead to occasional but widespread crop failures. The problem is that genetically engineered plant lines are sometimes produced from just one or a very few original embryonic plants that took up the gene of interest and then were divided over and over again in the laboratory. Such plants are clones—all of the individual plants are genetically identical. Therefore if a new pest or a brief change in environmental or climactic conditions were to damage the plants, the entire crop could fail. In a population of crop plants produced by sexual reproduction, genetic variation leads to variable responses to pests and environmental conditions because some plants are better able to withstand the challenge than others. However, sexual reproduction is not the method of choice for reproducing prized transgenic plant lines because it would tend to breed *out* the desired trait over time.

## Transgenic animals: A bigger challenge

Producing transgenic animals is even harder than producing transgenic plants. First, animal cells do not take up plasmids as do bacteria and plant cells, so introducing foreign DNA into an animal cell is a greater challenge. Second, the techniques for cloning animals from a single cell or group of cells are much more difficult than for cloning plants.

Producing a transgenic animal typically begins with inserting the DNA of interest into fertilized eggs. One way is to microinject DNA into each egg individually. Another is to agitate fertilized eggs in the presence of DNA and tiny silicon needles. The needles create holes in the eggs, allowing the DNA to enter. The eggs are then reimplanted into a female for gestation. The number of transgenic animals that can be produced at any one time is limited because usually only a few mature eggs are available at a time and fewer than 10% of the eggs incorporate the recombinant DNA into their own.

Despite these drawbacks, the production of transgenic animals is moving forward. To date, the gene for bovine growth hormone (bGH) has been inserted into cows, pigs, and sheep in order to create faster-growing and larger animals for food production. Transgenic animals are also used to study specific human diseases. For example, transgenic mice have been created that overexpress the beta-amyloid protein thought to be responsible for Alzheimer's disease in humans.

Pharmaceutical companies are inserting genes that code for useful human proteins into goats, sheep, and cows. Large animals are preferred because it may be possible to obtain sufficient quantities of the protein from the female's milk (Figure 20.9), rather than having to repeatedly bleed or even sacrifice the animal to obtain the protein from blood. The process of producing pharmaceuticals in farm animals is called "gene pharming," aptly enough (Figure 20.10).

**RECAP**

Transgenic plants and animals can provide new agricultural crops and useful human proteins. It is harder to create transgenic animals, because animal cells do not take up plasmids and the cloning techniques are more difficult. ■

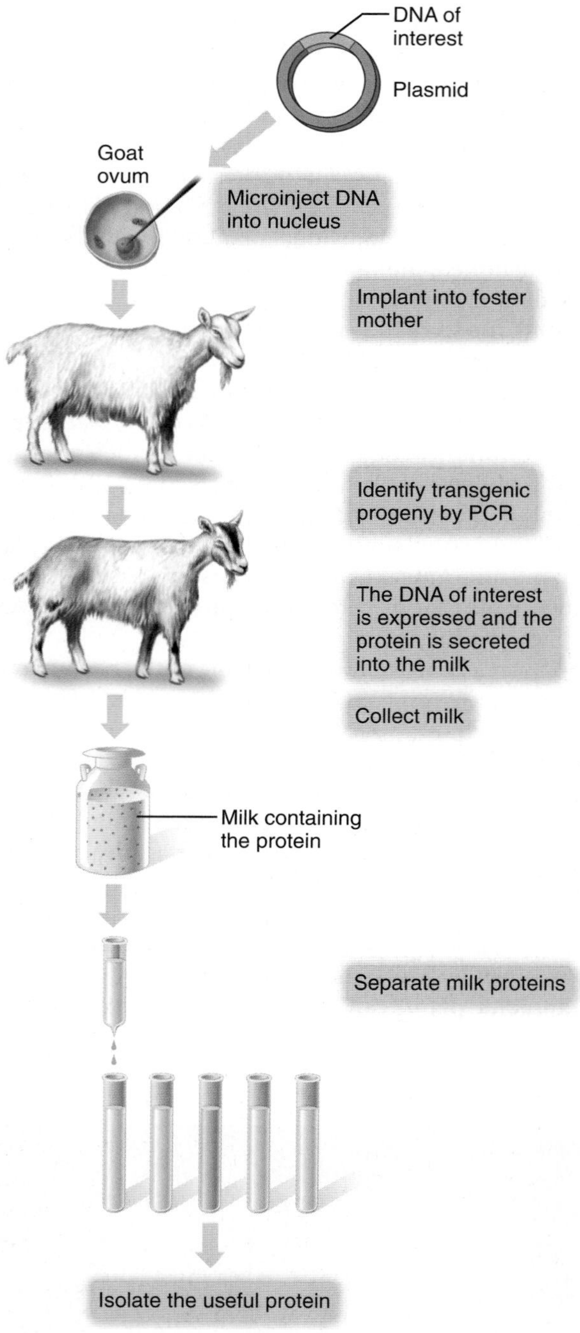


**Figure 20.9 Producing transgenic animals.** One way to produce a transgenic animal is to microinject the DNA of interest into an animal's egg and then implant the egg into another female for development. Genes that code for useful human proteins are inserted into the eggs of large mammals such as goats, and then the human protein of interest is collected from the animal's milk once the transgenic animal matures.

## 20.4 Gene therapy: The hope of the future?

Nothing quite fires the imagination like the notion of **gene therapy**—the insertion of human genes into human cells to treat or correct disease. The potential for successful gene therapy is often mentioned as one of the possible benefits of the Human Genome Project. We now know the chromosome and even the location on the chromosome where the gene mutations for many genetic diseases are located (Table 20.1). The great hope of the future is that with gene therapy, these mutations could be fixed.

But a word of caution is in order: despite considerable effort, successful gene therapy is still more of a dream than a reality. In this section we consider some of the obstacles to success and describe what has been accomplished so far.

### Gene therapy must overcome many obstacles

We have already discussed how difficult it is to produce an animal by genetic engineering. However, it is much easier to create an entire transgenic animal than to correct a genetic disease in a human adult, or even a child.

**Figure 20.10 Gene pharming.** These goats have been genetically engineered to produce milk containing antithrombin III, a human protein that can be used to prevent blood clots during surgery.

First, in an individual with trillions of already differentiated and matured cells, it has proven exceedingly difficult to get the recombinant DNA containing the gene of interest into enough of the right cells. Recall that transgenic animals are created by inserting the gene into a *single* cell (the fertilized egg) that has been isolated and is therefore available to the researcher for microinjection—and even then the procedure works less than 10% of the time. How would we ever insert the gene that codes for a single missing protein, for example, into every cell in the body, or at least into the cells that normally produce that protein? How would we deliver the gene that codes for a specific missing hormone into the millions of cells in a particular endocrine gland that normally produces that hormone? Ideally, what we need are delivery systems that deliver recombinant DNA efficiently to all body cells or to specific tissues or cell types. No such delivery systems exist yet.

Second, even if we could correct a specific genetic disorder in an individual, it does not follow that the disease would also be corrected in his or her offspring. If we managed to cure cystic fibrosis in an individual by inserting the appropriate normal gene into enough lung cells to make a difference, that person's children could still inherit the disease—unless we were also able to insert the normal gene into the germ cells in the testes or ovaries that produce sperm or eggs. In fact, if we *do* become able to treat genetic diseases in individuals who might otherwise die before reproductive age, we may well increase the prevalence of genetic diseases in the population. We might be forced to use genetic engineering to correct more and more people in the future.

**RECAP**

There are many obstacles to be overcome before human gene therapy will become commonplace. Even if we are able to correct genetic disease in an individual, that person's children could still inherit the disorder. ■

## Vectors transfer genes into human cells

Although in principle it would be ideal if we could deliver a gene so that it replaces a damaged or missing gene in all of a person's cells, in practice this is not necessary. All we really need to do is get the gene into enough living cells to produce

**Table 20.1 Some genetic diseases and their chromosomal locations.**

| Genetic Disease | Chromosome | Description |
|---|---|---|
| Huntington disease | 4 | Neurodegenerative disorder tending to strike people in their 30s and 40s. There is no cure. |
| Cystic fibrosis | 7 | Mucus fills up the lungs, interfering with breathing. |
| Melanoma | 9 | Malignant skin cancer. |
| Sickle-cell anemia | 11 | Chronic blood disease, primarily affecting African Americans. |
| Breast and ovarian cancers | 13 and 17 | BRCA2 and BRCA1 genes confer a high risk of breast and ovarian cancers. |
| Alzheimer's disease | 14 | Degenerative brain disease marked by premature senility. |
| Tay-Sachs disease | 15 | Rare fatal hereditary disorder involving lipid metabolism, most common among Eastern European Jews. |
| Familial hypercholesterolemia | 19 | Extremely high cholesterol levels. |
| Severe combined immunodeficiency disease (SCID) | 20 | Enzyme deficiency leads to severe susceptibility to infections. First hereditary condition treated by gene therapy. |
| Down syndrome | 21 | Congenital mental deficiency condition marked by three copies of chromosome 21 |
| Hemophilia | X | Blood defect making bleeding difficult to control. |

# Current Issue

## Should We Be Harnessing the Potential of GM Plants?

By now you have almost certainly eaten genetically modified (GM) food products. It is estimated that 70–75% of all processed foods in U.S. supermarkets contain GM ingredients. In 2007, 73% of the U.S. corn crop and a whopping 91% of the soybean crop came from GM plants. Should we continue to fear GM crops, or is it time to harness their potential?

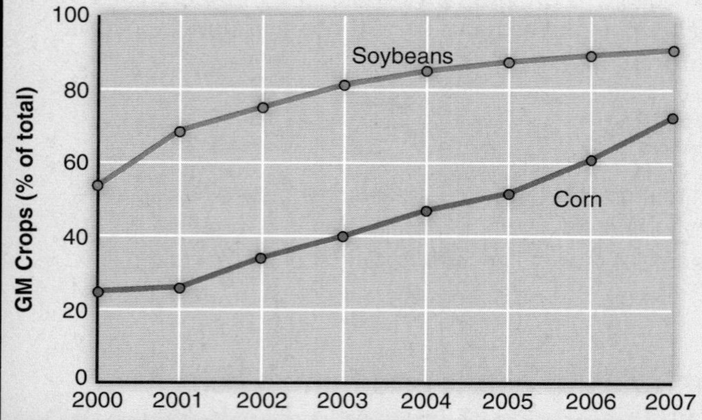


Percentage of U.S. soybean and corn crops from GM plants.

GM foods come from plants that have been genetically engineered for a specific purpose, such as to reduce the cost of crop production, increase crop yield, improve nutritional value, or even produce antibiotics. The first widely used GM plants were genetically engineered for increased resistance to insects or herbicides, reducing the need for costly and environmentally damaging sprays. More recently, plants have been genetically modified to grow under marginal environmental conditions or to produce vitamins, proteins, or even pharmaceuticals.

When it became apparent in the 1990s that scientists were successfully modifying plant genomes in the laboratory, people were rightly suspicious. There was widespread concern that GM crops might be dangerous to eat, or that they would damage the environment or produce a "superweed."

One of the very first GM crops ever to be planted in open fields was Starlink corn, genetically engineered to contain a novel protein that made it resistant to insects. Starlink was approved by the FDA in 1998 only for use as an animal feed, out of concern that some people might be allergic to the insecticidal protein it contained. But when traces of Starlink corn appeared in the human food supply in 2000 (most famously in Taco Bell taco shells), a huge public outcry ensued. Although no one claimed to have been injured, all products containing traces of Starlink corn were pulled from the market. Starlink corn was never grown again.

Healthy skepticism is a good thing, of course, but where does healthy skepticism end and irrational fear begin? Both the skepticism and the fear center on two general concerns—that GM foods may be dangerous to eat, and that GM plants have the potential to get out of control and damage ecosystems. What's the evidence so far?

### Are GM Foods Safe to Eat?

A major difficulty with safety testing is that by the very nature of science, one can never *prove* something to be 100% safe. All we can do is perform as many tests as possible to increase our level of confidence. In the U.S., GM food testing generally requires an assessment of *substantial equivalence*, coupled with the concept of *generally recognized as safe* (GRAS). If a plant or food is substantially equivalent to a non-GM food that is generally recognized as safe to eat, then the GM food does not have to undergo rigorous testing. However, if the GM plant has even one new feature that may be unsafe for some people (it might cause an allergic reaction, for example), then it is considered unsafe until further testing.

The safety of GM foods is monitored by the FDA. In assessing GM foods, FDA regulators focus on the novel protein that is expressed as a result of the recombinant DNA insertion. Although most proteins are broken down to amino acids in the human digestive tract, a few proteins manage to resist degradation by stomach acid. These stubborn proteins are often the cause of food allergies. Peanuts, for example, contain a protein that is hard to digest. For people with an allergy to that one peanut protein, eating peanuts can cause a life-threatening allergic reaction.

So far there is no scientific evidence that any currently approved GM food product is dangerous, despite the fact that millions of us are eating them every day. Nevertheless, we would be wise to remain vigilant. A recent report by the U.S. General Accounting Office concluded that the FDA's current regulation of GM foods is adequate but could be improved. Suggested improvements include making the FDA evaluation process more straightforward and less burdensome, and randomly checking the food companies' data.

## the facts...

- Genetically modified (GM) food plants contain genes from other plants, bacteria, or even animals.
- Almost 75% of processed foods in the U.S. contain GM ingredients.
- Some consumer and environmental groups oppose GM foods and plants on the grounds that they represent dangerous untested experiments.
- GM food testing and labeling requirements in some countries threaten the export of GM food crops from the U.S. and Canada.
- So far, GM food crops have not proven to be a threat to human health or the environment.

### Do GM Plants Endanger the Environment?

Some environmental concerns about GM plants are that they may endanger nonharmful insects, that they will cross-pollinate and contaminate the gene pool of conventional non-GM food plants, and that cross-pollination of

Genetically modified barley. A concern is that GM crops could cross-pollinate with non-GM crops.

herbicide-resistant GM plants with weeds will create "superweeds" resistant to herbicides.

Not all GM crops would endanger nonharmful insects, of course; only those crops genetically modified for insect resistance would do so. And although some nonharmful insects might be killed as a consequence of ingesting too much pollen from insect-resistant GM crops, that should be weighed against the benefits of not having to spray insecticides indiscriminately.

More problematic is the possibility of cross-pollination. In nature, the genes of a plant species are *supposed* to be redistributed in the next generation as pollination occurs, so it shouldn't be surprising that GM plants occasionally cross-pollinate with non-GM plants. Studies show that transgenes have already spread from GM corn in the U.S. to conventional maize in Mexico, and that other conventional food crops in the U.S. have been widely contaminated by their GM counterparts. Whether this might create a problem in the future is unknown. However, research is already beginning to address the issue. "Terminator technologies" are under development that could render the seeds of GM plants sterile in the second generation, or that could prevent GM plants from expressing the novel gene unless the plant is treated with a special "gene unlocking" chemical. However, these techniques have their own detractors. Social scientists worry that terminator technologies will prevent small, poor farmers from benefiting from GM crops because they will not be able to save seed for planting the next year—they'll have to buy GM seed (or the unlocking chemical) each year from the agribusiness that holds the patent.

### Public Resistance Inhibits GM Crop Development

Despite the general findings of a lack of significant harm by GM crops so far, public resistance remains high in some countries. In Europe, protesters still conduct raids on GM crops, destroying them before harvest. The European Union requires food producers to monitor GM crops at all stages of production, and any product that contains more than 0.9% GM ingredients must be labeled accordingly. In Australia and New Zealand, all GM foods intended for sale must undergo a premarket safety assessment by a government agency. In some cases these regulations effectively amount to trade barriers for GM food products, most of which come from the U.S. or Canada. The resistance has had a chilling effect on GM foods research, development, and commercialization. Remember golden rice (Figure 20.8)? Ten years after its development, golden rice *still* has not been commercialized. The patent holder has given up on it, claiming that it lacks economic potential.

Evidence of the safety of most GM crops continues to accumulate. Food prices are rising around the world and people are starving. What we need now are simplified but effective regulations that protect consumers and the environment from harmful practices and valid scientific research that convinces those who are skeptical that genetic engineering techniques are being used safely and responsibly.

*Some countries require that foods containing genetically modified ingredients be labeled.*

### Questions to consider

**1** *Do you approve of the widespread planting of genetically modified food crops? Do you feel comfortable eating them?* **2** *GM foods are created for a variety of reasons, from increasing a food's nutritional or medicinal value to providing no-tears onions that don't make cooks cry. Should we permit the development of some GM foods and not others, and if so, which ones? Defend your position.*

enough of the missing protein to prevent the disease. There are two strategies for doing this, both of which take advantage of transporters, or *vectors*, capable of delivering genes into human cells. The best vectors are a class of viruses called retroviruses. Retroviruses splice their own RNA-based genetic code permanently into the DNA of the cells they infect. This makes them ideal gene-transfer vectors as long as they are rendered harmless first.

In one gene-transfer method, human cells from a particular target tissue are removed from the body and exposed to retroviruses containing the human gene of interest. Then the cells are returned to the patient from whom they came (Figure 20.11). The hope is that the virus-infected cells will incorporate themselves back into the tissue from which they originated, except that now they will express the previously missing protein. In another technique, the retroviruses with their human gene payload are injected directly into the patient, or even directly into the desired tissue if possible.

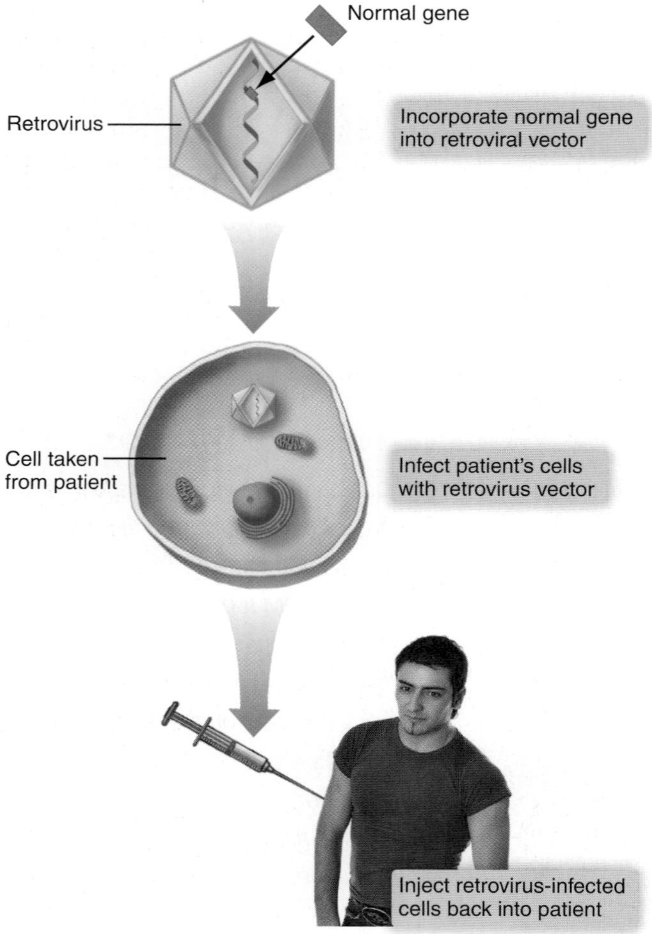


**Figure 20.11 Gene therapy using a retroviral vector.** Cells are removed from the human patient, exposed to retroviruses that contain the code for a human gene of interest, and then returned to the patient. The goal is for the "infected" cells to produce enough of the missing protein to correct symptoms of the disease.

Again, the hope is that some of the cells will take up the retroviruses and incorporate the human gene into the cell's own DNA.

Retroviruses have their drawbacks as gene delivery vectors, however. One problem is that retroviruses generally insert foreign DNA into a cell's DNA only when the cell is dividing. Another is that they insert their genetic material randomly in the genome, so they might disrupt the function of other human genes. To get around these drawbacks, some researchers are experimenting with nonviral methods of gene transfer. These methods include embedding plasmids containing the genes in small fatty spheres called liposomes, coating them with amino acid polymers, or even injecting plain ("naked") DNA. Such techniques are still highly experimental.

### Success with SCID gives hope

Given the technical problems associated with gene therapy, it's a wonder we have accomplished anything at all. Although failures have outnumbered successes so far, every small advance opens new avenues for research and increases the chances of success in the future.

The first patient treated for a disease by gene therapy was Ashanthi DeSilva (Figure 20.12). In 1990 Ashanthi, then 4 years old, suffered from severe combined immunodeficiency

**Figure 20.12 The first beneficiary of gene therapy.** Ashanthi DeSilva was the first patient to successfully receive gene therapy for severe combined immunodeficiency disease. The restoration of her immune system function was only partial, but the experience gained from her treatment paved the way for more recent advances in gene therapy for others. This photo was taken on the 10th anniversary of the event.

disease (SCID), an inherited disorder in which the lack of an enzyme called *adenosine deaminase (ADA)* leads to a marked deficiency of B and T cells of the immune system and an increased susceptibility to infections. In the landmark treatment of Ashanthi, T cells isolated from her blood were grown in the laboratory with a viral vector containing the gene for the enzyme. When the genetically engineered T cells were reintroduced into her blood they expressed the gene, ADA was produced, and her condition improved. However, the improvement was only temporary because mature T cells have a finite life span. Ashanthi and most other SCID patients treated by gene therapy have had to supplement their treatment with regular doses of ADA (now produced by genetic engineering techniques).

Other researchers have tried isolating and treating blood-forming stem cells from the umbilical cord of infants with SCID and then reintroducing them into the infants, in the hope of getting the stem cells themselves to produce corrected T cells throughout the patients' lives. The first results were only mildly encouraging: a few of the patients' T cells did produce the enzyme, but not enough to prevent the disease without additional treatment with regular doses of a synthetic form of the missing enzyme.

As of this writing, several SCID patients have finally been treated successfully with gene therapy alone. The time span from first attempt to first real success was approximately 10 years.

### Research targets cystic fibrosis and cancer

Recall that cystic fibrosis is a genetic disease caused by the lack of a single gene that codes for the transmembrane protein that transports chloride ions. Since the disease primarily affects the respiratory system, researchers are experimenting with delivering the normal gene in a viral vector via a nasal spray. The results so far have been only slightly encouraging. Although about 5% of the cells of the respiratory system take up the normal gene, that is not enough to prevent the disease. Nor is it clear that the gene will be expressed by those cells. Nevertheless, the results are promising enough to warrant the search for more effective delivery vectors.

Some types of cancer may soon be treatable by gene therapy. One promising approach is to add genes for interleukins (which activate the immune system) to cancer cells in the laboratory. The cancer cells are then returned to the patient. As the cancer cells divide, the interleukins they produce stimulate the patient's own immune system to recognize and attack the cancer cells. Another method is to incorporate the gene for a protein of a foreign cell into cancer cells so that they are specifically targeted for destruction by the immune system.

Another promising approach is based on an understanding of why cells die when they become damaged. When normal cells become damaged they undergo a process called apoptosis (programmed cell death). Apoptosis is nature's way of getting rid of damaged cells quickly. Scientists have discovered that certain proteins, including one called mda-7, are responsible for initiating apoptosis. However, cancer cells seem to avoid apoptosis. In one experiment, researchers inserted the mda-7 protein into a viral vector and injected it directly into malignant tumors. The tumors began to secrete mda-7, killing many cancerous cells and stimulating the patients' immune system.

Gene therapy of somatic cells holds the promise of treating specific diseases in specific individuals. As with any standard medical treatment, the effect would last only for the lifetime of the individual patient. However, gene therapy targeting the germ cells that lead to sperm and eggs would be another matter entirely, for it would alter the human genome for all future generations. We should start thinking about the legal, ethical, and moral implications of germ cell gene therapy now, before it becomes a real issue.

**RECAP**

Gene therapy depends on vectors to deliver corrected DNA into a patient's cells. Although there have been a few successes so far, gene therapy is still in its infancy. ■

## Chapter Summary

### DNA sequencing reveals structure of DNA *p. 465*

- DNA sequencing can now be done in the laboratory.
- The technique involves synthesizing a complementary new strand of DNA to a single strand that is to be sequenced, and then determining its sequence.
- An enzyme called DNA polymerase is used to add new nucleotides to the growing strand.
- A technique called *gel electrophoresis* is used to sort DNA strands by size.

### DNA can be modified in the laboratory *p. 466*

- Recombinant DNA technology refers to techniques for splicing segments of DNA into the DNA of other organisms.
- The technique involves cutting and splicing the DNA of interest into a plasmid, and then delivering the plasmid into the organism of interest.
- The *polymerase chain reaction* makes multiple copies of a short segment of DNA.

**Genetic engineering creates transgenic organisms** *p. 469*

- Bacteria are commonly used to make human proteins and hormones because they readily take up recombinant DNA plasmids and can be grown easily in the laboratory.
- Creating transgenic plant crops has proven easy because many plants can be regenerated from individual transgenic plant cells.
- Many transgenic plant crops are already in use in the agricultural industry. Their long-term safety is largely untested.
- Transgenic animals are more difficult to produce, and they can be produced only one at a time.

**Gene therapy: The hope of the future?** *p. 472*

- Human gene therapy has proven difficult because it is hard to deliver the appropriate recombinant DNA to the right human cells.
- Gene therapy has shown some success in treating SCID.
- Some cancers may be treatable by gene therapy techniques in the near future.

## Terms You Should Know

biotechnology, *465*
DNA ligase, *466*
DNA polymerase, *465*
gel electrophoresis, *465*
gene therapy, *472*
genetic engineering, *465*
plasmid, *466*
polymerase chain reaction (PCR), *467*
primer, *465*
recombinant DNA technology, *465*
restriction enzyme, *466*
transgenic, *469*

## Concept Review

1. Explain how DNA is sequenced.
2. Describe the enzymes used in recombinant DNA techniques.
3. Describe the process of producing recombinant DNA.
4. Discuss the polymerase chain reaction technique and explain its advantages.
5. Describe how one could insert a human gene into bacteria.
6. Explain why bacteria are so frequently used in the genetic engineering industry, and discuss some of the products that can result.
7. Give two reasons why it is harder to produce large numbers of transgenic animals than it is to produce transgenic plant crops.
8. Discuss the obstacles to successful gene therapy.
9. Discuss how gene therapy is presently used to treat genetic diseases.
10. List the diseases that gene therapy may be used to cure.

## Test Yourself

**Matching Exercise**

_____ 1. The process of creating molecules of DNA that did not previously exist
_____ 2. An enzyme that facilitates the addition of nucleotides to a growing DNA strand
_____ 3. Enzyme that cuts DNA at specific places
_____ 4. An enzyme that binds fragments of DNA together again after they have been cut
_____ 5. A technique for making copies of a specific fragment of DNA

a. restriction enzyme
b. polymerase chain reaction
c. DNA ligase
d. recombinant DNA technology
e. DNA polymerase

**Fill in the Blank**

6. A(n) ____________ organism is one that carries one or more foreign genes.
7. Bacteria that have been genetically engineered to contain a human gene can often be made to manufacture a human ____________.
8. Researchers are working on genetically engineering bananas so that they contain a(n) ____________ against the hepatitis B virus.
9. DNA ____________ is a technique for identifying a person from a small sample of his or her DNA.
10. A(n) ____________ is a small circular piece of self-replicating DNA found in bacteria.
11. Restriction enzymes cut at a specific ____________ DNA sequence.
12. Viruses are used as ____________ to deliver genes into human cells.

**True or False?**

13. Gel electrophoresis separates DNA fragments according to their size.
14. Genetically engineered corn has been proven unsafe for human consumption.
15. Cutting and splicing DNA is referred to as the polymerase chain reaction.

## References and Additional Reading

Bren, Linda. Genetic Engineering: The Future of Foods? *FDA Consumer Magazine*, November–December 2003. (An overview by a U.S. Food and Drug Administration publication of the advantages, safety concerns, and regulatory challenges presented by genetically modified foods.)

Enserink, Martin. Tough Lessons From Golden Rice. *Science*, April 25, 2008, pp. 268–471. (A lucid account of why golden rice is still not commercially available after 10 years in development.)

Lyon, Jeff, and Peter Gorner. *Altered Fates: Gene Therapy and the Retooling of Human Life.* New York: Norton, 1996. 636 pp. (A gripping account of the early scientific and political history of human gene therapy.)

Nicholl, Desmond S. T. *An Introduction to Genetic Engineering.* Cambridge University Press, 2002. (A straightforward introduction to this subject for the interested student.)

## Apply **What You Know**

1. What do you think are the chances that someone will try to use genetic engineering techniques to produce a biological weapon of mass destruction? Should this affect our research into genetic engineering, and if so how? Explain your reasoning.
2. Imagine a future in which the respiratory effects of cystic fibrosis, a genetic disorder, could be cured by a gene therapy technique in which the normal gene is delivered to the patient via a nasal spray. You are the patient's genetic counselor. Explain to the patient why the cure will not alter his or her future child's chances of having the disease.
3. Scientists in a Hollywood film used prehistoric dinosaur DNA to make real dinosaurs. Although recreating a complete dinosaur is not yet within the realm of possibility, with present techniques it would at least be feasible to analyze a dinosaur's DNA (if some were available). What techniques would be used for such an analysis?
4. Pharmaceutical companies produce human insulin using genetic engineering techniques. The drug Humulin was one of the first recombinant DNA drugs ever approved by the FDA. How would such a drug be produced?
5. Why are vaccines produced by genetic engineering techniques (such as the Recombivax vaccine against hepatitis B) safer than vaccines produced from killed or weakened (attenuated) viruses?
6. There is interest in producing vaccines in foods. What would be the advantages of having a vaccine embedded in food?
7. Transgenic plants have the potential to improve food production around the world. They also have the possibility of being more nutritious than their naturally occurring cousins. Still, there are drawbacks. How could global climate change affect transgenic crops?

*Answers can be found on the Human Biology Place.*

## Internet References

Find links to these Web sites at the Human Biology Place.

**American Society of Gene Therapy**
**www.asgt.org**
Medical professional association of researchers in gene therapy; click the Gene Therapy News topics to see press releases about new research.

**Council for Biotechnology Information**
**http://whybiotech.com**
A group of biotechnology companies and trade associations that offers articles emphasizing the benefits of agricultural and food biotechnology.

**DOE Joint Genome Institute**
**www.jgi.doe.gov**
A collaboration between the Department of Energy, University of California, and several laboratories. Click the Research Groups tab to read about research projects or the Education tab to read an introduction to genomics.

**U.S. Food and Drug Administration, FDA Consumer Magazine**
**www.fda.gov/fdac/features/2003/603_food.html**
Link to an article created by the Food and Drug Administration about the advantages, safety concerns, and regulatory challenges presented by genetically modified foods.

# 21 Development and Aging

1 How **long** does it usually take sperm to reach the egg after intercourse?
**a.** minutes **b.** hours **c.** days

2 Why can't human infants get up and **walk** within hours of birth, as a newborn calf can?

3 **True or False?** The hypothalamus of the human brain isn't fully **mature** until puberty.

4 **True or False?** One **hypothesis** for why we age is that our cells can only divide a certain number of times before they just quit dividing.

5 **True or False?** With modern medical equipment, it is relatively easy to determine the time of a person's **death**.

Staying fit may improve quality of life as we age.

**Life is a journey** that begins at fertilization and ends around the time of our last breath. It's an interesting and complicated process in which one developmental stage follows the next in a carefully choreographed dance.

The changes that occur during development are nothing short of amazing: in just nine months a single undifferentiated cell develops into a human baby with complex organ systems comprising more than 10 trillion cells. In less than 20 years, this helpless baby becomes a fully functioning adult capable of producing still more human babies. Then, starting at about age 40, there is a slow decline of function for reasons we don't yet fully understand, ending inevitably in death.

The amazing journey of life is what this chapter is all about. We begin at the beginning when sperm meets egg, and end at the ending when life finally ceases.

## 21.1 Fertilization occurs when sperm and egg unite

### The journeys of egg and sperm

It's remarkable that sperm and egg ever find each other at all, given the journey that each must take. An egg is released from one of the two ovaries at ovulation, and the sperm are deposited in the vagina near the cervix. The egg moves slowly and passively down the oviduct, propelled by cilia that line the tube and sweep it gently downward.

Sperm are not much more than a head containing the all-important DNA, a midpiece containing mitochondria for energy production during the sperm's long journey, and a flagellum for movement (Figure 21.1a). The several hundred million sperm encounter many hazards on their journey toward the egg. First they must pass through the mucus that blocks the cervical opening and cross the vast (to them) expanse of the uterus. Then they must locate and enter the correct oviduct (half don't). Sperm swim randomly at a rate of 1/4 inch per minute. Along the way they must tolerate the strongly acidic pH of the vagina, and avoid bacteria and the occasional white blood cells roaming the uterine lining.

A sperm's journey can take hours, and only a few thousand or a few hundred make it successfully to the upper oviduct; the rest are lost along the way and die. Fertilization typically takes place in the upper third of the oviduct approximately 6–24 hours after intercourse, provided that an egg is present (Figure 21.1b). If no egg is present, the sperm may live for a couple of days and then die. If no sperm arrive, the egg dies in about 24 hours.

**RECAP**

Sperm must swim from the vagina, where they are deposited, through the uterus and up the correct oviduct to meet the egg. Relatively few sperm survive the journey. ■

### One sperm fertilizes the egg

The odds of success for a single sperm are still not very good, for only one of the several hundred million sperm will fertilize the egg. This is important, for otherwise the **zygote** (fertilized cell) would end up with an abnormal number of chromosomes. The process of fertilization has evolved to ensure that only one sperm can succeed. Recall that before fertilization, the egg is really a secondary oocyte that has started but not finished the second stage of meiosis (Figure 21.1c). The second stage of meiosis is not completed until fertilization occurs. At this point the secondary oocyte is surrounded by a protective covering called the zona pellucida and by a layer of cells derived from the follicle called the corona radiata. The egg is relatively large (nearly 2,000 times the mass of a sperm) because it contains a great deal of cytoplasm. The cytoplasm of the egg must support nearly two weeks' worth of cell divisions until the "pre-embryo," as it is called, makes contact with the uterine lining and begins to receive nutrients from the mother.

When a sperm encounters the egg, the tip of the sperm head, called the acrosome, releases powerful enzymes (Figure 21.2). These enzymes digest a path for the sperm between the cells of the corona radiata and through the zona pellucida to the egg cell membrane. Several sperm may be

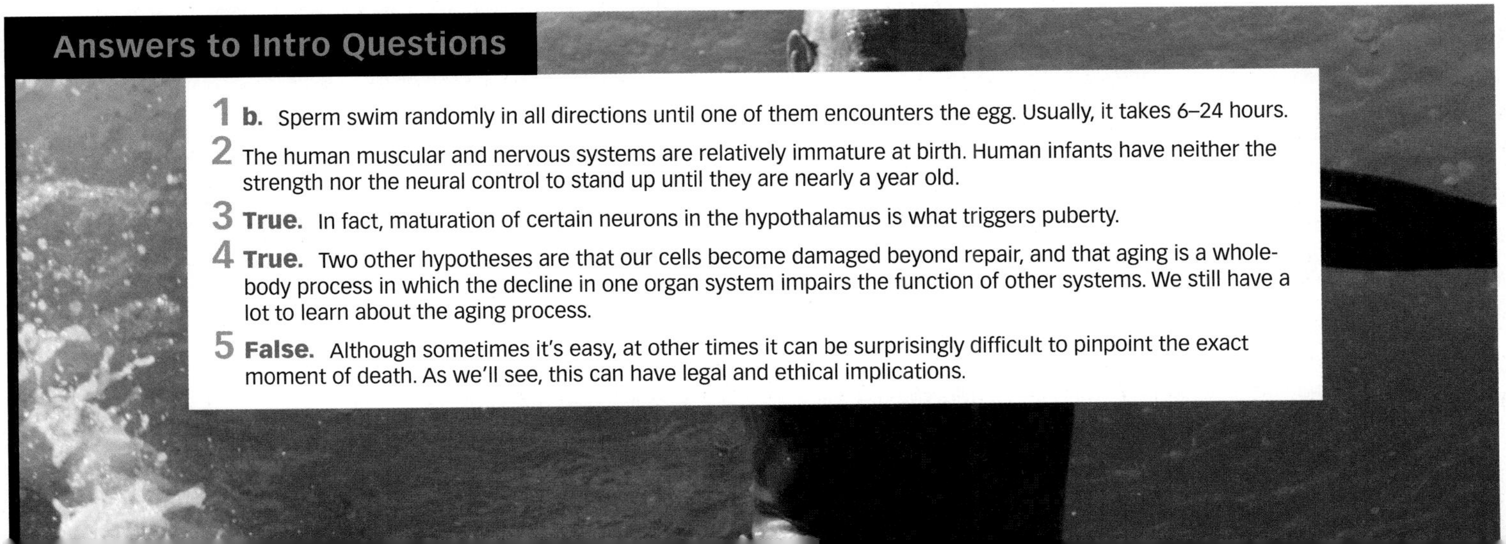

**Answers to Intro Questions**

1 **b.** Sperm swim randomly in all directions until one of them encounters the egg. Usually, it takes 6–24 hours.

2 The human muscular and nervous systems are relatively immature at birth. Human infants have neither the strength nor the neural control to stand up until they are nearly a year old.

3 **True.** In fact, maturation of certain neurons in the hypothalamus is what triggers puberty.

4 **True.** Two other hypotheses are that our cells become damaged beyond repair, and that aging is a whole-body process in which the decline in one organ system impairs the function of other systems. We still have a lot to learn about the aging process.

5 **False.** Although sometimes it's easy, at other times it can be surprisingly difficult to pinpoint the exact moment of death. As we'll see, this can have legal and ethical implications.

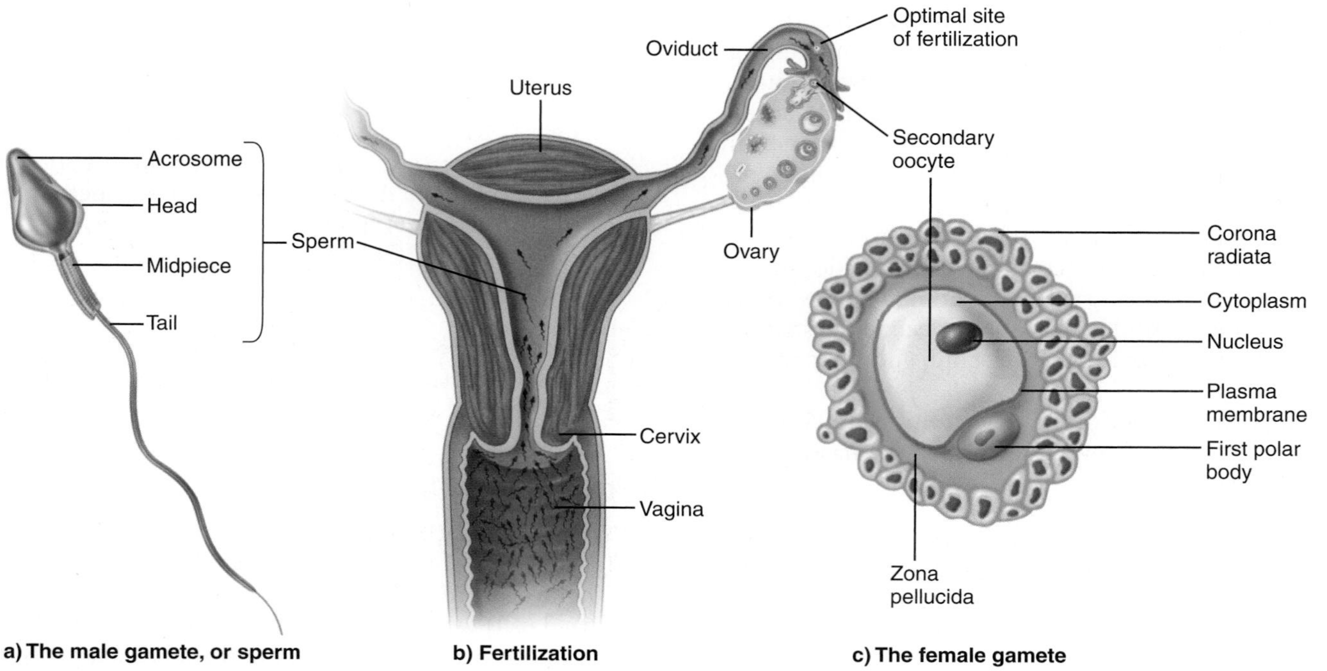


**Figure 21.1 Female and male gametes and fertilization. (a)** The size of a sperm relative to the secondary oocyte has been greatly exaggerated. **(b)** Fertilization generally takes place in the upper third of the oviduct. **(c)** The female gamete is a secondary oocyte that is in an arrested state of stage II of meiosis.

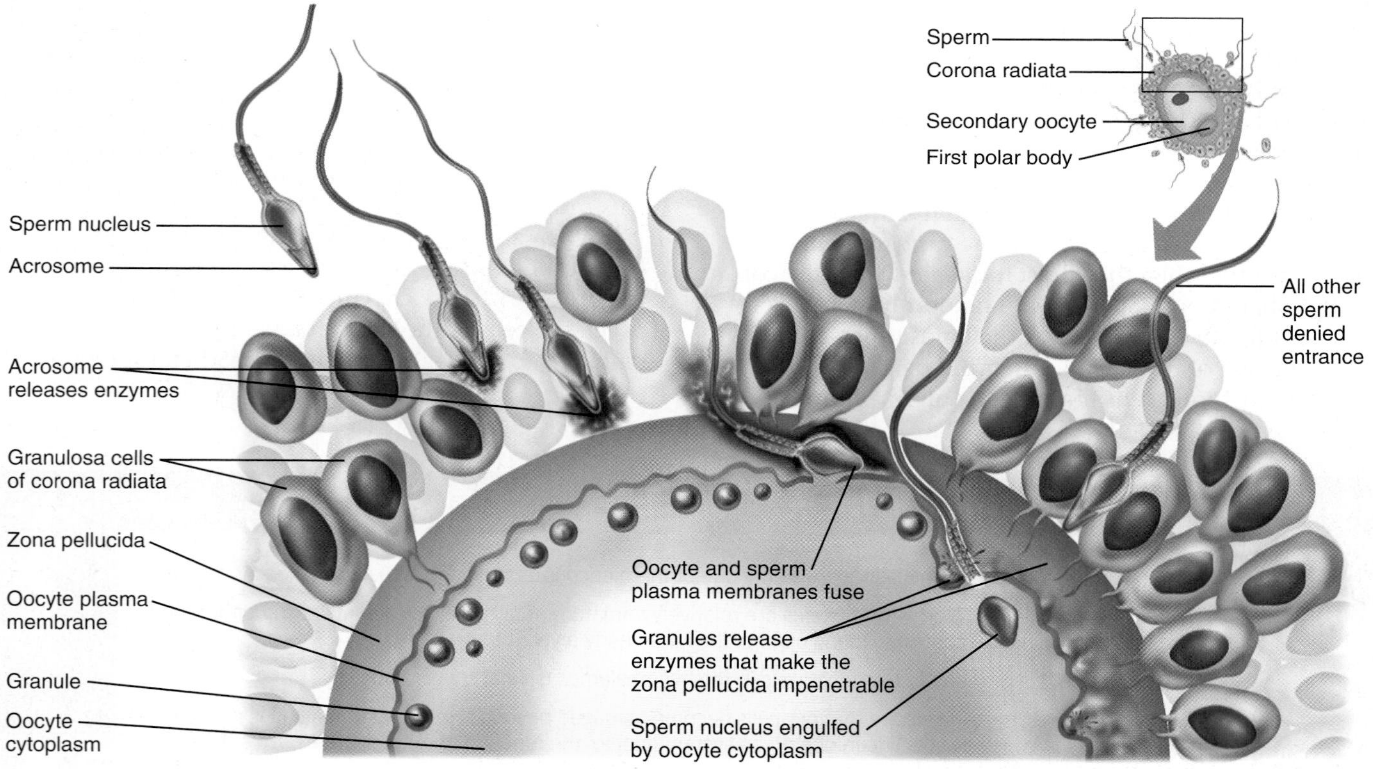


**Figure 21.2 Fertilization.** Fertilization begins when a sperm makes contact with the secondary oocyte and releases enzymes that digest a path through the zona pellucida. Once a sperm makes contact with the oocyte plasma membrane and enters the oocyte, granules are released from the oocyte that make the zona pellucida impenetrable to other sperm.

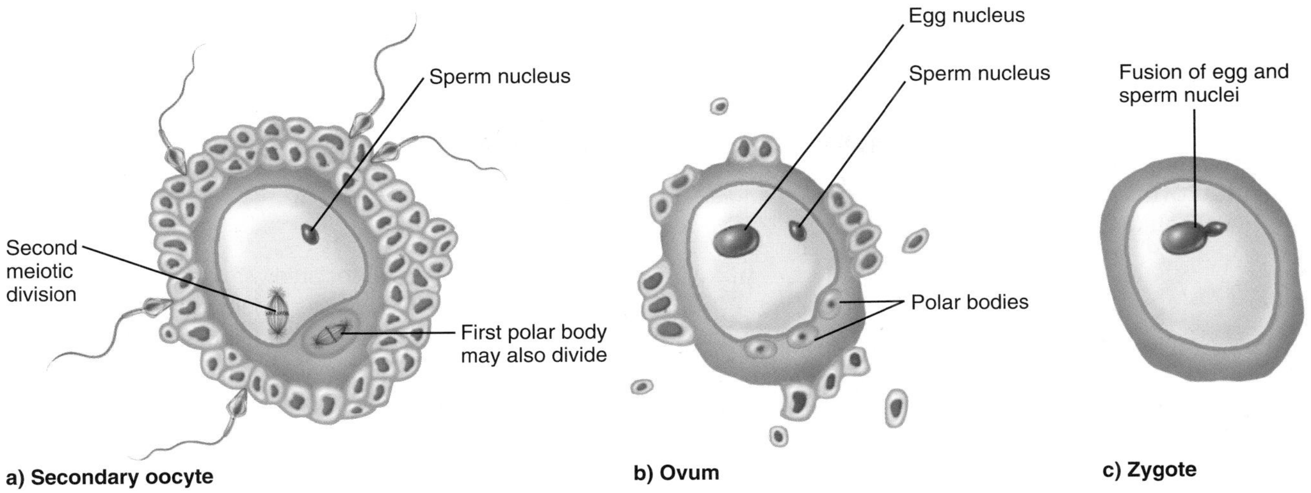


**Figure 21.3 Completion of fertilization. (a)** A sperm nucleus has just entered the secondary oocyte, triggering completion of meiosis II. **(b)** Completion of meiosis yields an ovum (egg) with a haploid nucleus and another polar body. If it has not already regressed, the original polar body may divide as well. **(c)** The nuclei of the ovum and sperm fuse, and the polar bodies die. A single diploid cell called the zygote is formed, and fertilization is complete.

making this journey at the same time. When the first sperm makes contact with the oocyte cell membrane, special protein "keys" of the sperm recognize receptor protein "locks" in the egg cell membrane, ensuring that only human sperm can penetrate a human egg. The combination of lock and key causes the cell membranes of egg and sperm to fuse so the nucleus of the sperm can enter the egg.

**Fertilization** begins when the sperm's nucleus enters the egg. The entry of one sperm triggers the release of enzymes from granules located just inside the egg. These enzymes produce changes in the zona pellucida that make it impenetrable to all other sperm. One sperm nucleus, and only one, will enter the egg.

The process of fertilization is not yet complete, however, because the "egg" is still a secondary oocyte. Entry of the sperm nucleus triggers the completion of meiosis II and formation of the haploid **ovum,** or mature egg, and another polar body. Fertilization is considered complete when the haploid nuclei of sperm and mature ovum join, forming a single diploid cell (the zygote) with 46 chromosomes (Figure 21.3). Some people refer to the end of fertilization as conception and to the product of conception as the conceptus. The follicular cells that surrounded the secondary oocyte are shed and the polar bodies die, leaving just the fertilized cell, or zygote.

**RECAP**

When sperm contact the egg they release enzymes that clear a path through the corona radiata and zona pellucida. Fertilization begins when one sperm's nucleus enters the oocyte and ends when the haploid nuclei of sperm and egg fuse, creating a new diploid cell. ■

## Twins may be fraternal or identical

Twins occur once in about every 90 births. Twins are the most common form of multiple births. Occasionally we hear of sextuplets or septuplets (six or seven newborns at once), but these are rare and almost always result from the use of fertility drugs. Even natural triplets are rare (1 in 8,000 births).

Two different processes lead to twins (Figure 21.4). **Fraternal twins** arise from the ovulation of more than one oocyte in a particular cycle. The oocytes are as different genetically as any two oocytes ovulated at different cycles, and each is fertilized by a different sperm. Fraternal twins are as different as any children by the same parents. Indeed, because they are derived from different sperm they can be of different genders.

**Figure 21.4 Twins. (a)** Fraternal twins arise when two eggs are ovulated and fertilized in the same monthly cycle. **(b)** Identical twins arise when a zygote divides in two during development.

**Identical twins,** sometimes called maternal twins, are always genetically identical. Identical twins arise from a single zygote. Recall that up until about the 16-cell stage, all cells of the developing pre-embryo are identical. If the ball of cells breaks into two groups before differentiation has begun, two complete and similar individuals may be formed. Identical twins are always of the same gender and are usually closely alike in phenotypic appearance.

**RECAP**

Fraternal twins result from the fertilization of two separate eggs. Identical twins occur when a single fertilized egg divides in two before differentiation has begun. ■

## 21.2 Development: Cleavage, morphogenesis, differentiation, and growth

During development, rapid and dramatic changes in size and form take place. This involves four processes:

- **Cleavage. Cleavage** is a series of cell divisions without cell growth or differentiation during the first four days following fertilization. Cleavage produces a ball of identical cells that is about the same size as the original zygote. Growth does not occur because the ball of cells is traveling down the oviduct at this time. With no attachment to the mother, the only energy available is that stored in the cytoplasm of the cells plus a little glycogen found within the oviduct itself.
- **Morphogenesis.** Throughout development the organism undergoes dramatic changes in shape and form. Starting as a ball of identical cells at day four, the organism becomes (in succession) several layers of different types of cells, a pre-embryo with a tail and head, an embryo with recognizable human features, and finally a fetus with a nearly complete human form. This process of physical change is called **morphogenesis** (*morpho* means "form; shape" and *genesis* means "origin; production").
- **Differentiation.** Individual cells, too, are beginning to take on specialized forms and functions, a process we know as differentiation (review Chapter 17). Differentiation of cells, and the development of organs and organ systems as a result of cell differentiation, is the primary cause of morphogenesis.
- **Growth.** Starting about the time that the developing organism becomes embedded in the endometrial lining of the uterus and begins to receive nutrients from the mother, the organism begins to grow in size. The growth of a human infant from fertilization to birth is truly spectacular—from a single cell too small to be seen to over 10 trillion cells with a combined weight of 6 or 7 pounds. Every time the cells divide, the two daughter cells double in mass to prepare for the next cell division. The only time cell division is not accompanied by cell growth is the initial period of cleavage.

Pregnancy is considered to comprise three periods called trimesters. Each trimester is approximately three months long, and characteristic events take place during each.

**RECAP**

The four processes associated with development are (1) cleavage, a series of cell divisions producing a ball of identical cells; (2) morphogenesis, a sequence of physical changes; (3) differentiation, as cells assume specialized forms and functions; and (4) growth in size. Pregnancy is divided into three trimesters. ■

## 21.3 Pre-embryonic development: The first two weeks

The period of prenatal ("before birth") human development can be divided into three stages called pre-embryonic, embryonic, and fetal development. Characteristic processes and changes take place in each stage.

During pre-embryonic development (the first two weeks), the conceptus makes its way down the oviduct, embeds itself in the endometrial lining of the uterus, begins to receive nutrients from the mother, and starts to grow. Cells differentiate into several tissue layers, and the first stages of morphogenesis begin.

Throughout the pre-embryonic period, the conceptus is known informally as a **pre-embryo** because many (if not most) of the cells are destined to become part of the placenta, not the embryo. While the conceptus is still in the oviduct, a series of successive cleavages yields a ball of about 32 identical cells called the **morula** (Figure 21.5). The term morula means "little mulberry," aptly describing its spherical, clustered appearance.

On about the fourth day the morula is swept into the uterus, where it undergoes the first stages of differentiation and morphogenesis. Over the next several days it becomes a **blastocyst,** a hollow ball comprising (1) an outer sphere of cells called a trophoblast, (2) a hollow central cavity, and (3) a group of cells called the inner cell mass. Only the inner cell mass is destined to become the embryo.

About day six or seven, the trophoblast cells make contact with the endometrial lining and secrete enzymes that digest endometrial cells. The creation of a path for the blastocyst causes it to burrow inward (Figure 21.6). The process by which the blastocyst becomes buried within the endometrium is called **implantation.**

During the second week the inner cell mass begins to separate from the surface of the blastocyst, creating a second hollow cavity. The second cavity will become the amniotic cavity filled with amniotic fluid. At this point the cell mass, now called the **embryonic disk,** differentiates into two cell types called ectoderm and endoderm. The appearance of an amniotic cavity and of ectoderm and endoderm in the embryonic disk marks the end of the pre-embryonic period.

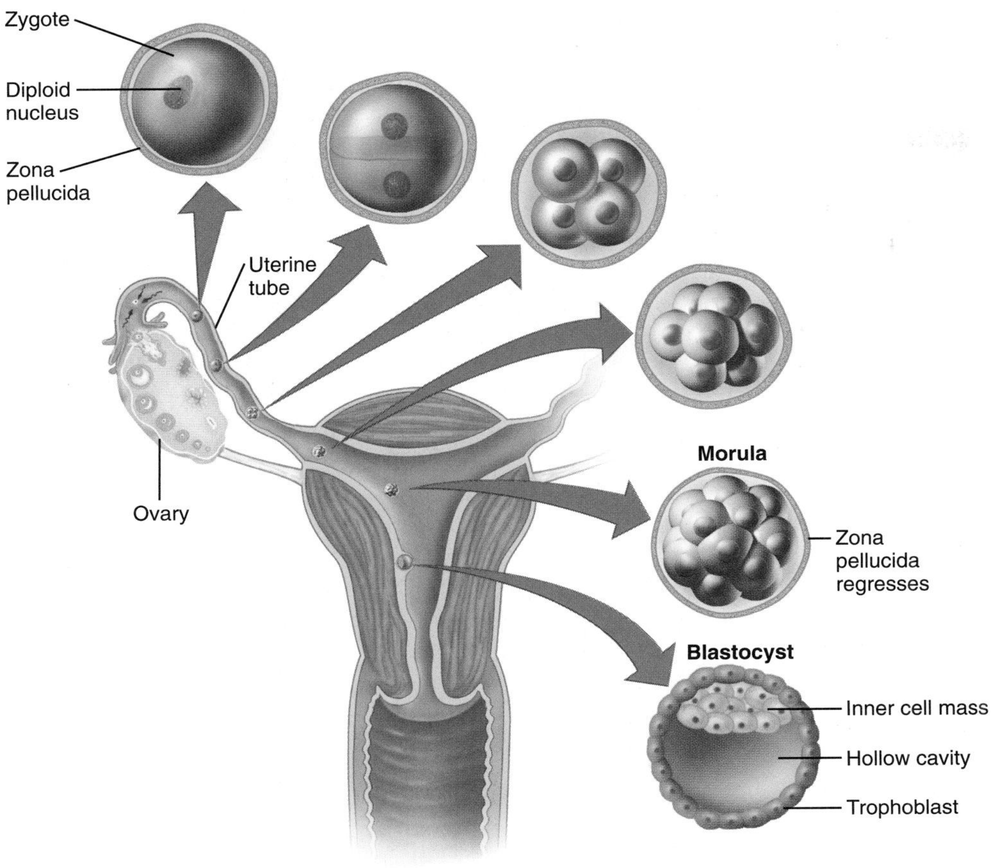


**Figure 21.5 Pre-embryonic development leading up to implantation.** After a series of cleavages the morula enters the uterus and develops into a blastocyst comprising an outer layer of cells called the trophoblast, a hollow cavity, and an inner mass of cells. The blastocyst attaches to the uterine wall.

Pre-embryonic development is a hazardous time in which a lot can go wrong. Usually a woman is not even aware that she is pregnant at this time, and so she may continue risky behaviors such as smoking and drinking alcohol.

On rare occasions the blastocyst implants in an oviduct before reaching the uterus, resulting in an **ectopic pregnancy.** An ectopic pregnancy can result in a healthy baby if watched carefully; however, the oviduct is not large enough to accommodate a full-term baby, nor is it a good site for placental development. If an ectopic pregnancy is not terminated early for the health of the mother, the infant generally is delivered surgically as soon as it is able to survive with intensive care in a hospital.

**RECAP**

During pre-embryonic development, successive cleavages yield a morula. Early stages of differentiation and morphogenesis cause the morula to become a blastocyst, which implants in the lining of the uterus. The embryonic disk is destined to become the embryo. ■

## 21.4 Embryonic development: Weeks three to eight

### Tissues and organs derive from three germ layers

From about the beginning of week three until the end of week eight the developing human is called an **embryo.** During this time growth, differentiation, and morphogenesis are especially rapid. All the organs and organ systems are established, though most of them are not fully functional. By the end of the embryonic period the embryo has taken on distinctly human features but is still only an inch long.

The embryonic period begins when a third cell layer, called the mesoderm appears between the other two in the embryonic disk (Figure 21.7). These three primary tissues, called the germ layers, represent the precursor (or germ) cells for the four basic tissue types introduced in Chapter 4 (epithelial, muscle, connective, and nervous) and all organs and organ systems in the body. Differentiation and morphogenesis follow a predictable pattern, so we know which tissues and organs are derived from each germ layer. The three germ layers are:

- **Ectoderm.** The ectoderm is the outermost layer, the one exposed to the amniotic cavity. Tissues derived from the ectoderm become the epidermis of the skin, the nervous system, hair, nails, enamel of teeth, parts of the eye, and several other organs and tissues (Table 21.1).
- **Mesoderm.** The middle layer, or mesoderm**,** becomes muscle, connective tissue and bone, kidneys and ureters, bone marrow, testes or ovaries, the lining of the blood vessels, and other organs and tissues.
- **Endoderm.** The innermost layer is the endoderm**.** It gives rise to the liver and pancreas, the alveoli of the lungs, the linings of the urinary bladder, urethra and vagina, and several glands.

**RECAP**

By the beginning of embryonic development the embryo comprises three primary germ layers, called ectoderm, mesoderm, and endoderm, that ultimately give rise to fetal tissues and organs. ■

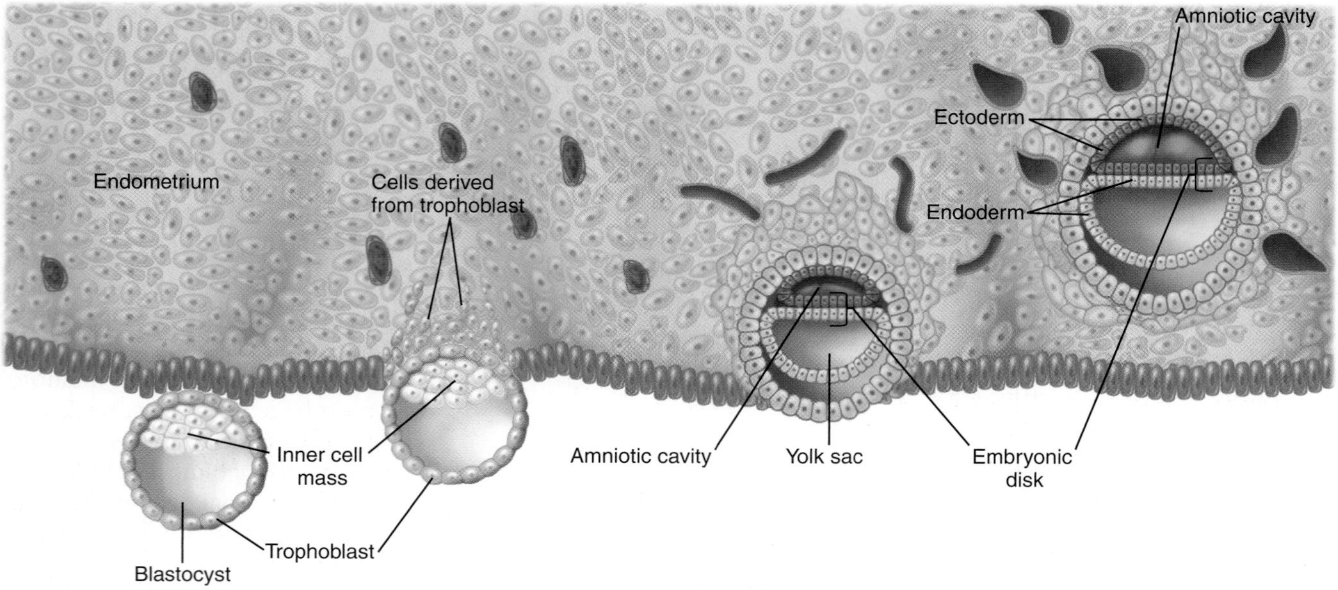


**Figure 21.6 Implantation and the end of pre-embryonic development.** Implantation takes place during days 7–14, at the same time that the inner cell mass of the blastocyst is developing into the embryonic disk. The inner cell mass separates from the outer ball to become the embryonic disk, comprising two cell types. The embryonic disk is destined to become the embryo.

## Extra-embryonic membranes and the placenta

Early in embryonic development, four different extra-embryonic membranes form that extend out from or surround the embryo: the amnion, allantois, yolk sac, and chorion. Most of the components of these membranes are either resorbed during later development or discarded at birth.

The innermost layer is the **amnion,** also known as the "bag of waters." The amnion lines the amniotic cavity, which is filled with **amniotic fluid.** The amniotic fluid is derived from the mother's interstitial fluid and is in continuous exchange with it. Later in development when the kidneys of the fetus form, the fetus will urinate into the amniotic fluid and the urine will be removed via exchange with the mother's blood. The amnion and amniotic fluid absorb physical shocks, insulate the fetus, and keep it from drying out.

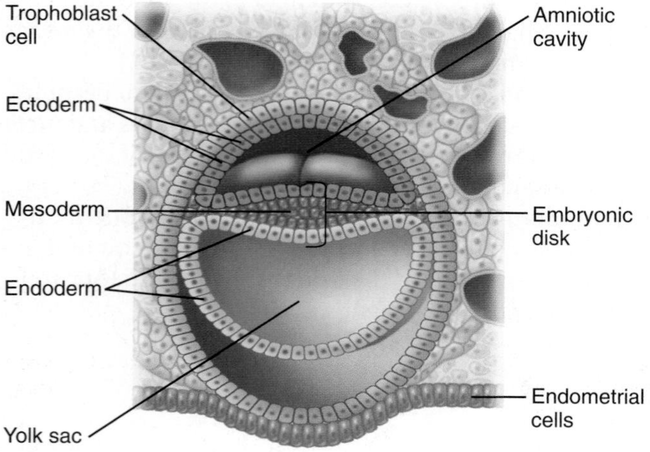


**Figure 21.7 The three primary germ layers.** The appearance of a third type of cell layer (mesoderm) between the ectoderm and endoderm in the embryonic disk marks the start of the embryonic period.

The allantois is a temporary membrane that helps form the blood vessels of the umbilical cord. It degenerates during the second month of development.

The yolk sac forms a small sac that hangs from the embryo's ventral surface. In many species the yolk sac serves a nutritive function, but in humans that function has been taken over by the placenta. Nevertheless, it is important in humans because it becomes part of the fetal digestive tract. It also produces fetal blood cells until that job is taken over by other tissues, and it is the source of the germ cells that migrate into the gonads and give rise to the gametes (sperm and eggs).

The outermost layer, the **chorion,** is derived primarily from the trophoblast of the early blastocyst. The chorion is the source of **human chorionic gonadotropin** (hCG), a hormone that supports pregnancy for the first three months until the placenta begins producing enough progesterone and estrogen. It also forms structures that will be part of the exchange mechanism in the placenta.

As the embryo grows and develops, its relationship with the mother becomes more complex. The embryo cannot supply itself with nutrients or get rid of its own wastes, so

**Table 21.1 Tissues, organs, and organ systems derived from the three primary germ layers**

| Ectoderm | Mesoderm | Endoderm |
|---|---|---|
| Epidermis of skin, including hair, nails, and glands | Dermis of skin | Epithelial tissues lining the digestive tract (except mouth and anus), vagina, bladder, and urethra |
| Mammary glands | All connective tissue, cartilage, and bone | Alveoli of lungs |
| The nervous system, including the brain, spinal cord, and all nerves | All muscle tissue (heart, skeletal, smooth) | Liver and pancreas |
| Cornea, retina, and lens of eye | Bone marrow (blood cells) | Thyroid, parathyroid, and thymus glands |
| Enamel of teeth | Kidneys and ureters | Anterior pituitary gland |
| Posterior pituitary gland | Testes, ovaries, and reproductive ducts | Tonsils |
| Adrenal medulla | Lining of blood vessels | Portions of the inner ear |
| Epithelial lining of nose, mouth, and anus | Lymphatic vessels | |

exchange vessels form between the embryo and the mother for the exchange of nutrients and wastes without direct mixing of their blood. This is the function of the placenta and the umbilical cord. The **placenta** (Figure 21.8) is the entire structure that forms from embryonic tissue (chorion and chorionic villi) and maternal tissue (endometrium). The **umbilical cord** is the two-way lifeline that connects the placenta to the embryo's circulation.

The placenta develops because the cells of the chorion, just like the cells of the trophoblast from which they derive, secrete enzymes that eat away at the endometrial tissues and capillaries in the vicinity of the embryo. These enzymes rupture the capillaries, causing the formation of small blood-filled cavities. The developing chorion extends finger-like processes called chorionic villi into these pools of maternal blood. Each chorionic villus contains small capillaries that are connected to umbilical arteries and veins that are part of the circulation of the fetus. In other words, the chorion damages the endometrium to cause local bleeding, and then it taps that bleeding as a source of nutrients and oxygen for the embryo and as a place to get rid of embryonic wastes, including carbon dioxide. In effect, an infant behaves like a parasite within the mother.

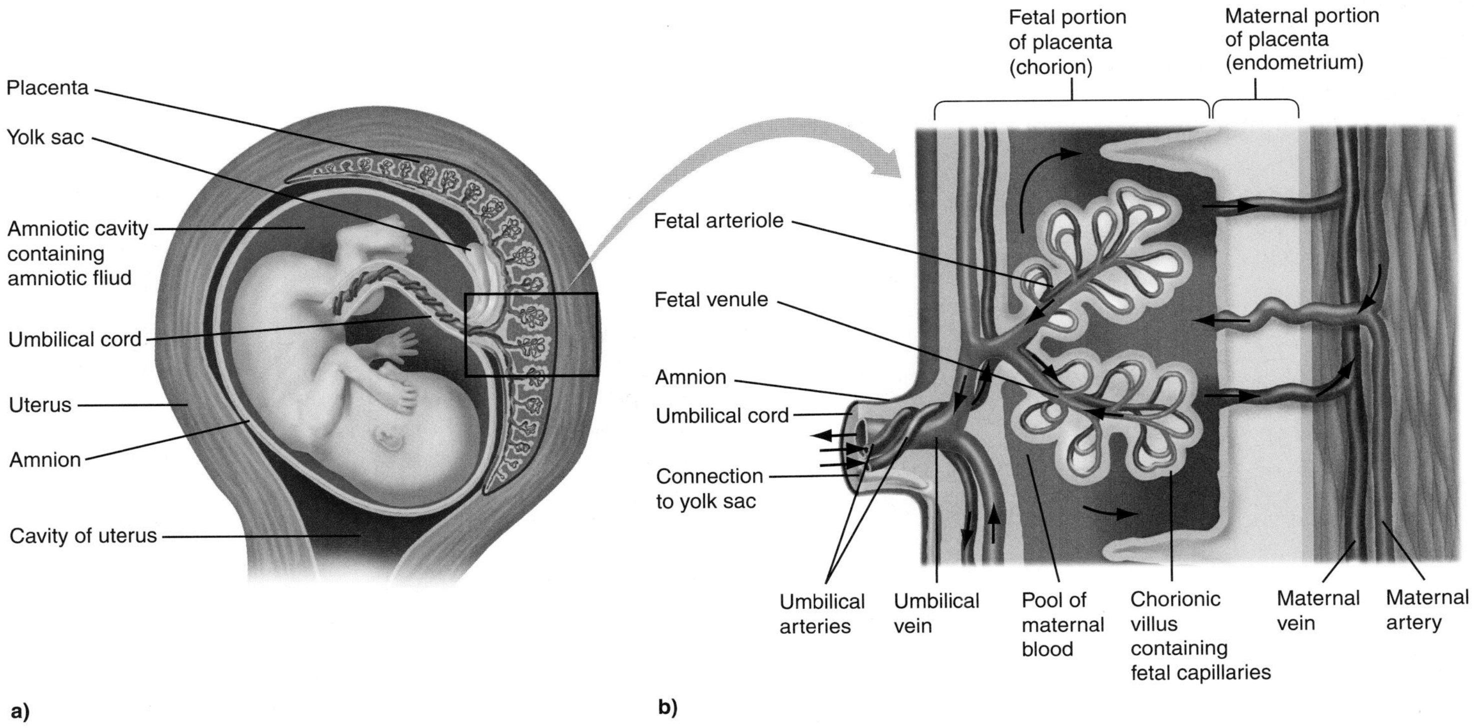


**Figure 21.8 The placenta and umbilical cord. (a)** The fetus is bathed in amniotic fluid within the amnion. Its only connection to the mother is the umbilical cord. **(b)** A closer view of portions of the placenta and umbilical cord, showing how nutrients and gases are exchanged between maternal and fetal blood without mixing.

The placenta is an effective filter. It permits the exchange of nutrients, gases, and antibodies between the maternal and embryonic circulations but not the exchange of large proteins or blood cells. The placenta allows the embryo to take advantage of the mother's organ systems until its own organs develop and become functional.

However, the placenta may permit certain toxic substances and agents of disease to cross over to the fetus as well. Examples include alcohol, cocaine, the HIV virus, and a wide variety of prescription and nonprescription drugs. Many of these substances can do a great deal of harm to the embryo when it is in the earliest stages of differentiation and morphogenesis, even though some of the prescription drugs may be therapeutic for the mother (review Chapter 17). Upon learning she is pregnant, a woman should review all her prescription and nonprescription drugs with her physician.

The placenta is also an endocrine organ. Initially the placenta secretes hCG so that the corpus luteum will continue to secrete the progesterone and estrogen necessary to maintain the pregnancy. Later the placenta secretes its own progesterone and estrogen, and the corpus luteum regresses. Progesterone and estrogen promote the growth of the myometrium in preparation for intense contractions at birth, maintain the endometrial lining so menstruation does not occur, inhibit uterine contractions during pregnancy, and help form a thick mucus plug over the cervix to inhibit uterine infections.

The two umbilical arteries and single umbilical vein are considered part of the embryonic circulation, meaning the umbilical vein carries blood *toward* the embryonic heart and the umbilical arteries carry blood *away* from the embryonic heart and back to the placenta. Because the exchange of nutrients by the placenta requires a functional embryonic heart, the placenta and umbilical vessels do not become fully functional until the embryonic heart develops at about five weeks. Until then the developing chorion supplies the nutrient needs of the embryo by diffusion.

**RECAP**

Four extra-embryonic membranes serve varying functions: (1) the amnion cushions the fetus and preserves it from dehydration; (2) the allantois forms blood vessels of the umbilical cord; (3) the yolk sac forms part of the digestive tract and produces fetal blood cells and reproductive germ cells; (4) and the chorion secretes hCG and forms structures that will become part of the placenta. The placenta is the site of nutrient and gas exchange between embryo and mother, and it secretes hormones. The umbilical cord joins the embryo to the placenta. ■

## The embryo develops rapidly

At three weeks the embryo is fully embedded in the endometrium, which provides it with nutrients via the developing chorion. At about this time the embryo begins to take shape as cells of the three primary tissue layers migrate to other locations and begin to form the rudimentary organs and organ systems. First a small groove called the primitive streak appears in the flat, round embryonic disk, and the embryonic disk begins to elongate along one axis (Figure 21.9).

Next, a neural groove of ectoderm forms that will later become the brain and spinal cord. Meanwhile, the mesoderm begins to separate into several segments called somites that will become most of the bone, muscle, and skin. Prominent bumps called the pharyngeal arches appear at one end; they are destined to become part of the face, neck, and mouth. By the end of week four the heart is beginning to

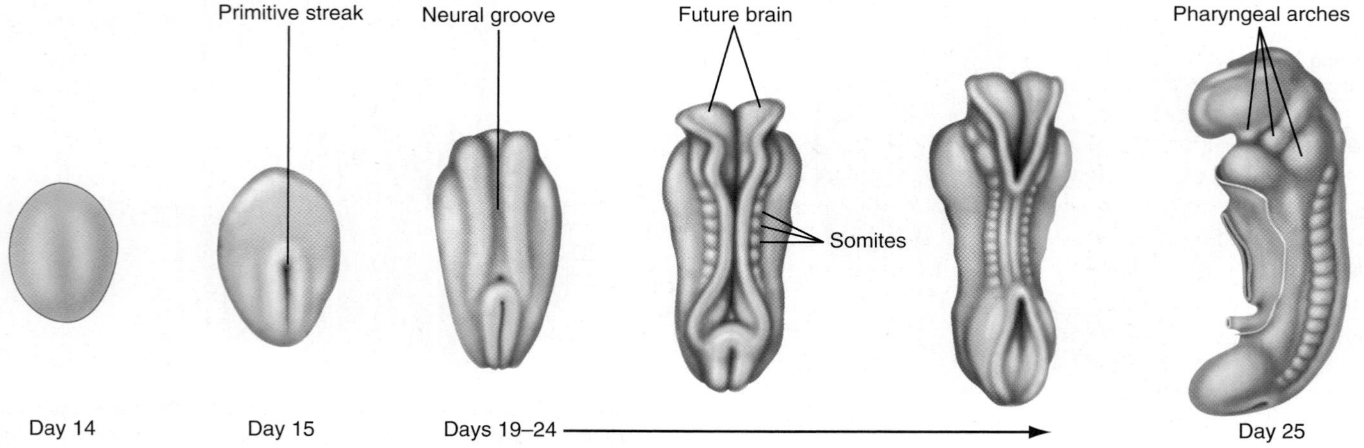


**Figure 21.9 Embryonic development during the third and early fourth week.** Day 14 represents the flat embryonic disk as it would look from above (from the amniotic cavity). On day 15 the embryo begins to elongate and the primitive streak of ectoderm appears. Days 19–23 mark the appearance of a neural groove of ectoderm. Somites develop in the mesoderm that will become bone, muscle, and skin. By days 24–25, pharyngeal arches that will contribute to structures of the head become visible. The embryo on days 24 and 25 is viewed from the side.

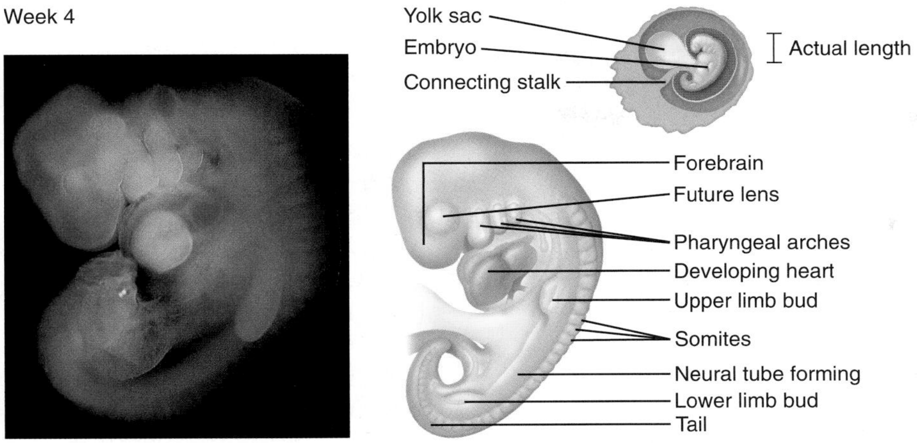


**Figure 21.10 Week four of development.** The future head is prominent, the position of the eyes becomes apparent, the heart and neural tube are forming, and limb buds appear.

develop, the head begins to take shape, the position of the eyes becomes apparent, the neural groove has closed into a neural tube, and four limb buds appear (Figure 21.10).

The patterns of cell differentiation and organism morphogenesis are so consistent among vertebrates that even an expert would have a hard time telling whether a four-week-old human embryo was destined to become a fish, a mammal, or a bird. Because early differentiation and morphogenesis follow such a common path, it is likely that these patterns developed early in the history of the vertebrates.

Weeks five through eight mark the transition from a general vertebrate form to one that is recognizably human. The head grows in relation to the rest of the body, the eyes and ears are visible, and the four limbs are formed with distinct fingers and toes. A cartilaginous skeleton forms. The heart and circulatory system complete their development and the umbilical cord and placenta become functional, so that now blood circulates throughout the fetus. However, the blood cells for the fetal blood are produced by the yolk sac because the blood-forming tissues of the fetus are not yet mature. Nutrients and wastes are now exchanged more efficiently and in greater quantities. The tail regresses. At the end of the embryonic period, the embryo is an inch long and weighs just 1 gram (Figure 21.11).

Although it is difficult to estimate how many embryos fail to survive to the end of the embryonic period, some estimates place the number as high as 20%. Spontaneous termination of pregnancy followed by expulsion of the embryo is called a **miscarriage,** or spontaneous abortion. Sometimes a woman never even realizes she was pregnant. Miscarriages are probably nature's way of weeding out embryos with genetic disorders that might prevent them from developing normally.

**RECAP**

Embryonic development is rapid and dramatic. By the fifth week the embryo is becoming distinctly human in form, and by eight weeks it is an inch long. The natural rate of miscarriages through eight weeks of development may be as high as 20%. ■

## 21.5 Gender development begins at six weeks

Male and female external and internal genitalia do not begin to develop until about six weeks. Until that time the embryo remains "sexually indifferent," meaning that it still has the capacity to develop into either a male or a female. However, the final outcome (male or female) is not in doubt; it was determined at the moment of conception by the single sperm that fertilized the egg.

The development of either male or female external genitalia is shown in Figure 21.12 on page 492. By six weeks an undifferentiated urogenital groove has developed, topped by a bud and surrounded by labioscrotal swellings. After six

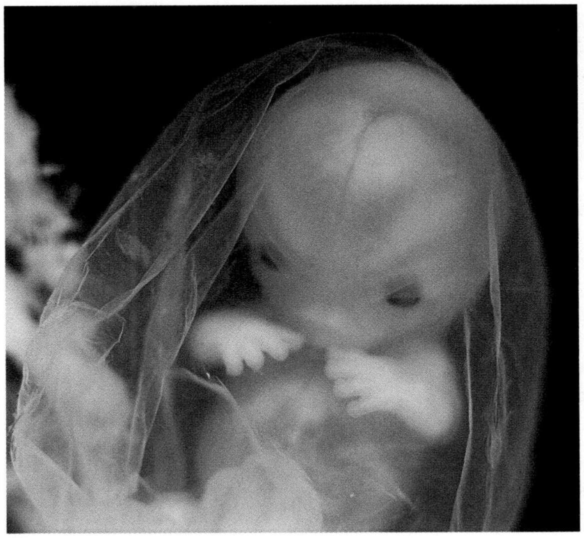

**Figure 21.11 Week eight of development.** The embryo is now distinctly human in appearance. The face, limbs, hands, and feet are well formed. The circulatory system is functional, and blood now circulates throughout the embryo and to and from the placenta. Actual length is 1 inch.

# Directions in Science

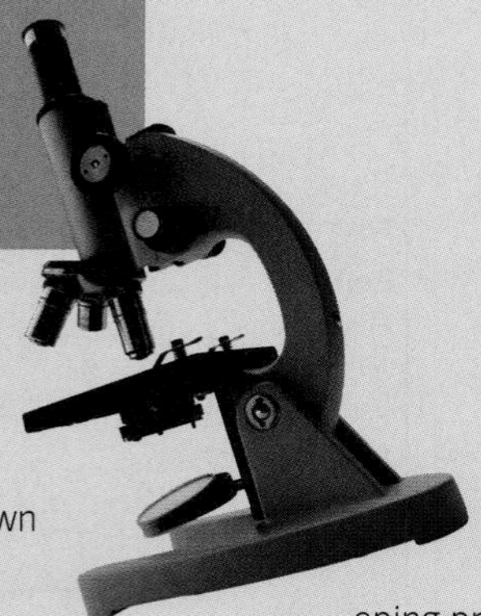

## Prenatal Diagnostic Techniques

Fewer than 40 years ago, when a woman became pregnant there was little that the parents or physician could do except hope that the baby would be born healthy. Late in pregnancy the physician could hear the fetal heartbeat, but that was about it. Given that nearly 7% of all newborns had a birth defect of some kind, pregnancy was a stressful period of wait-and-see.

The 1960s brought a new technique called **amniocentesis** (see Figure 1), in which a long hollow needle is inserted through the abdominal wall to take a sample of amniotic fluid. The technique takes advantage of the fact that fetal cells are sloughed off into amniotic fluid.

Amniocentesis generally is performed during the second trimester, between the 15th and 17th weeks of pregnancy. The harvested fetal cells are then grown in the laboratory for up to four weeks until there are enough of them to examine the chromosomes and perform certain biochemical tests.

Amniocentesis is relatively safe and may be recommended if there is a family history of a genetic disease or the risk of Down syndrome. Nearly 40 different fetal defects can be diagnosed using amniocentesis. A drawback is that test results may not be available until the middle of the second trimester, close to the time that termination of pregnancy will no longer be an option.

In the 1970s came **ultrasound,** a major advance in fetal imaging. Ultrasound does not test for genetic diseases. Rather, it provides a safe way to determine whether the fetus is developing properly by giving a real-time image of the fetus within the womb. High-frequency (ultrasound) sound waves aimed at the abdomen and uterus rebound when they hit hard tissues in the fetus. A computer analyzes and converts the reflected waves into an image.

Also in the 1970s, **chorionic villi sampling** (see Figure 2) was developed for collecting cells of the chorionic villi that originate from embryonic tissue. A thin flexible tube is inserted through the vagina and into the uterus under the guidance of an ultrasound image. When the tip of the tube reaches the

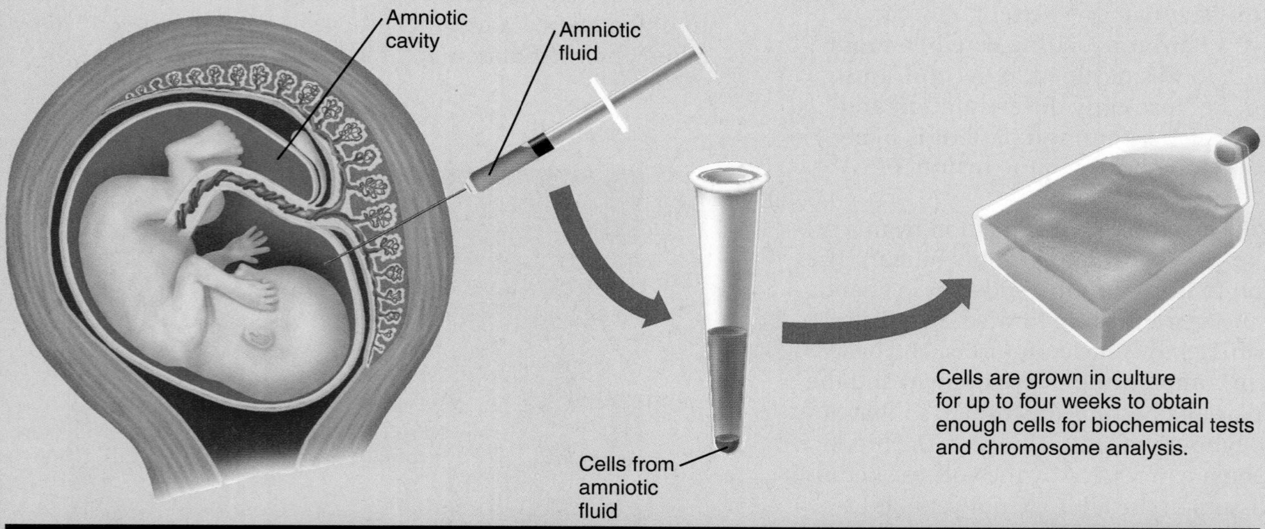


**Figure 1** Amniocentesis.

weeks, the presence of a Y chromosome causes the embryo to start developing male sexual characteristics. The process begins when a gene on the Y chromosome called SRY (for Sex-determining Region Y) is switched on. SRY encodes for a protein called *testis-determining factor* that directs the initial development of the testes internally. Shortly thereafter the testes begin to secrete testosterone, which in turn stimulates the development of the male internal ducts and external genitalia. (The embryonic testes also secrete a second hormone called anti-Mullerian hormone that suppresses the development of the female internal and external genitalia.) In males the undifferentiated urogenital groove closes up to become the urethra within the penis. The penis elongates, and the previously undifferentiated bud becomes the head of the penis. The urogenital swellings develop into the scrotum into which the testes later descend.

In the absence of a Y chromosome, female internal and external genitalia develop and the embryo becomes a female.

chorion, a small sample of chorionic villi tissue is taken for chromosomal and biochemical analysis.

The great advantage of chorionic villi sampling is that it can be done as early as five weeks of pregnancy. Because there is a slight but real risk of injury to the embryo, the technique is recommended only when a family history indicates a risk of genetic defects.

When information cannot be obtained by amniocentesis or the information is inconclusive, *percutaneous umbilical blood sampling (PUBS)*, a technique for collecting fetal blood directly from the umbilical cord, may be performed. Under ultrasound guidance, a needle is guided through the abdominal wall and into a vein in the umbilical cord. Cord blood obtained by PUBS can be tested for sickle-cell anemia, hemophilia, anemia, and Rh problems, as well as genetic abnormalities. The risk of miscarriage is slightly higher than with amniocentesis or chorionic villi sampling, so again, this technique may be advisable only when there is a known risk of certain diseases.

An experimental technique called *preimplantation genetic diagnosis (PGD)* screens embryos for specific genetic conditions such as cystic fibrosis, sickle-cell anemia, Tay-Sachs disease, and Franconi's anemia (see the Current Issue box in Chapter 16). This technique can be done only on embryos that are outside the body. First, eggs are harvested from a woman's uterus and fertilized in the laboratory. After two to three days, at the 6- to 10-cell stage, a single cell is removed from each embryo and tested for the presence of a gene that will give rise to a certain genetic disorder. An embryo that is free of this gene can then be inserted into the woman's uterus, where hopefully it will implant, leading to a normal pregnancy.

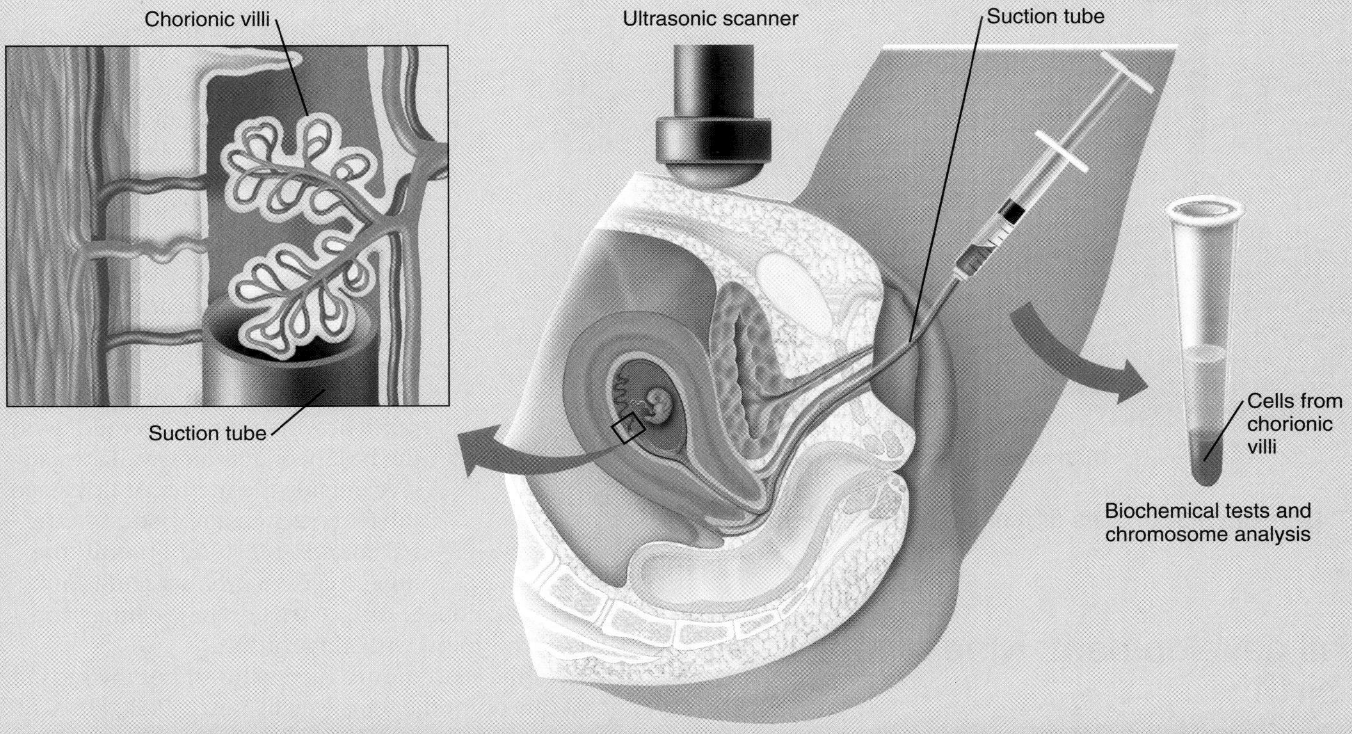


**Figure 2** Chorionic villi sampling.

The urogenital groove expands to become the vagina, and the undifferentiated bud becomes the clitoris. Meanwhile the ovaries, fallopian tubes, and uterus all develop internally. The development of female internal and external genitalia is the "default" condition; it occurs in the absence of any hormones, whenever a Y chromosome is *not* present. In other words, gender is determined by the presence or absence of a Y chromosome, not by whether the embryo has one or two X chromosomes.

**RECAP**

Gender development begins at about 6 weeks. The presence of a Y chromosome signals the embryo to develop into a male; the absence of a Y chromosome causes the embryo to develop into a female. ■

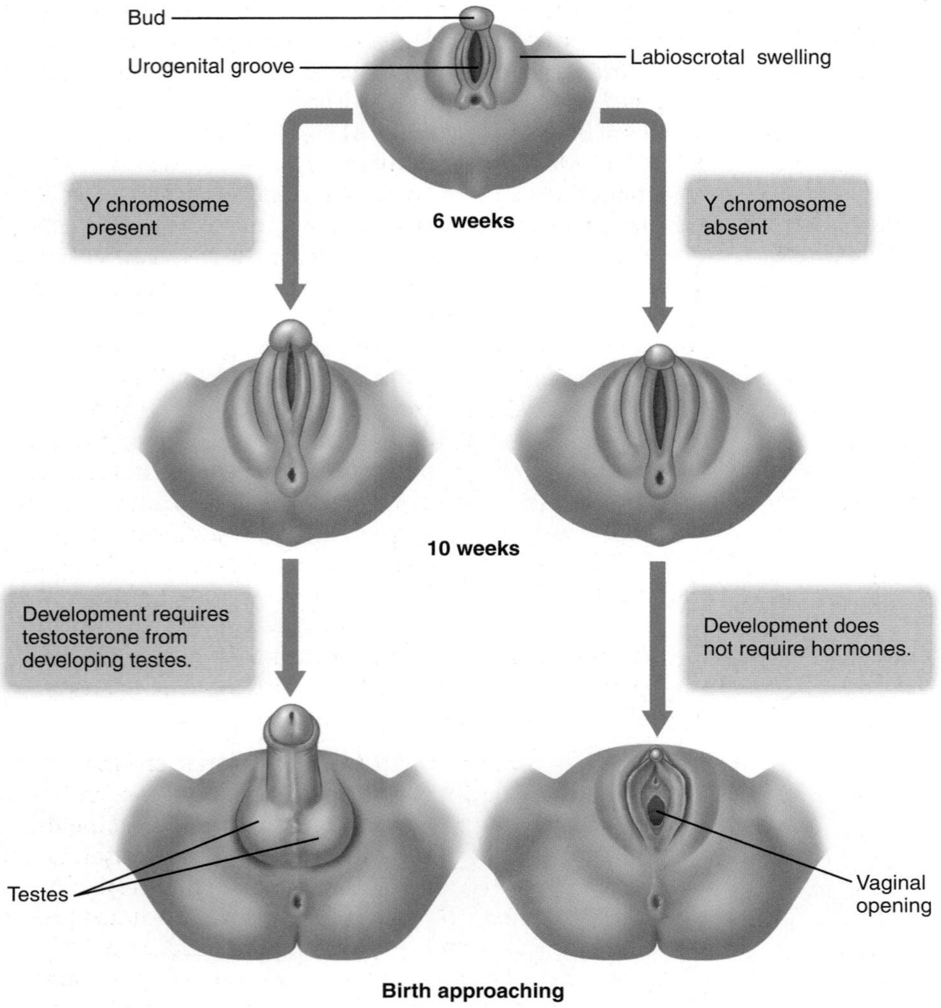


**Figure 21.12 Development of male or female external genitalia.**

## 21.6 Fetal development: Nine weeks to birth

After the eighth week the developing human is called a fetus. This is the time when fetal organ systems begin to function and the bones start to calcify. The mother, too, undergoes obvious changes in physical shape. Next, we examine each of these stages in detail.

### Months three and four

During the third month the kidneys develop sufficiently for the fetus to begin eliminating some wastes as urine into the amniotic fluid. The limbs are well developed, the cartilaginous skeleton begins to be replaced with bone, and the teeth form. The spleen participates briefly in the production of red blood cells, a job that will soon be taken over by the liver and bone marrow. The liver begins to function, and the genitalia are well enough developed that sex can be determined. The end of the third month marks the end of the first trimester.

During the fourth month the liver and bone marrow begin producing blood cells. The face takes on nearly its final form as the eyes and ears become fixed in their permanent locations (Figure 21.13). In the female fetus, follicles are forming in the ovaries.

Overall growth is rapid during this time. By the end of the fourth month the fetus is already 6 inches long and weighs about 170 grams (6 ounces).

### Months five and six

By the fifth month the nervous system and skeletal muscles are sufficiently mature for the fetus to begin moving. These movements are called quickening, and the mother may feel them for the first time. The skin, which is well formed although red and wrinkled, is covered by soft downy hair. The heartbeat is now loud enough to be heard with a stethoscope. Skeletal hardening continues.

The sixth month marks the first point at which the fetus could, with the best neonatal care available, survive outside the uterus. At this stage the fetus seems to respond to external sounds. Most importantly, the lungs begin to produce surfactant, the substance that reduces surface tension in the lungs and permits the alveoli to fill with air at birth.

The end of the sixth month marks the end of the second trimester. At this point the fetus weighs nearly 700 grams, or approximately 1½ pounds.

### Months seven through nine

The seventh through ninth months (the third trimester) are a period of continued rapid growth and maturation in preparation for birth. The eyes open and close spontaneously and can be conditioned to respond to environmental sounds. Activity increases, as if the fetus is seeking a more comfortable position in the increasingly restrictive space of the uterus. Usually the fetus moves to a position in which the head is positioned downward, near the cervix. The skin begins to lose some of its reddish color and its coat of downy hair. In the male the testes descend into the scrotal sac. Although neither the lungs nor the

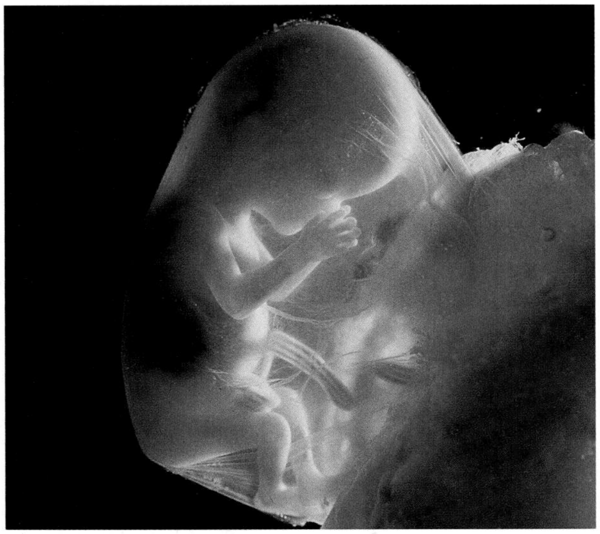

**Figure 21.13 The fetus and placenta at four months of development.** Note the amnion and the clear amniotic fluid surrounding the fetus. Actual length is 6 inches.

digestive systems have had a chance to function yet, both are now ready.

By nine months the fetus is about 20 inches long and weighs approximately 6–7½ pounds. Birth usually occurs at about 38 weeks of development.

**RECAP**

The period of fetal development extends from nine weeks to birth at 38 weeks. Growth is rapid, with the mature fetus weighing approximately 6–7½ pounds at birth. The fetus begins to move at about five months, and life outside the womb is at least possible by about six months when the lungs begin to produce surfactant. ■

## 21.7 Birth and the early postnatal period

Other than perhaps conception and death, there is no period in our lives marked by greater developmental change than the hours during and immediately after birth. Within minutes, the newborn makes the shift from relying solely on the maternal circulation for nutrient and gas exchange to depending on its own circulation and lungs. The digestive tract, too, starts to function with the first swallow of milk. Let's take a quick look at the changes that occur during birth and the postnatal ("after birth") period.

### Labor ends in delivery

Birth involves a sequence of events that we call labor (it's hard work!), which ends in the delivery of the newborn into the world.

Labor begins as a result of a series of events that is triggered by maturation of the fetal pituitary gland, which serves as the timing device to indicate that the fetus is now ready for birth.

The mature fetal pituitary gland begins to release ACTH, which stimulates the fetal adrenal gland to secrete steroid hormones that cause the placenta to increase its production of estrogen and decrease the production of progesterone. Estrogen, in turn, increases the number of oxytocin receptors and stimulates production of prostaglandins. Together, the increased estrogen, prostaglandins, and oxytocin receptors (along with the mother's oxytocin) stimulate the uterus to contract rhythmically.

A positive feedback cycle begins: rhythmic contractions of the uterus cause the release of still more oxytocin from the maternal pituitary, which increases contractions still further, and so on. As labor progresses the periods of contraction get closer together, last longer, and become stronger, creating enough force to push the fetus toward the cervix and eventually through the vagina.

The period of labor and delivery lasts about 24 hours for the first birth and slightly less time for subsequent births. Labor and delivery are divided into three phases: dilation, expulsion, and afterbirth (Figure 21.14).

- **Stage 1—dilation.** The first phase of labor can last 6–12 hours. During this time the rate, duration, and strength of contractions increase over time, pushing the head of the fetus against the cervix. The cervix itself is drawn back toward the uterus, widening the cervical opening and expelling the mucus plug. Continued pressure of the fetus against the cervix widens the cervical opening even further until eventually it is large enough to accommodate the baby's head, or about 10 centimeters. At about this time the pressure of the baby's head ruptures the amnion, releasing the amniotic fluid. This "breaking of the water" is a normal sign that delivery is proceeding. The physician keeps a close watch on the stage of dilation by measuring the degree of cervical dilation at regular intervals.
- **Stage 2—expulsion.** The period of expulsion extends from full cervical dilation through actual delivery. During this time uterine contractions strengthen and the woman experiences an intense urge to assist the expulsion with voluntary contractions as well. To make the birth easier, some women opt for a surgical incision called an episiotomy to enlarge the vaginal opening. The intense contractions push the baby slowly through the cervix, vagina, and surrounding pelvic girdle. The appearance of the baby's head at the labia is called crowning. As soon as the baby's head appears fully, an attendant removes mucus from the baby's nose and mouth to facilitate breathing. The rest of the body emerges rather quickly. When the baby has fully emerged, the umbilical cord is clamped and then cut. By this time the infant should be breathing on its own. The entire expulsion phase lasts less than an hour.

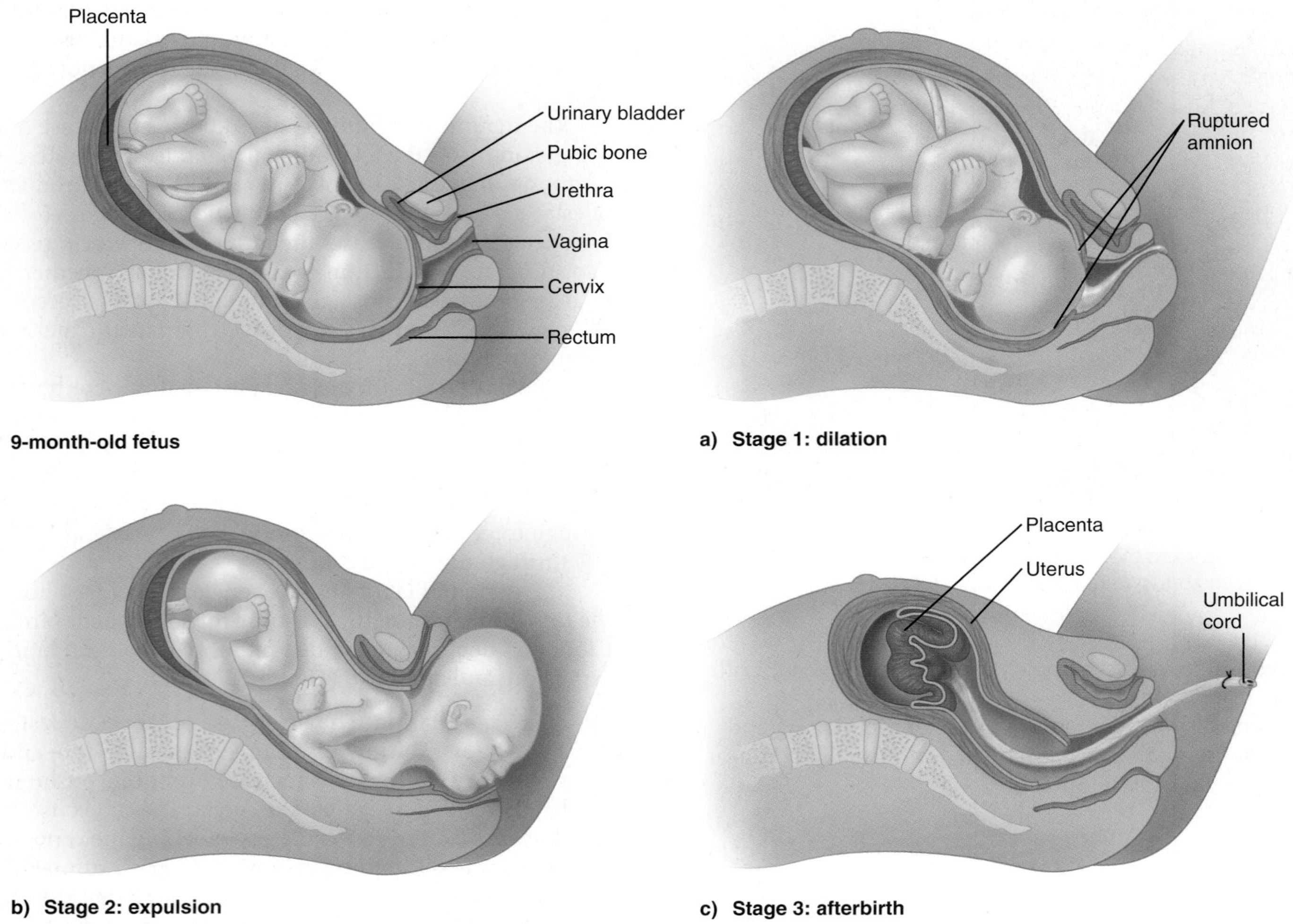


**Figure 21.14 The stages of birth.** As birth approaches, the fetus usually is positioned with the head down and toward the cervix. **(a)** Stage 1: dilation. The cervical opening widens. The amnion may break at this stage. **(b)** Stage 2: expulsion. The fetus passes headfirst through the cervical canal and the vagina. **(c)** Stage 3: afterbirth. The placenta detaches from the uterus and is expelled along with the remainder of the umbilical cord.

- **Stage 3—afterbirth.** Contractions do not stop with birth. Strong postdelivery contractions serve to detach the placenta from the uterus and expel the umbilical cord and placenta, collectively called the afterbirth. The afterbirth stage usually lasts less than half an hour after the birth of the infant.

**RECAP**

Labor and delivery take about 24 hours or less. The dilation phase is marked by widening of the cervix and increasingly frequent and strong uterine contractions. The fetus emerges in the shorter (one hour or less) expulsion phase. The placenta and umbilical cord are expelled during the afterbirth phase. ■

## Cesarean delivery: Surgical delivery of a baby

Some deliveries are not allowed to proceed as described above. Surgical delivery of a baby is called a **cesarean delivery,** or C-section. In a C-section, an incision is made through the abdominal wall and uterus so the baby can be removed quickly.

A C-section is often performed when the position or size of the fetus could make a vaginal delivery dangerous. Possible reasons include a fetus that is too large for the birth canal, improper position of the fetus with the legs near the cervix, maternal exhaustion from a long delivery, or signs of fetal distress such as an elevated fetal heart rate.

In the past, if a C-section was performed it was common practice to do all subsequent deliveries by C-section as well. Today most women who have a C-section can still opt for a vaginal delivery with the next child if they wish.

## The transition from fetus to newborn

Somewhere between the point when its head emerges and the umbilical cord is clamped, the fetus must become capable of sustaining life on its own. The first necessity is for the newborn (also called the neonate for the first 28 days) to start breathing, preferably even before its umbilical connection to the mother is severed. Second, over the first few days of life, its cardiovascular system undergoes a series of remarkable anatomical changes that reflect the loss of the placental connection for gas and nutrient exchange. The newborn is now entirely on its own.

**Taking the first breath** When the infant emerges, its lungs have never been inflated. After all, it essentially has been living underwater (more correctly, under amniotic fluid). The first inflation is critical and not all that easy. If you've ever tried to blow up a really stiff balloon, you know that it takes a lot of effort to start the inflation. The reason for this effect is that the surface tension generated by a small sphere is greater than the surface tension generated by a larger one. The first inflation in the infant is facilitated by substances called pulmonary surfactants that reduce surface tension in the lungs' alveoli.

But what causes the infant to take that first breath? During labor, the placental connection to the mother begins to separate, reducing gas exchange with the fetus. Clamping the umbilical cord stops gas exchange entirely. This situation is equivalent to someone covering your mouth and nose completely. Within seconds the carbon dioxide concentration in the fetus rises to the point that the respiratory centers in its brain stimulate respiration. With the enormous effort of one who is being smothered, the infant takes its first breath and begins to cry.

**Changes in the cardiovascular system** The fetal cardiovascular system is different from the cardiovascular system described in Chapter 8. Consider that the fetal lungs are not yet useful for gas exchange and that blood enters and leaves the fetus via the umbilical cord. Immediately after birth the umbilical circulation ceases, and pulmonary circulation becomes crucial to survival.

There are four major differences between the fetal cardiovascular system and the cardiovascular system of a newborn several weeks after birth (Figure 21.15):

- Blood enters the fetus via the umbilical vein. A small amount of umbilical vein blood flows through the liver, but most of it bypasses the liver and joins the inferior vena cava of the fetus via the ductus venosus (venous duct).
- Blood leaves the fetus via two umbilical arteries that originate from arteries in the legs.
- In the fetus there is a hole between the two atrial chambers of the heart called the foramen ovale (oval opening). The hole permits some blood to pass from right atrium to left atrium, bypassing the pulmonary circulation.
- In the fetus there is a shunt, or shortcut, from the pulmonary artery directly to the aorta called the ductus arteriosus (arterial duct). Consequently, most of the blood pumped by the right ventricle also bypasses the lungs.

Let us now follow the circulation of blood between fetus and mother and within the fetus. Oxygen-laden and nutrient-rich blood from the placenta enters the fetus via the umbilical vein. Some of the blood is carried to the developing liver either directly or via a branch of the umbilical vein that joins the hepatic portal vein. But the fetal liver is not yet fully developed and cannot handle the entire umbilical blood flow. Therefore, most of the blood bypasses the liver and is carried directly to the inferior vena cava by the ductus venosus. In the inferior vena cava, the nutrient-rich blood mixes with the venous blood of the fetus.

Most of the blood that enters the fetal heart must bypass the fetal lungs because they too are not fully developed. Some of the blood passes from the right atrium to the left atrium through the foramen ovale, and some is shunted from the pulmonary artery directly to the aorta via the ductus arteriosus.

Even though the fetal lungs are not yet functional and the digestive tract is not receiving nutrients, the aortic blood still has sufficient oxygen and nutrients (brought to the fetus via the umbilical vein) to supply all the fetal tissues. Some of the fetal arterial blood returns to the placenta via the umbilical arteries. In the placenta the blood again picks up nutrients and oxygen and gets rid of carbon dioxide generated by fetal metabolism.

The situation changes dramatically at birth, for the umbilical circulation is immediately cut off. Over time the umbilical vein, umbilical arteries, and ductus venosus regress to become vestigial connective tissue. The foramen ovale and ductus arteriosus close off in the first few days or weeks after birth as well, so that all the cardiac output passes through the lungs for efficient gas exchange. Nutrients are now absorbed by the newborn's digestive tract and pass through the liver via the hepatic portal vein. The only reminder of the intimate connection between fetus and mother is the umbilicus (navel).

## Lactation produces milk to nourish the newborn

The intimate relationship between mother and child does not end at birth, for the human infant must rely entirely on its mother (or someone else) for all its nutritional needs. During pregnancy, high concentrations of estrogen and progesterone cause the woman's breasts to enlarge in preparation for lactation (milk production). However, the breasts do not secrete milk before childbirth because estrogen and progesterone prevent the action of prolactin, the hormone that actually stimulates milk production.

During the first day or so after birth, the breasts produce a watery milk called **colostrum** that is rich in antibodies but low in fat and lactose. The antibodies help to protect the newborn until its own immune system matures. Later, the high fat and lactose content of milk help the infant to grow rapidly.

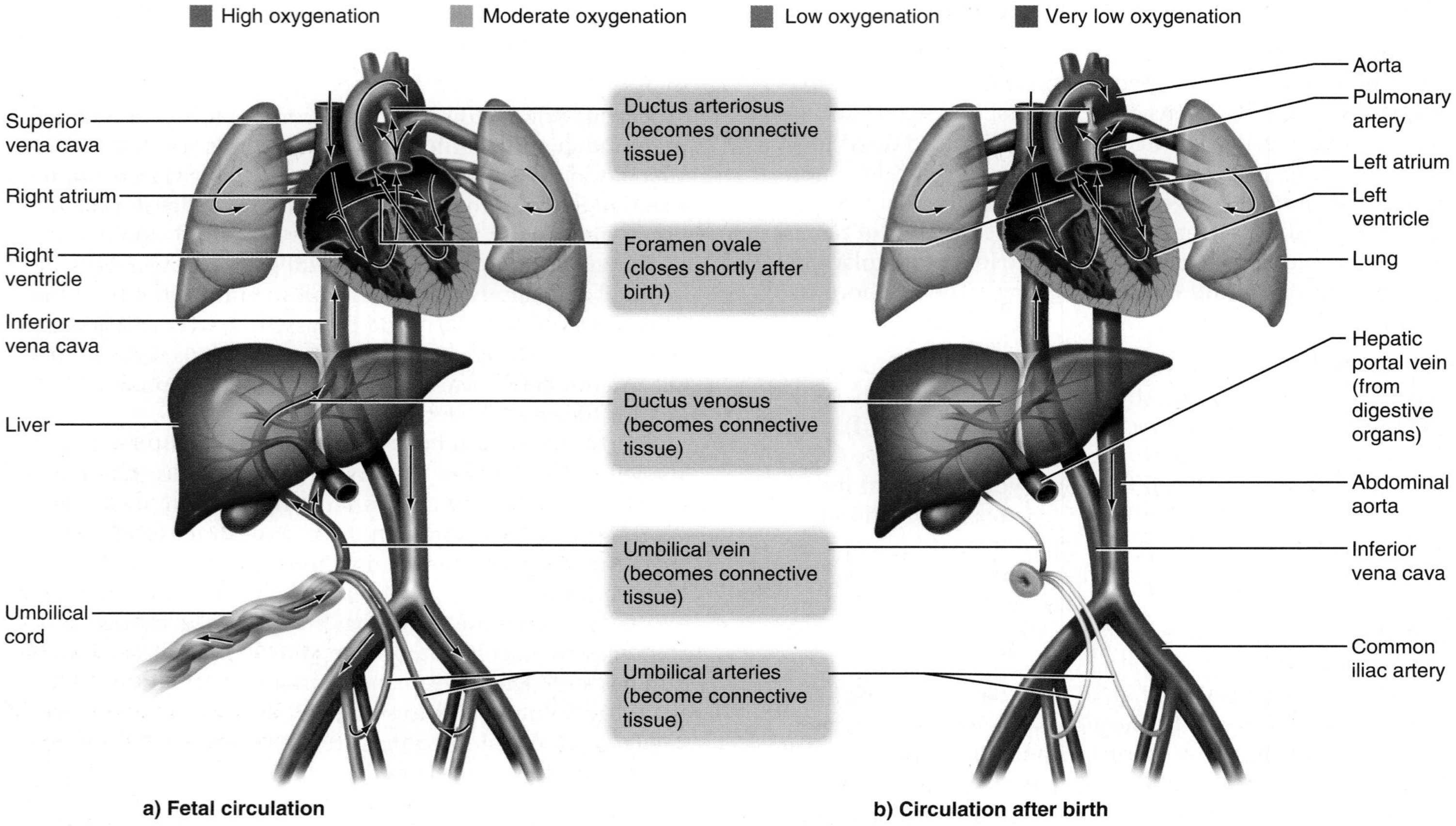


**Figure 21.15 The cardiovascular systems of the fetus and of the newborn.** In the fetus the immature lungs are not used for gas exchange, so most of the blood returning to the heart bypasses the lungs by flowing through either the foramen ovale or the ductus arteriosus. Gas exchange occurs via the placenta, so special fetal blood vessels connect the fetus to the placenta. These unique pathways for blood circulation in the fetus close shortly after birth.

A fourth hormone, oxytocin, is responsible for the contractions that deliver colostrum or milk only when needed. Oxytocin is released during childbirth and also as a result of a neural reflex every time the infant nurses. The expulsion of milk from the breast during suckling is called milk ejection.

**RECAP**

At birth a sharp increase in carbon dioxide causes the newborn to take the first breath. Shortly after birth the umbilical blood vessels and ductus arteriosus regress, and anatomical changes in the heart reroute all blood through the lungs. Prolactin stimulates lactation, and oxytocin stimulates the release of milk during suckling. ■

## 21.8 From birth to adulthood

The long process of human development continues after birth. Because development is a continuum, experts do not always agree on how to categorize its stages. Some categories may seem somewhat arbitrary, such as the distinction (if there is one) between adulthood and old age. At the risk of oversimplifying, we define the neonatal period as the first month, infancy as months 2–15, childhood as the period from infancy to adolescence, adolescence as the transitional period from childhood to adulthood (approximately 12 to 18 or 20 years of age), and adulthood as 20 years and beyond.

Table 21.2 summarizes the stages of human development. Bear in mind that these ages are approximate, intended as a guide to orient you with regard to your progression through life. We concentrate primarily on biophysical development, leaving human psychosocial and cognitive (learning) development to the fields of psychology and education. Figure 21.16 depicts the changes in body form that accompany human development to adulthood.

### The neonatal period: A helpless time

The human neonate (newborn) is fairly helpless. In particular, the nervous system and the muscular system are relatively immature at birth. Consequently, movements are uncoordinated, weak, and governed primarily by reflexes rather

**Table 21.2 A summary of the stages of human development**

| Stage | Age |
|---|---|
| *Prenatal (after fertilization)* | |
| Pre-embryo | From fertilization to 2 weeks |
| Zygote | Days 1–3 |
| Morula | Days 4–7 |
| Blastocyst | Days 8–14 |
| Embryo | Weeks 3–8 |
| Fetus | Weeks 9–40 (birth) |
| *Postnatal (after birth)* | |
| Neonate | The first month |
| Infant | Months 2–15 |
| Child | 16 months to 12 years |
| Adolescent | 12–20 years |
| Adult | Beyond 20 years |
| Old age | Aging accelerates after 40 years |

than conscious control. The neonate hardly has enough strength to hold its head up, so its head must be constantly supported whenever it is carried. The eyes are open but often they seem to wander about, unable to focus. Neonates are aware of their environment and can respond to it, but they are unable to retain any long-term memories. (What is *your* first memory?) They hear a narrower range of pitches than adults and are more sensitive to higher-pitched tones.

What neonates do best is suckle, urinate, and defecate. The digestive system can absorb the constituents of milk but is not yet ready for solid foods. The stools are soft, and defecation and urination occur as reflexes.

**RECAP**

The neonatal nervous and muscular systems are not well developed. Neonates are physically helpless and cannot form memories. ■

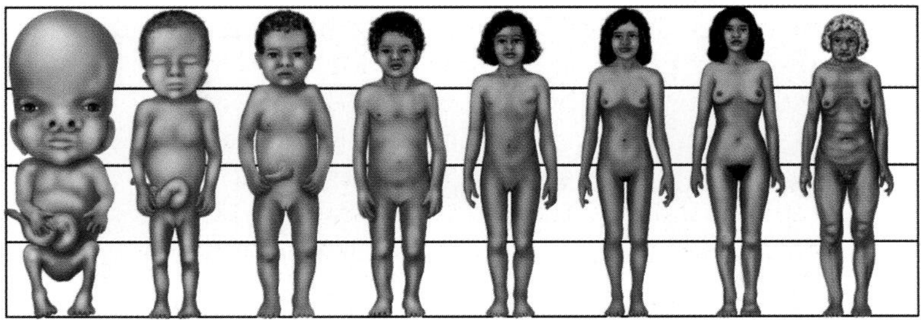


**Figure 21.16 Changes in body form and relative proportion throughout prenatal and postnatal growth and development.**

## Infancy: Rapid development and maturation of organ systems

Infancy is a time of rapid change. In just 15 months the infant more than triples in weight to about 22–24 pounds. The bones harden gradually, and there is a disproportionately large increase in muscle mass and strength. The brain also grows rapidly, with nearly half of all brain growth after birth occurring in infancy. Most of the growth occurs in the cerebral cortex, the area associated with sensory perception, motor function, speech, and learning. Most of the myelination of nerves occurs in infancy as well. The first teeth appear at about six months, and all 20 baby teeth are generally present by about one year. Most infants begin eating solid foods by about six months to a year.

By about 14 months the combined maturation of the musculoskeletal and nervous systems allows the human infant to begin to walk on its own. A rapidly growing body needs lots of rest, and infants sleep a lot. Infants can easily sleep 10 hours a night and still take several naps during the day.

The immune system consistently lags behind most other systems in its development. Most vaccinations are ineffective in infants because their immune systems cannot produce the appropriate antibodies. The schedule of vaccinations in infants and children is designed so that each vaccine is given only after the immune system becomes able to respond to that vaccine.

**RECAP**

Infancy is marked by rapid growth and continued maturation of organ systems. Infants begin to eat solid foods and to walk. The immune system develops more slowly than other organ systems. ■

## Childhood: Continued development and growth

The long period of childhood, from about 15 months to 12 years of age, involves continued growth of all systems. The brain grows to 95% of its final size during childhood. The immune system continues its slow process of maturation throughout childhood and even into adolescence. Body weight increases to an average of about 100 pounds in both boys and girls as the result of periods of slow growth interspersed with growth spurts. Both muscle strength and fine motor coordination improve.

In addition, body form alters as the long bones of the arms and legs lengthen. A lumbar curve develops in the small of the back, and abdominal musculature strengthens, so that the childhood "pot belly" disappears.

By the end of childhood the body form is distinctly adultlike, though still sexually immature. Most organ systems are fully functional or nearly so (although not necessarily their full adult size). The lone exceptions are the male and female reproductive systems, which have not yet matured.

**RECAP**

Brain growth is nearly complete by the end of childhood. Muscle strength and coordination improve, and body form changes to a more adult form. ■

### Adolescence: The transition to adulthood

One of the most challenging times of life is the transition from childhood to adulthood. The final growth spurt, one of the largest, occurs in adolescence. The growth spurt begins at different times in different individuals, so there is a wide range of normal body weights and degrees of sexual maturity in the 12- to 14-year-old age group. Rapid growth can lead to awkwardness and a temporary loss of coordination.

Both the skeletal and muscular systems experience their greatest rates of growth during adolescence. Other organs increase in size as well. Notably, the lungs more than double in mass, and the kidneys and stomach increase by more than 50%. The brain, however, gains only about 5%.

Adolescence is marked by maturation of the reproductive systems and the human sexual response, an event known as **puberty.** Puberty is defined as the onset of menstrual periods (menarche) in the female at some time between 9½ and 15½ years and by reflex discharge of semen during sleep (nocturnal emissions) in the male sometime between 11½ and 17½ years.

The concentrations of all the reproductive hormones are low in children, but they begin to rise during the period of sexual maturation (known as the pubertal period). The pubertal period is initiated by maturation of certain neurons of the hypothalamus, which begin to secrete a releasing hormone called GnRH (Gonadotropin Releasing Hormone). The initiation of GnRH secretion by the hypothalamus stimulates the secretion of luteinizing hormone (LH) and follicle-stimulating hormone (FSH) from the anterior pituitary, which in turn stimulate the production of sex hormones and the maturation of sex organs and secondary sexual characteristics.

**RECAP**

Adolescence is accompanied by a growth spurt and by maturation of the reproductive systems. Puberty begins when the hypothalamus matures and starts to secrete GnRH. ■

## 21.9 Aging takes place over time

Physiologically, at least, humans reach their peak in early adulthood at about 20 years of age. Most body systems are fairly stable from 20 to about 40, and then the process that we call aging seems to accelerate. No matter whether we exercise regularly, eat right, and in general take care of ourselves, there still seems to be at least some "natural" aging process, just like the carefully timed sequence of events that occur in human development. To be sure, exercise and a proper diet do help, but in the end we all must face the fact that we will not be the same at age 80 as we were at 20. The big question, of course, is why we age and whether the aging process can be halted or at least slowed.

**Aging** is the process of change associated with the passage of time (Figure 21.17). Although the word does not necessarily imply deterioration (after all, some wines get better as they age), human aging invariably leads in that direction. Aging as we use the term in biology could be used synonymously with senescence, the progressive deterioration of multiple organs and organ systems over time. Human senescence (or aging) has no apparent or obvious cause—that is, it cannot be blamed on a particular disease or event.

A common statistic is that the average life span in the United States has increased from 47 years in 1900 to the upper 70s today. Does that mean we are aging more slowly now? Not at all. **Longevity**—how long a person lives—does not depend solely on the aging process. Most experts believe that our increase in longevity is largely due to a reduction in deaths by accident or disease, not to a slowdown in the aging process itself.

In fact, it appears that nothing we have done (so far!) has decelerated the aging process. If we could solve every known disease and prevent every accidental death, would we still come face to face with a natural endpoint of life? Nobody knows for sure, but so far the answer seems to be a qualified yes. No one has beaten the aging process yet, and there are very few individuals with documented ages of over 100 years.

### What causes aging?

There are three hypotheses regarding the causes of aging. The first is that there is some sort of internal genetically determined program that dictates the timing of cell death. The second is that accumulated cell damage or errors eventually limit cells' ability to repair themselves. A third hypothesis is that the decline in function of a critical body system may

**a) Mick Jagger at age 23.** **b) Mick Jagger at age 60.**

**Figure 21.17 Aging. (a)** Rolling Stones' Mick Jagger at age 23, in 1967. **(b)** Jagger at age 60 on December 12, 2003, the night he became "Sir Mick."

lead to the parallel senescence of other systems. There is evidence to support each hypothesis.

**An internal cellular program counts cell divisions** It has long been known that even when cells are grown under laboratory conditions that are ideal for cell growth and division, most cells will not continue to divide indefinitely. Most cells go through approximately 50–90 successive divisions and then just stop. Cancer cells are the exception, for they will continue to divide indefinitely.

Why do normal cells stop dividing? Apparently every strand of DNA ends with a long tail of disposable bits of DNA called **telomeres** that do not code for any genes. The telomeres are like a roll of tickets, and the idea is that every time the DNA is replicated prior to cell division a ticket (telomere) is removed (Figure 21.18). When the cell runs out of telomeres, cell division begins to eat away at vital genetic information. Eventually enough vital genetic information is lost that the cell stops dividing and dies.

However, cancer cells manufacture an enzyme called telomerase that builds new telomeres to replace the ones lost during cell division. There has been a lot of excitement about telomerase lately as a result of these findings. Some researchers have even suggested that telomerase may be the magic bullet that could reverse or prevent the aging process, or that an antitelomerase substance might offer the cure for cancer.

These ideas remain far-fetched at the moment; understanding why a single cell stops dividing does not tell us how to arrest the aging process at the level of the whole body. After all, aging is not just a decline in cell division but in cell function as well.

**Cells become damaged beyond repair** The second hypothesis holds that over time, accumulated damage to DNA and errors in DNA replication become so great that they can no longer be countered by the cell's normal repair mechanisms. The damage is thought to be caused by certain toxic by-products of metabolism, such as oxygen free radicals. Eventually, like a ticking time bomb, the damage becomes too great to allow survival.

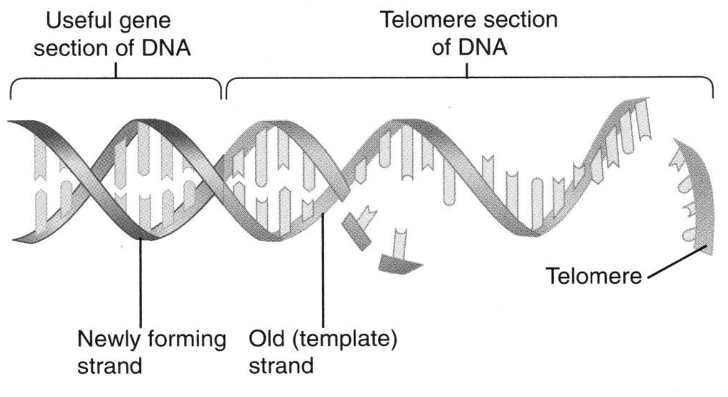


**Figure 21.18 Telomeres and aging.** Short terminal segments of DNA called telomeres are removed each time the DNA is replicated. As a result, the new strand will be shorter than the original strand. When all telomeres are gone, further cell divisions erode the useful genes.

According to proponents of this hypothesis, how long cells live is a function of the balance between how often damage occurs and how much of it can be repaired. Cells that undergo frequent injury and are slow to repair the damage have shorter lives than cells that are rarely damaged and repair themselves efficiently.

This hypothesis is supported by the finding that severe caloric restriction in certain experimental animals prolongs life. One possibility is that by lowering body temperature just a little, caloric restriction may slow metabolism and reduce the rate at which damaging metabolic by-products form. Some people believe that taking antioxidant vitamins may slow the aging process and prolong life, but there is not yet enough long-term evidence to know for sure if this is true.

**Aging is a whole-body process** Why does aging seem to happen to virtually all body systems at once, instead of just one or two systems? The third hypothesis of aging is that because all the organ systems in a complex organism are interdependent, a decline in the function of any one of them eventually impairs the function of the others.

For example, a decline in the secretion of growth hormone by the endocrine system could well tip the balance away from growth and replacement and toward a net loss of cells or organ function. Impaired function of the cardiovascular system would affect nutrient delivery to and waste removal from every cell in the body. A critical system in terms of aging may turn out to be the immune system. Indeed, the elderly have a higher incidence of cancer than the young, which may indicate that the immune system is not recognizing damaged cells as efficiently as it once did.

It is also possible that aging is due to a specific type of tissue change that affects many organ systems at once. One hallmark of aging is that a certain type of protein cross-linking increases with age. This cross-linking could contribute to multiple aging processes, ranging from decreased elasticity of tendons and ligaments to functional changes in lungs, heart, and blood vessels. Of course, this hypothesis still leaves unanswered the question of what initiates the aging process at the cellular level.

**RECAP**

Aging is a complex process that is still poorly understood. It appears that most cells are limited in how many times they can divide, and that damage may accumulate in cells until they no longer function properly. At the whole-organism level, declines in function of one organ or system may eventually impair other organ systems. ■

## Body systems age at different rates

What actually happens during aging is fairly well documented, even if we don't know exactly why. Next we describe important developments in each organ system.

**Musculoskeletal system and skin** Bone and muscle mass begin to decrease in early adulthood. Bone loss is more marked in women than in men, especially after menopause. The decline in muscle mass is a combination of a loss of muscle cells and a decrease in the diameter of remaining cells. By age 80 the average person has lost 30% of his or her muscle mass, and strength declines accordingly. Often the joints become stiff and painful because they secrete less joint fluid. Ligaments and tendons become less elastic.

The skin becomes thinner, less elastic, and wrinkled. There are fewer sweat glands, so it becomes harder to adjust to warm temperatures. Pigmentation may change as well, with the appearance of pigmented blotches called liver spots.

**Cardiovascular and respiratory systems** Lung tissue becomes less elastic, decreasing lung capacity. The heart walls become slightly stiffer due to an increase in the ratio of collagen to muscle, with the result that an aging heart generates less force. Blood vessels also lose elasticity, so the systolic pressure and pulse pressure may rise in elderly people. Overall there is a reduced capacity for aerobic exercise as aging progresses.

**Immune system** The thymus decreases to only 10% of its maximum size by age 60, and so there are fewer T cells. The activity, but not the number, of B cells declines as well. Wound healing slows, and susceptibility to infections increases—in the elderly, even the flu can become life-threatening. In addition the immune system fails to recognize "self" as well as it once did, leading to higher rates of autoimmune disorders.

**Nervous and sensory systems** Neurons in most areas of the brain do not divide in adults, so neurons that are lost throughout life generally are not replaced. The brain shrinks only slightly, however, because the neurons that remain tend to increase their connections with each other. Nevertheless, brain and sensory function do decline, in part because of degenerative changes that occur within the cell bodies of the remaining neurons. Virtually every neural activity is affected, including balance, motor skills, hearing, sight, smell, and taste. In addition to neural changes, sensory organs change as well. For example, hair cells in the inner ear stiffen, reducing hearing, and the lens of the eye stiffens, making it more difficult to focus on near objects. As a result of these many changes, elderly people become prone to injury. In addition, they may fail to eat properly because food seems less appealing.

**Reproductive and endocrine systems** Female reproductive capacity ceases when a woman reaches menopause, the cessation of menstruation, in her late 40s or early 50s. Menopause occurs because the ovaries lose their responsiveness to LH and FSH and slowly reduce their secretion of estrogen. The onset of menopause may be gradual, with menstrual periods becoming irregular over several years.

The symptoms of menopause are variable. As a result of the decline in estrogen, some women experience "hot flashes" (periods of sweating and uncomfortable warmth). There is a tendency for vaginal lubrication to decline after menopause, making intercourse potentially less comfortable. Mood swings are not uncommon. However, female sexual desire (libido) may be undiminished because the source of female androgens is the adrenal glands, not the ovaries. After menopause, women are at increased risk for cardiovascular disease and osteoporosis.

Hormone replacement therapy is sometimes prescribed for postmenopausal women to reduce menopausal symptoms and other health problems. However, new evidence indicates that hormone replacement therapy itself may be risky (see the Directions in Science box).

Men exhibit a long, slow decline in the number of viable sperm as they age. In addition, after age 50 men may take longer to achieve an erection. Nevertheless, both sexes can and do remain sexually active into old age.

The rate of decline of various components of the endocrine system varies widely. Notably, the secretion of growth hormone decreases substantially. However, there is not an appreciable decline in renin, TSH, ACTH, or ADH.

**Digestion and nutrition** The digestive system continues to function well except that some vitamins are not absorbed as efficiently. Nutritional requirements decline somewhat due to slower cellular metabolism, smaller muscle mass, and, often, less physical activity. Adequate nutrition can be a problem if the elderly fail to eat a balanced diet. Tooth loss varies widely among individuals, but people who have lost teeth may find it harder to eat fruit and other healthy but fibrous foods.

The liver's ability to detoxify and remove drugs from the body declines significantly. As a result, elderly people often require smaller doses of medications to achieve the appropriate therapeutic blood concentration.

**Urinary system** Kidney mass declines, and both blood flow and filtration rate may fall by as much as 50% by age 80. However, there is normally such a tremendous reserve of renal functional capacity that the decline is usually of little consequence. The elderly do lose some capacity to respond to extreme dehydration or overhydration, but otherwise the kidneys carry out their functions rather well.

The primary problem in men is usually prostate hypertrophy. The enlarged (hypertrophic) prostate presses against the ureter, making urination difficult. In women the most common problem is incontinence due to a weakened urethral sphincter.

**RECAP**

The actual pattern of aging in various organ systems is well documented even if we don't fully understand the underlying causes. All organs and organ systems decline in function with advancing age, though not necessarily at the same rate. ■

## Aging well

It would be easy to get depressed after reading the long list of declines in function that accompany aging. Bear in mind that not all of these developments occur to the same degree in everyone, nor do they all occur at the same age. The effects

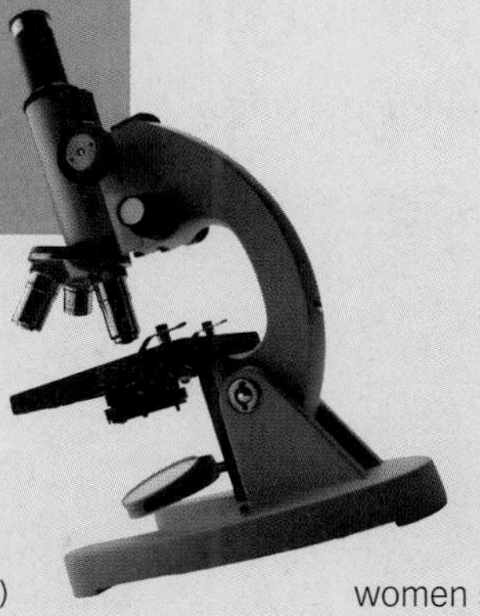

## Hormone Replacement Therapy: Helpful or Harmful?

During menopause, women's natural levels of the hormones estrogen and progesterone fall. After menopause, women have a greater incidence of heart disease, osteoporosis, cancer, and other health problems. Given these observations, it might seem logical that replenishing the hormones would be beneficial. But *is* hormone replacement therapy (HRT) beneficial?

The first estrogen pill came on the market in 1942. Doctors soon began prescribing estrogen for women at menopause and afterward, not only to relieve some of the symptoms of menopause—such as hot flashes and vaginal dryness—but also to promote long-term cardiovascular health and protect against osteoporosis. One drug company advertising campaign described estrogen as a "youth pill," implying that it would stave off wrinkles, depression, and the aging process in general. A 1966 book, *Feminine Forever,* advocated HRT for all postmenopausal women and dismissed any woman who did not take hormones as a "prematurely aging castrate."

Were the alleged health benefits of HRT supported by good scientific evidence? Not always. There *were* studies that concluded that women who took hormones seemed healthier than women who didn't. However, many of these studies were not well designed. In some studies the women were not randomly assigned to an experimental group or a control group—they decided on their own whether to take hormones. Consequently, factors in addition to the hormone therapy may have affected the outcome.

By the 1970s evidence was mounting that HRT with estrogen alone, known as unopposed estrogen, increased the risk of endometrial cancer. The addition of progesterone seemed to have a protective effect, so physicians began prescribing estrogen and progesterone together. (Unopposed estrogen therapy was still advised for women who had undergone a hysterectomy, as endometrial cancer would no longer be a concern.) However, questions about the benefits of long-term HRT began to mount when several studies in the 1980s failed to show that HRT was protective against cardiovascular disease and that estrogen might be linked to breast cancer.

In 1991 the National Heart, Lung, and Blood Institute launched the Women's Health Initiative (WHI) to investigate the most common causes of death, disability, and impaired quality of life in older women. Among its many studies were two randomized clinical trials, one to evaluate the long-term effects of estrogen-plus-progesterone therapy, and the other to evaluate the long-term effects of unopposed estrogen. Because it was designed to answer many questions about the health of older women, the WHI study was large (161,000 women) and long-term (scheduled to last 15 years).

The results of the WHI studies were a decided shock. After just five years, the women on estrogen-plus-progesterone showed a 26% increase in breast cancer, a 29% increase in heart attacks, and a 41% increase in strokes compared to those taking the placebo. They also had twice the incidence of blood clots in their legs and lungs, and twice the rate of dementia including Alzheimer's disease. The HRT users did experience some benefits—a 37% decrease in colorectal cancer and 34% fewer hip fractures. Nevertheless, the trial was discontinued in 2002 because the risks already appeared to outweigh the benefits for women who were otherwise healthy. The WHI also stopped the unopposed-estrogen trial early because the estrogen users showed a greater incidence of stroke compared to the control group, even though unopposed estrogen therapy did lower the risk of hip fracture and had little effect on the breast cancer rate.

Many postmenopausal women stopped taking HRT after the WHI reports came out, and prescriptions for HRT hormones fell dramatically. Significantly, the next year the incidence of breast cancer in the U.S. dropped by 6%. Some researchers still maintain that HRT may have long-term benefits in younger women, depending on the dose and the hormone administered. For example, studies have shown that mice receiving estradiol replacement therapy via subcutaneous (beneath the skin) implants consistently have lower rates of atherosclerosis than mice receiving no estradiol. In contrast, most human HRT pills flood the body with periodic bursts of hormones, including progesterone. Would continuous low-dose estradiol alone offer any long-term benefit? The other important factor is age: WHI participants were 63 on average at the beginning of the study. Detailed analysis of the WHI unopposed-estrogen data showed that participants aged 50 to 59 experienced *fewer* heart attacks and deaths from cardiovascular disease than comparably aged participants who took the placebo.

A new study, the Kronos Early Estrogen Prevention Study, will investigate whether beginning hormone therapy at an earlier age could protect postmenopausal women against atherosclerosis and heart disease. It will also compare the effects of administering estrogen via an oral pill versus continuous low-dose estradiol through a skin patch. It may be several years before the results are known.

As the HRT saga reminds us, science is a continuous process of discovery and rediscovery. Controversies and disagreements are healthy for science, for they lead to more refined hypotheses, more rigorous experiments, and ultimately more accurate information. It's just science at work. Stay tuned.

**Figure 21.19 Aging well.** Although it is not known for certain whether exercise and proper diet actually delay the aging process, they do improve performance and may provide an enhanced sense of wellness throughout life.

of aging are normal events in our long and exciting journey through life.

Will a healthy lifestyle that includes exercise and a proper diet slow the aging process? The answer is far from certain. However, regular exercise and healthy nutrition can certainly help us age better. Throughout human history, longevity has been determined primarily by the prevalence of disease, not by the "natural" length of a human life span (if indeed there is one). Exercise and a healthy diet improve cardiovascular and skeletomuscular fitness and reduce your risk of major killers such as cancer and cardiovascular disease. A healthy lifestyle also improves the quality of life, providing a heightened sense of well-being and increased energy and vigor (Figure 21.19).

With these benefits it really doesn't matter whether a healthy lifestyle can extend the "natural" human life span from 100 to, say, 105. If you can't live forever, you can at least age well and gracefully.

**RECAP**

Even if the aging process cannot be stopped, it is certainly possible to improve human health and wellness throughout life. Regular exercise and healthy nutrition are important factors in aging well. ■

## 21.10 Death is the final transition

The final transition in the journey of life is death. In terms of human biology, it is as natural as life itself.

Death is defined as the cessation of life. The death of a complex organism such as a human being is not necessarily accompanied by the immediate death of all its organs or cells. Death occurs when an organ system that is essential for life in the short term fails to function, making it impossible to sustain the life of other systems.

The critical organ systems whose failures lead to death very quickly are the brain (because it controls respiration), the respiratory system (without oxygen, life cannot be sustained), and the cardiovascular system (without oxygen and nutrient delivery to all cells, life ends). Failure of other organs with more long-term functions, such as the kidneys or digestive system, does not necessarily kill immediately. You can live without either of these systems for days as long as their loss does not cause one of the critical systems to fail.

The challenge of defining the precise moment of death, then, is that all of the organ systems don't necessarily die at the same time. Death is a process that begins with the failure of certain life-critical organ systems and then proceeds through the death of other organ systems, organs, and cells until the very last of the body's 100 trillion cells is no longer alive. That could take hours, days, or (with the assistance of life-support systems) even years.

Although death may occur gradually, our society requires a practical way to define the moment at which an individual dies. We need a definition of death so the living can begin to grieve and make plans, and so health care workers can stop the medical treatments that sustain life. We need a legal definition so that the police and courts can make a distinction between assault and murder, and so that estates can be settled. A precise definition of death is especially important because organs that might still be alive can be transplanted into another person and save a life.

Legal and medical criteria for declaring a person dead vary according to state law. Basically, all such criteria attempt to define the moment when, to the best of our knowledge and abilities, the person no longer has even a remote possibility of sustaining life. In general they define death as either (1) *irreversible cessation of circulatory and respiratory functions,* or (2) *irreversible cessation of all functions of the entire brain, including the brain stem.* Note that the definitions focus on critical systems that we cannot live without for more than a few minutes.

The key, of course, is the word "irreversible." Usually it is easy to tell when a person has had no respiration or blood flow for 10 minutes or so, long enough to cause brain death. Brain death alone, especially in a person on cardiopulmonary life support, is harder to define. Medical professionals generally run down a checklist of criteria that must be met in order to declare a person's brain nonfunctional, and even then they usually repeat the tests 6–12 hours later before they are willing to declare irreversible brain death. Even for the medical profession, the final transition in life can be difficult to define.

**RECAP**

Death is the termination of life. In a complex organism it is a process that can be gradual or brief. Death starts with the failure of one or more critical organ systems and ends ultimately with the inability to maintain an internal environment consistent with cellular life. ■

# Current Issue

## Who Should Make Life and Death Decisions for You?

If you suffered severe brain damage and could survive only on artificial life support, would you want to continue living? Who do you think will take care of you and make decisions related to your life—and death? If you think you're too young to worry about such issues, consider the story of Terri Schiavo.

In February 1990, 26-year-old Terri suffered cardiac arrest, possibly caused by potassium imbalance due to bulimia. She was rushed to a hospital. However, lack of oxygen had damaged her brain permanently, and she lapsed into a coma. A feeding tube was inserted through the skin and into her stomach to provide fluids and nutrition. Over the next 15 years Terri became the focus of a bitter court battle that escalated into a national debate about the right to live versus the right to die.

A supporter lights a prayer candle for Terri.

In June 1990 Michael Schiavo, Terri's husband, was appointed her legal guardian. Her parents, Robert and Mary Schindler, did not object. Over the next four years Terri was transferred to various medical centers, where she received ongoing testing, speech and occupational therapy, and other attempts at rehabilitation. In 1998, when Terri had been in a coma for eight years, Michael petitioned the court to authorize the removal of her feeding tube and allow her to die.

If Terri had made a "living will" (a legal document that expresses one's preferences regarding life support and resuscitation), the decision to terminate her life support might have been relatively straightforward. In this case, however, the decision became an immensely difficult undertaking. What would Terri have wanted? When a person's wishes are not clear, who should make the decision? Do we have an ethical obligation to keep someone alive as long as possible? And when, exactly, is someone no longer "alive"?

In Terri's case, Michael and two relatives testified that she had commented about a seriously ill person, "I wouldn't want to live like that. I would want to just die." Terri's parents opposed his petition. They told the court that Terri was a devout Catholic who would want to live. They insisted their daughter had the right to live; her husband insisted she had the right to die. A medical report indicated that Terri was in a "persistent vegetative state" with no chance of improvement.

*Family photo of Terri Schiavo before she had a heart attack.*

In 2000 a circuit court judge ruled that the feeding tube should be removed, on the grounds that Terri would have chosen to do so. Her parents initiated a series of legal appeals, countered by appeals from Michael Schiavo. In 2001 the feeding tube was removed, but it was reinserted two days later when the Schindlers filed a lawsuit.

By the time Terri's feeding tube was removed again in 2003, the case had caught the public's (and politicians') attention. Eventually the argument went all the way to the U.S. Supreme Court, which declined to hear the case.

Terri Schiavo's feeding tube was removed for the last time on March 18, 2005. On March 31, at age 41, she died. An autopsy showed that her brain had shrunk to 50% of its normal weight and confirmed the medical diagnosis of persistent vegetative state. She could not have recovered.

### the facts...

- In 1990, 26-year-old Terri Schiavo suffered a cardiac arrest, leading to permanent brain damage. She remained in a coma thereafter.
- In 1998, Michael Schiavo, her husband and legal guardian, asked to remove Terri's feeding tube on the basis that it was what she would have wanted. Her parents disagreed. They filed a lawsuit to block the removal of the feeding tube.
- The case escalated into a national legal and political battle over the right to live versus the right to die. Eventually it reached the U.S. Supreme Court, which refused to hear the case.
- Terri Schiavo died on March 31, 2005. An autopsy revealed that she could not have recovered.

### Questions to consider

*1 If you were in Terri Schiavo's situation, would you want to be allowed to die? 2 Do you have a living will? If not, who do you think will make decisions for you if you are unable to speak for yourself?*

# Chapter Summary

### Fertilization occurs when sperm and egg unite *p. 481*

- Sperm and egg meet (and fertilization occurs) in the upper third of the oviduct.
- Enzymes in the head of the sperm create a pathway through the corona radiata and the zona pellucida to the egg cell membrane.
- Entry of the sperm nucleus triggers the completion of meiosis II by the secondary oocyte. Thereafter the nuclei of sperm and egg fuse, creating a single diploid cell, the zygote.

### Development: Cleavage, morphogenesis, differentiation, and growth *p. 484*

- Development begins by a process called *cleavage* and then proceeds with morphogenesis, differentiation, and growth.
- The periods of development prior to birth are known as pre-embryonic (the first two weeks), embryonic (weeks three through eight), and fetal (weeks nine to birth).

### Pre-embryonic development: The first two weeks *p. 484*

- During the first two weeks of development, the single cell develops into a hollow ball with an embryonic disk in the center that will eventually become the embryo.
- At about one week the pre-embryo (now called a blastocyst) begins to burrow into the uterine wall, a process called implantation.

### Embryonic development: Weeks three to eight *p. 485*

- Embryonic development is marked by the presence of three primary germ layers (ectoderm, mesoderm, and endoderm) in the embryonic disk.
- During development the embryo is completely surrounded by two membranes. The amnion contains amniotic fluid, and the chorion develops into fetal placental tissue. Two other membranes (the allantois and the yolk sac) have temporary functions only.
- By the fifth week the embryo begins to take on distinctly human features.
- By the eighth week the placenta and umbilical cord circulation are fully functional, and male or female gonads have begun to develop.

### Gender development begins at six weeks *p. 489*

- Until six weeks an embryo is "sexually indifferent."
- The presence or absence of a Y chromosome determines whether the embryo will become phenotypically male or female.

### Fetal development: Nine weeks to birth *p. 492*

- Months 3–9 are marked by rapid growth and development of the organ systems. By the fifth month the fetus begins to move.
- By the sixth month, life outside the womb is possible with good medical care.

### Birth and the early postnatal period *p. 493*

- Birth occurs at about 38 weeks of development (nine months).
- The three phases of labor are dilation, expulsion, and afterbirth.
- Shortly after the newborn takes its first breath, the newborn's cardiovascular system undergoes substantial changes. Within hours or a few days the umbilical vessels regress and the ductus arteriosus and foramen ovale close, rerouting all blood through the pulmonary circulation.

### From birth to adulthood *p. 496*

- Human neonates are relatively helpless because the nervous and muscular systems are not yet mature.
- There is a disproportionate increase in the development of the musculoskeletal and nervous system during infancy. The immune system remains relatively immature.
- Body shape changes in childhood. The brain achieves 95% of its adult size.
- Adolescence is marked by the last spurt of rapid growth and the attainment of sexual maturity.

### Aging takes place over time *p. 498*

- Most cells have an internal mechanism that limits the number of times they can divide.
- Cumulative unrepaired cellular damage as a consequence of metabolic activity may limit the life of cells.
- Aging may affect all organ systems because a decline in one system will affect other systems.

### Death is the final transition *p. 502*

- Death is a process. Death begins with the failure of one or more critical organ systems, leading to the failure of other organ systems and eventually to the death of all cells.

# Terms You Should Know

amnion, *486*
amniotic fluid, *486*
blastocyst, *484*
cesarean delivery, *494*
chorion, *486*
colostrum, *495*
ectopic pregnancy, *485*
embryo, *485*
embryonic disk, *484*
endoderm, *485*
fertilization, *483*
fraternal twins, *483*
human chorionic gonadotropin (hCG), *486*
identical twins, *484*
miscarriage, *489*
morphogenesis, *484*
placenta, *487*
puberty, *498*
umbilical cord, *487*
zygote, *481*

# Concept Review

1. Why does only one sperm fertilize the egg, and why is this important?
2. What determines whether an embryo will develop into a male or a female?
3. Describe the function of the placenta and the hormones that it secretes.
4. Describe the stages of labor and delivery.
5. What causes the newborn to take its first breath immediately after birth?
6. Why aren't all of a child's vaccinations given in the first year?
7. What causes the onset of puberty (sexual maturation)?
8. Summarize the three main hypotheses of the causes of aging.
9. What has caused the increase in longevity of the U.S. population during the past 100 years?
10. Why is it sometimes so hard to define the moment when an individual dies?

# Test Yourself

### Matching Exercise

_____ 1. The outermost sphere of cells in a blastocyst
_____ 2. The germ layer that eventually develops into the epidermis, hair, nails, and tooth enamel
_____ 3. The germ layer that eventually develops into the liver, pancreas, and linings of the urinary bladder and urethra
_____ 4. The developing fetal cell mass that undergoes implantation
_____ 5. A structure that enables the exchange of nutrients and wastes between embryo and mother
_____ 6. The protective covering of the secondary oocyte

a. ectoderm
b. blastocyst
c. zona pellucida
d. trophoblast
e. placenta
f. endoderm

### Fill in the Blank

7. ____________________ begins when a single sperm enters the egg.
8. ____________________ twins derive from a single fertilized ovum.
9. ____________________ twins derive from two different oocytes.
10. If implantation occurs in an oviduct, this results in a(n) ____________________ pregnancy.
11. Labor is triggered by maturation of the fetal ____________________ gland.
12. Spontaneous termination of pregnancy or ____________________ likely happens to embryos that would not develop normally.

### True or False?

13. The placenta effectively blocks alcohol, drugs, and viruses from entering the embryonic circulation.
14. Until approximately four weeks of development, a human embryo resembles other vertebrate embryos.
15. The X chromosome encodes a protein that causes the development of the testes.

# References and Additional Reading

Austad, Stephen N. *Why We Age: What Science Is Discovering About the Body's Journey Through Life.* New York: Wiley, 1999. (A colorful and provocative look at aging for both laypeople and professionals.)

Moore, K. L., and T. V. N. Persaud. *Before We Are Born: Essentials of Embryology and Birth Defects.* Philadelphia: Saunders, 2003. (A more in-depth treatment of human embryology for the interested student.)

Ricklefs, R. E., and C. E. Finch. *Aging: A Natural History.* New York: Scientific American Library, 1995. 224 pp. (An exploration of patterns of aging among different species.)

## Apply What You Know

1. Why is it biologically impossible for humans and gorillas to mate and produce offspring?
2. Conjoined twins are twins that are attached to each other. They may even share limbs and organs. From what you know of early human development, how do you think conjoined twins come about?
3. Why are many sperm produced but only one egg in the process of fertilization? Would humans be able to reproduce if the cell numbers were inverted?
4. Each year it is estimated that over 40,000 newborn babies are impacted by the effects of alcohol consumed by the mother during pregnancy. Fetal alcohol syndrome is one of the leading causes of preventable birth defects. What is fetal alcohol syndrome, and why is alcohol more likely to damage the fetus than the mother?
5. What exactly do home pregnancy tests test for as an indication that a woman is pregnant?
6. Babies born before a full nine months of gestation (premature babies) are often at a high risk of death. What is the earliest a baby can be born and stand a good chance of survival, and which organ system is generally the limiting one?
7. How is it possible that one's life could be prolonged without slowing the aging process?

*Answers can be found on the Human Biology Place.*

# Internet References

Find links to these Web sites at the Human Biology Place.

**Women's Health Initiative**
**www.whi.org**
Web site for the large ongoing investigation of preventive measures for heart disease, cancer, and other chronic health problems in older women.

**New York Online Access to Health (NOAH)**
**www.noah-health.org**
Links to full-text consumer health information on pregnancy, parenting, aging, and many other topics. Selected by librarians and health professionals.

**Centers for Disease Control and Prevention: Healthy Aging**
**www.cdc.gov/aging**
Statistics, prevention guidelines, behavioral factors, chronic diseases, and advice for lifelong health.

**March of Dimes**
**www.marchofdimes.com**
Nonprofit organization that funds research and programs to protect babies from birth defects, premature birth, and low birth weight.

# 22 Evolution and the Origins of Life

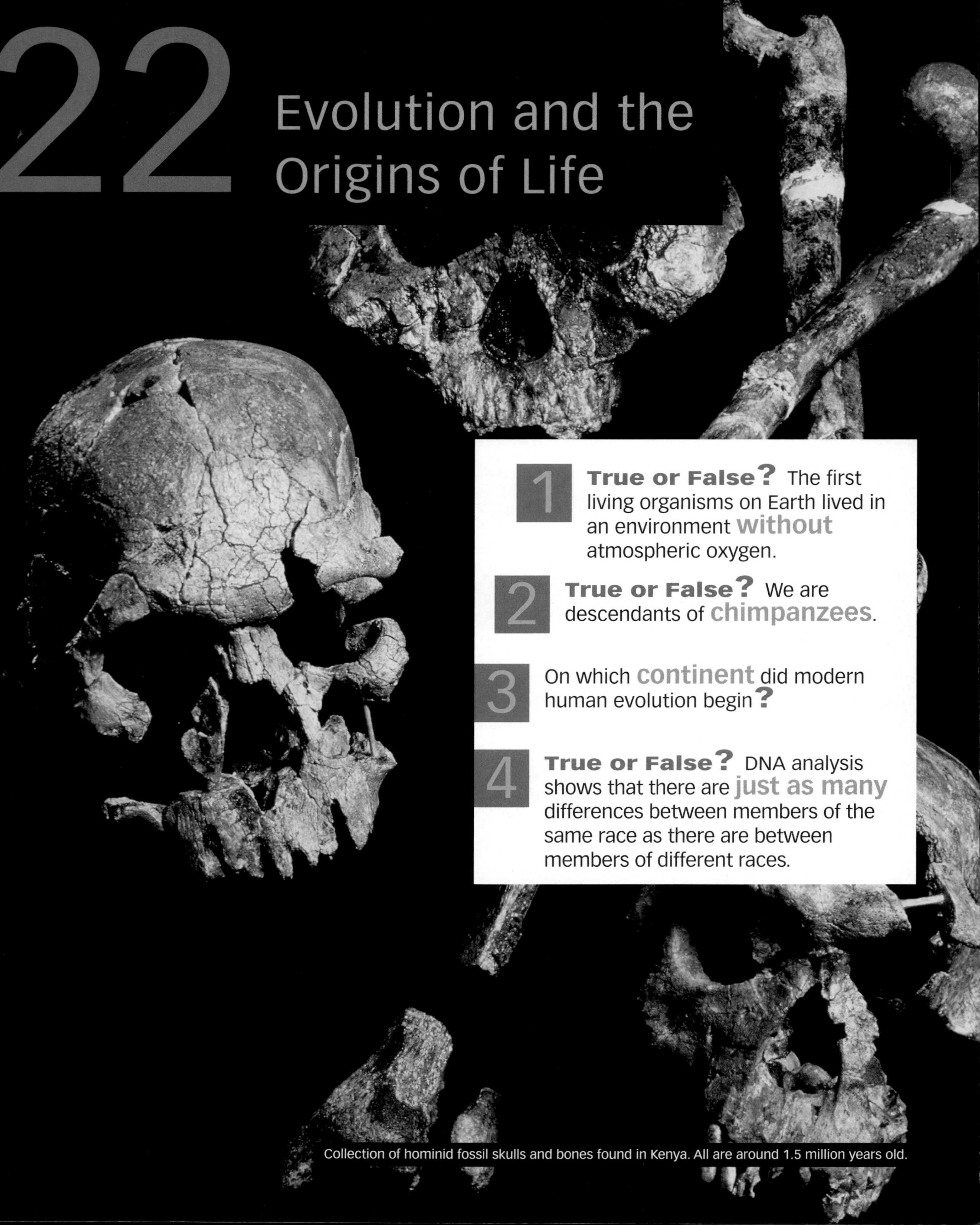

**1** **True or False?** The first living organisms on Earth lived in an environment **without** atmospheric oxygen.

**2** **True or False?** We are descendants of **chimpanzees**.

**3** On which **continent** did modern human evolution begin**?**

**4** **True or False?** DNA analysis shows that there are **just as many** differences between members of the same race as there are between members of different races.

Collection of hominid fossil skulls and bones found in Kenya. All are around 1.5 million years old.

**Look around and you'll be** impressed by the astounding variety of forms that life takes. From bacteria to beagles, hagfish to humans, living creatures come in a huge range of sizes, shapes, and colors. And yet, the evidence indicates that all living creatures on Earth are related. To the best of our knowledge, all of them descended from a single simple life-form that arose from the hot, steamy environment of Earth more than 3 billion years ago.

How did Earth's inhabitants come to be so different from each other? The diversity of life is thought to result from **evolution,** defined as an unpredictable and natural process of descent over time with genetic modification. The formal definition has three key elements:

- **Descent over time**. As one generation of organisms gives rise to the next, populations of organisms undergo slow change that makes them different from their ancestors. Sometimes a population becomes two populations that are so different from each other that they no longer interbreed, giving rise to new species.
- **Genetic modification.** The process of change depends on changes to the genes of the organisms.
- **Unpredictable and natural**. Evolution is affected by chance, *natural selection*, historical events, and changing environments.

**Microevolution** refers to evolution as a result of genetic changes that give rise to new species. **Macroevolution,** by contrast, describes large-scale evolutionary trends or changes that apply to whole groups of species, often as a result of changing environments or major historical events.

The theory that evolutionary processes shaped life on Earth is associated with Charles Darwin, a British naturalist of the mid-1800s. The heart of Darwin's hypothesis is that life arose only once, probably in the primordial sea long ago, and all life as we know it descended from that early life-form. Darwin actually used the word evolution sparingly, preferring instead "descent with change" or "descent with modification." Key to Darwin's hypothesis is the idea that descent with modification resulted from "natural selection," which we describe later in this chapter.

Scientists reserve the word "theory" for those few major concepts that offer the best explanation to fit a broad range of established facts. In that sense, scientists use the word "theory" very differently from opponents of evolution, who often say that evolution is "only a theory" as if the whole concept could be dismissed with a wave of the hand. Opponents of evolution also sometimes say "Darwin was wrong" by pointing to how specifics of his original explanation have had to be modified after extensive testing. Nevertheless, the *theory of evolution* remains the single most unifying concept in all of biology.

In this chapter we review the scientific evidence on which we base our understanding of evolution and discuss processes that affect evolutionary change. Then we pick up the intriguing question of life's origin on Earth. Finally, we trace the relatively recent evolution of human beings and consider the features that make us distinctively human.

**RECAP**

Evolution is a process of descent over time with genetic modification. First proposed by Charles Darwin in the 1800s, the theory of evolution remains the single most unifying concept in biology. ■

## 22.1 Evidence for evolution comes from many sources

The evidence that humans and all other life-forms have evolved over time comes from several sources, including the fossil record, comparative anatomy and embryology, biochemistry, and biogeography.

### The fossil record: Incomplete but valuable

**Fossils,** the preserved remnants of organisms, are one of our richest sources of information about life-forms that lived in the past. Soft tissues decay quickly, so most of the fossil record consists of bones, teeth, shells, and occasionally

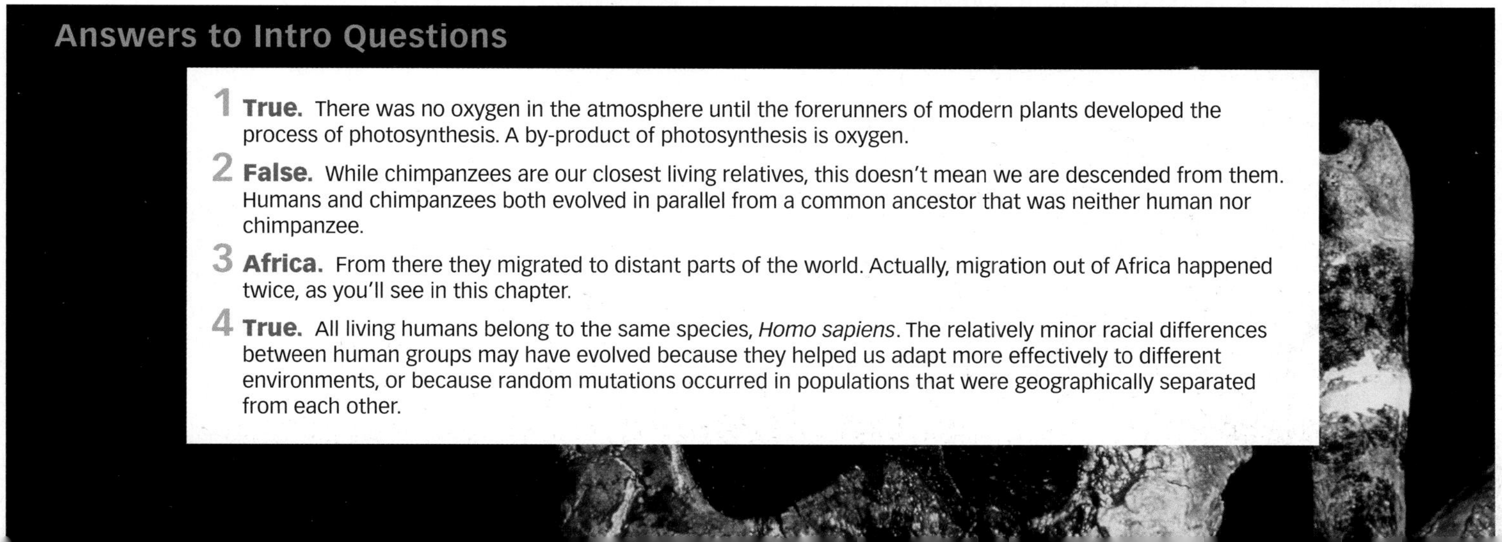

**Answers to Intro Questions**

1 **True.** There was no oxygen in the atmosphere until the forerunners of modern plants developed the process of photosynthesis. A by-product of photosynthesis is oxygen.

2 **False.** While chimpanzees are our closest living relatives, this doesn't mean we are descended from them. Humans and chimpanzees both evolved in parallel from a common ancestor that was neither human nor chimpanzee.

3 **Africa.** From there they migrated to distant parts of the world. Actually, migration out of Africa happened twice, as you'll see in this chapter.

4 **True.** All living humans belong to the same species, *Homo sapiens*. The relatively minor racial differences between human groups may have evolved because they helped us adapt more effectively to different environments, or because random mutations occurred in populations that were geographically separated from each other.

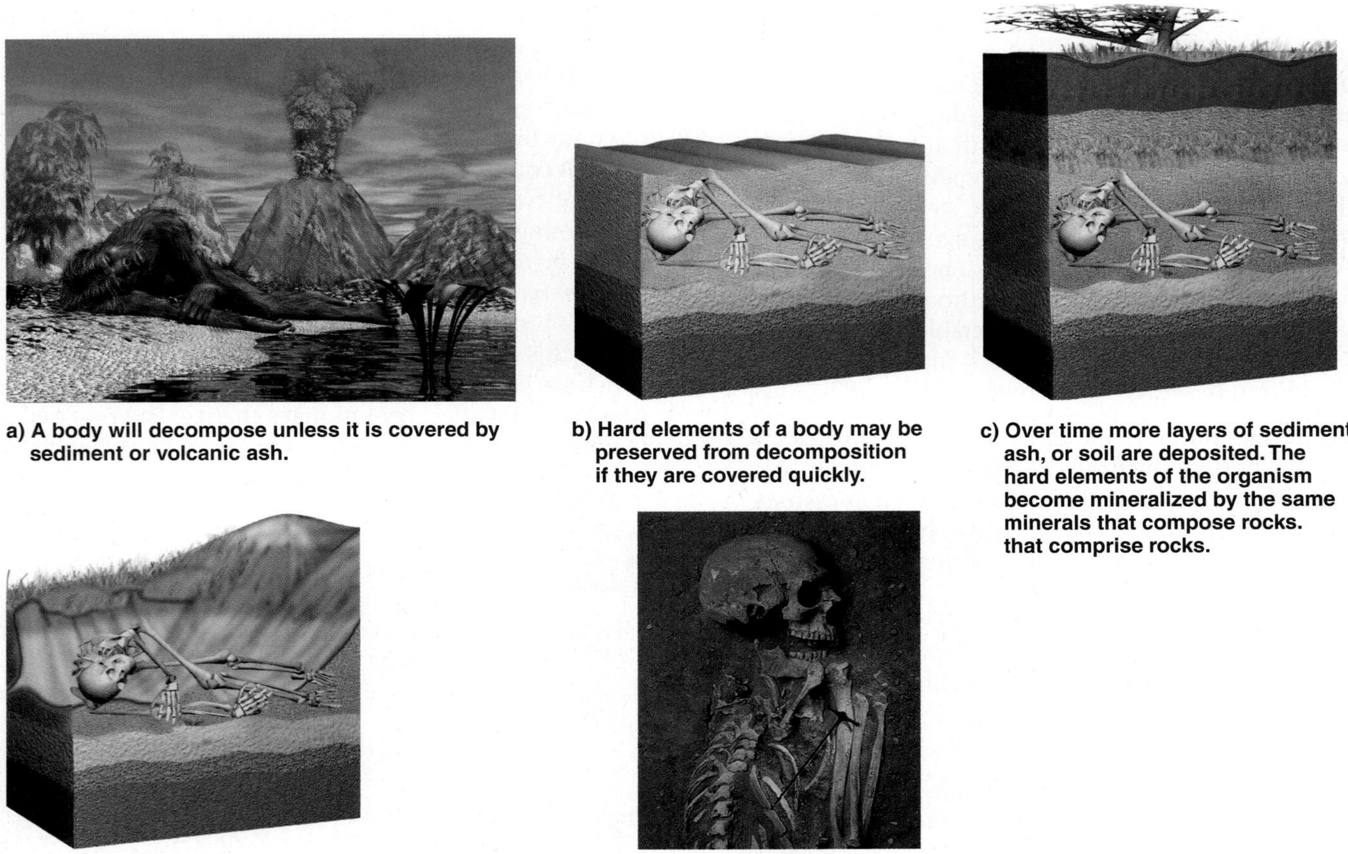

**a) A body will decompose unless it is covered by sediment or volcanic ash.**

**b) Hard elements of a body may be preserved from decomposition if they are covered quickly.**

**c) Over time more layers of sediment, ash, or soil are deposited. The hard elements of the organism become mineralized by the same minerals that compose rocks. that comprise rocks.**

**d) Occasionally erosion, uplifting of the earth's crust, or human excavation may expose fossils to the surface.**

**e) A fossilized human skeleton.**

**Figure 22.1 How fossils are formed.**

spores and seeds. Fossils of soft-tissue organisms such as jellyfish and bacteria do exist, but they are rare. In general, remnants of organisms are preserved only if they are covered soon after death with layers of sediment or volcanic ash (Figure 22.1). Over time the remains become mineralized with some of the same minerals that compose rocks, leaving a rocklike impression of the hard tissue of the organism, or a fossil.

Even though we have found fossils from over 200,000 species, there may be millions of species for which we will never have any record because they had no hard tissues. We have many fossils of ancient bony fishes, for example, but only a few fossils of jellyfish from the same time periods. We are also more likely to discover fossils on land (there may be many more, and possibly different, fossils deep under the sea) and to find fossils that were produced in great numbers. For example, we are more apt to find a seashell or spore from 100,000 years ago than to uncover the skeleton of an early human from the same time period. By its nature, then, the fossil record tends to be incomplete and heavily weighted toward fossils that are easy to find.

One of the most important pieces of information about a fossil is its age, which places it at a certain point in evolutionary history and shows how body structures have changed over time. Scientists know that sediment and volcanic ash are laid down layer upon layer, a process known as stratification. Where fossils exist in the same location in different layers, it is usually possible to tell which one came first. This helps scientists establish relative relationships between fossils over time (Figure 22.2).

In addition, radiometric dating and other techniques can be used to date rocks and fossils. Radiometric dating takes advantage of the fact that some atoms, called radioactive isotopes, are inherently unstable. Radioactive isotopes radiate or give off particles until they reach a more stable state, sometimes becoming a different, more stable atom.

The isotope most often used to date the oldest fossils is radioactive potassium, which is slowly converted to argon, a gas. The half-life of radioactive potassium is 1.3 billion years, meaning that it takes 1.3 billion years for half of the radioactive potassium in a fossil to become argon. It would take another 1.3 billion years for half of the remaining radioactive

**Figure 22.2 Stratification of sedimentary deposits.** The rock layers of the Grand Canyon were formed by sequential deposits of sediments. The oldest layers at the bottom of the canyon are over 1.2 billion years old.

potassium to become argon, and so on. The argon formed from the decay of radioactive potassium remains trapped in the fossil, so the ratio of radioactive potassium to argon in a fossil can be used to estimate the fossil's actual age, in billions of years. Radioactive potassium is of limited usefulness for dating most animal and plant fossils, however, because they are less than 600 million years old.

At the other end of the age spectrum, fossils newer than 50,000 years old are dated using carbon-14, the radioactive isotope of carbon, which decays with a half-life of only 5,700 years.

**RECAP**

Fossils are the mineralized remains of the hard tissues of past life-forms. Although the fossil record is incomplete, pieced together it provides compelling evidence for evolution. Radiometric dating can be used to date rocks and fossils. ■

## Comparative anatomy and embryology provide more evidence

Additional evidence for evolution comes from comparing the anatomy of animals and the development of their embryos. When examining them in the context of evolution, scientists describe anatomical structures as homologous, analogous, or vestigial.

When different organisms share similar anatomical features, often it is because they evolved from a common ancestor. For example, the forelimbs of all vertebrates (animals with backbones) seem to share roughly the same set of bones arranged in similar patterns. This is true even though vertebrate forelimbs have undergone numerous modifications so animals can use them in a variety of specialized ways, such as flying, swimming, running, or grasping objects (Figure 22.3). **Homologous structures** are body structures that share a common origin. The degree to which homologous structures resemble each other can be used to infer the closeness of evolutionary relatedness.

However, structures that share a common function may resemble each other even if they do not share a common origin. Good examples are the wings of birds and the wings of insects, both of which evolved for flight even though birds and insects are not closely related. Structures that share a common function but not necessarily a common ancestry are called **analogous structures** (Figure 22.4).

Finally, **vestigial structures** serve little or no function at all. Vestigial structures may be homologous to body parts in other organisms, where they do still have an important function. The human coccyx (tailbone) is the vestigial remnant of a tail, suggesting that we share a common ancestry with other vertebrates with tails. The muscles that enable you to wiggle your ears are vestigial in humans. Other animals, such as dogs and deer, still use these muscles to rotate their ears toward a sound so that they can hear it better.

Compelling evidence for evolution also comes from comparisons of the embryos of animals, especially vertebrates. The vertebrates are a varied group: fishes, amphibians, reptiles, birds, and mammals. Yet despite their diversity, their early embryonic development follows the same general pattern (Figure 22.5 on page 511). For example, all vertebrate embryos develop a primitive support structure called a notochord and a series of folds called somites that will become bone, muscle, and skin. But in addition, all vertebrate embryos develop a series of arches just below the head. In fishes and amphibians these are called gill arches because they develop into gills. In humans the homologous *pharyngeal arches* become parts of the face, middle ear, and mouth. The most likely explanation for these common embryonic structures with completely different functions is common ancestry. Later in embryonic and fetal development the paths of morphogenesis and differentiation diverge, giving us the variety of vertebrates we know today. It is almost as if embryonic and fetal development represent an acceleration of the entire evolutionary history of the vertebrates.

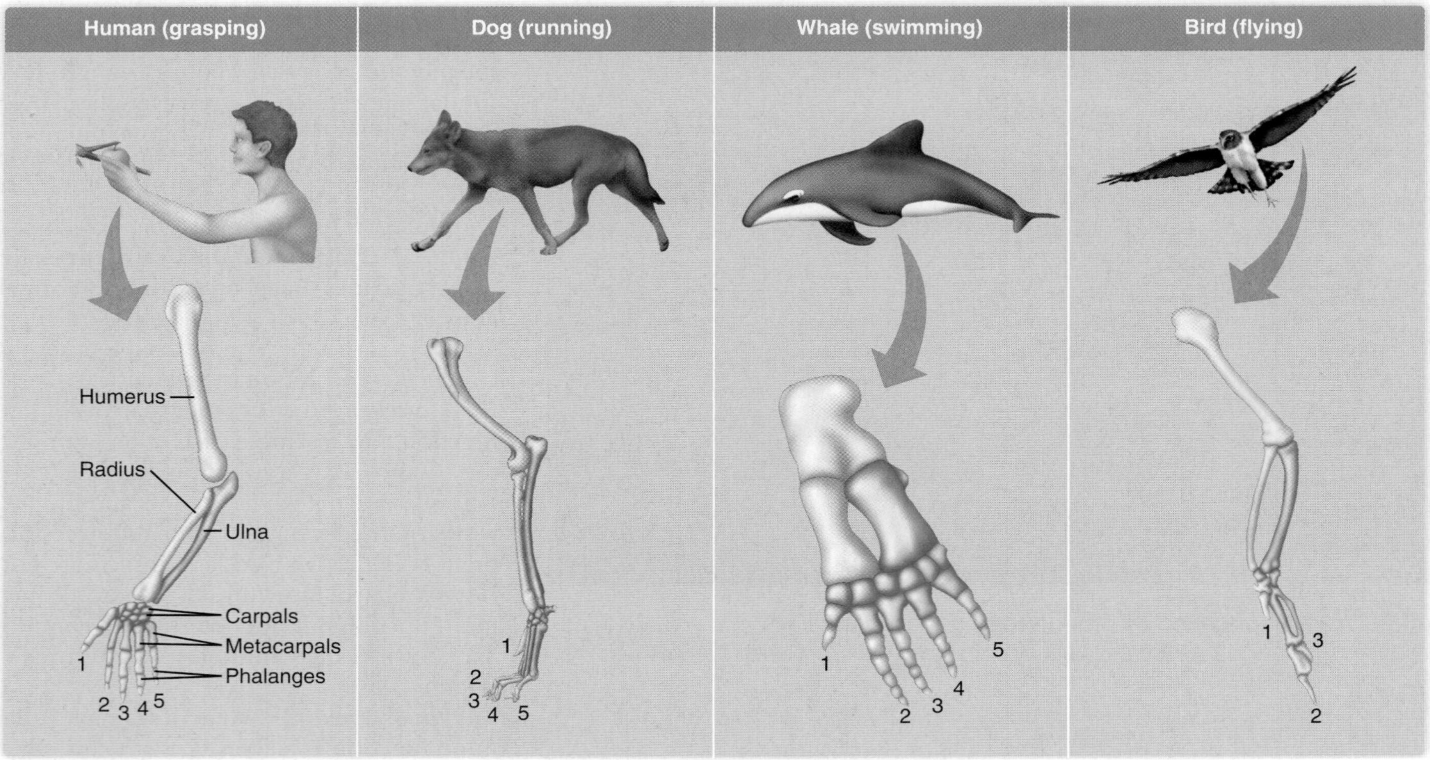


**Figure 22.3 Homologous structures.** Homologous structures evolve from a common structure. Numbers indicate digits. Notice how homologous bones (indicated by similar colors) have undergone modification in order to perform different functions in different vertebrates.

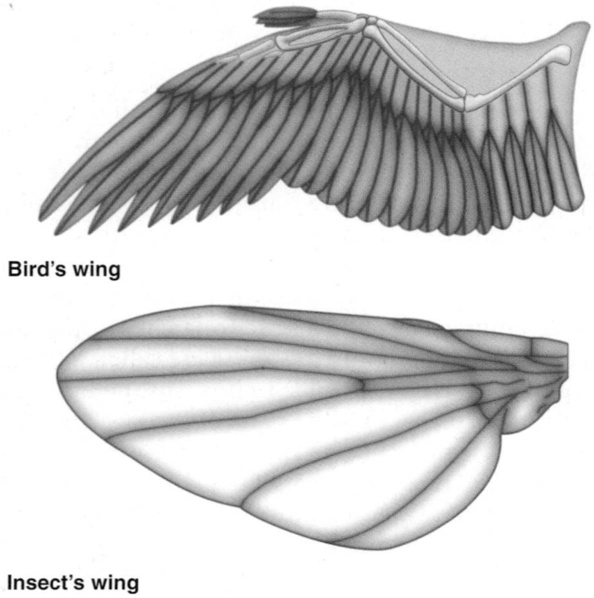


**Figure 22.4 Analogous structures.** The bird's wing and the insect's wing are both used for the same function, but they evolved from entirely different structures.

## Comparative biochemistry examines similarities between molecules

Proteins and genes also provide clues to the relationships among species. When two species possess identical or nearly identical biochemical molecules, common ancestry may be indicated. In principle, the two similar molecules are akin to homologous structures—you might call them "homologous molecules." They arise when evolutionary paths diverge, meaning that one species becomes two different species. Mutations occurring over long periods of time gradually modify the original molecule in each of the two new species. The greater the difference between two molecules serving the same function in two species, the earlier the two species probably diverged from a common ancestor.

For example, cytochrome *c*, an important protein in the metabolic pathways for energy exchange, is found in organisms ranging from yeast to humans. In humans, cytochrome *c* consists of 104 amino acids. A chimpanzee's cytochrome *c* is identical to that of a human, but it differs by 1 amino acid in rhesus monkeys, 16 amino acids in chickens, and over 50 amino acids in yeast. From this data you could hypothesize that humans are more closely related to chimpanzees than

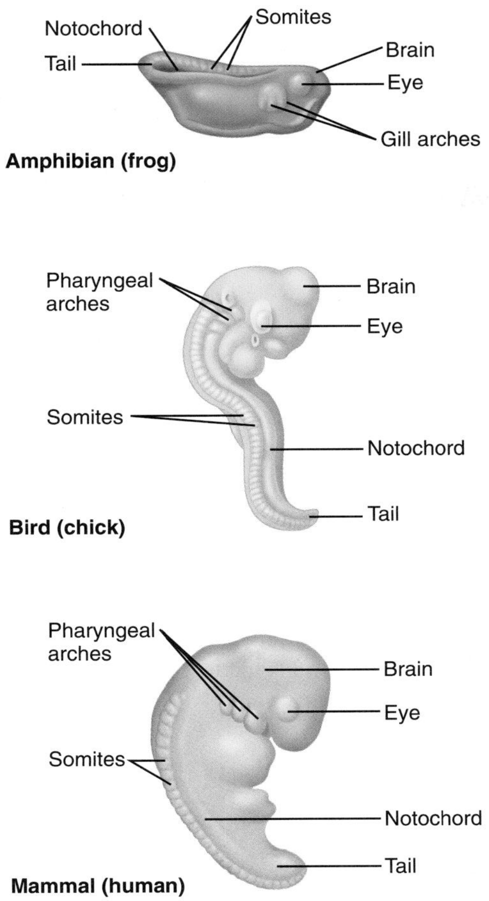


**Figure 22.5 Early developmental similarity among vertebrate embryos.** The embryos of all vertebrates tend to share certain developmental features, suggesting a common ancestry. In particular, all vertebrate embryos have either gill or pharyngeal arches. These arches ultimately have very different functions.

to rhesus monkeys, and also that humans are more closely related to other primates than to chickens or yeast.

Similarities in other protein sequences and in DNA are also used as indicators of common ancestry. The degree to which DNA base pair sequences resemble each other helps scientists infer ancestry and relationships between humans and other species.

**RECAP**

Comparisons of homologous structures and the course of embryologic development provide clues to how life-forms are related and give us additional evidence for the process of evolution. The degree of structural similarity between the DNA and proteins of different species can be used to estimate the closeness of evolutionary relationships. ■

## Biogeography: The impact of geographic barriers and continental drift on evolutionary processes

**Biogeography** is the study of the distribution of plants and animals around the world. Why do we find certain animals and plants in some locations on Earth and not in others? One explanation is that migrations are inhibited in regions isolated by barriers such as water, high mountain ranges, or deserts (Figure 22.6).

Where migrations of plants and animals were possible, the evidence indicates that closely related life-forms often evolved in one location and then spread to regions that were accessible to them at the time. Eventually their spread may have been blocked by physical barriers or by environments in which they could not survive, such as deserts or oceans. There are no snakes on the Hawaiian Islands, for example, because snakes evolved long before the volcanic islands existed, and the Pacific Ocean represents an effective barrier to snake migration. When we see how easily some plants and animals adapt (adjust to new conditions) when placed in new locations, we can appreciate the impact of geography on evolutionary processes and the distribution of life-forms.

Geologists tell us that Earth's continents are located on huge plates called tectonic plates, whose locations on the planet surface are not fixed. The plates slowly move over time, a process called **continental drift.** About 200 million years ago, however, all the continents were joined in one interconnected landmass called *Pangaea* (Figure 22.7). The continents drifted apart after the first animals and plants appeared. As a result, related groups of organisms that were isolated from each other evolved separately, but along almost parallel paths.

For instance, Australia separated from the other continents about 65 million years ago. Nevertheless, there are striking similarities between the unique marsupial (pouched) mammals of Australia and the predominant placental mammals (mammals that nourish their young

**Figure 22.6 Geographic barriers.** Animal and plant migrations are inhibited by barriers such as these mountains and desert sands in Death Valley, California.

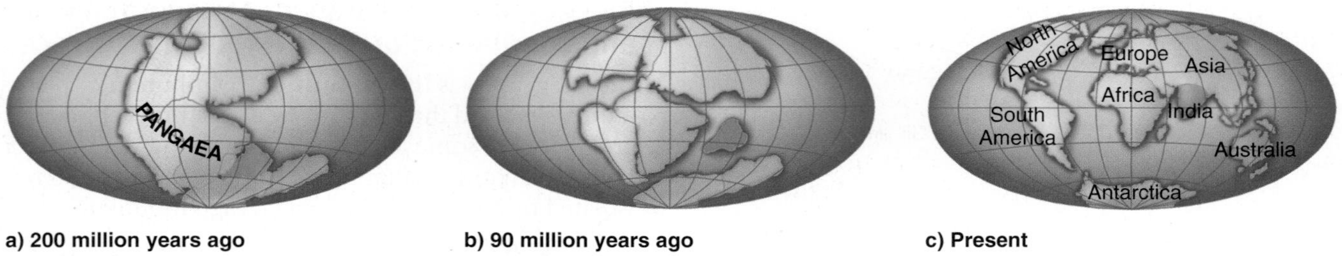


**Figure 22.7 The formation of Earth's continents from a common landmass.** The continents were once connected in one giant landmass called Pangaea.

with a true placenta) found on all other continents. These similarities exist because the two types of mammals evolved from common ancestors and also because evolution continued after separation, solving some of the same environmental challenges in the same way in both groups.

**RECAP**

The slow process of continental drift over the past 200 million years has had a major impact on evolutionary patterns and the worldwide distribution of life-forms. Within a continent, physical barriers such as mountain ranges and deserts also influence the evolution and distribution of life-forms. ■

## 22.2 Natural selection contributes to evolution

### Random mutations underlie evolution

Recall that an organism's DNA represents the set of instructions for all its life processes. If all creatures had an identical set of DNA they would all *be* identical in form and function. Differences in DNA account for the differences among species and even among individuals of a species.

A species' gene pool changes very slowly over time (measured in thousands to millions of years) as a result of random mutations to the genes of individual members of the species. Mutations are rare accidental events that produce a slightly different form of a gene, called an allele. Alleles that are not lethal may be passed on to future generations, to become part of the species' collective gene pool. Eventually these accumulating mutations may cause changes in the species' physical and functional traits. Ultimately, an accumulation of mutations may cause one species to diverge into two.

Without random mutations, there could be no evolution.

### Natural selection encourages changes in the gene pool

Mutations alone do not amount to evolution. Living organisms interact with their local environments, and as a consequence of that interaction, some live long enough to reproduce and some do not. The frequency with which any allele is found in the gene pool of a species depends critically on whether that allele confers survival value on its holder.

Darwin understood this principle even though he did not fully comprehend the genetic basis for it. He referred to it as "survival of the fittest" by means of natural selection. By **natural selection,** Darwin meant that individuals with certain traits are more fit for their local environment and therefore are more likely to survive and reproduce. Mutations coupled with natural selection produce changes in the gene pool of a population.

**RECAP**

Without mutations there would be no variation among life-forms. Mutations coupled with natural selection provide much of the basis for evolution. ■

### Genetic drift and gene flow alter populations

A **population** is a group of individuals of the same species that occupy the same geographical area. Darwin was convinced that the fittest members of a population were always the ones to survive. We now know that there are several other contributors to evolution besides natural selection. Other factors that affect the gene pool of a population include genetic drift, gene flow, and selective hunting.

**Genetic drift** refers to random changes in allele frequency because of chance events. One cause of genetic drift is the *bottleneck effect,* which occurs when a major catastrophe—such as a fire, a change in climate, or a new predator—wipes out most of a population without regard to any previous measure of fitness. When this happens the few genes left in the gene pool may no longer represent the original population, nor do they necessarily represent the most fit genes. An example of a species suffering from a severe bottleneck effect may be the cheetah. The 15,000 surviving cheetahs are all genetically similar, and their genomes include a few harmful alleles that affect fertility. It is not clear whether cheetahs will survive as a species.

Another cause of genetic drift, the *founder effect,* occurs when a few individuals leave the original group and begin a new population in a different location, or when some environmental change isolates a small population from a larger one. Again, the new gene pool may not be a representative sample of the original population.

Differences in the gene pool of a particular population are also affected by movement of individuals into (immigration) or out of (emigration) the population. This geographical redistribution of alleles, called **gene flow,** tends to mix pools of genes that might not otherwise mix. The prevalence of international travel today has markedly increased the possibility of gene flow in the human population.

A few events that have an impact on evolution may not be random at all. For example, the distinctly human practice of hunting big game animals for trophies specifically selects for larger, more fit males (Figure 22.8). How this practice might affect evolution is worth considering.

## Mass extinctions eliminate many species

An **extinction** occurs when a life-form dies out completely. Throughout evolutionary history, major catastrophic events have sometimes wiped out whole groups of species regardless of fitness. In the last 530 million years (the only period for which we have a good fossil record) there have been at least five mass extinctions, each of which destroyed more than 50% of the species existing at that time.

**Figure 22.8 Nonrandom impacts on evolution.** Big-game hunters specifically select the larger, more fit males in a population.

The largest mass extinction, called the Triassic, occurred around 200–250 million years ago. It was accompanied by a period of high carbon dioxide concentration and substantial global warming, and it killed 70% of all land-dwelling species and 90% of all ocean-dwelling species. The most recent and best-known mass extinction, called the Cretaceous, claimed all of the dinosaurs about 65 million years ago. Some scientists attribute the Cretaceous mass extinction to a dramatic change in climate after a comet or asteroid collided with Earth near what is now Cancun, Mexico.

## Evolutionary trees trace relationships between species

An **evolutionary tree** (also called a phylogenetic tree) illustrates evolutionary change and relationships among species. In an evolutionary tree each branch represents a point of divergence between two species (the creation of a new species), and the length of the branches represents time (Figure 22.9). If a species becomes extinct, the branch for that species ends short of the present time.

When conditions are right, many new species may develop in a relatively short time from a single ancestor. Such short bursts of evolutionary activity are called **adaptive radiation** and are shown as numerous branches from a single point on an evolutionary tree. Periods of adaptive radiation most commonly follow changes in the environment that create new habitats.

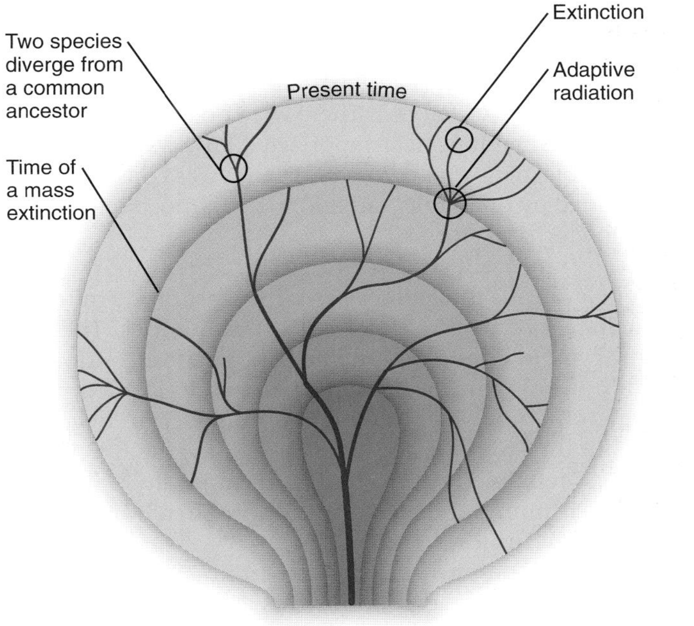


**Figure 22.9 An evolutionary (phylogenetic) tree.** Phylogenetic trees illustrate evolutionary change and relationships between species over time. Periods of mass extinctions are indicated by changes in color.

Populations of living creatures are constantly undergoing evolutionary change. Sometimes it is necessary to further subdivide species into subspecies that look slightly different but can still interbreed. At any given time some species are becoming extinct while others are in the process of diverging to become several new species. Evolutionary trees can be general, covering the entire history of all life-forms, or they can be detailed and focus on one species or one time period.

**RECAP**

In addition to mutations and natural selection, other events can change the course of evolution. The gene pool in a population can be affected by genetic drift, gene flow, and mass extinctions. An evolutionary tree visually depicts relationships between species. ■

## 22.3 The young Earth was too hot for life

To the best of our knowledge, Earth formed about 4.6 billion years ago. At one time our sun was surrounded by a swirling cloud of gases, dust, and debris. As the outer region of the cloud cooled, it condensed into solid masses that today we know as the planets, one of which was Earth.

Four and a half billion years ago Earth was an inhospitable place. Its tremendous heat melted the interior, which condensed as a core of liquid nickel, iron, and other metals. The solid but thin outer crust was constantly changing as frequent cracks in the surface and numerous volcanoes released molten rock and hot gases. The early atmosphere consisted primarily of carbon dioxide ($CO_2$), water vapor ($H_2O$), hydrogen ($H_2$), nitrogen ($N_2$), methane ($CH_4$), and ammonia ($NH_3$), but no oxygen ($O_2$). There were no oceans yet because the tremendous heat vaporized all the water. Earth was not yet protected by an ozone layer, so it was constantly bombarded by ultraviolet radiation. The atmosphere crackled with electrical storms.

Over time Earth cooled enough for water vapor at higher elevations to condense as rain. Most of the rain immediately vaporized again as it struck hot rock. The hot, steamy cycle of condensation and vaporization continued for millions of years until the planet's surface cooled enough to permit water to remain liquid. Oceans began to form, but they were warm, small, and not very salty. The land mass remained steamy, hot, and subject to frequent volcanic eruptions and electrical storms. There was still no oxygen in the atmosphere.

Somehow, despite this harsh environment, living organisms appeared about 3.8 billion years ago, less than a billion years after Earth was formed. Now we turn to the question of how life began, certainly one of the most intriguing questions in all of biology.

**RECAP**

Earth was formed about 4.6 billion years ago and life appeared about 3.8 billion years ago. The environment at the time was hot, steamy, and devoid of oxygen. ■

## 22.4 The first cells were able to live without oxygen

We know from the fossil record that by 3.5 billion years ago single-celled creatures resembling bacteria were present. Once life appeared, evolutionary processes over billions of years produced the varied life-forms that we know today, as well as many more that have long since become extinct.

### Organic molecules formed from atmospheric gases

Current scientific evidence indicates that the first step on the path to life was the creation of simple organic molecules from atmospheric gases (Figure 22.10). In today's living organisms the formation of organic molecules requires enzymes, but of course enzymes had not yet evolved. In fact, it appears that it was only *because* the early environment was so inhospitable (by our standards) that organic molecules were able to form. Apparently the intense heat, ultraviolet radiation, and electrical discharges produced an extreme amount of energy, enough to combine molecules in the atmosphere into simple organic compounds, even without enzymes. These compounds (amino acids, simple sugars, fatty acids) dissolved in the sea, so that over time the oceans became a warm soup containing organic molecules and a little salt. The absence of oxygen was important, because oxygen is highly reactive and would have broken down the organic molecules as they formed.

### Self-replicating RNA and DNA formed

The mere presence of organic molecules does not create a living organism that can grow and reproduce. How did these compounds join into molecules that could reliably reproduce themselves?

The problem we face in our understanding of this process is this: the only *self-replicating* molecules we know of are primitive single-stranded RNA and our modern double-stranded DNA, neither of which is likely to have formed spontaneously in the sea. Our best guess is that single-stranded self-replicating RNA first formed on templates of clay, in mudflats along the ocean's edge. Indeed, experiments have shown that, under the right conditions of moisture and heat, thin layers of clay can promote the formation of fairly complex molecules. Alternatively, the dry conditions and intense heat near volcanoes may have provided just the right environment for RNA formation.

**a) The primitive Earth was hot and steamy with small, warm oceans.**

**b) Simple organic molecules formed from atmospheric gases and dissolved in the oceans. The energy for their formation was provided by electrical storms, heat, and intense ultraviolet radiation.**

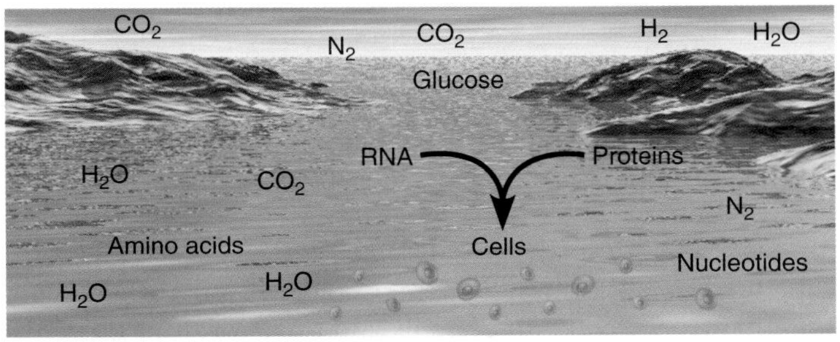


**c) Self-replicating RNA probably formed on clay templates in shallow waters along the shorelines of oceans. RNA and other organic molecules became enclosed in a cell membrane and the first self-replicating cells were formed.**

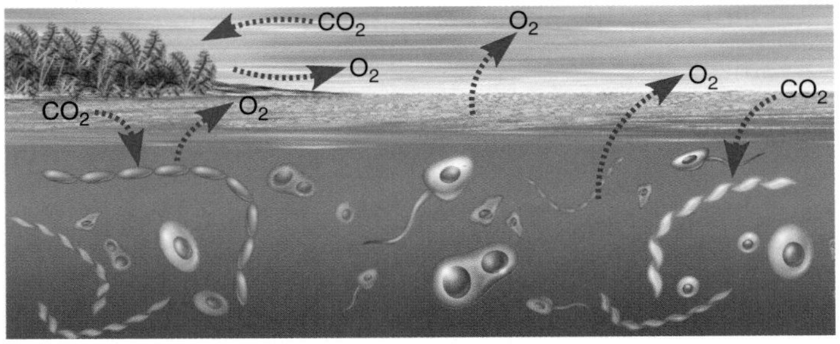


**d) The development of photosynthesis created oxygen gas. The presence of oxygen permitted the later development of aerobic forms of metabolism.**

Figure 22.10 **The origin and early evolution of life.**

If RNA was the first self-replicating molecule, the more stable DNA molecule must have developed from RNA very early in evolution. Modern cells use DNA as their self-replicating molecule and RNA to direct the synthesis of proteins, including enzymes. Only viruses use single-stranded RNA as their genetic material, and consequently viruses do not replicate on their own.

### The first living cells were anaerobic

At some point, self-replicating molecules and small organic molecules became enclosed within a lipid-protein membrane. We do not know exactly how this happened. However, experiments have demonstrated that, under the right conditions, certain mixtures of amino acids and lipids will spontaneously form hollow, water-filled spheres.

The first simple cells relied on anaerobic metabolism, meaning metabolism without oxygen. Their ability to synthesize compounds was limited, and so they relied on their immediate environment for the energy and raw materials they needed. When energy and raw materials were not available they died, or at least they did not replicate.

**RECAP**

As best we can surmise, the sequence of events leading to self-replicating living cells was (1) the formation of organic molecules from atmospheric gases, (2) the formation of self-replicating RNA on templates of clay, and (3) the enclosure of RNA and organic molecules inside a cell membrane. All early cells used an anaerobic form of metabolism. ■

## 22.5 Photosynthetic organisms altered the course of evolution

### Photosynthesis increased oxygen in the atmosphere

By about 3 billion years ago, certain cells had mutated and developed the ability to produce, internally, some of the molecules they needed. They drew on the abundant $CO_2$ and water in their environment and the energy available in sunlight to create complex organic molecules containing carbon. This process is called photosynthesis, and its by-product is oxygen. As a result, the oxygen concentration in the atmosphere began to rise. Note that oxygen appeared in Earth's atmosphere only after life began and as a direct consequence of life itself.

### Aerobic organisms evolved

The availability of oxygen changed everything. Oxygen was toxic to anaerobic cells. In addition, because it is highly reactive, the oxygen began to break down the energy-containing molecules in the sea that the anaerobic organisms relied on for energy. Consequently most of the anaerobic organisms that could not create their own organic molecules by photosynthesis died out.

In their place new cells evolved that could harness the reactive nature of oxygen. These cells extracted energy from the abundant organic molecules stored within the cell itself, using the now readily available oxygen. As you may recall, the ability to use oxygen to extract energy from organic molecules is called aerobic metabolism.

### The rise of animals and our human ancestors

Even from the brief description above, you can see that evolutionary processes are remarkably efficient at shaping life-forms to fit their environments. At the risk of condensing several billion years into a few sentences so that we can move to the recent evolution of human beings, here are some highlights:

- DNA became enclosed within a nucleus about 1.7 billion years ago. Cells with nuclei, called eukaryotes, became the dominant cell type.
- The first multicellular organism, a type of seaweed, appeared approximately 1.3 billion years ago.
- Animals appeared about 600 million years ago.
- Dinosaurs became extinct about 65 million years ago.
- Our first distinctly human ancestors appeared only about 5 million years ago.

Figure 22.11 presents a time line of biological milestones in the history of Earth as they relate to humans.

**RECAP**

Over time photosynthesis evolved, resulting in increased atmospheric concentrations of oxygen. Some organisms subsequently developed an aerobic form of metabolism. A cell nucleus formed to enclose the DNA in most cells, multicellular organisms arose, and animals appeared. Our first recognizably human ancestors emerged about 5 million years ago. ■

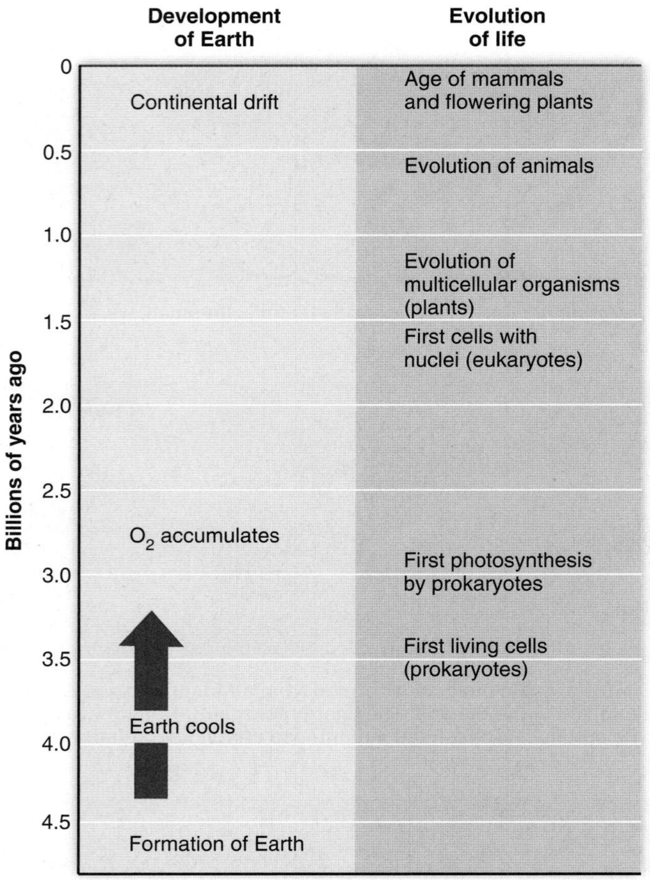


**Figure 22.11 A time line of the evolution of life since Earth's formation.** The entire span of human evolution lies within the horizontal line at the top of the figure.

## 22.6 Modern humans came from Africa

### Humans are primates

Taxonomy, the branch of science that focuses on classifying and naming life-forms, seeks a precise way to describe the relationships between all life-forms. The seven levels of the taxonomic classification system are *kingdom, phylum, class, order, family, genus,* and *species*. A **species** is defined as a group of organisms that under natural conditions tend to interbreed and produce fertile offspring.

Life-forms are generally referred to by their genus and species names. Names are italicized, with the genus name capitalized and listed first. Table 22.1 on page 518 shows the seven taxonomic categories as they apply to humans, or ***Homo sapiens.***

Humans belong to the class *Mammalia*. **Mammals** are vertebrates that have hair during all or part of their life, and mammary glands that produce milk. Within the class Mammalia we belong to the order *Primata*, more commonly called **primates.** Primates are mammals with five digits on their hands, fairly flat fingernails and toenails rather than hooves or claws, and forward-facing eyes adapted for stereoscopic vision. They include the lemurs (sometimes called pre-monkeys), monkeys, apes, and humans. The primate hand has a thumb that opposes four fingers. All of these features apparently evolved as adaptations for an arboreal lifestyle, that is, life in trees. The fossil record indicates that all present-day primates share a common ancestor that lived about 60 million years ago (Figure 22.12).

About 25 million years ago a subgroup of primates diverged from a common ancestor of the old-world monkeys to become the present-day apes (gibbons, orangutans, gorillas, chimpanzees) and humans (Figure 22.13). **Hominoids** differ from the rest of the primates in that they are larger and have bigger brains. They also lack tails, and their social behaviors are more complex. Based on the number of differences in DNA, it appears that orangutans diverged first, followed by gorillas, chimpanzees, and humans. In other words, chimpanzees are our closest living animal relatives among the hominoids. However, this does not mean that we descended from chimpanzees. It means that chimpanzees and humans apparently evolved from a common hominoid ancestor.

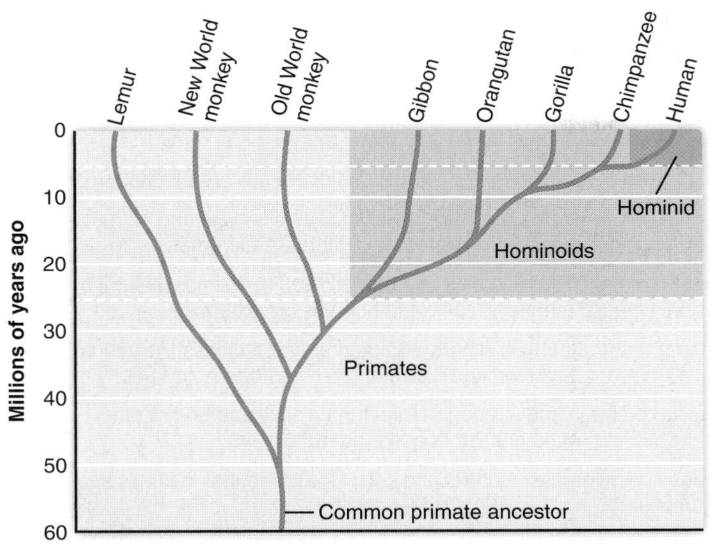


**Figure 22.12 Evolution of modern primates from a common primate ancestor.**

**RECAP**

A taxonomic system of seven categories classifies the relationship of any species to all others. Primates, an order of the class Mammalia, have flat fingernails and toenails, hands with five digits and an opposable thumb, and forward-facing eyes. A subset of the primates (the hominoids) became the present-day apes and humans. Chimpanzees appear to be our closest living animal relatives. ■

## Evolution of *Homo sapiens*

Although scientists disagree regarding specific dates and the classification of certain fossils, the general framework of human evolution is fairly well established. The story of the origins of modern humans begins in Africa.

***Australopithecus afarensis*: Our earliest ancestors walked upright** The fossil record indicates that the chimpanzee and human lines diverged from a common hominoid ancestor in Africa about 4–5 million years ago (review Figure 22.12). In the study of human origins, species of hominoids that are more like humans than chimpanzees are referred to as **hominids** (family Hominidae). One of the first hominids to appear was *Australopithecus.* Although all of the genus *Australopithecus* eventually became extinct, one of them, an African hominid named *Australopithecus afarensis,* is thought to be the direct ancestor of modern humans. A nearly complete 3.2-million-year-old skeleton of an *Australopithecus afarensis,* named Lucy by her discoverers, was found in Ethiopia in 1974 (Figure 22.14).

*Australopithecus afarensis* was still distinctly apelike in its anatomy and social structure, with just the beginnings of what we would call human features. Their brains were still relatively small relative to body size—more like chimpanzees than present-day humans. Their teeth had thick enamel, suggesting that they could grind hard foods; most likely they were vegetarian. The males were considerably larger than the females (*sexual dimorphism*), which suggests that *Australopithecus* had a social structure in which large, dominant males exerted control over small bands of females and less dominant males. Lucy, for example, was only about 1 meter tall. Their arms were long relative to their bodies, indicating that they still could travel from tree to tree (arboreal locomotion). But in terms of human evolution, the most important trait of *Australopithecus afarensis* was that they walked upright (Figure 22.15 on page 519).

***Homo habilis:* The first toolmaker** Our first distinctly human ancestor was ***Homo habilis,*** which first appeared about 2.4 million years ago in Africa. Brain enlargement

a) Gibbon b) Orangutan c) Gorilla d) Chimpanzee

**Figure 22.13 The hominoids.** Modern humans (not pictured) are also hominoids, of the family *Hominidae*. Chimpanzees are our closest living relatives.

**Table 22.1 The taxonomic classification system as it applies to modern humans**

| Taxonomic category | Scientific name | Characteristics and examples of life forms in each category |
|---|---|---|
| Kingdom | Animalia | Many-celled organisms with eukaryotic cells and a complex anatomy. Includes all animals: sponges, worms, insects, fish, birds, mammals, and many more. |
| Phylum | Chordata | Animal with a nerve cord and a backbone. Fish, birds, and mammals are examples. |
| Class | Mammalia | Members of the phylum Chordata with hair during part of their life cycle and mammary glands. Includes mice, dogs, cows, whales, kangaroos, primates, and humans. |
| Order | Primata | Members of the class Mammalia with five digits on the fore and hind limbs, flat fingernails, and stereoscopic vision. Lemurs, monkeys, apes, and humans are examples. |
| Family | Hominidae | Primates that walk upright and that have slightly enlarged brains. Includes the genus *Australopithecus* and our *Homo* ancestors (now all extinct) and modern humans. |
| Genus | *Homo* | Hominidae with an enlarged brain and a recognizable human skull and body form. Includes our extinct immediate *Homo* ancestors and modern humans. |
| Species | *sapiens* | *Homo* with large brains and a complex cultural and social structure that includes spoken language. Modern humans. |

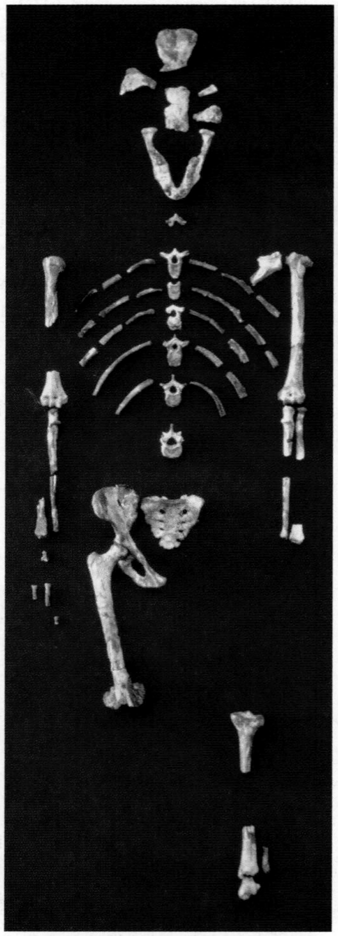

**a) The nearly complete skeleton of Lucy, a young female *Australopithecus afarensis* hominid who lived approximately 3.2 million years ago.**

**b) A reconstruction of Lucy on display at the Field Museum in Chicago.**

**Figure 22.14** ***Australopithecus afarensis*.**

continued in *Homo habilis*, along with changes in teeth and facial features, a decline in sexual dimorphism, and conversion to a diet that included meat. As the first stone tools appear about this time, *Homo habilis* (which means "handy man") may have been the first toolmaker.

***Homo erectus:* Out of Africa** The more human-looking ***Homo erectus*** (and its short-lived cousins *H. georgicus*, and *H. ergaster*) apparently arose from *Homo habilis* ancestors about 1.8 million years ago. *Homo erectus* migrated out of Africa to establish colonies as far away as Java and China. In the past, scientists thought that *Homo erectus* had been the direct ancestor of modern humans via populations that spread across Africa into Asia and Europe. However, *Homo erectus* died out in most locations by about 400,000 years ago. The very last *Homo erectus* lived in Java only 50,000 years ago, making them contemporary with modern humans.

With *Homo erectus* came even more brain enlargement (Figure 22.16), a longer period of infant development, a continued decline in sexual dimorphism, and the continuation and expansion of toolmaking. By 1.7 million years ago, *Homo erectus* had developed specialized stone tools such as hand axes and cleavers. There were probably changes in social structure as well, including male–female pair bonds, shared responsibilities for offspring, and the formation of hunting and gathering groups that shared food.

***Homo heidelbergensis:* "Archaic" humans** Scientists have discovered fossils that show characteristics of both *Homo erectus* and modern human skeletons. Ranging in age from about 800,000 to 200,000 years, these fossils are widely distributed geographically. Some scientists have grouped these so-called archaic humans into a single species, ***Homo heidelbergensis***, named for one of the early finds near Heidelberg, Germany. Whoever they were, these archaic humans created highly specialized stone tools, hunted cooperatively in groups, and may have had limited language skills.

It is possible that some European descendants of *Homo heidelbergensis* became the Neanderthals, a controversial group of humans whose fossils were first discovered in the Neander Valley of Germany. Some researchers assign the Neanderthals to a separate species *(Homo neanderthalensis)*, but this assignment remains controversial. Scientists have long debated whether the Neanderthals, who became extinct about 35,000 years ago, are related to modern humans or were replaced by modern humans and simply became an evolutionary dead end. Comparisons of modern human DNA with DNA extracted from Neanderthal fossils indicate that the Neanderthals were not our direct ancestors, but this conclusion is not universally accepted.

**Figure 22.15 Fossilized footprints of *Australopithecus afarensis*.** Found by Mary Leakey in Tanzania in 1978, these 3.6-million-year-old footprints provided evidence of patterns of early hominid upright posture and locomotion. The prints appear to be of two adults and a child.

***Homo sapiens:* Out of Africa again** The final phase of human development was marked by a substantial increase in brain size, the further development of spoken language, and the development of a physical structure that we would call thoroughly human. Although it is by no means certain, a current hypothesis receiving considerable support is that *Homo sapiens* evolved in Africa from *Homo erectus* between 140,000 and 100,000 years ago. About 50,000 years ago a small band of *Homo sapiens* crossed the sea to what is now Yemen, on the Arabian peninsula. From there they migrated to all parts of the world, reaching the tip of South America about 10,000 years ago.

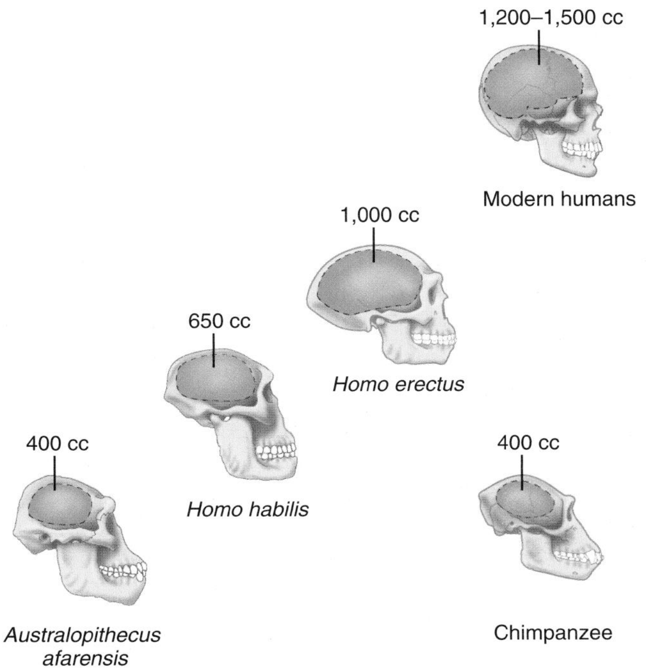


**Figure 22.16 Brain capacities of hominids and of modern chimpanzees.** Brain capacities are in units of cubic centimeters (cc).

A key point is that wherever they went, these new modern humans from Africa replaced all other existing *Homo* species. Ultimately *Homo heidelbergensis* and the Neanderthals vanished completely. Why? We don't know. Although some scientists speculate that there was interspecies violence, there is no evidence of it to date. It is just as likely that they fell victim to disease or were outcompeted for resources. Some researchers speculate that the Neanderthals interbred with *Homo sapiens*, but because they were so few in number compared to *Homo sapiens* their distinctive physical features eventually disappeared. Whatever the reason, the last Neanderthals disappeared about 35,000 years ago.

In what has been termed the greatest anthropological discovery in 50 years, archaeologists recently discovered evidence of what may have been yet another extinct human species, which they named *Homo floresiensis*. This latter group apparently existed as recently as 13,000 years ago, making them fully contemporary with modern humans. (See Current Issue: The Flores People Controversy Heats Up.)

*Homo sapiens* is the sole surviving human species (Figure 22.17 on page 522). At a mere 140,000 years, modern *Homo sapiens* have not been around all that long. To put our existence in perspective, if the history of life on Earth were compressed into a 24-hour day, the entire history of *Homo sapiens* would represent less than the last 3 seconds.

**RECAP**

Modern humans descended from a primate ancestor that began to walk upright nearly 5 million years ago. Over time the brain enlarged, and toolmaking skills and spoken language developed. The current best hypothesis is that modern humans first appeared in Africa about 140,000 years ago and that all present-day *Homo sapiens* descended from that African group. ■

## Differences within the human species

All humans belong to a single species. We are so similar that sometimes the sum of all humankind is called the human race. Nevertheless, there are certain distinct heritable physical differences between subpopulations of the human species that the dictionary defines as racial differences. How did these differences come about?

Throughout most of human history, the total human population existed mainly as smaller subpopulations that were geographically isolated from each other. Minor random mutations coupled with sexual reproduction within isolated subpopulations apparently led to slightly different human

# The Flores People Controversy Heats Up

Liang Bua Cave, where the discovery of the Flores skeleton was made.

In 2004, archaeologists unearthed a female skeleton from Liang Bua cave on the Indonesian island of Flores. They named the skeleton LB1, for Ling Bua #1. LB1 was barely 1 meter tall (about 3.3 feet) and weighed only about 25 kg (55 pounds). She was about 30 years old when she died.

Although similar in size and limb proportions to ancient hominids such as *Australopithecus afarensis*, LB1 bore an eerie resemblance to more recent members of the genus *Homo* in her upright walking posture and chewing ability. Her skull and brain were small, comparable to those of a chimpanzee. So archaeologists were astounded when her bones were dated to only 18,000 years ago—a time when *Homo sapiens* were thought to be the only modern humans living on Earth. Subsequently, bone fragments and teeth of seven other individuals were discovered in the same cave. The bones ranged in age from approximately 70,000 to 12,000 years, indicating a long and successful history in that area.

The Flores people, as the new people were dubbed, were not physically identical to *Homo sapiens*. Their arms were longer, their hands and feet were different, and they had heavier brow ridges, a sloping forehead, and a smaller chin. However, their behavior seemed intriguingly human. For instance, they would have had to cross at least two water barriers from mainland Asia to reach Flores Island. Furthermore, they crafted an impressive variety of stone tools. While most of the implements were relatively simple, some were complex tools comparable to those honed by prehistoric *Homo sapiens*. Many tools were found mingled with the bones of *Stegodon*, a 2,200-pound dwarf relative of modern elephants that—although small for an elephant—would have posed a significant challenge to hunters only 3 feet tall. This indicates that the Flores people engaged in group hunting activities that required planning and cooperation.

The discoverers proposed that the Flores people represent a new species descended from *Homo erectus*, which they named *Homo floresiensis*. They proposed that they became smaller than their *Homo erectus* ancestors as a result of an evolutionary adaptation to limited food supplies on the island, a phenomenon known as "Island dwarfism." Indeed, the ancestors of *Stegodon* were the size of modern elephants when they came to Flores Island, and they also grew smaller.

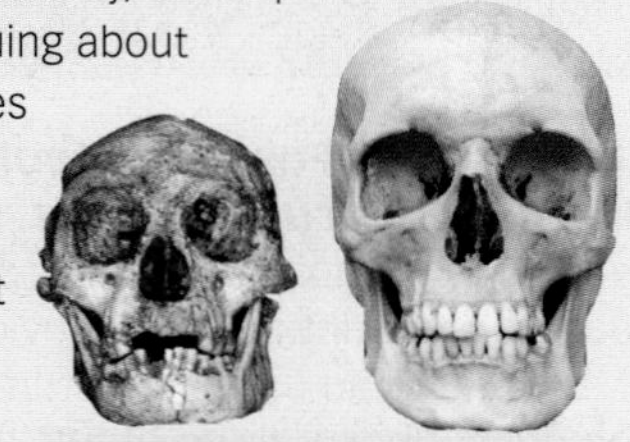

Skulls of Homo floresiensis (left) and Homo sapiens (right).

Almost immediately, anthropologists began arguing about whether the Flores people were, or were not, a new species. The most controversial aspect of LB1 was her brain size. The proposal that a hominid with that small a brain would be capable of making the sophisticated tools found with the Flores people came in direct conflict with most of what anthropologists believe about brain size and mental capacity. A large brain size, it had long been argued, was required for sophisticated tool-making and complex social organizations. How could a brain that small accomplish so much?

Several alternative hypotheses were proposed, all of them seeking to explain LB1's physical characteristics on the basis of known human diseases. Two disease possibilities were Laron syndrome, an inherited type of dwarfism marked by insensitivity to growth hormone, and myxoedematous endemic cretinism, a disorder caused by nutritional deficiencies. With no serious evidence to back them up, however, both of these hypotheses quickly fell out of favor. The best-supported hypothesis was that the Flores people were small-bodied *Homo sapiens* with microcephaly, a rare human condition marked by small brains and mental retardation. It turns out that LB1's skull is nearly the same size as skulls of modern human microcephalics. The lead author of a study making comparisons between LB1 and microcephalics concluded that LB1 was a modern human with microcephaly, saying "It is simply fanciful to imagine that this fossil represents anything other than a modern human."

## the **facts**...

- Archaeologists recently discovered partial remains of up to eight individuals of a small human species that became extinct only 12,000 years ago.
- Discoverers named this new species *Homo floresiensis*.
- The only skull found has a brain size comparable to that of a modern chimpanzee. However, these were intelligent people, as evidenced by their tools and their hunting abilities.
- The discovery challenges anthropologists' current beliefs about the relationship between brain size and human mental capacity and behavior.

Another completely independent observation also did not support the hypothesis that the Flores people descended from a larger-brained human ancestor such as *Homo erectus*. The observation is that as a human species becomes dwarfed from a larger ancestor, brain capacity doesn't necessarily decline. For example, there is not much difference in brain size between the 2-meter-tall Masai people of East Africa and the 1.4-meter-tall Bambuti people of the Congo. How, then, could the Flores people have descended from larger-brained ancestors and lost so much brain size?

Adding fuel to the controversy, shortly after the microcephalic study appeared a team of researchers led by Florida State University anthropologist Dean Falk hypothesized that the Flores people never had a big brain in the first place. Dr. Falk's team created three-dimensional reconstructions of nine microcephalic brains and the brains of 10 normal humans, and then looked closely for areas of significant difference. They found two areas of the brain that were completely different between healthy humans and microcephalics. And when they compared a reconstruction of LB1's brain to the healthy and microcephalic brains, they found that it had the two distinguishing characteristics of the healthy brains, except that the brain was smaller. Most importantly, the frontal lobes of the LB1 skull are large, consistent with higher cognitive processes. Dr. Falk's group believes that the Flores people represent a separate species that developed an unusually efficient small brain rather than a large brain. "It didn't get bigger, it got rewired and reorganized," says Dr. Falk. If this assertion is corroborated by additional evidence, we may need to abandon the presumption that a large brain is required for higher cognitive abilities and advanced tool-making.

Anthropologist Dean Falk believes that *Homo floresiensis* is not a microcephalic. "It's time to move on to other important questions," she says.

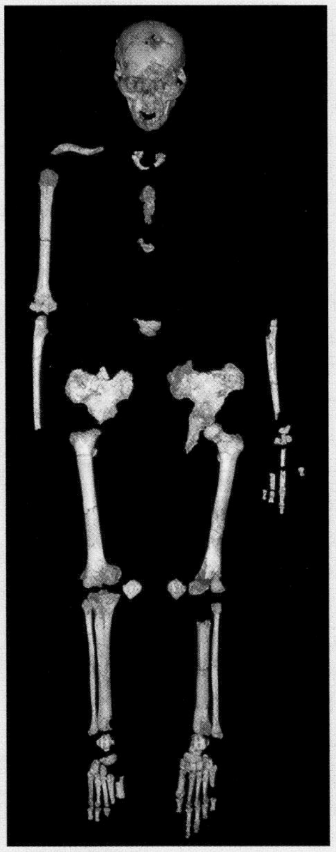

*LB1, the only nearly complete skeleton of Homo floresiensis.*

Additional evidence that *Homo floresiensis* is a separate species is the anatomy of LB1's hands and feet. Modern humans have a complex of five bones in the wrist that act as a shock absorber when we use the wrist forcefully, such as pounding with heavy tools or doing precision work. The shape of the wrist bones is very different in *Homo habilis*, the first toolmaker, who died out more than 1.6 million years ago. The wrist bones of LB1 closely resemble those of *Homo habilis* but not modern humans, even though she lived only 18,000 years ago, right along with modern humans. And her feet are much longer than the feet of modern humans—so long that the Flores people are hypothesized to have walked with a high-stepping gate and been poor runners. Taken together, the skull, hands, and feet of LB1 suggest that the Flores people were not diseased modern humans. Instead, they probably diverged from the line that became modern humans sometime back about the time of *Homo erectus*, and then managed to survive until almost the present day.

Although the pendulum seems to be swinging in favor of calling the Flores people a separate species, don't expect the controversy to be over any time soon. So far all we have is one skull, a partial skeleton, and bone and teeth fragments from about half a dozen individuals. It may be a while before we know for sure who the Flores people really were. In the meantime, it's likely to remain a contentious issue among anthropologists.

### Questions to consider

*1 Do you think the Flores people should be classified as a separate species? Why or why not? 2 Do you think it's important that we try to discover the evolutionary history of humans? Who should finance anthropological research, and why?*

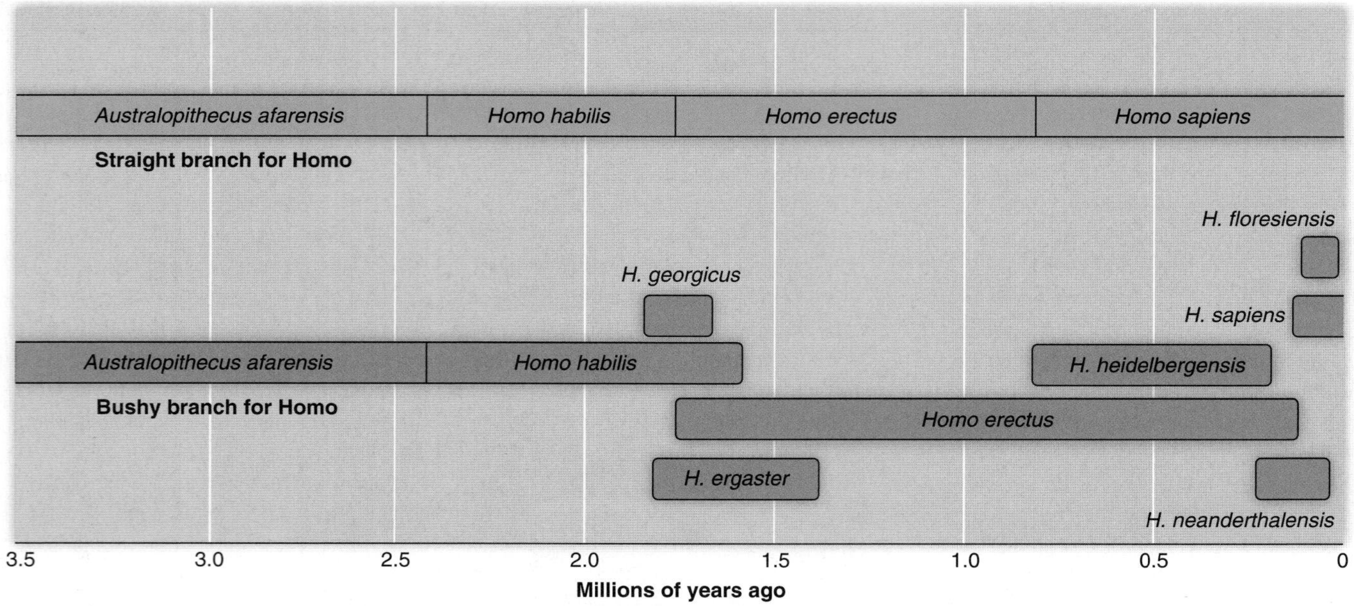


**Figure 22.17 Two versions of the family tree for *Homo sapiens*.** The straight branch version is the probable direct lineage. The bottom bushy branch shows our various extinct *Homo* relatives. The entire 3.5 million years shown in this figure corresponds to a sliver of the zero time line at the top of Figure 22.11.

group phenotypes (referred to as *races*) that are still observable today. Human racial differences are a testament to the effectiveness of evolution over tens of thousands of years.

Some racial differences may have helped humans adapt more effectively to their environment. For example, in a climate with intense sunlight a dark skin color would have offered protection against excessive ultraviolet radiation. But in a northern climate where sunlight was less intense a light skin color would have been helpful because small amounts of ultraviolet radiation are required to activate vitamin D. Facial features and even blood types may also have had their special advantages at the time. Other differences may simply have been neutral, meaning that they were the result of mutations that did no harm and so were retained in the population in which they arose.

In the final analysis, racial differences are nothing more than differences in phenotypes between subgroups of our common species. But then, individual phenotypes are all very different, too (Figure 22.18). In fact, DNA analysis reveals that there are as many differences between individuals of the same race as there are between individuals of different races. Given that there are no biological barriers to reproduction and that global travel and communication have recently become commonplace, human racial differences may disappear over the next 10,000 to 100,000 years, assuming we survive that long as a species.

**Figure 22.18 The human species.** Genotypic and phenotypic differences between individuals of the same race are as great as the differences between races.

**RECAP**

All human beings belong to the same species. Racial differences most likely arose as adaptations to different environments in geographically isolated human subpopulations. ■

# Chapter Summary

### Evidence for evolution comes from many sources *p. 507*

- The theory of evolution is the single most unifying concept in biology today.
- The fossil record provides a physical record of life-forms that lived in the past.
- Patterns of embryonic development and structures with common evolutionary origins can be used to determine relationships between life-forms.
- Structural similarities between proteins and DNA can be used to define closeness of evolutionary relationships.
- Geographical separations can affect the distributions of evolving life-forms.

### Natural selection contributes to evolution *p. 512*

- Mutations coupled with natural selection are the cause of most microevolution.
- The pool of alleles in a population is affected by chance events such as genetic drift and gene flow.
- At least five mass extinctions have altered the course of macroevolution.
- An evolutionary tree visually depicts relationships between species.

### The young Earth was too hot for life *p. 514*

- Earth was formed about 4.6 billion years ago. At first, it was a harsh environment with constant cycles of condensation and vaporization.
- Life began about 3.8 billion years ago.

### The first cells were able to live without oxygen *p. 514*

- Organic molecules formed from gases in Earth's atmosphere.
- The first self-replicating molecule was probably single-stranded RNA.
- The first cell was formed when RNA and organic molecules became enclosed in a membrane.
- The early atmosphere was devoid of oxygen, so the first living cells survived by anaerobic metabolism.

### Photosynthetic organisms altered the course of evolution *p. 515*

- Oxygen appeared only after certain life-forms developed the process of photosynthesis as a way to produce organic molecules inside the cell.
- With oxygen available, other cells developed the process of aerobic metabolism as a way to extract energy from organic molecules.
- Eukaryotes became the dominant cell type, and multicellular organisms evolved.

### Modern humans came from Africa *p. 516*

- Humans are a relatively recent development on Earth. Humans and modern chimpanzees evolved from a common ancestor that lived about 5 million years ago.
- *Australopithecus afarensis* and *Homo habilis* were early hominids in human evolution.
- Modern humans apparently first appeared in Africa about 140,000 years ago. From there they spread around the world.
- Heritable, observable, physical phenotype differences in human subpopulations are called racial differences. Racial differences are no more significant than differences between individuals. We all belong to the same human species.

# Terms You Should Know

adaptive radiation, *513*
analogous structures, *509*
evolution, *507*
evolutionary tree, *513*
extinction, *513*
fossil, *507*
gene flow, *513*
genetic drift, *512*
hominid, *517*
hominoid, *516*
*Homo habilis*, *517*
*Homo sapiens*, *516*
homologous structures, *509*
macroevolution, *507*
mammal, *516*
microevolution, *507*
natural selection, *512*
population, *512*
primate, *516*
species, *516*
vestigial structures, *509*

# Concept Review

1. Describe the three key elements of evolution.
2. Explain how a fossil is created.
3. List some of the main sources of evidence for evolution.
4. Describe how natural selection contributes to evolution.
5. Explain how genetic drift and gene flow affect populations.
6. Summarize the scientific theory of how life began on Earth.
7. Explain how rising atmospheric concentrations of oxygen affected life on Earth.
8. List the features that make Hominidae different from other families in the order Primata.
9. Describe the origins of *Homo sapiens*.
10. Explain why racial differences may disappear within the next 100,000 years.

# Test Yourself

### Matching Exercise

_____ 1. Organisms that do not require oxygen for their metabolic processes.
_____ 2. The term for a body structure that no longer has any function
_____ 3. These body structures serve similar functions but do not have the same evolutionary origin
_____ 4. The first of our human ancestors to use tools
_____ 5. An early human ancestor that walked upright
_____ 6. Geographical redistribution of alleles

a. vestigial
b. *Homo habilis*
c. analogous
d. anaerobic
e. gene flow
f. *Australopithecus afarensis*

**Fill in the Blank**

7. Body structures that share a common origin are said to be ____________________.
8. A(n) ____________________ is a group of individuals of the same species that occupies the same geographical area.
9. The first self-replicating molecule on Earth appears to have been ____________________.
10. ____________________ dating uses isotopes to determine the age of rocks.
11. ____________________ is the study of the planetary distribution of plants and animals.
12. Identify your genus and species: ____________________.

**True or False?**

13. Because of the nature of the fossilization process, the fossil record consists largely of soft tissues such as skin and internal organs.
14. When he coined the term *natural selection*, Darwin meant that individuals with traits that made them more fit for their local environments were more likely to survive and reproduce.
15. Even without random mutations evolution can occur.

## Apply **What You Know**

1. Because dogs are all one species, different breeds of dogs can mate and produce viable offspring. How, then, did different breeds of dogs with distinct characteristics evolve?
2. How would you expect an increase in gene flow in the human population to affect human phenotypes?
3. Critics of evolution often charge, correctly as it turns out, that the fossil record is incomplete and scientists cannot show how all living things evolved over time. Why don't we have a complete record?
4. Radiometric dating is a useful technique for identifying the age of fossils. Why does the suspected age of the fossil determine which isotope an investigator might use to try to date it?
5. There are species of fish that live in caves no longer connected to the surface. These fish have eye structures even though the fish are blind. Why do they have eyes even though the eyes don't function?
6. It is believed that humans evolved in Africa and then spread to all the other continents. If this is so, explain why the people of northern Europe do not have dark skin.
7. Throughout Earth's history many species, and perhaps even most of the species that ever existed, have become extinct. The causes are numerous: climate change, volcanic activity, the actions of oxygen producing organisms, changes in carbon dioxide concentration, and even asteroid impacts. Have humans ever caused extinctions?
8. Of all the great evolutionary advances of life on Earth, which organisms have contributed the most significant ones: simple organisms or complex multicellular organisms like plants and animals?

*Answers can be found on the Human Biology Place.*

## References and Additional Reading

Amigoni, D., and J. Wallace, eds. *Charles Darwin's Origin of Species—New Interdisciplinary Essays*. New York: Manchester University Press, 1995. (Essays in history, literature, sociology, and anthropology related to the work of Charles Darwin.)

Falk, Dean, *et. al.* Brain Shape in Human Microcephalics and *Homo floresiensis*. *Proceedings of the National Academy of Sciences of the United States*, February 13, 2007, pp. 2513–2518. (A research article by a leading paleoanthropologist which supports the hypothesis that *Homo floresiensis* is a new species, not a modern human with microcephaly.)

Stix, G. Traces of a Distant Past. *Scientific American*, July 2008, pp. 56–63. (A recent article that traces the paths of human migration from Africa, using modern DNA analysis techniques.)

Ward, P. The Greenhouse Extinction. *Discover*, August 1998, p. 54. (An examination of the possible cause of the largest mass extinction on Earth that occurred 250 million years ago.)

Wong, K. The Littlest Human. *Scientific American*, February 2005, p. 56. (An article about the discovery of the Flores people.)

Zimmer, Carl. What Is a Species? *Scientific American*, June 2008, p.72–79. (An examination of why a species is so hard to define.)

### Internet References

Find links to these Web sites at the Human Biology Place.

**Smithsonian Institution**
**http://anthropology.si.edu/humanorigins/ha/a_tree.html**
The "Early Human Phylogeny": A "family tree" of hominid ancestors, with descriptions and photos of fossils.

**Australian Museum**
**www.amonline.net.au/human_evolution/index.htm**
An overview of evolution, with photos and information about skulls, skeletons, and tools.

**Sibiloi National Park, Kenya**
**www.sibiloi.com**
Many important fossils have been discovered in Sibiloi Park; click the Prehistory link for more on its rich paleontological heritage.

**"Sue at the Field Museum"**
**www.fieldmuseum.org/sue/index.html**
All about Sue, the world's largest and most complete *T. rex* dinosaur fossil: 42 feet long, and the skull alone weighs 600 pounds.

# 23 Ecosystems and Populations

**1** **True or False?** Nearly all life on Earth is **solar-powered**.

**2** **True or false?** A population can continue to grow **indefinitely**.

**3** In the wild, plants rely on which of the following for their **nitrogen** requirements?

**a.** nitrogen-fixing bacteria in plant roots
**b.** gaseous nitrogen, taken directly from the air **c.** nitrogen from sediments
**d.** ammonium and nitrates in soil

**4** 75% of Earth's **surface** is covered by one substance. Which is it? **a.** Soil **b.** Rock **c.** Water **d.** Oil

**5** The oil we burn for **energy** comes from: **a.** decomposed plant and animal material. **b.** liquefied rocks. **c.** compressed gas.

Blue Wildebeest herd during migration, Masai Mara National Reserve, Kenya.

**Throughout this book,** we have focused on understanding enough basic biology to appreciate *human* biology. As you know by now, all living organisms have certain features in common. We all consist of one or more living cells, and we have the capacity to reproduce. We share a common origin and have evolved over time. And, perhaps most importantly, we share the same planet. Our futures are inextricably linked.

**Ecology** is the study of the relationships between organisms—including humans—and their physical environment. In this chapter we begin by describing general principles of ecology and of population dynamics. We also examine the rapid growth of the human population and the possible effects of this growth on our world in the future. The dynamics of our population on Earth are no different, conceptually, from those of a bacterial population in a laboratory dish—it's just that our world is slightly bigger (and our generation times are longer).

## 23.1 Ecosystems: Communities interact with their environment

The basic unit of study in ecology is an *ecosystem*. *Eco-* implies a connection to the environment, and *system* indicates that an ecosystem is a functional unit. An **ecosystem** consists of a community of organisms *and* the physical environment in which they live. An ecosystem comprises all the living things, all the matter, and all the energy. In an ecosystem we consider not only who eats whom, but how nonliving matter is recycled and how energy flows into and out of the system. The components of an ecosystem form a hierarchy that includes populations, communities, and the physical environment in which they live.

As discussed in Chapter 22, a **population** is a group of individuals of the same species that occupy the same geographic area and interact with each other. A population of elk inhabits a mountain valley, and a population of frogs inhabits a small pond.

A **community** consists of the populations of all the species that occupy the same geographic area and therefore interact. Some organisms serve as food or shelter for others. Insects feed on decaying wood. Woodpeckers feed on the insects and make nests in those same trees. Deer browse on shrubs, cougars hunt the deer, and so on. A community is the living part of an ecosystem.

Together, all of the ecosystems on Earth compose the **biosphere,** or planetary ecosystem (refer back to Figure 1.7 on p. 7). The biosphere is so complex that it is difficult to study as one entity. Studies of simpler ecosystems have, however, led to some interesting conclusions that may apply to the entire biosphere as well. Most importantly, it appears that ecosystems are delicately balanced self-sustaining units in which organisms interact with each other and their environment in complex ways. In the process, they can modify or control the physical and chemical nature of the ecosystem itself. Some ecologists suggest that disturbing the delicate balance of the biosphere could endanger the survival of the human species—and of all other species as well.

**RECAP**

An ecosystem consists of a community of organisms and their physical environment, and a community consists of all populations that interact within the same area. The biosphere comprises all ecosystems on Earth. ■

## 23.2 Populations: The dynamics of one species in an ecosystem

Characteristics of populations include habitat, range, size, actual growth rate, and potential capacity for growth.

### Where a species lives: Habitat and range

A species' **habitat** is the type of location where it chooses to live (Figure 23.1). Typically this is determined by its tolerance

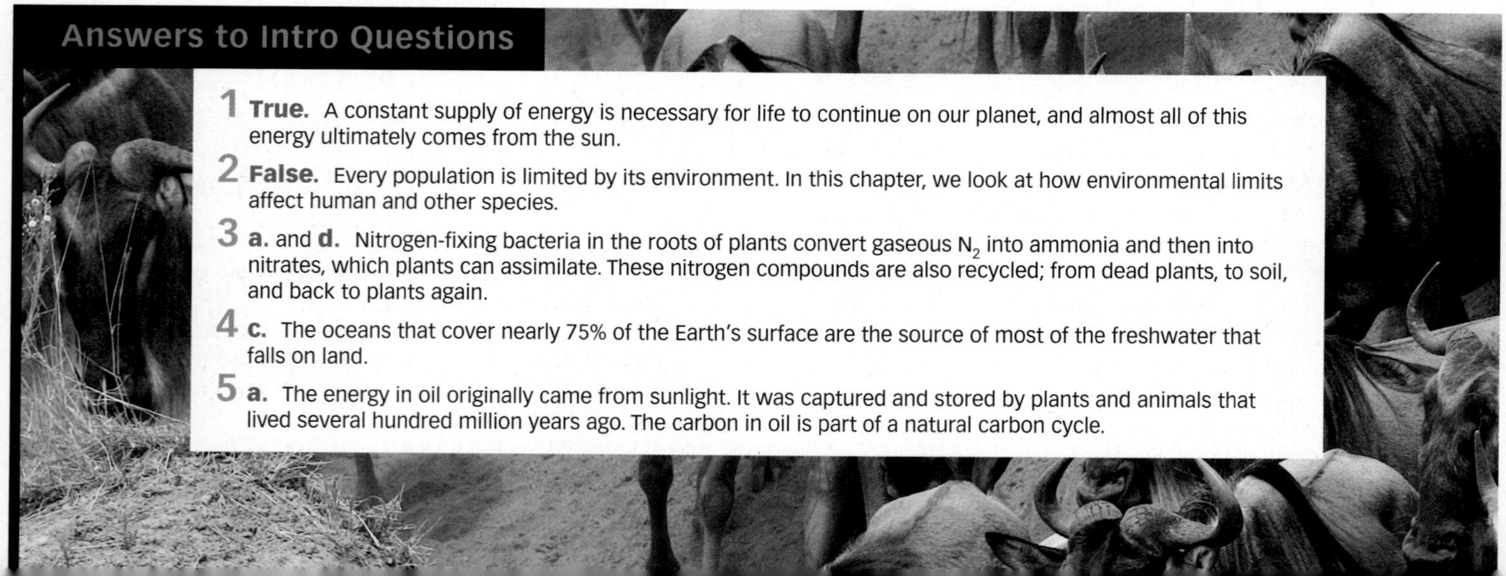

**Answers to Intro Questions**

1 **True.** A constant supply of energy is necessary for life to continue on our planet, and almost all of this energy ultimately comes from the sun.

2 **False.** Every population is limited by its environment. In this chapter, we look at how environmental limits affect human and other species.

3 **a.** and **d.** Nitrogen-fixing bacteria in the roots of plants convert gaseous $N_2$ into ammonia and then into nitrates, which plants can assimilate. These nitrogen compounds are also recycled; from dead plants, to soil, and back to plants again.

4 **c.** The oceans that cover nearly 75% of the Earth's surface are the source of most of the freshwater that falls on land.

5 **a.** The energy in oil originally came from sunlight. It was captured and stored by plants and animals that lived several hundred million years ago. The carbon in oil is part of a natural carbon cycle.

These red-eyed tree frogs inhabit the tree canopy of the Costa Rican rain forest.

**Figure 23.1 Habitats.** An organism's habitat is the place where it chooses to live.

for certain environmental conditions. For example, the habitat of the now rare northern spotted owl is mature evergreen forests, the habitat of the bison is grassland, and beavers prefer a habitat of mountain valleys with freshwater streams and small trees.

Each organism's habitat has certain chemical and physical characteristics that favor the organism's comfort and survival. Animals and plants that occupy the same or overlapping habitats form a community, competing with each other for resources in terms of matter or energy and using each other for food and/or shelter.

Note that a habitat refers to the specific part of an ecosystem that a particular population of organisms occupies and is therefore typically a subset of the whole. The sum of the populations and their habitats form the ecosystem. For example, the habitat of water-strider insects is the surface of a pond, and the pond and all its inhabitants constitute an ecosystem.

Because the availability of ideal habitats varies, each species also has a **geographic range** of distribution representing the area over which it may be found. An organism's range is limited by several factors: (1) competition for resources such as sunlight or nutrients, (2) intolerable conditions such as extreme temperatures or altitude, or (3) physical obstacles including mountain ranges, deserts, and bodies of water.

In the last few centuries the development of worldwide transportation has enabled some animals to expand their ranges beyond physical barriers. For example, innovations in navigation and shipbuilding allowed European humans to cross the Atlantic Ocean and expand their range into North and South America.

## Population growth rate tends toward biotic potential

One of the most important topics in ecology is how populations change in size over time. The maximum rate of growth of any population under ideal conditions is called its **biotic potential.** Biotic potential is a function of certain characteristics of the species itself, including:

- The number of offspring produced by each reproducing member (female, if reproduction is sexual)
- The time span before the offspring reach reproductive maturity
- The sex distribution if reproduction is sexual (ratio of males to females)
- The number of reproductive-age members of the population

Typically, the biotic potential of any organism follows an **exponential growth** curve with a characteristic J shape. For any species, the steepness of the growth curve, representing the biotic potential, is determined by the four factors above. The J shape reflects the fact that under ideal conditions, populations would double again and again over similar time periods. (See the Try It Yourself box on page 529 for a way to figure doubling time.)

## Environmental resistance limits biotic potential

In the real world of finite resources and competition, an opposing force called **environmental resistance** limits any species' ability to consistently realize its biotic potential (Figure 23.2). Environmental resistance consists of factors that kill organisms and/or prevent them from reproducing.

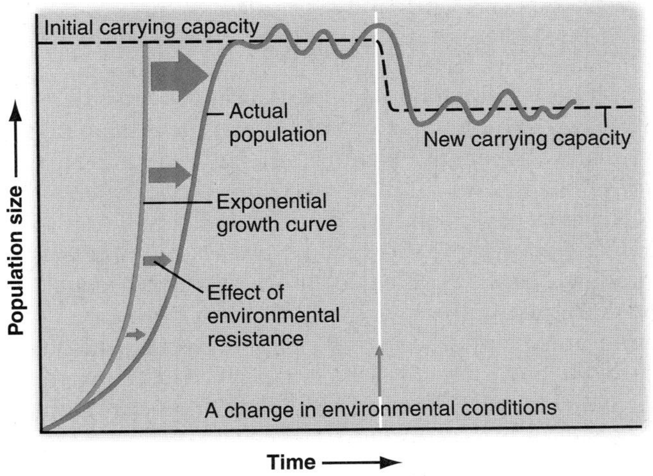


**Figure 23.2 Effects of environmental resistance and carrying capacity on population size.** As the population increases, the environmental resistance to continued ideal exponential growth increases. Eventually the population stabilizes near the carrying capacity. Changing environmental conditions can alter the carrying capacity.

Examples include limitations on nutrients, energy, and space; disease; predation by other organisms; and environmental toxins.

Even when conditions are ideal to begin with, eventually every growing population reaches a point where environmental resistance begins to increase. For bacteria in a petri dish or humans living on an island, it may be the food supply. For a population of mice it may be disease brought about by overcrowding. For a woodpecker it may be a lack of suitable nesting sites. Although we cannot always measure the specific environmental resistance, no population grows at its full biotic potential indefinitely.

Ultimately a population achieves an approximate balance between biotic potential and environmental resistance. At this point it stabilizes, reaching a steady state. The population that the ecosystem can support indefinitely is called the **carrying capacity.** Population sizes may vary around their carrying capacity from time to time. In addition, the carrying capacity can change if environmental conditions change. A wet spring might increase the carrying capacity of a prairie ecosystem for certain grasses and the animals that feed on those grasses, and three years of drought might reduce the carrying capacity to below its average value. But in the end, every population tends to stabilize near its carrying capacity.

**RECAP**

Every species has a preferred habitat and a geographic range over which it is distributed. Under ideal conditions a population grows exponentially according to its biotic potential. Under normal circumstances, however, environmental resistance limits growth. The population of a particular species that an ecosystem can sustain indefinitely is called its carrying capacity. ■

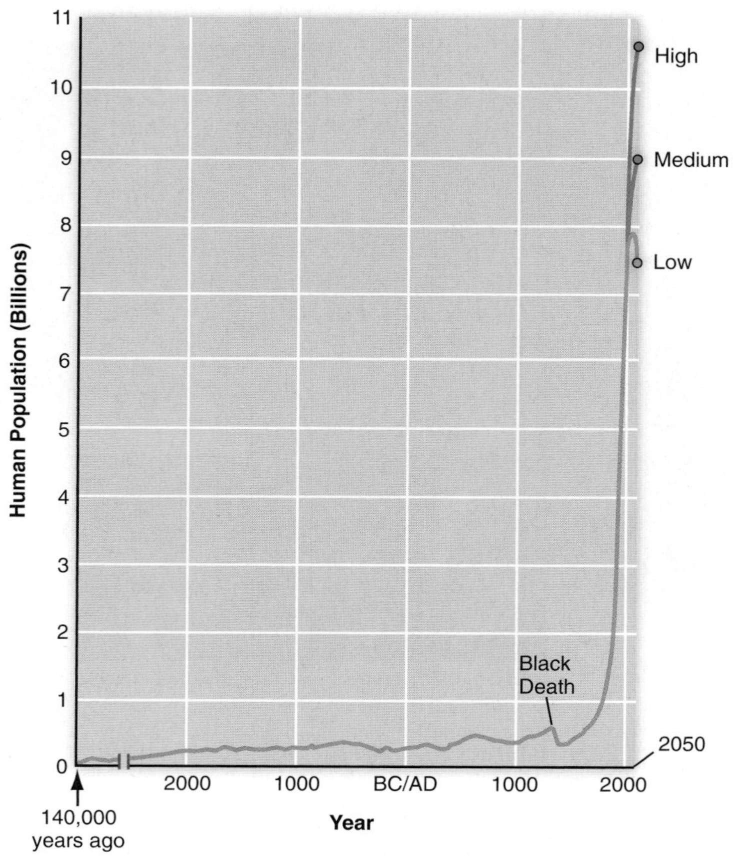


**Figure 23.3 Past and projected growth of the human population.** The human population currently is 6.7 billion. The dip in the population in the 1300s was caused by the Black Death, a bacterial plague that devastated the human population in Europe and Asia. The high, medium, and low world population projections are based on steady-state fertility rates of 2.6, 2.1, and 1.6 children per woman, respectively, by 2050.

*Data after 1950 from:* Population Division of the Department of Economic and Social Affairs at the United Nations Secretariat.

## 23.3 Human population growth

A graph of the global human population over just the past 4,000 years of human history shows that the human population is growing rapidly (Figure 23.3). How will this affect our world in the future?

For most of human history the global population remained relatively low and apparently stable, never exceeding 10 million people. People lived in widely dispersed small groups whose numbers were held in check by disease, famine, and a lack of tools and technology with which to control the environment or even to grow food. Apparently the environmental resistance was so high that our population was already at its carrying capacity.

About 4,000 years ago, the global human population began to rise slowly. The development of agriculture and the subsequent domestication of animals and plants for our own uses led to better conditions (a reduction in environmental resistance) and an increase in carrying capacity. Rapid growth began in the 1700s (barely 300 years ago) with the Industrial Revolution. Advances in communication, transportation, technologies for feeding and housing more people, and medical care, including the discovery of antibiotics and vaccines, have favored human reproduction and survival. As a result, the human population has entered a phase of explosive growth. Note that the human population curve in Figure 23.3 resembles a J-shaped curve, typical of a population that is increasing according to its biotic potential, without any apparent environmental resistance.

Can we continue this trend? We do not know how high the human carrying capacity might be or how much it could be raised by future discoveries that we can't even imagine. Some scientists believe that the concept of carrying capacity doesn't apply to humans, due to our seeming ability to increase our own carrying capacity by eliminating competing species, importing locally scarce resources, and developing new technologies.

Another view, taking into account our seemingly unlimited biotic potential, is to re-state the concept in terms of the maximum "load" that people can safely impose on the environment. In this case we have to take into account increasing per capita consumption of environmental resources. We then have to consider the possibility that we will inadvertently *lower* the carrying capacity of Earth through environmental degradation or other human actions, forcing a reduction in overall human population. At some time our population must stabilize at a point short of having a person standing on every square foot of Earth.

## Zero Population Growth Has Not Yet Been Achieved

The **growth rate** of a population is calculated as the number of births per year minus the number of deaths per year, divided by the total population. Currently the human population is growing about 1.2% per year. Although that doesn't sound like much, according to the "Rule of 72" (see the Try It Yourself box) at this rate the human population would double in the next 60 years.

**Zero population growth** is the point at which births equal deaths. To reach that point, of course, we would have to either decrease the birth rate or increase the death rate. Given that no one would advocate increasing the death rate on purpose, let's look at how we might reach a zero population growth through changing the birth rate.

The human **fertility rate** is the number of children born to each woman during her lifetime. Fertility experts agree that the average fertility rate required to achieve long-term zero population growth, called the **replacement fertility rate,** is about 2.1 children per woman. Those 2.1 children would exactly replace the equivalent of the two people (a woman and a man) who produced them. The replacement fertility rate is slightly higher than 2.0 because some children die before reaching their reproductive years.

The United Nations Population Division estimates that if replacement fertility rate is achieved by 2050, the world population would stabilize at about 9 billion. However, if fertility rates stabilize at lower or higher levels, the global population could range from a declining 7.4 billion to a rapidly increasing 10.6 billion (refer back to Figure 23.3). Note that the difference between the low and high projections is only one child per couple. (High, medium, and low population projections are based on fertility rates of 2.6, 2.1, and 1.6 children per couple.) Keep in mind that these graphs present global averages. Some areas, such as Africa and Asia, contribute to population growth more than others.

**RECAP**

The human population began to rise rapidly during the Industrial Revolution. Although we don't yet know Earth's human carrying capacity, eventually the human population must stop increasing. We will reach zero population growth when deaths equal births. This would mean the fertility rate would have to fall to the replacement fertility rate of 2.1 children per woman. ■

## Population age structure is linked to economic development

A nation's *age structure* describes the number of people in each age group within the population. As a nation develops, the age structure of its population undergoes a **demographic transition** (*demography* is the study of human populations). A demographic transition is a progression of population changes that are tied to the region's industrial development and the economic well-being of its citizens. The first stage of a demographic transition sees a shift from a society dominated by poor living conditions and a high death rate to one of rapidly improving economic conditions, declining death rate, and higher birth rate. In the final stages of transition the birth rate slowly declines until it equals the death rate, achieving zero population growth.

Demographic transitions have been underway around the world since the 1700s, with some countries further along in the transition than others. Demographers categorize nations with established industry-based economies as **more industrialized countries (MICs)** and those that are only just beginning to industrialize as **less industrialized countries (LICs).** The MICs, which include most countries of Europe, North America, northeastern Asia, and Australia, are in later stages of

**try it yourself**

### The Rule of 72

A human population growing at a rate of only 1.5% per year will double in just 48 years. How do we know that? You can calculate it yourself by applying a simple mathematical rule known as the rule of 72, which states that dividing the number 72 by the percentage increase per unit of time yields the time it will take for any number to double. In the human population example above, divide 72 by 1.5 and you get 48 years. The rule works for any time period and for any percentage increase, not just one relating to population. Try it yourself:

1. How long would it take the human population to double if it were increasing at a rate of 2% per year? (______ years)
2. How long would it take a bacterial population to double if it were increasing at a rate of 24% per hour? (______ hours)
3. How long would it take you to double your money if it were earning interest at a rate of 4% per year? (______ years) How about at 7.2% per year? (______ years)

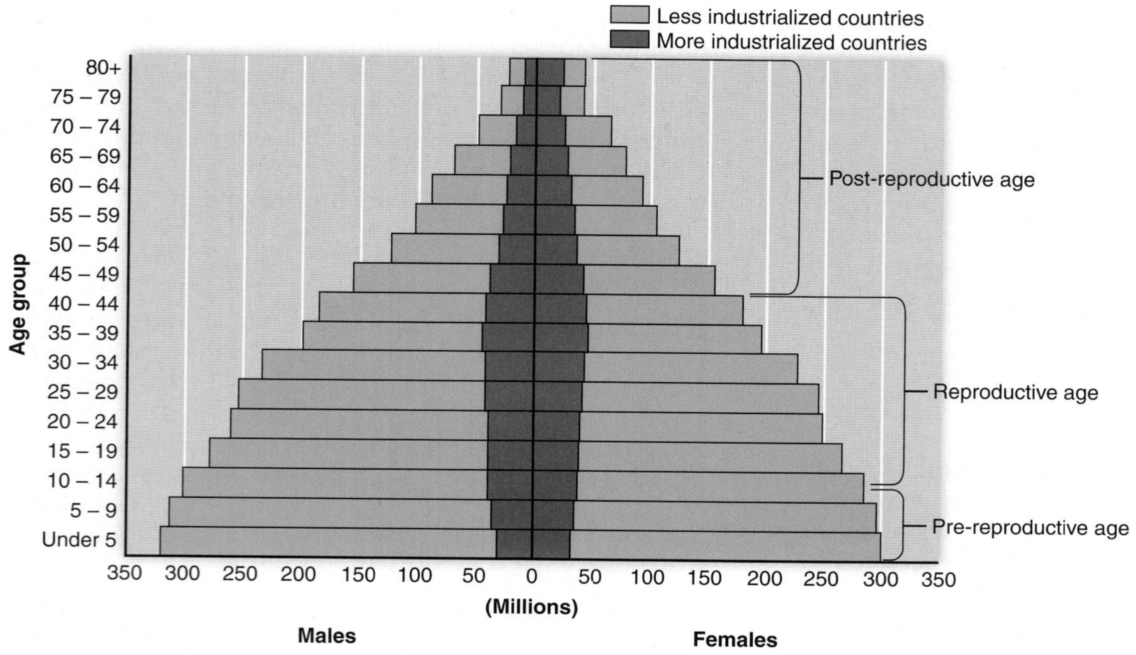


**Figure 23.4 Population age structures in the LICs and MICs.** The pyramid shape of the age structure of the LICs indicates that much of the population is younger than reproductive age. Therefore it is likely that their populations will continue to expand. The MICs have roughly the same number of people in each age group in and below the reproductive years, indicating a stable population in the future.

*Source:* U.S. Bureau of the Census, International Data Base.

demographic transition than the LICs, which include most nations of Africa, Latin America, and Asia. The demographic patterns suggest that industrialization raises the human carrying capacity and allows the population to expand to a new steady state.

Figure 23.4 depicts the population age structures of the LICs versus the MICs. Males within various age groups are shown on the left of the figure and females are shown on the right. The population of the less industrialized countries has a pyramid-like age structure, with a large proportion of young people still below reproductive age. In a stable population the age structure is more bullet-shaped, with roughly the same number of people in each age group through the reproductive years.

Although it may seem counterintuitive, the population of an LIC is likely to continue to grow even after the replacement fertility rate of 2.1 children per woman has been achieved. This is because an LIC typically has more young people entering their reproductive years than are leaving. In this case, the country's population will continue to grow for several more decades simply because there are more women in their reproductive years.

The problem, therefore, is that the largest increases in population over the next 50 years are likely to occur in the very nations that are least able to provide for their citizens. To prevent poverty and starvation in these countries, we must seek solutions that promote economic development while at the same time slowing their population growth rate. Family planning and other social programs that encourage delaying childbirth or reducing the number of children per couple would certainly help. Even government action has worked in some societies. In China, for example, it is against the law to have more than two children. In addition, substantial evidence supports the hypothesis that one of the most effective ways to reduce the birth rate is to improve the economic, social, and political standing of women in a society. Cultural norms and religious beliefs may conflict with this approach in some cultures, however.

**RECAP**

A population can continue to grow for decades after reaching the replacement fertility rate if it has a pyramid-shaped age structure with a large proportion of children under reproductive age. Such an age structure is typical of less industrialized countries as they become more industrialized. Consequently, most of the increase in human population during the next century will occur in LICs. ■

## 23.4 Communities: Different species living together

### Overlapping niches foster competition

An organism's **niche** is its role in the community—its functional relationship with all living and nonliving resources of its habitat (Figure 23.5). A woodpecker's habitat is woodland forests. Its niche is to rid trees of their insect infestations and serve as a food supply for hawks or raccoons, or ultimately for bacteria. A well-balanced ecosystem supports a wide variety of species, each with a different niche.

Although two species do not occupy exactly the same niche, niches can overlap enough that competition may occur between species for limited resources (Figure 23.6). Plants may compete for available sunlight or mineral nutrients, and animals often compete for similar food supplies

Figure 23.5 **An organism's role in its community is its niche.** A woodpecker's habitat is woodland forest, and its niche includes pest control. The woodpecker shown here is feeding on insects that damage trees.

Figure 23.6 **Competition.** Organisms within an ecosystem compete with each other for food and habitat. This bear is competing for food with other foragers of human trash such as raccoons and opossums, and for habitat with humans and other animals.

(for example, both foxes and hawks prey on mice). Depending on their particular niches, one species may be able to out-compete another in a given location, a phenomenon known as *competitive exclusion*. As the human population expands into new habitats, humans are increasingly excluding other species.

## Succession leads toward a climax community

Most natural communities undergo constant change. **Succession** is a natural sequence of change in terms of which organisms dominate in a community. Succession is determined by population growth rates, the niches occupied by various species, and the kinds of competition that exist between them.

If you have ever seen an abandoned field grow first to weeds, then to shrubs, and finally to trees, you have watched succession in action. Organisms that can reproduce and grow quickly under the prevailing conditions are the first to arrive in any area. These first organisms provide food and shelter for the next arrivals, which grow more slowly but occupy more specific niches. The number of species tends to increase as the succession advances and interrelationships between populations become ever more complex.

If the area suffers no major shocks, such as a fire, succession ends with the establishment of a *climax community*. Climax communities are the most efficient communities in terms of energy and nutrient utilization and also the most varied in terms of numbers of species. A climax community may take hundreds of years to develop, and retains its character for many hundreds to thousands of years.

The type of climax community found in any region is largely determined by the physical environment but can also be influenced by the organisms living in surrounding areas. In the Northeast United States, the typical climax community is dominated by large but slow-growing deciduous trees (broad-leaved trees such as oaks that lose their leaves each winter, then grow new leaves each spring). In the Midwest the climax community is prairie, in the Southwest it is semiarid desert, and in the mountainous West it is towering evergreen forests (Figure 23.7). Examples of climax communities in other parts of the world include the frozen tree-less Arctic tundra and tropical rainforests near the equator.

When climax communities are disturbed they do not recover easily. Consider the introduction of the giant reed, *Arundo donax*, to coastal stream communities in Southern California. The typical climax community in this area includes coast live oak and laurel sumac. However, since

Figure 23.7 **A climax community.** This old growth Douglas fir forest in Mt. Rainier National Park, Washington, is a climax community. The species present are those best adapted to the environment once the environment reaches a stable condition.

*A. donax* was brought to the U.S. in the 1800s for erosion control, its rapid growth characteristics have allowed it to supersede slower-growing native species until today it dominates these communities. The very complexity and slow growth characteristics of climax communities make them vulnerable.

### Ecosystems: Communities and their physical environment

An ecosystem, as mentioned earlier, has both living and nonliving components. The total living component of an ecosystem is called that ecosystem's **biomass.** The nonliving components consist of the *chemical elements* (the physical matter that makes up Earth) and the *energy* that drives all chemical reactions.

A constant supply of energy is essential for continued life because the transfer of nutrients and energy from one organism to the next is always an energy-absorbing process. Nearly all of Earth's energy comes from the sun, with only a tiny amount supplied by the residual heat of Earth itself (thermal vents and volcanoes). In contrast to energy, the chemical matter of Earth is recycled over and over again between Earth and the biomass. The next two sections discuss these two key concepts in more detail.

**RECAP**

Species with similar niches may be in competition with each other. Communities go through progressive changes over time, called succession, that increase overall efficiency and species variety. Left undisturbed, eventually they achieve a climax community. Ecosystems consist of biomass, energy, and nonliving matter. ■

## 23.5 Energy flows through ecosystems

### Producers capture and convert energy, consumers rely on stored energy

The flow of energy in an ecosystem demonstrates two key principles of physics, called the *laws of thermodynamics:*

- The *first law of thermodynamics* states that energy is neither created nor destroyed. However, energy can change form, and it can be stored.
- The *second law of thermodynamics* states that whenever energy changes form or is transferred, some energy is wasted (converted to nonuseful forms). Generally this wasted energy is lost as heat.

**Producer** organisms can make their own organic molecules. **Consumer** organisms get their organic molecules (and energy) by eating other organisms or dead and decaying material. Energy flows in one direction through an ecosystem, from the sun to producers to consumers.

Most producers are capable of **photosynthesis** (Figure 23.8). A few producers that live entirely in the dark, such as bacteria located near deep-ocean hydrothermal vents, rely on a process called *chemosynthesis*. Producers are also sometimes called *autotrophs,* meaning "self-nutritive" or "self-growing." On land the producers are mainly green plants, whereas in aquatic ecosystems they are primarily species of algae.

The ability of producers such as plants to harness the energy of the sun depends on small organelles called *chloroplasts* within certain plant cells. Chloroplasts contain a green light-absorbing pigment called *chlorophyll* that gives plants their green color. In the first stage of photosynthesis,

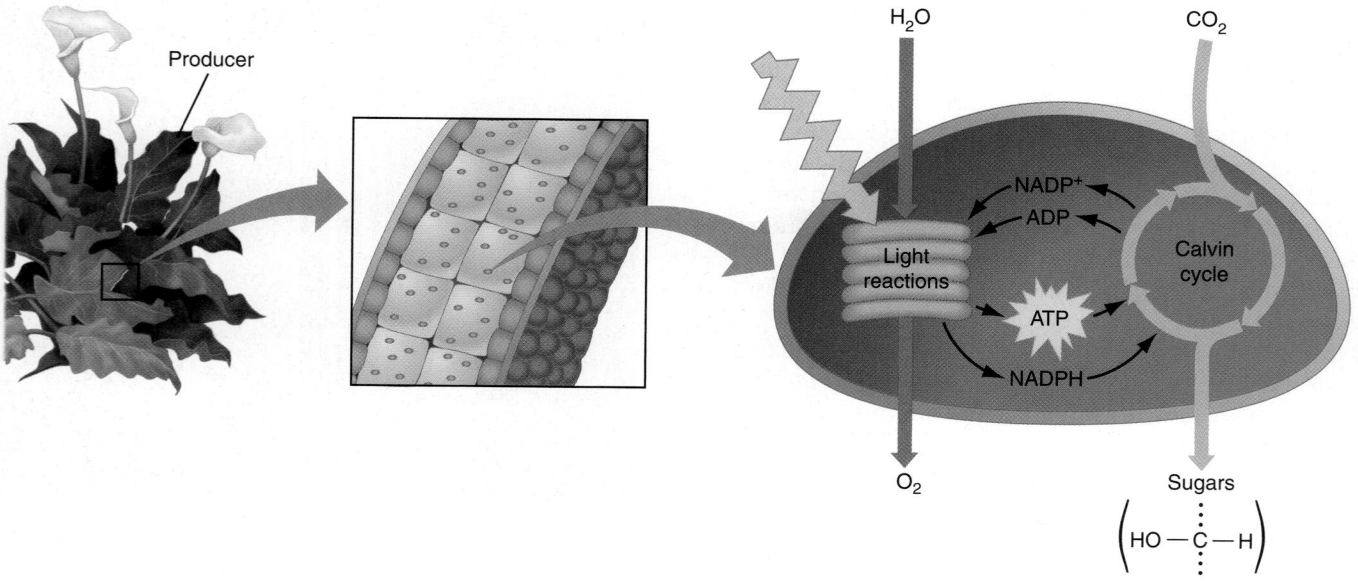


**Figure 23.8 Photosynthesis.** Producer organisms such as plants use the energy in sunlight, water, and $CO_2$ from the atmosphere to produce sugars. A by-product of photosynthesis is oxygen.

chlorophyll absorbs the energy of sunlight and then uses the energy to drive a chemical reaction in which water is disassembled and high-energy molecules of ATP and NADPH are produced. A by-product of the reaction is oxygen, which is released to the atmosphere. In the second stage of photosynthesis, ATP and NADPH are used to fuel a biochemical cycle called the Calvin cycle, in which $CO_2$ from the atmosphere is used to produce high-energy carbohydrate molecules (sugars) consisting of multiple $CH_2O$ units. Using the energy stored in the sugar and water and minerals obtained from the soil, plants are able to make all the other organic molecules they need, including proteins, lipids, and cellulose, a primary component of plant cell walls.

Notice how neatly the biochemical reactions of plants (producers) and animals (consumers) complement each other. Plants require $CO_2$ from the atmosphere for photosynthesis and produce $O_2$ as a by-product, whereas animals require $O_2$ for their metabolism and produce $CO_2$ as their waste product.

Most plants make more sugar than they need for their own use. The extra sugar is converted to starch, which is stored in the chloroplasts and in storage cells of roots, tubers, fruits, and seeds. On a global scale, it is estimated that photosynthesis accounts for the production of about 145 billion tons of carbohydrates per year, or nearly 23 tons for every person on Earth.

Animals, most bacteria, and fungi are *consumers* (also called *heterotrophs*). They cannot utilize the sun's energy to synthesize the molecules they need. Instead they must consume foods that already contain stored forms of energy. Consumers fall into four types depending on what they use as a food source:

- **Herbivores** feed on green plants. They are also called *primary* consumers because they eat only producers.
- **Carnivores** feed on other animals, and thus they are *secondary, tertiary* (third-level), and sometimes *quaternary* (fourth-level) consumers. The primary forms of stored energy in animals are fats and carbohydrates such as glycogen.
- **Omnivores** feed on both animals and plants. Humans, pigs, and bears are omnivores.
- **Decomposers** feed on *detritus*, the disintegrated matter of dead organisms. Bacteria, fungi, earthworms, and certain small arthropods (a phylum of organisms that includes insects and spiders) are all decomposers.

Figure 23.9 shows a pond ecosystem, where energy enters as sunlight and is converted to biomass by algae and aquatic plants (producers). Fish (consumers) eat the plant material, and when they die, bacterial or fungal decomposers (such as chytrids) return the nutrients to the water and soil for recycling. Heat is lost at each step.

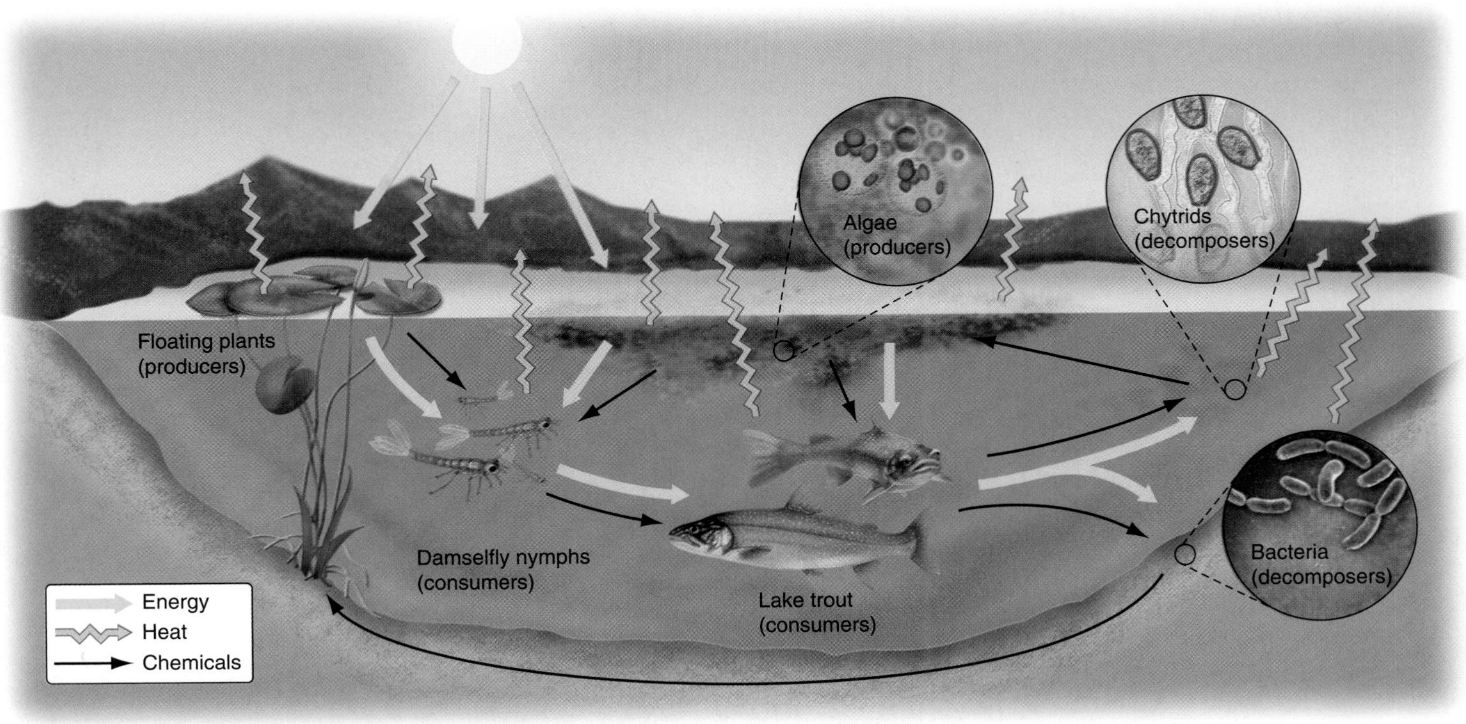


**Figure 23.9 Energy flows and chemical cycling in a pond ecosystem.** Energy flows in only one direction through ecosystems: from sunlight to producers and then to consumers. Most of the energy is eventually lost as heat. Chemicals are recycled continuously.

## A food web: Interactions among producers and consumers

Feeding relationships between producers and consumers are sometimes described by simple *food chains*, in which A (grass) is eaten by B (grasshopper), which is eaten by C (sparrow), which is eaten by D (fox). Although food chains are useful for presenting the relationships between types of consumers, they understate the degree of complexity in most ecosystems. Most organisms rely on more than one species for food and in turn may be eaten by more than one species.

A more accurate depiction of the complex balanced nature of the feeding relationships in an ecosystem is a **food web** (Figure 23.10). As a food web shows, a particular consumer may eat different foods at different times depending on what is available. For example, as the population of a particular species of secondary consumer rises, it provides a more abundant food supply for a tertiary consumer. These tertiary consumers then rely less on other secondary consumer species whose populations are low at the moment. Consequently, no single population ever gets completely out

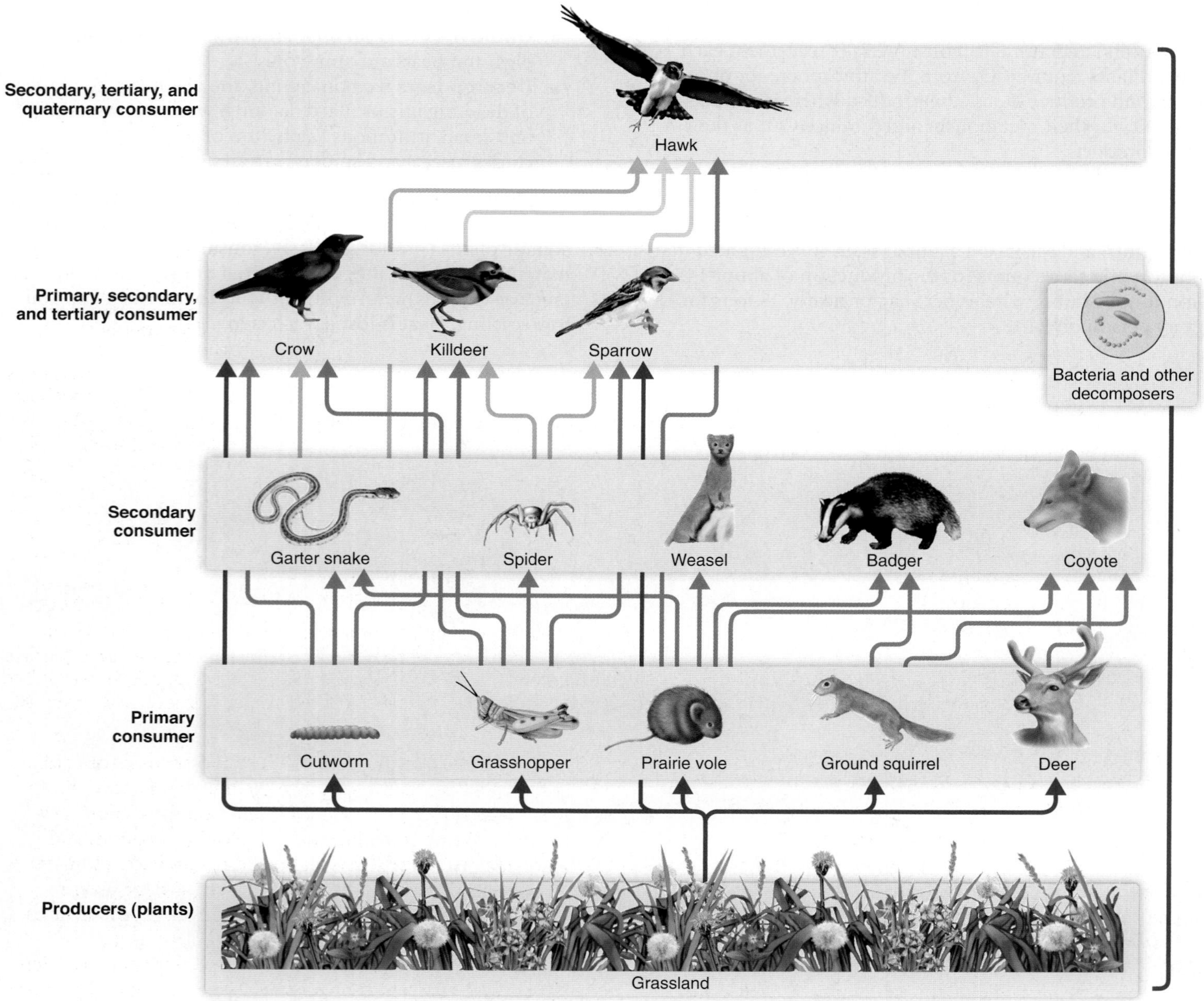


**Figure 23.10 A food web.** A food web shows the complexity of the feeding relationships among organisms in an ecosystem. Note that bacteria and other decomposers also play a role in the food web by feeding on dead organisms at all levels.

of hand, and rarely does any species become extinct. In a stable ecosystem every population rises and falls periodically as part of the normal ebb and flow of life. These variations in a species population are always near the carrying capacity of the ecosystem for that particular species.

**RECAP**

Producers are photosynthesizing organisms that use the sun's energy, available nutrients, and atmospheric carbon dioxide to produce energy-containing molecules. All other organisms, called consumers, obtain their energy from plants or other organisms. All organisms in an ecosystem form an interconnecting food web, and energy flows in one direction through the ecosystem. Populations may rise and fall, but generally they hover near the ecosystem's carrying capacity for each species. ■

## The lower levels of an ecological pyramid support consumer populations

The processes of energy conversion, transfer, and storage are remarkably inefficient at every level. For example, photosynthetic processes utilize and store in the biomass only 2% of the total energy in sunlight. The rest is reflected as light or heat energy. Only about 10% of the energy at one level of a food web can be found in the tissues of the consumers at the next level in the web. In other words, only about 10% of the stored energy available in plants is stored in herbivores, and only about 10% of that (or 1%) is stored in secondary consumers.

An **ecological pyramid** (Figure 23.11) depicts either the total amount of energy stored at each level of an ecosystem or the total biomass at each level. The total amount of energy represented by tertiary consumers at the top of the food chain is very small indeed. Ecological pyramids also generally indicate total biomass, as the amount of energy available usually defines how much biomass can be supported. To get a better image of the steepness of this pyramid, consider how many total pounds of large carnivores (wolves, bears, and eagles) there might be in a square mile of forest versus the total number of tons of grasses, shrubs, and trees.

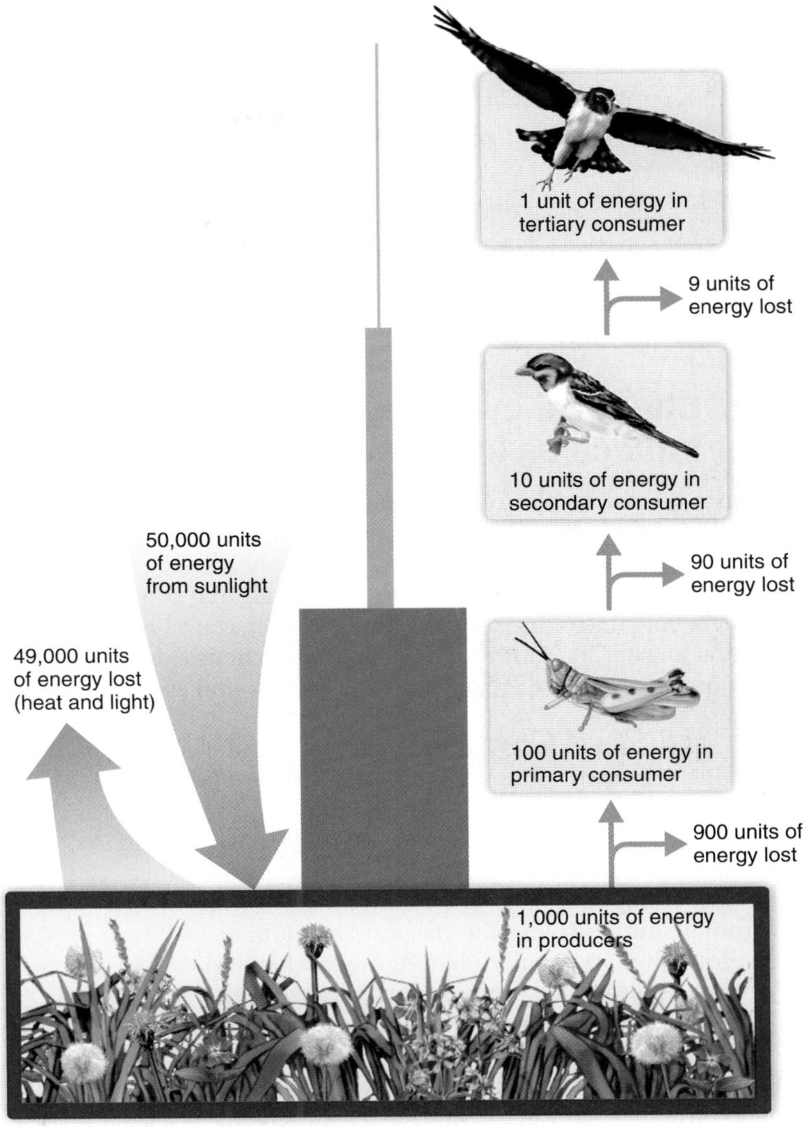


**Figure 23.11 An ecological pyramid.** This ecological pyramid depicts total energy stored in the biomass at each producer/consumer level. Because energy transfer is inefficient, only about 10% of the energy at one level can be found in the tissues of the consumer at the next highest level of the pyramid.

## Human activities disrupt ecological pyramids

Ecological pyramids illustrate that the population of consumers at any level depends critically on the populations of consumers directly below it. Tertiary consumers are especially vulnerable to ecosystem disruptions because the small amount of energy available to them depends on the energy transfers at all levels below them.

Humans can disrupt this balance rather easily with modern farming practices. When we create ecosystems with only one species of producer (mile after mile of wheat or corn), then harvest the entire crop, we exclude other species from their natural food web and their place on the ecological pyramid. We do this to feed more people, of course, and it works. But the short-term high yield comes with a long-term price in its effects on the field ecosystem and fertilizer requirements. In general, we must recognize that our actions affect other species on Earth.

Humans can be either primary or secondary consumers. We are secondary consumers when we eat meat and primary consumers when we eat plants. Eating meat is energetically expensive. When we feed grain to cattle and then eat the beef, we utilize only 10% of the energy that would otherwise be available to us in the grain. At some point, if we face hard choices about feeding the growing world population, scientists will surely point out that we can be more energy-efficient by eating plants rather than meat.

**RECAP**

Energy transfer is inefficient, so each consumer level can support fewer and fewer organisms than the level below it. The population at any consumer level depends on the size of the population below it. ■

## 23.6 Chemical cycles recycle molecules in ecosystems

In contrast to the continuous input of energy from the sun, the total mass of nutrient matter that makes up Earth and its biomass remains completely fixed. With only a finite amount of each element available, the chemicals that compose living organisms are recycled over and over again between organisms and Earth itself. Such **biogeochemical cycles** include living organisms, geologic events, and even weather events.

As shown in Figure 23.12, every molecule and element in a living organism cycles between three different pools: the exchange pool, biomass, and reservoir. Some of the elements or molecules are found in the *exchange pool* (water, soil, and atmosphere), from which the primary producers draw their nutrients. Using the energy of the sun, the primary producers incorporate nutrients into the *biomass*. The biomass is the only biotic (living) compartment in biogeochemical cycles, hence, molecules in the biomass are exchanged rapidly as organisms consume each other.

When an organism dies and decomposes, its nutrients return to the exchange pool, where they again become available to primary producers. Coupled to the exchange pool is a large but hard-to-access pool of nutrients called the *reservoir*. Nutrients in reservoirs include minerals in solid rock and in

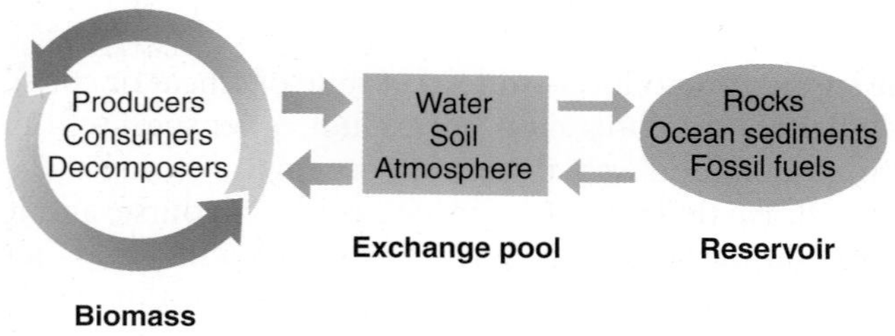


**Figure 23.12 The flow of nutrients in biogeochemical cycles.** The three components of a biogeochemical cycle are the biomass, the exchange pool, and the reservoir. The chemicals that compose living organisms are constantly recycled among the three components. The relative magnitudes of nutrient flow between nutrient pools and within the biomass are represented by differences in arrow thickness.

sediments deposited at the bottom of the oceans. Other important reservoirs are carbon-containing compounds in **fossil fuels** (coal, oil, and gas) that were created millions of years ago from the remains of living organisms, and were then covered by sediments. We turn now to the biogeochemical cycles for some of the most important molecules and elements of life—water, carbon, nitrogen, and phosphorus.

**RECAP**

A biogeochemical cycle describes how a chemical cycles between the biomass, exchange pool, and reservoir pool. Most nutrients cycle rapidly within the biomass pool, less rapidly with the exchange pool, and rarely with the reservoir pool. ■

### The water cycle is essential to other biogeochemical cycles

Water is probably more essential to life than any other molecule. It makes up about 60% of your body and covers approximately 75% of Earth's surface. However, freshwater—the kind that humans and most other organisms need in order to live—actually accounts for less than 3% of our planet's total water supply (and two-thirds of that is trapped in glaciers and polar ice caps. The remaining 97% of the Earth's water is salty ocean water). Water is the universal solvent for many other elements—indeed, without the water cycle, all other biogeochemical cycles would cease.

Figure 23.13 illustrates the water cycle. Both the water cycle and the biomass are important to the biogeochemical cycles for minerals. Rain and surface water runoff slowly erode rocks and leach the minerals from them. Plants take up these minerals and incorporate them into the biomass. If there are no plants, the temperature is higher due to decreased evaporative cooling, and the minerals wash into the sea instead. When forests or grasslands are destroyed, nutrients lost from the soil may not be replenished from the reservoir pool for hundreds of years.

Water cycles between the atmosphere, ocean, and land. Although evaporation and precipitation occur primarily over the ocean, on land evaporation is mostly from leaf surfaces and soil. Overuse of water can deplete underground stores, compromising deep-rooting, formerly drought-tolerant vegetation and decreasing available water for irrigation. A consequence of this overuse is the loss of wetlands worldwide: for example, Greek Macedonia in Northern Greece has lost 95% of its marshland since 1930, primarily due to diversion of water for irrigation. In addition, the combination of pollutants from human activities and changes in landcover due to urban development can degrade streams, rivers, and even the ocean. For more about the impact of human activities on water, see Chapter 24.

How much water do you use in a typical day? See the Try It Yourself box on page 538 to find out.

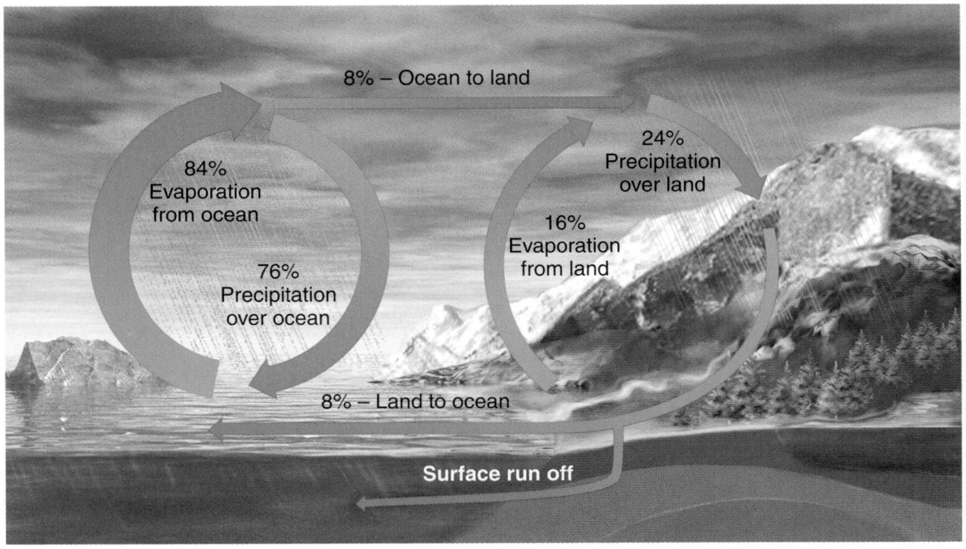


**Figure 23.13 The water cycle.** The amounts of water recycled relative to the total rates of evaporation and precipitation are indicated as percentages. Heat energy from the sun causes water to evaporate, primarily from oceans but also from leaf surfaces and soil on land. Most of the atmospheric water vapor precipitates as rain over the oceans, but approximately a quarter of it precipitates over land, replenishing surface water that was lost by evaporation and providing the extra water that becomes ponds, lakes, streams, and rivers.

**RECAP**

The amount of matter that makes up Earth and its biomass is fixed. The molecules that constitute living and nonliving things are constantly recycled. In the water cycle, water evaporates from the land and oceans. About a quarter of all water vapor precipitates over land, where it becomes surface water that either evaporates again or returns to the oceans. In the carbon cycle, plants use atmospheric $CO_2$ to make organic molecules, which cycle through the biomass of plants and animals. ■

## Nitrogen: An essential component of nucleic acids and proteins

Nitrogen is an essential component of proteins and nucleic acids. By far the largest reservoir of nitrogen is the nearly 79% of the air that is nitrogen gas ($N_2$).

## The carbon cycle: Organisms exchange $CO_2$ with the atmosphere

Carbon forms the backbone of organic molecules and the crystalline structure of bones and shells. Like the water cycle, the biogeochemical cycle for carbon (Figure 23.14) is called a *gaseous cycle* because carbon in living organisms is exchanged with atmospheric $CO_2$.

The carbon cycle is closely tied to photosynthesis by plants and aerobic respiration by both plants and animals. During photosynthesis, plants use the energy of sunlight to combine $CO_2$ with water, forming carbohydrates and releasing oxygen as a by-product. Both plants and animals then utilize aerobic respiration (metabolism in the presence of oxygen) to break down the carbohydrates, releasing the energy to make other complex molecules. In the process they produce $CO_2$ again.

$CO_2$ is also released through the actions of decomposers such as fungi and bacteria.

In the absence of human interference, utilization and production of atmospheric $CO_2$ by the biomass would be in approximate balance. However, as shown in Figure 23.14, burning of vegetation and combustion of fossil fuels are tipping the balance toward increased $CO_2$ production, raising atmospheric $CO_2$ levels. The result may be global warming, discussed in Chapter 24.

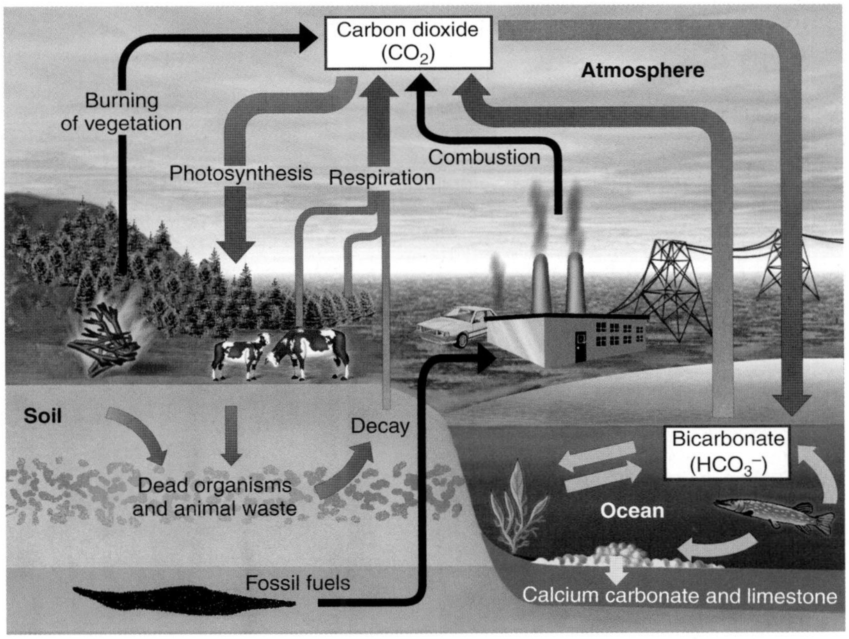


**Figure 23.14 The carbon cycle.** Carbon dioxide in the atmosphere and bicarbonate in the oceans constitute the exchange pool. The reservoir pool of carbon includes limestone and calcium carbonate from the shells of marine organisms and also fossil fuels formed several hundred million years ago from decomposed plant material. Fossil fuels represent a reservoir for carbon that would not normally be accessible to the exchange pool, but over the last several hundred years humans have tapped them for energy. The darker-colored arrows indicate the effect of human activities.

However, the nitrogen in air is unavailable to living organisms because the two nitrogen atoms are held tightly together by a triple covalent bond. Consequently plant growth is more often limited by a shortage of useful nitrogen than a shortage of any other nutrient.

Figure 23.15 illustrates the nitrogen cycle. The process of converting nitrogen gas to ammonium ($NH_4^+$) is called **nitrogen fixation** because the nitrogen becomes trapped, or "fixed," in a form that ultimately can be used by plants. Nitrogen fixation is carried out by certain bacteria in the root nodules of plants such as peas, alfalfa, and clover and also by modern fertilizer factories. Most of the ammonium is converted to nitrate ($NO_3^-$) before it is used by plants. The formation of nitrate is called **nitrification.** Modern fertilizer

**try it** *yourself*

## How Much Water Do You Use Each Day?

As we've seen in this chapter, fresh water is a scarce and crucial resource. How much of it do you use in a typical day? According to the American Water Works Association (AWWA), toilets are the biggest water consumers, averaging 26.7% of a U.S. household's total daily indoor use. Other water-draining appliances are clothes washers (21.7%), showers (16.8%), and faucets (15.7%). Do the calculations below to estimate your own usage.

| Appliances | Estimated use | Daily total in gallons |
|---|---|---|
| *Toilet* | | |
| **Vintage** (manufactured before 1978): 5 gallons per flush | Number of times you flush in a typical day: ______ | Daily subtotal: ______ |
| **Conventional** (manufactured 1978–1993): 3.5 gallons per flush | | |
| **Low consumption** (manufactured 1994 to present): 1.6 gallons per flush | | |
| *Clothes washer* | | |
| **Top-loading:** 48 gallons per load | Number of loads you wash in a typical week: ______ | Daily subtotal (divide the weekly total by 7): ______ |
| **Front-loading:** 24 gallons per load | | |
| *Shower* | | |
| **Conventional showerhead** (manufactured before 1978): 7 gallons per minute | Length in minutes of your typical shower: ______ | Daily subtotal: ______ |
| **Low-flow showerhead:** 2.5 gallons per minute | | |
| *Faucets* | | |
| **Faucet aerator** (manufactured before 1978): 5 gallons per minute | Number of minutes you run water from faucets in a typical day: ______ | Daily subtotal: ______ |
| **Flow regulating aerator:** 1.5 gallons per minute | | |
| | | **Daily total of gallons used:** ______ |

According to AWWA, the average American uses 18.5 gallons daily to flush toilets, 15 gallons to wash clothes, 11.6 gallons to take showers, and 10.9 gallons from faucets. How do you and your classmates compare to the average? Note that these figures are for only four indoor appliances; they do not include water used to wash cars or water lawns.

How can you conserve water? One way is to replace inefficient appliances; as you can see from the estimates above, newer appliances consume much less water. Also, pay attention to leaks: An estimated 9.5 gallons per person are wasted every day through leaking faucets and toilets.

plants use fossil fuels to manufacture nitrate from air, and lightning provides the energy for a small amount of nitrate formation as well.

Plants take up ammonium and nitrates from the soil and assimilate them into their proteins and nucleic acids in the course of their cellular metabolism. All other organisms must rely on plants or other animals for their usable nitrogen. When organisms die and decompose, the nitrogen compounds in their proteins and nucleic acids are converted again to ammonia, aided by bacteria. Most of the ammonia undergoes nitrification again and recycles through the biomass of living organisms. Similar nitrogen cycles occur on land and in the sea.

Finally, **denitrification** by certain denitrifying bacteria converts some nitrate back to atmospheric nitrogen gas. In a balanced ecosystem, denitrification should equal nitrogen fixation. The production of fertilizers by humans has tipped the balance in favor of nitrogen fixation. Excessive fertilizer runoff can pollute freshwater because the nitrates stimulate excessive growth of plants and algae.

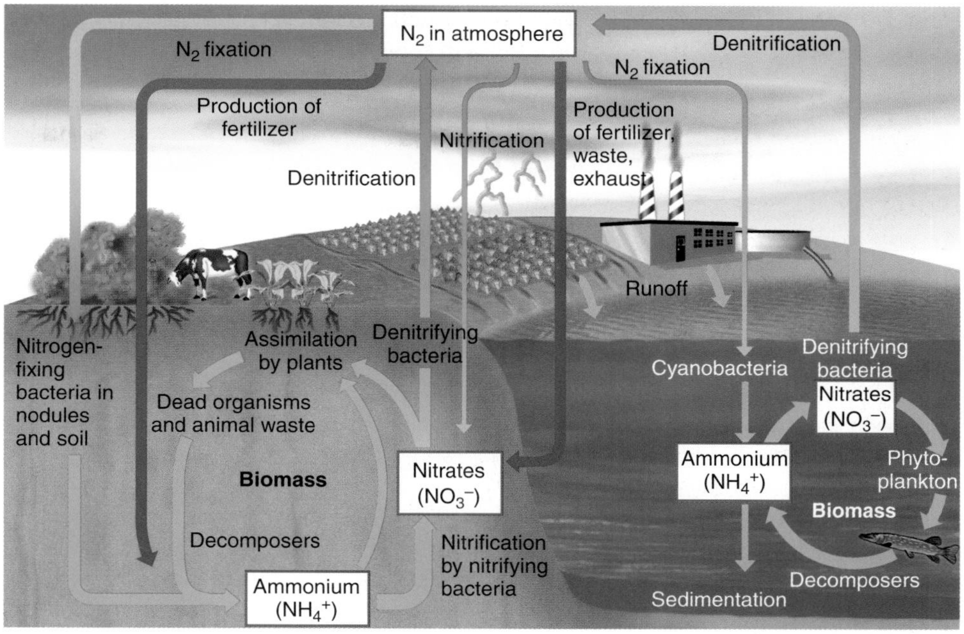


**Figure 23.15 The nitrogen cycle.** The nitrogen in nitrogen gas is not readily available to living organisms. Once it is "fixed" as ammonium or nitrified to nitrate, the nitrogen can be recycled over and over through the biomass. Nitrogen fixation is carried out by bacteria in the root nodules of certain plants and also by fertilizer factories. Cycles of nitrogen utilization occur both on land and in the sea. Under normal circumstances, the amount of nitrogen gas returned to the atmosphere by denitrification approximately balances nitrogen fixation. Humans upset this balance through the production of fertilizers from air, using fossil fuels as a source of energy.

## Phosphorus: A sedimentary cycle

Phosphorus is an essential element of life that most commonly exists as phosphate ions ($PO_4^{3-}$ and $HPO_4^{2-}$). Producer organisms use phosphate to make ATP for energy, phospholipids for cell membranes, and nucleotides for RNA and DNA. Consumer organisms that feed on the producers use phosphate for these purposes too, but they also incorporate phosphate into bones, teeth, and shells.

Figure 23.16 on page 542 shows the phosphorus cycle. It is called a *sedimentary cycle* because, unlike carbon or nitrogen, phosphorus never enters the atmosphere. Phosphate ions are deposited in sediments that over the course of millions of years are brought to Earth's surface. The phosphates in sedimentary rocks are mined by humans and weathered by the forces of nature.

Without human intervention, phosphates from sedimentary rock are exchanged with water and soil, providing needed minerals for plant growth. With urbanization, an increase in covered surface areas (roads, parking lots, and buildings) leads to increased water runoff into aquatic ecosystems, with less water absorption by soil and plants. Excess phosphates leached from rock reservoirs and phosphate from fertilizers or from human or animal wastes may also enter aquatic ecosystems, causing excessive algae growth. When the algae die, decomposers using them for food take up so much oxygen for metabolism that other organisms may suffocate.

In our discussion, we have focused on several major nutrients of life. There are similar biogeochemical cycles for all other nutrients, including oxygen, calcium, potassium, and sulfur. Pollutants and toxic substances such as heavy metals (mercury, cadmium, chromium, and lead), pesticides (DDT), and industrial chemicals (polychlorinated biphenyls or PCBs) also cycle between living organisms and Earth. Environmentalists need to understand these cycles to advise us on how to minimize the effects of pollution.

**RECAP**

Nitrogen gas in the atmosphere is not available to most living organisms until it undergoes nitrogen fixation to ammonia or to nitrates. Most phosphorus takes the form of phosphate that recycles within the biomass. The reservoir of phosphorus is in sedimentary rock. Similar biogeochemical cycles exist for all other nutrients as well as for toxic substances. ■

# Current Issue

## Bird Flu: Can We Stop Worrying Now?

In 1997, 18 people in Hong Kong developed a particularly deadly flu that killed a third of its victims within a week. The outbreak coincided with an outbreak of an equally deadly flu in domestic ducks and chickens. It was soon recognized that the virus, now known as *avian H5N1* for its particular H and N surface antigen subtypes, was responsible for both outbreaks. Apparently the disease was being transmitted from domestic birds to humans via bird fecal matter.

The Hong Kong government took quick action, killing millions of potentially infected domestic birds and probably preventing another outbreak among humans. However, the virus soon spread to the wild migratory bird population. Today it is the largest flu outbreak ever recorded in birds, and it shows no signs of abating.

The virus did not appear again in humans until 2003. Since that time it has infected nearly 400 people, killing more than half of its victims. Most of the human deaths have been in Asia, most notably in Indonesia (110 deaths), Vietnam (52), and China (20), but human deaths have also been reported as far east as Turkey, Egypt, and Nigeria in Eastern Africa. Although no human cases have been reported in Europe or the U.S. so far, bird flu has made its way into birds in Europe. Health officials worry that a variant of H5N1 could eventually cause a pandemic in humans as it has in birds, possibly killing millions of people.

### What Is a Pandemic?

A pandemic is a disease outbreak occurring over a wide geographical area and affecting a large part of the population. A viral pandemic occurs when a new virus subtype emerges that is both virulent (causes severe disease) and easily transmissible. H5N1 has already proven to be highly virulent in humans, but so far all human infections have come from direct and close contact with infected birds—there is not a single documented case of human-to-human transmission, though several are suspected.

There have been three influenza pandemics in the past 100 years. The worst was the 1918 Spanish flu, which killed 20–40 million people worldwide. More recently, the 1957 Asian flu and the 1968 Hong Kong flu each killed 1–4 million people. Each of these spread worldwide within a year of detection.

### Will H5N1 Ever Cause a Pandemic?

No one knows when, or even if, avian H5N1 will become easily transmissible between humans. All flu viruses undergo change over time, either by *genetic drift*—small incremental changes in the surface antigens that determine transmissibility—or by more dramatic and rapid *genetic shift*—wholesale re-assortment of viral genes when two different viruses infect a host cell at the same time.

It is the latter possibility that has health officials so concerned. The genome of flu viruses contains only eight separate gene segments, each of which can exchange with other flu viruses when two flu viruses infect the same cell at the same time. Humans who become infected with a bird flu virus and a human flu virus thus become mixing vessels for a new type of virus with a different combination of characteristics. Take, for example, a dual infection with the avian H5N1 virus and a human H1N2 virus. The result could be an entirely new combination of avian and human viral gene segments and a new virus that could have the virulence of the bird flu virus and the transmissibility of a seasonal human flu virus (see the illustration on the opposite page). So far it hasn't happened and indeed it may never happen. But the more people become infected with H5N1 directly from birds, the greater the chance that it will. And if it does, the result could be thousands or even millions of human deaths, similar to the effect that H5N1 has had on birds. That is why health officials are so worried about just a few hundred human H5N1 infections worldwide.

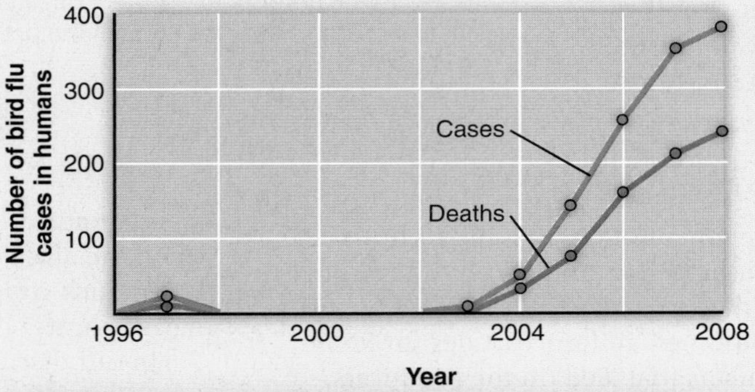


Cases and deaths from bird flu (cumulative since 2003) through June 2008.
*Data from:* WHO/Map Production: Public Health Mapping and GIS Communicable Diseases (CDS) World Health Organization

### What Is Being Done?

Several years ago, when human deaths were at their highest, the nations of the world were unprepared to treat a worldwide H5N1 pandemic. The fact that it hasn't happened (yet) has bought us some time. A concerted effort has been underway for several years now to prepare for the possibility of a pandemic. If it

## the facts...

- A virulent strain of influenza in birds can, under certain circumstances, infect humans.
- So far there is no evidence of human-to-human transmission of the virus.
- Health officials are worried that if the virus undergoes genetic shift and becomes easily transmissible between humans, a pandemic will occur in which millions of people could die.
- Efforts are now underway to contain the disease (if or when it occurs) and to prepare vaccines against it. It's a race against time and against a pandemic that may not occur at all.

All cases of bird flu in humans are thought to involve direct bird-human transmission.

were to strike now, the death toll may be high but it will certainly be less than might have been predicted several years ago. What is being done?

- **Communication.** In 2006 the World Health Organization (WHO) developed and issued a strategic action plan for pandemic influenza. The plan contained five points: reduce human flu exposure, strengthen early warning systems, intensify rapid containment, build capacity to cope with a pandemic, and coordinate global scientific research and development.
- **Detection.** Surveillance efforts are now underway in most countries that are currently affected by bird flu and in many that are not yet affected. Surveillance is particularly important in countries in the flight paths of migratory birds, so that the worldwide spread of the virus in birds can be tracked.
- **Response and containment.** If an outbreak in humans does occur, the first strategy will be to reduce exposure of noninfected persons to infected persons. However, if the outbreak is large, the sheer number of patients would quickly overwhelm health care systems. Worldwide or regional travel restrictions may have to be imposed and enforced.
- **Treatment of affected individuals.** Several antiviral drugs are currently available that might be used to treat individuals who develop symptoms of bird flu. Oseltamivir (Tamiflu) and zanamivir (Relenza) can reduce the severity of most seasonal influenzas, and have both recently been shown to be effective against H5N1. However, to be effective, Tamiflu and Relenza should be administered within 24 hours of the onset of symptoms.

### *What About a Vaccine?*

Vaccines are produced every year for new strains of seasonal flu viruses that evolve slowly by genetic drift. However, these vaccines are unlikely to protect against a virus that has undergone a dramatic genetic shift. If such a new, virulent, easily transmissible virus does emerge and a human pandemic begins, the disease could spread around the world in as little as three months. A specific vaccine against it would not likely be widely available for nearly six months. If nations cooperate to identify an outbreak early and contain its spread, they buy critical time for the development and production of a vaccine. And it appears that nations are cooperating with each other, in part because it is in their self-interest to do so. A worldwide pandemic could affect all of us. It would be ironic if something as small as a virus could bring about worldwide cooperation among humans.

### *Can We Stop Worrying Now?*

Health officials say "No." The pandemic in birds continues without signs of stopping, and humans continue to be infected and to die. Every time a human becomes infected, the possibility exists that an easily transmissible and highly virulent virus might emerge. Health officials worry that we are forgetting about bird flu, and that sooner or later we will choose not to invest our resources in preparing for a possible pandemic. Should we continue to worry and to direct our resources toward something that may *never* happen? On the other hand, what if we were to stop preparing for a bird flu pandemic and then one actually did emerge? There are consequences to being wrong either way.

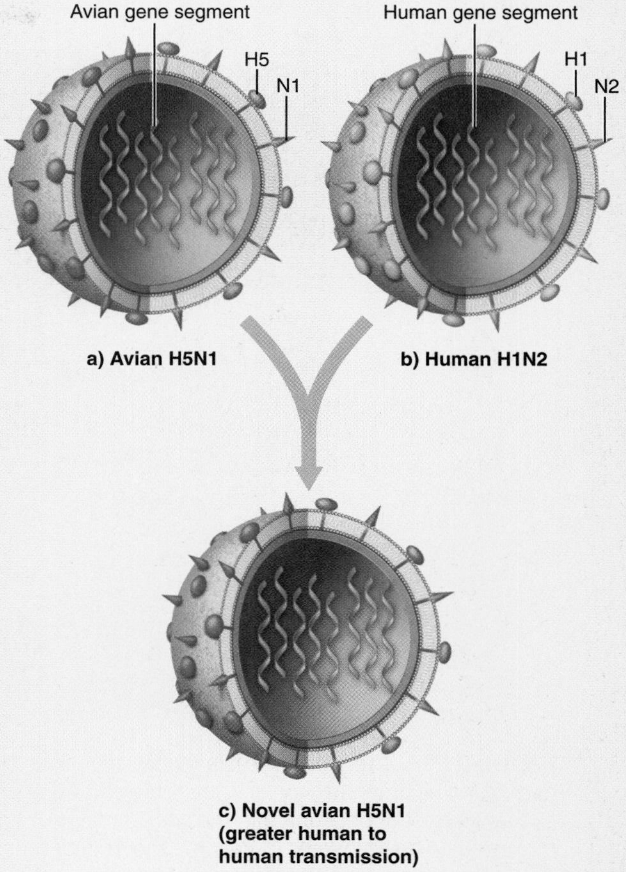


Segments of RNA from avian and human influenza viruses could recombine in humans to form a deadly new human strain.

Whether or not we can afford to stop worrying, it appears that we are losing interest anyway. Even the news media have lost interest. In 2006 there were 181 articles in *The New York Times* that referred to "avian flu"; in the first eight months of 2008 there were only 18.

We choose to forget at our peril.

### Questions to consider:

**1** *In the event of an initial outbreak of bird flu in another country, would you try to obtain Tamiflu for yourself and your family knowing that there was a worldwide shortage of the drug?* **2** *Does the possibility of a regional outbreak of disease affect your interest in world travel?*

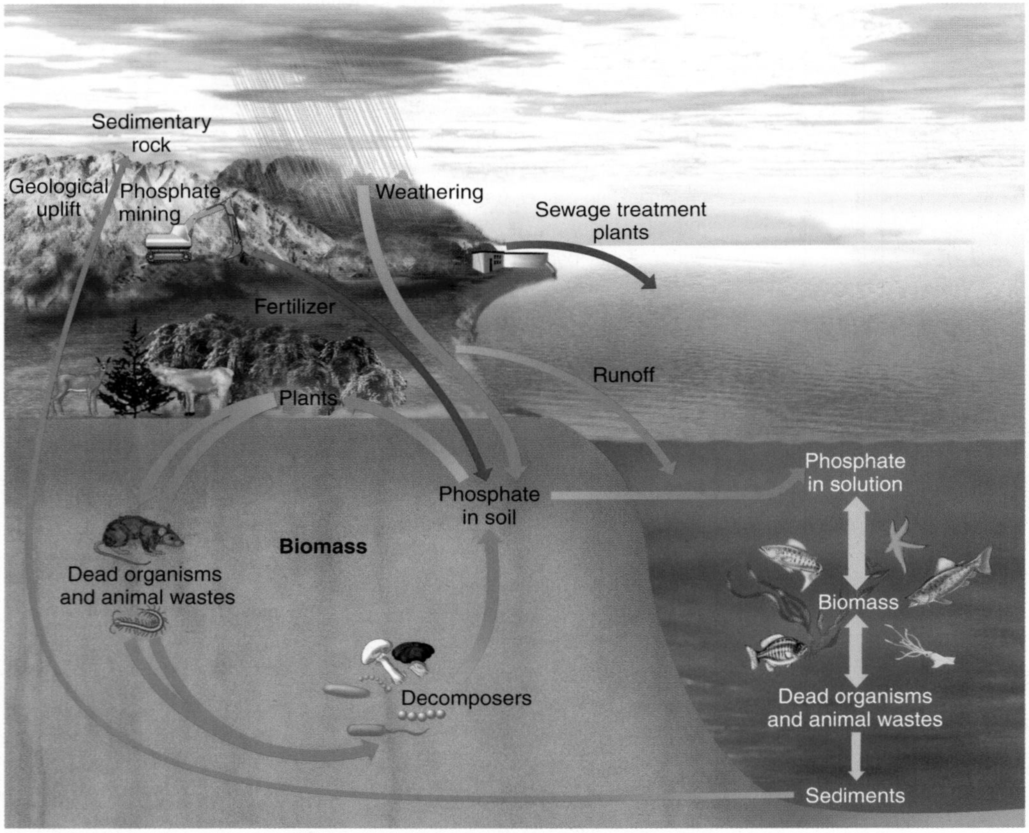


**Figure 23.16 The phosphorus cycle.** The reservoir pool for phosphorus is phosphate ions in sediments and sedimentary rocks. The slow weathering of rock makes "new" phosphate available to the exchange pool of phosphate in the soil. Some of this phosphate is taken up by plants and some runs off with the surface water to become the phosphorus supply for aquatic ecosystems. Eventually the phosphate ends up in sediments, where it may remain for millions of years until geologic upheaval brings the sedimentary rocks to the surface and a weathering process can begin again. Humans disturb the natural cycle by mining phosphate and applying it as fertilizer where it is in short supply. In urban areas, changes in land cover produce excess phosphate in runoff to streams and oceans. When organisms die the store of phosphate becomes available to producer organisms again.

# Chapter Summary

### Ecosystems: Communities interact with their environment *p. 526*

- The study of the relationships between organisms and their environment is called ecology.
- An ecosystem consists of a community of organisms and the physical environment in which they live.

### Populations: The dynamics of one species in an ecosystem *p. 526*

- When there are no restrictions to its growth, a population grows exponentially according to its biotic potential.
- Within an ecosystem, the stable size of the population of a particular species ultimately is determined by carrying capacity.

### Human population growth *p. 528*

- The human population has been growing rapidly since the Industrial Revolution, beginning in the 1700s.
- Currently there are wide differences in fertility rates between the more industrialized countries and the less industrialized countries.
- Even when (or if) the replacement fertility rate of 2.1 children per woman is reached, the world population will continue to grow for several more decades.

- Humans may be able to increase the magnitude of their carrying capacity using technology, but these activities may ultimately reduce that capacity.

### Communities: Different species living together *p. 530*

- Species that occupy overlapping niches may be in competition for limited resources.
- Communities go through a natural sequence of changes called succession that ends with the establishment of a stable climax community.

### Energy flows through ecosystems *p. 532*

- Because energy flows only one way through an ecosystem, a constant supply of energy (from the sun) is required.
- Producer organisms can utilize the energy of the sun through a process called photosynthesis. Consumer and decomposer organisms must rely on other organisms for energy.
- Less energy is available at each higher consumer level of a food web.

### Chemical cycles recycle molecules in ecosystems *p. 536*

- Chemicals (nutrients) recycle in an ecosystem, sometimes quickly, sometimes slowly.
- Water is constantly being recycled from the oceans to land and back to the oceans.
- In the carbon cycle, plants use $CO_2$ available in the atmosphere and animals obtain organic carbon molecules by consuming plants or other animals.
- Nitrogen gas in the atmosphere must be converted to $NH_4^+$ or $NO_3^-$ ("fixed") before it is useful to living organisms.
- The phosphorus cycle is a sedimentary cycle. Phosphorus from decaying organisms is available for reuse.

## Apply What You Know

1. Given absolutely no environmental resistance, how long would it take a population that was increasing by 8% a year to double?
2. Speculate as to what might eventually become the most important environmental resistance factor (or factors) determining the world's human carrying capacity.
3. Less industrialized countries tend to be poorer than more industrialized countries, and at the same time their populations are among the fastest growing. What sorts of interventions or assistance are likely to help less industiralized countries develop and prosper?
4. Both hawks and owls feed on small mammals to sustain their respective populations without causing competitive exclusion. How can this work when both species live in the same geographic area?
5. The introduction of the zebra mussel into the Great Lakes by oceangoing vessels has had a significant impact on the lake ecosystem. How could such a small organism have had such a large impact?
6. What would happen in an ecosystem if suddenly there were no decomposers?
7. The term "algae bloom" refers to rapid, excessive growth of algae. What might cause an algae bloom, and what would it cause?

*Answers can be found on the Human Biology Place.*

## Terms You Should Know

biogeochemical cycle, *536*
biomass, *532*
biosphere, *526*
biotic potential, *527*
carnivore, *533*
carrying capacity, *528*
community, *526*
consumer, *532*
decomposer, *533*
demographic transition, *529*
denitrification, *539*
ecological pyramid, *535*
ecology, *526*
ecosystem, *526*
environmental resistance, *527*
fertility rate, *529*
food web, *534*
fossil fuels, *536*
geographic range, *527*
habitat, *526*
herbivore, *533*
less industrialized countries (LICs), *529*
more industrialized countries (MICs), *529*
niche, *530*
nitrification, *538*
nitrogen fixation, *538*
omnivore, *533*
photosynthesis, *532*
population, *526*
producer, *532*
replacement fertility rate, *529*
succession, *531*
zero population growth, *529*

## Concept Review

1. What are the components of an ecosystem?
2. Describe the concept of an ecosystem's carrying capacity.
3. Describe what happens to a country as it undergoes demographic transition. Give examples of nations in early and late stages of transition.
4. Define zero population growth and explain why it has not been achieved.
5. Describe the concept of a climax community and why they are sensitive to disruption.
6. Why is a constant supply of energy needed to sustain life?
7. Discuss the interactions between producers and consumers in an ecosystem.
8. Explain why the water cycle is essential to all other biogeochemical cycles.
9. Discuss the importance of the carbon cycle.
10. Discuss the phosphorus cycle and its importance.

# Test Yourself

### Matching Exercise

_____ 1. Population pattern of a less industrialized country
_____ 2. Population pattern of a more industrialized country
_____ 3. The factors that oppose unrestricted population growth
_____ 4. A consumer organism that feeds on plants and animals
_____ 5. The maximum rate of growth a population can achieve under ideal conditions
_____ 6. Important reservoirs for carbon
_____ 7. In most populations undergoing industrialization, a predictable pattern in age structure that reflects the area's industrial development and economic well-being

a. environmental resistance
b. omnivore
c. fossil fuels
d. biotic potential
e. pyramid shaped
f. bullet shaped
g. demographic transition

### Fill in the Blank

8. A planetary ecosystem is known as a ____________________.
9. ____________________ is the sequence of changes that determines which organisms dominate in a community.
10. The role in a community that a species fills is its ____________________.
11. Organisms that can utilize the sun's energy to synthesize the molecules they need are called ____________________.
12. Organisms that must eat foods containing stored forms of energy are called ____________________.
13. In the biogeochemical cycle for any nutrient, the three types of nutrient pools are ____________________, ____________________, and ____________________.
14. By producing large amounts of nitrate-rich fertilizers, humans are enhancing the natural process of ____________________.

### True or False?

15. Plants use gaseous $N_2$ as their source of nitrogen.
16. A community consists of the populations of all of the species that live in the same geographical area.

# References and Additional Reading


Diamond, Jared. Easter's End. *Discover,* August 1995. (A fascinating and compelling look at an isolated human society that drove itself to extinction by resource depletion.)

Smith, Robert L., and Thomas M. Smith. *Elements of Ecology.* 7th Edn. San Francisco: Benjamin Cummings, 2009. (A more complete treatment of the subject of ecology for the interested student.)

Wilson, Edward O. The Bottleneck. *Scientific American,* February 2002. (A book excerpt that discusses the implications of the recent rapid growth in human population.)

*World Population Projections to 2150.* New York: United Nations, 1998. 41 pp. (World population trends, by region.)


## Internet References

Find links to these Web sites at the Human Biology Place.

**U.S. Geological Survey**
**www.usgs.gov**
Science arm of the federal Department of the Interior; gathers information and monitors natural resources.

**National Park Service**
**www.nature.nps.gov**
Federal agency that preserves and manages U.S. national parks.

**Smithsonian National Museum of Natural History**
**www.mnh.si.edu**
A world-class museum with exhibits and information on animals, plants, minerals, and fossils.

**National Wildlife Federation**
**www.nwf.org**
Largest member-supported conservation group in the U.S.

# 24 Human Impacts, Biodiversity, and Environmental Issues

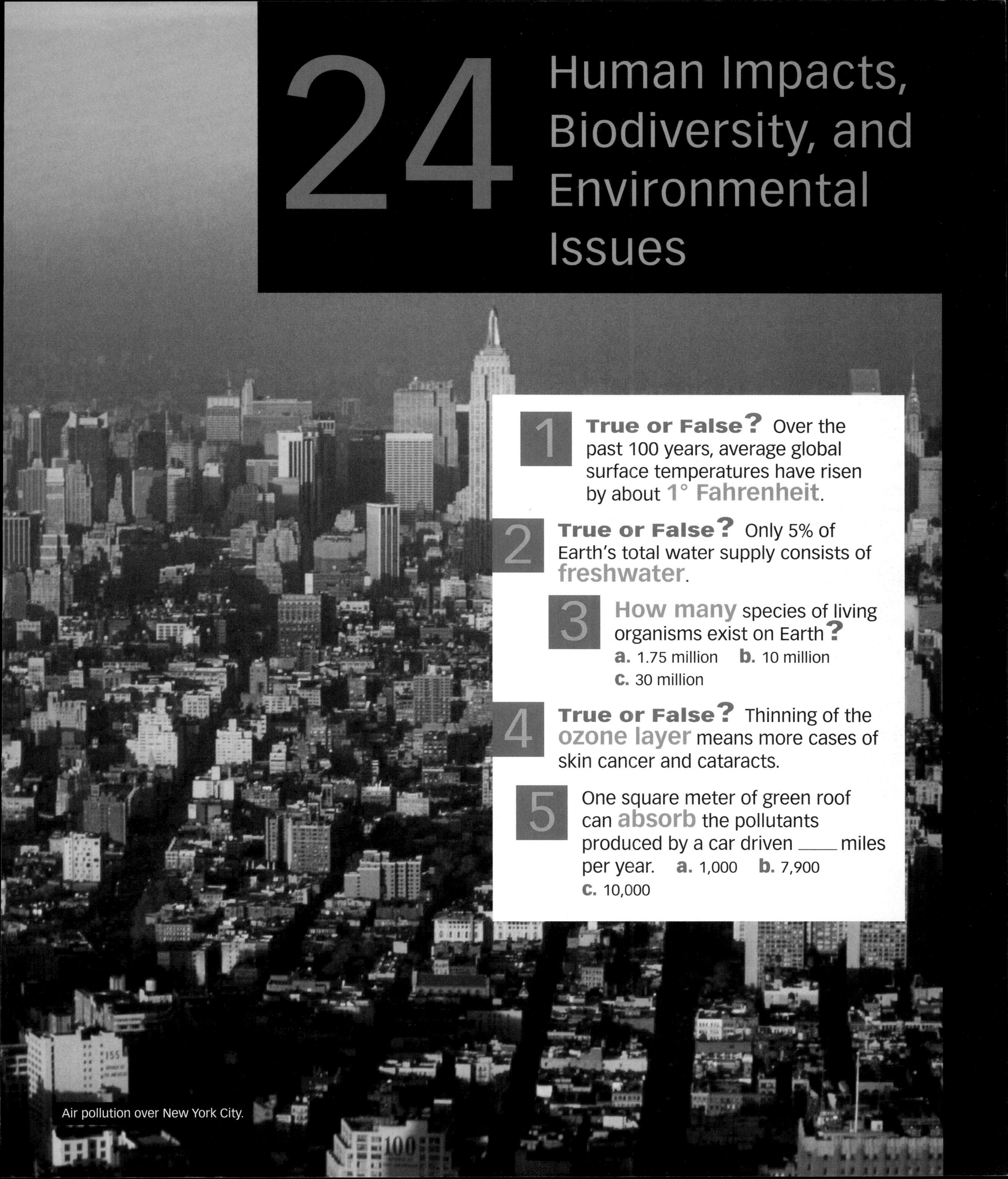

Air pollution over New York City.

**1** **True or False?** Over the past 100 years, average global surface temperatures have risen by about **1° Fahrenheit**.

**2** **True or False?** Only 5% of Earth's total water supply consists of **freshwater**.

**3** **How many** species of living organisms exist on Earth?
**a.** 1.75 million **b.** 10 million
**c.** 30 million

**4** **True or False?** Thinning of the **ozone layer** means more cases of skin cancer and cataracts.

**5** One square meter of green roof can **absorb** the pollutants produced by a car driven ____ miles per year. **a.** 1,000 **b.** 7,900
**c.** 10,000

**The human capacity** to shape the environment both creatively and destructively is causing global changes in biogeochemical cycles and affecting the populations of nearly all living species. Only humans live in houses that can be thousands of square feet per person. Only humans irrigate lands that otherwise could not grow crops, level entire mountains in search of minerals and fossil fuels, and spread herbicides, insecticides, and fertilizers over thousands of square miles. Our presence has altered air, water, and land quality not only in local ecosystems but globally as well. Along the way, we have favored the proliferation of some species while driving others to extinction.

This chapter examines how we *Homo sapiens* are altering our environment on a global scale. We will look at the causes and impacts of pollution on air, water, and land. We will discuss the benefits of biodiversity, examine the evidence for global warming, and look at steps we can take to build a sustainable future.

## 24.1 Pollutants impair air quality

The air we breathe is a mixture of primarily nitrogen (nearly 79%) and oxygen (nearly 21%), with trace amounts of carbon dioxide (0.03%). Air also contains trace amounts of thousands of chemicals or particles that have adverse effects on living organisms, collectively known as **pollution.** The major concerns regarding air pollution fall into four areas:

- Global warming
- Destruction of the ozone layer
- Acid precipitation
- Smog production

Figure 24.1 shows that for each of these issues there may be more than one contributing pollutant. Air pollution is difficult to remedy because it can be hard to determine who is responsible. Global problems require global solutions.

| Source | **Air pollutant:** Nitrogen oxides ($N_xO_x$) | Hydrocarbons (HC) | Carbon monoxide (CO) | Sulfur dioxide ($SO_2$) | Halons (contain bromine, Br) | Chlorofluorocarbons (CFCs) | Methane ($CH_4$) | Carbon dioxide ($CO_2$) | **Contributes to:** Ozone layer destruction | Global warming | Acid precipitation | Smog |
|---|---|---|---|---|---|---|---|---|---|---|---|---|
| Vehicle exhaust | ● | ● | ● | | | | ● | ● | | ● | ● | ● |
| Fossil fuel burning | ● | | | ● | | | | ● | | ● | ● | ● |
| Paints | | ● | | | | | | | | | | ● |
| Deforestation | | | ● | | | | | ● | | ● | | ● |
| Farms | | | | | | | ● | | | ● | | |
| Refrigerants | | | | | | ● | | | ● | ● | | |
| Fire extinguishers | | | | | ● | | | | ● | ● | | |
| Plastic foam | | | | | | ● | | | ● | ● | | |
| Pesticides | | ● | | | | | | | | | | ● |

**Figure 24.1 Major sources of air pollutants.** A single activity (such as driving a car) may produce more than one type of air pollutant.

### Excessive greenhouse gases could cause global warming

If you've ever been in a glass greenhouse on a sunny day you know that it permits sunlight to penetrate, but as sunlight is converted to heat energy, the greenhouse becomes warmer because the glass prevents the heat from escaping. Certain gases in the upper layer of the atmosphere (the stratosphere) act in much the same way for Earth; therefore they are called *greenhouse gases.*

The most significant greenhouse gas is water vapor, accounting for approximately 60% of the total. The remainder are human-made and consist of carbon dioxide ($CO_2$), methane ($CH_4$), nitrous oxide ($N_2O$), and small amounts of two other air pollutants: the chlorofluorocarbons (CFCs), used primarily as refrigerants, and gases called halons that

#### Answers to Intro Questions

1 **True.** While this may not sound like much of an increase, it can have surprisingly widespread effects on living organisms, including humans. In this chapter, we take a closer look at global warming and what it means for us.

2 **False.** Freshwater accounts for less than 1% of Earth's water. Water is more scarce than we realize, and human activities can easily pollute it.

3 **Actually, we don't know.** So far we have identified approximately 1.75 million species, but there are probably many more still undiscovered. Some scientists estimate that the total could be more than 30 million species.

4 **True.** We'll see why in this chapter.

5 **c.** 10,000 miles. Read the chapter to learn more about green roofs.

contain bromine, used in fire extinguishers. Together the greenhouse gases produce a **greenhouse effect,** allowing sunlight to pass but trapping most of the heat radiated from earth on its way to space (Figure 24.2). This is a natural and normal phenomenon. Without the greenhouse effect, most of the sun's heat would radiate away from Earth and the average temperature would be well below freezing. In other words, to maintain a normal surface temperature on Earth, a certain amount of greenhouse gases is needed in the stratosphere. Most of the $CO_2$ component of the greenhouse gases accumulated over millions of years, as a result of respiration.

In modern times, however, human activities have increased the levels of greenhouse gases, especially $CO_2$. Many scientists believe that excessive production of the greenhouse gases is increasing the greenhouse effect and raising the average global temperature, a phenomenon known as **global warming.** The two main human activities that have raised atmospheric levels of $CO_2$ are **deforestation** (removing trees from large areas of land) and the burning of fossil fuels. Deforestation by burning is doubly damaging—not only is $CO_2$ liberated as wood is burned, but with fewer plants, $CO_2$ uptake is reduced as well. A large tree, for example, absorbs approximately 50 lb of $CO_2$ per year through the process of photosynthesis. The burning of fossil fuels has returned $CO_2$ to the atmosphere that has been stored over millions of years. (See the Try It Yourself box on page 549 for an idea of how much $CO_2$ your car emits in a year.) Since global warming increases water evaporation and water vapor, a positive feedback loop may increase global warming still further.

Experts still debate the effects of global warming. For more on this controversy, see the Current Issue box at the end of the chapter.

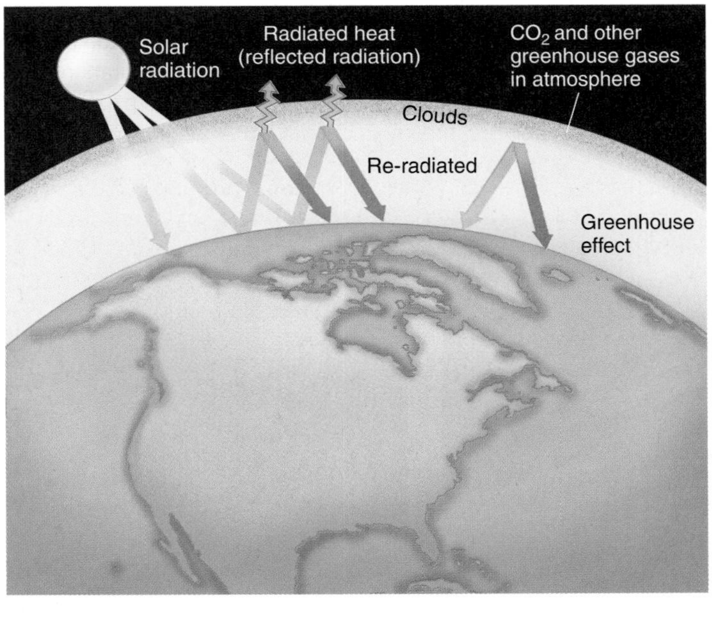


**Figure 24.2 The greenhouse effect.** A layer of stratospheric greenhouse gases consisting primarily of carbon dioxide ($CO_2$) allows sunlight to pass but traps most of the heat. An overabundance of greenhouse gases may contribute to global warming. Water vapor can also be a greenhouse gas, setting up a positive feedback loop: As global warming continues, more water will evaporate and be absorbed by clouds, which will reradiate heat back to Earth and cause further surface warming.

## CFCs deplete the ozone layer

**Ozone** ($O_3$) is found in two places in the atmosphere. In the atmospheric layer near the planet surface (the troposphere), ozone is an air pollutant formed by the reaction of oxygen with automobile exhaust and industrial pollution. Ozone is mildly toxic, causing plant damage and respiratory distress in animals, including humans.

Ozone is also found in the stratosphere, where it forms a thin layer that helps shield Earth from ultraviolet (UV) rays. UV rays contribute to skin cancer, suppress the immune system, and may cause cataracts. It now appears that the ozone layer has suffered significant damage due to CFCs, a group of chemicals that also contribute to global warming. CFCs released into the lower atmosphere migrate slowly toward the stratosphere and decompose, releasing chlorine atoms. The chlorine atoms combine with ozone and destroy it, producing oxygen (Figure 24.3). Because the chlorine molecule can be used over and over in the reaction, a single chlorine atom may destroy as many as 10,000 ozone molecules.

Already the stratospheric ozone layer has thinned noticeably, and "holes" have even developed at certain times of the year (Figure 24.4). As a result, researchers at the United Nations expect the incidence of cataracts and skin cancer to rise worldwide over the next several decades.

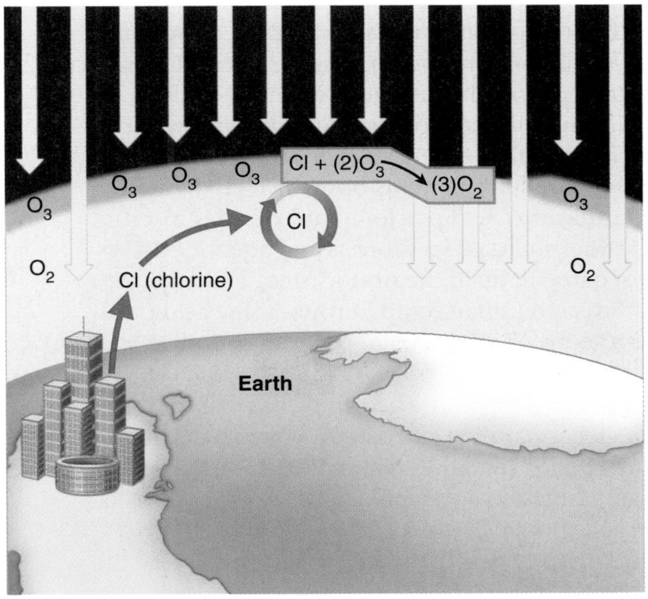


**Figure 24.3 Destruction of the ozone layer.** Chlorine released into the atmosphere reacts with ozone ($O_3$) to produce oxygen ($O_2$). Destruction of the ozone layer exposes Earth's surface to more ultraviolet radiation.

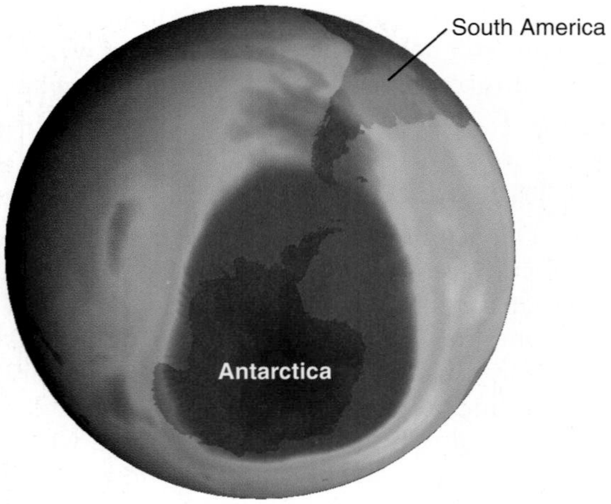


**Figure 24.4 Depletion of the ozone layer.** A hole (blue color) now appears in the stratospheric ozone layer over Antarctica at certain times of the year.

Fortunately, this is one area where action has been taken. In an international agreement signed in 1987, most industrialized nations are phasing out the production of CFCs. There will be a delay before we experience the full benefits of the phase-out, however, as it takes 10 to 20 years for CFCs to reach the stratosphere. Furthermore, CFC molecules can be highly stable, persisting for 100 years or more. Despite our progress so far, ozone depletion will continue to affect the atmosphere for years to come.

## Pollutants produce acid precipitation

The major source of acid precipitation is sulfur dioxide, which is released into the air as a result of burning high-sulfur coal and oil for power. A secondary source is nitrogen oxide in automobile exhaust. Sulfur dioxide and nitrogen oxides combine with water vapor in the air, become sulfuric acid and nitric acid, and dissolve in raindrops which fall as **acid precipitation.** Acid precipitation corrodes metal and stone and damages forests and aquatic ecosystems, particularly in the northeastern United States, southeastern Canada, and Europe. Some acid products also precipitate as solid particles of sulfate and nitrate salts.

Acid precipitation is becoming less of a concern than global warming and ozone depletion due to improved design (and thus reduced emissions) from power plants and automobiles.

## Smog blankets industrial areas

Several pollutants in air, most notably nitrogen oxides and hydrocarbons (chains of carbons linked to hydrogens), react with each other in the presence of sunlight and water vapor. They form a hazy brown or gray layer of **smog** that tends to hover over the region where it is produced (the term comes from "smoke" + "fog"). The burning of fossil fuels (coal and oil) and automobile exhausts is the primary culprit.

Smog also contains ozone and PANs (peroxyacyl nitrates), both of which irritate the eyes and lungs and may lead to chronic respiratory illnesses such as asthma and emphysema. Depending on the source, smog may also contain small oil droplets and particles of wood or coal ash, asbestos, lead, dust, and animal waste. It can become especially troublesome during a **thermal inversion,** when a warm stagnant upper layer of air traps a cooler air mass containing smog beneath it.

Like acid precipitation, the problem of smog has been reduced due to widespread cleanup efforts and reduced emissions of pollutants. For example, smog was once a significant health problem in London and Pittsburgh, but both of these cities have succeeded in major efforts to reduce smog (Figure 24.5). The state of California has passed strict automobile antipollution laws. Many regions of the United States now require the use of cleaner-burning oxygenated automobile fuels containing ethanol or methanol during certain winter months, and the use of lead as a fuel additive has been significantly reduced as well. Other areas, including cities such as Cairo and Mexico City, have not yet solved their smog problems.

**RECAP**

Air quality and air pollution are a worldwide concern. Human activities are destroying the protective layer of ozone around Earth, producing acid precipitation and smog, and may be causing a slow global warming trend. Remedial efforts are effective, as shown by the reduction of smog in some cities and the application of new technologies for reducing acid precipitation. Global initiatives to slow global warming and reduce ozone layer destruction are already underway. ■

a) b)

**Figure 24.5 Smog. (a)** Pittsburgh at the height of the steelmaking era, before smog cleanup efforts began. **(b)** Pittsburgh after programs were instituted to reduce smog.

## 24.2 **Pollution jeopardizes scarce water supplies**

Human activities have three major detrimental effects on water quality and availability. First, humans use excessive amounts of water, depleting freshwater supplies. Second, the replacement of natural vegetation with buildings and roads, especially in urban areas, prevents rainwater from soaking in, causing runoff. Third, human activities sometimes pollute precious sources of water.

### Water is scarce and unequally distributed

In one sense, water is a renewable resource because it evaporates continuously from the oceans and falls on land as rain or snow. However, all of the freshwater on the surface of the land and in **aquifers** (deep underground reservoirs) forms less than 1% of Earth's total water. Over 97% is salty ocean water and 2% is frozen in glaciers and polar ice caps.

In addition to general scarcity, water is not evenly distributed among human populations. Residents of the more industrialized countries use 10 to 100 times more water than people in less industrialized countries. Some desert and semiarid regions of the world have already reached their human carrying capacity as a result of water shortage. When we divert water for our purposes, we take it away from other species or limit their normal migration patterns. Water rights are a controversial subject in the western United States, where water is limited. Already, choices have to be made between irrigating crops, supplying growing cities, and encouraging the reproduction of Pacific salmon.

*try it yourself*

### Calculating the $CO_2$ Emissions of Your Vehicle

How much $CO_2$ does *your* vehicle release into the atmosphere? It's relatively easy to calculate because the combustion of every gallon of gasoline emits approximately 19.6 pounds of $CO_2$ regardless of the octane rating, your driving habits, or your vehicle. The $CO_2$ emissions weigh several times more than the gasoline burned because during combustion each carbon atom in gasoline combines with two atoms of oxygen that together weigh $2\frac{2}{3}$ times more than the carbon atom.

To calculate the yearly $CO_2$ emissions caused by your driving, you need only calculate how many gallons of gasoline you use per year and then multiply it by 19.6. Try it yourself:

1. Estimate how many miles you drive in a year: (______ miles/year).
2. Look up or estimate your vehicle's mileage/gallon of gas: (______ miles/gallon).
3. Divide the miles you drive per year by your mileage/gallon to get the number of gallons of gas you use per year: (______ gallons/year).
4. Multiply your gallons/year by 19.6 pounds of $CO_2$/gallon of gas consumed: (______ pounds of $CO_2$/year). This is *your* contribution to $CO_2$ emissions per year just from driving. It does not take into account the environmental cost of producing and later disposing of the vehicle itself or the environmental cost of the production and disposal of oil, tires, and batteries.

To see how you compare to your peers, as a class project create a graph with **Miles/Year** on the abscissa (horizontal axis) and **$CO_2$ Emissions** (pounds $CO_2$/year) on the ordinate (vertical axis). Then have each person put a dot on the graph corresponding to his/her vehicle. You will see that in general, the more miles driven, the higher the total yearly $CO_2$ emissions. However, fuel efficiency counts, too. A Ford Taurus driven 15,000 miles would produce 6.5 tons of $CO_2$, whereas a Lincoln Navigator driven the same distance would produce 9.9 tons.

### Urbanization increases storm water runoff

In urban areas, the shift from woodlands and fields to impermeable roads and buildings has caused major storm water runoff problems. In older cities on the U.S. east coast, storm water combines with sewage, leading to combined sewage overflow (CSO) which overwhelms receiving streams and oceans. Twenty-eight billion gallons of CSO impact the New York harbor each year. This CSO is the major source of pathogens in the area, causing gastroenteritis, eye and ear infections, skin rashes, respiratory infections, and hepatitis in swimmers and kayakers. Furthermore, the use of pipes to transport storm water runoff quickly from buildings and roads to streams leads to stream overflows during storms and insufficient water levels during dry periods. The result is erosion of stream beds and loss of aquatic life (Figure 24.6). Restoration of urban streams seeks to stabilize stream channels, reduce channel erosion, and restore aquatic wildlife populations.

### Human activities pollute freshwater

Human activities tend to pollute what freshwater there is. Untreated sewage, chemicals from factories, the runoff of pesticides, fertilizers, and rubber and oil from city streets, all must go somewhere. Either they degrade chemically according to their natural cycle of decomposition or they end up in water or soil.

Some water pollutants are *organic nutrients* that arise from sewage treatment plants, food-packing plants, and paper mills. When these nutrients are degraded by bacteria, the rapid growth rate of bacteria can deplete the water of oxygen, threatening aquatic animals. Others are *inorganic nutrients* such as nitrate and phosphate fertilizers and sulfates in laundry detergents. These cause prolific growth of algae, which die and are also decomposed by bacteria.

**Figure 24.6 Urban stream erosion.** Urbanization has adverse effects on streams due to excess and polluted runoff.

**Eutrophication** refers to the rapid growth of plant life and the death of animal life in a shallow body of water as a result of excessive organic or inorganic nutrients (Figure 24.7). Eutrophication is part of the normal process that converts freshwater into marsh and then dry land, but human activities can accelerate the process.

A special problem is *toxic pollutants*, including polychlorinated biphenyls (PCBs), oil and gasoline, pesticides, herbicides, and heavy metals. Most of these cannot be degraded by biological decomposition, so they remain in the environment for a long time. In addition, they tend to become more concentrated in the tissues of organisms higher up the food chain, a phenomenon known as **biological magnification** (Figure 24.8). Biological magnification occurs because each animal in a food chain consumes many times its own weight in food throughout its lifetime.

A classic example of biological magnification is the heavy metal, mercury. The primary sources of mercury in the environment are emissions from coal burning, gold production, smelters for nonferrous metal production, and cement production. Mercury released into the air or on land often ends up in aquatic ecosystems, where it accumulates by biological magnification in tertiary consumers such as shark, tuna, and whales. Exposure to mercury can result in diverse symptoms including loss of coordination, decreased memory and intellect, and poor immune system function. Pregnant women and young children are especially at risk since mercury affects nervous system development. Many countries now have regulations governing the maximum allowable mercury concentrations in fish destined for human consumption.

Other important water pollutants worldwide include *disease-causing organisms* like those that cause typhoid fever and hepatitis, *sediments* from soil erosion that clog waterways and fill in lakes and shipping canals, excess *nitrogen fertilizers* used on land to grow crops, and even *heat pollution* from power plants. Heat pollution reduces the amount of oxygen that water can carry. It also increases the oxygen demand by aquatic organisms whose activity level is temperature dependent. The resulting oxygen deprivation may suffocate them.

## Groundwater pollution may impair human health

Many of the same pollutants that taint surface water also pollute groundwater. However, groundwater pollution poses two additional concerns. First, groundwater is often used as drinking water, so its pollutants can quickly affect human health. Second, groundwater is a slowly exchanging pool. Once it becomes polluted it may stay polluted for a long time.

The U.S. Environmental Protection Agency estimates that as many as 50% of all water systems and rural wells contain some type of pollutant. The most common are organic solvents such as carbon tetrachloride, pesticides, and fertil-izers such as nitrates. We do not know the full effect of groundwater pollution because it is hard to separate from other possible causes of human disease. Public health officials suspect that some pollutants contribute to miscarriages, skin rashes, nervous disorders, and birth defects.

An issue of special concern regarding possible groundwater contamination is the disposal of radioactive wastes. Radioactive materials are used in nuclear power plants and in the diagnosis and treatment of human

**Figure 24.7 Eutrophication.** Water pollution accelerates the normal process of eutrophication, encouraging prolific growth of algae and plants at the expense of animal life.

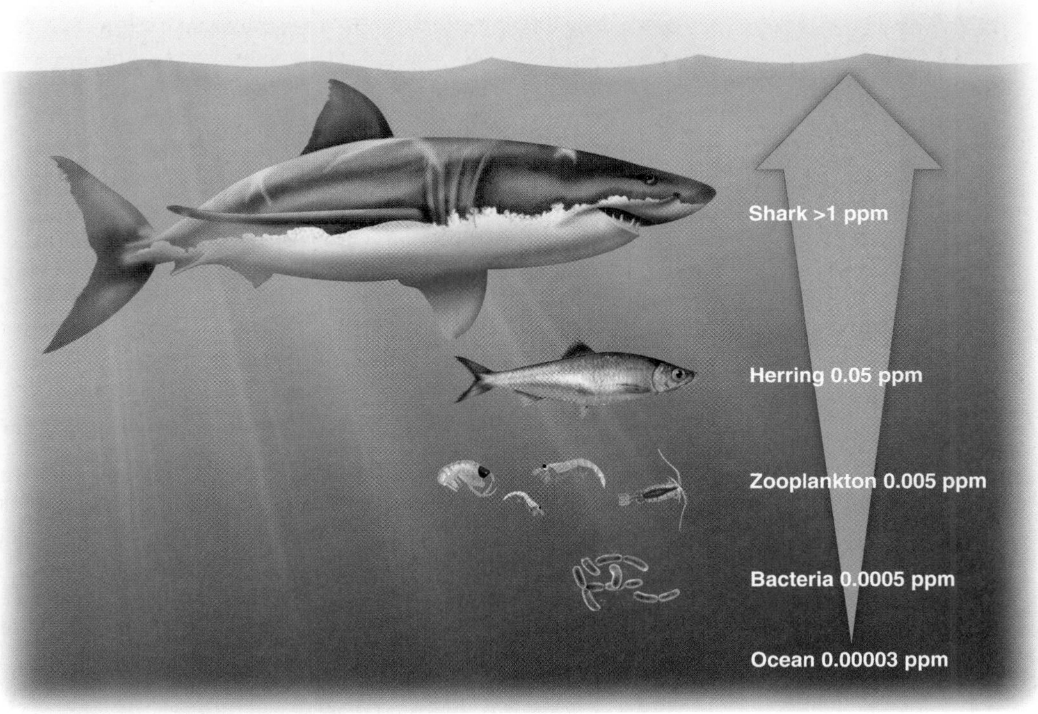


**Figure 24.8 Biological magnification.** The heavy metal mercury accumulates in body tissues as it moves up a food chain. Even though mercury may be present in only very trace amounts (about 0.00003 ppm or parts per million) in water, it becomes highly concentrated (more than 1 ppm) by the time it reaches top predators such as sharks and whales.

disease. Radioactive wastes are usually stored in some of the driest locations in the world because they remain radioactive for up to thousands of years. Some are so long-lived that they are dropped into molten glass, which cools and hardens before they are buried.

### Oil pollution damages oceans and shorelines

Pollution of freshwater rivers eventually ends up in the oceans. Human activities can also pollute oceans directly, and the most common and visible way is by spilling oil at sea.

Several million tons of oil enter the oceans each year. About 50% comes from natural seepage; therefore, some oil pollution is a natural phenomenon. However, 30% of total oceanic oil pollution is caused by oil disposal on land and its eventual washing to the sea in streams and rivers. The remaining 20% results from accidents at sea.

When oil is spilled at sea about a quarter evaporates, nearly half is degraded by bacteria, and the remaining quarter eventually settles to the ocean floor. Nevertheless, an oil spill can cause significant short-term damage to marine and shoreline ecosystems. Before the oil dissipates it coats living organisms, disrupting their ability to function and even choking smaller organisms (Figure 24.9). Shoreline ecosystems may show signs of damage for years. Although cleaning up an oil spill can help an ecosystem recover more quickly, it also shifts some of the pollution to a site on land.

**RECAP**

Freshwater is scarce and distributed unevenly. Freshwater can become polluted by surface water runoff from urban areas and by fertilizers, pesticides, and herbicides in rural areas. Pollution of rivers eventually reaches the oceans. Oil spills at sea are an example of how human activities directly pollute oceans. ■

## 24.3 Pollution and overuse damage the land

The main environmental issue with land may not be how we pollute it (though we do), but how much of it we use. Humans consume a lot, and we tend to alter the landscape to suit our own purposes. We dam river valleys to produce hydroelectric power, strip mountaintops to find coal, and cut down forests for lumber or to clear space for crops.

The economy of the United States alone accounts for the direct consumption of 44,000 pounds (22 tons) of fuels, metals, minerals, and biomass (food and forest products) for every person every year. Add to this number the amount of earth moved to build roads and waterways and to find energy, plus the erosion of soil by agricultural and forestry activities, and the total use of natural resources amounts to nearly 88 tons per U.S. citizen each year. It has been estimated that human activities have already altered a third of Earth's land mass, including removing nearly half of its original forest cover.

As the human population grows, a significant trend has been our migration toward cities. Cities often expand into farmland because it is nearby and because it is more economical to build where it is flat, even though only a fraction of Earth's surface will ever be suitable as farmland. Cities also require large quantities of water and power and generate waste and pollution in a relatively small area.

The problems of land use in rural areas are quite different but just as significant. More than half the people of the world live in rural poverty. Many rely almost entirely on their local environment to survive. It is not uncommon for impoverished rural communities to cut down all trees for fuel and shelter and overgraze communal lands with livestock. Stripping the biomass from fragile ecosystems leads to erosion

**Figure 24.9 An oil spill.** Oil spilled near a shoreline may wash up on shore. This oil spill was in Galveston, Texas.

**Figure 24.10 Desertification.** Many poor residents of rural areas must depend on local resources to survive. Stripping the biomass from the ecosystem causes desertification, as once productive land becomes eroded and barren. This photo was taken in Tanzania.

and **desertification**—the transformation of marginal lands into near-desert conditions unsuitable for future agriculture (Figure 24.10). Every year an estimated 15 million more acres of once-productive land become desert. Because the very survival of the rural poor is linked so closely to the use of the available resources, it is unlikely that we can halt land degradation in these regions without first doing something about rural poverty.

Wars cause environmental damage that is often overlooked. In Iraq, the draining of the marshlands of the Euphrates/Tigris delta during the 1980s and 1990s resulted in the loss of valuable farmland. More recently the oil spill at the Jiyyeh power station during the Israeli-Hizbollah conflict resulted in damage to 150 km of Lebanese and Syrian coastline, polluting beaches and coastal water.

And finally, there is the issue of how we should dispose of our garbage. Landfills, one solution, deserve our attention, perhaps because they are so clearly intentional and we are questioning our choices. It is wise that we *do* continually examine our choices, but it may be worth considering that landfills are not our biggest environmental problem—as long as they are well designed and do not contribute to ground or water pollution. Nevertheless, we could all seek ways to generate less garbage and recycle as much as possible.

**RECAP**

Land use and land pollution problems differ by region. In some areas humans alter the landscape in search of fossil fuels and minerals. Cities expand into productive land and place a burden on resources. In rural regions, deforestation and desertification damage ecosystems and limit their future productivity. ■

## 24.4 Energy: Many options, many choices

Energy—we just can't get enough of it. We want inexpensive fuel for automobiles weighing thousands of pounds. We heat our homes and even the water in our swimming pools. We need energy to refine raw materials, manufacture the products we use, and process and cook our food.

Energy use is tied to consumption, so we do have some choice in determining how much energy to use. We can also make choices about where to obtain our energy.

First, there are *fossil fuels*—coal, oil, and gas. We've already examined the environmental costs of retrieving and transporting them, and know that using them may contribute to greenhouse gases by releasing $CO_2$. In addition, coal in particular generates acid precipitation because it contains sulfur. Finally, we need to consider that fossil fuels are nonrenewable resources. Their formation took millions of years, but we could consume them all in a couple of centuries. One way to consume less fossil fuel is to use renewable biofuels for cars and airplanes. See the Directions in Science box on biofuels for more on this strategy.

Could *nuclear energy* fulfill our energy needs instead? In practice, nuclear energy has proved expensive because of all the safeguards necessary to ensure that the core of the energy plant does not become overheated, suffer a meltdown, and release radioactivity into the environment. In addition, nuclear power plants generate wastes that remain radioactive for thousands of years. How to store those wastes properly is a subject of current debate.

Many rural poor use *biomass fuels* such as wood and the dung of herbivores. These are renewable if they are not depleted too fast, but they pollute the air and are not always available. Some countries are experimenting with processes that burn waste material, including municipal garbage, to extract energy.

# Directions in Science

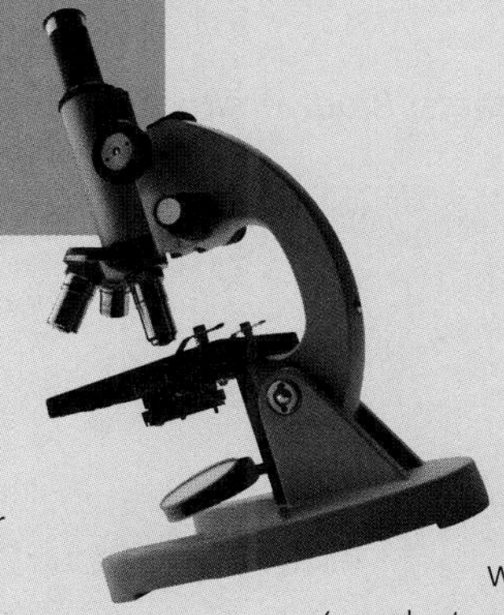

## Biofuels: the Fuels of the Future?

Biofuels are produced directly from living organisms or from their metabolic by-products. They must contain greater than 80% renewable materials to be considered biofuels, and can be in the form of solids, liquids, or gases. Although it may seem that the use of renewable materials for fuel is advantageous, there are pros and cons to be considered for each application.

One approach to biofuel development is the collection of methane gas from landfills. Waste in landfills is digested anaerobically (by bacteria inside the waste material) which generates methane gas. Since methane has more than 20 times the global warming capacity of $CO_2$, use of landfill methane as fuel provides a biofuel *and* reduces global warming by converting methane to $CO_2$. Methane can also be harvested from cow manure at dairy farms. While both of these are good ideas from an environmental standpoint, neither landfills nor dairy farms will ever produce enough methane to have much impact on our overall energy consumption.

The past several decades have seen increased emphasis on the use of corn-based ethanol for fuel in automobiles. The original intent behind producing ethanol from corn was not energy efficiency, but energy independence in the event that our sources of oil from abroad suffered a major disruption. However, in recent years scientists have begun to conclude that corn is not the best source of biofuel. Corn is a row-crop that requires large amounts of fertilizer, pesticides, and fuel to grow, harvest, and dry. It is usually grown in rotation with soy-beans, since soy-beans, like all legumes, add nitrogen to the soil. When grown for fuel, however, farmers may plant corn repeatedly on the same land, requiring more fertilizer and generating more nitrogen run-off. And compared to other energy crops like sugar cane, corn is not the most efficient source of biofuel energy because of the cost of growing it, harvesting it, and converting it to ethanol. There is also the food-versus-fuel debate: an average U.S. automobile traveling 10,000 miles a year on pure ethanol would need about 852 gallons of the corn-based fuel. The area of cropland required to produce this ethanol would feed seven Americans. We will probably see the use of corn-based ethanol as a fuel begin to decline within the next decade.

The use of cellulosic ethanol avoids the food-versus-fuel issue. Here the ethanol is derived from cellulose either using agricultural plant wastes (corn stover, cereal straws, sugarcane bagasse), plant wastes from industrial processes (sawdust, paper pulp), or energy crops grown specifically for fuel production, such as switchgrass or miscanthus. The crops used for cellosic ethanol are better suited to more marginal land than corn and therefore do not compete with food production. In addition, the production of cellosic ethanol may be less energy-intensive than corn-based ethanol. The stumbling block to commercialization has been finding efficient ways to break down the cellulose in plant walls. A number of microbe-derived enzymes are currently under investigation. Cellulose-derived sources of energy are likely to be a growth area in the years ahead.

A current new-concept industry is the production of "biodiesel" fuel from used cooking oils or other plant-based oils. Recipes for converting cooking oil to biodiesel fuel can be found on the Internet. The contribution of biodiesel to our overall energy supply is likely to be small, but who knows where the new technology will lead in the future?

Where water is readily available, *hydroelectric* power plants generate electricity. Hydroelectric power plants use the kinetic energy of water to turn turbines that drive electric generators. The environmental cost is the need to build dams that disrupt valley and river ecosystems.

Other types of renewable energy sources include "wind farms" that harness wind to generate electricity (Figure 24.11a), and geothermal power that uses heat from underground sources deep within the Earth. Both these power sources have the advantage of providing renewable energy without the need for cooling water, as compared to fossil or nuclear power plants. Wind farms allow rural areas to retain jobs and to transmit energy to urban centers via utility grids. Geothermal energy is most plentiful near active volcanoes: 5% of California's energy and 25% of El Salvador's are from geothermal sources.

Ultimately we may have to rely on the one original and renewable source, *solar power* (Figure 24.11b), just as plants do. Solar power uses photovoltaic panels to convert light directly into electricity, by absorbing light units (photons) and releasing electrons as direct current. At the moment, solar power technologies are less than 30% efficient at energy conversion, which makes them impractical to meet all our current energy demands. The efficiency of photovoltaic panels improves with each passing year, however. With the use of photovoltaic panels on residences (Figure 24.11c) and solar tracking mirrors at solar farms, solar power can make a significant contribution. Furthermore, the use of passive solar principles in building construction and site selection also adds to energy savings. Examples include the use of south-facing windows which can be shaded in the summer, and the use of building materials that offer thermal mass, or heat storage. Materials with thermal mass can store heat in winter and prevent heat gain in summer. With passive solar strategies and increases in energy conversion efficiency, the proportion of solar energy that can be utilized by humans continues to increase.

**a) A wind farm**

**b) A solar power plant**

**c) Photovoltaic panels power a home**

**Figure 24.11 Alternatives to fossil fuel. (a)** A wind farm. Wind farms are increasingly being used to generate power in areas that have sustained winds. **(b)** A solar power plant. Although solar energy holds great potential for energy production, the technology is not yet capable of generating sufficient power at low cost. This power plant is in Australia. **(c)** Photovoltaic panels.

**RECAP**

Humans consume a disproportionate amount of energy compared to other species. Most of the energy we use comes from nonrenewable fossil fuels that contribute to pollution. Other possible sources include nuclear energy, hydroelectric power, wind farms, geothermal energy, biomass fuels, and solar energy. ■

## 24.5 Human impacts are creating a biodiversity crisis

**Biodiversity** refers to species richness, the assortment of living organisms on Earth. One measure of biodiversity is the number of species: to date, we have identified approximately 1.75 million species, but many scientists estimate that the total could be closer to 10, 30, or even 80 million. Ultimately, biodiversity can be considered as the variety of all forms of life, from species all the way to ecosystems. In this sense, biodiversity is a measure of ecological "health."

Human impacts on the biosphere contribute to a reduction in biodiversity worldwide. Indeed, some scientists estimate that the global extinction rate is 50 times higher now than at any time during the past 100,000 years.

### Humans alter and destroy habitats

Pollution and overexploitation of natural resources are destroying whole habitats and driving many species of plants and animals toward extinction. Consider tropical rain forests. The African nation of Ivory Coast once possessed 70 million acres of pristine tropical rain forest. Today only 5 to 7 million acres remain, and even these may be gone in 10 years. One reason is population growth: Rural residents move to urban areas in search of better jobs and living conditions. As cities grow, land is cleared to make way for new buildings and roads.

Another cause of habitat destruction is farming, particularly in rain-forest areas. Millions of people around the world depend on subsistence farming to survive and feed their families. However, despite their lush vegetation, rain forests do not make good farmland—they are fragile ecosystems with little topsoil and scant soil nutrients. Several years of intensive farming deplete the nutrients from the soil. To continue raising enough crops to survive, farmers clear a fresh section of rain forest and start another destructive cycle. The clear-cut areas they leave behind are slow to recover, if they recover at all.

Exploitation of scarce forest resources poses another threat. In Brazil, poachers sneak into Itatiaia National Park and cut down 100-year-old palm trees for the tender heart of palm, found only at the top of the tree. Hearts of palm are a popular gourmet product, and there is a growing market for them in the U.S. and other countries. One tree yields enough heart to fill only two 14-ounce cans, but removing the heart kills the entire tree. It also endangers other wildlife, since the palm's small black fruit is a major food source for many animals.

Logging is also a factor. European and Middle Eastern logging companies harvest 800-year-old hardwood trees in Africa and ship them to other continents, where they are processed into furniture, floors, and buildings. In recent years the pace of logging has accelerated. Logging affects animals as well as plants, because logging destroys the animals' habitats and leaves behind roads that make once-remote areas accessible to poachers. Across Africa, illegal hunting of elephants, monkeys, and antelopes has soared.

The Forest Stewardship Council (FSC) promotes sustainable forestry through its certification process. The FSC supports forestry practices that are environmentally responsible, socially equitable, and economically viable. This means balancing logging with environmental outcomes, such as protecting biodiversity, sensitive aquatic habitats, and plant and animal communities. FSC-certified wood bears the FSC logo and can be obtained in more than 70 countries.

Deforestation and exploitation of resources are not confined to tropical rain forests, however. Much of the eastern half of the United States underwent considerable deforestation in the late 1800s, both for timber and to clear land for farming, and the trend continues today. The current destruction of the world's habitats cannot be blamed on just one people, country, continent, or industry. After all, the logging industry is supplying the demand from industrialized nations for paper, cardboard, and exotic woods. The hearts-of-palm poachers in Brazil are responding to American demand for this exotic delicacy.

### Urbanization is a major force for environmental change

The worldwide shift to urban living has widespread effects on ecosystems, including biodiversity. Human control of plant composition in cities results in fewer species overall, with decreased native species, uneven plant coverage, and more invasive and exotic plants. Urbanization also shrinks the biodiversity of animal populations, with a shift to predominantly birds and insects. Although cities cover less than 3% of the Earth's surface, they are responsible for 78% of carbon emissions, 60% of residential water usage, and 76% of wood used for industrial purposes. The resource consumption and waste management requirements of a city typically expand well beyond the city limits. For example, the land area or "ecological footprint" required to serve London's resources and wastes is 120 times the size of the actual city. Furthermore, there is evidence that urbanization may reduce native species diversity on a regional or even global scale. For instance, urban sprawl in northern latitudes appears to reduce the populations of some migratory birds in southern latitudes.

### Biodiversity is healthy for humans too

Biodiversity is healthy for all organisms, including *Homo sapiens,* and large-scale disruptions to the biosphere threaten human populations too. For example, we depend on plants for a healthy atmosphere. Through photosynthesis, plants consume carbon dioxide and produce oxygen, thereby removing $CO_2$ that might otherwise contribute to the greenhouse gases and producing oxygen for us to breathe.

We also depend on other species for clothing, shelter, food, and even medicine—25% of all prescription drugs sold in the U.S. are based on substances derived from fewer than 50 species of plants. It's estimated that there are 265,000 flowering plants in the world, and less than 1% have been tested so far for medicinal applications. By encouraging biodiversity, we maintain the potential to discover important new medicines in the future.

Healthy ecosystems offer other benefits that may not become apparent until they have been damaged. For instance, wetlands provide valuable flood control because they can hold large amounts of water; destroying them leaves metropolitan areas vulnerable to devastating floods. Biodiversity in the food supply is important for humans as well. Nutrition studies provide strong evidence that eating a varied diet, particularly a wide range of fruits and vegetables, is essential for optimal health. However, our current agriculture practices limit our food choices, since, for example, very few varieties of apples and tomatoes are typically available in U.S. supermarkets, and many leafy greens known to be high in antioxidants, such as arugula, watercress, and chard, can only be found in specialty stores or farmer's markets.

**RECAP**

Human impacts are leading to a global biodiversity crisis. Urbanization, pollution, habitat destruction, and overexploitation of natural resources are destroying habitats. Loss of biodiversity threatens human populations too, since humans depend on other species for oxygen, clothing, shelter, food, medicine, and other necessities. ■

## 24.6 Sustainable development supports future economic needs

In a sustainable world, humans would be an integral part of ecosystems so that those ecosystems (and we humans) could exist on the planet far into the future. This would mean practicing **sustainable development,** defined by the 1987 World Commission on Environment and Development as "development that meets the needs of the present without compromising the ability of future generations to meet their economic needs."

# The Debate over Global Warming

Few subjects have generated so much heated debate as the question of global warming (no pun intended). It's a sensitive political and economic issue with vital implications for the long-range future of Earth and all its inhabitants.

## Earth's Temperature Is Rising

Measurements taken from a worldwide network of thermometers on buoys, ships, and land-based weather stations over the past 125 years reveal that average global surface temperatures have increased by a rate of almost 0.6° Celsius (1.0° Fahrenheit) per century. Although temperatures vary from year to year, the overall trend is unmistakable, and since 1976 the pace has accelerated to 1.8°C (3.2°F) per century. Indeed, 1998 and 2005 set records for high temperatures. Although 2007 was only the eighth warmest year on record (exceeded by 1998, 2005, and 2006), the period 2001 to 2007 was 0.21°C warmer than 1991 to 2000. These data are supported by a 27-year record of temperature measurements taken by satellites circling the globe. The data indicate that the troposphere, the atmospheric layer that extends from Earth's surface to about 8 miles above sea level, has increased in temperature as well.

## Human Activities Affect Earth's Temperature

The mainstream scientific view is that most of the increase in temperature can be directly attributed to a sharp rise in atmospheric $CO_2$ concentrations from the burning of fossil fuels—coal, oil, and gas. Since the late 1800s when humans first began to use fossil fuels in large quantities, emissions of $CO_2$ into the atmosphere from the combustion of fossil fuels have increased to around 23.5 million metric tons per day. During this same period, atmospheric $CO_2$ concentration rose from 288 ppmv (parts per million by volume) to 377 ppmv. If the sharp upward trend of just the past 30 years continues, atmospheric $CO_2$ levels will be twice as high by the next century as they are today.

Evidence that all this $CO_2$ contributes to global warming comes from state-of-the-art climate models run by supercomputers. The models reveal that throughout the twentieth century, neither natural forces nor human activities alone could account for the observed climatic changes. Only when *both* natural forces and human activities were included did the model work with any reliability. The United Nations–sponsored Intergovernmental Panel on Climate Change has concluded that "most of the observed warming over the last 50 years is likely to have been due to the increase in greenhouse gas concentrations."

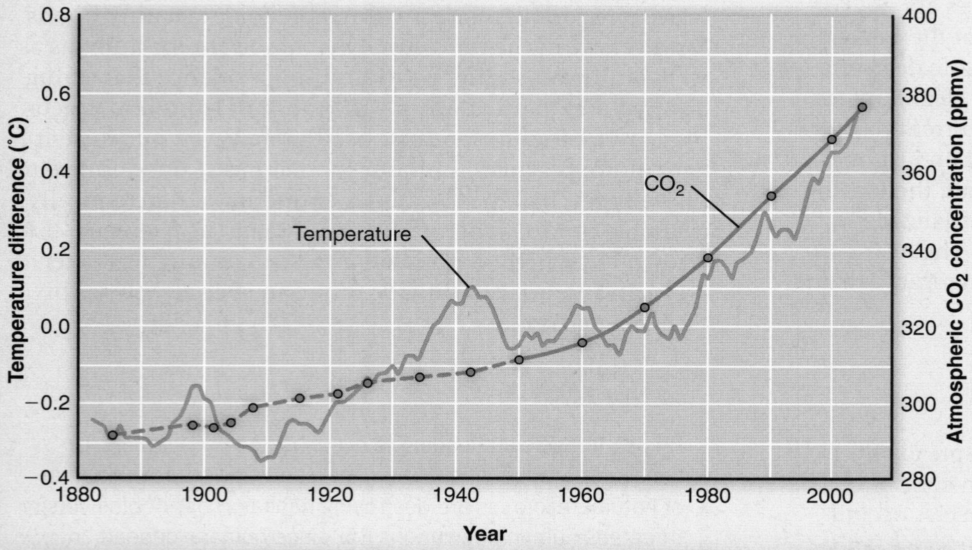


Global temperature differences (from a 1951–1980 base) and atmospheric $CO_2$ concentrations since 1880.
Data from National Aeronautics and Space Administration and Carbon Dioxide Information Analysis Center.

## How Might Global Warming Affect Us?

An average temperature change of only 1.1° Fahrenheit in the past century may not sound like much. However, if present trends continue, temperatures could rise another 3.6°F by 2100. Most experts agree that if global temperatures increase this much, we could expect a rise in sea level by several feet within several centuries due to increased loss of glacial ice. This would likely be enough to destroy coastal ecosystems and flood major cities. Evaporation could accelerate, increasing precipitation worldwide. In just the past century alone the sea level has risen 4–10 inches and global precipitation over land has increased 1%. The health of countless species of organisms on Earth, including humans, is likely to be affected.

## the facts...

- Global warming is likely to have profound effects on climate, weather, agriculture, and human health.
- Approaches to addressing global warming include establishing carbon emissions limits, trading carbon credits, and sequestering (storing) carbon to remove it from the atmosphere.
- Regardless of the approach taken to limit future global warming, we will almost certainly have to adapt to effects already caused by global warming.

### Why Is So Little Being Done?

The extent and causes of global warming are high-profile topics in the scientific community.

In 1997, 35 countries including the U.S. signed the Kyoto Protocol, an agreement that calls for signing countries to reduce their greenhouse gas emissions by an average of 5.2% below their 1990 levels by 2012. The United States later withdrew from the agreement, citing concerns over how it could affect the U.S. economy. Some countries have made concerted efforts to reduce their greenhouse gas emissions or at least slow their rate of increase, but overall their attempts have not yet been effective. Furthermore, developing countries in Asia that were not high emitters of greenhouse gases in the past continue to increase their emissions as they undergo industrialization. China now outranks the U.S. in total greenhouse gas emissions and is expected to increase its emissions significantly in the years to come.

The reasons for our failure to act are varied and complex. One reason is that many people have a hard time accepting that a change of only a few degrees over 100 years could alter the worldwide environment for tens of thousands of years to come. A second reason is that the effects of global warming, whatever they will be, are unlikely to affect those of us alive today. Why should we worry when it may take hundreds of years before the full effect of the recent rise in greenhouse gases is known? Third, virtually everyone contributes to the problem, but who among us is willing to sacrifice to solve it, especially when others don't seem to be doing their share? Reversing the global rise in $CO_2$ will be costly. If you were living in China today, would you volunteer to sacrifice your dream of prosperity to correct a problem largely caused by the industrialized nations over the past 150 years?

We all need to recognize that global warming is a serious problem and that it is in our collective best interest to solve it. Until that happens, we are unlikely to make much real progress. The problem is global and the solution will require international cooperation.

### Carbon Trading, Carbon Taxation, and Carbon Sequestration

Despite the failure of most nations to take effective action so far, scientists around the world continue to look for economically feasible solutions to global warming. There are several approaches to limiting greenhouse gases and eliminating the rise in $CO_2$ levels. One involves reducing emissions by trading carbon credits. Nations such as Great Britain, which produce less than their annual quota of $CO_2$ under the Kyoto Protocol, can sell their unused emissions "credits" to other countries. The goal is to reward countries that adopt "green" manufacturing technologies, thus motivating others to do the same. Another method is taxation; some countries levy heavy taxes for emitting $CO_2$ into the atmosphere.

Perhaps the most promising strategy is carbon sequestration; storing or burying $CO_2$ on the ocean floor or deep underground. Norway's Statoil company is already doing it at its Sleipner West gas field in the North Sea. The company taps a natural gas field more than two miles below the ocean floor, extracts $CO_2$ from the gas, liquefies it, and then pumps the $CO_2$ back into a sandstone formation that is almost half a mile below the ocean floor and under a solid rock layer. Scientists don't expect the $CO_2$ to escape for hundreds of years, and by that time humans will probably have converted to cleaner sources of energy. The company sequesters about 2,800 tons of $CO_2$ every day. It's expensive, but on the other hand if the company released the $CO_2$ into the atmosphere they would have to pay approximately $175,000 per day in Norwegian $CO_2$ tax. Sequestering the carbon costs about the same as paying the tax, it's environmentally friendly, and it has given the company a reputation as a global leader in carbon sequestration. At the moment, Sleipner West is the only facility in the world sequestering carbon on such a large scale.

### Adaptation Will Be Necessary

No matter what happens in the long run, the reality is that we'll have to adapt to environmental changes already certain to come. Possible adaptations include strengthening public health services and infrastructure, protecting natural environmental resources, relocating people away from coastal regions and regions prone to flooding, preparing for stronger and more frequent hurricanes, and developing crops that will fare better under conditions of drought, flooding, and stronger winds. What else we might have to do will be determined by the conditions we face at the time.

The Sleipner West natural gas platform.

### Questions to consider

*1 Is it possible to protect world economies and still address global warming? Is it necessary? Explain your answer. 2 In what ways might your own lifestyle choices contribute to global warming? Would you be willing to support legislation that would affect your lifestyle choices in order to reduce global warming?*

## Measuring sustainability and quality of life

How can we determine whether development is sustainable? Another way to think about this is to investigate the economics of sustainability. Economic progress is typically measured by the Gross Domestic Product (GDP), which is defined as the total market value of all goods and services produced within a country in a year. An alternative measure is the Genuine Progress Indicator (GPI). The GPI makes adjustments to the total market value of goods and services to account for environmental costs such as water and air pollution and loss of wetlands, as well as negative economic and social costs (crime, time spent commuting, loss of leisure time) associated with increased production. Quality of life is also taken into consideration by the GPI; it weighs the value of all goods and services produced against enjoyment of life, including such factors as family breakdown and loss of parklands.

## Strategies to support sustainable development

Given what we know today, let's focus on strategies that might help us reach a sustainable world.

**Consume less** This approach isn't popular, but by consuming less you automatically use fewer resources, generate less garbage, and cause less pollution. If you use less, it leaves more for another person or even another species. *What* to consume less of may be a very personal choice, but unfortunately it's the big-ticket items that have the most impact. You could do a lot for the environment, for example, by living in a house that is no larger than your needs, keeping your car an extra year before replacing it (thus purchasing fewer cars in your lifetime), and living closer to work. In some cases, we make decisions as a society that affect the environment (we have already chosen to use fewer chlorofluorocarbons, for example).

**Recycle more** This one is more popular. Recycling reusable materials such as paper, metal, and plastic reduces our consumption of raw materials. It also keeps the recycled substances from becoming either garbage or pollutants. We also need to consider not only how we recycle substances back into our manufacturing processes, but also how we recycle them back into the ecosystem. Some cities collect, compost, and then recycle leaves and organic material. Even landfills might be considered a slow form of recycling back into the ecosystem.

**Support sustainable agriculture** Current agriculture is based on an industrial model and is aptly referred to as "agribusiness" because it emphasizes high production. This approach has made food abundant and cheap but at the steep cost of degraded water and soil. In contrast, sustainable agriculture means developing systems to raise crops and livestock following the principles found in nature and hence not depleting the earth's resources. For example, shade-grown coffee involves coffee planted under shade trees. Larger trees and greater diversity of vegetation enhance the growth of coffee plants, while also allowing native plants and birds to flourish (Figure 24.12). Consider participating in Consumer Supported Agriculture (CSA) and connecting directly with a local farm. CSA members make a commitment to support a local farm, usually on a quarterly basis, by purchasing a share of the farm's harvest.

**Support green roofs** The replacement of conventional asphalt or tile with a living, vegetated roof system is a visually pleasing way to provide many benefits that support sustainability. Green roofs increase the energy efficiency of buildings, primarily due to evaporative cooling from the plant material and soil. Conventional roofs, along with roads and pavement, do not absorb rainwater, which results in large volumes of polluted runoff. Green roofs help restore the natural water cycle by filtering and retaining storm water. Green roofs absorb airborne particulate pollutants, and also absorb harmful nitrogen oxides and carbon dioxide for photosynthesis: 1 square meter of green roof absorbs the average amount of pollutants produced by an automobile driven 10,000 miles per year. Plants on green roofs typically consist of native species (for example, grasses in Scandinavia and succulents in California) and therefore require little irrigation or other maintenance (Figure 24.13).

**Lower the worldwide fertility rate** Translation: have fewer children. Fewer children means fewer cloth and disposable diapers. It means fewer cars and houses in North America, less deforestation in Brazil, fewer polluted rivers in India, less desertification in Africa. If the current fertility rate of the human species does not decline, eventually environmental degradation will reduce the human carrying capacity of

**Figure 24.12 Shade-grown coffee, an example of sustainable agriculture.**

**Figure 24.13 A green roof.** The roof of the new California Academy of Sciences building in San Francisco is covered with native plants and recycled materials.

Earth and the death rate will rise to equal the birth rate. We can already see this happening in certain areas of Africa where life expectancy is short and infant mortality is high.

**Reduce rural world poverty** People who are starving and without shelter must think of their immediate needs first. It is virtually impossible to convey the long-term impact of desertification to someone who relies on a few goats and trees for day-to-day survival. More and more of the world will become uninhabitable due to deforestation and desertification unless the poor people in those areas are given a viable economic alternative to destruction of their own habitat.

**Conserve energy in your home** Opt for renewable energy at home, such as installing photovoltaic panels, and use energy-efficient appliances. Install low emittance (low-E) glass windows to reduce heat loss in winter and heat gain in summer. Switch incandescent bulbs to compact fluorescents to increase lighting efficiency.

**Use environmentally preferable products** Whenever possible, choose environmental products that are less harmful to the environment than their alternatives, such as paints that are low in volatile organic compounds (VOC), composite wood made from recycled materials, and carpets that are both low in VOC and high in recycled content.

**Protect ecosystems that provide ecoservices** From an economic point of view, it makes sense to protect our ecosystems, since if they are destroyed we will lose crucial sources of food, new medicines, and many other benefits. For example, forests provide climate control, raw materials, and food. Since a forest is a natural asset that provides valuable services, it is a form of "natural capital." Similarly, the ozone layer provides protection from damaging ultraviolet radiation.

Will we be able to achieve a sustainable world? Given our history so far there is every reason for optimism, for we humans have a remarkable capacity for making intelligent decisions and shaping our own environment. Already we can see cooperation on a global scale with the problem of global warming. More choices will be made in the future and you will have a part in them. Your decisions will help to shape humankind's future.

**RECAP**

A sustainable world will require stabilizing the human population growth rate and the global environment. Strategies for doing this include consuming less, recycling more, supporting sustainable agriculture and green building practices, lowering the global fertility rate and poverty rate, utilizing renewable energy sources, and protecting ecosystems. Achieving this goal will test our capacity to make intelligent decisions on a worldwide scale. ■

# Chapter Summary

### Pollutants impair air quality *p. 546*

- Air pollution leads to excessive production of greenhouse gases, especially $CO_2$, and may be contributing to global warming.
- CFCs are thinning the ozone layer in the stratosphere. Although a number of nations are cooperating to reduce CFC emissions, ozone depletion remains a threat.
- Acid precipitation damages forests and aquatic ecosystems.
- Smog tends to hover over the area where it is produced and can cause chronic respiratory problems.

### Pollution jeopardizes scarce water supplies *p. 549*

- Water is scarce and often distributed unequally. Freshwater forms less than 1% of the world's total water supply.
- Pollution of surface freshwater can contaminate groundwater and ultimately pollute the oceans.
- Pollution can accelerate the process of eutrophication.
- Because of biological magnification, toxic substances become more concentrated in organisms higher up the food chain.

### Pollution and overuse damage the land *p. 551*

- Humans alter the landscape for their own purposes.
- Deforestation and desertification transform productive land into nonproductive land.

**Energy: Many options, many choices** *p. 552*

- Humans use a great deal of energy compared to other species.
- Most of the energy we consume comes from nonrenewable fossil fuels—coal, oil, and gas—that contribute to pollution.
- Other possible sources of energy include biomass fuels, nuclear power, hydroelectric power, wind farms, geothermal power, and solar power. Solar power is renewable, but current solar power technologies cannot fulfill all our energy demands.

**Human impacts are creating a biodiversity crisis** *p. 554*

- Pollution, urbanization, habitat destruction, and overexploitation of natural resources are damaging the biosphere and accelerating the global extinction rate. Human population growth, farming, logging, and exploitation of scarce resources are all factors.
- Humans depend on other species for clothing, shelter, food, medicine, oxygen and a healthy atmosphere, and other necessities of life. Loss of biodiversity places human populations at risk too.

**Sustainable development supports future economic needs** *p. 555*

- Strategies for achieving a sustainable future include: consuming less, recycling more, supporting sustainable agriculture, planting green roofs, lowering the worldwide fertility rate to the replacement fertility rate, reducing rural world poverty, conserving energy at home, using environmentally preferable products, and protecting ecosystems.
- Substituting the GPI (genuine progress indicator) for the GDP (gross domestic product) provides a measure of progress that takes into account our quality of life issues
- Humans can shape the environment. It's up to us to shape it wisely.

## Terms You Should Know

acid precipitation, *548*
aquifer, *549*
biodiversity, *554*
biological magnification, *550*
deforestation, *547*
desertification, *552*
eutrophication, *550*
global warming, *547*
greenhouse effect, *547*
ozone, *547*
pollution, *546*
smog, *548*
sustainable development, *555*
thermal inversion, *548*

## Concept Review

1. Describe the importance of maintaining the ozone layer that surrounds Earth.
2. Describe the effects of acid precipitation and smog.
3. Discuss how human activities pollute Earth's water supply.
4. Explain how pollution can increase the greenhouse effect, and how this might alter global temperatures.
5. Explain why tertiary consumers are more adversely affected by toxic pollutants than primary consumers.
6. Compare and contrast the various sources of energy that are available.
7. Describe the importance of biodiversity and impacts on human health.
8. Describe why sustainable development makes sense from an economic point of view.
9. List strategies that support sustainable development.

## Test Yourself

### Matching Exercise

_____ 1. Energy derived from the heat of the Earth.
_____ 2. The process by which marginal land is converted into barren land unsuitable for future agriculture.
_____ 3. The term that refers to the number and variety of species living on Earth.
_____ 4. Freshwater can be found in these deep underground reservoirs.
_____ 5. A hazy brown or gray layer of air pollution derived primarily from nitrogen oxides and hydrocarbons.

a. geothermal
b. aquifers
c. desertification
d. biodiversity
e. smog

### Fill in the Blank

6. ______________ are chemicals in the environment that have adverse effects on living organisms.
7. A "thermal ______________" occurs when a warm, stagnant upper layer of air traps a cooler air mass containing smog beneath it.
8. The gas called ______________ is found in two places: in the stratosphere and near Earth's surface.
9. ______________ power captures energy from the sun to generate electricity.
10. "Biological ______________" of toxic pollutants occurs because each animal in a food chain consumes many times its own weight in food during its lifetime, and toxic pollutants accumulate in animal tissues.

### True or False?

11. Carbon dioxide accounts for more than half of all greenhouse gases.
12. Smog generally appears over industrial areas, not rural areas.
13. About half of the oceans' oil pollution is due to natural seepage.

## References and Additional Reading

Broome, John. The Ethics of Climate Change. *Scientific American*, June 2008, pp. 97–102.

Carbon dioxide capture and storage: Summary for policymakers, IPCC Special Report 2005. www.ipcc.ch/pdf/ special-reports/srccs/srccs_summaryforpolicymakers.pdf

Fishetti, Mark. Living Cover. *Scientific American*, May 2008, pp. 104–105. (An introduction to the environmental benefits of green roofs.)

Gleick, Peter. Making Every Drop Count. *Scientific American*, February, 2001, pp. 40–45. (A discussion of how to cope with the increased demand on a constant water supply.)

## Apply **What You Know**

1. Your uncle in Iowa builds a farm pond and stocks it with bass and bluegill sunfish. At first the pond water is fairly clear and the bass grow to large size, but within five years the pond is covered with a thick green scum and all the fish are dead. Explain to your uncle what might have happened to the pond.
2. Human warfare can have a devastating effect on an ecosystem. One of the most recent large-scale wars occurred in the early 1990s when a coalition of forces fought Saddam Hussein's takeover of the tiny country of Kuwait. What unsuccessful plan did Saddam's forces employ to hamper the invasion, and what impact did it have on the southern Iraqi and Kuwaiti landscape?
3. How can the seemingly simple choices a person makes in decorating a home on one continent affect the habitats of distant continents?
4. Most humans would agree that they wouldn't want to intentionally destroy something useful or valuable. If that is so, what is driving humans to destroy what most agree are valuable rainforests?
5. In the 1970s the Black Forest of Germany experienced a period of damaged trees. The number of trees dying in the forest increased substantially in a relatively short period of time. In addition, some lakes in the region became increasingly acidic to the point that fish were beginning to die. What could have caused these problems?
6. During the recent Olympic games in Beijing, China, the government temporarily closed down many factories and mandated that people drastically reduce the use of their vehicles until the close of the Olympic games. What was the government concerned about?
7. After Hurricane Katrina, many citizens of New Orleans were not able to return to their homes. Even those homes with only moderate water damage were declared condemned and ultimately torn down. Why were so many homes declared unfit and torn down rather than repaired?
8. Many different energy sources can be used to generate electricity. Which ones do you favor as the energy sources of the future, at least in your lifetime?

*Answers can be found on the Human Biology Place.*

Grimm, Nancy B., et al. Global Change and the Ecology of Cities. *Science* 319(2008)756. (How urbanization is effecting global changes in land cover, biodiversity, and air quality.)

## Internet References

Find links to these Web sites at the Human Biology Place.

**National Sustainable Agriculture Information Service**
**www.attra.org/fundamental.html**
This site provides a wealth of publications that introduce the principles and practice of sustainable agriculture.

**Forest Stewardship Council**
**www.fsc.org**
Nonprofit organization devoted to encouraging responsible management of the world's forests.

**Center for Watershed Protection**
**www.cwp.org**
Nonprofit corporation that provides local governments, activists, and watershed organizations around the country with technical tools for protecting streams, lakes, and rivers.

**Earthwatch Institute**
**www.earthwatch.org**
International nonprofit organization that sponsors field research, education, and conservation efforts to build a sustainable future.

**Sustainable Ecosystems Institute**
**www.sei.org**
Organization of scientists dedicated to educating the public and providing technical expertise to preserve the environment.

**Intergovernmental Panel on Climate Change**
**www.ipcc.ch**
An international coalition that is studying the scientific evidence and socioeconomic issues related to global warming.

**U.S. Environmental Protection Agency**
**www.epa.gov**
Federal agency that conducts research, assessment, and education in environmental science.

**Greanseal**
**www.greanseal.org**
Information and sources for paints and sealants made from low VOC materials.

# Glossary

## A

**ABO blood typing** Technique for classifying blood according to the presence or absence of two protein markers, A and B.

**absorption** Process by which nutrients, water, and ions pass through the digestive tract mucosa and into the blood or lymph.

**accommodation** The process of adjusting the refractive power of the lens of the eye so that light rays are focused on the retina.

**acetylcholine (ACh)** (AS-uh-teel-KOL-een) Neurotransmitter released by some nerve endings in both the peripheral and central nervous systems.

**acid** A substance that releases hydrogen ions when in solution. A proton donor.

**acid rain** Rain that has become acidic as the result of the airborne environmental pollutants sulfur dioxide and nitrogen oxide.

**acromegaly** (AK-roh-MEG-uh-lee) A condition of enlargement of the bones and muscles of the head, hands, face, and feet caused by an excess of growth hormone in an adult.

**acrosome** (AK-roh-sohm) A cap containing enzymes that covers most of the head of a sperm. Helps sperm penetrate an egg.

**ACTH (adrenocorticotropic hormone)** (uh-DREE-noh-kort-ih-koh-TRO-pic) Anterior pituitary hormone that influences the activity of the adrenal cortex.

**actin** (AK-tin) A contractile protein of muscle. Forms the thin filaments in the myofibrils.

**action potential** A brief change in membrane potential of a nerve or muscle cell due to the movement of ions across the plasma membrane. Also called a nerve impulse.

**active immunization** The process of activation of the immune system in advance of the presence of a disease. Generally, active immunization is accomplished by administration of a vaccine.

**active transport** Process that transfers a substance into or out of a cell, usually against its concentration gradient. Requires a carrier and the expenditure of energy.

**adaptation** General term for the act or process of adjusting. In environmental biology, the process of changing to better suit a particular set of environmental conditions. In sensory neurons, a decline in the frequency of nerve impulses even when a receptor is stimulated continuously and without change in stimulus strength.

**adaptive radiation** A short burst of evolutionary activity in which many new life-forms develop in a brief span of time from a single ancestor.

**addiction** The need to continue obtaining and using a chemical substance despite one's better judgment and good intentions.

**Addison's disease** A condition caused by a failure of the adrenal cortex to secrete sufficient cortisol and aldosterone.

**adenosine diphosphate (ADP)** (uh-DEN-oh-seen dy-FOSS-fate) A nucleotide composed of adenosine with two phosphate groups. When ADP accepts another phosphate group it becomes the energy-storage molecule ATP.

**adenosine triphosphate (ATP)** (uh-DEN-oh-seen try-FOSS-fate) A nucleotide composed of adenosine and three phosphate groups. ATP is an important carrier of energy for the cell because energy is released when one of the phosphate groups is removed.

**ADH (antidiuretic hormone)** (AN-tih-dy-yu-RET-ik) Hormone produced by the hypothalamus and released by the posterior pituitary. Stimulates the kidneys to reabsorb more water, reducing urine volume.

**adipocyte** (AH-di-po-syt) An adipose (fat) cell.

**adipose tissue** (AH-di-pohs) A connective tissue consisting chiefly of fat cells.

**ADP (adenosine diphosphate)** (uh-DEN-oh-seen dy-FOSS-fate) A nucleotide composed of adenosine with two phosphate groups. When ADP accepts another phosphate group it becomes the energy-storage molecule ATP.

**adrenal cortex** (ah-DREE-nul KOR-teks) External portion of the adrenal gland. Its primary hormones, aldosterone and cortisol, influence inflammation, metabolism, interstitial fluid volume, and other functions.

**adrenal glands** (ah-DREE-nul) Hormone-producing glands located atop the kidneys. Each consists of medulla and cortex areas.

**adrenal medulla** (ah-DREE-nul meh-DUL-uh) Interior portion of the adrenal gland. Its hormones, epinephrine and norepinephrine, influence carbohydrate metabolism and blood circulation.

**adrenocorticotropic hormone (ACTH)** (uh-DREE-noh-kort-ih-koh-TRO-pic) Anterior pituitary hormone that influences the activity of the adrenal cortex.

**aerobic metabolism** (air-OH-bik) Metabolic reactions within a cell that utilize oxygen in the process of producing ATP.

**afferent** Directed to or toward a point of reference. In the kidney, an afferent arteriole carries blood to each glomerulus.

**agglutination** (uh-glue-tin-AY-shun) The clumping together of (foreign) cells induced by cross-linking of antigen-antibody complexes.

**aging** Progressive, cumulative changes in the body's structure and function that occur throughout a person's life span.

**agranular leukocyte** A white blood cell that does not contain distinctive granules. Includes lymphocytes and monocytes.

**AIDS (acquired immune deficiency syndrome)** Disease caused by human immunodeficiency virus (HIV). Symptoms include severe weight loss, night sweats, swollen lymph nodes, and opportunistic infections.

**albumins** (AL-byoo-mins) The most common group of proteins in blood plasma. Albumins have osmotic and transport functions.

**aldosterone** (al-DOS-ter-ohn or AL-do-STEER-ohn) Hormone produced by the adrenal cortex that regulates sodium reabsorption.

**allantois** (uh-LAN-toh-is) Embryonic membrane. Its blood vessels develop into blood vessels of the umbilical cord.

**alleles** (uh-LEELS) Genes coding for the same trait and found at the same locus on homologous chromosomes.

**allergen** (AL-ur-jen) Any substance that triggers an allergic response.

**allergy** (AL-ur-jee) Overzealous immune response to an otherwise harmless substance.

**all-or-none principle** The principle that muscle cells always contract completely each time they are stimulated by their motor neuron, and that they do not contract at all if they are not stimulated by their motor neuron.

**alveolus** (pl. alveoli) (al-VEE-oh-lus) One of the microscopic air sacs of the lungs.

**Alzheimer's disease** (AHLTZ-hy-merz) Degenerative brain disease resulting in progressive loss of motor control, memory, and intellectual functions.

**amino acid** (uh-MEE-no) Organic compound containing nitrogen, carbon, hydrogen, and oxygen. The 20 amino acids are the building blocks of protein.

**amniocentesis** A form of fetal testing in which a small sample of amniotic fluid is removed so that cells of the fetus can be examined for certain known diseases and genetic abnormalities.

**amnionic fluid** (am-nee-AHN-ik) A fluid similar to interstitial fluid that surrounds and protects the fetus during pregnancy. Amniotic fluid is in continuous exchange with maternal interstitial fluid.

**ampulla** (am-PULL-la) Base of a semicircular canal in the inner ear.

**anabolic steroid** Any one of over 100 synthetic and natural compounds, all of which are related to the male sex steroid hormone testosterone. Anabolic steroids increase muscle mass and contribute to the development and maintenance of masculine characteristics.

**anabolism** (ah-NAB-o-lizm) Energy-requiring building phase of metabolism, during which simpler substances are combined to form more complex substances.

**analogous structures** Structures that share a common function but not necessarily a common origin.

**anaphase** Third stage of mitosis, in which the two sets of daughter chromosomes move toward the poles of a cell.

**androgen** (AN-dro-jen) A hormone that controls male secondary sex characteristics, such as testosterone.

**anemia** (uh-NEE-mee-uh) A condition in which the blood's ability to carry oxygen is reduced because of a shortage of normal hemoglobin or too few red blood cells.

**aneurysm** (AN-yur-iz-um) A ballooning or bulging of the wall of an artery caused by dilation or weakening of the wall.

**angina pectoris** (AN-jin-uh PEK-tor-is) Sensation of severe pain and tightness in the chest caused by insufficient blood supply to the heart.

**angiogram** (AN-jee-oh-gram) An X-ray image of blood vessels.

**angiotensin II** (AN-jee-oh-TEN-sin TOO) A potent vasoconstrictor activated by renin. Also triggers the release of aldosterone from the adrenal gland.

**ANH (atrial natriuretic hormone)** (AY-tree-ul NAH-tree-u-RET-ik) A hormone secreted by the atria of the heart. Helps regulate blood pressure by causing the kidneys to excrete more salt.

**Animalia** The kingdom of life comprising animals.

**anorexia nervosa** (ah-nuh-REK-see-uh nur-VOH-suh) An eating disorder characterized by abnormally low body weight and unrealistic fear of becoming obese.

**antibiotic** (AN-tih-by-AH-tik) A substance that interferes with bacterial metabolism. Administered to cure bacterial diseases.

**antibody** A protein molecule released by a B cell or a plasma cell that binds to a specific antigen.

**antibody-mediated immunity** Mechanism of defense in which B cells and plasma cells produce antibodies that bind to specific antigens.

**anticodon** The three-base sequence in transfer RNA that pairs with a complementary sequence in messenger RNA.

**antidiuretic hormone (ADH)** (AN-tih-dy-yu-RET-ik) Hormone produced by the hypothalamus and released by the posterior pituitary. Stimulates the kidneys to reabsorb more water, reducing urine volume.

**antigen** (AN-tih-jen) A substance or part of a substance (living or nonliving) that the immune system recognizes as foreign. It activates the immune system and reacts with immune cells or their products, such as antibodies.

**antigen-presenting cell (APC)** A cell that displays antigen-MHC complexes on its surface. Triggers an immune response by lymphocytes.

**antioxidant** An agent that inhibits oxidation; specifically a substance that can neutralize the damaging effects of free radicals and other substances.

**anus** The outlet of the digestive tract.

**aorta** (ay-OR-tah) The main systemic artery. Arises from the left ventricle of the heart.

**aortic bodies** Receptors in the aorta that are sensitive primarily to the oxygen concentration of the blood. These receptors can also respond to $H^+$ and $CO_2$.

**appendicular skeleton** (ap-un-DIK-yuh-lur) The portion of the skeleton that forms the pectoral and pelvic girdles and the four extremities.

**aquaporins** Literally, water pores. Aquaporins are cell membrane proteins in certain specialized cells, especially the tubular cells in kidneys, that contain pores which permit the rapid diffusion of water.

**appendix** (uh-PEN-diks) A small finger-like pouch, with no known digestive function, that extends from the cecum of the large intestine.

**aqueous humor** (AY-kwee-us) Watery fluid between the cornea and the lens of the eye.

**aquifer** A deep underground reservoir of water.

**Archaea** (ar-KAY-uh) One of the three domains of life. The prokaryotes of Archaea have many of the features of eukaryotes, but they do not have true nuclei.

**arrhythmia** Irregular heart rhythm. Arrhythmias may be caused by defects in the cardiac conduction system or by drugs, stress, or cardiac disease.

**arteriole** (ar-TEER-ee-ohl) The smallest of the arterial blood vessels. Arterioles supply the capillaries, where nutrient and gas exchange takes place.

**artery** A blood vessel that conducts blood away from the heart and toward the capillaries.

**arthritis** Inflammation of the joints.

**artificial insemination** A technique to enhance fertility in which sperm are placed into the vagina or uterus with a syringe.

**asthma** (AZ-muh) A recurrent, chronic lung disorder characterized by spasmodic contraction of the bronchi, making breathing difficult.

**astigmatism** (uh-STIG-muh-tiz-um) An eye condition in which unequal curvatures in different parts of the lens (or cornea) lead to blurred vision.

**atherosclerosis** (ath-er-o-skler-OS-is) Buildup of fatty deposits on and within the inner walls of arteries. Atherosclerosis is a risk factor for cardiovascular disease.

**atom** Smallest particle of an element that exhibits the properties of that element. Atoms are composed of protons, neutrons, and electrons.

**ATP (adenosine triphosphate)** (uh-DEN-oh-seen try-FOSS-fate) A nucleotide composed of adenosine and three phosphate groups. ATP is an important carrier of energy for the cell because energy is released when one of the phosphate groups is removed.

**atrial natriuretic hormone (ANH)** (AY-tree-ul NAH-tree-u-RET-ik) A hormone secreted by the atria of the heart. Helps regulate blood pressure by causing the kidneys to excrete more salt.

**atrium** (pl. atria) (AY-tree-um) One of the two chambers of the heart that receive blood from veins and deliver it to the ventricles.

**auditory canal** Part of the outer ear. The auditory canal channels sounds to the eardrum.

**auditory tube** Hollow tube connecting the middle ear with the throat. The auditory tube is important for equalizing air pressure in the middle ear with atmospheric pressure.

**autoimmune disorder** A condition in which the immune system attacks the body's own tissues.

**autonomic division** Division of the peripheral nervous system composed of the sympathetic and parasympathetic divisions. The autonomic division carries signals from the central nervous system that control automatic functions of the body's internal organs. Sometimes referred to as the autonomic nervous system (ANS).

**autosomes** (AW-tow-sohms) Chromosomes 1 to 22. The term *autosome* applies to all chromosomes except the sex chromosomes.

**autotroph** An organism that uses carbon dioxide and energy from its physical environment to build its own large organic molecules.

**AV (atrioventricular) bundle** Bundle of specialized fibers that conduct impulses from the AV node to the right and left ventricles.

**AV (atrioventricular) node** Specialized mass of conducting cells located at the atrioventricular junction in the heart.

**AV (atrioventricular) valve** One of two heart valves located between the atria and the ventricles that prevents backflow into the atria when the ventricles are contracting.

**axial skeleton** (AK-see-ul) The portion of the skeleton that forms the main axis of the body, consisting of the skull, ribs, sternum, and backbone.

**axon** (AK-sahn) An extension of a neuron that carries nerve impulses away from the nerve cell body. The conducting portion of a nerve cell.

**axon bulb** One of many rounded tips at the end of an axon.

# B

**B cell (B lymphocyte)** (LIM-fo-syt) A white blood cell that matures in bone marrow and gives rise to antibody-producing plasma cells.

**bacteria** One of the three domains of life. Bacteria are prokaryotic microorganisms responsible for many human diseases.

**balloon angioplasty** Treatment to open a partially blocked blood vessel. The technique involves threading a small balloon into the blood vessel and then inflating the balloon, pressing the blocking material against the sides of the vessel.

**baroreceptor** Sensory receptor that is stimulated by increases in blood pressure.

**basal metabolic rate (BMR)** Rate at which energy is expended (heat produced) by the body per unit of time under resting conditions.

**base** A substance capable of binding with hydrogen ions. A proton acceptor.

**basement membrane** Layer of nonliving extracellular material that anchors epithelial tissue to the underlying connective tissue.

**basophil** (BAY-so-fil) White blood cell whose granules stain well with a basic dye. Basophils release histamine and other substances during inflammation.

**bile** Greenish-yellow or brownish fluid that is secreted by the liver, stored in the gallbladder, and released into the small intestine. Bile is important in emulsifying fat.

**biodiversity** The variety of living species on Earth.

**biogeochemical cycle** A cycle in which the chemicals that compose living organisms are recycled between organisms and Earth itself.

**biogeography** Study of the distribution of plants and animals around the world.

**biological magnification** Process by which nonexcreted substances become more concentrated in organisms that are higher in the food chain.

**biology** The study of living things and life's processes.

**biomass** Total living component of an ecosystem.

**biosphere** (BY-oh-sfeer) The portion of the surface of Earth (land, water, and air) inhabited by living organisms.

**biotechnology** The technical application of biological knowledge for human purposes.

**biotic potential** (by-AHT-ic) Maximum growth rate of a population under ideal conditions.

**birth control pill** Oral contraceptive containing hormones that inhibit ovulation.

**blastocyst** (BLAS-toh-sist) Stage of early embryonic development. The product of cleavage.

**blind spot** Region of the eye where the optic nerve passes through the retina. There are no photoreceptor cells in the blind spot.

**blood** A fluid connective tissue consisting of water, solutes, blood cells, and platelets that carries nutrients and waste products to and from all cells.

**blood-brain barrier** A functional barrier between the blood and the brain that inhibits passage of certain substances from the blood into brain tissues.

**blood doping** The practice of increasing a person's red blood cell production above normal by artificial means, for the purpose of increasing oxygen-carrying capacity.

**blood pressure** The force exerted by blood against blood vessel walls, generated by the pumping action of the heart.

**blood type** Classification of blood based on the presence of surface antigens on red blood cells, and the presence of antibodies to surface antigens other than one's own.

**BMR (basal metabolic rate)** Rate at which energy is expended (heat produced) by the body per unit of time under resting (basal) conditions.

**bone** A connective tissue that forms the bony skeleton. Bone consists of a few living cells encased in a hard extracellular matrix of mineral salts.

**bottleneck effect** Evolutionary effect that occurs when a major catastrophe wipes out most of a population without regard to any previous measure of fitness.

**botulism** A form of poisoning caused by a bacterium, *Clostridium botulinum*, occasionally found in inadequately cooked or preserved foods.

**Bowman's capsule** Double-walled cup at the beginning of a renal tubule. Bowman's capsule, also called the glomerular capsule, encloses the glomerulus.

**brain** Organ of the central nervous system that receives, stores, and integrates information from throughout the body and coordinates the body's responses.

**bronchiole** (BRAHNG-kee-ohl) Small airways within the lungs that carry air to the alveoli. The walls of bronchioles are devoid of cartilage.

**bronchitis** (brahng-KI-tis) Inflammation of the bronchi.

**bronchus** (pl. bronchi) (BRAHNG-kus) Any one of the larger branching airways of the lungs. The walls of bronchi are reinforced with cartilage.

**buffer** Chemical substance that minimizes changes in pH by releasing or binding hydrogen ions.

**bulbourethral gland** (bul-boh-yoo-REE-thral) One of a pair of male reproductive glands located below the prostate gland that secretes mucus into the urethra during sexual arousal.

**bulimia** (byoo-LEE-mee-uh) Eating disorder involving episodes of binging and purging.

## C

**C-section (cesarean section)** Surgical delivery of a baby.

**calcitonin** (kal-suh-TOW-nin) Hormone released by the thyroid glands that promotes a decrease in blood calcium levels.

**Calorie** Amount of energy needed to raise the temperature of 1 kilogram of water 1° Celsius.

**cancer** A malignant, invasive disease in which cells become abnormal and divide uncontrollably. May spread throughout the body.

**capillary** (KAP-uh-lair-ee) The smallest type of blood vessel. Capillaries are the site of exchange between the blood and tissue cells.

**carbaminohemoglobin** (kar-buh-MEE-noh-HEE-muh-gloh-bin) Hemoglobin molecule carrying carbon dioxide.

**carbohydrate** (kar-boh-HY-drayt) Organic compound composed primarily of $CH_2O$ groups. Includes starches, sugars, and cellulose.

**carbonic anhydrase** (kar-BAHN-ik an-HY-drase) Enzyme that facilitates the combination of carbon dioxide with water to form carbonic acid.

**carcinogen** (kar-SIN-o-jen) Cancer-causing agent.

**cardiac cycle** (KAR-dee-ak) Sequence of events encompassing one complete contraction and relaxation cycle of the atria and ventricles of the heart.

**cardiac muscle** Specialized muscle tissue of the heart.

**cardiac output** Amount of blood pumped out of a ventricle in one minute.

**cardiovascular system** The organ system composed of the heart and blood vessels.

**carnivore** (KAR-nih-vor) Organism that feeds only on animals.

**carotid bodies** (kuh-RAHT-id) Receptors in the carotid artery that are sensitive primarily to the oxygen concentration of the blood. These receptors can also respond to $H^+$ and $CO_2$. Carotid and aortic bodies are identical in function.

**carrier** In genetics, an individual who appears normal but who carries an allele for a genetic disorder. In cell physiology, a protein that binds with a specific substance and transports it across the plasma membrane.

**carrying capacity** The maximum number of individuals in a population that a given environment can sustain indefinitely.

**cartilage** (KAR-til-ij) White, semiopaque, flexible connective tissue.

**catabolism** (kah-TAB-o-lizm) The process whereby larger molecules are broken down to smaller ones and energy is released.

**catalyst** (KAT-uh-list) A substance that changes the rate of a chemical reaction without itself being altered or consumed by the reaction.

**cataracts** (KAT-uh-rakts) Clouding of the eye's lens. Cataracts are often congenital or age-related.

**CCK (cholecystokinin)** (kohl-uh-sis-tuh-KYN-in) An intestinal hormone that stimulates gallbladder contraction and the release of pancreatic juice.

**cecum** (SEE-kum) The blind-ended pouch at the beginning of the large intestine.

**cell** The smallest structure that shows all the characteristics of life. The cell is the fundamental structural and functional unit of all living organisms.

**cell body** Region of a nerve cell that includes the nucleus and most of the cytoplasmic mass, and from which the dendrites and axons extend.

**cell cycle** A repeating series of events in which a eukaryotic cell grows, duplicates its DNA, and then undergoes nuclear and cytoplasmic division to become two cells. Includes interphase (growth and DNA synthesis) and mitosis (cell division).

**cell doctrine** Theory consisting of three basic principles: (1) All living things are composed of cells and cell products. (2) A single cell is the smallest unit that exhibits all the characteristics of life. (3) All cells come only from preexisting cells.

**cell-mediated immunity** Immunity conferred by activated T cells, which directly lyse infected or cancerous body cells or foreign cells and release chemicals that regulate the immune response.

**cellular respiration** The collective term for all cellular metabolic processes that result in the production of ATP.

**central canal** In bone, the hollow central tube of an osteon that contains nerves and blood vessels.

**central nervous system (CNS)** The brain and spinal cord.

**centriole** (SEN-tree-ohl) Small organelle found near the nucleus of the cell, important in cell division.

**centromere** (SEN-troh-meer) Constricted region of a chromosome where sister chromatids are attached to each other and where they attach to the mitotic spindle during cell division.

**cerebellum** (ser-ah-BELL-um) Brain region most involved in producing smooth, coordinated skeletal muscle activity.

**cerebral cortex** (suh-REE-brul KOR-teks) The outer gray matter region of the cerebral hemispheres. Some regions of the cerebral cortex receive sensory information; others control motor responses.

**cerebral hemispheres** The large paired structures that together form most of the cerebrum of the brain.

**cerebrospinal fluid** (suh-REE-broh-SPY-nul) Plasmalike fluid that fills the cavities of the CNS and surrounds the CNS externally. Protects the brain and spinal cord.

**cerebrum** (suh-REE-brum) The cerebral hemispheres and nerve tracts that join them together. Involves higher mental functions.

**cesarean delivery (C-section)** Surgical delivery of a baby.

**chemical bonds** Attractive forces between atoms that cause atoms to be bound to each other.

**chemoreceptor** (KEE-moh-rih-sep-tur) Type of receptor sensitive to various chemicals.

**chemotherapy** The use of therapeutic drugs to selectively kill cancer cells.

**chlamydia** (kla-MID-ee-uh) Sexually transmitted disease involving infection by the bacterium *Chlamydia trachomatis.*

**cholecystokinin (CCK)** (kohl-uh-sis-tuh-KYN-in) An intestinal hormone that stimulates contraction of the gallbladder and the release of pancreatic juice.

**cholesterol** (ko-LES-ter-ahl) Steroid found in animal fats as well as in most body tissues. Made by the liver.

**chondroblast** A cartilage-forming cell. In the fetus, chondroblasts produce the hyaline cartilage that forms the rudimentary models of future bones.

**chorion** (KOR-ee-ahn) Outermost fetal membrane. Helps form the placenta.

**chorionic villi** (kor-ee-AHN-ik VIL-eye) Extensions of the fetal chorion that project into maternal tissues. Samples of chorionic villi are sometimes taken in early pregnancy to obtain fetal cells for diagnosis of fetal disease.

**choroid** (KOR-oyd) The vascular middle layer of the eye.

**chromatin** (KROH-muh-tin) Threadlike material in the nucleus composed of DNA and proteins.

**chromosome** (KROH-muh-som) Rodlike structure of tightly coiled chromatin. Visible in the nucleus during cell division.

**chyme** (kym) Semifluid mass consisting of partially digested food and gastric juice that is delivered from the stomach into the small intestine.

**cilium** (pl. cilia) (SIL-ee-um) A tiny hair-like projection on cell surfaces that moves in a wavelike manner.

**circadian cycle** (sur-KAY-dee-un) In many organisms, a repeating cycle of physiological events that occurs approximately once every 24 hours.

**cirrhosis** (sir-ROH-sis) Chronic disease of the liver, characterized by an overgrowth of connective tissue (fibrosis).

**citric acid cycle** The metabolic pathway within mitochondria in which acetyl groups are completely disassembled into $CO_2$ and high-energy compounds. Also called the Krebs cycle.

**cleavage** An early phase of embryonic development consisting of rapid mitotic cell divisions without cell growth.

**climax community** The stable result of ecological succession in a given environment.

**clitoris** (KLIT-uh-ris) In the female, a sensitive erectile organ located in the vulva.

**cloning** Production of identical copies of a gene, a cell, or an organism.

**clotting proteins** Collective term for a group of proteins in blood plasma that participate in the process of blood clotting. Two important clotting proteins are prothrombin and fibrinogen.

**cochlea** (KOK-lee-uh) Snail-shaped chamber in the inner ear that houses the organ of Corti.

**codominance** Pattern of inheritance in which both alleles of a gene are equally expressed even though the phenotypes they specify are different.

**codon** (KOH-dahn) The three-base sequence on a messenger RNA molecule that provides the code for a specific amino acid in protein synthesis.

**coenzyme** A small molecule that assists an enzyme by transporting small molecular groups. Most vitamins are coenzymes.

**coitus** (KOH-ee-tus; koh-EE-tus) Genital sexual intercourse.

**collagen fiber** Strong and slightly flexible type of connective tissue fiber, made of protein.

**colon** (KOH-lun) The region of the large intestine between the cecum and the rectum. The colon includes ascending, transverse, descending, and sigmoid portions.

**colostrum** (koh-LAHS-trum) Milky fluid secreted by the mammary glands shortly before and after delivery. Contains proteins and antibodies.

**community** Array of several different populations that coexist and interact within the same environment.

**compact bone** Type of dense bone tissue found on the outer surfaces and shafts of bones.

**complement system** A group of blood-borne proteins which, when activated, enhance the inflammatory and immune responses and may lead to lysis of pathogens.

**complete dominance** Pattern of genetic inheritance in which one allele completely masks or suppresses the expression of its complementary allele.

**conception** The end of fertilization, when a single diploid cell is produced from the union of sperm and egg nuclei.

**concussion** An injury to the brain resulting from a physical blow that may result in a brief loss of consciousness.

**condom** A contraceptive sheath, made of latex or animal membrane, that can be used to enclose the penis or line the vagina during sexual intercourse.

**cone cell** One of the two types of photoreceptor cells in the retina of the eye. Cone cells provide for color vision.

**congestive heart failure** Progressive condition in which the pumping efficiency of the heart becomes impaired. The result is often an inability to adequately pump the venous blood being returned to the heart, venous congestion, and body fluid imbalances.

**connective tissue** A primary tissue; form and function vary extensively. Functions include support, energy storage, and protection.

**constipation** (kahn-sti-PAY-shun) A condition in which chyme remains in the colon too long and the feces become dry and hard, making defecation difficult.

**consumer** In ecosystems, an organism that cannot produce its own food and must feed on other organisms. Also called a heterotroph.

**control center** In control system theory, a structure that receives input from a sensor, compares it to a correct, internally set value of the controlled variable, and sends an output to an effector. The most important control center in a living organism is the brain.

**control group** In scientific experiments, a group of subjects that undergoes all the steps in the experiment except the one being tested. The control group is used to evaluate all possible factors that might influence the experiment other than the experimental treatment. Compare *experimental group.*

**controlled variable** Any physical or chemical property that might vary from time to time and that must be controlled in order to maintain homeostasis. Examples of controlled variables are blood pressure, body temperature, and the concentration of glucose in blood.

**convergence** A coming together. In the nervous system, the phenomenon in which several presynaptic neurons form synapses with one postsynaptic neuron.

**core temperature** The body's internal temperature. In humans, normal core temperature is about 98.6 °F (37 °C).

**cornea** (KOR-nee-uh) The transparent anterior portion of the eyeball.

**coronary artery** (KOR-uh-nair-ee) One of the two arteries of the heart leading to capillaries that supply blood to cardiac muscle.

**coronary artery bypass graft (CABG)** Surgery to improve blood flow. A piece of blood vessel is removed from elsewhere in the body and grafted onto a blocked coronary artery to bypass the damaged region.

**corpus luteum** (KOR-pus LOOT-ee-um) Structure that develops from cells of a ruptured ovarian follicle. The corpus luteum secretes progesterone and estrogen.

**cortex** (KOR-teks) General term for the outer surface layer of an organ.

**cortisol** (KOR-tih-sahl) Glucocorticoid produced by the adrenal cortex, also called hydrocortisone.

**covalent bond** (koh-VAY-lent) Chemical bond created by electron sharing between atoms.

**coxal bones** The two large bones that connect the femur bones to the sacrum of the vertebral column. The coxal bones form our hips.

**cranial nerve** (KRAY-nee-ul) One of the 12 pairs of peripheral nerves that originate in the brain.

**creatinine** (kree-AT-uhn-een) A nitrogenous waste molecule excreted by the kidneys.

**crossing-over** Exchange of DNA segments between homologous chromosomes during prophase I of meiosis.

**cystic fibrosis** (SIS-tik fy-BRO-sys) Genetic disorder in which oversecretion of mucus clogs the respiratory passages. Cystic fibrosis can lead to fatal respiratory infections.

**cytokines** Signaling molecules secreted by helper T cells. Cytokines have a variety of functions, including promoting immune cell development, stimulating their activity, and attracting them to an area of infection.

**cytokinesis** (sy-tow-kih-NEE-sis) The division of cytoplasm that occurs after a cell nucleus has divided.

**cytoplasm** (SY-tow-plaz-um) The cellular material surrounding a cell nucleus and enclosed by the plasma membrane.

**cytoskeleton** A cell's internal "skeleton." The cytoplasm is a system of microtubules and other components that support cellular structures and provide the machinery to generate various cell movements.

**cytotoxic T cell** (sy-toh-TAHK-sik) A "killer T cell" that directly lyses foreign cells, cancer cells, or virus-infected body cells.

## D

**data** Facts derived from experiments and observations.

**decomposer** An organism that obtains energy by chemically breaking down the products, wastes, or remains of other organisms.

**defecation** (def-ih-KAY-shun) The movement of feces through the rectum and the anus, with their subsequent elimination from the body.

**deforestation** The loss of wooded areas due to harvesting trees and/or converting forestlands to other uses.

**dehydration synthesis** Process by which a larger molecule is synthesized by covalently bonding two smaller molecules together, with the subsequent removal of a molecule of water.

**deletion** In genetics, the loss of a piece of a chromosome due to chromosome breakage. Nearly all deletions are lethal to sperm, egg, or embryo.

**demographic transition** A progression of changes followed by many nations, in which the society gradually moves from poor living conditions and a high death rate to improved economic conditions and a declining death rate.

**denaturation** (dee-nay-chur-AY-shun) Loss of a protein's normal shape and function produced by disruption of hydrogen bonds and other weak bonds.

**dendrite** (DEN-dryt) Branching neuron extension that serves as a receptive or input region. Dendrites conduct graded potentials toward the cell body.

**denitrification** (dee-nyt-ruh-fih-KAY-shun) Process in which nitrate is converted to nitrogen gas ($N_2$). Denitrification is part of the nitrogen cycle.

**dental caries** (KAIR-eez) Tooth decay characterized by cavities.

**deoxyhemoglobin** Hemoglobin that has given up its oxygen.

**deoxyribonucleic acid (DNA)** (dee-OX-ee-RY-bo-new-CLAY-ik) A nucleic acid found in all living cells. Carries the organism's hereditary information.

**depolarization** Loss of a state of polarity. In nerve and muscle cells, the loss or reduction of the inside-negative membrane potential.

**dermis** Layer of skin underlying the epidermis. Consists mostly of dense connective tissue.

**desertification** (deh-ZERT-uh-fuh-KAY-shun) Process by which marginal lands are converted to desertlike conditions.

**detritus** (dih-TRY-tus) Nonliving organic matter.

**diabetes mellitus** (dy-uh-BEE-teez MEL-ih-tus) Disease characterized by a high blood sugar concentration and glucose in the urine, caused by either deficient insulin production (Type 1 diabetes) or insufficient glucose uptake by cells (Type 2 diabetes).

**dialysis** (dy-AL-ih-sis) General term for several techniques that attempt to take the place of kidney function in patients whose kidneys have failed by letting the patient's blood exchange waste materials with artificial fluids. Two dialysis techniques are *continuous ambulatory peritoneal dialysis (CAPD)* and *hemodialysis.*

**diaphragm** (DY-uh-fram) A dome-shaped sheet of muscle that separates the thoracic cavity from the abdominal cavity. Also, a contraceptive device inserted into the vagina to cover the cervical opening.

**diarrhea** (dy-uh-REE-uh) Watery feces. Can result from a number of factors.

**diastole** (dy-AS-toh-lee) Period of the cardiac cycle when a heart chamber is relaxed.

**diastolic pressure** (DY-uh-STAHL-ik) Lowest point of arterial blood pressure during a cardiac cycle. Diastolic pressure is the second of two numbers recorded by the health care provider, the first being systolic pressure.

**differentiation** Process by which a cell changes in form or function.

**diffusion** (dih-FYOO-shun) The movement of molecules from one region to another as the result of random motion. Net diffusion proceeds from a region of higher concentration to a region of lower concentration.

**digestion** Chemical or mechanical process of breaking down foodstuffs to substances that can be absorbed.

**diploid** The number of chromosomes in a body cell ($2n$), twice the chromosomal number ($n$) of a gamete. In humans, $2n = 46$.

**disaccharide** (dy-SAK-uh-ryd) Literally, a double sugar. A disaccharide consists of two monosaccharides linked together. Sucrose and lactose are disaccharides.

**diuretic** (dy-yoo-RET-ik) Any substance that enhances urinary output.

**divergence** Going in different directions from a common point. In the nervous system, the phenomenon in which one presynaptic neuron forms synapses with several postsynaptic neurons.

**DNA (deoxyribonucleic acid)** (dee-OX-ee-RY-bo-new-CLAY-ik) A nucleic acid found in all living cells. Carries the organism's hereditary information.

**DNA ligases** A class of enzymes that join fragments of DNA together.

**DNA polymerase** (poh-LIM-ur-ays) Enzyme that links separate nucleotides together as a new strand of DNA is formed.

**dominant allele** An allele that masks or suppresses the expression of its complementary allele.

**Down syndrome** A condition caused by inheriting three copies of chromosome 21.

**ductus deferens** (pl. ductus deferentia) (DUK-tus DEF-er-enz) Tube extending from the epididymis to the urethra through which sperm pass during a man's sexual climax and ejaculation. Also called the vas deferens.

**duodenum** (doo-oh-DEE-num) First part of the small intestine.

**dysplasia** (dis-PLAY-zhee-uh) Abnormal changes in the shape and/or organization of cells. Dysplasia may precede the development of cancer.

## E

**ECG (electrocardiogram)** Graphic record of the electrical activity of the heart.

**ecological pyramid** Graph representing the biomass, energy content, or number of organisms of each level in a food web. An ecological pyramid includes both producer and consumer populations.

**ecology** (ee-KAHL-uh-jee) Study of the relationships between organisms and their physical environment.

**ecosystem** (EEK-oh-sis-tem) All living organisms, all matter, and all energy in a given environment.

**ectoderm** Embryonic germ layer. Ectoderm forms the epidermis of the skin and its derivatives, and nerve tissues.

**ectopic pregnancy** (ek-TOP-ik) A pregnancy that results from implantation outside the uterus. The most common form of ectopic pregnancy is a tubal pregnancy.

**effector** In control system theory, a structure that can cause something to happen. The effector takes action in response to signals from the control center. In living organisms, muscles and endocrine glands are examples of effectors.

**efferent** Directed from or away from a point of reference. In the kidney, an efferent arteriole carries blood away from each glomerulus.

**egg** An ovum; a mature female gamete.

**ejaculatory duct** In the male, a short duct that carries sperm from the ductus deferens and seminal fluid from the seminal vesicle to the ureter.

**elastic fiber** Fiber formed from the protein elastin, which gives a rubbery and resilient quality to the matrix of connective tissue.

**electrocardiogram (ECG)** Graphic record of the electrical activity of the heart.

**electron** Negatively charged subatomic particle with almost no weight. Electrons orbit the atom's nucleus.

**electron transport system** A series of electron- and energy-transfer molecules in the inner membrane of mitochondria that provide the energy for the active transport of hydrogen ions across the membrane. The electron transport system is essential to the ability of the mitochondria to produce ATP for the cell.

**element** One of a limited number of unique varieties of matter that composes substances of all kinds. Elements each consist of just one kind of atom.

**embolus** (EM-bo-lus) Material, such as a blood clot, that floats in the bloodstream and may block a blood vessel.

**embryo** (EM-bree-oh) An organism in an early stage of development. In humans, the embryonic period extends from the beginning of week 3 to the end of week 8.

**embryonic disk** A flattened disk of cells that develops in the blastocyst shortly after implantation. The embryonic disk will develop into the embryo.

**emphysema** (em-fih-SEE-muh) Chronic respiratory disorder involving damage to the bronchioles and alveoli. In emphysema, loss of elastic tissue in the bronchioles causes them to collapse during expiration, trapping air in the alveoli and eventually damaging them as well.

**endocrine gland** (EN-duh-krin) Ductless gland that secretes one or more hormones into the bloodstream.

**endocrine system** Body system that includes all of the hormone-secreting organs and glands. Along with the nervous system, the endocrine system is involved in coordination and control of body activities.

**endocytosis** (en-do-sy-TO-sis) Process by which fluids, extracellular particles, or even whole bacteria are taken into cells. In endocytosis, the materials become enclosed by a vesicle composed of cell membrane material and then internalized within the cell. Phagocytosis is an example of endocytosis.

**endoderm** (EN-do-derm) Embryonic germ layer. Endoderm forms the lining of the digestive tube and its associated structures.

**endometriosis** (en-do-mee-tree-OH-sis) Condition in which endometrial tissue migrates up the oviduct during a menstrual period and implants on other organs such as ovaries, walls of the bladder, or colon.

**endometrium** (en-do-MEE-tree-um) Inner lining of the uterus. The endometrium becomes thickened and more vascular during the uterine cycle in preparation for pregnancy.

**endoplasmic reticulum (ER)** (en-do-PLAS-mik reh-TIK-yuh-lum) Membranous network of tubular or saclike channels in the cytoplasm of a cell. The endoplasmic reticulum is the site of most of the cell's production of proteins and other cell compounds.

**energy** The capacity to do work. Energy may be stored (potential energy) or in action (kinetic energy).

**environmental resistance** Factors in the environment that limit population growth in a particular geographic area.

**enzyme** (EN-zym) A protein that acts as a biological catalyst to speed up a chemical reaction.

**eosinophil** (ee-oh-SIN-oh-fil) Granular white blood cell whose granules stain readily with a red stain called eosin. Eosinophils attack parasites and function in allergic responses.

**epidermis** (ep-ih-DUR-mus) Outermost layer of the skin. The epidermis is composed of keratinized stratified squamous epithelium.

**epididymis** (ep-ih-DID-ih-mis) Portion of the male reproductive system in which sperm mature. The epididymis empties into the vas deferens.

**epiglottis** (ep-ih-GLAHT-is) Flaplike structure of elastic cartilage at the back of the throat that covers the opening of the larynx during swallowing.

**epilepsy** (EP-ih-lep-see) Condition involving abnormal electrical discharges of groups of brain neurons. Epilepsy may cause seizures.

**epinephrine** (ep-ih-NEF-rin) Primary hormone produced by the adrenal medulla, also called adrenaline.

**episiotomy** (ih-pee-zee-AHT-uh-mee) Surgical widening of the opening to the vagina during childbirth, performed to prevent tearing of tissues.

**epithelial tissue** (ep-ih-THEE-lee-ul) A primary tissue that covers the body's surface, lines its internal cavities, and forms glands.

**erythrocyte (red blood cell)** Blood cell that transports oxygen from the lungs to the tissues and carbon dioxide from the tissues to the lungs.

**erythropoietin** (ih-rith-roh-PO-ih-tin) Hormone that stimulates production of red blood cells.

**esophagus** (ih-SOF-uh-gus) Muscular tube extending from the throat to the stomach. The esophagus is collapsed when it does not contain food.

**essential amino acids** Group of eight amino acids that the body cannot synthesize. Essential amino acids must be obtained from the diet.

**estrogen** (ES-tro-jen) Female sex hormone that stimulates the development of female secondary sex characteristics, helps oocytes mature, and affects the uterine lining during the menstrual cycle and pregnancy.

**Eukarya** One of the three domains of life. Eukarya includes all life-forms whose cells have nuclei.

**eukaryote** (yoo-KAIR-ih-ot) An organism composed of cells with nuclei and internal membrane-bound organelles. Animals, plants, protists, and fungi are all eukaryotes.

**eutrophication** (yoo-troh-fih-KAY-shun) Process by which mineral and organic nutrients accumulate in a body of water, leading to plant overgrowth and loss of oxygen. Eutrophication may be accelerated by pollution.

**evolution** An unpredictable and natural process of descent over time with genetic modification. Evolution is influenced by natural selection, chance, historical events, and changing environments.

**evolutionary tree** Map that illustrates evolutionary change and relationships between life-forms.

**excretion** Elimination of waste products from the body.

**exocrine gland** Specialized epithelial tissue that secretes a product directly into a hollow organ or duct.

**exocytosis** (ex-oh-sy-TO-sis) Mechanism by which substances are moved from the cell interior to the extracellular space. In exocytosis, a membrane-bound secretory vesicle fuses with the plasma membrane and releases its contents to the exterior.

**exon** A nucleotide sequence of DNA that specifies a useful informational sequence. Compare *intron.*

**experiment** A procedure designed to test a working hypothesis. In a controlled experiment, all conditions of the environment are controlled except the specific factor dictated by the working hypothesis.

**experimental group** In a controlled experiment, the group of subjects that receives the experimental treatment. Compare *control group.*

**expiration** Act of exhaling or expelling air from the lungs.

**exponential growth** Growth pattern of a population that follows a characteristic J-curve. A population undergoing exponential growth will double repeatedly over similar time periods.

**extension** Movement that increases the angle of a joint, such as straightening a flexed knee.

**extinction** The loss of a particular life-form completely.

**extra-embryonic membranes** Membranes that are not part of an embryo's body but are essential for its growth and development (amnion, allantois, yolk sac, and chorion).

## F

**facilitated transport** Passive transport of a substance into or out of a cell along a concentration gradient. Facilitated transport requires a carrier protein.

**FAD** A transport molecule within mitochondria that can accept hydrogen ions and electrons liberated by the citric acid cycle, forming high-energy $FADH_2$.

**farsightedness** Condition in which the eyeball is too short, causing nearby objects to be focused behind the retina; also called hyperopia.

**fatigue** Condition of feeling tired or weary. In muscle physiology, a decreased capacity to function.

**fatty acid** Linear chain of carbon and hydrogen atoms (hydrocarbon chains) with an organic acid group at one end. Fatty acids are constituents of fats.

**fertility rate** Number of children that each female has during her lifetime.

**fertilization** Fusion of the nuclei of sperm and egg, thereby creating a zygote.

**fever** Body temperature that has risen above the normal set point (in humans, approximately 37 °C, or 98.6 °F). A fever often indicates illness.

**fiber** General term for a thin strand. A muscle fiber is a single muscle cell. A connective tissue fiber is a thin strand of extracellular material. In the digestive system, fiber refers to material that is indigestible but beneficial in the diet.

**fibrin** (FY-brin) Fibrous insoluble protein formed during blood clotting.

**fibrinogen** (fy-BRIN-oh-jen) A blood protein that is converted to fibrin during blood clotting.

**fibroblast** (FY-broh-blast) Young, actively mitotic cell that forms the fibers of connective tissue.

**fimbriae** (FYM-bree-ay) Fingerlike projections at the open end of an oviduct that help move an oocyte into the oviduct.

**flagellum** (pl. flagella) (flah-JEL-um) Long, whiplike extension of the plasma membrane used by sperm and some bacteria for propulsion.

**flexion** (FLEK-shun) Movement that decreases the angle of a joint, such as bending the knee from a straight to an angled position.

**flexor (withdrawal) reflex** Reflex initiated by a painful stimulus that causes automatic withdrawal of the threatened body part from the stimulus.

**follicle** (FAHL-ih-kul) Ovarian structure consisting of a developing egg surrounded by one or more layers of granulosa cells.

**follicle-stimulating hormone (FSH)** Hormone produced by the anterior pituitary that stimulates ovarian follicle production in females and sperm production in males.

**food web** Hierarchy consisting of numerous food chains. A food web depicts interactions between producers and consumers in an ecosystem.

**forebrain** Anterior portion of the brain that includes the cerebrum, the thalamus, and the hypothalamus.

**formed element** Portion of the blood consisting of cells or cell components. Formed elements include red blood cells, white blood cells, and platelets.

**fossil** Preserved remnant of an organism. The fossil record is one of our richest sources of information about life-forms that lived in the past.

**fossil fuel** A carbon-containing compound (coal, oil, or gas) that was formed millions of years ago by living organisms, then covered by sediments.

**fovea centralis** (FOH-vee-uh sen-TRA-lis) A small region of the retina that is responsible for the highest visual acuity. The fovea centralis consists of densely packed cone cells.

**fraternal twins** Twins resulting from the ovulation and fertilization of more than one oocyte in a particular cycle. Fraternal twins are as different as any two children by the same parents.

**free radicals** Highly reactive chemicals with unpaired electrons that can disrupt the structure of proteins, lipids, and nucleic acids.

**FSH (follicle-stimulating hormone)** Hormone produced by the anterior pituitary that stimulates ovarian follicle production in females and sperm production in males.

**fungi** (FUN-jy) One of the five kingdoms of life. The fungi include yeasts, molds, and mushrooms.

## G

**gallbladder** Organ located beneath the right lobe of the liver. The gallbladder stores and concentrates bile.

**gallstones** Hard crystals containing cholesterol, calcium, and bile salts that can obstruct the flow of bile from the gallbladder.

**gamete** (GAM-eet) Haploid sex or germ cell. Sperm and eggs are gametes.

**ganglion** (pl. ganglia) (GANG-lee-on) Collection of nerve cell bodies outside the central nervous system.

**gastric glands** Glands located beneath the stomach lining. Gastric glands secrete gastric juice.

**gastric juice** Collective term for the hydrochloric acid, pepsinogen, and fluid secreted by gastric glands.

**gastrin** (GAS-trin) Hormone secreted into the blood by cells located in the gastric glands. Gastrin regulates the secretion of gastric juice by stimulating production of hydrochloric acid.

**gastrointestinal (GI) tract** A hollow tube that extends from the mouth to the anus. The GI tract includes mouth, pharynx, esophagus, stomach, small intestine, large intestine, rectum, and anus.

**gel electrophoresis** A technique for separating fragments of DNA or protein according to size.

**gene** (JEEN) The unit of heredity. Most genes encode for specific polypeptides, and each gene has a specific location on a particular chromosome.

**gene flow** The physical movement of alleles caused by movement of individuals into (immigration) or out of (emigration) a population. Gene flow tends to mix pools of genes that might not otherwise mingle.

**gene therapy** Technique in which defective genes are repaired or replaced with their normal counterparts.

**genetic drift** Random changes in allele frequency because of chance events.

**genetic engineering** The planned alteration of the genetic makeup of an organism by modifying, inserting, or deleting genes or groups of genes.

**genital herpes** (JEN-ih-tul HUR-peez) A sexually transmitted disease that results from infection by the herpes simplex type 2 virus.

**genital warts** A sexually transmitted disease caused by the human papillomavirus (HPV). Genital warts are a potential risk factor for cancers of the cervix or penis.

**genome** (JEE-nohm) The complete set of DNA in the chromosomes of a particular species of organism.

**genotype** An individual's particular set of genes.

**genus** (JEE-nus) Level of taxonomic classification. Modern humans belong to the genus *Homo*.

**geographic range** The area of Earth over which a particular species is distributed.

**GIFT (gamete intrafallopian transfer)** Technique to enhance fertility in which unfertilized eggs and sperm are placed directly into an oviduct (Fallopian tube) through a small incision in a woman's abdomen.

**gigantism** Pituitary disorder caused by hypersecretion of growth hormone during childhood and adolescence.

**gingivitis** (jin-jih-VY-tis) Condition of inflamed gum tissue (gingiva), often caused by tooth decay and poor oral hygiene.

**gland** One or more epithelial cells that are specialized to secrete or excrete substances.

**glaucoma** (glaw-KO-muh) Eye condition caused by blockage of the ducts that drain the aqueous humor in the eye, resulting in high intraocular pressures and compression of the optic nerve. Glaucoma can result in blindness unless detected early.

**glial cells** (GLEE-ul) Cells in the nervous system that surround and protect neurons and supply them with nutrients. Glial cells do not generate action potentials.

**global warming** Increase in average global temperature.

**globulins** A group of proteins in blood plasma having transport and immune functions. Many antibodies are globulins.

**glomerular filtration** The process of filtering protein-free plasma fluid from the glomerular capillaries into Bowman's capsule.

**glomerulus** (glow-MAIR-yoo-lus) Cluster or tuft of capillaries inside the glomerular capsule in a kidney. The glomerulus is involved in the formation of the glomerular filtrate.

**glottis** (GLAHT-tis) Opening between the vocal cords in the larynx.

**glucagon** (GLOO-kah-gon) Hormone formed by alpha cells in the islets of Langerhans in the pancreas. Glucagon raises the glucose level of blood by stimulating the liver to break down glycogen.

**glucocorticoids** (gloo-kah-KOR-tih-koyds) Adrenal cortex hormones that increase blood glucose levels and help the body resist long-term stressors. The principal glucocorticoid is cortisol.

**glycogen** (GLY-ko-jen) Main carbohydrate stored in animal cells. A polysaccharide.

**glycolysis** (gly-KOL-ih-sis) Breakdown of glucose to pyruvic acid. Glycolysis is an anaerobic process.

**goiter** (GOY-tur) An enlarged thyroid, caused by iodine deficiency or other factors.

**Golgi apparatus** (GOHL-jee) Membranous system within a cell that packages proteins and lipids destined for export, packages enzymes into lysosomes for cellular use, and modifies proteins destined to become part of cellular membranes.

**gonad** (GOH-nad) An organ that produces sex cells. The gonads are the testes of the male and the ovaries of the female.

**gonadotropins** (goh-nad-o-TRO-pinz) Gonad-stimulating hormones produced by the anterior pituitary. The gonadotropins are FSH and LH.

**gonorrhea** (gahn-o-REE-uh) Sexually transmitted disease caused by the bacterium *Neisseria gonorrhoeae.*

**graded potential** A local change in membrane potential that varies directly with the strength of the stimulus. Graded potentials decline with distance from the stimulus.

**granular leukocyte** (GRAN-yoo-lur LOO-ko-syt) A type of white blood cell with granules that stain readily.

**Graves' disease** A disorder in which the thyroid gland produces too much thyroxine.

**gray matter** Area of the central nervous system that contains cell bodies and unmyelinated fibers of neurons. The gray matter is gray because of the absence of myelin.

**greenhouse effect** A natural phenomenon in which atmospheric gases allow sunlight to pass through but trap most of the heat that radiates outward from Earth's surface.

**greenhouse gases** Atmospheric gases, notably $CO_2$ and methane, responsible for the greenhouse effect.

**growth hormone** Hormone produced by the anterior pituitary that stimulates growth in general.

**growth plate** Cartilage plate located near the ends of bone. Bones become longer during childhood and adolescence because new cartilage is continually being added to the outer surface of the growth plates.

**growth rate** The percentage increase in a population per unit time. Growth rate is calculated as the number of births per year minus the number of deaths per year, divided by population number.

## H

**habitat** The type of location where an organism chooses to live. An organism's habitat typically is determined by its tolerance for certain environmental conditions.

**hair cells** The mechanoreceptor cells of the ear that lie between the tectorial and basilar membranes.

**haploid** (HAP-loyd) Half the diploid number of chromosomes; the number of chromosomes in a gamete.

**hCG (human chorionic gonadotropin)** (kor-ee-AHN-ik goh-nad-o-TRO-pin) A hormone secreted by the chorion that supports pregnancy for the first three months, until the placenta begins producing enough progesterone and estrogen.

**heart attack** Condition characterized by the death of heart tissue caused by inadequate oxygen supply. The medical term for a heart attack is *myocardial infarction.*

**helper T cell** Type of T lymphocyte that orchestrates cell-mediated immunity by direct contact with other immune cells and by releasing chemicals called lymphokines.

**hematocrit** (hee-MAHT-oh-krit) The percentage of blood that consists of red blood cells.

**hemoglobin** (HEE-moh-gloh-bin) Oxygen-transporting protein in red blood cells that gives the cells their characteristic red color.

**hemolytic disease of the newborn (HDN)** (hee-moh-LIT-ik) Potentially life-threatening disease in newborns characterized by reduced numbers of mature red blood cells and elevated blood levels of bilirubin.

**hemophilia** (hee-moh-FIL-ee-uh) Collective term for several different hereditary bleeding disorders with similar symptoms. Hemophilia is caused by a deficiency of one or more clotting factors.

**hemorrhoids** (HEM-oh-royds) Sometimes painful condition caused by swollen veins in the lining of the anus.

**hemostasis** (HEE-mo-STAY-sis) Stoppage of bleeding or of the circulation of blood to a part.

**hepatic portal system** (heh-PAT-ik) The system of blood vessels connecting the organs of the digestive tract to the liver.

**hepatitis** (hep-uh-TY-tis) General term for inflammation of the liver. Hepatitis is sometimes caused by viral infections.

**herbivore** (HUR-buh-vor) An organism that feeds on plants, utilizing the energy stored in them. Also called a primary consumer.

**heterotroph** (HET-ur-oh-trof) An organism that cannot utilize the sun's energy to synthesize the molecules it needs. Instead, it must consume foods that contain stored forms of energy. Also called a consumer.

**heterozygous** (HET-ur-oh-ZY-gus) Having different alleles at the same location (on a pair of homologous chromosomes).

**hindbrain** Region of brain connected to the spinal cord. The hindbrain comprises the medulla oblongata, cerebellum, pons, and part of the reticular formation.

**hippocampus** (hip-po-KAM-pus) In the brain, a region of the limbic system that plays a role in converting new information to long-term memories.

**histamine** (HIS-ta-meen) Substance produced by basophils and mast cells that causes vasodilation and increases vascular permeability.

**HIV (human immunodeficiency virus)** Virus that destroys helper T cells, thus depressing cell-mediated immunity. Symptomatic AIDS gradually appears when lymph nodes can no longer contain the virus.

**homeostasis** (ho-mee-oh-STAY-sis) State of body equilibrium characterized by a relatively constant and stable internal environment.

**hominids** (HAHM-ih-nids) Common name for members of the family *Hominidae*. Hominids include present-day humans (*Homo sapiens*) and all of their extinct ancestors of the genus *Australopithecus* and the genus *Homo*.

**hominoids** (HAHM-ih-noyds) A subgroup of primates that diverged from a common ancestor of old-world monkeys to become the great apes (gibbons, orangutans, gorillas, chimpanzees) and modern humans.

***Homo erectus*** (HOH-moh ih-REK-tus) A species of *Homo* that diverged from *Homo ergaster* and spread across Africa into Asia and Europe. *Homo erectus* died out only 50,000 years ago.

***Homo ergaster*** (HOH-moh er-GAS-tur) A species of *Homo* that arose from *Homo habilis* ancestors about 1.9 million years ago and migrated out of Africa to establish colonies as far away as Java and China.

***Homo habilis*** (HOH-moh HAB-ih-lus) First distinctly human ancestor. *Homo habilis* showed brain enlargement, changes in teeth and facial features, a decline in sexual dimorphism, and conversion to a diet that included meat. *Homo habilis* may also have used tools.

***Homo heidelbergensis*** (HOH-moh HY-del-bur-GEN-sus) Sometimes called "archaic" *Homo sapiens*, this species descended from *Homo ergaster* and eventually gave rise to modern humans, *Homo sapiens*.

***Homo sapiens*** (HOH-moh SAY-pee-enz) Genus and species of modern humans, thought to have evolved about 140,000 to 100,000 years ago.

**homologous chromosomes** (ho-MAHL-uh-gus) Chromosomes that look identical under the microscope. Homologous chromosomes have the same genes in the same locations.

**homologous structures** Body structures that share a common origin.

**homozygous** (hoh-moh-ZY-gus) Having identical alleles at the same location (on a pair of homologous chromosomes).

**hormone** (HOR-mohn) A chemical messenger molecule secreted by an endocrine gland or cell into the bloodstream that has effects on specific target cells throughout the body.

**human chorionic gonadotropin (hCG)** (kor-ee-AHN-ik goh-nad-o-TRO-pin) A hormone secreted by the chorion that supports pregnancy for the first three months, until the placenta begins producing enough progesterone and estrogen.

**human immunodeficiency virus (HIV)** Virus that destroys helper T cells, thus depressing cell-mediated immunity. Symptomatic AIDS gradually appears when lymph nodes can no longer contain the virus.

**human papillomavirus (HPV)** (pap-ih-LOH-ma-vy-rus) Virus that causes genital warts. HPV is a risk factor for cancers of the cervix or penis.

**hydrogen bond** Weak bond that forms between a hydrogen atom with a partial positive charge and a nearby atom with a partial negative charge.

**hydrolysis** (hy-DRAHL-ih-sis) Process in which water is used to split a molecule into two smaller molecules.

**hydrophilic** A substance that is attracted to water. Most polar and charged compounds are hydrophilic, and therefore they dissolve easily in water.

**hydrophobic** A substance that is not attracted to water or is repelled by water. Nonpolar compounds such as oils are hydrophobic.

**hyperopia** (hy-per-OH-pee-uh) Condition in which the eyeball is too short, causing nearby objects to be focused behind the retina; also called farsightedness.

**hyperplasia** (hy-per-PLAY-zhee-uh) An increase in the number of cells in a tissue caused by an increase in the rate of cell division.

**hyperpolarization** Transient local change in the resting potential of a neuron that makes it even more negative than usual.

**hypertension** High blood pressure. Clinically, hypertension is defined as a systolic blood pressure of 140 mm Hg or higher or a diastolic blood pressure of 90 mm Hg or higher.

**hypertonic** General term for above-normal tone or tension. In biology, a hypertonic solution is one with a higher solute concentration than plasma. Cells shrink when placed in a hypertonic solution.

**hypotension** Low blood pressure.

**hypothalamus** Region of the brain forming the floor of the third ventricle. The hypothalamus helps regulate the body's internal environment by secreting releasing factors that affect the secretion of the hormones of the anterior pituitary.

**hypothesis** An explanation or description of a proposed truth. A hypothesis is expressed as a testable statement about the natural world.

**hypotonic** General term for below-normal tone or tension. In biology, a hypotonic solution is one with a lower solute concentration than plasma. Cells swell when placed in a hypotonic solution.

## I

**identical twins** Twins that arise when a single fertilized ovum splits in two shortly after fertilization. Identical twins have identical genotypes.

**immune response** Collective term for the defense activities of the immune system.

**immune system** A complex group of cells, proteins, and structures of the lymphatic system that work together to provide the immune response.

**immunity** Resistance to disease and pathogens.

**immunization** (im-yoo-nuh-ZAY-shun) A strategy for causing the body to develop immunity to a specific pathogen. Immunization may be active (the administraion of a vaccine) or passive (the administration of specific antibodies).

**immunoglobulin (Ig)** (im-yoo-noh-GLAHB-yoo-lin) Blood plasma proteins (gamma globulins) that play a crucial role in immunity. There are five classes.

**immunosuppressive drugs** Medications that block the immune response. Examples are corticosteroid drugs to suppress inflammation and cytotoxic medications to block activated lymphocytes.

**immunotherapy** Treatments that promote the general responsiveness of the immune system so that it can fight cancer more effectively.

**incomplete dominance** A pattern of genetic inheritance in which the heterozygous genotype results in a phenotype that is intermediate between the two homozygous phenotypes.

**independent assortment** Mendelian principle that genetic factors separate completely independently of each other during the formation of sperm and egg. Independent assortment applies fully only to genes located on different chromosomes.

**inflammation** (in-fluh-MAY-shun) A nonspecific defensive response of the body to tissue injury characterized by dilation of blood vessels and an increase in vessel permeability. The presence of inflammation is indicated by redness, heat, swelling, and pain.

**inheritance** Characteristics or traits that are transmitted from parents to offspring via genes.

**inner cell mass** Accumulation of cells in the blastocyst from which the embryo develops.

**inner ear** Region of the ear consisting of the cochlea and the vestibular apparatus. The cochlea sorts sounds by tone and converts them into nerve impulses. The vestibular apparatus helps maintain balance.

**insertion** The end of a muscle attached to the bone that moves when the muscle contracts.

**inspiration** Inhalation; act of taking a breath.

**insulin** (IN-suh-lin) A hormone secreted by the pancreas that enhances the uptake of glucose by cells, thus lowering blood glucose levels.

**integration** General term for the process of combining into a complete and harmonious whole. In the nervous system, the process by which neurons receive multiple inputs and produce a coordinated output.

**interferon** (in-tur-FEER-ahn) Chemical that is able to provide some protection against virus invasion of the body. Interferon inhibits viral reproduction.

**interleukin** (in-tur-LOO-kin) A substance that promotes development of immune cells.

**internal environment** In a multicellular organism, the environment that surrounds the cells; the interstitial fluid.

**internal respiration** Exchange of gases between blood, interstitial fluid, and cells.

**interneuron** A neuron within the central nervous system located between two other neurons. Interneurons receive input from one or more neurons and influence the functioning of other neurons.

**interphase** One of two major periods in the cell life cycle. Includes the period from cell formation to cell division.

**interstitial fluid** (in-tur-STISH-ul) Fluid between body cells.

**intervertebral disk** (in-tur-vur-TEE-brul) A disk of fibrocartilage between vertebrae.

**intron** A noncoding nucleotide sequence of DNA. Compare *exon.*

**ion** (EYE-ahn) An atom or molecule with a positive or negative electric charge.

**ionic bond** (eye-AHN-ik) Chemical bond formed by the attractive force between oppositely charged ions.

**iris** (EYE-ris) A colored disk-shaped muscle that determines how much light enters the eye.

**isotonic** General term for normal tone or tension. In biology, an isotonic solution is one with the same solute concentration as plasma. Cells maintain their normal cell volume in isotonic solutions.

**isotopes** Different atomic forms of the same element, varying only in the number of neutrons they contain. The heavier forms tend to be radioactive.

**IUD (intrauterine device)** Contraceptive device that is inserted into the uterus by a health care provider.

**IVF (*in vitro* fertilization)** Fertilization outside the body. Eggs are harvested from a woman and fertilized, and the embryo is inserted into the woman's uterus through her cervix.

## J

**jaundice** (JAWN-dis) Yellowish color of the skin, mucous membranes, and sometimes the whites of the eyes. Jaundice is often caused by liver malfunction and high circulating levels of bilirubin.

**jejunum** (jeh-JOO-num) The part of the small intestine between the duodenum and the ileum.

**joint** The junction or area of contact between two or more bones; also called an articulation.

**juxtaglomerular apparatus** In the kidney, a region near the glomerulus where the afferent arteriole and the efferent arteriole make contact with the distal tubule. The hormone renin is secreted by specialized cells of the afferent arteriole of the juxtaglomerular apparatus.

## K

**karyotype** (KAIR-ee-oh-typ) The diploid chromosomal complement in any species. The human karyotype typically is shown as a composite display of the 22 pairs of autosomes arranged from longest to shortest, plus the sex chromosomes X and Y.

**keratinocyte** (kair-uh-TIN-oh-syt) Type of cell in the epidermis that produces a tough, waterproof protein called keratin.

**killer T cell** T lymphocyte that directly lyses foreign cells, cancer cells, or virus-infected body cells; also called a cytotoxic T cell.

**kinetic energy** Energy in motion; energy actually doing work.

**Klinefelter syndrome** A condition caused by an XXY genotype. People with Klinefelter syndrome show a tall male phenotype.

**Krebs cycle** See *citric acid cycle.*

## L

**labor** Collective term for the series of events that expel the infant from the uterus.

**lactation** Production and secretion of milk.

**lacteal** (LAK-tee-ul) Small lymphatic vessel in a villus of the small intestine that takes up lipids.

**lactose intolerance** (LAK-tohs) A common disorder of digestion and absorption caused by insufficient quantities of the enzyme lactase, which digests the lactose in milk and dairy products.

**large intestine** Portion of the digestive tract extending from the small intestine to the anus. Consists of the cecum, appendix, colon, rectum, and anal canal.

**larynx** (LAIR-inks) Cartilaginous organ containing the vocal cords, located between the trachea and pharynx. The larynx is also called the voice box.

**lens** A transparent, flexible, curved structure that focuses incoming light on the retina at the back of the eye.

**less industrialized countries (LICs)** Nations that are just beginning to industrialize.

**leukemia** (loo-KEE-mee-uh) Cancer of the cells that form white blood cells, resulting in overproduction of abnormal white blood cells.

**leukocyte (white blood cell)** One of several types of blood cells that are part of the body's defense system. Leukocytes are diverse in structure and specific function. They compose only about 1% of the volume of blood.

**Leydig cell** (LAY-dig) Cells located between the seminiferous tubules of the testes. Leydig cells produce testosterone.

**LH (luteinizing hormone)** (LOO-tee-in-eye-zing) Anterior pituitary hormone that aids maturation of cells in the ovary and triggers ovulation in females. In males, LH causes the interstitial cells of the testis to produce testosterone.

**ligament** Dense fibrous connective tissue that connects bone to bone.

**limbic system** Functional brain system involved in emotional responses.

**lipase** (LY-pace) Any lipid-digesting enzyme.

**lipid** (LIP-id) Organic compounds formed of carbon, hydrogen, and oxygen. Fats, oils, and cholesterol are lipids. Lipids are not very soluble in water.

**lipoprotein** (ly-poh-PRO-teen) A compound containing both lipid and protein. Two medically important lipoproteins are the low-density lipoproteins (LDLs) and high-density lipoproteins (HDLs) that transport cholesterol.

**liver** Large, lobed organ that overlies the stomach in the abdominal cavity. The liver produces bile to help digest fat, and serves other metabolic and regulatory functions.

**longevity** How long a person lives.

**loop of Henle** (HEN-lee) Hairpin-shaped tubular structure that extends into the medulla of a nephron. The loop of Henle (also called the loop of the nephron) is important in the ability of the kidney to form either concentrated or dilute urine.

**lumen** (LOO-men) Cavity inside a tube, blood vessel, or hollow organ.

**lupus erythematosis** (LOO-pus air-uh-them-uh-TOW-sis) An autoimmune disorder in which the body attacks its own connective tissue.

**luteinizing hormone (LH)** (LOO-tee-in-eye-zing) Anterior pituitary hormone that aids maturation of cells in the ovary and triggers ovulation. In males, LH causes the interstitial cells of the testis to produce testosterone.

**lymph** (LIMF) Fluid derived from interstitial fluid transported by lymphatic vessels.

**lymph nodes** Small masses of tissue and lymphatic vessels that contain macrophages and lymphocytes, which remove microorganisms, cellular debris, and abnormal cells from the lymph before it is returned to the cardiovascular system.

**lymphatic system** System consisting of lymphatic vessels, lymph nodes, and other lymphoid organs and tissues. The lymphatic system returns excess interstitial fluid to the cardiovascular system and provides a site for immune surveillance.

**lymphatic vessels** Lymphatic capillaries and larger conduits that transport lymph.

**lymphocyte** (LIM-foh-syt) One of several types of white blood cells (T cells and B cells) that participate in nonspecific and specific (immune) defense responses.

**lymphoma** General term for cancers of the lymphoid tissues.

**lysosome** (LY-soh-sohm) Organelle originating from the Golgi apparatus that contains strong digestive enzymes.

**lysozyme** (LY-soh-zym) Enzyme in saliva and tears that kills certain kinds of bacteria.

## M

**macroevolution** Large-scale evolutionary trends or changes that apply to whole groups of species, often as a result of changing environments or major historical events.

**macrophage** (MAK-roh-fayj) Large phagocytic white blood cell derived from a monocyte; it engulfs damaged tissue cells, bacteria, and other foreign debris. Macrophages are important as antigen presenters to T cells and B cells in the immune response.

**malignant tumor** A mass of cells that has metastasized to become invasive cancer.

**malnutrition** A nutritional condition in which human development and function are compromised by an unbalanced or insufficient diet. Malnutrition can be caused by overnutrition or undernutrition.

**mammal** Vertebrates that have hair during all or part of their lives, and mammary glands in the female that produce milk.

**mammary gland** Milk-producing gland of the breast.

**mass extinction** Catastrophic event that destroys more than 50% of the species existing at the time. The fossil record indicates Earth has experienced at least five mass extinctions.

**mast cell** Immune cell that detects foreign substances in the tissue spaces and releases histamine to initiate a local inflammatory response against them. Mast cells typically are clustered deep in an epithelium or along blood vessels.

**matter** The material substance, composed of elements, that makes up the natural world. Matter takes up space and has weight.

**mechanoreceptor** (meh-KAN-oh-ree-sep-tur) Receptor sensitive to mechanical pressure or distortion, such as that produced by touch, sound, or muscle contractions.

**medulla** (meh-DUL-uh) General term for the inner zone of an organ. In the kidney, an inner pyramid-shaped zone of dense tissue that contains the loops of Henle. The term is also used for an area of the brain (medulla oblongata) and for the inner zone of the adrenal glands.

**medulla oblongata** (meh-DUL-uh ahb-long-GAH-tah) Portion of the brain stem. Contains reflex centers for vital functions such as respiration and blood circulation.

**meiosis** (my-OH-sis) Nuclear division process that reduces the chromosomal number by half. Meiosis results in the formation of four haploid ($n$) cells. It occurs only in certain reproductive organs.

**melanocyte** (meh-LAN-oh-syt) Type of cell located near the base of the epidermis. Melanocytes produce a dark brown pigment called melanin that is largely responsible for skin color.

**melanoma** (mel-ah-NO-mah) Least common but most dangerous form of skin cancer.

**melatonin** (mel-ah-TON-in) A hormone secreted by the pineal gland that seems to synchronize our body's daily rhythms and may induce sleep. It may also play a role in determining the onset of puberty.

**memory** Storage of information for later retrieval as needed.

**memory cell** Members of T cell and B cell clones that provide for immunologic memory.

**meninges** (meh-NIN-jeez) Protective coverings of the central nervous system.

**meningitis** (meh-nin-JY-tis) Inflammation of the meninges.

**menopause** (MEN-oh-pawz) Period of a woman's life when, prompted by hormonal changes, ovulation and menstruation cease.

**menstrual cycle** (MEN-stroo-ul) Pattern of changes in the ovaries and uterus. The menstrual cycle lasts about 28 days and is controlled by hormones.

**menstruation** (men-stroo-AY-shun) Process in which the endometrial lining disintegrates, its small blood vessels rupture, and the tissue and blood are shed through the vagina.

**mesoderm** (MEEZ-oh-durm) Primary germ layer that forms the skeleton and muscles of the body.

**messenger RNA (mRNA)** Long nucleotide strand that complements the exact nucleotide sequence of genetically active DNA. Messenger RNA carries the genetic message to the cytoplasm.

**metabolism** Sum total of the chemical reactions occurring in body cells.

**metaphase** Second stage of mitosis, during which the chromosomes align themselves on one plane at the center of the cell.

**metastasis** (meh-TAS-tuh-sis) The spread of cancer from one organ or location to another not directly connected to it.

**MHC (major histocompatibility complex) proteins** A group of proteins on the cell surface that identify an individual's cells as "self" and normally signal the immune system to bypass the individual's cells.

**microevolution** Evolution as a result of genetic changes that give rise to new species.

**microvilli** (sing. microvillus) Tiny projections on the surface of some epithelial cells that function to increase a cell's surface area. Microvilli are often found on the luminal surface of cells involved in absorption of fluids, nutrients, and ions.

**midbrain** Region of the brain stem. The midbrain is a coordination center for reflex responses to visual and auditory stimuli.

**middle ear** Region of the ear consisting of an air-filled chamber within the temporal bone of the skull, bridged by the malleus, incus, and stapes. The middle ear amplifies sound.

**milk ejection** Expulsion of milk from the breast during suckling.

**mineral** An inorganic chemical compound found in nature. Some minerals must be in the diet because they are necessary for normal metabolic functioning.

**mineralocorticoid** (MIN-er-al-oh-KOR-tih-koyd) Steroid hormone of the adrenal cortex that regulates salt and fluid balance.

**miscarriage** Spontaneous termination of pregnancy followed by expulsion of the embryo.

**mitochondrion** (pl. mitochondria) (my-toh-KAHN-dree-ahn) A cytoplasmic organelle responsible for ATP generation for cellular activities.

**mitosis** (my-TOH-sis) Process of nuclear division during which duplicated chromosomes are distributed to two daughter nuclei, each with the same number of chromosomes as the parent cell. Mitosis consists of prophase, metaphase, anaphase, and telophase.

**mitral valve** (MY-trul) Left atrioventricular valve in the heart, also called the bicuspid valve.

**molecule** Particle consisting of two or more atoms joined together by chemical bonds.

**Monera** One of the five kingdoms of life, comprising the bacteria.

**monoclonal antibodies** Pure preparations of identical antibodies produced in the laboratory by a colony of genetically identical cells.

**monocyte** (MAHN-oh-syt) Large agranular leukocyte that can differentiate into a macrophage that functions as a phagocyte.

**mononucleosis** (mahn-oh-nu-klee-OH-sis) A contagious infection of lymphocytes in blood and lymph tissues, caused by the Epstein-Barr virus.

**monosaccharide** (mahn-oh-SAK-uh-ryd) Simplest type of carbohydrate with only one sugar unit. Glucose is a monosaccharide.

**more industrialized countries (MICs)** Nations with established industry-based economies.

**morphogenesis** (mor-foh-JEN-ih-sis) Process involving dramatic changes in shape and form that an organism goes through during development.

**motor neuron** A neuron in the peripheral nervous system that conducts nerve impulses from the central nervous system to body tissues and organs.

**motor unit** A somatic motor neuron and all the muscle cells that it stimulates.

**MRI (magnetic resonance imaging)** Technique that uses short bursts of a powerful magnetic field to produce cross-sectional images of body structures.

**mRNA (messenger RNA)** Long nucleotide strand that complements the exact nucleotide sequence of genetically active DNA. Messenger RNA carries the genetic message to the cytoplasm.

**mucosa** (myoo-KO-suh) The innermost tissue layer in the wall of the gastrointestinal tract.

**mucus** (MYOO-kus) A sticky, thick fluid secreted by mucous glands and mucous membranes. Mucus keeps the surfaces of certain membranes moist.

**multiple sclerosis** (skler-OH-sis) Progressive disorder of the central nervous system in which the myelin sheath around neuron axons disappears and is replaced by fibrous connective tissue.

**muscle spindle** Encapsulated receptor in skeletal muscles that is sensitive to stretch.

**muscle tension** The force exerted by a contracting muscle.

**muscle tissue** Tissue consisting of cells that are specialized to shorten or contract, resulting in movement of some kind. There are three types of muscle tissue: skeletal, cardiac, and smooth.

**muscular dystrophy** (DIS-trof-ee) A group of inherited muscle-destroying diseases.

**muscularis** One of the four tissue layers of the gastrointestinal tract wall. The muscularis consists primarily of smooth muscle.

**mutation** A change in the DNA base pair sequence of a cell.

**mutator gene** A class of gene that normally is involved in DNA repair during DNA replication. Mutated mutator genes may contribute to cancer because errors in DNA replication may not be corrected.

**myelin sheath** (MY-ih-lin) Fatty insulating sheath that surrounds the neuron axons of some types of neurons.

**myocardial infarction** (my-oh-KAR-dee-ul in-FAHRK-shun) Condition characterized by death of heart tissue caused by inadequate oxygen supply; also called a heart attack.

**myocardium** (my-oh-KAR-dee-um) Middle and largest layer of the heart wall, composed of cardiac muscle.

**myopia** (my-OH-pee-uh) A condition in which the eyeball is too long, causing distant visual objects to be focused in front of the retina. Also called nearsightedness.

**myosin** (MY-oh-sin) One of the principal contractile proteins found in muscle. Myosin is composed of thick filaments with cross-bridges.

## N

**$NAD^+$** A transport molecule within mitochondria that can accept hydrogen ions and electrons liberated by the citric acid cycle, forming high-energy NADH.

**nasal cavity** An internal space directly behind the external nose.

**natural killer (NK) cells** A type of lymphocyte that can lyse and kill cancer cells and virus-infected body cells before the immune system is activated.

**natural selection** The process by which, according to Darwin, individuals with traits that make them more fit for their local environments tend to survive and reproduce. Most changes in allele frequency in a population are the result of mutations coupled with natural selection.

**nearsightedness** A condition in which the eyeball is too long, causing distant visual objects to be focused in front of the retina; also called myopia.

**negative feedback** A homeostatic control mechanism in which a change in a controlled variable triggers a series of events that ultimately opposes (negates) the initial change, returning the controlled variable to its normal value, or set point.

**neonate** (NEE-oh-nayt) A newborn baby during its first 28 days after birth.

**neoplasm** (NEE-oh-plazm) Abnormal mass of proliferating cells; also called a tumor. Neoplasms may be benign or malignant.

**nephron** (NEF-rahn) Structural and functional unit of the kidney. A nephron consists of the renal tubule and the blood vessels that supply it.

**nerve** Cablelike bundle of many neuron axons, all wrapped together in a protective connective tissue sheath. Nerves carry nerve impulses to and from the central nervous system.

**nerve impulse** A self-propagating wave of depolarization, also called an action potential.

**nerve tract** A bundle of nerve axons in the central nervous system.

**nervous tissue** Tissue consisting of cells that are specialized for generating and transmitting nerve impulses throughout the body. Nervous tissue forms a rapid communication network for the body.

**neuroendocrine cell** A type of cell in the hypothalamus that essentially functions as both a nerve cell and an endocrine cell because it generates nerve impulses and releases a hormone into blood vessels.

**neuroglial cells** (noo-RAHG-lee-ul) Cells that provide physical support and protection to neurons and help maintain healthy concentrations of important chemicals in the fluid surrounding them.

**neuromuscular junction** Region where a motor neuron comes in close contact with a muscle cell. At the neuromuscular junction, neurotransmitter released by the motor neuron causes an electrical impulse to be generated in the muscle cell.

**neuron** (NYOOR-ahn, NOOR-ahn) Cell of the nervous system specialized to generate and transmit nerve impulses.

**neurotransmitter** A chemical released by a neuron that may stimulate or inhibit other neurons or effector cells.

**neutron** Uncharged subatomic particle found in the atomic nucleus.

**neutrophil** (NOO-truh-fil) Most abundant type of white blood cell. Neutrophils respond rapidly during an infection, surrounding and engulfing bacteria.

**niche** The role of an organism in its community.

**nitrification** The formation of nitrate ($NO_3^-$) by any of several means, including nitrifying bacteria, lightning, and nitrate-producing fertilizer factories.

**nitrogen fixation** The process whereby certain bacteria convert $N_2$ gas to ammonium ($NH_4^+$). Nitrogen fixation is an important part of the nitrogen cycle.

**node of Ranvier** (RAHN-vee-ay) A short unmyelinated gap between adjacent Schwann cells where the surface of a neuron axon is exposed.

**nondisjunction** Failure of sister chromatids to separate during mitosis or failure of homologous pairs to separate during meiosis. Nondisjunction causes abnormal numbers of chromosomes in the resulting daughter cells.

**nonsteroid hormone** A hormone that consists of, or at least is partly derived from, the amino acid building blocks of proteins. Nonsteroid hormones generally are lipid insoluble, so they tend to act by binding to a receptor on the cell surface rather than by entering the cell cytoplasm.

**norepinephrine** (NOR-ep-ih-NEF-rin) A neurotransmitter and adrenal medullary hormone, associated with sympathetic nervous system activation.

**nucleolus** (pl. nucleoli) (noo-KLEE-oh-lus) A dense spherical body in the cell nucleus involved with ribosomal subunit synthesis and storage.

**nucleotide** A structural unit consisting of a nitrogen base, a five-carbon sugar, and one or more phosphate groups. Nucleotides are the structural units of DNA and RNA. ATP and ADP are also nucleotides.

**nucleus** General term for a central or essential part. The nucleus of an atom consists of neutrons and protons and contains most of the atomic mass. The nucleus of a eukaryotic cell contains the cell's DNA.

**nutrient** A chemical substance taken in via the diet that is used for energy and for cell growth and reproduction.

## O

**obesity** The condition of weighing more than 20% above ideal body weight.

**olfactory receptor cell** A modified sensory neuron, located in the upper part of the nasal passages, that detects odors.

**oligosaccharide** A short string of monosaccharides (single sugars) linked together by dehydration synthesis.

**omnivore** (AHM-nih-vor) An organism that can derive energy from either plants or animals. Humans, pigs, and bears are omnivores.

**oncogene** (AHNG-koh-jeen) A mutated or damaged proto-oncogene that contributes to cancer.

**oocyte** An immature egg in the female ovary or newly released from the ovary.

**optic disk** The area of the retina where the axons of the optic nerve exit the eye. The optic disk has no photoreceptors, so its presence creates a "blind spot" in each eye.

**optic nerve** One of the two cranial nerves that transmit nerve impulses from the retina to the brain.

**organ** A part of the body formed of two or more tissues and adapted to carry out a specific function. The stomach and the heart are examples of organs.

**organ of Corti** Collective term for the hair cells and tectorial membrane of the inner ear. The organ of Corti converts pressure waves to nerve impulses.

**organ system** A group of organs that work together to perform a vital body function. The digestive system is an example of an organ system.

**organelle** (or-guh-NEL) One of many small cellular structures that perform specific functions for the cell as a whole.

**organic molecule** A molecule that contains carbon and other elements, held together by covalent bonds.

**orgasm** (OR-gazm) A brief, intensely pleasurable reflex event consisting of rhythmic, involuntary muscular contractions.

**origin** The end of a muscle that is attached to the bone that does not move during muscular contraction.

**osmosis** (ahz-MO-sis) The net diffusion of water across a selectively permeable membrane, such as a cell membrane.

**osteoblast** (AHS-tee-oh-blast) A bone-forming cell.

**osteoclast** (AHS-tee-oh-klast) A cell that resorbs or breaks down bone.

**osteocyte** (AHS-tee-oh-syt) A mature bone cell.

**osteodystrophy** (AHS-tee-oh-DIS-troh-fee) Progressive disorder in which the bones become weak because of an abnormal mineral composition of bone.

**osteon** (AHS-tee-ahn) A cylindrical structure in bone composed of layers of living bone cells and hard extracellular material, arranged like the layers of an onion. In the center is a central canal through which nerves and blood vessels pass.

**osteoporosis** (AHS-tee-oh-poh-ROH-sis) Progressive disorder involving increased softening and thinning of the bone. Osteoporosis results from an imbalance in the rates of bone resorption and bone formation.

**otoliths** (OH-toh-lith) Hard crystals of bonelike material embedded in gel in the inner ear. Otoliths contribute to sensations of head position and movement.

**outer ear** Region of the ear consisting of the pinna (visible portion) and the auditory canal. The outer ear channels sound waves to the eardrum.

**ovarian cycle** (oh-VAIR-ee-un) Monthly cycle of follicle development, ovulation, and corpus luteum formation in an ovary.

**ovaries** (OH-vair-eez) The two female sex organs (gonads) in which ova (eggs) are produced.

**oviduct** (OH-vih-dukt) Tube that leads from an ovary to the uterus, also called the Fallopian tube or uterine tube.

**ovulation** (AHV-yoo-LAY-shun) Ejection of an immature egg (oocyte) from the ovary.

**ovum** (pl. ova) (OH-vum) Female gamete, also called an egg.

**oxidative phosphorylation** The process of producing ATP from ADP plus a phosphate group ($P_i$), using the energy derived from the electron transport system within mitochondria. The process is called *oxidative* because it requires oxygen, and *phosphorylation* because a phosphate group is added (to ADP).

**oxygen debt** The amount of oxygen required after exercise to oxidize the lactic acid formed by anaerobic metabolism during exercise.

**oxyhemoglobin** (ahk-see-HEE-moh-gloh-bin) Oxygen-bound form of hemoglobin.

**oxytocin** (ahk-sih-TOH-sin) Hormone secreted from the posterior pituitary by neuroendocrine cells of the hypothalamus. Oxytocin stimulates contraction of the uterus during childbirth and the ejection of milk during nursing.

**ozone** In the stratosphere, a thin layer of $O_3$ gas that shields Earth from ultraviolet rays. Also an environmental pollutant near Earth's surface.

## P

**Pacinian corpuscle** (puh-SIN-ee-un) Type of encapsulated mechanoreceptor located in the dermis that responds to deep pressure or high-frequency vibration.

**pancreas** (PANG-kree-us) Organ located behind the stomach. The pancreas secretes digestive enzymes and bicarbonate into the small intestine and the hormones insulin and glucagon into the bloodstream.

**pancreatic amylase** (pang-kree-AT-ik AM-ih-lays) Pancreatic enzyme that continues the digestion of carbohydrates begun by salivary amylase.

**parasympathetic division** (par-uh-sym-puh-THET-ik) The division of the autonomic nervous system that generally promotes activities associated with the resting state, such as digestion and elimination.

**parathyroid glands** (par-uh-THY-royd) Small endocrine glands located on the thyroid gland that produce parathyroid hormone.

**parathyroid hormone (PTH)** Hormone released by the parathyroid glands that regulates blood calcium levels.

**Parkinson's disease** Progressive disorder of the nervous system involving death and degeneration of dopamine-containing nerve cells in the midbrain. Symptoms of Parkinson's disease include persistent tremor and rigid movements.

**partial pressure** The pressure exerted by one particular gas in a mixture of gases.

**passive immunization** The process of fighting an existing or anticipated infection by the administration of specific antibodies against the infective agent. The antibodies usually are isolated from a human or animal with immunity to the infective agent.

**passive transport** Membrane transport processes that do not require cellular energy. Diffusion is a form of passive transport.

**pathogen** (PATH-uh-jen) Disease-causing microorganism, such as a bacterium or virus.

**pectoral girdle** (PEK-tur-ul) Portion of the skeleton that attaches the upper limbs to the axial skeleton, composed of the clavicle and scapula.

**pelvic girdle** Portion of the skeleton that supports the weight of the upper body and attaches the lower limbs to the axial skeleton, composed of the two coxal bones and the sacrum and coccyx of the vertebral column.

**pelvic inflammatory disease (PID)** Infection of the internal female reproductive organs. PID can result in scarring that blocks the oviducts.

**penis** Male organ of sexual intercourse and urination.

**pepsin** (PEP-sin) Protein-digesting enzyme secreted by the gastric glands of the stomach.

**peptic ulcer** An open, sometimes bleeding sore that forms in the inner lining of the stomach, the esophagus, or the upper part of the small intestine.

**perception** The process or act of becoming aware of a sensation and attaching meaning to it.

**perforin** (PUR-for-in) A chemical released by secretory vesicles of a cytotoxic T cell that perforates the membrane of an abnormal or foreign cell and kills it.

**pericardium** (pair-ih-KAR-dee-um) Tough fibrous sac that encloses and protects the heart and prevents it from overfilling.

**periodontitis** (pair-ee-oh-dahn-TY-tus) Inflammation of the periodontal membrane lining the tooth socket.

**peripheral nervous system (PNS)** Portion of the nervous system that lies outside of the brain and spinal cord.

**peristalsis** (pair-ih-STAHL-sis) Progressive wavelike contractions of muscle in a tubular structure. Peristalsis moves food through the digestive tract and urine through the ureters.

**peritubular capillaries** (pair-ih-TOO-byoo-lur) Capillaries that form a network surrounding the proximal and distal tubules in the cortex of a nephron.

**peroxisome** (per-OX-ih-sohm) Membrane-bound vesicle in the cell cytoplasm containing powerful enzymes that detoxify harmful or toxic substances.

**PET (positron emission tomography)** Technique that employs radioactive substances to create three-dimensional images showing the metabolic activity of body structures.

**pH** The measure of the relative acidity or alkalinity of a solution. Any pH below 7 is acidic and any pH above 7 is basic.

**phagocyte** (FAG-uh-syt) A white blood cell that destroys foreign cells through the process of phagocytosis.

**phagocytosis** (fag-uh-sy-TOH-sis) Process by which phagocytes surround, engulf, and destroy foreign cells.

**pharynx** (FAIR-inks) The region of the digestive and respiratory systems that extends from behind the nasal cavities to the esophagus, also called the throat. Both air and food pass through the pharynx.

**phenotype** (FEE-noh-typ) The observable physical and functional traits of an organism.

**phospholipid** A modified lipid that has a polar (water-soluble) region containing a phosphate group. Phospholipids are the main structural components of the cell membrane.

**photodynamic therapy** A therapy for cancer. First, the patient takes light-sensitive drugs that are drawn into the rapidly dividing cancer cells. Then laser light is focused on the tumor, triggering a series of chemical changes in the light-sensitive drugs that kill malignant cells.

**photopigment** Any one of several proteins located in the rods and cones of the eye that changes its shape when exposed to energy in the form of light. The change in shape causes the rod or cone to alter the amount of neurotransmitter it releases.

**photoreceptor** A specialized receptor cell that responds to light energy.

**photosynthesis** The process by which plants capture the energy in sunlight and convert it into chemical energy for their own use.

**pineal gland** (PY-nee-ul) Endocrine gland thought to be involved in setting the biological clock and influencing reproductive function. The pineal gland secretes melatonin.

**pituitary gland** (pih-TOO-ih-tair-ee) Neuroendocrine gland located just below the hypothalamus of the brain. Together, the anterior and posterior lobes of the pituitary gland secrete eight hormones.

**pituitary portal system** A system of small blood vessels between the hypothalamus and anterior lobe of the pituitary gland.

**placebo** (pluh-SEE-bow) A false treatment in a controlled experiment, given or performed to minimize the possibility of bias by suggestion.

**placenta** (plah-SEN-tuh) Temporary organ formed from both fetal and maternal tissues that provides nutrients and oxygen to the developing fetus, removes fetal metabolic wastes, and produces the hormones of pregnancy.

**Plantae** The kingdom of life comprising plants.

**plasma** (PLAZ-muh) The fluid component of blood in which the formed elements are suspended.

**plasma cell** A cell derived from a B cell lymphocyte specifically to mass-produce and release antibodies.

**plasma membrane** Membrane surrounding the cell, consisting of a phospholipid bilayer with embedded cholesterol and proteins. The plasma membrane regulates the passage of substances into and out of the cell.

**plasmid** (PLAZ-mid) A small circular molecule of DNA found in the cytoplasm of some bacteria. Plasmids are used in recombinant DNA technology.

**platelets** (PLAYT-lets) Small cell fragments that are derived from certain cells in the bone marrow. Platelets are important in blood clotting.

**pleural membranes** (PLUR-ul) Membranes that line the thoracic cavity and cover the external surface of the lungs.

**pneumonia** (noo-MOHN-yuh) Respiratory condition involving inflammation and infection of the lungs. Pneumonia is usually caused by viruses or bacteria.

**polar body** Small nonfunctional cell with almost no cytoplasm that is formed when the primary oocyte completes stage I of meiosis.

**pollution** A general term for environmental contaminants that have adverse effects on living organisms. Pollution may be caused by natural events (dust and gases from volcanoes) or by human activities (hydrogen sulfide from coal-fired power plants).

**polygenic inheritance** (pahl-ee-JEN-ik) Pattern of inheritance in which a phenotypic trait depends on many genes. An example is eye color, controlled by three or more genes.

**polymerase chain reaction (PCR)** (poh-LIM-ur-ays) A technique for making multiple identical copies of DNA in a test tube.

**polypeptide** A chain of 3–100 amino acids (*poly* means "many"). Chains of more than 100 amino acids are generally referred to as proteins.

**polysaccharide** A chain of monosaccharides. Starch and glycogen are polysaccharides.

**population** A group of individuals of the same species that occupy the same geographic area and interact with each other.

**positive feedback** A control system in which a change in the controlled variable sets in motion a series of events that amplifies the original change. The process of childbirth once labor has started is an example of positive feedback.

**potential energy** Stored or inactive energy.

**precapillary sphincter** (SFINK-ter) Band of smooth muscle that controls blood flow into individual capillaries.

**pre-embryo** An organism during the first two weeks after fertilization. The term pre-embryo is used because many of the cells that result from cleavage and morphogenesis in the first two weeks will eventually not be part of the embryo at all, but will instead constitute extra-embryonic membranes and parts of the placenta.

**premenstrual syndrome (PMS)** Recurring episodes of discomfort during the menstrual cycle, generally beginning after ovulation and lasting until menstruation. PMS can include symptoms such as food cravings, mood swings, anxiety, back and joint pain, water retention, and headaches.

**presbyopia** (prez-bee-OH-pee-uh) Eye condition in which an increase in stiffness of the lens results in an inability to focus on near objects. Presbyopia typically begins after age 40.

**primary motor area** Region of the frontal lobe of the brain that initiates motor activity.

**primary somatosensory area** Region in the parietal lobe of the brain that receives sensory input from the skin.

**primate** (PRY-mayt) An order of mammals with five digits on their hands, fairly flat fingernails and toenails rather than hooves or claws, and forward-facing eyes adapted for stereoscopic vision. Primates include lemurs, monkeys, apes, and humans.

**primer** A short double-stranded piece of DNA used to initiate DNA synthesis during DNA sequencing.

**prion** (PREE-on) An infectious misfolded protein that replicates by causing a normal protein in the infected animal to misfold, producing another prion. Prions technically are not alive since they cannot reproduce on their own.

**producer** In ecosystems, an organism that makes its own organic molecules from inorganic compounds found in water, air, and soil, utilizing energy provided by the sun. Also called an autotroph. Green plants (on land) and algae (in water) are producers.

**product** In chemistry and biology, the end material of a chemical reaction.

**progesterone** (proh-JES-tur-ohn) Hormone partly responsible for preparing the uterus for the fertilized ovum. Progesterone is secreted by the corpus luteum of the ovary and by the placenta.

**prokaryote** (proh-KAIR-ee-oht) A single-celled organism that lacks the nucleus and the membrane-bound organelles characteristic of eukaryotes. Bacteria are prokaryotes.

**prolactin** (proh-LAK-tin) Hormone secreted by the anterior pituitary gland that stimulates the mammary glands to produce milk.

**promoter** A unique base sequence that marks the beginning of a gene.

**prophase** The first stage of mitosis. During prophase the chromosomes condense and thicken, the pairs of centrioles migrate to opposite sides of the cell, and the mitotic spindle forms.

**prostaglandins** (prahs-tuh-GLAN-dins) A group of lipid-based chemicals synthesized by most tissue cells that act as local messengers. Some prostaglandins dilate blood vessels and others constrict them.

**prostate gland** (PRAHS-tayt) Accessory reproductive gland in males that produces approximately one-third of the semen volume, including fluids that activate sperm.

**protein** One or more polypeptide chains of more than 100 amino acids. The three-dimensional structure of a protein is determined by the sequence of amino acids and by hydrogen bonds between different regions of the protein.

**proteinuria** (proh-tee-NYUR-ee-uh) Appearance of protein in urine. Persistent proteinuria may indicate glomerular damage.

**prothrombin** (proh-THRAHM-bin) A plasma protein that is converted to thrombin as part of the process of blood clot formation.

**prothrombin activator** Substance released by blood vessels and nearby platelets when blood vessels are damaged. Prothrombin activator activates the conversion of prothrombin into thrombin, facilitating the process of blood clotting.

**Protista** One of the five kingdoms of life, comprising unicellular and relatively simple multicellular eukaryotes such as protozoa, algae, and slime molds.

**proton** Positively charged subatomic particle in the nucleus of an atom.

**proto-oncogene** (proh-toh-AHNG-koh-jeen) Regulatory gene that promotes cell growth, differentiation, division, or adhesion. A proto-oncogene may contribute to cancer if it becomes mutated or damaged in such a way that it is turned on all the time.

**proximal tubule** Segment of a nephron that starts at Bowman's capsule and extends to the renal medulla.

**PTH (parathyroid hormone)** Hormone, released by the parathyroid gland, that regulates blood calcium levels.

**puberty** (PYOO-bur-tee) Period of life when reproductive maturity is achieved.

**pulmonary circuit** That part of the vascular system that takes deoxygenated blood to the lungs and returns oxygenated blood to the heart.

**pulmonary embolism** (EM-buh-liz-um) Condition that occurs when an embolus (blood clot) blocks an artery supplying blood to the lungs. A pulmonary embolism can cause sudden chest pain, shortness of breath, and even sudden death.

**pulse** Rhythmic expansion and recoil of arteries resulting from heart contraction that can be felt from the surface of the body.

**Punnett square** (PUN-et) A grid used for predicting patterns of inheritance and the probability that a particular genotype will be inherited.

**pupil** (PYOO-pul) Opening in the center of the iris through which light enters the eye.

**Purkinje fibers** (pur-KIN-jee) Modified cardiac muscle fibers that are part of the electrical conduction system of the heart.

**pyloric sphincter** (py-LOHR-ik SFINK-tur) A thickening of the circular layer of muscle at the distal end of the stomach that controls the rate at which the stomach empties.

**pyrogen** (PY-roh-jen) A fever-inducing agent. Macrophages and certain bacteria and viruses release pyrogens.

## R

**radiation** High-energy waves or particles emitted by radioactive isotopes.

**receptor** In sensory physiology, a specialized cell or nerve ending that receives a sensory signal such as touch, smell, light, or a chemical, and ultimately generates nerve impulses in a sensory neuron.

**receptor protein** A protein molecule of the cell membrane whose function is to transmit information across the cell membrane. Typically, when a particular molecule in the interstitial fluid binds to the receptor protein, a specific series of events is triggered within the cell.

**recessive allele** An allele that does not manifest itself in the presence of a more dominant allele. Two recessive alleles must be present in order for the recessive phenotypic trait to be expressed.

**recombinant DNA technology** Field of applied science that explores applications of cutting, splicing, and creating DNA.

**Recommended Daily Allowance (RDA)** The U.S. National Research Council's current best estimate of how much of each vitamin and mineral we need to maintain good health.

**red blood cell (RBC)** Blood cell that transports oxygen from the lungs to the tissues, and carbon dioxide from the tissues to the lungs. Also called an erythrocyte.

**reflex** An involuntary, automatic response to a stimulus.

**refractory period** (rih-FRAK-tuh-ree) Period immediately following a nerve impulse during which a neuron is unable to conduct another nerve impulse.

**regulatory gene** A gene that codes for a repressor or activator regulatory protein.

**REM (rapid eye movement) sleep** Stage of sleep in which rapid eye movements occur. REM sleep is accompanied by an alert EEG pattern and dreaming.

**renin** (REE-nin) An enzyme secreted into the bloodstream by the kidneys that leads to an increase in blood pressure and the secretion of aldosterone.

**replacement fertility rate** The fertility rate required to achieve long-term zero population growth. Replacement fertility rate is estimated to be an average of 2.1 children per woman.

**replication** The process of copying DNA prior to cell division.

**repolarization** In a nerve or muscle cell, return of the membrane potential to the initial resting (polarized) state after depolarization.

**reproductive system** Organ system that functions to produce offspring.

**residual volume** The amount of air remaining in the lungs even after a forceful, maximal expiration. Normal residual volume is approximately 1200 ml.

**respiratory center** Groups of nerve cells in the medulla oblongata near the base of the brain that are responsible for the cyclic nature of respiration.

**respiratory system** Organ system responsible for gas exchange. The respiratory system includes the nose, pharynx, larynx, trachea, bronchi, and lungs.

**resting potential** The slight difference in voltage (electrical potential) between the inside and outside of a cell.

**restriction enzyme** An enzyme found in bacteria that can be used to cut DNA at specific nucleotide sequences called restriction sites.

**reticular activating system (RAS)** (reh-TIK-yoo-lur) A group of neurons in the reticular formation that controls levels of sleep and wakefulness.

**reticular fibers** Thin, interconnecting fibers of collagen found in fibrous connective tissue. Reticular fibers provide an internal structural framework for soft organs such as the liver, spleen, and lymph nodes.

**reticular formation** Collective term for neurons in the pons that work with the cerebellum to coordinate the skeletal muscle activity required to maintain posture, balance, and muscle tone. The reticular formation is also responsible for maintaining the level of wakefulness.

**retina** (RET-ih-nuh) Layers of tissue at the back and sides of the eye. The retina is composed primarily of photoreceptor cells, neurons, and a few blood vessels.

**retrovirus** (REHT-roh-vy-rus) A class of viruses that replicate by using their RNA to produce double-stranded DNA, which is inserted into the host cell's DNA. The host cell then produces RNA for new viruses. HIV is a retrovirus.

**Rh factor** A red blood cell surface antigen, first discovered in rhesus monkeys, that is a crucial consideration in blood transfusions.

**rheumatoid arthritis** (ROO-muh-toyd) A type of chronic arthritis involving inflammation of the synovial membrane that lines certain joints.

**rhodopsin** (rho-DOP-sin) The photopigment found in the rods of the eye.

**rhythm method** Contraceptive technique based on the limited time available for fertilization in each menstrual cycle. The rhythm method requires avoiding intercourse from about five days before ovulation to three days after ovulation.

**ribonucleic acid (RNA)** Nucleic acid that contains ribose and the bases A, G, C, and U. RNA carries out DNA's instructions for protein synthesis. Types of RNA include mRNA, rRNA, and tRNA.

**ribosomal RNA (rRNA)** The RNA component of a ribosome. Ribosomal RNA assists in protein synthesis.

**ribosome** (RY-boh-sohm) A cellular structure consisting of rRNA and protein at which amino acids are assembled into proteins. Some ribosomes float freely within the cytoplasm; others are attached to the endoplasmic reticulum.

**rigor mortis** (RIG-ur MOR-tis) Period of time after death during which a body becomes stiff because it lacks the ATP required for muscle relaxation. Rigor mortis usually begins a few hours after death and ends several days later, when decomposition begins.

**RNA (ribonucleic acid)** Nucleic acid that contains ribose and the bases A, G, C, and U. RNA carries out DNA's instructions for protein synthesis. Types of RNA include mRNA, rRNA, and tRNA.

**RNA polymerase** (poh-LIM-ur-ays) One of several enzymes that recognizes a promoter (the starting point of transcription). RNA polymerase attaches to the promoter, starts the DNA unwinding process, and assists in attaching the appropriate RNA segments to the growing chain.

**rod cell** One of the two types of photosensitive cells in the retina.

**rRNA (ribosomal RNA)** The RNA component of a ribosome. Ribosomal RNA assists in protein synthesis.

## S

**SA (sinoatrial) node** (sy-noh-AY-tree-ul) Group of specialized myocardial cells in the wall of the right atrium that initiates the heartbeat. The SA node is called the pacemaker of the heart.

**salivary amylase** (SAL-ih-vair-ee AM-uh-layz) Enzyme in saliva that begins the process of digesting starch.

**salivary glands** Three pairs of glands that produce saliva to begin the process of digestion. The three pairs of salivary glands are the parotid, submandibular, and sublingual glands.

**saltatory conduction** Form of rapid transmission of a nerve impulse along a myelinated fiber, in which the nerve impulse leaps from node to node.

**sarcomere** (SAR-koh-mir) The smallest contractile unit of a muscle myofibril. A sarcomere extends from one Z-line to the next.

**sarcoplasmic reticulum** (sar-koh-PLAZ-mik reh-TIK-yuh-lum) Specialized endoplasmic reticulum of muscle cells that surrounds the myofibrils and stores the calcium needed for the initiation of muscle contraction.

**saturated fat** Type of fat with two hydrogen atoms for every carbon atom in the fatty acid tails. Saturated fats are found in meat and dairy products and in a few plant sources such as coconut and palm kernel oil.

**scanning electron microscope (SEM)** Microscope that bombards an object with beams of electrons to reveal what appears to be a three-dimensional view of the object's surface.

**Schwann cell** A type of supporting cell in the peripheral nervous system. Schwann cells form the myelin sheaths around myelinated neurons and are vital to peripheral nerve fiber regeneration.

**science** The study of the natural world.

**scientific method** The process of science; the way scientific knowledge is acquired.

**sclera** (SKLEAR-uh) White, opaque outer layer of the eyeball.

**scrotum** (SKROH-tum) External sac of skin enclosing the testes.

**second messenger** Any intracellular messenger molecule generated by the binding of a chemical messenger (hormone or neurotransmitter) to a plasma membrane receptor on a cell's outer surface. A second messenger mediates intracellular responses to an extracellular (first) messenger.

**secondary oocyte** The haploid female reproductive cell that is released from an ovary and begins traveling down the oviduct during the ovarian cycle. A secondary oocyte has completed stage I of meiosis but not stage II.

**secretin** (seh-KREE-tin) Hormone secreted by the duodenum into the bloodstream that stimulates the pancreas to secrete water and bicarbonate to neutralize acid.

**secretion** General term for the movement of a substance out of a cell of an endocrine or exocrine gland. Also, the substance secreted. The term is also used to denote the movement of any substance into the lumen of a tubule in the kidney.

**segmentation** Type of gastrointestinal motility in which short sections of smooth muscle contract and relax in seemingly random fashion, mixing the contents of the intestinal lumen.

**segregation** Mendelian principle that diploid organisms inherit two genes for each trait (on a pair of homologous chromosomes), and that during meiosis the two genes are distributed to different gametes.

**selective gene expression** The principle that, in any cell at any time, only a few of the genes are actually being expressed. Selective gene expression is responsible for differences in structure and function among different cells and for changes in cell function at different times.

**selectively permeable** The quality of allowing certain substances to pass while restricting the movement of others. The plasma membrane of a cell is selectively permeable.

**semen** (SEE-men) Thick, whitish fluid mixture containing sperm and the secretions of the male accessory reproductive glands.

**semicircular canals** Three fluid-filled canals in the vestibular apparatus of the inner ear that are important in sensing rotational movements of the head.

**semilunar valves** (sem-ee-LOO-nur) Heart valves located between the ventricles and the two major arteries of the body (pulmonary and aortic) that prevent blood from returning to the ventricles after contraction.

**seminal vesicles** (SEM-ih-nul) Male accessory reproductive structures that add fructose and prostaglandins to semen. Fructose serves as an energy source for sperm, and prostaglandins may induce muscle contractions in the female reproductive tract to help sperm travel more effectively.

**seminiferous tubules** (sem-ih-NIF-ur-us) Highly convoluted tubes within the testes in which sperm are formed.

**senescence** (seh-NES-ens) The progressive deterioration of multiple organs and organ systems over time; old age.

**sensation** The conscious awareness of a stimulus.

**sensor** In control system theory, any structure that monitors the current value of the controlled variable and sends the information to a control center. In biology, also called a receptor. Most receptors send information in the form of either action potentials in nerves or hormones in the bloodstream.

**sensory neuron** A neuron of the peripheral nervous system that is specialized to respond to a certain type of sensory stimulus, such as pressure or light. Sensory neurons conduct information about a stimulus to the central nervous system in the form of nerve impulses.

**septicemia** (sep-tih-SEE-mee-uh) Systemic disease caused by the spread of microorganisms or their toxins in blood. Also called blood poisoning or toxemia.

**septum** (SEP-tum) The muscular partition that separates the right and left sides of the heart.

**serosa** The outermost tissue layer of the gastrointestinal tract wall. It consists of a thin layer of connective tissue that surrounds the other three layers and attaches the gastrointestinal tract to the walls of the body cavities.

**Sertoli cells** Large cells that represent most of the bulk of seminiferous tubules in males. Also called *sustentacular cells,* they surround and nourish the developing sperm.

**set point** The internally set (expected, normal) value of a controlled variable.

**sex chromosomes** The chromosomes, X and Y, that determine gender (XXfemale, XYmale). The 23rd pair of chromosomes.

**sex-influenced trait** A trait not inherited with a sex gene but influenced by the actions of the sex genes. An example is the phenotypic trait of male baldness.

**sex-linked inheritance** Pattern of inheritance that depends on genes located on the sex chromosomes. Sex-linked inheritance is X-linked if the gene is located only on the X chromosome, and Y-linked if it is located only on the Y chromosome.

**sickle-cell anemia** An inherited disorder in which the red blood cells assume a sickle shape when the oxygen concentration is low.

**sickle-cell trait** A heterozygous condition for the sickle-cell allele, designated $Hb^A$-$Hb^S$. Unlike people with sickle-cell anemia, those with sickle-cell trait can generally lead normal lives because their condition is intermediate in severity.

**sinoatrial (SA) node** (sy-noh-AY-tree-ul) Group of specialized myocardial cells in the wall of the right atrium that initiates the heartbeat. The SA node is called the pacemaker of the heart.

**sinus** Mucous-membrane–lined, air-filled cavity in certain cranial bones.

**sister chromatids** The two identical chromosomes that remain attached at the centromere after replication. The centromere holds the sister chromatids together until they are physically pulled apart during the mitotic phase.

**skeletal muscle** Muscle composed of cylindrical multinucleate cells with obvious striations. Skeletal muscles attach to the body's skeleton.

**skeleton** The body's physical support system. The skeleton consists of bones and the various connective tissues that hold them together.

**skepticism** A questioning attitude. Good scientists combine creativity and imagination with skepticism.

**sliding filament mechanism** The mechanism of muscle contraction. Muscles contract when the thick and thin filaments slide past each other and sarcomeres shorten.

**smog** Hazy brown or gray layer of atmospheric pollution that tends to hover over the region where it is produced. The burning of fossil fuels (coal and oil) and automobile exhaust are the primary culprits.

**smooth muscle** Spindle-shaped muscle cells with one centrally located nucleus and no externally visible striations. Smooth muscle is found mainly in the walls of hollow organs.

**sodium-potassium pump** An active transport protein of the plasma membrane that simultaneously transports three sodium ions ($Na^+$) out of the cell and two potassium ions ($K^+$) in. The sodiumpotassium pump is important for maintaining cell volume and for generating the resting membrane potential.

**solute** Any substance dissolved in a liquid.

**solvent** A liquid in which other substances dissolve.

**somatic sensations** Sensations that arise from receptors located at many points throughout the body. The somatic sensations include temperature, touch, vibration, pressure, pain, and awareness of body movements and position.

**somatostatin** (soh-mah-toh-STAHT-in) Hormone secreted from several locations in the body. In the pancreas, somatostatin inhibits the secretion of glucagon and insulin.

**special senses** The five senses (taste, smell, hearing, balance, and vision) originating from receptors that are restricted to special areas of the body. The special senses deliver information about the external world to the central nervous system.

**species** The smallest classification category of life. A species is a group of organisms that under natural conditions tend to breed within that group.

**sperm** Male reproductive cell (gamete).

**sphincter** (SFINK-tur) General term for a ring of muscle around a hollow tube or duct that functions to restrict the passage of materials.

**sphygmomanometer** (SFIG-moh-mah-NOM-uh-tur) Device used to measure blood pressure.

**spinal cord** The portion of the central nervous system that lies outside the brain, extending from the base of the brain to about the second lumbar vertebra. The spinal cord provides a conduction pathway to and from the brain.

**spinal nerve** Any one of the 31 paired nerves that arise from the spinal cord.

**spinal reflex** An involuntary muscle response that is mediated at the level of the spinal cord, with little or no involvement of the brain.

**spleen** Largest lymphoid organ. The spleen removes old and damaged red blood cells and helps fight infections.

**spongy bone** Type of bone tissue characterized by thin, hard interconnecting bony elements enclosing hollow spaces. Red blood cells are produced in the spaces between the bony elements.

**starch** The storage polysaccharide utilized by plants.

**stem cells** General term for any cells that have not yet differentiated. Stem cells in bone marrow are the source of all blood cells and platelets.

**steroids** (STEER-oydz) Group of lipids having four interconnected rings that includes cholesterol and several hormones. Steroids are fat-soluble molecules.

**stimulus** An excitant or irritant. A chemical or physical form of energy such as heat, physical pressure, or sound waves that evokes a response in a nerve, muscle, gland, or receptor.

**stomach** Organ of the gastrointestinal tract where food is initially stored and where chemical breakdown of proteins begins.

**stretch reflex** Type of spinal reflex, important in maintaining upright posture and coordinating movement. Stretch receptors in a skeletal muscle stimulate sensory nerves when stretched, causing the sensory nerves to transmit nerve impulses to the spinal cord.

**stroke** Condition in which brain tissue is deprived of a blood supply, most often caused by blockage of a cerebral blood vessel. Also called a cerebrovascular accident.

**stroke volume** Volume of blood pumped out of a ventricle during one ventricular contraction.

**structural gene** A gene that codes for an enzyme or a structural protein.

**submucosa** The middle layer of the gastrointestinal tract wall. The submucosa is a layer of connective tissue that contains blood vessels, lymph vessels, and nerves.

**substrate** In chemistry and biology, the starting material of a chemical reaction.

**succession** A natural sequence of change in terms of which organisms dominate in a community.

**summation** Accumulation of effects, especially those of muscular or neural activity.

**suppressor T cell** Regulatory T lymphocyte that suppresses the immune response.

**surfactant** (sur-FAK-tant) Secretion produced by certain cells of the alveoli that reduces the surface tension of water molecules, preventing the collapse of the alveoli after each expiration.

**sustainable world** In theory, a world in which ecosystems are sustainable indefinitely.

**sympathetic division** The division of the autonomic nervous system that helps the body cope with stressors (danger, excitement, etc.) and with situations requiring high mental or physical activity.

**synapse** (SIN-aps) Functional junction or point of close contact between two neurons or between a neuron and an effector cell.

**synaptic cleft** (sih-NAP-tik) Fluid-filled space at a synapse.

**synaptic transmission** The process of transmitting information from a neuron to its target across a synapse.

**syndrome** Medical term for a group of symptoms that occur together.

**synovial joint** (sih-NO-vee-ul) A movable joint having a thin fluid-filled cavity between the bones.

**syphilis** (SIF-uh-lis) Sexually transmitted disease caused by infection with the bacterium *Treponema pallidum*.

**systemic circuit** The system of blood vessels that transport blood to all cells of the body except those served by the pulmonary circuit.

**systole** (SIS-toh-lee) Period when either the ventricles or the atria of the heart are contracting.

**systolic pressure** (sis-TOL-ik) The highest pressure reached in the arterial blood vessels during the cardiac cycle, and the first of two blood pressure numbers recorded by the health care provider. Systolic pressure is achieved during ventricular systole.

# T

**T cells (T lymphocytes)** Lymphocytes responsible for cell-mediated immunity, which depends on the actions of several types of T cells.

**taste bud** A cluster of taste receptor cells and supporting cells that respond to dissolved food chemicals in the mouth. The human tongue has about 10,000 taste buds.

**taxonomy** (tak-SAHN-uh-mee) The science of classifying and naming life-forms.

**technology** The application of science.

**tectorial membrane** (tek-TOR-ee-ul) The gelatinous noncellular material in which the mechanoreceptor hair cells of the inner ear are embedded. With the hair cells, the tectorial membrane forms the organ of Corti, which converts pressure waves to nerve impulses.

**telomerase** (tel-OH-mer-ays) An enzyme produced primarily by cancer cells and reproductive cells that builds new telomeres to replace telomeres lost during cell division.

**telomeres** (TEEL-oh-meer) Short segments of DNA at the end of each DNA molecule that do not encode for a protein. In most cells, telomeres are removed every time a cell divides until there are no telomeres left.

**telophase** In cell division, the last phase of mitosis in which the two new sets of chromosomes arrive at opposite poles of the cell, new nuclear membranes form around the chromosomes, and the chromosomes uncoil and are no longer visible under a microscope.

**TEM (transmission electron microscope)** Microscope that bombards a very thin sample with a beam of electrons, some of which pass through the sample. A TEM provides images that are two-dimensional but highly magnified.

**tendon** A cord of dense fibrous connective tissue attaching muscle to bone.

**teratogenic** (TAIR-uh-toh-JEN-ik) Capable of producing abnormal development of a fetus. Teratogenic substances are one cause of birth defects.

**testis** (pl. testes) The male primary sex organ (gonad); produces sperm.

**testosterone** (tes-TAHS-teh-rohn) Male sex hormone produced primarily by the testes. (The adrenal cortex produces a small amount of testosterone in both sexes.) Testosterone promotes the development of secondary sexual characteristics and is necessary for normal sperm production.

**tetanus** (TET-uh-nus) In a muscle, a sustained maximal muscle contraction resulting from high-frequency stimulation. In medicine, an infectious disease also called lockjaw that is caused by an anaerobic bacterium.

**thalamus** (THAL-uh-mus) A region of the forebrain that receives and processes sensory information and relays it to the cerebrum.

**theory** A main hypothesis that has been extensively tested over time and that explains a broad range of scientific facts with a high degree of reliability. An example is the theory of evolution.

**thermal inversion** A situation in which a warm stagnant upper layer of air traps a cooler air mass beneath it. Thermal inversions can cause air pollutants to accumulate close to the ground by preventing them from dissipating.

**thermoreceptor** Receptor sensitive to temperature changes.

**threshold** In an excitable cell such as a nerve or muscle, the membrane voltage that must be reached to trigger an action potential, or nerve impulse.

**thrombin** Enzyme that facilitates the conversion of fibrinogen into long threads of fibrin. Thrombin promotes blood clotting.

**thymus gland** Endocrine gland that contributes to immune responsiveness. T cells mature in the thymus.

**thyroid gland** An endocrine gland, located in the neck, that produces the hormones thyroxine, triiodothyronine, and calcitonin.

**thyroid-stimulating hormone (TSH)** Hormone produced by the anterior pituitary. TSH regulates secretion of thyroxine and triiodothyronine.

**thyroxine** (thy-RAHK-sin) A hormone containing four iodine molecules that is secreted by the thyroid gland. Thyroxine and a closely related three-iodine hormone (triiodothyronine) accelerate cellular metabolism in most body tissues.

**tidal volume** Volume of air inhaled and exhaled in a single breath. Normal tidal volume is approximately 500 milliliters, or about a pint.

**tissue** A group of similar cells (and their intercellular substance) specialized to perform a specific function. Primary tissue types of the body are epithelial, connective, muscle, and nervous tissue.

**tissue membranes** Flat, thin, structures consisting of a layer of epithelial tissue and a layer of connective tissue that line each body cavity and form the skin.

**tissue rejection** Situation in which the body's immune system attacks foreign tissues. Examples of tissue rejection are transfusion reactions and reactions to organ transplants.

**tonsillitis** Inflammation of the tonsils at the back of the throat.

**tonsils** Masses of lymphatic tissue near the entrance to the throat. Lymphocytes in the tonsils remove microorganisms that enter in food or in the air.

**trachea** (TRAY-kee-uh) Tube extending from the larynx to the bronchi that is the passageway for air to the lungs. Also called the windpipe.

**transcription** The production of a single strand of RNA from a segment (representing a gene) of one of the two strands of DNA. The base sequence of the RNA is complementary to that of the single strand of DNA.

***trans* fats** Vegetable oils that have been turned into solids by partial hydrogenation of their fatty acid tails. *Trans* fats increase the shelf life and stability of foods, but they also increase the risk of heart disease.

**transfer RNA (tRNA)** Short-chain RNA molecule that transfers amino acids to the ribosome.

**transfusion reaction** The adverse reaction that occurs in a recipient when a donor's red blood cells are attacked by the recipient's antibodies. During a transfusion reaction the donated cells may clump together (agglutinate), blocking blood flow in blood vessels.

**transgenic organism** A living organism that has had foreign genes inserted into it. Transgenic organisms are sometimes created to produce substances useful to humans, including human proteins.

**translation** The process by which the genetic code of mRNA is used to string together the appropriate amino acids to produce a specific protein.

**translocation** A change in chromosome location that occurs when a piece of a chromosome breaks off but reattaches at another site, either on the same chromosome or another chromosome. Translocations can result in subtle changes in gene expression and ability to function.

**transport protein** A protein molecule of the cell membrane whose function is to transport one or more molecules across the cell membrane.

**tricuspid valve** (try-KUS-pid) The right atrioventricular valve of the heart.

**triglyceride** A neutral fat molecule consisting of a molecule of glycerol and three fatty acid tails. Triglycerides are the body's most concentrated source of energy fuel.

**triiodothyronine** (try-i-oh-doh-THY-roh-neen) Hormone secreted by the thyroid gland, similar to thyroxine except that it contains three atoms of iodine instead of four. Like thyroxine, triiodothyronine accelerates cellular metabolism in most body tissues.

**triplet code** The genetic code of mRNA and tRNA in which three successive bases encode for one of the 20 amino acids.

**trisomy-X syndrome** (TRY-soh-mee) A condition caused by having three X chromosomes. Trisomy-X syndrome individuals are female phenotype, sometimes showing a tendency toward mild mental retardation.

**tRNA (transfer RNA)** Short-chain RNA molecule that transfers amino acids to the ribosome.

**trophoblast** Outer sphere of cells of the blastocyst.

**TSH (thyroid-stimulating hormone)** Hormone produced by the anterior pituitary. TSH regulates secretion of thyroxine and triiodothyronine.

**tubal ligation** Procedure for female sterilization in which each oviduct is cut and tied.

**tuberculosis** Infectious disease of the lungs caused by the bacterium *Mycobacterium tuberculosis.*

**tubular reabsorption** The movement of fluid and solutes (primarily nutrients) from the renal tubules into the blood.

**tubular secretion** The movement of solutes (primarily undesirable substances such as drugs, metabolic wastes, and excess ions) from the blood into the renal tubules.

**tumor** A mass of cells derived from a single cell that began to divide at an abnormally high rate. The cells of a benign tumor remain at the site of origin, whereas those of a malignant tumor travel to distant sites (metastasize).

**twitch** A complete cycle of contraction and relaxation in a muscle cell.

**tympanic membrane** (tim-PAN-ik) Membrane between the outer ear and inner ear that receives sound waves and transmits the vibrations to the bones of the middle ear. The eardrum.

## U

**ultrasound** Fetal imaging technique in which high-frequency (ultrasound) sound waves are aimed at the mother's uterus. The sound waves rebound when they hit hard tissues in the fetus. These reflecting waves are analyzed and converted to an image by a computer.

**umbilical cord** (um-BIL-uh-kul) Cablelike structure connecting the fetus to the mother, through which arteries and veins pass.

**unsaturated fat** Type of fat with fewer than two hydrogen atoms for every carbon atom in their fatty acid tails. Examples include plant oils—such as olive, safflower, canola, and corn oil—and fish oil.

**urea** (yoo-REE-uh) Main nitrogen-containing waste excreted in urine.

**ureter** (YUR-uh-tur) One of two tubes that transport urine from the kidneys to the urinary bladder.

**urethra** (yoo-REE-thruh) Tube through which urine passes from the bladder to the outside of the body.

**uterine cycle** (YOO-tur-in) A series of changes that occur in the uterus in preparation for the arrival of a fertilized egg. A complete cycle generally takes about 28 days.

**uterus** (YOO-tur-us) Hollow, thick-walled organ that receives, retains, and nourishes the fertilized egg. The uterus is the site of embryonic/fetal development.

## V

**vaccine** Antigens prepared in such a way that when injected or taken orally they induce active immunity without causing disease.

**vagina** (vah-JY-nuh) Hollow muscular female organ extending from the cervix to the body exterior. The vagina functions as an organ of sexual intercourse and as the birth canal.

**variable** Any factor that may vary. In scientific usage, any factor that may vary during the course of an experiment.

**varicose veins** (VAIR-ih-kohs) Permanently dilated veins, often caused by improperly functioning venous valves. Varicose veins can appear anywhere but are most common in the legs and feet.

**vasa recta** Long, straight capillaries that perfuse the inner (medullary) portion of the kidney, supplying the loops of Henle and collecting ducts.

**vasectomy** (vuh-SEK-tuh-mee) Procedure for male surgical sterilization in which the vas deferens (ductus deferens) is cut and tied in two places.

**vasoconstriction** A narrowing of blood vessel diameter caused by contraction of the smooth muscle in the vessel wall.

**vasodilation** A widening of blood vessel diameter caused by relaxation of the smooth muscle in the vessel wall.

**vein** A thin-walled blood vessel that returns blood toward the heart from the venules.

**ventilation** The movement of air into and out of the lungs. Also called breathing.

**ventricle** (VEN-trih-kul) A general term for a cavity. In the heart, one of the two chambers that receives blood from an atrium and pumps it into an artery. In the central nervous system, one of four hollow cavities in the brain.

**ventricular fibrillation** (ven-TRIK-yoo-lur fib-rih-LAY-shun) A type of abnormal heart rhythm involving rapid irregular ventricular contractions.

**venule** (VEEN-yool, VEN-yool) A small blood vessel that transports blood from capillaries to a vein.

**vertebral column** (VUR-tuh-brul) Structure of the axial skeleton formed of a number of individual bones (vertebrae) and two composite bones (sacrum and coccyx). Also called the spine or backbone.

**vertebrate** (VUR-tuh-brayt) Any animal with a backbone composed of vertebrae.

**vesicle** (VES-ih-kul) A small membrane-bound, fluid-filled sac that encloses and contains certain substances within a cell.

**vestibular apparatus** (ves-TIB-yoo-lur) A system of fluid-filled canals and chambers in the inner ear. The vestibular apparatus consists of three semicircular canals for sensing rotational movement of the head, and the vestibule for sensing static (nonmoving) position and linear acceleration and deceleration.

**vestigial structure** (ves-TIJ-ee-ul) A structure that may have had a function in some ancestor but which no longer serves any function. The human coccyx (tailbone) is a vestigial structure.

**villus** (pl. villi) (VIL-us) Fingerlike projection of the small intestinal mucosa that functions to increase the surface area for absorption.

**virus** A noncellular infectious agent that can replicate only within a host cell. Viruses consist only of one or more pieces of genetic material (DNA or RNA) surrounded by a protein coat.

**vital capacity** The maximum volume of air that can be expelled from the lungs by forcible expiration after the deepest inspiration.

**vitamin** Any one of more than a dozen organic compounds that the body requires in minute amounts but generally does not synthesize.

**vitreous humor** (VIT-ree-us) The clear fluid within the main chamber of the eye, between the lens and the retina.

**vocal cords** Two folds of connective tissue that extend across the airway. Audible sounds are heard when the vocal cords vibrate as air passes by.

**vulva** Female external genitalia that surround the opening of the vagina.

## W

**white blood cell (WBC)** One of several types of blood cells that are part of the body's defense system. WBCs are diverse in structure and specific function. They compose only about 1% of the volume of blood. Also called a leukocyte.

**withdrawal method** Birth control method in which the man withdraws his penis from the vagina immediately before ejaculation. In practice it may be difficult to time withdrawal correctly, and so the method is considered less effective than other contraceptive techniques.

## X

**X chromosome** One of the two human sex chromosomes. An embryo that inherits two X chromosomes will develop into a female.

## Y

**Y chromosome** One of the two human sex chromosomes. An embryo that inherits a Y chromosome will develop into a male.

**yolk sac** Extraembryonic membrane that serves as the first source for red blood cells for the fetus and as the source for primordial germ cells.

## Z

**zero population growth** The condition that exists in a population when the birth rate equals the death rate.

**ZIFT (zygote intrafallopian transfer)** (ZY-goht IN-trah-fuh-LO-pee-un) A technique for enhancing fertility in which an egg is fertilized outside the body, then inserted into an oviduct through a small incision in the abdomen.

**zona pellucida** (ZO-nuh peh-LOOS-ih-duh) A noncellular coating around an oocyte.

**zygote** (ZY-goht) The diploid cell formed by the union of the ovum and a sperm. The zygote is the product of fertilization.

# Answers to Test Yourself Questions

Answers to Apply What You Know Questions can be found on the Human Biology Place, www.humanbiology.com.

### Chapter 1 Human Biology, Science, and Society

**1.** d **2.** f **3.** a **4.** b **5.** c **6.** e **7.** species **8.** matter, energy **9.** inductive **10.** experiments **11.** experimental, control **12.** abcissa **13.** True **14.** False **15.** False

### Chapter 2 The Chemistry of Living Things

**1.** d **2.** a **3.** f **4.** b **5.** c **6.** e **7.** alkaline **8.** proteins **9.** glycogen **10.** enzymes **11.** fatty acids **12.** oils **13.** False **14.** True **15.** True

### Chapter 3 Structure and Function of Cells

**1.** c **2.** f **3.** a **4.** e **5.** d **6.** b **7.** cholesterol **8.** eukaryotes, prokaryotes **9.** endoplasmic reticulum **10.** ribosomes **11.** citric acid cycle **12.** lactic acid **13.** False **14.** True **15.** False

### Chapter 4 From Cells to Organ Systems

**1.** c **2.** d **3.** a **4.** b **5.** f **6.** e **7.** tissues **8.** hormones **9.** epidermis **10.** cranial **11.** keratinocytes **12.** set point **13.** True **14.** True **15.** False

### Chapter 5 The Skeletal System

**1.** c **2.** b **3.** e **4.** f **5.** a **6.** d **7.** flat **8.** chondroblasts **9.** axial **10.** pelvic **11.** periosteum **12.** synovial **13.** False **14.** False **15.** True

### Chapter 6 The Muscular System

**1.** c **2.** f **3.** a **4.** e **5.** b **6.** d **7.** involuntary **8.** antagonistic **9.** sarcomere **10.** acetylcholine **11.** motor **12.** gap **13.** False **14.** True **15.** False

### Chapter 7 Blood

**1.** c **2.** b **3.** a **4.** d **5.** f **6.** e **7.** thrombin **8.** hemophilia **9.** antigens **10.** stem **11.** spasm **12.** O **13.** True **14.** False **15.** True

### Chapter 8 Heart and Blood Vessels

**1.** d **2.** c **3.** f **4.** a **5.** b **6.** e **7.** aorta **8.** pulmonary semilunar valve **9.** right atrium **10.** right AV valve **11.** right ventricle **12.** left atrium **13.** left AV valve **14.** aortic semilunar valve **15.** left ventricle **16.** septum **17.** pulmonary embolus **18.** vasoconstriction **19.** cardiac output **20.** stroke

### Chapter 9 The Immune System and Mechanisms of Defense

**1.** f **2.** d **3.** b **4.** e **5.** a **6.** c **7.** virulent **8.** interferons **9.** allergen **10.** nodes; spleen **11.** autoimmune **12.** monoclonal **13.** True **14.** False **15.** False

### Chapter 10 The Respiratory System: Exchange of Gases

**1.** e **2.** b **3.** a **4.** d **5.** c **6.** f **7.** epiglottis **8.** larynx **9.** pleural **10.** respiratory center **11.** diaphragm **12.** carotid; aortic **13.** False **14.** True **15.** False

### Chapter 11 The Nervous System: Integration and Control

**1.** d **2.** b **3.** e **4.** f **5.** a **6.** c **7.** axon terminals **8.** neuroglial **9.** synaptic cleft **10.** central **11.** sympathetic, parasympathetic **12.** limbic **13.** False **14.** False **15.** True

### Chapter 12 Sensory Mechanisms

**1.** c **2.** a **3.** b **4.** d **5.** f **6.** e **7.** chemoreceptors **8.** sweet, sour, salty, bitter, (umami) **9.** fast **10.** tectorial **11.** rods, cones **12.** lens **13.** True **14.** True **15.** True

### Chapter 13 The Endocrine System

**1.** c **2.** f **3.** a **4.** e **5.** b **6.** d **7.** ADH, oxytocin **8.** nonsteroid **9.** FSH / LH **10.** aldosterone **11.** insulin **12.** epinephrine **13.** False **14.** True **15.** True

### Chapter 14 The Digestive System and Nutrition

**1.** c **2.** a **3.** d **4.** b **5.** f **6.** e **7.** liver **8.** canines **9.** carbohydrates **10.** minerals **11.** intake **12.** lactose **13.** True **14.** False **15.** True

### Chapter 15 The Urinary System

**1.** f **2.** d **3.** c **4.** a **5.** b **6.** e **7.** erythropoietin **8.** renin **9.** urea **10.** Henle **11.** sodium **12.** increase **13.** False **14.** False **15.** True

### Chapter 16 Reproductive Systems

**1.** c **2.** a **3.** f **4.** e **5.** b **6.** d **7.** seminiferous **8.** bulbourethral **9.** endometrium **10.** corpus luteum **11.** clitoris **12.** FSH **13.** True **14.** True **15.** False

### Chapter 17 Cell Reproduction and Differentiation

**1.** a **2.** e **3.** c **4.** f **5.** b **6.** d **7.** prophase **8.** gene **9.** transfer RNA (tRNA) **10.** differentiation **11.** cytokinesis **12.** homologous **13.** True **14.** True **15.** False

### Chapter 18 Cancer: Uncontrolled Cell Division and Differentiation

**1.** a **2.** c **3.** f **4.** e **5.** b **6.** d **7.** melanoma **8.** surgery, radiation, chemotherapy **9.** lung, breast, colon/rectum **10.** carcinogen **11.** leukemia **12.** neoplasm **13.** True **14.** False **15.** True

### Chapter 19 Genetics and Inheritance

**1.** c **2.** a **3.** b **4.** e **5.** f **6.** d **7.** gene **8.** translocation **9.** Punnett **10.** heterozygous **11.** phenotype **12.** genotype **13.** False **14.** True **15.** False

## Chapter 20 DNA Technology and Genetic Engineering

**1.** d **2.** e **3.** a **4.** c **5.** b **6.** transgenic **7.** protein **8.** vaccine **9.** fingerprinting **10.** plasmid **11.** palindromic **12.** vectors **13.** True **14.** False **15.** False

## Chapter 21 Development and Aging

**1.** d **2.** a **3.** f **4.** b **5.** e **6.** c **7.** fertilization **8.** identical **9.** fraternal **10.** ectopic (tubal) **11.** pituitary **12.** miscarriage **13.** False **14.** True **15.** False

## Chapter 22 Evolution and the Origins of Life

**1.** d **2.** a **3.** c **4.** b **5.** f **6.** e **7.** homologous **8.** population **9.** RNA **10.** radiometric **11.** biogeography **12.** *Homo sapiens* **13.** False **14.** True **15.** False

## Chapter 23 Ecosystems and Populations

**1.** e **2.** f **3.** a **4.** b **5.** d **6.** c **7.** g **8.** biosphere **9.** succession **10.** niche **11.** producers **12.** consumers **13.** exchange pool; biomass; reservoir **14.** nitrogen fixation **15.** False **16.** True

## Answers to Try It Yourself: The Rule of 72

**1.** 36 years **2.** 3 hours **3.** 18 and 10 years

## Chapter 24 Human Impacts, Biodiversity, and Environmental Issues

**1.** a **2.** c **3.** d **4.** b **5.** e **6.** Pollutants **7.** inversion **8.** ozone **9.** solar **10.** magnification **11.** False **12.** True **13.** True

# Credits

The following illustrations were rendered by Electronic Publishing Services: 3.14, 3.15, 3.16, 3.17, 3.18, 3.19, 3.20, 4.1, 4.2, 4.8, 4.9, UN 4.1, 5.7, 5.12, 6.1, 6.2, 6.3, 6.9, 8.1, 8.5, 8.6, 8.7, 8.9, 8.10, 8.13, 8.19, 9.2, 9.3, 9.12, 9.13, 9.14, 10.1, 10.2, 10.8, 10.13, 11.7, 11.8, 11.10, 11.12, 11.14, 12.1, 12.4, 12.9, 12.10, 12.18, 13.1, 13.5, 14.1, 14.5, 14.6, 14.7, 14.11, 15.2, 15.6, 15.7, 15.10, 15.11, 15.14, 16.2, 16.4c, 16.8. 17.9, 17.11, 21.12, 21.14, 21.15, 23.CI.O3, 23.09, 24.08.

All other illustrations were rendered by Rolin Graphics, Inc. unless otherwise noted.

### Chapter 1

**Opener:** Gary I. Rothstein/epa/Corbis; **Fig. 1.1 clockwise from top left:** NASA; Frank Siteman/PhotoEdit; M. Gunther /BIOS/Peter Arnold; Norbert Wu/Minden Pictures; **Fig. 1.2a–b:** Oliver Meckes/Photo Researchers; **Fig. 1.3 left:** Philip Schermeister/Getty images; **Fig. 1.3 right:** Stem Jems/Photo Researchers; **Fig. 1.3 bottom:** Tim Fitzharris /Minden Pictures; **Fig. 1.6:** Corbis; **Fig. 1.9:** Digital Vision/Getty Images; **Fig. 1.12a:** Corbis; **Fig. 1.12b:** Gerald Davis /Phototake NYC; **Fig. 1.12c:** NASA; **Current Issue p. 16:** Cordelia Molloy/Photo Researchers; **Current Issue p. 17 top left:** Brian Hagiwara/Foodpix/Jupiter Images; **top right:** Corbis; **center:** Ruaridh Stewart/ZUMA/Corbis; **bottom:** Wally Eberhart/Botanica/Jupiter Images; **Health Watch p. 18:** Scott Camazine/Alamy; **Fig. 1.13:** Michael Rosenfeld/Stone/Getty Images.

### Chapter 2

**Opener:** Jeff Tompkinson/SPL/Photo Researchers; **Fig. 2.1a:** Custom Medical Stock Photo; **Fig. 2.1b:** Richard Megna /Fundamental Photographs, NYC; **Fig. 2.4a:** All Sport Photography, USA/Getty Images; **Fig. 2.4b:** All Sport Photography, USA/Getty Images; **Fig. 2.9:** Masterfile; **Fig. 2.11a:** Peter/Stef Lamberti/Stone/Getty Images; **Fig. 2.11b:** Court Mast /Photographer's Choice/Getty Images; **Fig. 2.15c:** Don Fawcett /Visuals Unlimited; **Current Issue p. 42 left:** Marco Cristofori /AGE Fotostock; **right:** Corbis; **Current Issue p. 43 left:** Photocuisine/Corbis; **right:** Kristin Piljay.

### Chapter 3

**Opener:** Dr. Torsten Wittmann/SPL/Photo Researchers; **Fig. 3.1a:** Gopal Murti/Visuals Unlimited; **Fig. 3.1b:** Photo Researchers; **Fig. 3.2a:** David M. Philips/Photo Researchers; **Fig. 3.2b:** Dr. Dennis Kunkel/Phototake NYC; **Fig. 3.2c:** Ed Reschke; **Fig. 3.3a:** Michael Abbey/Photo Researchers; **Fig. 3.3b:** Biophoto Associates/Science Source/Photo Researchers; **Fig. 3.3c:** Oliver Meckes/Photo Researchers; **Fig. 3.6:** Erik Schweitzer, M.D., Ph.D; **Fig. 3.10c:** M. Schliwa/Visuals Unlimited; **Fig. 3.13b left:** Stanley Flagler/Visuals Unlimited; **Fig. 3.13b middle & right:** David M. Phillips/Visuals Unlimited; **Fig. 3.15:** Don W. Fawcett/Visuals Unlimited; **Fig. 3.17:** Photo Researchers; **Fig. 3.19b:** Bill Longcore/Photo Researchers; **Directions in Science p. 66:** Photo Researchers; **Fig. 3.29b:** Corbis; **Current Issue p. 72 left:** Ron Sachs/Sygma/Corbis; **right:** Science Photo Library/Photo Researchers; **Current Issue p. 73 top:** David McNew/Getty Images; **right:** Chris Pizzello/AP Wide World Photos.

### Chapter 4

**Opener:** Steve Gschmeissner/Photo Researchers; **Fig. 4.4a-b:** Ed Reschke/Peter Arnold; **Fig. 4.5a:** Ed Reschke/Peter Arnold; **Fig. 4.5b:** Allen Bell; **Fig. 4.6a:** Eric Graves/Photo Researchers; **Fig. 4.6b:** Ed Reschke/Peter Arnold; **Fig. 4.6c:** Allen Bell; **Fig. 4.7:** Ed Reschke/Peter Arnold; **Health Watch p. 93 left:** Dr. P. Marazzi/Science Picture Library/Photo Researchers; **right:** Sonda Dawes/The Image Works; **Current Issue p. 94 left:** Quest/Photo Researchers; **right:** Liu Jin/Getty Images; **Current Issue p. 95:** Image Source/Getty Images.

### Chapter 5

**Opener:** GustoImages/SPL/Photo Researchers; **Fig 5.1c:** Gene Cox/Photo Researchers; **Current Issue p. 114 left:** Corbis; **right:** Mauro Fermariello/Photo Researchers; **Current Issue p. 115 top:** District Attorneys Office/AP Wide World Photos; **bottom:** Mauro Fermariello/Photo Researchers; **Fig. 5.14:** Larry Mulvehill/Science Source/Photo Researchers; **Fig 5.15a–b:** Reproduced from the J Bone Miner Res 1986; 1:15-21 with permission of the American Society for Bone and Mineral Research.

### Chapter 6

**Opener:** John Burcham/National Geographic Creative/Getty Images; **Fig. 6.4b:** R. Calentine/Visuals Unlimited; **Fig. 6.5c:** Biophoto Associates/Science Source/Photo Researchers; **Fig. 6.5d:** K. G. Murti/Visuals Unlimited; **Fig. 6.9b:** Fred Hossler/Visuals Unlimited; **Fig. 6.11a:** Andersen Ross/Getty Images; **Fig. 6.11b:** Lothar Schulz/Getty Images; **Directions in Science p. 132:** Joel Saget/AFP/Getty Images; **Current Issue p. 134 left:** Scott Barbour/Getty Images; **right:** Hiroko Masuike/Getty Images; **Current Issue p. 135 top left:** George Gojkovich/Getty Images; **top right:** Dilip Vishwanat/Getty Images; **bottom:** Custom Medical Stock Photo.

### Chapter 7

**Opener:** Juergen Berger/SPL/Photo Researchers; **Fig. 7.2c:** Klaus Guldbrandsen/Science Photo Library/Photo Researchers; **Fig. 7.3:** Phototake NYC; **Fig. 7.7:** Dr. Kari Lounatmaa/Photo Researchers; **Fig. 7.9:** Volker Steger/Peter Arnold; **Fig. 7.10:** St. Mary's Hospital Medical School/Science Photo Library/Photo Researchers; **Fig. 7.14:** Jack Scanlon, Holyoke Community College; **Current Issue p. 154 left:** Jaclyn Albanese; **right:** Tissuepix/Photo Researchers; **Current Issue p. 155 left:** Steve Gschmeissner/Photo Researchers; **right:** Burger/Photo Researchers; **Health Watch p. 156:** Larry Mulvehill/Photo Researchers.

### Chapter 8

**Opener:** SPL/Photo Researchers; **Fig. 8.3a:** Matthew A. Boegehold, Ph.D.; **Fig. 8.3b:** Lennart Nilsson/Albert Bonniers Forlag AB; **Fig. 8.6a:** Visuals Unlimited; **Fig. 8.12a:** Jean Claude Revy/Phototake NYC; **Fig. 8.12b:** SIU/Visuals Unlimited; **Fig. 8.14a:** MacNeal Hospital/David Joel/Stone/Getty Images; **Fig. 8.18:** ISM/Phototake NYC; **Health Watch p. 179, a–b:** Visuals Unlimited; **Fig. 8.20:** Jupiter Images **Current Issue p. 182 left:** Mike Segar/Reuters/Corbis; **middle:** Leonard Lessin/Photo Researchers; **right:** Eff Zelevansky/Reuters/Corbis; **Current Issue p. 183 top:** Jamie-Andrea Yanak/AP Wide World Photos; **bottom:** Shutterstock

### Chapter 9

**Opener:** Institut Pasteur/Phototake NYC; **Fig. 9.1a:** S. Lowry /University of Ulster/Stone/Getty Images; **Fig. 9.1b:** Dr. Dennis Kunkel/Phototake NYC; **Fig. 9.1c:** S. Lowry /University of Ulster/Stone/Getty Images; **Fig. 9.4:** Steve Gschmeissner/Photo Researchers; **Fig. 9.5:** Tim Vernon, LTH NHS Trust/Photo Researchers; **Fig. 9.6a:** Visuals Unlimited; **Fig. 9.8 both:** Photo Lennart Nilsson/Albert Bonniers Forlag AB; **Fig. 9.15a:** Jean Claude Revy/Phototake NYC; **Fig. 9.19 top:** SIU/Visuals Unlimited; **bottom:** CNRI/Science Photo Library/Photo Researchers; **Current Issue p. 212:** Aurora & Quanta Productions; **Current Issue p. 213 left:** Joel Stettenheim/Corbis; **right:** Reuters/Corbis.

### Chapter 10

**Opener:** Dennis Kunkel/Phototake NYC; **Fig. 10.4a–b:** CNRI/Phototake NYC; **Fig. 10.6a:** Visuals Unlimited; **Fig. 10.6b:** Andrew P. Evan; **Fig. 10.8b:** Dr. Richard Kessel & Dr. Randy Kardon/Tissues & Organs/Visuals Unlimited; **Fig. 10.10b:** L. Steinmark/Custom Medical Stock Photo; **Current Issue p. 236 left:** Sean Gallup/Getty Images; **right:** Graeme Robertson/Getty Images; **Current Issue p. 237:** Robert W. Ginn/Alamy; **Fig. 10.14a:** John D. Cunningham/Visuals Unlimited; **Fig. 10.14b:** John Burbidge/Science Photo Library/Photo Researchers.

### Chapter 11

**Opener:** David McCarthy/Photo Researchers; **Fig. 11.7b:** C. Raines/Visuals Unlimited; **Fig. 11.8 top right:** E. Lewis, T. Everhart, and Y. Zaevi/Visuals Unlimited; **center left:** CNRI/Science Photo Library/Photo Researchers; **Fig. 11.11:** Jose Luis Pelaez/Corbis; **Fig. 11.14c:** Manfred Kage/Peter Arnold; **Fig. 11.15:** Martin Rotker/Phototake NYC; **Health Watch p. 266:** KJ/Icon SMI/Corbis; **Fig. 11.21a–b:** Photo Researchers; **Current Issue p. 268 left:** Morry Gash/AP Wide World Photos; **right:** Mark J. Terrill/AP Wide World Photos.

### Chapter 12

**Opener:** Dennis Kunkel/Phototake NYC; **Fig. 12.5b:** Omikron/Science Source/Photo Researchers; **Fig. 12.5c:** Astrid & Hanns-Frieder Michler/Science Photo Library/Photo Researchers; **Fig. 12.7:** Corbis; **Fig. 12.10d:** Photo Researchers; **Fig. 12.12c:** Richard J. Mount, Auditory Science Laboratory, The Hospital for Sick Children, Toronto, Canada; **Fig. 12.13d:** Photo Lennart Nilsson/Albert Bonniers Forlag AB; **Fig. 12.18b:**

Ralph C. Eagle/Photo Researchers; **Fig. 12.19a–b:** Scanning electron micrographs by Robert Preston and Joseph E. Hawkins, Kresge Hearing Research Institute, University of Michigan; **Fig. 12.20a:** Sue Ford /Science Photo Library/Photo Researchers; **Fig. 12.20b:** Western Opthamalmic Hospital/ Science Photo Library/Photo Researchers; **Fig. 12.21a–b:** National Eye Institute, National Institutes of Health; **Current Issue p. 293 left:** Alamy Images; **right:** D. Hurst/Alamy Images.

## Chapter 13

**Opener:** Quest/Photo Researchers; **Fig. 13.8:** Science Photo Library/Photo Researchers; **Fig. 13.9 all:** Reproduced by permission from American Journal of Medicine 20:133, © 1956 by Elsevier Science Ltd; **Fig. 13.14:** Bettmann/Corbis; **Current Issue p. 314 left:** Jules Frazier/PhotoDisc/Getty Images; **right:** Bubbles Photolibrary/Alamy; **Current Issue p. 315 top:** Roche Diagnostics Corporation; **bottom:** AJ Photos/Photo Researchers; **Fig. 13.16a–b:** Courtesy of Dr. Charles B. Wilson, Neurological Surgery, University of California Medical Center, San Francisco.

## Chapter 14

**Opener:** Steve Gschmeissner/Photo Researchers; **Fig. 14.4c:** David Scharf/Peter Arnold; **Fig. 14.7c:** Fred Hossler/Visuals Unlimited **Directions in Science p. 328:** Eye of Science /Photo Researchers; **Fig. 14.9e:** Fred Hossler/Visuals Unlimited; **Fig. 14.19:** Martin Rotker/Phototake NYC; **Fig. 14.21:** Sipa Press; **Current Issue p. 346:** Daniel Berehulak/Getty Images; **Current Issue p. 347:** Chris Pizzello/Reuters/Corbis.

## Chapter 15

**Opener:** Steve Gschmeissner/Photo Researchers; **Fig. 15.7a:** Dennis Kunkel/Phototake NYC; **Fig. 15.7b:** Dr. William Kriz, Ruprecgt-Karls-Universitat Heidelberg, Institut fur Anatomie und Zellbiologie; **Fig. 15.8a:** Fred Hossler/Visuals Unlimited; **Current Issue p. 368 left:** Will and Deni McIntyre/Photo Researchers; **right:** Argus Fotoarchiv/Peter Arnold; **Current Issue p. 369:** James A. Finley/AP Photo; **Fig. 15.17:** BSIP /Phototake USA.

## Chapter 16

**Opener:** Yorgos Nikas/Getty Images; **Fig. 16.2c:** Ed Reschke /Peter Arnold; **Health Watch p. 385:** Saturn Stills/Photo Researchers; **Fig. 16.9:** Photo Researchers; **Fig. 16.11a:** Getty Images; **Fig. 16.11b:** NuvaRing Inc., Organon USA Inc.; **Fig. 16.11c:** Habel/Maritius, GMBH /Phototake NYC; **Fig. 16.11d:** Cordelia Malloy/Photo Researchers; **Fig. 16.11e:** SIU/Photo Researchers; **Fig. 16.11f:** Scott Camazine/Sue Trainor /Photo Researchers; **Fig. 16.11g:** M. Long/Visuals Unlimited; **Fig. 16.11h:** Cordelia Molloy /Photo Researchers; **Fig. 16.12:** SGO/BSIP/Photo Researchers; **Fig. 16.14:** Richard G. Rawlins, Ph.D./Custom Medical Stock Photo; **Directions in Science p. 394 left:** AP Photo; **right:** LookatSciences/ PhototakeUSA; **Current Issue p. 396 left:** Chad Ehlers/Alamy Images; **right:** Photodisc Blue/Getty Images; **Current Issue p. 397 left:** AP Wide World Photos; **right:** Getty Images; **Fig. 16.17a:** Science Source/SPL/Photo Researchers; **Fig. 16.17b:** Mediscan/Visuals Unlimited; **Fig. 16.17c:** CNRI/Phototake NYC; **Fig. 16.18:** Photo Researchers.

## Chapter 17

**Opener:** Dr. Alexey Khodjakov/Photo Researchers; **Fig. 17.2:** Biophoto Associates/Photo Researchers; **Fig. 17.9 all:** Michael Abbey/Photo Researchers; **Fig. 17.10:** David M. Phillips/Visuals Unlimited; **Current Issue p. 416:** Mauro Fermariello/Photo Researchers; **Current Issue p. 417:** Gusto/Photo Researchers; **Current Issue p. 418 left:** Seoul National University/Getty Images; **right:** Simon Thong/AP Wide World Photos.

## Chapter 18

**Opener:** Dr. M. Brauner/Photo Researchers; **Fig. 18.3:** Dr. P. Marazzi/Photo Researchers; **Fig. 18.4:** Richard R. Hansen/Photo Researchers; **Fig. 18.5:** Myrleen Ferguson Cate/PhotoEdit; **Fig. 18.8:** Chris Bjornberg/Photo Researchers; **Fig. 18.9:** Simon Fraser/Science Photo Library/ Photo Researchers; **Fig. 18.10:** National Cancer Institute/Photo Researchers; **Fig. 18.11a:** James Stevenson/Photo Researchers; **Fig. 18.11b:** CNRI/ Photo Researchers; **Fig. 18.11c:** Dr. P. Marazzi/ Photo Researchers; **Fig. 18.11d:** ISM/Phototake NYC; **Fig. 18.12:** David M. Martin, M.D./Photo Researchers; **Current Issue p. 437:** Newscom.

## Chapter 19

**Opener:** Andrew Syred/Photo Researchers; **Fig. 19.3 left:** Corbis; **right:** Image100/Jupiter Images; **Fig. 19.4a left:** Jennifer Graylock/AP Wide World Photos; **right:** Chris Jackson/Getty Images; **Fig. 19.4b:** Bert Krages/Visuals Unlimited; **Fig. 19.5a:** SPL/Photo Researchers; **Fig. 19.5b:** Paul Bricknell/Dorling Kindersley; **Health Watch p. 447:** A. Menashe/Humanistic-photography .com; **Fig. 19.8 left:** Comstock Images/Jupiter Images; **top right:** Photos.com; **bottom right:** Comstock Images/Jupiter Images; **Fig. 19.10b:** Oliver Meckes and Nicole Ottawa/Photo Researchers; **Fig. 19.11 top left:** George Hausman/ Stock Market/Corbis; **top right:** David A. Wagner/ Phototake NYC; **bottom left:** Pete Saloutos/Stock Market/Corbis; **bottom right:** Zhang Xiao Qiu/iStockphoto; **Fig. 19.14:** Phototake NYC; **Fig. 19.18:** Richard Hutchings/Photo Researchers; **Fig. 19.19a–b:** Courtesy of Dr. Nadler/Children's Memorial Hospital, Chicago, Illinois; **Current Issue p. 458 left:** John Gress /Reuters/Corbis; **right:** Phanie/Photo Researchers; **Current Issue p. 459:** Phototake NYC.

## Chapter 20

**Opener:** Mauro Fermariello/SPL/Photo Researchers; **Fig. 20.1:** Tek Image/Photo Researchers; **Fig. 20.5:** Maximilian Stock Ltd/SPL/Photo Researchers; **Fig. 20.6:** Michael L. Simpson; **Fig. 20.7:** Monsanto/Visuals Unlimited; **Fig. 20.8:** Courtesy Syngenta; **Fig. 20.10:** Genzyme Transgenics Corp. **Current Issue p. 475 left:** Chris Knapton /Photo Researchers; **right:** Robert Brook/Photo Researchers; **Fig. 20.11:** jazzikov/Shutterstock; **Fig. 20.12:** AP Wide World Photos.

## Chapter 21

**Opener:** Joe McBride/Taxi/Getty Images; **Fig. 21.4a–b:** Barbara Penoya/Getty Images, Inc. **Fig. 21.10:** Photo Lennart Nilsson /Albert Bonniers Forlag AB. A CHILD IS BORN, Dell Publishing Company; **Fig. 21.11:** Photo Lennart Nilsson/Albert Bonniers Forlag AB. A CHILD IS BORN, Dell Publishing Company; **Fig. 21.13:** Photo Lennart Nilsson/Albert Bonniers Forlag AB. A CHILD IS BORN, Dell Publishing Company; **Fig. 21.17a:** The Image Works; **Fig. 21.17b:** Matthew Fern/Pool/Corbis; **Fig. 21.19:** Ariel Skelley/Corbis; **Current Issue p. 503 left:** David Kadlubowski/Corbis; **right:** Schindler Family/AP Wide World Photos.

## Chapter 22

**Opener:** John Reader/Photo Researchers; **Fig. 22.1e:** Kenneth Garrett/Kenneth Garrett Photography; **Fig. 22.2:** Harvey Lloyd /The Stock Market/Corbis; **Fig. 22.6:** Geoffrey Clifford/ Woodfin Camp & Associates; **Fig. 22.8:** Jack Ballard/Visuals Unlimited; **Fig. 22.13a:** Manoj Shah/Image Bank/Getty Images; **Fig. 22.13b:** Anup Shah/Image Bank/Getty Images; **Fig. 22.13c:** Rod Williams /Nature Picture Library; **Fig. 22.13d:** John Giustina/Taxi/Getty Images; **Fig. 22.14a:** The Natural History Museum of London; **Fig. 22.14b:** Tim Boyle/Getty Images; **Fig. 22.15:** John Reader /Science Photo Library/Photo Researchers; **Current Issue p. 520 left:** Peter Brown; **right:** Ho New; **Current Issue p. 521 left:** Ray Stanyard; **right:** Dr. William L. Jungers; **Fig. 22.18 top row left to right:** Photos.com; Comstock Complete; Andi Berger /Shutterstock; Photos.com; Photos.com; **second row left to right:** Robert Kneschke/ iStockphoto; Comstock Complete; Phil Date/ Shutterstock; Comstock Complete; Photos.com; **third row left to right:** Comstock Complete; Comstock Complete; Comstock Complete; Photos.com; Photos.com; **bottom row left to right:** Photos.com; Photos.com; Comstock Complete; Yuri Arcurs/Shutterstock; Comstock Complete.

## Chapter 23

**Opener:** Suzi Eszterhas/Minden Pictures; **Fig. 23.1 top left:** Joseph Van Os/Getty Images; **top right:** Jeremy Woodhouse /Getty Images; **bottom:** R. Andrew Odum/Peter Arnold; **Fig. 23.5:** Dr. Harvey Barnett/Peter Arnold; **Fig. 23.6:** Daniel Cox/Photolibrary; **Fig. 23.7:** Tim Fitzharris/ Minden Pictures; **Current Issue p. 541:** Hoang Dinh Nam/Agence France Presse/Getty Images.

## Chapter 24

**Opener:** Novastock/Photo Researchers; **Fig. 24.4:** NASA /Goddard Space Flight Center; **Fig. 24.5a:** Bettmann/Corbis; **Fig. 24.5b:** Mark E. Gibson/ Visuals Unlimited; **Fig. 24.6:** Alamy; **Fig. 24.7:** John Sohlden/Visuals Unlimited; **Fig. 24.9:** Jim Olive/Peter Arnold; **Fig. 24.10:** Frans Lanting/ Minden Pictures; **Fig. 24.11a:** Simon Harris/Robert Harding World Imagery; **Fig. 24.11b:** Klein/ Hubert/Bios/Peter Arnold; **Fig. 24.11c:** Russell Illig/PhotoLibrary; **Current Issue p. 557 left:** Science Magazine; **right:** Hydro-Handout/ epa/Corbis; **Fig. 24.12:** Russell Gordon/Alamy; **Fig. 24.13:** California Academy of Sciences.

**Recurring features photos:**
**Try It Yourself**: Thomas Northcut/Photodisc/Getty Images; Vladimir Pcholkin/Photographers's Choice/Getty Images.
**Current Issue:** Ryan McVay/Photodisc/Getty Images.
**Health Watch:** khz/Shutterstock.
**Directions in Science:** TRBfoto/Photodisc/Getty Images.

# Index

Italicized page numbers indicate information in tables or figures.